EVERYMAN,
I WILL GO WITH THEE,
AND BE THY GUIDE,
IN THY MOST NEED
TO GO BY THY SIDE

MICHEL DE MONTAIGNE

The Complete Works

Essays, Travel Journal, Letters

Translated by Donald M. Frame
with an Introduction by Stuart Hampshire

EVERYMAN'S LIBRARY

259

The Essays of Montaigne first included in Everyman's Library, 1910
This translation of the Complete Works first included in Everyman's
Library, 2003
© 1943 by Donald M. Frame. © 1948 by the Board of Trustees of
the Leland Stanford Junior University. Copyright renewed 1971,
1976 by Donald M. Frame. © 1957, 1958 by the Board of Trustees of
the Leland Stanford Junior University. All rights reserved.
Reprinted and published by arrangement with
Stanford University Press.
Introduction, Bibliography and Chronology © Everyman's Library,
2003
Typography by Peter B. Willberg

ISBN 1-85715-259-X

A CIP catalogue record for this book is available from the
British Library

Published by Everyman's Library,
Gloucester Mansions, 140A Shaftesbury Avenue,
London WC2H 8HD

Distributed by Random House (UK) Ltd.,
20 Vauxhall Bridge Road, London SW1V 2SA

Printed and bound in Germany
by GGP Media, Pössneck

CONTENTS

ESSAYS

With approximate dates of composition

BOOK I

CONTENTS

MONTAIGNE

CONTENTS

BOOK III

TRAVEL JOURNAL

MONTAIGNE

LETTERS

CONTENTS

INTRODUCTION

Michel de Montaigne was born in 1533 into the minor nobility on his family's estate near Bordeaux. He always loved and admired his father, Pierre Eyquem de Montaigne, who was the strongest influence on his early life. His mother was of Spanish Jewish origin. Montaigne was brought up as a Catholic and he never deserted this faith, although one of his brothers and two sisters became Protestants. His father, a man of ideas, entrusted his early education to a tutor who spoke only Latin and no French. Until he was six years old Latin was Montaigne's native language.

Montaigne's father was elected Mayor of Bordeaux and the son entered what may be called municipal politics as a councillor in the Chambre des Enquêtes. He was bored by the routine of the work but endured it for thirteen years. In the Parlement in Bordeaux he met Etienne de La Boétie, with whom he formed an intense and complete friendship, based on unqualified admiration. 'If you press me to tell why I loved him, I feel that this cannot be expressed, except by answering: "Because it was he, because it was I."' La Boétie died of a fever in 1563, aged thirty-two. He had written a treatise against tyranny and he recognized freedom of conscience as a supreme value. There can be no doubt that intimate friendship with Etienne de La Boétie was the great emotional experience of Montaigne's life, alongside his relation to his father. He commemorated La Boétie in the famous chapter in the Essays under the title 'Of Friendship'. In 1565 he married the daughter of a colleague who brought him six children, only one of whom survived beyond infancy: a daughter to whom he was later devoted. In the Essays he expresses little enthusiasm or warmth about his marriage or about marriage in general.

In 1568 he duly inherited the title and estate after the death of his father. He soon sold his public position, having failed to find work which he could consider useful. He announced his retirement in a Latin inscription on the wall of his study:

MONTAIGNE

'At the age of thirty-eight, on the last day of February, his birthday, Michel de Montaigne, long weary of the servitude of the court and of public employments, while still entire, retired to the bosom of the learned virgins.' But retirement proved not as easy and delightful as he had expected, and he turned to writing to combat his depression. Early in his writing career he wrote the 'Apology for Raymond Sebond'. Sebond had tried to prove the nature and existence of God by what he called 'Natural Theology'. Montaigne's scepticism emerged in the Preface to his translation of this work. He was gradually discovering the true and endless subject of his work: himself. He found that the exploration of this absorbing subject relieved his depression, and that the continued exploration of its complexities had its effect in changing the subject. He was gradually becoming less strict in his moral views and less interested in stoic and ancient virtues, more tolerant of his own inconsistencies, more diffuse and easygoing both in his writing and in his life.

In 1580 the first two books of the Essays were published. He travelled to Italy (keeping an account of the trip in a Travel Journal). During the 1570s he had acted as an agent in negotiations for Henry of Navarre, later Henry IV, in attempting, unsuccessfully, a reconciliation with the Catholic Guise family. In 1581 he entered into office as Mayor of Bordeaux, and he was to serve for four years. He escaped the plague, which killed nearly half the inhabitants of the city. He took refuge in travel, which he greatly enjoyed as he observed human varieties in different populations. He was always proud of the fact that he did not close his house and estate to visitors in spite of the wars of religion that raged around them. With the publication in 1588 of the first three-book edition of the Essays, he resumed his political activities in Paris and in the court on behalf of Henry of Navarre, but he also continued to work on his book, as if compulsively, introducing many minor additions and corrections. The additions appeared in the margins of a copy of the 1588 edition, which has subsequently become known as the Bordeaux copy. He continued working in his own peculiar way, rather like Proust, until the end, and added a cheerful epigraph – 'He acquires strength

as he goes.' In spite of the murderous environment of his time and place, he greatly and evidently enjoyed living. He took pleasure in recording this fact, as also in recording everything else about himself.

*

Montaigne himself remarked that his 'foolish enterprise', as he described writing about himself, was utterly unique and without precedent in history. There had been Confessions, as by Saint Augustine, and there had been many treatises and learned studies of the workings of the mind. But in the Essays he was not studying the human mind, unless accidentally and by implication along the way. He states firmly and clearly that he is writing about one individual, Michel de Montaigne, recognizing his individuality, and not treating him as a former Mayor of Bordeaux, or as a representative, or as an instance of any type or class of person. 'The world always looks straight ahead; as for me, I turn my gaze inward, I fix it there and keep it busy. Everyone looks in front of him; as for me, I look inside of me; I have no business but with myself; I continually observe myself, I take stock of myself, I taste myself. Others always go elsewhere, if they stop to think about it; they always go forward ... as for me, I roll about in myself.' This is precisely what he does in the Essays, making experiments with the form – works of 'apprenticeship', as he calls then – following no beaten path of an established genre, but inventing it for himself.

This entirely original topic in literature, Montaigne on Montaigne, demanded for its full development a new literary form, the loose, unstructured, discursive essay, replete with deliberate irrelevances, antiquarian references and classical quotations, with snippets of autobiography and fragments of philosophy and with speculations about the relations between mind and body. The final product, always and necessarily unfinished and open-ended, was to be the confused picture of this single confused consciousness at one passing moment in its unique history. Montaigne's mind in its very nature could not stand still and could not sit for its portrait. 'I paint transience' ('je peins le passage') he wrote, and the flickering uncertainties and contradictions of intermingling thought and

feeling are the true gait and stride of his mind; perhaps also of all minds to some degree, as far as he could tell. 'Each man bears the entire form of man's estate', and instability of mood and attitude is part of the human condition. For Montaigne there was a clear division between the realm of eternal realities and eternal truths, and the natural order of perpetually changing things to which we have access through the senses and through introspection. About transient things we can have 'options', but he refuses to have options about eternal things. He defers without question to the theology of the Catholic Church and he rejects Christian reformers and Protestants who intrude with their reasoning into a realm where they can have no direct access to the truth apart from the Church. He does not meddle with theology. Written and published at a time when there was savage fighting in France, and throughout Europe, about theological issues, the Essays will be found to include not a word of theological speculation. The traditional authority of the Catholic Church, an overarching dome of certainty, was enough for Montaigne, and he anticipated thinkers in the eighteenth century in his dislike and distrust of any form of metaphysical and religious enthusiasm. 'The most beautiful lives to my taste,' he wrote, 'are those which frame themselves to the common model, the human model, with order but without miracles and without extravagance.' This quotation comes from the third volume of the Essays and it is delightful that it should have the words 'to my taste', a typical qualification in Montaigne, always reporting on himself.

Everywhere in the Essays one encounters a strong moral taste, coolly and sometimes ironically expressed, but immensely vivid and dominant. Montaigne's preference for moderation in all things led him to hate cruelty and violence. 'Among other vices, I cruelly hate cruelty, both by nature and by judgment, as the extreme of all vices. But this is to such a point of softness that I do not see a chicken's neck wrung without distress ...' Worst of all is the cruelty which often supports mere opinions. 'Should the regular means [of support] be lacking, we support them with commands, force, fire, and sword ...' 'There is a certain strong and generous ignorance that concedes nothing to knowledge in honor and courage, an

ignorance that requires no less knowledge to conceive it than does knowledge.' 'After all, it is putting a very high price on one's conjectures to have a man roasted alive because of them.' In education, 'Away with violence and compulsion! There is nothing to my mind which so depraves and stupefies a wellborn nature.' He habitually left his house open on principle and did not defend it with force against roaming bands of robbers and fanatics. He was horrified by the then recently revealed savagery of the conquistadores in Latin America. In several discussions in the Essays he rejects the idea that so-called primitive people appear barbaric, or morally primitive, when compared with the so-called civilized populations of Europe. On the contrary, the moral advantage goes the other way. The simpler and less artificial the social system, the less the oppression and cruelty. Even within his own society he respected and admired craftsmen and working men for their good sense and decency and distrusted the more polished and educated members of professional classes, each with their own pretences. He lambasts the whole medical profession in a long passage in the Essays. Their claims to knowledge are mostly fraudulent and their alleged cures are generally not cures at all. They are merely 'opinions', that is, theories which generally are neither tested nor testable. 'Everyone competes in plastering up and confirming this accepted belief, with all the power of their reason, which is a supple tool, pliable, and adaptable to any form. Thus the world is filled and soaked with twaddle and lies.' This is his light-hearted polemic against doctors.

Appeals to theory do not convince Montaigne. But while never claiming to be a philosopher he gradually discloses a philosophical position in the Essays. Within Nature, and in the sight of God, we are very small creatures, with humble and limited powers. 'It seems to me,' he writes, 'that we can never be despised as much as we deserve ... I do not think there is as much unhappiness in us as vanity, nor as much malice as stupidity. We are not so full of evil as inanity; we are not as wretched as we are worthless.' Admittedly there had been supermen such as Alexander and Julius Caesar and, among writers, at least Virgil, Lucretius and Plutarch. But

looking into ordinary humanity, in the person of Montaigne, we must admit that 'We are all patchwork, and so shapeless and diverse in composition that each bit, each moment, plays its own game.' The form and style of the Essays were meant to illustrate this natural unsteadiness and incoherence of their author's consciousness. He flits within a few paragraphs from a discussion of the relation between mind and body – the conjugal relationship that composes a whole person – to mere anecdotes about heroes and villains in ancient Greece and Rome. In his restless inquiry Montaigne's purpose was to tell the unvarnished truth about Montaigne, after he retired from public life, surrounded by books in his tower. In his idleness he was liable to melancholy, that popular disease of his age, and he resolved to write the only book of its kind in the world and in its conception wild and fantastically eccentric. He decided that he would 'reserve a back shop [arrière-boutique] all our own, entirely free, in which to establish our real liberty and our principal retreat and solitude'.

This famous image of the back shop makes precisely the point about the composition of the Essays that he needs to make. They are the product of solitary introspection and of delving into past experiences recaptured in memory and re-assessed. Most men are absorbed in dealing with persons and things in the external world and in maintaining their contacts there. They have occupations and careers and they must move forward in their business. Therefore they remain in the front of the shop, looking out to the street and talking to buyers and passers by. Montaigne thought of his own personality as including an inner world and an inner self and an outside self and a comparatively public world. For the sake of his writing and for the sake of himself he had turned decisively inward. He did not doubt that other men also had back shops to which they could retreat in solitude if they wanted and that in the secret and concealed parts of themselves and of their minds they could find features of humanity which were not recognized in the public domain. But he was reluctant to generalize, and he preferred to study only a single individual, Montaigne, and to cultivate his powers of reflection.

There is one comparison which cannot be avoided: Marcel

Proust also believed, generalizing, that every man has a secret and concealed self which constitutes his true identity and that he misguidedly allows the conventions of public and social life to distract him from exploring his inner nature. But in revealing the intermittences of the heart and the unavoidable disappointments of desire in social life Proust conveyed a prophetic message about art and the imagination which is not to be found in Montaigne. Montaigne is interested only in his own subjectivity. 'What I write here is not my teaching, but my study; it is not a lesson for others, but for me.' 'It is a thorny undertaking, and more so than it seems, to follow a movement so wandering as that of our mind, to penetrate the opaque depths of its innermost folds ...' There are those who 'touch themselves no more than superficially; who observe themselves only after taking care of their business; who call it daydreaming and idleness to be concerned with oneself, and making castles in Spain to furnish and build oneself; who think themselves something alien and foreign to themselves'. Again: 'We must untie these bonds that are so powerful, and henceforth love this and that, but be wedded only to ourselves ... The greatest thing in the world is to know how to belong to oneself.'

In strong contrast with Proust's pessimism, Montaigne confesses that he can do nothing without gaiety: 'continuation and too strong contention dazes, depresses, and wearies my judgment.' He praises a relaxed will, an easygoing enjoyment of living and its contingencies, and he dislikes erudition if it is painfully acquired. 'We would be much better off if we dropped our inquiries and let ourselves be moulded by the natural order of the world.' 'The natural order of the world' gives us the essence of Montaigne. Ecstasies and visions that may involve escaping from our corporeal selves are dangerous and not to be trusted. We cannot bootstrap ourselves into some elevated state which is not our natural setting. Each one of us has his own idiosyncrasies, both of body and of mind, his own forma mentis, and the idiosyncrasies are the result of countless causes and influences, which will never be traced. Therefore it is foolish to publish rules and disciplines for all humanity as the Stoics did, since humanity consists of endlessly varying and diverse

individuals, whose needs must be endlessly varying also. Montaigne is delighted by the variety of individual tempera- ments and by the diversity of the customs and cultures from which they spring. This is the philosophical foundation of his pleas for toleration.

Tolerance is not for Montaigne, as it is for many modern liberals, a virtuous disposition that he must constrain himself to acquire and to exercise. On the contrary, no constraint is required, just because enjoyment of human variety comes to him naturally as one of his greatest sources of pleasure, particu- larly if he travels to Italy or to Paris, which 'has had my heart since my childhood'. Paris is great above all places and in- comparable in the variety and diversity of its attractions; it is 'the glory of France, and one of the noblest ornaments of the world'. A great city – Paris, New York, Rome, London – makes it impossible to think of mankind as dully uniform: the city at its best is a bazaar of clashing cultures, which its citizens expect to pass through day by day. In his achieved self-knowledge, Montaigne finally admits, 'I know well that if you take it liter- ally, this pleasure in traveling is a testimony of restlessness and irresolution . . . Yes, I confess, I see nothing, even in a dream or a wish, that I could hold myself to; variety alone satisfies me, and the enjoyment of diversity, at least if anything satisfies me.'

There is a deeper reason for Montaigne's enjoyment of human diversity: he was aware of, and he recounts in the Essays, the many contraries, contradictions and ambivalences that enter into his own dispositions and make up his character. It is in the nature of an *in*tolerant man that he will wholeheart- edly support his own cause, moral or religious, whatever it may be, and that he will never yield anything in the struggle against those who oppose him. How could Montaigne, whose soul was divided into a tangle of contradictory attitudes and conflicting impulses and ambivalent affections, ever pull himself together to become an unyielding supporter of a single, undivided cause against all its enemies? He could do no such thing: he knows that he could never be unwavering, unyielding and undivided in his sympathies when any 'important issue is at stake'. 'Not only does the wind of accident move me at will, but, besides, I am moved and disturbed as a result merely of

my own unstable posture; and anyone who observes carefully can hardly find himself twice in the same state. I give my soul now one face, now another, according to which direction I turn it. If I speak of myself in different ways, that is because I look at myself in different ways. All contradictions may be found in me by some twist and in some fashion. Bashful, insolent; chaste, lascivious; talkative, taciturn ... all this I see in myself to some extent according to how I turn; and whoever studies himself really attentively finds in himself, yes, even in his judgment, this gyration and discord. I have nothing to say about myself absolutely, simply, and solidly, without confusion and without mixture, or in one word.' Diversity is therefore built into the most intimate experience that we enjoy in our own souls, and we have no reason to look for or to require uniformity and stability outside ourselves and in the soul of others. 'I do not at all hate opinions contrary to mine. I am so far from being vexed to see discord between my judgments and others', and from making myself incompatible with the society of men because they are of a different sentiment and party from mine, that on the contrary, since variety is the most general fashion that nature has followed ... I find it much rarer to see our humors and plans agree. And there were never in the world two opinions alike, any more than two hairs or two grains. Their most universal quality is diversity.'

Montaigne's version of Nature, of a type usually associated with Heraclitus, was not only a vision of constant flux and change, but also of the irreducible individualities of distinct but similar things. He was a particularist because of his observation of himself. He belongs to a phase of thought that preceded by many years Galileo's discoveries of possible uniformities in Nature. His primary access to Nature was through the sustained attention in watching his own body and soul which writing the Essays required. He could not envisage the later conception of Nature, already discernible in Hobbes, as the domain of universal laws of motion and of the type of causality which is explained by such laws. For him, human souls and bodies (and animals and plants too), being individuals, have to be understood through their individual

natures, sometimes minutely differentiated, which are the out-
come of chance encounters and influences. Medical theories,
and the attempted cures based on them, come to grief on
the particularities of individual cases. Montaigne studying
Montaigne, in virtue of his method of inquiry, has already
eschewed the generalizations which tempt doctors into talking
nonsense at an exalted level.

When Montaigne sallied forth on his horse to visit distant
places, he was ready to observe with delight the minutiae of
contrasting customs which he met along the way. He gloried
in the variety and sought historical explanations for the differ-
ences, explanations that sometimes stretched back to the
ancient world of Greece and Rome. He was an ideal tourist
because he could see in the landscape the history that formed
it, and he always wanted to tell you, the reader, what he saw,
while a later, more scientific traveller might have seen only
the physical effects and the effects of climate which had formed
the landscape. Montaigne hated to be confined and limited in
his range of observation, and he considered any such con-
finement as a blow to his personal freedom. Anticipating the
eighteenth century again, he liked to think of China, 'whose
history teaches me that the world is more abundant and
diverse than either we or the ancients ever realized'. Historical
information, travelling backwards in time, was by itself for
him a form of liberation, a relief from the burden of wearing
always one uniform.

Praise of love and of friendship fits exactly and beautifully
into an account dwelling on individuality and on the differen-
tiations involved in the observation of individuality rather
than of the general case. A list of personal qualities, however
specific, could never convey the reality of the perfect and
intimate friendship between La Boétie and himself nor explain
their coming together. 'It is not one special consideration, nor
two, nor three, nor four, nor a thousand: it is I know not what
quintessence of all this mixture, which ... seized my whole
will,' he writes, making a point which is familiar but need not
be so obscurely expressed. Loving a place, a landscape, a
painting, a view, a poem or a line of poetry, or, finally, a
person, it is typically impossible to name the features of the

object which first generated the love and which later sustain it. In the case of loved persons, intimate friends and lovers and members of a family, unobvious and perhaps unique features of a person, their manner of walking or of talking, the angle at which they hold their head, their smile, or perhaps the sound of their voice, may enchant the lover. A third party cannot tell and cannot anticipate the impression.

In the Essays Montaigne celebrated, in classical style and before the world, his friendship with La Boétie and he asserted that the friendship was without blemish and without qualification. The ancient Greek word φιλια as in Aristotle, may in different translated contexts be either love or friendship and embraces both. Montaigne reviews the occasional sexual passions of youth, and the tranquil harbour of his marriage, together with the great emotional experience of his life, which was his falling in love, spiritually and immediately, with his friend. The joy of friendship and of talk among friends are both vividly recaptured in the Essays.

In his famous chapter on the art of conversation, Montaigne roundly asserts, 'The most fruitful and natural exercise of our mind, in my opinion, is discussion. I find it sweeter than any other action of our life.' Talk – often continuous talk – stands at the top of the pyramid of all human activities: above writing and a long way above reading. In their cultivated discontinuities, in their unexpected division into chapters, in their lightness of tone, in their allusiveness and their tumbling into anecdote and into historical gossip, his essays have brought writing as near as it can come to talk among friends. Montaigne revelled in discussion and debate, even in its contrariness. Once again he seems to anticipate in his tastes the *esprits forts* of the eighteenth century in everything except their hostility to religion and to the Church. Diderot is the supreme master who takes up the conversational, sceptical and the pleasure-loving tone, and, speaking across the terrible century of religious wars, Montaigne and Diderot seem to confirm each other in intellectual gaiety.

Pleasure, like freedom, was one of the supreme values for Montaigne: a certain lightness of being was his aim both in writing and in day-to-day living. 'I have naturally a humorous

and familiar style,' he writes, 'but of a form all my own, inept for public negotiations, as my language is in every way, being too compact, disorderly, abrupt, individual.' He also writes, 'I love the poetic gait, by leaps and gambols.' His delight was in the sudden movements of life and of language, in the aggravated sensation of being alive. Dismissing 'exquisite subtleties' that 'are only fit for preaching,' he asserted, 'Life is a material and corporeal movement, an action which by its very essence is imperfect and irregular; I apply myself to serving it in its own way.' The three great monuments of French secular sensibility – Montaigne, Diderot and Stendhal – all thought of themselves as serving life and with it the unending hunt for the feeling of happiness.

Stuart Hampshire

My aim in translating Montaigne has been to capture in modern English not only his meaning but also the living, natural quality of his style. I have deliberately chosen to retain, as he did, as many as possible of the idiosyncrasies that portray him: the vivid, bold images; the epigrammatic word play; the meandering, associative order, often disdainful of logical connectives; the obscenity, which is a studied protest against man's rejection of the body. I have smoothed the rough spots over only when they seemed less characteristic of Montaigne than of his time or when the claims of intelligible English seemed clearly to outweigh those of scrupulous fidelity. I have tried, in short, to express Montaigne as I think he would have expressed himself had he been writing in English today.

The basic text of the Essays followed here is the Bordeaux Copy, a copy of the 1588 (5th) edition which Montaigne, in his own hand, marked '6th edition' and covered, in the margins, with additions. This volume, preserved in the Municipal Library of Bordeaux, has been reproduced phototypically by Fortunat Strowski (Paris: Hachette, 1912). A copy of the additions was sent to Montaigne's literary executrix, Marie de Gournay, and served as a basis for her first edition of 1595. This 1595 text, though not always wholly trustworthy, is useful in two ways: it gives readings that were later cut from the margins of the Bordeaux Copy by a heedless binder in trimming the pages, and also readings that Montaigne may have relegated to separate slips of paper which have since been lost. Readings of the former type from the 1595 edition are included in the present translation without comment; those of other types have usually been either noted in the text or relegated to footnotes with the other variants.

Variants from earlier editions of the Essays (1580, 1582, 1587), as well as post-1588 additions that were deleted after being written, have been given in the footnotes whenever they seemed interesting enough to warrant mention.

Montaigne's text abounds in quotations in prose and verse,

mainly Latin but also Italian, Greek and French, without indication of source. In the present translation these have been given solely in English, italicized when in prose, and with the author's name added. The translations of the verse quotations are my own. They represent the form that Montaigne quotes, even when he adapts or misquotes. I have tried to be faithful to their meaning in the context Montaigne gives them, in which precision is often important.

Originally each chapter of the Essays was set as a single paragraph. The present translation follows modern usage in breaking up these long paragraphs. Bracketed subheads are introduced for the reader's convenience into the huge 'Apology for Raymond Sebond' (II: 12).

The superscript letters ABC in the text serve to distinguish the three certain strata in which the Essays were composed:

A designates material published before 1588 (generally in 1580 unless otherwise noted);

B designates material published in 1588;

C designates material published after 1588.

This device is a variant of those used in the editions by Strowski, Villey, Plattard and Thibaudet, and in the translations by Ives and Zeitlin. It is necessary for almost any serious study of Montaigne and often for the simplest comprehension. Often in the same chapter – I: 14, II:6 and II:18 are good examples – additions of 1588 or later show a very different attitude from that of the original text in which they are set. An attentive reader unaware of these strata is likely to find Montaigne puzzling and may write him off as irresponsibly inconsistent. The Essays are intended to be a record of change, and the strata indicators help to make this change clear.

Montaigne sometimes alters his original phrasing but keeps his sentence structure, with the result that it is not always possible to read the earlier strata continuously. When changes of this sort are substantive, the revised passage has usually been attached entirely to the later stratum, in order to avoid the danger of attributing later remarks to an earlier period.

The texts used for the translation of the Travel Journal and Letters are discussed in the notes preceding those sections of

TRANSLATOR'S NOTE

this volume (pp. 1049–51, 1273). A list of the most important French editions and English translations can be found in the Select Bibliography (pp. xxx–xxxi).

Several chapters of the Essays – here considerably revised – were published in another form in 1943 by Walter J. Black, Inc. and in 1948 by F. S. Crofts & Co., Inc.

I wish to take this opportunity to thank the staff of Stanford University Press – especially Jesse C. Bell, Jr. and J. Christopher Herold – for their constructive criticism, counsel and suggestions, in helping to prepare this volume for publication. An especially cherished debt is to my wife, Katharine Mailler Frame, for constant encouragement, ready advice and a willing ear.

<div align="right">

Donald M. Frame
1957

</div>

SELECT BIBLIOGRAPHY

EDITIONS

Essais. Ed. by Fortunat Strowski *et al.* 5 vols. Bordeaux: Pech, 1906–33. 'Edition Municipale'. Gives all variants of all six basic editions.

Essais. Ed. by Fortunat Strowski. Hachette,[1] 1912. Phototypic reproduction of 'Bordeaux Copy', showing all Montaigne's handwritten additions of 1588–92.

Essais. Ed. by Pierre Villey. 3 vols. Alcan, 1922–23. Gives strata indications and dates of composition of essays.

Essais. Ed. by Pierre Villey. 3 vols. Alcan, 1930–31. Superb scholarly reader's edition. Gives strata indications and dates of composition.

Essais. Ed. by Jean Plattard. 6 vols. Roches, 1931–33. Reprinted by the Société Les Belles Lettres in 1946–48. Gives strata indications.

Essais. Ed. by Albert Thibaudet. Gallimard, 1934; reprinted with different pagination, 1950. Pléiade edition. The handiest of all and the best all-round edition currently available. Gives strata indications.

L'Italia alla fine del secolo XVI. Giornale del Viaggio di Michele di Montaigne in Italia nel 1580 e 1581. Ed. by Alessandro d'Ancona. Città di Castello: Lapi, 1889. French text, valuable notes in Italian on persons and places mentioned.

Journal de Voyage. Ed. by Louis Lautrey. Hachette, 1906. Offers bold and useful conjectural emendations to text.

Journal de Voyage. Ed. by Arthur Armaingaud. 2 vols. Conard, 1928–29. (Vols. VII–VIII of *Œuvres complètes.*) Accurate text.

Journal de Voyage. Ed. by Silvestre de Sacy. Club Français du Livre, 1954.

Lettres. Ed. by Arthur Armaingaud. Conard, 1939. (Vol. XI, pp. 159–266 of *Œuvres complètes.*) Accurate complete text.

TRANSLATIONS

The Essayes. Tr. by John Florio. London: V. Sims for E. Blount, 1603. First English version, often reprinted.

The Essays. Tr. by Charles Cotton. 3 vols. London: T. Basset, M. Gilliflower and W. Hensman, 1685–86. Often reprinted and revised in the eighteenth and nineteenth centuries.

The Works. Essays tr. by Charles Cotton, revised by the younger William

[1] All books listed in this Bibliography are published in Paris unless otherwise noted.

Hazlitt; 'Diary of a Journey and Letters' tr. by the younger William Hazlitt. London: Templeman, 1842. Contains ten letters. Reprinted several times.

The Works. Essays tr. by Charles Cotton, revised by William Carew Hazlitt; Letters revised by William Carew Hazlitt. 10 vols. New York: Edwin C. Hill, 1910. Thirty-five letters, one of them dubious.

The Essays. Tr. by George B. Ives; introductions by Grace Norton. 4 vols. Cambridge, Mass.: Harvard University Press, 1925. Gives strata indications. Leaves all coarse passages untranslated.

The Essays. Tr. by E. J. Trechmann. 2 vols. Oxford: Oxford University Press, 1927.

The Essays. Tr. by Jacob Zeitlin. 3 vols. New York: Knopf, 1934–36. Excellent Introduction and Notes. Gives strata indications.

The Complete Essays. Tr. by M. A. Screech. London and New York: Penguin, 1993.

The Journal of Montaigne's Travels. Tr. by W. G. Waters. 3 vols. London: John Murray, 1903.

The Diary of Montaigne's Journey to Italy in 1580 and 1581. Tr. by E. J. Trechmann. London: Hogarth Press, 1929.

RECENT STUDIES IN ENGLISH

BURKE, PETER, *Montaigne.* Oxford: Oxford University Press, 1981.

FRAME, DONALD M., *Montaigne: A Biography.* New York: Harcourt/London: Hamish Hamilton, 1965.

——*Montaigne's Discovery of Man: The Humanization of a Humanist.* New York: Columbia University Press, 1955.

FRIEDRICH, HUGO, *Montaigne.* Berkeley: University of California Press, 1991.

SAYCE, RICHARD A., *The Essays of Montaigne.* London: Weidenfeld and Nicolson, 1972.

SCREECH, M. A., *Montaigne and Melancholy.* London: Duckworth, 1983.

There are also classic essays on Montaigne to be found in Virginia Woolf's *The Common Reader* (1925), Eric Auerbach's *Mimesis* (1953) and Emerson's *Representative Men* (1850).

CHRONOLOGY

DATE	AUTHOR'S LIFE	LITERARY CONTEXT
1530		Zwingli: *De providentia Dei*; *Fideo ratio*. Tyndale: *The Practice of Prelates*.
1531		Machiavelli: *Discourses* (posthumous publication).
1532		Machiavelli: *The Prince* (posthumous publication). Rabelais: *Pantagruel*. Calvin's first published work, a commentary on Seneca's *De Clementia*.
1533	Birth of Michel de Montaigne (28 February), the eldest son of Pierre Eyquem de Montaigne, a Gascon gentleman, and Antoinette de Loupes of Toulouse, who was of Spanish Jewish descent, at the château de Montaigne in south-west France, some 30 miles east of Bordeaux. The Eyquem family, wine merchants, had purchased their estate, and the minor nobility it conferred, as recently as 1477. Montaigne's upbringing	Death of Ariosto. 1530s and 40s: Circle of court writers active under patronage of Margaret of Navarre, producing poetry, collections of stories, and translations: these include Clément Marot, Bonaventure des Périers, Antoine Héroët and Margaret herself.
1534	was overseen by his father: he was given peasant godparents in order that he should feel close to the common people, and was sent out to nurse in a nearby village. But he was also educated from infancy by a German	Rabelais: *Gargantua*.
1535	tutor who spoke no French. French was forbidden in the Montaigne household and Michel consequently acquired Latin as his first language.	Erasmus: *Ecclesiastes* (treatise on preaching).

Francis I founds France's first non-theological school of higher learning, the future Collège de France. Diet of Augsburg; Melanchthon draws up Confession of Augsburg, an attempt to conciliate German Catholics and Protestants.

Beginning of period of relative success of 'evangelicals' in France, protected by Margaret of Navarre. Death of Zwingli at the battle of Kappel. Alliance of France and England. Jean du Bellay, moderate reformer, becomes Bishop of Paris. Revival of old College of Arts in Bordeaux under the name Collège de Guyenne, which becomes a centre for the church reform movement (Montaigne letter attends this school). Religious Peace of Nürnberg. Inquisition first established in Lisbon. Conquest of Peru.

The future Henry II of France marries Catherine de' Medici. Nicolas Cop, Rector of the Sorbonne, publicly expounds doctrine of Justification by Faith in a discourse written by Calvin; Francis I enjoins the Paris Parlement to proceed against the 'accursed heretic Lutheran sect'. In England, Thomas Cranmer, Archbishop of Canterbury, grants annulment of Henry VIII's marriage to Catherine of Aragon, and marries him to Anne Boleyn; Henry excommunicated by Pope Clement VII. Advance of Turks into Europe continues: Hungary partitioned between Habsburg and Ottomon empires.

Persecutions cease while Francis I negotiates alliance with German Protestant princes; Guillaume du Bellay, Governor of Piedmont, in conference with Melanchthon. October: 'Affaire des placards'; temporary repression and flight of evangelicals. Twenty-three burnt for heresy 1534–5. Calvin leaves France for Basel, eventually settling in Geneva (1540). Ignatius Loyola founds the Society of Jesus (Jesuits) in Paris. Act of Supremacy confirms Henry VIII as Supreme Head of Church of England. Execution of Sir Thomas More in England. French negotiations with Protestant Princes resume; Guillaume du Bellay in Germany. By the Edict of Coucy, persecutions of Protestants suspended in France.

DATE	AUTHOR'S LIFE	LITERARY CONTEXT
1536	Together with seven siblings, he was brought up a Catholic, but three of them later converted to Protestantism. Somewhat unusually for the time, the family attitude to religion appears to have been tolerant.	Calvin: *Christianae religionis Institutio* (sets out principles of Calvinism, which is embraced by French Protestants). Death of Erasmus.
1537		
1538		Marot: *Collected Works* (and 1544).
1539–46	Michel sent to the Collège de Guyenne in Bordeaux, where his Latin fluency confounds some of the greatest Latinists in France. His teachers include humanists who later became famous – Marc-Antoine Muret and the Scotsman George Buchanan. He enjoys taking leading roles in some of their Latin plays, but otherwise derives little pleasure or satisfaction from his formal schooling.	Antonio de Guevara: *Contempt for the Court and Praise of the Country* (1539). Calvin: *Letter to Cardinal Sadoleto*; *Commentary on the Romans* (1539). Vesalius: *De Humani Corporis Fabrica* (1543). Marot's French translation of the Psalms banned by the Sorbonne (1543). Death of Marot (1544). New French translation of Boccaccio's *Decameron* by Antoine Le Maçon (1545).
1540s		
1546–54	It is generally assumed that Montaigne was a law student at either Bordeaux or Toulouse, though his career has not been firmly established.	Rabelais: *Third Book* (1546).
1547		First published poem of Pierre de Ronsard. Birth of Cervantes.

CHRONOLOGY

HISTORICAL EVENTS

War between France and the Empire (to 1538). Death of Lefèvre d'Etaples, foremost of the early church reformers in France. Dissolution of monasteries begins in England. Tyndale, at the instigation of Henry VIII, burnt at the stake at Vilvorde, near Brussels. European colonization of North America begins with the founding of Montreal by Breton sailor Jacques Cartier.

Pope Paul III commissions enquiry into church reform: Consilium de emendanda ecclesia. Danish and Norwegian churches become Protestant. Completion of the magnificent Château of Chambord for Francis I. Anne, duc de Montmorency, becomes Constable of France (banished from court 1541).
1542 Inquisition established in Rome. France and the Empire at war again (to 1544).
1543 The Sorbonne's Twenty-Six Articles ratified by royal ordinance. Copernicus: *On the Revolution of the Heavenly Spheres* puts forward theory that the earth and planets revolve around the sun.
1544 Calvin's *Institutio* burnt by order of the Paris Parlement.
1545 Opening of the Council of Trent, commisioned by Pope Paul III to define Catholic doctrine and instigate (conservative) reforms in ecclesiastical structure and policy (sits, with interruptions, until 1563). Massacre of the Waldenses in Provence.

Benvenuto Cellini spends five years in the service of Francis I (1540–45); Francis I begins converting the Louvre from a medieval castle to a royal palace, employing the architect Pierre Lescot (1541); François Clouet becomes court painter (1545–72).
Death of Luther. Execution of the 'Fourteen of Meaux' (members of first French Protestant church); in Paris, Etienne Dolet, leading humanist and printer, is among those to suffer the same fate (1546).

Death of Francis I: succeeded by his son, Henry II. Montmorency resumes control of affairs. La Chambre Ardente, a special criminal court for trial of heretics, set up by the Paris Parlement: in the following two years it condemns at least 100 people to death. Other provincial parlements are similarly active. In spite of this, there is no province in France except Brittany in which Protestantism does not gain a foothold.
Death of Henry VIII of England and accession of Edward VI under regency of Protector Somerset. Emperor Charles V defeats German Protestants.

DATE	AUTHOR'S LIFE	LITERARY CONTEXT
1548		Ignatius Loyola: *Spiritual Exercises.* Rabelais: *Fourth Book* (and 1552).
1549		Joachim du Bellay: *Deffence et illustration de la langue françoyse* (programme for renewal of French poetry); *L'Olive* (first French sonnet sequence).
1550		Ronsard: *Odes.* Vasari: *Lives of the most eminent Painters, Sculptors and Architects.*
1552		Ronsard: *Amours.* Etienne Jodelle: *Cléopâtre captive* performed at court (often regarded as the starting point of French classical tragedy).
1553		Servetus: *Christianismi Restitutio* (contains first printed description of pulmonary circulation). Death of Rabelais.
1554	Pierre de Montaigne purchases position in the Cour des Aides of Périgeuex, newly created by Henry II. Shortly afterwards he is elected Mayor of Bordeaux, and passes his councillorship to his son.	Sebastian Castello: *De Haereticis.* Crespin: *Martyrology.*
1555		Ronsard: *Continuation des Amours*; *Les Hymnes.* Birth of François Malherbe.
1556		Ronsard coins the term 'Pléiade' to describe the group of seven poets – himself, Du Bellay, Pontus de Tyard, Baïf, Jodelle, Belleau and Daurat – who were all inspired by the literature of antiquity and of the Italian Renaissance, and who shared

HISTORICAL EVENTS

Betrothal of Mary Stuart to the Dauphin Francis. Architect Philibert
Delorme put in charge of building the palace of Fontainebleau (begun under
Francis I); Italian Mannerist artists Rosso Fiorentino and Primaticcio are
later brought in to assist with the interior decoration.
Act of Uniformity in England: Book of Common Prayer published (and
1552). Death of Margaret of Navarre. War between France and England
(to 1550). The anti-Lutheran *Consensus Tigurinus* of Calvin and Bullinger
unites Protestant Switzerland.

Treaty of Chambord between Henry II and Protestant German princes.
French invasion of Lorraine and occupation of the bishoprics of Metz, Toul
and Verdun.

Execution of the 'Five Scholars of Lausanne' at Lyons. Spanish physician
and theologian Servetus, who had escaped a death sentence pronounced by
the Catholic Inquisitor-General in Lyons, is instead burnt as a heretic by
Calvin in Geneva. In England, death of Edward VI: succeeded by Catholic
Mary I. Prayer Book declared illegal.
Marriage of Philip II of Spain and Mary I. Wyatt's rebellion. Execution of
Lady Jane Grey. Roman Catholicism restored in England.

First Protestant church established in Paris, followed by many others
throughout France (1555–8), largely under Calvin's supervision. Religious
Peace of Augsburg in Germany. Abdication of Emperor Charles V in
favour of his brother Ferdinand I. Renewal of war (to 1559) between France
(in alliance with Pope Paul IV) and the Empire (under Philip II of Spain,
Charles's son and Lord of the Low Countries). Persecution of Protestants in
England: Bishops Hooper, Ridley and Latimer burnt at the stake.
Archbishop Cranmer burnt.

DATE	AUTHOR'S LIFE	LITERARY CONTEXT
1556 *cont.*		a common aim: to elevate contemporary French literature to the same level. In particular they were responsible for the adoption of the sonnet form in France and for establishing the alexandrine as the dominant metrical form in later French poetry. Ronsard: *Nouvelle Continuations des Amours.*
1557	The new court, strongly opposed by existing administrative bodies, is disbanded and incorporated into the Parlement of Bordeaux. Montaigne serves for thirteen tedious years in this body as a *conseiller* (magistrate) in the Chambre des Enquêtes. Forms a close friendship with fellow member Etienne de La Boétie. Makes many trips to Paris and the court in a futile attempt to find more useful and congenial employment.	Pedro Mexia: *Silva* (120 essays dealing with many of the same subjects as Montaigne) translated into French. Du Bellay: *Les Antiquetez de Rome*; *Les Regrets.*
1558		Margaret of Navarre's *Heptameron* first printed posthumously. Du Bellay: *Divers jeux rustiques.* Guy de Bruès: *Dialogues against the New Academics.* John Knox: *First Blast of the Trumpet against the Monstrous Regiment of Women.*
1559		Jacques Amyot: French translation of Plutarch's *Lives.* Du Bellay: *Le poète courtesan.* Pierre Boaystuau: *Theatre of the World.* Calvin: *Confessio Gallicana.*

CHRONOLOGY

England declares war on France. Spaniards defeat French at battle of St Quentin. French crown declared bankrupt. First papal Index of prohibited books (revised 1559 and 1564).

French capture Calais from English. Marriage of Mary Stuart and the Dauphin Francis. Anti-heretical Edict of Compiègne effectively establishes an Inquisition in France. Death of Mary I and accession of Elizabeth I in England.
Death of influential French composer Clément Jannequin (works include *Les Oiseaux*, *Les Cris de Paris* and *La Bataille de Marignan*).

Treaty of Cateau-Cambrésis ends war between France and Empire: French withdraw from Italy but retain the three frontier bishoprics seized in 1552; marriage arranged between Philip II of Spain and Elisabeth of France. Henry II killed in a tournament: accession of his son Francis II, aged 15. Struggle for domination begins between two aristocratic factions, the Catholic House of Guise, led by Charles, Cardinal of Lorraine, and a Huguenot (Protestant) party, led by Louis Bourbon, Prince of Condé. First Protestant Synod held in Paris. Execution of Anne du Bourg, for opposing persecution of Protestants in the Parlement of Paris.
In England, Act of Supremacy declares Elizabeth I Supreme Governor of the Church; Act of Uniformity restores 1552 Prayer Book. In Scotland Protestants rebel against the French regent (Mary of Guise).

DATE	AUTHOR'S LIFE	LITERARY CONTEXT
1560		Death of Joachim du Bellay.
1561		Francesco Guicciardini: *The History of Italy*. Jean Antoine de Baïf: *Twelve Hymns or Spiritual Songs*. Birth of Francis Bacon.
1562		Tasso: *Rinaldo*. Ronsard: *Discours des misères de ce temps*. Birth of Lope de Vega.
1563	Death of La Boétie leaves Montaigne devastated.	John Foxe: *Book of Martyrs*.
1564		Birth of Shakespeare and Marlowe.
1565	After two years of distracting himself from his grief in various love affairs, Montaigne takes his father's advice and marries. His wife is Françoise de La Chassaigne, the daughter of a colleague. Of their six children, only one daughter survives infancy.	Rémy Belleau: *La Bergerie*.
1566		Jean Bodin: *Method for the Easy Understanding of History*.
1567		Baïf founds an 'Académie de poésie et de musique' in Paris (to 1584) – the first of its kind.

HISTORICAL EVENTS

'Tumult of Amboise': Huguenot plot to capture Francis II and arrest the Guises is brutally suppressed. By the influence of Catherine de' Medici, the Queen Mother, the moderate Michel de L'Hôpital is appointed Chancellor of France. Assembly of Notables called, at which a senior statesman, Admiral Gaspard Coligny, is among those who champion the Protestant cause. A further Huguenot rebellion in the south enables the Guises to regain their ascendancy. Condé condemned to death but reprieved by death of Francis II. Catherine de' Medici becomes regent for her second son, the 10-year-old Charles IX: summons French Estates at Orléans.

In Scotland, Calvinism becomes sole established religion.

Royal edict orders religious amnesty. Second Protestant Synod held at Poitiers. French Estates meet at Pontoise. Catherine de' Medici sets up Colloquy of Poissy, attended by leading Catholics and Protestants and the royal family: fails to reach compromise. Her own discussions with Theodore Beza, rector of Calvin's Geneva Academy, arouse Catholic suspicions: Montmorency, François, duc de Guise and Marshal St André form alliance known as the Triumvirate, to counter this threat. Civil disturbances fuelled by religion continue throughout 1561 and 1562.

Mary Stuart returns to Scotland.

Catherine de' Medici summons Conference of St Germain to settle religious differences: edict issued which obliged Protestants to surrender their churches but gave them, for the first time, legal recognition. The Edict of St Germain pleased no one. Beginning of first war of religion (to 1563). Close of the Council of Trent. Antoine de Bourbon, king-consort of Navarre (and father of the future Henry IV), killed at the siege of Rouen (formerly Protestant, he died fighting against them). Murder of the duc de Guise by a Huguenot at the siege of Orléans. Pacification of Amboise: Huguenots allowed to worship within their houses and in certain churches.

Death of Calvin: Beza becomes head of reformed church in France and Geneva. Death of Michelangelo. Birth of Galileo.

Catherine de' Medici commissions building of the Tuileries palace in Paris. Both Philibert Delorme and Jean Bullant work on this project.

Revolt of the Netherlands against Spanish rule. Bullinger draws up Second Helvetic Confession (first in 1536), a full formation of Calvinist doctrines which is influential beyond Switzerland.

Botched attempt by Huguenots to capture the king – 'the Conspiracy of Meaux'. Second French war of religion (to 1568). Montmorency fatally wounded at St Denis.

Death of Monteverdi.

DATE	AUTHOR'S LIFE	LITERARY CONTEXT
1568	Death of his beloved father, Pierre de Montaigne. Title and estate pass to Michel.	
1569	Publishes his translation of *Natural Theology*, by the 15th-century Catalan writer Raymond Sebond. Also edits the works of Etienne de La Boétie.	St Teresa of Avila: *Libro de su vida.* Martin and Guillaume du Bellay: *Memoirs.*
1570	Resigns his office in the Parlement. Visits Paris for publication of La Boétie's works.	Palladio: *Four Books of Architecture.*
1571	Retires to his estate to devote himself to study. Spends 'most of his days, and most hours of the day' in his library.	
1572	Falls into a melancholic depression, to combat which he begins to write the first of his Essays.	Amyot: French translation of Plutarch's *Moral Essays.* Birth of John Donne.
1572–6	Montaigne remains involved in public life, in spite of his retirement. At some point during these years he makes a vain attempt to mediate between Henri de Guise and Henry of Navarre. He receives the Order of Saint Michel and is made a gentleman-in-ordinary of the king's chamber by Charles IX (and later by Henry III and Henry of Navarre). His only surviving daughter, Léonor, is born between 1572 and 1574.	Tasso: *Aminta* (1573). Baïf: *Oeuvres en rime*; *Les Jeux* (1573). Jodelle: *Oeuvres et meslanges poétiques* (1574). French translations of Seneca's *Letters to Lucilius* by Montaigne's brother-in-law Pressac (1574) and the Calvinist nobleman Mornay (1576). Louis Le Roy: *Vicissitude, or Variety of Things in the Universe* (1575).

CHRONOLOGY

Third French war of religion (to 1570). L'Hôpital resigns as chancellor in protest against violence and corruption. Mary Queen of Scots deposed and escapes to England. William Allen founds English Catholic College at Douai. Peace of Adrianople between Habsburgs and Turks.
Condé killed and Huguenots defeated at Jarnac. Huguenots suffer a further defeat and only survive as a group under the leadership of Coligny. English Catholic Northern Rebellion.

Huguenot party re-establishes its strength in the south under Coligny and gains favourable terms at the Treaty of St Germain. Marriage of Charles IX and Elisabeth of Austria. Charles's patronage of Coligny arouses jealousy of Catherine de' Medici and the Guises.
Allied fleet under Don John of Austria defeats Turks at battle of Lepanto. Ridolfi Plot.

Marriage of Margaret of Valois, the king's sister, to Henry of Navarre, now the leader of the Huguenot party. Attempted murder of Coligny at the instigation of the Guises and of Catherine de' Medici: the latter persuades the king to forestall Huguenot reprisals by ordering the massacre of St Bartholomew's Day (23–24 August). Probably intended to be a select killing of Huguenot leaders (Coligny is among them), it escalates into large-scale slaughter: estimates of the numbers killed vary between 2,000 and 20,000 in Paris alone; the killing also spreads to Lyons, Toulouse, Bordeaux and elsewhere. On hearing the news, Pope Gregory XIII publicly celebrates a *Te Deum*. Navarre converts temporarily to Catholicism. Fourth war of religion (to 1573). Siege of La Rochelle by Henry of Anjou, later Henry III. Dutch rebels capture Holland and Zeeland.

Death of Charles IX (1574) and accession of his younger brother, Henry III. Huguenots create an independent state in the south (1574): controlled by the duc de Montmorency-Damille, it incorporates Poitou, Languedoc, Bearn and Provence and has its own army, law courts and system of taxation. The king's younger brother, the duc d'Alençon withdraws there, as does Henry of Navarre (now Protestant again). Death of Charles, Cardinal of Lorraine (1574). Fifth French war of religion (1575–6) ends with Treaty of Monsieur, which grants Huguenots the most generous terms to date.

DATE	AUTHOR'S LIFE	LITERARY CONTEXT
1576	The longest essay, 'Apology for Raymond Sebond', composed. This is considered to mark the end of his 'stoical period' and the beginning of a more sceptical one.	Belleau: *Amours et nouveaux eschanges des pierres précieuses.*
1577		Tycho Brahe: *De Nova Stella.*
1578	Suffers from a kidney stone, the disease that killed his father. At first fearful, he is delighted to find that life is still bearable.	Ronsard: *Sonnets pour Hélène.* Jean de Léry: *Story of a Voyage to Brazil.*
1579		*Defence of Liberty against Tyrants* (Huguenot manifesto). George Buchanan: *The Law of the Kingdom in Scotland* (a justification of the deposition of Mary Queen of Scots, written *c.* 1570, published in 1579 because of its relevance to the situation in France). Spenser: *The Shepherd's Calendar.*
1580	First two books of the Essays published in Bordeaux. They are much admired and go through five editions between 1580 and 1588. Montaigne travels to Paris where he presents a copy to the king. Takes part in the siege of Protestant-held La Fère. Embarks on a trip to Rome (June) for both pleasure and health, travelling via the mineral baths of Germany, Switzerland, Austria and Italy. He is accompanied by his brother and several friends. Keeps a travel journal. Meets Torquato Tasso in Ferrara and Pope Gregory XIII in Rome.	Tasso: *Jerusalem Delivered.*

CHRONOLOGY

Formation of nationwide Catholic League with Henri, duc de Guise (son of François) at its head, in response to the government's return to a policy of concession towards the Huguenots. Local Catholic leagues were already in existence. Treaty of Monsieur rejected at the Estates General, held at Blois. Death of Titian.

For fear of being isolated, Henry III puts himself at head of the Catholic League. Sixth French war of religion. Successful campaign against Huguenots (who were led by Henry of Navarre) ends with Treaty of Bergerac (at which Huguenot gains of Monsieur are withdrawn).
Drake's circumnavigation of the world. Birth of Rubens.
Union of Arras: the ten southern provinces of the Netherlands accept Spanish rule.

Seventh French war of religion (to 1580). Union of Utrecht: the seven northern provinces of the Netherlands declare independence and form the Dutch United Provinces.

Edict of Poitiers ends seventh war of religion and reconfirms terms made at Bergerac in 1577. Spanish conquest of Portugal.

DATE	AUTHOR'S LIFE	LITERARY CONTEXT
1581	Summoned back from Italy to take up office as Mayor of Bordeaux. He had been elected in his absence and originally declined the honour until Henry III commanded him to accept. He arrives home in November.	Francisco Sanchez: *Quod Nihil Scitur* ('Nothing is Known'). Adam Blackwood: *Apologia for Kings*.
1582		
1583	Montaigne is elected for a second two-year term. Bordeaux was Catholic and loyal to Henry III but Montaigne had to contend with ultra-Catholic extremists within the city and Protestant forces nearby. Working closely with the Marshal de Matignon, the king's lieutenant-general in Guienne, he is successful in keeping the peace. Also continues to keep communications open between Protestant Navarre and Catholic France.	
1584	Henry of Navarre and his court stay for two days at Montaigne.	Guillaume Bouchet: *Serées*. Etienne Tabourot: *Bigarrures* (both collections of essays).
1585	At the end of his mayoralty, a serious outbreak of plague in Bordeaux kills nearly half the population. Montaigne, out of town at the time, returns only to the outskirts of the city for the election of his successor, for which he was later criticized.	Death of Ronsard. Nicholas Cholières: *Matinées* (essays). In the Netherlands, Justus Lipsius, an admirer of Montaigne, publishes his edition of Seneca's letters and his own treatise, 'On Constancy'.
1586	Montaigne retires to his estate once more, where he is harassed as a loyal moderate by extremists on both sides during the siege of nearby Protestant-held Castillon by the Catholic League. He is finally driven from his home when plague spreads from the besieged city, and he and his family spend six months on the road.	

CHRONOLOGY

Execution of Edmund Campion, Jesuit missionary, in England.

Reform of the calendar by Pope Gregory XIII.

Death of the duc d'Alençon, Henry III's younger brother and heir.
Protestant Henry of Navarre becomes heir to French throne and is accepted
as such by Henry III. Henri de Guise allies with Spain in support of a
Catholic claimant, the Cardinal de Bourbon. Assassination of William of
Orange. The completion of El Escorial in Spain.
Eighth French war of religion (to 1589). Catholic League revived, at its
strongest and most extreme in Paris, where it attracts support from lawyers,
clerics and artisans alike. A secret council, 'The Sixteen', effectively governs
the city. Henry III, isolated once more, re-allies himself with the Guises and
accepts Cardinal de Bourbon as his heir. Henry of Navarre
excommunicated by Pope Sixtus V.
England sends military aid to Dutch rebels under command of the Earl of
Leicester. Sir Walter Ralegh organizes colonization of Virginia.

DATE	AUTHOR'S LIFE	LITERARY CONTEXT
1587	Writes a great part of Book III of the Essays, plus about 600 additions to Books I and II. Visited by Henry of Navarre at his château on 23 October, following his victory at Coutras (it is thought that the advice of Montaigne, amongst others, may have restrained Navarre from following up this victory with a counter-attack).	Marlowe: *Tamburlaine* (part 1) acted (part II in 1588).
1588	First three-book edition of the Essays published in Paris. Montaigne visits the city for the occasion, but also for political reasons: he was to represent Henry of Navarre, on the instructions of Marshal de Matignon, in negotiations with Henry III, and was the adviser of Navarre's influential mistress, Diane d'Andoins de Gramont. On 10 July he is arrested on the orders of the Catholic League, but promptly released at the command of Catherine de' Medici. Remains with the court for most of the year, but also goes to Picardy to visit the family of his admirer and later literary executrix, Marie de Gournay.	Thomas Kyd: *The Spanish Tragedy.* Lope de Vega, serving with the Armada, writes some of *The Beauty of Angelica.*
1589–92	After the assassination of Henry III, to whom he had remained loyal, Montaigne supports Henry of Navarre who succeeds him as Henry IV. Ill health, however, prevents him from going to court. While writing no new essays, Montaigne continues to revise those already published (in the margins of a 1588 edition now known as the 'Bordeaux Copy') and adds about a thousand new passages. Ill with quinsy and other ailments, he dies peacefully in his bed, listening to Mass, on 13 September 1592.	Shakespeare's first plays written and performed (1589–92). Marlowe: *The Jew of Malta* (1589); *Doctor Faustus* performed (1592). Malherbe: 'Consolation à Monsieur du Périer' (*c.* 1590). Spenser: *The Faerie Queene* (Books I–III) (1590). Sidney: *Arcadia* (1590); *Astrophel and Stella* (1591).

CHRONOLOGY

Navarre defeats Henry III at the battle of Coutras, but his other army (of mercenaries, paid for by the English) is defeated by an army of Guise. Execution of Mary, Queen of Scots. Drake's raid on Cadiz.

Day of Barricades: Henri de Guise marches on Paris and the Sixteen rise up in his support. Royal troops are driven from the city and the king withdraws to Chartres. Henry III forced to sign Edict of Union, once more recognizing Cardinal de Bourbon as his heir and making Guise Lieutenant-General of France. States General meets at Blois (Montaigne was present): Henry III disappointed in his hope for support against the League. He instigates murder of Henri de Guise and his brother, Louis, Cardinal Guise, and tries to come to terms with Henry of Navarre, whom he recognizes as his successor. The League, however, now headed by Charles de Guise, duc de Mayenne, remains in the ascendancy and commands popular support. By the end of 1588, royal power is at a nadir.

1589 Catherine de' Medici dies. Henry III assassinated by a fanatical monk. Ninth French war of religion (to 1598). Catholic League refuses to accept Navarre as lawful king of France. Navarre wins battle of Arques.
1590 Death of Bourbon. Navarre wins battle of Ivry. Paris, however, remains staunchly pro-League. Siege of Paris begins: the Sixteen, with Spanish aid, drive off Huguenot forces.
1591 Earl of Essex commands an English army in France in support of Henry IV. The Sixteen begin fighting among themselves; Mayenne first orders execution of the extremist element, then disbands the group.

DATE	AUTHOR'S LIFE	LITERARY CONTEXT
1593		Shakespeare: *Venus and Adonis*. Marlowe: *Massacre of Paris*. John Donne writing his early poems, the Satires and Elegies (to 1596). Death of Marlowe.
1594		Shakespeare: *The Rape of Lucrece*. Spenser: *Amoretti*; *Epithalamion*.
1595	Marie de Gournay's first complete edition of the Essays.	Soldier-turned-historian Pierre de Bourdeilles de Brantôme embarks upon his *Memoirs*. Sidney: *Defence of Poetry*. Ralegh: *The Discovery of the Empire of Guiana*. Death of Tasso and Kyd.
1598		
1603	First translation of Montaigne's Essays into English, by John Florio.	

CHRONOLOGY

ESSAYS

To the Reader

ᴬThis book was written in good faith, reader. It warns you from the outset that in it I have set myself no goal but a domestic and private one. I have had no thought of serving either you or my own glory. My powers are inadequate for such a purpose. I have dedicated it to the private convenience of my relatives and friends, so that when they have lost me (as soon they must), they may recover here some features of my habits and temperament, and by this means keep the knowledge they have had of me more complete and alive.

If I had written to seek the world's favor, I should have bedecked myself better, and should present myself in a studied posture. I want to be seen here in my simple, natural, ordinary fashion, without straining or artifice; for it is myself that I portray. My defects will here be read to the life, and also my natural form, as far as respect for the public has allowed. Had I been placed among those nations which are said to live still in the sweet freedom of nature's first laws, I assure you I should very gladly have portrayed myself here entire and wholly naked.

Thus, reader, I am myself the matter of my book; you would be unreasonable to spend your leisure on so frivolous and vain a subject.

So farewell. Montaigne, this first day of March, fifteen hundred and eighty.

BOOK ONE

I

By diverse means we arrive at the same end

^AThe commonest way of softening the hearts of those we have
offended, when, vengeance in hand, they hold us at their mercy, is
by submission to move them to commiseration and pity. However,
audacity and steadfastness – entirely contrary means – have some-
times served to produce the same effect.

Edward, prince of Wales, the one who governed our Guienne so
long (a person whose traits and fortune have in them many notable
elements of greatness), having suffered much harm from the
Limousins, and taking their city by force, could not be halted by
the cries of the people and of the women and children abandoned to
the butchery, who implored his mercy and threw themselves at his
feet – until, going farther and farther into the city, he saw three
French gentlemen who with incredible boldness were holding out
alone against the assault of his victorious army. Consideration and
respect for such remarkable valor first took the edge off his anger;
and he began with these three men to show mercy to all the
inhabitants of the city.

As Scanderbeg, prince of Epirus, was pursuing one of his soldiers
in order to kill him, this soldier, after trying by every sort of humility
and supplication to appease him, resolved in the last extremity
to await him sword in hand. This resoluteness of his put a sudden
stop to the fury of his master, who, having seen him take such an
honorable stand, received him into his favor. This example may
suffer another interpretation from those who have not read about
the prodigious strength and valor of that prince.

Emperor Conrad III, having besieged Guelph, duke of Bavaria,
would not come down to milder terms, no matter what vile and
cowardly satisfactions were offered him, than merely to allow the
gentlewomen who were besieged with the duke to go out, their
honor safe, on foot, with what they could carry away on them. They,
great-heartedly, decided to load their husbands, their children, and
the duke himself on their shoulders. The Emperor took such great
pleasure in the nobility of their courage that he wept with delight
and wholly subdued the bitter and deadly hatred which he had

3

borne against this duke, and from that time forward treated him and
his humanely.

^BEither one of these two ways would easily win me, for I am
wonderfully lax in the direction of mercy and gentleness. As a matter
of fact, I believe I should be likely to surrender more naturally
to compassion than to esteem. Yet to the Stoics pity is a vicious
passion; they want us to succor the afflicted, but not to unbend and
sympathize with them.

^ANow these examples seem to me more to the point, inasmuch as
we see these souls, assailed and tested by these two means, hold up
unshaken against one and bow beneath the other. It may be said that
to subdue your heart to commiseration is the act of easygoing
indulgence and softness, which is why the weaker natures, such as
those of women, children, and the common herd, are the most
subject to it; but that, having disdained tears and prayers, to surren-
der simply to reverence for the sacred image of valor is the act of
a strong and inflexible soul which holds in affection and honor
a masculine and obstinate vigor.

However, in less lofty souls, astonishment and admiration
can engender a like effect. Witness the people of Thebes: having
put their generals on trial for their lives for continuing in their
posts beyond the time prescribed and foreordained for them, they
just barely absolved Pelopidas, who bowed under the weight of
such accusations and used only pleas and supplications to protect
himself; whereas with Epaminondas, who came out and related
proudly the things done by him and reproached the people
with them in a haughty ^cand arrogant ^Amanner, they did not
have the heart even to take the ballots into their hands, and
the assembly broke up, greatly praising the loftiness of this man's
courage.

^cDionysius the Elder, having taken the city of Rhegium after
extreme delays and difficulties, and in it the captain Phyto, a first-
rate man, who had defended it most obstinately, decided to make
him a tragic example of vengeance. First he told him how the day
before he had had his son and all his relatives drowned. To which
Phyto replied only that they were thereby happier than he by one
day. After that he had him stripped and seized by executioners, who
dragged him through the town, whipping him very ignominiously
and cruelly and, in addition, heaping on him slanderous and insult-
ing words. But Phyto kept his courage steadfast, not letting himself
go, and with a firm countenance persisted in recalling loudly the

honorable and glorious cause of his death – that he had refused to surrender his country into the hands of a tyrant – and in threatening that tyrant with prompt punishment by the gods. Instead of growing angry at this defiance of a conquered enemy, the rank and file of Dionysius' army showed in their countenance that, disregarding their leader and his triumph, they were softened by astonishment at such rare valor; so that, seeing them on the point of mutiny and about to snatch Phyto from the hands of his sergeants, Dionysius had his martyrdom stopped and secretly sent him to be drowned in the sea.

[A]Truly man is a marvelously vain, diverse, and undulating object. It is hard to found any constant and uniform judgment on him. Here is Pompey pardoning the whole city of the Mamertines, against which he was greatly incensed, in consideration of the valor and magnanimity of the citizen Stheno, who took the fault of the people upon himself alone and asked no other favor but to bear the punishment alone. Yet Sulla's host, who displayed similar valor in the city of Praeneste, got nothing out of it, either for himself or for the others.

[B]And directly contrary to my first examples, the bravest of men and one very gracious to the vanquished, Alexander, forcing the city of Gaza after many great difficulties, came upon Betis – who was in command there and of whose valor he had experienced marvelous proofs during this siege – now alone, abandoned by his men, his armor cut to pieces, all covered with blood and wounds, still fighting on in the midst of many Macedonians who were attacking him from all sides. Stung by such a dearly won victory – for among other damage Alexander had received two fresh wounds on his person – he said to him: "You shall not die as you wanted, Betis; prepare yourself to suffer every kind of torment that can be invented against a captive." The other, with a look not only confident but insolent and haughty, stood without saying a word to these threats. Then Alexander, seeing his proud and obstinate silence: "Has he bent a knee? Has any suppliant cry escaped him? I'll conquer your muteness yet; and if I cannot wring a word from it, at least I'll wring a groan." And turning his anger into rage, he ordered Betis' heels to be pierced through and had him thus dragged alive, torn, and dismembered, behind a cart.

Could it be that hardihood was so common to Alexander that, not marveling at it, he respected it the less? [C]Or did he consider it so peculiarly his own that he could not bear to see it at this

height in another without passionately envious spite? Or was the natural impetuosity of his anger incapable of brooking opposition? In truth, if it could have been bridled, it is probable that it would have been in the capture and desolation of the city of Thebes, at the sight of so many valiant men, lost and without any further means of common defense, cruelly put to the sword. For fully six thousand of them were killed, of whom not one was seen fleeing or asking for mercy, but who were on the contrary seeking, some here, some there, through the streets, to confront the victorious enemy and to provoke an honorable death at his hands. Not one was seen so beaten down with wounds as not to try even in his last gasp to avenge himself, and with the weapons of despair to assuage his death in the death of some enemy. Yet the distress of their valor found no pity, and the length of a day was not enough to satiate Alexander's revenge. This slaughter went on to the last drop of blood that could be shed, and stopped only at the unarmed people, old men, women, and children, so that thirty thousand of them might be taken as slaves.

2
Of sadness

^BI am one of those freest from this passion. ^CI neither like it nor respect it, although everyone has decided to honor it, as if at a fixed price, with particular favor. They clothe wisdom, virtue, conscience with it: a stupid and monstrous ornament! The Italians, more appropriately, have baptized malignancy with its name. For it is always a harmful quality, always insane; and, as being always cowardly and base, the Stoics forbid their sages to feel it.

But ^Athe story goes that when Psammenitus, king of Egypt, after his defeat and capture by Cambyses, king of Persia, saw his daughter pass before him as a prisoner, dressed as a servant and on her way to draw water, while all his friends around him were weeping and lamenting, he himself neither moved nor spoke a word, his eyes fixed on the ground. And further, seeing his son presently being led to his death, he held himself to this same demeanor. But having seen one of his friends led along among the captives, he began to beat his head and manifest extreme grief.

This could be compared with what was seen lately of one of our princes,[1] who, hearing at Trent the news of the death of his older brother – a brother in whom lay the support and honor of his whole house – and soon afterward that of a younger brother, his second hope, withstood these two assaults with exemplary steadfastness; but when a few days afterward one of his men came to die, he let himself go at this last accident and, abandoning his resoluteness, gave himself up to sorrow and mourning, so that some argued that he had been touched to the quick only by this last shock. But the truth was that since he was already brimful of sadness, the slightest overload broke down the barriers of his endurance.

One might, I think, make the same judgment of our story, if it did not add that when Cambyses inquired of Psammenitus why, though unmoved by the misfortune of his son and daughter, he lacked the patience to bear that of one of his friends, he answered: "It is because this last grief alone can be signified by tears; the first two far surpass any power of expression."

Perhaps related to this remark is the idea of the ancient painter who, being obliged to represent the grief of the spectators at the sacrifice of Iphigenia according to the degrees of their concern over the death of this beautiful innocent girl, and having exhausted the utmost powers of his art, when he came to the girl's father portrayed him with his face covered, as if no countenance could represent that degree of grief. That is why the poets show that wretched mother Niobe, overwhelmed by losing first seven sons and then soon after as many daughters, as having been at last transformed into a rock –

<div align="center">

Petrified by her woes

OVID

</div>

– to represent that bleak, dumb, and deaf stupor that benumbs us when accidents surpassing our endurance overwhelm us.

In truth, the impact of grief, to be extreme, must stun the whole soul and impede its freedom of action; as it happens to us, at the hot alarm of some very bad news, to feel ourselves caught, benumbed, and as it were paralyzed from any movements, so that the soul,

1 Charles de Guise, cardinal of Lorraine. The two brothers are François de Lorraine, duke of Guise, assassinated on February 24, 1563, and François de Lorraine, abbot of Cluny, who died on March 6, 1563.

relaxing afterward into tears and lamentations, seems to unbend, extricate itself, and gain more space and freedom.

> ^BAnd grief at long hard last breaks a way for the voice.
>
> <div align="right">VIRGIL</div>

^CIn the war that King Ferdinand waged around Buda against the widow of John, king of Hungary, Raisciac, a German captain, seeing the body of a horseman brought in, whom all had seen doing extremely well in the melee, lamented him with an ordinary lament; but, being curious, like the others, to recognize who he was, he found, after they had taken his armor off, that it was his son. And amid the general tears, he alone remained without giving vent to cries or weeping, erect on his feet, his eyes motionless, staring at him fixedly; until the impact of sorrow, freezing his vital spirits, dropped him in this condition stone dead on the ground.

> ^AHe who can say how he burns, burns little,
>
> <div align="right">PETRARCH</div>

say lovers who want to express an unbearable passion:

> Alas, my senses, dazed,
> Are snatched away. For soon as I have gazed
> On thee, Lesbia, my wits depart amazed,
> I can say nothing.
>
> My tongue is numb, a subtle fire runs round
> Throughout my every limb, my ears resound
> With ringing all their own, both eyes are drowned
> In blackest night.
>
> <div align="right">CATULLUS</div>

^BNor is it in the live and most ardent heat of passion that we are fit to set forth our amorous complaints and pleadings; the soul is then burdened with deep thoughts, and the body weighed down and languishing with love.

^AAnd from that is sometimes engendered the accidental failing that surprises lovers so unseasonably, and that frigidity that seizes them by the force of extreme ardor in the very lap of enjoyment.[2] All

2 The 1588 edition here shows an addition that Montaigne later crossed out: "an accident that is not unknown to me."

passions that allow themselves to be savored and digested are only mediocre.

> Light cares can speak, but heavy ones are dumb.
>
> <div align="right">SENECA</div>

[B]The surprise of an unexpected pleasure stuns us in the same way:

> When, dazed, she saw me come, and with me all around
> Trojans and Trojan arms, wonder made her afraid,
> She stiffened in mid gaze, the warmth out of her fled.
> She crumples, and much later with difficulty speaks.
>
> <div align="right">VIRGIL</div>

[A]Besides the Roman woman who died overcome with gladness to see her son back from the rout at Cannae, Sophocles and Dionysius the tyrant, who passed away for gladness, and Talva, who died in Corsica reading the news of the honors that the Senate of Rome had decreed for him, we understand that in our time Pope Leo X, upon being advised of the taking of Milan, which he had ardently desired, fell into such an excess of joy that a fever got him and he died. And as a more remarkable testimony of human frailty, it was noted by the ancients that Diodorus the dialectician died on the spot, seized with an extreme passion of shame, for not having been able to shake loose, in his own school and in public, from an argument that had been put to him.

[B]I am little subject to these violent passions. My susceptibility is naturally tough; and I harden and thicken it every day by force of reason.

<div align="center">3

Our feelings reach out beyond us</div>

[B]Those who accuse men of always gaping after future things, and teach us to lay hold of present goods and settle ourselves in them, since we have no grip on what is to come (indeed a good deal less than we have on what is past), put their finger on the commonest of human errors – if they dare to call an error something to which Nature herself leads us in serving the continuation of her work, [C]and which, more zealous for our action than for our knowledge, she imprints in us like many other false notions. [B]We are never at home, we are always beyond. Fear, desire, hope, project us toward

the future and steal from us the feeling and consideration of what is, to busy us with what will be, even when we shall no longer be. ^C*A soul anxious about the future is most vulnerable* [Seneca].

This great precept is often cited in Plato: "Do thy job and know thyself." Each of its two parts generally includes our whole duty, and likewise includes its fellow. He who would do his job would see that his first lesson is to know what he is and what is proper for him. And he who knows himself no longer takes extraneous business for his own; he loves and cultivates himself before anything else; he refuses superfluous occupations and useless thoughts and projects. *As folly, though it has gotten what it wanted, yet never thinks it has obtained enough; so wisdom is always content with the present and never displeased with itself* [Cicero]. Epicurus dispenses his sage from foresight and concern for the future.

^BAmong the laws that concern the dead, this one seems to me as solid as any, which obliges the actions of princes to be examined after their death. They are equals with, if not masters of, the laws; what justice could not do to their persons, it should rightfully be able to do to their reputations and to the property of their successors – things that we often prefer to life. It is a custom that brings singular advantages to the nations in which it is observed, and desirable to all good princes, ^Cwho have reason to complain that the memory of the wicked is honored like their own.

We owe subjection and obedience equally to all kings, for that concerns their office; but we do not owe esteem, any more than affection, except to their virtue. Let us make this concession to the political order: to suffer them patiently if they are unworthy, to conceal their vices, to abet them by commending their indifferent actions if their authority needs our support. But, our dealings over, it is not right to deny to justice and to our liberty the expression of our true feelings, and especially to deny good subjects the glory of having reverently and faithfully served a master whose imperfections were so well known to them, and thus to deprive posterity of such a useful example. And those who out of respect for some private obligation unjustly espouse the memory of a blameworthy prince, do private justice at the expense of public justice. Livy says truly that the language of men brought up under royalty is always full of foolish ostentation and vain testimonies, each man indiscriminately raising his king to the highest level of worth and sovereign greatness.

One may reprove the fine candor of those two soldiers who answered Nero to his beard. One, asked by him why he wished him ill: "I loved you when you were worthy of it; but since you have become a parricide, a firebug, a mountebank, a charioteer, I hate you as you deserve." The other, asked why he wanted to kill him: "Because I find no other remedy against your continual wicked deeds." But as for the public and universal testimonies to his vile and tyrannical deportment that were given after his death and will be given for all time, what man of sound understanding can reprove them?

I dislike the fact that in such a saintly government as the Lacedaemonian should be found such a hypocritical ceremony as this: At the death of the kings all the confederates and neighbors, all the Helots, men, women, and all, would cut their foreheads as a token of mourning and say in their cries and lamentations that that one, whatever he may have been, was the best king they ever had; attributing to rank the praise that belonged to merit, and the praise that belonged to the highest merit to the latest and lowest rank.

Aristotle, who discusses and stirs up everything, inquires in connection with Solon's saying that no man can be called happy before his death, whether even a man who has lived and died in good order can be called happy if his reputation is in bad shape or if his posterity is miserable. While we move about, we transport ourselves by anticipation wherever we please; but once out of being, we have no communication with what is; and it would be better to say to Solon that man is never happy, then, since he is so only after he is no more.

> [B]A man does not
> Uproot himself from life, and cast his self away;
> Unconsciously he dreams some part of him will stay...
> Nor from his cast-off body does he depart enough
> And free himself.
>
> LUCRETIUS

[A]Bertrand du Guesclin died commanding the siege of the castle of Randon, near Le Puy in Auvergne. The besieged, when they surrendered after his death, were obliged to place the keys of the fortress on the dead man's body.

When Bartolomeo Alviano, general of the Venetian army, had died in the service of the wars Venice waged against Brescia, and his body had to be brought back to Venice through the enemy territory

of Verona, most of the army thought they should ask the people of Verona for safe-conduct to pass through. But Teodoro Trivulzio opposed this, and chose rather to pass by main force with the risks of battle; it was not fitting, he said, that he who in life had never been afraid of his enemies should have the appearance of fearing them in death.

[B]Indeed, in a related matter, by Greek laws he who asked the enemy for a body to bury it renounced the victory, and it was no longer lawful for him to erect a trophy. To him who was asked this, it was proof of winning. Thus Nicias lost the advantage that he had clearly gained over the Corinthians, and conversely, Agesilaus ensured the one which he had very doubtfully won over the Boeotians.

[A]These actions might seem strange if it were not an accepted practice in all ages to extend the concern we have for ourselves beyond this life, and even to believe that very often celestial favors accompany us to the tomb and continue to operate in our bones. Of which there are so many ancient examples, leaving aside our own, that there is no need for me to elaborate. Edward I, king of England, found in his long wars with King Robert of Scotland how much advantage his presence gave to his affairs, so that he always carried off the victory in what he undertook in person. Accordingly, when he came to die, he obliged his son by a solemn oath to have his body boiled to detach his flesh from the bones. The flesh should be interred; the bones his son should save, to carry with him in his army every time he should happen to be at war against the Scots. As if destiny had fatally attached victory to his limbs.

[B]John Vischa [Zizka], who troubled Bohemia in defense of Wiclif's errors, willed to be flayed after his death and to have a drum made of his skin to carry into war against his enemies; thinking that this would help continue the advantages he had obtained in the wars he had conducted against them. Thus certain Indians carried into combat against the Spaniards the bones of one of their captains, in consideration of the success he had had when alive. And other peoples in this same New World bring to war the bodies of the valiant men who have died in their battles to serve them as good luck and encouragement.

[A]The first examples reserve for the tomb only the reputation acquired by their past actions; but these want to add even the power to act.

Of a finer temper is the deed of Captain Bayard, who, feeling himself wounded to death by a harquebus shot in the body, and advised to withdraw from the fight, replied that he would not begin at the end of his life to turn his back on the enemy. Having fought as long as he had strength, and feeling himself faint and slipping from his horse, he ordered his steward to lay him down at the foot of a tree, but in such a way that he should die with his face turned toward the enemy; as he did.

I must add this other example, as remarkable for the present consideration as any of the preceding ones. Emperor Maximilian, the great-grandfather of the present King Philip, was a prince superabundantly endowed with great qualities, and among others with singular bodily beauty. But among his humors was this one, very contrary to that of the princes who to dispatch their most important affairs make their throne of their toilet seat: that he never had a personal servant so familiar that he would allow him to see him in his privy. He would hide to make water, as scrupulous as a virgin not to uncover, either to a doctor or to anyone else whatever, the parts that are customarily kept hidden. [B]I, who am so bold-mouthed, am nevertheless by nature affected by this shame. Except under great stress of necessity or voluptuousness, I hardly communicate to the sight of anyone the members and acts that our custom orders us to cover up. I suffer from more constraint in this than I consider becoming to a man, and especially to a man of my profession.[1] But Emperor Maximilian reached [A]such a point of superstition that he ordered in so many words in his will that they should put underdrawers on him when he was dead. He should have added a codicil that the man who put them on should be blind-folded.

[C]The order that Cyrus gave his children, that neither they nor any other should see or touch his body after the soul had left it, I attribute to some devout feeling of his. For both his historian [Xenophon] and himself, among their great qualities, disseminated through the whole course of their lives a singular concern and reverence for religion.

[B]I did not like this story that a great personage told me of a connection of mine, a man pretty well known both in peace and war. It is that, dying at a very old age in his court, tormented with

1 As a nobleman and one who had borne arms, Montaigne considered his profession to be that of soldier.

acute pain from the stone, he occupied all his last hours with a vehement concern about arranging the pomp and ceremony of his funeral, and pressed all the noblemen that visited him to give him their word to be present at the procession. Even to this prince, who saw him in this final stage, he made urgent entreaty that his household be ordered to be there, using many examples and reasons to prove that it was something due to a man of his condition; and he seemed to die content, having extracted this promise and ordered the arrangement and plan of his funeral to his taste. I have scarcely seen any vanity so persevering.

The opposite kind of preoccupation, of which also I have no lack of examples close to home, seems to me germane to this one: to fret and fuss at this last stage over planning one's funeral so as to effect some trifling and unusual economy – one servant and one lantern. I see this humor praised, as was the command of Marcus Aemilius Lepidus, who forbade his heirs to employ for him the ceremonies that had been customary in such matters. Is it still temperance and frugality to avoid expenses and pleasures whose use and knowledge are imperceptible to us? An easy way to reform and a cheap one!

ᶜIf it were necessary to make an ordinance about it, I should judge that in this, as in all actions of life, each man should relate his rule to the shape of his fortune. The philosopher Lyco wisely instructed his friends to place his body where they should judge best, and as for the funeral, to make it neither extravagant nor mean. ᴮI shall let custom order this ceremony entirely, and shall leave it to the discretion of the first people into whose charge I fall. ᶜ*This care is to be entirely despised for ourselves, but not neglected for ours* [Cicero]. And it is a saintly saying of a saint: *The arranging of funerals, the conditions of burials, the pomp of obsequies, are rather a consolation for the living than any help to the dead* [Saint Augustine]. Therefore Socrates, to Crito, who at the hour of his death asks him how he wants to be buried, answers: "As you wish."

ᴮIf I had to become more involved in this matter, I should find it more sprightly to imitate those who undertake, while alive and breathing, to enjoy the arrangement and honor of their obsequies, and who take pleasure in seeing their dead countenance in marble. Happy are those who can delight and gratify their sense by insensibility, and live by their death.

ᶜI am almost ready to vow irreconcilable hatred against all democratic rule, although it seems to me the most natural and equitable, when I remember that inhuman injustice of the Athenian

people, who killed their brave captains without remission and without even consenting to hear them in their own defense, because after their victory over the Lacedaemonians in the naval battle near the Arginusian Isles – the most sharply contested and the greatest battle that the Greeks ever fought at sea with their own forces – they had pursued the chances that the rules of war offered them rather than stopping to gather up and bury their dead. And the behavior of Diomedon makes this execution still more odious. He was one of the condemned men, a man of notable virtue, both military and political. Coming forward to speak after hearing the sentence that condemned them, and finding only then a chance for a peaceable hearing, instead of using this for his own cause and for exposing the evident injustice of so cruel a decision, he expressed only concern for the continued safety of his judges. He prayed the gods to turn this judgment to their advantage, and informed them of what vows he and his companions had made in gratitude for such a glorious success, lest by failing to fulfill those vows the people should draw down the wrath of the gods upon them. And without saying another thing and without hesitating, he went directly and courageously to his death.

Fortune, a few years after, punished them with a taste of their own medicine. For after Chabrias, commander in chief of the naval forces of the Athenians, had had the upper hand in combat against Pollis, admiral of Sparta, at the island of Naxos, he clean and clear lost the fruits of his victory, a very important one for their affairs, in order not to incur the same misfortune. And so as not to lose a few dead bodies of his friends which were floating on the sea, he let a whole world of living enemies sail away in safety, who later made the Athenians pay dear for this importunate superstition.

> You ask where you will lie after your death?
> Where lie the souls unborn.
> SENECA

Another man restores the sense of repose to a body without a soul:

> And let him have no tomb, no haven of repose,
> To give his lifeless body respite from his woes.
> ENNIUS, QUOTED BY CICERO

Even so nature shows us that many dead things still have occult relations to life. Wine alters in the cellars according to certain seasonal changes in its vine. And venison changes its condition

and flavor in the salting tubs according to the laws of the live flesh, so they say.[2]

4
How the soul discharges its passions on false objects when the true are wanting

[A]One of our gentlemen who was wondrously subject to the gout, on being urged by the doctors to give up entirely the use of salt meats, used to answer them very humorously that in the agonies and torments of the illness he wanted to have something to blame, and by crying out and cursing now the sausage, now the ox tongue and the ham, he felt just that much relieved. But in all seriousness, just as when the arm is raised to strike, it hurts us if the blow does not land and is wasted on the air; also as the sight, to make a pleasant view, must not be lost and led away in the vague reaches of the air, but must have some bound to sustain it at a reasonable distance;

[B]As wind loses its strength, diffused in empty space,
 Unless some strong dense wood resists its forward pace;

LUCAN

[A]so it seems that the soul, once stirred and set in motion, is lost in itself unless we give it something to grasp; and we must always give it an object to aim at and act on. Plutarch says of those who grow fond of monkeys and little dogs that the loving part that is in us, lacking a legitimate object, rather than remain idle, thus forges itself a false and frivolous one. And we see that the soul in its passions will sooner deceive itself by setting up a false and fantastical object, even contrary to its own belief, than not act against something.

[B]Thus animals are carried away by their rage to attack the stone or the metal that has wounded them and to take revenge tooth and nail on themselves for the pain they feel.

So the Pannonian bear, made fiercer by the sting,
When struck by the dart from the Lybian hunter's sling,

2 This last paragraph of the chapter appears in the 1595 edition by Marie de Gournay but not in the Bordeaux Copy, nor is there any trace of it there. Most editors accept it as probably written by Montaigne.

Turns on the wound enraged, attacks the buried spear,
Which whirls as she whirls after, flees as she draws near.

<div align="right">LUCAN</div>

^AWhat causes do we not invent for the misfortunes that befall us?
On what do we not place the blame, rightly or wrongly, so as to have
something at which to thrust? It is not those blond tresses that you
are tearing, nor the whiteness of that bosom that in your anger
you beat so cruelly, that have made you lose by an unlucky bullet that
well-loved brother: place the blame elsewhere. ^CLivy, speaking of
the Roman army in Spain after the loss of the two brothers,[1] their
great captains, says: *Immediately all began to weep and beat their
heads.* It is a common practice. And was it not amusing of the
philosopher Bion to say about that king who was tearing his hair
for grief, "Does this man think that baldness relieves grief?" ^AWho
has not seen people chew and swallow the cards or stuff themselves
with a set of dice to avenge the loss of their money? Xerxes whipped
the waters ^Cof the Hellespont, put irons on it and had a thousand
insults hurled at it, ^Aand wrote a challenge to Mount Athos. Cyrus
wasted a whole army's time for several days taking vengeance on the
river Gyndus for the fright he had had crossing it. And
Caligula ruined a very beautiful house for the displeasure[2] that his
mother had had there.

^CIn my youth the people used to say that one of our neighboring
kings, having received a beating from God, swore to take revenge;
and ordered that for ten years no one should pray to God, or speak of
him, or, as far as the king's authority could prevent it, believe in him.
By which they wanted to portray not so much the folly as the
vainglory natural to the nation about whom the story was told.
These are vices that always go together; but in truth such actions
spring from presumption even more than from stupidity.

^AAugustus Caesar, having been battered by a tempest at sea, set
about defying the god Neptune, and in the celebration of the circus
games had his image removed from the place where it was among
the other gods, to take vengeance on him. Wherein he is still less
excusable than the preceding ones, and less than he was later, when,
having lost a battle under Quintilius Varus in Germany, he went

1 Publius and Cnaeus Scipio.
2 Montaigne's text reads "pleasure," but apparently this is oversight, not para-
dox; for the passage in Seneca tells the story about a place where Caligula's
mother had been a prisoner.

about in anger and despair banging his head against the wall and crying: "Varus, give me back my soldiers." For those surpass all madness who, adding impiety to folly, turn their blame against God himself, or against Fortune, as if she had ears susceptible to our assault; ^Clike the Thracians who, when there is thunder or lightning, start shooting at the heavens with a Titan's vengeance, to bring God to reason by arrow shots. ^ANow, as that ancient poet says in Plutarch,

> Anger at things that happen shows small wit;
> For all our wrath concerns them not a bit.
>
> AUTHOR UNKNOWN

^BBut we shall never heap enough insults on the unruliness of our mind.

5
Whether the governor of a besieged place should go out to parley

^ALucius Marcius, legate of the Romans in the war against Perseus, king of Macedonia, wishing to gain the time he still needed to get his army fully ready, made some propositions pointing to an agreement, which lulled the king into granting a truce for a few days and thereby furnished his enemy with opportunity and leisure to arm. As a result, the king incurred his final ruin. Yet the old men of the Senate, remembering the mores of their fathers, condemned this practice as hostile to their old way – ^Cwhich was, said they, to fight in valor, not in trickery, or by surprises and night encounters, or by pretended flights and unexpected countercharges; starting war only after having announced it, and often after having assigned the time and place of the battle. Because of this scrupulousness they had sent back to Pyrrhus his treacherous doctor, and to the Faliscans their evil schoolmaster. These were truly Roman ways, not those of Greek subtlety and Punic cunning, according to which it was less glorious to conquer by force than by fraud. Deceit may serve for the moment; but only that man considers himself overcome who knows he was downed neither by trick nor by luck but by valiance, man to man, in a fair and just war. ^AIt clearly appears from the language of these good men that they had not yet accepted this fine saying:

Courage or ruse – against an enemy, who cares?
<div align="right">VIRGIL</div>

^CThe Achaeans, says Polybius, detested all manner of deceit in their wars, seeing no victory except where the courage of the enemy was subdued. *The pure and wise man will know only that victory to be real which is obtained with faith unbroken and dignity intact*, says another [Florus].

> Whether 'tis Fortune's will that you shall rule, or I,
> Or what, let us test by valor.
> <div align="right">ENNIUS, QUOTED BY CICERO</div>

In the kingdom of Ternate,[1] among those nations that we so smugly call barbarians, custom has it that they never start a war without having first announced it, adding to this an ample declaration of the means that they have to employ in it: what sort of men and how many, what supplies, what offensive and defensive weapons. But also, that being done, if their enemies do not yield and come to an agreement, they give themselves the right to do their worst, and do not think they can be reproached for treason, ruse, and any other means whatever that serves to conquer.

The ancient Florentines were so far from wanting to gain an advantage over their enemies by surprise that they used to warn them a month before putting their army in the field by the continual ringing of the bell they called Martinella.

^AAs for us, who, less superstitious, hold that the man who has the profit of war has the honor of it, and who say, after Lysander, that where the lion's skin will not suffice we must sew on a bit of the fox's, the most usual chances for surprise are derived from this practice of trickery. And there is no time, we say, when a leader must be more on the watch than that of parleys and peace treaties. And for that reason there is a rule in the mouth of all military men of our time, that the governor of a besieged place must never go out himself to parley. In our fathers' day the seigneurs de Montmord and de Lassigny, defending Mouzon against the count of Nassau, were blamed for this. But also, by this reckoning, a man would be excusable who went out in such a way that the security and advantage remained on his side; as Count Guido Rangone did at the city of Reggio (if we are to believe Du Bellay, for Guicciardini says it was

1 Island in Indonesia, east of Celebes.

he himself) when the seigneur de l'Escut approached to parley. For he stayed so close to his fort that when trouble broke out during this parley, Monsieur de l'Escut not only found himself and his accompanying troop the weaker, so that Alessandro Trivulzio was killed there, but was constrained, for greater security, to follow the count and trust himself to his good faith, taking shelter from the shots inside the town.

^BAntigonus, who was besieging Eumenes in the town of Nora, urged him to come out and talk, alleging after several other attempts that it was right that Eumenes should come to him, seeing that he, Antigonus, was the greater and stronger. To which Eumenes made this noble answer: "I will never consider any man greater than I as long as I have my sword within my power"; and he would not consent until Antigonus had given him his own nephew Ptolomaeus as a hostage, as he asked.

^AYet it is true that there are some who have done very well by coming out on the attacker's word. Witness Henri de Vaux, a knight of Champagne, who was besieged in the castle of Commercy by the English. Barthélemy de Bonnes, who commanded the siege, after having the greater part of the castle sapped from outside, so that nothing remained but setting fire in order to overwhelm the besieged beneath the ruins, asked the aforesaid Henri to come out and parley for his own good; this Henri did, preceded by three other men. And, convinced by what he was shown that he would have been ruined without fail, he felt remarkably obliged to his enemy, to whose discretion he surrendered himself and his forces. After this, the fire was set to the mine, the wooden props gave way, and the castle was demolished from top to bottom.

^BI put my trust easily in another man's word. But I should do so reluctantly whenever I would give the impression of acting from despair and want of courage rather than freely and through trust in his honesty.

6
Parley time is dangerous

^AHowever, I saw recently in my neighborhood at Mussidan that those who were forcibly driven out from there by our army, and others of their party, screamed as at treachery because during the

discussion of terms, and while the treaty was still in effect, they had been surprised and cut to pieces: a complaint which might have had some plausibility in another century. But as I have just said, our ways are utterly remote from these rules; and parties should not trust one another until the last binding seal has been set. Even then there is plenty of room for wariness.

^CAnd it has always been a hazardous plan to trust to the license of a victorious army the observance of a promise given to a town that has just surrendered on mild and favorable terms, and to allow the soldiers free entry in the heat of victory. L. Aemilius Regillus, the Roman praetor, after wasting his time trying to take the city of Phocaea by force, because of the singular prowess of the inhabitants in defending themselves stoutly, made a pact with them to accept them as friends of the Roman people and to enter theirs as a confederate city, taking from them all fear of hostile action. But having brought his army in with him, to display himself in greater pomp, he was unable, for all the efforts he put forth, to keep his men in check; and he saw a good part of the city sacked before his eyes, the claims of avarice and vengeance trampling under foot those of his authority and of military discipline.

^ACleomenes used to say that whatever harm you could do to your enemies in war was above justice and not subject to it in respect to either gods or men. And, after making a truce with the Argives for seven days, on the third night he went and attacked them as they all slept and killed them, alleging that in his truce there had been no mention of the nights. But the gods avenged this perfidious subtlety.

^CDuring a parley and while its inhabitants were daydreaming about their security, the town of Casilinum was taken by surprise, and that in the age of the justest captains and the most perfect Roman discipline. For it is not said that, at a given time and place, it is not permissible for us to take advantage of the stupidity of our enemies, as we do of their cowardice. And indeed war has by nature many privileges that are reasonable even at the expense of reason. And here the rule breaks down, *that no one should do a thing that will prey on another's ignorance* [Cicero]. But I am astonished at the range that Xenophon gives these privileges, both by the statements and by various exploits of his perfect emperor; he an author of marvelous weight in such matters, as a great captain and a philosopher among the first disciples of Socrates. And I do not agree to the extent of his dispensation, in all things and throughout.

^A When Monsieur d'Aubigny was besieging Capua and had given it a furious battering, and Signor Fabrizio Colonna, governor of the town, had begun to parley from on top of a bastion and his men relaxed their guard, our men took possession of the place and cut the enemy to pieces. And in more recent memory at Yvoy, Signor Giuliano Romero, having made the novice's blunder of going out to parley with the Constable, on his return found his place seized. But so as not to leave us without our side of the story: when the marquis of Pescara was besieging Genoa, where Duke Ottaviano Fregoso was in command under our protection, the agreement between them had been pushed forward so far that they considered it completed; but on the point of its conclusion the Spaniards, having slipped inside, made use of their advantage as if it had been a full-fledged victory. And since then, when Ligny-en-Barrois was being besieged by the Emperor in person, its commander, the count of Brienne, sent his lieutenant, Bertheville, out to parley, and during the bargaining the town was taken.

> To conquer always was a glorious thing,
> Whether achieved by fortune or by skill,
>
> ARIOSTO

so they say. But the philosopher Chrysippus would not have been of that opinion, and I just as little. For he used to say that those who run a race should indeed employ their whole strength for speed but that, nevertheless, it was not in the least permissible for them to lay a hand on their adversary to stop him, or to stick out a leg to make him fall.

^B And still more generously that great Alexander answered Polypercon, who was trying to persuade him to take advantage of the darkness of night to attack Darius: "I will not," he said; "I am not the man to steal my victories"; *I would rather be sorry for my fortune than ashamed of my victory* [Quintus Curtius].

> Nor did he deign to knock down from the rear
> Fleeing Orodes with an unseen spear:
> He passes, veers, and man to man, in fight,
> He proves the better, not by stealth but might.
>
> VIRGIL

7

That intention is judge of our actions

ᴬDeath, they say, acquits us of all our obligations. I know those who have taken this in a strange sense. Henry VII, king of England, made an agreement with Don Philip, son of Emperor Maximilian – or, to place him more honorably, father of Emperor Charles V – that the said Philip would deliver into his hands the duke of Suffolk of the White Rose, his enemy, who had escaped and withdrawn to the Low Countries, in exchange for which Henry promised to make no attempt on the life of the said duke. However, nearing death, Henry ordered in his will that his son should have the duke killed as soon as he, Henry, was dead.

Recently, in the tragedy that the duke of Alva showed us in Brussels involving the counts of Horn and of Egmont, there were plenty of noteworthy events, among them that the said count of Egmont, on whose faith and assurance the count of Horn had come and given himself up to the duke of Alva, demanded most insistently that he should himself be killed the first, so that his death should free him from his obligation to the said count of Horn.

It seems to me that death did not discharge King Henry from his promise, and that the count of Egmont was quit of his even without dying. We cannot be bound beyond our powers and means. For this reason – that we have no power to effect and accomplish, that there is nothing really in our power but will – all man's rules of duty are necessarily founded and established in our will. Thus the count of Egmont, considering his soul and will in debt to his promise, though the power to carry it out was not in his hands, was certainly absolved of his duty even had he survived the count of Horn. But the king of England, in intentionally breaking his word, cannot be excused merely on the ground that he delayed the execution of his dishonest plan until after his death; any more than Herodotus' mason, who, having loyally kept during his life the secret of the treasures of his master the king of Egypt, revealed it to his children as he died.

ᶜI have seen several in my time, convicted by their conscience of keeping other people's goods, plan to make restitution in their will after death. By delaying a thing so urgent and wishing to right a wrong with so little feeling and sacrifice, they do no good. They owe a part of what is most their own. And the more onerous and

inconvenient their restitution, the more just and deserving it is. Penitence demands a burden.

They do still worse who save till their dying wish the revelation of some hateful intent against those near to them, which they have hidden during their life. They show they have small care for their own honor, by irritating the offended person against their memory, and less for their conscience, by failing to kill their ill will, even out of respect for death, and by extending its life beyond their own. Unjust judges, who put off judging till they no longer know the case!

If I can, I shall keep my death from saying anything that my life has not already said.

8
Of idleness

AJust as we see that fallow land, if rich and fertile, teems with a hundred thousand kinds of wild and useless weeds, and that to set it to work we must subject it and sow it with certain seeds for our service; and as we see that women, all alone, produce mere shapeless masses and lumps of flesh, but that to create a good and natural offspring they must be made fertile with a different kind of seed; so it is with minds. Unless you keep them busy with some definite subject that will bridle and control them, they throw themselves in disorder hither and yon in the vague field of imagination.

> BThus, in a brazen urn, the water's light
> Trembling reflects the sun's and moon's bright rays,
> And, darting here and there in aimless flight,
> Rises aloft, and on the ceiling plays.
>
> VIRGIL

AAnd there is no mad or idle fancy that they do not bring forth in this agitation:

> Like a sick man's dreams,
> They form vain visions.
>
> HORACE

The soul that has no fixed goal loses itself; for as they say, to be everywhere is to be nowhere:

> BHe who dwells everywhere, Maximus, nowhere dwells.
>
> MARTIAL

[A]Lately when I retired to my home, determined so far as possible to bother about nothing except spending the little life I have left in rest and seclusion, it seemed to me I could do my mind no greater favor than to let it entertain itself in full idleness and stay and settle in itself, which I hoped it might do more easily now, having become weightier and riper with time. But I find –

> Ever idle hours breed wandering thoughts
> LUCAN

– that, on the contrary, like a runaway horse, it gives itself a hundred times more trouble than it took for others, and gives birth to so many chimeras and fantastic monsters, one after another, without order or purpose, that in order to contemplate their ineptitude and strangeness at my pleasure, I have begun to put them in writing, hoping in time to make my mind ashamed of itself.

9
Of liars

[A]There is no man who has less business talking about memory. For I recognize almost no trace of it in me, and I do not think there is another one in the world so monstrously deficient. All my other faculties are low and common; but in this one I think I am singular and very rare, and thereby worthy of gaining a name and reputation.

[B]Besides the natural inconvenience that I suffer by this – [C]for certainly, in view of its necessity, Plato is right to call memory a great and powerful goddess – [B]if in my part of the country they want to say that a man has no sense, they say he has no memory. And when I complain of the defectiveness of mine, they argue with me and do not believe me, as if I were accusing myself of witlessness. They see no distinction between memory and understanding. This makes me look a lot worse than I am.

But they do me wrong. For rather the opposite is seen by experience: that excellent memories are prone to be joined to feeble judgments. They do me wrong also in this, I who know how to do nothing so well as be a friend: that by the very words they use to denounce my malady they also make me look ungrateful. They blame my feelings for my want of memory, and of a natural lack they make a lack of conscience. "He has forgotten," they say, "this request or that promise. He does not remember his friends. He did

not remember to say, or do, or be silent about such and such a thing, for my sake." Certainly I may easily forget; but careless about the charge with which my friend has entrusted me, that I am not. Let them be content with my infirmity, without making it into a sort of malice, and a malice so alien to my nature.

I have some consolation. First, because ^Cit is an evil that has shown me the way to correct a worse evil which would easily have developed in me – to wit, ambition; for lack of memory is intolerable in anyone who is involved in public negotiations. Because, as several similar examples of nature's processes demonstrate, nature has tended to strengthen other faculties in me in proportion as my memory has grown weaker; and I might easily rest my mind and judgment and let them grow languid following on others' traces, as everyone does, without exercising their own strength, if other men's discoveries and opinions were always present to me by virtue of my memory. ^BMy speech is the briefer for it. For the magazine of memory is apt to be better furnished with matter than that of invention. ^C(If my memory had stood me in good stead, I would have deafened all my friends with babble; for topics arouse the faculty, such as it is, that I have of handling and treating them, warming up my arguments and leading them on.) ^BThis is a pity.[1] I see it confirmed by the example of some of my close friends: to the extent that memory supplies them with the thing as present and entire, they push their narrative so far back and load it with such pointless circumstances, that if the story is good they smother its goodness; if it is not, you are left cursing either the felicity of their memory or the infelicity of their judgment. ^CAnd it is a difficult thing to close a train of speech and cut it short once you are under way. There is nothing in which the strength of a horse is better recognized than in making a full sharp stop. Even among people who speak to the point I see some who want to break off their run and cannot. While they are looking for the point at which to halt their steps, they go on fiddle-faddling and dragging along like men fainting from weakness. Old men especially are dangerous, whose memory of things past remains, but who have lost the memory of their repetitions. I have seen some very amusing stories become very boring in the mouth of one nobleman, everyone present having been sated with them a hundred times.

1 That we remember more readily than we think. (The sentence just before this one is a later interpolation by Montaigne.)

[B]My second consolation is that I remember injuries received less, as that ancient said; [C]I should need a prompter, like Darius, who, so as not to forget the harm he had received from the Athenians, had a page come every time he sat down to table and sing three times in his ear: "Sire, remember the Athenians." [B]And the places and books that I revisit always smile at me with a fresh newness.

[A]It is not unreasonably said that anyone who does not feel sufficiently strong in memory should not meddle with lying. I know very well that the grammarians make this distinction between telling a lie and lying: that telling a lie means saying something false but which we have taken for true; and that lying – as defined in Latin, from which our French is taken – implies going against our conscience, and thus applies only to those who say what is contrary to what they know: those of whom I am speaking. Now liars either invent everything out of whole cloth, or else disguise and alter something fundamentally true. When they disguise and change a story, if you put them back onto it often enough they find it hard not to get tangled up. For since the thing as it is has become lodged first in the memory and has imprinted itself there by way of consciousness and knowledge, it is difficult for it not to present itself to the imagination, dislodging the falsehood, which cannot have so firm and secure a foothold. Likewise, the circumstances that were learned first, slipping into the mind every moment, tend to weaken the memory of the false or corrupted parts that have been added. In what liars invent completely, inasmuch as there is no contrary impression which clashes with the falsehood, they seem to have the less reason to fear making a mistake. Nevertheless even this, since it is an empty thing without a grip, is prone to escape any but a very strong memory.

[B]I have often seen the proof of this, and amusingly, at the expense of those who make a profession of fashioning their words only to suit the affairs they are negotiating and to please the great to whom they are speaking. For these circumstances, to which they are willing to enslave their honor and their conscience, being subject to many changes, their words must vary accordingly. Whence it happens that they describe the same thing as now gray, now yellow; to one man one way, to another another. And if by chance these men compare notes on such contrary reports, what becomes of this fine art? Let alone the fact that so often they imprudently entangle themselves; for what memory could suffice them to remember all the many different shapes into which they have cast the same subject? I have

seen many in my time envy someone's reputation for this fine sort of prudence, who do not see that if the reputation is there, the effect cannot be.

^CIn truth lying is an accursed vice. We are men, and hold together, only by our word. If we recognized the horror and the gravity of lying, we would persecute it with fire more justly than other crimes. I find that people ordinarily fool around chastising harmless faults in children very inappropriately, and torment them for thoughtless actions that leave neither imprint nor consequences. Only lying, and a little below it obstinacy, seem to me to be the actions whose birth and progress one should combat insistently. They grow with the child. And once the tongue has been put on this wrong track, it cannot be called back without amazing difficulty. Whence it happens that we see otherwise honest men subject to this vice and enslaved by it. I have a fine lad of a tailor whom I have never heard speak a single truth, not even one that is right there ready to serve his advantage.

If falsehood, like truth, had only one face, we would be in better shape. For we would take as certain the opposite of what the liar said. But the reverse of truth has a hundred thousand shapes and a limitless field. The Pythagoreans make out the good to be certain and finite, evil infinite and uncertain. A thousand paths miss the target, one goes to it.

Truly I am not sure that I could bring myself to ward off even an evident and extreme danger by a shameless and solemn lie. An ancient Church Father [Saint Augustine] says that we are better off in the company of a dog we know than in that of a man whose language we do not know. *So that to man a foreigner is not like a man* [Pliny]. And how much less sociable is false speech than silence.

^AKing Francis I boasted that he had trapped by this means[2] Francesco Taverna, ambassador of Francesco Sforza, duke of Milan, a man very famous for skill in talking. This man had been dispatched to present his master's excuses to His Majesty about a matter of great consequence, which was this. The king, in order to maintain some intelligence service in Italy, from which he had lately been driven out, and especially in the duchy of Milan, had decided to keep one of his own gentlemen near the duke, an ambassador in effect but in appearance a private person, who

2 By providing every chance for the liar to entangle himself in his lies and contradict himself.

pretended to be there for his personal affairs; inasmuch as the duke, who had grown increasingly dependent on the Emperor (especially at that time, when he was negotiating a marriage with his niece, daughter of the king of Denmark, now dowager of Lorraine), could not openly deal or confer with us without great damage to himself. For this commission a Milanese gentleman named Merveille, equerry to the king, was found suitable. Dispatched with secret credentials and instructions as ambassador, and with other letters of recommendation to the duke regarding his personal affairs for mask and show, this man stayed so long with the duke that some inkling of it came to the Emperor, who, so we think, brought about what followed after: which was that on the pretext of some murder, the duke goes and has his head cut off one fine night, with his trial completed in two days. Sir Francesco, having come ready with a long counterfeit account of this affair – for the king had addressed himself, to demand satisfaction, to all the princes of Christendom and to the duke himself – was heard during the morning's business. After he had established as the basis of his case, and prepared to that end, several plausible explanations of the fact – that his master had never taken our man for anything but a private gentleman and subject of his own, who had come to do business at Milan and had never lived there in any other guise; denying even having known that he was in the service of the king's household or known to him, so far was he from taking him for an ambassador – the king in his turn, pressing him with various objections and questions and attacking him from all sides, finally cornered him on the matter of the execution performed by night, and as it were by stealth. To which the poor man, embarrassed, answered, to play the honest man, that out of respect for His Majesty, the duke would have been very reluctant to have such an execution performed by day. Anyone may imagine how he was picked up for having contradicted himself so clumsily, and that before such a nose as that of King Francis.

Pope Julius II sent an ambassador to the king of England to incite him against the French king. When the ambassador had had his audience, and the king of England had dwelt in his reply on the difficulties he found in making the preparations that would be needed to combat so powerful a king, and stated some of the reasons for those difficulties, the ambassador inappropriately replied that he for his part had also considered them and indeed had mentioned them to the Pope. From this speech, so far removed from his mission, which was to urge him headlong into war, the king of

England got the first inkling of what he later actually found out, that this ambassador in his private intent leaned toward the side of France. And when the man's master had been informed of this, the man's goods were confiscated and he barely avoided losing his life.

10
Of prompt or slow speech

^Never to all men were all graces given.
LA BOÉTIE

So we see that in the gift of eloquence some have facility and promptness, and, as they say, can get it out so easily that at every turn they are ready; whereas others, slower, never speak except with elaboration and premeditation.

As they instruct ladies to select games and bodily exercises that will set off to advantage what is most beautiful about them, so if I had to give advice regarding these two diverse abilities in eloquence, which seems in our time to be the profession principally of preachers and lawyers, the slow man would do better as a preacher, it seems to me, and the other better as a lawyer. For the former's calling gives him all the leisure he pleases to prepare himself, and then his course is run in a straight continuous line, without interruption; whereas the opportunities of the lawyer press him at every moment to enter the lists, and the unforeseen replies of his adversary force him off his course, so that he must immediately take up a new line.

Yet at the interview between Pope Clement and King Francis at Marseilles, quite the contrary happened. Monsieur Poyet, a man trained all his life at the bar, with a great reputation, having the task of making the harangue to the Pope, thought it through long beforehand and indeed, so they say, brought it ready-made from Paris. On the very day that it was to be delivered, however, the Pope, fearing that someone's speech might give offense to the other princes' ambassadors who were around him, notified the king of the theme that seemed to him the most appropriate to the time and place, a theme by chance wholly different from the one on which Monsieur Poyet had labored; so that his harangue was useless, and he had to draft another promptly. Since he felt himself incapable of this, Cardinal du Bellay had to take on the job.

[B]The lawyer's part is harder than the preacher's; and yet we find, it seems to me, more passable lawyers than preachers, at least in France.

[A]It seems to be more peculiar to the mind to be prompt and sudden in its operation, and more peculiar to the judgment to be slow and deliberate. But a man who remains completely mute unless he has leisure to prepare, and also one to whom leisure gives no advantage for speaking better, are both abnormal cases. They tell of Severus Cassius that he spoke better without having thought about what he was going to say; that he owed more to fortune than to diligence; that it was an advantage to him to be interrupted in speaking, and that his adversaries were afraid to goad him, for fear that anger would redouble his eloquence.

I know by experience this sort of nature that cannot bear vehement and laborious premeditation. If it doesn't go along gaily and freely, it goes nowhere worth going. We say of certain works that they smell of oil and the lamp, because of a certain harshness and roughness that labor imprints on productions in which it has a large part. But besides this, the anxiety to do well, and the tension of straining too intently on one's work, put the soul on the rack, break it, and make it impotent; as happens with water, which because of the very pressure of its violence and abundance cannot find a way out of an open bottle-neck.

It is no less peculiar to the kind of temperament I am speaking of, that it wants to be stimulated: not shaken and stung by such strong passions as Cassius' anger (for that emotion would be too violent); not shocked; but roused and warmed up by external, present, and accidental stimuli. If it goes along all by itself, it does nothing but drag and languish. Agitation is its very life and grace.

[B]I have little control over myself and my moods. Chance has more power here than I. The occasion, the company, the very sound of my voice, draw more from my mind than I find in it when I sound it and use it by myself. [A]Thus its speech is better than its writings, if there can be choice where there is no value.

[C]This also happens to me: that I do not find myself in the place where I look; and I find myself more by chance encounter than by searching my judgment. I will have tossed off some subtle remark as I write. (I mean, of course, dull for anyone else, sharp for me. But let's leave aside all these amenities. Each man states this kind of thing according to his powers.) Later I have lost the point so thoroughly that I do not know what I meant; and sometimes

a stranger has discovered it before I do. If I erased every passage
where this happens to me, there would be nothing left of myself. At
other times, chance will show me the light clearer than noonday and
make me astonished at my hesitation.

II
Of prognostications

[A]As for oracles, it is certain that they had begun to lose credit a good
while before the coming of Jesus Christ; for we see that Cicero
goes to a lot of trouble to find the cause of their weakening. [C]And
these words are his: *Why are oracles of this sort no longer given at
Delphi, not only in our day but for a long time already, so that now
nothing could be more despised?* [A]But as for the other prognostications
– those drawn from the anatomy of animals at sacrifices [C](to which
use Plato attributes in part the natural constitution of their internal
organs), [A]from the scratching of chickens and the flight of birds [C](we
think that certain birds were born for the sake of augury* [Cicero]),
[A]from lightning and from the windings of rivers [C](the soothsayers
discern many things, the augurs foresee many, many are revealed by
oracles, many by divinations, many by dreams, many by portents*
[Cicero]), [A]and the like on which the ancients relied for most of
their public and private enterprises – all these our religion has
abolished. True, there remain among us some means of divination
by the stars, by spirits, bodily traits, dreams, and the like – a notable
example of the frenzied curiosity of our nature, which wastes its
time anticipating future things, as if it did not have enough to do
digesting the present:

> [B]Ruler of Olympus, why didst thou see fit
> To add this anguish to man's other woes:
> Foreknowledge by grim signs of future blows? ...
> Strike by surprise, and shroud our fate in night;
> Even in terror, let hope remain man's right;
>
> LUCAN

[C]*there is no use in knowing what is to be; for it is wretched to be
tormented to no purpose* [Cicero] – [A]nevertheless it is a fact that
divination is of much less authority now.

That is why I find remarkable the example of Francis, marquis of Saluzzo, a lieutenant of King Francis in his army beyond the mountains, a man infinitely favored in our court and obligated to the king for the marquisate itself, which had been confiscated from his brother. This marquis, for no reason and even against his own affections, let himself be so very terrified, it was reported, by the fine prognostications that were then being circulated on all sides to the advantage of Emperor Charles V and to our disadvantage – especially in Italy, where these insane prophecies were so widely accepted that in Rome a great amount of money was put on the exchange to back them – that after repeatedly lamenting to his intimates the evils he regarded as being inevitably prepared for the crown of France and for the friends he had there, he revolted and changed sides: to his own great misfortune, as it happened, whatever constellation may have been in the ascendant. But he went about it like a man torn by conflicting passions. For having both cities and forces in hand, the enemy army under Antonio de Leyva three steps away, and us without a suspicion of his action, he could have done worse than he did. For by his treason we lost neither a man, nor a town except Fossano, and that only after having resisted for a long time.

> God hides within night's blackest folds,
> Most wisely, what the future holds,
> And laughs if a man takes fright
> More than is right.
>
> HORACE

> Happy the man,
> And master of himself, who can
> Each day say: "I have lived. Let Jove
> Tomorrow fill the sky above
> With clouds, or sunlight pure."
>
> HORACE

> Our soul, happy in the present,
> Cares not what lies beyond.
>
> HORACE

^cAnd those who believe the following remark to the contrary are wrong to believe it: *These things are thus reciprocal, so that if there is*

divination, there are gods, and if there are gods, there is divination
[Cicero]. Pacuvius writes, much more wisely:

> For those who understand the speech of birds,
> And learn from others' inwards more than from their own:
> We may well hear, but not attend, their words.

That much-celebrated art of divination of the Tuscans origi-
nated in this way: A laborer, piercing the ground deeply with his
plough, saw Tages emerge from it, a demigod with the face of a child
but the wisdom of an old man. Everyone came on the run, and his
words and knowledge, containing the principles and methods of
this art, were collected and preserved for many centuries. A birth in
conformity with its development.

ᴮI would much rather regulate my affairs by the chance of the
dice than by such dreams. ᶜAnd indeed in all commonwealths a good
share of authority has always been left to chance. Plato, in the
government that he forges as he pleases, has it decide many impor-
tant matters, and among other things wills that marriages between
good people shall be made by lot. And he gives great weight to this
accidental selection, to the point of ordaining that children born of
it shall be brought up in the community, and those born of the
wicked shall be thrust out. However, if one of these exiles should
happen by any chance to show good promise as he grows up, he can
be recalled; and if any one of those retained shows little promise in
his adolescence, he can be exiled.

ᴮI see some who study and comment on their almanacs and cite
their authority in current events. With all they say, they necessarily
tell both truth and falsehood. ᶜ*For who is there who, shooting all day,
will not sometime hit the mark?* [Cicero.] ᴮI think none the better of
them to see them sometimes happen to hit the truth; there would be
more certainty in it, if it were the rule and the truth that they always
lied. ᶜBesides, no one keeps a record of their mistakes, inasmuch as
these are ordinary and numberless; and their correct divinations are
made much of because they are rare, incredible, and prodigious. In
this way Diagoras, who was surnamed the Atheist, replied to the
man in Samothrace, who, showing him in the temple many votive
offerings and tablets of those who had escaped shipwreck, said to
him: "Well, you who think that the gods care nothing about human
affairs, what do you say about so many men saved by their grace?"
"This is how it happens," Diagoras answered. "Those who were
drowned, in much greater number, are not portrayed here." Cicero

says that only Xenophanes of Colophon, out of all the philosophers who have acknowledged the gods, tried to eradicate every kind of divination. It is therefore the less amazing that [B]we have occasionally seen some of our princely souls linger on these vanities to their disadvantage.

[C]I would certainly like to have seen with my own eyes these two marvels: the book of Joachim, the Calabrian abbot, which predicted all the future popes, their names and appearance; and that of the Emperor Leo, which predicted the emperors and patriarchs of Greece. This I have seen with my own eyes, that in public disorders men stunned by their fate will throw themselves back, as on any superstition, on seeking in the heavens the ancient causes and threats of their misfortune. And they have been so strangely fortunate in this in my time as to persuade me that since divination is an amusement of sharp and idle minds, those who are trained in this subtle trick of tying and untying knots would be capable of finding, in any writings, whatever they want. But what gives them an especially good chance to play is the obscure, ambiguous, and fantastic language of the prophetic jargon, to which their authors give no clear meaning, so that posterity can apply to it whatever meanings it pleases.

[B]The daemon of Socrates was perhaps a certain impulse of the will that came to him without awaiting the advice of his reason. In a well-purified soul such as his, prepared by a continual exercise of wisdom and virtue, it is likely that these inclinations, although instinctive and undigested, were always important and worth following. Everyone feels within himself some likeness of such stirrings [C]of a prompt, vehement, and accidental opinion. It is my business to give them some authority, since I give so little to our wisdom. [B]And I have had some [C]as weak in reason as violent in persuasiveness – or in dissuasiveness, as was more ordinary in Socrates – [B]by which I let myself be carried away so usefully and fortunately that they might be judged to have in them something of divine inspiration.

12

Of constancy

[A]The precepts of resoluteness and constancy do not state that we must not protect ourselves as much as it lies in our power from

the evils and troubles that threaten us; nor consequently that we should not fear being taken by surprise. On the contrary, all honorable means of safeguarding ourselves from evils are not only permitted but laudable. And constancy's part is played principally in bearing troubles patiently where there is no remedy. So that there is neither any bodily suppleness, nor any move with hand weapons, that we should despise if it serves to safeguard us from the blow that is struck at us.

ᶜMany very warlike nations used flight as a principal resource in their armed encounters, and were more dangerous with their backs to the enemy than facing him. The Turks retain something of this. And Socrates in Plato, making fun of Laches, who had defined fortitude as "standing firm in rank against the enemy," said: "What? then would it be cowardice to beat them by giving ground?" He then cites Homer to him, who praises the science of flight in Aeneas. And when Laches, on second thought, concedes this practice in the Scythians and finally in cavalry in general, Socrates cites further the example of the infantry of the Lacedaemonians, a nation trained above all others to fight standing their ground, who at the battle of Plataea, being unable to break open the Persian phalanx, thought of the plan of loosening ranks and falling back, in order by their supposed flight to break up and disperse this solid mass in the pursuit. Whereby they gained the day.

Regarding the Scythians, they say that when Darius went to subjugate them, he sent their king many reproaches because he saw him always retreating before him and avoiding battle. To which Indathyrsus, for that was his name, made reply that it was not that they were afraid of him or of any man alive, but that this was his nation's way of campaigning, having neither cultivated land, nor town, nor house to defend and to fear for, lest the enemy profit by it. But that if he was so hungry for battle, let him come near to see the place of their ancient burials, and there he would find someone to talk to.

ᴬHowever, in cannonades, once you are in the line of fire, as the chances of war often bring about, it is unbecoming to move because of the threat of the shot, inasmuch as because of its violence and speed we consider it unavoidable. And there is many a one who, for having either lifted his hand or ducked his head, has at least given a laugh to his companions.

Yet in the campaign Emperor Charles V made against us in Provence, the marquis de Guast, on his way to reconnoiter

the city of Arles, having emerged from the shelter of a windmill under cover of which he had approached, was spotted by the seigneur de Bonneval and the seneschal d'Agenois, who were walking on top of the city's amphitheater. They pointed him out to the seigneur de Villiers, head of the artillery, who aimed a culverin so accurately that if the said marquis, seeing the match applied, had not sprung aside, it was thought that he would have got it in the body. And likewise a few years before, Lorenzo de' Medici, duke of Urbino and father of the Queen Mother, besieging Mondolfo, a place in Italy in the territories that they call the Vicariate, seeing the match applied to a piece that pointed right at him, did well to duck; for otherwise the shot, which only grazed the top of his head, would undoubtedly have hit him in the stomach.

To tell the truth about it, I do not think that these movements are deliberate; for how can you judge whether the aim is high or low in such a sudden thing? It is much easier to believe that fortune favored their fright, and that another time this would be just as good a way to jump into the shot as to avoid it.

[B]I cannot help starting if the bang of a harquebus hits my ears unexpectedly, in a place where I should not expect it; and I have seen this happen also to others who are better men than I.

[C]Nor do the Stoics mean that the soul of their sage can resist the first visions and fancies that come upon him; rather they consent that he give in, as to a natural subjection, to the great noise of the heavens or of a falling building, for example, to the point of turning pale and tightening up. Likewise for the other passions, provided that his judgment remains sound and entire, that the seat of his reason suffers no injury or alteration, and that he lends no consent to his fright and suffering. For the man who is not a sage it goes the same way for the first part, but entirely differently for the second. For the impression of the passions does not remain superficial in him, but penetrates right to the seat of reason, infecting and corrupting it. He judges according to them and conforms to them. Here very eloquently and fully is the state of the Stoic sage:

> The mind remains unmoved, the tears all useless flow.
>
> VIRGIL

The Peripatetic sage does not exempt himself from perturbations, but he moderates them.

13
Ceremony of interviews between kings

ᴬThere is no subject so vain that it does not deserve a place in this rhapsody. According to our ordinary rules, it would be a notable discourtesy, both toward an equal and even more so toward one of the great, to fail to be at home when he had notified you that he was to come. Indeed, Queen Margaret of Navarre added on this subject that it was incivility for a gentleman to leave his house, as is done most often, in order to go to meet the person who is coming to see him, however great he may be; that it is more respectful and civil to wait to receive him, were it only for fear of missing him on the way; and that it is enough to accompany him when he leaves.

ᴮAs for me, I often forget both of these vain formalities, just as I cut out all ceremony in my house. Someone takes offense: I can't help it. It is better for me to offend him once than myself every day; that would be perpetual slavery. What is the use of fleeing the servitude of courts if we drag some of it right home to our lair?

ᴬAnother common rule in all assemblies is that the lesser should be first at an appointment, since it is more reasonable that the more prominent should make others wait for them. Nevertheless, at the interview arranged between Pope Clement and King Francis at Marseilles, the king, having ordered the necessary preparations there, left the city, and gave the Pope two or three days' leisure for his entry and to refresh himself before he came to see him. And likewise at the entry of the Pope and the Emperor at Bologna, the Emperor gave the Pope the chance to be there first, and came on after him. It is, they say, an ordinary ceremony at the interviews of such princes that the greater should be at the assigned place before the others, even before the person on whose territory the meeting is being held. The argument is that this show serves to demonstrate that it is the greater whom the lesser ones come to see and seek out, and not the greater who comes to the lesser.

ᶜNot only each country but each city has its particular forms of civility, and so has each occupation. I was brought up in this carefully enough in my youth, and have lived in good enough company, not to be ignorant of the laws of our French civility; I could run a school of it. I like to follow these laws, but not so timidly that my life would remain constrained. They have some troublesome forms, which a man may forget, provided he does so

by discretion and not by mistake, without losing grace by his behavior. I have often seen men uncivil by too much civility, and importunate in courtesy.

Moreover it is a very useful knowledge, this knowledge of social dexterity. Like grace and beauty, it acts as a moderator at the first approaches of sociability and familiarity, and consequently opens the door for us to learning by the examples of others, and to bringing forth and displaying our own example, if it has anything instructive and communicable about it.

14
That the taste of good and evil depends in large part on the opinion we have of them

^Men, says an old Greek maxim, are tormented by the opinions they have of things, not by the things themselves. There would be a great point gained for the relief of our wretched human lot if someone could prove this statement true in every case. For if evils have no entry into us but by our judgment, it seems to be in our power to disdain them or turn them to good use. If things give themselves up to our mercy, why shall we not dispose of them and arrange them to our advantage? If what we call evil and torment is neither evil nor torment in itself, if it is merely our fancy that gives it this quality, it is in us to change it. And having the choice, if no one forces us, we are strangely insane to tense ourselves for the course that is more painful to us, and to give sicknesses, poverty, and slights a bitter and unpleasant taste if we can give them a good one and if, fortune furnishing merely the material, it is for us to give it form. But let us see whether this can be maintained: that what we call evil is not evil in itself – or at least, whatever it is, that it depends on us to give it a different savor and a different complexion; for all this comes to the same thing.

If the original essence of the things we fear had power to lodge in us of its own authority, it would lodge alike in everyone; for men are all of a kind, and are furnished, though some more and some less, with similar tools and instruments for thought and judgment. But the diversity of the opinions we have of these things shows clearly that they enter us only by mutual agreement; one man perchance lodges them in himself in their true essence, but in a thousand other men they are given a new and contrary essence.

We consider death, poverty, and pain our principal adversaries. Now this death, which some call the most horrible of horrible things, who does not know that others call it the only haven from the torments of this life, the sovereign good of nature, the sole support of our freedom, and the common and prompt remedy for all evils? And even as some await it trembling and afraid, others ^Cendure it more easily than life. ^BOne man complains of its ease:

> Death, would that you scorned to take the coward's life,
> And came only to valor!

<div align="right">LUCAN</div>

^CNow let us leave aside these men of proud courage. Theodorus replied to Lysimachus, who was threatening to kill him: "You will do a great deed in matching the strength of a poisonous fly!" Most philosophers have either deliberately anticipated or hastened and abetted their own death. ^AHow many low-born people do we see led to death – and not a simple death, but mingled with shame and sometimes with grievous torments – bringing to it such assurance, some through stubbornness, others through natural simplicity, that we see no change from their ordinary manner: settling their domestic affairs, commending themselves to their friends, singing, preaching, and keeping up a conversation with the people; sometimes even joking and drinking to their friends, yielding in nothing to Socrates. One man who was being led to the gallows said they must not go by a certain street, since there was a danger that a certain merchant might have him collared for an old debt. Another told the hangman not to touch him on the throat for fear of making him shake with laughter, he was so ticklish. Another replied to his confessor, who was promising him that he should sup that day with Our Lord: "You go there yourself; for my part, I'm fasting." Another, having asked for a drink and seeing the hangman drink first, said he would not drink after him for fear of catching the pox. Everyone has heard the story of the man of Picardy to whom, on the scaffold, they presented a wench, offering (as our justice sometimes allows) to save his life if he would marry her. He, having looked at her a while and noticed that she was lame, said: "Tie up, tie up! She limps." And likewise they say that in Denmark a man condemned to have his head cut off, being offered similar terms when he was on the scaffold, turned it down because the girl they offered him had sagging cheeks and too sharp a nose. A servant at Toulouse, accused of heresy, made no other defense of his belief than to refer himself to that of his master,

a young student in prison with him, and preferred to die rather than let himself be persuaded that his master could err. We read of the people of Arras, when King Louis XI took that town, that there were many ordinary folk who let themselves be hanged rather than say "Long live the king!"

ᶜIn the kingdom of Narsinga even today the wives of the priests are buried alive with their dead husbands. All other wives endure being burned alive, not only with fortitude but gaily, at their husbands' funerals. And when they burn the body of their deceased king, all his wives and concubines, his favorites and all sorts of officers and servants – a whole nation in themselves – run so blithely to this fire to throw themselves in it with their master, that they seem to take honor in being companions of his death.

ᴬAnd among those base souls the buffoons there have been some who would not give up their clowning even in death. One, as the hangman set him swinging, cried out, "Let 'er rip!" which was his usual refrain. And another who, on the point of death, had been laid in a bed of straw along the hearthstone, replied to the doctor, when he asked him where his pain got him: "Between the bench and the fire." And when the priest, to give him extreme unction, tried to find his feet, which his illness had made him draw up to him cramped, he said: "You will find them at the end of my legs." When a man exhorted him to commend himself to God, he asked, "Who is going there?" And the other replying, "It will soon be you, if He pleases," he rejoined: "I'd really like to be there tomorrow evening." "Just commend yourself to Him," went on the other; "you'll be there soon." "Then," he said, "it is better for me to make my compliments in person."

During our late Milanese wars, with so many captures and recaptures, the people, unable to bear such varied changes of fortune, became so firmly resolved on death that I have heard my father say he saw a count made of fully twenty-five heads of houses who had done away with themselves in a week. An incident not unlike that which befell the city of the Xanthians, who, besieged by Brutus, flew pell-mell, men, women, and children, into such a frenzied craving for death that there is nothing done to escape death which they did not do to escape life; so that only with difficulty could Brutus save a very small number of them.

ᶜAny opinion is strong enough to make people espouse it at the price of life. The first article in that fine oath that Greece swore and kept in the Median war was that each man would sooner exchange

life for death than his country's laws for those of Persia. How many
people we see in the war between the Turks and the Greeks accept
a cruel death rather than abandon circumcision for baptism! An
example of which no sort of religion is incapable.

When the kings of Castile banished the Jews from their terri-
tories, King John of Portugal for eight crowns a head sold them
refuge in his, on condition that on a certain day they should move
out; and promised to furnish them ships to transport them to Africa.
The day having come, past which it was stated that those who had
not obeyed would remain slaves, too few vessels were furnished; and
those who embarked in them were treated roughly and villainously
by the sailors, who, besides many other indignities, kept them at sea,
sailing back and forth, until they had used up their victuals and were
constrained to buy some from their captors at such high prices and
over so long a period that they were set ashore with nothing left but
their shirts. When this inhumanity was reported to those who had
remained on land, most of them resolved on slavery; some made
a show of changing religion. Manuel, when he came to the throne,
first set them free, and then, changing his mind, gave them time to
leave his country, assigning three ports for their passage. He hoped,
says Bishop Osorius, the best Latin historian of our era, that though
the favor he had done them by granting them liberty had failed to
convert them to Christianity, their fear of committing themselves
like their comrades to the thievery of the sailors, and of leaving their
great riches and a country to which they were accustomed in order
to go and cast themselves into an unknown and foreign region,
would bring them to it. But seeing himself disappointed in his
hope, and finding that they were all set on the voyage, he cut off
two of the ports he had promised them, so that the length and
difficulty of the trip should make some change their minds; or else
so as to pile them all up in one place for the greater convenience of
the plan he had decided on. This was to have all the children under
fourteen snatched from the hands of their fathers and mothers, and
taken elsewhere to be brought up in our religion.

They say that this act produced a horrible spectacle, the natural
affection between fathers and children, and also the zeal for their
former belief, fighting against this violent decree. It was common to
see fathers and mothers doing away with themselves, and, what is
a still more austere example, through love and compassion throwing
their children into wells to escape the law. As for the remainder,
when the stipulated term had expired they could do nothing but

return to slavery. Some turned Christians; of their faith, or of that of their descendants, even today, a hundred years later, few Portuguese are sure, though custom and length of time are far stronger coun-selors than any other compulsion.[1] *How often have not only our leaders*, says Cicero, *but even whole armies rushed to certain death*.

[B]I have seen one of my intimate friends chase death with a real affection, rooted in his heart by various plausible arguments that I could not rid him of, and rush headlong for no apparent reason, with bitter and burning hunger, to the first death that came his way crowned with a gleam of honor.

[A]We have many examples in our time of people, even children, who, for fear of some slight inconvenience, have given themselves up to death. And in this connection, what shall we not fear, says an ancient, if we fear what cowardice itself has chosen for its refuge? If I were to string together here a long list of those of all sexes and conditions and sects in happier times who have either awaited death resolutely or sought it voluntarily, and sought it not only to flee the ills of this life, but some simply to flee satiety with living and others for the hope of a better condition elsewhere, I should never have done. Their number is so infinite that in truth I should make a better bargain to count up those who have feared death. So just this one. Pyrrho the philosopher, being one day in a boat in a great tempest, showed the most frightened among his companions a pig that was there, not at all concerned at this storm, and encouraged them by its example. Shall we then dare to say that this advantage, reason, that we make such a fuss about, and on account of which we think ourselves masters and emperors of the rest of creation, has been put in us for our torment? What good is the knowledge of things if by it we lose the repose and tranquillity we should enjoy without it, and if it puts us into a worse condition than Pyrrho's pig? The intelligence that has been given us for our greatest good, shall we use it for our ruin, combating the plan of nature and the universal order of things, which says that each man shall use his tools and means for his advantage?

Very well, someone will tell me, let your rule hold for death, but what will you say of want? And what will you say of pain, which

1 Here the 1595 edition adds the following sentence: "In the town of Castelnau Darry fifty Albigensian heretics together, with determined courage, endured being burned alive in the same fire rather than renounce their opinions."

ᶜAristippus, Hieronymus, and ᴬmost of the sages have thought the
ultimate evil? And those who have denied it in word have admitted
it in practice. When Posidonius was extremely tormented by an
acute and painful malady, Pompey went to see him, and excused
himself for having chosen so poor a time to hear him talk about
philosophy. "God forbid," said Posidonius, "that pain should gain
such power over me as to keep me from such a subject!" And he
threw himself into this same topic, the contempt of pain. But
meanwhile it was playing its part and pressing him incessantly. At
which he cried: "You may do your worst, pain, yet I will not say that
you are an evil." This tale that they make so much of, what has it to
do with contempt of pain? He is only arguing about the word; and
meanwhile if these pangs do not move him, why does he interrupt
his talk for their sake? Why does he think he is doing a lot by not
calling pain an evil?

Here all does not consist in imagination. We have opinions
about the rest; here it is certain knowledge that plays its part.
Even our senses are judges of it.

> And if these be not true, all reason then is false.
>
> LUCRETIUS

Shall we make our skin believe that the lashes of a stirrup strap tickle
it, and our palate that aloes is Graves wine? Here Pyrrho's pig is in
the same boat with us. To be sure, he is unafraid in the presence of
death, but if you beat him he will squeal and wriggle. Shall we
violate the general law of nature, which can be observed in all that
lives under heaven, that we shall tremble under pain? The very trees
seem to groan at the blows that are given them.

Death is felt only by the mind, since it is a momentary passage:

> 'Tis past or future, nought in it is now.
>
> LA BOÉTIE

> Death holds less pain than does the wait for death.
>
> OVID

A thousand beasts, a thousand men, are sooner dead than threa-
tened. And in truth what we say we principally fear in death is pain,
its customary forerunner.

ᶜHowever, if we are to believe a Church Father, *Death is not an
evil, unless that which follows it is* [Saint Augustine]. And I should
say, still more probably, that neither what goes before nor what

comes after is an appurtenance of death. We are making false excuses. And I find by experience that it is rather our inability to stand the idea of death that makes us unable to stand pain, and that we feel pain doubly painful because it threatens us with death. But since reason accuses our cowardice of fearing a thing so sudden, so inevitable, so imperceptible, we take this other more excusable pretext.

All pains whose only danger is their pain we call free from danger; toothache and the gout, painful as they are, inasmuch as they are not fatal, who lists them as illnesses? But let us suppose that in death we principally consider the pain, ᴬas likewise poverty has nothing to be feared but this, that it delivers us into the hands of pain, by the thirst, hunger, cold, heat, and sleepless nights that it makes us endure.

Thus let us deal only with pain. I grant them, and that willingly, that it is the worst accident of our being; for in all the world I am the man who bears it the most ill will and who flees it the most, the more so because until now, thank God, I have had no great association with it. But it is in us, if not to annihilate it, at least to lessen it by patience, and, even should the body be disturbed by it, to maintain nevertheless our soul and reason in good trim.

And if this were not so, who would have brought into credit among us virtue, valor, strength, magnanimity, and resolution? Where would these play their part, if there were no more pain to defy? *Courage is greedy of danger* [Seneca]. If we need not sleep on hard ground, sustain fully armed the heat of noon, feed on a horse or an ass, watch ourselves being sliced open and a bullet torn out from between our bones, let ourselves be sewn up again, cauterized, and probed, how shall we acquire the advantage that we wish to have over the common herd? It is a far cry from fleeing evil and pain to what the sages say, that among equally good actions the most desirable to do is the one in which there is most trouble: ᶜ*For people are happy not in hilarity or sensuality or laughter, nor in games, the comrades of levity, but often even in sadness through firmness and constancy* [Cicero]. ᴬAnd for that reason it has proved impossible to persuade our fathers that conquests made by main force with the risks of war were no more advantageous than those made in complete safety by diplomatic maneuvers:

There is most joy in virtue when 'tis hardest won.
LUCAN

Furthermore, this should console us, that in the course of nature, if the pain is violent, it is short; if it is long, it is light: ^c*if heavy, short; if long, light* [Cicero]. ^AYou will not feel it very long, if you feel it too much; it will put an end to itself, or to you; both come to the same thing. ^cIf you cannot bear it, it will bear you off. *Remember that death ends the greatest ills, that the small ones have many intervals of respite, and that we are masters of the moderate ones; so that if they are bearable we shall bear them; if not, we can leave life as we leave a theater when the play ceases to please us* [Cicero].

^AWhat makes us endure pain so poorly is that we are not accustomed to find our principal contentment in the soul, ^cand that we do not concentrate enough on it; for the soul is the one and sovereign mistress of our condition and conduct. The body has, except for differences of degree, only one gait and one posture. The soul may be shaped into all varieties of forms, and molds to itself and to its every condition the feelings of the body and all other accidents. Therefore we must study the soul and look into it, and awaken in it its all-powerful springs. There is no reason, prescription, or might that has power against its inclination and its choice. Out of the many thousands of attitudes at its disposal, let us give it one conducive to our repose and preservation, and we shall be not only sheltered from all harm, but even gratified and flattered, if it please, by ills and pains. The soul profits from everything without distinction. Error and dreams serve it usefully, being suitable stuff for giving us security and contentment.

It is easy to see that what makes pain and pleasure keen in us is the sharpness of our mind. The animals, who keep the mind on a leash, leave to their bodies their own feelings, free and natural and therefore almost exactly alike within each species, as we see by the uniformity of their movements. If we did not disturb within our members the jurisdiction which belongs to them in this matter, it is probable that we should be better off, and that nature has given them a just and measured temperance toward pleasure and toward pain. Indeed it cannot fail to be just, being equal and common in all. But since we have emancipated ourselves from nature's rules to abandon ourselves to the vagabond freedom of our fancies, at least let us help ourselves by turning them in the most agreeable direction.

Plato fears our hard bondage to pain and pleasure, since it obligates and attaches the soul too much to the body; I, on the contrary, because it detaches and unbinds it.

^AEven as the enemy grows keener at our flight, so pain waxes proud to see us tremble beneath it. It will make itself far easier to deal with to those who stand up against it. We must resist it and tense ourselves against it. By turning tail and retreating we call upon us the ruin that threatens us. ^CAs the body is firmer against attack when stiffened, so is the soul.

^ABut let us come to those examples (which are really the quarry for weak-backed people like myself) in which we shall find that it is with pain as with the stones which take on a brighter or duller color according to the foil they are set in, and that it occupies in us only as much room as we give it. *They have suffered just so much as they have given in to pain*, says Saint Augustine. We feel a surgeon's cut with the razor more than ten sword strokes in the heat of combat. The pains of childbirth, considered great by the doctors and by God himself, and which we surround with so many cere-monies: there are whole nations that take no account of them. I leave aside the Lacedaemonian women; but in the Swiss women among our foot soldiers, what change do you find, except that as they trot after their husbands you see them today carrying around their neck the child that they had yesterday in their belly? And those counterfeit Egyptian women[2] who have shown up in our midst go themselves and wash their newborn children and take a bath in the nearest river. ^CBesides so many wenches who every day hide their children in their delivery just as in their conception, that fine wife of Sabinus, a Roman patrician, for the sake of others endured the labor of bearing twins alone, without help, and without a cry or a groan.

^AA simple Spartan boy, after stealing a fox and putting it under his cape, endured its gnawing his stomach rather than betray him-self (for they feared even more the shame of clumsiness in stealing than we fear its punishment). And another, offering incense at a sacrifice, when the coal fell into his sleeve, let himself be burned to the bone rather than disturb the mystery. And many of them have been seen who, merely to test their manliness, according to their habits of upbringing, have at the age of seven endured being whipped to death, without changing expression. ^CAnd Cicero saw men fighting in troops, with fists, feet, and teeth, until they lost consciousness, rather than admit themselves beaten. *Never could custom conquer nature, for it is invincible; but we have corrupted our*

2 Gypsies.

soul with shaded ease, luxuries, idleness, languor, sloth; we have softened it by evil opinions and habits [Cicero].

[A]Everyone knows the story of Scaevola, who, having slipped into the enemy's camp to kill their leader and having failed in his attempt, in order to make good his purpose by a still stranger device and free his country, not only confessed his plan to Porsena, the king he wanted to kill, but added that there were in his own camp a great number of Romans, accomplices in the undertaking, just like him. And to show the stuff he was made of, having had a brazier brought him, he saw and suffered his arm to be grilled and roasted, until the enemy himself, struck with horror, ordered the brazier to be taken away.

What of the man who did not deign to interrupt the reading of his book while he was being cut open? And the one who persisted in matching his ridicule and laughter against the pains inflicted on him, so that the exasperated cruelty of the executioners who were holding him, and all their inventing of redoubled tortures, one upon the other, acknowledged him the winner. But he was a philosopher. What of Caesar's gladiator, who, laughing all the while, endured the probing and cutting open of his wounds? [C]*What common gladiator ever groaned? Which of them ever changed expression? Which stood up or even fell shamefully? Which, when downed and ordered to take the fatal sword stroke, drew back his neck?* [Cicero.]

[A]Let us bring in the women. Who has not heard tell in Paris of the one who had herself flayed just to gain the fresher complexion of a new skin? There are some who have had live healthy teeth yanked out so as to make their voice softer and richer, or to arrange their other teeth in better order. How many examples of the contempt for pain we have in this sex! What can they not do, what do they fear, if only they may hope for some increase in their beauty?

> [B]Their labor is to pluck the white hairs from their place,
> And, stripping off the skin, to make them a new face.
>
> TIBULLUS

[A]I have seen some of them swallow sand and ashes, and work deliberately to ruin their stomach, so as to get pale complexions. To get a slim body, Spanish style, what torture do they not endure, tight-laced and braced, until they suffer great gashes in their sides, right to the live flesh – yes, sometimes even until they die of it?

ᶜIt is a common practice in many nations of our time for people to wound themselves intentionally to give credit to their word; and our king³ tells of notable examples of this among those he saw in Poland, performed in dealing with himself. But besides the cases I know where these were imitated in France by some people, I have seen a girl, to show the ardor of her promises, and also her constancy, strike herself, with the bodkin she wore in her hair, four or five lusty stabs in the arm, which broke the skin and made her bleed in good earnest.⁴ The Turks give themselves great scars for their ladies; and, so that the mark shall remain, they instantly apply fire to the wound and hold it there an incredibly long time to stop the blood and form the scar. People who have seen this have written it down and sworn it to me. But for ten aspers⁵ some one of them may be found every day who will give himself a really deep cut in the arm or the thighs.

ᴬI am very glad that we have witnesses nearer at hand, where we need them more; for Christendom provides us with plenty. And after the example of our holy guide, there are many who out of piety have willed to bear the cross. We learn by a witness most worthy of belief [Joinville] that King Louis the Saint wore the hair shirt until, in his old age, his confessor gave him dispensation; and that every Friday he had his priest flog his shoulders with five little iron chains, which he always carried about for that purpose in a box. William, our last duke of Guienne, father of the Eleanor who transmitted that duchy to the houses of France and England, wore continually, for the last ten or twelve years of his life, a corselet under a monk's dress, for penance. Fulk, count of Anjou, went all the way to Jerusalem to have himself scourged there by two of his servants, a rope around his neck, before the sepulcher of Our Lord. But do we not see every Good Friday in various places a large number of men and women beating themselves until they tear their flesh and cut it to the bone? That I have often seen, and without enchantment; and it was said that there were some (for they go masked) who for money undertook in this way to ensure other people's religion, with a contempt for pain all the greater as the spurs of piety are greater than those of avarice.

3 Henry III, who was king of Poland before his accession in France.
4 Further indications in the 1595 edition of the *Essays* seem to show that the girl was Marie de Gournay.
5 Turkish coins worth about two cents each.

[C]Q. Maximus buried his son, a consul; M. Cato his, a praetor-elect; and L. Paulus both of his, within a few days, with a calm face that bore no sign of grief. Once in my time I said of someone jokingly that he had cheated divine justice: for the violent death of three grown-up children having been sent him in one day as a bitter scourge, as may well be believed, he all but took it as a favor. And I have lost two or three (but while they were still nursing), if not without grief, at least without repining. Yet there is hardly any accident that touches men more to the quick. I see enough other common occasions for affliction which I should scarcely feel if they happened to me, and I have disdained some, when they came to me, to which the world has given such an atrocious appearance that I wouldn't dare boast of my indifference to them to most people without blushing: *Whence it is understood that grief lies not in nature, but in opinion* [Cicero].

[B]Opinion is a powerful performer, bold and immoderate. Who ever with such hunger sought security and repose as Alexander and Caesar sought unrest and difficulties? Teres, the father of Sitalces, was wont to say that when he was not making war it seemed to him that there was no difference between him and his groom.

[C]When Cato the consul merely forbade the inhabitants of certain towns in Spain to bear arms, so that he might be sure of them, a large number killed themselves: *a fierce race to whom life without arms was not life* [Livy]. [B]How many we know who have fled the sweetness of a tranquil life in their homes, among their friends, to seek the horror of uninhabitable deserts; who have flung themselves into humiliation, degradation, and the contempt of the world, and have enjoyed these and even sought them out. Cardinal Borromeo, who died lately in Milan, held to so austere a way of life in the midst of the debauchery to which his nobility, his great riches, the atmosphere of Italy, and his youth invited him, that the same robe that served him in summer served him in winter. He slept on straw only; and the hours he had left from the duties of his position he spent in continual study, planted on his knees, having a little bread and water beside his book, but no other food and no other time for eating. I know those who knowingly have derived profit and advancement from cuckoldry, the mere name of which frightens so many people.

If sight is not the most necessary of our senses, it is at least the most pleasant; but the most pleasant and useful of our members seem to be those which serve to beget us; yet many people have conceived a mortal hatred for them, merely because they were too

likable, and have rejected them because we prize and value them so highly. And this was the opinion about his eyes of the man who put them out. ᶜThe commonest and healthiest sort of men consider an abundance of children a great happiness; I and some others regard the lack of them as equally fortunate. And when Thales is asked why he does not marry, he answers that he does not like to leave any descendants.

That our opinion gives value to things is seen by the many things that we do not think about even to appraise them, preferring to think about ourselves instead. We consider neither their qualities nor their uses, but only the cost to us of getting them, as if that were some part of their substance; and we call value in them not what they bring, but what we bring to them. At which point I note that we are great economizers of our expenditure. According as it weighs, it serves by the very fact that it weighs. Our opinion never lets it run at a false valuation. Purchase gives value to the diamond, and difficulty to virtue, and pain to piety, and harshness to medicine.

ᴮOne man, to achieve poverty, cast his money into the same sea that so many others ransack up and down to fish out riches. Epicurus says that being rich is not an alleviation, but a change, of troubles. In truth, it is not want, but rather abundance, that breeds avarice. I want to tell my experience in this matter.

I have lived in three kinds of situation since I came out of childhood. The first period, which lasted nearly twenty years, I spent with none but casual means and dependent on the authority and help of others, without rule or fixed revenue. My spending was done the more joyously and carelessly for being all at the hazard of fortune. I was never better off. I never had the experience of finding my friends' purses closed, since I had enjoined on myself beyond all other necessities the necessity of not failing to pay up at the time I had chosen. This they have extended a thousand times, seeing the effort I made upon myself to satisfy them; so that I repaid them with a thrifty and somewhat deceptive honesty. I feel naturally a certain sensual pleasure in paying, as if I were unburdening my shoulders of a troublesome weight and of that image of slavery; besides, there is a certain satisfaction which tickles me when I do a just action and make others content. I except the payments where you must come to bargain and haggle, for if I do not find someone to give this chore to, I put them off shamefully and unjustly as long as I can, for fear of the sort of altercation with which my humor and my way of speaking are wholly incompatible. There is nothing I hate like bargaining. It is

a pure interchange of trickery and shamelessness: after an hour of disputing and haggling both men go back on their word and their oath for a gain of five sous. And so I used to borrow at a disadvantage; for having no heart to make my request in the other's presence, I trusted its chances to paper, which is a poor advocate and lends a helping hand to refusal. I referred the handling of my need more gaily to the stars, and more freely, than I have ever referred it since to my foresight and sense.

Most good managers think it horrible to live thus in uncertainty, and do not realize that in the first place, most people live thus. How many good men have cast away all their security, and do so every day, to pursue the wind of royal favor and of fortune. Caesar went into debt for more than a million in gold beyond what he was worth, to become Caesar. And how many merchants begin their traffic by the sale of their farms, which they send to the Indies

> Across so many stormy seas!
> CATULLUS

In our present great drought of devotion, we have thousands and thousands of congregations[6] which spend life comfortably, expecting every day from the liberality of heaven what they need for dinner.

In the second place, these good managers do not consider that this certainty on which they rely is scarcely less uncertain and chancy than chance itself. I see misery as close from beyond two thousand crowns of income as if it were right next to me. For besides that fate has power to open up a hundred breaches through our riches to poverty, ᶜthere being often no middle ground between the highest and lowest fortune –

> Fortune is glass; it shatters when it shines –
> PUBLILIUS SYRUS

ᴮand to turn all our defenses and ramparts topsy-turvy, I find that for various reasons poverty is seen dwelling as commonly in those who have property as in those who have nothing; and that perhaps it is somewhat less uncomfortable when it is alone than when it is met in company with riches. ᶜRiches come rather from management than from revenue: *Each man is the maker of his fortune* [Sallust]. ᴮAnd more wretched to me seems an uneasy, hard-up, over-busy rich man,

6 Orders of mendicant monks.

than he who is simply poor. ᶜ*They are poor in the midst of riches, which is the worst kind of poverty* [Seneca]. The greatest and richest princes are through poverty and want commonly driven to extreme need: for is there any need more extreme than the one that makes men become tyrants and unjust usurpers of their subjects' property?

ᴮMy second situation was to have money. Having taken to this, I soon laid by considerable reserves, for my circumstances; thinking that a man owns only as much as he has beyond his ordinary expenses, and that he cannot rely on what as yet he merely hopes to receive, however clear his hope. For what, I would say, if I were surprised by such or such an accident? And in the wake of these vain and pernicious imaginings I would go and exercise my ingenuity to provide by this superfluous reserve for all emergencies; and still could reply to him who pointed out that the number of emergencies was too infinite, that if I could not provide for all, I could for some, and many. This did not go on without painful worry. ᶜI made a secret of it; and I, who dare say so much about myself, spoke of my money only to lie, as do the others who, rich, make out to be poor, or poor, make out to be rich, and dispense their conscience from ever testifying sincerely to what they have: a ridiculous and shameful prudence. ᴮWas I going on a journey, I never thought I was sufficiently provided. And the bigger my load of money, the bigger my load of fear: now about the safety of the roads, now about the fidelity of those who had charge of my baggage, of which, like some others I know, I was never sure enough unless I had it before my eyes. Did I leave my strongbox at home, how many suspicions, how many thorny and, what is worse, incommunicable thoughts! My mind was always turned in that direction. ᶜAll things considered, there is more trouble in keeping money than in getting it. ᴮIf I did not do literally everything I say, at least it cost me dear to keep myself from doing it.

I got little or no advantage from this; ᶜthough I had more means for spending, it weighed no less heavily on me. ᴮFor, as Bion used to say, the man with hair is as angry as the bald man if you pull one out. And once you are accustomed to a certain pile and set your fancy on it, it is no longer at your service: ᶜyou wouldn't dare to make a dent in it. ᴮIt is a building which seems to you ready to crumble altogether at a touch. Necessity must take you by the throat before you will cut into it. And earlier I would pawn my clothes and sell a horse with much less reluctance and less regret, than I would then make a breach in that beloved purse that I had laid by. But the danger

lay in the fact that one cannot easily set fixed limits to this desire
^C(they are hard to find in the things we consider good) ^Band put
a check on frugality. We go on ever fattening this pile and increasing
it with one sum after another, until we deprive ourselves sordidly of
the enjoyment of our own possessions and place our only joy in
keeping them and not using them. ^CAccording to this way of using
things, the men richest in money are those who have charge of
guarding the gates and walls of a good city. Every rich man is
avaricious, in my opinion.

Plato ranks corporal or human goods in this order: health,
beauty, strength, riches. And riches, he says, are not blind, but
very clear-sighted when illuminated by wisdom. ^BDionysius the
Younger did a graceful thing in this connection. He was informed
that one of his Syracusans had hidden a treasure in the ground. He
told him to bring it to him, which he did, furtively holding back for
himself a part of it, with which he went off to another town, where,
having lost this appetite for hoarding, he began to live more liber-
ally. Hearing this, Dionysius had the rest of the man's treasure
returned to him, saying that since he had learned how to use his
money, he was welcome to the rest of it.

I was in this state for a few years.[7] I know not what good daemon
cast me out of it – most usefully, like the Syracusan – and sent
into abandonment all this saving, the pleasure of a certain trip at
great expense having overthrown this stupid fancy. This way I fell
into a third kind of life (I say what I feel about it) certainly much
more pleasant and more regulated, which is that I make my expense
run abreast with my receipts; now one is ahead, now the other,
but they are never far apart. I live from day to day, and content
myself with having enough to meet my present and ordinary needs;
for the extraordinary, all the provision in the world could not suffice.
^CAnd it is madness to expect fortune itself ever to arm us adequately
against itself. It is with our own weapons that we must combat
fortune; the accidental ones will betray us at the vital point. ^BIf
I amass money, it is only in the hope of using it soon; not to
buy lands ^Cthat I have no use for, ^Bbut to buy pleasure. ^C*Not to be
covetous is money, not to be avid to buy is revenue* [Cicero]. ^BI have
neither any real fear that my money will run out, nor any desire
of increasing it: ^C*The fruit of riches is abundance, and sufficiency
declares abundance* [Cicero]. ^BAnd I am singularly gratified that

7 The 1588 edition reads: "four or five years."

this correction has come to me at an age naturally inclined to avarice, and that I see myself rid of this malady so common in old men, and the most ridiculous of all human manias.

^CPheraulas, who had passed through both kinds of fortune and found that increase of possessions was not increase in appetite for drinking, eating, sleeping, and embracing his wife, and who further-more felt the trouble of running his household weighing on his shoulders, as it does on mine, decided to gratify a poor young man, his faithful friend, who was ever baying after riches, by making him a present of all his own, which were great and extensive, and of those also that he was accumulating every day through the liberality of his good master Cyrus and through war; on condition that he should undertake to support and feed him honorably as his guest and his friend. Thus they lived thereafter very happily and equally glad of the change in their lot. That is a change that I would imitate with all my heart.

And I highly praise the fortune of an old prelate, whom I know to have given up so completely his purse, his revenue, and his expenses, now to one chosen servant, now to another, that he has let many years flow by, ignorant as a stranger of his own household affairs. Confidence in the goodness of others is no slight testimony to one's own goodness; and so God gladly favors it. And as regards this prelate, I see no household run more worthily or with greater regularity than his. Happy the man who has regulated his needs in such just measure that his wealth can satisfy them without his care and trouble and without the spending or acquiring of it interrupting his pursuit of other occupations better suited to him, more tranquil, and more congenial.

^BThus ease and indigence depend on each man's opinion; and neither riches, glory, nor health has any more beauty and pleasure than its possessor lends it. ^CEach man is as well or as badly off as he thinks he is. Not the man of whom it is thought, but the one who thinks it of himself, is happy. And by just this fact belief gains reality and truth.

Fortune does us neither good nor harm; she only offers us the material and the seed of them, which our soul, more powerful than she, turns and applies as it pleases, sole cause and mistress of its happy or unhappy condition.

^BExternal circumstances take their savor and color from the inner constitution, just as clothes keep us warm not by their heat but by our own, which they are fitted to foster and nourish; he who would

shelter a cold body with them would get the same service for cold; thus are snow and ice preserved.

^AIndeed, just as study is a torment to a lazy man, abstinence from wine to a drunkard, frugality to the luxurious man, and exercise to a delicate idler, so it is with the rest. Things are not that painful or difficult of themselves; it is our weakness and cowardice that make them so. To judge of great and lofty things we need a soul of the same caliber; otherwise we attribute to them the vice that is our own. A straight oar looks bent in the water. What matters is not merely that we see the thing, but how we see it.

Well then, why, out of so many arguments which in various ways persuade men to despise death and endure pain, do we not find one that will do for us? And of all the many kinds of fancies which have persuaded others, why doesn't each man apply to himself the one that best suits his humor? If he cannot digest the strong purgative drug to root out the trouble, at least let him take a palliative one to relieve it. ^c*There is a certain weak and effeminate attitude shown in pleasure as much as in pain, whereby, when softness has reduced us to a liquid flow, we cannot endure a bee sting without crying out. The whole thing is to be master of yourself* [Cicero].

^AFor the rest, we do not escape philosophy by stressing immoderately the sharpness of pain and the weakness of man. For we force her to fall back on these unanswerable replies:

If it is bad to live in need, at least there is no need to live in need.

^cNo one suffers long except by his own fault.

He who has not the courage to suffer either death or life, who will neither resist nor flee, what can we do with him?

15
One is punished for defending a place obstinately without reason

^AValor has its limits like the other virtues, and these limits once transgressed, we find ourselves on the path of vice; so that we may pass through valor to temerity, obstinacy, and madness, unless we know its limits well – and they are truly hard to discern near the borderlines. From this consideration is derived the custom, which we have in wars, of punishing even with death those who obstinately defend a place which by the rules of war cannot be held. Otherwise,

in the hope of impunity, there would not be a chicken coop that would not hold up an army. Monsieur de Montmorency, Constable of France, at the siege of Pavia, was commissioned to cross the Ticino and take quarters in the suburb of San Antonio; finding himself hindered by a tower at the end of the bridge which obstinately resisted until it was overcome, he had everyone who was in it hanged. And the same man later, with the Dauphin in the campaign beyond the Alps, when our soldiers had taken the castle of Villano by force and in their fury cut everyone inside to pieces except the captain and the ensign, had these two hanged and strangled for this same reason. Captain Martin du Bellay, then governor of Turin in this same country, did the same to Captain de Saint-Bony, the rest of whose men were massacred at the taking of the place.

But the judgment of the strength or weakness of a place is formed by estimating the comparative strength of the forces attacking it; a man might properly hold out against two culverins who would be crazy to resist thirty cannon. Moreover, there comes into account also the greatness of the conquering prince, his reputation, the respect that is owed to him, whence there is danger that the balance will be weighted a bit heavily on the side of the attackers. And it happens because of these same conditions that some have so great an opinion of themselves and their power that, since it seems unreasonable to them that there should be anything worthy to stand up against them, they put everyone to the sword wherever they find resistance, as long as their fortune lasts; as is seen in the forms of summoning and challenging, fierce, haughty, and full of barbaric imperiousness, which were in use among Oriental princes and are still among their successors.

ᶜAnd in that part of the world where the Portuguese made inroads in the Indies, they found some states with this universal and inviolable law, that any enemy vanquished by the king with the king or his lieutenant present is beyond consideration for ransom or mercy.

ᴮThus above all we must beware, if we can, of falling into the hands of an enemy judge who is victorious and armed.

16
Of the punishment of cowardice

ᴬI once heard a prince, a very great captain, maintain that a soldier could not be condemned to death for faintheartedness; he had just

been told the story at table of the trial of the seigneur de Vervins, who was condemned to death for having surrendered Boulogne.

In truth it is right to make a great distinction between the faults that come from our weakness and those that come from our malice. For in the latter we have tensed ourselves deliberately against the rules of reason that nature has imprinted in us; and in the former it seems that we can call on this same nature as our warrantor, for having left us in such imperfection and weakness. Thus many people have thought that we could not be blamed except for what we do against our conscience; and on this rule is partly based the opinion of those who condemn capital punishment for heretics and unbelievers, and the belief that an advocate or a judge cannot be held responsible for having failed in his charge because of ignorance.

But as for cowardice, it is certain that the commonest way to chastise it is by shame and ignominy. And they say that this rule was first put into practice by the legislator Charondas; and that before his time the laws of Greece punished by death those who had fled from a battle, whereas he ordained merely that they should be placed in the public square for three days, dressed in women's clothes; hoping still to be able to use them after having brought back their courage by this shame. ^C*Rather bring the blood to a man's cheeks than shed it* [Tertullian].

^AIt seems also that in ancient times the Roman laws condemned to death those who had fled. For Ammianus Marcellinus relates that Emperor Julian condemned ten of his soldiers, who had turned their backs in a charge against the Parthians, to be degraded and afterward to suffer death, according, he says, to the ancient laws. Elsewhere, however, for a similar fault, he condemns others merely to stay among the prisoners under the baggage ensign. ^CThe harsh sentences passed by the Roman people on the soldiers who had escaped from Cannae, and on those who accompanied Cn. Fulvius to his defeat, in that same war, did not go so far as death.

Yet it is to be feared that shame may make them desperate, and not merely cold, but enemies.

^AIn our fathers' time the seigneur de Franget, formerly lieutenant of Marshal de Chastillon's company, having been made governor of Fuenterrabía by the Marshal de Chabannes in place of Monsieur du Lude, and having surrendered the place to the Spaniards, was condemned to be deprived of his nobility, and both he and his posterity were declared commoners, taxable, and unfit to bear arms; this rough sentence was executed at Lyons. Later, all the

noblemen who were in Guise when the count of Nassau entered it suffered the same punishment; and still others since.

At all events, if there should be such gross and apparent ignorance or cowardice as to surpass all ordinary examples, it would be right to take it as sufficient proof of wickedness and malice and to punish it as such.

17
A trait of certain ambassadors

^AIn order always to be learning something by communication with others (which is one of the finest schools there can be), I observe in my travels this practice: I always steer those I talk with back to the subjects they know best.

> To winds the sailor should confine his words,
> The farmer to his oxen. Let the man of war
> Tell of his wounds, the shepherd of his herds.
> PROPERTIUS[1]

For most often the opposite happens: each man chooses to hold forth on another man's occupation rather than his own, thinking that this is so much new reputation acquired; witness the reproach Archidamus made to Periander, that he was abandoning the glory of a good doctor for that of a bad poet.

^CSee how broadly Caesar spreads himself to make us understand his inventions for building bridges and machines, and how he restricts himself where he speaks of the functions of his profession, of his valor and his military conduct. His exploits sufficiently prove him an excellent captain; he wants to make himself known as an excellent engineer, a somewhat different matter.

The other day, a man of the legal profession, when shown a study furnished with all sorts of books of his trade and of every other sort, found in it no occasion for remark. But he stopped to comment rudely and magisterially upon a barricade placed at the head of the winding stair to the study, which a hundred captains and soldiers encountered every day without remark and without offense.

Dionysius the Elder was a very great leader in war, as befitted his rank; but he labored to recommend himself principally by poetry, about which he knew nothing.

1 Quoted by Montaigne in Guazzo's Italian translation.

^AThe slow ox wants the saddle, the horse wants to plow.
 HORACE

^COn that track you never do anything worth while.

^AThus we must always throw the architect, the painter, the shoemaker and the rest each back to his quarry. And apropos of this, in the reading of history, which is everybody's business, I make it a habit to consider who are the authors. If they are people who have no other profession than letters, I learn mainly their style and language; if they are doctors, I believe them most readily in what they tell us about the temperature of the air, the health and constitution of princes, and wounds and maladies; if they are lawyers, we must take what they say on controversies over rights, the laws, the establishment of governments, and things like that; if theologians, Church affairs, ecclesiastical censures, dispensations, and marriages; if courtiers, manners and ceremonies; if men of war, what belongs to their business, and principally the accounts of the great actions at which they were present in person; if ambassadors, negotiations, understandings, and diplomatic practices, and the way to conduct them.

For this reason, what I should have passed over in another without stopping, I noticed and considered in the history of the seigneur de Langey, a very wise man in such matters. He first relates the edifying remonstrances delivered by Emperor Charles V in the Roman Consistory in the presence of the bishop of Mâcon and the seigneur du Velly, our ambassadors, in which were interspersed many outrageous remarks against us – among others, that if his captains, soldiers, and subjects were not very different from those of the king of France in fidelity and military ability, he would instantly tie a rope around his neck and go beg the king for mercy (it seems that he meant something of this, for two or three times thereafter it befell him to repeat these same words), and also that he challenged the king to fight him in his shirt with sword and dagger in a boat. After relating which, the aforesaid seigneur de Langey, continuing his history, adds that when these ambassadors sent the king a dispatch about these matters, they disguised the greater part and especially concealed from him the two preceding items.

Now I found it very strange that it should be in the power of an ambassador to make his choice of the information that he should give his master, especially in material of such consequence, coming from such a personage, and spoken in so great an assembly. It seems

to me that the function of a servant is to represent things faithfully in their entirety just as they happened, leaving to his master the liberty to arrange, judge, and choose. For to alter the truth or hide it from another for fear he might take it otherwise than he should and that it might push him into some bad course, and meanwhile to leave him ignorant of his affairs – such conduct seems to me proper for him who gives the law, not for him who receives it; for the man in charge and the schoolmaster, not for the man who ought to think himself inferior in prudence and good counsel as well as in authority. However this may be, I should not like to be served in this way, in my little doings.

ᶜWe are so eager to get out from under command, under some pretext, and to usurp mastery; each man aspires so naturally to liberty and authority, that to a superior no useful quality in those who serve him should be so dear as their natural and simple obedience.

We corrupt the function of command when we obey through discretion, not subjection. P. Crassus, whom the Romans considered five times happy, when he was consul in Asia, commanded a Greek engineer to fetch him the bigger of two ship's masts that he had seen in Athens for some battering machine he wanted to make. The engineer, on the strength of his knowledge, permitted himself to choose otherwise, and fetched the smaller one, the more suitable according to the rules of his craft. Crassus, after listening patiently to his reasons, had him well whipped, respecting the interests of discipline more than the interests of the job.

On the other hand, however, one might also consider that such constrained obedience belongs only to precise and stated commands. Ambassadors have a freer commission, which in many areas depends in the last resort on their judgment; they do not simply carry out, but also by their counsel form and direct their master's will. I have in my time known people in command to be reprimanded for having obeyed the words of the king's letters rather than the demands of the situation they were in. Men of understanding still condemn the practice of the kings of Persia, who gave such minutely detailed instructions to their agents and lieutenants that in the slightest matters they had to have recourse to these instructions; so that the resulting delay, in so vast an area of dominion, often did notable harm to their affairs. And did not Crassus, when he wrote to an expert and advised him of the use for which that mast was destined, seem to consult his judgment and invite him to interpose his opinion?

18
Of fear

ᴬI stood stunned, my hair rose, the voice stuck in my throat.
 VIRGIL

I am not a good "naturalist" (as they call it) and I hardly know by what springs fear acts in us; but at all events it is a strange passion, and the doctors say that there is none which carries our judgment away sooner from its proper seat. In truth, I have known many people to become insane from fear; and even in the most stable, it is certain that while the fit lasts it engenders terrible bewilderment. I leave aside the common herd, whom it causes to imagine now great-grandfathers issued from the tomb wrapped in their shrouds, now werewolves, goblins, and chimeras. But even among soldiers, in whom it should have less room, how many times has it changed a flock of sheep into a squadron of armed men, reeds and rushes into men-at-arms and lancers, friend into foe, and the white cross into the red!

When Monsieur de Bourbon took Rome, a standard-bearer on guard at the fort of San Pietro was seized with such a fright at the first alarm that he threw himself through a ruined part of the wall, standard in hand, out of the city right toward the enemy, thinking that he was heading toward the center of town. And only with great effort, at the last moment, seeing Monsieur de Bourbon's men, who thought this was a sortie made by those in the city, take their positions to resist him, he came to himself and, facing about, re-entered the city by that same breach, from which he had come out more than three hundred paces into the open field.

It did not turn out so fortunately for the ensign of Captain Juille when Saint-Pol was taken from us by the count de Bures and Monsieur du Reu; for, being so utterly lost from fright as to rush with his colors out of the town through an embrasure, he was cut to pieces by the assailants. And at the same siege, memorable was the fear that so powerfully seized, constricted, and froze the heart of a gentleman, that he fell to the ground in the breach stone dead of it, without a single wound.

ᴮA similar fear sometimes seizes a whole multitude. In one of the encounters of Germanicus with the Germans, two large bodies of men, out of fright, took two opposite directions, the one fleeing from where the other was running from.

^ANow fear gives wings to our heels as in the above examples; now it nails down and fetters our feet. Thus we read that Emperor Theophilus, in a battle he lost against the Agarenes, became so stunned and paralyzed that he could not make up his mind to flee – ^B*so much is fear afraid even of help* [Quintus Curtius] – ^Auntil Manuel, one of the principal leaders of his army, having tugged and shaken him as if to wake him from a deep sleep, said to him: "If you do not follow me, I will kill you; for it is better for you to lose your life than, by being taken prisoner, to lose your empire."

^CFear expresses its utmost power when, in its own service, it throws us back upon the courage that it has snatched away from our sense of duty and honor. In the first pitched battle that the Romans lost against Hannibal under the consul Sempronius, a body of at least ten thousand infantrymen, having taken fright and seeing no other way out for their cowardice, threw themselves into the main body of the enemy, which by a marvelous effort they pierced, slaughtering a great many of the Carthaginians and purchasing a shameful flight at the same price they would have paid for a glorious victory.

The thing I fear most is fear.

Moreover, it exceeds all other disorders in intensity. What anger could be more bitter and more just than that of Pompey's friends, who were in his ship, spectators of that horrible massacre?[1] Yet their fear of the Egyptian sails, which were beginning to approach them, stifled this feeling, so that commentators have noted that they did nothing but spur the sailors to make haste and escape by plying their oars; until, having arrived at Tyre, free from fear, they had a chance to turn their thoughts to the loss they had just suffered and to give free rein to the lamentations and tears that this other stronger passion had suspended.

> Then fear drives out all wisdom from my mind.
>
> ENNIUS, QUOTED BY CICERO[2]

1 The treacherous murder of Pompey by one of his old centurions as he sought refuge in Egypt (48 B.C.).

2 The passage above, from "What anger could..." on, is not found in the Bordeaux Copy, but only in the 1595 edition. Most modern editors accept it because a mark in the Bordeaux Copy calls for an insertion, perhaps on a piece of paper now lost. However, there was room enough on the margins of that page for Montaigne to have written it there, as was his practice.

Those who have been well drubbed in some battle, and who are still all wounded and bloody – you can perfectly well bring them back to the charge the next day. But those who have conceived a healthy fear of the enemy – you would never get them to look him in the face. Those who are in pressing fear of losing their property, of being exiled, of being subjugated, live in constant anguish, losing even the capacity to drink, eat, and rest; whereas the poor, the exiles, and the slaves often live as joyfully as other men. And so many people who, unable to endure the pangs of fear, have hanged themselves, drowned themselves, or leaped to their death, have taught us well that fear is even more unwelcome and unbearable than death itself.

The Greeks recognize another kind of fear, which comes, they say, not from any failure of our reason, but without any apparent cause and by divine impulsion. Whole peoples are often seen to be seized by it, and whole armies. Such was the fear which brought incredible desolation upon Carthage. You heard nothing there but frightened cries and exclamations. You saw the inhabitants running out of their houses as at a call to arms, and charging, wounding, and killing each other, as if they were enemies coming to occupy their city. Everything there was in disorder and tumult, until, by prayers and sacrifices, they had appeased the anger of the gods. They call these panic terrors.

19
That our happiness must not be judged until after our death

ᴬNo man should be called happy till his death;
Always we must await his final day,
Reserving judgment till he's laid away.

OVID

Children know the story of King Croesus in this connection, who, having been captured by Cyrus and condemned to death, on the point of execution cried out: "O Solon, Solon!" When this was reported to Cyrus, he inquired what it meant, and was given to understand that Croesus was now verifying at his own expense the warning that Solon once had given him: that men, however fortune may smile on them, cannot be called happy until they have been seen to spend the last day of their lives, because of the uncertainty and

variability of human affairs, which the slightest shift changes from one state to another entirely different.

And therefore Agesilaus said to someone who called the king of Persia happy because he had come very young to such a powerful estate: "Yes, but Priam at his age was not unhappy." Kings of Macedon, successors to the great Alexander, are made into carpenters and clerks at Rome; tyrants of Sicily, into schoolmasters at Corinth. A conqueror of half the world and emperor of many armies becomes a miserable suppliant before the good-for-nothing officers of a king of Egypt: so much did it cost the great Pompey to prolong his life five or six months. And in our fathers' time, Ludovico Sforza, tenth duke of Milan, whose will moved all Italy for so long, was seen to die a prisoner at Loches – and that only after living there ten years, which is the worst part of his bargain. ^CThe fairest of queens,¹ widow of the greatest king in Christendom, has she not just died by the hand of an executioner? ^AAnd there are a thousand such examples.

For it seems that, as storms and tempests are provoked to humble the pride and loftiness of our buildings, so there are spirits up above who are envious of grandeurs here below:

> Such havoc on human things some hidden power wreaks,
> Tramples the gleaming rods, fierce axes, all that speaks
> Of human eminence, and laughs them all to scorn.
>
> LUCRETIUS

And it seems that Fortune sometimes lies in wait precisely for the last day of our life, to show her power to overturn in a moment what she has built up over many years, and makes us cry out after Laberius: *Truly this day I have lived one day longer than I should have* [Macrobius].

In this sense Solon's good advice may reasonably be taken. But inasmuch as Solon is a philosopher, one of those to whom the favors and disfavors of fortune rank as neither happiness nor unhappiness, and grandeurs and powers are accidents of almost indifferent quality, I find it likely that he was looking further, and meant that this same happiness of our life, which depends on the tranquillity and contentment of a well-born spirit and the resolution and assurance of a well-ordered soul, should never be attributed to a man until he has been seen to play the last act of his comedy, and beyond doubt

1 Mary Stuart, widow of Francis II, decapitated on February 8, 1587.

the hardest. In everything else there may be sham: the fine reason-
ings of philosophy may be a mere pose in us; or else our trials, by
not testing us to the quick, give us a chance to keep our face always
composed. But in the last scene, between death and ourselves,
there is no more pretending; we must talk plain French, we
must show what there is that is good and clean at the bottom of
the pot:

> At last true words surge up from deep within our breast,
> The mask is snatched away, reality is left.

<div align="right">LUCRETIUS</div>

That is why all the other actions of our life must be tried and
tested by this last act. It is the master day, the day that is judge of all
the others. "It is the day," says one of the ancients [Seneca], "that
must judge all my past years." I leave it to death to test the fruit of my
studies. We shall see then whether my reasonings come from
my mouth or from my heart.

ᴮI know of many who by their death gave their whole life
a good or a bad reputation. Scipio, the father-in-law of Pompey,
redressed, by dying well, the bad opinion that people had had
of him until then. Epaminondas, asked which of the three he
esteemed most, Chabrias or Iphicrates or himself, said: "You must
see us die before you can decide." In truth you would rob a man
of much if you weighed him without the honor and greatness of
his end.

God has willed it as he pleased; but in my time three of the most
execrable and most infamous persons I have known in every abom-
ination of life have had deaths that were ordered and in every
circumstance composed to perfection.

ᶜThere are gallant and fortunate deaths. I have seen death bring
a wonderfully brilliant career, and that in its flower, to such
a splendid end that in my opinion the dead man's ambitions and
courageous designs had nothing so lofty about them as their inter-
ruption. He arrived where he aspired to without going there, more
grandly and gloriously than he had desired or hoped. And by his fall
he went beyond the power and the fame to which he had aspired by
his career.

ᴮIn judging the life of another, I always observe how it ended;
and one of my principal concerns about my own end is that it shall
go well, that is to say quietly and insensibly.

20
That to philosophize is to learn to die

^ACicero says that to philosophize is nothing else but to prepare for death. This is because study and contemplation draw our soul out of us to some extent and keep it busy outside the body; which is a sort of apprenticeship and semblance of death. Or else it is because all the wisdom and reasoning in the world boils down finally to this point: to teach us not to be afraid to die. In truth, either reason is a mockery, or it must aim solely at our contentment, and the sum of its labors must tend to make us live well and at our ease, as Holy Scripture says. All the opinions in the world agree on this – ^Cthat pleasure is our goal – ^Athough they choose different means to it. Otherwise they would be thrown out right away; for who would listen to a man who would set up our pain and discomfort as his goal?

^CThe dissensions of the philosophic sects in this matter are merely verbal. *Let us skip over such frivolous subtleties* [Seneca]. There is more stubbornness and wrangling than befits such a sacred profession. But whatever role man undertakes to play, he always plays his own at the same time. Whatever they say, in virtue itself the ultimate goal we aim at is voluptuousness. I like to beat their ears with that word, which so goes against their grain. And if it means a certain supreme pleasure and excessive contentment, this is due more to the assistance of virtue than to any other assistance. This voluptuousness, for being more lusty, sinewy, robust, and manly, is only the more seriously voluptuous. And we should have given virtue the name of pleasure, a name more favorable, sweet, and natural; not that of vigor, as we have named it. That other baser sort of voluptuousness, if it deserved that beautiful name, should have acquired it in competition, not as a privilege. I find it less free of inconveniences and obstacles than virtue. Besides the fact that its enjoyment is more momentary, watery, and weak, it has its vigils, its fasts, and its hardships, its sweat and blood; and, more particularly, its poignant sufferings of so many kinds, and an accompanying satiety so heavy that it is the equivalent of penance. We are very wrong to suppose that these disadvantages act as a spur and a spice to its sweetness, as in nature a thing is enlivened by its opposite, and to say, when we come to virtue, that similar consequences and difficulties oppress it, make it austere and inaccessible; whereas, much more than in the case of voluptuousness, they ennoble, whet,

and heighten the divine and perfect pleasure that virtue affords us. That man is surely very unworthy of its acquaintance who balances its cost against its fruits; he knows neither its graces nor its use. Those who go on teaching us that the quest of it is rugged and laborious, though the enjoyment of it is agreeable, what are they doing but telling us that it is always disagreeable? For what human means ever attained the enjoyment of virtue? The most perfect have been quite content to aspire to it and to approach it, without possessing it. But those others are wrong; since in all the pleasures that we know, even the pursuit is pleasant. The attempt is made fragrant by the quality of the thing it aims at, for it is a good part of the effect, and consubstantial with it. The happiness and blessedness that shines in virtue fills all its appurtenances and approaches even to the first entrance and the utmost barrier.

Now among the principal benefits of virtue is disdain for death, a means that furnishes our life with a soft tranquillity and gives us a pure and pleasant enjoyment of it, without which all other pleasures are extinguished. ᴬThat is why all rules meet and agree at this point. And though they all with one accord lead us also to scorn pain, poverty, and other accidents to which human life is subject, it is not with equal insistence; partly because these accidents are not so inevitable (most men spend their life without tasting poverty, and some also without feeling pain and illness, like Xenophilus the musician, who lived a hundred and six years in complete health), and also because at worst, whenever we please, death can put an end, and deny access, to all our other woes. But as for death itself, it is inevitable.

> ᴮWe are all forced down the same road. Our fate,
> Tossed in the urn, will spring out soon or late,
> And force us helpless into Charon's bark,
> Passengers destined for eternal dark.
>
> HORACE

ᴬAnd consequently, if it frightens us, it is a continual source of torment which cannot be alleviated at all. ᶜThere is no place from which it may not come to us; we may turn our heads constantly this way and that as in a suspicious country: *death always hangs over us, like the stone over Tantalus* [Cicero]. ᴬOur law courts often send criminals to be executed at the place where the crime was committed. On the way, take them past beautiful houses, give them as good a time as you like –

> [B]Not even a Sicilian feast
> Can now produce for him a pleasant taste,
> Nor song of birds, nor music of the lyre
> Restore his sleep
> HORACE

– [A]do you think that they can rejoice in these things, and that the final purpose of their trip, being steadily before their eyes, will not have changed and spoiled their taste for all these pleasures?

> [B]He hears it as it comes, counts days, measures the breath
> Of life upon their length, tortured by coming death.
> CLAUDIAN

[A]The goal of our career is death. It is the necessary object of our aim. If it frightens us, how is it possible to go a step forward without feverishness? The remedy of the common herd is not to think about it. But from what brutish stupidity can come so gross a blindness! They have to bridle the ass by the tail,

> Who sets his mind on moving only backward.
> LUCRETIUS

It is no wonder they are so often caught in the trap. These people take fright at the mere mention of death, and most of them cross themselves at that name, as at the name of the devil. And because death is mentioned in wills, don't expect them to set about writing a will until the doctor has given them their final sentence; and then, between the pain and the fright, Lord knows with what fine judgment they will concoct it.

[B]Because this syllable struck their ears too harshly and seemed to them unlucky, the Romans learned to soften it or to spread it out into a periphrasis. Instead of saying "He is dead," they say "He has ceased to live," "He has lived." Provided it is life, even past life, they take comfort. We have borrowed from them our "late Mr. John."[1]

[A]Perhaps it is true that, as the saying goes, the delay is worth the money. I was born between eleven o'clock and noon on the last day of February, 1533, as we reckon time now,[2] beginning the year in

1 The French for *late* in this sense is *feu*, from Latin *fatutus*. Montaigne seems to think it comes from Latin *fuit* (*was*), Old French *feut*.

2 In 1563 Charles IX set January 1 as the beginning of the year, and this decree took full effect in 1567. Until then the year had officially begun at Easter.

January. It was only just two weeks ago that I passed the age of
thirty-nine years, and I need at least that many more; but to be
bothered meanwhile by the thought of a thing so far off would be
folly. After all, young and old leave life on the same terms. ^CNone
goes out of it otherwise than as if he had just entered it. ^AAnd
besides, there is no man so decrepit that as long as he sees Methu-
selah ahead of him, he does not think he has another twenty years
left in his body. Furthermore, poor fool that you are, who has
assured you the term of your life? You are building on the tales of
doctors. Look rather at facts and experience. By the ordinary run of
things, you have been living a long time now by extraordinary favor.
You have passed the accustomed limits of life. And to prove this,
count how many more of your acquaintances have died before your
age than have attained it. And even for those who have glorified
their lives by renown, make a list, and I'll wager I'll find more of
them who died before thirty-five than after. It is completely reason-
able and pious to take our example from the humanity of Jesus
Christ himself; now he finished his life at thirty-three. The greatest
man that was simply a man, Alexander, also died at that age.

How many ways has death to surprise us!

> Man never can plan fully to avoid
> What any hour may bring.
>
> HORACE

I leave aside fevers and pleurisies. Who would ever have thought
that a duke of Brittany would be stifled to death by a crowd, as that
duke was at the entrance of Pope Clement, my neighbor,[3] into
Lyons? Haven't you seen one of our kings killed at play? And did
not one of his ancestors die from the charge of a hog? Aeschylus,
threatened with the fall of a house, takes every precaution – in vain:
he gets himself killed by a sort of roof, the shell of a tortoise dropped
by a flying eagle. Another dies from a grape seed; an emperor from
the scratch of a comb, while combing his hair; Aemilius Lepidus
through stumbling against his threshold, and Aufidius through
bumping against the door of the council chamber on his way in;
and between women's thighs, Cornelius Gallus the praetor, Tigilli-
nus, captain of the watch at Rome, Ludovico, son of Guido de

3 Clement V (Bertrand de Got), Pope from 1305 to 1314, who transferred the
papal seat to Avignon, had earlier been archbishop of Bordeaux and hence
Montaigne's "neighbor."

Gonzaga, marquis of Mantua – and still worse, the Platonic philosopher Speusippus, and one of our Popes. Poor Bebius, a judge, in the act of granting a week's postponement to a litigant, has a seizure, his own term of living having expired; and Caius Julius, a doctor, is anointing the eyes of a patient, when along comes death and closes his. And, if I must bring myself into this, a brother of mine, Captain Saint-Martin, twenty-three years old, who had already given pretty good proof of his valor, while playing tennis was struck by a ball a little above the right ear, with no sign of contusion or wound. He did not sit down or rest, but five or six hours later he died of an apoplexy that this blow gave him. With such frequent and ordinary examples passing before our eyes, how can we possibly rid ourselves of the thought of death and of the idea that at every moment it is gripping us by the throat?

What does it matter, you will tell me, how it happens, provided we do not worry about it? I am of that opinion; and in whatever way we can put ourselves in shelter from blows, even under a calf's skin, I am not the man to shrink from it. For it is enough for me to spend my life comfortably; and the best game I can give myself I'll take, though it be as little glorious and exemplary as you like:

> If but my faults could trick and please
> My wits, I'd rather seem a fool at ease,
> Than to be wise and rage. HORACE

But it is folly to expect to get there that way. They go, they come, they trot, they dance – of death no news. All that is fine. But when it comes, either to them or to their wives, children, or friends, surprising them unprepared and defenseless, what torments, what cries, what frenzy, what despair overwhelms them! Did you ever see anything so dejected, so changed, so upset? We must provide for this earlier; and this brutish nonchalance, even if it could lodge in the head of a man of understanding – which I consider entirely impossible – sells us its wares too dear. If it were an enemy we could avoid, I would advise us to borrow the arms of cowardice. But since that cannot be, ᴮsince it catches you just the same, whether you flee like a coward or act like a man –

> ᴬAs surely it pursues the man that flees,
> Nor does it spare the haunches slack
> Of warless youth, or its timid back
> HORACE

– ^Band since no kind of armor protects you –

> Hide as he will, cautious, in steel and brass,
> Still death will drag his head outside at last
>
> PROPERTIS

– ^Alet us learn to meet it steadfastly and to combat it. And to begin to strip it of its greatest advantage against us, let us take an entirely different way from the usual one. Let us rid it of its strangeness, come to know it, get used to it. Let us have nothing on our minds as often as death. At every moment let us picture it in our imagination in all its aspects. At the stumbling of a horse, the fall of a tile, the slightest pin prick, let us promptly chew on this: Well, what if it were death itself? And thereupon let us tense ourselves and make an effort. Amid feasting and gaiety let us ever keep in mind this refrain, the memory of our condition; and let us never allow ourselves to be so carried away by pleasure that we do not sometimes remember in how many ways this happiness of ours is a prey to death, and how death's clutches threaten it. Thus did the Egyptians, who, in the midst of their feasts and their greatest pleasures, had the skeleton of a dead man brought before them, to serve as a reminder to the guests.

> Look on each day as if it were your last,
> And each unlooked-for hour will seem a boon.
>
> HORACE

It is uncertain where death awaits us; let us await it everywhere. Premeditation of death is premeditation of freedom. He who has learned how to die has unlearned how to be a slave. Knowing how to die frees us from all subjection and constraint. ^CThere is nothing evil in life for the man who has thoroughly grasped the fact that to be deprived of life is not an evil. ^AAemilius Paulus replied to the messenger sent by that miserable king of Macedon, his prisoner, to beg him not to lead him in his triumph: "Let him make that request of himself."

In truth, in all things, unless nature lends a hand, it is hard for art and industry to get very far. I am by nature not melancholy, but dreamy. Since my earliest days, there is nothing with which I have occupied my mind more than with images of death. Even in the most licentious season of my life,

> ^BWhen blooming youth enjoyed a gladsome spring,
>
> CATULLUS

^Aamid ladies and games, someone would think me involved in digesting some jealousy by myself, or the uncertainty of some hope, while I was thinking about I don't remember whom, who had been overtaken a few days before by a hot fever and by death, on leaving a similar feast, his head full of idleness, love, and a good time, like myself; and thinking that the same chance was hanging from my ear:

^BAnd soon it will have been, past any man's recall.

LUCRETIUS

^AI did not wrinkle my forehead any more over that thought than any other. It is impossible that we should fail to feel the sting of such notions at first. But by handling them and going over them, in the long run we tame them beyond question. Otherwise for my part I should be in continual fright and frenzy; for never did a man so distrust his life, never did a man set less faith in his duration. Neither does health, which thus far I have enjoyed in great vigor and with little interruption, lengthen my hope of life, nor do illnesses shorten it. Every minute I seem to be slipping away from myself. ^CAnd I constantly sing myself this refrain: Whatever can be done another day can be done today. ^ATruly risks and dangers bring us little or no nearer our end; and if we think how many million accidents remain hanging over our heads, not to mention this one that seems to threaten us most, we shall conclude that lusty or feverish, on sea or in our houses, in battle or in rest, death is equally near us. ^C*No man is frailer than another, no man more certain of the morrow* [Seneca]. ^ATo finish what I have to do before I die, even if it were one hour's work, any leisure seems short to me.

Someone, looking through my tablets the other day, found a memorandum about something I wanted done after my death. I told him what was true, that although only a league away from my house, and hale and hearty, I had hastened to write it there, since I could not be certain of reaching home. ^CSince I am constantly brooding over my thoughts and settling them within me, I am at all times about as well prepared as I can be. And the coming of death will teach me nothing new.

^AWe must be always booted and ready to go, so far as it is in our power, and take especial care to have only ourselves to deal with then:

^BWhy aim so stoutly at so many things
In our short life?

HORACE

^AFor we shall have enough trouble without adding any. One man complains not so much of death as that it interrupts the course of a glorious victory; another, that he must move out before he has married off his daughter or supervised the education of his children; one laments losing the company of his wife, another of his son, as the principal comforts of his life.

^CI am at this moment in such a condition, thank God, that I can move out when he chooses, without regret for anything at all, unless for life, if I find that the loss of it weighs on me. I unbind myself on all sides; my farewells are already half made to everyone except myself. Never did a man prepare to leave the world more utterly and completely, nor detach himself from it more universally, than I propose to do.

> ^B"Wretch that I am," they say, "one all-destroying day
> Takes every last reward of all my life away!"
>
> LUCRETIUS

^AAnd the builder says:

> The works remain suspended,
> And the high looming walls.
>
> VIRGIL

We must not plan anything that takes so long, or at least not with the idea of flying into a passion if we cannot see it accomplished.

We are born to act:

> When death comes, let it find me at my work.
>
> OVID

I want a man to act, ^Cand to prolong the functions of life as long as he can; ^Aand I want death to find me planting my cabbages, but careless of death, and still more of my unfinished garden. I saw a man die who, in his last extremity, complained constantly that destiny was cutting short the history, on which he was at work, of the fifteenth or sixteenth of our kings.

> ^BBut this they fail to add: that after you expire
> Not one of all these things will fill you with desire.
>
> LUCRETIUS

^AWe must rid ourselves of these vulgar and harmful humors. Just as we plant our cemeteries next to churches, and in the most frequented parts of town, in order (says Lycurgus) to accustom

the common people, women and children, not to grow panicky at the sight of a dead man, and so that the constant sight of bones, tombs, and funeral processions should remind us of our condition –

 ᴮTo feasts, it once was thought, slaughter lent added charms,
 Mingling with foods the sight of combatants in arms,
 And gladiators fell amid the cups, to pour
 Onto the very tables their abundant gore
 SILIUS ITALICUS

– ᶜand as the Egyptians, after their feasts, had a large image of death shown to the guests by a man who called out to them: "Drink and be merry, for when you are dead you will be like this"; ᴬso I have formed the habit of having death continually present, not merely in my imagination, but in my mouth. And there is nothing that I investigate so eagerly as the death of men: what words, what look, what bearing they maintained at that time; nor is there a place in the histories that I note so attentively. ᶜThis shows in the abundance of my illustrative examples; I have indeed a particular fondness for this subject. If I were a maker of books, I would make a register, with comments, of various deaths. He who would teach men to die would teach them to live. Dicearchus made a book with such a title, but with a different and less useful purpose.

ᴬPeople will tell me that the reality of death so far exceeds the image we form of it that, when a man is faced with it, even the most skillful fencing will do him no good. Let them talk; beyond question forethought is a great advantage. And then, is it nothing to go at least that far without disturbance and fever? What is more, Nature herself lends us her hand and gives us courage. If it is a quick and violent death, we have no leisure to fear it; if it is otherwise, I notice that in proportion as I sink into sickness, I naturally enter into a certain disdain for life. I find that I have much more trouble digesting this resolution to die when I am in health than when I have a fever. Inasmuch as I no longer cling so hard to the good things of life when I begin to lose the use and pleasure of them, I come to view death with much less frightened eyes. This makes me hope that the farther I get from life and the nearer to death, the more easily I shall accept the exchange. Even as I have experienced in many other occasions what Caesar says, that things often appear greater to us from a distance than near, so I have found that when I was healthy I had a much greater horror of sicknesses than when I felt them. The good spirits, pleasure, and strength I now

enjoy make the other state appear to me so disproportionate to this one, that by imagination I magnify those inconveniences by half, and think of them as much heavier than I find they are when I have them on my shoulders. I hope I shall have the same experience with death.

^BLet us see how, in those ordinary changes and declines that we suffer, nature hides from us the sense of our loss and decay. What has an old man left of the vigor of his youth, and of his past life?

> Alas! how scant a share of life the old have left!
>
> MAXIMIANUS

^CCaesar, observing the decrepit appearance of a soldier of his guard, an exhausted and broken man, who came to him in the street to ask leave to kill himself, replied humorously: "So you think you're alive." ^BIf we fell into such a change suddenly, I don't think we could endure it. But, when we are led by Nature's hand down a gentle and virtually imperceptible slope, bit by bit, one step at a time, she rolls us into this wretched state and makes us familiar with it; so that we feel no shock when youth dies within us, which in essence and in truth is a harder death than the complete death of a languishing life or the death of old age; inasmuch as the leap is not so cruel from a painful life to no life as from a sweet and flourishing life to a grievous and painful one.

^AThe body, when bent and bowed, has less strength to support a burden, and so has the soul; we must raise and straighten her against the assault of this adversary. For as it is impossible for the soul to be at rest while she fears death, so, if she can gain assurance against it, she can boast of a thing as it were beyond man's estate: that it is impossible for worry, torment, fear, or even the slightest displeasure to dwell in her:

> ^BThe fierce look of a tyrant brings no fright
> To his firm mind, nor yet the south wind's might,
> That drives the Adriatic on command,
> Nor Jupiter's great thunder-hurling hand.
>
> HORACE

^AShe is made mistress of her passions and lusts, mistress over indigence, shame, poverty, and all other wounds of fortune. Let us gain this advantage, those of us who can; this is the true and sovereign liberty, which enables us to thumb our noses at force and injustice and to laugh at prisons and chains:

> "I'll keep you bound
> Both hand and foot, in savage custody."
> – "Whene'er I please, a god will set me free."
> I think he meant: I'll die. For death is final.

HORACE

Our religion has no surer human foundation than contempt for life. Not only do the arguments of reason invite us to it; for why should we fear to lose a thing which once lost cannot be regretted? And since we are threatened by so many kinds of death, is there not more pain in fearing them all than in enduring one?[4]

ᶜWhat does it matter when it comes, since it is inevitable? To the man who told Socrates, "The thirty tyrants have condemned you to death," he replied: "And nature, them."

What stupidity to torment ourselves about passing into exemption from all torment! As our birth brought us the birth of all things, so will our death bring us the death of all things. Wherefore it is as foolish to lament that we shall not be alive a hundred years from now as it is to lament that we were not alive a hundred years ago. Death is the origin of another life. Just so did we weep, just so did we struggle against entering this life, just so did we strip off our former veil when we entered it.

Nothing can be grievous that happens only once. Is it reasonable so long to fear a thing so short? Long life and short life are made all one by death. For there is no long or short for things that are no more. Aristotle says that there are little animals by the river Hypanis that live only a day. The one that dies at eight o'clock in the morning dies in its youth; the one that dies at five in the afternoon dies in its decrepitude. Which of us does not laugh to see this moment of duration considered in terms of happiness or unhappiness? The length or shortness of our duration, if we compare it with eternity, or yet with the duration of mountains, rivers, stars, trees, and even of some animals, is no less ridiculous.

ᴬBut Nature forces us to it.[5] Go out of this world, she says, as you entered it. The same passage that you made from death to life,

4 Montaigne's argument is that not only reason but also nature urges us to accept death gracefully. The following three paragraphs, which interrupt his movement, are additions to the original version.

5 Nature's speech, which extends to "the last one reaches it" almost at the end of this chapter (p. 81), is largely a paraphrase of Seneca and Lucretius, and especially Lucretius.

without feeling or fright, make it again from life to death. Your death is a part of the order of the universe; it is a part of the life of the world.

> ^BOur lives we borrow from each other...
> And men, like runners, pass along the torch of life.
> LUCRETIUS

^AShall I change for you this beautiful contexture of things? Death is the condition of your creation, it is a part of you; you are fleeing from your own selves. This being of yours that you enjoy is equally divided between death and life. The first day of your birth leads you toward death as toward life:

> The hour which gave us life led to its end.
> SENECA

> Even in birth we die; the end is there from the start.
> MANILIUS

^CAll the time you live you steal from life; living is at life's expense. The constant work of your life is to build death. You are in death while you are in life; for you are after death when you are no longer in life. Or, if you prefer it this way, you are dead after life; but during life you are dying; and death affects the dying much more roughly than the dead, and more keenly and essentially.

^BIf you have made your profit of life, you have had your fill of it; go your way satisfied:

> Why, like a well-filled guest, not leave the feast of life?
> LUCRETIUS

If you have not known how to make good use of it, if it was useless to you, what do you care that you have lost it, what do you still want it for?

> Why do you seek to add more years
> Which too would pass but ill, and vanish unawares?
> LUCRETIUS

^CLife is neither good nor evil in itself: it is the scene of good and evil according as you give them room.

^AAnd if you have lived a day, you have seen everything. One day is equal to all days. There is no other light, no other night. This sun, this moon, these stars, the way they are arranged, all is the very same your ancestors enjoyed and that will entertain your grandchildren:

> ^CYour ancestors beheld no other one, nor shall
> Your nephews see another.
> MANILIUS

^AAnd at worst, the distribution and variety of all the acts of my comedy runs its course in a year. If you have taken note of the revolution of my four seasons, they embrace the infancy, the youth, the manhood, and the old age of the world. It has played its part. It knows no other trick than to begin again. It will always be just this:

> ^BWe turn in the same circle, and never leave;
> LUCRETIUS

> And on itself the year revolves along its track.
> VIRGIL

^AI am not minded to make you any other new pastimes:

> I can contrive, to please you, nothing more;
> All things remain as they have been before.
> LUCRETIUS

Make room for others, as others have for you. ^CEquality is the principal part of equity. Who can complain of being included where all are included? ^AAnd so, live as long as you please, you will strike nothing off the time you will have to spend dead; it is no use; you shall be as long in that state which you fear as if you had died nursing:

> So live victorious, live long as you will,
> Eternal death shall be there waiting still.
> LUCRETIUS

^BAnd furthermore, I shall put you in such a condition as will give you no cause for complaint:

> Do you not know that when death comes, there'll be
> No other you to mourn your memory,
> And stand above you prostrate?
> LUCRETIUS

Nor will you wish for the life you now lament so much:

> Then none shall mourn their person or their life...
> And all regret of self shall cease to be.
> LUCRETIUS

Death is to be feared less than nothing, if there is anything less than nothing:

> For us far less a thing must death be thought,
> If ought there be that can be less than nought.
>
> LUCRETIUS

^CIt does not concern you dead or alive: alive, because you are; dead, because you are no more.

^ANo one dies before his time. The time you leave behind was no more yours than that which passed before your birth, ^Band it concerns you no more.

> Look back and see how past eternities of time
> Are nothing to us.
>
> LUCRETIUS

^AWherever your life ends, it is all there. ^CThe advantage of living is not measured by length, but by use; some men have lived long, and lived little; attend to it while you are in it. It lies in your will, not in the number of years, for you to have lived enough. ^ADid you think you would never arrive where you never ceased going? ^CYet there is no road but has its end. ^AAnd if company can comfort you, does not the world keep pace with you?

^BAll things, their life being done, will follow you.

> LUCRETIUS

^ADoes not everything move with your movement? Is there anything that does not grow old along with you? A thousand men, a thousand animals, and a thousand other creatures die at the very moment when you die:

> ^BNo night has ever followed day, no day the night,
> That has not heard, amid the newborn infants' squalls,
> The wild laments that go with death and funerals.
>
> LUCRETIUS

^CWhy do you recoil, if you cannot draw back? You have seen enough men who were better off for dying, thereby avoiding great miseries. Have you found any man that was worse off? How simpleminded it is to condemn a thing that you have not experienced yourself or through anyone else. Why do you complain of me and of destiny? Do we wrong you? Is it for you to govern us, or us you? Though your age is not full-grown, your life is. A little man is

a whole man, just like a big one. Neither men nor their lives are measured by the ell.

Chiron refused immortality when informed of its conditions by the very god of time and duration, his father Saturn. Imagine honestly how much less bearable and more painful to man would be an everlasting life than the life I have given him. If you did not have death, you would curse me incessantly for having deprived you of it. I have deliberately mixed with it a little bitterness to keep you, seeing the convenience of it, from embracing it too greedily and intemperately. To lodge you in that moderate state that I ask of you, of neither fleeing life nor fleeing back from death, I have tempered both of them between sweetness and bitterness.

I taught Thales, the first of your sages, that life and death were matters of indifference; wherefore, to the man who asked him why then he did not die, he replied very wisely: "Because it is indifferent."

Water, earth, air, fire, and the other parts of this structure of mine are no more instruments of your life than instruments of your death. Why do you fear your last day? It contributes no more to your death than each of the others. The last step does not cause the fatigue, but reveals it. All days travel toward death, the last one reaches it.

^Such are the good counsels of our mother Nature. Now I have often pondered how it happens that in wars the face of death, whether we see it in ourselves or in others, seems to us incomparably less terrifying than in our houses – otherwise you would have an army of doctors and snivelers – and, since death is always the same, why nevertheless there is much more assurance against it among villagers and humble folk than among others. I truly think it is those dreadful faces and trappings with which we surround it, that frighten us more than death itself: an entirely new way of living; the cries of mothers, wives, and children; the visits of people dazed and benumbed by grief; the presence of a number of pale and weeping servants; a darkened room; lighted candles; our bedside besieged by doctors and preachers; in short, everything horror and fright around us. There we are already shrouded and buried. Children fear even their friends when they see them masked, and so do we ours. We must strip the mask from things as well as from persons; when it is off, we shall find beneath only that same death which a valet or a mere chambermaid passed through not long ago

without fear. Happy the death that leaves no leisure for preparing such ceremonies!

21
Of the power of the imagination

^A*A strong imagination creates the event*, say the scholars. I am one of those who are very much influenced by the imagination. ^CEveryone feels its impact, but some are overthrown by it. Its impression on me is piercing. And my art is to escape it, not to resist it. I would live solely in the presence of gay, healthy people. The sight of other people's anguish causes very real anguish to me, and my feelings have often usurped the feelings of others. A continual cougher irritates my lungs and throat. I visit less willingly the sick toward whom duty directs me than those toward whom I am less attentive and concerned. I catch the disease that I study, and lodge it in me. I do not find it strange that imagination brings fevers and death to those who give it a free hand and encourage it.

Simon Thomas was a great doctor in his time. I remember that one day, when he met me at the house of a rich old consumptive with whom he was discussing ways to cure his illness, he told him that one of these would be to give me occasion to enjoy his company; and that by fixing his eyes on the freshness of my face and his thoughts on the blitheness and overflowing vigor of my youth, and filling all his senses with my flourishing condition, he might improve his constitution. But he forgot to say that mine might get worse at the same time.

^AGallus Vibius strained his mind so hard to understand the essence and impulses of insanity that he dragged his judgment off its seat and never could get it back again; and he could boast of having become mad through wisdom. There are some who through fear anticipate the hand of the executioner. And one man who was being unbound to have his pardon read him dropped stone dead on the scaffold, struck down by his mere imagination. We drip with sweat, we tremble, we turn pale and turn red at the blows of our imagination; reclining in our feather beds we feel our bodies agitated by their impact, sometimes to the point of expiring. And boiling youth, fast asleep, grows so hot in the harness that in dreams it satisfies its amorous desires:

So that as though it were an actual affair,
They pour out mighty streams, and stain the clothes they wear.
LUCRETIUS

And although it is nothing new to see horns grow overnight on someone who did not have them when he went to bed, nevertheless what happened to Cippus, king of Italy, is memorable; having been in the daytime a very excited spectator at a bullfight and having all night in his dreams had horns on his head, he grew actual horns on his forehead by the power of his imagination. Passion gave the son of Croesus the voice that nature had refused him. And Antiochus took fever from the beauty of Stratonice too vividly imprinted in his soul. Pliny says he saw Lucius Cossitius changed from a woman into a man on his wedding day. Pontanus and others report similar metamorphoses as having happened in Italy in these later ages. And through his and his mother's vehement desire,

Iphis the man fulfilled vows made when he was a girl.
OVID

[B]Passing through Vitry-le-François, I might have seen a man whom the bishop of Soissons had named Germain at confirmation, but whom all the inhabitants of that place had seen and known as a girl named Marie until the age of twenty-two. He was now heavily bearded, and old, and not married. Straining himself in some way in jumping, he says, his masculine organs came forth; and among the girls there a song is still current by which they warn each other not to take big strides for fear of becoming boys, like Marie Germain. It is not so great a marvel that this sort of accident is frequently met with. For if the imagination has power in such things, it is so continually and vigorously fixed on this subject that in order not to have to relapse so often into the same thought and sharpness of desire, it is better off if once and for all it incorporates this masculine member in girls.

[A]Some attribute to the power of imagination the scars of King Dagobert and of Saint Francis. It is said that thereby bodies are sometimes removed from their places. And Celsus tells of a priest who used to fly with his soul into such ecstasy that his body would remain a long time without breath and without sensation. [C]Saint Augustine names another who whenever he heard lamentable and plaintive cries would suddenly go into a trance and get so carried

away that it was no use to shake him and shout at him, to pinch him and burn him, until he had come to; then he would say that he had heard voices, but as if coming from afar, and he would notice his burns and bruises. And that this was no feigned resistance to his senses was shown by the fact that while in this state he had neither pulse nor breath.

^AIt is probable that the principal credit of miracles, visions, enchantments, and such extraordinary occurrences comes from the power of imagination, acting principally upon the minds of the common people, which are softer. Their belief has been so strongly seized that they think they see what they do not see.

I am still of this opinion, that those comical inhibitions by which our society is so fettered that people talk of nothing else are for the most part the effects of apprehension and fear. For I know by experience that one man, whom I can answer for as for myself, on whom there could fall no suspicion whatever of impotence and just as little of being enchanted, having heard a friend of his tell the story of an extraordinary impotence into which he had fallen at the moment when he needed it least, and finding himself in a similar situation, was all at once so struck in his imagination by the horror of this story that he incurred the same fate. ^CAnd from then on he was subject to relapse, for the ugly memory of his mishap checked him and tyrannized him. He found some remedy for this fancy by another fancy: which was that by admitting this weakness and speaking about it in advance, he relieved the tension of his soul, for when the trouble had been presented as one to be expected, his sense of responsibility diminished and weighed upon him less. When he had a chance of his own choosing, with his mind unembroiled and relaxed and his body in good shape, to have his bodily powers first tested, then seized and taken by surprise, with the other party's full knowledge of his problem, he was completely cured in this respect.[1] A man is never after incapable, unless from genuine impotence, with a woman with whom he has once been capable.

^AThis mishap is to be feared only in enterprises where our soul is immoderately tense with desire and respect, and especially if the opportunity is unexpected and pressing; there is no way of recovering from this trouble. I know one man who found it helpful to bring to it a body that had already begun to be sated

[1] Thibaudet suggests that the man in question is Montaigne himself.

elsewhere, ^cso as to lull his frenzied ardor, and who with age finds himself less impotent through being less potent. And I know another who was helped when a friend assured him that he was supplied with a counterbattery of enchantments that were certain to save him. I had better tell how this happened.

A count, a member of a very distinguished family, with whom I was quite intimate, upon getting married to a beautiful lady who had been courted by a man who was present at the wedding feast, had his friends very worried and especially an old lady, a relative of his, who was presiding at the wedding and holding it at her house. She was fearful of these sorceries, and gave me to understand this. I asked her to rely on me. I had by chance in my coffers a certain little flat piece of gold on which were engraved some celestial figures, to protect against sunstroke and take away a headache by placing it precisely on the suture of the skull; and, to keep it there, it was sewed to a ribbon intended to be tied under the chin: a kindred fancy to the one we are speaking of. Jacques Peletier had given me this singular present. I thought of making some use of it, and said to the count that he might incur the same fate as others, there being men present who would like to bring this about; but that he should boldly go to bed and I would do him a friendly turn and would not, if he needed it, spare a miracle which was in my power, provided that he promised me on his honor to keep it most faithfully secret; he was only to make a given signal to me, when they came to bring him the midnight meal, if things had gone badly with him. He had had his soul and his ears so battered that he did find himself fettered by the trouble of his imagination, and gave me his signal. I told him then that he should get up on the pretext of chasing us out, and playfully take the bathrobe that I had on (we were very close in height) and put it on him until he had carried out my prescription, which was this: when we had left, he should withdraw to pass water, say certain prayers three times and go through certain motions; each of these three times he should tie the ribbon I was putting in his hand around him and very carefully lay the medal that was attached to it on his kidneys, with the figure in such and such a position; this done, having tied this ribbon firmly so that it could neither come untied nor slip from its place, he should return to his business with complete assurance and not forget to spread my robe over his bed so that it should cover them both. These monkey tricks are the main part of the business, our mind being unable to get free of

the idea that such strange means must come from some abstruse science. Their inanity gives them weight and reverence. All in all, it is certain that the characters on my medal proved themselves more venereal than solar, more useful for action than for prevention. It was a sudden and curious whim that led me to do such a thing, which was alien to my nature. I am an enemy of subtle and dissimulated acts and hate trickery in myself, not only for sport but also for someone's profit. If the action is not vicious, the road to it is.

Amasis, king of Egypt, married Laodice, a very beautiful Greek girl; and he, who showed himself a gay companion everywhere else, fell short when it came to enjoying her, and threatened to kill her, thinking it was some sort of sorcery. As is usual in matters of fancy, she referred him to religion; and having made his vows and promises to Venus, he found himself divinely restored from the first night after his oblations and sacrifices.

Now women are wrong to greet us with those threatening, quarrelsome, and coy countenances, which put out our fires even as they light them. The daughter-in-law of Pythagoras used to say that the woman who goes to bed with a man should put off her modesty with her skirt and put it on again with her petticoat. ^The soul of the assailant, when troubled with many various alarms, is easily discouraged; and when imagination has once made a man suffer this shame – and it does so only at the first encounters, inasmuch as these are more boiling and violent, and also because in this first intimacy a man is much more afraid of failing – having begun badly, he gets from this accident a feverishness and vexation which lasts into subsequent occasions.

^CMarried people, whose time is all their own, should neither press their undertaking nor even attempt it if they are not ready; it is better to fail unbecomingly to handsel the nuptial couch, which is full of agitation and feverishness, and wait for some other more private and less tense opportunity, than to fall into perpetual misery for having been stunned and made desperate by a first refusal. Before taking possession, the patient should try himself out and offer himself, lightly, by sallies at different times, without priding himself and obstinately insisting on convincing himself definitively. Those who know that their members are naturally obedient, let them take care only to counteract the tricks of their fancies.

People are right to notice the unruly liberty of this member, obtruding so importunately when we have no use for it, and failing so importunately when we have the most use for it, and struggling for mastery so imperiously with our will, refusing with so much pride and obstinacy our solicitations, both mental and manual.

If, however, in the matter of his rebellion being blamed and used as proof to condemn him, he had paid me to plead his cause, I should perhaps place our other members, his fellows, under suspicion of having framed this trumped-up charge out of sheer envy of the importance and pleasure of the use of him, and of having armed everyone against him by a conspiracy, malignantly charging him alone with their common fault. For I ask you to think whether there is a single one of the parts of our body that does not often refuse its function to our will and exercise it against our will. They each have passions of their own which rouse them and put them to sleep without our leave. How many times do the forced movements of our face bear witness to the thoughts that we were holding secret, and betray us to those present. The same cause that animates this member also animates, without our knowledge, the heart, the lungs, and the pulse; the sight of a pleasing object spreading in us imperceptibly the flame of a feverish emotion. Are there only these muscles and these veins that stand up and lie down without the consent, not only of our will, but even of our thoughts? We do not command our hair to stand on end or our skin to shiver with desire or fear. The hand often moves itself to where we do not send it. The tongue is paralyzed, and the voice congealed, at their own time. Even when, having nothing to put in to fry, we should like to forbid it, the appetite for eating and drinking does not fail to stir the parts that are subject to it, no more nor less than that other appetite; and it likewise abandons us inopportunely when it sees fit. The organs that serve to discharge the stomach have their own dilatations and compressions, beyond and against our plans, just like those that are destined to discharge the kidneys. To vindicate the omnipotence of our will, Saint Augustine alleges that he knew a man who commanded his behind to produce as many farts as he wanted, and his commentator Vives goes him one better with another example of his own time, of farts arranged to suit the tone of verses pronounced to their accompaniment; but all this does not really argue any pure obedience in this organ; for is there any that is ordinarily more

indiscreet or tumultuous? Besides, I know one so turbulent and unruly, that for forty years it has kept its master farting with a constant and unremitting wind and compulsion, and is thus taking him to his death.[2]

But as for our will, on behalf of whose rights we set forth this complaint, how much more plausibly may we charge it with rebellion and sedition for its disorderliness and disobedience! Does it always will what we would will it to will? Doesn't it often will what we forbid it to will, and that to our evident disadvantage? Is it any more amenable than our other parts to the decisions of our reason?

To conclude, I would say this in defense of the honorable member whom I represent: May it please the court to take into consideration that in this matter, although my client's case is inseparably and indistinguishably linked with that of an accessory, nevertheless he alone has been brought to trial; and that the arguments and charges against him are such as cannot – in view of the status of the parties – be in any manner pertinent or relevant to the aforesaid accessory.[3] Whereby is revealed his accusers' manifest animosity and disrespect for law. However that may be, Nature will meanwhile go her way, protesting that the lawyers and judges quarrel and pass sentence in vain. Indeed, she would have done no more than is right if she had endowed with some particular privilege this member, author of the sole immortal work of mortals. Wherefore to Socrates generation is a divine act; and love, a desire for immortality and itself an immortal daemon.

ᴬPerhaps it is by this effect of the imagination that one man here gets rid of the scrofula which his companion carries back to Spain.[4] This effect is the reason why, in such matters, it is customary to demand that the mind be prepared. Why do the doctors work on the

2 Here the 1595 edition adds: "And would God I knew only from the history books how many times our stomach, by refusing one single fart, brings us to the gates of a very anguished death; and that the Emperor who gave us the liberty to fart anywhere had given us the power to." Suetonius reports that the Emperor Claudius had contemplated such a decree as this.
3 Here the 1595 edition adds: "for it is indeed in the nature of my client to solicit inopportunely at times, but never to refuse; and to solicit wordlessly and silently at that."
4 Scrofula, or king's evil, was supposed to be curable by the touch of the kings of France. In Montaigne's time great numbers of Spaniards came to France for this purpose.

credulity of their patient beforehand with so many false promises of a cure, if not so that the effect of the imagination may make up for the imposture of their decoction? They know that one of the masters of the trade left them this in writing, that there have been men for whom the mere sight of medicine did the job.

And this whole caprice[5] has just come to hand apropos of the story that an apothecary, a servant of my late father, used to tell me, a simple man and Swiss, of a nation little addicted to vanity and lying. He had long known a merchant at Toulouse, sickly and subject to the stone, who often needed enemas, and ordered various kinds from his doctors according to the circumstances of his illness. Once they were brought to him, nothing was omitted of the accustomed formalities; often he tested them by hand to make sure they were not too hot. There he was, lying on his stomach, and all the motions were gone through – except that no injection was made. After this ceremony, the apothecary having retired and the patient being accommodated as if he had really taken the enema, he felt the same effect from it as those who do take them. And if the doctor did not find its operation sufficient, he would give him two or three more, of the same sort. My witness swears that when to save the expense (for he paid for them as if he had taken them) this sick man's wife sometimes tried to have just warm water used, the effect revealed the fraud; and having found that kind useless, they were obliged to return to the first method.

A woman, thinking she had swallowed a pin with her bread, was screaming in agony as though she had an unbearable pain in her throat, where she thought she felt it stuck; but because externally there was neither swelling nor alteration, a smart man, judging that it was only a fancy and notion derived from some bit of bread that had scratched her as it went down, made her vomit, and, on the sly, tossed a crooked pin into what she threw up. The woman, thinking she had thrown it up, felt herself suddenly relieved of her pain. I know that one gentleman, having entertained a goodly company at his house, three or four days later boasted, as a sort of joke (for there was nothing in it), that he had made them eat cat in a pie; at which one lady in the party was so horrified that she fell into a violent stomach disorder and fever, and it was impossible to save her. Even animals are subject like ourselves to the power of

5 The benevolent trick that Montaigne played with the medal upon his friend. (See pp. 85–6.)

imagination. Witness dogs, who let themselves die out of grief for the loss of their masters. We also see them yap and twitch in their dreams, and horses whinny and writhe.

But all this may be attributed to the narrow seam between the soul and body, through which the experience of the one is communicated to the other. Sometimes, however, one's imagination acts not only against one's own body, but against someone else's. And just as a body passes on its sickness to its neighbor, as is seen in the plague, the pox, and soreness of the eyes, which are transmitted from one body to the other –

> By looking at sore eyes, eyes become sore:
> From body into body ills pass o'er
>
> OVID

– likewise the imagination, when vehemently stirred, launches darts that can injure an external object. The ancients maintained that certain women of Scythia, when animated and enraged against anyone, would kill him with their mere glance. Tortoises and ostriches hatch their eggs just by looking at them, a sign that their sight has some ejaculative virtue. And as for sorcerers, they are said to have baleful and harmful eyes:

> Some evil eye bewitched my tender lambs.
>
> VIRGIL

To me, magicians are poor authorities. Nevertheless, we know by experience that women transmit marks of their fancies to the bodies of the children they carry in their womb; witness the one who gave birth to the Moor.[6] And there was presented to Charles, king of Bohemia and Emperor, a girl from near Pisa, all hairy and bristly, who her mother said had been thus conceived because of a picture of Saint John the Baptist hanging by her bed.

With animals it is the same: witness Jacob's sheep, and the partridges and hares that the snow turns white in the mountains. Recently at my house a cat was seen watching a bird on a treetop, and, after they had locked gazes for some time, the bird let itself fall

6 Saint Jerome tells of a woman who, accused of adultery for giving birth to a black child, was absolved when Hippocrates explained that she had a picture of a dark man hanging in her room by her bed. Montaigne may have taken the example, as he did many of these hereabouts, from any of various contemporaries: Bouaystuau, Rhodiginus, Mexia, or Paré.

as if dead between the cat's paws, either intoxicated by its own imagination or drawn by some attracting power of the cat. Those who like falconry have heard the story of the falconer who, setting his gaze obstinately upon a kite in the air, wagered that by the sole power of his gaze he would bring it down, and did. At least, so they say – for I refer the stories that I borrow to the conscience of those from whom I take them. [B]The reflections are my own, and depend on the proofs of reason, not of experience; everyone can add his own examples to them; and he who has none, let him not fail to believe that there are plenty, in view of the number and variety of occurrences. [C]If I do not apply them well, let another apply them for me.

So in the study that I am making of our behavior and motives, fabulous testimonies, provided they are possible, serve like true ones. Whether they have happened or no, in Paris or Rome, to John or Peter, they exemplify, at all events, some human potentiality, and thus their telling imparts useful information to me. I see it and profit from it just as well in shadow as in substance. And of the different readings that histories often give, I take for my use the one that is most rare and memorable. There are authors whose end is to tell what has happened. Mine, if I could attain it, would be to talk about what can happen. The schools are justly permitted to suppose similitudes when they have none at hand. I do not do so, however, and in that respect I surpass all historical fidelity, being scrupulous to the point of superstition. In the examples that I bring in here of what I have heard, done, or said, I have forbidden myself to dare to alter even the slightest and most inconsequential circumstances. My conscience does not falsify one iota; my knowledge, I don't know.

In this connection, I sometimes fall to thinking whether it befits a theologian, a philosopher, and such people of exquisite and exact conscience and prudence, to write history. How can they stake their fidelity on the fidelity of an ordinary person? How be responsible for the thoughts of persons unknown and give their conjectures as coin of the realm? Of complicated actions that happen in their presence they would refuse to give testimony if placed under oath by a judge; and they know no man so intimately that they would undertake to answer fully for his intentions. I consider it less hazardous to write of things past than present, inasmuch as the writer has only to give an account of a borrowed truth.

Some urge me to write the events of my time, believing that I see them with a view less distorted by passion than another man's, and from closer, because of the access that fortune has given me to the

heads of different parties. What they forget is that even for all the glory of Sallust, I would not take the trouble, being a sworn enemy of obligation, assiduity, perseverance; and that there is nothing so contrary to my style as an extended narration. I cut myself off so often for lack of breath; I have neither composition nor develop-ment that is worth anything; I am more ignorant than a child of the phrases and terms that serve for the commonest things. And so I have chosen to say what I know how to say, accommodating the matter to my power. If I took a subject that would lead me along, I might not be able to measure up to it; and with my freedom being so very free, I might publish judgments which, even according to my own opinion and to reason, would be illegitimate and punishable. Plutarch might well say to us, concerning his accomplishments in this line, that the credit belongs to others if his examples are wholly and everywhere true; but that their being useful to posterity, and presented with a luster which lights our way to virtue, that is his work. There is no danger – as there is in a medicinal drug – in an old story being this way or that.

22
One man's profit is another man's harm

ᴬDemades the Athenian condemned a man of his city whose trade was to sell things necessary for burials, on the ground that he demanded too much profit, and that this profit could not come to him without the death of many people. This judgment seems to be badly taken, inasmuch as no profit is made except at the expense of others, and by this reckoning you would have to condemn every sort of gain.

The merchant does good business only by the extravagance of youth; the plowman by the high cost of grain; the architect by the ruin of houses; officers of justice by men's lawsuits and quarrels; the very honor and function of ministers of religion is derived from our death and our vices. No doctor takes pleasure in the health even of his friends, says the ancient Greek comic writer, no soldier in the peace of his city; and so for the rest. And what is worse, let each man sound himself within, and he will find that our private wishes are for the most part born and nourished at the expense of others.

Considering which, it strikes me how nature in this does not belie her general policy. For students of natural law hold that the

birth, nourishment, and growth of each thing is the alteration and corruption of another:

> Whenever anything is changed and leaves its bounds,
> Instantly this brings death to that which was before.
> LUCRETIUS

23
Of custom, and not easily changing an accepted law

^AThat man seems to me to have very well understood the power of habit[1] who first invented this story: that a village woman, having learned to pet and carry in her arms a calf from the hour of its birth, and continuing always to do so, gained this by habit, that even when he was a great ox she still could carry him. For in truth habit is a violent and treacherous schoolmistress. She establishes in us, little by little, stealthily, the foothold of her authority; but having by this mild and humble beginning settled and planted it with the help of time, she soon uncovers to us a furious and tyrannical face against which we no longer have the liberty of even raising our eyes. We see her at every turn forcing the rules of nature. ^C*Habit is the most effective teacher of all things* [Pliny].

^AFor this I hold with ^CPlato's cave in his *Republic*, and I trust ^Athe doctors who so often abdicate the reasonings of their art to the authority of habit. I refer to that king who trained his stomach to feed on poison; and the girl whom Albertus reports as having accustomed herself to live on spiders. ^BAnd in that world of the new Indies there were found great nations, and in very varied climates, who lived on spiders, made provision of them, and raised and fattened them, as they did also with grasshoppers, ants, lizards, and bats; and a toad was sold for six crowns during a food shortage. They cook them and prepare them with various sauces. Other nations were found to whom our meats and foods were fatally poisonous. ^C*The force of habit is great. Hunters spend the night in the snow; they endure the burning sun in the mountains. Boxers bruised by the cestuses do not even groan* [Cicero].

1 The French word *coutume* here, in the title, and throughout the chapter, has either of its usual meanings of *custom* or *habit*.

These examples from strange lands are not strange if we consider what we regularly experience: how much habit stupefies our senses. We do not need to go and find out what they say of those who live near the cataracts of the Nile, and what the philosophers believe about the music of the heavenly spheres – that the bodies of these spheres, being solid, and coming to touch and rub on one another as they roll, cannot fail to produce a marvelous harmony, whose rhythms and modulations regulate the circles and the changing figures of the dances of the stars; but that the sense of hearing of all the creatures of the universe, put to sleep, like that of the Egyptians, by the continuousness of this sound, cannot perceive it, however great it be. Smiths, millers, armorers could not endure the noise that strikes them if they were stunned by it as we are.

My perfumed doublet is pleasant to my nose, but after I have worn it three days in a row it is pleasant only to the noses of others. It is even more strange that, notwithstanding long intervals and inter-missions, habit can combine and establish the effect of its impression on our senses, as those people experience who live near belfries. At home I live in a tower where at dawn and at sunset every day a very big bell rings out the *Ave Maria*. This jangling frightens my very tower; to me, it seems unendurable at first, but in a short time it has me tamed, so that I hear it without disturbance and often without awaking.

Plato scolded a child who was playing at cobnuts. He answered him: "You scold me for a small matter." "Habit," replied Plato, "is no small matter."

I find that our greatest vices take shape from our tenderest childhood, and that our most important training is in the hands of nurses. It is a pastime for mothers to see a child wring the neck of a chicken or amuse itself by hurting a dog or a cat; and there are fathers stupid enough to take it as a good omen of a martial soul when they see a son unjustly striking a peasant or a lackey who is not defending himself, and as a charming prank when they see him trick his playmate by a bit of malicious dishonesty and deceit. Never-theless these are the true seeds and roots of cruelty, tyranny, and treason; they sprout there, and afterward shoot up lustily, and flourish mightily in the hands of habit. And it is a very dangerous educational policy to excuse our children for these ugly inclinations on the grounds of their tender age and the triviality of the subject. In the first place, it is nature speaking, whose voice then is all the purer and stronger because it is more tenuous. Second, the ugliness of

cheating does not depend on the difference between crown pieces and pins: it depends on itself. I find it much more just to come to this conclusion: "Why would he not cheat for crowns, since he cheats for pins?" than, as they do: "It is only for pins, he would never do it for crowns." Children must be carefully taught to hate vices for their own sake, and taught the natural deformity of vices, so that they will shun them not only in their actions but above all in their heart, so that the very thought of them may be odious, whatever mask they wear.

I know very well from having trained myself in my childhood always to walk in my own straight open road, and having had an aversion for mixing trickery or ruse in my childish games – as indeed it must be noted that children's games are not games, and must be judged in children like their more serious actions – that there is no pastime so trivial that I do not bring to it, from within, by a natural and unstudied propensity, an extreme repugnance to cheating. I handle the cards and keep score for a couple of pennies just as for double doubloons; when winning or losing, against my wife and daughter, is indifferent to me, just as when playing for keeps. In all things and all places my own eyes are enough to keep me in line; there are none that watch me so carefully, nor that I respect more.

^AI have just seen in my house a little man, a native of Nantes, born without arms, who has so well adapted his feet for the service his hands owed him that in truth they have half forgotten their natural function. Moreover he calls them his hands; he carves, he loads a pistol and fires it, he threads his needle, he sews, he writes, he doffs his hat, he combs his hair, he plays cards and dice, and moves them with as much dexterity as any other could do. The money I gave him – for he gains his living by exhibiting himself – he carried off in his foot as we do in our hand. I saw another when I was a child who handled a two-handed sword and a halberd in the crook of his neck for lack of hands, threw them in the air and caught them again, hurled a dagger, and cracked a whip as well as any wagoner in France.

But you discover the effects of habit much better in the strange impressions she makes in our souls, where she does not find so much resistance. What power does she not have in our judgments and in our beliefs? Is there any opinion so bizarre – I leave aside the gross impostures of religions, with which so many great nations and so many able men have been seen to be besotted, for since this matter is beyond the scope of our human reason, it is more excusable for

anyone who is not extraordinarily enlightened by divine favor to be lost in it; but of other opinions is there any so strange – that habit has not planted and established it by law in the regions where she saw fit to do so? ^CAnd that ancient exclamation is very just: *The natural philosopher, who should be the observer and quester of nature, brazenly seeks the proof of truth from minds imbued with habit* [Cicero].

^BI think that there falls into man's imagination no fantasy so wild that it does not match the example of some public practice, and for which, consequently, our reason does not find a stay and a foundation. There are countries where they turn their back to the person they greet, and never look at the one they wish to honor. There are some where, when the king spits, the most favored of the ladies of his court holds out her hand; and in another nation the most eminent persons around him stoop to the ground to pick up his ordure in a linen cloth.

^CLet us here steal room for a story. One French gentleman always used to blow his nose in his hand, a thing very repugnant to our practice. Defending his action against this reproach (and he was famous for his original remarks), he asked me what privilege this dirty excrement had that we should prepare a fine delicate piece of linen to receive it, and then, what is more, wrap it up and carry it carefully on us; for that should be much more horrifying and nauseating than to see it dropped in any old place, as we do all other excrements. I found that what he said was not entirely without reason; and habit had led me not to perceive the strangeness of this action, which nevertheless we find so hideous when it is told us about another country.

Miracles arise from our ignorance of nature, not from the essence of nature. Habituation puts to sleep the eye of our judgment. Barbarians are no more marvelous to us than we are to them, nor for better cause; as everyone would admit if everyone knew how, after perusing these new examples, to reflect on his own and compare them sanely. Human reason is a tincture infused in about equal strength in all our opinions and ways, whatever their form: infinite in substance, infinite in diversity.

To come back to the point. There are countries where, ^Bexcept for his wife and children, no one speaks to the king except through a tube. In one and the same nation the virgins openly show their pudenda, and the married women carefully cover and conceal them. To which another custom that exists elsewhere has some relation:

chastity is prized there only in attendance to marriage, for girls may abandon themselves as they like and, if pregnant, have abortions by suitable drugs, as a matter of public knowledge. And in another place, if it is a merchant that is getting married, all the merchants invited to the wedding lie with the bride before him; and the more there are, the more honor and commendation she has for endurance and capacity. If an officer marries, it is the same; the same if it is a nobleman, and so for all others, except if it is a plowman or someone of the lowest class, for then the privilege is for the lord. And yet there they do not fail strictly to recommend fidelity during marriage.

There are places where there are public brothels of males, and even marriages between them; where the women go to war alongside their husbands, and take their place not only in the combat but also in command. Where they not only wear rings on the nose, lips, cheeks, and toes, but also have very heavy gold rods thrust through their breasts and buttocks. Where in eating they wipe their fingers on their thighs, on the pouch of their genitals, and on the soles of their feet. Where it is not the children that are the heirs, but the brothers and nephews; and elsewhere the nephews only, except in the succession of the prince. Where to regulate the community of goods that is observed, certain sovereign magistrates have universal charge of the cultivation of lands and the distribution of crops, according to each man's need. Where they mourn the death of children and celebrate that of old men. Where they sleep ten or twelve together in beds, husbands and wives. Where the wives who lose their husbands by violent death may remarry, the others no. Where they have such a bad opinion of the condition of women that they kill the females that are born, and buy wives from neighboring nations to satisfy their needs. Where husbands can repudiate their mates without alleging any cause, the wives not for any cause whatever. Where the husbands have the right to sell them if they are sterile.

Where they cook the body of the deceased and then crush it until a sort of pulp is formed, which they mix with their wine, and drink it. Where the most desirable sepulture is to be eaten by dogs, elsewhere by birds. Where they believe that happy souls live in all liberty, in pleasant fields, furnished with all comforts; and that it is they who make the echo that we hear. Where they fight in the water, and shoot accurately with their bows while swimming. Where for a sign of subjection you must shrug your shoulders and lower your

head, and take off your shoes when you enter the king's dwelling. Where the eunuchs who guard the religious women also lack nose and lips, so that they cannot be loved; and the priests put out their eyes in order to communicate with their demons and receive their oracles. Where each man makes a god of what he likes – the hunter of a lion or a fox, the fisherman of a certain fish – and idols of each human action or passion; the sun, the moon, and the earth are the principal gods; the form of swearing an oath is to touch the ground while looking at the sun; and they eat flesh and fish raw.

ᶜWhere the great oath is to swear by the name of some dead man who has had a good reputation in the country, while touching his tomb with the hand. Where the king's annual present to his vassal princes is fire: when the envoy who brings it arrives, the old fire is extinguished throughout the house, and from this new fire the people who depend on this prince must come to take some, each for himself, on pain of the crime of lèse-majesté. Where, when the king retires from his office to devote himself completely to piety (as they often do), his immediate successor is obliged to do as much, and the right to the kingdom passes to the third in line. Where they vary the form of government according as affairs require: depose the king when it seems good, and substitute elders to assume the governing of the state, and also sometimes leave it in the hands of the people. Where men and women are circumcised as well as baptized. Where the soldier who in one or several battles has succeeded in presenting to the king seven enemies' heads is made a noble.

ᴮWhere they live in the belief, so rare and uncivilized, in the mortality of souls. Where the women bear children without complaint or fright. ᶜWhere the women wear copper greaves on both legs; and, if a louse bites them, they are bound by the code of bravery to bite it back; and they dare not marry until they have offered their king their virginity, if he wants it. ᴮWhere people greet one another by putting their finger to the ground and then raising it to heaven. Where the men carry their burdens on their head; the women, on their shoulders; and where women piss standing, men squatting. Where they send some of their blood as a sign of friendship, and burn incense to the men they wish to honor, as to gods. Where kinship is forbidden in marriages not only to the fourth degree, but to some even more remote one. Where children are four years nursing, and often twelve; and in that very place, it is

considered fatal to give the child suck throughout the first day. Where the fathers have charge of the punishment of the male children, and the mothers, separately, of the females; and where the punishment is to hang them by the heels and smoke them. Where they have women circumcised. Where they eat every kind of herbs with no discrimination except to refuse those that seem to them to have a bad odor. Where everything is open, and the houses, however beautiful and rich they may be, without a door, without a window, without a strongbox that locks; and there robbers are punished twice as severely as elsewhere. Where they kill lice with their teeth like monkeys, and think it horrible to see them crushed between the fingernails. Where in all their lives they cut neither hair nor nails; another place where they cut only the nails of the right hand, and those of the left are grown as a sign of nobility. ᶜWhere they grow all the hair of the body on the right side as much as it can grow, and keep the hair on the other side clean-shaven. And one of two neighboring provinces grows the hair in front, the other in back, and they shave the opposite side. ᴮWhere the fathers lend their children, the husbands their wives, to their guests to enjoy, for money. Where a man can respectably have children by his mother, and fathers have sexual relations with their daughters, and with their sons. ᶜWhere at their festival assemblies they lend their children to one another.

ᴬHere they live on human flesh; there it is an act of piety to kill one's father at a certain age; elsewhere the fathers ordain, while the children are still in their mothers' wombs, which ones they want to have brought up and kept, and which abandoned and killed. Elsewhere old husbands lend their wives to the young for their use; and elsewhere still they are had in common, without sin: indeed, in one country they wear as a mark of honor as many fine tassels as a fringe at the edge of their dresses as there are men they have lain with. Did not custom also make a commonwealth of women alone? Did it not put weapons in their hands, make them raise armies and fight battles?

And what all philosophy cannot implant in the head of the wisest men, does not custom by her sole ordinance teach the crudest common herd? For we know whole nations where death was not merely scorned, but celebrated; where seven-year-old children endured being whipped to death without changing expression; where riches were in such contempt that the most wretched

citizen of the town would not have deigned to lower his arm to pick up a purse of crowns. And we know regions very fertile in all forms of foods where nevertheless the most usual and savory dishes were bread, cress, and water. ^BDid not custom also perform this miracle in Chios, that seven hundred years passed with no memory that woman or maid ever failed of her honor?

^AIn short, to my way of thinking, there is nothing that custom will not or cannot do; and with reason Pindar calls her, so I have been told, the queen and empress of the world.

^CThe man whom they found beating his father replied that it was the custom of his house: that his father had beaten his grandfather thus, his grandfather his great-grandfather; and, pointing to his son: "And this one will beat me when he has come to my present age."

And the father whom his son was dragging and bumping along the street ordered him to stop at a certain door, for he had dragged his own father only that far; this was the limit of the hereditary rough treatment that the sons traditionally practiced upon the fathers in their family. By custom as often as by derangement, says Aristotle, women tear out their hair, gnaw their nails, eat coals and earth; and as much by custom as by nature do males have sexual relations with males.

The laws of conscience, which we say are born of nature, are born of custom. Each man, holding in inward veneration the opinions and the behavior approved and accepted around him, cannot break loose from them without remorse, or apply himself to them without self-satisfaction.

^BWhen the Cretans in times past wanted to curse someone, they would pray the gods to entice him into some bad habit.

^ABut the principal effect of the power of custom is to seize and ensnare us in such a way that it is hardly within our power to get ourselves back out of its grip and return into ourselves to reflect and reason about its ordinances. In truth, because we drink them with our milk from birth, and because the face of the world presents itself in this aspect to our first view, it seems that we are born on condition of following this course. And the common notions that we find in credit around us and infused into our soul by our fathers' seed, these seem to be the universal and natural ones. ^CWhence it comes to pass that what is off the hinges of custom, people believe to be off the hinges of reason: God knows how unreasonably, most of the time.

If, as we who study ourselves have learned to do, each man who hears a true statement immediately considered how it properly pertains to him, each man would find that it is not so much a good saying as a good whiplash to the ordinary stupidity of his judgment. But men receive the advice of truth and its precepts as if addressed to the common people, never to themselves; and each man, instead of incorporating them into his behavior, incorporates them into his memory, very stupidly and uselessly. Let us return to the sovereignty of custom.

Nations brought up to liberty and to ruling themselves consider any other form of government monstrous and contrary to nature. Those who are accustomed to monarchy do the same. And whatever easy chance fortune offers them to change, even when with great difficulties they have rid themselves of the importunity of one master, they run to supplant him with another, with similar difficulties, because they cannot make up their minds to hate domination itself.[2]

[A]Darius asked certain Greeks for how much they would adopt the Indian custom of eating their dead fathers (for that was their way, considering that they could not give them a more favorable sepulture than in themselves); they answered him that not for anything in the world would they do it. And when he tried to persuade the Indians to give up their practice and adopt that of Greece, which was to burn their fathers' bodies, he horrified them still more. Everyone acts the same way, inasmuch as usage robs us of the true appearance of things.

> There's nothing seems at first so wonderful, so great,
> But that men's wonder will not presently abate
> Little by little.
>
> LUCRETIUS

Once, having to justify one of our observances, which was received with steadfast authority far and wide around us, and preferring to establish it, not as is usually done, merely by force of laws and examples, but by tracking it to its origin, I there found its foundation so weak that I nearly became disgusted with it, I who was supposed to confirm it in others.

2 Here the 1595 edition adds: "It is by the mediation of custom that every man is content with the place where nature has planted him, and the savages of Scotland have no concern with Touraine, nor the Scythians with Thessaly."

^CThis is the prescription by which Plato undertakes to drive out the unnatural loves of his time, and which he considers supreme and fundamental: to wit, that public opinion must condemn them, that the poets and everyone should tell bad stories about them. Thanks to this same prescription even the most beautiful daughters no longer attract their fathers' amorousness, nor do brothers whose beauty is outstanding attract the amorousness of their sisters; for the very fables of Thyestes, Oedipus, and Macareus have, through the pleasure of their song, infused this useful belief into the tender brains of children.

In truth, chastity is a fine virtue, whose utility is well enough known; but to treat it and justify it according to nature is as hard as it is easy to justify it according to custom, laws, and precepts. The first and universal reasons are hard to scrutinize, and our masters either skim over them lightly or, not even daring to touch them at all, cast themselves immediately into the protection of custom, where they puff themselves up and enjoy a cheap triumph. Those who will not let themselves be dragged out of this original source err even more and bind themselves to barbarous opinions, like Chrysippus, who in so many places strewed his writings with remarks displaying the little account he took of incestuous unions, of whatever kind they might be.

^AWhoever wants to get rid[3] of this violent prejudice of custom will find many things accepted with undoubting resolution, which have no support but in the hoary beard and the wrinkles of the usage that goes with them; but when this mask is torn off, and he refers things to truth and reason, he will feel his judgment as it were all upset, and nevertheless restored to a much surer status. For example, I shall ask him then, what can be stranger than to see a people obliged to obey laws that they never understood, bound in all their domestic affairs, marriages, donations, wills, sales, and purchases, to rules that they cannot know, since they are neither written nor published in their language, and whose interpretation and use they must of necessity purchase? ^CNot according to the ingenious notion of Isocrates, who advises his king to make the trades and negotiations of his subjects free, gratuitous, and lucrative, and their disputes and quarrels onerous, by loading these with heavy taxes; but according to a monstrous idea, that of putting reason itself on

3 In all the versions of this passage except the final one, it reads: "And whoever wants to essay himself in the same way, and get rid..."

the market, and treating laws as merchandise. ^AI am grateful to fortune that, so our historians say, it was a Gascon gentleman, and from my part of the country, who first opposed Charlemagne when he wanted to give us Latin and imperial laws.

What is more barbarous to see than a nation where by lawful custom the charge of judging is sold, and judgments are paid for in ready cash, and where justice is lawfully refused to whoever has not the wherewithal to pay; and where this merchandise has such good credit that in a government a fourth estate is formed of people handling lawsuits, to add to the three ancient ones of Church, Nobility, and People; which estate, having charge of the laws and sovereign authority over property and life, forms a body apart from that of the nobility? (Whence it comes about that there are two sets of laws, those of honor and those of justice, in many matters quite opposed. The former condemn as rigorously a man's enduring being given the lie as the latter condemn his avenging it.) What could be more barbarous than that by the code of arms the man who endures an insult should be degraded from honor and nobility, and by the civil code he who avenges an insult should incur capital punishment? (He who appeals to the laws to get satisfaction for an offense to his honor, dishonors himself; and he who does not appeal to them is therefore punished and chastised by the laws.) And that of these two bodies,[4] so different but nevertheless joined to a single head, one should have charge of peace, the other of war; one should have gain as its share, the other honor; one knowledge, the other virtue; one words, the other action; one justice, the other valor; one reason, the other force; one the long robe, the other the short?

As for indifferent things such as clothes, if any man wants to restore them to their true purpose, which is the service and comfort of the body, on which depend their original grace and fitness, I will offer him, among other examples, as in my opinion the most monstrous that can be imagined, our square bonnets, that long tail of pleated velvet that hangs from our women's heads with its many-colored trappings, and that empty and useless model of a member that we cannot even decently mention by name, which however we show off and parade in public.

These considerations, however, do not deter a man of understanding from following the common style. On the contrary, it seems to me that all peculiar and out-of-the-way fashions come

4 The men of justice and the nobles.

rather from folly and ambitious affectation than from true reason,
and that the wise man should withdraw his soul within, out of the
crowd, and keep it in freedom and power to judge things freely; but
as for externals, he should wholly follow the accepted fashions and
forms. Society in general can do without our thoughts; but the rest –
our actions, our work, our fortunes, and our very life – we must lend
and abandon to its service and to the common opinions, just as the
great and good Socrates refused to save his life by disobedience to
the magistrate, even to a very unjust and very iniquitous magistrate.[5]
For it is the rule of rules, and the universal law of laws, that each man
should observe those of the place he is in:

> It is a fine thing to obey your country's laws.
> CRISPIN

Here is something from another vat. It is very doubtful whether
there can be such evident profit in changing an accepted law, of
whatever sort it be, as there is harm in disturbing it; inasmuch as
a government is like a structure of different parts joined together in
such a relation that it is impossible to budge one without the whole
body feeling it. The lawmaker of the Thurians ordained that who-
ever should want either to abolish one of the old laws or to establish
a new one should present himself to the people with a rope around
his neck; so that if the innovation were not approved by each and
every man, he should be promptly strangled. And the one of Lace-
daemon employed his life to draw from his citizens a certain pro-
mise not to infringe any of his ordinances. The ephor who so rudely
cut out the two strings that Phrynis had added to music does not
worry whether music is the better for their addition or whether the
chords are richer; for him to condemn them, it is enough that they
represent an alteration of the old fashion. That was the meaning of
that rusty sword of justice in Marseilles.

^BI am disgusted with innovation, in whatever guise, and with
reason, for I have seen very harmful effects of it. The one that has
been oppressing us for so many years[6] is not the sole author of our
troubles, but one may say with good reason that it has accidentally
produced and engendered everything, even the troubles and ruins
that have been happening since without it, and against it; it has itself
to blame.

5 This clause, from "just as the" to "magistrate" is an addition of 1582.
6 The Reformation.

Alas, I smart from wounds that my own darts have made.

<div align="right">OVID</div>

Those who give the first shock to a state are apt to be the first ones swallowed up in its ruin. ᶜThe fruits of the trouble rarely go to the one who has stirred it up; he beats and disturbs the water for other fishermen. ᴮThe unity and contexture of this monarchy, this great structure, having been dislocated and dissolved, especially in its old age, by this innovation, as wide an entry as one could wish is opened to similar attacks. ᶜThe majesty of kings, says an ancient, declines less easily from the summit to the middle than it plunges from the middle to the bottom.

But if the inventors have done more harm, the imitators[7] are more vicious in that they wholeheartedly follow examples whose horror and evil they have felt and punished. And if there is some degree of honor even in evil-doing, they must concede to the others the glory of invention and the courage of making the first effort.

ᴮAll sorts of new depravity gleefully draw, from this first and fertile source, examples and models to trouble our government. Men read in our very laws, made for the remedy of this first evil, an apprenticeship and excuse for all sorts of wicked enterprises; and we are experiencing what Thucydides says of the civil wars of his time, that men baptized public vices with new milder names to excuse them, adulterating and softening their true titles. Yet the purpose of this is to reform our conscience and belief. *The plea is fair* [Terence]. But even the best pretext for innovation is very dangerous: ᶜ*so true it is that no change from the ancient ways is to be approved* [Livy]. ᴮThus it seems to me, to speak frankly, that it takes a lot of self-love and presumption to have such esteem for one's own opinions that to establish them one must overthrow the public peace and introduce so many inevitable evils, and such a horrible corruption of morals, as civil wars and political changes bring with them in a matter of such weight – and introduce them into one's own country. ᶜIsn't it bad management to encourage so many certain and known vices in order to combat contested and debatable errors? Is there any worse kind of vices than those which attack our conscience and our understanding of one another?

7 The inventors are the Protestants, the imitators the intransigent Catholic party of the League.

The Senate, in its dispute with the people over the administration of their religion, was bold enough to give them this evasion as payment: *that this concerned the gods rather than themselves, and the gods would see that their rites were not profaned* [Livy] – modeling itself on the reply made by the oracle to the men of Delphi in the Median war. Fearing the invasion of the Persians, they had asked the god what they were to do with the sacred treasures of his temple, whether to hide them or carry them off. He answered that they should not budge a thing; that they should take care of themselves; that he was capable of looking after what belonged to him.

ᴮThe Christian religion has all the marks of the utmost justice and utility, but none more apparent than the precise recommendation of obedience to the magistrate and maintenance of the government. What a marvelous example of this the divine wisdom has left us, which, to establish the salvation of the human race and to conduct its glorious victory over death and sin, willed to do so only with the sanction of our political order; and subjected its progress, and the conduct of such a lofty and salutary action, to the blindness and injustice of our observances and usages; letting flow the innocent blood of so many of its beloved elect, and suffering a long loss of years in ripening this priceless fruit!

There is a great difference between the cause of the man who follows the forms and laws of his country and that of the one who undertakes to control and change them. The former pleads, as his excuse, simplicity, obedience, and example; whatever he may do, it cannot be malice, it is at most misfortune. ᶜ*For who is the man who is not swayed by an antiquity attested and certified by the clearest records?* [Cicero] – quite apart from what Isocrates says: that deficiency has a greater share of moderation than excess.

ᴮThe other man is in a much rougher position. ᶜFor whoever meddles with choosing and changing usurps the authority to judge, and he must be very sure that he sees the weakness of what he is casting out and the goodness of what he is bringing in. The following very vulgar consideration has confirmed me in my position and kept me in check even during my rasher youth: not to burden my shoulders with so heavy a load as the responsibility for a knowledge of such importance, and not to dare to do in this area what in sane judgment I could never dare to do even in the easiest of the disciplines in which I had been instructed and in which rashness of judgment does no harm. For it seems to me very iniquitous to want to subject public and immutable institutions

and observances to the instability of a private fancy (private reason has only a private jurisdiction), and to attempt against divine laws what no government would endure against civil laws. These last, although human reason has much more to do with them, are still supremely the judges of their judges; and the utmost ability serves at best to expound and extend their accepted use, not to turn it aside and innovate.

If sometimes divine Providence has passed over the rules to which it has necessarily constrained us, the intention was not to give us any dispensation from them. These are strokes of the divine hand, which we must not imitate but admire: extraordinary examples, marked with an express and particular sign, of the same nature as the miracles which it offers us as evidence of its omnipotence, above our categories and our powers. These it is folly and impiety to try to reproduce; we must not follow them, but contemplate them with awe: acts of its character, not of ours.

Cotta protests very opportunely: *When it is a question of religion, I follow T. Coruncanius, P. Scipio, P. Scaevola, the sovereign pontiffs, not Zeno or Cleanthes or Chrysippus* [Cicero].

[B]God knows, in our present quarrel, where there are a hundred articles to remove and replace, great and deep articles, how many there are who can boast of having exactly understood the reasons and grounds of both parties. It is a number, if it is any number, that would not have much power to disturb us. But all this other mob, where are they going? Under what colors are they breaking away? Their medicine has the same effect as other medicines that are weak and ill applied: the humors that it wanted to purge in us it has heated, exasperated, and embittered by the conflict, and still it has remained in our body. It has not been able to purge us because of its weakness, and yet it has weakened us so that we cannot evacuate it either; and all we get from its operation is long intestinal pains.

[A]Yet it is true that Fortune, always reserving her authority above our reasonings, sometimes presents us with such an urgent necessity that the laws must needs give some place to it.

[B]And when you resist the growth of an innovation that has come to introduce itself by violence, it is a dangerous obligation and a handicap to keep yourself in check and within the rules, in all matters and places, against those who are free as air, to whom everything is permissible that can advance their plan, who have neither law nor order except to follow their advantage:

^CFaith in a faithless man can give him means to harm.
SENECA

^BFor the ordinary discipline of a state that is in a healthy
condition does not provide for these extraordinary accidents;
it presupposes a body that holds together in its principal parts
and functions, and a common consent to its observance and obedi-
ence. ^CThe law-abiding pace is a cold, deliberate, and constrained
one, and is not the kind that can hold up against a lawless and
unbridled pace.

^AIt is well known that those two great personages, Octavius[8] and
Cato, one in the civil war with Sulla, the other in the civil war with
Caesar, are still reproached for having let their country incur the last
extremities rather than disturb things by rescuing it at the expense of
the laws. For in truth, in these ultimate necessities where there is
nothing more to hold on to, it would perhaps be more wisely done to
lower your head and give way a little to the blow, than, by struggling
to let nothing go when this is impossible, to give violence an
occasion to trample everything underfoot; and it would be better
to make the laws will what they can do, since they cannot do what
they will. Thus did the man who ordered that the laws should sleep
for twenty-four hours, and he who for one occasion removed a day
from the calendar, and that other who of the month of June made
a second month of May. The Lacedaemonians themselves, such
religious observers of the ordinances of their country, being ham-
pered by a law that forbade them to elect the same man admiral
twice, but finding it absolutely necessary to their affairs that Lysan-
der should take this office again, did indeed make one Aracus
admiral, but made Lysander superintendent of the navy. And by
the same subtlety, one of their ambassadors, being sent to the
Athenians to obtain a change of some ordinance, and hearing
from Pericles that it was forbidden to remove the tablet on which
a law had once been inscribed, advised him simply to turn it over,
inasmuch as that was not forbidden. This is what Plutarch praises
Philopoemen for: that, being born to command, he knew not only
how to command according to the laws, but how to command the
laws themselves, when the public necessity required.

8 Cnaeus Octavius, a consul who supported Marius against Sulla. Plutarch tells
about him in his "Life of Marius."

24
Various outcomes of the same plan

^AJacques Amyot, Grand Almoner of France, one day told me the following story to the honor of one of our princes[1] (and he was ours by very good tokens, even though his extraction was foreign). During our first troubles, at the siege of Rouen, this prince was warned by the Queen Mother of a plot against his life and particularly informed by her letters of the person who was to carry it out, a gentleman of Anjou or Maine who was then for that purpose regularly frequenting this prince's house. He told no one of this warning; but when walking the next day on the Mont Sainte-Catherine, from which our battery was firing on Rouen (for it was at the time when we held it besieged), having beside him the said Grand Almoner and another bishop, he saw this man, who had been pointed out to him, and had called him over. Upon his arrival, the prince, seeing him already turn pale and tremble from the alarms of his conscience, spoke to him thus: "Monsieur So-and-So, you certainly suspect what I want with you, and your face shows it. You have nothing to hide from me, for I am so thoroughly informed about your business that you would only make your plight worse by trying to conceal it. You very well know such-and-such matters (which were the ins and outs of the most secret parts of this undertaking); do not fail, as you value your life, to confess to me the truth about this whole plan." When this poor man found himself caught and convicted (for the whole thing had been revealed to the queen by one of the accomplices), there was nothing for him but to clasp his hands and pray for grace and mercy from this prince, at whose feet he tried to throw himself. But the prince kept him from doing so, and continued his talk thus: "Come here. Have I ever done anything against you? Have I harmed one of your family through private hatred? I haven't known you three weeks; what reason can have moved you to undertake my death?" To that the gentleman replied in a trembling voice that it was no personal cause that he had for it, but the interest of the general cause of his party; and that some persons had persuaded him that it would be an act of piety to extirpate by any means whatever so powerful an enemy of their religion. "Now," went on this prince, "I want to show you how much gentler is the religion I hold than the one that you profess.

1 François, duke of Guise.

Yours has advised you to kill me without a hearing, having received no harm from me; and mine commands me to pardon you, convicted though you are of having wanted to murder me without reason. Go away, get out, don't let me see you here again; and if you are wise, henceforth take more decent counselors for your enterprises."

The Emperor Augustus, while in Gaul, received certain warning of a conspiracy that Lucius Cinna was brewing against him. He decided to take revenge, and to that effect summoned a council of his friends for the next day. But the night between he spent in great agitation, considering that he was to put to death a young man of good family and nephew to the great Pompey; and in complaint he uttered several different arguments. "What then," he said, "shall it be said that I am to live in fear and alarm, and meanwhile let my murderer walk about at his ease? Shall he go free after attacking my head, which I have brought back safe from so many civil wars, so many battles by sea and land? And after I have established the universal peace of the world, shall he be absolved when he has decided not merely to murder me but to sacrifice me?" For the conspiracy was formed to kill him while he was performing some sacrifice. After that, having kept quiet for some time, he began again in a louder voice and took himself to task: "Why do you live, if it is important to so many people that you should die? Shall there be no end to your vengeances and cruelties? Is your life worth all the harm done to preserve it?" His wife Livia, sensing that he was in this anguish, said to him: "Are women's counsels to be admitted? Do what the doctors do when the accustomed prescriptions will not serve: they try the opposite. By severity up to now you have not gained a thing: Lepidus has followed Salvidienus, Murena Lepidus, Caepio Murena, Egnatius Caepio. Now try how gentleness and clemency will succeed. Cinna is convicted; pardon him; harm you henceforth he cannot, and it will profit your glory."

Augustus was well pleased to have found an advocate of his own humor; and having thanked his wife and countermanded the summons to his friends, he ordered Cinna to be brought to him all alone. After sending everyone from the room and giving Cinna a chair, he spoke to him in this manner: "In the first place, Cinna, I ask you to hear me peaceably. Do not interrupt my speech; I shall give you time and opportunity to answer it. You know, Cinna, that although I took you in the camp of my enemies, and although you had not merely become my enemy but were born so, I spared

you and restored your property, and in short made you so well and comfortably off that the victors are envious of the condition of the vanquished. The priestly office that you asked of me I granted you, having refused it to others whose fathers had always fought for me. Despite such strong obligations, you have undertaken to kill me."

At which Cinna exclaimed that he was far removed from so wicked a thought. "You are not keeping your promise to me, Cinna," Augustus went on; "you assured me that I should not be interrupted. Yes, you undertook to kill me, in such and such a place, such and such a day, in such and such company, and such and such a fashion." And seeing him stupefied by this news, and silent, no longer in order to keep his bargain to remain so, but from the pressure of his conscience, Augustus continued: "Why are you doing it? Is it to be Emperor? Truly, the commonwealth is in very bad shape if there is nothing but myself that keeps you from gaining the Empire. You cannot even defend your own house, and lately you lost a lawsuit through the influence of a mere freedman. What, have you neither means nor power for anything but to take on Caesar? I give up the Empire, if I am the only one who stands in the way of your hopes. Do you think that Paulus, that Fabius, that the Cossii and the Servilii will endure you, and such a great host of nobles, not only noble in title but by their virtue honoring their nobility?"

After many other remarks (for he talked to him more than two full hours), "Now go," he said to him. "I give you, Cinna, the life as traitor and parricide that I once gave you as enemy. Let friendship begin from this day between us; let us see which is in better faith, my giving you your life or your receiving it." And he parted from him in this manner. Some time afterward he gave Cinna the consulate, complaining that he had not dared to ask him for it. From then on they were great friends, and Cinna made Augustus sole heir to his property.

Now from the time of this incident, which happened to Augustus in his fortieth year, there was never a conspiracy or attempt against him, and he received a just reward for this clemency of his. But it did not turn out the same way for our prince;[2] for his mildness was not able to protect him from falling later into the toils of a similar treason. So vain and frivolous a thing is human prudence;

2 On February 18, 1563, only a few months after the episode recounted above, François de Guise was assassinated by Poltrot de Méré.

and athwart all our plans, counsels, and precautions, Fortune still maintains her grasp on the results.

We call doctors fortunate when they attain some good end, as if their art alone could not stand on its own feet and had too weak a foundation to support itself by its own strength; and as if no other needed a helping hand from Fortune. Of medicine I believe all the bad or the good you like, for we have, thank God, no dealings whatever. I am at the opposite pole from others; for indeed, I despise it always, but when I am sick, instead of making peace overtures, I begin also to hate and fear it; and I reply to those who urge me to take medicine that they should wait at least until I am restored to my strength and health, so that I may have more resources to withstand the impact and the hazards of their potion. I let Nature act, and assume that she is provided with teeth and claws to defend herself against the attacks that come upon her and to maintain this contexture[3] whose dissolution she shuns. I am afraid that instead of helping her when she is at close grips with the illness, we may rather aid her adversary, and burden her with fresh tasks.

Now, I say that not only in medicine but in many more certain arts Fortune has a large part. Poetic sallies, which transport their author and ravish him out of himself, why shall we not attribute them to his good luck? He himself confesses that they surpass his ability and strength, and acknowledges that they come from something other than himself and that he does not have them at all in his power, any more than orators say they have in theirs those extraordinary impulses and agitations that push them beyond their plan. It is the same with painting: sometimes there escape from the painter's hand touches so surpassing his conception and his knowledge as to arouse his wonder and astonishment. But Fortune shows still more evidently the part she has in all these works by the graces and beauties that are found in them, not only without the workman's intention, but even without his knowledge. An able reader often discovers in other men's writings perfections beyond those that the author put in or perceived, and lends them richer meanings and aspects.

As for military enterprises, everyone sees how large a part Fortune has in them. Even in our counsels and our deliberations there must certainly be some chance and good luck mixed in; for all that

3 The body.

our wisdom can do is not much; the sharper and livelier it is, the more weakness it finds in itself and the more it mistrusts itself. I am of Sulla's opinion; when I scrutinize closely the most glorious exploits of war, I see, it seems to me, that those who conduct them make use of deliberation and counsel only for form; they abandon the better part of the enterprise to Fortune, and, in the confidence they have in her help, go beyond the limits of all reason at every turn. There occur amid their deliberations fortuitous rejoicings and extraneous frenzies which impel them most of the time to choose the least likely course and which swell their courage beyond reason. Whence it has happened that many great ancient captains, in order to give these rash plans credit, have alleged to their men that they were impelled by some inspiration, some sign and prognostication.

That is why, when the various details and circumstances of a matter have so perplexed us that we are powerless to see and choose what is most advantageous, I find the surest thing to do, even if no other consideration invited us to it, is this: to cast ourselves into the course in which there is the most decency and justice, and since we are in doubt about the shortest path, to hold always to the straight path. Thus, in the two examples I have just advanced, it was clearly finer and more generous in the man who had received the offense to pardon it than to do otherwise. If the first one came to grief, this good plan of his must not be blamed for it; and no one knows whether, if he had taken the opposite course, he would have escaped the end to which his destiny called him; and thus he would have lost the glory of such exceptional kindness.

You see in the histories many people prone to this fear, and most of them have followed the course of running to meet conspiracies against them with vengeance and punishment; but I see very few whom this remedy has served, witness so many Roman emperors. A man who finds himself in this danger should not expect much from his strength or his vigilance. For how hard it is to protect ourselves from an enemy who is concealed behind the face of the most assiduous friend we have, and to know the inmost wills and thoughts of those who serve us! In vain he employs foreigners as a guard and is always surrounded with a hedge of armed men: whoever holds his own life in scorn will always be master of that of others. And then that continual suspicion that puts a prince in fear of everybody must be an extraordinary torment to him.

[B]Therefore Dion, being warned that Callippus was on the watch for ways to have him killed, never had the heart to look into the

matter, saying that he would rather die than live in the misery of
having to guard himself not only against his enemies but also against
his friends. This Alexander represented much more vividly in
action, and more daringly, when, after reading in a letter from
Parmenio that Philip, his most beloved doctor, had been corrupted
by Darius' money and was planning to poison him, he gave Philip
the letter to read and at the same time swallowed the drink that
Philip had brought him. Wasn't that expressing this resolve, that if
his friends wanted to kill him, he was willing to let them? This
prince is the supreme model of hazardous acts; but I do not know if
there is an episode in his life that shows more courage than this one,
or a beauty shining in so many aspects.

Those who preach to princes such an attentive distrust, under
the guise of preaching them security, preach them their ruin and
their shame. Nothing noble is done without risk. I know a man,[4] [c]of
a very martial courage by nature, and enterprising, [B]whose fine
career is being corrupted every day by such persuasions: that he
should stay in close among his own people; that he should hear of no
reconciliation with his former enemies, should keep apart and not
trust himself to hands stronger than his own, whatever promise may
be made him, whatever advantage he may see in it. [c]I know another[5]
who has advanced his fortune beyond all expectations by following
a wholly opposite plan.

Boldness, the glory of which they seek so avidly, displays itself,
when necessary, as magnificently in a doublet as in armor, in a room
as in a camp, with arm hanging as with arm raised.

[B]Such tender and circumspect prudence is a mortal enemy of
lofty actions. [c]Scipio, to win Syphax to his own side, had the vision
to leave his army, to abandon Spain, which was still uncertain under
its fresh conquest, to pass over into Africa in two small ships, and to
entrust himself in enemy country to the power of a barbarian king
and to an untried faith – without obligation, without a hostage,
under the sole security of the greatness of his own courage, his good
fortune, and the promise of his high hopes: *our own trust generally
wins the trust of others* [Livy].

[B]For an ambitious and famous life, on the contrary, we must give
way little to suspicions, and keep a tight rein on them: fear and
mistrust attract and invite attack. The most mistrustful of our kings

4 Henry of Navarre.
5 Henri de Guise.

consolidated his affairs mainly by having voluntarily abandoned and committed his life and liberty into the hands of his enemies, showing that he had complete trust in them, so that they might pick up this trust from him. To his legions, mutinous and in arms against him, Caesar opposed only the authority of his countenance and the pride of his words; and he trusted himself and his fortune so much that he did not fear to abandon his person and commit his fate to a seditious and rebellious army.

> [C]Intrepid and erect,
> On a grassy mound he stood, deserving to be feared,
> Since he feared nothing.
>
> <div align="right">LUCAN</div>

[B]But it is quite true that this strong assurance cannot be displayed truly entire and natural except by those who do not take fright at the notion of death, and of the worst that can happen after all; for to display it trembling, still doubtful and uncertain, in attempting an important reconciliation, is to do nothing worth while. To submit and entrust oneself to others is an excellent way to win their heart and will, provided it be done freely and without the constraint of any necessity, and that the situation be such that we bring to it a pure and clean confidence, and at least a countenance free of any misgiving.

I saw, when I was a boy, a gentleman,[6] the military governor of a great city, hard pressed by the commotion of a frenzied populace. To quell the incipient riot, he decided to leave a very safe place that he was in and commit himself to this seditious mob; whereby it went ill with him, and he was killed miserably. But it seems to me that his mistake was not so much that he went out, which is the ordinary reproach to his memory, as that he took a course of submission and softness and tried to lull the people's rage rather by following than by guiding, and by beseeching rather than remonstrating. And I think that a gracious severity, with a martial command full of security and confidence, suitable to his rank and to the dignity of his position, would have succeeded better for him, or at least would have been more honorable and proper. There is nothing less to be hoped for from this monster thus agitated than humanity and gentleness; it is much more accessible to reverence and fear.

6 Monsieur de Moneins, the King's lieutenant in Guienne, killed in Bordeaux in 1548 during the rioting in protest at the salt tax.

I should also reproach him because, having made a resolution, in my opinion rather brave than rash, to cast himself, weak and without armor, into the midst of this tempestuous sea of madmen, he should have swallowed the whole cup and not abandoned his role; whereas what happened to him was that after having seen the danger close up, he lost his nerve and changed once again that deflated and fawning countenance that he had assumed into a frightened one, filling his voice and his eyes with astonishment and penitence. Trying to hole up and hide, he inflamed them and called them down on himself.

Once it was planned to have a general review of various troops under arms. That is an excellent occasion for secret vengeances; never can they be executed with greater security. There were public and notorious evidences that things would go badly for some who had the principal and necessary responsibility for the reviewing.[7] Various plans were proposed, since the matter was difficult and had much weight and consequence. Mine was that they should above all avoid giving any sign of this fear, and should show up and mingle in the ranks, head high and countenance open, and that instead of cutting out anything (as the other opinions mostly aimed to do), they should on the contrary urge the captains to instruct their soldiers to make their volleys fine and lusty in honor of the spectators, and not spare their powder. This served to gratify the suspected troops, and engendered from then on a useful mutual confidence.

[A]The course that Julius Caesar took seems to me the finest that can be taken. First he tried, by clemency and mildness, to make himself loved even by his enemies, contenting himself, in conspiracies that were revealed to him, with simply declaring that he was informed of them. That done, he adopted a very noble resolution to await without fear and without solicitude whatever might come of it, abandoning and entrusting himself to the protection of the gods and of fortune. For certainly this was the state he was in when he was killed.

[B]A stranger stated and proclaimed everywhere that he could teach Dionysius, tyrant of Syracuse, a way to smell out and reveal

7 Montaigne, in his second term (1583–85) as mayor of Bordeaux, had this duty. Not long before, he had helped Marshal de Matignon, the king's lieutenant, oust the Leaguer Vaillac from the dangerous Château Trompette in the city; and reprisals were feared.

with complete certainty any machinations of his subjects against him if he would give him a good sum of money. Dionysius, being informed of this, had the man summoned to enlighten him about an art so necessary to his preservation. This stranger told him that there was no art except this: that Dionysius should have one talent delivered to him and should boast of having learned from him a singular secret. Dionysius found this device good, and had six hundred crowns counted out to him. It was not likely that he would have given so great a sum to an unknown man except as a reward for learning something very useful; and this notion served to keep his enemies in fear.

Therefore princes are wise to publish the information they receive about plots that are set up against their lives, so as to make people believe that they are well informed, and that nothing can be undertaken that they do not get wind of. ᶜThe duke of Athens did many stupid things in establishing his recent tyranny over Florence; but this was the most notable, that having received the first warning of the conspiracies that the people were forming against him from Matteo di Morozo, one of the accomplices, he had him killed, to suppress this information and not to let it be known that anyone in the city could be annoyed by his just government.

ᴬI remember having read once the story of some Roman, a personage of dignity, who, fleeing the tyranny of the Triumvirate, had a thousand times escaped the hands of his pursuers by the subtlety of his devices. It happened one day that a troop of horsemen who had orders to take him passed right next to a thicket where he had hidden and just missed discovering him. But at that point, considering the trouble and hardships which he had already so long endured to save himself from the continual careful searches that were made for him everywhere, the little pleasure he could hope for from such a life, and how much better it was for him to take the step once and for all than to remain always in this apprehension, he himself called them back and betrayed his hiding place to them, voluntarily abandoning himself to their cruelty in order to rid them and himself of further trouble. To call out for the hand of the enemy is a rather extreme measure, yet a better one, I think, than to remain in continual fever over an accident that has no remedy. But since all the precautions that a man can take are full of uneasiness and uncertainty, it is better to prepare with fine assurance for the worst that can happen, and derive some consolation from the fact that we are not sure that it will happen.

25
Of pedantry

[A]I was often annoyed in my childhood to see a teacher always the butt in Italian comedies; and the title of Magister used to have scarcely a more honorable significance among us Frenchmen. For since I had been given into their tutelage and charge, was it not the least I could do to be jealous of their reputation? I sought indeed to excuse them on account of the natural incompatibility that exists between the common herd and people of rare and excellent judgment and knowledge, inasmuch as these two groups go entirely different ways. But I was wasting my Latin, since the finest gentlemen were those who held teachers most in contempt, witness our good Du Bellay:

> But I hate above all pedantic learning.

[B]And this custom is an ancient one; for Plutarch says that *Greek* and *student* were terms of reproach and contempt among the Romans.

[A]Since then, as I grew older, I found that they had a very good reason for this, and that *the greatest scholars are not the wisest men* [proverb quoted by Rabelais]. But how it is possible that a soul rich in the knowledge of so many things should not thereby become keener and more alert, and that a crude and commonplace mind can harbor within itself, without being improved, the reasonings and judgments of the greatest minds that the world has produced – that still has me puzzled.

[B]"To take in so many other brains, and such great and powerful ones," a young lady,[1] the first of our princesses, said to me, speaking of a certain person, "our own must crowd itself down, confine itself, and make itself small, to make room for the others."

[A]I should be inclined to say that as plants are stifled with too much moisture, and lamps with too much oil, so too much study and matter stifles the action of the mind, which, being caught and entangled in a great variety of things, may lose the ability to break loose, and be kept bent and huddled down by its burden.

But it works the other way, for the more our soul is filled, the larger it becomes. And in the examples from olden times, we see as

1 Probably Catherine de Bourbon, sister of Henry of Navarre; but quite possibly Henry's wife, Margaret of Valois, sister of Henry III.

further proof to the contrary that able men in the handling of public matters, great captains, and great counselors in affairs of state, have at the same time been very learned.

And as for the philosophers, who are remote from all public occupation, they have also in truth sometimes been mocked by the comic license of their times, ᶜtheir opinions and ways making them ridiculous.

Do you want to make them judge the merits of a case, the actions of a man? They are well prepared indeed. They are still trying to find out whether there is life, whether there is movement, whether man is something other than an ox, what it is to act and to be acted on, what kind of animals laws and justice are. Do they speak of the magistrate, or speak to him? They do so with an irreverent and uncivil liberty. Do they hear their prince or a king praised? He is just a shepherd to them, idle as a shepherd, occupied in milking and fleecing his flocks, but much more roughly than a shepherd. Do you consider someone greater for owning two thousand acres of land? They mock him, being accustomed to embrace the whole world as their possession. Do you boast of your nobility because you can count seven rich ancestors? They think little of you, as one not conceiving the universal image of nature or how many predecessors each of us has had: rich, poor, kings, servants, Greeks, and barbarians. And though you were the fiftieth in descent from Hercules, they find you vain to make capital of this gift of fortune.

Thus the common herd disdained them as ignorant of the elementary and common things, as presumptuous and insolent. But this Platonic picture is far removed from the one we need for our folk. ᴬThose men were envied as being above the common fashion, as disdaining public actions, as having set up a particular and inimitable way of life regulated by certain lofty and extraordinary principles; these are despised as being beneath the common fashion, as incapable of public responsibilities, as dragging along behind the common herd their base life and ways.

> ᶜI hate men base in deeds but wise in words.
>
> PACUVIUS

ᴬAs for those philosophers, I say, as they were great in knowledge, so they were greater still in every kind of action. And just as they tell of that geometrician of Syracuse² that having been diverted

2 Archimedes.

from his contemplation to put some of it into practice for the defense of his country, he immediately put into operation frightful machines and effects surpassing all human belief, though all the while himself disdaining all this handiwork and thinking that he had thereby besmirched the dignity of his art, of which his inventions were but the apprentice work and playthings; so they, if at any time they were put to the test of action, were seen to soar on such a lofty wing that it clearly appeared that their heart and soul had been marvelously enlarged and enriched by the understanding of things.

But ᶜsome of them, seeing the citadel of political government seized by incapable men, have withdrawn from it. And the man who asked Crates how long it was necessary to philosophize received this answer: "Until it is no longer donkey drivers who lead our armies." Heraclitus resigned the kingdom to his brother, and said to the Ephesians who were reproaching him for spending his time playing with children in front of the temple: "Isn't it better to be doing this than to be governing the affairs of state in your company?" ᴬOthers, whose imagination was set above fortune and the world, found the seats of justice, and even the thrones of kings, low and vile. ᶜAnd Empedocles refused the throne that the Agrigentines offered him. ᴬAfter Thales had several times criticized people's concern with managing a household and getting rich, they reproached him, saying that he was doing so like the fox, because he could not attain these things. He decided, for fun, to test this out; and making his learning stoop for this once to the service of profit and gain, he set up a traffic which within a year brought in such riches that hardly in their whole lifetime could the most experienced in that trade make as much.

ᶜWhat Aristotle relates of some who called both Thales and Anaxagoras and the likes of them wise but not prudent, because they cared not enough for the more useful things – aside from the fact that I do not very well digest this distinction in terms – does not serve to excuse the people I have in mind; rather, seeing the base and necessitous fortune with which they are content, we would be justified in saying both things, that they are both not wise and not prudent.

ᴬI leave this first explanation, and think it better to say that this evil comes from the bad way that men of learning have of going at the sciences; and that the way we are instructed, it is no wonder if neither the students nor the masters grow in ability, although they

do make themselves more learned. In truth, the care and expense of our fathers aims only at furnishing our heads with knowledge; of judgment and virtue, little news. ^CExclaim to our people about a passer-by "Oh, what a learned man!" and about another "Oh, what a good man!" They will not fail to turn their eyes and their respect toward the first. There should be a third exclamation: "Oh, what blockheads!" ^AWe are eager to inquire: "Does he know Greek or Latin? Does he write in verse or in prose?" But whether he has become better or wiser, which would be the main thing, that is left out. We should have asked who is better learned, not who is more learned.

We labor only to fill our memory, and leave the understanding ^Cand the conscience ^Aempty. Just as birds sometimes go in quest of grain, and carry it in their beak without tasting it to give a beakful to their little ones, so our pedants go pillaging knowledge in books and lodge it only on the end of their lips, in order merely to disgorge it and scatter it to the winds.

^CIt is wonderful how appropriately this folly fits my case. Isn't it doing the same thing, what I do in most of this composition? I go about cadging from books here and there the sayings that please me, not to keep them, for I have no storehouses, but to transport them into this one, in which, to tell the truth, they are no more mine than in their original place. We are, I believe, learned only with present knowledge, not with past, any more than with future.

^ABut what is worse, their students and their little ones are not nourished and fed with their learning either; it passes from hand to hand for the sole purpose of making a show of it, talking to others and telling stories about it; like chits that have no other value and use than to be counted and thrown away. ^C*They have learned to speak among others, not with themselves* [Cicero]. *Not talking, but steering, is needed* [Seneca].

Nature, to show that there is nothing barbarous in what is under her guidance, often brings forth, in the nations least cultivated by art, productions of the mind that vie with the most artistic productions. How nice for my purpose is the Gascon proverb, *We may blow and blow, but we still have to move our fingers*, taken from a shepherd's song.

^AWe know how to say: "Cicero says thus; such are the morals of Plato; these are the very words of Aristotle." But what do we say ourselves? What do we judge? What do we do? A parrot could well say as much.

This habit makes me think of that rich Roman who went to much trouble and very great expense to procure men learned in every field of knowledge, whom he kept continually around him, so that when there should befall among his friends some occasion to speak of one thing or another, they should fill his place and all be ready to furnish him, one with an argument, one with a verse of Homer, each one according to his quarry; and he thought that this knowledge was his own because it was in the heads of his men, as those also do whose ability dwells in their sumptuous libraries.

^CI know a man who, when I ask him what he knows, asks me for a book in order to point it out to me, and wouldn't dare tell me that he has an itchy backside unless he goes immediately and studies in his lexicon what is itchy and what is a backside.

^AWe take the opinions and the knowledge of others into our keeping, and that is all. We must make them our own. We are just like a man who, needing fire, should go and fetch some at his neighbor's house, and, having found a fine big fire there, should stop there and warm himself, forgetting to carry any back home. What good does it do us to have our belly full of meat if it is not digested, if it is not transformed into us, if it does not make us bigger and stronger? Do we think that Lucullus, whom books, without experience, made and fashioned into such a great captain, used them in our manner?

^BWe let ourselves lean so heavily on the arms of others that we annihilate our own powers. Do I want to arm myself against the fear of death? I do so at Seneca's expense. Do I want to draw consolation for myself or for another? I borrow it from Cicero. I would have got it in myself if I had been trained to. I don't like this dependent and mendicant ability.

^AEven if we could be learned with other men's learning, at least wise we cannot be except by our own wisdom.

> I hate the wise man who is not wise for himself.
>
> EURIPIDES

^C*Whence Ennius: The wise man is wise to no purpose who can do himself no good* [quoted by Cicero].

> ^BIf greedy, vain, and viler than a Euganean lamb.
>
> JUVENAL

^C*For we must not only acquire wisdom, but profit by it* [Cicero].

Dionysius used to make fun of the grammarians who are at pains to inquire about the troubles of Ulysses and are ignorant of their own; the musicians who attune their flutes and do not attune their morals; the orators who study to talk justice, not to do it.

^AIf our soul does not go at a better gait, if we do not have sounder judgment for all our learning, I had just as lief my student had spent his time playing tennis: at least his body would be the blither. See him come back from there, after fifteen or sixteen years put in: there is nothing so unfit for use. All the advantage you recognize is that his Latin and Greek have made him more conceited and arrogant than when he left home. ^CHe should have brought back his soul full; he brings it back only swollen; he has only inflated it instead of enlarging it.

These schoolmasters, as Plato says of their cousins the Sophists, are of all men those who promise to be the most useful to men, and who, alone of all men, not only do not improve what is committed to them, as does a carpenter or a mason, but make it worse, and take pay for having made it worse.

If the rule that Protagoras proposed to his pupils were followed – that they should either pay him on his terms, or swear in the temple how much they valued the profit that they had received from his teachings and compensate his pains accordingly – my pedagogues would find themselves disappointed, if they trusted the sworn testimony of my experience.

^AMy Perigordian patois very comically calls these little men of learning *Lettre-ferits*, as if to say *lettre-ferus*[3] (letter-struck), men whom letters have dealt a hammer blow, as they say. In truth, most of the time they seem to have sunk even beneath common sense. For you see the peasant and the shoemaker go their way simply and naturally talking about what they know; while these men, through wanting to exalt themselves and swagger around with this learning that is floating on the surface of their brain, are perpetually getting confused and tangled up in their own feet. Fine words escape them, but let another man apply them. They know Galen well, but the patient not at all. They have already filled your head with laws, and still have not yet grasped the crux of the case. They know the theory of all things; *you* find someone who will put it in practice.

I have seen a friend of mine, in my house, when he had to deal with one of these people, invent for fun a jargon of windy nonsense,

3 *Ferit* and *feru* both are past participles of the verb *ferir*, to strike.

remarks without sequence, a tissue of borrowed fragments, except that it was often interlarded with words appropriate to their dispute, and thus keep this fool busy all day debating and always thinking he was answering the objections that were made against him; and yet this was a man of letters and reputation, [B]and wore a fine gown.

> Oh you, patrician race, whose skulls are blind,
> Watch for the grimaces that lurk behind.
>
> PERSIUS

[A]Whoever will closely observe this sort of people, who are very widespread, will find, as I have, that most of the time they understand neither themselves nor others, and that they have a full enough memory but an entirely hollow judgment, unless their nature has of itself fashioned it otherwise: as I have seen in Adrianus Turnebus, who, having had no other profession but letters, in which, in my opinion, he was the greatest man that has been in a thousand years, had nevertheless nothing pedantic about him but the gown he wore and a certain external mannerism that might not be civilized by a courtier's standard, which are things of no importance. [B]And I hate our people who find it harder to tolerate a gown awry than a soul awry, and judge a man by his bow, his bearing, and his boots. [A]For inside he was the most polished soul in the world. I have often deliberately launched him on topics remote from his practice; he saw into them so clearly, with so quick an apprehension, so sound a judgment, that it seemed as if he had never practiced any other profession than war and affairs of state. Those are fine strong natures –

> [B]For whom, with art benign,
> Prometheus shaped a heart of clay more fine
>
> PERSIUS

– [A]which hold fast through a bad education. Now it is not enough for our education not to spoil us; it must change us for the better.

There are some of our Parlements which, when they have to admit members, examine them only on their learning; the others add also a test of their sense, by presenting them with a case for judgment. These seem to me to have a much better method; and even though both parts are necessary, and both must be present, still in truth it is a fact that learning is less valuable than judgment. The

latter can do without the former, and not the former without the latter. For as that Greek verse says –

Knowledge is nothing if the mind's not there
STOBAEUS

– what is the use of learning, if understanding is absent? Would God that, for the good of our justice, those bodies were as well furnished with understanding and conscience as they are with learning! ᶜ*We learn not for life but for the schoolroom* [Seneca]. ᴬNow we must not attach learning to the mind, we must incorporate it; we must not sprinkle, but dye. And if learning does not change the mind and improve its imperfect state, certainly we do much better to let it alone. Learning is a dangerous sword that will hamper and hurt its master, if it is in a weak hand that does not know how to use it – ᶜ*so that it were better not to have learned* [Cicero].

ᴬPerhaps this is the reason why neither we nor theology require much learning of women; and why Francis, duke of Brittany, son of John V, when they were talking to him about his marriage with Isabel, a princess of Scotland, and told him that she had been brought up simply and without any instruction in letters, replied that he loved her the better for it, and that a woman was learned enough when she knew how to distinguish between her husband's shirt and his doublet.

And so it is not so great a wonder as they claim that our ancestors took no great account of letters, and that even today they come in only by chance in the principal councils of our kings; and if the aim of getting rich by them, which alone is set before us today, by means of jurisprudence, medicine, teaching, and even theology, did not maintain them in credit, you would undoubtedly see them in as wretched condition as they ever were. And what loss would that be, if they teach us neither to think well nor to do well? ᶜ*Now that the learned have appeared, good men are wanting* [Seneca]. Any other knowledge is harmful to a man who has not the knowledge of goodness.

But perhaps the reason that I was just looking for comes also from this, that our studies in France have almost no other aim but profit, except for those whom nature brought into the world for offices more noble than lucrative and who devote themselves to letters for such a short time, withdrawing, before they have acquired a taste for them, to a profession that has nothing in common with books; hence there ordinarily remain none to involve themselves

completely in study but people of humble means, who seek a living in it. And the souls of those people, being both by nature and by home upbringing and example of the basest alloy, bring forth false fruits of learning. For learning is not there to give light to the soul that has none, or to make a blind man see. Her business is not to furnish him with sight but to direct the sight he has, to regulate its steps, provided it has straight and capable feet and legs of its own.

Knowledge is a good drug; but no drug is strong enough to preserve itself without alteration and corruption, according to the taint of the vessel that contains it. A given man sees clear but not straight, and consequently sees the good and does not follow it, and sees knowledge and does not use it. The principal ordinance of Plato in his *Republic* is to give his citizens their jobs according to their nature. Nature can do all and does all. Cripples are ill-suited to bodily exercises, and crippled souls to mental exercises; bastard and vulgar souls are unworthy of philosophy. When we see a man ill-shod, we say it is no wonder, if he is a shoemaker. Likewise it seems that experience often shows us a doctor worse doctored, a theologian less reformed, a scholar less competent, than anyone else.

Aristo of Chios had reason to say long ago that philosophers harmed their listeners, inasmuch as most souls are not fit to profit by such instruction, which, if it does not work for good, works for evil: *debauchees came out of the school of Aristippus, boors from that of Zeno* [Cicero].

ᴬIn that fine education that Xenophon attributes to the Persians, we find that they taught their children virtue as other nations do letters. ᶜPlato says that the eldest son in their royal succession was brought up as follows: After his birth he was given over not to women but to eunuchs of the highest authority with their kings because of their virtue. These took charge of making his body fair and healthy, and after seven years trained him to ride a horse and to go hunting. When he had reached fourteen, they put him in the hands of four men: the wisest, the most just, the most temperate, and the most valiant in the nation. The first taught him religion; the second, to be always truthful; the third, to make himself master of his appetites; the fourth, to fear nothing.

ᴬIt is a thing worthy of very great consideration in that excellent form of government of Lycurgus, one in truth prodigious in its

perfection, that despite the emphasis on the education of children as the state's principal responsibility, and that in the very seat of the Muses, there is so little mention made of learning; as if those high-souled youths, disdaining any other yoke than that of virtue, had to be furnished merely with masters of valor, wisdom, and justice, instead of with our masters of knowledge: ᶜan example that Plato followed in his *Laws*. ᴬThe method of their teaching was to ask them questions on their judgment of men and their actions; and if they condemned or praised this person or that deed, they had to reason out what they said; and by this means they both sharpened their understanding and at the same time learned what was right.

Astyages, in Xenophon, asks Cyrus for an account of his last lesson. "It was this," he says. "In our school a big boy who had a small coat gave it to one of his schoolmates who was smaller and took away his coat, which was larger. Our teacher having made me judge of this dispute, I judged that things should be left in that state, and that both seemed to be better suited in this way; whereupon he pointed out to me that I had done badly, for I had stopped at considering fitness, whereas I should first of all have taken care of justice, which willed that no one should be forced in regard to what belonged to him." And he says that he was whipped for it, just as we are in our villages for having forgotten the first aorist of τύπτω.

My schoolmaster would make me a fine harangue *in genere demonstrativo* before he would persuade me that his school is worth that one. They wanted to take a short cut; and since it is a fact that learning, even when it is taken most directly, can only teach us *about* wisdom, integrity, and resolution, they wanted to put their children from the first in contact with deeds, and instruct them, not by hearsay, but by the test of action, forming and molding them in a living way, not only by precepts and words, but principally by examples and works; so that learning might be not merely a knowledge in their soul, but its character and habit; not an acquisition but a natural possession. In this connection, some-one asked Agesilaus what he thought children should learn. "What they should do when they are men," he replied. It is no wonder if such an education has produced such admirable results.

They used to go, it is said, to the other cities of Greece to look for rhetoricians, painters, and musicians; but to Lacedaemon for legislators, magistrates, and army generals. At Athens they learned to

speak well, here to do well; there to disentangle themselves from a sophistical argument and to overthrow the imposture of words captiously interlaced, here to disentangle themselves from the lures of sensual pleasure, and with great courage to overthrow the threats of fortune and death; those men busied themselves with words, these with things; there it was a continual exercise of the tongue, here a continual exercise of the soul. Wherefore it is not strange if, when Antipater demanded of them fifty children for hostages, they answered, quite contrary to what we should do, that they would rather give up twice as many grown men, so important did they consider the loss of their country's education. When Agesilaus invites Xenophon to send his children to be brought up in Sparta, it is not to learn rhetoric or dialectic there, but to learn, as he says, the finest science there is, namely, the science of obeying and commanding.

ᶜIt is very amusing to see Socrates, after his manner, making fun of Hippias – who tells him how he earned a good sum of money teaching school, especially in certain little towns in Sicily, and that at Sparta he didn't earn a cent – by saying that they are idiots, who don't know how to measure or count and who set no store by either grammar or rhythm, busying themselves merely with knowing the succession of kings, the founding and decadence of states, and such a jumble of tales. And at the end of all this, Socrates, making Hippias admit step by step the excellence of their form of public government, the happiness and virtue of their life, leaves it to him to guess the conclusion: that his own arts are useless.

Examples teach us, both in that martial government and in all others like it, that the pursuit of knowledge makes men's hearts soft and effeminate more than it makes them strong and warlike. The strongest state that we see in the world at present is that of the Turks, a people equally trained to esteem arms and despise letters. I consider Rome more valiant before she was learned. The most warlike nations in our day are the most crude and ignorant. The Scythians, the Parthians, Tamerlane, serve as a proof of this. When the Goths ravaged Greece, what saved all the libraries from being set afire was that one of the invaders spread the opinion that this item might well be left intact to the enemy, to divert them from military exercises and keep them busy in sedentary and idle occupations. When our King Charles VIII, without drawing his sword from its scabbard, saw himself master of the

kingdom of Naples and a good part of Tuscany, the noblemen in his suite attributed the unhoped-for ease of this conquest to the fact that the princes and nobles of Italy were more involved in making themselves ingenious and learned than vigorous and warlike.

26
Of the education of children

TO MADAME DIANE DE FOIX, COMTESSE DE GURSON

^AI have never seen a father who failed to claim his son, however mangy or hunchbacked he was. Not that he does not perceive his defect, unless he is utterly intoxicated by his affection; but the fact remains that the boy is his. And so I myself see better than anyone else that these are nothing but reveries of a man who has tasted only the outer crust of sciences in his childhood, and has retained only a vague general picture of them: a little of everything and nothing thoroughly, French style. For to sum up, I know that there is such a thing as medicine, jurisprudence, four parts in mathematics, and roughly what they aim at. ^CAnd perhaps I also know the service that the sciences in general aim to contribute to our life. ^ABut as for plunging in deeper, or gnawing my nails over the study of Aristotle, ^Cmonarch of modern learning, ^Aor stubbornly pursuing some part of knowledge, I have never done it; ^Cnor is there an art of which I could sketch even the outlines. There is not a child halfway through school who cannot claim to be more learned than I, who have not even the equipment to examine him on his first lesson, at least according to that lesson. And if they force me to, I am constrained, rather ineptly, to draw from it some matter of universal scope, on which I test the boy's natural judgment: a lesson as strange to them as theirs is to me.

I have not had regular dealings with any solid book, except Plutarch and Seneca, from whom I draw like the Danaïds, incessantly filling up and pouring out. Some of this sticks to this paper; to myself, little or nothing.

^AHistory is more my quarry, or poetry, which I love with particular affection. For as Cleanthes said, just as sound, when pent up in the narrow channel of a trumpet, comes out sharper and stronger, so it seems to me that a thought, when compressed into the numbered

feet of poetry, springs forth much more violently and strikes me
a much stiffer jolt. As for the natural faculties that are in me, of
which this book is the essay, I feel them bending under the load. My
conceptions and my judgment move only by groping, staggering,
stumbling, and blundering; and when I have gone ahead as far as
I can, still I am not at all satisfied: I can still see country beyond, but
with a dim and clouded vision, so that I cannot clearly distinguish it.
And when I undertake to speak indiscriminately of everything
that comes to my fancy without using any but my own natural
resources, if I happen, as I often do, to come across in the good
authors those same subjects I have attempted to treat – as in
Plutarch I have just this very moment come across his discourse
on the power of imagination – seeing myself so weak and puny, so
heavy and sluggish, in comparison with those men, I hold myself in
pity and disdain.

 Still I am pleased at this, that my opinions have the honor of
often coinciding with theirs, ᶜand that at least I go the same way,
though far behind them, saying "How true!" ᴬAlso that I have this,
which not everyone has, that I know the vast difference between
them and me. And nonetheless I let my thoughts run on, weak and
lowly as they are, as I have produced them, without plastering
and sewing up the flaws that this comparison has revealed to me.
ᶜOne needs very strong loins to undertake to march abreast of those
men. ᴬThe undiscerning writers of our century who amid their
nonexistent works scatter whole passages of the ancient authors to
do themselves honor, do just the opposite. For this infinite differ-
ence in brilliance gives so pale, tarnished, and ugly an aspect to the
part that is their own that they lose in this way much more than
they gain.

 ᶜThere were two contrasting fancies. The philosopher Chrysip-
pus mixed into his books, not merely passages, but entire works
of other authors, and in one the *Medea* of Euripides; and Apollo-
dorus said that if you cut out of them all the foreign matter,
the paper he used would be left blank. Epicurus, on the contrary,
in three hundred volumes that he left, put in not a single
borrowed quotation.

 ᴬI happened the other day to come upon such a passage. I had
dragged along languidly after French words so bloodless, fleshless,
and empty of matter and sense that they really were nothing but
French words. At the end of a long and tedious road I came upon
a bit that was sublime, rich, and lofty as the clouds. If I had found

the slope gentle and the climb a bit slower, it would have been excusable; but it was a precipice so straight and steep that after the first six words I realized that I was flying off into another world. From there I saw the bog I had come out of, so low and deep that I never again had the stomach to go back down into it. If I stuffed one of my chapters with these rich spoils, it would show up too clearly the stupidity of the others.

ᶜTo criticize my own faults in others seems to me no more inconsistent than to criticize, as I often do, others' faults in myself. We must denounce them everywhere and leave them no place of refuge. Still, I well know how audaciously I always attempt to match the level of my pilferings, to keep pace with them, not without a rash hope that I may deceive the eyes of the judges who try to discover them. But this is as much by virtue of my use of them as by virtue of my inventiveness or my power. And then, I do not wrestle with those old champions wholesale and body against body; I do so by snatches, by little light attacks. I don't go at them stubbornly; I only feel them out; and I don't go nearly as much as I think about going. If I were a match for them I would be a good man, for I take them on only at their stiffest points.

As for doing what I have discovered others doing, covering themselves with other men's armor until they don't show even their fingertips, and carrying out their plan, as is easy for the learned in common subjects, with ancient inventions pieced out here and there – for those who want to hide their borrowings and appropriate them, this is first of all injustice and cowardice, that, having nothing of their own worth bringing out, they try to present themselves under false colors; and second, it is stupid of them to content themselves with gaining deceitfully the ignorant approbation of the common herd, while discrediting themselves in the eyes of men of understanding, whose praise alone has any weight, and who turn up their nose at our borrowed incrustations. For my part, there is nothing I want less to do. I do not speak the minds of others except to speak my own mind better. This does not apply to the compilations that are published as compilations; and I have seen some very ingenious ones in my time; among others, one under the name of Capilupus, besides the ancients. The minds of these authors are such that they stand out in this sort of writing as well as in other kinds, as does Lipsius in the learned and laborious web of his *Politics*.

ᴬHowever that may be, I mean to say, and whatever these absurdities may be, I have had no intention of concealing them,

any more than I would a bald and graying portrait of myself, in which the painter had drawn not a perfect face, but mine. For likewise these are my humors and opinions; I offer them as what I believe, not what is to be believed. I aim here only at revealing myself, who will perhaps be different tomorrow, if I learn something new which changes me. I have no authority to be believed, nor do I want it, feeling myself too ill-instructed to instruct others.

Well, someone who had seen the preceding article[1] was telling me at my home the other day that I should have enlarged a bit on the subject of the education of children. Now, Madame, if I had some competence in this matter, I could not use it better than to make a present of it to the little man who threatens soon to come out so bravely from within you (you are too noble-spirited to begin otherwise than with a male). For having had so great a part in bringing about your marriage, I have a certain rightful interest in the greatness and prosperity of whatever comes out of it; besides that, the ancient claim that you have on my servitude is enough to oblige me to wish honor, good, and advantage to all that concerns you. But in truth I understand nothing about it except this, that the greatest and most important difficulty in human knowledge seems to lie in the branch of knowledge which deals with the upbringing and education of children.

ᶜJust as in agriculture the operations that come before the planting, as well as the planting itself, are certain and easy; but as soon as the plant comes to life, there are various methods and great difficulties in raising it; so it is with men: little industry is needed to plant them, but it is quite a different burden we assume from the moment of their birth, a burden full of care and fear – that of training them and bringing them up.

ᴬThe manifestation of their inclinations is so slight and so obscure at that early age, the promises so uncertain and misleading, that it is hard to base any solid judgment on them. ᴮLook at Cimon, look at Themistocles and a thousand others, how they belied themselves. The young of bears and dogs show their natural inclination, but men, plunging headlong into certain habits, opinions, and laws, easily change or disguise themselves.

ᴬStill it is difficult to force natural propensities. Whence it happens that, because we have failed to choose their road well, we often spend a lot of time and effort for nothing, training children for

1 The chapter "Of Pedantry".

things in which they cannot get a foothold. At all events, in this difficulty, my advice is to guide them always to the best and most profitable things, and to pay little heed to those trivial conjectures and prognostications which we make from the actions of their childhood. ᶜEven Plato, in his *Republic*, seems to me to give them too much authority.

ᴬMadame, learning is a great ornament and a wonderfully serviceable tool, notably for people raised to such a degree of fortune as you are. In truth, it does not receive its proper use in mean and lowborn hands. It is much prouder to lend its resources to conducting a war, governing a people, or gaining the friendship of a prince or a foreign nation, than to constructing a dialectical argument, pleading an appeal, or prescribing a mass of pills. Thus, Madame, because I think you will not forget this element in the education of your children, you who have tasted its sweetness and who are of a literary race (for we still have the writings of those ancient counts of Foix from whom his lordship the count your husband and yourself are descended; and François, Monsieur de Candale, your uncle, every day brings forth others, which will extend for many centuries the knowledge of this quality in your family), I want to tell you a single fancy of mine on this subject, which is contrary to common usage; it is all that I can contribute to your service in this matter.

The task of the tutor that you will give your son, upon whose choice depends the whole success of his education, has many other important parts, but I do not touch upon them, since I cannot offer anything worth while concerning them; and in this matter on which I venture to give him advice, he will take it only as far as it seems good to him. For a child of noble family who seeks learning not for gain (for such an abject goal is unworthy of the graces and favor of the Muses, and besides it looks to others and depends on them), or so much for external advantages as for his own, and to enrich and furnish himself inwardly, since I would rather make of him an able man than a learned man, I would also urge that care be taken to choose a guide with a well-made rather than a well-filled head; that both these qualities should be required of him, but more particularly character and understanding than learning; and that he should go about his job in a novel way.

Our tutors never stop bawling into our ears, as though they were pouring water into a funnel; and our task is only to repeat what has been told us. I should like the tutor to correct this practice, and right

from the start, according to the capacity of the mind he has in hand, to begin putting it through its paces, making it taste things, choose them, and discern them by itself; sometimes clearing the way for him, sometimes letting him clear his own way. I don't want him to think and talk alone, I want him to listen to his pupil speaking in his turn. ^CSocrates, and later Arcesilaus, first had their disciples speak, and then they spoke to them. *The authority of those who teach is often an obstacle to those who want to learn* [Cicero].

It is good that he should have his pupil trot before him, to judge the child's pace and how much he must stoop to match his strength. For lack of this proportion we spoil everything; and to be able to hit it right and to go along in it evenly is one of the hardest tasks that I know; it is the achievement of a lofty and very strong soul to know how to come down to a childish gait and guide it. I walk more firmly and surely uphill than down.

If, as is our custom, the teachers undertake to regulate many minds of such different capacities and forms with the same lesson and a similar measure of guidance, it is no wonder if in a whole race of children they find barely two or three who reap any proper fruit from their teaching.

^ALet him be asked for an account not merely of the words of his lesson, but of its sense and substance, and let him judge the profit he has made by the testimony not of his memory, but of his life. Let him be made to show what he has just learned in a hundred aspects, and apply it to as many different subjects, to see if he has yet properly grasped it and made it his own, ^Cplanning his progress according to the pedagogical method of Plato. ^AIt is a sign of rawness and indigestion to disgorge food just as we swallowed it. The stomach has not done its work if it has not changed the condition and form of what has been given it to cook.

^BOur mind moves only on faith, being bound and constrained to the whim of others' fancies, a slave and a captive under the authority of their teaching. We have been so well accustomed to leading strings that we have no free motion left; our vigor and liberty are extinct. ^C*They never become their own guardians* [Seneca]. ^BI had a private talk with a man at Pisa, a good man, but such an Aristotelian that the most sweeping of his dogmas is that the touchstone and measure of all solid speculations and of all truth is conformity with the teaching of Aristotle; that outside of this there is nothing but chimeras and inanity; that Aristotle saw everything and said everything. This proposition, having been interpreted a little too

broadly and unfairly, put him once, and kept him long, in great danger of the Inquisition at Rome.

^ALet the tutor make his charge pass everything through a sieve and lodge nothing in his head on mere authority and trust: let not Aristotle's principles be principles to him any more than those of the Stoics or Epicureans. Let this variety of ideas be set before him; he will choose if he can; if not, he will remain in doubt. ^COnly the fools are certain and assured.

^AFor doubting pleases me no less than knowing.

DANTE

For if he embraces Xenophon's and Plato's opinions by his own reasoning, they will no longer be theirs, they will be his. ^CHe who follows another follows nothing. He finds nothing; indeed he seeks nothing. *We are not under a king; let each one claim his own freedom* [Seneca]. Let him know that he knows, at least. ^AHe must imbibe their ways of thinking, not learn their precepts. And let him boldly forget, if he wants, where he got them, but let him know how to make them his own. Truth and reason are common to everyone, and no more belong to the man who first spoke them than to the man who says them later. ^CIt is no more according to Plato than according to me, since he and I understand and see it in the same way. ^AThe bees plunder the flowers here and there, but afterward they make of them honey, which is all theirs; it is no longer thyme or marjoram. Even so with the pieces borrowed from others; he will transform and blend them to make a work that is all his own, to wit, his judgment. His education, work, and study aim only at forming this.

^CLet him hide all the help he has had, and show only what he has made of it. The pillagers, the borrowers, parade their buildings, their purchases, not what they get from others. You do not see the gratuities of a member of a Parlement, you see the alliances he has gained and honors for his children. No one makes public his receipts; everyone makes public his acquisitions.

The gain from our study is to have become better and wiser by it.

^AIt is the understanding, Epicharmus used to say, that sees and hears; it is the understanding that makes profit of everything, that arranges everything, that acts, dominates, and reigns; all other things are blind, deaf, and soulless. Truly we make it servile and cowardly, by leaving it no freedom to do anything by itself. Who ever asked his pupil what he thinks ^Bof rhetoric or grammar, or ^Aof such-and-such a saying of Cicero? They slap them into our

memory with all their feathers on, like oracles in which the letters and syllables are the substance of the matter. ^CTo know by heart is not to know; it is to retain what we have given our memory to keep. What we know rightly we dispose of, without looking at the model, without turning our eyes toward our book. Sad competence, a purely bookish competence! I intend it to serve as decoration, not as foundation, according to the opinion of Plato, who says that steadfastness, faith, and sincerity are the real philosophy, and the other sciences which aim at other things are only powder and rouge.

^AI wish Paluel or Pompey,[2] those fine dancers of my time, could teach us capers just by performing them before us and without moving us from our seats, as those people want to train our understanding without setting it in motion; ^Cor that we could be taught to handle a horse, or a pike, or a lute, or our voice, without practicing at it, as those people want to teach us to judge well and to speak well, without having us practice either speaking or judging.

^ANow, for this apprenticeship, everything that comes to our eyes is book enough: a page's prank, a servant's blunder, a remark at table, are so many new materials.

For this reason, mixing with men is wonderfully useful, and visiting foreign countries, not merely to bring back, in the manner of our French noblemen, knowledge of the measurements of the Santa Rotonda, or of the richness of Signora Livia's[3] drawers, or, like some others, how much longer or wider Nero's face is in some old ruin there than on some similar medallion; but to bring back knowledge of the characters and ways of those nations, and to rub and polish our brains by contact with those of others. I should like the tutor to start taking him abroad at a tender age, and first, to kill two birds with one stone, in those neighboring nations where the language is farthest from our own and where the tongue cannot be bent to it unless you train it early.

Likewise it is an opinion accepted by all, that it is not right to bring up a child in the lap of his parents. This natural love makes them too tender and lax, even the wisest of them. They are capable neither of chastising his faults nor of seeing him brought up roughly, as he should be, and hazardously. They could not endure his

2 Ludovico Palvalli and Pompeo Diobono, two famous Milanese dancing masters at the French court.
3 Probably a Roman dancer of Montaigne's time.

returning sweating and dusty from his exercise, ^cdrinking hot, drinking cold, ^Aor see him on a skittish horse, or up against a tough fencer, foil in hand, or with his first harquebus. For there is no help for it: if you want to make a man of him, unquestionably you must not spare him in his youth, and must often clash with the rules of medicine:

^BLet him live beneath the open sky
And dangerously.

<div align="right">HORACE</div>

^CIt is not enough to toughen his soul; we must also toughen his muscles. The soul is too hard pressed unless it is seconded, and has too great a task doing two jobs alone. I know how much mine labors in company with a body so tender and so sensitive, which leans so hard upon it. And I often perceive in my reading that in their writings my masters give weight, as examples of great spirit and stoutheartedness, to acts that are likely to owe more to thickness of skin and toughness of bones. I have seen men, women, and children naturally so constituted that a beating is less to them than a flick of the finger to me; who move neither tongue nor eyebrow at the blows they receive. When athletes imitate philosophers in endurance, their strength is that of sinews rather than of heart.

Now practice at enduring work is practice at enduring pain: *Work hardens one against pain* [Cicero]. The boy must be broken in to the pain and harshness of exercises, to build him up against the pain and harshness of dislocation, colic, cauterization, and the dungeon, and torture. For he may yet be a prey to the last two, which threaten the good as well as the bad in a time like this. We have proof of this right now. Whoever fights the laws threatens even the best of men with the scourge and the noose.

^AAnd besides, the authority of the tutor, which should be sovereign over the pupil, is interrupted and hampered by the presence of the parents. Add the fact that the respect the whole household pays the boy, and the consciousness of the power and greatness of his house, are in my opinion no slight drawbacks at that age.

In this school of dealing with men I have often noticed this flaw, that instead of gaining knowledge of others we strive only to give knowledge of ourselves, and take more pains to peddle our wares than to get new ones. Silence and modesty are very good qualities for social intercourse. This boy will be trained to be sparing and thrifty with his ability when he has acquired it; not to take exception to the stupid things and wild tales that will be told in his presence,

for it is uncivil and annoying to hit at everything that is not to our taste. ᶜLet him be content with correcting himself, and not seem to reproach others for everything that he refuses to do, or set himself up against common practices. *A man may be wise without ostentation, without arousing envy* [Seneca]. Let him shun these domineering and uncivil airs, and this childish ambition to try to seem more clever by being different and to gain reputation by finding fault and being original. As it is becoming only to great poets to indulge in poetic license, so it is tolerable only for great and illustrious souls to take unusual liberties. *If Socrates and Aristippus have done something contrary to the rules of behavior and custom, let him not think that he has a right to do the same; for they have gained that privilege by great and divine merits* [Cicero].

ᴬHe will be taught not to enter into discussion or argument except when he sees a champion worth wrestling with, and even then not to use all the tricks that can help him, but only those that can help him most. Let him be made fastidious in choosing and sorting his arguments, and fond of pertinence, and consequently of brevity. Let him be taught above all to surrender and throw down his arms before truth as soon as he perceives it, whether it be found in the hands of his opponents, or in himself through reconsideration. For he will not be set in a professor's chair to deliver a prepared lecture. He is pledged to no cause, except by the fact that he approves of it. Nor will he take up the trade in which men sell for ready cash the liberty to repent and acknowledge their mistakes. ᶜ*Nor is he forced by any necessity to defend everything that has been prescribed and commanded* [Cicero].

If his tutor is of my disposition, he will form his will to be a very loyal, very affectionate, and very courageous servant of his prince; but he will cool in him any desire to attach himself to that prince otherwise than by sense of public duty. Besides several other disadvantages which impair our freedom by these private obligations, the judgment of a man who is hired and bought is either less whole and less free, or tainted with imprudence and ingratitude. A courtier can have neither the right nor the will to speak and think otherwise than favorably of a master who among so many thousands of other subjects has chosen him to train and raise up with his own hand. This favor and advantage corrupt his freedom, not without some reason, and dazzle him. Therefore we generally find the language of those people different from any other language in a state, and little to be trusted in such matters.

^ALet his conscience and his virtue shine forth in his speech, ^Cand be guided only by reason. ^ALet him be made to understand that to confess the flaw he discovers in his own argument, though it be still unnoticed except by himself, is an act of judgment and sincerity, which are the principal qualities he seeks; ^Cthat obstinacy and contention are vulgar qualities, most often seen in the meanest souls; that to change his mind and correct himself, to give up a bad position at the height of his ardor, are rare, strong, and philosophical qualities.

^AHe will be warned, when he is in company, to have his eyes everywhere; for I find that the chief places are commonly seized by the least capable men, and that greatness of fortune is rarely found in combination with ability. While people at the upper end of a table were talking about the beauty of a tapestry or the flavor of the malmsey, I have seen many fine sallies wasted at the other end. He will sound the capacity of each man: a cowherd, a mason, a passer-by; he must put everything to use, and borrow from each man according to his wares, for everything is useful in a household; even the stupidity and weakness of others will be an education to him. By taking stock of the graces and manners of others, he will create in himself desire of the good ones and contempt for the bad.

Put into his head an honest curiosity to inquire into all things; whatever is unusual around him he will see: a building, a fountain, a man, the field of an ancient battle, the place where Caesar or Charlemagne passed:

> ^BWhich land is parched with heat, which numb with frost,
> What wind drives sails to the Italian coast.

PROPERTIUS

^AHe will inquire into the conduct, the resources, and the alliances of this prince and that. These are things very pleasant to learn and very useful to know.

In this association with men I mean to include, and foremost, those who live only in the memory of books. He will associate, by means of histories, with those great souls of the best ages. It is a vain study, if you will; but also, if you will, it is a study of inestimable value, ^Cand the only study, as Plato tells us, in which the Lacedae-monians had kept a stake for themselves. ^AWhat profit will he not gain in this field by reading the *Lives* of our Plutarch? But let my guide remember the object of his task, and let him not impress on

his pupil so much ^cthe date of the destruction of Carthage as the characters of Hannibal and Scipio, nor so much ^Awhere Marcellus died as why his death there showed him unworthy of his duty. Let him be taught not so much the histories as how to judge them. ^cThat, in my opinion, is of all matters the one to which we apply our minds in the most varying degree. I have read in Livy a hundred things that another man has not read in him. Plutarch has read in him a hundred besides the ones I could read, and perhaps besides what the author had put in. For some it is a purely grammatical study; for others, the skeleton of philosophy, in which the most abstruse parts of our nature are penetrated.

^AThere are in Plutarch many extensive discussions, well worth knowing, for in my judgment he is the master workman in that field; but there are a thousand that he has only just touched on; he merely points out with his finger where we are to go, if we like, and sometimes is content to make only a stab at the heart of a subject. We must snatch these bits out of there and display them properly. ^BJust as that remark of his, that the inhabitants of Asia served one single man because they could not pronounce one single syllable, which is "No," may have given the matter and the impulsion to La Boétie for his *Voluntary Servitude*. ^AJust to see him pick out a trivial action in a man's life, or a word which seems unimportant: that is a treatise in itself. It is a pity that men of understanding are so fond of brevity; doubtless their reputation gains by it, but we lose by it. Plutarch would rather we praised him for his judgment than for his knowledge; he would rather leave us wanting more of him than satiated. He knew that even of good things one may say too much, and that Alexandridas justly reproached the man who was talking sensibly but too long to the Ephors: "O stranger, you say what you should, but otherwise than you should." ^cThose who have a thin body fill it out with padding; those who have slim substance swell it out with words.

^AWonderful brilliance may be gained for human judgment by getting to know men. We are all huddled and concentrated in ourselves, and our vision is reduced to the length of our nose. Socrates was asked where he was from. He replied not "Athens," but "The world." He, whose imagination was fuller and more extensive, embraced the universe as his city, and distributed his knowledge, his company, and his affections to all mankind, unlike us who look only at what is underfoot. When the vines freeze in my village, my priest infers that the wrath of God is upon the human

race, and judges that the cannibals already have the pip. Seeing our civil wars, who does not cry out that this mechanism is being turned topsy-turvy and that the judgment day has us by the throat, without reflecting that many worse things have happened, and that ten thousand parts of the world, to our one, are meanwhile having a gay time? [B]Myself, considering their licentiousness and impunity, I am amazed to see our wars so gentle and mild. [A]When the hail comes down on a man's head, it seems to him that the whole hemisphere is in tempest and storm. And a Savoyard said that if that fool of a French king had known how to play his cards right, he would have had it in him to become chief steward to the duke of Savoy. His imagination conceived no higher dignity than that of his master. [C]We are all unconsciously in this error, an error of great consequence and harm. [A]But whoever considers as in a painting the great picture of our mother Nature in her full majesty; whoever reads such universal and constant variety in her face; whoever finds himself there, and not merely himself, but a whole kingdom, as a dot made with a very fine brush; that man alone estimates things according to their true proportions.

This great world, which some multiply further as being only a species under one genus, is the mirror in which we must look at ourselves to recognize ourselves from the proper angle. In short, I want it to be the book of my student. So many humors, sects, judgments, opinions, laws, and customs teach us to judge sanely of our own, and teach our judgment to recognize its own imperfection and natural weakness, which is no small lesson. So many state disturbances and changes of public fortune teach us not to make a great miracle out of our own. So many names, so many victories and conquests, buried in oblivion, make it ridiculous to hope to perpetuate our name by the capture of ten mounted archers and some chicken coop known only by its fall. The pride and arrogance of so many foreign displays of pomp, the puffed-up majesty of so many courts and dignities, strengthens our sight and makes it steady enough to sustain the brilliance of our own without blinking. So many millions of men buried before us encourage us not to be afraid of joining such good company in the other world. And likewise for other things.

[C]Our life, Pythagoras used to say, is like the great and populous assembly at the Olympic games. Some exercise their bodies to win glory in the games, others bring merchandise to sell for gain. There are some, and not the worst, who seek no other profit than to see

how and why everything is done, and to be spectators of the life of other men in order to judge and regulate their own.

^ATo the examples may properly be fitted all the most profitable lessons of philosophy, by which human actions must be measured as their rule. He will be told:

> ^BWhat you may justly wish; the use and ends
> Of hard-earned coin; our debt to country and to friends;
> What heaven has ordered us to be, and where our stand,
> Amid humanity, is fixed by high command;
> What we now are, what destiny for us is planned;
>
> PERSIUS

^Awhat it is to know and not to know, and what must be the aim of study; what are valor, temperance, and justice; what the difference is between ambition and avarice, servitude and submission, license and liberty; by what signs we may recognize true and solid contentment; how much we should fear death, pain, and shame;

> ^BWhat hardships to avoid, what to endure, and how;
>
> VIRGIL

^Awhat springs move us, and the cause of such different impulses in us. For it seems to me that the first lessons in which we should steep his mind must be those that regulate his behavior and his sense, that will teach him to know himself and to die well and live well. ^CAmong the liberal arts, let us begin with the art that liberates us. They are all somewhat useful for the edification and service of our life, just as everything else is somewhat useful. But let us choose the one that is directly and professedly useful for it.

If we knew how to confine the appurtenances of our life to their just and natural limits, we should find that the better part of the sciences that are now in use are no use to us; and that even in those which are, there are very useless stretches and depths that we would do better to leave alone, in accord with the teaching of Socrates, limiting the extent of our study in those regions where utility is lacking.

> ^ADare to be wise! Begin!
> The man who would reform, but hesitates, is kin
> Unto the boor who waits until the stream is gone;
> But ever flows the stream, and ever will flow on.
>
> HORACE

It is very silly to teach our children

> [B]What effect have Pisces and Leo, fierce and brave,
> Or Capricorn, that bathes in the Hesperian wave,
>
> PROPERTIUS

the knowledge of the stars and [A]the movement of the eighth sphere, before the knowledge of themselves and their movements:

> What are the Pleiades to me,
> And what to me Boötes' stars?
>
> ANACREON

[C]Anaximenes, writing to Pythagoras: "What sense have I if I can amuse myself with the secret of the stars, having death or slavery ever present before my eyes?" For at that time the kings of Persia were preparing to make war on his country. Everyone should speak thus: "When I am battered by ambition, avarice, temerity, and superstition, and have other such enemies of life within me, shall I go dreaming about the revolutions of the earth?"

[A]After the tutor has told his pupil what will help make him wiser and better, he will explain to him the meaning of logic, physics, geometry, rhetoric; and the science he chooses, now that his judgment is already formed, he will soon master. His lesson will be now in talk, now in a book; now his tutor will give him straight from the author some passage that is suitable to this purpose in his education, now he will give him the marrow and the substance predigested. And if the tutor himself is not familiar enough with books to find all the fine passages that are in them for his purpose, some man of letters may be associated with him, who as each need arises shall supply him with the material he requires, which he may then sort out and dispense to his nursling. And who can doubt that this kind of teaching is easier and more natural than that of Gaza?[4] There we find thorny and unpleasant precepts and empty and fleshless words that you cannot get a hold on, nothing that rouses your mind. Here the mind finds something to bite and feed on. The fruit of it is incomparably greater, and also it will be sooner ripe.

It is a strange fact that things should be in such a pass in our century that philosophy, even with people of understanding, should be an empty and fantastic name, a thing of no use and no value,

4 A fifteenth-century translator of Aristotle and author of a Greek grammar.

^Cboth in common opinion and in fact. ^AI think those quibblings which have taken possession of all the approaches to her are the cause of this. It is very wrong to portray her as inaccessible to children, with a surly, frowning, and terrifying face. Who has masked her with this false face, pale and hideous? There is nothing more gay, more lusty, more sprightly, and I might almost say more frolicsome. She preaches nothing but merry-making and a good time. A sad and dejected look shows that she does not dwell there. Demetrius the grammarian, finding a group of philosophers seated together in the temple of Delphi, said to them: "Either I am mistaken, or, judging by your peaceful and gay countenances, you are not engaged in any deep discussion." To which one of them, Heracleon the Megarian, replied: "It is for those who are inquiring whether the verb βάλλω has a double λ, or seeking the derivation of the comparatives χεῖρον and βέλτιον and the superlatives χείριστον and βέλτιστον, to knit their brows when discussing their science. But as for the teachings of philosophy, they are wont to delight and rejoice those who discuss them, not to make them sullen and sad."

> ^BYou'll find the hidden torments of the mind
> Shown in the body, and the joys you'll find;
> The face puts on a cloak of either kind.
> JUVENAL

^AThe soul in which philosophy dwells should by its health make even the body healthy. It should make its tranquillity and gladness shine out from within; should form in its own mold the outward demeanor, and consequently arm it with graceful pride, an active and joyous bearing, and a contented and good-natured countenance. ^CThe surest sign of wisdom is constant cheerfulness; her state is like that of things above the moon, ever serene. ^AIt is *Baroco* and *Baralipton*[5] that make their disciples dirt-caked and smoky, and not she; they know her only by hearsay. Why, she makes it her business to calm the tempests of the soul and to teach hungers and fevers to laugh, not by some imaginary epicycles, but by natural and palpable reasons. ^CShe has virtue as her goal, which is not, as the schoolmen say, set on the top of a steep, rugged, inaccessible mountain. Those who have approached virtue maintain, on the contrary,

5 Artificial words in scholastic logic whose vowels represent forms of syllogisms.

that she is established in a beautiful plain, fertile and flowering, from where, to be sure, she sees all things beneath her; but you can get there, if you know the way, by shady, grassy, sweetly flowering roads, pleasantly, by an easy smooth slope, like that of the celestial vaults. It is because they have not associated with this virtue – this supreme, beautiful, triumphant, loving virtue, as delightful as she is courageous, a professed and implacable enemy of sourness, displeasure, fear, and constraint, having nature for her guide, fortune and pleasure for companions – that there are men who in their weakness have made up this stupid, sad, quarrelsome, sullen, threatening, scowling image and set it on a rock, in a solitary place, among the brambles: a phantom to frighten people.

My tutor, who knows he must fill his pupil's mind as much, or more, with affection as with reverence for virtue, will be able to tell him that the poets agree with the common view, and to set his finger on the fact that the gods make men sweat harder in the approaches to the chambers of Venus than of Pallas. And when he begins to feel his oats, and the choice is offered him between Bradamante and Angelica as a mistress to be enjoyed – a natural, active, spirited, manly but not mannish beauty, next to a soft, affected, delicate, artificial beauty; one disguised as a boy, wearing a shining helmet, the other dressed as a girl, wearing a headdress of pearls – the tutor will think his pupil manly even in love if he chooses quite differently from that effeminate shepherd of Phrygia.[6]

He will teach him this new lesson, that the value and height of true virtue lies in the ease, utility, and pleasure of its practice, which is so far from being difficult that children can master it as well as men, the simple as well as the subtle. Virtue's tool is moderation, not strength. Socrates, her prime favorite, deliberately gives up his strength, to slip into the naturalness and ease of her gait. She is the nursing mother of human pleasures. By making them just, she makes them sure and pure. By moderating them, she keeps them in breath and appetite. By withdrawing the ones she refuses, she makes us keener for the ones she allows us; and she allows us abundantly all those that nature wills, even to satiety, in maternal fashion, if not to the point of lassitude (unless perchance we want to say that the regimen that stops the drinker short of drunkenness, the

6 Paris, whose award of the golden apple, the prize of beauty, to Aphrodite instead of Hera or Athene led to the Trojan War. Bradamante and Angelica are two heroines of Ariosto's *Orlando Furioso*.

eater short of indigestion, the lecher short of baldness, is an enemy of our pleasures). If she lacks the fortune of ordinary men, she rises above it or does without it, and makes herself a different sort of fortune that is all her own, and no longer fluctuating and unsteady. She knows how to be rich and powerful and learned, and lie on perfumed mattresses. She loves life, she loves beauty and glory and health. But her own particular task is to know how to enjoy those blessings with temperance, and to lose them with fortitude: a task far more noble than harsh, without which the course of any life is denatured, turbulent, and deformed, and fit to be associated with those dangers, those brambles, and those monsters.

If this pupil happens to be of such an odd disposition that he would rather listen to some idle story than to the account of a fine voyage or a wise conversation when he hears one; if, at the sound of the drum that calls the youthful ardor of his companions to arms, he turns aside to another that invites him to the tricks of the jugglers; if, by his own preference, he does not find it more pleasant and sweet to return dusty and victorious from a combat than from tennis or a ball with the prize for that exercise, I see no other remedy than for his tutor to strangle him early, if there are no witnesses, or apprentice him to a pastry cook in some good town, even though he were the son of a duke; in accordance with Plato's precept that children should be placed not according to the faculties of their father, but according to the faculties of their soul.

^ASince it is philosophy that teaches us to live, and since there is a lesson in it for childhood as well as for the other ages, why is it not imparted to children?

> ^BHe still is yielding clay; now, now, ere he congeal,
> Tirelessly we must shape him on the potter's wheel.
> PERSIUS

^AThey teach us to live, when life is past. A hundred students have caught the syphilis before they came to Aristotle's lesson on temperance. ^CCicero used to say that even if he lived the lives of two men, he would not take the time to study the lyric poets. And I find these quibblers still more pathetically useless. Our child is in much more of a hurry: he owes to education only the first fifteen or sixteen years of his life; the rest he owes to action. Let us use so short a time for the necessary teachings. ^AThe others are abuses: away with all those thorny subtleties of dialectics, by which our lives cannot be amended. Take the simple teachings of philosophy, know how to

choose them and treat them at the right time; they are easier to understand than a tale of Boccaccio. A child is capable of that when he leaves his nurse, much more than of learning to read and write. Philosophy has lessons for the birth of men as well as for their decrepitude.

I am of Plutarch's opinion, that Aristotle did not amuse his great pupil so much with the trick of constructing syllogisms or with the principles of geometry, as by instructing him in the good precepts concerning valor, prowess, magnanimity, and temperance, and the security of fearing nothing; and with this ammunition he sent him, still a child, to subjugate the empire of the whole world with only thirty thousand foot, four thousand horse, and forty-two thousand crowns. As for the other arts and sciences, says Plutarch, Alexander indeed honored them and praised their excellence and prettiness; but for all the pleasure he found in them, he was not easily overcome by a desire to practice them.

> [B]Young men and old, seek here a purpose for the soul,
> And comfort for the woes that over gray hairs roll.
>
> PERSIUS

[C]It is what Epicurus says in the beginning of his letter to Meniceus: "Neither let the youngest refuse to study philosophy, nor the oldest weary of it." He who does otherwise seems to say that it is not yet time to live happily, or that it is no longer time.

[A]For all this education I do not want the boy to be made a prisoner. I do not want him to be given up to the surly humors of a choleric schoolmaster. I do not want to spoil his mind by keeping him in torture and at hard labor, as others do, fourteen or fifteen hours a day, like a porter. [C]Nor would I think it good, if by virtue of some solitary and melancholy streak he were found to be addicted to the study of books with too undiscerning application, for him to be encouraged in that direction; such application makes them unfit for social intercourse and diverts them from better occupations. And how many men I have seen in my time made stupid by rash avidity for learning! Carneades became so mad about it that he had no time left to take care of his hair and nails.

[A]Nor do I want to spoil his noble manners by the incivility and barbarism of others. French wisdom was proverbial of old as a wisdom that took hold early, and lost its hold soon. Indeed we still see that there is nothing as fine as the little children in France; but ordinarily they disappoint the hopes that have been conceived

for them, and as grown men they have no distinction. I have heard intelligent men maintain that these schools they are sent to, of which there are plenty, make them so brutish.

For our boy, a closet, a garden, the table and the bed, solitude, company, morning and evening, all hours will be the same, all places will be his study; for philosophy, which, as the molder of judgment and conduct, will be his principal lesson, has this privilege of being everywhere at home. When the orator Isocrates was entreated at a feast to speak of his art, everyone agrees that he was right to answer: "It is not the time now for what I can do; what it is time for now, I cannot do." For to deliver harangues or rhetorical disputations to a company assembled to laugh and make merry would produce too discordant a mixture. And as much could be said of all the other sciences. But as for philosophy, in the part where she treats of man and his duties and functions, it has been the common judgment of all the sages that because of the sweetness of her society she should not be excluded either from feasts or from games. And Plato having invited her to his Symposium, we see how she entertains the company in a mellow manner suited to the time and the place, though this is one of his loftiest and most salutary treatises:

> Upon the rich and poor alike its blessings flow,
> And its neglect to young and old alike brings woe.
>
> HORACE

Thus he will doubtless be less idle than others. But, as the steps we take walking back and forth in a gallery, though there be three times as many, do not tire us like those we take on a set journey, so our lesson, occurring as if by chance, not bound to any time or place, and mingling with all our actions, will slip by without being felt. Even games and exercises will be a good part of his study: running, wrestling, ^cmusic, ^Adancing, hunting, handling horses and weapons. I want his outward behavior and social grace ^cand his physical adaptability ^Ato be fashioned at the same time with his soul. It is not a soul that is being trained, not a body, but a man; these parts must not be separated. And, as Plato says, they must not be trained one without the other, but driven abreast like a pair of horses harnessed to the same pole. ^cAnd, to hear him, does he not seem to give more time and care to exercises of the body, and to think that the mind gets its exercise at the same time, and not the other way around?

^AFor the rest, this education is to be carried on with severe gentleness, not as is customary. Instead of being invited to letters, children are shown in truth nothing but horror and cruelty. Away with violence and compulsion! There is nothing to my mind which so depraves and stupefies a wellborn nature. If you would like him to fear shame and chastisement, don't harden him to them. Harden him to sweat and cold, wind and sun, and the dangers that he must scorn; wean him from all softness and delicacy in dressing and sleeping, eating and drinking; accustom him to everything. Let him not be a pretty boy and a little lady, but a lusty and vigorous youth.

^CAs a boy, a man, and a graybeard, I have always thought and judged in the same way. But, among other things, I have always disliked the discipline of most of our schools. They might have erred less harmfully by leaning toward indulgence. They are a real jail of captive youth. They make them slack, by punishing them for slackness before they show it. Go in at lesson time: you hear nothing but cries, both from tortured boys and from masters drunk with rage. What a way to arouse zest for their lesson in these tender and timid souls, to guide them to it with a horrible scowl and hands armed with rods! Wicked and pernicious system! Besides, as Quintilian very rightly remarked, this imperious authority brings on dangerous consequences, and especially in our manner of punishment. How much more fittingly would their classes be strewn with flowers and leaves than with bloody stumps of birch rods! I would have portraits there of Joy and Gladness, and Flora and the Graces, as the philosopher Speusippus had in his school. Where their profit is, let their frolic be also. Healthy foods should be sweetened for the child, and harmful ones dipped in gall.

It is wonderful how solicitous Plato shows himself in his *Laws* about the gaiety and pastimes of the youth of his city, and how much he dwells upon their races, games, songs, jumping, and dancing, whose conduct and patronage he says antiquity gave to the gods themselves: Apollo, the Muses, and Minerva. He extends this to a thousand precepts for his gymnasiums; as for the literary studies, he wastes little time on them, and seems to recommend poetry in particular only for the sake of the music.

^AAny strangeness and peculiarity in our conduct and ways is to be avoided as inimical to social intercourse, ^Cand unnatural. Who would not be astonished at the constitution of Demophon,

Alexander's steward, who sweated in the shade and shivered in the sun? ᴬI have seen men flee from the smell of apples more than from harquebus fire, others take fright at a mouse, others throw up at the sight of cream, and others at the plumping of a feather bed; and Germanicus could not endure either the sight or the crowing of cocks. There may perhaps be some occult quality in this; but a man could exterminate it, in my opinion, if he set about it early. Education has won this much from me – it is true that it was not without some trouble – that, except for beer, my appetite adapts itself indiscriminately to everything people eat.

While the body is still supple, it should for that reason be bent to all fashions and customs. And provided his appetite and will can be kept in check, let a young man boldly be made fit for all nations and companies, even for dissoluteness and excess, if need be. ᶜLet his training follow usage. ᴬLet him be able to do all things, and love to do only the good. The philosophers themselves do not think it praiseworthy in Callisthenes to have lost the good graces of his master Alexander the Great by refusing to keep pace with him in drinking. He will laugh, he will carouse, he will dissipate with his prince. Even in dissipation I want him to outdo his comrades in vigor and endurance; and I want him to refrain from doing evil, not for lack of power or knowledge, but for lack of will. ᶜ*There is a great difference between not wishing to do evil and not knowing how* [Seneca].

ᴬI thought I was doing honor to a lord who was as far removed from such excesses as any lord in France, by asking him, in good company, how many times in his life he had got drunk in the interest of his king's affairs in Germany. He took it as it was intended, and answered that he had done so three times, which he related. I know some who for lack of this faculty have made themselves a lot of trouble when they had to deal with that nation. I have often noticed with great admiration the wonderful nature of Alcibiades, who could change so easily to suit such different fashions, without damage to his health; now outdoing the Persians in luxury and pomp, now the Lacedaemonians in austerity and frugality; as pure in Sparta as he was voluptuous in Ionia.

> Any dress, rank, or state, Aristippus bore well.
>
> HORACE

So I would make my pupil.

Him I admire whom patience clothes in shabby dress,
If he can grace a different way of life no less,
And if he plays both parts with equal comeliness.

<div align="right">HORACE</div>

These are my lessons. ᶜHe whose conduct shows them has profited by them better than he who merely knows them. If you see him, you hear him; if you hear him, you see him.

God forbid, says someone in Plato, that philosophizing should mean learning a number of things and discussing the arts! *This most valuable of all arts, the art of living well, they followed rather in their lives than in their writings* [Cicero]. When Leon, prince of the Phliasians, asked Heraclides Ponticus what science or art he professed, he replied: "I know neither art nor science; but I am a philosopher." Someone reproached Diogenes for meddling, though ignorant, with philosophy. "I meddle with it," he said, "all the more appropriately." Hegesias begged him to read him some book. "You are jesting," he replied; "you choose real and natural figs, not painted ones; why don't you also choose real and natural exercises, not written ones?"

He will not so much say his lesson as do it. He will repeat it in his actions. ᴬWe shall see if he shows prudence in his enterprises, if he shows goodness and justice in his conduct, ᶜif he shows judgment and grace in his speaking, fortitude in his illnesses, modesty in his games, temperance in his pleasures, ᴬunconcern in his tastes, whether flesh or fish, wine or water, ᶜorder in his economy: *Who makes his learning not a display of knowledge, but the law of his life; who obeys himself and submits to his own injunctions* [Cicero]. The true mirror of our discourse is the course of our lives.

ᴬZeuxidamus replied to a man who asked him why the Lacedaemonians did not draw up in writing the rules of prowess and give them to their young men to read, that it was because they wanted to accustom them to deeds, not words. Compare with our pupil, after fifteen or sixteen years, one of your school Latinizers, who has spent that much time merely learning to speak. The world is nothing but babble, and I never saw a man who did not say rather more than less than he should. And yet half of our life is wasted on that. They keep us for four or five years learning to understand words and stitch them into sentences; as many more, to mold them into a great body, extending into four or five parts; and another five, at least, learning

how to mix and interweave them briefly in some subtle way. Let us leave that to those who make a special profession of it.

Going to Orléans one day, I met, in that plain this side of Cléry, two teachers coming to Bordeaux, about fifty yards apart. Further off, behind them, I perceived a company and a lord at the head, who was the late Count de La Rochefoucauld. One of my men inquired of the first of these teachers who was the gentleman that came behind him. He, not having seen the retinue that was following him, and thinking that my man was talking about his companion, replied comically: "He is not a gentleman; he is a grammarian, and I am a logician."

Now, we who are trying on the contrary to make not a grammarian or a logician, but a gentleman, let us allow them to misuse their free time; we have business elsewhere. Provided our pupil is well equipped with substance, words will follow only too readily; if they won't follow willingly, he will drag them. I hear some making excuses for not being able to express themselves, and pretending to have their heads full of many fine things, but to be unable to express them for lack of eloquence. That is all bluff. Do you know what I think those things are? They are shadows that come to them of some shapeless conceptions, which they cannot untangle and clear up within, and consequently cannot set forth without: they do not understand themselves yet. And just watch them stammer on the point of giving birth; you will conclude that they are laboring not for delivery, but ^cfor conception, and ^Athat they are only trying to lick into shape this unfinished matter. For my part I hold, ^cand Socrates makes it a rule, ^Athat whoever has a vivid and clear idea in his mind will express it, if necessary in Bergamask dialect, or, if he is dumb, by signs:

Master the stuff, and words will freely follow.
HORACE

And as another said just as poetically in his prose: *When things have taken possession of the mind, words come thick and fast* [Seneca]. ^cAnd another: *The things themselves carry the words along* [Cicero].

^AHe knows no ablatives, conjunctives, substantives, or grammar; nor does his lackey, or a fishwife of the Petit Pont, and yet they will talk your ear off, if you like, and will perhaps stumble as little over the rules of their language as the best master of arts in France. He does not know rhetoric, or how in a preface to capture the benevolence of the gentle reader; nor does he care to know it. In truth,

all this fine painting is easily eclipsed by the luster of a simple natural truth. These niceties serve only to amuse the common herd, who are incapable of taking their meat tougher or in bigger morsels, as Aper very clearly shows in Tacitus. The ambassadors of Samos had come to Cleomenes, king of Sparta, ready with a fine long oration, to incite him to war against the tyrant Polycrates. After letting them have their say, he replied to them: "As for your beginning and exordium, I no longer remember it, nor consequently the middle; and as for your conclusion, I will do nothing of the sort." There we have a fine answer, it seems to me, and speechifiers well snubbed.

^BAnd what about this other? The Athenians were to choose between two architects to build a big structure. The first, more affected, came forward with a fine prepared speech on the subject of this job, and was winning the judgment of the people in his favor. But the other, in three words: "Athenian lords, what this man has said, I will do."

^AWhen Cicero's eloquence was at its height, many were struck with admiration; but Cato only laughed and said: "We have an amusing consul." Before or after, a useful maxim or a fine touch is always in season. ^CIf it does not suit what precedes or what follows, it is good in itself. ^AI am not one of those who think that good rhythm makes a good poem. Let him make a short syllable long if he wants, that doesn't matter; if the inventions are pleasant, if wit and judgment have done their work well, I shall say: There is a good poet, but a bad versifier.

> ^BHis taste is keen, although his verse is harsh.
>
> HORACE

^ALet his work, says Horace, lose all its seams and measures –

> ^BThe rhythm and the measure; and what goes
> Foremost, make last, and last to first transpose;
> Yet still the poet's scattered limbs it shows
>
> HORACE

^A– he will not belie himself for all that; the very fragments will be beautiful. This is what Menander answered, when, as the day drew near for which he had promised a comedy, he was chided for not having set his hand to it yet: "It is composed and ready; it remains only to add the verses." Having the substance and the materials arranged in his mind, he took little account of the rest. Since

Ronsard and Du Bellay have brought honor to our French poetry, I never see a little apprentice who doesn't swell his words and arrange his rhythms almost as they do. ᶜ*It makes more sound than sense* [Seneca]. ᴬIn the eyes of the common people, there never were so many poets. But just as it was very easy for them to reproduce their rhythms, just so they fall far short of imitating the rich descriptions of the one and the delicate inventions of the other.

True, but what will he do if someone presses him with the sophistic subtlety of some syllogism? "Ham makes us drink; drinking quenches thirst; therefore ham quenches thirst." ᶜLet him laugh at it; it is subtler to laugh at it than to answer it.

Let him borrow from Aristippus this amusing counterthrust: "Why shall I untie it, since it gives me so much trouble tied?" Someone was using dialectical tricks against Cleanthes, when Chrysippus said to him: "Play those tricks with children, and don't divert the thoughts of a grown man to that stuff." ᴬIf those silly quibbles, ᶜ*tortuous and thorny sophisms* [Cicero], ᴬare intended to convince him of a lie, that is dangerous; but if they remain without effect and only make him laugh, I do not see why he need be on his guard against them.

There are some men so stupid that they go a mile out of their way to chase after a fine word, ᶜ*or who do not fit words to things, but seek irrelevant things which their words may fit* [Quintilian]. And as another says, *There are some who are led by the charm of some attractive word to write something they had not intended* [Seneca]. I much more readily twist a good saying to sew it on me than I twist the thread of my thought to go and fetch it. ᴬOn the contrary, it is for words to serve and follow; and let Gascon get there if French cannot. I want the substance to stand out, and so to fill the imagination of the listener that he will have no memory of the words. The speech I love is a simple, natural speech, the same on paper as in the mouth; a speech succulent and sinewy, brief and compressed, ᶜnot so much dainty and well-combed as vehement and brusque:

The speech that strikes the mind will have most taste;
 EPITAPH OF LUCAN

ᴬrather difficult than boring, remote from affectation, irregular, disconnected and bold; each bit making a body in itself; not pedantic, not monkish, not lawyer-like, but rather soldierly, as Suetonius calls Julius Caesar's speech; ᶜand yet I do not quite see why he calls it so.

^BI have been prone to imitate that disorder in dress which we see in our young men – a cloak worn like a scarf, the hood over one shoulder, a neglected stocking – which shows a pride disdainful of these foreign adornments and careless of art. But I think it is even better employed in our form of speech. ^CAny affectation, especially in the gaiety and freedom of French, is unbecoming to a courtier. And in a monarchy every gentleman should be trained in the manner of a courtier. Wherefore we do well to lean a little in the direction of naturalness and negligence.

^AI do not like a fabric in which the seams and stitches show, just as in a handsome body we must not be able to count the bones and veins: ^C*Let the language devoted to truth be plain and simple. Who speaks carefully unless he wants to speak affectedly?* [Seneca]. The eloquence that diverts us to itself harms its content.

As in dress it is pettiness to seek attention by some peculiar and unusual fashion, so in language the search for novel phrases and little-known words comes from a childish and pedantic ambition. Would that I might use only those that are used in the markets of Paris! Aristophanes the grammarian did not know what he was talking about when he criticized Epicurus for the simplicity of his words and the aim of his oratorical art, which was simply lucidity of speech. The imitation of speech, because of its facility, may be quickly picked up by a whole people; the imitation of judgment and invention does not come so fast. Most readers, because they have found a similar robe, think very wrongly that they have hold of a similar body. Strength and sinews are not to be borrowed; the attire and the cloak may be borrowed. Most of the people who frequent me speak like these Essays; but I don't know whether they think like them.

^AThe Athenians, says Plato, give their attention to fullness and elegance in speech, the Lacedaemonians to brevity, and the Cretans to fertility of thought rather than of language; the last are the best. Zeno used to say that he had two kinds of disciples: some that he called φιλολόγους, curious to learn things, who were his favorites; the others, λογοφίλους, who cared only for the language. This is not to say that it is not a fine and excellent thing to speak well, but it is not as fine as they make it out; and I am vexed that we keep busy all our life at that. I would want first to know my own language well, and that of my neighbors, with whom I have the commonest dealings. There is no doubt that Greek and Latin are great and handsome ornaments, but we buy them too dear. I shall tell you here a way

to get them cheaper than usual, which was tried out on myself.
Anyone who wants to can use it.

My late father, having made all the inquiries a man can make,
among men of learning and understanding, about a superlative
system of education, became aware of the drawbacks that were
prevalent; and he was told that the long time we put into learning
languages ^Cwhich cost the ancient Greeks and Romans nothing
^Awas the only reason we could not attain their greatness in soul
and in knowledge. I do not think that that is the only reason. At all
events, the expedient my father hit upon was this, that while I was
nursing and before the first loosening of my tongue, he put me in
the care of a German, who has since died a famous doctor in France,
wholly ignorant of our language and very well versed in Latin.[7] This
man, whom he had sent for expressly, and who was very highly paid,
had me constantly in his hands. There were also two others with
him, less learned, to attend me and relieve him. These spoke to me
in no other language than Latin. As for the rest of my father's
household, it was an inviolable rule that neither my father himself,
nor my mother, nor any valet or housemaid, should speak anything
in my presence but such Latin words as each had learned in order to
jabber with me.

It is wonderful how everyone profited from this. My father
and mother learned enough Latin in this way to understand it, and
acquired sufficient skill to use it when necessary, as did also the
servants who were most attached to my service. Altogether, we
Latinized ourselves so much that it overflowed all the way to our
villages on every side, where there still remain several Latin names
for artisans and tools that have taken root by usage. As for me, I was
over six before I understood any more French or Perigordian than
Arabic. And without artificial means, without a book, without
grammar or precept, without the whip and without tears, I had
learned a Latin quite as pure as what my schoolmaster knew, for
I could not have contaminated or altered it. If as a test they wanted
to give me a theme in the school fashion, where they give it to others
in French, they had to give it to me in bad Latin, to turn it into good.
And Nicholas Grouchy, who wrote *De Comitiis Romanorum*, Guil-
laume Guerente, who wrote a commentary on Aristotle, George
Buchanan, that great Scottish poet, ^BMarc-Antoine Muret, ^Cwhom

7 Doctor Horstanus, later a professor at the Collège de Guyenne at
Bordeaux.

France and Italy recognize as the best orator of his time, [A]my private tutors, have often told me that in my childhood I had that language so ready and handy that they were afraid to accost me. Buchanan, whom I afterward saw in the suite of the late Marshal de Brissac, told me that he was writing on the education of children and that he was taking my education as a model; for he was then in charge of that Count de Brissac who later showed himself so valorous and brave.

As for Greek, of which I have practically no knowledge at all, my father planned to have me taught it artificially, but in a new way, in the form of amusement and exercise. We volleyed our conjugations back and forth, like those who learn arithmetic and geometry by such games as checkers and chess. For among other things he had been advised to teach me to enjoy knowledge and duty by my own free will and desire, and to educate my mind in all gentleness and freedom, without rigor and constraint. He did this so religiously that because some hold that it troubles the tender brains of children to wake them in the morning with a start, and to snatch them suddenly and violently from their sleep, in which they are plunged much more deeply than we are, he had me awakened by the sound of some instrument; and I was never without a man to do this for me.

This example will be enough to let you judge the rest, and also to commend both the prudence and the affection of so good a father, who is not at all to be blamed if he reaped no fruit corresponding to such an excellent cultivation. Two things were the cause of this: first, the sterile and unfit soil; for though my health was sound and complete and my nature gentle and tractable, I was withal so sluggish, lax, and drowsy that they could not tear me from my sloth, not even to make me play. What I saw, I saw well, and beneath this inert appearance nourished bold ideas and opinions beyond my years. I had a slow mind, which would go only as far as it was led; a tardy understanding, a weak imagination, and on top of all an incredible lack of memory. It is no wonder if he could get nothing worth while from all this.

Second, just as people frantically eager to be cured will try any sort of advice, that good man, being extremely afraid of failing in a thing so close to his heart, at last let himself be carried away by the common opinion, which always follows the leader like a flock of cranes, and fell in line with custom, having no longer about him the men who had given him those first plans, which he had brought from Italy. And he sent me, when I was about six, to the Collège de

Guyenne, which was then very flourishing and the best in France. And there, nothing could be added to the care he took, both to choose me competent personal tutors and in all the other aspects of my education, in which he held out for certain particular practices contrary to school usage. But for all that, it was still school. My Latin promptly degenerated, and since then, for lack of practice, I have lost all use of it. And all this novel education of mine did for me was to make me skip immediately to the upper classes; for when I left the school at thirteen, I had finished my course (as they call it), and in truth without any benefit that I can place in evidence now.

The first taste I had for books came to me from my pleasure in the fables of the *Metamorphoses* of Ovid. For at about seven or eight years of age I would steal away from any other pleasure to read them, inasmuch as this language was my mother tongue, and it was the easiest book I knew and the best suited by its content to my tender age. For as regards the Lancelots of the Lake, ᴮthe Amadises, ᴬthe Huons of Bordeaux, and such books of rubbish on which children waste their time, I did not know even their names, and I still do not know their substance, so strict was my discipline. Thereby I grew more careless in the study of my other prescribed lessons. At that point, I happened by remarkable good fortune to come in contact with a tutor who was an understanding man, who knew enough to connive cleverly at this frivolity of mine and others like it. For by this means I went right through Virgil's *Aeneid*, and then Terence, and then Plautus, and some Italian comedies, always lured on by the pleasantness of the subject. If he had been foolish enough to break this habit, I think I should have got nothing out of school but a hatred of books, as do nearly all our noblemen. He went about it cleverly. Pretending to see nothing, he whetted my appetite, letting me gorge myself with these books only in secret, and gently keeping me at my work on the regular studies. For the chief qualities my father sought in those he put in charge of me were good nature and an easygoing disposition. Correspondingly, my own character had no other vice than inertia and laziness. The danger was not that I should do ill, but that I should do nothing. No one predicted that I should become wicked, but only useless. They foresaw loafing, not knavery.

ᶜI realize that it has turned out that way. The complaints that ring in my ears are of this sort: "Idle. Cool in the duties of friendship and kinship, and in public duties. Too self-centered." The most

insulting do not say, "Why did he take what he did? Why didn't he pay for it?" but "Why doesn't he cancel what is owed him? Why doesn't he give more?"

I should take it as a favor that men should find me wanting only in such acts of supererogation. But they are unjust to demand what I do not owe, much more rigorously than they demand of themselves what they do owe. By condemning me to an action they wipe out all the gratification of it and the gratitude that would be due me for it; whereas the good that I do should have greater weight coming from me, considering that I have none at all done me. I may dispose of my fortune the more freely the more it is my own. However, if I were a great blazoner of my own actions, perhaps I might well throw back these reproaches. And I might inform some people that they are not so much offended that I do not do enough, as that I could do a lot more than I do.

ᴬMeanwhile, for all that, my mind was not lacking in strong stirrings of its own, ᶜand certain and open-minded judgments about the things it understood; ᴬand it digested them alone, without communication. And, among other things, I really do believe that it would have been wholly incapable of submitting to force and violence.

ᴮShall I include in my account this faculty of my boyhood, assurance in expression and flexibility in voice and gesture, in adapting myself to the parts I undertook to act? For before the usual age,

Scarce had my twelfth year snatched me from the year before,
 VIRGIL

I played the leading parts in the Latin tragedies of Buchanan, Guerente, and Muret, which were performed with dignity in our Collège de Guyenne. In this matter, as in all other parts of his job, Andreas Goveanus, our principal, was incomparably the greatest principal of France; and I was considered a master craftsman. Acting is an exercise that I do not at all disapprove of for young children of good family; and since then I have seen our princes take part in it in person, honorably and commendably, after the example of some of the ancients.

ᶜIt was even permissible for people of quality to make a profession of it in Greece. *He revealed the matter to the tragic*

actor Ariston. This man was distinguished in both birth and fortune; nor did his art spoil his position, since nothing of that sort is considered a disgrace by the Greeks [Livy].

[B]For I have always blamed as undiscerning those who condemn these recreations, and as unjust those who refuse entry into our good towns to the comedians who deserve it, and begrudge the people these public amusements. Good governments take care to assemble the citizens and bring them together for sports and amusements as well as for the serious functions of piety; sociability and friendliness are thereby increased. And besides, they could not be granted more orderly pastimes than those that take place in the presence of everyone and right in the sight of the magistrate. And I should think it reasonable that the magistrate and the prince, at their own expense, should sometimes give the people this treat, out of a sort of paternal goodness and affection; [C]and that in populous cities there should be places intended and arranged for these spectacles – a diversion from worse and hidden doings.

[A]To return to my subject, there is nothing like arousing appetite and affection; otherwise all you make out of them is asses loaded with books. By dint of whipping, they are given their pocketful of learning for safekeeping; but if learning is to do us any good, we must not merely lodge it within us, we must espouse it.

27
It is folly to measure the true and false by our own capacity

[A]Perhaps it is not without reason that we attribute facility in belief and conviction to simplicity and ignorance; for it seems to me I once learned that belief was a sort of impression made on our mind, and that the softer and less resistant the mind, the easier it was to imprint something on it. [C]*As the scale of the balance must necessarily sink under the weight placed upon it, so must the mind yield to evident things* [Cicero]. The more a mind is empty and without counterpoise, the more easily it gives beneath the weight of the first persuasive argument. [A]That is why children, common people, women, and sick people are most subject to being led by the ears. But then, on the other hand, it is foolish presumption to go around disdaining and condemning as false whatever does not seem likely to us; which is an ordinary vice in those who think they have more than common ability. I used to do so once; and if I heard of returning

spirits, prognostications of future events, enchantments, sorcery, or some other story that I could not swallow,

> Dreams, witches, miracles, magic alarms,
> Nocturnal specters, and Thessalian charms,
>
> HORACE

I felt compassion for the poor people who were taken in by these follies. And now I think that I was at least as much to be pitied myself. Not that experience has since shown me anything surpassing my first beliefs, and that through no fault of my curiosity; but reason has taught me that to condemn a thing thus, dogmatically, as false and impossible, is to assume the advantage of knowing the bounds and limits of God's will and of the power of our mother Nature; and that there is no more notable folly in the world than to reduce these things to the measure of our capacity and competence. If we call prodigies or miracles whatever our reason cannot reach, how many of these appear continually to our eyes! Let us consider through what clouds and how gropingly we are led to the knowledge of most of the things that are right in our hands; assuredly we shall find that it is rather familiarity than knowledge that takes away their strangeness,

> [B]But no one now, so tired of seeing are our eyes,
> Deigns to look up at the bright temples of the skies,
>
> LUCRETIUS

[A]and that if those things were presented to us for the first time, we should find them as incredible as any others, or more so.

> If they were here for the first time for men to see,
> If they were set before us unexpectedly,
> Nothing more marvelous than these things could be told,
> Nothing more unbelievable for men of old.
>
> LUCRETIUS

He who had never seen a river thought that the first one he came across was the ocean. And the things that are the greatest within our knowledge we judge to be the utmost that nature can do in that category.

> [B]A fair-sized stream seems vast to one who until then
> Has never seen a greater; so with trees, with men.
> [A]In every field each man regards as vast in size
> The greatest objects that have come before his eyes.
>
> LUCRETIUS

^C*The mind becomes accustomed to things by the habitual sight of them, and neither wonders nor inquires about the reasons for the things it sees all the time* [Cicero].

The novelty of things incites us more than their greatness to seek their causes.

^AWe must judge with more reverence the infinite power of nature, and with more consciousness of our ignorance and weakness. How many things of slight probability there are, testified to by trustworthy people, which, if we cannot be convinced of them, we should at least leave in suspense! For to condemn them as impossible is to pretend, with rash presumption, to know the limits of possibility. ^CIf people rightly understood the difference between the impossible and the unusual, and between what is contrary to the orderly course of nature and what is contrary to the common opinion of men, neither believing rashly nor disbelieving easily, they would observe the rule of "nothing too much," enjoined by Chilo.

^AWhen we find in Froissart that the count of Foix, in Béarn, learned of the defeat of King John of Castile at Juberoth the day after it happened, and the way he says he learned it, we can laugh at it; and also at the story our annals tell, that Pope Honorius performed public funeral rites for King Philip Augustus and commanded them to be performed throughout Italy on the very day he died ^Bat Mantes. ^AFor the authority of these witnesses has perhaps not enough rank to keep us in check. But if Plutarch, besides several examples that he cites from antiquity, says that he knows with certain knowledge that in the time of Domitian, the news of the battle lost by Antonius in Germany was published in Rome, several days' journey from there, and dispersed throughout the whole world, on the same day it was lost; and if Caesar maintains that it has often happened that the report has preceded the event – shall we say that these simple men let themselves be hoaxed like the common herd, because they were not clear-sighted like ourselves? Is there anything more delicate, clearer, and more alert than Pliny's judgment, when he sees fit to bring it into play, or anything farther from inanity? Leaving aside the excellence of his knowledge, which I count for less, in which of these qualities do we surpass him? However, there is no schoolboy so young but he will convict him of falsehood, and want to give him a lesson on the progress of nature's works.

When we read in Bouchet about the miracles done by the relics of Saint Hilary, let it go: his credit is not great enough to take away our right to contradict him. But to condemn wholesale all similar stories seems to me a singular impudence. The great Saint Augustine testifies that he saw a blind child recover his sight upon the relics of Saint Gervase and Saint Protasius at Milan; a woman at Carthage cured of a cancer by the sign of the cross that a newly baptized woman made over her; Hesperius, a close friend of his, cast out the spirits that infested his house with a little earth from the sepulcher of our Lord, and a paralytic promptly cured by this earth, later, when it had been carried to church; a woman in a procession, having touched Saint Stephen's shrine with a bouquet, and rubbed her eyes with this bouquet, recover her long-lost sight; and he reports many other miracles at which he says he himself was present. Of what shall we accuse both him and two holy bishops, Aurelius and Maximinus, whom he calls upon as his witnesses? Shall it be of ignorance, simplicity, and credulity, or of knavery and imposture? Is there any man in our time so impudent that he thinks himself comparable to them, either in virtue and piety, or in learning, judgment, and ability? ^c*Who, though they brought forth no proof, might crush me by their mere authority* [Cicero].

^AIt is a dangerous and fateful presumption, besides the absurd temerity that it implies, to disdain what we do not comprehend. For after you have established, according to your fine understanding, the limits of truth and falsehood, and it turns out that you must necessarily believe things even stranger than those you deny, you are obliged from then on to abandon these limits. Now, what seems to me to bring as much disorder into our consciences as anything, in these religious troubles that we are in, is this partial surrender of their beliefs by Catholics. It seems to them that they are being very moderate and understanding when they yield to their opponents some of the articles in dispute. But, besides the fact that they do not see what an advantage it is to a man charging you for you to begin to give ground and withdraw, and how much that encourages him to pursue his point, those articles which they select as the most trivial are sometimes very important. We must either submit completely to the authority of our ecclesiastical government, or do without it completely. It is not for us to decide what portion of obedience we owe it.

Moreover, I can say this for having tried it. In other days I exercised this freedom of personal choice and selection, regarding with negligence certain points in the observance of our Church which seem more vain or strange than others; until, coming to discuss them with learned men, I found that these things have a massive and very solid foundation, and that it is only stupidity and ignorance that make us receive them with less reverence than the rest. Why do we not remember how much contradiction we sense even in our own judgment? How many things were articles of faith to us yesterday, which are fables to us today? Vainglory and curiosity are the two scourges of our soul. The latter leads us to thrust our noses into everything, and the former forbids us to leave anything unresolved and undecided.

28
Of friendship

^AAs I was considering the way a painter I employ went about his work, I had a mind to imitate him. He chooses the best spot, the middle of each wall, to put a picture labored over with all his skill, and the empty space all around it he fills with grotesques, which are fantastic paintings whose only charm lies in their variety and strangeness. And what are these things of mine, in truth, but grotesques and monstrous bodies, pieced together of divers members, without definite shape, having no order, sequence, or proportion other than accidental?

> A lovely woman tapers off into a fish.
>
> HORACE

I do indeed go along with my painter in this second point, but I fall short in the first and better part; for my ability does not go far enough for me to dare to undertake a rich, polished picture, formed according to art. It has occurred to me to borrow one from Etienne de La Boétie, which will do honor to all the rest of this work. It is a discourse to which he gave the name *La Servitude Volontaire*; but those who did not know this have since very fitly rebaptized it *Le Contre Un.*[1] He wrote it by way of essay in his early youth, in honor

1 *La Servitude Volontaire*, "Voluntary Servitude." *Le Contre Un*, "Against One Man."

of liberty against tyrants. It has long been circulating in the hands of
men of understanding, not without great and well-merited com-
mendation; for it is a fine thing, and as full as can be. Still, it is far
from being the best he could do; and if at the more mature age when
I knew him, he had adopted a plan such as mine, of putting his ideas
in writing, we should see many rare things which would bring us
very close to the glory of antiquity; for particularly in the matter of
natural gifts, I know no one who can be compared with him. But
nothing of his has remained except this treatise – and that by
chance, and I think he never saw it after it left his hands – and
some observations on that Edict of January, made famous by our
civil wars, which will perhaps yet find their place elsewhere. That
was all I could recover of what he left – ^CI, to whom in his will, with
such loving recommendation, with death in his throat, he
bequeathed his library and his papers – ^Aexcept for the little volume
of his works which I have had published.

And yet I am particularly obliged to this work, since it served as
the medium of our first acquaintance. For it was shown to me long
before I had seen him, and gave me my first knowledge of his name,
thus starting on its way this friendship which together we fostered,
as long as God willed, so entire and so perfect that certainly you
will hardly read of the like, and among men of today you see no
trace of it in practice. So many coincidences are needed to build
up such a friendship that it is a lot if fortune can do it once in
three centuries.

There is nothing to which nature seems to have inclined us more
than to society. ^CAnd Aristotle says that good legislators have had
more care for friendship than for justice. ^ANow the ultimate point in
the perfection of society is this. For ^Cin general, all associations that
are forged and nourished by pleasure or profit, by public or private
needs, are the less beautiful and noble, and the less friendships, in so
far as they mix into friendship another cause and object and reward
than friendship itself. Nor do the four ancient types – natural, social,
hospitable, erotic – come up to real friendship, either separately
or together.

^AFrom children toward fathers, it is rather respect. Friendship
feeds on communication, which cannot exist between them because
of their too great inequality, and might perhaps interfere with
the duties of nature. For neither can all the secret thoughts of fathers
be communicated to children, lest this beget an unbecoming inti-
macy, nor could the admonitions and corrections, which are one of

the chief duties of friendship, be administered by children to fathers. There have been nations where by custom the children killed their fathers, and others where the fathers killed their children, to avoid the interference that they can sometimes cause each other; and by nature the one depends on the destruction of the other. There have been philosophers who disdained this natural tie, witness ^CAristippus: ^Awhen pressed about the affection he owed his children for having come out of him, he began to spit, saying that that had come out of him just as well, and that we also bred lice and worms. And that other, whom Plutarch wanted to reconcile with his brother, said: "I don't think any more of him for having come out of the same hole."

Truly the name of brother is a beautiful name and full of affection, and for that reason he and I made our alliance a brotherhood. But that confusion of ownership, the dividing, and the fact that the richness of one is the poverty of the other, wonderfully softens and loosens the solder of brotherhood. Since brothers have to guide their careers along the same path and at the same rate, it is inevitable that they often jostle and clash with each other. Furthermore, why should the harmony and kinship which begets these true and perfect friendships be found in them? Father and son may be of entirely different dispositions, and brothers also. He is my son, he is my kinsman, but he is an unsociable man, a knave, or a fool. And then, the more they are friendships which law and natural obligation impose on us, the less of our choice and free will there is in them. And our free will has no product more properly its own than affection and friendship. Not that I have not experienced all the friendship that can exist in that situation, having had the best father that ever was, and the most indulgent, even in his extreme old age, and being of a family famous and exemplary, from father to son, in this matter of brotherly concord:

> ^BKnown to others
> For fatherly affection toward my brothers.
> HORACE

^ATo compare this brotherly affection with affection for women, even though it is the result of our choice – it cannot be done; nor can we put the love of women in the same category. Its ardor, I confess –

> Of us that goddess is not unaware
> Who blends a bitter sweetness with her care
> CATULLUS

– is more active, more scorching, and more intense. But it is
an impetuous and fickle flame, undulating and variable,
a fever flame, subject to fits and lulls, that holds us only by one
corner. In friendship it is a general and universal warmth, moderate
and even, besides, a constant and settled warmth, all gentleness and
smoothness, with nothing bitter and stinging about it. What
is more, in love there is nothing but a frantic desire for what flees
from us:

> Just as a huntsman will pursue a hare
> O'er hill and dale, in weather cold or fair;
> The captured hare is worthless in his sight;
> He only hastens after things in flight.
>
> ARIOSTO

As soon as it enters the boundaries of friendship, that is to say
harmony of wills, it grows faint and languid. Enjoyment destroys
it, as having a fleshly end, subject to satiety. Friendship, on the
contrary, is enjoyed according as it is desired; it is bred, nourished,
and increased only in enjoyment, since it is spiritual, and the soul
grows refined by practice. During the reign of this perfect friendship
those fleeting affections once found a place in me, not to speak of my
friend, who confesses only too many of them in these verses. Thus
these two passions within me came to be known to each other, but to
be compared, never; the first keeping its course in proud and lofty
flight, and disdainfully watching the other making its way far, far
beneath it.

As for marriage, for one thing it is a bargain to which only the
entrance is free – its continuance being constrained and forced,
depending otherwise than on our will – and a bargain ordinarily
made for other ends. For another, there supervene a thousand
foreign tangles to unravel, enough to break the thread and trouble
the course of a lively affection; whereas in friendship there are no
dealings or business except with itself. Besides, to tell the truth, the
ordinary capacity of women is inadequate for that communion and
fellowship which is the nurse of this sacred bond; nor does their soul
seem firm enough to endure the strain of so tight and durable a knot.
And indeed, but for that, if such a relationship, free and voluntary,
could be built up, in which not only would the souls have this
complete enjoyment, but the bodies would also share in the alliance,
^cso that the entire man would be engaged, ^Ait is certain that the
resulting friendship would be fuller and more complete. But this sex

in no instance has yet succeeded in attaining it, ^cand by the common agreement of the ancient schools is excluded from it.

^AAnd that other, licentious Greek love is justly abhorred by our morality. ^cSince it involved, moreover, according to their practice, such a necessary disparity in age and such a difference in the lovers' functions, it did not correspond closely enough with the perfect union and harmony that we require here: *For what is this love of friendship? Why does no one love either an ugly youth, or a handsome old man?* [Cicero.] For even the picture the Academy paints of it will not contradict me, I think, if I say this on the subject: that this first frenzy which the son of Venus inspired in the lover's heart at the sight of the flower of tender youth, in which they allow all the insolent and passionate acts that immoderate ardor can produce, was simply founded on external beauty, the false image of corporeal generation. For it could not be founded on the spirit, the signs of which were still hidden, which was only at its birth and before the age of budding. If this frenzy seized a base heart, the means of his courtship were riches, presents, favor in advancement to dignities, and other such base merchandise, which were generally condemned. If it fell on a nobler heart, the means were also noble: philosophical instruction, precepts to revere religion, obey the laws, die for the good of the country; examples of valor, prudence, justice; the lover studying to make himself acceptable by the grace and beauty of his soul, that of his body being long since faded, and hoping by this mental fellowship to establish a firmer and more lasting pact.

When this courtship attained its effect in due season (for whereas they do not require of the lover that he use leisure and discretion in his enterprise, they strictly require it of the loved one, because he had to judge an inner beauty, difficult to know and hidden from discovery), then there was born in the loved one the desire of spiritual conception through the medium of spiritual beauty. This was the main thing here, and corporeal beauty accidental and secondary; quite the opposite of the lover. For this reason they prefer the loved one, and prove that the gods also prefer him, and strongly rebuke the poet Aeschylus for having, in the love of Achilles and Patroclus, given the lover's part to Achilles, who was in the first beardless bloom of his youth, and the handsomest of all the Greeks.

After this general communion was established, the stronger and worthier part of it exercising its functions and predominating, they

say that there resulted from it fruits very useful personally and to the public; that it constituted the strength of the countries which accepted the practice, and the principal defense of equity and liberty: witness the salutary loves of Harmodius and Aristogeiton. Therefore they call it sacred and divine. And, by their reckoning, only the violence of tyrants and the cowardice of the common people are hostile to it. In short, all that can be said in favor of the Academy is that this was a love ending in friendship; which corresponds pretty well to the Stoic definition of love: *Love is the attempt to form a friendship inspired by beauty* [Cicero].

I return to my description of a more equitable and more equable kind of friendship. *Only those are to be judged friendships in which the characters have been strengthened and matured by age* [Cicero].

^AFor the rest, what we ordinarily call friends and friendships are nothing but acquaintanceships and familiarities formed by some chance or convenience, by means of which our souls are bound to each other. In the friendship I speak of, our souls mingle and blend with each other so completely that they efface the seam that joined them, and cannot find it again. If you press me to tell why I loved him, I feel that this cannot be expressed, ^cexcept by answering: Because it was he, because it was I.

^ABeyond all my understanding, beyond what I can say about this in particular, there was I know not what inexplicable and fateful force that was the mediator of this union. ^cWe sought each other before we met because of the reports we heard of each other, which had more effect on our affection than such reports would reasonably have; I think it was by some ordinance from heaven. We embraced each other by our names. And at our first meeting, which by chance came at a great feast and gathering in the city, we found ourselves so taken with each other, so well acquainted, so bound together, that from that time on nothing was so close to us as each other. He wrote an excellent Latin satire, which is published, in which he excuses and explains the precipitancy of our mutual understanding, so promptly grown to its perfection. Having so little time to last, and having begun so late, for we were both grown men, and he a few years older than I, it could not lose time and conform to the pattern of mild and regular friendships, which need so many precautions in the form of long preliminary association. Our friendship has no other model than itself, and can be compared only with itself. ^AIt is not one special consideration, nor two, nor three, nor four, nor a thousand: it is I know not what quintessence of all this mixture,

which, having seized my whole will, led it to plunge and lose itself in his; ^cwhich, having seized his whole will, led it to plunge and lose itself in mine, with equal hunger, equal rivalry. ^AI say lose, in truth, for neither of us reserved anything for himself, nor was anything either his or mine.

When Laelius, in the presence of the Roman consuls – who, after condemning Tiberius Gracchus, prosecuted all those who had been in his confidence – came to ask Caius Blossius, who was Gracchus' best friend, how much he would have been willing to do for him, he answered: "Everything." "What, everything?" pursued Laelius. "And what if he had commanded you to set fire to our temples?" "He would never have commanded me to do that," replied Blossius. "But what if he had?" Laelius insisted. "I would have obeyed," he replied. If he was such a perfect friend to Gracchus as the histories say, he did not need to offend the consuls by this last bold confession, and he should not have abandoned the assurance he had of Gracchus' will. But nevertheless, those who charge that this answer is seditious do not fully understand this mystery, and fail to assume first what is true, that he had Gracchus' will up his sleeve, both by power over him and by knowledge of him. ^cThey were friends more than citizens, friends more than friends or enemies of their country or friends of ambition and disturbance. Having committed themselves absolutely to each other, they held absolutely the reins of each other's inclination; and if you assume that this team was guided by the strength and leadership of reason, as indeed it is quite impossible to harness it without that, Blossius' answer is as it should have been. If their actions went astray, they were by my measure neither friends to each other, nor friends to themselves.

For that matter, ^Athis answer has no better ring than would mine if someone questioned me in this fashion: "If your will commanded you to kill your daughter, would you kill her?" and I said yes. For that does not bear witness to any consent to do so, because I have no doubt at all about my will, and just as little about that of such a friend. It is not in the power of all the arguments in the world to dislodge me from the certainty I have of the intentions and judgments of my friend. Not one of his actions could be presented to me, whatever appearance it might have, that I could not immediately find the motive for it. Our souls pulled together in such unison, they regarded each other with such ardent affection, and with a like affection revealed themselves to each other to the very depths of our hearts, that not only did I know his soul as well as mine,

but I should certainly have trusted myself to him more readily than to myself.

Let not these other, common friendships be placed in this rank. I have as much knowledge of them as another, and of the most perfect of their type, ^Bbut I advise you not to confuse the rules of the two; you would make a mistake. You must walk in those other friendships bridle in hand, with prudence and precaution; the knot is not so well tied that there is no cause to mistrust it. "Love him," Chilo used to say, "as if you are to hate him some day; hate him as if you are to love him." This precept, which is so abominable in this sovereign and masterful friendship, is healthy in the practice of ordinary ^Cand customary ^Bfriendships, ^Cin regard to which we must use the remark that Aristotle often repeated: "O my friends, there is no friend."

^AIn this noble relationship, services and benefits, on which other friendships feed, do not even deserve to be taken into account; the reason for this is the complete fusion of our wills. For just as the friendship I feel for myself receives no increase from the help I give myself in time of need, whatever the Stoics say, and as I feel no gratitude to myself for the service I do myself; so the union of such friends, being truly perfect, makes them lose the sense of such duties, and hate and banish from between them these words of separation and distinction: benefit, obligation, gratitude, request, thanks, and the like. Everything actually being in common between them – wills, thoughts, judgments, goods, wives, children, honor, and life – ^Cand their relationship being that of one soul in two bodies, according to Aristotle's very apt definition, ^Athey can neither lend nor give anything to each other. That is why the lawmakers, to honor marriage with some imaginary resemblance to this divine union, forbid gifts between husband and wife, wishing thus to imply that everything should belong to each of them and that they have nothing to divide and split up between them.

If, in the friendship I speak of, one could give to the other, it would be the one who received the benefit who would oblige his friend. For, each of them seeking above all things to benefit the other, the one who provides the matter and the occasion is the liberal one, giving his friend the satisfaction of doing for him what he most wants to do. ^CWhen the philosopher Diogenes was short of money, he used to say that he asked it back of his friends, not that he asked for it. ^AAnd to show how this works in practice, I will tell you an ancient example that is singular.

Eudamidas of Corinth had two friends, Charixenus, a Sicyonian, and Aretheus, a Corinthian. When he came to die, he being poor and his two friends rich, he made his will thus: "I leave this to Aretheus, to feed my mother and support her in her old age; this to Charixenus, to see my daughter married and give her the biggest dowry he can; and in case one of them should chance to die, I substitute the survivor in his place." Those who first saw this will laughed at it; but his heirs, having been informed of it, accepted it with singular satisfaction. And when one of them, Charixenus, died five days later, and the place of substitute was opened to Aretheus, he supported the mother with great care, and of five talents he had in his estate, he gave two and a half to his only daughter for her marriage, and two and a half for the marriage of the daughter of Eudamidas, holding their weddings on the same day.

This example is quite complete except for one circumstance, which is the plurality of friends. For this perfect friendship I speak of is indivisible: each one gives himself so wholly to his friend that he has nothing left to distribute elsewhere; on the contrary, he is sorry that he is not double, triple, or quadruple, and that he has not several souls and several wills, to confer them all on this one object. Common friendships can be divided up: one may love in one man his beauty, in another his easygoing ways, in another liberality, in one paternal love, in another brotherly love, and so forth; but this friendship that possesses the soul and rules it with absolute sovereignty cannot possibly be double. ᶜIf two called for help at the same time, which one would you run to? If they demanded conflicting services of you, how would you arrange it? If one confided to your silence a thing that would be useful for the other to know, how would you extricate yourself? A single dominant friendship dissolves all other obligations. The secret I have sworn to reveal to no other man, I can impart without perjury to the one who is not another man: he is myself. It is a great enough miracle to be doubled, and those who talk of tripling themselves do not realize the loftiness of the thing: nothing is extreme that can be matched. And he who supposes that of two men I love one just as much as the other, and that they love each other and me just as much as I love them, multiplies into a fraternity the most singular and unified of all things, of which even a single one is the rarest thing in the world to find.

^AThe rest of this story fits in very well with what I was saying, for Eudamidas bestows upon his friends the kindness and favor of using them for his need. He leaves them heirs to this liberality of his, which consists of putting into their hands a chance to do him good. And without doubt the strength of friendship is shown much more richly in his action than in that of Aretheus.

In short, these are actions inconceivable to anyone who has not tasted friendship, ^Cand which make me honor wonderfully the answer of that young soldier to Cyrus, who asked him for how much he would sell a horse with which he had just won the prize in a race, and whether he would exchange him for a kingdom: "No indeed, Sire, but I would most willingly let him go to gain a friend, if I found a man worthy of such an alliance." That was not badly spoken, "if I found one"; for it is easy to find men fit for a superficial acquaintance. But for this kind, in which we act from the very bottom of our hearts, which holds nothing back, truly it is necessary that all the springs of action be perfectly clean and true.

In the relationships which bind us only by one small part, we need look out only for the imperfections that particularly concern that part. The religion of my doctor or my lawyer cannot matter. That consideration has nothing in common with the functions of the friendship they owe me. And in the domestic relationship between me and those who serve me, I have the same attitude. I scarcely inquire of a lackey whether he is chaste; I try to find out whether he is diligent. And I am not as much afraid of a gambling mule driver as of a weak one, or of a profane cook as of an ignorant one. I do not make it my business to tell the world what it should do – enough others do that – but what I do in it.

That is my practice: do as you see fit.
TERENCE

For the familiarity of the table I look for wit, not prudence; for the bed, beauty before goodness; in conversation, competence, even without uprightness. Likewise in other matters.

^AJust as the man who was found astride a stick, playing with his children, asked the man who surprised him thus to say nothing about it until he was a father himself, in the belief that the passion which would then be born in his soul would make him an equitable judge of such an act, so I should like to talk to people who have

experienced what I tell. But knowing how far from common usage and how rare such a friendship is, I do not expect to find any good judge of it. For the very discourses that antiquity has left us on this subject seem to me weak compared with the feeling I have. And in this particular the facts surpass even the precepts of philosophy:

> Nothing shall I, while sane, compare with a dear friend.
>
> <div align="right">HORACE</div>

The ancient Menander declared that man happy who had been able to meet even the shadow of a friend. He was certainly right to say so, especially if he spoke from experience. For in truth, if I compare all the rest of my life – though by the grace of God I have spent it pleasantly, comfortably, and, except for the loss of such a friend, free from any grievous affliction, and full of tranquillity of mind, having accepted my natural and original advantages without seeking other ones – if I compare it all, I say, with the four years which were granted me to enjoy the sweet company and society of that man, it is nothing but smoke, nothing but dark and dreary night. Since the day I lost him,

> Which I shall ever recall with pain,
> Ever with reverence – thus, Gods, did you ordain –
>
> <div align="right">VIRGIL</div>

I only drag on a weary life. And the very pleasures that come my way, instead of consoling me, redouble my grief for his loss. We went halves in everything; it seems to me that I am robbing him of his share,

> Nor may I rightly taste of pleasures here alone,
> – So I resolved – when he who shared my life is gone.
>
> <div align="right">TERENCE</div>

I was already so formed and accustomed to being a second self everywhere that only half of me seems to be alive now.

> ^BSince an untimely blow has snatched away
> Part of my soul, why then do I delay,
> I the remaining part, less dear than he,
> And not entire surviving? The same day
> Brought ruin equally to him and me.
>
> <div align="right">HORACE</div>

^There is no action or thought in which I do not miss him, as indeed he would have missed me. For just as he surpassed me infinitely in every other ability and virtue, so he did in the duty of friendship.

> Why should I be ashamed or exercise control
> Mourning so dear a soul?
>
> HORACE

> Brother, your death has left me sad and lone;
> Since you departed all our joys have gone,
> Which while you lived your sweet affection fed;
> My pleasures all lie shattered, with you dead.
> Our soul is buried, mine with yours entwined;
> And since then I have banished from my mind
> My studies, and my spirit's dearest joys.
> Shall I ne'er speak to you, or hear your voice?
> Or see your face, more dear than life to me?
> At least I'll love you to eternity.
>
> CATULLUS

But let us listen a while to this boy of sixteen.

Because I have found that this work has since been brought to light, and with evil intent, by those who seek to disturb and change the state of our government without worrying whether they will improve it, and because they have mixed his work up with some of their own concoctions, I have changed my mind about putting it in here.[2] And so that the memory of the author may not be damaged in the eyes of those who could not know his opinions and actions at close hand, I beg to advise them that this subject was treated by him in his boyhood, only by way of an exercise, as a common theme hashed over in a thousand places in books. I have no doubt that he believed what he wrote, for he was so conscientious as not to lie even in jest. And I know further that if he had had the choice, he would

2 La Boétie's *Voluntary Servitude* was published in a revolutionary context by Protestants, in part in 1574 (*Le Reveille – Matin des François*), and in its entirety in 1576 (*Mémoires de l'Estat de France sous Charles Neufiesme*). Montaigne had presumably written most of this chapter before 1574 and changed his mind about publishing La Boétie's discourse when he learned of these publications.

In the 1580–88 editions of the *Essays*, Montaigne speaks of La Boétie as eighteen, not sixteen.

rather have been born in Venice than in Sarlat, and with reason. But he had another maxim sovereignly imprinted in his soul, to obey and submit most religiously to the laws under which he was born. There never was a better citizen, or one more devoted to the tranquillity of his country, or more hostile to the commotions and innovations of his time. He would much rather have used his ability to suppress them than to give them material that would excite them further. His mind was molded in the pattern of other ages than this.

Now, in exchange for this serious work, I shall substitute another, produced in that same season of his life, gayer and more lusty.

29
Twenty-nine sonnets of Etienne de La Boétie

TO MADAME DE GRAMONT, COMTESSE DE GUISSEN

^AMadame, I offer you nothing of my own, either because it is already yours, or because I find none of it worthy of you. But I did want these verses, wherever they might be seen, to bear your name at their head, for the honor that it will be to them to have the great Corisande d'Andoins[1] as their sponsor. This present seemed to me suited to you because there are few ladies in France who are better judges of poetry than you and handle it more aptly, and none who can make it alive and animated as you do by those beautiful rich tones with which, among a million other beauties, nature has endowed you. Madame, these verses deserve that you should cherish them; for you will agree with me that none have come out of Gascony that have more originality and beauty or that give evidence of having come from a richer hand. And do not be jealous because you have only the remainder of what I published some time ago under the patronage of your good kinsman Monsieur de Foix; for certainly these have about them I know not what that is livelier and more ebullient, written as they were in his greenest youth, when he was inflamed by a fine and noble ardor whose details, Madame, I will one of these days whisper in your ear. The others were written later, for his wife, when he was suing for her hand, and they already

1 Diane d'Andoins, comtesse de Guiche (or Guissen) et de Gramont (1555–1621), mistress and counselor of Henry of Navarre before he became Henry IV of France, some of whose good advice to him came from Montaigne. In her fondness for the pastoral *Amadis de Gaule*, she took the name Corisande.

smack of a certain marital coolness. And I am one of those who hold that poetry is never so blithe as in a wanton and irregular subject.

ᶜThese verses may be seen elsewhere.²

30
Of moderation

ᴬAs if our touch were infectious, we by our handling corrupt things that of themselves are beautiful and good. We can grasp virtue in such a way that it will become vicious, if we embrace it with too sharp and violent a desire. Those who say that there is never any excess in virtue, inasmuch as it is no longer virtue if there is excess in it, are playing with words:

> The fair man should be termed unfair, the wise unsound,
> If he seeks even virtue beyond the proper bound.

HORACE

This is a subtle consideration of philosophy. A man may both love virtue too much, and perform excessively in a just action. The Holy Writ fits this bias: "Be not wiser than you should, but be soberly wise."¹

ᶜI have known a man of high rank² to injure his reputation for religion by making a display of religion beyond all example of men of his sort.

I like temperate and moderate natures. Immoderation, even in the direction of the good, if it does not offend me, astonishes me and gives me trouble to name it. The mother of Pausanias, who gave the first information and brought the first stone for her son's death, and the dictator Posthumius, who had his son killed because his youthful ardor had driven him successfully against the enemy

2 These sonnets appeared in all the editions of the *Essays* published during Montaigne's lifetime. Presumably someone else published them between 1588 and 1592, thereby leading Montaigne to remove them from here; but no such edition has been found.

1 Romans 12:3. The King James version is this: "For I say, through the grace given unto me, to every man that is among you, not to think of himself more highly than he ought to think; but to think soberly…" In its Latin form – "Nolite esse prudentes apud vos metipsos" – this was one of the inscriptions on the rafters of the ceiling of Montaigne's library.

2 Probably Henry III of France.

a little in advance of his rank, seem to me not so much just as strange. And I like neither to advise nor to follow a virtue so savage and costly.

The archer who overshoots the target misses as much as the one who does not reach it. And my eyes trouble me as much when I raise them suddenly to a strong light as when I drop them into the shadow. Callicles, in Plato, says that the extremity of philosophy is harmful, and advises us not to plunge into it beyond the limits of profit; that, taken with moderation, it is pleasant and advantageous, but that in the end it makes a man wild and vicious, disdainful of common religions and laws, an enemy of social intercourse, an enemy of human pleasures, incapable of any political administration and of helping either others or himself, fit to be slapped with impunity. He speaks truly, for in its excess it enslaves our natural freedom and, by importunate subtlety, leads us astray from the fine and level road that nature has traced for us.

ᴬThe affection we bear to our wives is very legitimate; yet theology does not fail to bridle and restrain it. It seems to me I once read in Saint Thomas, in a place where he is condemning marriages of relatives within the forbidden degrees, this reason among others, that there is a danger that the affection a man bears to such a wife will be immoderate; for if conjugal love is whole and perfect, as it should be, and you add to it also that which is due to kinship, there is no doubt that this increase will carry such a husband beyond the barriers of reason.

The branches of knowledge that regulate men's morals, like theology and philosophy, enter in everywhere. There is no action so private and secret that it escapes their cognizance and jurisdiction. ᶜVery immature are those who criticize this liberty of theirs. They are like women who expose their parts all you like for whoring; but for being medically treated, shame forbids them. ᴬSo, on behalf of theology and philosophy, I want to teach husbands this – ᶜif there still are any who are too vehement: ᴬthat even the pleasures they get in making love to their wives are condemned, unless moderation is observed; and that it is possible to err through licentiousness and debauchery, just as in an illicit affair. ᶜThose shameless excesses that our first heat suggests to us in this sport are not only indecently but detrimentally practiced on our wives. Let them at least learn shamelessness from another hand. They are always aroused enough for our need. I have never followed in that any but the simple instruction of nature.

^AMarriage is a religious and holy bond. That is why the pleasure we derive from it should be a restrained pleasure, serious, and mixed with some austerity; it should be a somewhat discreet and conscientious voluptuousness. And because its principal end is generation, there are some who raise a doubt whether, when we have no hope of such a fruit, as when women are beyond the age, or pregnant, it is permissible to seek their embraces. ^CIt is homicide according to Plato. ^BCertain nations, ^Cthe Mohammedan among others, ^Babominate all copulation with pregnant women; many also with those who are menstruating. Zenobia would receive her husband for only one encounter, and, that done, she let him run free all the time of her conception, allowing him only then to begin again: a fine and noble example of marriage.

^CIt was from some poet in need of this delight and famished for it that Plato borrowed this story: that Jupiter went after his wife one day so hotly that, unable to be patient until she had reached her couch, he threw her on the floor, and in the vehemence of his pleasure forgot the great and important resolutions that he had just taken with the other gods in his celestial court; and boasted that he had enjoyed it as much that time as when he first deflowered her, hiding from their parents.

^AThe kings of Persia used to invite their wives to join them at their feasts; but when the wine began to heat them in good earnest and they had to give completely free rein to sensuality, they sent them back to their private rooms, so as not to make them participants in their immoderate appetites, and sent for other women in their place, to whom they did not have this obligation of respect.

^BNot all pleasures or all gratifications are well conferred on all people. Epaminondas had had a young debauchee imprisoned; Pelopidas asked that the man be set free as a favor to himself. Epaminondas refused, and granted this to a wench of his who also asked him, saying that it was a gratification due to a mistress, not to a captain. ^CSophocles, when he shared the praetorship with Pericles, happening to see a handsome boy go by, said to Pericles: "Oh, what a handsome boy that is!" "That would be all right," said Pericles, "for anyone but a praetor, who must have not only chaste hands but also chaste eyes."

^AThe Emperor Aelius Verus, when his wife complained that he indulged in the chase after other women's love, answered that he did so from conscientious motives, since the word marriage meant

honor and dignity, not wanton and lascivious lust. ᶜAnd our ancient ecclesiastical authors make honorable mention of a woman who repudiated her husband because she would not be a partner to his too lascivious and immoderate lovemaking. ᴬIn short there is no sensual pleasure so just that excess and intemperance in it are not a matter of reproach.

But to speak in good earnest, isn't man a miserable animal? Hardly is it in his power, by his natural condition, to taste a single pleasure pure and entire, and still he is at pains to curtail that pleasure by his reason: he is not wretched enough unless by art and study he augments his misery:

> ᴮWe have increased by art the troubles of our lot.
>
> PROPERTIUS

ᶜHuman wisdom very stupidly exercises its ingenuity to reduce the number and the sweetness of the sensual pleasures that belong to us, just as she does favorably and industriously in using her artifices to trick out and disguise our ills and to alleviate our sense of them. If the decision had been up to me, I should have taken another course, one that would have been more natural – which is to say, true, practicable, and holy; and I might perhaps have made myself strong enough to set bounds to it.

ᴬWhat of the fact that our spiritual and bodily physicians, as if by a conspiracy, find no way to a cure, no remedy for the diseases of the body and the soul, but by torment, misery, and pain? Vigils, fasts, hair shirts, remote and solitary exiles, perpetual imprisonments, scourges, and other afflictions have been introduced to this end; but on this condition, that they shall really be afflictions involving bitterness and sting, ᴮand that it shall not come out as it did to one Gallio, who had been sent in exile to the island of Lesbos. News came to Rome that he was giving himself a good time, and that what had been imposed on him as a penalty was turning out to be a pleasure; wherefore they changed their minds and recalled him to his home with his wife, and ordered him to stay there; suiting their punishment to his feeling of it. ᴬFor if fasting sharpened a man's health and blitheness, if fish were more appetizing to him than flesh, these would no longer be salutary prescriptions; just as in the other sort of medicine drugs have no effect on a man who takes them with appetite and pleasure. The bitterness and the difficulty are circumstances helping their operation. A nature that would accept rhubarb as something

familiar would spoil its usefulness; it must be something that hurts the stomach in order to cure it; and here the common rule fails, that things are cured by their opposites, for here the evil cures the evil.

ᴮThis idea has some relation to that other very ancient one, which consists of thinking that we gratify heaven and nature by committing massacre and homicide, a belief universally embraced in all religions. ᶜEven in the time of our fathers, Murad, at the taking of the Isthmus, immolated six hundred young Greeks to his father's soul, so that this blood should serve as a propitiation to expiate the sins of the deceased. ᴮAnd in these new lands discovered in our time, still pure and virgin compared with ours, this practice is to some extent accepted everywhere: all their idols are drenched with human blood, often with horrible cruelty. They burn the victims alive, and take them out of the brazier half roasted to tear their heart and entrails out. Others, even women, are flayed alive, and with their bloody skins they dress and disguise others. And there are no fewer examples of constancy and resolution. For these poor people that are to be sacrificed, old men, women, children, themselves go about, some days before, begging alms for the offering at their sacrifice, and present themselves to the slaughter singing and dancing with the spectators.

The ambassadors of the king of Mexico, to give Hernando Cortez an idea of the greatness of their master, after having told him that he had thirty vassals, each of whom could assemble a hundred thousand fighting men, and that he lived in the most beautiful and strongest city under heaven, added that he had to sacrifice to the gods fifty thousand men a year. Indeed, they say he fostered war with certain great neighboring peoples, not only to exercise the youth of his country, but principally to have enough prisoners of war to supply his sacrifices. Elsewhere, in a certain town, as a welcome to the said Cortez, they sacrificed fifty men all at the same time.

I will tell this one story more. Some of these people, having been beaten by him, sent to acknowledge him and seek his friendship. The messengers offered him three sorts of presents, in this manner: "Lord, here are five slaves; if you are a cruel god that feeds on flesh and blood, eat them, and we will bring you more. If you are a good-natured god, here are incense and plumes. If you are a man, take these birds and fruits."

31
Of cannibals

^AWhen King Pyrrhus passed over into Italy, after he had reconnoitered the formation of the army that the Romans were sending to meet him, he said: "I do not know what barbarians these are" (for so the Greeks called all foreign nations), "but the formation of this army that I see is not at all barbarous." The Greeks said as much of the army that Flaminius brought into their country, ^cand so did Philip, seeing from a knoll the order and distribution of the Roman camp, in his kingdom, under Publius Sulpicius Galba. ^AThus we should beware of clinging to vulgar opinions, and judge things by reason's way, not by popular say.

I had with me for a long time a man who had lived for ten or twelve years in that other world which has been discovered in our century, in the place where Villegaignon landed, and which he called Antarctic France.¹ This discovery of a boundless country seems worthy of consideration. I don't know if I can guarantee that some other such discovery will not be made in the future, so many personages greater than ourselves having been mistaken about this one. I am afraid we have eyes bigger than our stomachs, and more curiosity than capacity. We embrace everything, but we clasp only wind.

Plato brings in Solon, telling how he had learned from the priests of the city of Saïs in Egypt that in days of old, before the Flood, there was a great island named Atlantis, right at the mouth of the Strait of Gibraltar, which contained more land than Africa and Asia put together, and that the kings of that country, who not only possessed that island but had stretched out so far on the mainland that they held the breadth of Africa as far as Egypt, and the length of Europe as far as Tuscany, undertook to step over into Asia and subjugate all the nations that border on the Mediterranean, as far as the Black Sea; and for this purpose crossed the Spains, Gaul, Italy, as far as Greece, where the Athenians checked them; but that some time after, both the Athenians and themselves and their island were swallowed up by the Flood.

It is quite likely that that extreme devastation of waters made amazing changes in the habitations of the earth, as people maintain that the sea cut off Sicily from Italy –

1 In Brazil, in 1557.

> [B]'Tis said an earthquake once asunder tore
> These lands with dreadful havoc, which before
> Formed but one land, one coast
> VIRGIL

– [A]Cyprus from Syria, the island of Euboea from the mainland of
Boeotia; and elsewhere joined lands that were divided, filling the
channels between them with sand and mud:

> A sterile marsh, long fit for rowing, now
> Feeds neighbor towns, and feels the heavy plow.
> HORACE

But there is no great likelihood that that island was the
new world which we have just discovered; for it almost touched
Spain, and it would be an incredible result of a flood to have
forced it away as far as it is, more than twelve hundred leagues;
besides, the travels of the moderns have already almost revealed
that it is not an island, but a mainland connected with the East
Indies on one side, and elsewhere with the lands under the
two poles; or, if it is separated from them, it is by so narrow
a strait and interval that it does not deserve to be called an island
on that account.

[B]It seems that there are movements, [c]some natural, others
[B]feverish, in these great bodies, just as in our own. When
I consider the inroads that my river, the Dordogne, is making in
my lifetime into the right bank in its descent, and that in twenty
years it has gained so much ground and stolen away the foundations
of several buildings, I clearly see that this is an extraordinary dis-
turbance; for if it had always gone at this rate, or was to do so in the
future, the face of the world would be turned topsy-turvy. But rivers
are subject to changes: now they overflow in one direction, now in
another, now they keep to their course. I am not speaking of
the sudden inundations whose causes are manifest. In Médoc,
along the seashore, my brother, the sieur d'Arsac, can see an estate
of his buried under the sands that the sea spews forth; the tops of
some buildings are still visible; his farms and domains have changed
into very thin pasturage. The inhabitants say that for some time the
sea has been pushing toward them so hard that they have lost four
leagues of land. These sands are its harbingers; [c]and we see great
dunes of moving sand that march half a league ahead of it and keep
conquering land.

^AThe other testimony of antiquity with which some would con-
nect this discovery is in Aristotle, at least if that little book *Of
Unheard-of Wonders* is by him. He there relates that certain Cartha-
ginians, after setting out upon the Atlantic Ocean from the Strait of
Gibraltar and sailing a long time, at last discovered a great fertile
island, all clothed in woods and watered by great deep rivers, far
remote from any mainland; and that they, and others since, attracted
by the goodness and fertility of the soil, went there with their wives
and children, and began to settle there. The lords of Carthage,
seeing that their country was gradually becoming depopulated,
expressly forbade anyone to go there any more, on pain of death,
and drove out these new inhabitants, fearing, it is said, that in course
of time they might come to multiply so greatly as to supplant their
former masters and ruin their state. This story of Aristotle does not
fit our new lands any better than the other.

This man I had was a simple, crude fellow² – a character fit to
bear true witness; for clever people observe more things and more
curiously, but they interpret them; and to lend weight and convic-
tion to their interpretation, they cannot help altering history a little.
They never show you things as they are, but bend and disguise them
according to the way they have seen them; and to give credence to
their judgment and attract you to it, they are prone to add some-
thing to their matter, to stretch it out and amplify it. We need a man
either very honest, or so simple that he has not the stuff to build up
false inventions and give them plausibility; and wedded to no
theory. Such was my man; and besides this, he at various times
brought sailors and merchants, whom he had known on that trip, to
see me. So I content myself with his information, without inquiring
what the cosmographers say about it.

We ought to have topographers who would give us an exact
account of the places where they have been. But because they have
over us the advantage of having seen Palestine, they want to enjoy
the privilege of telling us news about all the rest of the world. I would
like everyone to write what he knows, and as much as he knows, not
only in this, but in all other subjects; for a man may have some
special knowledge and experience of the nature of a river or
a fountain, who in other matters knows only what everybody
knows. However, to circulate this little scrap of knowledge, he will

2 The traveler Montaigne spoke of at the beginning of the chapter.

undertake to write the whole of physics. From this vice spring many great abuses.

Now, to return to my subject, I think there is nothing barbarous and savage in that nation, from what I have been told, except that each man calls barbarism whatever is not his own practice; for indeed it seems we have no other test of truth and reason than the example and pattern of the opinions and customs of the country we live in. *There* is always the perfect religion, the perfect government, the perfect and accomplished manners in all things. Those people are wild, just as we call wild the fruits that Nature has produced by herself and in her normal course; whereas really it is those that we have changed artificially and led astray from the common order, that we should rather call wild. The former retain alive and vigorous their genuine, their most useful and natural, virtues and properties, which we have debased in the latter in adapting them to gratify our corrupted taste. ^CAnd yet for all that, the savor and delicacy of some uncultivated fruits of those countries is quite as excellent, even to our taste, as that of our own. ^AIt is not reasonable that art should win the place of honor over our great and powerful mother Nature. We have so overloaded the beauty and richness of her works by our inventions that we have quite smothered her. Yet wherever her purity shines forth, she wonderfully puts to shame our vain and frivolous attempts:

> ^BIvy comes readier without our care;
> In lonely caves the arbutus grows more fair;
> No art with artless bird song can compare.
>
> PROPERTIUS

^AAll our efforts cannot even succeed in reproducing the nest of the tiniest little bird, its contexture, its beauty and convenience; or even the web of the puny spider. ^CAll things, says Plato, are produced by nature, by fortune, or by art; the greatest and most beautiful by one or the other of the first two, the least and most imperfect by the last.

^AThese nations, then, seem to me barbarous in this sense, that they have been fashioned very little by the human mind, and are still very close to their original naturalness. The laws of nature still rule them, very little corrupted by ours; and they are in such a state of purity that I am sometimes vexed that they were unknown earlier, in the days when there were men able to judge them better than we.

I am sorry that Lycurgus and Plato did not know of them; for it seems to me that what we actually see in these nations surpasses not only all the pictures in which poets have idealized the golden age and all their inventions in imagining a happy state of man, but also the conceptions and the very desire of philosophy. They could not imagine a naturalness so pure and simple as we see by experience; nor could they believe that our society could be maintained with so little artifice and human solder. This is a nation, I should say to Plato, in which there is no sort of traffic, no knowledge of letters, no science of numbers, no name for a magistrate or for political superiority, no custom of servitude, no riches or poverty, no contracts, no successions, no partitions, no occupations but leisure ones, no care for any but common kinship, no clothes, no agriculture, no metal, no use of wine or wheat. The very words that signify lying, treachery, dissimulation, avarice, envy, belittling, pardon – unheard of. How far from this perfection would he find the republic that he imagined: ^C*Men fresh sprung from the gods* [Seneca].

^BThese manners nature first ordained.
 VIRGIL

^AFor the rest, they live in a country with a very pleasant and temperate climate, so that according to my witnesses it is rare to see a sick man there; and they have assured me that they never saw one palsied, bleary-eyed, toothless, or bent with age. They are settled along the sea and shut in on the land side by great high mountains, with a stretch about a hundred leagues wide in between. They have a great abundance of fish and flesh which bear no resemblance to ours, and they eat them with no other artifice than cooking. The first man who rode a horse there, though he had had dealings with them on several other trips, so horrified them in this posture that they shot him dead with arrows before they could recognize him.

Their buildings are very long, with a capacity of two or three hundred souls; they are covered with the bark of great trees, the strips reaching to the ground at one end and supporting and leaning on one another at the top, in the manner of some of our barns, whose covering hangs down to the ground and acts as a side. They have wood so hard that they cut with it and make of it their swords and grills to cook their food. Their beds are of a cotton weave, hung from the roof like those in our ships, each man having his own; for the wives sleep apart from their husbands.

They get up with the sun, and eat immediately upon rising, to last them through the day; for they take no other meal than that one. Like some other Eastern peoples, of whom Suidas tells us, who drank apart from meals, they do not drink then; but they drink several times a day, and to capacity. Their drink is made of some root, and is of the color of our claret wines. They drink it only lukewarm. This beverage keeps only two or three days; it has a slightly sharp taste, is not at all heady, is good for the stomach, and has a laxative effect upon those who are not used to it; it is a very pleasant drink for anyone who is accustomed to it. In place of bread they use a certain white substance like preserved coriander. I have tried it; it tastes sweet and a little flat.

The whole day is spent in dancing. The younger men go to hunt animals with bows. Some of the women busy themselves meanwhile with warming their drink, which is their chief duty. Some one of the old men, in the morning before they begin to eat, preaches to the whole barnful in common, walking from one end to the other, and repeating one single sentence several times until he has completed the circuit (for the buildings are fully a hundred paces long). He recommends to them only two things: valor against the enemy and love for their wives. And they never fail to point out this obligation, as their refrain, that it is their wives who keep their drink warm and seasoned.

There may be seen in several places, including my own house, specimens of their beds, of their ropes, of their wooden swords and the bracelets with which they cover their wrists in combats, and of the big canes, open at one end, by whose sound they keep time in their dances. They are close shaven all over, and shave themselves much more cleanly than we, with nothing but a wooden or stone razor. They believe that souls are immortal, and that those who have deserved well of the gods are lodged in that part of heaven where the sun rises, and the damned in the west.

They have some sort of priests and prophets, but they rarely appear before the people, having their home in the mountains. On their arrival there is a great feast and solemn assembly of several villages – each barn, as I have described it, makes up a village, and they are about one French league from each other. The prophet speaks to them in public, exhorting them to virtue and their duty; but their whole ethical science contains only these two articles: resoluteness in war and affection for their wives. He prophesies to them things to come and the results they are to expect from their

undertakings, and urges them to war or holds them back from it; but this is on the condition that when he fails to prophesy correctly, and if things turn out otherwise than he has predicted, he is cut into a thousand pieces if they catch him, and condemned as a false prophet. For this reason, the prophet who has once been mistaken is never seen again.

^CDivination is a gift of God; that is why its abuse should be punished as imposture. Among the Scythians, when the soothsayers failed to hit the mark, they were laid, chained hand and foot, on carts full of heather and drawn by oxen, on which they were burned. Those who handle matters subject to the control of human capacity are excusable if they do the best they can. But these others, who come and trick us with assurances of an extraordinary faculty that is beyond our ken, should they not be punished for not making good their promise, and for the temerity of their imposture?

^AThey have their wars with the nations beyond the mountains, further inland, to which they go quite naked, with no other arms than bows or wooden swords ending in a sharp point, in the manner of the tongues of our boar spears. It is astonishing what firmness they show in their combats, which never end but in slaughter and bloodshed; for as to routs and terror, they know nothing of either.

Each man brings back as his trophy the head of the enemy he has killed, and sets it up at the entrance to his dwelling. After they have treated their prisoners well for a long time with all the hospitality they can think of, each man who has a prisoner calls a great assembly of his acquaintances. He ties a rope to one of the prisoner's arms, ^Cby the end of which he holds him, a few steps away, for fear of being hurt, ^Aand gives his dearest friend the other arm to hold in the same way; and these two, in the presence of the whole assembly, kill him with their swords. This done, they roast him and eat him in common and send some pieces to their absent friends. This is not, as people think, for nourishment, as of old the Scythians used to do; it is to betoken an extreme revenge. And the proof of this came when they saw the Portuguese, who had joined forces with their adversaries, inflict a different kind of death on them when they took them prisoner, which was to bury them up to the waist, shoot the rest of their body full of arrows, and afterward hang them. They thought that these people from the other world, being men who had sown the knowledge of many vices among their neighbors and were much greater masters than themselves in every sort of wickedness, did not adopt this sort of vengeance without some reason, and that it

must be more painful than their own; so they began to give up their old method and to follow this one.

I am not sorry that we notice the barbarous horror of such acts, but I am heartily sorry that, judging their faults rightly, we should be so blind to our own. I think there is more barbarity in eating a man alive than in eating him dead; and in tearing by tortures and the rack a body still full of feeling, in roasting a man bit by bit, in having him bitten and mangled by dogs and swine (as we have not only read but seen within fresh memory, not among ancient enemies, but among neighbors and fellow citizens, and what is worse, on the pretext of piety and religion), than in roasting and eating him after he is dead.

Indeed, Chrysippus and Zeno, heads of the Stoic sect, thought there was nothing wrong in using our carcasses for any purpose in case of need, and getting nourishment from them; just as our ancestors, when besieged by Caesar in the city of Alesia, resolved to relieve their famine by eating old men, women, and other people useless for fighting.

> [B]The Gascons once, 'tis said, their life renewed
> By eating of such food.
>
> JUVENAL

[A]And physicians do not fear to use human flesh in all sorts of ways for our health, applying it either inwardly or outwardly. But there never was any opinion so disordered as to excuse treachery, disloyalty, tyranny, and cruelty, which are our ordinary vices.

So we may well call these people barbarians, in respect to the rules of reason, but not in respect to ourselves, who surpass them in every kind of barbarity.

Their warfare is wholly noble and generous, and as excusable and beautiful as this human disease can be; its only basis among them is their rivalry in valor. They are not fighting for the conquest of new lands, for they still enjoy that natural abundance that provides them without toil and trouble with all necessary things in such profusion that they have no wish to enlarge their boundaries. They are still in that happy state of desiring only as much as their natural needs demand; anything beyond that is superfluous to them.

They generally call those of the same age, brothers; those who are younger, children; and the old men are fathers to all the others. These leave to their heirs in common the full possession of their property, without division or any other title at all than just the one that Nature gives to her creatures in bringing them into the world.

If their neighbors cross the mountains to attack them and win a victory, the gain of the victor is glory, and the advantage of having proved the master in valor and virtue; for apart from this they have no use for the goods of the vanquished, and they return to their own country, where they lack neither anything necessary nor that great thing, the knowledge of how to enjoy their condition happily and be content with it. These men of ours do the same in their turn. They demand of their prisoners no other ransom than that they confess and acknowledge their defeat. But there is not one in a whole century who does not choose to die rather than to relax a single bit, by word or look, from the grandeur of an invincible courage; not one who would not rather be killed and eaten than so much as ask not to be. They treat them very freely, so that life may be all the dearer to them, and usually entertain them with threats of their coming death, of the torments they will have to suffer, the preparations that are being made for that purpose, the cutting up of their limbs, and the feast that will be made at their expense. All this is done for the sole purpose of extorting from their lips some weak or base word, or making them want to flee, so as to gain the advantage of having terrified them and broken down their firmness. For indeed, if you take it the right way, it is in this point alone that true victory lies:

> [c]It is no victory
> Unless the vanquished foe admits your mastery.
> CLAUDIAN

The Hungarians, very bellicose fighters, did not in olden times pursue their advantage beyond putting the enemy at their mercy. For having wrung a confession from him to this effect, they let him go unharmed and unransomed, except, at most, for exacting his promise never again to take up arms against them.

[A]We win enough advantages over our enemies that are borrowed advantages, not really our own. It is the quality of a porter, not of valor, to have sturdier arms and legs; agility is a dead and corporeal quality; it is a stroke of luck to make our enemy stumble, or dazzle his eyes by the sunlight; it is a trick of art and technique, which may be found in a worthless coward, to be an able fencer. The worth and value of a man is in his heart and his will; there lies his real honor. Valor is the strength, not of legs and arms, but of heart and soul; it consists not in the worth of our horse or our weapons, but in our own. He who falls obstinate in his courage, [c]*if he has fallen, he fights*

on his knees [Seneca]. [A]He who relaxes none of his assurance, no matter how great the danger of imminent death; who, giving up his soul, still looks firmly and scornfully at his enemy – he is beaten not by us, but by fortune; he is killed, not conquered.

[B]The most valiant are sometimes the most unfortunate. [C]Thus there are triumphant defeats that rival victories. Nor did those four sister victories, the fairest that the sun ever set eyes on – Salamis, Plataea, Mycale, and Sicily – ever dare match all their combined glory against the glory of the annihilation of King Leonidas and his men at the pass of Thermopylae.

Who ever hastened with more glorious and ambitious desire to win a battle than Captain Ischolas to lose one? Who ever secured his safety more ingeniously and painstakingly than he did his destruction? He was charged to defend a certain pass in the Peloponnesus against the Arcadians. Finding himself wholly incapable of doing this, in view of the nature of the place and the inequality of the forces, he made up his mind that all who confronted the enemy would necessarily have to remain on the field. On the other hand, deeming it unworthy both of his own virtue and magnanimity and of the Lacedaemonian name to fail in his charge, he took a middle course between these two extremes, in this way. The youngest and fittest of his band he preserved for the defense and service of their country, and sent them home; and with those whose loss was less important, he determined to hold this pass, and by their death to make the enemy buy their entry as dearly as he could. And so it turned out. For he was presently surrounded on all sides by the Arcadians, and after slaughtering a large number of them, he and his men were all put to the sword. Is there a trophy dedicated to victors that would not be more due to these vanquished? The role of true victory is in fighting, not in coming off safely; and the honor of valor consists in combating, not in beating.

[A]To return to our story. These prisoners are so far from giving in, in spite of all that is done to them, that on the contrary, during the two or three months that they are kept, they wear a gay expression; they urge their captors to hurry and put them to the test; they defy them, insult them, reproach them with their cowardice and the number of battles they have lost to the prisoners' own people.

I have a song composed by a prisoner which contains this challenge, that they should all come boldly and gather to dine off him, for they will be eating at the same time their own fathers and grandfathers, who have served to feed and nourish his body. "These

muscles," he says, "this flesh and these veins are your own, poor fools that you are. You do not recognize that the substance of your ancestors' limbs is still contained in them. Savor them well; you will find in them the taste of your own flesh." An idea that certainly does not smack of barbarity. Those that paint these people dying, and who show the execution, portray the prisoner spitting in the face of his slayers and scowling at them. Indeed, to the last gasp they never stop braving and defying their enemies by word and look. Truly here are real savages by our standards; for either they must be thoroughly so, or we must be; there is an amazing distance between their character and ours.

The men there have several wives, and the higher their reputation for valor the more wives they have. It is a remarkably beautiful thing about their marriages that the same jealousy our wives have to keep us from the affection and kindness of other women, theirs have to win this for them. Being more concerned for their husbands' honor than for anything else, they strive and scheme to have as many companions as they can, since that is a sign of their husbands' valor.

ᶜOur wives will cry "Miracle!" but it is no miracle. It is a properly matrimonial virtue, but one of the highest order. In the Bible, Leah, Rachel, Sarah, and Jacob's wives gave their beautiful handmaids to their husbands; and Livia seconded the appetites of Augustus, to her own disadvantage; and Stratonice, the wife of King Deiotarus, not only lent her husband for his use a very beautiful young chambermaid in her service, but carefully brought up her children, and backed them up to succeed to their father's estates.

ᴬAnd lest it be thought that all this is done through a simple and servile bondage to usage and through the pressure of the authority of their ancient customs, without reasoning or judgment, and because their minds are so stupid that they cannot take any other course, I must cite some examples of their capacity. Besides the warlike song I have just quoted, I have another, a love song, which begins in this vein: "Adder, stay; stay, adder, that from the pattern of your coloring my sister may draw the fashion and the workmanship of a rich girdle that I may give to my love; so may your beauty and your pattern be forever preferred to all other serpents." This first couplet is the refrain of the song. Now I am familiar enough with poetry to be a judge of this: not only is there nothing barbarous in this fancy, but it is altogether Anacreontic. Their language, moreover, is a soft language, with an agreeable sound, somewhat like Greek in its endings.

Three of these men, ignorant of the price they will pay some day, in loss of repose and happiness, for gaining knowledge of the corruptions of this side of the ocean; ignorant also of the fact that of this intercourse will come their ruin (which I suppose is already well advanced: poor wretches, to let themselves be tricked by the desire for new things, and to have left the serenity of their own sky to come and see ours!) – three of these men were at Rouen, at the time the late King Charles IX[3] was there. The king talked to them for a long time; they were shown our ways, our splendor, the aspect of a fine city. After that, someone asked their opinion, and wanted to know what they had found most amazing. They mentioned three things, of which I have forgotten the third, and I am very sorry for it; but I still remember two of them. They said that in the first place they thought it very strange that so many grown men, bearded, strong, and armed, who were around the king (it is likely that they were talking about the Swiss of his guard) should submit to obey a child, and that one of them was not chosen to command instead. Second (they have a way in their language of speaking of men as halves of one another), they had noticed that there were among us men full and gorged with all sorts of good things, and that their other halves were beggars at their doors, emaciated with hunger and poverty; and they thought it strange that these needy halves could endure such an injustice, and did not take the others by the throat, or set fire to their houses.

I had a very long talk with one of them; but I had an interpreter who followed my meaning so badly, and who was so hindered by his stupidity in taking in my ideas, that I could get hardly any satisfaction from the man. When I asked him what profit he gained from his superior position among his people (for he was a captain, and our sailors called him king), he told me that it was to march foremost in war. How many men followed him? He pointed to a piece of ground, to signify as many as such a space could hold; it might have been four or five thousand men. Did all his authority expire with the war? He said that this much remained, that when he visited the villages dependent on him, they made paths for him through the underbrush by which he might pass quite comfortably.

All this is not too bad – but what's the use? They don't wear breeches.

3 In 1562.

32
We should meddle soberly with judging divine ordinances

^AThe true field and subject of imposture are things unknown.
Because in the first place strangeness itself lends credit; and then,
not being subject to our ordinary reasoning, such things take away
our means of combating them. ^CFor this reason, says Plato, it is
much easier to give satisfaction when speaking of the nature of the
gods than when speaking of the nature of men, because the ignor-
ance of one's audience affords a fine broad range and full liberty in
handling so obscure a subject.

^AThence it happens that nothing is so firmly believed as what is
least known, nor are any people so confident as those who tell us
fables, such as alchemists, prognosticators, astrologers, palmists,
doctors – *that whole breed* [Horace]. To whom I would be prone to
add, if I dared, a whole pile of people, interpreters and controllers-
in-ordinary of God's designs, claiming to find the causes of every
incident and to see in the secrets of the divine will the incompre-
hensible motives of his works; and although the variety and con-
tinual discordance of events tosses them from corner to corner
and from east to west, yet they do not stop chasing their ball and
painting black and white with the same pencil.

^BIn one Indian nation there is this laudable observance: when
things have come out badly for them in some encounter or battle,
they publicly ask pardon of the sun, which is their god, as for an
unjust act; attributing their good or bad fortune to the divine reason,
and submitting to it their judgment and reasonings.

^AIt is enough for a Christian to believe that all things come from
God, to receive them with acknowledgment of his divine and
inscrutable wisdom, and therefore to take them in good part, in
whatever aspect they may be sent to him. But I think that the
practice I see is bad, of trying to strengthen and support our religion
by the good fortune and prosperity of our enterprises. Our belief has
enough other foundations; it does not need events to authorize it.
For when the people are accustomed to these arguments, which are
plausible and suited to their taste, there is a danger that when in turn
contrary and disadvantageous events come, this will shake their
faith. Thus, in the wars we are engaged in for the sake of religion,
those who had the advantage in the encounter at La Rochelabeille
make much ado about this incident and use their good fortune as
a sure approbation of their party; but when they come later to excuse

their misfortunes at Moncontour and Jarnac[1] as being fatherly scourges and chastisements, unless they have their following completely at their mercy, they make the people sense readily enough that this is getting two grinding fees for one sack, and blowing hot and cold with the same mouth. It would be better to tell them the true foundations of the truth.

It was a fine naval battle that was won these past months against the Turks, under the leadership of Don John of Austria;[2] but it has certainly pleased God at other times to let us see others like it, at our expense.

In short, it is difficult to bring down divine things to our scale without their suffering loss. And if someone wanted to give the reason why Arius and Leo, his Pope,[3] the principal leaders of the Arian heresy, died at different times of such similar and strange deaths (for a bellyache having forced them to withdraw from the disputation to the toilet, they both suddenly gave up the ghost there), and were minded to dramatize this divine vengeance by the circumstance of the place, he could indeed further add the death of Heliogabalus, who was also killed in a privy. But what does this prove? Irenaeus happens to have suffered the same fate.

^cGod, wishing to teach us that the good have something else to hope for, and the wicked something else to fear, than the fortunes and misfortunes of this world, handles and allots these according to his occult disposition, and deprives us of the means of foolishly making our profit of them. And those people delude themselves who try to take advantage of them by human reason. They never score one hit but they receive two. Saint Augustine gives a fine proof of this against his adversaries. It is a conflict that is decided by the weapons of memory more than by those of reason.

1 After their victory of La Rochelabeille (May, 1569) the Protestants used these arguments, forgetting their loss at Jarnac (March, 1569), until they were defeated again at Moncontour (October, 1569).
2 The battle of Lepanto (October 7, 1571), won by the combined fleets of Spain, Venice, and the Pope.
3 Montaigne took this story from the *Annales d'Aquitaine* of the sixteenth-century chronicler Jean Bouchet. Writing about Saint Hilary of Poitiers, Bouchet tells how two of his enemies, Arius (in A.D. 341; modern opinion prefers 336) and his follower the antipope Leo (in 364) met miraculous and ignominious deaths in the nearly identical manner that Montaigne describes. The precise identity of this Leo is still an enigma today, as it was in Bouchet's time.

^AWe must be content with the light that it pleases the sun to communicate to us by its rays; and if anyone raises his eyes to gain a greater light from its very body, let him not find it strange if as a penalty for his presumption he loses his sight. ^C*What man can know the counsel of God? or who can think what is the will of the Lord?* [Apocrypha: Book of Wisdom.]

33
To flee from sensual pleasures at the price of life

^AI had indeed seen that most ancient opinions agree on this, that it is time to die when there is more evil than good in living; and that to preserve our life to our torment and discomfort is to bump up against the very laws of nature, as these old rules say:

> Either a painless life, or else a happy death.
> To die is good for those whom life brings misery.
> 'Tis better not to live than live in wretchedness.
>
> GREEK GNOMIC POETS

But as for pushing the contempt of death to the point of using it to withdraw ourselves from the honors, riches, dignities, and other favors and goods which we call those of fortune, as if reason had not enough to do to persuade us to abandon them without adding this new burden on her, I had never seen this either commanded or practiced until I came across that passage in which Seneca advises Lucilius, a powerful personage and a man of great authority with the emperor, to give up his voluptuous and pompous existence and retire from worldly ambition to some solitary, tranquil, and philosophical life. Lucilius alleged some difficulties, to which Seneca replied: "My advice is that you either quit that life you lead, or quit life altogether. I do indeed counsel you to follow the milder way, and untie rather than break the knot you have so badly tied; provided that if it cannot be otherwise untied, you break it. No man is such a coward that he would not rather fall once than remain forever tottering." I should have found this advice in keeping with Stoical harshness; but it is more strange that it should be borrowed from Epicurus, who writes things just like it on this subject to Idomeneus.

Yet I think I have noticed something like it among our people, but with Christian moderation. When Saint Hilary, bishop of Poitiers, that famous enemy of the Arian heresy, was in Syria, he

was informed that Abra, his only daughter, whom he had left at home with her mother, was being sought in marriage by the most eminent lords of the country, as a girl well brought up, beautiful, rich, and in the flower of her youth. He wrote to her (as we see) that she should withdraw her affection from all these pleasures and advantages that were being offered her; that in his travels he had found her a much greater and worthier match, with a husband of far different power and magnificence, who would present her with robes and jewels of inestimable price. His design was to make her lose the desire and habit of worldly pleasures in order to unite her wholly to God; but as the shortest and surest means to this end seemed to him to be the death of his daughter, he did not cease, by vows, prayers, and orisons, to request God to take her from this world and call her to himself. And so it happened; for soon after his return she died, at which he exhibited a singular joy.

This man seems to outdo the others, in that he addresses himself from the first to this means, which the others adopt only as a subsidiary; and besides, it concerns his only daughter.

But I do not want to omit the end of this story, even though it is not to my point. When Saint Hilary's wife heard from him how the death of their daughter had been brought about by his design and will, and how much happier she was to be dislodged from this world than to be in it, she conceived such a lively sense of eternal celestial beatitude that she begged her husband with extreme insistence to do as much for her. And, God having soon after taken her to him in response to their unanimous prayers, hers was a death embraced with singular unanimous contentment.

34
Fortune is often met in the path of reason

ᴬThe inconstant and variable movement of Fortune makes her necessarily present all sorts of faces. Is there a more express act of justice than this one? The duke of Valentinois,[1] having resolved to poison Adrian, cardinal of Corneto, with whom he and his father, Pope Alexander VI, were going to sup at the Vatican, sent ahead of him a certain bottle of poisoned wine and ordered the butler to watch over it very carefully. When the Pope arrived before his son

1 Cesare Borgia.

and asked for drink, the butler, who thought that this wine had been recommended to his care only for its excellence, served him some of it; and the duke himself, arriving just in time for the meal and trusting to it that his bottle would not have been touched, took some in turn: so that the father died immediately, and the son, after having been long tormented by sickness, was preserved for another and worse fate.

Sometimes it seems that Fortune deliberately plays with us. The seigneur d'Estrées, then ensign to Monsieur de Vendôme, and the seigneur de Licques, lieutenant in the company of the duke of Ascot, were both suitors of the sister of the sieur de Fouquerolle, though of opposite parties (as happens with frontier neighbors). The sieur de Licques won her; but on the very day of the marriage, and, what is worse, before going to bed, the bridegroom, wanting to break a lance in honor of his new bride, went out to a skirmish near Saint-Omer, where the sieur d'Estrées, finding himself the stronger, made him his prisoner. And, to get full value from his advantage, the lady was obliged –

> Forced to give up her new-wed groom's embrace
> Until two winters, following apace,
> With their long nights sated her eager love
>
> CATULLUS

– herself to request him to give up his prisoner to her out of courtesy, which he did; for the French nobility never refuses anything to the ladies.

ᶜDoesn't this seem to be an artistic fate? Constantine, son of Helen, founded the Empire of Constantinople; and so many centuries later, Constantine, son of Helen, ended it.

ᴬSometimes Fortune is pleased to vie with our miracles. We are told that when King Clovis was besieging Angoulême, the walls fell of themselves by divine favor. And Bouchet borrows this from some author, that when King Robert was besieging a city, he stole away from the siege to go to Orléans to celebrate the feast of Saint Aignan; and while he was at his devotions at a certain point of the Mass, the walls of the besieged city fell in ruins without any attack. She did just the opposite in our wars with Milan when Captain Renzo, who was besieging the city of Arona for us, set a mine under a big section of wall; the wall was suddenly blown into the air, but fell down again in one piece, so straight into its foundation that the besieged were none the worse off.

Sometimes she practices medicine. Jason of Pheres, given up by the doctors because of an abscess in his chest, wished to get rid of it by death if necessary, and threw himself bodily into the thick of the enemy in a battle, where he was wounded through the body so exactly that his abscess burst and he was cured.

Did she not surpass the painter Protogenes in the knowledge of his art? He had completed the picture of a tired and panting dog to his satisfaction in all parts but one: he was unable to show the foam and slaver to suit himself. Vexed with his work, he took his sponge, which was soaked with various colors, and threw it at the picture to blot it out completely. Fortune guided the throw with perfect aptness right to the dog's mouth, and accomplished what art had been unable to attain.

Does she not sometimes direct our counsels and correct them? Isabel, queen of England, having to lead an army across from Zeeland to her kingdom to support her son against her husband, would have been lost if she had arrived at the port she had planned to land at, where she was awaited by her enemies; but Fortune cast her elsewhere against her will, and she landed in entire safety. And that ancient who, throwing a stone at a dog, hit and killed his stepmother, was he not right to pronounce this verse:

> Chance decides matters better than ourselves
>
> MENANDER

– "Fortune is better advised than we"?

ᶜIcetes had worked on two soldiers to kill Timoleon, who was staying at Adrana in Sicily. They chose a time when Timoleon was performing some sacrifice, and mingled with the multitude. As they were making signs to one another that the occasion was suitable for their job, up comes a third man who hits one of them a hard blow on the head with his sword and stretches him dead on the ground, and then runs away. The companion, thinking himself discovered and lost, ran to the altar to beg sanctuary, promising to tell the whole truth. As he was telling the story of the conspiracy, enter the third man, who had been caught and whom, as a murderer, the people were pushing and dragging through the crowd toward Timoleon and the most eminent men in the assembly. There he cried for mercy, saying he had rightfully killed his father's assassin and proving on the spot, by witnesses whom his good fortune provided for him most appropriately, that in the city of the Leontines his father had in truth been killed by the man on whom he had

taken revenge. They awarded him ten Attic minae for having had the good fortune, in taking satisfaction for the death of his father, to have saved from death the common father of the Sicilians. This fortune is more equitable than the equity of human wisdom.

ᴮA final example. Does not the fact which is about to be related reveal a very express act of Fortune's favor, of her singular kindness and piety? The Egnatii, father and son, proscribed by the triumvirs at Rome, resolved on the noble device of giving up their lives at each other's hands, in order to frustrate the cruelty of the tyrants. They ran upon each other sword in hand. Fortune directed the points and made two equally mortal wounds, and granted in honor of such a beautiful affection that both men should have just enough strength to withdraw their weapons from the wounds and, with bloodied arms, clasp each other in so strong an embrace that the executioners cut off both their heads together, leaving the bodies still held in this noble bond, and the wounds so joined that they lovingly drank in each other's blood and what was left of each other's life.

35
Of a lack in our administrations

ᴬMy late father, a man of very clear judgment for one who was aided only by experience and nature, once told me that he had wanted to arrange that towns should have a certain designated place where those who needed something could go and have their business registered by an officer appointed for that purpose. As, for example: ᶜ"I want to sell some pearls; I want to buy some pearls. ᴬSo-and-so wants company to go to Paris; so-and-so is looking for a servant with such-and-such qualifications; so-and-so wants a master; so-and-so a workman; one man this, another man that, each according to his need." And it seems that this means of informing one another would be of no slight advantage to public commerce; for all the time there are people with congruous needs who are looking for one another, and, for lack of knowing one another, are left in extreme need.

I hear, with great shame for our century, that under our very eyes two personages most outstanding in learning have died so poor that they had not enough to eat: Lilius Gregorius Giraldus in Italy and Sebastianus Castalio in Germany. And I believe there are a thousand

men who would have sent for them on very advantageous terms, ^cor helped them where they were, ^Aif they had known.

The world is not so generally corrupted but that I know a man who would wish with all his heart to use what he has inherited from his ancestors, as long as Fortune is pleased to let him enjoy it, to put beyond the reach of want persons rare and remarkable in any way, whom misfortune persecutes at times to the last extremity – a man who would at least set them up in such a way that it would be unreasonable of them not to be content.

^cIn his domestic administration my father had this system, which I can praise but not follow: besides the record of household affairs kept by his steward, in which were entered petty accounts, payments, and transactions not requiring the notary's hand, he ordered the servant whom he used as his secretary to keep a journal and insert in it all occurrences of any note, and the memorabilia of his family history day by day. A record very pleasant to look at when time begins to efface the memory of events, and very well suited to get us out of perplexity: When was such and such a thing begun? When completed? What retinues came? How long did they stay? Our trips, our absences; marriages; deaths; the receipt of happy or unhappy news; the change of principal servants; such matters. An ancient custom, which I think it would be good to revive, each man in each man's home. And I think I am a fool to have neglected it.

<div align="center">

36
Of the custom of wearing clothes

</div>

^AWherever I want to turn, I have to force some barrier of custom, so carefully has it blocked all our approaches. I was wondering in this shivery season whether the fashion of going stark naked in these lately discovered nations is forced on them by the warm temperature of the air, as we say of the Indians and Moors, or whether it is the original way of mankind. Inasmuch as all things under heaven, as Holy Writ says,[1] are subject to the same laws, men of understanding, in considerations like these (where we must distinguish natural from artificial laws), are wont to have recourse

1 Ecclesiastes 9:3.

to the general order of the world, in which there can be nothing counterfeit.

Now, since everything else is furnished with the exact amount of thread and needle required to maintain its being, it is in truth incredible that we alone should be brought into the world in a defective and indigent state, in a state such that we cannot maintain ourselves without external aid. Thus I hold that, just as plants, trees, animals, all things that live, are naturally equipped with sufficient covering to defend themselves against the injury of the weather,

> And therefore everything is covered o'er
> With either hide, silk, shells, thick skin, or bark,
>
> LUCRETIUS

so were we; but like those who by artificial light extinguish the light of day, we have extinguished our own means by borrowed means. And it is easy to see that it is custom that makes impossible for us what is not impossible in itself; for of those nations that have no knowledge of clothes, there are some situated under much the same sky as ours; and besides, our most delicate parts are those that are always kept uncovered: ᶜeyes, mouth, nose, ears; with our peasants, as with our ancestors, the chest and belly. ᴬIf we had been born with natural petticoats and breeches, there can be no doubt but that Nature would have armed with a thicker skin the parts she intended to expose to the beating of the seasons, as she has done for the fingertips and the soles of the feet.

ᶜWhy does this seem hard to believe? Between my way of dressing and that of a peasant of my region I find far more distance than there is between his way and that of a man dressed only in his skin.

How many men, especially in Turkey, go naked as a matter of religion!

ᴬSomeone or other was asking one of our beggars whom he saw in the depth of winter as cheery in his shirt as someone muffled to the ears in sables, how he could endure it. "And you, sir," he answered, "you have your face uncovered; now, I am all face." The Italians tell this story of the duke of Florence's fool, I think it was: that on his master's inquiring how, so poorly clad, he could bear the cold which he himself had trouble bearing, the fool replied, "Follow my rule, and pile on you all the garments you have, as I do, and you won't suffer from the cold any

more than I do." King Massinissa, even in his extreme old age, could not be induced to go with his head covered, however cold, stormy, or rainy it might be. ^CThis is also said of the Emperor Severus.

In the battles fought between the Egyptians and the Persians, Herodotus says it was remarked both by others and by himself that of those who remained dead on the field, the skulls of the Egyptians were incomparably harder than those of the Persians, because the latter kept their heads always covered, first with caps and then with turbans, whereas the former kept theirs shaven and bare from infancy.

^AAnd King Agesilaus observed until his decrepitude the habit of wearing the same clothing in winter as in summer. Caesar, says Suetonius, always marched at the head of his army, most of the time on foot, head bare, whether it was sunny or raining; and they say as much of Hannibal:

> Then with bare head
> He met the frenzy of the storm, the falling sky.
> SILIUS ITALICUS

^CA Venetian who stayed in the kingdom of Pegu a long time and has only just come back writes that the men and women there always go barefoot, even on horseback, and with the other parts of the body clothed.

And Plato gives this wonderful advice, for the health of the whole body: to give the head and feet no other covering than that which nature has provided.

^AThe man whom the Poles chose for their king after ours,[2] and who is in truth one of the greatest princes of our century, never wears gloves, or changes, for winter or any weather whatever, the bonnet that he wears indoors.

^BWhereas I cannot bear to go unbuttoned and untied, the laborers in my neighborhood would feel fettered if they were otherwise. Varro maintains that when it was ordained that we should keep our head uncovered in the presence of the gods or the magistrate, it was done more for our health, and to harden us against the attacks of the weather, than on account of reverence.

^AAnd since we are on the subject of cold, and Frenchmen, accustomed to array ourselves in varied colors (not I, for I scarcely

2 Henry III was the elected king of Poland before he became king of France. He was succeeded in Poland in 1574 by Stephen Bathori.

wear anything but black or white, in imitation of my father), let us add in another connection that Captain Martin du Bellay says he saw, on the march to Luxemburg, frosts so severe that the supply of wine was cut with hatchets and axes, distributed to the soldiers by weight, and carried away in baskets. And Ovid, very close:

> Uncasked, the wines retain the shape of casks,
> And lumps are passed around instead of flasks.
>
> OVID

[B]The frosts are so bitter at the mouth of Lake Maeotis[3] that in the same place where Mithridates' lieutenant had fought the enemy dry-footed and defeated them in the winter, he won a naval battle against them the next summer.

[C]The Romans suffered a great disadvantage in their combat with the Carthaginians near Placentia, because they went to the charge with their blood congealed and limbs benumbed with cold, whereas Hannibal had passed out fire throughout his host to warm his soldiers, and distributed oil among each company, so that by anointing themselves they might render their sinews more supple and limber, and encrust their pores against the assault of the air and the freezing wind that was blowing.

The retreat of the Greeks from Babylon into their country is famous for the difficulties and hardships that they had to overcome. This was one: they were met by a terrible blizzard in the mountains of Armenia, and lost all knowledge of the country and the roads. Being quite simply besieged by the storm, they were a day and a night without eating or drinking, most of their animals dead, many of themselves dead, many blinded by the driving hail and the glare of the snow, many crippled in their extremities, many stiff, numb, and immobilized with cold, though still in possession of all their senses.

Alexander saw a nation in which they bury their fruit trees in winter to protect them from the frost.

[B]On the subject of clothing, the king of Mexico changed his clothes four times a day and never put them on again, using his castoffs for his continual liberalities and rewards; likewise neither pot, nor dish, nor any kitchen or table utensil was ever put before him twice.

3 The Sea of Azov.

37
Of Cato the Younger

^I do not share that common error of judging another by myself. I easily believe that another man may have qualities different from mine. ^CBecause I feel myself tied down to one form, I do not oblige everybody to espouse it, as all others do. I believe in and conceive a thousand contrary ways of life; and in contrast with the common run of men, I more easily admit difference than resemblance between us. I am as ready as you please to acquit another man from sharing my conditions and principles. I consider him simply in himself, without relation to others; I mold him to his own model. I do not fail, just because I am not continent, to acknowledge sincerely the continence of the Feuillants and the Capuchins, and to admire the manner of their life. I can very well insinuate myself by imagination into their place, and I love and honor them all the more because they are different from me. I have a singular desire that we should each be judged in ourselves apart, and that I may not be measured in conformity with the common patterns.

^My weakness in no way alters my necessarily high regard for the strength and vigor of those who deserve it. ^C*There are men who praise nothing except what they are confident they can imitate* [Cicero]. ^ACrawling in the slime of the earth, I do not fail to observe, even in the clouds, the inimitable loftiness of certain heroic souls. It is a great deal for me to have my judgment regulated, if my actions cannot be, and to maintain at least this sovereign part free from corruption. It is something to have my will good when my legs fail me. This century in which we live, at least in our part of the world, is so leaden that not only the practice but even the idea of virtue is wanting; and it seems to be nothing else but a piece of school jargon –

> ^CThey think that virtue's just a word,
> And a sacred grove mere sticks HORACE

– *something they should revere even if they cannot understand it* [Cicero]. It is a trinket to hang in a cabinet, or as an ornament on the end of the tongue, like an earring on the tip of the ear.

^AThere are no more virtuous actions to be seen; those that wear virtue's appearance do not for all that have its essence; for profit, glory, fear, habit, and other such extraneous causes lead us to

perform them. The justice, the valor, the good nature that we then exercise may be so called in consideration of others and of the appearance they bear in public, but in the doer this is not virtue at all; there is another end proposed, ^Canother motivating cause. ^ANow virtue will avow nothing but what is done by and for itself alone.

^CIn that great battle of Potidaea that the Greeks under Pausanias won against Mardonius and the Persians, the victors, according to their custom, when they came to divide among themselves the glory of the exploit, attributed to the Spartan nation the preeminence of valor in this combat. The Spartans, excellent judges of valor, when they came to decide to what particular man should go the honor of having done best on that day, found that Aristodemus had hazarded his life the most courageously; but they did not give him the prize, because his valor had been incited by the desire to purge himself of the reproach he had incurred in the Thermopylae action, and by a craving to die courageously in order to make up for his past shame.

^AOur judgments are still sick and follow the depravation of our morals. I see most of the wits of my time using their ingenuity to obscure the glory of the beautiful and noble actions of antiquity, giving them some vile interpretation and conjuring up vain occasions and causes for them. ^BWhat great subtlety! Give me the most excellent and purest action, and I will plausibly supply fifty vicious motives for it. God knows what a variety of interpretations may be placed on our inward will, for anyone who wants to elaborate them. ^CIn their calumny they play at ingenuity not so much maliciously as clumsily and crudely.

The same pains that they take to detract from these great names, and the same license, I would willingly take to lend them a shoulder to raise them higher. These great figures, whom the consensus of the wise has selected as examples to the world, I shall not hesitate to restore to their places of honor, as far as my ingenuity allows me to interpret them in a favorable light. But we are forced to believe that our powers of conception are far beneath their merit. It is the duty of good men to portray virtue as being as beautiful as possible; and it would not be unbecoming to us if passion carried us away in favor of such sacred models.

What these people do to the contrary, ^Athey do either out of malice, or from that vice of dragging down their belief to their capacity, which I have just spoken of; or, as I rather think, from not having their sight strong enough and clear enough, or properly trained, to conceive of the splendor of virtue in its native purity. So

Plutarch is rightly annoyed that in his time some people attributed the cause of the younger Cato's death to his fear of Caesar; and we may judge from this how much more offended Plutarch would have been with those who have attributed Cato's death to ambition. ᶜFools! He would actually have preferred to perform a beautiful, noble, and just action with ignominy than for the sake of glory. ᴬHe was truly a model chosen by nature to show how far human virtue and constancy could go.

But I am not equipped to treat this rich subject here. I want only to put in contention the lines of five Latin poets in praise of Cato, ᶜboth in Cato's interest, and, incidentally, in their own also. Now a well-educated youngster should find the first two languid compared with the others, the third lustier, but overcome by the extravagance of his own power. He should think that there would be room for one or two more degrees of inventiveness before coming to the fourth, at whose work he will clasp his hands in admiration. At the last one – who is first by quite a space, and a space which our youth will swear no human mind can fill – he will be stunned and speechless.

Here is a wonder: we have many more poets than judges and interpreters of poetry. It is easier to create it than to understand it. On a certain low level it can be judged by precepts and by art. But the good, supreme, divine poetry is above the rules and reason. Whoever discerns its beauty with a firm, sedate gaze does not see it, any more than he sees the splendor of a lightning flash. It does not persuade our judgment, it ravishes and overwhelms it. The frenzy that goads the man who can penetrate it also strikes a third person on hearing him discuss it and recite it, as a magnet not only attracts a needle but infuses into it its own faculty of attracting others. And it is seen more clearly in the theater that the sacred inspiration of the muses, after first stirring the poet to anger, sorrow, and hatred and transporting him out of himself wherever they will, then through the poet strikes the actor, and through the actor consecutively a whole crowd. It is the chain of our needles, hanging one from the other.[1]

From my earliest childhood poetry has had that power to transpierce and transport me. But this very lively feeling that is natural in me has been variously affected by a variety of forms, not so much higher or lower (for they were always of the highest in each kind) as

1 By the effect of the magnet.

different in color: first a gay and ingenious fluency; then a keen and lofty subtlety; finally a mature and constant power. The examples will express it better: Ovid, Lucan, Virgil. But here are our poets in the lists.

> ^ALet Cato outdo even Caesar, while he lives,

says one [Martial].

> Cato unvanquished, having vanquished death,

says another [Manilius]. And another, speaking of the civil wars between Caesar and Pompey,

> The gods chose the victorious cause, Cato the vanquished.
>
> LUCAN

And the fourth, in praise of Caesar:

> This earth of ours he subjugated whole,
> Excepting Cato's unrelenting soul.
>
> HORACE

And the master of the choir, after displaying in his painting the names of the greatest Romans, ends in this wise:

> And Cato, giving them their laws.
>
> VIRGIL

38
How we cry and laugh for the same thing

^AWe read in the history books that Antigonus was very angry with his son for having presented him with the head of his enemy King Pyrrhus, who that very moment had been killed fighting against him, and that upon seeing it he began to weep very hard; and that Duke René of Lorraine also lamented the death of Duke Charles of Burgundy, whom he had just defeated, and wore mourning at his burial; and that in the battle of Auray, which the count of Montfort won against Charles of Blois, his rival for the duchy of Brittany, the victor, coming upon the body of his dead enemy, showed great sorrow over it. But in reading of these events we should not immediately exclaim:

> And thus it happens that each soul conceals,
> Showing the opposite, now gay, now sad,
> The passion that it genuinely feels.
>
> PETRARCH

When they presented Caesar with the head of Pompey, the histories say, he turned his eyes away as from an ugly and unpleasant sight. There had been such a long understanding and association between them in the management of public affairs, such great community of fortunes, so many mutual services and so close an alliance, that we must not believe that Caesar's countenance was entirely false and counterfeit, as this man supposes:

> And now he saw
> 'Twas safe to be a good father-in-law;
> Out came false tears, groans from his happy breast.
>
> LUCAN

For although most of our actions are indeed only mask and make-up, and it may sometimes be true that

> An heir's tears are a laugh behind the mask,
>
> PUBLILIUS SYRUS

yet in judging these accidents we must consider how our soul is often agitated by diverse passions. And just as in our body they say there is an assemblage of diverse humors, of which that one is master which most ordinarily rules within us, according to our constitution; so in our soul, though various impulses stir it, there must be one that remains master of the field. Its advantage is not complete, however; because of the volatility and pliancy of our soul, the weaker ones on occasion regain the lost ground and make a brief attack in their turn. Hence we see children, who quite spontaneously follow nature, often cry and laugh at the same thing. And not only that, but not one of us can boast, however much he wants to make a trip, that on parting from his family and friends he does not feel a tremor in his heart; if he does not actually shed tears, at least he puts his foot in the stirrup with a sad and mournful face. And however sweet the flame that warms the heart of wellborn maidens, still they have to be pulled by force from their mother's neck to be delivered over to their husband, no matter what this good companion says:

> Is Venus really hateful to each blushing bride,
> Or false those tears which dash their parents' joy and pride,

When on the bedroom threshold they pour out like rain?
Heaven help me, no; not from the heart do they complain.

 CATULLUS

Thus it is not strange to lament a person dead whom one would not
in the least want to have alive.

ᴮWhen I scold my valet, I scold him with all my heart; my
imprecations are real, not feigned. But when the smoke has blown
away, let him need my help, and I am glad to do him a service;
I instantly turn over the leaf. ᶜWhen I call him a clown or a calf, I do
not undertake to sew those labels on him forever; nor do I think
I contradict myself when I presently call him a fine fellow.

No quality embraces us purely and universally. If it did not seem
crazy to talk to oneself, there is not a day when I would not be heard
growling at myself: "Confounded fool!" And yet I do not intend that
to be my definition.

ᴮWhoever supposes, to see me look sometimes coldly, sometimes
lovingly, on my wife, that either look is feigned, is a fool. Nero,
taking leave of his mother, whom he was sending to be drowned,
nevertheless underwent the emotion of this maternal farewell, and
had a feeling of horror and pity.

ᴬThey say that the sun does not give off a continuous light, but
that it incessantly darts new rays so thick on one another that we
cannot perceive the intervals between them:

ᴮFor the ethereal sun, great source of liquid light,
Assiduously with fresh radiance floods the sky,
Adding new light to light in ever-fresh supply.

 LUCRETIUS

Just so our soul diversely and imperceptibly darts its rays.

ᶜArtabanus came on his nephew Xerxes by surprise and chided
him for his sudden change of countenance. Xerxes had been con-
sidering the immeasurable greatness of his forces at the crossing of
the Hellespont for the expedition against Greece. At first he quiv-
ered with joy to see so many thousands of men in his service, and
showed his feelings by the happiness and delight on his face. And
quite suddenly, at the same instant, as his thought suggested to him
how all those lives would give out within a century at the latest, he
knit his brows and was saddened even to tears.

ᴬWe have with resolute will sought revenge for an injury, and felt
singular satisfaction in gaining it, and yet we weep. It is not for our
victory that we weep, there is nothing changed; but our soul looks

on the thing with a different eye, and represents it to itself in another aspect, for each thing has many angles and many lights. Kinship, old acquaintance, and friendship seize our imagination and get it passionately involved for the moment, according to their character; but the turn is so quick that it escapes us.

> [B]Nothing is known to match in lightning speed
> The mind of man, passing from thought to deed.
> Whatever nature shows to human sight
> Is not so swift as is the soul in flight.
>
> LUCRETIUS

[A]And for this reason we are wrong to try to compose a continuous body out of all this succession of feelings. When Timoleon weeps for the murder he has committed with such mature and high-minded deliberation, he is not weeping for the liberty restored to his country, he is not weeping for the tyrant; he is weeping for his brother. One part of his duty is performed; let us allow him to perform the other.

39
Of solitude

[A]Let us leave aside the usual long comparison between the solitary and the active life; and as for that fine statement under which ambition and avarice take cover – that we are not born for our private selves, but for the public – let us boldly appeal to those who are in the midst of the dance. Let them cudgel their conscience and say whether, on the contrary, the titles, the offices, and the hustle and bustle of the world are not sought out to gain private profit from the public. The evil means men use in our day to push themselves show clearly that the end is not worth much. Let us reply to ambition that it is she herself that gives us a taste for solitude. For what does she shun so much as society? What does she seek so much as elbowroom? There is opportunity everywhere for doing good or evil. However, if Bias' statement is true, that the wicked are in the majority, or what Ecclesiastes says, that not one in a thousand is good –

> [B]The good are rare: if all their numbers you compile,
> They'll scarcely match the gates of Thebes, the mouths of Nile
>
> JUVENAL

– [A]contagion is very dangerous in the crowd. One must either imitate the vicious or hate them. Both these things are dangerous: to imitate them because they are many, and to hate many of them because they are unlike us.

[C]Merchants who go to sea are right to be careful that those who embark on the same ship are not dissolute, blasphemous, or wicked, and to regard such company as unlucky. Wherefore Bias said humorously to those who were undergoing with him the danger of a great tempest and calling on the gods for help: "Be quiet, so they may not realize that you are here with me." And in a more pressing case, Albuquerque, viceroy in the Indies for King Manuel of Portugal, when in great peril of shipwreck at sea, took a young boy upon his shoulders for this purpose alone, that in their common danger the boy's innocence might serve him as a guarantee and a recommendation to divine favor, and bring him to safety.

[A]It is not that the wise man cannot live anywhere content, yes, and alone in a palace crowd; but if he has the choice, says he, he will flee even the sight of a throng. He will endure it, if need be, but if it is up to him, he will choose solitude. He does not feel sufficiently rid of vices if he must still contend with those of other men. [B]Charondas chastised as evil those who were convicted of keeping evil company.

[C]There is nothing so unsociable and so sociable as man; the one by his vice, the other by his nature. And Antisthenes does not seem to me to have given a satisfactory answer to the man who reproached him for associating with wicked men, when he said that doctors lived well enough among the sick; for if they improve the health of the sick, they impair their own by contagion, and by the constant sight and treatment of diseases.

[A]Now the aim of all solitude, I take it, is the same: to live more at leisure and at one's ease. But people do not always look for the right way. Often they think they have left business, and they have only changed it. There is scarcely less trouble in governing a family than in governing an entire state: whatever the mind is wrapped up in, it is all wrapped up in it, and domestic occupations are no less importunate for being less important. Furthermore, by getting rid of the court and the market place we do not get rid of the principal worries of our life:

> Reason and sense remove anxiety,
> Not villas that look out upon the sea.
> HORACE

Ambition, avarice, irresolution, fear, and lust do not leave us when we change our country.

> Behind the horseman sits black care.
>
> HORACE

They often follow us even into the cloisters and the schools of philosophy. Neither deserts, nor rocky caves, nor hair shirts, nor fastings will free us of them:

> The fatal shaft sticks in her side.
>
> VIRGIL

Someone said to Socrates that a certain man had grown no better by his travels. "I should think not," he said; "he took himself along with him."

> Why should we move to find
> Countries and climates of another kind?
> What exile leaves himself behind?
>
> HORACE

If a man does not first unburden his soul of the load that weighs upon it, movement will cause it to be crushed still more, as in a ship the cargo is less cumbersome when it is settled. You do a sick man more harm than good by moving him. You imbed the malady by disturbing it, as stakes penetrate deeper and grow firmer when you budge them and shake them. Wherefore it is not enough to have gotten away from the crowd, it is not enough to move; we must get away from the gregarious instincts that are inside us, we must sequester ourselves and repossess ourselves.

> B"At last," you'll say, "I've snapped my chains."
> A fleeing dog may well have snapped his, at great pains,
> Yet dangling from his neck the greater part remains.
>
> PERSIUS

We take our chains along with us; our freedom is not complete; we still turn our eyes to what we have left behind, our fancy is full of it.

> Unless the heart is purged, what must we undergo!
> What battles and what perils, to our fruitless woe!
> How great the bitter cares of lust that rend apart,

With terrors in their train, an agitated heart!
What ruin, what disasters, follow in the path
Of pride, and lust, and luxury, and sloth, and wrath!

<div style="text-align:right">LUCRETIUS</div>

^AOur illness grips us by the soul, and the soul cannot escape from itself:

The soul's at fault, which ne'er escapes itself.

<div style="text-align:right">HORACE</div>

Therefore we must bring it back and withdraw it into itself: that is the real solitude, which may be enjoyed in the midst of cities and the courts of kings; but it is enjoyed more handily alone.

Now since we are undertaking to live alone and do without company, let us make our contentment depend on ourselves; let us cut loose from all the ties that bind us to others; let us win from ourselves the power to live really alone and to live that way at our ease.

After Stilpo escaped the burning of his city, in which he had lost wife, children, and property, Demetrius Poliorcetes, seeing him unperturbed in expression amid the great ruin of his country, asked him if he had not suffered loss. No, he replied; thanks to God he had lost nothing of his own. ^CThe philosopher Antisthenes expressed the same idea humorously: that man should furnish himself with provisions that would float on water and could swim ashore with him from a shipwreck.

^ACertainly a man of understanding has lost nothing, if he has himself. When the city of Nola was ruined by the barbarians, Paulinus, the bishop of the city, who had lost everything and had been taken prisoner, prayed God thus: "Lord, keep me from feeling this loss; for Thou knowest that they have yet touched nothing of what is mine." The riches that made him rich and the goods that made him good were still entire. That is what it is to choose wisely the treasures that can be secured from harm, and to hide them in a place where no one may go and which can be betrayed only by ourselves.

We should have wife, children, goods, and above all health, if we can; but we must not bind ourselves to them so strongly that our happiness depends on them. We must reserve a back shop all our own, entirely free, in which to establish our real liberty and our principal retreat and solitude. Here our ordinary conversation must be between us and ourselves, and so private that no outside

association or communication can find a place; here we must talk and laugh as if without wife, without children, without possessions, without retinue and servants, so that, when the time comes to lose them, it will be nothing new to us to do without them. We have a soul that can be turned upon itself; it can keep itself company; it has the means to attack and the means to defend, the means to receive and the means to give: let us not fear that in this solitude we shall stagnate in tedious idleness:

> ^BIn solitude be to thyself a throng.
>
> TIBULLUS

^CVirtue, says Antisthenes, is content with itself, without rules, without words, without deeds.

^AAmong our customary actions there is not one in a thousand that concerns ourselves. The man you see climbing atop the ruins of that wall, frenzied and beside himself, a mark for so many harquebus shots; and that other, all scarred, pale and faint with hunger, determined to die rather than open the gates to him – do you think they are there for their own sake? They are there for the sake of a man whom perhaps they never saw, who is not in the least concerned about their doings, and who at that very moment is plunged in idleness and pleasures.

This fellow, all dirty, with running nose and eyes, whom you see coming out of his study after midnight, do you think he is seeking among his books how to make himself a better, happier, and wiser man? No such news. He is going to teach posterity the meter of Plautus' verses and the true spelling of a Latin word, or die in the attempt. Who does not willingly exchange health, rest, and life for reputation and glory, the most useless, worthless, and false coin that is current among us? Our own death does not frighten us enough? Let us burden ourselves also with that of our wives, our children, and our servants. Our own affairs don't give us enough trouble? Let us also torment ourselves and get headaches over those of our neighbors and friends.

> What! Shall a man establish in his soul, or prize
> Anything dearer than himself in his own eyes?
>
> TERENCE

^CSolitude seems to me more appropriate and reasonable for those who have given to the world their most active and flourishing years, following the example of Thales.

^AWe have lived enough for others; let us live at least this remaining bit of life for ourselves. Let us bring back our thoughts and plans to ourselves and our well-being. It is no small matter to arrange our retirement securely; it keeps us busy enough without mixing other undertakings with it. Since God gives us leisure to make arrangements for moving out, let us make them; let us pack our bags; let us take an early leave of the company; let us break free from the violent clutches that engage us elsewhere and draw us away from ourselves. We must untie these bonds that are so powerful, and henceforth love this and that, but be wedded only to ourselves. That is to say, let the other things be ours, but not joined and glued to us so strongly that they cannot be detached without tearing off our skin and some part of our flesh as well. The greatest thing in the world is to know how to belong to oneself.

^CIt is time to untie ourselves from society, since we can contribute nothing to it. And he who cannot lend, let him keep from borrowing. Our powers are failing us; let us withdraw them and concentrate them on ourselves. He who can turn the offices of friendship and fellowship around and fuse them into himself, let him do so. In this decline, which makes him useless, burdensome, and troublesome to others, let him keep from being troublesome to himself, and burdensome, and useless. Let him indulge and care for himself, and especially govern himself, respecting and fearing his reason and his conscience, so that he cannot make a false step in their presence without shame. *For it is rare for anyone to respect himself enough* [Quintilian].

Socrates says that the young should get instruction; that grown men should practice doing good; and that old men should withdraw from all civil and military occupations and live at their own discretion, without being tied down to any fixed office.

^AThere are some temperaments more suited to these precepts ^Cfor retirement ^Athan others. Those whose susceptibility is weak and lax, and whose affection and will are fastidious and slow to enter service or employment – of whom I am one, both by natural disposition and by conviction – will comply with this advice better than will the active and busy souls who embrace everything and engage themselves everywhere, who grow passionate about all things, who offer, present, and give themselves on all occasions. We should use these accidental and external conveniences, so far as they are agreeable to us, but without making them our mainstay; they are not; neither reason nor nature will have it so. Why should

we, contrary to their laws, enslave our contentment to the power of others? Moreover, to anticipate the accidents of fortune; to deprive ourselves of the commodities that are in our hands, as many have done through piety and some philosophers through reason; to wait on ourselves; to sleep on the hard ground; to put out our eyes; to throw our riches into the river; to seek pain, some in order to win bliss in another life by torment in this, others to make themselves safe from a new fall by settling on the lowest step – these are the acts of an excessive virtue. Let the sturdier and stronger natures make even their hiding place glorious and exemplary:

> When riches fail, I praise
> The safe and simple life, content with humble ways;
> But then, when better, richer fortune smiles on me,
> I say that only they live well and sensibly
> Whose wealth in country manors glistens brilliantly.

> HORACE

I have enough on my hands without going that far. It is enough for me while under fortune's favor, to prepare for its disfavor, and while I am well off, to picture the evil that is to come, as far as my imagination can reach; just as we accustom ourselves to jousts and tournaments, and imitate war in the midst of peace.

ᶜI do not consider the philosopher Arcesilaus less virtuous because I know that he used gold and silver vessels as much as his fortune allowed him to; and I esteem him more highly for having used them moderately and liberally than if he had given them up.

ᴬI see to what limits natural necessity goes; and, thinking about the poor beggar at my door, often merrier and healthier than myself, I put myself in his place, I try to fit my mind to his bias. And running over the other examples in the same way, though I may think that death, poverty, contempt, and disease are at my heels, I easily resolve not to take fright at what a lesser man than I accepts with such patience. I cannot believe that meanness of understanding can do more than vigor, or that the effects of reason cannot match the effects of habit. And knowing how precarious these incidental comforts are, I do not fail, while in full enjoyment of them, to make it my sovereign request of God that he make me content with myself and the good things I bring forth. I see hearty young men who never fail to carry in their baggage a mass of pills to take when afflicted with a cold, which they fear the less because they think they have the remedy at hand. Thus we must do; and further, if we feel ourselves subject to

some graver malady, we must provide ourselves with the drugs that benumb and put to sleep the affected part.

The occupation we must choose for such a life must be neither laborious nor annoying; otherwise there would be no point in having come to it in search of rest. This depends on each man's particular taste: mine is not at all adaptable to household management. Those who like it should apply themselves to it with moderation:

> Try to bend things to them, not them to things.
>
> HORACE

Besides, the care of an estate is a job for slaves, as Sallust calls it. Some parts of it are more excusable, like the care of gardens, which Xenophon attributes to Cyrus; and a mean may be found between that base and sordid concern, tense and full of anxiety, which is seen in men who plunge themselves deep into it, and that profound and extreme negligence, letting everything go to seed, which we see in others:

> Democritus' herds devour his season's yield,
> While his swift soul without his body roams afield.
>
> HORACE

But let us hear the counsel that the younger Pliny gives his friend Cornelius Rufus on this matter of solitude: "I advise you, in this full and prosperous retreat of yours, to leave to your servants the sordid and abject care of the household, and to devote yourself to the study of letters, in order to derive from them something that is all your own." He means reputation, being of a like temper with Cicero, who says he wants to use his solitude and rest from public affairs to gain by his writings immortal life:

> [B]Is knowledge naught to you
> Unless another knows that you know all you do?
>
> PERSIUS

[C]It seems reasonable, when a man talks of retiring from the world, that he should set his gaze outside of it. These men do so only halfway. They indeed arrange their affairs for the time when they will no longer be there; but by a ridiculous contradiction they still aspire to reap the fruit of their plan from the world when they have left it.

The idea of those who seek solitude for religious reasons, filling their hearts with the certainty of divine promises for the other life, is much more sane and consistent. They set before their eyes God, an object infinite both in goodness and in power; in him the soul has the wherewithal to satisfy its desires abundantly in complete freedom. Afflictions, sufferings, come to them as profit, being used for the acquisition of eternal health and rejoicing; death is to be desired, being the passage to so perfect a state. The harshness of their rules is promptly smoothed by habit; and the carnal appetites are frustrated and then put to sleep by denial, for nothing keeps them up but use and exercise. Only this one goal of another life, happily immortal, rightly deserves that we abandon the comforts and pleasures of this life of ours. And he who can really and constantly kindle his soul with the flame of that living faith and hope, builds himself in solitude a life that is voluptuous and delightful beyond any other kind of life.

^AtTherefore I am satisfied with neither the purpose nor the means of Pliny's advice; we still would merely fall out of an ague into a burning fever. This occupation with books is as laborious as any other, and as much an enemy to health, which should be our chief consideration. And we must not let ourselves be lulled to sleep by the pleasure we take in it; it is the same pleasure that ruins the frugal man, the miser, the voluptuous man, and the ambitious man. The sages teach us often enough to beware of the treachery of our appetites, and to distinguish true and entire pleasures from pleasures that are mixed and streaked with a preponderance of pain. For most pleasures, they say, caress and embrace us only to strangle us, like those thieves that the Egyptians called Philistas. If we got our headache before getting drunk, we should take care not to drink too much; but pleasure, to deceive us, walks ahead and hides her sequel from us. Books are pleasant; but if by associating with them we end by losing gaiety and health, the best parts of us, let us leave them. I am one of those who think that their benefits cannot counterbalance this loss.

As men who have long felt weakened by some indisposition at last give themselves up to the mercy of medicine and have certain rules of living prescribed for them by art, rules which are nevermore to be transgressed; so he who retires, annoyed and disgusted with the common way of life, must model his new life on the rules of reason, order it and arrange it by premeditation and

reflection. He must have taken leave of every kind of labor, whatever aspect it may bear; he must flee in general the passions that prevent tranquillity of body and soul, [B]and choose the way that suits his humor best:

> Let each one know the way that he should go.
>> PROPERTIUS

[A]In household management, in study, in hunting, and in all other pursuits, we should take part up to the utmost limits of pleasure, but beware of engaging ourselves further, where it begins to be mingled with pain. We must reserve only so much business and occupation as we need to keep us in trim and protect ourselves from the inconveniences that the other extreme, slack and sluggish idleness, brings in its train.

There are sterile and thorny sciences, for the most part created for the busy life; we must leave them to those who are in the service of the world. For myself, I like only pleasant and easy books, which entertain me, or those that console me and counsel me to regulate my life and my death:

> To saunter silent through the wholesome wood,
> Bent on thoughts worthy of the wise and good.
>> HORACE

Wiser men, having a strong and vigorous soul, can make for themselves a wholly spiritual repose. But I, who have a commonplace soul, must help support myself by bodily comforts; and since age has lately robbed me of those that were more to my fancy, I train and sharpen my appetite for those that remain and are more suitable to this present season. We must hold on, tooth and nail, to our enjoyment of the pleasures of life, which our years tear, one after the other, from our hands:

> [B]Let us seize pleasures; life is ours to claim;
> Too soon we shall be ashes, ghosts, a name.
>> PERSIUS

[A]Now, as for glory, the goal that Pliny and Cicero set up for us, it is very far from my reckoning. The humor most directly opposite to retirement is ambition. Glory and repose are things that cannot lodge in the same dwelling. As far as I can see, these men have only their arms and legs outside the crowd; their souls, their intentions, are more than ever in the thick of it:

B Old man, do you cull scraps for others' ears?
 PERSIUS

A They have only stepped back to make a better jump, to get a stronger impetus wherewith to plunge deeper into the crowd. Do you want to see how they shoot a grain's length too short? Let us put into the scales the advice of two philosophers [Epicurus and Seneca] of two very different sects, one writing to Idomeneus, the other to Lucilius, their friends, to persuade them to give up handling affairs and withdraw from their high positions into solitude.

"You have," they say, "lived until now swimming and floating; come away and die in port. You have given the rest of your life to light; give this part to the shade. It is impossible to abandon occupations if you do not abandon the fruits of them; therefore rid yourself of all care for reputation and glory. There is danger that the gleam of your past actions may give you only too much light and follow you right into your lair. Abandon with the other pleasures that which comes from the approbation of others; and as for your knowledge and ability, don't worry, it will not lose its effect if it makes you yourself a better man. Remember the man who, when asked why he took so much pains in an art which could come to the knowledge of so few people, replied: 'Few are enough for me, one is enough for me, none at all is enough for me.' He spoke truly: you and one companion are an adequate theater for each other, or you for yourself. Let the people be one to you, and let one be a whole people to you. It is a base ambition to want to derive glory from our idleness and our concealment. We must do like the animals that rub out their tracks at the entrance to their lairs.

"Seek no longer that the world should speak of you, but how you should speak to yourself. Retire into yourself, but first prepare to receive yourself there; it would be madness to trust in yourself if you do not know how to govern yourself. There are ways to fail in solitude as well as in company. Until you have made yourself such that you dare not trip up in your own presence, and until you feel both shame and respect for yourself, C let true ideals be kept before your mind [Cicero], A keep ever in your mind Cato, Phocion, and Aristides, in whose presence even fools would hide their faults; make them controllers of all your intentions; if these intentions get off the track, your reverence for those men will set them right again. They will keep you in a fair way to be content with yourself, to

borrow nothing except from yourself, to arrest your mind and fix it on definite and limited thoughts in which it may take pleasure; and, after understanding the true blessings, which we enjoy in so far as we understand them, to rest content with them, without any desire to prolong life and reputation."

That is the counsel of true and natural philosophy, not of an ostentatious and talky philosophy like that of Pliny and Cicero.

40
A consideration upon Cicero

^AOne more note on the comparison of these pairs.[1] We may gather from the writings of Cicero and of this Pliny (who in my opinion bears little resemblance in temperament to his uncle) numberless proofs of their immeasurably ambitious nature: among others that they openly solicit the historians of their time not to forget them in their annals; and Fortune, as if in spite, has made the vanity of these requests endure to our day, long after the annals in question dropped from sight. But this surpasses all baseness of heart in persons of such rank: to have wanted to derive some great glory from mere babble and talk, to the point of publishing their private letters written to their friends; and even though some of these failed to be sent, they were published nonetheless, with this worthy excuse, that the writers did not want to lose their labor and their vigils. Is it not a fine thing for two Roman consuls, sovereign magistrates of the republic that was empress of the world, to employ their leisure in arranging and dressing up a pretty missive, in order to gain a reputation for a good knowledge of the language of their nurse? What worse would a simple schoolmaster do who gained his living by it? If the deeds of Xenophon and Caesar had not far surpassed their eloquence, I do not believe they would ever have written them down. They sought to recommend not their sayings but their doings.

And if the perfection of fine speaking could bring any glory suitable to a great personage, certainly Scipio and Laelius would not have resigned the credit for their comedies, and all the elegance and charms of their Latin, to an African slave; for that the work is theirs its beauty and excellence sufficiently demonstrates, and

1 The last part of the preceding chapter compared Cicero and Pliny the Younger with Epicurus and Seneca on the subject of retirement.

Terence himself admits it. [B]I would be unhappy to be dislodged from this belief.

[A]It is a kind of mockery and insult to praise a man's worth for qualities unbecoming his rank, though they be otherwise laudable, and for qualities also which ought not to be his principal ones; as if you praised a king for being a good painter, or a good architect, or else a good shot with a harquebus or a good tilter at the ring. These praises do no honor unless they are presented in mass and after those that befit him: to wit, justice and the science of leading his people in peace and war. In this way agriculture does honor to Cyrus; and to Charlemagne, eloquence and the knowledge of good letters. [C]To put this in stronger terms, I have known in my time distinguished men who derived their titles and calling from writing, to disown their apprenticeship; to corrupt their style; and to affect ignorance of so commonplace a faculty, which our people believe is scarcely ever to be found among the learned, and seek to recommend themselves by better qualities.

[B]The companions of Demosthenes in the embassy to Philip praised that prince as being handsome, eloquent, and a good drinker. Demosthenes said that those were praises more appropriate to a woman, a lawyer, and a sponge, than to a king.

> Let him show mastery over a fighting foe,
> And clemency when he has brought him low.
>
> HORACE

It is not his profession to be either a good hunter or a good dancer:

> Others will plead cases, measure the sky with bars;
> Others will tell us of the gleaming stars.
> Let him know only how to rule his empire.
>
> VIRGIL

[A]Plutarch says further that to appear so excellent in these less necessary qualities is to testify that one has misspent one's leisure and study, which should have been employed in more necessary and useful things. So that King Philip of Macedon, after hearing the great Alexander, his son, sing at a feast in an attempt to vie with the best musicians, said to him: "Aren't you ashamed to sing so well?" And to this same Philip a musician, with whom he was arguing about his art, said: "God forbid, Sire, that you should ever have the misfortune to understand these things better than I."

[B] A king should be able to reply as Iphicrates replied to the orator who was assailing him in his invective with these questions: "Well, what are you, to play so brave? Are you a man-at-arms? Are you an archer? Are you a pikesman?" "I am none of these, but I am the man who knows how to command them all."

[A] And Antisthenes took it as evidence of the little worth of Ismenias that he was praised for being an excellent flute player.

[C] I know well that when I hear someone dwell on the language of these essays, I would rather he said nothing. This is not so much to extol the style as to depreciate the sense; the more galling for being more oblique. Yet I am much mistaken if many other writers offer more to take hold of in their material than I do, and, whether for better or for worse, if any writer has sown his materials more substantially or at least more thickly on his paper. In order to get more in, I pile up only the headings of subjects. Were I to add on their consequences, I would multiply this volume many times over. And how many stories have I spread around which say nothing of themselves, but from which anyone who troubles to pluck them with a little ingenuity will produce numberless essays. Neither these stories nor my quotations serve always simply for example, authority, or ornament. I do not esteem them solely for the use I derive from them. They often bear, outside of my subject, the seeds of a richer and bolder material, and sound obliquely a subtler note, both for myself, who do not wish to express anything more, and for those who get my drift.

Coming back to the subject of wordy prowess, I find no great choice between knowing how to speak only badly and knowing only how to speak well. *Elegance of style is not a manly ornament* [Seneca]. [A] The sages say that as regards knowledge only philosophy, and as regards actions only virtue, are generally suited to all ranks and all classes.

There is something similar in those two other philosophers [Epicurus and Seneca], for they also promise eternity to the letters they write to their friends, but in a different fashion: they accommodate themselves, for a good end, to the vanity of others. For they write their friends that if the concern with making themselves known to the ages to come, and with renown, keeps them at the management of affairs and makes them fear the solitude and retirement to which the two philosophers want to call them, they should give themselves no more trouble; inasmuch as Epicurus and Seneca have enough credit with posterity to guarantee them

that, by virtue of these letters alone, they will become as well known and famous as their own public actions could make them. Moreover, these are not mere empty and fleshless letters, holding together only by a delicate choice of words piled up and arranged in precise cadence, but letters stuffed full of the fine arguments of wisdom, by which a man becomes not more eloquent but wiser, letters that teach us not to speak well but to do well. Fie on the eloquence that leaves us craving itself, not things! Unless we say that Cicero's, being of such extreme perfection, gives itself body and substance.

I shall add one more story that we read about Cicero in this connection, to make us put our finger on his nature. He had to make an oration in public and was a little pressed for time to prepare himself at leisure. Eros, one of his slaves, came and notified him that the meeting was postponed until the next day. He was so delighted that he gave him his freedom for the good news.

^BOn the subject of letter writing, I want to say this: that it is a kind of work in which my friends think I have some ability. ^CAnd I would have preferred to adopt this form to publish my sallies, if I had had someone to talk to. I needed what I once had, a certain relationship to lead me on, sustain me, and raise me up. For to talk to the winds, as others do, is beyond me except in dreams; nor could I fabricate fictitious names to talk with on a serious matter, being a sworn enemy of any falsification. I would have been more attentive and confident, with a strong friend to address, than I am now, when I consider the various tastes of a whole public. And if I am not mistaken, I would have been more successful.

^BI have naturally a humorous and familiar style, but of a form all my own, inept for public negotiations, as my language is in every way, being too compact, disorderly, abrupt, individual; and I have no gift for letters of ceremony that have no other substance than a fine string of courteous words. I have neither the faculty nor the taste for those lengthy offers of affection and service. I do not really believe all that, and I dislike saying much of anything beyond what I believe. That is a far cry from present practice, for there never was so abject and servile a prostitution of complimentary addresses: life, soul, devotion, adoration, serf, slave, all these words have such vulgar currency that when letter writers want to convey a more sincere and respectful feeling, they have no way left to express it.

I mortally hate to seem a flatterer; and so I naturally drop into a dry, plain, blunt way of speaking, which, to anyone who does not

know me otherwise, verges a little on the disdainful. ^CI honor most those to whom I show least honor; and where my soul moves with great alacrity, I forget the proper steps of ceremony. ^BI offer myself meagerly and proudly to those to whom I belong. ^CAnd I tender myself least to those to whom I have given myself most; ^Bit seems to me that they should read my feelings in my heart, and see that what my words express does an injustice to my thought. ^CIn welcoming, in taking leave, in thanking, in greeting, in offering my services, in all those verbose compliments imposed by the ceremonial laws of our etiquette, I know no one so stupidly barren of words as myself. And I have never been made use of to write letters of favor and recommendation but that the man for whom they were written found them dry and weak.

^BThe Italians are great printers of letters. I think I have a hundred different volumes of them; those of Annibal Caro seem to me the best. If all the paper I once bedaubed for the ladies when my hand was really carried away by my passion were now in existence, there might perhaps be found some page worthy to be communicated to our idle youth that is infatuated with this mania.

I always write my letters posthaste, and so precipitously that although my handwriting is intolerably bad, I prefer to write with my own hand rather than employ another, for I find no one who can follow me, and I never have them copied. I have accustomed high personages who know me to put up with scratchings and crossings-out, and a paper without fold or margin. The letters that cost me most are those that are worth least; as soon as I begin to drag them out, it is a sign that I am not there. I am prone to begin without a plan; the first remark brings on the second. The letters of this age consist more in embroideries and preambles than in substance. Just as I would rather compose two letters than close and fold one, and always resign that job to someone else; so, when the substance is finished, I would gladly give someone else the charge of adding those long harangues, offers, and prayers that we place at the end, and I wish some new custom would relieve us of it, as well as that of stringing out a whole series of qualities and titles in the address. In order not to stumble in these I have many times refrained from writing, especially to jurists and financiers. There are so many new offices, such a difficult distribution and arrangement of various titles of honor, which, being so dearly bought, cannot be exchanged or

forgotten without offense. I also consider it in bad taste to load with these the frontispiece and title page of the books we print.[2]

41
Of not communicating one's glory

[A]Of all the illusions in the world, the most universally received is the concern for reputation and glory, which we espouse even to the point of giving up riches, rest, life, and health, which are effectual and substantial goods, to follow that vain phantom and mere sound that has neither body nor substance:

> The fame that charms proud mortals with sweet sound,
> And seems so fair, is but an echo, a dream,
> The shadow of a dream, beyond repair
> Dispersed and scattered by a puff of air.
>
> TASSO

And of the irrational humors of men, it seems that even the philosophers get rid of this one later and more reluctantly than any other.

[B]It is the most contrary and stubborn of all, [C]*because it does not cease to tempt even souls that are making good progress* [Saint Augustine]. [B]There is hardly any other illusion whose vanity reason condemns so clearly; but it has such live roots in us that I do not know whether anyone yet has ever been able to get clean rid of it. After you have said everything and believed everything to disown it, it produces such an ingrained inclination against your arguments that you have little power to withstand it. [A]For as Cicero says, even those who combat it still want the books that they write about it to bear their name on the title page, and want to become glorious for having despised glory.

All other things can be traded; we lend our goods and our lives to the need of our friends; but to communicate one's honor and endow another with one's glory, that is hardly ever seen.

Catalus Luctatius, in the war against the Cimbrians, after making every effort to stop his soldiers from fleeing before the enemy, himself joined the fugitives and played the coward, so that they

2 Montaigne suppressed these in the 1588 edition of the *Essays* after using them in earlier editions.

should seem rather to be following their captain than fleeing from the enemy. That was abandoning his reputation to cover the shame of others.

When the Emperor Charles V came into Provence in the year 1537, they say that Antonio de Leyva, seeing his master resolved on this expedition and believing that it would add wonderfully to his glory, nevertheless expressed a contrary opinion and advised him against it; to this end, that all the glory and honor of this plan should be attributed to his master, and that it might be said that his good judgment and foresight had been such that, against the opinion of everyone, he had carried out such a splendid enterprise: which for de Leyva, was to honor his master at his own expense.

When the Thracian ambassadors, in consoling Argileonis, the mother of Brasidas, for the death of her son, praised him so highly as to say that he had not left his like behind him, she refused this private and particular praise and gave it back to the public: "Don't tell me that," she said; "I know that the city of Sparta has many citizens greater and more valiant than he was."

In the battle of Crécy the prince of Wales, still a very young man, was in charge of the vanguard. The principal stress of the encounter was at that point. The lords who were with him, finding themselves in a tough fight, sent word to King Edward to come up and help them. He inquired about the condition of his son, and being answered that he was alive and on his horse, he said: "I should be doing him wrong to go now and rob him of the honor of victory in this combat that he has sustained so long; whatever risk there may be, this shall be all his own." And he would not go or send to him, knowing that if he went, it would be said that all would have been lost without his help, and that the credit for this exploit would be attributed to him: ᶜ*for it is always what is thrown in last that seems to have accomplished the whole thing* [Livy].

ᴮMany in Rome thought, and it was commonly said, that the principal great deeds of Scipio were due ᶜin part ᴮto Laelius, who was always promoting and seconding Scipio's greatness and glory without any care for his own. And Theopompus, king of Sparta, to the man who told him that the republic remained on its feet because he knew how to command well, said: "It is rather because the people know how to obey well."

ᶜAs women who succeeded to peerages, in spite of their sex, had the right to attend and deliberate in cases pertaining to the jurisdiction of peers, so the ecclesiastical peers, in spite of their profession,

were obliged to assist our kings in their wars, not only with their friends and retainers, but also in person. The bishop of Beauvais, finding himself with Philip Augustus at the battle of Bouvines, participated very courageously in the action; but it seemed to him he should not touch the fruit and glory of this bloody and violent activity. With his own hand he got the better of several of the enemy that day; and he would give them to the first gentleman he found, to cut their throats or take them as prisoners, letting him handle them as he chose; and he so delivered William, earl of Salisbury, to Messire Jean de Nesle. With a like subtlety of conscience he was willing to club a man to death but not to wound him, and therefore fought only with a mace.

Someone in my day, being reproached by the king for having laid hands on a priest, strongly and stoutly denied it: the fact was that he had cudgeled and kicked him.

42
Of the inequality that is between us

^A^Plutarch says somewhere that he does not find so much difference between one animal and another as he does between one man and another. He is talking about the capacity of the soul and the inward qualities. In truth, I find Epaminondas, as I imagine him, so remote from some men I know – I mean men capable of common sense – that I would willingly outdo Plutarch and say that there is more distance from a given man to a given man than from a given man to a given animal:

> ^C^How far one man excels another!
>
> TERENCE

and that there are as many degrees in minds as there are fathoms from here to heaven, and as innumerable.

^A^But apropos of judging men, it is a wonder that, ourselves excepted, nothing is evaluated except by its own qualities. We praise a horse because it is vigorous and skillful –

> ^B^Thus we praise the steed
> Who wins the highest palms with easy speed,
> Amid the raucous plaudits of the Circus
>
> JUVENAL

– ^not for his harness; a greyhound for his speed, not for his collar; a bird for his wing, not for his jesses and bells. Why do we not likewise judge a man by what is his own? He has a great retinue, a beautiful palace, so much influence, so much income: all that is around him, not in him. You don't buy a cat in a bag. If you are bargaining for a horse, you take off his trappings, you see him bare and uncovered. Or if he is covered, as in olden days they used to offer horses to princes for sale, the covering covers only the least important parts, and is there so that you may not waste time on the beauty of his coat or the breadth of his crupper, but linger principally over considering his legs, eyes, and feet, which are the most useful parts:

> When kings want to buy horses, this is ever their way:
> To see them covered up, lest they be led astray
> And buy a soft lame foot, paired with a handsome face,
> Fine cruppers, a short head, a neck of arching grace.
>
> HORACE

Why in judging a man do you judge him all wrapped up in a package? He displays to us only parts that are not at all his own, and hides from us those by which alone one can truly judge of his value. It is the worth of the blade that you seek to know, not of the scabbard; perhaps you will not give a penny for it if you have unsheathed it. You must judge him by himself, not by his finery. And as one of the ancients [Seneca] says very comically: "Do you know why you think him tall? You are counting in the height of his heels." The pedestal is not part of the statue. Measure him without his stilts; let him put aside his riches and honors, let him present himself in his shirt. Has he a body fit for its functions, healthy and blithe? What sort of soul has he? Is it beautiful, capable, and happily furnished with all its parts? Is it rich of its own riches, or of others'? Has fortune nothing to do with it? If open-eyed he awaits the drawn swords; if he cares not whether his life expires by the mouth or the neck; if his soul is composed, equable, and content: this is what we must see, and by this judge the extreme differences that are between us. Is he

> Wise, and master of himself,
> Fearing not death, or chains, or lack of wealth,
> Disdaining honors, firm against desire,
> Within himself well-rounded and entire,

> Beyond the reach of all external pain,
> Against whom even fortune strikes in vain?
>> HORACE

Such a man is five hundred fathoms above kingdoms and duchies; he is himself his own empire.

> ^CIndeed the wise man his own fortune shapes.
>> PLAUTUS

^AWhat is there left for him to desire?

> Do we not
> See nature crave but this, a body wholly free
> From pain, a mind we can enjoy delightfully,
> Remote from care and fear?
>> LUCRETIUS

Compare with him the common run of men today, stupid, base, servile, unstable, and continually tossed about by the tempest of the diverse passions that drive them to and fro; depending entirely on others. There is more distance between them than between heaven and earth. And yet our practice is so blind that we make little or no account of it; whereas if we consider a peasant and a king, ^Ca nobleman and a plebeian, a magistrate and a private citizen, a rich man and a pauper, ^Athere immediately appears to our eyes an extreme disparity between them, though they are different, so to speak, only in their breeches.

^CIn Thrace the king was distinguished from his people in an amusing and very exaggerated manner. He had a religion apart, a god all to himself – Mercury – whom his subjects had no right to worship, and he disdained their gods, Mars, Bacchus, Diana.

Yet these things are only coats of paint, which make no essential difference. ^AFor like actors in a comedy – you see them on the stage assume the mien of a duke or an emperor, but immediately afterward, there they are, turned back into miserable valets and porters, which is their natural and original condition – so the emperor, whose pomp dazzles you in public –

> ^BAnd, brightly green, great emeralds glow in golden mounting,
> And raiment of sea-purple, rich beyond our counting,
> Grows worn with constant soaking in the sweat of love
>> LUCRETIUS

– [A]see him behind the curtain: he is nothing but an ordinary man, and perhaps viler than the least of his subjects. [C]*This man is inwardly happy. That man's happiness is a veneer* [Seneca]. [A]Cowardice, irresolution, spite, and envy drive him like anyone else:

> For treasures cannot keep away,
> Nor consul's lictors hold at bay,
> The mind's sad storms, or cares that fly
> Round paneled ceilings high;
>
> HORACE

[B]and anxiety and fear hold him by the throat in the midst of his armies:

> And truly, human fears, and consequent alarms
> Neither dread cruel swords nor shun the clash of arms,
> But fix on kings and potentates their clutches bold,
> And show no reverence for all the gleam of gold.
>
> LUCRETIUS

[A]Do fever, migraine, and gout spare him any more than us? When old age weighs on his shoulders, will the archers of his guard relieve him of it? When the terror of death paralyzes him, will he be reassured by the presence of the gentlemen of his chamber? When he is in a jealous and capricious mood, will our taking off our hat set him right? That canopy over his bed, all bloated with gold and pearls, has no virtue to appease the gripings of an acute colic:

> Nor is a burning fever more rapidly brought down
> Tossing on purple, with embroidered counterpane,
> Than lying on a bed that's commonplace and plain.
>
> LUCRETIUS

The flatterers of Alexander the Great were getting him to believe he was the son of Jupiter. One day, being wounded and watching the blood flow from his wound, he said: "Well, what do you say to this? Isn't this blood crimson and purely human? It is not the sort that Homer makes to flow from the wounds of the gods." Hermodorus the poet had composed some verses in honor of Antigonus, in which he called him son of the sun. Antigonus contradicted him, saying: "The man who empties my chamber pot knows very well that I am nothing of the sort."

All in all, he is a man; and if of himself he is ill-born, the empire of the universe could not dress him up.

> [B]For him let maidens come to blows;
> Beneath his every step let there spring up a rose:
> PERSIUS

What of it, if he is a coarse and stupid soul? Even voluptuousness and happiness are not felt without vigor and spirit:

> These things reflect the owner's mind. Bad for the man
> Who cannot use them, they are good for him who can.
> TERENCE

[A]The goods of fortune, even such as they really are, still need taste to enjoy them. It is the enjoying, not the possessing, that makes us happy:

> Not house and land, not heaps of gold or brass
> Can make the fevers from the master pass,
> Nor cares vacate his soul. He must have health
> Who would enjoy accumulated wealth.
> The man who lusts or fears, his goods help out
> As pictures cheer the blind or baths the gout.
> HORACE

He is a fool, his taste is dull and numb; he enjoys things no more than a man with a cold enjoys the sweetness of Greek wine, or a horse the richness of the harness with which they have adorned him. [C]Just as health, beauty, strength, riches, and all that is called good, as Plato says, are as much an evil to the unjust man as a good to the just; and the evil contrariwise.

[A]And then, where body and mind are in bad shape, what is the use of these external advantages, seeing that the slightest pinprick, or passion of the soul, is sufficient to deprive us of the pleasure of being monarch of the world? At the first twinge of the gout, [B]there is no comfort in his being Sire and Majesty,

> All swollen both with silver and with gold:
> TIBULLUS

[A]does he not lose the memory of his palaces and grandeurs? If he is angry, does his princedom keep him from turning red or pale, from

grinding his teeth like a madman? Now if he is an able and wellborn
man, royalty adds little to his happiness:

> If stomach, side, and feet are all in perfect health,
> Nothing more can be had, for all a monarch's wealth;
>
> HORACE

he sees that it is only illusion and trickery. Indeed, perhaps he will be
of King Seleucus' opinion, that a man who knew the weight of
a scepter would not deign to pick it up if he found it on the ground.
He said this because of the great and troublesome charges incum-
bent on a good king.

Truly it is no small thing to have to rule others, since in ruling
ourselves so many difficulties occur. As for commanding, which
seems to be so sweet: considering the imbecility of human judgment
and the difficulty of choice in new and doubtful things, I am
strongly of this opinion, that it is much easier and pleasanter to
follow than to guide, and that it is a great rest for the mind to have
only to hold to a mapped-out path and to be answerable only
for oneself:

> [B]Quiet obedience is better far
> Than hunger after empire.
>
> LUCRETIUS

Moreover, Cyrus used to say that no man is fit to command who is
not better than those he commands.

[A]But King Hiero, in Xenophon, says further that even in the
enjoyment of pleasures kings are worse off than private citizens,
since ease and facility take from them the bittersweet tang that we
find in them:

> [B]Love that's too mighty loses all its charm,
> And palls, as sweet food does the stomach harm.
>
> OVID

[A]Do we think that choirboys take great pleasure in music? Not
so; satiety makes it boring to them. Feasts, dances, masquerades,
tourneys, delight those who do not see them often and who
have looked forward to seeing them; but to anyone who makes
them an ordinary pastime, the taste of them becomes insipid
and unpleasant. Nor do ladies titillate the man who enjoys his
fill of them. He who does not give himself leisure to be thirsty
cannot take pleasure in drinking. The farces of the mountebanks

delight us, but to the players they are a chore. And the proof of this is that it is the delight of princes, and a holiday for them, to be able sometimes to disguise themselves and stoop to a low and plebeian way of living:

> Often the great choose for a change to roam:
> A simple meal, a poor man's humble home,
> No purple, no display –
> These waft their cares away. HORACE

ᶜThere is nothing so hampering, so cloying, as abundance. What appetite would not balk to see three hundred women at its mercy, such as the Grand Turk has in his seraglio? And what appetite for hunting, and appearance of it, did that one of his ancestors reserve for himself who never went out to the fields with fewer than seven thousand falconers?

ᴬAnd besides, I believe that this luster of greatness brings no slight drawbacks to the enjoyment of the sweeter pleasures: they are too much in the limelight and exposed to view.

ᴮAnd, I know not why, the great are more obliged than we to hide and cover up their faults. For what in us is indiscretion, in them the people judge to be tyranny, contempt, and disdain for the laws; and it is true that besides their normal pleasure from vice, it seems that they take an added pleasure in insulting public observances and trampling them underfoot. ᶜIndeed Plato, in his *Gorgias*, defines a tyrant as one who has license to do anything he pleases in a city. ᴮAnd often, for that reason, the public display of their vice gives more offense than the vice itself. Everyone fears to be spied on and watched, and the great are watched even to their expressions and thoughts, since all the people think they have a right and an interest to judge them; moreover, blemishes are magnified according to the eminence and brightness of the place where they are located, and a mole or a wart on the forehead shows more than a scar elsewhere.

ᴬThat is why the poets imagine Jupiter's amours to have been conducted under other guises than his own. And of all the amorous undertakings that they attribute to him, there is only one, it seems to me, in which he appears in his grandeur and majesty.

But let us return to Hiero. He also tells how many disadvantages he feels in his royalty, since he cannot go about and travel freely, being like a prisoner within the limits of his country, and since in all

his actions he finds himself surrounded by an annoying crowd. Indeed, seeing our kings all alone at table, besieged by so many unknowns talking and staring, I have often felt more pity than envy of them.

^BKing Alfonso used to say that in this respect asses were better off than kings: their masters let them eat in peace, whereas kings cannot obtain that favor of their servants.

^AAnd it has never struck me that it was any special advantage in the life of a man of understanding to have some twenty people watching him go to the toilet, nor that the services of a man with an income of ten thousand pounds, or who has taken Casale or defended Siena, are more convenient and acceptable to him than those of a good and experienced valet.

^BThe advantages of princes are quasi-imaginary advantages. Every degree of fortune has in it some semblance of the princely. Caesar calls all the lords having jurisdiction in France in his time kinglets. In truth, except for the title of Sire, some people keep pace quite a way with our kings. Notice, in the provinces remote from the court, let's say Brittany for example, the retinue, the subjects, the officers, the occupations, the service and ceremony of a retired and stay-at-home lord, brought up among his servants. And also see the flight of his imagination: there is nothing more kingly. He hears speak of his master once a year, as if of the king of Persia, and acknowledges him only by some ancient cousinship of which his secretary keeps a record. In truth, our laws are free enough, and the weight of sovereignty scarcely touches a French nobleman twice in his life. The real and essential subjection is only for those among us who go seeking it and who like to gain honors and riches by such service; for anyone who wants to ensconce himself by his hearth, and who can manage his house without quarrels and lawsuits, is as free as the Doge of Venice: ^C*Slavery holds but few; many hold fast to slavery* [Seneca].

^ABut above all Hiero emphasizes the fact that he finds himself deprived of all mutual friendship and society, wherein consists the sweetest and most perfect fruit of human life. For what testimony of affection and good will can I extract from a man who, willy-nilly, owes me everything he can do? Can I take any stock in his humble speech and courteous reverence, seeing that it is not in his power to refuse me them? The honor we receive from those who fear us is not honor; these respects are due to royalty, not to me:

^BThe greatest thing in rule is this,
That subjects are required not only to endure
But to applaud their master's deeds. SENECA

^ADo I not see that the wicked and the good king, the one they hate and the one they love, are honored equally? With the same show, the same ceremony, my predecessor was served, and my successor will be. If my subjects do not harm me, that is no evidence of their good will; why should I take it as such, since they could not harm me even if they would? No one follows me for any friendship there may be between him and me; for no friendship can be knit where there is so little relation and correspondence. My elevation has placed me outside of human association: there is too much disparity and disproportion. They follow me by countenance and custom, or, rather than me, my fortune, to increase their own. All they say to me and do for me is only powder and paint. Their liberty being bridled on all sides by the great power I have over them, I see nothing around me except what is covered and masked.

One day the Emperor Julian's courtiers were praising him for being so just. "I would readily take pride in these praises," he said, "if they came from people who dared to accuse or dispraise my unjust actions, if there should be any."

^BAll the real advantages that princes have are shared by men of moderate fortune (it is for the gods to ride winged horses and feed on ambrosia): they have no other sleep or other appetite than ours; their steel is of no better temper than what we use for our armor; their crown covers them from neither the sun nor the rain. Diocletian, who wore a crown so revered and so favored by fortune, resigned it to retire to the pleasure of private life; and some time after, the exigencies of public affairs requiring that he return and resume his charge, he replied to those who were begging him to do so: "You would not ask this of me if you had seen the beautiful rows of trees that I myself have planted at home, and the fine melons I have sown."

In the opinion of Anacharsis, the best government would be one in which, all other things being equal, precedence was measured out according to virtue, and rejection according to vice.

^AWhen King Pyrrhus was undertaking his expedition into Italy, Cyneas, his wise counselor, wanting to make him feel the vanity of his ambition, asked him: "Well, Sire, to what purpose are you

setting up this great enterprise?" "To make myself master of Italy,"
he immediately replied. "And then," continued Cyneas, "when that
is done?" "I shall pass over into Gaul and Spain," said the other. "And
after that?" "I shall go and subdue Africa; and finally, when I have
brought the world under my subjection, I shall rest and live content
and at my ease." "In God's name, Sire," Cyneas then retorted, "tell
me what keeps you from being in that condition right now, if that is
what you want. Why don't you settle down at this very moment in
the state you say you aspire to, and spare yourself all the intervening
toil and risks?"

> Because he does not know the bounds of gain,
> And where true pleasure stops, and starts to wane.
>
> LUCRETIUS

I will conclude this piece with this old line that I think is
singularly fine and to the purpose: *Each man's character shapes his
fortune* [Cornelius Nepos].

43
Of sumptuary laws

^A^The way in which our laws try to regulate vain and insane expen-
ditures for the table and for clothes seems to be opposed to
their purpose. The real way would be to engender in men contempt
for gold and silk, as vain and useless things; whereas we increase
their honor and value, which is a very inept way to make men
lose their taste for them. For to say that none but princes ^c^shall
eat turbot, or ^A^shall be allowed to wear velvet and gold braid,
and to forbid them to the people, what else is this but to give
prestige to these things and increase everyone's desire to enjoy
them? Let kings boldly abandon these marks of greatness;
they have enough others; such excesses are more excusable in any
other than in a prince. From the example of many nations we may
learn enough better ways of distinguishing ourselves and our
rank externally (which I truly believe to be very necessary in
a state), without for this purpose fostering such manifest corruption
and harm.

It is amazing how easily and quickly custom, in these indifferent
things, establishes the footing of its authority. It is a fact that when
we had hardly been a year wearing broadcloth at court in mourning

for King Henry II, silks had already sunk so low in everyone's opinion that if you saw anyone dressed in them you immediately set him down as a bourgeois. They had been left to the physicians and surgeons; and although everyone was dressed about alike, still in other ways there were plenty of obvious distinctions between men's ranks.

[B]How quickly are dirty doublets of chamois and linen coming into honor in our armies, and elegance and richness of dress into reproach and contempt!

[A]Let kings begin to abandon these expenses, and all will be done with in a month, without edict or ordinance: we shall all go along after. The law should say, contrary to what it says now, that gold ornaments and crimson are forbidden to all kinds of people except mountebanks and courtesans. With such a device Zaleucus corrected the corrupted manners of the Locrians. His ordinances were these: that a free woman may not be attended by more than one chambermaid except when she is drunk, nor may she go outside the city at night, or wear gold jewels about her person, or an embroidered dress, unless she is a public whore; and that except for pimps, no man is allowed to wear a gold ring on his finger, or a dainty robe of the sort made of the cloth woven in the city of Miletus. And thus, by these shameful exceptions, he ingeniously diverted his citizens from pernicious superfluities and luxuries. [B]This was a very useful way of attracting men to obedience by honor and ambition.

Our kings can do anything they want in such outer reforms: their inclination serves as law. [C]*Whatever princes do, they seem to command* [Quintilian]. [B]The rest of France takes as its rule the rule of the court. Let them get sick of that ugly codpiece that so openly shows our secret parts; of that heavy stuffing of doublets that makes us look completely different than we are, and that is so inconvenient for putting on armor; those long effeminate tresses of hair; of that custom of kissing whatever we present to our friends and kissing our hands in greeting them, a ceremony formerly due to princes alone; of seeing a gentleman appear, in a place calling for respect, without his sword at his side, all slovenly and untidy, as if he were coming from the toilet; and of our standing bareheaded – contrary to the ways of our fathers and the particular privilege of the nobility of this kingdom – at a long distance around our kings, wherever they may be, and not only around them but around a hundred others, so many kinglets and semi-kinglets do we have;

and so with other, similar newly introduced and vicious practices: they will soon be seen to vanish and be decried. These are superficial errors, but still they augur badly; we are warned that the solid masonry is crumbling when we see the plaster and coating of our walls cracking.

^cPlato, in his *Laws*, considers no plague in the world more harmful to his city than this: to let the young change at will from one fashion to another in dress, gestures, dances, exercises, and songs, shifting their judgment now to this position, now to that, running after novelties and honoring their inventors; whereby morals are corrupted and all ancient institutions come into disdain and contempt. In all things except those that are simply bad, change is to be feared: change of seasons, winds, food, and humors. And no laws are held in their true honor except those to which God has given some ancient duration, so that no one knows their origin or that they were ever different.

44
Of sleep

^AReason orders us always to go on the same path, but not always at the same pace. And whereas the sage should not allow human passions to make him deviate from the right course, he may well, without prejudice to his duty, let them hasten or retard his steps, and not plant himself like an immobile and impassible Colossus. Even if Virtue herself were incarnate, I think her pulse would beat stronger going to the attack than going to dinner; indeed it is necessary that she should be heated and stirred. For this reason it has struck me as a rare thing to see sometimes that great men remain so entirely poised, in the loftiest undertakings and most important affairs, as not even to curtail their sleep.

Alexander the Great, on the day appointed for that furious battle against Darius, slept so deeply and so late in the morning that Parmenio was forced to enter his chamber, and, approaching his bed, to call him two or three times by name to wake him, the hour of battle being at hand.

The Emperor Otho resolved one day to kill himself that very night. After putting his domestic affairs in order, dividing his money among his servants, and sharpening the edge of the sword he intended to use, and while waiting only to hear that all his friends

had retired in safety, he fell into so deep a sleep that his chamber servants heard him snore.

The death of that emperor has about it many things like that of the great Cato, and this point especially. For while Cato, who was ready to do away with himself, was waiting to be informed whether the senators he was sending away had got clear of the port of Utica, he fell so sound asleep that they could hear him breathing from the next room; and when the man he had sent to the port waked him to tell him that a storm was keeping the senators from setting sail conveniently, he sent still another man there, and snuggling back into bed, fell asleep again and slept until this last man assured him of their departure.

And in that great and dangerous storm that the sedition of the tribune Metellus brought down upon Cato, we may again compare him to Alexander. Metellus insisted on publishing the decree recalling Pompey to the city with his army at the time of Catiline's conspiracy; which decree Cato alone opposed, and Metellus and he exchanged strong words and great threats in the Senate. But it was on the next day that the plan was to be executed, in the public square. Metellus would arrive there accompanied not only by the favor of the people and of Caesar, who was then conspiring in Pompey's interest, but also by many foreign slaves and gladiators who would stop at nothing; Cato would come fortified with his courage alone. In consequence his relations, his household, and many good people were very anxious about him, and there were some who spent the night together without wanting to rest, or eat or drink, because of the danger they saw in store for him; his wife and sisters in particular did nothing but weep and torment themselves in his house. He, on the contrary, comforted everybody; and after having supped as usual, went to bed and slept very soundly until morning, when one of his fellow tribunes came and woke him to go to the skirmish. The knowledge we have of the greatness of this man's courage from the rest of his life enables us to judge with complete certainty that his behavior proceeded from a soul elevated so far above such accidents that he did not deign to let them worry him any more than ordinary disturbances.

In the naval battle that Augustus won against Sextus Pompeius in Sicily, on the point of going into battle, he found himself overcome by such a deep sleep that his friends had to wake him to give the signal for battle. That gave Mark Antony occasion to reproach him afterward for not having had the courage even to look with

open eyes at the array of his army, and for not having dared to present himself to his soldiers until Agrippa came to announce to him the news of the victory he had won over his enemies.

But as for young Marius, he did even worse – for on the day of his last battle against Sulla, after drawing up his army and giving the word and signal for battle, he lay down under a tree in the shade to rest, and fell so fast asleep that he could hardly be awakened by the rout and flight of his men, and saw nothing of the combat. They say this happened because he was so extremely weighed down from work and lack of sleep that nature could hold out no longer.

And in this connection, let the doctors determine whether sleep is so necessary that our life depends on it. For we certainly find that they put to death King Perseus of Macedonia, when he was a prisoner in Rome, by preventing him from sleeping; but Pliny instances people who lived a long time without sleep. ᶜIn Herodotus there are nations in which the men sleep and wake by half-years. And those who write the life of the sage Epimenides say that he slept for fifty-seven years on end.

45
Of the battle of Dreux

ᴬThere were plenty of unusual incidents in our battle of Dreux; but those who do not strongly favor the reputation of Monsieur de Guise are fond of averring that he cannot be excused for having halted and temporized with the forces under his command while the Constable, the commander-in-chief of the army, was being smashed by the artillery; and that it would have been better for him to take the risk of attacking the enemy by the flank, than to suffer so heavy a loss by waiting for the advantage of catching them from the rear. But besides what the outcome proved, whoever will discuss this without passion will readily confess, in my opinion, that the goal and aim not only of a captain but of every soldier must be the victory as a whole, and that no particular occurrences, of whatever interest to himself, should divert him from that goal.

When Philopoemen, in an encounter with Machanidas, sent ahead a good force of archers and darters to begin the skirmish, the enemy, after bowling them over, wasted their time pursuing them at full speed, and after their victory passed right by the

battalion where Philopoemen was. Though his soldiers were impatient, he thought it best not to budge from his position or face the enemy to succor his men; but after letting them be chased and cut to pieces before his eyes, he began his attack on the enemy by charging their infantry battalion, when he saw them completely abandoned by their cavalry. And although they were Lacedaemonians, nonetheless, because he caught them at a moment when they thought the battle won, and were beginning to fall into disorder, he easily got the better of them, and, that done, started in pursuit of Machanidas. This case is germane to that of Monsieur de Guise.

[B]In the bitter battle of Agesilaus against the Boeotians, which Xenophon, who was there, said was the toughest he had ever seen, Agesilaus refused the advantage which fortune presented to him of letting the Boeotian battalion pass and charging them from the rear. Though he foresaw certain victory in this course, he felt that there was more craft than valor in it; and to show his prowess, he chose rather with astonishingly ardent courage to attack them head on. But he was well beaten and wounded in the process, and finally constrained to disengage himself and take the course he had refused at the beginning; he opened his ranks to give passage to the torrent of Boeotians; then, when they had passed, noting that they were marching in disorder like people who certainly thought they were out of all danger, he pursued them and charged them on the flanks. But for all that, he could not put them to flight and rout them completely; rather they retreated slowly, always showing their teeth, until they had reached safety.

46
Of names

[A]Whatever variety of herbs there may be, the whole thing is included under the name of salad. Likewise, under the consideration of names, I am here going to whip up a hodgepodge of various items.

Each nation has certain names which, I know not why, are taken in a bad sense: with us, Jean, Guillaume, Benoît.

Item, in the genealogy of princes there seem to be certain names earmarked by fate, as that of the Ptolemies in Egypt, the Henrys in England, the Charleses in France, the Baldwins in Flanders, and in our ancient Aquitania the Williams (*Guillaumes*), from whom the

name of Guienne is said to come; by a strained coincidence, were
there not as crude ones in Plato himself.

Item, it is a trifling thing, but nevertheless worth remembering
for its strangeness, and written down by an eyewitness, that Henry,
duke of Normandy, son of Henry II, king of England, held a feast in
France where the assembly of nobles was so great that when they
divided up for sport into groups according to the similarity of
names, in the first company, that of the Williams, there were seated
at table a hundred and ten knights bearing that name, without
counting the ordinary gentlemen and servants.

[B]This idea of assigning the tables according to the guests' names
is as amusing as that of the Emperor Geta, who based the distribu-
tion of his courses on the first letters of the various dishes' names:
they served together those that began with M, mutton, mackerel,
mallard, mushrooms; and so with the rest.

[A]Item, there is a saying that it is a good thing to have a good
name, that is to say credit and reputation. But also, in truth, it is
advantageous to have a handsome name and one that is easy to
pronounce and retain, for thereby kings and grandees recognize us
more easily and are less apt to forget us; and even with our own
servants, we more ordinarily call on and employ those whose names
come easiest to the tongue. I have observed that King Henry II could
never call by his right name a gentleman from this part of Gascony;
and to one of the queen's maids of honor he even proposed to give
the general name of her family, because that of her father's house
seemed to him too awkward. [C]And Socrates considers it worthy of
a father's care to give his children attractive names.

[A]Item, they say that the foundation of Notre-Dame la Grand' at
Poitiers took its origin from the fact that a dissipated young man
living on that spot, having picked up a wench and promptly asked
her name, which was Marie, felt himself so violently smitten with
religion and awe of that sacrosanct name of the Virgin Mother of
our Savior, that he not only sent the girl away but reformed all the
rest of his life; and that in consideration of this miracle there was
built, on the spot where this young man's house was, a chapel in the
name of Our Lady, and, later on, the church that we see there.

[C]This vocal and auricular reproof, of a religious sort, went
straight to the soul. This other, of the same kind, insinuated itself
through the bodily senses: Pythagoras, being in company with some
young men who were heated with feasting, and whom he perceived
to be conspiring to go and violate a house of chaste women,

commanded the minstrel girl to change her tone, and by a solemn, grave, and spondaic music gently cast a spell on their ardor and put it to sleep.

[A]Item, will not posterity say that our present-day reformation has been fastidious and precise, not only to have combated errors and vices and filled the world with devotion, humility, obedience, peace, and every sort of virtue, but to have gone so far as to combat our ancient baptismal names, Charles, Louis, François, in order to populate the world with Methuselahs, Ezekiels, and Malachis, which smack much more of the faith? A gentleman neighbor of mine, estimating the advantages of the olden times in comparison with ours, did not forget to place in account the pride and magnificence of the names of the nobility of those days, Don Grumedan, Quedragan, Agesilan, and the fact that in merely hearing them sounded he felt that they had been very different people from Pierre, Guillot, and Michel.

Item, I am very grateful to Jacques Amyot for having left the Latin names entire in the course of a work in French, without coloring and changing them to give them a French cadence. This seemed a little harsh at first, but already usage, by the authority of his Plutarch, has taken away all its strangeness for us. I have often wished that those who write histories in Latin would leave us all our names just as they are; for when they make Vallemontanus out of Vaudemont, and metamorphose them to dress them out Greek or Roman style, we don't know where we are, and lose our knowledge of them.

To close our account, it is a base practice, and of very bad consequence in our France, to call everyone by the name of his land and lordship; nothing in the world causes more confusion and misconceptions about families. A younger son of good family cannot honorably abandon an estate that has been settled on him and by whose name he has been known and honored. Ten years after his death the estate goes to a stranger, who does the same with it: guess where this leaves us when it comes to knowing who these men are. We need seek no other examples than those of our own royal family: so many divisions, so many surnames; meanwhile the original of the stock has escaped us.

[B]There is so much liberty in these mutations that in my time I have not seen anyone elevated by fortune to any extraordinary greatness who has not promptly taken on new genealogical titles not known to his father, and been grafted onto some illustrious

stock. And, by good luck, the most obscure families are the best suited to falsification. How many gentlemen have we in France who are of royal blood by their account? More, I believe, than the others.

Was not this well said by one of my friends? There were several gentlemen assembled to discuss a dispute between two of their number, one of whom had in truth some precedence in titles and alliances that raised him above the ordinary nobility. On the subject of this precedence, everyone, trying to make himself this gentleman's equal, alleged, one man one origin, another another, one a resemblance in name, another in coat of arms, another some old family document; and the least of them found himself great-grandson of some king from beyond the seas. When it was time for dinner, my friend, instead of taking his place, retreated with deep bows, begging the company to excuse him for having, in his temerity, lived with them until then as a companion; but saying that now, having been recently informed of their ancient quality, he was beginning to honor them according to their rank, and that it was not for him to sit among so many princes. After this farce, he abused them freely: "Be content, in God's name, with ᶜwhat contented our fathers, and with ᴮwhat we are. We are good enough, if we know how to maintain our rank properly. Let us not disown the fortune and condition of our forefathers, and let us put away these stupid pretensions, which no one can lack who has the impudence to put them forward."

Coats of arms have no more security than surnames. I bear azure powdered with trefoils or, with a lion's paw of the same, armed gules in fesse. What privilege has this design to remain privately in my house? A son-in-law will transport it into another family; some paltry buyer will make of it his first coat of arms; there is nothing in which more change and confusion is found.

ᴬBut this consideration draws me perforce into another field. Let us probe a little closer, and in God's name consider to what foundation we attach this glory and reputation for which the world is turned upside down. On what do we establish this renown that we go seeking with such great pains? After all, it is Peter or William who bears it, guards it, and is concerned with it. ᶜOh, what a brave faculty is hope, which, in a mortal subject and in a moment, usurps infinity, immensity, eternity! Nature has given us an amusing toy there. ᴬAnd this Peter or William, what is that, when all is said and

done, but a sound, or three or four strokes of a pen, so easy to vary in the first place that I would like to ask who received the honor of so many victories, Guesquin, Glesquin, or Gueaquin?[1] There would be a lot better grounds here than in Lucian for Σ to bring suit against T, for

> Not for slight or merely sporting stakes
> Do they compete.
> VIRGIL

This is a serious business. The question is which of these letters is to be paid for so many sieges, battles, wounds, prisons, and so many services performed for the crown of France by that famous Constable of hers.

Nicolas Denisot concerned himself only with the letters of his name, and changed their whole arrangement to make of them the Conte d'Alsinois, whom he endowed with the glory of his poetry and painting. And the historian Suetonius liked only the meaning of his, and having deprived it of Lenis, which was his father's surname, left Transquillus successor to the reputation of his writings. Who would believe that Captain Bayard had no honor but what he borrowed from the deeds of Pierre Terrail? And that Antoine Escalin should let himself be robbed right under his eyes of so many navigations and commands on sea and land by Captain Poulin and Baron de la Garde?

Second, these are pen strokes common to a thousand men. How many people are there in every family with the same name and surname? ^CAnd in different families, centuries, and countries, how many? History has known three Socrateses, five Platos, eight Aristotles, seven Xenophons, twenty Demetriuses, twenty Theodores; and just guess how many it has not known.

^AWhat prevents my groom from calling himself Pompey the Great? But after all, even if he does, what means or powers exist that can attach and join this glorious sound or the honored pen strokes that represent this name to my groom when he is dead, or to that other Pompey who had his head cut off in Egypt, in such a way that they can get advantage out of them?

> Do you think buried ghosts, or ashes, care for this?
> VIRGIL

[1] These are a few of the known forms of the name of Bertrand du Guesclin, a great French commander in the Hundred Years' War.

ᶜWhat perception have the two who share the leadership in valor among men, Epaminondas of this glorious verse in his praise that is current in our mouths,

> And by my plans was Sparta's glory shorn,
> QUOTED BY CICERO

and Africanus of this other:

> From where the sun rises o'er Lake Maeotis' reeds
> There is no man alive able to match my deeds.
> QUOTED BY CICERO

Survivors, tickled by the sweetness of words like these and incited by them to emulation and desire, unthinkingly transfer to the deceased, in their imagination, this feeling of their own, and delude themselves into believing that they will be capable of such a feeling in their turn. God knows!

ᴬAt all events,

> To this end
> Roman, barbarian, Greek chiefs did contend,
> Endured all risks and labors with this aim,
> So much more burning is the thirst for fame
> Than that for virtue.
> JUVENAL

47
Of the uncertainty of our judgment

ᴬIt is just as this verse says:

> Wide is the range of words, on one side and the other,
> HOMER

there is much to be said on all matters, both for and against. For example:

> Hannibal conquered, but he never knew
> How best to profit by his victories.
> PETRARCH

Whoever wants to take this side and bring out to our people the mistake of not having pursued our advantage recently at

Moncontour, or accuse the king of Spain of not having known how to use the advantage he had over us at Saint-Quentin, may say that these mistakes proceeded from a soul intoxicated with its good fortune, and from that spirit in which a man, filled to the brim with the beginning of success, loses his appetite for increasing it, being already too much involved in digesting what he has. He has his arms full, he can grasp no more, unworthy that fortune should have placed such a prize in his hands. For what profit does he realize if nevertheless he gives his enemy the means of recovering? What hope can one have that another time he will dare attack them when they have rallied and recovered and are armed anew with anger and revenge, when he dared not, or did not know enough to, pursue them when they all were routed and terrified?

> While fortune glows, while terror weakens all.
>
> LUCAN

But after all, what better can he expect than what he has just lost? It is not like in fencing, where the number of hits decides the victory: as long as the enemy is on his feet, you have to start over again; it is not a victory if it does not end the war. In that skirmish where Caesar got the worst of it near the city of Oricum, he made this criticism to Pompey's soldiers, that he would have been lost if their captain had known how to conquer; and he put on Pompey's spurs for him in a very different way when it was his turn.

But why not add the contrary: that it is the act of a hasty and insatiable spirit not to know how to set a limit to its greed; that it is abusing God's favors to try to stretch them beyond the measure that he has prescribed for them; that to rush back into danger after victory is to place it once again at the mercy of fortune; and that one of the greatest pieces of wisdom in the art of war is not to drive one's enemy to despair. Sulla and Marius, after defeating the Marsi in the Social War, seeing one last troop of them returning in despair to charge them like infuriated beasts, did not think it best to await them. If Monsieur de Foix had not been carried away by his ardor to pursue too fiercely the stragglers from the victory of Ravenna, he would not have sullied it by his death. However, the memory of his recent example did serve to save Monsieur d'Enghien from the same misfortune at Ceresole.

It is dangerous to attack a man whom you have deprived of every other means of escape but that of weapons; for necessity is a violent

schoolmistress: ᶜ*most grievous are the bites of enraged necessity* [Porcius Latro].

ᴮThe man prepared to die will not be beaten cheaply.

LUCAN

ᶜThat is why Pharax prevented the king of Lacedaemon, who had just won the day against the Mantineans, from going and provoking a thousand Argives who had escaped intact from the defeat, and instead had him let them slip away freely so as not to test a valor goaded and infuriated by misfortune. ᴬClodomir, king of Aquitania, pursuing after his victory Gondemar, king of Burgundy, who was conquered and fleeing, forced him to face about; but his obstinacy deprived him of the fruit of his victory, for he was killed.

Likewise, if one had to choose whether to keep one's soldiers richly and sumptuously armed or armed only for necessity, it could be advanced in favor of the first course – which was that of Sertorius, Philopoemen, Brutus, Caesar, and others – that it is always a spur to honor and glory for a soldier to see himself adorned, and a stimulus to greater obstinacy in combat, since he has to save his arms as his property and inheritance: ᶜthe reason, says Xenophon, why the Asiatics in their wars took along wives and concubines with their dearest jewels and treasures.

ᴬIt could be argued on the other side, however, that a soldier's care for self-preservation should be rather diminished than increased; for the richly arrayed soldier will be doubly afraid of risking himself. Besides, these rich spoils increase the enemy's craving for victory; and it has been noted that in other days this wonderfully encouraged the Romans against the Samnites. ᴮAntiochus, showing Hannibal the army that he was preparing against them, pompous and magnificent in all sorts of equipment, asked him: "Will the Romans be content with this army?" "Will they be content?" he replied. "I should certainly think so, however greedy they may be." ᴬLycurgus forbade his soldiers not only sumptuousness in their equipment, but also to despoil their conquered enemies, wanting, he said, their poverty and frugality to shine as bright as everything else in the battle.

In sieges and other situations where the occasion brings us close to the enemy, we are prone to give the soldiers license to defy, taunt, and insult them with all sorts of abuse, and not without apparent reason. For it is no small accomplishment to deprive our men of all hope of mercy and conciliation by showing them that there is no

further reason to expect these from anyone whom they have so strongly outraged, and that no remedy remains except victory. Yet his turned out badly for Vitellius when he encountered Otho, though Otho's soldiers were weaker in quality, being long unaccustomed to war and softened up by the pleasures of the city. Vitellius finally irritated them so much by his stinging words, reproaching them with their pusillanimity and their regret for the ladies and feasts that they had just left behind in Rome, that he put hearts back into their stomachs again, as no exhortations had been able to do, and himself brought them down upon him, whither no one had been able to push them. And indeed, when they are insults that touch to the quick, they can easily make a man whose labors in his king's quarrel were fainthearted go to it with a different sort of temper for his own quarrel.

Considering how important it is to safeguard the leader of an army, and that the enemy's aim is chiefly directed at this head, whom all the others hold to and depend on, it seems that one cannot question this course, which we see has been adopted by many great leaders, of changing attire and disguising themselves on the point of battle. However, the disadvantage incurred by this means is no less than the one which we think to avoid; for, when the captain is unrecognized by his men, the courage they derive from his example and presence fails them; and losing sight of his customary marks and insignia, they judge him either to be dead or to have fled in despair of success. And as for experience, we see it favor now one side, now the other. What happened to Pyrrhus in the battle he fought against the consul Laevinus in Italy serves for both points of view; for by having decided to hide under the armor of Demogacles [Megacles] and given him his own, he indeed and unquestionably saved his life, but at the same time he nearly incurred the other misfortune of losing the battle. ^cAlexander, Caesar, and Lucullus liked to be marked in battle by rich arms and accouterments of a particular shining color; Agis, Agesilaus, and the great Gylippus, on the contrary, used to go to war obscurely covered and without the trappings of command.

^AAmong other criticisms made against Pompey at the battle of Pharsalia is that he halted his army and awaited the enemy at a standstill. "Because" (here I shall steal Plutarch's very words, which are better than mine) "that weakens the violence which running gives to the first blows and at the same time takes away that rush of the combatants against one another which usually more

than anything else fills them with impetuosity and fury when they come to clash hard, increasing their courage by the shouting and the running; and it makes the soldiers' ardor chilled and congealed, so to speak." This is what he says on that subject. But if Caesar had lost, might not the contrary have been said just as well: that the strongest and stiffest posture is that in which a man stands planted without budging, and that whoever has stopped in his march, holding in and saving up his strength within himself for the time of need, has a great advantage over one who is in motion and has already wasted half his breath in running? Besides, an army, being a body made up of so many different parts, cannot possibly move with such precision in this fury as not to alter or break up its battle array, or in such a way that the swiftest will not be at grips before his companion comes to support him.

ᶜIn that ugly battle between the two Persian brothers, Clearchus, a Lacedaemonian, who commanded the Greeks of Cyrus' side, led them deliberately to the charge without hurrying; but at fifty paces away he put them on the run, hoping in that short distance to keep both their order and their breath, while giving them the advantage of the impetus both for themselves and for their missiles. ᴬOthers have settled this doubt by instructing their army in this manner: if the enemies rush upon you, await them with firm foot; if they await you with firm foot, rush upon them.

When the Emperor Charles V made his expedition into Provence, King Francis was in a position to choose between going to meet him in Italy and awaiting him in his own territories. To be sure, he considered how much of an advantage it is to keep one's house pure and clear of the troubles of war, so that, intact in its resources, it can continually furnish money and help when needed; and how the necessity of war involves laying waste at every turn, which cannot be done to good purpose in our own properties; and moreover how the peasant does not endure as mildly this ravaging by those of his own side as by the enemy, so that seditions and troubles might thereby be easily kindled among us. He further reflected that the license to rob and pillage, which cannot be tolerated in one's own country, is a great support against the hardships of war, and that it is hard to keep a man to his duty who has no other hope of gain than his pay when he is only two steps away from his wife and home; that he who lays the tablecloth always pays the bill; that there is more alacrity to attack than to defend; that the shock of the loss of a battle in our country's

entrails is so violent that it is hard for it not to bring down the whole body, seeing that there is no passion so contagious as that of fear, nor so easily caught on faith, nor quicker to spread; and that cities that have heard the roar of this tempest at their gates, that have taken in their captains and soldiers still trembling and out of breath, are in danger, in the heat of the moment, of rushing into some ill-chosen course of action. Nonetheless, he chose to recall the forces he had beyond the mountains and to watch the enemy come to him.

For he may have imagined on the other hand that being at home and among his friends, he could not fail to have plenty of all commodities (the rivers and passes, being his, would bring him both provisions and money safely and without need of escort); that his subjects would be the more devoted to him, the nearer the danger was to them; and that with so many towns and barriers to protect him, he could give battle according to his own opportunity and advantage. And moreover, that if it pleased him to temporize, he could remain at ease and under cover, and watch his enemies get chilled and defeat themselves by reason of the difficulties that would beset them, being engaged in a hostile country, with nothing before or behind or on either side that would not make war on them; with no way to refresh or free their army if diseases broke out, or to lodge their wounded in safety; with no money, no food, except at lance-point; no leisure to rest and catch their breath; no knowledge of the places or the terrain to secure them from ambushes and surprises; and if they should lose a battle, no way to save the remains of their army. And there was no lack of examples on both sides.

Scipio thought it much better to go and attack his enemy's territory in Africa than to defend his own and fight in Italy where he was; and this worked out well for him. On the other hand, Hannibal, in that same war, ruined himself by abandoning the conquest of a foreign country to go and defend his own. The Athenians, having left the enemy in their territory to go over into Sicily, had Fortune against them; but Agathocles, king of Syracuse, found her favorable when he crossed over into Africa and left the war at home.

Thus we are quite wont to say, with reason, that events and outcomes depend for the most part, especially in war, on Fortune, who will not fall into line and subject herself to our reason and foresight, as these lines say:

The ill-advised may win; the wise may lose;
Fortune cares not what cause prevails, or whose,
But wanders in our midst, unheeding, free.
Something beyond, whatever it may be,
Commands and rules, and bends us to its laws.

MANILIUS

But if you take it rightly, it seems that our counsels and deliberations depend just as much on Fortune, and that she involves our reason also in her confusion and uncertainty. ^C"We reason rashly and inconsiderately," says Timaeus in Plato, "because, like ourselves, our reason has in it a large element of chance."

48
Of war horses

^AHere I am turned grammarian, I who never learned a language except by rote, and who still do not know what is an adjective, subjunctive, or ablative. I seem to have heard that the Romans had horses that they called *funales* or *dextrarios*, which were led on the right or used in relays, so as to get them quite fresh when needed; whence it comes that we call service horses *destriers*. And our romances ordinarily say *adestrer* for accompany. They also had *desultorios equos*, horses trained in such a way that, while they were running at top speed side by side without bridle or saddle, the Roman nobles, even fully armed, would throw themselves back and forth from one to the other in full career. ^CThe Numidian men-at-arms would lead by hand a second horse to change in the heat of the melee: *whose custom it was, in the manner of circus-riders, leading two horses, in the heat of battle often to jump fully armed from a tired horse to a fresh one: such was the agility of the men and the docile breed of horses* [Livy].

There are many horses trained to help their masters, to rush upon anyone who wields a drawn sword at them, to hurl themselves with feet and teeth on those who attack and confront them; but they turn out to hurt their friends more often than their enemies. Besides, you cannot call them off at will when they once have come to grips, and you remain at the mercy of their combat. It turned out very grievously for Artybius, general of the Persian army, who was fighting man to man against Onesilus, king of Salamis, to

be mounted on a horse trained in this school, for it was the cause of his death; the squire of Onesilus met the horse with a falchion between the shoulders as it reared up against his master. And what the Italians report, that in the battle of Fornova the king's horse, by volleys of kicks, freed him from the enemies that were pressing upon him, and that otherwise he would have been lost – that was a great stroke of luck, if it is true.

The Mamelukes boast of having the cleverest cavalry horses in the world. And it is said that by nature and habit they are trained, at certain signals and words, to pick up lances and darts with their teeth and offer them to their master in the midst of the melee, and to know and distinguish the enemy.[1]

^AThey say of Caesar, and also of Pompey the Great, that among their other excellent qualities they were very good horsemen; and of Caesar that in his youth, mounted bareback, without a bridle, and with his hands behind his back, he would make a horse run full speed. As Nature willed to make of that man and Alexander two miracles of military art, so you would say that she also made an effort to arm them extraordinarily: for everyone knows that Alexander's horse Bucephalus had a head resembling that of a bull, that he would allow no one but his master to mount him, could be broken only by him, was honored after his death, and had a city built in his name. Caesar too had one whose forefeet were like a man's, with the hoof divided in the shape of toes, a horse which could be mounted and broken only by Caesar, who after his death dedicated his statue to the goddess Venus.

I do not like to dismount when I am on horseback, for that is the position in which I feel best, healthy or sick. ^CPlato recommends it for health; ^APliny, too, says that it is good for the stomach and the joints. Let's go on then, since we are here.

We read in Xenophon a law forbidding any man who had a horse to travel on foot. Trogus and Justinus say that the Parthians mounted horses not only to make war, but also for all their public and private business, trading, negotiating, conversing, and taking the air; and that the most notable difference between free men and slaves among them was that the former went on horseback, the latter on foot: ^Can institution born of King Cyrus.

[1] The Bordeaux Copy is slightly clipped here and incomplete. The 1595 edition slightly rearranges the material in this paragraph, and adds, after "the enemy": "on whom they must hurl themselves with teeth and feet."

^AThere are several examples in Roman history (and Suetonius notes it most particularly of Caesar) of captains who on pressing occasions would command their horsemen to dismount, to deprive the soldiers of all hope of flight, ^Cand for the advantage they hoped for in this sort of combat, *in which the Roman soldier undoubtedly excels*, says Livy. Yet the first thing the Romans did to bridle the rebellion of newly conquered peoples was to take away their arms and horses; wherefore we see so often in Caesar: *he orders the arms to be delivered, the horses produced, hostages given.* The Grand Turk to this day permits no Christian or Jew, of those who are under his rule, to have his own horse.

^AOur ancestors, especially in the time of the wars with the English, in all serious engagements and pitched battles, fought most of the time on foot, so as to trust to nothing but their own strength and the vigor of their courage and their limbs for anything as dear as honor and life. ^CNo matter what Chrysanthas in Xeno-phon says, ^Ayou stake your valor and your fortune on that of your horse; his wounds and his death bring on yours as a consequence; his fright or his impetuosity make you either rash or cowardly; if he fails to respond to bit or spur, it is your honor that must answer for it. For that reason I do not find it strange that those infantry engage-ments were stouter and more furious than those that are fought on horseback:

> ^BTogether they drew back, together charged,
> Victors and vanquished both knew naught of flight.
>
> VIRGIL

^CWe can see that their battles were much better contested; today there are nothing but routs: *the first shout and onset decides the affair* [Livy]. ^AAnd a thing that we call on to share such great risks with us must be in our power as much as possible. Just as I should advise the choice of the shortest weapons, and those that we can answer for best. It is much more sensible to rely on a sword that we hold in our hand than on the bullet that escapes out of our pistol, in which there are many parts – the powder, the flint, the lock – the least of which, by failing, will make your fortune fail. ^BYou strike with little cer-tainty the blow that the air carries for you:

> Let the winds waft their blows where'er they will.
> A sword has strength; and every manly race
> Makes war with swords.
>
> LUCAN

[A]But as for the pistol, I shall speak of it more amply when I make a comparison of ancient arms with ours; and except for the shock to the ear, with which by now everyone has become familiar, I think it is a weapon of very little effect, and hope that some day we shall abandon the use of it.

[C]The one the Italians used as a missile and a firearm was more frightful. They called *phalarica* a certain type of javelin, armed at the point with three feet of iron, so that it could pierce an armed man through and through; and it was hurled sometimes by hand in the field, sometimes by machines in defense of besieged places. The shaft, covered with flax soaked in pitch and oil, caught fire in its flight, and, sticking into a man's body or buckler, took away all use of weapons or limbs. However, it seems to me that for coming to close quarters, it would also give hindrance to the assailant, and that the field, strewn with these burning stumps, would bring a disadvantage to both sides in the melee:

> But, hissing loud, a whirled phalarica
> Sped like a thunderbolt.
> VIRGIL

They had other devices, in which custom made them skillful, and which seem incredible to us through our inexperience, whereby they made up for the lack of our powder and bullets. They hurled their javelins with such power that they often transfixed two bucklers and two armed men with them, and pinned them together. The shots of their slings were no less accurate and far-reaching: *shooting round stones from their sling over the open sea and being trained to hit a circle of moderate circumference at a great distance, they could not only wound their enemies in the head, but hit any part of the head they pleased* [Livy]. Their battering machines produced the din as well as the effect of ours: *at the battering of the walls, inflicted with a terrible noise, fear and trepidation seized them* [Livy]. The Gauls, our cousins in Asia, hated these treacherous flying weapons, being trained to fight hand to hand with greater courage. *They are not so much moved by gaping wounds. When the wound is more wide than deep, they think they have fought the more gloriously; but when the point of an arrow or a sling shot buries itself in their flesh and shows only a slight trace on the surface, then in rage and shame at having to perish of such a small hurt, they roll their bodies on the ground* [Livy]: a description much like a harquebus shot.

The ten thousand Greeks in their long and famous retreat met a nation that did them marvelous damage with shots from great and strong bows, and arrows so long that when you picked them up in your hand you could throw them back like a dart; and they would pierce a buckler and an armed man through and through. The engines that Dionysius invented at Syracuse to shoot massive bolts and stones of terrible size, with such great range and speed, came very close to our inventions.

^AStill we must not forget the comical posture on his mule of one Master Pierre Pol, doctor in theology, who, Monstrelet reports, was accustomed to ride around the city of Paris seated sidesaddle, like a woman. He also says elsewhere that the Gascons had terrible horses, accustomed to turn around on the run, which the French, Picards, Flemings, and Brabanters considered a great miracle, "not being accustomed to see such things": these are his words.

Caesar, speaking of the men of Sweden,[2] says: "In the encounters that take place on horseback, they often jump to the ground to fight on foot, having trained their horses not to budge meanwhile from their place, to which they run back promptly if they need to; and according to their custom, there is nothing so base and cowardly as to use saddles or pads, and they despise those who use them so much that, even if they themselves are few in number, they do not fear to attack many of them."

^BWhat I have marveled at in other days, to see a horse trained to go through all sorts of paces at the touch of a rod, with the reins hanging down over his ears, was the rule among the Massilians, who rode their horses without saddle or bridle.

> And the Massilian tribe all ride their horses bareback,
> And, ignorant of bridles, guide them with a switch.
>
> LUCAN

^CAnd without reins the Numidians ride:
>
> VIRGIL

their horses are without bridles, and their running is ungainly, with neck rigid and head thrust forward [Livy].

^AKing Alfonso, he who instituted in Spain the Order of the Knights of the Band, or Scarf, gave them this rule, among others, never to ride a mule, male or female, on pain of a fine of a silver mark, as I have just learned in Guevara's Letters, of which those who

2 Montaigne's mistake for the Suevi or people of Swabia.

have called them "Golden" had a very different judgment than mine. ᶜThe Courtier[3] says that before his time it was a disgrace for a gentleman to ride one. The Abyssinians, on the other hand, the greater they are and the closer to Prester John, their master, the more they affect riding mules as an honor.

Xenophon tells us that the Assyrians kept their horses always hobbled in the stable, they were so vicious and untamed; and thus it took so much time to untie and harness them that they never stayed in a camp that was not protected by ditches and ramparts, lest this delay should harm them in war if they came to be taken by surprise and unprepared by the enemy.

His Cyrus, such a grand master in the art of horsemanship, held his horses to the same reckoning as himself, and never gave them food until they had earned it by the sweat of some exercise.

ᴮThe Scythians, when the need pressed them in war, drew blood from their horses and used it for food and drink.

> Comes the Sarmatian, fed on horse's blood.
>
> MARTIAL

The people of Crete, besieged by Metellus, were in such want of any other drink that they had to use their horses' urine.

ᶜTo show how much more cheaply the Turkish armies are led and maintained than ours, they say that besides the fact that the soldiers drink nothing but water and eat nothing but rice and powdered salt meat, of which each man easily carries on him a month's provision, they can also live on their horses' blood, like the Tartars and Muscovites, and they salt it.

ᴮThese new people of the Indies, when the Spaniards arrived, judged that both the men and the horses were either gods or animals of a nobler nature than their own. Some, after being vanquished, coming to ask for peace and pardon of the men and bring gold and food, did not fail to go and offer the same to the horses, with a harangue just like the one for the men, taking their neighing for a language of conciliation and truce.

In the nearer Indies, it was in ancient times the principal and royal honor to ride an elephant, the second to go in a coach drawn by four horses, the third to ride a camel, the last and meanest degree to be borne or drawn by a single horse. ᶜSomeone of our time writes

3 *Il Libro del Cortegiano* (1528), by Baldassare Castiglione, which was extremely popular and influential in France.

that he saw in that zone countries where they ride oxen with little packsaddles, stirrups, and bridles, and that he found such mounts very comfortable.

Quintus Fabius Maximus Rutilianus, fighting the Samnites, saw that his horsemen in two or three charges had failed to break into the enemy's battalion, and adopted this plan, that they should unbridle their horses and clap their spurs with all their might; with the result that, since nothing could stop them, through weapons and prostrate men they opened the way for their foot soldiers, who completed a very bloody defeat.

Quintus Fulvius Flaccus gave a similar command against the Celtiberians: *You will get more power from your horses if you spur them unbridled upon the enemy; which it is recorded that the Roman cavalrymen have often done with great glory. Their bits removed, they twice charged right through the enemy and back again, inflicting great slaughter on them and breaking off all their spears* [Livy].

[B]The duke of Muscovy in ancient days owed the Tartars this homage: when they sent ambassadors to him, he went to meet them on foot and presented them with a goblet of mare's milk (a drink in which they delight); and if, while they were drinking it, any drop of it fell on their horses' mane, he was bound to lick it off with his tongue.

In Russia, the army that the Emperor Bajazet had sent there was overwhelmed by such a dreadful blizzard that in order to shelter and save themselves from the cold, many resorted to killing and disemboweling their horses, to plunge inside and enjoy that vital heat.

[C]Bajazet, after that fierce battle in which he was routed by Tamerlane, would have escaped at top speed on an Arabian mare, if he had not been obliged to let her drink her fill in crossing a stream, which made her so flabby and chilled that afterward he was very easily overtaken by his pursuers. Indeed they say that we make horses slack by letting them piss; but drinking I should rather have expected to refresh and strengthen her.

Croesus, passing by the city of Sardis, found some waste land where there was a great quantity of snakes which the horses of his army ate with good appetite: a bad omen for his affairs, says Herodotus.

[B]We call a horse entire that has a mane and ears, and the others do not pass muster. The Lacedaemonians, after defeating the Athenians in Sicily, returning in pomp from the victory into the city of Syracuse, among other acts of bravado had the conquered horses

shorn and led them thus in triumph. Alexander fought a nation called the Dahae; they went to war, two armed men to a horse, but in the melee one of these alighted, and the two fought now on foot, now on horseback, in turn.

[C]I do not think that any nation surpasses us in ability and grace on horseback. "A good horseman," in our parlance, seems to refer more to courage than to skill. The most expert horseman, the surest and most graceful at breaking a horse that I have known, was in my opinion the sieur de Carnevalet, who performed this service for our King Henry II.

I have seen a man ride full speed with both feet on the saddle, take off his saddle, and on his return pick it up again, readjust it, and reassume his seat, racing all the time with loose reins; ride over a cap and shoot back at it with his bow and hit it repeatedly; pick up anything he wanted by putting one foot on the ground while keeping the other in the stirrup; and other similar monkey tricks, by which he made his living.

[B]In Constantinople in my time there have been seen two men on one horse who, at the top of its speed, would by turns leap to the ground and then back into the saddle. And one who bridled and harnessed his horse with just his teeth. Another who rode full tilt between two horses, one foot on one saddle and one on the other, carrying another man standing bolt upright on his arms who made very accurate bowshots as they went. Many who, feet in the air, rode with head planted on the saddle between the points of scimitars attached to the harness. In my boyhood the prince of Sulmona, in Naples, putting a tough horse through all sorts of paces, held reals[4] under his knees and toes as if they had been nailed there [C]to show the firmness of his seat.

49
Of ancient customs

[A]I should be prone to excuse our people for having no other pattern and rule of perfection than their own manners and customs; for it is a common vice, not of the vulgar only but of almost all men, to fix their aim and limit by the ways to which they were born. I am content that when they see Fabricius or Laelius they should find

4 Spanish coins.

their countenance and bearing barbaric, since they are neither clothed nor fashioned according to our mode. But I do complain of their particular lack of judgment in letting themselves be so thoroughly fooled and blinded by the authority of present usage that they are capable of changing opinion and ideas every month, if custom pleases, and that they judge themselves so diversely.

When they wore the busk of their doublet between their breasts, they maintained with heated arguments that it was in its proper place; some years after, it has slipped down between the thighs, and they laugh at their former custom and find it absurd and intolerable. The present fashion in dress makes them promptly condemn the old, with such great positiveness and such universal agreement that you would think it was a kind of mania that thus turns their understanding upside down. Because we change so suddenly and promptly that the inventiveness of all the tailors in the world could never furnish us enough novelties, it is inevitable that the despised fashions very often return into favor, and these very ones soon after fall back again into contempt; and that one and the same judgment, in the space of fifteen or twenty years, may be so incredibly inconsistent and frivolous as to adopt two or three opinions that are not merely different but contrary. ᶜThere is no one of us so clever as not to let this contradiction make a monkey out of him and insensibly dazzle both his inward and his outward eyes.

ᴬI want to pile up here some ancient fashions that I have in my memory, some like ours, others different, to the end that we may strengthen and enlighten our judgment by reflecting upon this continual variation of human things.

What we call fighting with rapier and cloak was already practiced among the Romans, says Caesar: *they wrap their cloaks around their left arms and draw their swords*. And even then he notes in our nation this vice, which is still in us, of stopping passers-by whom we meet on the road and forcing them to tell us who they are, and taking it as an insult and reason for a quarrel if they refuse to answer us.

At the baths, which the ancients took every day before their meals, and as ordinarily as we take water to wash our hands, at first they washed only their arms and legs; but later, by a custom that has lasted for many centuries and in most of the nations of the world, they washed stark naked in water mixed with perfume, so that they considered washing in plain water as evidence of great simplicity. The most affected and delicate perfumed their whole body a good three or four times a day. They often had all the hair of the body

plucked, just as French women have for some time been in the habit of plucking the hair from their forehead:

> You pluck the hair from breast and thighs and arms;
>
> MARTIAL

although they had ointments suited for that purpose:

> Gleaming with oil or swathed in vinegar-and-chalk.
>
> MARTIAL

They loved to lie soft, and alleged sleeping on a mattress as proof of endurance. They ate reclining on couches in about the same posture as the Turks of our time.

> Then from his lofty couch Aeneas thus began.
>
> VIRGIL

And they say of Cato the Younger that after the battle of Pharsalia, when he was in mourning over the evil state of public affairs, he always ate seated, adopting a more austere way of life.

They kissed the hands of the great to show them honor and affection; and among friends they kissed one another in salutation, as the Venetians do:

> I'd mix, to wish you joy, kisses with dulcet words.
>
> OVID

^CAnd to supplicate or salute a grandee they would touch his knees. Pasicles the philosopher, brother of Crates, instead of placing his hand on the knee, placed it on the genitals. When the man he was addressing repelled him rudely, he said: "What, isn't this yours just as much as the knees?"

^AThey ate fruit, as we do, at the end of the meal.

They wiped their ass (we must leave that vain squeamishness about words to women) with a sponge – that is why *spongia* is an obscene word in Latin – and this sponge was attached to the end of a stick, as is shown by the story of the man who was being taken to be thrown to the beasts in front of the people, and who asked permission to go and do his business; and having no other way to kill himself, he stuffed the stick and sponge down his throat and choked himself. They wiped their prick with perfumed wool after using it:

> I'll do nothing to you till it is washed with wool.
>
> MARTIAL

At the street crossings in Rome there were vessels and little tubs for
the passers-by to piss in:

> And overcome by sleep, young children often think
> They raised their dress beside some public urinal.
>
> <div align="center">LUCRETIUS</div>

They used to have snacks between meals. And in summer there
were vendors of snow to cool the wine; and there were some who
used snow in winter, not finding the wine cold enough even then.
The great had their cupbearers and carvers, and their buffoons to
give them pleasure. Their food was served them in winter on
chafing dishes that were brought to the table; and they had portable
kitchens, ^csuch as I have seen, ^Ain which everything needed to serve
a meal was carried with them:

> Epicures, you can have this kind of feast;
> We are offended by these walking meals.
>
> <div align="center">MARTIAL</div>

In summer in their lower rooms they often had clear fresh water run
in open channels underneath, in which there were a lot of live fish,
which the guests would select and catch in their hands to be
prepared to the taste of each. Fish has always had this privilege, as
it still does, that the great have pretensions of knowing how to
prepare it; and indeed its taste is much more exquisite than that of
flesh, at least to me.

But in every sort of magnificence, debauchery, voluptuous inven-
tions, luxury, and sumptuousness, we do in truth what we can to
equal them, for our will is quite as corrupt as theirs; but our ability
cannot make it. Our powers are no more capable of matching them
in these vicious parts than in the virtuous ones; for both proceed
from a vigor of soul which was incomparably greater in them than it
is in us; and the weaker the soul, the less its power to do either very
well or very ill.

The seat of honor with them was the middle. Before or after, in
writing and speaking, carried no implication of greater or lesser, as is
evident in their writings: they will say "Oppius and Caesar" as
readily as "Caesar and Oppius," and indifferently "me and you" or
"you and me." That is why I once noted, in the "Life of Flaminius"
in the French translation of Plutarch, a passage where the author,
speaking of the jealousy of the Aetolians and the Romans for the
glory of victory in a battle that they had won together, seems to lend

some weight to the fact that in Greek songs they named the
Aetolians before the Romans, unless there is some ambiguity in
the French words.

The ladies, when in the steam baths, used to receive men, and
employed menservants to rub and anoint them:

> A slave, his middle girt in black, stands by,
> While you bathe, nude, under his watchful eye.
>
> MARTIAL

They sprinkled themselves with some kind of powder to check
perspiration.

The ancient Gauls, says Sidonius Apollinaris, wore their hair long
in front and the back of the head shaven, a fashion that has just been
revived by the lax and effeminate practice of this century.

The Romans used to pay the boatmen their fare as soon as they
entered the boat; which we do after coming to port:

> While the mule is harnessed, the fare paid,
> A whole hour passes by.
>
> HORACE

Women slept on the side of the bed next to the wall: that is
why they called Caesar *the inner side of King Nicomedes' bed*
[Suetonius].

ᴮThey took breath in drinking. They watered their wine:

> To cool Falernian wine
> What active boy will go and bring
> Fresh water from the nearby spring?
>
> HORACE

And those impudent faces of our lackeys were there too:

> O Janus, behind whose back no jokester sneers,
> No mocking hands form storks or asses' ears,
> No tongue is thrust out like the Apulian hound's.
>
> PERSIUS

Argive and Roman ladies wore white mourning, as ours used to
and should have continued to do, if they had taken my advice.

ᴬBut there are entire books written about this question.

50
Of Democritus and Heraclitus

^AJudgment is a tool to use on all subjects, and comes in everywhere. Therefore in the tests[1] that I make of it here, I use every sort of occasion. If it is a subject I do not understand at all, even on that I essay my judgment, sounding the ford from a good distance; and then, finding it too deep for my height, I stick to the bank. And this acknowledgment that I cannot cross over is a token of its action, indeed one of those it is most proud of. Sometimes in a vain and nonexistent subject I try to see if it will find the wherewithal to give it body, prop it up, and support it. Sometimes I lead it to a noble and well-worn subject in which it has nothing original to discover, the road being so beaten that it can walk only in others' footsteps. There it plays its part by choosing the way that seems best to it, and of a thousand paths it says that this one or that was the most wisely chosen.

I take the first subject that chance offers. They are all equally good to me. And I never plan to develop them completely. ^CFor I do not see the whole of anything; nor do those who promise to show it to us. Of a hundred members and faces that each thing has, I take one, sometimes only to lick it, sometimes to brush the surface, sometimes to pinch it to the bone. I give it a stab, not as wide but as deep as I know how. And most often I like to take them from some unaccustomed point of view. I would venture to treat some matter thoroughly, if I knew myself less well. Scattering a word here, there another, samples separated from their context, dispersed, without a plan and without a promise, I am not bound to make something of them or to adhere to them myself without varying when I please and giving myself up to doubt and uncertainty and my ruling quality, which is ignorance.

Every movement reveals us. ^AThat same mind of Caesar's which shows itself in ordering and directing the battle of Pharsalia, shows itself also in arranging idle and amorous affairs. We judge a horse not only by seeing him handled on a racecourse, but also by seeing him walk, and even by seeing him resting in the stable.

^CAmong the functions of the soul there are some lowly ones; he who does not see that side of her also, does not fully know her. And

1 In the French, *essais*; hence, *tests* or *essays*.

perhaps she is best observed when she goes at her simple pace. The winds of passion seize her more strongly on her lofty flights. Moreover, she gives all her being to each matter, and concentrates all her strength on it, and never treats more than one at a time. And she treats a matter not according to itself, but according to herself.

Things in themselves may have their own weights and measures and qualities; but once inside, within us, she allots them their qualities as she sees fit. Death is frightful to Cicero, desirable to Cato, a matter of indifference to Socrates. Health, conscience, authority, knowledge, riches, beauty, and their opposites – all are stripped on entry and receive from the soul new clothing, and the coloring that she chooses – brown, green, bright, dark, bitter, sweet, deep, superficial – and which each individual soul chooses; for they have not agreed together on their styles, rules, and forms; each one is queen in her realm. Wherefore let us no longer make the external qualities of things our excuse; it is up to us to reckon them as we will. Our good and our ill depend on ourselves alone. Let us offer our offerings and vows to ourselves, not to Fortune; she has no power over our character; on the contrary, it drags her in its train and molds her in its own form.

Why shall I not judge Alexander at table, talking and drinking his fill, or when he was playing chess? What sinew of his soul is not touched and employed in this silly and puerile game? I hate it and avoid it, because it is not enough a game, and too serious an amusement; I am ashamed to devote to it the attention that would suffice to accomplish something good. He was no more absorbed when he prepared his glorious expedition to India; nor is this other in unraveling a passage on which depends the salvation of the human race. See how our mind swells and magnifies this ridiculous amusement; how all its muscles grow tense; what ample opportunity it here gives everyone to know himself, and to judge himself rightly. In no other situation do I see and check up on myself more thoroughly. What passion does not excite us in this game: anger, vexation, hatred, impatience, and a vehement ambition to win in a thing in which ambition to be beaten would be more excusable. For rare and extraordinary excellence in frivolous things is unbecoming a man of honor. What I say of this example may be said of all others: each particle, each occupation, of a man betrays him and reveals him just as well as any other.

^ADemocritus and Heraclitus were two philosophers, of whom the first, finding the condition of man vain and ridiculous, never went out in public but with a mocking and laughing face; whereas Heraclitus, having pity and compassion on this same condition of ours, wore a face perpetually sad, and eyes filled with tears:

> ^BOne always, when he o'er his threshold stepped,
> Laughed at the world; the other always wept.
>
> JUVENAL

^AI prefer the first humor; not because it is pleasanter to laugh than to weep, but because it is more disdainful, and condemns us more than the other; and it seems to me that we can never be despised as much as we deserve. Pity and commiseration are mingled with some esteem for the thing we pity; the things we laugh at we consider worthless. I do not think there is as much unhappiness in us as vanity, nor as much malice as stupidity. We are not so full of evil as of inanity; we are not as wretched as we are worthless.

Thus Diogenes, who pottered about by himself, rolling his tub and turning up his nose at the great Alexander, considering us as flies or bags of wind, was really a sharper and more stinging judge, and consequently juster, to my taste, than Timon, who was surnamed the hater of men. For what we hate we take seriously. Timon wished us ill, passionately desired our ruin, shunned association with us as dangerous, as with wicked men depraved by nature. Diogenes esteemed us so little that contact with us could neither disturb him nor affect him, and avoided our company, not through fear of association with us, but through disdain of it; he considered us incapable of doing either good or evil.

Of the same stamp was the reply of Statilius, whom Brutus asked to join the conspiracy against Caesar. He considered the enterprise just, but he did not believe that men were worth taking any trouble about. ^CAnd this is in conformity with the teachings of Hegesias, who said that the wise man should do nothing except for himself, since he alone is worth having anything done for him; and that of Theodorus, that it is unjust for a wise man to risk his life for the good of his country, and endanger wisdom for the sake of fools.

Our own peculiar condition is that we are as fit to be laughed at as able to laugh.

51
Of the vanity of words

^AA rhetorician of times past said that his trade was to make little things appear and be thought great. ^BThat's a shoemaker who can make big shoes for a small foot. ^AThey would have had him whipped in Sparta for professing a deceitful and lying art. ^BAnd I believe that Archidamus, who was king of Sparta, did not hear without astonishment the answer of Thucydides[1] when he asked him who was better in wrestling, Pericles or he: "That," he said, "would be hard to establish; for when I have thrown him in wrestling, he persuades those who saw it happen that he did not fall, and he wins the prize." ^AThose who mask and make up women do less harm, for it is a matter of small loss not to see them in their natural state; whereas the other men make a profession of deceiving not our eyes but our judgment, and of adulterating and corrupting the essence of things. The commonwealths that kept themselves regulated and well governed, like the Cretan and the Lacedaemonian, made little account of orators.

^CAristo wisely defines rhetoric as the science of persuading the people; Socrates and Plato, as the art of deceiving and flattering. And those who deny this in the general definition verify it everywhere in their precepts. The Mohammedans forbid its being taught to their children, because of its uselessness. And the Athenians, perceiving its perniciousness, for all its complete prestige in their city, ordained that the principal part of it, which is to stir the emotions, should be eliminated, together with the exordiums and perorations.

^AIt is an instrument invented to manipulate and agitate a crowd and a disorderly populace, and an instrument that is employed only in sick states, like medicine. To those states where the vulgar, or the ignorant, or all men held all power – such as Athens, Rhodes, and Rome – and where things were in perpetual turmoil, there orators flocked. And in truth, we see few persons in those republics who have pushed themselves into great credit without the aid of eloquence. Pompey, Caesar, Crassus, Lucullus, Lentulus, Metellus, derived from it the great strength needed to rise to the height of authority that they finally attained, and helped themselves by it more than by arms; ^Ccontrary to the opinion of the best times. For L. Volumnius, speaking publicly in favor of the election of Q. Fabius

1 Not the historian, but a political rival of Pericles.

and P. Decius to the consulship, said: "They are men born for war, great in deeds; at combat in prattle, clumsy; truly consular minds. The subtle, eloquent, and learned are good for city life, as praetors to administer justice."

[A]Eloquence flourished most at Rome when affairs were in the worst state and agitated by the storm of civil wars; as a free and untamed field bears the lustiest weeds. From that it seems that monarchical governments need it less than others: for the stupidity and facility that is found in the common people, which makes them subject to be led by the ears to the sweet sound of this harmony without weighing things and coming to know their truth by force of reason – this facility, I say, is not so easily found in a single ruler; it is easier to safeguard him, by good education and advice, from the effects of that poison. No orator of renown was ever seen to come out of Macedon or Persia.

What I have been saying was suggested by an Italian with whom I have just been talking, who served the late Cardinal Caraffa as chief steward until his death. I asked him about his job, and he replied with a discourse on the science of guzzling, delivered with magisterial gravity and demeanor as if he had been expounding some great point of theology. He spelled out to me the difference in appetites: the one we have before eating, the one we have after the second and third course; the means, now of simply gratifying it, now of arousing it and stimulating it; the organization of his sauces, first in general, and then particularizing the qualities of the ingredients and their effects; the differences in salads according to the season, which one should be warmed up and which served cold, the way of adorning and embellishing them to make them also pleasant to the sight. After that he entered upon the order of serving, full of beautiful and important considerations:

> [B]Nor is it any light affair
> How one should carve a hen, and how a hare.
>
> JUVENAL

[A]And all this swollen with rich and magnificent words, and the very ones we use to talk about the government of an empire. I was reminded of a man I like:

> "This is too salty, this is burned, this full of grime,
> That is just right; remember it another time."
> I warn them carefully, as wisely as I can.

> I tell them, Demea, to look in every pan
> As in a glass. In short, I tell them everything.
> TERENCE

To be sure, even the Greeks highly praised the order and arrangement that Paulus Aemilius observed in the feast he offered them on his return from Macedon. But I am not speaking of actions, I am speaking of words.

I don't know whether it happens with others as with me; but when I hear our architects puffing themselves out with those big words like pilasters, architraves, cornices, Corinthian and Doric work, and suchlike jargon, I cannot keep my imagination from immediately seizing on the palace of Apollidon; and in reality I find that these are the paltry parts of my kitchen door.

[B]When you hear people talk about metonymy, metaphor, allegory, and other such names in grammar, doesn't it seem that they mean some rare and exotic form of language? They are terms that apply to the babble of your chambermaid.

[A]It is an imposture akin to this one to call the offices of our state by the superb titles of the Romans, even though they have no resemblance in function, and still less in authority and power. And this device too, which in my opinion will one day serve as testimony of a singular ineptitude in our century, of unworthily assigning the most glorious surnames of antiquity to whoever we think fit, surnames with which the ancients honored one or two personages every several centuries. Plato has won by universal consent the epithet of *divine*, which no one has presumed to begrudge him; but the Italians, who boast, and with reason, of generally having more alert minds and sounder judgments than the other nations of their time, have just conferred it on Aretino, in whom, except for a turgid style, bubbling over with conceits, ingenious indeed but farfetched and fantastic – in short besides his eloquence, such as it may be – I see nothing superior to the ordinary authors of his time; so far is he from approaching that ancient divinity. And the epithet of *great* we apply to princes who have nothing above the greatness of the common people.

52
Of the parsimony of the ancients

[A]Attilius Regulus, general of the Roman army in Africa, in the midst of his glory and his victories against the Carthaginians,

wrote to the Republic that a farm laborer whom he had left in
sole charge of his estate, which was seven acres of land in all, had
run away and stolen his farming tools; and he asked leave to return
and look after this matter, for fear that his wife and children would
suffer from it. The Senate provided another man to manage his
property, caused what had been stolen to be returned to him, and
ordered that his wife and children should be maintained at the
public expense.

The elder Cato, returning as consul from Spain, sold his service
horse to save the money it would have cost to bring him back by
sea to Italy; and when he was governor of Sardinia he made his
rounds on foot, having with him no retinue but an officer of the
Republic, who carried his robe and a vase for offering sacrifices; and
most of the time he carried his trunk himself. He boasted that he
had never had a robe that cost more than ten crowns, and had never
sent more than ten sous to market for one day's food; and that not
one of his houses in the country was coated and plastered on the
outside.

Scipio Aemilianus, after two triumphs and two consulships,
went on a diplomatic mission with only seven servants. They say
Homer never had more than one; Plato, three; Zeno, chief of the
Stoic sect, not one.

[B]Tiberius Gracchus was allowed only five and a half sous a day
when he went on a mission for the Republic, although he was then
the first man among the Romans.

53
Of a saying of Caesar's

[A]If we sometimes spent a little consideration on ourselves, and
employed in probing ourselves the time we put into checking up
on others and learning about things that are outside us, we would
easily sense how much this fabric of ours is built up of feeble and
failing pieces. Is it not a singular evidence of our imperfection that
we cannot establish our contentment in any one thing, and that even
in desire and imagination it is beyond our power to choose what we
need? A good proof of this is the great dispute that has always gone
on between the philosophers over the sovereign good of man, and
that still goes on and will go on eternally, without solution
and without agreement:

> [B]Lacking the thing we want, it seems more grave
> Than anything; that got, there's something else we crave,
> Consumed with equal thirst.
>
> LUCRETIUS

[A]Everything, no matter what it is, that falls within our knowledge and enjoyment, we find unsatisfactory; and we go gaping after things to come and unknown, inasmuch as things present do not satiate us. Not, in my opinion, that they do not have the wherewithal to satiate us, but that we seize them with a sick and disordered grasp:

> [B]For when he saw that nearly all that use demands
> Already was prepared for use by mortal hands,
> That men were powerful in honor and in fame,
> In riches affluent, proud in their sons' good name,
> Yet nonetheless within were anxious in their heart,
> In painful quarrels of the mind forced to take part:
> Then Epicurus knew the vessel caused the vice;
> That all good things that enter, of whatever price,
> Within us, by that vessel's vice, became corrupt.
>
> LUCRETIUS

[A]Our appetite is irresolute and uncertain: it does not know how to keep anything or enjoy anything in the right way. Man, thinking that it is the fault of these things, fills and feeds himself on other things that he does not know and does not understand, to which he applies his desires and his hopes, and which he holds in honor and reverence; as Caesar says, *it happens by a common vice of nature that we trust more, and fear more violently, things to us unseen, hidden, and unknown.*

54
Of vain subtleties

[A]There are some subtleties that are frivolous and vain, by means of which men sometimes seek commendation, like the poets who compose entire works in which every verse begins with the same letter. We see eggs, balls, wings, hatchets, shaped by the Greeks of old with the measure of their verses, by lengthening some lines and shortening others so as to represent one or another of

these figures. Such was the knowledge of the man who amused himself by counting in how many ways the letters of the alphabet could be arranged, and found that incredible number that we see in Plutarch.

A man who had learned to throw a grain of millet through the eye of a needle with unfailing accuracy performed this feat for another man, whose response to it I applaud. He was asked afterward for some present as a reward for such a rare ability; whereupon he ordered, very humorously and in my opinion justly, that this performer should be given two or three bushels of millet, so that so fine an art should not remain unexercised. It is a marvelous testimony of the weakness of our judgment that it recommends things for their rarity or novelty, or even for their difficulty, even if they are neither good nor useful.

We have just now at my house been playing a game to see who could find the most things that meet at their two extremes: as Sire is a title that is given to the loftiest person in our state, the king, and is also given to the vulgar, as to tradesmen, and applies to no one in between. Women of quality are called *dames*; those of the middle class, *damoiselles*; and *dames* again, those of the lowest station.

^BThe canopies that are spread over tables are allowed only in princes' houses and in taverns.

^ADemocritus used to say that gods and animals had more acute senses than men, who are on a middle level. The Romans wore the same attire on days of mourning and on feast days. It is certain that extreme fear and extreme ardor of courage equally trouble and relax the bowels.

^CThe nickname of "the Trembler" with which Sancho, the twelfth king of Navarre,[1] was surnamed, teaches us that boldness as well as fear makes our limbs quake. And another man, whose skin quivered so while his attendants were arming him that they tried to reassure him by minimizing the danger he was going to face, said to them: "You don't know me. If my flesh knew where my courage will shortly take it, it would fall flat, paralyzed."

^AThe weakness that comes to us from coldness and disgust in the exercises of Venus comes to us also from too vehement a desire and inordinate heat. Extreme cold and extreme heat cook and roast. Aristotle says that pigs of lead will melt and run with the cold and

1 The twelfth king of Navarre, and the one called "the Trembler," was not Sancho but Garcia V.

the rigor of winter as with intense heat. ᶜDesire and satiety fill the stages above and below pleasure with pain.

ᴬStupidity and wisdom meet at the same point of feeling and of resolving to endure human accidents. The wise curb and control the evil; the others are not aware of it. The latter are, so to speak, on this side of accidents, the former beyond them; for the wise man, after having well weighed and considered their qualities and measured and judged them for what they are, springs above them by the power of a vigorous courage. He disdains them and tramples them underfoot, having a strong and solid soul, against which the arrows of fortune, when they come to strike, must necessarily bounce off and be blunted, meeting a body on which they can make no impression. The ordinary and middle condition of men lodges between these two extremes; which is that of those who perceive evils, feel them, and cannot endure them. Infancy and decrepitude meet in weakness of the brain; avarice and extravagance, in a like desire to take in and acquire.

ᴮIt may be said with some plausibility that ᶜthere is an abecedarian ignorance that comes before knowledge, and another, doctoral ignorance that comes after knowledge: an ignorance that knowledge creates and engenders, just as it undoes and destroys the first.

ᴮOf simple souls, less curious and less learned, are made good Christians, who, through reverence and obedience, believe simply and live under the laws. In the middle range of mental vigor and ability, error in opinion is engendered; those in this range follow the first plausible meaning, and have some claim to regard our sticking to the old ways – those of us who are not versed in these matters by study – as simplicity and stupidity. Great minds, more settled and clear-sighted, make up another type of good believers, who, by long and religious investigation, penetrate to a deeper and more abstruse light on the Scriptures and sense the mysterious and divine secret of our ecclesiastical polity. However, we see some who have arrived at this last stage by way of the second, with marvelous profit and confirmation, as at the extreme limit of Christian intelligence, and who enjoy their victory with consolation, active gratitude, reformed conduct, and great modesty. And I do not mean to place in this rank those others who, to cleanse themselves of the suspicion of their past error and make us sure of them, become extreme, injudicious, and unjust in the conduct of our cause, and stain it with infinite reproaches of violence.

ᶜThe simple peasants are good men, and good men the philoso-
phers, at least what passes for philosophers in our time: strong and
clear natures, enriched by a broad education in useful knowledge.
The half-breeds who have disdained the first seat, ignorance of
letters, and have not been able to reach the other – their rear end
between two saddles, like me and so many others – are dangerous,
inept, and importunate: these men trouble the world. Therefore for
my part I draw back as much as I can into the first and natural stage,
which for naught I attempted to leave.

Popular and purely natural poetry has spontaneous effects and
charms by which it may be compared with the principal beauty of
poetry as perfected according to art; as is seen in the villanelles
of Gascony and the songs that are brought back to us from the
nations that have no knowledge of any science, or even of writing.
Mediocre poetry, which stops between the two, is disdained, with-
out honor and without value.

ᴬBut I find again, as ordinarily happens after the mind
has opened up a passage, that we have taken for a difficult exercise
and a rare subject what is not so at all; and that after our inventive-
ness has been warmed up, it discovers an infinite number of
similar examples. And so I shall add only this one: that if
these essays were worthy of being judged, I think they might not
be much liked by common and vulgar minds, or by singular
and excellent ones; the former would not understand enough
about them, the latter too much. But they might get by in the
middle region.

55
Of smells

ᴬIt is said of some, as of Alexander the Great, that their sweat
emitted a sweet odor, owing to some rare and extraordinary con-
stitution of theirs, of which Plutarch and others seek the cause. But
the common make-up of bodies is the opposite, and the best con-
dition they may have is to be free of smell. The sweetness even of the
purest breath has nothing more excellent about it than to be without
any odor that offends us, as is that of very healthy children. That is
why, says Plautus,

A woman smells good when she does not smell.

The most perfect smell for a woman is to smell of nothing, ^Bas they say that her actions smell best when they are imperceptible and mute. ^AAnd perfumes are rightly considered suspicious in those who use them, and thought to be used to cover up some natural defect in that quarter. Whence arise these nice sayings of the ancient poets: To smell good is to stink:

> You laugh at us because we do not smell.
> I'd rather smell of nothing than smell sweet.
>
> MARTIAL

And elsewhere:

> Men who smell always sweet, Posthumus, don't smell good.
>
> MARTIAL

^BHowever, I like very much to be surrounded with good smells, and I hate bad ones beyond measure, and detect them from further off than anyone else:

> My scent will sooner be aware
> Where goat-smells, Polypus, in hairy arm-pits lurk,
> Than keen hounds scent a wild boar's lair.
>
> HORACE

^CThe simplest and most natural smells seem to me the most agreeable. And this concern chiefly affects the ladies. Amid the densest barbarism, the Scythian women, after washing, powder and plaster their whole body and face with a certain odoriferous drug that is native to their soil; and having removed this paint to approach the men, they find themselves both sleek and perfumed.

^BWhatever the odor is, it is a marvel how it clings to me and how apt my skin is to imbibe it. He who complains of nature that she has left man without an instrument to convey smells to his nose is wrong, for they convey themselves. But in my particular case my mustache, which is thick, performs that service. If I bring my gloves or my handkerchief near it, the smell will stay there a whole day. It betrays the place I come from. The close kisses of youth, savory, greedy, and sticky, once used to adhere to it and stay there for several hours after. And yet, for all that, I find myself little subject to epidemics, which are caught by communication and bred by the contagion of the air; and I have escaped those of my time, of which there have been many sorts in our cities and our armies. ^CWe read of

Socrates that though he never left Athens during many recurrences of the plague which so many times tormented that city, he alone never found himself the worse for it.

[B]The doctors might, I believe, derive more use from odors than they do; for I have often noticed that they make a change in me and work upon my spirits according to their properties; which makes me approve of the idea that the use of incense and perfumes in churches, so ancient and widespread in all nations and religions, was intended to delight us and arouse and purify our senses to make us more fit for contemplation.

[C]I should like, in order to judge of it, to have shared the art of those cooks who know how to add a seasoning of foreign odors to the savor of foods, as was particularly remarked in the service of the king of Tunis, who in our time landed at Naples to confer with the Emperor Charles. They stuffed his foods with aromatic substances, so sumptuously that one peacock and two pheasants came to a hundred ducats to dress them in that manner; and when they were carved, they filled not only the dining hall but all the rooms in his palace, and even the neighboring houses, with sweet fumes which did not vanish for some time.

[B]The principal care I take in my lodgings is to avoid heavy, stinking air. Those beautiful cities Venice and Paris weaken my fondness for them by the acrid smell of the marshes of the one and of the mud of the other.

56
Of prayers

[A]I put forward formless and unresolved notions, as do those who publish doubtful questions to debate in the schools, not to establish the truth but to seek it. And I submit them to the judgment of those whose concern it is to regulate not only my actions and my writings, but even my thoughts. Equally acceptable and useful to me will be condemnation or approval, [C]since I hold it as execrable if anything is found which was said by me, ignorantly or inadvertently, against the holy prescriptions of the Catholic, Apostolic, and Roman Church, in which I die and in which I was born. [A]And therefore, always submitting to the authority of their censure, which has absolute power over me, I meddle rashly with every sort of subject, as I do here.

I may be wrong, I don't know; but since by a particular favor of divine goodness a certain form of prayer has been prescribed and dictated to us word for word by the mouth of God, it has always seemed to me that its use should be more ordinary with us than it is. And if I had my way, on sitting down to table and rising from it, on getting up and going to bed, and on all particular actions with which we are accustomed to associate prayers, I should like it to be the Lord's Prayer that Christians employ, ^Cif not exclusively, at least always. ^AThe Church may extend and diversify prayers according to the need of our instruction, for well I know that it is always the same substance and the same thing. But we ought to have given that one this privilege, that the people should have it continually in their mouths; for it is certain that it says all that is necessary and that it is very proper for all occasions. ^CIt is the only prayer I use in every circumstance; and I repeat it instead of changing. Whence it happens that I have none in my memory as well as that one.

^AI was just now thinking about where that error of ours comes from, of having recourse to God in all our designs and enterprises, ^Band calling on him in every kind of need and in whatever spot our weakness wants help, without considering whether the occasion is just or unjust, and invoking his name and his power, in whatever condition or action we are involved, however vicious it may be.

^AHe is indeed our sole and unique protector, ^Cand can do anything to help us; ^Abut although he deigns to honor us with that sweet fatherly relationship, nevertheless he is as just as he is good ^Cand as he is powerful. But he exercises his justice much more often than his power, ^Aand favors us according to its dictates, not according to our requests.

^CPlato, in his *Laws*, makes three kinds of belief concerning the gods offensive: that there are none; that they do not concern themselves in our affairs; that they refuse nothing to our vows, offerings, and sacrifices. The first error, in his opinion, never remained immutable in any man from his childhood until his old age. The other two may permit of constancy.

^AHis justice and his power are inseparable. For naught do we implore his power in an evil cause. We must have our soul clean, at least in that moment in which we pray to him, and rid of vicious passions; otherwise we ourselves present to him the rods with which to chastise us. Instead of redressing our fault, we redouble it when we offer feelings full of irreverence and hatred to him whom we are to ask for pardon. That is why I am not inclined to praise those

whom I see praying to God most often and habitually, if the actions surrounding the prayer do not show me evidence of some amendment and reform:

> [B]If, an adulterer by night,
> You cover up your forehead with a Gaulish cowl.
> JUVENAL

[C]And the state of a man who mixes piety with an execrable life seems to be rather more damnable than that of a man consistent with himself and dissolute throughout. Wherefore our Church every day refuses the favor of entry and fellowship to those who stubbornly adhere to any striking wickedness.

[A]We pray out of habit and custom, or to speak more correctly, we read or pronounce our prayers. All in all, it is only an act. [B]And I dislike to see a man cross himself three times at the Benedicite, and as often at the Grace[1] (and I dislike it the more because it is a sign that I revere and continually use, [C]even when I yawn), [B]and meanwhile see him all the other hours of the day occupied with hatred, avarice, and injustice. To vices their hour, to God his hour, as if by compensation and compromise. It is a miracle to see actions so opposite follow each other so smoothly that no interruption or alteration is felt even at their confines and in the transition from one to the other.

[C]What prodigy of a conscience can be at rest, while harboring under the same roof, in such harmonious and peaceful association, both the crime and the judge?

A man whose head is incessantly ruled by lechery and who judges it to be very odious in the sight of God, what does he say to God when he speaks to him about it? He pulls himself back, but immediately relapses. If the fact and the presence of divine justice struck and chastised his soul, as he claims, however short his repentance might be, the very fear would throw back his thoughts to it so often that he would promptly see himself master of those vices that are habitual and ingrained in him.

But what of those who base an entire life on the fruit and emolument of a sin they know to be mortal? How many trades and vocations have we seen accepted, the essence of which is vicious! And the man who, confessing himself to me, told me that for ages he had professed and practiced a religion damnable in his own

1 The blessing of food before, and the thanksgiving after, a meal.

opinion and contradictory to what he had in his heart, so as not to lose his credit and the honor of his offices: how did he reconcile this statement in his heart? With what language do they converse with divine justice on this subject? Their repentance consisting in a visible and palpable reparation, they lose the means of affirming it, both in the sight of God and in ours. Are they so bold as to ask for pardon without satisfaction and without repentance? I hold that it is the same with the first ones[2] as with these, but the obstinacy there is not so easy to overcome. This contradictoriness and fickleness of opinion that they feign, so sudden and so violent, savors to me of the miraculous. They portray to us a state of indigestible conflict.

How fantastic seemed to me the imagination of those who in recent years had the habit of reproaching each and every man in whom there gleamed some light of intelligence and who professed the Catholic religion, with dissimulation; and who even maintained, thinking to do him honor, that whatever he said for appearance, he could not help having his belief within reformed according to their measure. An annoying malady, to think yourself so wise that you persuade yourself that no one can believe the contrary! And still more annoying, to persuade yourself that a person of such intelligence would prefer I know not what disparity of present fortune to the hopes and threats of eternal life. They may take my word for it: if anything were to have tempted my youth, ambition for the risk and difficulties that attended this recent enterprise[3] would have played a good part in it.

[A]It is not without good reason, it seems to me, that the Church forbids the promiscuous, reckless, and indiscreet use of the holy and divine songs which the Holy Spirit dictated to David. We must not mix God into our actions except with reverence and with devout and respectful attention. His word is too divine to have no other use than to exercise our lungs and please our ears; it should be uttered from the conscience and not from the tongue. It is not right that a shop apprentice, amid his vain and frivolous thoughts, should entertain himself and play with it.

[B]Nor assuredly is it right to see the holy book of the sacred mysteries of our belief bandied about a hall or a kitchen. [C]Formerly they were mysteries; at present they are sports and pastimes. [B]It is

2 Those like the lecherous man in the previous paragraph.
3 The Reformation.

not in passing and in whirlwind fashion that we should handle so serious and venerable a study. It must be a premeditated and sober action, to which we should always add this preface of our service, *sursum corda*,[4] and always bring even the body disposed in a demeanor that attests a particular attention and reverence.

^CIt is not everyone's study; it is the study of the persons who are dedicated to it, whom God calls to it. The wicked, the ignorant, grow worse by it. It is not a story to tell, it is a story to revere, fear, and adore. Comical folk, those who think they have made it fit for the people to handle because they have put it into the language of the people! Is it just a matter of the words, that they do not understand all they find in writing? Shall I say more? By bringing it this little bit closer to the people, they remove it farther. Pure ignorance that relied entirely on others was much more salutary, and more learned, than this vain and verbal knowledge, the nurse of presumption and temerity.

^BI also believe that this freedom for everyone to disperse a word so sacred and important into so many kinds of idioms has in it much more danger than utility. The Jews, the Mohammedans, and almost all others have espoused, and revere, the language in which their mysteries were originally conceived; and any alteration or change in them is forbidden, not without reason. Are we quite sure that in the Basque country or Brittany there are enough competent judges to warrant this translation made into their language? The universal Church has no judgment more arduous and solemn to make. In preaching and speaking, the interpretation is vague, free, mutable, and piecemeal; so it is not the same thing.

^COne of our Greek historians justly accuses his age because the secrets of the Christian religion were scattered about the market place in the hands of the merest artisans, so that anyone might argue and talk about them according to his lights; and he thinks that it was shameful of us, who, by the grace of God, enjoy the pure mysteries of piety, to let them be profaned in the mouths of ignorant and common people, seeing that the Gentiles forbade Socrates, Plato, and the wisest men to speak of and inquire into the things committed to the priests of Delphi. He says also that the factions of princes in theological disputes are armed not with zeal but with anger; that zeal takes after divine reason and

4 Lift up your hearts.

justice when it guides itself with order and moderation, but changes into envious hatred and produces tares instead of wheat and nettles instead of grapes when it is guided by human passion.

And that other man also, advising the Emperor Theodosius, said rightly that disputes did not so much put to sleep the schisms of the Church as wake them up and stir up heresies; that therefore they should avoid all contentions and dialectical argumentations and fall back purely on the prescriptions and formulas of faith established by the ancients. And the Emperor Andronicus, coming upon two great men in his palace at verbal grips with Lopadius over one of our points of great importance, scolded them to the point of threatening to throw them into the river if they continued.

Women and children nowadays lecture the oldest and most experienced men about the ecclesiastical laws; whereas the first of Plato's laws forbids them to inquire even into the reason of the civil laws, which are to be respected as divine ordinances. And Plato, while he allows the old men to talk about these matters among themselves or with the magistrate, adds: provided it is not in the presence of young or profane persons.

A bishop has left it in writing that at the other end of the world there is an island that the ancients called Dioscorides, an island delightful for its salubrious climate and its fertility, for it abounds in all sorts of trees and fruits. The people of this island are Christians, having churches and altars which are adorned only with crosses, without any other images. They are great observers of fasts and holidays, pay their tithes exactly to the priests, and are so chaste that not one of them may have more than one woman in all his life; for the rest, so content with their fortune that in the middle of the sea they do not know the use of ships, and so simple that of the religion they observe so scrupulously they understand not a single word: a thing incredible to anyone who is unaware that the pagans, who are such devout idolaters, know nothing about their gods except simply their names and statues.

The old beginning of *Menalippus*, a tragedy of Euripides, ran thus:

> O Jupiter! for to me is known
> Nothing of thee but thy name alone.[5]

5 Montaigne quotes this couplet in French from Amyot's translation of Plutarch's *Moral Essays*.

[B]In my time I have also heard certain writings reproached as being purely human and philosophical, with no admixture of theology. Nevertheless, it would not be wholly unreasonable to say the contrary: that the divine doctrine keeps her rank better apart, as queen and mistress; that she must be sovereign everywhere, not deputy and subsidiary, and that examples for grammar, rhetoric, and logic might perhaps be drawn more suitably elsewhere than from so sacred a matter, as also subjects for theaters, games, and public spectacles; that divine reasons are regarded with greater veneration and reverence by themselves and in their own style than when coupled with human reasonings; that it is a more common fault for theologians to write too humanly than for humanists to write too untheologically: philosophy, says Saint Chrysostom, has long been banished from the holy schools as a useless handmaid, and considered unworthy to peer, even in passing and from the doorway, into the sanctuary of the holy treasures of the celestial doctrine; that human speech has lower forms, and should not make use of the dignity, majesty, and authority of divine speech. I for my part allow it to say, [C]*in unsanctioned terms* [Saint Augustine], [B]"fortune," "destiny," "accident," "good luck," and "bad luck," "the gods," and other phrases, in its own way.

[C]I set forth notions that are human and my own, simply as human notions considered in themselves, not as determined and decreed by heavenly ordinance and permitting neither doubt nor dispute; matter of opinion, not matter of faith; what I reason out according to me, not what I believe according to God; as children set forth their essays to be instructed, not to instruct; in a lay manner, not clerical, but always very religious.

[B]And might it not reasonably be said that an order against writing on religion, unless very reservedly, for any but those who make this their express profession, would have some appearance of utility and justice; as perhaps would an order to me, at the same time, to hold my peace about it?

[A]I have been told that even those who are not of our Church nevertheless forbid the use of the name of God among themselves in their ordinary talk. They do not want it to be used by way of interjection or exclamation, or for testimony or comparison; in which I think they are right. In whatever way we call God to our company and society, it should be seriously and religiously.

There is, it seems to me, a certain passage in Xenophon where he shows that we should pray to God more rarely, since it is not likely

that we can restore our soul so often to that orderly, reformed, and devout state in which it must be for that purpose; otherwise our prayers are not only vain and useless, but vicious. "Forgive us," we say, "as we forgive those who have trespassed against us." What do we mean by that, if not that we offer him our soul free from vengeance and rancor? However, we call on God and his aid to conspire in our faults, ᶜand invite him to our injustice.

> ᴮWhich you will reveal to the gods only in private.
>
> PERSIUS

ᴬThe miser prays to him for the vain and superfluous conservation of his treasures; the ambitious man, for his victories and the guidance of this passion; the thief uses his help to pass through the risks and difficulties that oppose the execution of his wicked enterprises, or thanks him for having found it easy to cut a passer-by's throat. ᶜStanding beside the house they are going to scale or blow up, they say their prayers, with their intentions and hopes full of cruelty, lust, and avarice.

> ᴮThe thing you want to say into Jove's private ear,
> Come on, say it to Staius. He'll cry: "Jove, didst thou hear?"
> Then will not Jove himself likewise utter a cry?
>
> PERSIUS

ᴬMargaret, queen of Navarre, tells of a young prince – and although she does not name him, his greatness has made him recognizable enough[6] – that when he went to an amorous assignation to sleep with the wife of a Paris advocate, his route leading through a church, he never passed through that holy place in going to or coming from his enterprise without making his prayers and orisons. His soul filled with that fine thought, I leave you to judge for what purpose he employed the divine favor; yet she cites this as evidence of singular devotion. But it is not by this proof only that one could demonstrate that women are hardly fit to treat theological matters.

A true prayer and religious reconciliation of ourselves to God cannot occur in an impure soul, subject even then to the domination of Satan. He who calls God to his assistance while he is in the very act of vice acts like a cutpurse who would call justice to his aid, or like those who put forward the name of God as witness to a lie:

6 King Francis I, Margaret's brother.

> [B]Our evil prayers we say
> In a quiet whisper.
>
> LUCAN

[A]There are few men who would dare place in evidence the secret requests they make of God:

> 'Tis hard for any man to quit the low-voiced whispers
> Within the shrine, and bare his prayers to the world.
>
> PERSIUS

That is why the Pythagoreans wanted them to be public and heard by everyone, so that God should not be asked for anything indecent or unjust, as by this man:

> Aloud he cries "Apollo!" to the air.
> Then his lips move inaudibly: "Laverna fair,
> Grant me to cheat, but seem pious and just; and shroud
> My sins and frauds within a black protecting cloud."
>
> HORACE

[C]The gods grievously punished the iniquitous prayers of Oedipus by granting them. He had prayed that his children should settle the succession to his state by arms among themselves. He was so unfortunate as to see himself taken at his word. We must not ask that all things should obey our will, but that our will should obey wisdom.

[A]It seems, in truth, that we use our prayers [C]as a jargon, and [A]like those who use holy and divine words for sorceries and magical effects; and that we count on their effect depending on the texture, sound, or sequence of the words, or on our bearing. For with our soul full of lust, untouched by repentance or by any fresh reconciliation with God, we go and offer him these words that memory lends to our tongue, and hope from them to derive expiation for our sins. There is nothing so easy, so gentle, and so favorable as the divine law; she calls us to herself, sinful and detestable as we are; she stretches out her arms to us and takes us to her bosom, no matter how vile, filthy, and besmirched we are now and are to be in the future. But still, in return, we must look on her in the right way. We must receive this pardon with thanksgiving, and, at least for that instant when we address ourselves to her, have a soul remorseful for its sins and at enmity with the passions that have driven us to offend her. [C]Neither the gods nor good men, says Plato, accept the wicked man's present.

^ABrought to the altar by unspotted hand,
A sacred cake and sparkling salt command
From grim Penates treatment far more nice
Than does the most extravagant sacrifice.

<div align="right">HORACE</div>

57
Of age

^AI cannot accept the way in which we establish the duration of our life. I see that the sages, as compared with popular opinion, make it a great deal shorter. "What," said the younger Cato to those who wanted to keep him from killing himself, "am I now at an age where I can be reproached for abandoning life too soon?" Yet he was only forty-eight. He regarded that age as quite ripe and quite advanced, considering how few men reach it. And those who delude themselves with the idea that some course or other which they call natural promises a few years beyond, might do so properly if they had a privilege to exempt them from the many accidents to which we are all naturally subject, and which can interrupt this course that they promise themselves.

What an idle fancy it is to expect to die of a decay of powers brought on by extreme old age, and to set ourselves this term for our duration, since that is the rarest of all deaths and the least customary! We call it alone natural, as if it were contrary to nature to see a man break his neck by a fall, be drowned in a shipwreck, or be snatched away by the plague or a pleurisy, and as if our ordinary condition did not expose us to all these mishaps. Let us not flatter ourselves with these fine words: we ought perhaps rather to call natural what is general, common, and universal.

Death of old age is a rare, singular, and extraordinary death, and hence less natural than the others; it is the last and ultimate sort of death; the further it is from us, the less it is to be hoped for. It is indeed the bourn beyond which we shall not go, and which the law of nature has prescribed as not to be passed; but it is a very rare privilege of hers to make us last that long. It is an exemption which she grants by special favor to a single person in the space of two or three centuries, relieving him of the misfortunes and difficulties that she has cast in the way of others during this long period.

Thus my idea is to consider the age we have reached as one few people reach. Since in the ordinary course of things men do not come thus far, it is a sign that we are well along. And since we have passed the customary limits which are the true measure of our life, we must not hope to go much further. Having escaped so many occasions of dying, at which we see everyone stumble, we must recognize that an extraordinary fortune, and one out of the usual, like the one that is keeping us going, is not due to last much longer.

It is a defect in the very laws to hold this false idea: they have it that a man is not capable of the management of his estate until he is twenty-five, whereas he will hardly keep the management of his life that long. Augustus cut off five years from the ancient Roman ordinances, and declared that it was enough for those assuming the office of judge to be thirty. Servius Tullius released the knights who had passed forty-seven from service in war; Augustus set this back to forty-five. To send men back into retirement before the age of fifty-five or sixty seems not very reasonable to me. I should be of the opinion that our employment and occupation should be extended as far as possible, for the public welfare; I find the fault in the other direction, that of not putting us to work soon enough. Augustus had been universal judge of the world at nineteen, and yet would have a man be thirty in order to pass judgment on the position of a gutter.

As for me, I think our souls are as developed at twenty as they are ever to be, and give the promise of all they ever can do. No soul which at that age has not given very evident earnest of its strength has given proof of it later. The natural qualities and virtues give notice within that term, or never, of whatever vigor or beauty they possess:

> [B]If the thorn will not prick at birth,
> It never will prick on earth,

they say in Dauphiné.

[A]If I were to enumerate all the beautiful human actions, of whatever kind, that have come to my knowledge, I should think I would find that the greater part were performed, both in ancient times and in our own, before the age of thirty, rather than after. [C]Yes, often even in the lives of the same men.

May I not say that with all assurance about those of Hannibal and of Scipio, his great adversary? They lived a good half of their life on the glory acquired in their youth: great men afterward in

comparison with all others, but by no means in comparison with themselves.

^AAs for me, I hold it as certain that since that age my mind and my body have rather shrunk than grown, and gone backward rather than forward. It is possible that in those who employ their time well, knowledge and experience grow with living; but vivacity, quickness, firmness, and other qualities much more our own, more important and essential, wither and languish.

> ^BWhen age has crushed the body with its might,
> The limbs collapse with weakness and decay,
> The judgment limps, and mind and speech give way.
>
> LUCRETIUS

Sometimes it is the body that first surrenders to age, sometimes, too, it is the mind; and I have seen enough whose brains were enfeebled before their stomach and legs; and inasmuch as this is a malady hardly perceptible to the sufferer and obscure in its symptoms, it is all the more dangerous. For the time, ^AI complain of the laws, not that they leave us at work too long, but that they set us to work too late. It seems to me that considering the frailty of our life and how many ordinary natural reefs it is exposed to, we should not allot so great a part of it to birth, idleness, and apprenticeship.

END OF BOOK ONE

BOOK TWO

I
Of the inconsistency of our actions

^AThose who make a practice of comparing human actions are never so perplexed as when they try to see them as a whole and in the same light; for they commonly contradict each other so strangely that it seems impossible that they have come from the same shop. One moment young Marius is a son of Mars, another moment a son of Venus. Pope Boniface VIII, they say, entered office like a fox, behaved in it like a lion, and died like a dog. And who would believe that it was Nero, that living image of cruelty, who said, when they brought him in customary fashion the sentence of a condemned criminal to sign: "Would to God I had never learned to write!" So much his heart was wrung at condemning a man to death!

Everything is so full of such examples – each man, in fact, can supply himself with so many – that I find it strange to see intelligent men sometimes going to great pains to match these pieces; seeing that irresolution seems to me the most common and apparent defect of our nature, as witness that famous line of Publilius, the farce writer:

> Bad is the plan that never can be changed.
>
> PUBLILIUS SYRUS

^BThere is some justification for basing a judgment of a man on the most ordinary acts of his life; but in view of the natural instability of our conduct and opinions, it has often seemed to me that even good authors are wrong to insist on fashioning a consistent and solid fabric out of us. They choose one general characteristic, and go and arrange and interpret all a man's actions to fit their picture; and if they cannot twist them enough, they go and set them down to dissimulation. Augustus has escaped them; for there is in this man throughout the course of his life such an obvious, abrupt, and continual variety of actions that even the boldest judges have had to let him go, intact and unsolved. Nothing is harder for me than to believe in men's consistency, nothing easier than to believe in their inconsistency. He who would judge them in detail ^cand distinctly, bit by bit, ^Bwould more often hit upon the truth.

^AIn all antiquity it is hard to pick out a dozen men who set their lives to a certain and constant course, which is the principal goal of wisdom. For, to comprise all wisdom in a word, says an ancient [Seneca], and to embrace all the rules of our life in one, it is "always to will the same things, and always to oppose the same things." I would not deign, he says, to add "provided the will is just"; for if it is not just, it cannot always be whole.

In truth, I once learned that vice is only unruliness and lack of moderation, and that consequently consistency cannot be attributed to it. It is a maxim of Demosthenes, they say, that the beginning of all virtue is consultation and deliberation; and the end and perfection, consistency. If it were by reasoning that we settled on a particular course of action, we would choose the fairest course – but no one has thought of that:

> He spurns the thing he sought, and seeks anew
> What he just spurned; he seethes, his life's askew.
>
> HORACE

Our ordinary practice is to follow the inclinations of our appetite, to the left, to the right, uphill and down, as the wind of circumstance carries us. We think of what we want only at the moment we want it, and we change like that animal which takes the color of the place you set it on. What we have just now planned, we presently change, and presently again we retrace our steps: nothing but oscillation and inconsistency:

> Like puppets we are moved by outside strings.
>
> HORACE

We do not go; we are carried away, like floating objects, now gently, now violently, according as the water is angry or calm:

> ^BDo we not see all humans unaware
> Of what they want, and always searching everywhere,
> And changing place, as if to drop the load they bear?
>
> LUCRETIUS

^AEvery day a new fancy, and our humors shift with the shifts in the weather:

> Such are the minds of men, as is the fertile light
> That Father Jove himself sends down to make earth bright.
>
> HOMER

^CWe float between different states of mind; we wish nothing freely, nothing absolutely, nothing constantly. ^AIf any man could prescribe and establish definite laws and a definite organization in his head, we should see shining throughout his life an evenness of habits, an order, and an infallible relation between his principles and his practice.

^CEmpedocles noticed this inconsistency in the Agrigentines, that they abandoned themselves to pleasures as if they were to die on the morrow, and built as if they were never to die.

^AThis man[1] would be easy to understand, as is shown by the example of the younger Cato: he who has touched one chord of him has touched all; he is a harmony of perfectly concordant sounds, which cannot conflict. With us, it is the opposite: for so many actions, we need so many individual judgments. The surest thing, in my opinion, would be to trace our actions to the neighboring circumstances, without getting into any further research and without drawing from them any other conclusions.

During the disorders of our poor country,[2] I was told that a girl, living near where I then was, had thrown herself out of a high window to avoid the violence of a knavish soldier quartered in her house. Not killed by the fall, she reasserted her purpose by trying to cut her throat with a knife. From this she was prevented, but only after wounding herself gravely. She herself confessed that the soldier had as yet pressed her only with requests, solicitations, and gifts; but she had been afraid, she said, that he would finally resort to force. And all this with such words, such expressions, not to mention the blood that testified to her virtue, as would have become another Lucrece. Now, I learned that as a matter of fact, both before and since, she was a wench not so hard to come to terms with. As the story says: Handsome and gentlemanly as you may be, when you have had no luck, do not promptly conclude that your mistress is inviolably chaste; for all you know, the mule driver may get his will with her.

Antigonus, having taken a liking to one of his soldiers for his virtue and valor, ordered his physicians to treat the man for a persistent internal malady that had long tormented him. After his cure, his master noticed that he was going about his business

1 The disciplined man in the sentence before last.
2 The religious civil wars between Catholics and Protestants, which lasted intermittently from 1562 to 1594.

much less warmly, and asked him what had changed him so and made him such a coward. "You yourself, Sire," he answered, "by delivering me from the ills that made my life indifferent to me." A soldier of Lucullus who had been robbed of everything by the enemy made a bold attack on them to get revenge. When he had retrieved his loss, Lucullus, having formed a good opinion of him, urged him to some dangerous exploit with all the fine expostulations he could think of,

> With words that might have stirred a coward's heart.
>
> HORACE

"Urge some poor soldier who has been robbed to do it," he replied;

> Though but a rustic lout,
> "That man will go who's lost his money," he called out;
>
> HORACE

and resolutely refused to go.

ᶜWe read that Sultan Mohammed outrageously berated Hassan, leader of his Janissaries, because he saw his troops giving way to the Hungarians and Hassan himself behaving like a coward in the fight. Hassan's only reply was to go and hurl himself furiously – alone, just as he was, arms in hand – into the first body of enemies that he met, by whom he was promptly swallowed up; this was perhaps not so much self-justification as a change of mood, nor so much his natural valor as fresh spite.

ᴬThat man whom you saw so adventurous yesterday, do not think it strange to find him just as cowardly today: either anger, or necessity, or company, or wine, or the sound of a trumpet, had put his heart in his belly. His was a courage formed not by reason, but by one of these circumstances; it is no wonder if he has now been made different by other, contrary circumstances.

ᶜThese supple variations and contradictions that are seen in us have made some imagine that we have two souls, and others that two powers accompany us and drive us, each in its own way, one toward good, the other toward evil; for such sudden diversity cannot well be reconciled with a simple subject.

ᴮNot only does the wind of accident move me at will, but, besides, I am moved and disturbed as a result merely of my own unstable posture; and anyone who observes carefully can hardly find himself twice in the same state. I give my soul now one face, now

another, according to which direction I turn it. If I speak of myself in different ways, that is because I look at myself in different ways. All contradictions may be found in me by some twist and in some fashion. Bashful, insolent; ^Cchaste, lascivious; ^Btalkative, taciturn; tough, delicate; clever, stupid; surly, affable; lying, truthful; ^Clearned, ignorant; liberal, miserly, and prodigal: ^Ball this I see in myself to some extent according to how I turn; and whoever studies himself really attentively finds in himself, yes, even in his judgment, this gyration and discord. I have nothing to say about myself absolutely, simply, and solidly, without confusion and without mixture, or in one word. *Distinguo* is the most universal member of my logic.

^AAlthough I am always minded to say good of what is good, and inclined to interpret favorably anything that can be so interpreted, still it is true that the strangeness of our condition makes it happen that we are often driven to do good by vice itself – were it not that doing good is judged by intention alone.

Therefore one courageous deed must not be taken to prove a man valiant; a man who was really valiant would be so always and on all occasions. If valor were a habit of virtue, and not a sally, it would make a man equally resolute in any contingency, the same alone as in company, the same in single combat as in battle; for, whatever they say, there is not one valor for the pavement and another for the camp. As bravely would he bear an illness in his bed as a wound in camp, and he would fear death no more in his home than in an assault. We would not see the same man charging into the breach with brave assurance, and later tormenting himself, like a woman, over the loss of a lawsuit or a son. ^CWhen, though a coward against infamy, he is firm against poverty; when, though weak against the surgeons' knives, he is steadfast against the enemy's swords, the action is praiseworthy, not the man.

Many Greeks, says Cicero, cannot look at the enemy, and are brave in sickness; the Cimbrians and Celtiberians, just the opposite; *for nothing can be uniform that does not spring from a firm principle* [Cicero].

^BThere is no more extreme valor of its kind than Alexander's; but it is only of one kind, and not complete and universal enough. ^CIncomparable though it is, it still has its blemishes; ^Bwhich is why we see him worry so frantically when he conceives the slightest suspicion that his men are plotting against his life, and why he behaves in such matters with such violent and indiscriminate

injustice and with a fear that subverts his natural reason. Also superstition, with which he was so strongly tainted, bears some stamp of pusillanimity. ^CAnd the excessiveness of the penance he did for the murder of Clytus is also evidence of the unevenness of his temper.

^AOur actions are nothing but a patchwork – ^C*they despise pleasure, but are too cowardly in pain; they are indifferent to glory, but infamy breaks their spirit* [Cicero] – ^Aand we want to gain honor under false colors. Virtue will not be followed except for her own sake; and if we sometimes borrow her mask for some other purpose, she promptly snatches it from our face. It is a strong and vivid dye, once the soul is steeped in it, and will not go without taking the fabric with it. That is why, to judge a man, we must follow his traces long and carefully. If he does not maintain consistency for its own sake, ^C*with a way of life that has been well considered and preconcerted* [Cicero]; ^Aif changing circumstances make him change his pace (I mean his path, for his pace may be hastened or slowed), let him go: that man goes before the wind, as the motto of our Talbot says.

It is no wonder, says an ancient [Seneca], that chance has so much power over us, since we live by chance. A man who has not directed his life as a whole toward a definite goal cannot possibly set his particular actions in order. A man who does not have a picture of the whole in his head cannot possibly arrange the pieces. What good does it do a man to lay in a supply of paints if he does not know what he is to paint? No one makes a definite plan of his life; we think about it only piecemeal. The archer must first know what he is aiming at, and then set his hand, his bow, his string, his arrow, and his movements for that goal. Our plans go astray because they have no direction and no aim. No wind works for the man who has no port of destination.

I do not agree with the judgment given in favor of Sophocles, on the strength of seeing one of his tragedies, that it proved him competent to manage his domestic affairs, against the accusation of his son. ^CNor do I think that the conjecture of the Parians sent to reform the Milesians was sufficient ground for the conclusion they drew. Visiting the island, they noticed the best-cultivated lands and the best-run country houses, and noted down the names of their owners. Then they assembled the citizens in the town and appointed these owners the new governors and magistrates, judging that they, who were careful of their private affairs, would be careful of those of the public.

^AWe are all patchwork, and so shapeless and diverse in composition that each bit, each moment, plays its own game. And there is as much difference between us and ourselves as between us and others. ^C*Consider it a great thing to play the part of one single man* [Seneca]. ^AAmbition can teach men valor, and temperance, and liberality, and even justice. Greed can implant in the heart of a shop apprentice, brought up in obscurity and idleness, the confidence to cast himself far from hearth and home, in a frail boat at the mercy of the waves and angry Neptune; it also teaches discretion and wisdom. Venus herself supplies resolution and boldness to boys still subject to discipline and the rod, and arms the tender hearts of virgins who are still in their mothers' laps:

> ^BFurtively passing sleeping guards, with Love as guide,
> Alone by night the girl comes to the young man's side.
> TIBULLUS

^AIn view of this, a sound intellect will refuse to judge men simply by their outward actions; we must probe the inside and discover what springs set men in motion. But since this is an arduous and hazardous undertaking, I wish fewer people would meddle with it.

2
Of drunkenness

^AThe world is nothing but variety and dissimilarity. Vices are all alike in that they are all vices, and perhaps this is the way the Stoics understand it. But although they are equally vices, they are not equal vices. And it is not credible that the man who has transgressed the limits by a hundred paces,

> Short of which or beyond which there is no right path,
> HORACE

is in as good condition as the one who is only ten paces beyond; nor is it credible that sacrilege is no worse than the theft of a cabbage from our garden:

> Nor will reason convince me that the sin's the same
> To trample someone's cabbages, as without shame
> To rob by night the sacred temples of the gods.
> HORACE

There is as much diversity in this as in anything else.

[B]Confusion about the order and measurement of sins is danger-ous. Murderers, traitors, tyrants, gain too much by it. It is not right that their conscience should be relieved because some other man is indolent, or lascivious, or less assiduous in his devotions. Each man lays weight on his neighbor's sin and lightens his own. Even our teachers often rank sins badly, in my opinion.

[C]As Socrates used to say that the principal function of wisdom was to distinguish good things from bad, so we lesser men, who even at our best are always tainted with vice, should say the same thing about the science of distinguishing among the vices; if we do not make this distinction very nicely, the virtuous man and the wicked man will remain confused and unrecognized.

[A]Now drunkenness, among the others, seems to me a gross and brutish vice. The mind has more of a part in the others; and there are vices that have about them something indefinably noble, if we must call it that. There are some that involve knowledge, diligence, valor, prudence, skill, and subtlety; this one is all bodily and earthy. Thus the grossest nation in existence today is the only one that holds it in esteem. The other vices affect the understanding; this one overturns it, [B]and stuns the body:

> When we are conquered by the strength of wine,
> Our limbs grow heavy, our legs intertwine;
> With sodden mind, slow tongue, and swimming eyes,
> We reel amid the hiccups, brawls and cries.
>
> LUCRETIUS

[C]The worst condition of man is when he loses knowledge and control of himself.

[A]And they say among other things that just as must, fermenting in a vessel, pushes to the top all there is on the bottom, so wine, in those who have taken it in excess, uncorks the most intimate secrets:

> [B]In Bacchic revel
> The sage to you his cares
> And secret counsel bares.
>
> HORACE

[A]Josephus tells how he wormed the secrets out of a certain ambassador that the enemy had sent to him by having him drink his fill. However, Augustus confided his most private affairs to Lucius Piso, who conquered Thrace, and never found himself

mistaken about him; nor was Tiberius mistaken about Cossus, to whom he unburdened himself of all his plans; though we know both to have been so subject to wine that they often had to be carried drunk out of the Senate,

> His veins, as always, swol'n with wine of yesterday.
> VIRGIL

^CAnd they confided the plan to kill Caesar as trustingly to Cimber, although he often got drunk, as to Cassius, a water drinker. Wherefore he retorted wittily: "I should bear up under a tyrant, I who cannot bear up under my wine!" ^AWe see our Germans, drowned in wine, remember their quarters, the watchword, and their rank:

> ^BSteeped though they are in wine, drunk, staggering,
> Beating them down is still no easy thing. JUVENAL

^CI should not have believed in a drunkenness so deep, so dead and buried, if I had not read of this instance of it in the histories. Attalus, having invited Pausanias to supper in order to do him some notable indignity – that same Pausanias who for this same reason later killed Philip, king of Macedon, a king who by his fine qualities bore witness to the education he had received in the house and company of Epaminondas – made him drink so much that he could abandon his body insensibly, like the body of some whore under a hedge, to the muleteers and a number of vile slaves of Attalus' household. And I learned from a lady whom I hold in singular honor and esteem that near Bordeaux (toward Castres, where her house is) a village woman, a widow of chaste reputation, feeling the first inklings of pregnancy, told her neighbors that she would think she was with child if she had a husband. But as the occasion of this suspicion grew from day to day and finally became evident, she brought herself to have it announced at the service in her church that if anyone would admit the deed, she promised to pardon him and, if he saw fit, to marry him. A young farmhand of hers, emboldened by this proclamation, declared that he had found her, one holiday when she had taken her wine very freely, so fast asleep by her fireplace, and in so indecent a posture, that he had been able to enjoy her without waking her. They are still alive and married to each other.

^AIt is certain that antiquity did not strongly decry this vice. Indeed, the writings of several philosophers speak of it very mildly,

and even among the Stoics there are some who recommend that we allow ourselves sometimes to drink our fill, and get drunk in order to relax the soul:

> ^BIn this contest like others, so they say,
> The great Socrates bore the prize away.
>
> MAXIMIANUS

^CThat censor and corrector of others,[1] ^ACato, was reproached for drinking well:

> ^BOld Cato's virtue drew from wine,
> So we are told, a glow more fine.
>
> HORACE

^ACyrus, such a renowned king, to put himself ahead of his brother Artaxerxes, alleged among other things in his own praise that he could drink much better. And in the best-regulated and best-governed nations this test of drinking one's fill was much in use. I have heard Silvius, an excellent doctor from Paris, say that to keep the digestive powers from getting lazy, it is good to rouse them once a month by this excess, and stimulate them to keep them from getting sluggish. ^BAnd they say that the Persians used to consult about their principal affairs after wine.

^AMy taste and constitution are more inimical to this vice than my reason. For, quite aside from the fact that I easily submit my beliefs to the authority of ancient opinions, I find it indeed a loose and stupid vice, but less malicious and harmful than the others, which almost all clash more directly with society in general. And if we cannot give ourselves pleasure without its costing us something, as they maintain, I find that this vice costs our conscience less than the others. Moreover, it is not hard to prepare for and find: a consideration not to be despised.

^CA man advanced in dignity and age counted drink among the three principal comforts that he used to say he had left in life. But he took it in the wrong way. Fastidiousness is to be avoided in it, and careful selection of wines. If you make your pleasure depend on drinking good wine, you condemn yourself to the pain of sometimes drinking bad wine. We must have a less exacting and freer taste. To be a good drinker, one must not have so delicate a palate.

1 Instead of this phrase, in the editions published during his lifetime, Montaigne had written: "The true image of Stoic virtue ..."

The Germans drink almost all wines with equal pleasure. Their aim is to swallow rather than to taste. They have much the better of the bargain. Their pleasure is much more plentiful and ready at hand.

Second, to drink French style, at two meals and moderately, for fear of your health, is to restrain the god's favor too much. You need more time and persistence. The ancients spent whole nights at this exercise, and often added the days. And so we should make our daily drinking habits more expansive and vigorous. I have seen a great lord in my time, a personage of high enterprises and famous successes, who, without effort and in the course of his ordinary meals, used to drink scarcely fewer than ten quarts of wine, and showed himself on leaving only too wise and circumspect, at the expense of our affairs.

The pleasure we want to reckon on for the course of our life should occupy more space in it. Like shop apprentices and workmen, we should refuse no chance to drink, and have this desire always in our head. It seems that every day we cut down on our eating and drinking, and that in our houses, as I remember from my childhood, lunches, suppers, and collations used to be much more frequent and usual than they are now. Could it be that in some respects we are moving toward improvement? Surely not. The fact is that we are much more addicted to lechery than were our fathers. These two occupations interfere with each other in their vigor. Lechery has weakened our stomach on the one hand; and on the other hand, sobriety serves to make us more lively and lusty for the exercise of love.

It is marvelous what stories I have heard my father tell of the chastity of his day. He was the man to tell them, being very well suited to the service of the ladies, both by nature and by art. He spoke little and well, and sprinkled his language with ornamental expressions from books in the modern vernaculars, especially Spanish; and among the Spanish his usual reading was the book they call Marcus Aurelius.[2] His bearing was one of gentle, humble, and very modest gravity. A singular care for neatness and propriety of person and dress, whether afoot or on horseback. A prodigious fidelity in keeping his word, and a general conscientiousness and scrupulousness leaning rather toward than away from superstition. For a small man, full of vigor, and straight and well-proportioned in stature. An

2 *The Golden Book of Marcus Aurelius*, by Antonio de Guevara (1490–1545), a historical romance popular in France, Italy, and England as well as Spain.

attractive face, inclining to brown. Adroit and distinguished in all gentlemanly exercises. I have even seen some canes filled with lead, with which they say he exercised his arms to prepare for throwing the bar or the stone, or for fencing, and some shoes with leaded soles to train him to be lighter in running and jumping. Of his vaulting, he has left some small miracles in people's memory. I have seen him, past sixty, put our agility to shame: leap into the saddle in his furred gown, do a turn over the table on his thumb, hardly ever go up to his room without taking three or four steps at a time. On this subject of mine, he used to say that in a whole province there was scarcely one woman of quality who had a bad reputation; and he would tell of remarkable intimacies, especially of his own, with respectable women, free from any suspicion. And of himself he solemnly swore that he had come to his marriage a virgin. And yet he had taken a very long part in the Italian wars, of which he has left a diary in his own hand, following what happened point by point, in both public and his own private matters. Consequently he married well along in age, in the year 1528, which was his thirty-third, on his return from Italy. Let's get back to our bottles.

ᴬThe discomforts of old age, which need some support and refreshment, might reasonably make me wish to be a better drinker; for drinking is almost the last pleasure that the years steal from us. Natural liveliness, good fellows say, first starts in the feet: this is true of children. From there it rises to the middle region, where it plants itself for a long time, and produces there, in my opinion, the only true pleasures of bodily life; ᶜthe other pleasures are asleep by comparison. ᴬToward the end, like a vapor that rises upward and is exhaled, it arrives at the gullet, where it makes its last stop.

ᴮI cannot understand, for all that, how people come to prolong the pleasure of drinking beyond their thirst, and forge themselves in their imagination an artificial and unnatural appetite. My stomach would not go that far; it has enough trouble taking care of what it takes for its need. ᶜMy disposition is not to set store by drinking except after eating; and for that reason my last drink is almost always the biggest. Anacharsis was amazed that the Greeks drank in bigger glasses at the end of the meal than at the beginning. That was, I suppose, for the same reason that the Germans do it, who then begin their drinking bouts.

Plato forbids children to drink wine before eighteen, and to get drunk before forty; but those who have passed forty he orders to enjoy drinking, and to mix freely in their banquets the influence of

Dionysus, that good god who restores gaiety to all men and youth to the old, who softens and mollifies the passions of the soul as iron is softened by fire. And in his *Laws* he finds such drinking parties useful, provided there is a leader of the group to control and regulate them. For drunkenness to Plato is a good and certain test of each and every man's nature, and at the same time suited to give older people the courage to make merry in dances and music, useful pastimes that they shy away from in a sober mood. He adds that wine is capable of giving temperance to the soul and health to the body. However, he likes these restrictions, borrowed partly from the Carthaginians: that it be used sparingly on a military expedition; that every magistrate and every judge abstain from it when he is on the point of carrying out his duties and consulting on public affairs; that the day, a time due to other occupations, should not be spent in drinking, or a night when we intend to beget children.

They say that the philosopher Stilpo, weighed down with old age, deliberately hastened his end by drinking undiluted wine. The same cause, but not by his own design, also stifled the worn-out vital forces of the philosopher Arcesilaus.

^ABut it is an old and amusing question whether the soul of the sage is such that it would yield to the power of wine,

> If wine can storm the very fort of wisdom.
>
> HORACE

To how much vanity are we driven by the high opinion we have of ourselves! The best-regulated soul in the world has only too much to do to stay on its feet and keep itself from collapsing to the ground through its own weakness. Out of a thousand souls, there is not one that is straight and composed for a single moment in a lifetime; and it may be questioned, given the soul's natural condition, whether it can ever be so. But when straightness and composure are combined with constancy, then the soul attains its ultimate perfection; I mean even if nothing should jar it, which a thousand accidents can do.

Look at Lucretius, that great poet; all his philosophizing and self-discipline cannot prevent him from being driven insane by an aphrodisiac. Is there anybody who believes that an apoplexy will not stun Socrates as well as a porter? Some have been driven by an illness to forget their very name, and a slight wound has overturned the judgment of others.

For all his wisdom, the sage is still a man: what is there more vulnerable, more wretched, and more null? Wisdom does not overcome our natural limitations:

> [B]Over the whole body therefore we see arise
> Pallor and sweat; the tongue is tied, and the voice dies,
> The eyes grow dim, ears ring, the limbs give way; the whole
> At last collapses from the terror of the soul.
> LUCRETIUS

[A]The sage must blink his eyes at the blow that threatens him; if you set him on the edge of a precipice, he must shudder [C]like a child. Nature has willed to reserve to herself these slight marks of her authority, invincible to our reason and to Stoic virtue, in order to teach man his mortality and frailty. [A]He pales with fear, he reddens with shame; he complains at a sharp attack of the colic, if not in a desperate and clamorous voice, at least with a voice broken and hoarse:

> Let him think nothing human foreign to him.
> ADAPTED FROM TERENCE

The poets, [C]who invent everything as they please, [A]do not dare to exempt their heroes even from tears:

> Thus weeping does he speak, and bids his fleet depart.
> VIRGIL

Enough for the sage to curb and moderate his inclinations; for to do away with them is not in him.

Even that Plutarch of ours, so perfect and excellent a judge of human actions, on seeing Brutus and Torquatus kill their children, came to doubt whether virtue could go that far, and to wonder whether those personages had not rather been motivated by some other passion. All actions outside the ordinary limits are subject to sinister interpretation, inasmuch as our taste responds no more to what is above it than to what is below.

[C]Let us leave aside that other sect that makes an express profession of pride. But even in the sect[3] that is considered the softest, we hear these boasts of Metrodorus: *Fortune, I have anticipated you and seized you; I have cut off all your access, so that you cannot come near me* [Cicero]. Anaxarchus, who had been laid in a stone trough by the

3 The Epicureans. The "other sect" is the Stoics.

orders of Nicocreon, tyrant of Cyprus, and fatally beaten with an iron mallet, does not stop saying: "Strike, break; it is not Anaxarchus but his shell that you are pounding." ^Our martyrs were heard crying out to the tyrant in the midst of the flame: "It's roasted enough on that side, chop it up, eat it, it's cooked, start on the other side!" And that boy in Josephus, all torn by biting pincers and pierced by the awls of Antiochus, still defied him, crying out with a firm and steady voice: "Tyrant, you're wasting your time, here I am still at ease; where is that pain, where are those torments, with which you were threatening me? Is this all you know how to do? My constancy gives you more pain than I feel from your cruelty. O cowardly wretch, you are giving up, and I am growing stronger; make me complain, make me bend, make me yield, if you can; give your satellites and your executioners courage; see, they have lost heart, they can do no more; arm them, goad them!" When we hear such defiance, surely we must confess that in these souls there is some alteration, some frenzy, however holy it be.

When we come to such Stoic sallies as *I would rather be insane than voluptuous,* ^c^a saying of Antisthenes; ^when Sextius tells us that he would rather be pierced through by pain than by sensual pleasure; when Epicurus undertakes to be caressed by the gout, refuses rest and health, cheerfully defies ills, and, scorning the less severe pains and disdaining to struggle with them, invokes and wishes for pains strong, biting, and worthy of him –

> Among his harmless flocks, it is his prayer to meet
> A foaming boar, or tawny lion from the hills

<div align="right">VIRGIL</div>

– who does not judge that these are the sallies of a runaway courage? Our soul from its abode could not reach so high. It must leave its dwelling place and rise, and, taking the bit in its teeth, abduct its man and carry him off so far that afterward he is himself astonished at his deeds; as, in exploits of war, the heat of combat often impels high-souled soldiers to go through such dangers that when they have come back to themselves they are the first to be struck with amazement; as also poets are often rapt in wonder at their own works and no longer recognize the track over which they ran so fine a race. That is what is called poetic frenzy and madness. And as Plato says that a sedate man knocks in vain on the door of poetry, so Aristotle says that no excellent soul is free from an admixture of madness. And he is right to call madness any transport, however

laudable, that transcends our own judgment and reason; inasmuch as wisdom is an orderly management of our soul, which she conducts with measure and proportion and is responsible for.

^CPlato argues thus: that the faculty of prophecy is above us; that we must be outside of ourselves when we exercise it; that our wisdom must be obscured either by sleep or by some illness, or lifted from its place by some celestial rapture.

3
A custom of the island of Cea

^AIf to philosophize is to doubt, as they say, then to play the fool and follow my fancies, as I do, is all the more to doubt. For it is for the learners to inquire and dispute, and for the master to decide. My master is the authority of the divine will, which rules us without contradiction and has its place above these vain and human wranglings.

When Philip had entered the Peloponnesus with an armed force, someone said to Damidas that the Lacedaemonians would have much to suffer if they did not regain his favor. "Coward," he answered, "and what can people suffer who do not fear death?" Also Agis was asked how a man could live free. "By despising death," he said.

These sayings, and a thousand like them that we come across on this subject, evidently have a ring of something beyond patiently waiting for the end when death comes to us. For there are many accidents in life worse to suffer than death itself. Witness that Lacedaemonian boy, taken by Antigonus and sold as a slave, who, when pressed by his master to perform some mean service, replied: "You shall see whom you have bought; it would be shameful for me to be a servant, with freedom so ready at hand." And so saying, he threw himself from the top of the house. When Antipater harshly threatened the Lacedaemonians to make them fall in with some demand of his, they answered: "If you threaten us with worse than death, we shall die the more willlingly." ^CAnd to Philip, who had written them that he would hinder all their enterprises: "What, will you also hinder us from dying?"

^AThat is what they mean by saying that the sage lives as long as he should, not as long as he can; and that the most beneficent present Nature has given us, a present which takes from us any reason for

complaining about our condition, is the gift of the key to the fields.
She has ordained only one entry into life, and a hundred thousand
exits. ᴮWe may lack land to live on, but land to die on we cannot
lack, as Boiocalus replied to the Romans. ᴬWhy do you complain of
this world? It does not hold you: if you live in pain, your cowardice is
the cause; to die all that is needed is the will:

> For death is everywhere. Gracious is this, God's plan:
> That though our life may be destroyed by any man,
> No one can take our death; a thousand roads lead there.
> SENECA

And death is not the remedy for just one malady, but the remedy
for all ills. It is a very sure haven, which is never to be feared, and
often to be sought. It all comes to the same thing whether man gives
himself his death or suffers it, whether he runs to meet his day or
awaits it; wherever it comes from, it is still his; wherever the thread
breaks, it is all there, that's the end of the skein.

The most voluntary death is the fairest.

Life depends on the will of others; death, on our own.

In nothing should we suit our own humor as much as in this.
Reputation is not concerned in such an enterprise; it is folly to
consider it.

Life is slavery if the freedom to die is wanting.

The ordinary course of a cure is carried on at the expense of
life: they incise us, they cauterize us, they amputate our limbs,
they deprive us of food and blood. One step further, and we are
completely cured. Why is not the jugular vein as much at our
disposal as the median vein? For the most violent diseases the
most violent remedies.

Servius the grammarian, having the gout, found no better plan
for it than to apply poison and kill his legs. ᶜLet them be as gouty as
they liked, provided they were insensitive. ᴬGod gives us leave
enough when he puts us in such a state that it is worse to live than
to die. ᶜIt is weakness to yield to ills, but it is madness to foster them.

The Stoics say that it is living in conformity with nature for the
sage to part with life even in full happiness, if he does so oppor-
tunely, and for the fool to cling to his life, even though he is
miserable – the essential thing, for both men, is to be in general
harmony with nature.

Just as I do not violate the laws against thieves when I carry away
my own money and cut my own purse, or those against firebugs

when I burn my own wood, so I am not bound by the laws against murderers for having taken my own life.

Hegesias used to say that like the condition of life, the condition of death ought to depend on our choice. And when Diogenes met the philosopher Speusippus, long afflicted with the dropsy and being carried in a litter, who called out to him "Good health to you, Diogenes!" he replied "No health to you, who endure life, being in such a state." Indeed, some time after, Speusippus killed himself, weary of such a painful condition of life.

^AThis does not pass without contradiction. For many hold that we cannot abandon this garrison of the world without the express command of him who has placed us in it; and that it is for God, who has sent us here not for ourselves alone, but for his glory and the service of others, to give us leave when he pleases, not for us to take it. ^CWe are not born for ourselves, it is said, but also for our country; the laws demand of us, for their interest, an accounting of ourselves, and can take action for homicide against us. ^AOtherwise, as deserters from our post, we are punished in both this and the other world:

> Next we see the abode of those sad innocents
> Whose own hands took their lives, who, weary of the light,
> Did cast away their souls.
>
> VIRGIL

There is much more fortitude in wearing out the chain that binds us than in breaking it, and more proof of strength in Regulus than in Cato. It is lack of judgment and of patience that hastens our pace. Virtue, if energetic, never turns its back under any circumstances; it seeks out evils and pain for nourishment. The threats of tyrants, the rack and the scaffold, put spirit and life into it:

> Just like the oak, lopped by the axe's blows,
> In fertile Algidus, of its dark boughs,
> He does not seem the cuts and strokes to feel,
> But draws his strength and spirit from the steel.
>
> HORACE

And as another says:

> It is not virtue, father, as you think,
> To be afraid of life, but to oppose
> Firmly, not giving way, the greatest woes.
>
> SENECA

'Tis easy in bad times to look on death with scorn;
Braver is he who proves that misery can be borne.
 MARTIAL

It is an act of cowardice, not of virtue, to go and hide in a hole, under a massive tomb, in order to avoid the blows of fortune. Virtue does not stop on the road or slow its pace for any storm that blows:

If shattered falls the heavenly sphere,
Its ruins strike him, but not fear.
 HORACE

Most commonly flight from other misfortunes drives us to this one. Indeed, sometimes flight from death makes us run into it –

ᶜIs it not mad, I ask, to die for fear of death?
 MARTIAL

– ᴬlike those who, for fear of a precipice, throw themselves over it:

Fear of ills to come has sent
Many into great dangers; bravest is the man
Who, ready to endure the ills at hand, yet can
Also defer them.
 LUCAN

Further, when death strikes men with fright,
Possessed by deep disgust of vision, life, and light,
They do themselves to death, full of unhappiness,
Forgetting that this fear produces their distress.
 LUCRETIUS

ᶜPlato, in his *Laws*, ordains an ignominious burial for the man who has deprived his closest and best friend, namely himself, of life and of his destined course when constrained not by public judgment, or by some sad and unavoidable accident of fortune, or by unbearable shame, but by the cowardice and weakness of a timorous soul.

ᴬAs for the opinion that disdains our life, it is ridiculous. For after all, life is our being, it is our all. Things that have a nobler and richer being may accuse ours; but it is against nature that we despise ourselves and care nothing about ourselves. It is a malady peculiar to man, and not seen in any other creature, to hate and disdain himself.

It is by a similar vanity that we wish to be something other than we are. The object of such a desire does not really affect us,

inasmuch as the desire contradicts and hinders itself within. A man who wishes to be made into an angel does nothing for himself; ^che would never benefit from the change. ^AFor when he is no more, who will feel and rejoice in this improvement for him?

> ^BFor if a man's to suffer malady or pain,
> He needs must be on hand in person at the time
> When the blow falls.
> LUCRETIUS

^AThe security, the freedom from pain and suffering, the exemption from the ills of this life, that we purchase at the price of death, bring us no advantage. To no purpose does the man avoid war who cannot enjoy peace, and to no purpose does the man flee from trouble who does not have what it takes to relish repose.

Among those of the first opinion there has been much doubt over this point: What occasions are sufficient to justify a man's decision to kill himself? They call it *a reasonable exit* [Diogenes Laertius]. For although they say that often we must die for trivial reasons since the reasons that keep us living are not very strong, still some moderation is necessary. There are fantastic and irrational humors that have driven not only individual men but nations to do away with themselves. I have cited examples of this earlier.[1] And besides, we read of the virgins of Miletus that in a mad conspiracy they hanged themselves one after the other until the authorities put a stop to this by ordering that those who were found thus hanged should be dragged with the same rope stark naked through the city.

When Cleomenes had fled from an honorable death in a battle he had just lost, Therycion urged him to kill himself because of the bad state of his affairs and to accept this other death which was second to the first in honor, in order not to give the victors the chance to make him suffer either a shameful death or a shameful life. Cleomenes, with Spartan and Stoic courage, refused this counsel as cowardly and effeminate. "That is a remedy," he said, "which can never fail me, and which must not be used as long as there is an inch of hope remaining." And he added that sometimes it is constancy and valor to live; that he wanted even his death to serve his country, and desired to make it an act of honor and virtue. Therycion then followed his own advice and killed himself. Cleomenes did the same

1 *Essays* I: 14, pp. 40–43.

later, but that was after experiencing the ultimate test of fortune. Not all troubles are worth our wanting to die to avoid them.

And then, there being so many sudden changes in human affairs, it is hard to judge just at what point we are at the end of our hope:

> [B]The gladiator too has hope, prone on the sand,
> Although the thumb is down on every threatening hand.
>
> PENTADIUS, QUOTED BY JUSTUS LIPSIUS

[A]A man may hope for anything, says an old adage, as long as he is alive. "Yes," replies Seneca, "but why should I keep in mind this fact, that fortune can do anything for one who is alive, rather than this other fact, that fortune can do nothing to one who knows how to die?" We see Josephus caught in a danger so clear and so imminent – a whole nation had risen up against him – that logically there could be no way out. However, as he says, although he was advised by one of his friends at this point to do away with himself, he did well to hang on stubbornly to his hopes; for fortune, beyond all human reason, so reversed this situation that he saw himself delivered from it without any mishap.

And Cassius and Brutus, on the contrary, demolished the last remnants of Roman liberty, of which they were the protectors, by the rash haste with which they killed themselves before the proper time and occasion.[2]

[C]I have seen a hundred hares escape from the very teeth of the greyhounds. *Some men have survived their executioners* [Seneca].

> [B]Time, and the work of changing days, has made
> Many a bad thing good; fortune has played
> With many men, and set them firm again.
>
> VIRGIL

[A]Pliny says that there are only three kinds of diseases that a man may rightfully kill himself to escape from:[3] the fiercest of all is the

2 Here the 1595 edition adds: "At the battle of Ceresole, Monsieur d'Enghien tried twice to cut his throat with his sword, being desperate over the fortunes of the combat, which went badly in the place where he was; and by his precipitation nearly deprived himself of the enjoyment of so fine a victory." This passage may have been inserted into the Bordeaux Copy three paragraphs earlier, after "ultimate test of fortune."

3 The editions published in Montaigne's lifetime read: "that people have been accustomed to escape from by killing themselves."

kidney stone when the urine is held back by it.[4] ^CSeneca allows only those which for a long time disturb the functions of the soul.

^ATo avoid a worse death, there are some who decide to take theirs at their discretion. ^CDamocritus, leader of the Aetolians, being brought prisoner to Rome, found a way to escape by night. But, finding himself pursued by his guards, he ran himself through with his sword rather than let himself be retaken.

Antinous and Theodotus, when their city in Epirus had been reduced to extremity by the Romans, advised all its people to kill themselves; but, finding their counsel spurned in favor of surrender, they went to seek death, hurling themselves upon the enemy intent only on striking, and not on defending themselves. When the Turks took the island of Gozo by storm a few years ago, a Sicilian, who had two beautiful daughters ready for marriage, killed them with his own hand, and after them their mother, who came running up at their death. This done, he went out into the street with a crossbow and a harquebus, and with two shots killed the first two Turks who approached his door; and then, taking sword in hand, he went furiously into the melee, where he was immediately surrounded and cut to pieces, thus saving himself from slavery after delivering his family from it.

^AThe Jewish women, after having their children circumcised, went and threw themselves with them to their death to escape the cruelty of Antiochus.

I have been told a story about a prisoner of quality in one of our jails, whose relatives, being informed that he would certainly be condemned and wishing to avoid the shame of such a death, had a priest tell him that to be delivered he need only commend himself to such-and-such a saint, with such-and-such a vow, and go eight days without taking any nourishment, whatever faintness and weakness he might feel inside. He took this advice, and by this means unintentionally rid himself of his life and the danger.

Scribonia, advising her nephew Libo to kill himself rather than await the hand of justice, told him that to preserve his life for those who would come to seek it three or four days later was to do other people's business, and that he was serving his enemies by keeping his blood only to make it their quarry.

4 The editions published in Montaigne's lifetime add: "the second, pain in the stomach; the third, a headache."

We read in the Bible that Nicanor, the persecutor of the law of
God, sent his satellites to seize the good old man Razis, in honor
of his virtue surnamed the father of the Jews. This good man, seeing
there was no remedy, his gate burned down and his enemies ready to
seize him, chose rather to die nobly than fall into the hands of the
wicked and be humiliated to the dishonor of his rank, and struck
himself with his sword. Having dealt the blow badly in his haste,
he ran and threw himself from the top of a wall into the midst of
the troop, and when they moved apart and made room for him,
he fell right on his head. Nevertheless, still feeling some bit of
life left in him, he rekindled his courage, and getting up all bloody
and weighed down with blows, pierced his way through the crowd.
He got to a certain steep, precipitous rock, where, unable to do
anything more, he plucked out his entrails with both hands through
one of his wounds, tearing and mangling them, and threw them
among the pursuers, calling down and attesting divine vengeance
upon them.

Of acts of violence against the conscience, the most to be
avoided, in my opinion, is that against the chastity of women,
inasmuch as they naturally derive some physical pleasure from it;
and for this reason their want of consent cannot be so complete but
that, it seems, force meets with a certain willingness. Pelagia and
Sophronia both have been canonized; Pelagia threw herself in the
river with her mother and sisters to escape being raped by
some soldiers, and Sophronia killed herself to escape the violence
of the Emperor Maxentius. ᶜChurch history holds in reverence
several such examples of devout people who called on death to
protect them against outrages that tyrants were preparing against
their conscience.

ᴬIt will perhaps be to our honor in the centuries to come that
a learned author of this day, and a Parisian at that, takes pains to
persuade the ladies of our time to make up their minds to anything
rather than adopt the horrible counsel of such despair. I am sorry
that he did not know and insert among his stories the good one
I heard at Toulouse of a woman who had passed through the hands
of some soldiers: "God be praised," she said, "that at least once in my
life I have had my fill without sin!" In truth, these cruelties are
not worthy of the gentle ways of France; and so, thank God, our
atmosphere has been thoroughly purged of them by that man's good
advice. Enough for them to say No while doing it, following the rule
of our good Marot.

History is chock full of those who in a thousand ways have changed a painful life for death.

[B]Lucius Aruntius killed himself, he said, to escape both the future and the past.

[C]Granius Silvanus and Statius Proximus, after being pardoned by Nero, killed themselves, either in order not to live by the grace of so wicked a man, or in order not to go through the ordeal of a second pardon at some future time, in view of his readiness to suspect and accuse good men.

Spargapises, son of Queen Tomyris, being a prisoner of war of Cyrus, used the first favor that Cyrus did him, that of having him unbound, to kill himself; for he had aspired to no other benefit from his freedom than to avenge on himself the shame of his capture.

Boges, governor in Eion for King Xerxes, when besieged by the army of the Athenians under the leadership of Cimon, refused an offer that would have let him return safely to Asia with all his possessions, as he was unwilling to survive the loss of what his master had given into his keeping. And after defending his town to the last extremity, there being nothing left to eat, he first threw into the river Strymon all the gold and everything he thought the enemy might best make into booty. He then ordered a great pyre to be lit, and saw to it that his wife, children, concubines, and servants had their throats cut; after which he cast them into the fire, and then himself.

When Ninachetuen, an Indian lord, first got wind of the Portuguese viceroy's apparently reasonless determination to deprive him of his position in Malacca and give it to the king of Campar, he resolved on the following course of action. He had a scaffold erected, longer than it was wide, supported on columns and royally adorned with tapestry, flowers, and perfumes in abundance. He then put on a robe of cloth of gold heavy with many precious stones of great price, and went out into the street and up the steps onto the scaffold, in one corner of which there was a pyre of aromatic woods lit. The people ran up to see what these unaccustomed preparations were for. Ninachetuen, with a bold and angry countenance, pointed out how much the Portuguese nation was obligated to him; how faithfully he had acted in his office; that having so often borne arms on others' behalf to prove that he held honor much dearer than life, he was not the man to abandon its defense in his own behalf; that though his fortune prevented him from resisting the affront that they wanted to offer him, at least his courage ordered him to

cease feeling it, and to avoid serving as a laughingstock to the people and as a cause of triumph to men less worthy than himself. So saying, he threw himself into the fire.

[B]Sextilia, wife of Scaurus, and Paxea, wife of Labeo, to encourage their husbands to avoid the dangers that pressed them, in which they themselves had no share except by virtue of conjugal affection, voluntarily sacrificed their own lives so as to serve in this extremity as example and company to their husbands. What these women did for their husbands, Cocceius Nerva did for his country, less usefully but with equal love. This great jurist, flourishing in health, riches, reputation, and credit with the Emperor, had no other reason to kill himself than compassion for the miserable state of the Roman republic.

Nothing can be added to the delicacy of the death of the wife of Fulvius, a close friend of Augustus. Augustus, having discovered that Fulvius had aired an important secret he had confided to him, treated him bleakly one morning when he came to see him. Fulvius went back to his house full of despair, and said most piteously to his wife that because of this misfortune he was resolved to kill himself. She said very frankly: "You will only be doing the right thing, seeing that for all your experience of the incontinence of my tongue you did not guard against it. But here, let me kill myself first." And without further ado she ran a sword through her body.

[C]Vibius Virius despaired of saving his city, which was being besieged by the Romans, and of any mercy from them; and so, in the last deliberation of the city's senate, he concluded, after offering many representations to support his conclusion, that the finest thing was for them to escape fortune by their own hands. The enemy would honor them for it, and Hannibal would feel what faithful friends he had abandoned. Vibius invited those who approved his plan to come and have a good supper that had been prepared at his house, where, after making good cheer, they should drink together of what would be offered to him – "a drink that will deliver our bodies from the tortures, our souls from the insults, our eyes and ears from the many ugly evils that the vanquished have to suffer from cruel and offended conquerors. I have arranged," he said, "that there shall be suitable people to throw us onto a pyre in front of my door when we have expired."

Many approved this lofty resolution; few imitated it. Twenty-seven senators followed him, and, after trying to drown their unpleasant thoughts in wine, finished their meal with this fatal

draught. After embracing one another and together deploring their country's misfortune, some retired to their houses and the others stayed to be buried with Vibius in his fire. And they all were so long in dying, for wine fumes had filled their veins and retarded the effect of the poison, that some were within an hour of seeing the enemy in Capua, which was taken the next day, and of incurring the miseries that they had fled at such cost.

Taurea Jubellius, another citizen from Capua, when the consul Fulvius was returning from his shameful butchery of two hundred and twenty-five senators, called him back fiercely by name and, having stopped him, said: "Order me to be massacred also after so many others, so that you may boast of having killed a much more valiant man than yourself." When Fulvius disdained him as a madman, and also because he had just that very moment received letters from Rome opposing the inhumanity of his execution, which tied his hands, Jubellius continued: "My country has been taken, my friends are dead, and I have with own hand killed my wife and children to save them from the desolation of this ruin. Since I am forbidden to die the death of my fellow citizens, let me borrow from virtue vengeance on this hateful life." And drawing a blade that he had hidden, he thrust it through his chest, and fell on his back, dying, at the consul's feet.

[B]Alexander was besieging a city in India. Those inside, finding themselves hard pressed, vigorously resolved to deprive him of the pleasure of this victory, and burned themselves all together, with their city, in spite of his humanity. A new sort of war: the enemy fought to save them, they to destroy themselves; and to ensure their death they did all the things that people do to ensure their life.

[C]The men of Astapa, a city of Spain, finding their city too weak in walls and defenses to withstand the Romans, made a pile of their riches and furniture in the public square, placed their women and children on top of this heap, and surrounded it with wood and material that would catch fire quickly. This done, they left fifty young men to carry out their resolution, and made a sally in which, according to a vow they had made, being unable to conquer, they died to a man. The fifty, after massacring every living soul they could find in the city, set fire to the pile and flung themselves into it also, ending their high-minded liberty in insensibility rather than in pain and shame; and showing the enemy that if fortune had willed, they would have been as brave in winning the victory as they were in making their defeat frustrating and hideous for their conquerors.

Yes, and fatal to those who, lured by the glitter of the gold melting in the flame, approached it in good numbers and were suffocated and burned, retreat being denied them by the crowd at their heels.

The Abydeans, pressed by Philip, made the same resolution. But they were caught short of time, and Philip, horrified at the frantic precipitation with which they were carrying out their plan (they already had seized the treasures and furniture which they had condemned to be burned or thrown into the water), withdrew his soldiers and granted them three days to kill themselves at leisure; which days they filled with blood and slaughter, beyond any enemy's cruelty, and not a single person of them escaped who had power over himself.

There are countless examples of similar mass resolves, which seem all the more grim as their effect is more universal. But they are in effect less grim when taken in a mass than individually. What persuasion would not do in each man singly, it does in all, the ardor of association stealing away the individual judgment.

^BIn the time of Tiberius, condemned men awaiting execution lost their property and were denied the rites of sepulture; those who anticipated it by killing themselves were buried and could make their will.

^ABut also men sometimes desire death in the hope of a greater good. "I desire," says Saint Paul, "to be dissolved, to be with Jesus Christ." And "Who will deliver me from these bonds?" Cleombrotus of Ambracia, having read Plato's *Phaedo*, gained such an appetite for the life to come that, without any other reason, he went and threw himself into the sea. ^CWhence it appears how improperly we call "despair" that voluntary dissolution to which we are often borne by the ardor of hope, and often by a tranquil and deliberate inclination of our judgment.

^AJacques du Chastel, bishop of Soissons, in the expedition overseas made by Saint Louis, seeing the king and the whole army preparing to return to France leaving the affairs of religion unfinished, resolved rather to go to paradise. And having said adieu to his friends, he charged alone, in the sight of all, into the enemy's army, where he was cut to pieces.

^CIn a certain kingdom of these new regions,[5] on the day of a solemn procession in which the idol they worship is paraded in

5 Not America, as one might suppose, but the Far East. The reference is to the car of Juggernaut.

public on a car of marvelous size, not only are many seen cutting off pieces of their living flesh to offer to it, but a number of others are seen who prostrate themselves in the public square and get themselves crushed and broken under the wheels, thereby to acquire after their death the veneration for holiness, which in fact is paid them. The death of our bishop, arms in hand, is more high-minded and less felt, since the ardor of combat diverts some of the feeling.

ᴬThere are governments that have taken it upon themselves to determine the justice and opportuneness of voluntary deaths. In our own Marseilles in the past there was kept, at public expense, some poison prepared with hemlock for those who wanted to hasten their days, which they could use after having first had the reasons for their enterprise approved by the Six Hundred, their senate; and it was not lawful to lay hands on oneself otherwise than by leave of the authorities and for legitimate reasons. This law also existed elsewhere.

Sextus Pompeius, going to Asia, stopped off at the island of Cea, off Negropont. It happened by chance while he was there, as one of his company informs us, that a woman of great authority, after rendering an account to her fellow citizens of why she was resolved to end her life, asked Pompeius to lend his presence to her death in order to make it more honorable; which he did. And after trying in vain for a long time by force of eloquence, of which he had a marvelous command, and of persuasion, to turn her from this design, he at last suffered her to have her will. She had spent ninety years in a very happy state of mind and body; but now, reclining on her bed, which was better adorned than usual, and leaning on her elbow, she said: "May the gods, O Sextus Pompeius, and rather those I am leaving than those I am going to meet, be gracious to you for not disdaining to be both counselor to my life and witness of my death! For my part, having always experienced the favorable face of Fortune, lest the desire to live too long may make me see one of her contrary faces, I am going to dismiss the remains of my soul by a happy end, leaving two daughters of my own and a legion of grandchildren." This done, she adjured and exhorted her family to live in unity and peace, divided her possessions among them, commended her household gods to her elder daughter, took the cup that held the poison with a steady hand, and after making her vows to Mercury and praying that she might be led to some happy abode in the other world, quickly swallowed the fatal potion. Then she entertained the company with an account of its progress and how

she felt the parts of her body seized one after the other with cold, until, saying finally that it was reaching her heart and entrails, she called her daughters to perform the last office and close her eyes for her.

Pliny tells of a certain Hyperborean nation in which, because of the mild temperature of the air, the inhabitants' lives are ordinarily ended only by their own will; when they are weary and satiated with living after reaching an advanced age, it is their custom, after making good cheer, to throw themselves into the sea from the top of a certain rock reserved for that use.

^CUnendurable ^Bpain and fear of a worse death seem to me the most excusable motives for suicide.

4
Let business wait till tomorrow

^AI give, and it seems to me with reason, the palm to Jacques Amyot over all our French writers, and not only for the naturalness and purity of his language, in which he surpasses all others; or for his perseverance in so long a work; or for the depth of his knowledge, for having been able to interpret so successfully an author so thorny and compact (for they may tell me what they will, I understand nothing of Greek; but I see throughout his translation a sense so beautiful, coherent, and sustained, that either he has clearly understood the real thought of the author, or at least, having by long acquaintance implanted vividly in his own soul a general idea of Plutarch's soul, he has attributed to him nothing that belies or contradicts him). But above all I am grateful to him for having had the wit to pick out and choose a book so worthy and appropriate to present to his country. We ignoramuses would have been lost if this book had not lifted us out of the quagmire; thanks to it, we now dare to speak and write; from it the ladies give lessons to the schoolmasters; it is our breviary.

If this good man is living, I offer him Xenophon to do as much with; it is an easier occupation, and all the better suited to his old age; and then it somehow seems to me that although Amyot gets out of bad situations very briskly and neatly, still his style is more at home when it is not under pressure and rolls at its ease.

I was just now on that passage where Plutarch tells us on his own that Rusticus, while attending one of his lectures at Rome, received

a packet from the Emperor, and delayed opening it until the lecture was all over, for which, says Plutarch, all the audience highly praised his composure. In truth, since Plutarch was on the subject of curiosity – and specifically that greedy and gluttonous passion for news that makes us so indiscreetly and impatiently abandon everything to talk with a newcomer, or tear open immediately the letters that are brought to us, no matter where we are and without regard to respect and decorum – he was right to praise the composure of Rusticus; and he might also have added praise for his civility and courtesy in not having wanted to interrupt the course of his lecture. But I doubt if he can be praised for wisdom: for one who receives letters unexpectedly, and especially from an emperor, it might well be very harmful to defer reading them.

The vice contrary to curiosity is nonchalance, [B]toward which I clearly lean by temperament, and [A]in which I have known some men so extreme that three or four days afterward you would still find in their pocket unopened letters that had been sent them.

[B]I have never opened anyone else's, and I speak not only of letters entrusted to me but even of those which passed by chance through my hands. And I am conscience-stricken if, when I am with a great man, my eyes steal inadvertently some knowledge of important letters that he is reading. Never did a man do less inquiring or less ferreting into other people's affairs.

[A]In our fathers' time Monsieur de Boutières nearly lost Turin because, while supping in good company, he put off reading a warning given him of the treason that was being plotted against this city, in which he was in command. And this same Plutarch has taught me that Julius Caesar would have saved his life if, in going to the Senate on the day when he was killed there by the conspirators, he had read a memorandum that was handed to him. And he also tells this story about Archias, tyrant of Thebes: On the evening before Pelopidas carried out his plot to kill him in order to restore his country to freedom, Archias was sent information in writing by another Archias, an Athenian, of what was being prepared for him, point by point. This packet having been delivered to him during his supper, he put off opening it, making this remark, which later became a proverb in Greece: "Let business wait till tomorrow."

A wise man may in my opinion, out of consideration for others – for example, in order not to break company unbecomingly, like Rusticus, or not to interrupt some other affair of importance – put off hearing the news that is brought to him; but to do so for his own

personal interest or pleasure, in order not to interrupt his dinner or indeed his sleep, especially if he is a man holding public office, is inexcusable. And in ancient times in Rome the consular place, as they called it, was the most honorable at table, being more free and accessible to those who should come in to talk to the person seated there. This shows that even at table the Romans did not shut themselves off from the encroachment of other affairs and contingencies.

But when all is said, it is hard in human actions to arrive by reasoning at any rule so exact as to exclude Fortune from her rights in the matter.

5
Of conscience

ᴬTraveling one day – my brother the sieur de la Brousse and I – during our civil wars, we met a gentleman of good appearance. He was of the opposing party, but I knew nothing of it, for he pretended otherwise; and the worst of these wars is that the cards are so shuffled that your enemy is distinguished from yourself by no apparent mark either of language or of bearing, and has been brought up in the same laws and customs and the same atmosphere, so that it is hard to avoid confusion and disorder. This fact made me afraid, for my part, of meeting our troops in a place where I was not known, lest I have trouble getting a chance to give my name, or perhaps something worse. ᴮSuch a misunderstanding had happened to me once before: I lost both men and horses, and they killed miserably, among others, an Italian page of mine, a gentleman, whom I was bringing up carefully; and in him was extinguished a very fine young life full of great promise.

ᴬBut this man was so desperately afraid and seemed so nearly dead at each meeting with horsemen and each passage through towns that were holding fast for the king, that I finally guessed that his alarms were caused by his conscience. It seemed to this poor man that right through his mask and the crosses on his cassock people would read the secret intentions in his heart. So marvelous is the power of conscience! It makes us betray, accuse, and fight ourselves, and, in the absence of an outside witness, it brings us forward against ourselves:

Plying a secret whip, our soul as torturer.
 JUVENAL

This story is in the mouths of children. Bessus, a Paeonian, reproached for having wantonly knocked down a nest full of sparrows and killed them, said he had reason to, because these little birds would not stop accusing him falsely of the murder of his father. This parricide until then had been concealed and unknown; but the avenging furies of conscience made the very man bring it out who was to bear the penalty for it.

Hesiod corrects the saying of Plato, that punishment follows close after sin; for he says that it is born at the same instant with the sin. Whoever expects punishment already suffers it; and whoever has deserved it expects it. Wickedness forges torments against itself:

He who plans evil suffers from it most;
 PROVERB QUOTED BY AULUS GELLIUS

as the wasp stings and hurts others, but itself most, for there it loses its sting and its strength forever,

In the wound they make they leave their lives.
 VIRGIL

The Spanish fly has in itself something that serves as an antidote to its own poison, by a contrariety of nature. So, even while we take pleasure in vice, there is engendered in our conscience a contrary displeasure which torments us, waking and sleeping, with many painful imaginings:

ᴮOften, indeed, by speaking in their dreams
Or in delirious fever, men betray
Their darkest deeds, long hidden from the day.
 LUCRETIUS

ᴬApollodorus dreamed that he saw himself being flayed by the Scythians and then boiled in a caldron, and that his heart kept murmuring, "I am the cause of all these woes." No hiding place avails the wicked, Epicurus used to say, because they cannot be sure of being hidden, since their conscience discovers them to themselves:

The main revenge is this: himself as judge,
No guilty man can ever be absolved.
 JUVENAL

As conscience fills us with fear, so also it fills us with assurance and confidence. ᴮAnd I can say that in many perils I have walked with a much firmer step by virtue of the secret knowledge I had of my own will and the innocence of my intentions.

> ᴬAccording as we have our inmost conscience clear
> Or troubled, we feel hope or fear.
> OVID

There are a thousand examples of this; it will be enough to cite three about the same man.

When Scipio was accused one day before the Roman people of an important charge, instead of excusing himself or flattering his judges, he said to them: "It will become you well to presume to pass judgment on the head of the man by whose means you have the authority to pass judgment on the whole world!" And another time, as his only answer to the imputations cast upon him by a tribune of the people, instead of pleading his cause, he said: "Come, my fellow citizens, let us go and give thanks to the gods for the victory they gave me over the Carthaginians on a day like this one"; and as he started to walk ahead toward the temple, behold the whole assembly and even his accuser following him. And when Petilius was incited by Cato to ask him for an account of the money he had handled in the province of Antioch, Scipio, having come to the Senate for this purpose, produced the account book, which he had under his robe, and said that this book contained precisely the receipts and expenditures in question. But when asked to give it to the recording clerk, he refused, saying that he would not put himself to this shame; and with his own hands, in the presence of the Senate, he tore it to pieces. I do not believe that a cauterized soul could counterfeit such assurance. ᶜHe had a heart too great by nature and accustomed to too lofty a fortune, says Livy, to know how to play the part of a criminal and stoop to the depths of defending his innocence.

ᴬTortures are a dangerous invention, and seem to be a test of endurance rather than of truth. ᶜBoth the man who can endure them and the man who cannot endure them conceal the truth. ᴬFor why shall pain rather make me confess what is, than force me to say what is not? And on the other hand, if the man who has not done what he is accused of is patient enough to endure these torments, why shall the man who has done it not be also, when so fair a reward as life is set before him? I think that the basis of this invention rests on the consideration of the power of conscience. For the guilty

man's conscience seems to abet the torture in making him confess his fault, and to weaken him; whereas the innocent man's conscience seems to fortify him against his torture.

To tell the truth, torture is a means full of uncertainty and danger. [B]What would a man not say, what would a man not do, to escape such grievous pains?

> [C]Pain forces even the innocent to lie.
> PUBLILIUS SYRUS

Whence it happens that the man whom the judge has tortured so as not to make him die innocent, is made to die both innocent and tortured. [B]Thousands and thousands have thus loaded their head with false confessions. Among these I place Philotas, considering the circumstances of the suit Alexander brought against him and the progress of his torture.

[A]But at all events, [C]they say, [A]it is the least ineffective[1] way that human weakness has been able to invent. [C]Very inhumanly, however, and very uselessly, in my opinion. Many nations, less barbarous in this respect than the Greeks and Romans who call them barbarians, consider it horrible and cruel to torture and break in pieces a man of whose guilt you are still in doubt. What more can he do about your ignorance? Are you not unjust when, in order not to kill him without cause, you do worse to him than kill him? As proof that this is so, see how many times he would rather die without reason than go through this investigation that is more painful than the execution, and which by its cruelty often anticipates the execution and carries it out.

I don't know where I got this story, but it represents exactly the conscience of our justice. A village woman was accusing a soldier before an army general, a great doer of justice, of having snatched from her small children the little broth she had left to sustain them with, the army having ravaged all the villages round about. Of proof there was none. The general called upon the woman to consider well what she was saying, since she would be guilty of false accusation if she was lying; when she persisted, he had the soldier's stomach opened up to get light on the truth of the matter. And it seems the woman was right. An instructive condemnation!

1 In the editions prior to 1588, this read "most effective."

6
Of practice

^AReasoning and education, though we are willing to put our trust in them, can hardly be powerful enough to lead us to action, unless besides we exercise and form our soul by experience to the way we want it to go; otherwise, when it comes to the time for action, it will undoubtedly find itself at a loss. That is why, among the philosophers, those who have wanted to attain some greater excellence have not been content to await the rigors of Fortune in shelter and repose, for fear she might surprise them inexperienced and new to the combat; rather they have gone forth to meet her and have flung themselves deliberately into the test of difficulties. Some of them have abandoned riches to exercise themselves in a voluntary poverty; others have sought labor and a painful austerity of life to toughen themselves against toil and trouble; others have deprived themselves of the most precious parts of the body, such as sight and the organs of generation, for fear that their services, too pleasant and easy, might relax and soften the firmness of their soul.

But for dying, which is the greatest task we have to perform, practice cannot help us. A man can, by habit and experience, fortify himself against pain, shame, indigence, and such other accidents; but as for death, we can try it only once: we are all apprentices when we come to it.

In ancient times there were men who husbanded their time so excellently that they tried to taste and savor it even at the point of death, and strained their minds to see what this passage was; but they have not come back to tell us news of it:

No man awakes
Whom once the icy end of living overtakes.
LUCRETIUS

Canius Julius, a Roman nobleman of singular virtue and firmness, after being condemned to death by that scoundrel Caligula, gave this among many prodigious proofs of his resoluteness. As he was on the point of being executed, a philosopher friend of his asked him: "Well, Canius, how stands your soul at this moment? What is it doing? What are your thoughts?" "I was thinking," he replied, "about holding myself ready and with all my powers intent to see whether in that instant of death, so short and brief, I shall be able to perceive any dislodgment of the soul, and whether it will have any

feeling of its departure; so that, if I learn anything about it, I may return later, if I can, to give the information to my friends." This man philosophizes not only unto death, but even in death itself. What assurance it was, and what proud courage, to want his death to serve as a lesson to him, and to have leisure to think about other things in such a great business!

> [B]Such sway he had over his dying soul.
>
> LUCAN

[A]It seems to me, however, that there is a certain way of familiarizing ourselves with death and trying it out to some extent. We can have an experience of it that is, if not entire and perfect, at least not useless, and that makes us more fortified and assured. If we cannot reach it, we can approach it, we can reconnoiter it; and if we do not penetrate as far as its fort, at least we shall see and become acquainted with the approaches to it.

It is not without reason that we are taught to study even our sleep for the resemblance it has with death. [C]How easily we pass from waking to sleeping! With how little sense of loss we lose consciousness of the light and of ourselves! Perhaps the faculty of sleep, which deprives us of all action and all feeling, might seem useless and contrary to nature, were it not that thereby Nature teaches us that she has made us for dying and living alike, and from the start of life presents to us the eternal state that she reserves for us after we die, to accustom us to it and take away our fear of it.

[A]But those who by some violent accident have fallen into a faint and lost all sensation, those, in my opinion, have been very close to seeing death's true and natural face. For as for the instant and point of passing away, it is not to be feared that it carries with it any travail or pain, since we can have no feeling without leisure. Our sufferings need time, which in death is so short and precipitate that it must necessarily be imperceptible. It is the approaches that we have to fear; and these may fall within our experience.

Many things seem to us greater in imagination than in reality. I have spent a good part of my life in perfect and entire health; I mean not merely entire, but even blithe and ebullient. This state, full of verdure and cheer, made me find the thought of illnesses so horrible that when I came to experience them I found their pains mild and easy compared with my fears.

[B]Here is what I experience every day: if I am warmly sheltered in a nice room during a stormy and tempestuous night, I am appalled

and distressed for those who are then in the open country; if I am myself outside, I do not even wish to be anywhere else.

^The mere idea of being always shut up in a room seemed to me unbearable. Suddenly I had to get used to being there a week, or a month, full of agitation, alteration, and weakness. And I have found that in time of health I used to pity the sick much more than I now think I deserve to be pitied when I am sick myself; and that the power of my apprehension made its object appear almost half again as fearful as it was in its truth and essence. I hope that the same thing will happen to me with death, and that it is not worth the trouble I take, the many preparations that I make, and all the many aids that I invoke and assemble to sustain the shock of it. But at all events, we can never be well enough prepared.

During our third civil war, or the second (I do not quite remember which), I went riding one day about a league from my house, which is situated at the very hub of all the turmoil of the civil wars of France. Thinking myself perfectly safe, and so near my home that I needed no better equipage, I took a very easy but not very strong horse. On my return, when a sudden occasion came up for me to use this horse for a service to which it was not accustomed, one of my men, big and strong, riding a powerful work horse who had a desperately hard mouth and was moreover fresh and vigorous – this man, in order to show his daring and get ahead of his companions, spurred his horse at full speed up the path behind me, came down like a colossus on the little man and little horse, and hit us like a thunderbolt with all his strength and weight, sending us both head over heels. So that there lay the horse bowled over and stunned, and I ten or twelve paces beyond, dead, stretched on my back, my face all bruised and skinned, my sword, which I had had in my hand, more than ten paces away, my belt in pieces, having no more motion or feeling than a log. It is the only swoon that I have experienced to this day.

Those who were with me, after having tried all the means they could to bring me round, thinking me dead, took me in their arms and were carrying me with great difficulty to my house, which was about half a French league from there. On the way, and after I had been taken for dead for more than two full hours, I began to move and breathe; for so great an abundance of blood had fallen into my stomach that nature had to revive its forces to discharge it. They set me up on my feet, where I threw up a whole bucketful of clots of pure blood, and several times on the way I had to do the same thing.

In so doing I began to recover a little life, but it was bit by bit and over so long a stretch of time that my first feelings were much closer to death than to life:

> [B]Because the shaken soul, uncertain yet
> Of its return, is still not firmly set.
>
> TASSO

[A]This recollection, which is strongly implanted on my soul, showing me the face and idea of death so true to nature, reconciles me to it somewhat.

When I began to see anything, it was with a vision so blurred, weak, and dead, that I still could distinguish nothing but the light,

> As one 'twixt wakefulness and doze,
> Whose eyes now open, now again they close.
>
> TASSO

As for the functions of the soul, they were reviving with the same progress as those of the body. I saw myself all bloody, for my doublet was stained all over with the blood I had thrown up. The first thought that came to me was that I had gotten a harquebus shot in the head; indeed several were being fired around us at the time of the accident. It seemed to me that my life was hanging only by the tip of my lips; I closed my eyes in order, it seemed to me, to help push it out, and took pleasure in growing languid and letting myself go. It was an idea that was only floating on the surface of my soul, as delicate and feeble as all the rest, but in truth not only free from distress but mingled with that sweet feeling that people have who let themselves slide into sleep.

I believe that this is the same state in which people find themselves whom we see fainting with weakness in the agony of death; and I maintain that we pity them without cause, supposing that they are agitated by grievous pains or have their soul oppressed by painful thoughts. This has always been my view, against the opinion of many, and even of Etienne de La Boétie, concerning those whom we see thus prostrate and comatose as their end approaches, or overwhelmed by the length of the disease, or by a stroke of apoplexy, or by epilepsy –

> [B]This do we often see:
> A man, struck, as by lightning, by some malady,
> Falls down all foaming at the mouth, shivers and rants;

> He moans under the torture, writhes his muscles, pants,
> And in fitful tossing exhausts his weary limbs
>
> LUCRETIUS

– ^Aor wounded in the head: When we hear them groan and from time to time utter poignant sighs, or see them make certain movements of the body, we seem to see signs that they still have some consciousness left; but I have always thought, I say, that their soul and body were buried in sleep.

> ^BHe lives, and is unconscious of his life.
>
> OVID

^AAnd I could not believe that with so great a paralysis of the limbs, and so great a failing of the senses, the soul could maintain any force within by which to be conscious of itself; and so I believed that they had no reflections to torment them, nothing able to make them judge and feel the misery of their condition, and that consequently they were not much to be pitied.

^BI can imagine no state so horrible and unbearable for me as to have my soul alive and afflicted, without means to express itself. I should say the same of those who are sent to execution with their tongue cut out, were it not that in this sort of death the most silent seems to be the most becoming, if it goes with a firm, grave countenance; and the same of those miserable prisoners who fall into the hands of the villainous murdering soldiers of these days, who torture them with every kind of cruel treatment to force them to pay some excessive and impossible ransom, keeping them meanwhile in a condition and in a place where they have no means whatever of expressing or signifying their thoughts and their misery.

^AThe poets have portrayed some gods as favorable to the deliverance of those who thus drag out a lingering death:

> I bear to Pluto, by decree,
> This lock of hair, and from your body set you free.
>
> VIRGIL

Nonetheless, the short and incoherent words and replies that are extorted from them by dint of shouting about their ears and storming at them, or the movements that seem to have some connection with what is asked them, are not evidence that they are alive, at least fully alive. So it happens to us in the early stages of sleep, before it has seized us completely, to sense as in a dream what is happening around us, and to follow voices with a blurred and uncertain hearing

which seems to touch on only the edges of the soul; and following the last words spoken to us, we make answers that are more random than sensible.

Now I have no doubt, now that I have tried this out by experience, that I judged this matter rightly all along. For from the first, while wholly unconscious, I was laboring to rip open my doublet with my nails (for I was not in armor); and yet I know that I felt nothing in my imagination that hurt me; for there are many movements of ours that do not come from our will:

> [B]And half-dead fingers writhe and seize the sword again.
>
> VIRGIL

[A]Thus those who are falling throw out their arms in front of them, by a natural impulse which makes our limbs lend each other their services [B]and have stirrings apart from our reason:

> They say that chariots bearing scythes will cut so fast
> That severed limbs are writhing on the ground below
> Before the victim's soul and strength can ever know
> Or even feel the pain, so swift has been the hurt.
>
> LUCRETIUS

[A]My stomach was oppressed with the clotted blood; my hands flew to it of their own accord, as they often do where we itch, against the intention of our will.

There are many animals, and even men, whose muscles we can see contract and move after they are dead. Every man knows by experience that there are parts that often move, stand up, and lie down, without his leave. Now these passions which touch only the rind of us cannot be called ours. To make them ours, the whole man must be involved; and the pains which the foot or the hand feel while we are asleep are not ours.

As I approached my house, where the alarm of my fall had already come, and the members of my family had met me with the outcries customary in such cases, not only did I make some sort of answer to what was asked me, but also (they say) I thought of ordering them to give a horse to my wife, whom I saw stumbling and having trouble on the road, which is steep and rugged. It would seem that this consideration must have proceeded from a wide-awake soul; yet the fact is that I was not there at all. These were idle thoughts, in the clouds, set in motion by the sensations of the eyes and ears; they did not come from within me. I did not know, for all

that, where I was coming from or where I was going, nor could I weigh and consider what I was asked. These are slight effects which the senses produce of themselves, as if by habit; what the soul contributed was in a dream, touched very lightly, and merely licked and sprinkled, as it were, by the soft impression of the senses.

Meanwhile my condition was, in truth, very pleasant and peaceful; I felt no affliction either for others or for myself; it was a languor and an extreme weakness, without any pain. I saw my house without recognizing it. When they had put me to bed, I felt infinite sweetness in this repose, for I had been villainously yanked about by those poor fellows, who had taken the pains to carry me in their arms over a long and very bad road, and had tired themselves out two or three times in relays. They offered me many remedies, of which I accepted none, holding it for certain that I was mortally wounded in the head. It would, in truth, have been a very happy death; for the weakness of my understanding kept me from having any judgment of it, and that of my body from having any feeling of it. I was letting myself slip away so gently, so gradually and easily, that I hardly ever did anything with less of a feeling of effort.

When I came back to life and regained my powers,

> [B]When my senses at last regained their strength,
>
> OVID

[A]which was two or three hours later, I felt myself all of a sudden caught up again in the pains, my limbs being all battered and bruised by my fall; and I felt so bad two or three nights after that I thought I was going to die all over again, but by a more painful death; and I still feel the effect of the shock of that collision.

I do not want to forget this, that the last thing I was able to recover was the memory of this accident; I had people repeat to me several times where I was going, where I was coming from, at what time it had happened to me, before I could take it in. As for the manner of my fall, they concealed it from me and made up other versions for the sake of the man who had been the cause of it. But a long time after, and the next day, when my memory came to open up and picture to me the state I had been in at the instant I had perceived that horse bearing down on me (for I had seen him at my heels and thought I was a dead man, but that thought had been so sudden that I had no time to be afraid), it seemed to me that a flash of lightning was striking my soul with a violent shock, and that I was coming back from the other world.

This account of so trivial an event would be rather pointless, were it not for the instruction that I have derived from it for myself; for in truth, in order to get used to the idea of death, I find there is nothing like coming close to it. Now as Pliny says, each man is a good education to himself, provided he has the capacity to spy on himself from close up. What I write here is not my teaching, but my study; it is not a lesson for others, but for me.

^cAnd yet it should not be held against me if I publish what I write. What is useful to me may also by accident be useful to another. Moreover, I am not spoiling anything, I am using only what is mine. And if I play the fool, it is at my expense and without harm to anyone. For it is a folly that will die with me, and will have no consequences. We have heard of only two or three ancients who opened up this road, and even of them we cannot say whether their manner in the least resembled mine, since we know only their names. No one since has followed their lead. It is a thorny undertaking, and more so than it seems, to follow a movement so wandering as that of our mind, to penetrate the opaque depths of its innermost folds, to pick out and immobilize the innumerable flutterings that agitate it. And it is a new and extraordinary amusement, which withdraws us from the ordinary occupations of the world, yes, even from those most recommended.

It is many years now that I have had only myself as object of my thoughts, that I have been examining and studying only myself; and if I study anything else, it is in order promptly to apply it to myself, or rather within myself. And it does not seem to me that I am making a mistake if – as is done in the other sciences, which are incomparably less useful – I impart what I have learned in this one, though I am hardly satisfied with the progress I have made in it. There is no description equal in difficulty, or certainly in usefulness, to the description of oneself. Even so one must spruce up, even so one must present oneself in an orderly arrangement, if one would go out in public. Now, I am constantly adorning myself, for I am constantly describing myself.

Custom has made speaking of oneself a vice, and obstinately forbids it out of hatred for the boasting that seems always to accompany it. Instead of blowing the child's nose, as we should, this amounts to pulling it off.

> Flight from a fault will lead us into crime.
> HORACE

I find more harm than good in this remedy. But even if it were true that it is presumptuous, no matter what the circumstances, to talk to the public about oneself, I still must not, according to my general plan, refrain from an action that openly displays this morbid quality, since it is in me; nor may I conceal this fault, which I not only practice but profess. However, to say what I think about it, custom is wrong to condemn wine because many get drunk on it. We can misuse only things which are good. And I believe that the rule against speaking of oneself applies only to the vulgar form of this failing. Such rules are bridles for calves, with which neither the saints, whom we hear speaking so boldly about themselves, nor the philosophers, nor the theologians curb themselves. Nor do I, though I am none of these. If they do not write about themselves expressly, at least when the occasion leads them to it they do not hesitate to put themselves prominently on display. What does Socrates treat of more fully than himself? To what does he lead his disciples' conversation more often than to talk about themselves, not about the lesson of their book, but about the essence and movement of their soul? We speak our thoughts religiously to God, and to our confessor, as our neighbors[1] do to the whole people. But, someone will answer, we speak only our self-accusations. Then we speak everything: for our very virtue is faulty and fit for repentance.

My trade and my art is living. He who forbids me to speak about it according to my sense, experience, and practice, let him order the architect to speak of buildings not according to himself but according to his neighbor; according to another man's knowledge, not according to his own. If it is vainglory for a man himself to publish his own merits, why doesn't Cicero proclaim the eloquence of Hortensius, Hortensius that of Cicero?

Perhaps they mean that I should testify about myself by works and deeds, not by bare words. What I chiefly portray is my cogitations, a shapeless subject that does not lend itself to expression in actions. It is all I can do to couch my thoughts in this airy medium of words. Some of the wisest and most devout men have lived avoiding all noticeable actions. My actions would tell more about fortune than about me. They bear witness to their own part, not to mine, unless it be by conjecture and without certainty: they are samples which display only details. I expose myself entire: my portrait is

1 The Protestants.

a cadaver on which the veins, the muscles, and the tendons appear at a glance, each part in its place. One part of what I am was produced by a cough, another by a pallor or a palpitation of the heart – in any case dubiously. It is not my deeds that I write down; it is myself, it is my essence.

I hold that a man should be cautious in making an estimate of himself, and equally conscientious in testifying about himself – whether he rates himself high or low makes no difference. If I seemed to myself good and wise or nearly so, I would shout it out at the top of my voice. To say less of yourself than is true is stupidity, not modesty. To pay yourself less than you are worth is cowardice and pusillanimity, according to Aristotle. No virtue is helped by falsehood, and truth is never subject to error. To say more of yourself than is true is not always presumption; it too is often stupidity. To be immoderately pleased with what you are, to fall therefore into an undiscerning self-love, is in my opinion the substance of this vice. The supreme remedy to cure it is to do just the opposite of what those people prescribe who, by prohibiting talking about oneself, even more strongly prohibit thinking about oneself. The pride lies in the thought; the tongue can have only a very slight share in it.

It seems to them that to be occupied with oneself means to be pleased with oneself, that to frequent and associate with oneself means to cherish oneself too much. That may be. But this excess arises only in those who touch themselves no more than super-ficially; who observe themselves only after taking care of their business; who call it daydreaming and idleness to be concerned with oneself, and making castles in Spain to furnish and build oneself; who think themselves something alien and foreign to themselves.

If anyone gets intoxicated with his knowledge when he looks beneath him, let him turn his eyes upward toward past ages, and he will lower his horns, finding there so many thousands of minds that trample him underfoot. If he gets into some flattering presumption about his valor, let him remember the lives of the two Scipios, so many armies, so many nations, all of whom leave him so far behind them. No particular quality will make a man proud who balances it against the many weaknesses and imperfections that are also in him, and, in the end, against the nullity of man's estate.

Because Socrates alone had seriously digested the precept of his god – to know himself – and because by that study he had come to

despise himself, he alone was deemed worthy of the name *wise*.
Whoever knows himself thus, let him boldly make himself known
by his own mouth.

7
Of honorary awards

^AThose who write the life of Augustus Caesar note this in his
military discipline: that of gifts he was wonderfully liberal toward
those who deserved it, but that of purely honorary awards he was
equally sparing. Yet he himself had been gratified by his uncle with
all the military awards before he had ever been to war.

It was a fine invention, and one taken up by most of the govern-
ments of the world, to establish certain vain and valueless marks to
honor and reward virtue, as do the crowns of laurel, oak, and myrtle,
the form of a certain garment, the privilege of riding in a coach
through the city or with a torch by night, some particular seat in
public assemblies, the prerogative of certain surnames and titles,
certain marks on coats of arms, and things like that, which have
been variously dealt with according to the opinions of nations, and
are still in use.

We for our part, and many of our neighbors, have the orders of
knighthood, which are established only for this purpose. In truth, it
is a very good and profitable custom to find a means of recognizing
the worth of rare and excellent men, and of contenting and satisfy-
ing them by payments which are no load on the public and cost the
prince nothing. And what has always been known by ancient
experience, and what we have also been able to see among us in
other times, that men of quality were more jealous of such rewards
than of those in which there was gain and profit – that is not without
reason and great justification. If with the prize that should be simply
one of honor you mingle other advantages and riches, this admix-
ture, instead of augmenting the original prestige, lowers it and cuts
it down.

The Order of Saint Michael,[1] which was so long in honor among
us, had no greater advantage than this, that it had no connection
with any other advantage. The result was that formerly there was no

1 Montaigne was a knight of this order. He tells us (*Essays* II: 12, p. 528) that he
long desired this honor, but received it only after it had been devalued.

office or status whatever that the nobility aspired to with as much desire and longing as this order, and no distinction that carried with it more respect and grandeur; since virtue more readily embraces and aspires to a reward that is purely her own, and more glorious than useful.

For in truth, other gifts do not have so dignified an employment, inasmuch as they are used for all sorts of occasions. With money we pay for the services of a valet, the diligence of a courier, dancing, rope-walking, speaking, and the meanest duties that we receive; yes, and even vice is paid for with money, and flattery, pandering, treachery. It is no wonder if virtue is less eager to receive and desire this sort of common coin than that which is proper and peculiar to it, and wholly noble and generous. Augustus was right to be much more thrifty and sparing of this than of the other, since honor is a privilege that derives its principal essence from rarity; and so does virtue itself:

> To him who thinks none bad, whoever can seem good?
>
> MARTIAL

We do not note in commendation of a man that he cares for the education of his children, since this is a common action, however just, ^cany more than we note a great tree when all the forest is like it. ^AI do not think that any citizen of Sparta gloried either in his valor, for that was a universal virtue in their nation, or in his fidelity and contempt for riches. No reward falls due to a virtue, however great, that has passed into a custom; and for that matter I do not know whether we would ever call it great when it was common.

So since these honorary awards have no other value and prestige than this, that few people enjoy them, in order to annihilate them we have only to be lavish with them. Even if there were more men now than in past times who deserved our order, its prestige should not be degraded just for that reason. And it can easily happen that more deserve it, for there is no other virtue that spreads so easily as military valor.

There is another kind of valor, true, perfect, and philosophical, of which I do not speak (and I employ this word according to our usage), a valor much greater than ours and fuller, a valor that is a strength and assurance of the soul, equally despising all sorts of adverse accidents, equable, uniform, and constant, a valor of which ours is only a very feeble ray. Habit, education, example, and custom can do all they want in establishing the valor of which I do speak,

and they easily make it common, as is easy to see by the experience of it which our civil wars afford us. ^BAnd if anyone could unite us at this moment and arouse our whole nation to a common enterprise, we would make our ancient military reputation flourish again.

^AIt is quite certain that the award of the Order of Saint Michael in times past was not contingent on this consideration alone; it looked further. It was never the payment of a valiant soldier, but that of a famous captain. The science of obeying did not merit so honorable a reward. In the old days they required for it a more universal expertness in war, which embraced the broadest and the greatest qualities of a military man – ^C*for the qualities of a soldier and those of a general are not the same* [Livy] – ^Awho should also be, besides that, of a rank suitable to such a dignity. But I say that even if more people were worthy of it than in other times, it should not for that reason have been handed out more liberally; it would have been better to err by not presenting it to all those to whom it was due, than to lose forever, as we have just done, the use of so valuable an invention. No man of spirit deigns to pride himself on what he has in common with many; and the men of today who have least deserved this reward make the most show of disdaining it, in order thereby to place themselves in the rank of those who have been wronged by the unworthy spread and debasement of this distinction, which was their particular due.

Now, to obliterate and abolish this order, in the expectation of thereby restoring this kind of institution to its former credit and of renewing it in another form, is not an undertaking suitable to a period as licentious and sick as the one in which we now find ourselves; and the result will be that the latest[2] will incur right from its birth the troubles that have just ruined the other. The rules for dispensing this new order would need to be extremely tight and strict to give it any authority; and this tumultuous period is incapable of a short and firm rein. Besides, before this one can be brought into repute, people must needs have lost their memory of the first, and of the contempt into which it has fallen.

This might be the place to insert some discussion on the subject of valor, and the difference between this virtue and the others; but since Plutarch has often returned to this theme, I should be meddling to no purpose in reporting here what he says about it. It is worth considering, however, that our nation gives valor the highest

2 The Order of the Holy Ghost, founded by Henry III in 1578.

rank among the virtues, as its name shows, which comes from *value*; and that according to our usage, when we say *a very valuable man*, or *a worthy man*, in the language of our court and our nobility, we are saying nothing else than *a valiant man*, as in the Roman fashion; for the Romans took the general term *virtue* from their word for *strength*. The proper, the only, the essential, form of nobility in France is the military profession.

It is probable that the first virtue that manifested itself among men and gave some the advantage over others was this one, by which the strongest and most courageous made themselves masters of the weaker and acquired particular rank and reputation; whence it has retained this linguistic honor and dignity. Or else that these nations, being very warlike, gave the prize and the worthiest title to the one virtue which was most familiar to them.

Just so our passion, combined with the feverish solicitude that we have for the chastity of women, brings it about that *a good woman*, *a worthy woman*, *a woman of honor and virtue*, means in effect nothing else to us than *a chaste woman*; as if, to obligate them to that duty, we were indifferent to all the rest, and gave them free rein for any other fault provided they abandon this one.

8
Of the affection of fathers for their children

TO MADAME D'ESTISSAC[1]

^A Madame, if strangeness and novelty, which customarily give value to things, do not save me, I shall never get out of this stupid enterprise with honor; but it is so fantastic and appears so remote from common usage that that may enable it to pass. It was a melancholy humor, and consequently a humor very hostile to my natural disposition, produced by the gloom of the solitude into which I had cast myself some years ago, that first put into my head this daydream of meddling with writing. And then, finding myself entirely destitute and void of any other matter, I presented myself to

[1] A friend and neighbor of Montaigne, whose son Charles accompanied him on his trip to Italy in 1580–81. Born Louise de La Béraudière, she has long been identified with a contemporary of the same name whose lively youth made her notorious as *la belle Rouet*. M. Roger Trinquet has recently shown that this identification is false.

myself for argument and subject. It is ᶜthe only book in the world of its kind, a book with ᴬa wild and eccentric plan. And so there is nothing in this job worth noting but its bizarreness; for a subject so vain and mean could not have been fashioned by the best workman in the world into something worthy of notice.

Now, Madame, having here to portray myself to the life, I would have forgotten one important feature if I had not represented the honor that I have always paid to your merits. And I wanted to say this particularly at the head of this chapter, since among your other good qualities the love you have shown your children holds one of the first ranks. Anyone who knows at what age Monsieur d'Estissac, your husband, left you a widow; the great and honorable matches that have been offered you, as many as to any lady in France of your rank; the constancy and firmness with which you sustained, for so many years and through so many thorny difficulties, the burden and the conduct of their affairs, which have driven you through all corners of France and still keep you besieged; the happy direction you have given them solely by your prudence or good fortune – such a person will readily say with me that we have in our time no clearer example of maternal affection than yours.

I praise God, Madame, that it has been so well employed: for the good hopes that your son Monsieur d'Estissac gives of himself are assurance enough that when he comes of age you will draw from him the obedience and gratitude of a very good son. But since, because of his youth, he could not notice the supreme services that he has received from you in such great number, I want him, if these writings happen to fall into his hands some day when I shall have neither mouth nor speech left that can say it, to receive from me in all truth this testimony, which will be attested to him even more vividly by the good results which, if it please God, he will feel: that there is not a gentleman in France who owes more to his mother than he does, and that he cannot in the future give any more certain proof of his goodness and virtue than by recognizing you for what you are.

If there is any truly natural law, that is to say, any instinct that is seen universally and permanently imprinted in both the animals and ourselves (which is not beyond dispute), I may say that in my opinion, after the care every animal has for its own preservation and the avoidance of what is harmful, the affection that the begetter has for his begotten ranks second. And because Nature seems to have recommended it to us with a view to extending and advancing the

successive parts of this machine of hers, it is no wonder if, turning backward, the affection of children for their fathers is not so great.

^CAdd to that this other Aristotelian consideration, that he who does good to someone loves him better than he is loved by him; and that he to whom something is owed loves better than he who owes; and that every workman loves his work better than he would be loved by it, if the work had feeling. For being is something we hold dear, and being consists in movement and action. Wherefore each man in some sort exists in his work. He who does good performs a beautiful and honorable action; he who receives performs only a useful one. Now, the useful is much less lovable than is the honorable. The honorable is stable and permanent, furnishing the man who has done it with a constant gratification. The useful easily escapes and is lost, and the memory of it is neither so fresh nor so sweet. Those things are dearest to us that have cost us most; and it is more difficult to give than to take.

^ASince it has pleased God to give us some capacity for reason, so that we should not be, like the animals, slavishly subjected to the common laws, but should apply ourselves to them by judgment and voluntary liberty, we must indeed yield a little to the simple authority of Nature, but not let ourselves be carried away tyrannically by her: reason alone must guide our inclinations.

I, for my part, have a taste strangely blunted to these propensities that are produced in us without the command and mediation of our judgment. For example, on this subject that I am talking about, I cannot entertain that passion which makes people hug infants that are hardly born yet, having neither movement in the soul nor recognizable shape to the body by which they can make themselves lovable. ^CAnd I have not willingly suffered them to be brought up near me.

^AA true and well-regulated affection should be born and increase with the knowledge children give us of themselves; and then, if they are worthy of it, the natural propensity going along with reason, we should cherish them with a truly paternal love; and we should likewise pass judgment on them if they are otherwise, always submitting to reason, notwithstanding the force of nature. It is very often the reverse; and most commonly we feel more excited over the stamping, the games, and the infantile tricks of our children than we do later over their grown-up actions, as if we had loved them for our pastime, ^Clike monkeys, not like men. ^AAnd some supply toys very liberally for their childhood, who tighten up at the slightest

expenditure they need when they are of age. Indeed it seems that the jealousy we feel at seeing them appear in the world and enjoy it when we are about to leave it makes us more stingy and tight with them; it vexes us that they are treading on our heels, ^Cas if to solicit us to leave. ^AAnd if we had that to fear, then since in the nature of things they cannot in truth either be or live except at the expense of our being and our life, we should not have meddled with being fathers.

As for me, I think it is cruelty and injustice not to receive them into a share and association in our goods, and as companions in the understanding of our domestic affairs, when they are capable of it, and not to cut down and restrict our own comforts in order to provide for theirs, since we have begotten them to that end. It is an injustice that an old, broken, half-dead father should enjoy alone, in a corner of his hearth, possessions that would suffice for the advancement and maintenance of many children, and let them meanwhile, for lack of means, lose their best years without making progress in public service and the knowledge of men. They are cast into the desperate plight of seeking by any means, however unjust, to provide for their need; as I have seen in my time several young men of good family so addicted to stealing that no correction could turn them from it. I know one, well-connected, to whom, at the request of a brother of his, a very honorable and brave gentleman, I once spoke to this purpose. He answered me and confessed quite roundly that he had been set on this filthy path by the rigor and avarice of his father, but that now he was so accustomed to it that he could not keep out of it. And he had then just been caught stealing the rings of a lady at whose levee he had been present with many others. He made me remember the story I had heard of another gentleman, so formed and fashioned to this fine trade in the time of his youth that when he came later to be master of his estate and determined to abandon this traffic, nevertheless, if he passed by a shop where there was something he needed, he could not keep himself from stealing it, on pain of sending to pay for it later. And I have seen several so trained and schooled to this that even among their comrades they regularly stole things which they intended to return.

^BI am a Gascon, and yet there is no vice in which I am less expert than this. I hate it a little more by temperament than I condemn it by reason: even in desire, I take nothing away from anyone. ^AThis province is indeed a little more decried in this respect than the

others of the French nation; yet we have seen in our day at various times men of good families from other provinces in the hands of justice, convicted of many horrible robberies. I fear that this depravity must be blamed to some extent on the avarice of fathers.

Someone may answer me as one lord of good understanding did one day. From hoarding his riches, he said, he expected to derive no other benefit and use than to make himself honored and sought after by his dependents, since when age had deprived him of all other powers, he would have only this way left to maintain his authority in his family and to avoid incurring everyone's scorn and disdain. ᶜIn truth not old age alone, but every weakness, according to Aristotle, is a promoter of avarice. ᴬThere is something to be said for this; but it is medicine for a disease whose birth we should have prevented.

A father is very miserable who holds his children's affection only by the need they have of his help – if that is to be called affection. He should make himself worthy of respect by his virtue and by his ability, and of love by his goodness and the kindness of his behavior. The very ashes of a rich material have their value; and we are accustomed to hold in respect and reverence the bones and relics of persons of honor. No old age can be so decrepit and rancid in a person who has passed his life in honor as not to be venerable, especially to his children, whose souls he ought to have trained to their duty by reason, not by necessity and need nor by harshness and force:

> In my opinion he is wrong who thinks
> That an authority by power attained
> Is more secure than that by friendship gained.
>
> TERENCE

ᴮI condemn all violence in the education of a tender soul which is being trained for honor and liberty. There is a sort of servility about rigor and constraint; and I hold that what cannot be done by reason, and by wisdom and tact, is never done by force. I was brought up that way. They say that in all my childhood I felt the rod only twice, and that very softly. I have owed the same to the children I have had; they all die on me at nurse; but ᶜLéonor, ᴮone single daughter who escaped that misfortune, is over six years old now, and has never been guided or punished for her childish faults – her mother's indulgence easily concurring – by anything but words, and very gentle ones. And even if my wishes should be frustrated, there are

enough other causes on which to place the blame without reproaching my system, which I know to be just and natural. I should have been much more scrupulous still in this respect toward boys, who are less born to serve and of a freer condition: I should have loved to swell their hearts with ingenuousness and frankness. I have seen no other effect of whips except to make souls more cowardly or more maliciously obstinate.

^ADo we want to be loved by our children? Do we want to take away from them the occasion for desiring our death (though no occasion for so horrible a wish can be either just or excusable: ^c*no crime is based on reason* [Livy])? ^ALet us furnish their life reasonably with what is in our power. For that purpose, we should not marry so young that our age comes to be almost confounded with theirs. For this inconvenience casts us into many great difficulties. I am referring especially to the nobility, which is a leisure class and lives, as they say, only on its private income. For with other groups, where a living must be earned, the plurality and company of children is an advantage to the household; they are so many new tools and instruments for getting rich.

^BI married at thirty-three, and approve the suggestion of thirty-five, which they say is Aristotle's. ^CPlato does not want people to marry before thirty; but he is right to laugh at those who perform the works of marriage after fifty-five; and he condemns their offspring as unworthy of nourishment and life. Thales sets its truest limits. When young, he answered his mother, who was urging him to marry, that it was not yet time; and, when he was getting old, that it was no longer time. We must deny that there is any appropriate time for any inappropriate action.

^AThe ancient Gauls considered it extremely reprehensible for a man under twenty to have had knowledge of a woman, and particularly recommended to the men who wanted to train for war to keep their virginity until well along in years, since courage is softened and diverted by intercourse with women.

> Happy in children, wed to a young wife,
> For exploits he had lost his predilection
> Through fatherly and marital affection.
> TASSO

^CGreek history observes of Iccus of Tarentum, of Chryson, of Astylus, of Diopompus and others, that to keep their bodies strong for the races in the Olympic games, for wrestling, and for other

exercises, they denied themselves any sort of sexual act as long as their training lasted. Muley Hassan, king of Tunis, the one whom the Emperor Charles V restored to his estate, reproached the memory of his father for his frequentation of his wives, and called him slack, effeminate, maker of children. [B]In a certain country of the Spanish Indies, they did not permit men to marry until after forty, and yet they permitted girls to do so at ten.

[A]When a gentleman is thirty-five, it is not time for him to give place to his son who is twenty: he is himself in the midst of appearing on military expeditions and in the court of his prince; he needs his resources, and should certainly share them, but not so as to forget himself for others. And such a man may justifiably use the reply that fathers have ordinarily in their mouths: "I do not want to strip myself before I go to bed."

But a father prostrated by years and infirmities, deprived by his weakness and lack of health of the common society of men, wrongs himself and his family by uselessly brooding over a great heap of riches. He is pretty well in shape, if he is wise, to want to strip himself for bed, not down to his shirt, but to a good warm night-shirt. The remaining pomps, for which he has no more use, he should willingly present to those to whom by the order of nature they should belong. It is right that he should leave the enjoyment of these things to them, since nature deprives him of it; if he does otherwise, there is malice and envy involved without a doubt.

The finest act of Emperor Charles V was this: that he was able to recognize, [C]in imitation of certain ancients of his caliber, [A]that reason commands us to strip ourselves when our robes become a burden and a hindrance to us, and to go to bed when our legs fail us. He resigned his possessions, his greatness, and his power to his son when he felt himself failing in the firmness and strength to conduct affairs with the glory he had acquired in them.

> Set free the aging horse before it is too late,
> Lest he go stumbling broken-winded at the end.
> HORACE

This fault of not being able to recognize oneself early and not feeling the impotence and extreme alteration that age naturally brings to both body and soul, and in my opinion equally, unless the soul receives more than half of it, has ruined the reputation of most of the world's great men. I have seen in my time, and known intimately, persons of great authority who, it was easy to see, had

declined marvelously from their former ability, which I knew of by the reputation they had acquired for it in their better years. I could readily, for their honor, have wished them retired, living at home at their ease and unburdened with public and warlike occupations that were no longer suited to their shoulders.

I was once an intimate in the house of a gentleman, a widower and very old, yet of a pretty green old age. He had several daughters to marry off and a son old enough to appear in the world. This burdened his house with many expenses and visits of strangers, in which he took little pleasure, not only out of concern for economy, but even more because he had adopted, owing to his age, a mode of life far removed from ours. I told him one day a little boldly, as is my custom, that it would become him better to make room for us younger folk, to leave his principal house (for that was the only one he had that was well furnished and fitted out) to his son and retire to a neighboring estate of his where no one would trouble his repose, since he could not otherwise avoid being disturbed by us in view of the situation of his children. He took my advice later and was well off for it.

This is not to say that we should so obligate ourselves to our children that we can no longer retract what we give them. I, who am ready to play this role, would leave my children the enjoyment of my house and possessions, but with liberty to repent if they gave me occasion to. I would leave them the use of it because that would no longer be convenient to me; and of authority over affairs in general, I would reserve for myself as much as I pleased. For I have always judged that it must be a great contentment to an old father himself to give his children a start in managing his affairs, and during his lifetime to be able to oversee their conduct, furnishing them with instruction and advice according to the experience he has of them, directing their efforts to uphold the ancient honor and order of his house, and thereby finding firm ground for the hopes he may conceive of their future conduct.

And for this purpose I would not avoid their company; I would observe them close up, and enjoy their fun and festivities within the limitations of my age. If I did not live among them (as I could not without spoiling their gatherings by being fretful as old men are and a slave to my infirmities, and without also doing violence to the rules and ways of living that I should then have), I should at least want to live near them in a part of my house, not the most showy but the most comfortable. Not like a dean of the church of Saint Hilary at

Poitiers whom I saw, some years ago, so cut off by his gloomy disagreeableness that when I entered his room it had been twenty-two years since he had gone one step out of it; and yet he was free and easy in all his functions, except for a cold that was going down into his stomach. Hardly once a week would he permit anyone to come in to see him; he kept himself always locked up in his chamber alone, except that a servant, who only came in and went out, brought him something to eat once a day. His occupation was to walk around and read some book (for he had a certain knowledge of letters); moreover, he was obstinately set on dying in this routine, as he did soon after.

I would try by pleasant relations to foster in my children a lively and unfeigned affection and good will toward me, which is easily won in a wellborn nature; for if they are raging beasts, ^csuch as our time produces in profusion, ^Awe must hate and shun them as such.

I loathe the custom ^cof forbidding children to use the name of father and enjoining upon them some strange address, as being more respectful; as if nature had not readily provided sufficiently for our authority. We call God Almighty father, and disdain to have our children call us that. It is also wrong and foolish ^Ato prohibit children who have come of age from being familiar with their fathers, and to prefer to maintain an austere and disdainful gravity toward them, hoping thereby to keep them in fear and obedience. For that is a very futile farce, which makes fathers annoying to their children and, what is worse, ridiculous. They have in their hands youth and vigor, and consequently the wind and favor of the world behind them; and they receive with mockery these fierce and tyrannical looks from men who have no blood left in either heart or veins – real scarecrows in a hemp field. Even if I could make myself feared, I would much rather make myself loved.

^BThere are so many sorts of defects in old age, so much impotence, it is so liable to contempt, that the best acquisition it can make is the love and affection of our family: command and fear are no longer its weapons. I know one old man[2] whose youth was very

2 According to Florimond de Raemond, this man is Montaigne's neighbor and sponsor, the former ambassador to England, German-Gaston de Foix, marquis de Trans. It was he who presented Montaigne with the Order of Saint Michael. Brantôme's claim that he did so to make fun of Montaigne is implausible, because Trans was probably instrumental in Montaigne's receipt of two other honors: that of gentleman-in-ordinary of the king's chamber and that of mayor of Bordeaux.

imperious. Now that age has come on, although he is as healthy
as can be, he strikes, he bites, he swears: ^Cthe most tempestuous
master in France. ^BHe is eaten up by care and vigilance. All that is
just a farce in which the family itself conspires: of the storeroom,
the cellar, and even of his purse, others have the best share of the
enjoyment, while he holds the keys in his pouch more dearly than if
they were his eyes. While he is happy over the frugality and nig-
gardliness of his table, everybody is living it up in various corners
of his house, gaming, spending, and exchanging stories about his
vain anger and foresight. Everyone is on guard against him. If, by
chance, some wretched servant devotes himself to him, promptly
he falls under his suspicion, a trait on which old age is so prone to
bite of its own accord. How many times has he boasted to me of the
check he kept on his household and the strict obedience and rever-
ence he received from them, and how clearly he saw into his
own affairs!

> He alone is ignorant of all things.
> TERENCE

I know no man who can bring to bear more qualities, both natural
and acquired, fit to preserve mastery, than he does; and yet he has
fallen from authority like a child. Therefore I have chosen him from
among several I know in that condition, as the best example.

^CIt would be a matter for a scholastic dispute whether he is better
off thus or otherwise. In his presence, all things yield to him. They
allow his authority this vain course: they never resist him; they take
his word, they fear him, they give him his bellyful of respect. Does
he dismiss a servant? He packs his bundle, there he is gone – but
only out of his presence. The steps of old age are so slow, the senses
so blurred, that he will live and do his job in the same house for a year
without being perceived. And when the time comes, they have
letters arrive from far away, piteous, suppliant, full of promises to
do better, whereby he is restored to grace. Does Monsieur take some
step or send some dispatch that displeases? They suppress it, soon
afterward forging causes enough to excuse the lack of execution or
reply. No letters from outside are brought to him first; he sees only
those that it seems convenient for him to know. If by accident he
gets hold of one, the person on whom he relies to read his letters to
him promptly finds in it whatever he chooses; and all the time they
have someone asking his pardon who is really insulting him in this
very letter. In fine, he sees his affairs only in an image arranged,

designed, and made just as satisfactory as possible, so as not to rouse his bad humor and anger. I have seen, under different forms, plenty of long, constant domestic economies with exactly the same result.

ᴮWives always have a proclivity for disagreeing with their husbands. ᶜThey seize with both hands every pretext to go contrary to them; the first excuse serves them as plenary justification. I have known one who robbed her husband wholesale in order, so she told her confessor, to give fatter alms. Just trust that pious almsgiving! No responsibility seems to them to have sufficient dignity if it comes by the husband's concession. They have to usurp it either by cunning or by insolence, and always unjustly, to give it grace and authority. As in the case I am speaking of, ᴮwhen they act against a poor old man and for the sake of children, then they seize this pretext and glory in making it serve their passion, ᶜand, as if they were slaves making a common cause, readily conspire against his domination and government. ᴮAs for sons, grown and vigorous, they also promptly suborn, either by force or by favor, both steward and receiver and all the rest.

Those who have neither wife nor son fall into this misfortune less easily, but also more cruelly and shamefully. ᶜCato the Elder used to say in his time: "So many servants, so many enemies." Consider whether, in keeping with the difference in purity between his age and ours, he did not mean to warn us that wife, son, and servant are so many enemies to us. ᴮIt is well that our declining years bring with them the sweet benefits of imperceptiveness and ignorance, and a facility for letting ourselves be deceived. If we got stirred up over this, what would become of us, especially in this age in which the judges who have to decide our controversies are commonly partisans of the young, and interested parties?

ᶜIn case this deception escapes my sight, at least it does not escape my sight that I am very deceivable.[3] And will it ever be said enough how precious is a friend, and how different a thing from

3 The Bordeaux Copy shows an addition here: "Three and four times happy the man who can entrust his pitiful old age into a friendly hand." And at the end of the paragraph: "Am I better off for having had the taste of it [friendship], or am I worse off? Certainly I am better off. My regret for him consoles and honors me. Is it not a pious and pleasant duty of my life to be forever performing his obsequies? Is there an enjoyment that is worth this privation? I could easily let myself be lulled into idleness by such a flattering notion."

these civil bonds?[4] Even the image of friendship that I see in the animals, so pure, how religiously I respect it!

If others deceive me, at least I do not deceive myself, either by thinking myself capable of guarding against their deception, or by racking my brains to make myself capable. I escape from such betrayals in my own bosom not by a restless and tumultuous curiosity, but rather by diversion and resolution.

When I hear tell of someone's condition, I do not dwell on him; I promptly turn my eyes to myself to see how it is with me. Everything that affects him concerns me. His mishap warns me and rouses me in that direction. Every day and every hour we say things about another that we would more properly say about ourselves, if we knew how to turn our attention inward as well as extend it outward.

And many authors in this manner injure their cause, running rashly forward to meet the one they are attacking, and hurling shafts at their enemies that are suited to being hurled back at them.

ᴬAfter the late Marshal de Monluc lost his son – in truth a brave gentleman and one of great promise, who died on the island of Madeira – he used to stress greatly to me, among his other regrets, the sorrow and heartbreak he felt for never having opened up to him. He had lost, he said, by that habit of paternal gravity and stiffness, the comfort of appreciating his son and knowing him well, and also of declaring to him the extreme affection that he bore him and the high opinion he had of his virtue. "And that poor boy," he would say, "saw nothing of me but a scowling and disdainful countenance, and took with him the belief that I knew neither how to love him nor how to esteem him according to his merit. For whom was I keeping the revelation of that singular affection that I bore him in my soul? Wasn't he the one who should have had all the pleasure of it and all the gratitude? I constrained and tortured

Both these passages are crossed out, but in a different way (with many cross lines instead of one strong one) and apparently a different hand from nearly all Montaigne's other manuscript deletions. The second passage (but not the first) appears in the 1595 edition, with the last sentence omitted, and preceded by "O my friend!" in a later position, four paragraphs later, after "perfect and entire communication with them."

Some scholars suppose that Montaigne retained but moved the passage on the copy he sent to Mlle de Gournay for the 1595 edition, and later crossed it out on his own copy.

4 Marriage.

myself to maintain this vain mask, and thereby lost the pleasure of association with him, and of his good will along with it, for he could not be other than very cool toward me, having never had anything but harshness from me or experienced any but a tyrannical bearing." I think this lament was well taken and reasonable; for, as I know by too certain experience, there is no consolation so sweet in the loss of our friends as that which comes to us from the knowledge of not having forgotten to tell them anything and of having had perfect and entire communication with them.[5]

[B]I open myself to my family as much as I can, and very readily signify to them the state of my will and my judgment toward them, as toward everyone. I hasten to bring myself out and put myself forth: I do not want people to be mistaken about me, whether for better or for worse.

[A]Among other peculiar customs of our ancient Gauls, from what Caesar says, was this one: that children did not appear before their fathers or dare to be found in their company in public until they were beginning to bear arms; as if they meant that only then was it time for the fathers to receive their sons into their familiarity and acquaintance.

I have observed still another sort of error of judgment in some fathers of my time, who are not content with depriving their children during their long lifetime of the share they naturally ought to have had in their fortunes, but afterward also leave to their wives this same authority over all their possessions and the right to dispose of them according to their fancy. And I have known one lord, one of the first officers of our crown, a man with an income of more than fifty thousand crowns in prospect by right of succession, who died needy and overwhelmed with debts at over fifty years of age, while his mother in her extreme decrepitude was still enjoying all his property by the will of his father, who for his part had lived nearly eighty years. This does not seem at all reasonable to me.

[B]However, I find it of little advantage for a man whose affairs are going well to go looking for a wife who will burden him with a big dowry; there is no outside debt that brings more ruin on houses. My predecessors have generally followed this counsel to good advantage, and so have I. [C]But those who advise us against rich wives for fear they may be less tractable and grateful are wrong to

5 See note 3 above.

make us lose some real profit for so frivolous a conjecture. It costs an unreasonable woman no more to override one reason than another. They love themselves best wherever they are most in the wrong. Unfairness allures them, as the honor of their virtuous actions allures good women; and the richer these are, the nicer they are, as they are the more willingly and proudly chaste because they are beautiful.

^AIt is right to leave the administration of affairs to mothers while the children are not yet of legal age to take over on their own. But the father has brought them up very badly if he cannot hope that at that age they will have more wisdom and ability than his wife, seeing the ordinary weakness of the sex. However, in truth, it would be much more contrary to nature to make mothers dependent on the discretion of their children. They should be given plentiful means to maintain themselves according to the standing of their house and their age, since necessity and indigence are much more unbecoming and hard to bear for them than for men: this should be borne by the children rather than by the mother.

^CIn general the soundest distribution of our estate when we die seems to me the one prescribed by the custom of the country. The laws have thought about this better than we; and it is better to let them err in their choice than rashly to run the risk of erring in ours. The estate is not properly ours, since by a civil ordinance and independently of us it is destined to certain successors. And although we have some liberty beyond that, I hold that we need a very great and apparent cause to make us take away from anyone that which his fortune has won him and to which common justice entitles him; and that it is abusing this liberty unreasonably to make it serve our frivolous and private fancies. My lot has been gracious to me in not having offered me occasions that could tempt me and divert my affection from the common and legitimate arrangement.

I see some on whom it is wasted time to take long pains in doing good services: one word taken amiss wipes out the merit of ten years. Happy the man who is there on the spot to anoint their good will at this last passage. The nearest action carries the day; not the best and most frequent services, but the most recent and present, do the job. Such men play with their wills as with apples or rods, to gratify or chastise every action of those who claim an interest in them. A will is a thing of too great consequence and weight to be thus trotted out at every instant; wise men take their stand on it once for all, having regard to reason and public observances.

We take these male entails too much to heart. And we look forward to a ridiculous eternity for our names.[6] We also weigh too heavily the vain conjectures about the future that we draw from childish minds. They might perhaps have done an injustice by displacing me from my rank for having been the most sluggish and leaden, the slowest and most reluctant, in my lesson, not only of all my brothers, but of all the boys of my province, whether the lesson was in mental or bodily exercise. It is folly to make extraordinary selections on the faith of these divinations in which we are so often deceived. If one may violate this rule and correct the destinies in the choice they have made of our heirs, it is somewhat more reasonable to do so on grounds of some remarkable and enormous physical deformity, a constant, irremediable defect, and, according to us who greatly esteem beauty, a very harmful one.

The amusing dialogue between Plato's lawgiver and his fellow citizens will do honor to this passage. "What," say they, feeling the end approaching, "may we not dispose of what is ours to whom we please? Ye gods, what cruelty that it should not be lawful for us, according as our people have served us in our illnesses, in our old age, in our affairs, to give them more or less according to our fancies!" To which the lawgiver replies in this manner: "My friends, who no doubt have soon to die, it is hard both for you to know yourselves and for you to know what is yours, according to the Delphic inscription. I who make the laws hold that neither are you your own nor is what you enjoy your own. Both your goods and yourselves belong to your family, past as well as future. But even more do both your family and your goods belong to the public. Wherefore if some flatterer in your old age or in your illness, or some passion, solicits you at a bad time to make an unjust will, I will guard you against it. But, having regard to both the general interest of the city and that of your family, I shall establish laws and make it felt, as is reasonable, that the private interest must yield to the public interest. Go your way then peacefully and with good will where human necessity calls you. It is for me, who do not regard one thing more than the other, who, as much as I can, look after the general interest, to take care of what you leave."

6 Despite these remarks, Montaigne yielded to this very temptation and in his will entailed his estate and his name to the younger descendant of his daughter Léonor, who married twice and had children by both marriages. The result was two centuries of litigation.

To return to my subject, ^it seems to me, I know not why, that no kind of mastery is due to women over men except the maternal and natural, unless it is for the punishment of those who, by some feverish humor, have voluntarily submitted themselves to them. But that does not concern old women, of whom we are speaking here. It is the reasonableness of this consideration that has made us create and so readily give force to this law, which no one has ever seen, that deprives women of the succession to our crown; and there is hardly a sovereignty in the world where it is not alleged, as it is here, by some appearance of reason that gives it authority; but fortune has given it more credit in certain places than in others.

It is dangerous to leave the disposal of our succession to women's judgment, according to the choice they will make among the children, which is at all times unfair and capricious. For that disordered appetite and sick taste that they have at the time of their pregnancies they have in their soul at all times. We commonly see them devote themselves to the weakest and most ill-favored, or to those, if they have any, who are still hanging about their necks. For, not having enough force of reason to choose and embrace what deserves it, they most readily let themselves be carried away where the impressions of nature stand most alone; like the animals, who have no knowledge of their young except while they cling to their dugs.

Moreover, it is easy to see by experience that this natural affection, to which we give so much authority, has very weak roots. Every day we take their own children out of the arms of mothers, and make them take charge of ours, for a very slight profit. We make them abandon their own to some wretched nurse to whom we do not want to entrust our own, or to some goat; forbidding them not only to give them suck, whatever danger they may thereby incur, but even to take any care of them, that they may be entirely employed in the service of ours. And we see in most of them a bastard affection soon engendered by habit, more vehement than the natural, and a greater solicitude for the preservation of the borrowed children than for their own.

And what I said about goats I said because it is ordinary around where I live to see village women, when they cannot feed their children from their breasts, call goats to their aid; and I have at this moment two lackeys who never sucked woman's milk for more than a week. These goats are promptly trained to come and suckle these little children; they recognize their voices when they call out, and come running. If any other than their nursling is presented to them,

they refuse it; and the child does the same with another goat. I saw one the other day whose goat they took away because his father had only borrowed her from a neighbor of his; he never could take to the other that they presented to him, and doubtless died of hunger. Animals alter and corrupt their natural affection as easily as we.

^CHerodotus relates of a certain district of Libya that intercourse with women is promiscuous, but that the child, when he has the strength to walk, finds to be his father the one toward whom, in the crowd, natural inclination bears his first steps. I believe that this must lead to frequent mistakes.

^ANow when we consider this simple reason for loving our children – that we begot them, wherefore we call them our other selves – it seems to me that there is indeed another production proceeding from us that is no less commendable. For what we engender by the soul, the children of our mind, of our heart and our ability, are produced by a nobler part than the body and are more our own. We are father and mother both in this generation. These cost us a lot more, and bring us more honor, if they have any good in them. For the worth of our other children is much more theirs than ours; the share we have in it is very slight; but of these all the beauty, all the grace and value, is ours. Thus they represent and report us much more to the life than the others. ^CPlato adds that these are immortal children who immortalize their fathers and even deify them, as with Lycurgus, Solon, and Minos.

^ANow, since the histories are full of examples of that common affection of fathers toward their children, it seemed to me not inappropriate to pick out also some of this other kind.

^CHeliodorus, that good bishop of Tricca, preferred to lose the dignity, the profit, and the piety of so venerable a prelacy rather than lose his daughter[7] – a daughter who still lives on, very nice, but for all that perhaps a little too curiously and loosely tricked out, and in too amorous a fashion, for the daughter of a churchman and a priest.

^AThere was one Labienus in Rome, a person of great worth and authority, and, among other qualities, excelling in every sort of literature. He was, I believe, the son of that great Labienus, the first of the captains who were under Caesar in the Gallic war, and who

7 The Greek romance *Theagenes and Chariclea*, very popular in France in Jacques Amyot's translation, was then attributed to this Heliodorus (bishop of Tricca), but is now attributed to Heliodorus of Emesa in Syria.

later, after throwing himself to the great Pompey's side, maintained himself there so valorously until Caesar defeated him in Spain. The virtue of this Labienus aroused many people's envy; and, as seems likely, the courtiers and favorites of the emperors of his time opposed him for his independence and for the feelings against tyranny which he had from his father, which he still retained, and with which we may believe he had colored his books and writings. His adversaries prosecuted him before the magistrate in Rome and succeeded in having several of his published works condemned to be burned. It was with him that this new sort of penalty began, which was later continued in Rome against many others, of punishing by death even writings and studies. There was not enough means and matter for cruelty unless we brought in things which nature has exempted from all feeling and all suffering, such as reputation and the inventions of our mind, and unless we communicated corporal punishments to the teachings and monuments of the muses.

Now Labienus could not endure this loss nor survive that dear progeny of his; he had himself taken and shut up alive in the tomb of his ancestors, where he contrived to kill and bury himself at the same time. It is hard to show any more vehement paternal affection than that. Cassius Severus, a very eloquent man and his intimate friend, seeing his books burning, cried out that by the same sentence they should have condemned him to be burned alive with them; for he carried and preserved in his memory what they contained.

[B]A like fate befell Greuntius Cordus, accused of having praised Brutus and Cassius in his books. That vile, servile, and corrupt Senate, worthy of a worse master than Tiberius, condemned his writings to the fire. He was content to keep them company in their death, and killed himself by abstaining from food.

[A]In the last moments of the good Lucan's life, after he was condemned by that scoundrel Nero, when most of his blood had already flowed out through the veins of his arms, which he had had his doctor cut open so as to die, and when the cold had seized on his extremities and was beginning to approach his vital parts, the last thing he had in his memory was some of the verses of his book on the battle of Pharsalia, which he recited; and he died with those last words in his mouth. What was that but a tender and paternal leave he was taking of his children, representing the farewells and close embraces that we give to ours when we die, and an effect of that natural inclination that recalls to our memory in this extremity the things we have held dearest during our life?

Do you think that Epicurus, who (while dying in torment, as he says, from the utmost pains of colic) had all his consolation in the beauty of the doctrine he was leaving to the world, would have received as much contentment from a number of wellborn and well-brought-up children, if he had had any, as he did from the production of his rich writings? And that if he had had to choose between leaving behind a deformed and ill-born child and leaving behind a stupid and inept book, he would not rather have chosen, and not only he but any man of like ability, to incur the former misfortune than the other? It would perhaps be impiety in Saint Augustine, for example – if it were proposed to him on the one hand to bury his writings, from which our religion receives such great fruit, or else to bury his children, in case he had any – if he did not prefer to bury his children.

[B]And I do not know whether I would not like much better to have produced one perfectly formed child by intercourse with the muses than by intercourse with my wife.

[C]To this child, such as it is, what I give I give purely and irrevocably, as one gives to the children of one's body. The little good I have done for it is no longer at my disposal. It may know a good many things that I no longer know and hold from me what I have not retained and what, just like a stranger, I should have to borrow from it if I came to need it. If I am wiser than it, it is richer than I.

[A]There are few men devoted to poetry who would not be prouder to be the father of the *Aeneid* than of the handsomest boy in Rome, and who would not more easily suffer the loss of the one than of the other. [C]For, according to Aristotle, of all craftsmen the poet in particular is the most in love with his own work.

[A]It is hard to believe that Epaminondas, who boasted of leaving as his entire posterity daughters who would one day do their father honor (these were the two noble victories he had won over the Lacedaemonians), would willingly have consented to exchange these for the most gorgeous daughters of all Greece, or that Alexander and Caesar ever wanted to be deprived of the grandeur of their glorious deeds of war for the satisfaction of having children and heirs, however perfect and accomplished they might be.

Indeed I very much doubt that Phidias or any other excellent sculptor would be so pleased with the preservation and long life of his natural children as with that of an excellent statue that his long labor and study had brought to artistic perfection. And as for those

vicious and frenzied passions which have sometimes inflamed fathers with love for their daughters, or mothers for their sons, the like even of these are found in this other sort of parenthood: witness what they tell of Pygmalion, who after building a statue of a woman of singular beauty, became so madly and frantically smitten with love of this work that the gods, for the sake of his passion, had to bring it to life for him:

> Its hardness gone, the ivory softens, yields
> Beneath his fingers.
>
> OVID

9
Of the arms of the Parthians

ᴬIt is a vicious practice of the nobility of our time, and full of softness, to put on armor only on the point of extreme need and to take it off as soon as there is the slightest appearance that the danger has gone. Whence come many disorders. For with everyone shouting and running for his arms at the last moment before the attack, some are still lacing their cuirass when their comrades are already routed. Our fathers used to give their headpiece, lance, and gauntlets to be carried, and did not abandon the rest of their equipment as long as the job lasted. Our troops nowadays are all mixed up and thrown into disorder by the confusion of the baggage and the servants, who cannot leave their masters because they have their arms.

ᶜLivy, speaking of our people: *Their bodies, utterly incapable of toil, could scarcely carry their armor on their shoulders.*

ᴬSeveral nations formerly went, and still go, to war without wearing armor, or wore things useless for defense:

> ᴮWearing helmets made of bark stripped from the cork-tree.
>
> VIRGIL

Alexander, the most daring commander that ever was, rarely wore armor. ᴬAnd those of us who despise it scarcely get the worse of the bargain for it. If we see some man killed for want of a harness, there is hardly a smaller number who have been lost by the encumbrance of their armor, trapped beneath its weight, or bruised and broken, either by a counterblow or otherwise. For it seems in truth, to see the weight and thickness of ours, that we seek only to defend

ourselves; ^cand we are more burdened by it than protected. ^AWe have enough to do to sustain its weight, fettered and constrained, as if we had to fight only with the shock of our armor, and as if we had not the same obligation to defend it as it has to defend us.

^BTacitus comically portrays the warriors of our ancient Gaul thus armed only to hold their ground, having no way either to harm or to be harmed, or to get up again if knocked down. Lucullus, seeing certain Median men-at-arms who formed the front of the army of Tigranes heavily and awkwardly armed as if in an iron prison, concluded that he could easily defeat them, and began his charge and his victory with them.

^AAnd now that our musketeers are so esteemed, I believe people will find some invention to immure us in order to protect us from them, and have us dragged to war shut up in bastions, like those that the ancients had their elephants carry.

This humor is far removed from that of the younger Scipio, who bitterly blamed his soldiers for having scattered caltrops under water in the part of the moat by which the people of a town he was besieging could make sorties against him; saying that those who were attacking should think of being enterprising, not of fearing; ^cand being rightly afraid that this provision might lull his soldiers' vigilance in guarding themselves.

^BHe also said to a young man who was showing off his handsome buckler to him: "It is really beautiful, my son; but a Roman soldier should put more trust in his right hand than in his left."

^ANow it is only habit that makes the burden of our armor insupportable to us:

> Helmet on head and coat of mail on chest
> Both warriors of whom I sing then wore.
> By night or day, since entering their rest,
> They never took them off or gave them o'er;
> For these to wear were easy as a vest,
> So trained the men were to the arms they bore.
>
> ARIOSTO

^cThe Emperor Caracalla used to go about the country on foot, fully armed, leading his army. ^ARoman foot soldiers bore not only a helmet, sword, and shield (for as for armor, says Cicero, they were so accustomed to have it on their back that it impeded them no more than their limbs: ^c*for they say that arms are the limbs of a soldier*), ^Abut also at the same time whatever provisions they needed for two weeks

and a certain quantity of stakes to make their ramparts, ^Bup to sixty pounds' weight. And the soldiers of Marius, thus laden, were trained to do five leagues in five hours, and six if there was any haste. ^ATheir military discipline was much tougher than ours, and so it produced very different results. This is admirably illustrated by the episode of a Lacedaemonian soldier who was reproached because on an expedition to war he had been seen under cover of a house. They were so toughened to hardship that it was shameful to be seen under any other roof than the sky, whatever the weather. ^CThe younger Scipio, reforming his army in Spain, ordered his soldiers to eat only standing and nothing cooked. ^AWe should not lead our men very far at that price.

Moreover Marcellinus, a man brought up in the Roman wars, carefully notes the way the Parthians had of arming themselves, and notes it because it was different from the Roman way.[1] "They had," he says, "armor woven in the manner of little feathers, which did not hinder the movement of their body, and yet was so strong that our darts bounced off when they came to strike it." (These are the scales that our ancestors were much in the habit of using.) And in another place he says: "They had strong sturdy horses, covered with stout leather; and they themselves were armed from head to foot with thick iron plates arranged with such artifice that at the joints of the limbs they lent themselves to movement. You would have said that they were men of iron; for they had head accouterments so neatly fitted and naturally representing the form and parts of the face that there was no way to hit them except through little round holes corresponding with their eyes, which gave them a little light, and slits at the place of the nostrils, through which with some difficulty they drew breath."

> ^BThe supple metal leaf is brought to life by limbs
> Within, a fearful sight; statues of steel, you'd say,
> Are moved, and through this steel breathe in a human way.

[1] The editions published in Montaigne's lifetime here included the following passage: "Now, because it seems very close to our own, I intended to take this passage from its author, having once taken the trouble to say very amply what I knew about the comparison of our armor with Roman armor. But this scrap of my notes having been stolen from me with several others by a man in my service, I will not deprive him of the profit he hopes to make from it; also it would be very hard for me to chew over the same meat twice."

The horses, likewise armed, threaten with iron brow,
And move their iron flanks, secure from any blow.
<div align="right">CLAUDIAN</div>

^AThere is a description that very strongly resembles the equipment of a French man-at-arms with all his trappings.

Plutarch says that Demetrius had made for himself and for Alcinus, the leading warrior that was with him, a complete suit of armor for each weighing six score pounds, whereas the ordinary suits weighted only sixty.

<div align="center">

10

Of books

</div>

^AI have no doubt that I often happen to speak of things that are better treated by the masters of the craft, and more truthfully. This is purely the essay of my natural faculties, and not at all of the acquired ones; and whoever shall catch me in ignorance will do nothing against me, for I should hardly be answerable for my ideas to others, I who am not answerable for them to myself, or satisfied with them. Whoever is in search of knowledge, let him fish for it where it dwells; there is nothing I profess less. These are my fancies, by which I try to give knowledge not of things, but of myself. The things will perhaps be known to me some day, or have been once, according as fortune may have brought me to the places where they were made clear. But I no longer remember them. ^CAnd if I am a man of some reading, I am a man of no retentiveness.

^AThus I guarantee no certainty, unless it be to make known to what point, at this moment, extends the knowledge that I have of myself. Let attention be paid not to the matter, but to the shape I give it.

^CLet people see in what I borrow whether I have known how to choose what would enhance my theme. For I make others say what I cannot say so well, now through the weakness of my language, now through the weakness of my understanding. I do not count my borrowings, I weight them. And if I had wanted to have them valued by their number, I should have loaded myself with twice as many. They are all, or very nearly all, from such famous and ancient names that they seem to identify themselves enough without me. In the reasonings and inventions that I transplant into my soil and confound with my own, I have sometimes deliberately not indicated

the author, in order to hold in check the temerity of those hasty condemnations that are tossed at all sorts of writings, notably recent writings of men still living, and in the vulgar tongue, which invites everyone to talk about them and seems to convict the conception and design of being likewise vulgar. I want them to give Plutarch a fillip on my nose and get burned insulting Seneca in me. I have to hide my weakness under these great authorities. I will love anyone that can unplume me, I mean by clearness of judgment and by the sole distinction of the force and beauty of the remarks. For I who, for lack of memory, fall short at every turn in picking them out by knowledge of their origin, can very well realize, by measuring my capacity, that my soil is not at all capable of producing certain too rich flowers that I find sown there, and that all the fruits of my own growing could not match them.

^For this I am obliged to be responsible: if I get myself tangled up, if there is vanity and faultiness in my reasonings that I do not perceive or that I am not capable of perceiving when pointed out to me. For faults often escape our eyes; but infirmity of judgment consists in not being able to perceive them when another reveals them to us. Knowledge and truth can lodge in us without judgment, and judgment also without them; indeed the recognition of ignorance is one of the fairest and surest testimonies of judgment that I find.

I have no other marshal but fortune to arrange my bits. As my fancies present themselves, I pile them up; now they come pressing in a crowd, now dragging single file. I want people to see my natural and ordinary pace, however off the track it is. I let myself go as I am. Besides, these are not matters of which we are forbidden to be ignorant and to speak casually and at random.

I should certainly like to have a more perfect knowledge of things, but I do not want to buy it as dear as it costs. My intention is to pass pleasantly, and not laboriously, what life I have left. There is nothing for which I want to rack my brain, not even knowledge, however great its value.

I seek in books only to give myself pleasure by honest amusement; or if I study, I seek only the learning that treats of the knowledge of myself and instructs me in how to die well and live well:

^B This is the goal toward which my sweating horse should strain.
 PROPERTIUS

^AIf I encounter difficulties in reading, I do not gnaw my nails over them; I leave them there, after making one or two attacks on them. ^BIf I planted myself in them, I would lose both myself and time; for I have an impulsive mind. What I do not see at the first attack, I see less by persisting. I do nothing without gaiety; continuation ^Cand too strong contention ^Bdazes, depresses, and wearies my judgment. ^CMy sight becomes confused and dispersed. ^BI have to withdraw it and apply it again by starts, just as in order to judge the luster of a scarlet fabric, they tell us to pass our eyes over it several times, catching it in various quickly renewed and repeated glimpses.

^AIf this book wearies me, I take up another; and I apply myself to it only at the moments when the boredom of doing nothing begins to grip me. I do not take much to modern books, because the ancient ones seem to me fuller and stronger; nor to those in Greek, because my judgment cannot do its work with a childish and apprentice understanding.

Among the books that are simply entertaining, I find, of the moderns, the *Decameron* of Boccaccio, Rabelais, and *The Kisses* of Johannes Secundus, if they may be placed under this heading, worth reading for amusement. As for the Amadises and writings of that sort, they did not have the authority to detain even my childhood. I will also say this, whether boldly or rashly, that this heavy old soul of mine no longer lets itself be tickled, not merely by Ariosto, but even by the good Ovid: his facility and inventions, which once enchanted me, hardly entertain me at all now.

I speak my mind freely on all things, even on those which perhaps exceed my capacity and which I by no means hold to be within my jurisdiction. And so the opinion I give of them is to declare the measure of my sight, not the measure of things. When I feel a distaste for Plato's *Axiochus* as a work without power considering such an author, my judgment does not trust itself: it is not so stupid as to oppose itself to the authority of so many other famous ^Cancient ^Ajudgments, ^Cwhich it considers its tutors and masters, and with which it is rather content to err. ^AIt blames and condemns itself either for stopping at the outer bark, not being able to penetrate to the heart, or for looking at the thing by some false light. It is content with simply securing itself from confusion and disorder; as for its weakness, it readily recognizes and admits it. It thinks it gives a correct interpretation to the appearances that its conception presents to it; but these are weak and imperfect.

Most of Aesop's Fables have many meanings and interpretations. Those who take them allegorically choose some aspect that squares with the fable, but for the most part this is only the first and superficial aspect; there are others more living, more essential and internal, to which they have not known how to penetrate; this is how I read them.

But, to pursue my path, it has always seemed to me that in poetry Virgil, Lucretius, Catullus, and Horace hold the first rank by very far, and especially Virgil in his *Georgics*, which I consider the most accomplished work in poetry; in comparison with it one can easily recognize that there are passages in the *Aeneid* which the author would have brushed up still a little more if he had had the chance. ^BAnd the fifth book of the *Aeneid* seems to me the most perfect. ^AI also love Lucan and enjoy his company, not so much for his style as for his own worth and the truth of his opinions and judgments. As for the good Terence, the very refinement and charm of the Latin language, I find him admirable at representing to the life the movements of the soul and the state of our characters; ^Cat every moment our actions throw me back to him. ^AI cannot read him so often as not to find in him some new beauty and grace.

Those who lived near Virgil's time used to complain that some compared Lucretius to him. I am of the opinion that that is in truth an unequal comparison; but I have much to do to confirm myself in this belief when I find myself fixed on one of the beautiful passages in Lucretius. If they were stung by this comparison, what would they say of the barbarous brutishness and stupidity of those who nowadays compare Ariosto to him? And what would Ariosto himself say?

O foolish and dull-witted age!
CATULLUS

I think the ancients had still more reason to complain of those who compared Plautus to Terence (the latter savors much more of the gentleman) than of those who compared Lucretius to Virgil. ^CIt does much ^Afor the esteem and preference of Terence ^Cthat the father of Roman eloquence[1] has him, and him alone of his class, so often in his mouth; and also the verdict that the first judge among the Roman poets[2] gives of his fellow.

1 Cicero.
2 Horace.

^AIt has often struck my mind how in our time those who set themselves to write comedies (like the Italians, who are rather happy at it) use three or four plots from Terence or Plautus to make one of their own. They pile up in a single comedy five or six stories from Boccaccio. What makes them so load themselves with material is the distrust they have of being able to sustain themselves by their own graces; they have to find a body to lean on; and not having enough of their own to detain us, they want the story to amuse us. It is quite the contrary with my author: the perfections and beauties of his style of expression make us lose our appetite for his subject. His distinction and elegance hold us throughout; he is everywhere so delightful,

> Clear flowing and most like a crystal stream,
>
> HORACE

and so fills our soul with his charms, that we forget those of his plot.

This same consideration draws me on further. I observe that the good ancient poets avoided the affectation and the quest, not only of the fantastic Spanish and Petrarchian flights, but even of the milder and more restrained conceits that are the adornment of all the poetic works of the succeeding centuries. Yet there is no good judge who misses them in those ancients, and who does not admire incomparably more the even polish and that perpetual sweetness and flowering beauty of Catullus' epigrams than all the stings with which Martial sharpens the tails of his. This is for the same reason that I was stating just now, as Martial says of himself: *he had less need for the labor of wit, since his subject matter took the place of wit.* The former, without getting excited and without goading themselves, make themselves sufficiently felt: they have matter enough for laughter everywhere, they don't have to tickle themselves. The latter need outside help: the less wit they have, the more body they need. ^BThey mount on horseback because they are not strong enough on their legs.

^AJust as at our balls these men of low condition who keep dancing schools, not being able to imitate the bearing and fitness of our nobility, seek to recommend themselves by perilous leaps and other strange mountebank's antics. ^BAnd the ladies can more cheaply show off their carriage in the dances where there are various contortions and twistings of the body, than in certain other formal dances where they need only walk with a natural step and display

a natural bearing and their ordinary grace. ^As I have also seen excellent clowns, in their ordinary dress and usual face, give us all the pleasure that can be derived from their art, while the apprentices and those who are not so highly skilled need to flour their faces, dress up, and counterfeit wild movements and grimaces in order to make us laugh.

This idea of mine is easier to recognize in the comparison of the *Aeneid* and the *Orlando Furioso* than anywhere else. We see the former on outspread wings in lofty and sustained flight always pursuing his point; the latter fluttering and hopping from tale to tale as from branch to branch, not trusting his wings except for a very short hop, and alighting at every turn for fear his breath and strength should fail:

> He tries his wings in short excursions.
>
> VIRGIL

These, then, in this sort of subjects, are the authors I like best.

As for my other reading, which mingles a little more profit with the pleasure, and by which I learn to arrange my humors and my ways, the books that serve me for this are Plutarch, since he exists in French, and Seneca. They both have this notable advantage for my humor, that the knowledge I seek is there treated in detached pieces that do not demand the obligation of long labor, of which I am incapable. Such are the *Moral Essays* of Plutarch and the *Epistles* of Seneca, which are the finest part of his writings, and the most profitable. I need no great enterprise to get at them, and I leave them whenever I like. For they have no continuity from one to the other.

These authors agree in most of the opinions that are useful and true; and so were their fortunes similar: they were born at about the same time, each tutored a Roman Emperor, both came from foreign countries, both were rich and powerful. Their teaching is the cream of philosophy, and presented in simple and pertinent fashion. Plutarch is more uniform and constant, Seneca more undulating and diverse. The latter labors, strains, and tenses himself to arm virtue against weakness, fear, and vicious appetites; the other seems not to esteem their power so much, and to disdain to hurry his step or stand on guard for them. Plutarch's opinions are Platonic, mild, and accommodated to civil society; the other's are Stoic and Epicurean, more remote from common use, but in my opinion more suitable ^cfor private life ^and more sturdy. In Seneca it seems that he

concedes a little to the tyranny of the emperors of his time, for I hold it for certain that it is by a forced judgment that he condemns the cause of those high-minded murderers of Caesar; Plutarch is free throughout. Seneca is full of witty points and sallies, Plutarch of things. The former heats you and moves you more; the latter contents you more and pays you better. ᴮHe guides us, the other pushes us.

ᴬAs for Cicero, the works of his that can best serve my purpose are those that treat of philosophy, especially moral. But to confess the truth boldly (for once you have crossed over the barriers of impudence there is no more curb), his way of writing, and every other similar way, seems to me boring. For his prefaces, definitions, partitions, etymologies, consume the greater part of his work; what life and marrow there is, is smothered by his long-winded preparations. If I have spent an hour in reading him, which is a lot for me, and I remember what juice and substance I have derived, most of the time I find nothing but wind; for he has not yet come to the arguments that serve his purpose and the reasons that properly touch on the crux, which I am looking for.

For me, who ask only to become wiser, not more learned ᶜor eloquent, ᴬthese logical and Aristotelian arrangements are not to the point. I want a man to begin with the conclusion. I understand well enough what death and pleasure are; let him not waste his time anatomizing them. I look for good solid reasons from the start, which will instruct me in how to sustain their attack. Neither grammatical subtleties nor an ingenious contexture of words and argumentations are any use for that. I want reasonings that drive their first attack into the stronghold of the doubt; his languish around the pot. They are good for the school, for the bar, and for the sermon, where we have leisure to nap and are still in time a quarter of an hour later to pick up the thread of the discourse. It is necessary to speak thus to judges, whom we want to win over rightly or wrongly, to children, and to the common herd, ᶜto whom we have to say everything to see what will carry.

ᴬI do not want a man to use his strength making me attentive and to shout at me fifty times "*Or oyez!*" in the manner of our heralds. The Romans used to say in their religion "*Hoc age*," ᶜas we say in ours "*Sursum corda*":³ ᴬthese are so many words lost on me. I come fully

3 "*Or oyez*" – "Now listen." "*Hoc age*" – "Give heed." "*Sursum corda*" – "Lift up your hearts."

prepared from my house; I need no allurement or sauce; I can perfectly well eat my meat quite raw; and instead of whetting my appetite by these preparations and preliminaries, they pall and weary it.

ᶜWill the license of the times excuse my sacrilegious audacity in considering that even Plato's dialogues drag and stifle his substance too much, and in lamenting the time put into these long vain preliminary interlocutions by a man who had so many better things to say? My ignorance will excuse me better in that I have no perception of the beauty of his language. In general I ask for books that make use of learning, not those that build it up.

ᴬThe first two, and Pliny, and their like, have no *Hoc age*; they want to have to do with men who themselves have told themselves this; or if they have one, it is a substantial *Hoc age* that has a body of its own.

I also like to read the *Letters to Atticus*,[4] not only because they contain a very ample education in the history and affairs of his time, but much more because in them I discover his personal humors. For I have a singular curiosity, as I have said elsewhere, to know the soul and the natural judgments of my authors. We must indeed judge their capacity, but not their character nor themselves, by that display of their writings that they expose on the stage of the world. I have regretted a thousand times that we have lost the book that Brutus had written on virtue: for it is a fine thing to learn the theory from those who well know the practice. But since the preachings are one thing and the preacher another, I am as glad to see Brutus in Plutarch as in a book of his own. I would rather choose to know truly the conversation he held in his tent with some one of his intimate friends on the eve of a battle than the speech he made the next day to his army; and what he was doing in his study and his chamber than what he was doing in the public square and in the Senate.

As for Cicero, I am of the common opinion, that except for learning there was not much excellence in his soul. He was a good citizen, of an affable nature, as all fat jesting men, such as he was, are apt to be; but of softness and ambitious vanity he had in truth a great deal. And moreover I do not know how to excuse him for having considered his poetry worth being published. It is not a great imperfection to write verses badly; but it is a lack of judgment in

4 By Cicero.

him not to have felt how unworthy they were of the glory of his name. As for his eloquence, it is entirely beyond comparison; I believe that no man will ever equal him.

The younger Cicero, who resembled his father only in name, while commanding in Asia, had several strangers at his table one day, and among others Cestius, seated at the lower end, as people often push in to the open tables of the great. Cicero inquired who he was of one of his men, who told him his name. But like a man whose thoughts were elsewhere and who kept forgetting what they answered him, he asked him that again two or three more times. The servant, in order not to have the trouble of repeating the same thing so often to him, and to make him know him by some circumstance, said to him: "It is that Cestius of whom you were told that he sets no great store by your father's eloquence in comparison with his own." Cicero, suddenly stung by this, ordered them to lay hold of this poor Cestius and had him very soundly whipped in his presence. That was a discourteous host!

Even among those who, all things considered, esteemed this eloquence of his as incomparable, there were some who did not fail to note some faults in it; thus the great Brutus, his friend, used to say that it was a broken and weak-loined eloquence, *fractam et elumbem*. The orators who lived near his time also reprehended in him his sedulous care for a certain long cadence at the end of his periods, and noted the words *esse videatur*[5] which he uses so often. As for me, I prefer a cadence that falls shorter, cut into iambics. To be sure, he does sometimes mix up his rhythms quite roughly, but rarely. My ears have noted this passage: "Ego vero me minus diu senem esse mallem, quam esse senem, antequam essem."[6]

The historians come right to my forehand. They are pleasant and easy; and at the same time, ^cman in general, the knowledge of whom I seek, appears in them more alive and entire than in any other place – the diversity and truth of his inner qualities in the mass and in detail, the variety of the ways he is put together, and the accidents that threaten him. ^ANow those who write biographies, since they spend more time on plans than on events, more on what comes from within than on what happens without, are most suited to me. That is why in every way Plutarch is my man. I am very sorry that we do

5 "It would seem to be."
6 "For my part, in truth, I would rather be old less long than be old before I am old."

not have a dozen Laertiuses, or that he is not either more receptive
^cor more perceptive. ^AFor I consider no less curiously the fortunes
and the lives of these great teachers of the world than the diversity of
their doctrines and fancies.

In this kind of study of history we must leaf without distinction
through all sorts of authors, both old and new, both gibberish and
French, in order to learn in them the things of which they variously
treat. But it seems to me that Caesar singularly deserves to be
studied, not only for the knowledge of history, but for himself, so
much perfection and excellence he has above all the others, although
Sallust is one of their number. Indeed I read this author with a little
more reverence and respect than one reads human works: now
considering him in himself by his actions and the miracle of his
greatness, now the purity and inimitable polish of his language,
which surpassed not only all the historians, as Cicero says, but
^cperhaps ^ACicero himself. With so much sincerity in his judgments
when speaking of his enemies, that except for the false colors with
which he tries to cover his evil cause and the filthiness of his
pestilential ambition, I think the only fault that can be found in
him is that he has been too sparing in speaking of himself. For so
many great things cannot have been performed by him without
much more of himself having gone into them than he sets down.

I like historians who are either very simple or outstanding. The
simple, who have not the wherewithal to mix in anything of their
own, and who bring to it only the care and diligence to collect all
that comes to their attention and to record everything faithfully
without choice or discrimination, leave our judgment intact to
discern the truth. Such, for example, among others, is the good
Froissart, who has gone along in his undertaking with such frank
simplicity that having made a mistake he is not at all afraid to
recognize it and correct it at the spot where he has been made
aware of it; and who presents to us even the diversity of the rumors
that were current and the different reports that were made to him.
This is the material of history, naked and unformed; each man can
make his profit of it according to his understanding.

The really outstanding ones have the capacity to choose what is
worth knowing; they can pick out of two reports the one that is more
likely. From the nature and humors of princes they infer their
intentions and attribute appropriate words to them. They are right
to assume the authority to regulate our belief by their own; but
certainly this privilege belongs to very few people.

Those in between (which are the commonest sort) spoil every-thing for us. They want to chew our morsels for us; they give themselves the right to judge, and consequently to slant history to their fancy; for once the judgment leans to one side, one cannot help turning and twisting the narrative to that bias. They undertake to choose the things worth knowing, and often conceal from us a given word, a given private action, that would instruct us better; they omit as incredible the things they do not understand, and perhaps also some things because they do not know how to say them in good Latin or French. Let them boldly display their eloquence and their reasonings, let them judge all they like; but let them also leave us the wherewithal to judge after them, and not alter or arrange by their abridgments and selection anything of the sub-stance of the matter, but pass it on to us pure and entire in all its dimensions.

Most of the time, especially in these days, people are selected for this work from among the common herd for the sole considera-tion of knowing how to speak well; as if here we were trying to learn grammar! And having been hired only for that and having put on sale only their babble, they are right accordingly to care chiefly only about that part. Thus with many fine words they go and cook up a fine concoction of the rumors they pick up in the city squares.

The only good histories are those that have been written by the very men who were in command in the affairs, or who were parti-cipants in the conduct of them, ᶜor who at least have had the fortune to conduct others of the same sort. ᴬSuch are almost all the Greek and Roman histories. For when several eyewitnesses have written about the same subject (as it happened in those days that greatness and learning usually met), if there is a mistake, it must be very slight, and on a very doubtful incident. What can you expect of a doctor discussing war, or a schoolboy discussing the intentions of princes? If we want to note the scruples the Romans had in this, we need only this example. Asinius Pollio found in the histories even of Caesar some mistake into which he had fallen through not having been able to keep his eyes on every part of his army and having believed individuals who often reported to him things insuf-ficiently verified; or else through not having been carefully enough informed by his lieutenants about what they had done in his absence. We can see by this example whether this quest of truth is delicate, when we cannot trust the commander's knowledge of

a battle his soldiers have fought, or the soldiers' knowledge of what happened near them, unless, in the manner of a judicial inquiry, we confront the witnesses and hear the objections about the evidence in the slightest details of each incident. Truly, the knowledge we have of our own affairs is much looser. But this has been sufficiently treated by Bodin, and according to my way of thinking.

To compensate a little for the treachery and weakness of my memory, so extreme that it has happened to me more than once to pick up again, as recent and unknown to me, books which I had read carefully a few years before and scribbled over with my notes, I have adopted the habit for some time now of adding at the end of each book (I mean of those that I intend to use only once) the time I finished reading it and the judgment I have derived of it as a whole, so that this may represent to me at least the sense and general idea I had conceived of the author in reading it. I want to transcribe here some of these annotations.

Here is what I put some ten years ago in my Guicciardini (for whatever language my books speak, I speak to them in my own): "He is a diligent historiographer from whom, in my opinion, one can learn the truth about the affairs of his time as exactly as from any other: and indeed in most of them he was an actor himself, and of honorable rank. There is no appearance that through hatred, favor, or vanity, he disguised things; which is attested by the free judgments he gives of the great, and especially of those by whom he had been advanced and employed in responsibilities, like Pope Clement VII. As for the part he seems to want to make most of, which is his digressions and discourses, there are some good ones and enriched with fine traits, but he is too fond of them. For by not wanting to leave anything unsaid, having a subject so full and ample and almost infinite, he becomes diffuse and smacking a bit of scholastic prattle. I have also noted this, that of so many souls and actions that he judges, so many motives and plans, he never refers a single one to virtue, religion, and conscience, as if these qualities were wholly extinct in the world; and of all actions, however fair in appearance they may be of themselves, he throws the cause back onto some vicious motive or some profit. It is impossible to imagine that among the infinite number of actions that he judges there was not a single one produced by the way of reason. No corruption can have seized men so universally that someone would not escape the contagion. This makes me fear that his taste was a bit corrupted; and it may have happened that he judged others by himself."

In my Philippe de Commines there is this: "Here you will find the language pleasant and agreeable, of a natural simplicity; the narrative pure, and the author's good faith showing through it clearly, free from vanity in speaking of himself, and of partiality or envy in speaking of others; his ideas and exhortations accompanied more by good zeal and truth than by any exquisite capacity; and, throughout, authority and gravity, representing the man of good background and brought up in great affairs."

On the *Memoirs* of Monsieur du Bellay:[7] "It is always a pleasure to see things written by people who have experienced how they should be conducted; but it cannot be denied that there is clearly revealed in these two lords a great falling off from the frankness and freedom of writing that shine forth in the ancients of their class, such as the sire de Joinville, intimate friend of Saint Louis; Eginhard, chancellor of Charlemagne; and, of more recent memory, Philippe de Commines. This is rather a plea for King Francis against the Emperor Charles V, than a history. I will not believe that they have changed anything in the main facts; but as for turning the judgment of events to our advantage, often contrary to reason, and omitting everything that is ticklish in the life of their master, they make a practice of it: witness the disgrace of Messieurs de Montmorency and de Brion, which are forgotten; indeed the very name of Madame d'Estampes is not to be found. One may cover up secret actions; but to be silent about what all the world knows, and about things that have led to public results of such consequence, is an inexcusable defect. In short, to get a complete knowledge of King Francis and the events of his time, a man should turn elsewhere, if he takes my advice. The profit one can make here is from the detailed narrative of the battles and exploits of war at which these gentlemen were present; some private words and actions of certain princes of their time; and the dealings and negotiations carried on by the seigneur de Langey, in which there are plenty of things worth knowing, and ideas above the ordinary."

7 These *Memoirs*, which cover the years 1513–47 and were first published in 1569, are presented by Martin du Bellay but include three books (out of ten) by his brother Guillaume du Bellay, seigneur de Langey. This explains Montaigne's reference to "these two lords."

II

Of cruelty

^AIt seems to me that virtue is something other and nobler than the inclinations toward goodness that are born in us. Souls naturally regulated and wellborn follow the same path, and show the same countenance in their actions, as virtuous ones. But virtue means something greater and more active than letting oneself, by a happy disposition, be led gently and peacefully in the footsteps of reason. He who through a natural mildness and easygoingness should despise injuries received would do a very fine and praiseworthy thing; but he who, outraged and stung to the quick by an injury, should arm himself with the arms of reason against this furious appetite for vengeance, and after a great conflict should finally master it, would without doubt do much more. The former would do well, and the other virtuously; one action might be called goodness, the other virtue. For it seems that the name of virtue presupposes difficulty and contrast, and that it cannot be exercised without opposition. Perhaps this is why we call God good, strong, liberal, and just, but we do not call him virtuous: his operations are wholly natural and effortless.

Of the philosophers, not only Stoics but even the Epicureans[1] –

And this gradation I borrow from the common opinion, which is false, ^Cdespite Arcesilaus' witty rejoinder to the man who reproached him that many people passed from his school to the Epicureans, but never the other way: "I should think so. Plenty of capons are made out of cocks, but cocks are never made out of capons." ^AFor truly, in firmness and rigor of opinions and precepts the Epicurean sect in no way yields to the Stoic. And a Stoic – showing more honesty than these disputants who, to combat Epicurus and give themselves a good hand to play, make him say what he never even thought of, twisting his words awry, arguing by the laws of grammar another sense into his way of speaking and another belief than the one they know he had in his soul and in his conduct – says that he has given up being an Epicurean for this consideration,

1 The following paragraph is a vast parenthetical insert in the original, within a single sentence starting with "Of the philosophers" and ending with "put them to the proof." Montaigne rather often indulges in long sentences of this sort, as one of his devices for portraying himself and the movement of his thought by his style as well as his content.

among others, that he finds their road too lofty and inaccessible: *and those who are called lovers of pleasure are lovers of beauty and lovers of justice, and they both cultivate and retain all the virtues* [Cicero] –

*Of the Stoic and Epicurean philosophers, I say, there were many who judged that it was not enough to have the soul in a good posture, well regulated and well disposed to virtue, that it was not enough to have our resolutions and our ideas set above all the attacks of fortune; but that we also had to seek occasions to put them to the proof. They want to seek pain, need, and contempt, in order to combat them and to keep their soul in trim: *virtue when challenged takes on much strength* [Seneca].

*This is one of the reasons why Epaminondas, who was of yet a third sect, refuses the riches that fortune puts into his hand in a very legitimate way, in order, he says, to have to duel with poverty, in which extreme he always persisted. Socrates, it seems to me, tested himself still more roughly, keeping for his exercise the malignity of his wife, which is a test with the naked blade.

Metellus alone, of all the Roman senators, undertook by the power of his virtue to withstand the violence of Saturninus, tribune of the people at Rome, who wanted at all costs to get an unjust law passed in favor of the common people, and thereby incurred the capital penalties that Saturninus had established against the refractory. To those who, in this extremity, were escorting him to the public square, he spoke in such terms as these: That it was too easy and too cowardly a thing to do evil, and that to do good where there was no danger was common; but to do good where there was danger was the proper duty of a virtuous man.

These words of Metellus represent to us very clearly what I was trying to prove: that virtue refuses facility for her companion; and that the easy, gentle, and sloping path that guides the footsteps of a good natural disposition is not the path of true virtue. It demands a rough and thorny road; it wants to have either external difficulties to struggle with, like those of Metellus, by means of which fortune takes pleasure in breaking up the unwaveringness of a man's career; or internal difficulties created by the disordered appetites *and imperfections *of our nature.

I have come this far quite at my ease. But at the end of this discourse it comes into my mind that the soul of Socrates, which is the most perfect that has come to my knowledge, would be, by my reckoning, a soul deserving little commendation: for I cannot conceive, in that person, any power of vicious lust. In the movement

of his virtue I cannot imagine any difficulty or any constraint. I know his reason to be so powerful and so much the master in him that it would never so much as let a vicious appetite be born. I can put nothing up against a virtue as lofty as his. I seem to see it marching with a victorious and triumphant step, in pomp and at ease, without impediment or disturbance.

If virtue can shine only by clashing with opposing appetites, shall we then say that it cannot do without the assistance of vice, and that it owes to vice its repute and its honor? Also what would become of that brave and noble Epicurean *voluptas*, which undertakes to bring up virtue softly in her bosom and make it frolic, giving it as its playthings shame, fevers, poverty, death, and tortures? If I define perfect virtue as dependent upon combating pain, upon bearing it patiently, upon supporting attacks of the gout without giving way; if I assign it unpleasantness and difficulty as its necessary condition; then what will become of the virtue which has climbed so high that it not only despises pain but rejoices in it and feels tickled by the pangs of a bad colic, the kind of virtue introduced by the Epicureans, of which many of them by their actions have left us incontestable proof? As have many others, who, I find, have surpassed in action the very rules of their discipline.

Witness the younger Cato. When I see him dying and tearing out his entrails, I cannot be content to believe simply that he then had his soul totally free from disturbance and fright; I cannot believe that he merely maintained himself in the attitude that the rules of the Stoic sect ordained for him, sedate, without emotion, and impassible; there was, it seems to me, in that man's virtue too much lustiness and verdancy to stop there. I believe without any doubt that he felt pleasure and bliss in so noble an action, and that he enjoyed himself more in it than in any other action of his life. ^c*He so departed from life, as if he rejoiced in having found a reason for dying* [Cicero].

^AI go so far in that belief that I begin to doubt whether he would have wanted to be deprived of the occasion for so fine an exploit. And if his goodness, which made him embrace the public advantage more than his own, did not hold me in check, I should easily fall into this opinion, that he was grateful to fortune for having put his virtue to so beautiful a test and for having favored that brigand[2] in treading underfoot the ancient liberty of his country. I seem to read in that action I know not what rejoicing of his soul, and an emotion of

2 Caesar.

extraordinary pleasure and manly exultation, when it considered the nobility and sublimity of its enterprise:

[B]Prouder for having chosen death.

HORACE

[A]This enterprise was not spurred by some hope of glory, as the plebeian and effeminate judgments of some men have judged (for that consideration is too base to touch a heart so noble, so lofty, and so unbending), but was undertaken for the beauty of the very thing in itself, which he, who handled the springs of it, saw much more clearly in its perfection than we can see it.

[C]Philosophy has given me pleasure by judging that so beautiful an action would have been unbecomingly located in any other life than Cato's, and that it belonged to his alone to end thus. Therefore it was according to reason that he ordered his son and the senators who accompanied him to make some other provision for themselves. *Cato, since nature had endowed him with incredible firmness, and he had himself strengthened it by perpetual constancy, and had always remained in the plan he had set himself, had to die rather than look upon the face of a tyrant* [Cicero].

Every death should correspond with its life. We do not become different for dying. I always interpret the death by the life. And if they tell me of a death strong in appearance, attached to a feeble life, I maintain that it is produced by a feeble cause corresponding with the life.

[A]So the ease of this death and the facility that he had acquired through the strength of his soul, shall we say that it should cut down something of the luster of his virtue? And who that has a mind howsoever little tinctured with true philosophy can be satisfied with imagining Socrates as merely free from fear and passion in the incident of his imprisonment, his fetters, and his condemnation? And who does not recognize in him not only firmness and constancy (that was his ordinary attitude), but also I know not what new contentment, and a blithe cheerfulness in his last words and actions?

[C]By that quiver of pleasure that he feels in scratching his leg after the irons were off, does he not betray a like sweetness and joy in his soul at being unfettered by past discomforts and prepared to enter into the knowledge of things to come? [A]Cato will pardon me, if he please; his death is more tragic and tense, but this one is still, I know not how, more beautiful. [C]Aristippus said to those who were deploring it: "May the gods send me one like it!"

ᴬWe see in the souls of these two persons and their imitators (for as for rivals, I doubt very much that there have been any) so perfect a habituation to virtue that it has passed into their nature. It is no longer a laborious virtue, or one formed by the ordinances of reason and maintained by a deliberate stiffening of the soul; it is the very essence of their soul, its natural and ordinary gait. They have made it so by a long exercise of the precepts of philosophy, coming upon a fine rich nature. The vicious passions that come to life in us can find nowhere to enter these men; the strength and rigidity of their soul stifles and extinguishes lusts as soon as they begin to stir.

Now I do not think there is any doubt that it is finer to prevent the birth of temptations by a lofty and divine resolution, and to have so formed oneself to virtue that the very seeds of the vices are rooted out, than to prevent their progress by main force, and, having let oneself be surprised by the first commotions of the passions, to arm and tense oneself to stop their course and conquer them; and that this second action still is finer than to be simply provided with a nature easy and affable and having an inborn distaste for debauchery and vice. For it certainly seems that this third and last type makes a man innocent, but not virtuous; exempt from doing ill, but not apt enough to do good. Besides, this condition is so close to imperfection and weakness that I do not very well know how to separate their confines and distinguish them. The very names of goodness and innocence are for this reason to some extent terms of contempt. I see that several virtues, like chastity, sobriety, and temperance, can come to us through bodily failing. Firmness in dangers (if firmness it should be called), contempt for death, endurance in misfortunes, can come to men, and are often found in them, through failure to judge such accidents rightly, and through not conceiving them as they are. Thus want of apprehension and stupidity sometimes counterfeit virtuous actions; as I have often seen it happen that people have praised men for something for which they deserved blame.

An Italian lord once maintained this theme in my presence, to the disadvantage of his nation: that the subtlety of the Italians and the liveliness of their imaginations were so great, that they foresaw the dangers and accidents that could happen to them from so far off, that it should not be thought strange if in war they were often seen providing for their security even before having recognized the peril; that we and the Spaniards, who were not so sharp, went further, and had to be made to see the danger with our

own eyes and touch it with our hands before taking fright, and that then we too no longer had any control; but that the Germans and Swiss, coarser and heavier, had hardly the sense to reconsider even when they were overwhelmed under the blows.

Perhaps this was only for a laugh. Yet it is quite true that novices in the business of war very often hurl themselves into dangers more recklessly than they will later, after they have been scalded:

> [B]Knowing well the power of new-found pride
> In arms, and the sweet spell of the first armed encounter.
>
> VIRGIL

[A]That is why when we judge a particular action we must consider many circumstances and the whole man who performed it, before we give it a name.

To say a word about myself. [B]I have sometimes seen my friends call prudence in me what was merely fortune, and consider as an advantage of courage and patience what was an advantage of judgment and opinion, and attribute to me one title for another, now to my gain, now to my loss. Moreover, [A]I am so far from having arrived at that first and most perfect degree of excellence where virtue becomes a habit, that even of the second degree I have hardly given any proof. I have not put myself to great effort to curb the desires by which I have found myself pressed. My virtue is a virtue, or I should say an innocence, that is accidental and fortuitous. If I had been born with a more unruly disposition, I fear it would have gone pitifully with me. For I have not experienced much firmness in my soul to withstand passions, if they are even the least bit vehement. I do not know how to foster quarrels and conflict within me. Thus I cannot give myself any great thanks because I find myself free from many vices:

> If few and modest vices mar my soul,
> Otherwise sound, as you may find a mole
> Here and there even on the fairest body;
>
> HORACE

I owe it more to my fortune than to my reason. It had me born of a race famous for integrity, and of a very good father. I do not know whether he infused into me a part of his humors, or else whether the home examples and the good education of my childhood insensibly contributed to it, or whether for some other reason I was born so:

> [B]Whether 'twas Liber on my birth looked down,
> Dread Scorpio, with woe-betiding frown,
> Or Capricorn, who rules the western sea
> With tyrant hand;
>
> HORACE

[A]but the fact is that of myself I hold most vices in horror.

[C]The answer of Antisthenes to the man who asked him what was the best apprenticeship, "To unlearn evil," seems to dwell on this idea.

I hold them in horror, I say, [A]from an attitude so natural and so much my own that the same instinct and impression that I brought away from my nurse I have still retained. Nothing has been able to make me alter it, not even my own reasonings, which, having in some things broken away from the common road, would easily give me license for actions which this natural inclination makes me hate.

[B]It is a monstrous thing that I will say, but I will say it all the same: I find in that area, in many things, more restraint and order in my morals than in my opinions, and my lust less depraved than my reason.

[C]Aristippus affirmed such bold opinions in favor of sensual pleasure and riches that he put all philosophy in an uproar against him. But as for his morals, when the tyrant Dionysius offered him three beautiful wenches to choose from, he replied that he chose all three, and that Paris had got into trouble for preferring one to her companions; but having brought them to his house, he sent them back without touching them. When his valet found himself overloaded on the road with the money he was carrying, he ordered him to throw away and get rid of as much as bothered him.

And Epicurus, whose doctrines are irreligious and effeminate, in his way of living bore himself very devoutly and laboriously. He writes to a friend of his that he lives on nothing but coarse bread and water, and for him to send him a little cheese for when he wants to make some sumptuous repast. Could it be true that to be wholly good we must be so by some occult, natural, and universal property, without law, without reason, without example?

[A]The excesses in which I have found myself involved are not, thank God, of the worst. I have indeed condemned them in myself according as they deserve; for my judgment has not been infected by them. On the contrary, it accuses them more vigorously in myself

than in another. But that is all, for otherwise I bring to them too
little resistance and let myself lean too easily toward the other side of
the balance; except to regulate them and keep them from mixing
with other vices, which for the most part hold together and inter-
twine, if you are not careful. Mine I have cut down and constrained
to be as solitary and simple as I could:

> [B]Nor beyond this
> Do I indulge my faults.
> JUVENAL

[A]The Stoics say that the wise man operates, when he operates,
by all the virtues together, although one of them will always
stand out according to the nature of the action – and the comparison
of the human body could serve them somewhat for this, for
the action of anger cannot be exercised unless all the humors assist
us in it, although anger predominates. But if from that they want
to draw a like consequence, that when the sinner sins he sins
by all the vices together, I do not believe them so simply or else
I do not understand them, for in fact I feel the contrary. [C]These
are sharp, insubstantial subtleties, on which philosophy some-
times lingers.

I ply some vices, but I fly others as much as a saint could do.
Moreover, the Peripatetics do not accept this indissoluble connec-
tion and bond; and Aristotle holds that a wise and just man may be
both intemperate and incontinent. [A]Socrates admitted to those who
recognized in his face some inclination to vice that that was in truth
his natural propensity, but that he had corrected it by discipline.
[C]And the intimates of the philosopher Stilpo said that, having been
born susceptible to wine and women, he had by study made himself
very abstinent from both.

[A]What good I have in me I have, on the contrary, by the chance
of my birth. I have gotten it neither from law, nor from precept, nor
from any other apprenticeship. [B]The innocence that is in me is
a childish innocence: little vigor and no art.

[A]Among other vices, I cruelly hate cruelty, both by nature and by
judgment, as the extreme of all vices. But this is to such a point of
softness that I do not see a chicken's neck wrung without distress,
and I cannot bear to hear the scream of a hare in the teeth of my
dogs, although the chase is a violent pleasure.

Those who have to combat sensual pleasure like to use this
argument to show that it is wholly vicious and unreasonable: that

when it is at its greatest pitch it masters us to such an extent that reason can have no access. And they cite the experience of it that we feel in intercourse with women,

> Anticipated joy the body feels,
> And Venus now prepares to sow the woman's fields;
> LUCRETIUS

where it seems to them that the pleasure transports us so far beyond ourselves that our reason could not possibly then perform its function, being all crippled and ravished away in pleasure.

I know that it can go otherwise, and that we may sometimes, if we will, cast our soul back to other thoughts at this very instant. But we must tense and stiffen it vigilantly. I know that it is possible to master the onset of this pleasure; and ^CI am well versed in this; and I have not found Venus so imperious a goddess as many chaster men than I attest her. ^AI do not take it for a miracle, as does the queen of Navarre in one of the tales of her *Heptameron* (which is a nice book for one of its substance), or for an extremely difficult thing, to spend entire nights with every opportunity and in all freedom, with a long-desired mistress, keeping the faith one has pledged to her, to be content with kisses and simple contacts.

I think the example of the chase would be more appropriate. Even as there is less pleasure in it, so there is more transport and surprise, whereby our reason, stunned, loses the leisure to prepare and brace itself against it, when after a long quest the beast starts up suddenly and appears in a place where perhaps we were least expecting it. This shock, and the ardor of the hue and cry, strike us so that it would be hard for those who love this sort of hunt to withdraw their thought elsewhere at that point. And the poets make Diana victorious over the torch and arrows of Cupid:

> Who amid these does not forget the stings
> And all the cares love brings?
> HORACE

To return to my subject, I sympathize very tenderly with the afflictions of others, and would readily weep to keep others company, if I could weep for any occasion whatever. ^CThere is nothing that tempts my tears but tears, not only real ones, but all sorts, even the feigned or the painted. ^AThe dead I hardly pity, and I should rather envy them; but I very greatly pity the dying. Savages do not shock me as much by roasting and eating the bodies of

the dead as do those who torment them and persecute them living. Even the executions of the law, however reasonable they may be, I cannot witness with a steady gaze.

Someone having occasion to testify to Julius Caesar's clemency said: "He was mild in his revenges. Having forced the pirates to surrender to him, whom they had formerly taken prisoner and put to ransom, since he had threatened to crucify them he condemned them to that punishment, but only after having them strangled." Philemon, his secretary, who had tried to poison him, he punished no more harshly than simply by death. Even without the name of the Latin author[3] who dares to allege as evidence of clemency the mere killing of those by whom one has been injured, it is easy to guess that he is struck by the ugly and horrible examples of cruelty that the Roman tyrants put into practice.

As for me, even in justice, all that goes beyond plain death seems to me pure cruelty, and especially for us who ought to have some concern about sending souls away in a good state; which cannot happen when we have agitated them and made them desperate by unbearable tortures.

ᶜThese past days an imprisoned soldier, perceiving from his tower that carpenters were beginning to erect their structures in the square and that the people were assembling, concluded that it was for him, and, in desperation, having nothing else to kill himself with, seized an old rusty cart nail that fortune put in his way and with it gave himself two big blows around the throat; and seeing that he had not thus been able to budge his life, he soon after gave himself another in the stomach, from which he fell in a faint. And in this state he was found by the first of his guards who came in to see him. They brought him round; and to make use of the time before he expired, they at once had his sentence read to him, which was to have his head cut off; with which he was infinitely delighted, and consented to take some wine, which he had refused; and thanking the judges for the unhoped-for mildness of their condemnation, he said that this resolve to kill himself had come to him through the horror of some more cruel punishment, the fear of which had been increased in him by the preparations [which he had seen made in the square. He had conceived the idea that they wanted to torment him with some horrible torture. He had decided to summon death to

3 Suetonius.

escape a more unbearable one. And he seemed to be delivered from death for having changed it.]⁴

ᴬI would advise that these examples of severity, by means of which they want to keep the people at their duty, be exercised against the corpses of criminals. For to see them deprived of burial, to see them boiled and quartered, would affect the common people just about as much as the punishments they make the living suffer, although in reality it is little or nothing, ᶜas God says: *they kill the body, and after that have no more that they can do* [Saint Luke]. And the poets bring out remarkably the horror of this picture, as something beyond death:

> Alas! a king's remains, half-burned, covered with blood,
> Torn to the bone, and dragged in shame amid the mud!
> ENNIUS, QUOTED BY CICERO

ᴬI happened to be in Rome one day at the moment when they were doing away with Catena, a notorious robber. They strangled him without any emotion among the crowd; but when they came to quarter him, the executioner struck no blow that the people did not follow with a plaintive cry and exclamation, as if everyone had lent his own sense of feeling to that carcass.⁵

ᴮThese inhuman excesses should be exercised against the shell, not against the living core. Thus Artaxerxes, in a somewhat similar case, softened the harshness of the ancient laws of Persia by ordaining that the lords who had failed in their charge, instead of being whipped, as was the custom, should be stripped, and their clothes whipped in their place; and that whereas they used to tear out their hair, they should only take away their high headgear. ᶜThe Egyptians, who were so devout, thought they satisfied divine justice well by sacrificing effigies and pictures of hogs: a bold idea, to try to pay God, a substance so essential, with painting and shadow.

4 The part bracketed here is taken from the 1595 edition, with a minor change in order (the position of the sentence "He had decided . . . unbearable one") which is necessitated by the fact that the 1595 reading is quite different in detail from that in the Bordeaux Copy. The reason for using the 1595 reading here is that the edge of the page in the Bordeaux Copy is cut and with it two-thirds of a line in Montaigne's hand, between "by the preparations" and "a more unbearable one."

5 This paragraph is an addition of 1582 and refers to an incident of Montaigne's Italian trip. See *Travel Journal*, pp. 941–42.

^A I live in a time when we abound in incredible examples of this vice, through the license of our civil wars; and we see in the ancient histories nothing more extreme than what we experience of this every day. But that has not reconciled me to it at all. I could hardly be convinced, until I saw it, that there were souls so monstrous that they would commit murder for the mere pleasure of it; hack and cut off other men's limbs; sharpen their wits to invent unaccustomed torments and new forms of death, without enmity, without profit, and for the sole purpose of enjoying the pleasing spectacle of the pitiful gestures and movements, the lamentable groans and cries, of a man dying in anguish. For that is the uttermost point that cruelty can attain. ^C *That man should kill man not in anger, not in fear, but only to watch the sight* [Seneca].

^A For myself, I have not even been able without distress to see pursued and killed an innocent animal which is defenseless and which does us no harm. And as it commonly happens that the stag, feeling himself out of breath and strength, having no other remedy left, throws himself back and surrenders to ourselves who are pursuing him, asking for our mercy by his tears,

> ^B Bleeding, with moans
> Like some imploring creature,
>
> VIRGIL

^A that has always seemed to me a very unpleasant spectacle.

^B I hardly take any animal alive that I do not give it back the freedom of the fields. Pythagoras used to buy them from fishermen and fowlers, to do the same:

> ^A I think 'twas slaughtered animals first made
> The blood run hot upon the spotted blade.
>
> OVID

Natures that are bloodthirsty toward animals give proof of a natural propensity toward cruelty.

^B At Rome, after they had become accustomed to the spectacle of the slaughter of animals, they proceeded to that of men and of gladiators. Nature herself, I fear, attaches to man some instinct for inhumanity. No one takes his sport in seeing animals play with and caress one another, and no one fails to take it in seeing them tear apart and dismember one another.

^A And so that people will not laugh at this sympathy that I have with them, Theology herself orders us to show some favor in their

regard; and considering that one and the same master has lodged us in this place for his service, and that they, like ourselves, are of his family, she is right to enjoin upon us some respect and affection toward them. Pythagoras borrowed his metempsychosis from the Egyptians; but it has since been accepted by many nations, and notably by our Druids:

> Souls do not die; they leave their first abodes, alive,
> And in new habitations dwell and ever thrive.
>
> OVID

The religion of our ancient Gauls held that souls, being eternal, never ceased moving and changing places from one body to another. Moreover, their religion combined with this fancy some consideration of divine justice; for according to the behavior of the soul while it had been in Alexander's body, they said that God ordained for it another body to inhabit, more or less disagreeable, and conforming to its condition:

> [B]He makes them suffer
> The silent chains of brutes; the fierce he plants in bears;
> The thief a wolf's, the cheat a fox's body wears;
> And when through varied years and myriad shapes they've passed,
> He purges them in Lethe's stream, and then at last
> He calls them back to their primordial human form.
>
> CLAUDIAN

[A]If it had been valiant, they lodged it in the body of a lion; if voluptuous, in that of a hog; if cowardly, in that of a stag or a hare; if malicious, in that of a fox; and so for the rest; until, purified by this chastisement, it resumed the body of some other man.

> And in the Trojan War, for I remember well,
> I myself was Euphorbus, Pantheus' son.
>
> OVID

As for that cousinship between us and the animals, I do not put much stock in it; nor in the fact that many nations, and notably some of the most ancient and noble, have not only received animals into their society and company, but given them a rank very far above themselves, sometimes esteeming them as intimates and favorites of the gods, and holding them in more than human respect and reverence. And other nations recognized no other god or

divinity but animals: ᶜ*beasts were made sacred by the barbarians on account of the benefits they bestowed* [Cicero].

> ᴮThis land adores the crocodile,
> That one the snake-gorged Ibis as divine;
> Here golden images of monkeys shine;
>
>
>
> . . . while here
> A fish, and there a dog, whole towns revere.
>
> JUVENAL

ᴬAnd even the well-conceived interpretation that Plutarch gives of this error is still honorable for them. For he says that it was not the cat or the ox, for example, that the Egyptians worshiped in those animals, but some image of the divine faculties: in the ox patience and usefulness, in the cat liveliness – ᶜ or, like our neighbors the Burgundians, together with all of Germany, impatience at being confined, the cat thus signifying liberty, which they loved and worshiped beyond any other divine faculty – ᴬand so for the rest. But when among the more moderate opinions I meet with arguments that try to show the close resemblance between us and the animals, and how much of a share they have in our greatest privileges, and with how much probability they are likened to us, truly I beat down a lot of our presumption and willingly resign that imaginary kingship that people give us over the other creatures.

Even if all this were lacking, still there is a certain respect, and a general duty of humanity, that attaches us not only to animals, who have life and feeling, but even to trees and plants. We owe justice to men, and mercy and kindness to other creatures that may be capable of receiving it. There is some relationship between them and us, and some mutual obligation. ᶜI am not afraid to admit that my nature is so tender, so childish, that I cannot well refuse my dog the play he offers me or asks of me outside the proper time.

ᴮThe Turks have alms and hospitals for animals. ᴬThe Romans made a public charge of the feeding of geese, by whose vigilance their Capitol had been saved. The Athenians ordained that the mules which had served in building the temple called Hecatompedon should be set free, and that they should be allowed to graze anywhere without hindrance.

ᶜThe Agrigentines commonly gave a solemn burial to animals they had held dear, such as horses of some rare merit, dogs, and useful birds, even those which had served only as a pastime

for their children. And the magnificence that was ordinary with them in all other things was also singularly apparent in the sumptuousness and number of the monuments they raised to animals, monuments which have endured in their splendor for many centuries after. The Egyptians buried wolves, bears, crocodiles, dogs, and cats in sacred places, embalmed their bodies, and wore mourning at their death.

^ACimon gave honorable burial to the mares with which he had three times won the prize for the race at the Olympic games. The ancient Xantippus had his dog buried on a headland on the seacoast which has since retained its name. And Plutarch had scruples, he says, about selling and sending to the slaughterhouse, for a slight profit, an ox that had long served him.

12
Apology for Raymond Sebond

This chapter, by far the longest of the *Essays*, has been the most influential and remains one of the most perplexing. Its extreme skepticism, summed up in the famous motto *Que sçay-je?* (What do I know?), has been accepted by centuries of readers as the center of Montaigne's thought, although recent scholars have seen it rather as a step on his way to the psychological and moral convictions of Book Three.

It is perplexing mainly because it belies its title. Sebond, whose "Natural Theology" Montaigne had translated at his father's request, had argued that man could learn all about God and religion by reading in the book of God's creation, the world. Montaigne shows his complete disagreement here, as he already had when he translated Sebond's Preface. He is the most apologetic of apologists. The best he can bring himself to say in the page or two that can be called a defense is that Sebond means well; that thanks to Sebond's faith (though by implication in spite of his method) the book may have some limited merit and use; and that anyway the bad state of religion in Montaigne's time shows that few men, if any, receive their religion in the right way.

Less than one-tenth of the chapter deals with Sebond at all. Primarily it is a sustained argument of the impotence of unaided human reason, here set in the form of a counterattack against one group of objectors to Sebond and his book.

Understandably enough, the "Apology for Raymond Sebond" has given rise to varied interpretations. Some readers, like Sainte-Beuve, have seen in it a perfidious attack on Christianity; some argue that Montaigne merely forgot Sebond. The present translator prefers the theory that most of the

chapter was written with no thought of Sebond, as a treatise on human presumption and the vanity of human reason; that the princess to whom Montaigne addresses his warning, almost certainly Margaret of Valois, asked him to defend the author he had translated; and that he built upon his attack on human reason a superstructure designed to make of it the best apology he could honestly make for his author.

In the version that follows, the main parts of the chapter are shown by bracketed subheads which are not Montaigne's, but interpolations by the present editor.

^AIn truth, knowledge is a great and very useful quality; those who despise it give evidence enough of their stupidity. But yet I do not set its value at that extreme measure that some attribute to it, like Herillus the philosopher, who placed in it the sovereign good, and held that it was in its power to make us wise and content. That I do not believe, nor what others have said, that knowledge is the mother of all virtue, and that all vice is produced by ignorance. If that is true, it is subject to a long interpretation.

[SEBOND AND HIS BOOK]

My house has long been open to men of learning, and is well known to them. For my father, who ruled it for fifty years and more, inflamed with that new ardor with which King Francis I embraced letters and brought them into credit, sought with great diligence and expense the acquaintance of learned men, receiving them at his house like holy persons having some particular inspiration of divine wisdom, collecting their sayings and discourses like oracles, and with all the more reverence and religion as he was less qualified to judge them; for he had no knowledge of letters, any more than his predecessors. Myself, I like them well enough, but I do not worship them.

Among others, Pierre Bunel, a man of great reputation for learning in his time, after staying a few days at Montaigne in the company of my father with other men of his sort, made him a present, on his departure, of a book entitled "Natural Theology, or Book of Creatures, by Master Raymond de Sabonde."¹ And because the Italian and Spanish languages were familiar to my father, and this book was composed in a Spanish scrambled up

1 Raymond de Sebond, Sebond, Sabaude, Sebeyde, Sabonde, etc., as his name is variously spelled, was a professor of medicine, theology, and philosophy at Toulouse around 1430. His "Natural Theology" was published in 1484.

with Latin endings, Bunel hoped that with a very little help he could make his profit of it, and recommended it to him as a very useful book and suited to the time in which he gave it to him; this was when the innovations of Luther were beginning to gain favor and to shake our old belief in many places.

In this he was very well advised, rightly foreseeing by rational inference that this incipient malady would easily degenerate into an execrable atheism. For the common herd, not having the faculty of judging things in themselves, let themselves be carried away by chance and by appearances, when once they have been given the temerity to despise and judge the opinions that they had held in extreme reverence, such as are those in which their salvation is concerned. And when some articles of their religion have been set in doubt and upon the balance, they will soon after cast easily into like uncertainty all the other parts of their belief, which had no more authority or foundation in them than those that have been shaken; and they shake off as a tyrannical yoke all the impressions they had once received from the authority of the laws or the reverence of ancient usage –

^BFor eagerly is trampled what once was too much feared

LUCRETIUS

–^Adetermined from then on to accept nothing to which they have not applied their judgment and granted their personal consent.

Now some days before his death, my father, having by chance come across this book under a pile of other abandoned papers, commanded me to put it into French for him. It is nice to translate authors like this one, where there is hardly anything but the matter to reproduce; but those who have given much care to grace and elegance of language are dangerous to undertake, ^cespecially to render them into a weaker idiom.[2] ^AIt was a very strange and a new occupation for me; but being by chance at leisure at the time, and being unable to disobey any command of the best father there ever was, I got through it as best I could; at which he was singularly pleased, and ordered it to be printed; and this was done after his death.

I found the ideas of this author fine, the arrangement and sequence of his work good, and his plan full of piety. Because many people are busy reading it, and especially the ladies, to

2 French, which was still considered weaker than Latin.

whom we owe additional help, I have often found myself in a position to help them by clearing their book of two principal objections that are made against it. His purpose is bold and courageous, for he undertakes by human and natural reasons to establish and prove against the atheists all the articles of the Christian religion; wherein, to tell the truth, I find him so firm and felicitous that I do not think it is possible to do better in that argument, and I think that no one has equaled him.

Since this work seemed to me too rich and splendid for an author whose name is so little known, and of whom all we know is that he was a Spaniard professing medicine at Toulouse about two hundred years ago, I once inquired of Adrianus Turnebus, who knew everything, what could be the truth about this book. He replied that he thought it was some quintessence extracted from Saint Thomas Aquinas; for in truth that mind, full of infinite erudition and admirable subtlety, was alone capable of such ideas. At all events, whoever is the author and inventor (and it is not reasonable, without greater occasion, to rob Sebond of that title), he was a very able man with many fine qualities.

[FIRST OBJECTION TO SEBOND:
DEFENSE]

The first criticism that they make of his work is that Christians do themselves harm in trying to support their belief by human reasons, since it is conceived only by faith and by a particular inspiration of divine grace. In this objection there seems to be a certain pious zeal, and for this reason we must try with all the more mildness and respect to satisfy those who advance it. This would be rather the task for a man versed in theology than for myself, who know nothing about it.

However, I think thus, that in a thing so divine and so lofty, and so far surpassing human intelligence, as is this truth with which it has pleased the goodness of God to enlighten us, it is very necessary that he still lend us his help, by extraordinary and privileged favor, so that we may conceive it and lodge it in us. And I do not think that purely human means are at all capable of this; if they were, so many rare and excellent souls, so abundantly furnished with natural powers, in ancient times, would not have failed to arrive at this knowledge through their reason. It is faith alone that embraces vividly and surely the high mysteries of our religion.

But this is not to say that it is not a very fine and very laudable enterprise to accommodate also to the service of our faith the natural and human tools that God has given us. There can be no doubt that this is the most honorable use that we could put them to, and that there is no occupation or design more worthy of a Christian man than to aim, by all his studies and thoughts, to embellish, extend, and amplify the truth of his belief. We do not content ourselves with serving God with mind and soul, we also owe and render him a bodily reverence; we apply even our limbs and movements and external things to honor him. We must do the same here, and accompany our faith with all the reason that is in us, but always with this reservation, not to think that it is on us that faith depends, or that our efforts and arguments can attain a knowledge so supernatural and divine.

If it does not enter into us by an extraordinary infusion; if it enters, I will not say only by reason, but by human means of any sort, it is not in us in its dignity or in its splendor. And yet I am afraid that we enjoy it only in this way. If we held to God by the mediation of a living faith, if we held to God through him and not through ourselves, if we had a divine foothold and foundation, human accidents would not have the power to shake us as they do. Our fort would not be prone to surrender to so weak a battery; the love of novelty, the constraint of princes, the good fortune of one party, a heedless and accidental change in our opinions, would not have the power to shake and alter our belief; we would not allow it to be troubled by every new argument or by persuasion, not even by all the rhetoric there ever was; we should withstand those waves with inflexible and immobile firmness,

> As a vast rock repels the dashing seas
> And sprays the roaring waves into the breeze
> With its great bulk.
> AUTHOR UNKNOWN

If this ray of divinity touched us at all, it would appear all over: not only our words, but also our works would bear its light and luster. Everything that came from us would be seen to be illuminated by this noble brightness. We ought to be ashamed that in human sects there never was a partisan, whatever difficult and strange thing his doctrine maintained, who did not to some extent conform his conduct and his life to it; and so divine and celestial a teaching as ours marks Christians only by their words.

[B]Do you want to see this? Compare our morals with a Mohammedan's, or a pagan's; we always fall short of them. Whereas, in view of the advantage of our religion, we should shine with excellence at an extreme and incomparable distance, and people ought to say: "Are they so just, so charitable, so good? Then they are Christians."

[C]All other signs are common to all religions: hope, trust, events, ceremonies, penitence, martyrs. The peculiar mark of our truth should be our virtue, as it is also the most heavenly and difficult mark, and the worthiest product of truth.

[B]Therefore our good Saint Louis was right, when that Tartar king who had turned Christian planned to come to Lyons to kiss the Pope's feet and witness the sanctity he expected to find in our morals, to dissuade him insistently, for fear that on the contrary our dissolute way of living should make him disgusted with so sacred a belief. Although it later came out quite differently for that other, who went to Rome for the same purpose, and, seeing there the dissoluteness of the prelates and people of that time, became all the more firmly established in our religion, from considering how much power and divinity it must have to maintain its dignity and splendor amid so much corruption and in such vicious hands.

[A]If we had a single drop of faith, we should move mountains from their place, says the Holy Word. Our actions, which would be accompanied and guided by the divinity, would not be simply human; they would have something miraculous about them like our belief. [C]*Brief is the task of starting an honorable and happy life, if you believe* [Quintilian].

Some make the world believe that they believe what they do not believe. Others, in greater number, make themselves believe it, being unable to penetrate what it means to believe.

[A]And we think it strange if, in the wars which at this moment are oppressing our state, we see events fluctuating and varying in a common ordinary manner. That is because we contribute nothing to them that is not in ourselves. The justice that is in one of the parties is there only as an ornament and a covering; it is indeed alleged, but it is neither received, nor lodged, nor espoused; it is there as in the mouth of the advocate, not as in the heart and affection of the party. God owes his extraordinary help to faith and religion, not to our passions. Men are the leaders here, and make use of religion; it ought to be quite the contrary.

[C]See if it is not by our hands that we lead it, drawing, as if from wax, so many contrasting figures from a rule so straight and so firm. When has this been seen better than in France in our day? Those who have taken it to the left, those who have taken it to the right, those who call it black, those who call it white, use it so similarly for their violent and ambitious enterprises, conduct themselves in these with a procedure so identical in excesses and injustice, that they render doubtful and hard to believe that there really exists, as they claim, a difference of opinion between them in a thing on which depends the conduct and law of our life. Can one see conduct more uniform, more at one, issue from the same school and teaching?

See the horrible impudence with which we bandy divine reasons about, and how irreligiously we have both rejected them and taken them again, according as fortune has changed our place in these public storms. This proposition, so solemn, whether it is lawful for a subject to rebel and take arms against his prince in defense of religion – remember in whose mouths, this year just past, the affirmative of this was the buttress of one party, the negative was the buttress of what other party; and hear now from what quarter comes the voice and the instruction of both sides, and whether the weapons make less din for this cause than for that.[3] And we burn the people who say that truth must be made to endure the yoke of our need. And how much worse France does than say it!

[A]Let us confess the truth: if anyone should sift out of the army, even the average loyalist army, those who march in it from the pure zeal of affection for religion, and also those who consider only the protection of the laws of their country or the service of their prince, he could not make up one complete company of men-at-arms out of them. Whence comes this, that there are so few who have maintained the same will and the same pace in our public movements, and that we see them now going only at a walk, now riding with free rein, and the same men now spoiling our affairs by their violence and asperity, now by their coolness, sluggishness, and heaviness, if it is not that they are driven to it by private [C]and accidental [A]considerations according to whose diversity they are stirred?

[C]I see this evident, that we willingly accord to piety only the services that flatter our passions. There is no hostility that excels

3 Before the death of the Catholic king Henry III, assassinated in 1589, the Protestants claimed the right to revolt, and the Catholics denied it. When the Protestant king Henry IV succeeded Henry III, both parties did an about-face.

Christian hostility. Our zeal does wonders when it is seconding our leaning toward hatred, cruelty, ambition, avarice, detraction, rebellion. Against the grain, toward goodness, benignity, moderation, unless as by a miracle some rare nature bears it, it will neither walk nor fly.

Our religion is made to extirpate vices; it covers them, fosters them, incites them.

ᴬWe must not give God chaff for wheat, as they say. If we believed in him, I do not say by faith, but with a simple belief; in fact (and I say it to our great confusion), if we believed in him just as in any other history, if we knew him like one of our comrades, we would love him above all other things, for the infinite goodness and beauty that shines in him. At least he would march in the same rank in our affection as riches, pleasures, glory, and our friends.

ᶜThe best of us does not fear to outrage him as he fears to outrage his neighbor, his kinsman, his master. Is there any mind so simple that, having on one side the object of one of our vicious pleasures and on the other in equal knowledge and conviction the state of immortal glory, he would trade the one for the other? And yet we often renounce immortal glory out of pure disdain; for what taste leads us to blaspheme, unless perhaps the very taste of the offense?

When the philosopher Antisthenes was being initiated into the mysteries of Orpheus, and the priest told him that those who vowed themselves to that religion were to receive after death eternal and perfect blessings, he said to him: "Why, then, do you not die yourself?"

Diogenes, more brusquely according to his manner, and outside of our subject, to the priest who was urging him in the same way to join his order so as to attain the blessings of the other world: "Do you want me to believe that Agesilaus and Epaminondas, such great men, will be miserable, and that you, who are only a calf, will be blessed because you are a priest?"

ᴬThese great promises of eternal beatitude – if we accorded them the same authority as a philosophic discourse, we would not hold death in such horror as we do.

> ᴮThen would the dying man not wail about his death,
> But gladly leave behind his body and his breath
> As the snake sheds his skin, the aged stag his horns.
> LUCRETIUS

^AI would be dissolved, we would say, and be with Jesus Christ. The power of Plato's discourse on the immortality of the soul indeed impelled some of his disciples to death, to enjoy more promptly the hopes he gave them.

All this is a very evident sign that we receive our religion only in our own way and with our own hands, and not otherwise than as other religions are received. We happen to have been born in a country where it was in practice; or we regard its antiquity or the authority of the men who have maintained it; or we fear the threats it fastens upon unbelievers, or pursue its promises. Those considerations should be employed in our belief, but as subsidiaries; they are human ties. Another region, other witnesses, similar promises and threats, might imprint upon us in the same way a contrary belief.

^BWe are Christians by the same title that we are Perigordians or Germans.

^AAnd as for what Plato says, that there are few men so firm in their atheism that a pressing danger will not bring them back to recognition of the divine power; this is not the role of a true Christian. It is for mortal and human religions to be accepted by human guidance. What kind of faith must be that which cowardice and faintheartedness implant and establish in us? ^CA nice faith, that believes what it believes only through not having the courage to disbelieve it! ^ACan a vicious passion, like that of inconstancy and terror, produce in our soul anything regulated?

^CThe atheists establish, says Plato, by the reason of their judgment, that what is said about hell and future punishments is fiction. But when the chance to test this is offered as old age or illnesses bring them near their death, the terror of it fills them with a new belief through horror at their coming condition. And because such impressions make hearts fearful, he forbids in his *Laws* all teaching of such threats and all persuasion that any harm can come to man from the gods, except for his greater good and for a medicinal effect. They tell of Bion that, infected with the atheisms of Theodorus, he had long been a scoffer at religious men; but that when death surprised him, he gave himself up to the most extreme superstitions, as if the gods were removed and replaced according to Bion's situation.

Plato and these examples would conclude that we are brought back to the belief in God either by love or by force. Atheism being a proposition as it were unnatural and monstrous, difficult too and not easy to establish in the human mind, however insolent

and unruly it may be, plenty of men have been seen, out of vanity and pride in conceiving opinions that are not common and that reform the world, to affect to profess it outwardly; who, if they are mad enough, are not strong enough nevertheless to have implanted it in their conscience. They will not fail to clasp their hands to heaven if you stick them a good sword-thrust in the chest. And when fear or illness has beaten down the licentious ardor of that flighty humor, they will not fail to come back to themselves and very discreetly let themselves be managed by the common faith and examples. A doctrine seriously digested is one thing; another thing is these superficial impressions, which, born of the disorder of an unhinged mind, swim about heedlessly and uncertainly in the imagination. Miserable and brainless men indeed, who try to be worse than they can be!

^BThe error of paganism, and ignorance of our sacred truth, allowed that great soul Plato (but great with human greatness only) to fall also into this neighboring fallacy, that children and old men are more susceptible to religion, as if it was born and derived its credit from our imbecility.

^AThe knot that should bind our judgment and our will, that should clasp and join our soul to our creator, should be a knot taking its twists and its strength not from our considerations, our reasons and passions, but from a divine and supernatural clasp, having only one form, one face, and one aspect, which is the authority of God and his grace. Now, our heart and soul being ruled and commanded by faith, it is right that faith should bring to the service of its plan all our other parts according to their capacity.

And it is not credible that this whole machine should not have on it some marks imprinted by the hand of this great architect, and that there should not be some picture in the things of this world that somewhat represents the workman who has built and formed them. He has left the stamp of his divinity on these lofty works, and it is only because of our imbecility that we cannot discover it. It is what he says himself, that his invisible operations he manifests to us by the visible.

Sebond has labored at this worthy study, and shows us how there is no part of the world that belies its maker. It would be doing a wrong to divine goodness if the universe did not assent to our belief. The sky, the earth, the elements, our body and our soul, all things conspire in this; we have only to find the way to use them. They instruct us, if we are capable of understanding. ^BFor this world

is a very holy temple, into which man is introduced to contemplate statues, not statues wrought by mortal hand, but those which the divine thought has made perceptible – the sun, the stars, the waters, and the earth – to represent to us intelligible things. ^The invisible things of God, says Saint Paul, appear by the creation of the world, when we consider his eternal wisdom and his divinity by his works.[4]

> And even God himself does not begrudge the world
> The sight of heaven; revolving ever, he displays
> His face and form; he shows, imprints himself indeed,
> That he may be well known, and teach us as we gaze
> To know his ways and nature, and his laws to heed.
> MANILIUS

[FIRST OBJECTION TO SEBOND:
CONCLUSION]

Now our human reasons and arguments are as it were the heavy and barren matter; the grace of God is their form; it is that which gives them shape and value. Just as the virtuous actions of Socrates and Cato remain vain and useless because they did not direct them toward the end of loving and obeying the true creator of all things, and because they did not know God; so it is with our ideas and reasonings: they have a certain body, but it is a shapeless mass, without form or light, if faith and divine grace are not added to it.

Faith, coming to color and illumine Sebond's arguments, makes them firm and solid; they are capable of serving as a start and a first guide to an apprentice to set him on the road to this knowledge; they fashion him to some extent and make him capable of the grace of God, by means of which our belief is afterward completed and perfected. I know a man of authority, nurtured in letters, who confessed to me that he had been brought back from the errors of unbelief through the medium of Sebond's arguments. And even if we strip them of this ornament and of the help and approbation of faith, and take them as purely human fancies, to combat those who are precipitated into the frightful and horrible darkness of irreligion, they will still be found as solid and as firm as any others of the same

4 Here Montaigne is translating Romans 1:20, which is rendered in the King James version as follows: "For the invisible things of him [God] from the creation of the world are clearly seen, being understood by the things that are made, even his eternal power and Godhead."

type that may be opposed to them; so that we shall be in a position to say to our adversaries –

> If you have better, bring it out; if not, give in
>> HORACE

– that they must admit the force of our proofs, or show us elsewhere and on some other subject proofs better woven and of better stuff.

[SECOND OBJECTION TO SEBOND: THE OBJECTORS]

I have already, without thinking about it, half involved myself in the second objection which I had proposed to answer for Sebond.

Some say that his arguments are weak and unfit to prove what he proposes, and undertake to shatter them with ease. These must be shaken up a little more roughly, for they are more dangerous and malicious than the others. ^cPeople are prone to apply the meaning of other men's writings to suit opinions that they have previously determined in their minds; and an atheist flatters himself by reducing all authors to atheism, infecting innocent matter with his own venom. ^AThese men have some prepossession in judgment that makes their taste jaded for Sebond's reasons. Furthermore, it seems to them that they are given an easy game when set at liberty to combat our religion by purely human weapons, which they would not dare attack in its authoritative and commanding majesty.

The means I take to beat down this frenzy, and which seems fittest to me, is to crush and trample underfoot human arrogance and pride; to make them feel the inanity, the vanity and nothingness, of man; to wrest from their hands the puny weapons of their reason; to make them bow their heads and bite the ground beneath the authority and reverence of divine majesty. It is to this alone that knowledge and wisdom belong; it alone that can have some self-esteem, and from which we steal what we account and prize ourselves for:

> For God allows great thoughts to no one else.
>> HERODOTUS

^cLet us beat down this presumption, the first foundation of the tyranny of the evil spirit. *For God resisteth the proud, and giveth grace to the humble* [Saint Peter]. Intelligence is in all gods, says Plato, and in very few men.

[SECOND OBJECTION TO SEBOND: DEFENSE]

^A^Now it is nevertheless a great consolation to the Christian to see our frail mortal tools so properly suited to our holy and divine faith, that when they are used on subjects that are by their nature frail and mortal, they are no more completely and powerfully appropriate. Let us see then if man has within his power other reasons more powerful than those of Sebond, or indeed if it is in him to arrive at any certainty by argument and reason.

^C^For Saint Augustine, arguing against these people, has good cause to reproach them for their injustice in that they hold those parts of our belief to be false which our reason fails to establish. And to show that there can be and can have been plenty of things whose nature and causes our reason cannot possibly establish, he puts before his adversaries certain known and indubitable experiences into which man confesses he has no insight; and this he does, like all other things, with careful and ingenious research. We must do more, and teach them that to convict our reason of weakness, there is no need to go sifting out rare examples, and that she is so lame and so blind that there is nothing so clear and easy as to be clear enough to her; that the easy and the hard are one to her; that all subjects alike, and nature in general, disavow her jurisdiction and mediation.

^A^What does truth preach to us, when she exhorts us to flee worldly philosophy, when she so often inculcates in us that our wisdom is but folly before God; that of all vanities the vainest is man; that the man who is presumptuous of his knowledge does not yet know what knowledge is; and that man, who is nothing, if he thinks he is something, seduces and deceives himself? These statements of the Holy Spirit express so clearly and so vividly what I wish to maintain, that no other proof would be needed against men who would surrender with all submission and obedience to its authority. But these men insist on being whipped to their own cost and will not allow us to combat their reason except by itself.

[COUNTERATTACK: THE VANITY OF MAN AND OF MAN'S KNOWLEDGE WITHOUT GOD]

Let us then consider for the moment man alone, without outside assistance, armed solely with his own weapons, and deprived of divine grace and knowledge, which is his whole honor, his strength,

and the foundation of his being. Let us see how much presence he
has in this fine array. Let him help me to understand, by the force of
his reason, on what foundations he has built these great advantages
that he thinks he has over other creatures. Who has persuaded
him that that admirable motion of the celestial vault, the eternal
light of those torches rolling so proudly above his head, the fearful
movements of that infinite sea, were established and have lasted so
many centuries for his convenience and his service? Is it possible to
imagine anything so ridiculous as that this miserable and puny
creature, who is not even master of himself, exposed to the attacks
of all things, should call himself master and emperor of the universe,
the least part of which it is not in his power to know, much less to
command? And this privilege that he attributes to himself of being
the only one in this great edifice who has the capacity to recognize
its beauty and its parts, the only one who can give thanks for it to
the architect and keep an account of the receipts and expenses of the
world: who has sealed him this privilege? Let him show us his letters
patent for this great and splendid charge.

 ᶜHave they been granted in favor of the wise only? Then they do
not touch many people. Are the fools and the wicked worthy of such
extraordinary favor, and, being the worst part of the world, of being
preferred to all the rest?

 Shall we believe this man? *For whom then shall a man say that the
world was made? Naturally, for those souls who have the use of reason.
These are gods and men, to whom certainly nothing is superior* [Cicero,
quoting Balbus]. We shall never have flouted enough the impu-
dence of this coupling.

 ᴬBut, poor wight, what has he in himself worthy of such an
advantage? When we consider the incorruptible life of the celestial
bodies, their beauty, their greatness, their continual motion by so
exact a rule;

> When the vaults of heaven meet our sight,
> Infinite worlds above, ether with stars alight;
> And when the course of sun and moon come to our mind;
> LUCRETIUS

when we consider the dominion and power that those bodies have,
not only over our lives and the conditions of our fortune,

> For on the stars men's deeds and lives depend,
> MANILIUS

but over our very inclinations, our reasonings, our wills, which they
govern, drive, and stir at the mercy of their influences, as our reason
finds and teaches us;

> He learns that stars remotely seen
> Govern by silent laws, and intervene;
> To move the universe they alternate,
> And rule by certain signs the twists of fate;
>
> MANILIUS

when we see that not merely a man, nor a king, but kingdoms,
empires, and all this world below move in step with the slightest
movements of the heavens;

> How great a change the slightest motion brings:
> So great this kingdom is that governs kings;
>
> MANILIUS

if our virtue, our vices, our competence and knowledge, and this
very dissertation that we are making about the power of the stars
and this comparison of them to us, comes, as our reason judges, by
their medium and their favor;

> One, in love's delirium,
> Can cross the sea and conquer Ilium;
> Another man is destined laws to build;
> Fathers kill sons, fathers by sons are killed,
> And brother wounds armed brother in the fray.
> This war is not of ours; Fate makes men stray,
> Punish themselves, their members lacerate.
>
> This too is fated, that I write of fate;
>
> MANILIUS

if we hold by the dispensation of heaven this portion of reason that
we have, how can our reason make us equal to heaven? How subject
its essence and conditions to our knowledge? All that we see in those
bodies astonishes us. ^c*What preparations, what instruments, what
levers, what machines, what workmen performed so great a work?*
[Cicero.]

^AWhy do we deny them soul, and life, and reason? Have we
recognized in them some inert, insensible stupidity, we who have no
dealings with them except obedience? ^cShall we say that we have
seen in no other creature than man the exercise of a rational soul?

Well, have we seen anything like the sun? Does it fail to exist, because we have seen nothing like it, and its movements to exist, because there are none like them? If what we have not seen does not exist, our knowledge is marvelously shrunk: *How narrow are the limits of our mind!* [Cicero.]

^AAre these not dreams of human vanity, to make the moon a celestial earth, ^Cto imagine mountains and valleys there, like Anaxagoras; ^Ato plant habitations and human dwellings there, and set up colonies for our convenience, as Plato and Plutarch do; and to make our earth a bright star lighting the moon? ^C*Among other human infirmities is this one also, mental fog, and not so much the need to err as the love of errors* [Seneca]. *The corruptible body weighs down the soul, and the earthy tabernacle oppresses the much pondering mind* [The Book of Wisdom, quoted by Saint Augustine].

[MAN IS NO BETTER THAN THE ANIMALS]

^APresumption is our natural and original malady. The most vulnerable and frail of all creatures is man, and at the same time the most arrogant. He feels and sees himself lodged here, amid the mire and dung of the world, nailed and riveted to the worst, the deadest, and the most stagnant part of the universe, on the lowest story of the house and the farthest from the vault of heaven, with the animals of the worst condition of the three;[5] and in his imagination he goes planting himself above the circle of the moon, and bringing the sky down beneath his feet. It is by the vanity of this same imagination that he equals himself to God, attributes to himself divine characteristics, picks himself out and separates himself from the horde of other creatures, carves out their shares to his fellows and companions the animals, and distributes among them such portions of faculties and powers as he sees fit. How does he know, by the force of his intelligence, the secret internal stirrings of animals? By what comparison between them and us does he infer the stupidity that he attributes to them?

^CWhen I play with my cat, who knows if I am not a pastime to her more than she is to me?[6] Plato, in his picture of the golden age under Saturn, counts among the principal advantages of the man of that time the communication he had with the beasts; inquiring

5 Those that walk, those that fly, those that swim.
6 The 1595 edition adds: "We entertain each other with reciprocal monkey tricks. If I have my time to begin or to refuse, so has she hers."

of them and learning from them, he knew the true qualities and differences of each one of them; whereby he acquired a very perfect intelligence and prudence, and conducted his life far more happily than we could possibly do. Do we need a better proof to judge man's impudence with regard to the beasts? That great author opined that in most of the bodily form that Nature gave them, she considered solely the use of prognostications that were derived from them in his time.

[A]This defect that hinders communication between them and us, why is it not just as much ours as theirs? It is a matter of guesswork whose fault it is that we do not understand one another; for we do not understand them any more than they do us. By this same reasoning they may consider us beasts, as we consider them. It is no great wonder if we do not understand them; neither do we understand the Basques and the Troglodytes.[7] However, some have boasted of understanding them, like Apollonius of Tyana, [B]Melampus, Tiresias, Thales, [A]and others. [B]And since it is a fact, as the cosmographers say, that there are nations that accept a dog as their king, they must give a definite interpretation to his voice and motions. [A]We must notice the parity there is between us. We have some mediocre understanding of their meaning; so do they of ours, in about the same degree. They flatter us, threaten us, and implore us, and we them.

Furthermore, we discover very evidently that there is full and complete communication between them and that they understand each other, not only those of the same species, but also those of different species.

> [B]Even dumb cattle and the savage beasts
> Varied and different noises do employ
> When they feel fear or pain, or thrill with joy.
> LUCRETIUS

[A]In a certain bark of the dog the horse knows there is anger; at a certain other sound of his he is not frightened. Even in the beasts that have no voice, from the mutual services we see between them we easily infer some other means of communication; [C]their motions converse and discuss:

> [B]Likewise in children, the tongue's speechlessness
> Leads them to gesture what they would express.
> LUCRETIUS

7 Cave-dwellers on the western shore of the Red Sea.

^AWhy not; just as well as our mutes dispute, argue, and tell stories by signs? I have seen some so supple and versed in this, that in truth they lacked nothing of perfection in being able to make themselves understood. Lovers grow angry, are reconciled, entreat, thank, make assignations, and in fine say everything, with their eyes:

> And silence too records
> Our prayers and our words.
> TASSO

^CWhat of the hands? We beg, we promise, call, dismiss, threaten, pray, entreat, deny, refuse, question, admire, count, confess, repent, fear, blush, doubt, instruct, command, incite, encourage, swear, testify, accuse, condemn, absolve, insult, despise, defy, vex, flatter, applaud, bless, humiliate, mock, reconcile, commend, exalt, entertain, rejoice, complain, grieve, mope, despair, wonder, exclaim, are silent, and what not, with a variation and multiplication that vie with the tongue. With the head: we invite, send away, avow, disavow, give the lie, welcome, honor, venerate, disdain, demand, show out, cheer, lament, caress, scold, submit, brave, exhort, menace, assure, inquire. What of the eyebrows? What of the shoulders? There is no movement that does not speak both a language intelligible without instruction, and a public language; which means, seeing the variety and particular use of other languages, that this one must rather be judged the one proper to human nature. I omit what necessity teaches privately and promptly to those who need it, and the finger alphabets, and the grammars in gestures, and the sciences which are practiced and expressed only by gestures, and the nations which Pliny says have no other language.

^BAn ambassador of the city of Abdera, after speaking at length to King Agis of Sparta, asked him: "Well, Sire, what answer do you wish me to take back to our citizens?" "That I allowed you to say all you wanted, and as much as you wanted, without ever saying a word." Wasn't that an eloquent and thoroughly intelligible silence?

^AMoreover, what sort of faculty of ours do we not recognize in the actions of the animals? Is there a society regulated with more order, diversified into more charges and functions, and more consistently maintained, than that of the honeybees? Can we imagine so orderly an arrangement of actions and occupations as this to be conducted without reason and foresight?

Some, by these signs and instances inclined,
Have said that bees share in the divine mind
And the ethereal spirit.

 VIRGIL

Do the swallows that we see on the return of spring ferreting in all
the corners of our houses search without judgment, and choose
without discrimination, out of a thousand places, the one which is
most suitable for them to dwell in? And in that beautiful and
admirable texture of their buildings, can birds use a square rather
than a round figure, an obtuse rather than a right angle, without
knowing their properties and their effects? Do they take now water,
now clay, without judging that hardness is softened by moistening?
Do they floor their palace with moss or with down, without fore-
seeing that the tender limbs of their little ones will lie softer and
more comfortably on it? Do they shelter themselves from the rainy
wind and face their dwelling toward the orient without knowing the
different conditions of these winds and considering that one is more
salutary to them than the other? Why does the spider thicken her
web in one place and slacken it in another, use now this sort of knot,
now that one, unless she has the power of reflection, and thought,
and inference?

We recognize easily enough, in most of their works, how much
superiority the animals have over us and how feeble is our skill to
imitate them. We see, however, in our cruder works, the faculties
that we use, and that our soul applies itself with all its power; why do
we not think the same thing of them? Why do we attribute to some
sort of natural and servile inclination these works which surpass all
that we can do by nature and by art? Wherein, without realizing it,
we grant them a very great advantage over us, by making Nature,
with maternal tenderness, accompany them and guide them as by
the hand in all the actions and comforts of their life; while us she
abandons to chance and to fortune, and to seek by art the things
necessary for our preservation, and denies us at the same time the
power to attain, by any education and mental straining, the natural
resourcefulness of the animals: so that their brutish stupidity sur-
passes in all conveniences all that our divine intelligence can do.

Truly, by this reckoning, we should be quite right to call her a very
unjust stepmother. But this is not so; our organization is not so
deformed and disorderly. Nature has universally embraced all her
creatures; and there is none that she has not very amply furnished

with all powers necessary for the preservation of its being. For these vulgar complaints that I hear men make (as the license of their opinions now raises them above the clouds, and then sinks them to the antipodes) that we are the only animal abandoned naked on the naked earth, tied, bound, having nothing to arm and cover ourselves with except the spoils of others; whereas all other creatures Nature has clothed with shells, husks, bark, hair, wool, spikes, hide, down, feathers, scales, fleece, and silk, according to the need of their being; has armed them with claws, teeth, or horns for attack and defense; and has herself instructed them in what is fit for them – to swim, to run, to fly, to sing – whereas man can neither walk, nor speak, nor eat, nor do anything but cry, without apprenticeship –

> [B]The infant, like a sailor tossed ashore
> By raging seas, lies naked on the earth,
> Speechless, helpless for life, when at his birth
> Nature from out the womb brings him to light.
> He fills the place with wailing, as is right
> For one who through so many woes must pass.
> Yet flocks, herds, savage beasts of every class
> Grow up without the need for any rattle,
> Or for a gentle nurse's soothing prattle;
> They seek no varied clothes against the sky;
> Lastly they need no arms, no ramparts high
> To guard their own – since earth itself and nature
> Amply bring forth all things for every creature
>
> LUCRETIUS

– [A]those complaints are false, there is a greater equality and a more uniform relationship in the organization of the world. Our skin is provided as adequately as theirs with endurance against the assaults of the weather: witness so many nations who have not yet tried the use of any clothes. [B]Our ancient Gauls wore hardly any clothes; nor do the Irish, our neighbors, under so cold a sky. [A]But we may judge this better by ourselves; for all the parts of the body that we see fit to expose to the wind and air are found fit to endure it: face, feet, hands, legs, shoulders, head, according as custom invites us. For if there is a part of us that is tender and that seems as though it should fear the cold, it should be the stomach, where digestion takes place; our fathers left it uncovered, and our ladies, soft and delicate as they are, sometimes go half bare down to the navel. Nor are the bindings and swaddlings of infants necessary either; and the Lacedaemonian

mothers raised their children in complete freedom to move their limbs, without wrapping or binding them. Our weeping is common to most of the other animals; and there are scarcely any who are not observed to complain and wail long after their birth, since it is a demeanor most appropriate to the helplessness that they feel. As for the habit of eating, it is, in us as in them, natural and needing no instruction:

> ^BFor each one feels his powers and his needs.
>
> LUCRETIUS

^AWho doubts that a child, having attained the strength to feed himself, would be able to seek his food? And the earth produces and offers him enough of it for his need, with no other cultivation or artifice; and if not in all weather, neither does she for the beasts: witness the provisions we see the ants and others make for the sterile seasons of the year. These nations that we have just discovered to be so abundantly furnished with food and natural drink, without care or preparation, have now taught us that bread is not our only food, and that without plowing, our mother Nature had provided us in plenty with all we needed; indeed, as seems likely, more amply and richly than she does now that we have interpolated our artifice:

> At first and of her own accord the earth
> Brought forth sleek fruits and vintages of worth,
> Herself gave harvests sweet and pastures fair,
> Which now scarce grow, despite our toil and care,
> And we exhaust our oxen and our men;
>
> LUCRETIUS

the excess and unruliness of our appetite outstripping all the inventions with which we seek to satisfy it.

As for weapons, we have more that are natural than most other animals, and more varied movements of our limbs; and we get more service out of them, naturally and without lessons. Those who are trained to fight naked are seen to throw themselves into dangers like our own men. If some animals surpass us in this advantage, we surpass many others. And the skill to fortify and protect the body by acquired means, we possess by a natural instinct and precept. As proof that this is so, the elephant sharpens and whets the teeth which he uses in war (for he has special ones for this purpose, which he spares, and does not use at all for his other functions).

When bulls go into combat, they spread and toss the dust around them; boars whet their tusks; and the ichneumon, when he is to come to grips with the crocodile, arms his body, coats it, and crusts it all over with mud, well pressed and well kneaded, as with a cuirass. Why shall we not say that it is just as natural to arm ourselves with wood and iron?

As for speech, it is certain that if it is not natural, it is not necessary. Nevertheless, I believe that a child who had been brought up in complete solitude, remote from all association (which would be a hard experiment to make), would have some sort of speech to express his ideas. And it is not credible that Nature has denied us this resource that she has given to many other animals: for what is it but speech, this faculty we see in them of complaining, rejoicing, calling to each other for help, inviting each other to love, as they do by the use of their voice? ᴮHow could they not speak to one another? They certainly speak to us, and we to them. In how many ways do we not speak to our dogs? And they answer us. We talk to them in another language, with other names, than to birds, hogs, oxen, horses; and we change the idiom according to the species:

> ᴬSo ants amidst their sable-colored band
> Greet one another, and inquire perchance
> The road each follows, and the prize in hand.
> DANTE

It seems to me that Lactantius attributes to beasts not only speech but also laughter. And the difference of language that is seen between us, according to the difference of countries, is found also in animals of the same species. Aristotle cites in this connection the various calls of partridges according to the place they are situated in,

> ᴮAnd various birds ...
> Utter at different times far different cries ...
> And some change with the changing of the skies
> Their raucous songs.
> LUCRETIUS

ᴬBut it is yet to be known what language this child would speak; and what is said about it by conjecture has not much appearance of truth. If they allege to me, against this opinion, that men naturally deaf do not speak at all, I reply that it is not only because they could not be taught speech by ear, but rather because the sense of hearing, of which they are deprived, is related to that of speech, and they hold

together by a natural tie: so that what we speak we must speak first
to ourselves, and make it ring on our own ears inwardly, before we
send it to other ears.

I have said all this to maintain this resemblance that exists to
human things, and to bring us back and join us to the majority. We
are neither above nor below the rest: all that is under heaven, says
the sage, incurs the same law and the same fortune,

> [B]All things are bound by their own chains of fate.
>
> LUCRETIUS

[A]There is some difference, there are orders and degrees; but it is
under the aspect of one and the same nature:

> [B]And all things go their own way, nor forget
> Distinctions by the law of nature set.
>
> LUCRETIUS

[A]Man must be constrained and forced into line inside the barriers of
this order. The poor wretch is in no position really to step outside
them; he is fettered and bound, he is subjected to the same obliga-
tion as the other creatures of his class, and in a very ordinary
condition, without any real and essential prerogative or preemi-
nence. That which he accords himself in his mind and in his fancy
has neither body nor taste. And if it is true that he alone of all the
animals has this freedom of imagination and this unruliness in
thought that represents to him what is, what is not, what he
wants, the false and the true, it is an advantage that is sold him
very dear, and in which he has little cause to glory, for from it springs
the principal source of the ills that oppress him: sin, disease, irreso-
lution, confusion, despair.

So I say, to return to my subject, that there is no apparent reason
to judge that the beasts do by natural and obligatory instinct the
same things that we do by our choice and cleverness. We must infer
from like results like faculties,[8] and consequently confess that this
same reason, this same method that we have for working, is also that
of the animals.[9] Why do we imagine in them this compulsion of
nature, we who feel no similar effect? Besides, it is more honorable,
and closer to divinity, to be guided and obliged to act lawfully by

8 The 1595 edition adds: "and from richer results, richer faculties."
9 The 1595 edition reads, instead of "is also that of the animals," "the animals
have it also, or some better one."

a natural and inevitable condition, than to act lawfully by accidental and fortuitous liberty; and safer to leave the reins of our conduct to nature than to ourselves. The vanity of our presumption makes us prefer to owe our ability to our powers than to nature's liberality; and we enrich the other animals with natural goods and renounce them in their favor, in order to honor and ennoble ourselves with goods acquired: a very simple notion, it seems to me, for I should prize just as highly graces that were all mine and inborn as those I had gone begging and seeking from education. It is not in our power to acquire a fairer recommendation than to be favored by God and nature.

Take for example the fox, whom the inhabitants of Thrace use when they want to undertake to cross some frozen stream over the ice, turning him loose ahead of them for this reason. If we saw him at the edge of the water bring his ear very near the ice, to hear whether the water running beneath sounds near or far away, and draw back or advance according as he finds the ice too thin or thick enough, would we not have reason to suppose that there passes through his head the same reasoning that would pass through ours, and that it is a ratiocination and conclusion drawn from natural common sense: "What makes a noise, moves; what moves is not frozen; what is not frozen is liquid; and what is liquid gives way under a weight"? For to attribute this simply to a keenness of the sense of hearing, without reasoning or inference, is a chimera, and cannot enter our imagination. We must make the same supposition about the many sorts of ruses and tricks by which the animals protect themselves from the attacks we make upon them.

And if we wish to derive some advantage from this very fact, that it is in our power to seize them, to use them and do what we like with them, this is only the same advantage that we have over one another. We have our slaves on this condition. ᴮAnd were there not the Climacides, women in Syria who, crouching on all fours, served as a footstool and a stepladder for ladies to climb into their coach? ᴬAnd most free people, for very slight advantages, abandon their life and their being to the power of others. ᶜThe wives and concubines of the Thracians plead each to be chosen to be killed at their husband's tomb.

ᴬHave tyrants ever failed to find enough men vowed to devote themselves to them, some of them adding further the obligation to accompany them in death as in life? ᴮWhole armies have thus bound themselves to their captains. The formula of the oath in that tough

school of the gladiators who fought to the death bore these pro-
mises: "We swear to let ourselves be chained, burned, beaten, and
killed with the sword, and to suffer all that legitimate gladiators
suffer from their master, most religiously engaging body and soul in
his service":

> Burn, if you will, my head, pierce me with sword,
> And scourge my shoulders with a twisted cord.
>
> TIBULLUS

That was a real obligation; and yet there were ten thousand in a given
year who entered into it and were lost.

ᶜWhen the Scythians interred their king, they strangled upon his
body the most favored of his concubines, his cupbearer, groom,
chamberlain, room usher, and cook. And on his anniversary they
killed fifty horses mounted by fifty pages whom they had impaled by
the spine up to the throat, and left them thus planted on parade
around the tomb.

ᴬThe men that serve us do so more cheaply, and for a treatment
less careful and favorable than the one we give our birds, horses, and
dogs. ᶜTo what care do we not stoop for the comfort of these? It does
not seem to me that the most abject servants do willingly for their
masters what princes take honor in doing for these animals.

Diogenes, seeing his parents at pains to redeem him from slavery,
said: "They are mad: it is the man who keeps and feeds me who is my
slave." And those who keep animals should be said rather to serve
them than to be served by them.

ᴬAnd yet they are more noble in this way, that never did a lion
enslave himself to another lion, nor a horse to another horse, for lack
of heart. As we go hunting beasts, so the tigers and lions go hunting
men; and they have the same practice toward one another: dogs after
hares, pikes after tench, swallows after grasshoppers, sparrow hawks
after blackbirds and larks:

> ᴮThe stork brings to her brood
> From lonely spots, lizards and snakes for food;
> Jove's eagle and the nobles of the air
> Hunt down the kid and hare.
>
> JUVENAL

We share the result of our hunt with our dogs and birds, as well as
the pains and skill; and above Amphipolis in Thrace, hunters and
wild falcons divide the booty exactly in half; just as, along the

marshes of Lake Maeotis,[10] if the fisherman does not honestly leave the wolves an equal share of his catch, they immediately go and tear his nets.

^AAnd as we have a kind of hunting that is conducted more by subtlety than by force, like that of snares and hook and line, so are similar ones seen among the beasts. Aristotle says that the cuttlefish throws out of her neck a long gut as a line, which she extends at full length in releasing it, and draws back to her when she wishes. As she perceives some little fish approaching, she lets him nibble the end of this gut, being herself hidden in the sand or the mud, and little by little draws it in until the little fish is so near her that with one leap she can catch it.

As for strength, there is no animal in the world exposed to so many injuries as man. We do not need a whale, an elephant or a crocodile, or other such animals, just one of which is capable of destroying a large number of men; lice are enough to vacate Sulla's dictatorship; and the heart and life of a great and triumphant emperor is the breakfast of a little worm.

Why do we say that in man it is science and knowledge built up by art and reason, to distinguish the things useful for his living and for help in his illnesses from those which are not, for knowing the power of rhubarb and fern? And when we see the goats of Candia, if they have received an arrow wound, go and pick out dittany out of a million herbs for their cure; and the tortoise, when it has eaten viper meat, immediately look for marjoram to purge itself; the dragon rub and clear his eyes with fennel; storks give themselves enemas with sea water; elephants pull out, not only from their own and their companions' bodies, but also from the bodies of their masters (witness the elephant of King Porus, whom Alexander defeated), the javelins and darts cast at them in combat, and pull them out so dexterously that we could not possibly do it with so little pain: why do we not say likewise that that is science and wisdom? For to assert, to disparage them, that it is solely by the instruction and tutelage of nature that they know this, is not to take away from them the claim to science and wisdom; it is to attribute it to them by a better reason than to ourselves, because of the honor of so sure a schoolmistress.

Chrysippus, although in all other things as disdainful a judge of the condition of animals as any other philosopher, considering the

10 The Sea of Azov.

movements of the dog, who, coming upon a crossroad with three roads, either in search of his master whom he has lost, or in pursuit of some prey fleeing before him, goes and tries one road after the other, and, after having made sure of two and not having found in them the trace of what he is looking for, darts into the third without hesitation, is forced to confess that in that dog some such reasoning as this takes place: "I have traced my master to this crossroad; he must necessarily be going by one of these three roads; it is not by this one or that one; so he must infallibly be going by this other"; and that assured by this inference and reasoning, he no longer uses his sense of smell on the third road or tests it any further, but lets himself be swept on by the force of his reason. This act of pure logic, and this use of propositions divided and conjoined and of the adequate enumeration of the parts, is it not as valuable for the dog to know it by himself as to learn it from Trapezuntius?[11]

Yet the animals are not incapable of being taught also in our way. Blackbirds, ravens, magpies, and parrots we teach to speak; and that facility with which we see them rendering their voice and breath so supple and manageable for us, to form and constrain it to a certain number of letters and syllables, testifies that they have an inward power of reason which makes them so teachable and determined to learn.

Everybody is satiated, I think, with seeing so many sorts of monkey tricks that mountebanks teach their dogs: the dances in which they do not miss a single cadence of the sound they hear, many various motions and jumps that they are made to do by a word of command. But I observe with more amazement the behavior, which is nevertheless common enough, of the dogs that blind men use both in the fields and in town; I have noticed how they stop at certain doors where they have been accustomed to receive alms, how they avoid being hit by coaches and carts, even when for their part they have enough room to pass; I have seen one, along a town ditch, leave a smooth flat path and take a worse one, to keep his master away from the ditch. How can this dog have been made to understand that it was his responsibility to consider solely the safety of his master and to despise his own comforts in order to serve him? And how did he know that a given road was quite broad enough for

11 Georgius Trapezuntius or George of Trebizond (1396–1486), logician. He translated and annotated Aristotle.

himself, which would not be so for a blind man? Can all this be understood without reasoning and intelligence?

We must not forget what Plutarch says that he and the Emperor Vespasian, the father, saw done by a dog in Rome at the theater of Marcellus. This dog served a mountebank who was acting a play in several scenes and with several parts, and the dog had his part in it. He had among other things to play dead for a while as having eaten a certain drug; after swallowing the bread that represented this drug, he promptly began to tremble and shake as if he were dizzy; finally, stretching out and stiffening himself as if dead, he let himself be pulled and dragged from one place to another, as the subject of the play demanded; and then, when he knew it was time, he began at first to stir very gently, as if he had come out of a deep sleep, and, raising his head, looked around here and there in a way that astonished all the spectators.

The oxen that served in the royal gardens of Susa to water them and turn certain great wheels for drawing water, to which there were buckets attached (like many that are to be seen in Languedoc), had been ordered to draw up to one hundred turns a day; they were so accustomed to this number that it was impossible by any force to make them draw one turn more, and having done their task, they stopped short. We are in our adolescence before we know how to count up to a hundred, and we have just discovered nations which have no knowledge of numbers.

There is still more intelligence needed to teach others than to be taught. Now, leaving aside what Democritus concluded and proved, that the animals have taught us most of the arts, as the spider to weave and sew, the swallow to build, the swan and the nightingale music, and many animals, through imitation of them, to practice medicine; Aristotle maintains that the nightingales teach their young to sing, and spend time and care on it, whence it happens that those that we bring up in a cage, who have had no chance to go to school under their parents, lose much of the charm of their song. [B]We may judge from this that it improves by teaching and study. And even among the free birds it is not uniform and the same; each one has learned according to his capacity; and in the jealousy of their apprenticeship they vie with each other and contend so bravely that sometimes the vanquished falls dead, his breath failing him rather than his voice. The youngest ruminate pensively and take certain couplets of song to imitate; the disciple listens to the lesson of his teacher and gives him back a very careful account of it; they are

quiet, first one, then the other; you hear the mistakes corrected, and you sense occasional reprehensions by the teacher.

"I once saw," says Arrius, "an elephant who had a cymbal hanging from each thigh, and another attached to his trunk, to the sound of which all the others danced in a circle, rising and bending at certain cadences, as the instrument guided them; and it was pleasant to listen to this harmony." [A]In the spectacles in Rome one ordinarily saw elephants trained to move and dance, to the sound of the voice, dances with many intricate and interrupted steps and many cadences very hard to learn. Some of them have been seen in private going over their lesson and practicing with care and study, so as not to be scolded and beaten by their masters.

But this story of the magpie, for which we have Plutarch himself as sponsor, is strange. She was in a barber's shop in Rome, and did wonders in imitating with her voice all that she heard. One day it happened that certain trumpeters stopped and blew a long time in front of this shop. After that and all the next day here was this magpie pensive, mute, and melancholy, at which everyone marveled, and thought that the sound of the trumpets had stunned her and deafened her, and that her voice had been snuffed out together with her hearing. But they found in the end that it was a profound study and a withdrawal within herself, while her mind was practicing and preparing her voice to represent the sound of these trumpets; so that the first voice she used was that one, expressing perfectly their runs, pitches, and variations; and for this new acquirement she abandoned and scorned all she had learned to say before.

I do not want to omit citing also this other example of a dog that the same Plutarch says he saw (for as for the order, I fully realize that I am disturbing it; but I observe none in arranging these examples any more than in the rest of my work) when he was on a ship. This dog, having trouble getting some oil that was in the bottom of a pitcher, where he could not get at it with his tongue because of the narrow mouth of the vessel, went and fetched some pebbles and put some in this pitcher until he had made the oil rise nearer the edge, where he could reach it. What is that if not the work of a very subtle mind? They say that the Barbary crows do the same thing when the water they want to drink is too low.

This action is somewhat akin to what was told of the elephants by a king of their country, Juba, that when by the craft of their hunters one of them finds himself caught in certain deep pits that

they prepare for them and cover with brush to fool them, his comrades arrive posthaste with many stones and logs to help him get out. But this animal in so many other actions approaches human capacity that if I wanted to trace in detail what experience has taught us about him, I should easily win the argument that I ordinarily maintain, that there is more difference between a given man and a given man than between a given animal and a given man.

The keeper of an elephant, in a private house in Syria, used to rob him at all his meals of half the ration ordered for him. One day the master of the house decided to take care of him himself, and poured into his manger the proper measure of barley that he had prescribed for his feeding; the elephant, looking at his keeper with an evil eye, separated one half of it with his trunk and set it aside, revealing in that way the wrong that was being done him. And another, having a keeper who mixed stones into his feed to increase the measure, approached the pot where he was cooking his meat for his dinner and filled it with ashes for him.

These are particular actions; but what everyone has seen and what everyone knows is that in all the armies that were brought from the East one of the strongest elements consisted of elephants, from which they derived results incomparably greater than we do at present from our artillery, which more or less takes their place in the order of battle (this is easy to judge for those who know ancient history):

> [B]Their sires served Tyrian Hannibal,
> Pyrrhus, and many a Roman general,
> Upon their mighty backs whole cohorts bore,
> And took their place amidst the thick of war.
>
> JUVENAL

[A]They must have relied knowingly on the confidence they placed in these animals and in their intelligence, abandoning to them the leading place in battle, where the slightest stop they might have made, because of the size and weight of their body, or the slightest fear that might have made them face about against their own men, would have been enough to ruin everything. And they have less often been known to fall back upon their own troops than our troops to fall back upon those behind them and thus rout their own side. They entrusted to elephants not a simple movement, but many different functions in combat; [B]as the Spaniards in the recent

conquest of the Indies did to their dogs, to whom they gave pay and a share in the booty; and these animals showed as much skill and judgment in pursuing their victory and holding back, in charging or withdrawing according to the occasion, in distinguishing friends from enemies, as they did ardor and fierceness.

ᴬWe admire more, and value more, foreign things than ordinary ones; and but for that I should not have spent my time on this long list. For in my opinion, if anyone studies closely what we see ordinarily of the animals that live among us, there is material there for him to find facts just as wonderful as those that we go collecting in remote countries and centuries. ᶜIt is one and the same nature that rolls its course. Anyone who had formed a competent judgment of its present state could infer from this with certainty both all the future and all the past.

ᴬI once saw among us some men brought by sea from a far country. Because we did not understand their language at all, and because their ways, moreover, and their bearing and their clothes were totally remote from ours, which of us did not consider them savages and brutes? Who did not attribute it to stupidity and brutishness to see them mute, ignorant of the French language, ignorant of our hand kissings and our serpentine bows, our deport- ment and our bearing, which human nature must take as its pattern without fail?

Everything that seems strange to us we condemn, and every- thing that we do not understand; as happens in our judgment of the animals. They have many qualities that are related to ours; from these by comparison we can draw some conjecture; but as for what is peculiar to them, what do we know about it? Horses, dogs, oxen, sheep, birds, and most of the animals that live with us recognize our voice and let themselves be guided by it; so also, indeed, did Crassus' lamprey, which came to him when he called it; and so also do the eels that are found in the fountain of Arethusa. ᴮAnd I have seen enough ponds where the fish come hurrying up to eat at a certain call from those who tend them:

> ᴬThey have their names, and each and all
> Come at the summons of their master's call.
> MARTIAL

That we can judge. We can also say that the elephants have some participation in religion, since after many ablutions and purifica- tions we see them, raising their trunks like arms and keeping their

eyes fixed toward the rising sun, stand still a long time in meditation and contemplation at certain hours of the day, by their own inclination, without instruction and without precept. But because we do not see any such signs in other animals, we cannot thereby prove that they are without religion and cannot grasp any part of what is hidden from us. Just as we see something in this action which the philosopher Cleanthes observed, because it resembles our own. He saw, says he, some ants leave their anthill bearing the body of a dead ant toward another anthill, from which several other ants came to meet them as if to speak to them; and after they had been together for a time, the second group returned to consult, you may suppose, with their fellow citizens, and in this way made two or three trips because of the difficulty of coming to terms. Finally the last-comers brought the first ones a worm out of their den, as if for the ransom of the dead one, which worm the first ones loaded on their back and carried home, leaving to the others the body of the deceased. That is the interpretation that Cleanthes gave to it, testifying thereby that those creatures who have no voice nevertheless have mutual intercourse and communication, in which it is our fault that we cannot participate; and for this reason we are meddling foolishly by expressing our opinion in the matter.

Now they do still other things which are far beyond our capacity, which we are so far from being able to imitate that we cannot even imagine them. Many maintain that in that great and final naval battle that Antony lost to Augustus, his admiral's galley was stopped in the middle of its course by that little fish that the Latins call *remora*,[12] because of that property it has of stopping every sort of vessel to which it attaches itself. And when the Emperor Caligula was sailing with a great fleet along the coast of Romania, his galley alone was stopped short by this same fish, which he caused to be caught, attached as it was to the keel of his vessel. He was thoroughly irritated that such a little animal could overpower the sea and the winds and the violence of all his oars, by being simply attached to his galley by the beak (for it is a shellfish); and he was further astonished, not without good reason, that when it was brought to him inside the boat it no longer had the power that it had outside.

12 *Remorari* in Latin means "to delay."

A citizen of Cyzicus once acquired the reputation of being a good mathematician by learning this habit of the hedgehog: that it builds its burrow open to various quarters and various winds, and, foreseeing from which quarter the wind will blow, stops up the hole on that side. After observing which, this citizen brought to his town sure predictions of how the wind would blow next.

The chameleon takes the color of the place where he is set; but the octopus himself assumes the color he likes, according to the occasion, to hide from what he fears and catch what he hunts; in the chameleon it is a passive change, but in the octopus it is an active change. We have some changes of color in fear, anger, shame, and other passions that alter our complexion, but it is a passive effect, as with the chameleon: it is indeed in the power of jaundice to make us turn yellow, but it is not in the power of our will. Now these effects which we recognize in the other animals, greater than our own, testify to some more excellent faculty in them which is concealed from us, as are in all likelihood many others of their properties and powers ᶜof which no signs come through to us.

ᴬOf all the predictions in times past, the most ancient and the most certain were those drawn from the flight of birds. We have nothing like it and nothing so wonderful That rule and order in the flapping of their wings by which men draw conclusions about things to come, must certainly be led by some excellent means to so noble an operation; for it is playing with words to go and attribute this great effect to some natural ordinance, without the intelligence, consent, and reason of the creature that produces it; and this is an opinion evidently false.

As proof of this, the torpedo[13] has the property, not only of putting to sleep the limbs that directly touch her, but of transmitting through nets and seines a sort of numbed heaviness to the hands of those who move and handle them. Indeed they say further that if you pour water upon her, you feel this sensation which climbs uphill to the hand and numbs the touch through the water. This power is marvelous, but it is not useless to the torpedo: she senses it and uses it, in this way, that to catch the prey she seeks, you see her hide under the mud, so that the other fish, gliding past above, struck and benumbed by this chill of hers, fall into her power.

Cranes, swallows, and other birds of passage, changing their residence according to the seasons of the year, show well enough

13 Electric ray.

the knowledge they have of their faculty of divination, and put it to use.

Hunters assure us that in order to choose out of a number of puppies the one that you should save as the best, all you need is to put the mother in a position to choose him herself; since, if you carry them out of their kennel, the first one she brings back will always be the best; or else, if you pretend to surround their kennel with fire on all sides, it will be the puppy that she runs to rescue first. Whence it appears that they have a power of prognostication that we have not, or that they have some ability to judge their young which is different and keener than ours.

Since animals are born, beget, feed, act, move, live, and die in a manner so close to our own, all that we detract from their motive powers, and all that we add to ours to raise our state above theirs, can in no way proceed from the judgment of our reason. As a rule for our health, doctors propose to us the example of the way the animals live and act; for this saying has in all times been in the mouth of the people:

> Keep your head warm, and your feet;
> For the rest, live like a beast.

Generation is the principal of the natural actions. We have a certain disposition of members which to us is more suitable for this; however, they order us to conform to the posture and arrangement of the brutes, as being more effectual:

> And they say
> That wives conceive best in the wild beasts' way,
> Like quadrupeds; for thus, loins high, breasts low,
> The seeds can to their destination go.
> LUCRETIUS

And they condemn as harmful those indecent and unusual motions which the women have brought into it on their own, recalling them to the more modest and sedate example and practice of the animals of their sex:

> For thus a woman may oppose conception,
> If, writhing in her joy, she makes improvements,
> Draws back his part from hers, upsets his movements.
> For thus she turns the plowshare from its way
> And sends the vital spurt of seed astray.
> LUCRETIUS

If it is justice to give each his due, the beasts which serve, love, and defend their benefactors, and pursue and attack strangers and those who hurt them, represent by this a certain image of our justice; as also in observing a very equitable equality in the distribution of their goods to their young.

As for friendship, theirs is without comparison more alive and more constant than that of men. Hyrcanus, King Lysimachus' dog, when his master was dead, remained obstinately on his bed, refusing to eat or drink; and the day they burned the body he took a run and threw himself into the fire, where he was burned. As did also the dog of a man named Pyrrhus, for he did not budge off his master's bed after he was dead; and when they took his master away he let himself be carried away with him, and finally sprang into the pyre on which they were burning his master's body.

There are certain affectionate leanings which sometimes arise in us without the advice of our reason, which come from an unpremeditated accident that others call sympathy: the animals are as capable of it as we are. We see horses forming a certain familiarity with one another, until we have trouble making them live or travel separately; we see them apply their affection to a certain color in their companions, as we might to a certain type of face, and, when they encounter this color, approach it immediately with joy and demonstrations of good will, and take a dislike and hatred of some other color. Animals, like us, exercise choice in their amours and make a certain selection among their females. They are not exempt from our jealousies, or from extreme and irreconcilable envy.

Desires are either natural and necessary, like eating and drinking; or natural and not necessary, like intercourse with females; or neither natural nor necessary. Of this last type are nearly all those of men; they are all superfluous and artificial. For it is marvelous how little Nature needs to be content, how little she has left us to desire. The dressings of our cooking have nothing to do with her ordaining. The Stoics say that a man could stay alive on one olive a day. The delicacy of our wines is no part of her teaching, nor the embellishments that we add to our amorous appetites:

> Nor does she require
> A wench who claims a consul as her sire.
> HORACE

These extraneous desires, which ignorance of the good and a false opinion have insinuated into us, are in such great number that they

drive out almost all the natural ones; neither more nor less than if there were such a great number of foreigners in a city that they put out the natural inhabitants, or extinguished their ancient authority and power, completely usurping it and taking possession of it.

Animals are much more self-controlled than we are, and restrain themselves with more moderation within the limits that nature has prescribed to us; but not so strictly that they do not still have something comparable to our debauch. And just as there have been furious desires that have driven men to the love of beasts, so they too are sometimes smitten with love of us and entertain unnatural affections between one species and another. Witness the elephant who was rival to Aristophanes the grammarian in the love of a young flower girl in the city of Alexandria, and who yielded no ground to him in the attentions of a very passionate suitor; for walking through the market where they sold fruits he would take some with his trunk and carry them to her; he lost sight of her only as little as was possible for him, and would sometimes put his trunk into her bosom under her collar and feel her breasts. They tell also of a dragon in love with a girl, and a goose smitten with the love of a boy in the town of Asopus, and a ram that was suitor to the minstrel girl Glaucia; and every day are seen monkeys furiously in love with women. We also see certain animals addicted to the love of males of their own sex. Oppianus and others relate certain examples to show the reverence that beasts in their marriages have for laws of kinship, but experience very often shows us the contrary:

> The heifer unashamed upon her takes
> Her sire; the stallion of his filly makes
> His mate; goats pair with their begotten young;
> Birds breed with birds from whom themselves are sprung.
> OVID

Of sly trickery is there a clearer example than that of the philosopher Thales' mule? Fording a river while loaded with salt, and having happened to stumble, so that the sacks he carried were all wet through, and having perceived that the salt melted by this means had made his burden lighter, he never failed, as soon as he came to any stream, to plunge in with his load; until his master, discovering his knavery, ordered him to be loaded with wool, whereupon, his calculations upset, he stopped using that trick.

There are many who naturally portray the image of our avarice; for we see in them an extreme solicitude to snatch all they can and hide it carefully, although they make no use of it at all.

As for domestic management, not only do they surpass us in their foresight in piling up and saving for the time to come, but they also possess many parts of the knowledge necessary for it. The ants spread their grains and seeds outside their threshing floor to air them, freshen them, and dry them, when they see that they are beginning to molder and smell rancid, for fear they may spoil and rot. But the caution and foresight they use in gnawing the grains of wheat surpasses anything imagined by human prudence. Because the wheat does not always remain dry and sound, but grows soft and soggy and dissolves as in milk, when it is on the way to germinate and produce; for fear it may sprout and lose its nature and property as a storehouse for their food, they nibble off the end by which it usually sprouts.

As for war, which is the greatest and most pompous of human actions, I should be glad to know whether we want to use it as an argument for some preeminence, or, on the contrary, as testimony of our imbecility and imperfection; as indeed the science of undoing and killing one another, of ruining and destroying our own species, seems to have little to make it alluring to the beasts who do not have it:

> [B]When did a lion kill
> A weaker lion? In what forest strife
> Did one boar's tusks destroy another's life?
>
> JUVENAL

[A]But yet they are not universally exempt from this; witness the furious encounters of the honeybees and the enterprises of the princes of the two opposing armies:

> Often disputes arise
> Between two kings, and uproar fills the skies;
> The passion of the mob is heard afar,
> And hearts that throb for war.
>
> VIRGIL

I never read that divine description without seeming to read in it human absurdity and vanity portrayed. For these warlike movements that ravish us with their horror and terror, this tempest of sounds and shouts,

[B]Skyward rises the gleam, and all around
The earth glitters with brass; a mighty sound
Starts 'neath the feet of stalwart men; the cries
Re-echo from the hills to starry skies;

LUCRETIUS

[A]this frightful array of so many thousands of armed men, so much fury, ardor, and courage – it is comical to consider by what inane causes it is stirred up and by what trivial causes extinguished:

All because Paris loved another's wife,
Greeks and barbarians clashed in baneful strife.

HORACE

All Asia was ruined and consumed in wars for Paris' lechery. The envy of one single man, a spite, a pleasure, a domestic jealousy, causes which should not move two fishwives to scratch one another – that is the soul and motive of all this great turmoil. Will we believe the very ones who are the principal authors and movers of wars? Let us listen to the greatest, the most victorious emperor, and the most powerful that ever was, very comically and very cleverly making a sport and a laughingstock of many battles hazarded on land and sea, the blood and the lives of five hundred thousand men who followed his fortunes, and the power and riches of both parts of the world exhausted in the service of his enterprises:

Since Antony took Glaphyra to his bed,
Fulvia wills that she to mine be led.
I must have Fulvia? Then if Manius pray
I do the same to him? No thanks, I say.
Make love or fight, she says. Supposing, though,
Dearer than life's my member? . . . Bugles, blow!

AUGUSTUS, QUOTED BY MARTIAL

(I use my Latin with a free conscience, and with the permission you have given me.)[14]

Now this great body, with so many aspects and movements, which seems to threaten heaven and earth:

14 This essay is addressed to a lady of quality, almost certainly Margaret of Valois. See below, pp. 508–10.

^BAs waves roll numberless upon the Libyan sea
When fierce Orion in the wintry deep goes down,
Or as thick ears of wheat, by the young sun scorched brown,
Grow ripe on Hermus' plain or Lycia's golden fields,
The earth quakes 'neath the tramp of feet, the clash of shields;

 VIRGIL

^Athis furious monster with so many arms and so many heads is still
man, feeble, calamitous, and miserable. It is only an anthill stirred
and wrought up,

 The black column moves across the plain.

 VIRGIL

A contrary breath of wind, the croaking of a flight of ravens, a horse's
stumble, the accidental passing of an eagle, a dream, a word, a sign,
a morning mist, are enough to overthrow him and bring him to the
ground. Just give him a sunbeam on his face, and he has melted and
fainted; just blow a little dust in his eyes, as with the bees of our poet,
and there are all our flags, our legions, and great Pompey himself at
their head, broken and shattered. For it was he, it seems to me,
whom Sertorius beat in Spain with this splendid weapon,[15] ^Bwhich
has also served others, such as Eumenes against Antigonus, and
Surena against Crassus:

 ^AThese passions and these mighty fights are quelled
 And by the merest pinch of dust dispelled.

 VIRGIL

 ^CTurn loose even some of our flies after them, and they will have
the power and the courage to disperse an army. In recent memory,
when the Portuguese were besieging the town of Tamly in the
territory of Xiatine, the inhabitants of the town carried upon
the walls a large quantity of hives, in which they are rich, and with
fire drove the bees so fiercely upon their enemies that they were put
to rout, being unable to withstand the assaults and stings. Thus the
victory and the freedom of their town remained to these novel
rescuers, with such good fortune that on their return from combat
not a single bee was missing.
 ^AThe souls of emperors and cobblers are cast in the same mold.
Considering the importance of the actions of princes and their

15 A cloud of dust.

weightiness, we persuade ourselves that they are produced by some causes equally weighty and important. We are wrong: they are led to and fro in their movements by the same springs as we are in ours. The same reason that makes us bicker with a neighbor creates a war between princes; the same reason that makes us whip a lackey, when it happens in a king makes him ruin a province. ^BTheir will is as frivolous as ours, but their power is greater. ^ALike appetites move a mite and an elephant.

As for fidelity, there is no animal in the world as treacherous as man. Our histories tell of the keen pursuit that some dogs have made after the murderers of their masters. King Pyrrhus, encountering a dog who was guarding a dead man, and hearing that he had been performing that function for three days, ordered the body to be buried, and took the dog along with him. One day when he was attending a general review of his army, this dog, perceiving his master's murderers, ran at them with loud barking and fierce anger, and by this first indication set in motion vengeance for this murder, which was accomplished soon afterward by the path of justice. The dog of the sage Hesiod did as much, in convicting the sons of Ganistor of Naupactus of the murder committed on the person of his master.

Another dog, guarding a temple in Athens, perceiving a sacrilegious thief who was carrying away the finest jewels, began to bark at him as hard as he could; and when this did not wake the wardens, he proceeded to follow him, and, when day came, kept a little farther from him, without ever losing sight of him. If the man offered him anything to eat, he refused it, but wagged his tail at the other passers-by that he met on his way, and took from their hands whatever they gave him to eat. If his thief stopped to sleep, he stopped with him in the same place. News of this dog having come to the wardens of this church, they set themselves to follow in his tracks, inquiring for news of the color of the dog, and finally came upon him in the town of Cromyon, and the robber also, whom they took back to the city of Athens, where he was punished. And the judges, in recognition of this good service, ordered a certain measure of wheat at public expense to feed the dog, and ordered the priests to take care of him. Plutarch testifies to this story as a thing well confirmed and happening in his time.

As for gratitude (for it seems to me that we need to bring this word into favor), this one example will suffice, which Apion tells as having been a spectator of it himself. One day, he says, when the

people in Rome were being given the pleasure of combats between many strange beasts, principally lions of unusual size, there was one among others who, by his furious demeanor, the strength and size of his limbs, and an arrogant and frightful roar, attracted the glances of all the spectators. Among other slaves that were presented to the people in this combat with beasts was one Androdus,[16] of Dacia, who belonged to a Roman lord of consular rank. This lion, having perceived him afar off, first stopped short, as if struck with wonder, and then approached very gently, in a mild and peaceable fashion, as if to try to renew acquaintance with him. This done, and having made sure of what he was looking for, he began to wag his tail in the manner of dogs making up to their master, and to kiss and lick the hands and thighs of this poor wretch, who was completely petrified with fear and beside himself. When Androdus had recovered his spirits thanks to the friendliness of this lion, and reassured his eyes enough to look at him and recognize him, it was a singular pleasure to see the caresses and greetings that they lavished upon each other. Whereat the people having raised cries of joy, the Emperor sent for this slave to hear from him the cause of such a strange event. He told him a novel and wonderful story.

"When my master," he said, "was proconsul in Africa, I was constrained, by the cruelty and rigor with which he treated me – he had me beaten daily – to steal away from him and take flight. And to hide safely from a personage having such great authority in the province, I decided my shortest way was to gain the lonely places and the sandy and uninhabitable regions of that country, resolved, if the means of sustenance came to fail me, to find some way of killing myself. The sun being extremely fierce around noon and the heat insupportable, when I stumbled upon a hidden and inaccessible cave, I threw myself inside. Soon afterward in came this lion, with a bleeding and wounded paw, complaining and groaning at the pain he suffered. At his arrival I took great fright; but he, seeing me cowering in a corner of his den, approached me very gently, holding out to me his injured paw, and showing it to me as if to ask for help. I then took out a great splinter that was in it, and having become a little accustomed to him, squeezed his wound, got out the dirt that was accumulating in it, wiped it, and scoured it as clean as I could. He, feeling himself eased of his trouble and relieved of this pain, lay down to rest and sleep, still keeping his paw between my hands.

16 Sometimes referred to as Androclus, most often as Androcles.

From then on, he and I lived together in this cave three whole years, on the same food; for of the animals he killed in his hunting, he brought me the best parts, which I cooked in the sun for lack of fire and fed on. At length, weary of this wild and brutish life, when the lion one day had gone on his accustomed hunt, I left there, and on the third day was caught by the soldiers, who took me from Africa to my master in this city, and he immediately condemned me to death and to be abandoned to the beasts. Now, from what I see, this lion was also caught soon after, and he has now tried to repay me for the good deed and cure he received from me."

That is the story that Androdus told the Emperor, which he also voiced abroad from one to another among the people. Wherefore, at the request of all, he was set at liberty and absolved from his sentence, and by the order of the people he was made a present of this lion. Since then, says Apion, we would see Androdus leading this lion on a little leash, strolling through the taverns in Rome to receive the money that was given to him, while the lion let himself be covered with the flowers they threw to him, and everyone would say on meeting them: "There is the lion, host to the man; there is the man, doctor to the lion."

[B]We often weep for the loss of the animals we love, and so do they for ours:

> His war horse Aethon, trappings gone, appears,
> Weeping, and wets his face with heavy tears.
>
> VIRGIL

As some of our nations have wives in common, some each man his own; do we not see this also among the beasts, and marriages better kept than ours?

[A]As for the society and confederation that they form among themselves to league together and assist one another, it may be seen of oxen, hogs, and other animals that at the call of the one you injure, all the herd runs up to his aid and rallies in his defense. When the parrot fish has swallowed the fisherman's hook, his comrades gather in a swarm around him and gnaw through the line; and if by chance there is one that has got into the net, the others offer him their tail from outside, and he grips it as tight as he can with his teeth; thus they drag him out and take him away. Barbels, when one of their comrades is caught, set the line against their back, raising a spine they have which is toothed like a saw, and with which they saw it and cut it.

As for the particular aids we receive from one another in the service of life, many similar examples are seen among them. They maintain that the whale never moves unless it has ahead of it a little fish resembling the sea gudgeon, which for this reason is called the *guide*. The whale follows it, letting itself be led and turned as easily as the tiller turns the boat; and in recompense for this, whereas everything else, whether beast or vessel, that enters the horrible chaos of this monster's mouth, is straightway engulfed and lost, this little fish retires into it in all security and sleeps there, and during its sleep the whale does not budge. But as soon as it comes out, the whale starts in to follow it without stopping, and if by chance it loses the guide, it goes wandering here and there, and often bruising itself against the rocks, like a vessel that has no rudder; which Plutarch testifies to having seen on the island of Anticyra.

There is a similar association between the little bird they call the wren and the crocodile: the wren serves as a sentinel for this great animal. And if the ichneumon, his enemy, approaches to fight him, this little bird, for fear it may surprise him asleep, goes and wakes him up and warns him of his danger by his song and his pecking. It lives on the leavings of this monster, who receives it familiarly in his mouth and allows it to peck in his jaws and between his teeth and collect bits of flesh that have remained there. And if he wants to close his mouth, he first warns it to leave, by closing it little by little, without squeezing or hurting it.

The shellfish they call the nacre also lives in this way with the pinnothere, a little animal of the crab class, who serves him as usher and doorkeeper, sitting in the opening of this shell that he keeps continually ajar and open, until he sees some little fish enter that is suitable for their catch; then he enters the nacre, and pinches the living flesh, and makes him close his shell; then the two of them together eat the prey shut up in their fort.

In the way the tunnies live we observe a singular knowledge of three parts of mathematics. As for astrology, they teach it to man; for they stop in the place where the winter solstice overtakes them, and do not stir from there until the following equinox; that is why Aristotle himself willingly concedes them this science. As for geometry and arithmetic, they always form their school in a cubic figure, square on every side, and make it a solid battalion, closed and surrounded on all sides with six surfaces all equal; then they swim in this square order, as wide behind as in front, so that whoever

sees and counts one row can easily number the whole troop, since the number in depth is equal to the width, and the width to the length.

As for magnanimity, it is hard to give a more evident example of it than in this action of the big dog that was sent from the Indies to King Alexander. They first offered him a stag to fight with, and then a boar, and then a bear; he took no account of them and did not deign to stir from his place. But when he saw a lion, he promptly stood up on his feet, showing clearly that he declared him alone worthy to enter into combat with him.

^BRegarding repentance and acknowledgment of faults, they tell of an elephant who, having killed his keeper by the impetuosity of his anger, conceived such extreme grief that thereafter he never would eat again and let himself die.

^AAs for clemency, they tell of a tiger, the most inhuman beast of all, that when a kid was given him, he suffered hunger for two days rather than harm it, and on the third he broke the cage in which he was confined to go and seek other food, not wanting to attack the kid, his friend and his guest.

And as for the rights of the familiarity and agreement that is formed by association, it happens quite ordinarily that we bring up cats, dogs, and hares to live together.

But what experience teaches those who travel by sea, and notably on the sea of Sicily, of the condition of the halcyons, surpasses all human notions. What species of animal has nature ever so honored in its conception, birth, and delivery? For the poets say indeed that the one island of Delos, being formerly afloat, was made firm for the sake of the lying-in of Latona; but God willed that the entire ocean should be stilled, made firm and smooth, without waves, without winds and without rain, while the halcyon makes its young, which is just about the solstice, the shortest day of the year; and by his privilege, we have seven days and seven nights, in the very heart of winter, when we can navigate without danger. Their females acknowledge no other male than their own, and attend him all their life without ever abandoning him; if he becomes debilitated and broken, they load him on their shoulders, carry him everywhere, and serve him until death.

But no cleverness has yet been able to attain the knowledge of the marvelous workmanship by which the halcyon builds the nest for her young, or to guess the material of it. Plutarch, who saw

and handled several of them, thinks that they are the bones of some fish that she joins and binds together, interlacing them, some lengthwise, the others crosswise, and adding ribs and hoops so that at last it forms a round vessel ready to float. Then, when she has finished constructing it, she carries it to the wash of the beach, where the sea, beating it very gently, teaches her to repair what is not well joined, and to strengthen the places where she sees that her construction is loosening and coming apart under the blows of the sea. And on the contrary, what is well joined is compressed and tightened by the beating of the sea so that it can neither break, nor dissolve, nor be damaged by blows with stone or iron, except with great difficulty. And what is more admirable is the proportion and shape of the cavity inside; for it is put together and proportioned in such a way that it cannot receive or admit anything but the bird who built it. For to anything else it is impenetrable, closed and shut so that nothing can get in, not even the sea water.

That is a very clear description of this structure, and borrowed from a good source; nevertheless it seems to me that it still does not sufficiently clear up for us the difficulty of this architecture. Now, from what vanity can it come that we place beneath us, and interpret scornfully, achievements that we can neither imitate nor comprehend?

To pursue yet a little further this equality and correspondence between us and the beasts: the privilege in which our soul glories, of reducing to her condition all that she conceives, of stripping all that comes to her of its mortal and corporeal qualities, of constraining all the things that she considers worthy of her acquaintance to put off and divest themselves of their corruptible properties, and making them leave aside as base and superfluous garments their thickness, length, depth, weight, color, odor, roughness, smoothness, hardness, softness, and all accidents of sense, in order to accommodate them to her immortal and spiritual condition; so that the Rome and Paris that I have in my soul, the Paris that I imagine, I imagine and conceive it without size and without place, without stone, without plaster, and without wood – this same privilege, I say, seems very evidently to belong to the beasts. For a horse accustomed to trumpets, harquebus fire, and battles, whom we see tremble and quiver in his sleep, stretched out on his litter, as if he were in the fray: it is certain that in his soul he conceives a drum beat that has no sound, an army that has no weapons or body:

> Indeed you'll see strong horses sweat and pant,
> Although in sleep their limbs lie stretched full length,
> And strain, as for a prize, their utmost strength.
>
> LUCRETIUS

That hare that a greyhound imagines in a dream, after which we see him pant in his sleep, stretch out his tail, wriggle his legs, and reproduce perfectly the motions of running, is a hare without fur or bones:

> And often hunters' hounds in soft repose,
> Suddenly bark, toss wildly to and fro,
> And sniff the air repeatedly, as though
> To hold some wild beast's spoor that they have found.
> And even when awakened, still they hound
> Their phantom stags, and still their flight discern;
> At last the spell is gone, and they return.
>
> LUCRETIUS

The watchdogs that we often see growl in their sleep, and then bark outright and wake up with a start, as if they saw some stranger coming – this stranger that their soul sees is a bodiless and imperceptible man, without dimension, without color, and without being:

> House-bred affectionate young dogs will rise,
> Shake off their fitful slumbers from their eyes,
> And from the ground spring up expectantly,
> As though some stranger's countenance they see.
>
> LUCRETIUS

As for bodily beauty, before going any further, I ought to know if we are agreed about its description. It is likely that we know little about what beauty is in nature and in general, since to our own human beauty we give so many different forms. ^CIf there was any natural prescription for it, we should recognize it in common, like the heat of fire. We imagine its forms to suit our fancy.

> ^BA Belgian's color mars a Roman face.
>
> PROPERTIUS

^AThe Indies paint it black and dusky, with large swollen lips and a wide flat nose. ^BAnd they load the cartilage between the nostrils with big gold rings, to make it hang down to the mouth; as also the lower lip with large hoops enriched with precious stones, so that it falls down over their chin; and their charm is to show their teeth

down to the base of the roots. In Peru, the biggest ears are the fairest, and they stretch them artificially as much as they can; ᶜand a man of this day says he saw in one oriental nation this care for enlarging them and loading them with heavy jewels in such favor, that time and again he could pass his arm, fully clothed, through the hole in an ear. ᴮElsewhere there are nations that blacken their teeth with great care, and scorn to see white ones; elsewhere they stain them red.

ᶜNot only in the Basque country do women consider themselves more beautiful with heads shaven, but in plenty of other places, and what is more, in certain glacial countries, so Pliny says. ᴮMexican women count among their beauties a small forehead; and whereas they trim their hair on all other parts of the body, on their forehead they cultivate it and increase it by art; and they have such great esteem for large breasts, that they aspire to be able to suckle their children over their shoulder. ᴬWe would represent ugliness that way.

The Italians make beauty plump and massive, the Spaniards hollow and gaunt; and among us, one man makes it fair, the other dark; one soft and delicate, the other strong and vigorous; one demands daintiness and sweetness, another pride and majesty. ᶜEven as the preference in beauty, which Plato attributes to the spherical figure, the Epicureans give rather to the pyramidal or the square, and cannot swallow a god in the shape of a ball.

ᴬBut, however that may be, nature has no more privileged us in this above her common laws than in the rest. And if we judge ourselves rightly, we shall find that if there are some animals less favored in this respect than ourselves, there are others, and in great number, who are more so – ᶜ*by many animals we are surpassed in beauty* [Seneca] – even among the terrestrial ones, our compatriots. For as for those of the sea – leaving aside the figure, in which comparison is impossible, so different is it from ours – in color, sheen, polish, symmetry, we yield to them enough; and no less, in all qualities, to those of the air. ᴬAnd that prerogative that the poets make much of, our erect stature, looking toward heaven, its origin,

> While other animals face down to earth,
> To man he gave a face raised to the skies,
> And to the stars he bade him lift his eyes,
>
> OVID

it is truly poetic, for there are many little creatures whose sight is wholly overturned to the sky; and I find that camels and ostriches have their necks set even higher and more erect than ours.

^CWhat animals do not have their face up high and in front, and do not look straight forward like ourselves, and do not discover, in their proper posture, as much of heaven and earth as man? And what qualities of our corporeal constitution, in Plato and Cicero, cannot apply to a thousand kinds of beasts? ^AThose that resemble us most are the ugliest and most abject of the whole band: for in external appearance and shape of the face, it is the apes:

> ^CHow similar the simian, ugliest of beasts!
> ENNIUS, QUOTED BY CICERO

^Afor the insides and vital parts, it is the hog.

Indeed, when I imagine man quite naked, yes, even in that sex which seems to have the greater share of beauty, his blemishes, his natural subjection, and his imperfections, I think we had more reason than any other animal to cover ourselves. We can be excused for having borrowed from those whom nature had favored more than ourselves in this, to adorn ourselves with their beauty and hide ourselves beneath their spoils – wool, feathers, fur, silk.

Let us observe moreover that we are the only animal whose defectiveness offends our own fellows, and the only ones who have to hide, in our natural actions, from our own species. Truly it is also a fact worthy of consideration that the masters of the craft order as a remedy to amorous passions the entire and open sight of the body that we pursue; that to cool our love, we need only see freely what we love:

> His loved one's private parts, bared to his sight,
> Checked the man's passion in its headlong flight.
> OVID

And although this recipe may perhaps proceed from a somewhat cooled and delicate temperament, still it is a wonderful sign of our defectiveness that acquaintance and familiarity disgust us with one another. ^BIt is not so much modesty as artfulness and prudence that makes our ladies so circumspect in refusing us entry to their boudoirs before they are painted and dressed up for public display:

> ^AOf this our Venuses are well aware;
> Wherefore they hide the backstage with great care
> From those they wish to hold in love's sweet snare;
> LUCRETIUS

whereas in many animals there is nothing that we do not love and that does not please our senses, so that from their very excretions and discharges we derive not only tidbits to eat, but our richest ornaments and perfumes.

This dissertation concerns only the common run of us, and is not so sacrilegious as to mean to include those divine, supernatural, and extraordinary beauties that we sometimes see shine among us like stars under a corporeal and terrestrial veil.

Moreover, the very share of the favors of nature that we concede to the animals, by our own confession, is much to their advantage. We attribute to ourselves imaginary and fanciful goods, goods future and absent, for which human capacity by itself cannot answer, or goods which we attribute to ourselves falsely through the license of our opinion, like reason, knowledge, and honor. And to them for their share we leave essential, tangible, and palpable goods: peace, repose, security, innocence, and health – health, I say, the finest and richest present that nature can give us. So much so that philosophy, even the Stoic, dares to say that if Heraclitus and Pherecydes could have exchanged their wisdom for health and by this bargain delivered themselves, one from the dropsy, the other from the disease of lice that oppressed him, they would have done well. By which they set a still greater price on wisdom, comparing it and balancing it with health, than they do in this other proposition, which is also one of theirs. They say that if Circe had offered Ulysses two potions, one to make a fool a wise man, the other a wise man a fool, Ulysses should rather have accepted the cup of folly than consent to Circe's changing his human figure to that of a beast; and they say that Wisdom herself would have spoken to him in this manner: "Forsake me, leave me alone, rather than lodge me in the shape and body of an ass."

What? So our philosophers abandon this great and divine wisdom for this corporeal and terrestrial veil? Then it is no longer by our reason, our intelligence, and our soul that we are superior to the beasts; it is by our beauty, our fair complexion, and the fine symmetry of our limbs, for which we should abandon our intelligence, our wisdom, and all the rest.

Well, I accept this naïve, frank confession. Indeed, they knew that those qualities about which we make so much ado are but idle fancy. Even if the beasts, then, had all the virtue, knowledge, wisdom, and capability of the Stoics, they would still

be beasts; nor would they for all that be comparable to a wretched, wicked, senseless man. ^CIn short, whatever is not as we are is worth nothing. And God himself, to make himself appreciated, must resemble us, as we shall presently declare. Whereby it is apparent that ^Ait is not by a true judgment, but by foolish pride and stubbornness, that we set ourselves before the other animals and sequester ourselves from their condition and society.

[MAN'S KNOWLEDGE CANNOT MAKE HIM HAPPY]

But to return to my subject, we have as our share inconstancy, irresolution, uncertainty, grief, superstition, worry over things to come, even after our life, ambition, avarice, jealousy, envy, unruly, frantic, and untamable appetites, war, falsehood, disloyalty, detraction, and curiosity. Indeed we have strangely overpaid for this fine reason that we glory in, and this capacity to judge and know, if we have bought it at the price of this infinite number of passions to which we are incessantly a prey. ^BUnless we like to make much, as indeed Socrates does, of this notable prerogative over the other animals, that whereas Nature has prescribed to them certain seasons and limits to the pleasures of Venus, she has given us free rein at all hours and occasions.

^C*As with wine for sick men, since it is rarely good and often bad, it is better not to use it at all, than in the hope of a doubtful benefit to incur a manifest risk; so I hardly know whether it would not have been better for the human race if this swift movement of thought, this acumen, this cleverness, which we call reason, had not been given to man at all, since it is a plague to many and salutary only to a few, rather than given so abundantly and so lavishly* [Cicero].

^AWhat good can we suppose it did Varro and Aristotle to know so many things? Did it exempt them from human discomforts? Were they freed from the accidents that oppress a porter? Did they derive from logic some consolation for the gout? For knowing how this humor lodges in the joints, did they feel it less? Were they reconciled to death for knowing that some nations rejoice in it, and with cuckoldry for knowing that wives are held in common in some region? On the contrary, though they held the first rank in knowledge, one among the Romans, the other among the Greeks, and in the period when knowledge flourished most, we have not for all that heard that they had any particular excellence in their lives; in fact the Greek has a hard time to clear himself of some notable spots in his.

[B]Have they found that sensual pleasure and health are more savory to him who knows astrology and grammar?

> Does the illiterate's tool stand less erect?
>
> HORACE

And are shame and poverty less troublesome?

> Disease and weakness you of course will miss,
> Escape both grief and pain, and possibly
> Win longer life, a better destiny.
>
> JUVENAL

I have seen in my time a hundred artisans, a hundred plowmen, wiser and happier than rectors of the university, and whom I would rather resemble. Learning, in my opinion, has a place among things necessary for life, like glory, nobility, dignity, [C]or at best like beauty, riches, [A]and such other qualities which are really useful for it, but remotely, and a little more in fancy than in nature.

[C]We hardly need any more offices, rules, and laws of living, in our community than do the cranes and ants in theirs. And nevertheless we see that they conduct themselves in a very orderly manner without erudition. If man were wise, he would set the true price of each thing according as it was most useful and appropriate for his life.

[A]If anyone will sum us up by our actions and conduct, a greater number of excellent men will be found among the ignorant than among the learned: I mean in every sort of virtue. The old Rome seems to me to have borne men of greater worth, both for peace and for war, than that learned Rome that ruined itself. Even if the rest were exactly equal, at least worth and innocence would remain on the side of the old, for they dwell singularly well with simplicity.

But I leave this subject, which would lead me farther than I would follow. I will add only this, that humility and submissiveness alone can make a good man. The knowledge of his duty should not be left to each man's judgment; it should be prescribed to him, not left to the choice of his reason. Otherwise, judging by the imbecility and infinite variety of our reasons and opinions, we would finally forge for ourselves duties that would set us to eating one another, as Epicurus says.

The first law that God ever gave to man was a law of pure obedience; it was a naked and simple commandment about which man had nothing to know or discuss; [C]since to obey is the principal

function of a reasonable soul, recognizing a heavenly superior and benefactor. From obeying and yielding spring all other virtues, as from presumption all sin. ᴮAnd on the contrary, the first temptation that came to human nature from the devil, its first poison, insinuated itself into us through the promises he made us of knowledge and intelligence: *Ye shall be as gods, knowing good and evil* [Genesis]. ᶜAnd the sirens, in Homer, to trick Ulysses and lure him into their dangerous and ruinous snares, offer him the gift of knowledge. ᴬThe plague of man is the opinion of knowledge. That is why ignorance is so recommended by our religion as a quality suitable to belief and obedience. ᶜ*Beware lest any man spoil you through philosophy and vain deceit, after the rudiments of the world* [Colossians].

ᴬOn this there is general agreement among all the philosophers of all sects, that the sovereign good consists in tranquillity of soul and body. ᴮBut where do we find it?

> ᴬIn short, 'neath Jove alone the wise man dwells:
> A king of kings, free, honored, handsome, wealthy;
> Save when he has a cold, above all healthy.
>
> HORACE

It seems in truth that nature, for the consolation of our miserable and puny condition, has given us as our share only presumption. This is what Epictetus says, that man has nothing properly his own but the use of his opinions. We have nothing but wind and smoke for our portion. ᴮThe gods have health in reality, says philosophy, sickness in thought; man, on the contrary, possesses his goods in fancy, his ills in reality. ᴬWe have been right to make much of the powers of our imagination, for all our goods exist only in dreams.

Hear this poor calamitous animal boast: "There is nothing," says Cicero, "so sweet as the occupation of letters, of those letters, I mean, by means of which the infinity of things, the immense grandeur of nature, the heavens in this very world, the lands and the seas, are revealed to us. It is they that have taught us religion, moderation, greatheartedness, and that have wrested our soul out of the shadows to make it see all things, high, low, first, last, and middling. It is they that furnish us with means to live well and happily, and guide us to pass our age without displeasure and without pain." Does not this man seem to be talking about the condition of God, ever-living and almighty? And as for the facts, a thousand little women in their villages have lived a more equable, sweeter, and more consistent life than his.

> A god it was, great Memmius, a god,
> Who was the first that way of life to find
> Which we call wisdom now; whose artful mind
> Brought life from such great storms, such depths of night,
> Safe into such a haven, such clear light.
> LUCRETIUS

Those are very magnificent and beautiful words; but a very slight accident put this man's understanding into a worse state than that of the lowest shepherd, notwithstanding that Teacher-God[17] of his and that divine wisdom.

Of like impudence is ᶜthis promise of the book of Democritus, "I am going to speak of all things"; and that stupid title that Aristotle lends us of "mortal gods"; and ᴬthat judgment of Chrysippus, that Dion was as virtuous as God. And my Seneca acknowledges, he says, that God has given him life, but that the good life he got from himself; ᶜin conformity with this other: *We rightly glory in virtue; which would not happen if we had it as a gift from God, not from ourselves* [Cicero]. This also is of Seneca, that the sage has courage like unto God, but set in human frailty; whereby he excels him.

ᴬNothing is so common as to encounter cases of similar temerity. There is not one of us who is so offended to see himself compared to God as he is to see himself brought down to the rank of the other animals: so much more jealous are we of our own interest than of that of our creator.

But we must tread this stupid vanity underfoot, and sharply and boldly shake the ridiculous foundations on which these false opinions are built. As long as he thinks he has some resources and power by himself, never will man recognize what he owes to his master; he will always make chickens of his eggs, as they say. He must be stripped to his shirt.

Let us look at some notable examples of the effect of his philosophy.

Posidonius, being oppressed by a malady so painful that it made him twist his arms and gnash his teeth, actually thought he was thumbing his nose at pain by crying out against it: "Do what you will, still I will not say you are an evil." He feels the same pains as my lackey, but he prides himself that he restrains at least his tongue

17 Epicurus.

within the laws of his sect.[18] ^C*It was wrong to brag in words and yield in deeds* [Cicero].

Arcesilaus was sick with the gout; when Carneades, who had come to visit him, was going away very sorry, he called him back, and, pointing to his feet and his breast, said: "Nothing has come from there to here." This man has somewhat better grace, for he feels that he has pain and would like to be rid of it, but nevertheless his heart is not beaten down or weakened by this pain. The other stands in his rigidity, which, I fear, is more verbal than real. And Dionysius of Heraclea, afflicted with a violent smarting of the eyes, was forced to abandon these Stoical resolutions.

^ABut even if knowledge would actually do what they say, blunt and lessen the keenness of the misfortunes that pursue us, what does it do but what ignorance does much more purely and more evidently? The philosopher Pyrrho, incurring the peril of a great storm at sea, offered those who were with him nothing better to imitate than the assurance of a pig that was traveling with them, and that was looking at this tempest without fear. Philosophy, at the end of her precepts, sends us back to the examples of an athlete or a muleteer, in whom we ordinarily see much less feeling of death, pain, and other discomforts, and more firmness than knowledge ever supplied to any man who had not been born and prepared for it on his own by natural habit.[19] What is the reason that the tender limbs of a child are incised and cut more easily than ours, if it is not ignorance? ^CAnd those of a horse? ^AHow many men have been made sick by the mere power of imagination? We see them regularly, having themselves bled, purged, and physicked, to cure ills that they feel only in their mind. When real evils fail us, knowledge lends us hers: That color and that complexion presage some catarrhal fluxion; this hot season threatens you with a feverish disturbance; this break in the life line of your left hand warns you of some notable and impending indisposition. And finally she addresses herself unblushingly to health itself: This sprightliness and vigor of youth cannot stay in the same state; we must bleed it and weaken it, for fear it may turn against yourself. Compare the life of a man enslaved to such imaginings with that of a plowman letting himself

18 The editions published in Montaigne's lifetime here add: "It is nothing but wind and words. But ... "
19 The editions published in Montaigne's lifetime here add: "Knowledge rather sharpens our feeling of troubles than relieves it."

follow his natural appetites, measuring things only by the present sensation, without knowledge and without prognostication, who has pain only when he has it; whereas the other often has the stone in his soul before he has it in his loins. As if he were not in time to suffer the pain when he is in it, he anticipates it in imagination and runs to meet it.

What I say of medicine may be applied generally to all knowledge. Thence came that ancient opinion of the philosophers who located the sovereign good in the recognition of the weakness of our judgment. My ignorance affords me as much occasion for hope as for fear; and having no other rule for my health than that of the examples of others and of the results that I see in others in similar cases, I find all sorts, and dwell on the comparisons that are the most favorable for me. I welcome health with open arms, free, full, and entire, and whet my appetite to enjoy it, the more so as it is at present rarer and less ordinary with me; so far am I from troubling its repose and sweetness with the bitterness of a new and constrained way of life. The animals show us well enough how many maladies the agitation of our mind brings us.

ᶜWhat they tell us of the Brazilians, that they died only of old age, which is attributed to the serenity and tranquillity of their air, I attribute rather to the tranquillity and serenity of their souls, unburdened with any tense or unpleasant passion or thought or occupation, as people who spent their life in admirable simplicity and ignorance, without letters, without law, without king, without religion of any kind.

ᴬAnd how does this happen, which we see by experience, that the grossest and coarsest men are the most sturdy and desirable in amorous performances, and that the love of a muleteer often makes itself more acceptable than that of a gentleman; if not that in the latter the agitation of his soul troubles his bodily strength, breaks it and tires it? As it also usually tires and troubles itself.

What unseats it, what casts it most commonly into insanity, but its quickness, its keenness, its agility, and in short its very strength? ᴮOf what is the subtlest madness made, but the subtlest wisdom? As great enmities are born of great friendships, and mortal maladies of vigorous health, so are the greatest and wildest manias born of the rare and lively stirrings of our soul; it is only a half turn of the peg to pass from the one to the other. ᴬIn the actions of the insane we see how neatly madness combines with the most vigorous operations of our soul. Who does not know how imperceptibly near is madness to

the lusty flights of a free mind and the effects of supreme and extraordinary virtue? Plato says that melancholy minds are the most teachable and excellent: likewise there are none with so much propensity to madness.

Countless minds have been ruined by their very power and suppleness. What a leap has just been taken, because of the very restlessness and liveliness of his mind, by one of the most judicious and ingenious of men, a man more closely molded by the pure poetry of antiquity than any other Italian poet has been for a long time![20] Does he not have reason to be grateful to that murderous vivacity of his mind? to that brilliance that has blinded him? to that exact and intent apprehension of his reason, which has deprived him of reason? to the careful and laborious pursuit of the sciences, which has led him to stupidity? to that rare aptitude for the exercises of the mind, which has left him without exercise and without mind? I felt even more vexation than compassion to see him in Ferrara in so piteous a state, surviving himself, not recognizing himself or his works, which, without his knowledge and yet before his eyes, have been brought out uncorrected and shapeless.

Do you want a man to be healthy, do you want him disciplined and firmly and securely poised? Wrap him in darkness, idleness, and dullness. ᶜWe must become like the animals in order to become wise, and be blinded in order to be guided.

ᴬAnd if they tell me that the advantage of being but coldly and dully sensitive to pains and woes brings with it as a consequence the disadvantage of making us also less keen and eager for the enjoyment of good things and pleasures, that is true; but the wretchedness of our condition makes us have less to enjoy than to avoid, and makes the extremest pleasure not touch us so much as a slight pain. ᶜ*Men feel good things more dully than evils* [Livy]. ᴬWe do not feel perfect health as we do the slightest of illnesses,

> A scratch affects the body like a wound,
> While no one feels his health when it is sound.

20 Torquato Tasso, who for many years was confined for insanity. Montaigne must have seen him in Italy in 1580–81, though, surprisingly, he does not mention him in his *Travel Journal*. This whole A passage, from "In the actions of the insane" to "Wrap him in darkness, idleness, and dullness," first appeared in the 1582 edition, as did the preceding A lines, from "As it also" to "in short its very strength."

> I'm glad to have no pain in foot or side.
> But of our health, awareness is denied.
> LA BOÉTIE

Our well-being is but the privation of being ill. That is why the sect
of philosophy that set the greatest value on voluptuousness still
ranked it with mere freedom from pain. To have no ill is to have
the most good that man can hope for; ᶜas Ennius said:

> Who has no ill has only too much good.

ᴬFor that very tickling and sting that is found in certain pleasures
and seems to raise us above simple health and absence of pain, that
active, stirring, and somehow or other burning and biting voluptu-
ousness, even that itself points only to freedom from pain as its goal.
The appetite that sweeps us away into intercourse with women
seeks only to drive out the pain that ardent and furious desire brings
us, and asks only to assuage it and to be set at rest and exempted
from this fever. And so for the rest.

So I say that if simplicity leads us on the way to having no pain,
it leads us to a very happy state for our condition. ᶜYet we must
not imagine it so leaden as to be totally without feeling. For Crantor
was quite right to combat the apathy of Epicurus, if it was built
so deep that even the approach and birth of evils were lacking. I have
no praise for the insensibility that is neither possible nor desirable.
I am glad not to be sick; but if I am, I want to know I am; and if
they cauterize or incise me, I want to feel it. In truth, he who would
eradicate the knowledge of evil would at the same time extirpate
the knowledge of pleasure, and in fine would annihilate man: *this
insensibility does not come without a great price: in humanity of the soul,
torpor of the body* [Cicero].

Evil is in its turn a good to man. Neither is pain always some-
thing for him to flee, nor pleasure always for him to pursue.

ᴬIt is a very great triumph for the honor of ignorance
that knowledge herself throws us back into its arms when she
finds herself powerless to strengthen us against the weight of ills;
she is constrained to come to this compromise, to give us free
rein and permission to take refuge in its bosom and by its favor
gain shelter from the blows and injuries of fortune. For what else
does she mean when she preaches to us to ᶜwithdraw our thoughts
from the ills that grip us, and entertain them with lost pleasures; and
to ᴬtake consolation for present ills from the remembrance of past

joys; and to call to our aid a vanished contentment to oppose what oppresses us: *he finds relief from griefs in calling the mind away from burdensome thoughts and back to the contemplation of pleasures* [Cicero]? ^Unless that where she lacks strength she will use cunning, and nimbly trip her opponent up when vigor of body and arms fails her. For when not even a philosopher, but simply a sound man, feels in reality the burning thirst of a high fever, what kind of coin to pay him in is the memory of the sweetness of Greek wine? ^BThis would rather make his bargain worse,

> For to recall the joy doubles the pain.
> ADAPTED FROM DANTE

^Of the same sort is that other advice that philosophy gives, to keep in our memory only past happiness, and to efface from it the troubles we have suffered; as if the science of forgetfulness were in our power.

^It is advice, moreover, that makes worse men of us.

> Sweet is the memory of bygone woes.
> EURIPIDES

^For how is it that philosophy, which should put arms in my hand to fight fortune, which should stiffen my courage to tread all human adversities underfoot, comes to such a state of weakness as to have me duck out of sight by these cowardly dodges, which are also ridiculous?

For memory sets before us, not what we choose, but what it pleases. Indeed there is nothing that imprints a thing so vividly on our memory as the desire to forget it: a good way to give our mind something to guard, and to impress it on her, is to solicit her to lose it. ^And this is false: *It is in our power both to bury our adversities in almost perpetual oblivion, and to remember our prosperities with pleasure and delight* [Cicero]. And this is true: *I remember even what I would not; I cannot forget what I would* [Cicero]. ^And whose is this advice? ^His *who alone dared to profess himself wise* [Cicero, speaking of Epicurus],

> ^Who in his genius topped mankind by far,
> Eclipsed them as the sun dims every star.
> LUCRETIUS, SPEAKING OF EPICURUS

To empty and strip the memory, is that not the true and proper road to ignorance? *Ignorance is a poor remedy for ills* [Seneca].

ᴬWe see many similar precepts by which we are allowed to borrow frivolous delusions from the common herd where strong live reason is not powerful enough, provided that these afford us contentment and consolation. Where they cannot cure the wound, they are content to benumb it and alleviate it. I think they will not deny me this, that if they could add order and constancy to a man's state of life and maintain it in pleasure and tranquillity by some weakness or infirmity of judgment, they would accept:

> I shall begin to scatter flowers, and drink.
> And if men think me witless, let them think.
>
> HORACE

Many philosophers would be of Lycas' mind. This man, though otherwise of very regular conduct, living quietly and peacefully in his family, failing in no part of his duty toward his own and toward strangers, preserving himself very well from harm, by some alteration of his senses had stamped in his imagination this hallucination: he thought he was perpetually at the amphitheaters watching entertainments, spectacles, and the finest comedies in the world. After being cured of this peccant humor by the doctors, he nearly sued them to make them restore him to the pleasure of these fancies.

> Alas, you have not saved me, friends, quoth he,
> But murdered me, my pleasure snatched away,
> And that delusion that made life so gay.
>
> HORACE

His delusion was like that of Thrasylaus, son of Pythodorus, who tricked himself into believing that all the ships that put out from the port of Piraeus and came in there were working only in his service; he rejoiced in the good fortune of their voyages and welcomed them with joy. When his brother Crito had had him restored to his better senses, he regretted that state of mind in which he had lived full of joy and free from all trouble. It is what this old Greek verse says, that there is great advantage in not being so wise,

> In heeding nothing lies the sweetest life.
>
> SOPHOCLES

And Ecclesiastes: "In much wisdom is much grief; and he that acquires knowledge acquires travail and torment."

Even that in which philosophy in general agrees, that last remedy that she prescribes for all kinds of necessities, which is to

put an end to the life that we cannot endure: *^CDo you like it? Bear it. Don't you like it? Leave it any way you like* [adapted from Seneca]. *Does grief prick you? Nay, does it stab you? If you are naked, offer your throat; if you are covered by the armor of Vulcan, that is, by fortitude, resist* [Cicero]. And that saying of the Greek banqueters, which they apply to it: *Let him drink or leave*; which sounds more appropriate in the tongue of a Gascon, who is prone to change the B to V,²¹ than in that of Cicero:

> ^AIf you know not right living, then give way
> To those that do; you've had enough of play,
> Of food and drink; 'tis time you left with grace,
> Lest lusty youth expel you from the place.
> HORACE

What is all that but philosophy confessing her impotence, and sending us back not merely to ignorance, to be under cover, but to stupidity itself, to insensibility and nonexistence?

> Democritus, by his advancing years
> Warned of the growing torpor of his mind,
> Offered himself to death, his soul resigned.
> LUCRETIUS

It is what Antisthenes used to say, that we must provide ourselves either with sense to understand, or with a rope to hang ourselves; and what Chrysippus used to quote on the subject from the poet Tyrtaeus,

> We must draw near to virtue, or to death.
> QUOTED BY PLUTARCH

^CAnd Crates said that love was cured by hunger; if not, by time; and in him who liked neither method, by the halter.

^BThe Sextius of whom Seneca and Plutarch speak with such great commendation, after abandoning everything and throwing himself into the study of philosophy, decided to cast himself into the sea, finding the progress of his studies too slow and tedious. He hastened to death in default of knowledge. Here are the words of the law on this subject: If by chance there comes some great misfortune that cannot be remedied, the haven is near, and you can escape by swimming out of the body as out of a leaking skiff; for it is

21 Thus *bibat* ("let him drink") would become *vivat* ("let him live").

the fear of dying, not the desire to live, that keeps the fool attached
to his body.

[MAN'S KNOWLEDGE CANNOT MAKE HIM GOOD]

^AAs by simplicity life becomes pleasanter, so also does it become
better and more innocent, as I was starting to say a while back. The
simple and ignorant, says Saint Paul, raise themselves to heaven,
and take possession of it; and we, with all our learning, plunge
ourselves into the infernal abyss. I do not stop to consider either
Valentinian, a declared enemy of knowledge and letters, or Licinius,
Roman emperors both, who called them the poison and plague of
any political state; or Mohammed, who, ^cso I have heard, ^Aforbade
learning to his followers. But the example of the great Lycurgus, and
his authority, should certainly have great weight, and the reverence
of that divine Lacedaemonian government, so great, so admirable,
and so long flourishing in virtue and good fortune without
any teaching or practice of letters. Those who return from that
new world which was discovered in our fathers' time by the
Spaniards can testify to us how much more lawfully and regulatedly
these nations live, without magistrates and without law, than
ours, where there are more officers and laws than there are other
men and actions:

> Their hands are full of motions and petitions,
> Their pockets stuffed with reams of briefs and writs,
> With powers of attorney, depositions,
> Decisions, and opinions, and *op. cit.*'s,
> Designed to rob, with maximum efficiency,
> The simple folk of their remaining wits;
> Before, behind, no matter where they turn is
> A host of lawyers, notaries, attorneys.
> ARIOSTO

It is what a Roman senator of the late period said, that their
predecessors had a breath stinking of garlic, and a stomach per-
fumed with a good conscience; and that on the contrary those of his
time smelled outwardly of nothing but perfume, though stinking
within of every kind of vice. That is to say, so I think, that they had
great learning and ability, and a great lack of integrity. Uncouthness,
ignorance, simplicity, and crudity are prone to go with innocence;
curiosity, subtlety, and learning bring malice in their train; humility,
fear, obedience, and amenability (which are the principal qualities

for the preservation of human society) require a soul that is open, docile, and with little presumption.

Christians have a particular knowledge of the extent to which curiosity is a natural and original evil in man. The urge to increase in wisdom and knowledge was the first downfall of the human race; it was the way by which man hurled himself into eternal damnation. Pride is his ruin and his corruption; it is pride that casts man aside from the common ways, that makes him embrace novelties and prefer to be the leader of an erring troop that has strayed into the path of perdition, prefer to be a teacher and tutor of error and falsehood, rather than to be a disciple in the school of truth, led and guided by another's hand, on the straight and beaten path. This is perhaps the meaning of that old Greek saying, that superstition follows pride and obeys it as if it were its father.[22]

[c]O presumption, how you hinder us! When Socrates was advised that the God of wisdom had given him the title of Sage, he was astonished; and, examining and searching himself through and through, he found no basis for this divine judgment. He knew of men as just, as temperate, as valiant, as learned as himself, and more eloquent, handsomer, and more useful to their country. Finally he concluded that he was distinguished from the others, and wise, only in that he did not think himself so; and that his God considered the opinion that we possess learning and wisdom a singular piece of stupidity in man; and that his best knowledge was the knowledge of his ignorance, and simplicity his best wisdom.

[A]Holy Writ declares those of us wretches who think well of ourselves: "Dust and ashes," it says to them, "what hast thou to glory in?" And elsewhere: "God has made man like the shadow, of which who shall judge when, with the passing of the light, it shall have vanished away?"[23] In truth we are nothing.

Our powers are so far from conceiving the sublimity of God, that of the works of our creator those bear his stamp most clearly, and are most his, that we understand least. To Christians it is an occasion for belief to encounter something incredible. It is the

22 This quotation from Stobaeus is one of the sentences inscribed on the ceiling of Montaigne's library. Here he translates it before quoting it in the original Greek.

23 The first quotation is from Ecclesiasticus 10:9, the second apparently inspired by Ecclesiastes, especially 6:12. Both are among the Latin sentences inscribed on the ceiling of Montaigne's library.

more according to reason as it is contrary to human reason. ᴮIf it were according to reason, it would no longer be a miracle; and if it were according to some example, it would no longer be singular. ᶜ*God is better known by not knowing*, says Saint Augustine; and Tacitus, *It is more holy and reverent to believe in the works of the gods than to know them.*

And Plato thinks there is some sinful impiety in inquiring too curiously into God and the world, and the first causes of things. *And it is difficult to discover the parent of this universe; and when once you have discovered him, it is sinful to reveal him to the vulgar*, says Cicero.

ᴬWe say indeed "power," "truth," "justice"; they are words that mean something great; but that something we neither see nor conceive at all. ᴮWe say that God fears, that God is angry, that God loves,

> Marking in mortal words immortal things.

LUCRETIUS

These are all feelings and emotions that cannot be lodged in God in our sense, nor can we imagine them according to his. ᴬIt is for God alone to know himself and to interpret his works.

ᶜAnd he does it improperly in our human language, in order to stoop and descend to us, who are on the ground, prostrate. How can wisdom, which is the choice between good and evil, fit him, seeing that no evil touches him? What has he to do with reason and intelligence, which we use to arrive at apparent things from things obscure, seeing that there is nothing obscure to God? Justice, which distributes to each man what belongs to him, created for the society and community of men – how can it be in God? And what of temperance, which is moderation in bodily pleasures, which have no place in divinity? Fortitude in bearing pain, toil, and dangers, appertains to him as little, since these three things have no access to him.[24] Wherefore Aristotle holds him equally exempt from virtue and vice. *He is susceptible neither to favor nor to anger, for all that are so are weak* [Cicero].

ᴬThe participation that we have in the knowledge of truth, whatever it may be, has not been acquired by our own powers. God has taught us that clearly enough by the witnesses that he has chosen from the common people, simple and ignorant, to

24 This whole passage, from "How can wisdom" on, is taken from Cicero *Of the Nature of the Gods* III. xv.

instruct us in his admirable secrets. Our faith is not of our own acquiring, it is a pure present of another's liberality. It is not by reasoning or by our understanding that we have received our religion; it is by external authority and command. The weakness of our judgment helps us more in this than its strength, and our blindness more than our clear-sightedness. It is by the mediation of our ignorance more than of our knowledge that we are learned with that divine learning. It is no wonder if our natural and earthly powers cannot conceive that supernatural and heavenly knowledge; let us bring to it nothing of our own but obedience and submission. For, as it is written, "I will destroy the wisdom of the wise, and will bring to nothing the understanding of the prudent. Where is the wise? where is the scribe? where is the disputer of this world? hath not God made foolish the wisdom of this world? For after that the world by wisdom knew not God, it pleased God by the foolishness of preaching to save them that believe" [I Corinthians].

[MAN HAS NO KNOWLEDGE]

Yet must I see at last whether it is in the power of man to find what he seeks, and whether that quest that he has been making for so many centuries has enriched him with any new power and any solid truth.

I think he will confess to me, if he speaks in all conscience, that all the profit he has gained from so long a pursuit is to have learned to acknowledge his weakness. The ignorance that was naturally in us we have by long study confirmed and verified.

To really learned men has happened what happens to ears of wheat: they rise high and lofty, heads erect and proud, as long as they are empty; but when they are full and swollen with grain in their ripeness, they begin to grow humble and lower their horns. Similarly, men who have tried everything and sounded everything, having found in that pile of knowledge and store of so many various things nothing solid and firm, and nothing but vanity, have renounced their presumption and recognized their natural condition.

It is what Velleius reproaches Cotta and Cicero for, that they learned from Philo that they had learned nothing.

Pherecydes, one of the Seven Sages, writing to Thales as he was dying, said: "I have ordered my friends, after they have buried me, to bring you my writings. If they satisfy you and the other sages,

publish them; if not, suppress them: they contain no certainty that satisfies myself. Nor do I profess to know the truth and to attain it. I uncover things more than I discover them."

^AThe wisest man that ever was, when they asked him what he knew, answered that he knew this much, that he knew nothing. He was verifying what they say, that the greatest part of what we know is the least of those parts that we do not know; that is to say that the very thing we think we know is a part, and a very small part, of our ignorance.

^CWe know things in a dream, says Plato, and we are ignorant of them in reality.

Almost all the ancients have said that nothing can be understood, nothing perceived, nothing known; that our senses are narrow, our minds weak, the course of our life short [Cicero].

^AAs for Cicero himself, who owed all his worth to learning, Valerius says that in his old age he began to lose his esteem for letters. ^CAnd while he practiced them, it was without obligation to any party, following what seemed probable to him now in one sect, now in another, keeping himself always in Academic doubt. *I must speak, but in such a way as to affirm nothing; I shall search into all things, doubting most of them and mistrusting myself* [Cicero].

^AI should have too easy a time if I wanted to consider man in his ordinary condition and in the mass; and yet I could do so according to his own rule, which judges the truth not by the weight of votes but by the number. Let us leave the people aside,

> Who waking snore …
> Whose life is dead, although they live and see,
>
> LUCRETIUS

who are not conscious of themselves, who do not judge themselves, who leave most of their natural faculties idle.

I wish to take man in his highest estate. Let us consider him in that small number of excellent and select men who, having been endowed with fine and particular natural ability, have further strengthened and sharpened it by care, by study, and by art, and have raised it to the highest pitch ^Cof wisdom ^Athat it can attain. They have fashioned their soul to all directions and all angles, supported and propped it with all the outside assistance that was fit for it, and enriched and adorned it with all they could borrow, for its advantage, from the inside and the outside of the world; it is in them that the utmost height of human nature is found. They have

regulated the world with governments and laws; they have instructed it with arts and sciences, and instructed it further by the example of their admirable conduct.

I shall take into account only these people, their testimony, and their experience. Let us see how far they have gone and where they have halted. The infirmities and defects that we shall find in this assembly the world may well boldly acknowledge as its own.

Whoever seeks anything comes to this point: he says either that he has found it, or that it cannot be found, or that he is still in quest of it. All philosophy is divided into these three types. Its purpose is to seek out truth, knowledge, and certainty.

The Peripatetics, Epicureans, Stoics, and others thought they had found it. These established the sciences that we have, and treated them as certain knowledge.

Clitomachus, Carneades, and the Academics despaired of their quest, and judged that truth could not be conceived by our powers. The conclusion of these men was man's weakness and ignorance. This school had the greatest following and the noblest adherents.

Pyrrho and other Skeptics or Epechists[25] – ᶜwhose doctrines, many of the ancients maintained, were derived from Homer, the Seven Sages, Archilochus, and Euripides, and were held by Zeno, Democritus, Xenophanes – ᴬsay that they are still in search of the truth. These men judge that those who think they have found it are infinitely mistaken; and that there is also an overbold vanity in that second class that assures us that human powers are not capable of attaining it. For this matter of establishing the measure of our power, of knowing and judging the difficulty of things, is a great and supreme knowledge, of which they doubt that man is capable:

> Whoever thinks that we know nothing does not know
> Whether we know enough to say that this is so.
>
> LUCRETIUS

Ignorance that knows itself, that judges itself and condemns itself, is not complete ignorance: to be that, it must be ignorant of itself. So that the profession of the Pyrrhonians is to waver, doubt, and inquire, to be sure of nothing, to answer for nothing. Of the three functions of the soul, the imaginative, the appetitive, and the consenting, they accept the first two; the last they suspend

25 From ἐπέχω, "I abstain."

and keep it ambiguous, without inclination or approbation, however
slight, in one direction or the other.

^cZeno pictured in a gesture his conception of this division of the
faculties of the soul: the hand spread and open was appearance;
the hand half shut and the fingers a little hooked, consent; the
closed fist, comprehension; when with his left hand he closed his
fist still tighter, knowledge.

^ANow this attitude of their judgment,[26] straight and inflexible,
taking all things in without adherence or consent, leads them to
their Ataraxia, which is a peaceful and sedate condition of life,
exempt from the agitations we receive through the impression of
the opinion and knowledge we think we have of things. Whence are
born fear, avarice, envy, immoderate desires, ambition, pride, super-
stition, love of novelty, rebellion, disobedience, obstinacy, and most
bodily ills. Indeed, they free themselves thereby from jealousy on
behalf of their doctrine. For they dispute in a very mild manner.
They do not fear contradiction in their discussion. When they say
that heavy things go down, they would be very sorry to have anyone
take their word for it; and they seek to be contradicted, so as to
create doubt and suspension of judgment, which is their goal. They
advance their propositions only to combat those they think we
believe in.

If you accept their proposition, they will just as gladly take the
opposite one to maintain; it is all one to them; they have no
preference in the matter. If you postulate that snow is black, they
argue on the contrary that it is white. If you say that it is neither one
nor the other, it is up to them to maintain that it is both. If you
maintain with certain judgment that you know nothing about it,
they will maintain that you do. Yes, and if by an affirmative axiom
you assure them that you are in doubt about it, they will go and
argue that you are not, or that you cannot judge and prove that you
are in doubt. And by this extremity of doubt that shakes its own
foundations, they separate and divide themselves from many opi-
nions, even from those which in many ways have upheld doubt
and ignorance.

^BWhy, they say, since among the dogmatists one is allowed to say
green, the other yellow, are they not also allowed to doubt? Is there
anything that can be proposed for you to admit or deny, which it is
not legitimate to consider ambiguous? And where others are swept

26 The Pyrrhonians.

– either by the custom of their country, or by their parental upbring-
ing, or by chance – as by a tempest, without judgment or choice,
indeed most often before the age of discretion, to such or such
an opinion, to the Stoic or Epicurean sect, to which they find
themselves pledged, enslaved, and fastened as to a prey they have
bitten into and cannot shake loose –*to whatever doctrine they have
been driven, as by a storm, to it they cling as to a rock* [Cicero] – *why
shall it not be granted similarly to these men to maintain
their liberty, and to consider things without obligation and servi-
tude? *The more free and independent because their power to judge is
intact* [Cicero].

Is it not an advantage to be freed from the necessity that curbs
others? *Is it not better to remain in suspense than to entangle
yourself in the many errors that the human fancy has produced? Is
it not better to suspend your conviction than to get mixed up in
these seditious and quarrelsome divisions?

*What am I to choose? What you like, provided you choose!
There is a stupid answer, to which nevertheless all dogmatism
seems to come, by which we are not allowed not to know what we
do not know.

*Take the most famous theory, it will never be so sure but that in
order to defend it you will have to attack and combat hundreds of
contrary theories. Is it not better to keep out of this melee? You are
permitted to espouse, as you would your honor and your life,
Aristotle's belief about the eternity of the soul, and to contradict
and give the lie to Plato on the matter; and shall they be forbidden to
doubt it?

*If it is lawful for Panaetius to suspend his judgment about
auspices, dreams, oracles, vaticinations, about which the Stoics
have no doubt at all, why shall a wise man not dare in all things
what this man dares in those he has learned from his masters,
which are established by the common consent of the school that
he follows and professes? *If it is a boy that judges, he does not know
what it is about; if it is a scholar, he is prejudiced.

The Pyrrhonians have kept themselves a wonderful advantage in
combat, having rid themselves of the need to cover up. It does not
matter to them that they are struck, provided they strike; and they
do their work with everything. If they win, your proposition is lame;
if you win, theirs is. If they lose, they confirm ignorance; if you lose,
you confirm it. If they prove that nothing is known, well and good; if
they do not know how to prove it, just as good. *So that, since equal*

reasons are found on both sides of the same subject, it may be the easier to suspend judgment on each side [Cicero].

And they set store by the fact that they can find much more easily why a thing is false than that it is true; and what is not than what is; and what they do not believe than what they believe.

^ATheir expressions are: "I establish nothing; it is no more thus than thus, or than neither way; I do not understand it; the appearances are equal on all sides; it is equally legitimate to speak for and against. ^CNothing seems true, which may not seem false." ^AThieir sacramental word is ἐπέχω, that is to say, "I hold back, I do not budge."[27] Those are their refrains, and others of similar substance. Their effect is a pure, complete, and very perfect postponement and suspension of judgment. They use their reason to inquire and debate, but not to conclude and choose. Whoever will imagine a perpetual confession of ignorance, a judgment without leaning or inclination, on any occasion whatever, he has a conception of Pyrrhonism.

I express this point of view as well as I can, because many find it difficult to conceive; and its authors themselves represent it rather obscurely and diversely.

As for the actions of life, they are of the common fashion in that. They lend and accommodate themselves to natural inclinations, to the impulsion and constraint of passions, to the constitutions of laws and customs, and to the tradition of the arts. ^CFor God wished us not to know, but only to use, those things [Cicero]. ^AThey let their common actions be guided by those things, without any taking sides or judgment. Which is why I cannot very well reconcile with this principle what they say of Pyrrho. They portray him as stupid and immobile, adopting a wild and unsociable way of life, waiting for carts to hit him, risking himself on precipices, refusing to conform to the laws. That is outdoing his doctrine. He did not want to make himself a stump or a stone; he wanted to make himself a living, thinking, reasoning man, enjoying all natural pleasures and comforts, employing and using all his bodily and spiritual faculties ^Cin regular and upright fashion. ^AThe fantastic, imaginary, false privileges that man has arrogated to himself, of regimenting, arranging, and fixing truth, he honestly renounced and gave up.

27 This and most of the expressions and sayings that precede it were inscribed in Greek on the ceiling of Montaigne's library.

^CMoreover, there is no sect that is not constrained to permit its sage to conform in a number of things that are not understood, or perceived, or accepted, if he wants to live. And when he goes to sea, he follows this course, not knowing if it will be useful to him, and relies on the vessel being good, the pilot experienced, the season suitable – merely probable circumstances. He is bound to follow them and to let himself be swayed by appearances, provided that they show no express contrariness. He has a body, he has a soul; his senses impel him, his mind stirs him. Even though he does not discover in himself that peculiar and singular mark of the right to judge, and perceives that he must not pledge his consent, since there may be some falsehood resembling this truth, he does not fail to carry on the functions of his life fully and comfortably.

How many arts there are that profess to consist of conjecture more than of knowledge, that do not decide on the true and the false and merely follow what seems to be! There are, they say, both a true and a false, and there is in us the means to seek it, but not to test it by a touchstone. We are much better if we let ourselves be led without inquisitiveness in the way of the world. A soul guaranteed against prejudice is marvelously advanced toward tranquillity. People who judge and check their judges never submit to them as they ought. How much more docile and easily led, both by the laws of religion and by political laws, are the simple and incurious minds, than those minds that survey divine and human causes like pedagogues!

^AThere is nothing in man's invention that has so much verisimilitude and usefulness.[28] It presents man naked and empty, acknowledging his natural weakness, fit to receive from above some outside power; stripped of human knowledge, and all the more apt to lodge divine knowledge in himself, ^Bannihilating his judgment to make more room for faith; ^Cneither disbelieving ^Anor setting up any doctrine ^Bagainst the common observances; humble, obedient, teachable, zealous; a sworn enemy of heresy, ^Aand consequently free from the vain and irreligious opinions introduced by the false sects. ^BHe is a blank tablet prepared to take from the finger of God such forms as he shall be pleased to engrave on it. The more we cast ourselves back on God and commit ourselves to him, and renounce ourselves, the better we are. ^A"Receive things thankfully," says the Preacher, "in the aspect and taste that they are offered to

28 As Pyrrhonism.

thee, from day to day; the rest is beyond thy knowledge."[29] ᶜ*The Lord knoweth the thoughts of man, that they are vanity* [Psalms].

ᴬThat is how, of three general sects of philosophy, two make express profession of doubt and ignorance; and in that of the dogmatists, which is the third, it is easy to discover that most of them have put on the mask of assurance only to look better. They have not thought so much of establishing any certainty for us as of showing us how far they had gone in this pursuit of the truth: ᶜ*which the learned suppose rather than know* [Livy].

Timaeus, having to instruct Socrates in what he knows of the gods, of the world, and of men, proposes to speak of them as man to man, and says it is enough if his reasons are as probable as another man's; for the exact reasons are not in his hand or in any mortal hand. Which one of his followers has imitated thus: *As well as I can, I will explain; however, I shall not declare certain and fixed things, like Pythian Apollo, but shall speak like a puny man, pursuing probabilities by conjecture* [Cicero]. And this was on the subject of contempt for death, a natural and popular subject. Elsewhere he translated this word for word from Plato: *If by chance, discoursing on the nature of the gods and the origin of the world, we do not attain the goal we have in mind, no wonder. You should rightly remember that both I who shall be discoursing and you who will be judging are men; so that if probabilities are stated, you will ask for nothing more.*

ᴬAristotle ordinarily piles up for us a great number of other opinions and other beliefs, to compare with his own and show us how much further he has gone and how much closer he has come to verisimilitude. For truth is not judged by the authority and on the testimony of another. ᶜAnd therefore Epicurus scrupulously avoided quoting other opinions in his writings. ᴬThe former is the prince of dogmatists; and yet we learn from him that knowing much gives occasion for doubting more. We see him often deliberately covering himself with such thick and inextricable obscurity that we cannot pick out anything of his opinion. It is in fact a Pyrrhonism in an affirmative form.

ᶜHear Cicero's protest, explaining the conception of others by his own: *They who inquire what we personally think about each matter are more curious than is necessary. This method in philosophy of arguing*

29 This passage closely resembles one which Montaigne had inscribed on the ceiling of his library, there ascribing it to "ECCL." However, it is not found in Ecclesiastes or in Ecclesiasticus.

against everything and making no open judgment of anything, started by Socrates, repeated by Arcesilaus, confirmed by Carneades, flourishes still even in our time. We are those who say that some falsehood is mixed with every truth, with so much similarity that there is no criterion in them by which we can judge and assent with certainty.

^BWhy did not only Aristotle but most philosophers affect difficulty, if not to bring out the vanity of the subject, and keep the curiosity of our mind amused by giving it fodder in gnawing on this hollow and fleshless bone? ^CClitomachus declared that he never could understand from the writings of Carneades what his opinion was. ^BWhy did Epicurus in his writings avoid clarity, and was Heraclitus for the same reason surnamed the Shadowy? Difficulty is a coin ^Cthat the learned employ, like conjurors, in order not to reveal the vanity of their art, and ^Bwhich human stupidity readily accepts as payment:

> Praised for his cryptic speech, mostly by fools;
> For those things best appeal to the obtuse
> Which they see hidden under words abstruse.
> LUCRETIUS

^CCicero reproves some of his friends for being accustomed to spend on astrology, law, dialectic, and geometry more time than these arts deserved; and because that diverted them from the more useful and honorable duties of life. The Cyrenaic philosophers equally despised physics and dialectic. Zeno, at the very beginning of the books of his *Republic*, declared all the liberal studies useless.

^AChrysippus said that what Plato and Aristotle had written about logic they had written as a game and for exercise, and could not believe that they had spoken seriously of such an empty matter. ^CPlutarch says the same of metaphysics. ^AEpicurus would have said it also of rhetoric, grammar, ^Cpoetry, mathematics, and all the sciences except physics. ^AAnd Socrates also of all except only that which treats of morals and life. ^CWhatever they asked him about, he always brought the inquirer back first of all to give an account of the conditions of his present and past life, which he examined and judged, considering any other learning subordinate to that and superfluous.

That learning would please me little which brought its teachers no closer to virtue [Sallust]. ^AMost of the arts have been thus despised by learning itself. But they did not think it inappropriate to exercise and amuse their minds on things in which there was no solid profit.

Moreover, some have considered Plato a dogmatist, others a doubter; others, in certain things the one, in certain things the other. ^CThe leader of his dialogues, Socrates, is always asking questions and stirring up discussion, never concluding, never satisfying; and says he has no other knowledge than that of opposing. Homer, their author, laid the foundations equally for all schools of philosophy, to show how indifferent he was about which way we went. From Plato arose ten different sects, they say. And indeed, in my opinion, never was teaching wavering and noncommittal if his is not.

Socrates used to say that the wise women,[30] on taking up the practice of making others give birth, abandon the practice of giving birth themselves; that he, by the title of wise man that the gods conferred on him, has also done away, in his virile and mental love, with his faculty of begetting, and contents himself with aiding and favoring with his help those who are in labor, opening their organs, greasing their conduits, facilitating the issue of their offspring, judging it, baptizing it, nursing it, strengthening it, swaddling and circumscribing it;[31] exercising and employing his skill upon the perils and fortunes of others.

^AIt is the same[32] with most of the others of this third type, ^Bas the ancients remarked of the writings of Anaxagoras, Democritus, Parmenides, Xenophanes, and others. ^ATheir way of writing is doubtful in substance, and their plan is to inquire rather than to instruct, even though they sprinkle their style with dogmatic cadences. Do we not see this as well in ^Cboth Seneca and ^APlutarch? ^CHow much they say now one way, now another, for those who study them closely! And those who reconcile jurists with each other should first reconcile each one with himself.

Plato seems to me to have favored this form of philosophizing in dialogues deliberately, to put more fittingly into diverse mouths the diversity and variation of his own ideas.

To treat matters diversely is as good as to treat them uniformly, and better: to wit, more copiously and usefully. Let us take an example from ourselves. Judicial sentences form the ultimate point of dogmatic and decisive speaking. Yet the most exemplary ones which our highest courts present to the people, fitted to foster in

30 *Sages femmes*: midwives.
31 The 1595 and later editions read "circumcising."
32 As with Plato.

them the reverence they owe to the dignity of those bodies, princi-
pally because of the ability of the persons who form them, derive
their beauty, not so much from the conclusion, which to them is
everyday, and which is common to every judge, as from the discus-
sion and stirring up of the diverse and contrary reasonings which the
matter of the law allows.

And the widest field for reprehensions of philosophers among
one another is derived from the contradictions and differences in
which each one of them finds himself entangled, either on purpose,
to show the vacillation of the human mind around all matters,
or unwittingly, forced by the mobility and incomprehensibility of
all matters.

ᴬWhat is the meaning of this refrain: "In a slippery and treacher-
ous place let us suspend our belief"? For, as Euripides says,

> The works of God in various ways
> Cross us and leave us in a daze.[33]

ᴮLike the refrain that Empedocles scattered often in his books, as if
agitated with a divine frenzy and forced by the truth: "No, no, we
sense nothing, we see nothing; all things are hidden from us;
we cannot establish what any one of them is"; ᶜin keeping with
this divine saying: *The thoughts of mortal men are miserable, and our
devices and plannings but uncertain* [Book of Wisdom].

ᴬIt must not be thought strange if people despairing of the
capture have yet taken pleasure in the chase; study being in itself
a pleasant occupation, so pleasant that among other pleasures the
Stoics forbid also that which comes from the exercise of the mind,
want a curb on it, ᶜand find intemperance in knowing too much.

ᴬDemocritus, having eaten at his table some figs that tasted of
honey, immediately began to seek out in his mind whence came this
unaccustomed sweetness; and to clear up the matter, he was about to
get up from the table to see the situation of the place where these
figs had been gathered. His maidservant, having heard the cause of
this stir, laughed and told him not to trouble himself about it, for the
reason was that she had put them in a vessel where there had been
some honey. He was vexed that she had deprived him of this
occasion for research and robbed him of matter for curiosity: "Go
along," he said to her, "you have made me angry; I will not for all
that give up seeking the cause as if it was a natural one." ᶜAnd he

33 Montaigne quotes this couplet in French from Amyot's translation.

willfully sought and found some "true" reason for a false and supposed effect.

^AThis story of a great and famous philosopher shows us very clearly this passion for study, which keeps us amused in pursuit of things of whose gain we have no hope. Plutarch tells a similar case of someone who did not want to be enlightened about something he was in doubt about, so as not to lose the pleasure of seeking it; like the other who did not want his doctor to rid him of the thirst of the fever, so as not to lose the pleasure of quenching it by drinking. ^C*It is more satisfactory to learn superfluous things than nothing* [Seneca].

Just as in all feeding there is often the pleasure alone, and not all we take that is pleasant is always nutritious and healthful; so what our mind derives from learning does not fail to be voluptuous even though it be neither nourishing nor salutary.

^BHere is what they say: "The consideration of nature is a food fit for our minds; it uplifts us and swells us, makes us disdain base and earthly things by comparison with higher and heavenly things. The very search for great and occult things is very pleasant, even to him who gains from it nothing but reverence and fear of judging them." Those are words of their profession.

The vain picture of this morbid curiosity is seen still more expressly in that other example that they have so often in their mouth as an honor. Eudoxus wished and prayed the gods that he might once see the sun from close by and comprehend its form, its greatness, and its beauty, even on penalty of being immediately burned up by it. He wants, at the price of his life, to acquire a knowledge whose use and possession will be at the same instant taken away, and for the sake of this momentary and fleeting knowledge to lose all other knowledge that he has and that he may afterward acquire.

^AI cannot easily persuade myself that Epicurus, Plato, and Pythagoras gave us their Atoms, their Ideas, and their Numbers as good coin of the realm. They were too wise to establish their articles of faith on anything so uncertain and so debatable. But into the obscurity and ignorance of this world, each one of those great men labored to bring some semblance of light, such as it was; and they exercised their minds on such conceptions as had at least a pleasant and subtle appearance, ^Cprovided that, false though they might be, they could hold their own against opposing ideas. *These are created by each man's imaginative genius, not by the power of his knowledge* [Seneca].

^AAn ancient who was reproached for professing philosophy, of which nevertheless in his own mind he took no great account, replied that this was being a true philosopher. They wanted to consider everything, to weigh everything, and they found that occupation suited to the natural curiosity that is in us. Some things they wrote for the needs of society, like their religions; and on that account it was reasonable that they did not want to bare popular opinions to the skin, so as not to breed disorder in people's obedience to the laws and customs of their country.

^CPlato treats this mystery with his cards pretty much on the table. For where he writes on his own, he makes no certain prescriptions. When he plays the lawgiver, he borrows a domineering and assertive style, and yet mixes in boldly the most fantastic of his inventions, which are as useful for persuading the common herd as they are ridiculous for persuading himself; knowing how apt we are to accept any impressions, and most of all the wildest and most monstrous.

And therefore, in his *Laws*, he takes great care that they shall sing in public only poems whose fabulous fictions tend to some useful purpose; and, it being so easy to imprint all sorts of phantasms on the human mind, he thought it an injustice not to feed it rather on profitable lies than on lies that were either useless or harmful. He says quite shamelessly in his *Republic* that it is often necessary to trick men for their own good.

It is easy to discern that some sects have rather followed truth, others utility; whereby the latter have gained credit. It is the bane of our condition that often what appears to our imagination as most true does not appear to it as most useful for our life. The boldest sects, Epicurean, Pyrrhonian, and New Academic, are still constrained, when all is said and done, to bow to civil law.

^AThere are other subjects that they have sifted and tossed, some to the left, some to the right, each one laboring to give them some appearance, right or wrong. For, having found nothing so occult that they did not want to talk about it, they often had to forge weak and foolish conjectures; not that they themselves took them for a foundation, or to establish any truth, but for the exercise of their study. ^C*They seemed not so much to believe what they said as to want to exercise their wits on the difficulty of the matter* [Quintilian].

^AAnd if we did not take it this way, how could we defend such great inconsistency, variety, and vanity in the opinions that we see were produced by these admirable and excellent souls? For what is there, for example, more vain than to try to divine God by our

analogies and conjectures, to regulate him and the world by our
capacity and our laws, and to use at the expense of the Deity this
little shred of ability that he was pleased to allot to our natural
condition? And, because we cannot stretch our vision as far as his
glorious throne, to have brought him here below to our corruption
and our miseries?

Of all the ancient human opinions concerning religion, that one,
it seems to me, was most probable and most excusable which
recognized God as an incomprehensible power, origin and preserver
of all things, all goodness, all perfection, accepting and taking in
good part the honor and reverence that human beings rendered him,
under whatever aspect, under whatever name, in whatever manner:

> ^cAlmighty Jupiter, of things and kings and gods
> Begetter and conceiver.
> VALERIUS SORANUS

This zeal has been regarded universally with favor by heaven.
All governments have reaped fruit from their piety: impious men
and impious deeds have always come out appropriately. Pagan
histories recognize dignity, order, justice, and prodigies and oracles
used for their profit and instruction, in their fabulous religions;
God, in his mercy, perhaps deigning to foster by these temporal
benefits the tender beginnings of a rough knowledge of him, how-
ever feeble, that natural reason has given us amid the false images of
our dreams.

Not only false, but also impious and harmful, are those that man
has fabricated of his own invention.

^AAnd of all the religions that Saint Paul found in credit at
Athens, the one that they had dedicated to a hidden and unknown
Deity seemed to him the most excusable.

^cPythagoras adumbrated truth more closely in judging that the
knowledge of this first cause, and being of beings, must be unde-
fined, unprescribed, undeclared; that it was nothing else but the
utmost effort of our imagination toward perfection, each man
amplifying the idea of it according to his capacity. But if
Numa undertook to make the piety of his people conform to this
plan, to attach it to a purely intellectual religion, without any
predetermined object or any material admixture, he undertook
something unusable. The human spirit cannot keep on floating in
this infinity of formless ideas; they must be compiled for it into
a definite picture after its own pattern.

The divine majesty has thus let itself be somewhat circumscribed within corporeal limits on our behalf; his supernatural and heavenly sacraments show signs of our earthly condition; his worship is expressed by perceptible rituals and words; for it is man that believes and prays.

I leave aside the other arguments that are employed on this subject. But I could hardly be made to believe that the sight of our crucifixes and the pictures of that piteous agony, the ornaments and ceremonious movements in our churches, the voices attuned to the piety of our thoughts, and that stirring of the senses, do not warm the souls of the people with religious emotion very beneficial in effect.

^AOf the divinities that have been given a body, as necessity required, in the midst of this universal blindness, it seems to me I would most willingly have joined those who worshiped the sun –

> the common light,
> Eye of the world; and if our God has eyes,
> They are the sun's bright rays that light the skies,
> That give us life, guard and maintain us all,
> And watch man's actions on this earthly ball;
> The sun, who makes our seasons' alteration
> By entering another habitation;
> Whose well-known virtues fill the universe;
> Who with a glance can sullen clouds disperse;
> The world's spirit and soul, ablaze, alight,
> Circling all heaven in his daily flight;
> Immensely great, wandering, firm and round,
> Who holds the world beneath him as his bound;
> At rest without rest, idle without stay,
> First-born of nature, father of the day
>
> RONSARD

– inasmuch as besides this, its grandeur and beauty, it is the part of this machine that we find farthest from us, and therefore so little known that they were to be pardoned for regarding it with wonder and reverence.

^CThales, who first inquired into this matter, thought God a spirit who made all things of water.

Anaximander, that the gods were dying and being born at various seasons, and that they were worlds infinite in number.

Anaximenes, that the air was a god, that he was created and immense, ever moving.

Anaxagoras was the first to hold that the form and manner of all things was directed by the power and reason of an infinite mind.

Alcmaeon granted divinity to the sun, the moon, the stars, and the soul.

Pythagoras made God a spirit diffused throughout the nature of all things, from which our souls are derived.

Parmenides, a circle surrounding the sky and sustaining the world by the glow of its light.

Empedocles said the four elements, of which all things are made, were gods.

Protagoras, that he had nothing to say about whether they are or not, or what they are.

Democritus, now that images and their circular movements are gods, now this nature that sends out these images, and now our knowledge and intelligence.

Plato scatters his belief in various images. He says in the *Timaeus* that the father of the world cannot be named; in the *Laws*, that we must not inquire into his nature; and elsewhere in these same books he makes world, heaven, stars, earth, and our souls gods, and accepts besides those accepted by ancient teaching in each commonwealth.

Xenophon reports a similar confusion in the teaching of Socrates: now we must not inquire into the form of God, then again he makes him prove that the sun is God, and the soul God; that there is only one, then again that there are many.

Speusippus, nephew of Plato, makes God a certain power that governs things, and is animate.

Aristotle says now that it is the mind, now the world; now he gives this world another master, and now makes God the heat of heaven.

Xenocrates makes eight of them: five named among the planets, the sixth composed of all the fixed stars as his members, the seventh and eighth the sun and moon.

Heraclides Ponticus does nothing but waver between opinions, and finally deprives God of feeling, and makes him change from one form to another; and then says that he is heaven and earth.

Theophrastus rambles with similar irresoluteness among all his fancies, attributing the superintendence of the world now to understanding, now to heaven, now to the stars.

Strato says that it is nature, with the power to engender, to increase, and to diminish, without form or feeling.

Zeno, the law of nature, commanding good and prohibiting evil, which law is an animate being; and he abolishes the customary gods, Jupiter, Juno, Vesta.

Diogenes of Apollonia, that it is age.[34]

Xenophanes makes God round, seeing, hearing, nonbreathing, having nothing in common with human nature.

Aristo thinks the form of God incomprehensible, deprives him of senses, and does not know if he is animate or something else.

Cleanthes, now reason, now the world, now the soul of nature, now the supreme heat enfolding and enveloping everything.

Perseus, a disciple of Zeno, held that those who had brought some notable contribution to human life, and the profitable things themselves, were given the surname of gods.

Chrysippus made a confused accumulation of all the preceding statements, and also numbered, among the thousand forms of gods that he creates, men who have been immortalized.

Diagoras and Theodorus denied quite flatly that there were gods.

Epicurus makes the gods shining, transparent, pervious to air, lodged between two worlds as between two forts, sheltered from blows, invested in human form and limbs like ours, which limbs are of no use to them.

> That there are gods I'll always claim, I've always thought;
> But what men do, so I believe, to them is nought.
>
> ENNIUS, QUOTED BY CICERO

Now trust to your philosophy; boast that you have found the bean in the cake,[35] when you consider the clatter of so many philosophical brains!

The confusion in the ways of the world has gained this from me, that conduct and fancies different from mine do not so much displease me as instruct me, do not so much swell my pride as humble me when I compare them; and any choice other than that which comes from the hand of God direct seems to me a choice of little advantage. (I leave aside monstrous and unnatural ways of life.)

34 Presumably a misprint for *air*, as we read in Cicero.
35 The person who found the bean in the Twelfth Night cake became King of the Bean.

The governments of the world are no less contradictory in this respect than the schools; whereby we may learn that Fortune herself is no more diverse and variable than our reason, nor more blind and unthinking.

^AThe least-known things are the fittest to be deified; ^cwherefore to make gods of ourselves, ^Alike antiquity, passes the utmost bounds of feeble-mindedness. I would even rather have followed those who worshiped the serpent, the dog, and the ox; inasmuch as their nature and being is less known to us, and we have more chance to imagine what we please about those animals and attribute extraordinary faculties to them. But to have made gods of our condition, the imperfection of which we should know; to have attributed to them desire, anger, vengeances, marriages, generation, kinships, love and jealousy, our limbs and our bones, our fevers and our pleasures, ^cour deaths, our burials – ^Athis must have come from a marvelous intoxication of the human intelligence:

> ^BWhich, far removed from any touch divine,
> Do not deserve amid the gods to shine.
> LUCRETIUS

^c*Their shapes, ages, clothing, ornaments, are known; their genealogies, marriages, kinships, and all are translated into a likeness of human weakness. For troubled minds are ascribed to them; for we accept the lusts, the griefs, the angers, of the gods* [Cicero].

^AThis is like attributing divinity ^cnot only to faith, virtue, honor, concord, liberty, victory, and piety, but also to voluptuousness, fraud, death, envy, old age, misery, ^Afear, fever, and bad fortune, and other troubles of our frail and perishable life.

> ^BWhy then profane the temples with our ways?
> O souls empty of heaven, that earthward gaze!
> PERSIUS

^cThe Egyptians, with unwise wisdom, forbade, under pain of hanging, that anyone should say that Serapis and Isis, their gods, had once been men; and no one was unaware that they had been. And their statues representing them with a finger to their lips signified, says Varro, that mysterious ordinance to their priests to hush up their mortal origin as if it annulled as a necessary consequence all the veneration paid them.

^ASince man desired so greatly to liken himself to God, he would have done better, says Cicero, to bring the qualities of the Deity

down here to his own level, than to send his corruption and his wretchedness up there; but if you take it rightly, he has done both in many ways, with equally vain conceit.

When the philosophers dissect the hierarchy of their gods and go about eagerly distinguishing their alliances, their functions, and their power, I cannot believe that they are speaking in earnest. When Plato describes Pluto's orchard to us, and the bodily comforts and pains that still await us after the destruction and annihilation of our bodies, and adapts them to the senses we have in this life –

> In hidden paths, in myrtle groves they hide;
> For even after death their cares abide
>
> VIRGIL

– when Mohammed promises his followers a paradise tapestried, adorned with gold and precious stones, peopled with wenches of surpassing beauty, with rare wines and foods, I can easily see that they are mockers stooping to our folly to honey us and attract us by these ideas and hopes appropriate to our mortal appetites.

^CYet some of our fellows have fallen into a similar error, promising themselves after the resurrection a terrestrial and temporal life accompanied with all sorts of worldly pleasures and comforts.

^AAre we to believe that Plato – he who had such celestial conceptions, and such great acquaintance with divinity, that the surname Divine remains with him – thought that man, that poor creature, had anything in him applicable to that incomprehensible power? And that he believed that our feeble grasp was able, or the power of our sense robust enough, to participate in eternal beatitude or pain? We should say to him on behalf of human reason:

"If the pleasures that you promise us in the other life are of the kind I have tasted here below, that has nothing in common with infinity. Even if all my five natural senses were filled to overflowing with delight, and this soul possessed of all the contentment it can desire and hope for, we know what it is capable of: that would still be nothing.

"If there is anything of mine in it, there is nothing divine. If it is nothing but what can pertain to this present condition of ours, it cannot be counted. ^CAll contentment of mortals is mortal.

^A"The gratitude of our parents, our children, and our friends – if it can touch us and please us in the other world, if we still cling to such a pleasure, we are among earthly and finite goods.

"We cannot worthily conceive the grandeur of those sublime and divine promises, if we can conceive them at all; to imagine them worthily, we must imagine them unimaginable, ineffable, and incomprehensible, ^cand completely different from those of our miserable experience. ^A'Eye cannot see,' says Saint Paul, 'neither can it have entered into the heart of man, the happiness which God hath prepared for them that love him' [I Corinthians].

"And if, to make us capable of it, they reform and change our being (as you mean, Plato, by your purifications), it must be by so extreme and universal a change that, according to the teachings of physics, it will no longer be ourselves:

> ^BHector was he, bending on war his force;
> Hector he was not, dragged by Achilles' horse.
>
> OVID

^AIt will be something else that will receive these rewards:

> ^BWhat changes, decomposes, and so dies;
> Its parts transposed, their former order flies.
>
> LUCRETIUS

^AFor in the Metempsychosis of Pythagoras, the change of habitation that he imagined for our souls, do we think that the lion, in whom is the soul of Caesar, espouses the passions that moved Caesar, ^cor that he is Caesar? If it were still he, those men would be right who, combating this opinion against Plato, reproach him because the son might find himself riding his mother, she being invested with the body of a mule; and similar absurdities.

"And do we think ^Athat in the transformations that make the bodies of animals into others of the same species, the newcomers are not other than their predecessors? From the ashes of a phoenix, they say, is engendered a worm, and then another phoenix: this second phoenix, who can imagine that he is not other than the first? The worms that make our silk, we see them, as it were, die and dry up, and from this same body is produced a butterfly, and from that another worm, which it would be ridiculous to think is still the first. What has once ceased to be, is no more:

> Even if after death time should collect
> Our matter, and our bodies resurrect;
> If light of life were given us again;

> To us that process still would not pertain,
> When once the thread of memory had been cut.
>
> LUCRETIUS

And when you say elsewhere, Plato, that it will be for the spiritual part of man to enjoy the rewards of the other life, you tell us a thing of as little likelihood:

> [B]Just as without the body, torn away,
> The eye cannot behold the light of day.
>
> LUCRETIUS

[A]For by that reckoning, it will no longer be man, nor consequently ourselves, whom this enjoyment will concern; for we are built of two principal essential parts, whose separation is the death and destruction of our being:

> [B]A pause has come in life's experience,
> When movement wandered, unperceived by sense.
>
> LUCRETIUS

[A]We do not say that man suffers when the worms nibble his limbs, whereby he lived, and when the earth consumes them:

> And this is naught to us, who form one whole
> Because our body's wedded to our soul.
>
> LUCRETIUS

"Moreover, on what grounds of their justice can the gods give recognition and recompense to man, after his death, for his good and virtuous actions, since it is they themselves who have furthered and produced them in him? And why do they take offense and vengeance on him for his misdeeds, since they themselves have brought him forth in this faulty condition, and since with a single flick of their will they can keep him from erring?"

Might not Epicurus bring up all this against Plato with every appearance of human reason, [C]if he did not often cover himself by this saying: "That it is impossible to establish anything certain about immortal nature from mortal nature"?

[A]Reason does nothing but go astray in everything, and especially when it meddles with divine things. Who feels this more evidently than we? For even though we have given it certain and infallible principles, even though we light its steps with the holy lamp of the truth which it has pleased God to communicate to us, nevertheless

we see daily how, when it strays however little from the beaten path and deviates or wanders from the way traced and trodden by the Church, immediately it is lost, it grows embarrassed and entangled, whirling round and floating in that vast, troubled, and undulating sea of human opinions, unbridled and aimless. As soon as it loses that great common highroad it breaks up and disperses onto a thousand different roads.

Man can be only what he is, and imagine only within his reach. [B]It is greater presumption, says Plutarch, for those who are mere men to venture to talk and discourse about the gods and demigods than it is for a man ignorant of music to want to judge singers, or for a man who was never in a camp to want to argue about arms and warfare, presuming to understand by some flimsy conjecture the products of an art that is outside his knowledge.

[A]Antiquity thought, I believe, that it was doing something for divine greatness by likening it to man, investing it with his faculties, and presenting it with his fine humors [C]and his most shameful needs; [A]offering it our food to eat, [C]our dances, mummeries, and farces to amuse it, [A]our clothes to cover it, and our houses to live in; cajoling it with the odor of incense and the sounds of music, with festoons and bouquets; [C]and, to reconcile it to our vicious passions, flattering its justice with inhuman vengeance, delighting it with the destruction and dispersion of things by it created and preserved – like Tiberius Sempronius, who burned, as a sacrifice to Vulcan, the rich spoils and arms he had won from the enemy in Sardinia; and Paulus Emilius, those of Macedonia to Mars and Minerva; and Alexander, on reaching the Indian Ocean, cast into the sea, in honor of Thetis, many great gold vases – filling its altars, besides, with butchery, not only of innocent animals, but also of men, [A]as was the ordinary practice in many nations, among others our own. And I think no nation is innocent of having tried this:

> [B]Four young men
> Of Sulmo town, from Ufens' stream as many again,
> He takes and sacrifices to the shades below.
>
> VIRGIL

[C]The Getae think themselves immortal, and their dying but a journey toward their god, Zamolxis. Every five years they dispatch toward him some one among them to ask him for necessary things. This deputy is chosen by lot. And the manner of dispatching him, after they have notified him orally of his charge, is this: of those who

are with him, three hold upright as many javelins, on which the others hurl him with all their might. If he happens to be pierced in a vital spot and dies instantly, that is to them a certain proof of divine favor; if he escapes, they consider him wicked and execrable, and depute still another in the same way.

Amestris, mother of Xerxes, in her old age, at one time had fourteen youths of the best houses in Persia buried alive, following the religion of the country, to gratify some subterranean god.

Even today, the idols of Themistitan are cemented with the blood of little children, and love no sacrifice but that of these pure and childish souls: a justice athirst for the blood of innocence,

> So many grievous crimes religion has inspired!
>
> LUCRETIUS

The Carthaginians immolated their own children to Saturn; [B]and whoever had none bought some, the father and mother being bound meanwhile to watch this ceremony with a gay and happy countenance.

[A]It was a strange fancy to try to pay for divine goodness with our affliction, like the Lacedaemonians who wheedled their Diana by the torture of young boys, whom they had whipped for her sake, often to death. It was a savage impulse to try to gratify the architect by the overthrow of his building, and to try to cover the penalty due to the guilty by the punishment of the guiltless; and to think that poor Iphigenia, at the port of Aulis, would by her death and sacrifice clear the army of the Greeks in the eyes of God of the offenses they had committed:

> [B]Pure maid impurely sacrificed, she lay
> Slain by her father on her wedding day;
>
> LUCRETIUS

[C]and that those two beautiful and generous souls, the two Decii, father and son, to propitiate the favor of the gods toward the affairs of Rome, should go and throw themselves headlong into the thick of the enemy. *What iniquity of the gods was so great that they could not be reconciled to the Roman people unless such men died?* [Cicero.]

[A]Besides, it is not up to the criminal to have himself whipped at his own rate and time; it is up to the judge, [B]who counts as chastisement nothing but the penalty he orders, [C]and cannot regard as

punishment what comes to him who suffers it at his own will. Divine vengeance presupposes our absolute dissent, for its justice and our punishment.

^BAnd it was a ridiculous notion of Polycrates, tyrant of Samos, who, to interrupt the course of his continual happiness and to compensate for it, went and threw into the sea the dearest and most precious jewel he had, thinking that by this calculated misfortune he was satisfying the turning and vicissitude of Fortune; ^Cand she, to mock his futility, made this same jewel return again into his hands, found in the belly of a fish.

^AAnd then ^Cwhat is the use of the mutilations and dismemberings of the Corybantes, the Maenads, and in our own time the Mohammedans, who scar their face, their stomach, and their genitals to please their prophet; since ^Athe offense is in the will, not ^Cin the chest, the eyes, the genitals, the belly, ^Athe shoulders, or the throat? ^C*Such is the frenzy of their disordered and unsettled mind that they placate their gods with a savagery unsurpassed by men* [Saint Augustine].

The treatment of this natural structure³⁶ concerns not only ourselves, but also the service of God and of other men; it is unjust to damage it deliberately, as it is to kill ourselves on any pretext whatsoever. It seems a great cowardice and treachery to mistreat and corrupt the functions of the body, which are stupid and servile, in order to spare the soul the bother of directing them according to reason. *At what point do they fear the anger of the gods, they who think to propitiate them thus? . . . Some have been castrated to please the lust of kings; but no one ever emasculated himself with his own hand at his master's command* [Saint Augustine].

^AThus they filled their religion with many evil deeds:

> Too often, in past times,
> Religion has brought forth impiety and crimes.
> LUCRETIUS

Now nothing of ours can be likened or compared in any way whatsoever to the divine nature without staining and marking it with just that much imperfection. That infinite beauty, power, and goodness – how can it allow any correspondence or likeness with anything as abject as we are, without an extreme loss and fall of its

36 Our body.

divine greatness? ᶜ*The weakness of God is stronger than men, and the foolishness of God is wiser than men* [I Corinthians].

Stilpo the philosopher, asked whether the gods rejoice in our honors and sacrifices, replied: "You are indiscreet; let us draw aside, if you want to talk about that."

ᴬHowever, we prescribe limits to God, we hold his power besieged by our reasons (I am calling reason our reveries and dreams, with the dispensation of philosophy, which says that even the crazy man and the wicked man are mad with reason, but it is a particular sort of reason); we want to enslave him to the vain and feeble approximations of our understanding, him who has made both us and our knowledge.

"Because nothing is made of nothing, God cannot have built the world without material." What! Has God placed in our hands the keys and ultimate springs of his power? Has he pledged himself not to overstep the bounds of our knowledge? Put the case, O man, that you have been able to observe here some traces of his deeds; do you think that he has used all his power and put all his forms and all his ideas into this work? You see only the order and government of this little cave you dwell in, at least if you do see it. His divinity has infinite jurisdiction beyond; this part is nothing in comparison with the whole:

> The sky, the land, the sea, and all
> Are nothing to the universal whole.
> LUCRETIUS

It is a municipal law that you allege; you do not know what the universal law is. Attach yourself to what you are subject to, but not him; he is not your colleague, or fellow citizen, or companion; if he has communicated himself at all to you, it is not in order to lower himself to your smallness, nor to give you surveillance over his power.

The human body cannot fly up to the clouds: this is a law that affects you. The sun runs its ordinary course without rest; the limits of seas and land cannot be confounded; water is unstable and without firmness; a wall without a breach is impenetrable to a solid body; man cannot keep alive in the flames; he cannot be bodily both in heaven and on earth, and in a thousand places at the same time.

It is for you that he has made these rules; it is you that they bind. He has proved to Christians that he has overstepped them all when he pleased. Why, in truth, all-powerful as he is, would he have

restricted his powers to a certain measure? In whose favor would he have renounced his privilege?

Your reason is never more plausible and on more solid ground than when it convinces you of the plurality of worlds:

> [B]That earth, and sun, and moon, and all that we behold
> Are not unique, but infinitely manifold.
> LUCRETIUS

[A]The most famous minds of times past have believed this, and even some of our contemporaries, forced by the probabilities of human reason; inasmuch as in this structure that we see, there is nothing single and unique,

> [B]Since in the whole of things no thing is one,
> Nothing is born or grows unique and lone,
> LUCRETIUS

[A]and since all the species are multiplied to some number. Whence it does not seem likely that God has made this one work without a companion, and that the material of this form has been all exhausted in this single individual:

> [B]Wherefore we must conclude on every ground
> That elsewhere other piles of matter, bound
> Like this one by the ether, do exist;
> LUCRETIUS

[A]especially if it is an animate being, as its motions make so credible [C]that Plato assures us of it, and many of our fellows either confirm it or do not dare deny it; no more than that ancient belief that the sky, the stars, and other parts of the world are creatures composed of body and soul, mortal in consideration of their composition, but immortal by the decree of the creator.

[A]Now if there are many worlds, as [C]Democritus, [A]Epicurus, and almost all philosophy has thought, how do we know whether the principles and rules of this one apply similarly to the others? Perchance they have a different appearance and different laws. [C]Epicurus imagines some similar, some dissimilar. [A]We see in this world an infinite difference and variety due solely to distance in place. Neither wheat nor wine is seen, nor any of our animals, in these new lands that our fathers have discovered; everything there is different. [C]And in times past, see in how many parts of the world they had no acquaintance with either Bacchus or Ceres.

[A]If we want to believe Pliny [C]and Herodotus, [A]there are species of men in certain places who have very little resemblance to our kind. [B]And there are half-breed and ambiguous forms between human and brutish nature. There are countries where the men are born without heads, wearing their eyes and mouth in their chest; where they are all androgynous; where they walk on all fours; where they have only one eye in their forehead, and a head more like a dog's than like ours; where they are half fish underneath and live in the water; where the women give birth at the age of five and live only till eight; where their head and the skin of their forehead is so hard that iron cannot cut it and is blunted by it; where the men are beardless; [C]nations without use or knowledge of fire; others that give black-colored sperm.

[B]What of those who naturally change into wolves, [C]into mares, [B]and then back into men? And if it is so, [A]as Plutarch says, that in some place in the Indies there are men without mouths, feeding on the smell of certain odors, how many of our descriptions are false? Man is no longer capable of laughter, nor perhaps of reason or society. The arrangement and the cause of our internal construction would be for the most part inapplicable.

Besides, how many things there are within our knowledge which defy these fine rules that we have cut out and prescribed to nature! And we shall undertake to bind even God to them! How many things we call miraculous and contrary to nature! [C]This is done by each man and each nation according to the measure of his ignorance. [A]How many occult properties and quintessences we discover! For to us, to go according to nature is only to go according to our intelligence, as far as it can follow and as far as we can see; what is beyond is monstrous and disordered.

Now by this reckoning, to the most knowing and ablest men everything will therefore be monstrous; for human reason has convinced those men that she has no footing or foundation whatever, not even enough to be sure [C]whether snow is white (Anaxagoras said it was black); whether there is anything, or whether there is nothing; whether there is knowledge or ignorance (Metrodorus of Chios denied that man could tell); or [A]whether we live, since Euripides is in doubt whether the life we live is life, or whether it is what we call death that is life:

> Who knows but life is that which is called death,
> And death what is called life?
> EURIPIDES, QUOTED BY STOBAEUS

ᴮAnd not without plausibility. For why do we claim title to existence, on account of that instant that is only a flash in the infinite course of an eternal night, and so brief an interruption of our perpetual and natural condition; ᶜdeath occupying all that is before and all that is behind that moment, and also a good part of that moment?

ᴮOthers swear that there is no movement, that nothing stirs, ᶜlike the followers of Melissus (for if there is only one, neither spherical movement can serve it, nor movement from place to place, as Plato proves); ᴮthat there is neither generation nor corruption in nature.

ᶜProtagoras says that there is nothing in nature but doubt; that about all things we may equally dispute, and even about this, whether we may equally dispute about all things. Nausiphanes, that of things that seem to be, nothing is, any more than it is not; that there is no other certainty but uncertainty. Parmenides, that of what seems to be, there is no one thing in general; that it is but one. Zeno, that even one is not, and that there is nothing.

If one were, it would be either in another or in itself: if it is in another, there are two; if it is in itself, there are still two, the comprising and the comprised.

According to these doctrines, the nature of things is only a false or an empty shadow.

ᴬIt has always seemed to me that for a Christian this sort of talk is full of indiscretion and irreverence: "God cannot die, God cannot go back on his word, God cannot do this or that." I do not think it is good to confine the divine power thus under the laws of our speech. And the probability that appears to us in these propositions should be expressed more reverently and religiously.

Our speech has its weaknesses and its defects, like all the rest. Most of the occasions for the troubles of the world are grammatical. Our lawsuits spring only from debate over the interpretation of the laws, and most of our wars from the inability to express clearly the conventions and treaties of agreement of princes. How many quarrels, and how important, have been produced in the world by doubt of the meaning of that syllable *Hoc!*[37]

37 Much of the dispute over transubstantiation, especially between Catholics and Protestants, centers on the interpretation of Christ's words: "Hoc est corpus meum..."

[B]Let us take the sentence that logic itself offers us as the clearest. If you say "It is fine weather," and if you are speaking the truth, then it is fine weather. Isn't that a sure way of speaking? Still it will deceive us. To show this let us continue the example. If you say "I lie," and if you are speaking the truth, then you lie. The art, the reason, the force, of the conclusion of this one are the same as in the other; yet there we are stuck in the mud.

[A]I can see why the Pyrrhonian philosophers cannot express their general conception in any manner of speaking; for they would need a new language. Ours is wholly formed of affirmative propositions, which to them are utterly repugnant; so that when they say "I doubt," immediately you have them by the throat to make them admit that at least they know and are sure of this fact, that they doubt. Thus they have been constrained to take refuge in this comparison from medicine, without which their attitude would be inexplicable: when they declare "I do not know" or "I doubt," they say that this proposition carries itself away with the rest, no more nor less than rhubarb, which expels evil humors and carries itself off with them.

[B]This idea is more firmly grasped in the form of interrogation: "What do I know?"[38] – the words I bear as a motto, inscribed over a pair of scales.

[A]See how people take advantage of this wholly irreverent way of speaking. In the disputes we have at present in our religion, if you press your adversaries too hard, they will tell you quite shamelessly that it is not in God's power to make his body be in paradise and on earth, and in several places at the same time. And that ancient scoffer,[39] how he takes advantage of it! At least, he says, it is no slight consolation to man to see that God cannot do everything: for he cannot kill himself even if he wished, which is the greatest privilege we have in our condition; he cannot make mortals immortal, or the dead live again, nor can he arrange that the man who has lived shall not have lived, or that the man who has had honors shall not have had them; he has no other power over the past than that of oblivion. And, to bind this association of man to God further by comical examples, he cannot make two times ten not be twenty.

38 The famous "*Que sçay-je?*" which many consider Montaigne's central idea.
39 Pliny the Elder.

That is what he says, and what a Christian should avoid having pass out of his mouth. Whereas, on the contrary, men seem to seek out this mad arrogance of speech, to bring God down to their measure:

> Whether tomorrow Jove
> With blackest clouds shall fill the sky above
> Or with the purest radiance of the sun;
> Still can he not annul whate'er is done,
> Spoil or undo one thing, however slight,
> That time has carried past us in its flight.
>
> HORACE

When we say that the infinity of the centuries both past and to come is to God but an instant, that his goodness, wisdom, power, are the same thing as his essence – our tongues say it, but our intelligence does not apprehend it. And yet our overweening arrogance would pass the deity through our sieve. And from that are born all the delusions and errors with which the world is possessed, reducing and weighing in its scales a thing so far from its measure. ^c*It is a wonder how far the depravity of the human heart will go when encouraged by the slightest success* [Pliny].

How insolently the Stoics rebuke Epicurus because he holds that to be truly good and happy belongs only to God, and that the wise man has only a shadow and semblance of it! ^AHow rashly have they bound God to destiny (I would that none bearing the surname of Christian would still do it!), and Thales, Plato, and Pythagoras have made him a slave to necessity!

This arrogance of trying to discover God with our eyes made a great man of our religion[40] give the deity bodily form. ^BAnd it is the cause of what happens to us every day, to attribute events of importance, by particular assignment, to God. Because they weigh with us, it seems as though they weigh with him also, and that he considers them with more undivided attention than the events that to us are slight or of ordinary occurrence. ^c*The gods take care about great things, and neglect small things* [Cicero]. Listen to his example, it will make his reason clear to you: *Nor do kings in their rule take care about all the trifles* [Cicero].

As if it were more or less to him to move an empire or the leaf of a tree; and as if his providence were exercised otherwise in deciding

40 Tertullian.

the outcome of a battle than the jump of a flea! The hand with which he governs lends itself to all things with the same tenor, the same power, and the same order; the effect on us adds nothing to it; our movements and our measures do not touch him. *God, so great a craftsman in great things, is no less so in small* [Saint Augustine].

Our arrogance is always proposing to us this blasphemous comparison. Because our occupations burden us, Strato endowed the gods with total immunity from duties, like their priests. He makes nature produce and maintain all things, and with her weights and motions constructs the parts of the world, relieving human nature of the fear of divine judgments. *What is blessed and eternal has no business itself, nor gives any to another* [Cicero]. Nature wills that in like things there be a like relation. So the infinite number of mortals indicates a like number of immortals. The infinity of things that kill and harm presupposes as many that preserve and benefit. As the souls of the gods, without tongue, without eyes, without ears, have each a feeling of what the other feels, and judge our thoughts; so the souls of men, when they are free and released from the body by sleep or some trance, divine, prognosticate, and see things that they could not see when mingled with the body.

^A"Men," says Saint Paul, "professing themselves to be wise, became fools, and changed the glory of the incorruptible God into an image made like to corruptible man."

^BJust take a look at the hocus-pocus of the ancient deifications. After the grand and superb pomp of the burial, as the fire was about to reach the top of the pyramid and catch the bed of the deceased, at the same time they let loose an eagle, which, flying upward, signified that the soul was departing to paradise. We have a thousand medals, and particularly of that virtuous woman Faustina, wherein this eagle is represented carrying these deified souls pickaback toward heaven. It is a pity that we fool ourselves with our own monkey tricks and inventions –

> They fear their own imaginings
> LUCAN

– like children who take fright at that very face that they have smeared and blackened for their playmate. ^C*As if anything was more unhappy than a man dominated by the figments of his imagination* [Saint Augustine].

It is far from honoring him who made us, to honor him whom we have made. ^BAugustus had more temples than Jupiter, served with as

much religion and belief in miracles. The Thasians, in recompense for the benefits they had received from Agesilaus, came to tell him that they had canonized him. "Does your nation," he said to them, "have this power to make a god of whomever they choose? Make one of one of yourselves, so I can see; and then, ^cwhen I see how he likes it, ^BI will thank you very much for your offer."

^CMan is certainly crazy. He could not make a mite, and he makes gods by the dozen.

Listen to Trismegistus[41] praising our capacity: "Of all wonderful things, this has surpassed wonder, that man has been able to discover the divine nature and to make it, too."

^BHere are some arguments of the very school of philosophy,

> To which alone 'tis granted gods to know
> Or whether they are knowable or no.
> LUCAN

"If God is, he is animal; if he is animal, he is sentient; and if he is sentient, he is subject to corruption. If he is without body, he is without soul, and consequently without action; and if he has a body, he is perishable." Isn't that a triumph?

^C"We are incapable of having made the world; so there is some more excellent nature that has set its hand to it. It would be stupid arrogance to esteem ourselves the most perfect thing in this universe: so there is something better; that is God. When you see a rich and pompous dwelling, even though you do not know who is the master of it, still you will not say that it was made for rats. And this divine structure of the heavenly palace that we see, do we not have to believe that it is the abode of some master greater than we are? Isn't the highest always the worthiest? And we are placed at the bottom.

"Nothing without soul and without reason can produce an animate being capable of reason. The world produces us, so it has soul and reason.

"Each part of us is less than ourselves. We are part of the world. So the world is furnished with wisdom and reason, and more abundantly than we are.

"It is a fine thing to have a great government. So the government of the world belongs to some happy nature.

"The stars do us no harm, so they are full of goodness.

41 Hermes Trismegistus, the name given by Greek mystics to the Egyptian god Thoth, was also applied to the author of various Neoplatonic writings.

[B]"We need food, therefore so do the gods, and they feed on the fumes from here below.

[C]"Worldly goods are not goods to God; so they are not goods to us.

"To harm and to be harmed are alike signs of weakness; so it is madness to fear God.

"God is good by his nature; man, by his cleverness, which is a bigger thing.

"Divine wisdom and human wisdom have no other distinction except that the former is eternal. Now duration is no accession to wisdom; wherefore we are fellows.

[B]"We have life, reason, and liberty, we esteem goodness, charity, and justice; so these qualities are in him."[42]

In short, the construction and the destruction of the deity, and its conditions, are wrought by man, on the basis of a relationship to himself. What a pattern and what a model! Let us stretch, exalt, and magnify human qualities all we please; inflate yourself, poor man, and more, and more, and more:

> Not even if you burst, said he.[43]
>
> HORACE

[C]*In truth it is not God, whom they cannot conceive, conceiving themselves in his stead, not him but themselves whom they compare, not with him, but with themselves* [Saint Augustine].

[B]In natural things, the effects only half reflect their causes: What about this cause? It is above the order of nature; its condition is too lofty, too distant, and too much in authority to suffer our conclusions to tie and bind it. It is not through ourselves that we reach it; that route is too low. We are no nearer heaven at the top of Mont Cenis than at the bottom of the sea; consult your astrolabe and see.

They bring God down even to having carnal knowledge of women, to how many times and how many begettings. Paulina, wife of Saturninus, a matron of great repute in Rome, thinking she was sleeping with the god Serapis, found herself in the arms of a suitor of hers through the pandering of the priests of his temple.

[C]Varro, the most subtle and the most learned Latin author, writes in his books on theology that the sacristan of Hercules, casting lots for himself with one hand and for Hercules with the other, bet him

42 The above arguments are taken from Cicero, *Of the Nature of the Gods.*
43 Allusion to the fable of the frog who wanted to be as big as the ox.

a supper and a wench: if he won, at the expense of the offerings; if he lost, at his own. He lost, paid for his supper and his girl. Her name was Laurentina, and that night she saw this god in her arms, telling her into the bargain that the next day the first man she met would pay her her wages in heavenly fashion. This was Taruntius, a rich young man, who took her to his house, and in time made her his heiress. She in her turn, hoping to do something agreeable to this god, left the Roman people as her heirs; wherefore they conferred divine honors upon her.

As if it was not enough that Plato, on both sides, was originally descended from the gods, and had Neptune as the common author of his race, it was held for certain at Athens that Aristo, having wanted to enjoy the beauteous Perictione, had not been able to, and was warned in a dream by the god Apollo to leave her unpolluted and intact until she gave birth. These were the father and mother of Plato.

How many such cuckoldries are there in the histories, procured by the gods at the expense of the poor humans! And husbands unjustly decried in favor of the children!

In the religion of Mohammed, according to popular belief, plenty of Merlins are found: to wit, children without fathers, spiritual, divinely born in the womb of virgins; and they bear a name which signifies this in their language.

ᴮIt must be noted that to every creature there is nothing dearer and more estimable than its own being: ᶜthe lion, the eagle, the dolphin, prize nothing above their own species; ᴮand each relates the qualities of all other things to its own qualities. Which indeed we can extend or shorten, but that is all; for beyond this relation and this principle our imagination cannot go; it can divine nothing different; and it is impossible for it to go outside of this and pass beyond it. ᶜWhence arise these ancient conclusions: Of all forms, the most beautiful is that of man; so God is of that form. No man can be happy without virtue, nor can virtue be without reason, and no reason can dwell elsewhere than in the human form; therefore God is clothed in human form. *There is a conception, a prejudice in our minds such that when a man thinks of God, a human form occurs to him* [Cicero].

ᴮWherefore Xenophanes used to say wittily that if the animals make gods for themselves, as it is likely they do, they certainly make them like themselves, and glorify themselves as we do. For why shall a gosling not say thus: "All the parts of the universe have me in view:

the earth serves for me to walk on, the sun to give me light, the stars
to breathe their influences into me; I gain this advantage from the
winds, that from the waters; there is nothing that the heavenly vault
regards so favorably as me; I am the darling of nature. Is it not man
that treats me, houses me, serves me? It is for me that he sows and
grinds. If he eats me, so indeed does he eat his fellow man, and so do
I eat the worms that kill and eat him." A crane would say as much,
and still more magnificently, because of the freedom of its flight and
the possession of that beautiful and lofty region: *c such an alluring
matchmaker and such a procuress to herself is nature!* [Cicero.]

B Now then, by this same reasoning, for us are the destinies, for us
the world; it shines, it thunders for us; both the creator and the
creatures, all are for us. We are the end and the goal at which
the universality of things aims. Look at the register that philosophy
has kept, for two thousand years and more, of heavenly affairs. The
gods have acted, have spoken only for man; she attributes to them
no other consideration and no other function.

Here they are against us in war:

> And the earth-born brood,
> By the Herculean hand subdued,
> Who yet imperiled the bright abode
> Of ancient Saturn.
>
> HORACE

Here they are partisans in our troubles, *c* to repay us in kind for being
so many times partisans in theirs:

> *B* The walls and the foundations Neptune shakes
> With his vast trident, and the city entire
> He overturns. Juno, with rage afire,
> Seizes the Scaean gates.
>
> VIRGIL

c The Caunians, out of jealousy for the dominance of their own
gods, take arms on their backs on the day of their devotions, and go
running about all the neighborhood, smiting the air in all directions
with their swords, thus pursuing to the death and banishing from
their territory all foreign gods.

B The powers of the gods are detailed according to our need: one
cures horses, one men, *c* one the plague, *B* one the scurvy, one the
cough, *c* one one sort of itch, one another: *for a corrupt religion drags
the gods into the smallest matters* [Livy]; *B* one makes grapes grow, one

garlic; one has charge of lechery, one of business – ^cto each race of artisans its god; ^Bone has his province and credit in the Orient, one in the Occident:

> Here were her arms,
> Here her chariot.
>
> VIRGIL

^cSacred Apollo, lodged in the earth's fixed navel.

CICERO

> The sons of Cecrops worship at Pallas' shrine;
> To Minos' Crete Diana's most divine;
> To Lemnos, Vulcan; Juno to a man
> Of Sparta or Mycenae; pine-crowned Pan
> To Maenalus; to Latium, Mars.
>
> OVID

^BOne god has but one borough or one family in his possession; ^canother lives alone; another in company, either voluntary or imposed.

> Great-grandsire's temples are by grandson's joined.
>
> OVID

^BThere are some so puny and common (for their number amounts to thirty-six thousand) that you have to accumulate fully five or six to produce an ear of wheat, and from that they take their various names. ^cThree for a door, the one for the board, the one for the hinge, the one for the threshold; four for a child, protectors of his swaddling clothes, his drinking, his eating, his nursing; some certain, some uncertain and doubtful; some that do not yet enter paradise:

> Since yet we do not deem them worthy of heaven,
> At least we let them dwell in lands we've given.
>
> OVID

There are some that are physicians, some poets, some politicians; some midway between divine and human nature, mediators and go-betweens between us and God, worshiped with a sort of secondary and diminutive order of worship. Some are infinite in titles and offices; some are good, some bad. ^BThere are some that are old and broken, and some that are mortal; for Chrysippus thought that

in the last conflagration of the world all the gods were to perish except Jupiter.

ᶜMan fabricates a thousand ridiculous associations between God and himself. Is he not his compatriot?

> Crete, cradle of Jove.
>
> OVID

Here is the excuse that is given us, upon consideration of this matter, by Scaevola, a great pontiff, and Varro, a great theologian, in their day: "That it is necessary for the people to be ignorant of many true things and to believe many false ones." *Since he seeks the truth whereby he may be free, let us believe that it is expedient for him to be deceived* [Saint Augustine].

ᴮHuman eyes can perceive things only in the forms that they know. ᶜAnd we do not remember what a fall the wretched Phaeton took for having tried to manage the reins of his father's horses with a mortal hand. Our mind falls to the same depth, is shattered and bruised in the same way, through its temerity.

ᴮIf you ask philosophy of what material are the sky and the sun, what will she reply to you except of iron, or ᶜwith Anaxagoras ᴮof stone, or such-and-such a material that we use? ᶜYou ask Zeno what nature is? "A fire," he says, "craftsmanlike, able to create, proceeding by rule." ᴮArchimedes, master of that science which attributes to itself precedence over all the others in truth and certainty, says: "The sun is a god of flaming iron." Isn't that a fine bit of imagination, produced by the beauty and inevitable necessity of geometrical demonstrations? Yet not so inevitable ᶜand useful but that Socrates considered that it was sufficient if a man knew enough geometry to be able to measure the land he gave or received; and ᴮthat Polyaenus, who had been a famous and illustrious geometrician, took them in scorn as full of falsity and obvious vanity, after he had tasted the sweet fruits of the enervating gardens of Epicurus.

ᶜSocrates, in Xenophon, concerning that statement of Anaxagoras, who was esteemed by antiquity as wise above all others in things celestial and divine, says that his brain became troubled, as happens to all men who probe too deeply into knowledge that does not belong to them. As for his making the sun a glowing stone, he did not stop to think that a stone does not shine in the fire, and, what is worse, that it is consumed in it. As for his making the sun and fire one, he did not stop to think that fire does not blacken those

whom it looks on; that we can look fixedly at fire; that fire kills plants and herbs. In Socrates' opinion, and in mine too, the wisest way to judge heaven is not to judge it at all.

Plato, having to discuss daemons in the *Timaeus*, says: "That is an undertaking that is beyond our reach. We must believe those ancients who have said they were begotten by them. It is contrary to reason to refuse to have faith in the children of the gods, even though their statement is not established by necessary or plausible reasons, since they give us their word that they are speaking of domestic and family matters."

^A Let us see if we have the least bit more clarity in our knowledge of human and natural things.

Is it not a ridiculous undertaking, in those things which by our own confession our knowledge cannot reach, to go and forge another body for them and lend them a false shape of our invention; as is seen in the movement of the planets, wherein, since our mind cannot reach it nor imagine its natural course, we lend them, on our own part, material, gross, physical springs:

> Golden wheel rims, golden beam,
> And radiating spokes that silver gleam. OVID

You would think we had had coach makers, carpenters, and painters that went up there and set up machines with various movements, ^c and arranged the wheelwork and interlacings of the heavenly bodies, in motley colors, around the spindle of necessity, according to Plato:

> ^B The world is the tremendous home of things,
> Girt by five zones with lofty thunderings,
> Traversed obliquely by a fringe bedight
> With twice six constellations shining bright,
> Accepting the two coursers of the moon.
> VARRO

These are all dreams and fanatical follies. Why does it not please nature some day to open her bosom to us and reveal to us properly the means and conduct of her movements, and prepare our eyes for them? O Lord, what abuses, what mistakes we should find in our poor science! ^c I am mistaken if it grasps one single thing straight as it is; and I shall depart hence more ignorant of everything else than of my own ignorance.

Have I not seen in Plato this divine remark, that nature is nothing but an enigmatic poem?[44] As you might say a veiled and shadowy picture, shining through here and there with an infinite variety of false lights to exercise our conjectures. *All those things lie hidden and enveloped in such thick shadows that no human genius is keen enough to be able to penetrate into heaven or descend into the earth* [Cicero].

And indeed philosophy is but sophisticated poetry. Whence do these ancient authors derive all their authority, but from the poets? And the first ones were themselves poets, and treat of philosophy in their style. Plato is but a disconnected poet. Timon calls him, as an insult, a great miracle maker.

[A]Just as women wear ivory teeth where their natural ones are lacking, and in place of their real complexion fabricate one of some foreign matter; as they make themselves hips of cloth and felt, and flesh of cotton, and in the sight and knowledge of everyone, embellish themselves with a false and borrowed beauty; so does science [B](and even our law has, they say, legitimate fictions on which it founds the truth of its justice). [A]She gives us in payment and as presuppositions the things that she herself teaches us are invented; for those epicycles, eccentrics, concentrics, which astrology calls to its aid to conduct the movement of its stars, it gives us as the best it has succeeded in inventing on that subject. As also, for that matter, philosophy offers us not what is, or what it believes, but the most plausible and pleasant thing it forges.

[C]Plato, on the subject of the state of our body and that of the beasts: "We would state surely that what we have said is true if we had the confirmation of an oracle on the matter; we will state surely only that this is the most probable thing we could say."

[A]It is not to heaven alone that she sends her ropes, her machines, and her wheels. Let us consider a little what she says of ourselves and our make-up. There is no more retrogradation, trepidation, accession, recession, reversal, in the stars and heavenly bodies, than they have fabricated in this poor little human body. Truly they had good reason therefore to call it the little world,[45] so many pieces and facets have they used to plaster it and build it. To accommodate the impulses they see in man, the diverse functions and faculties that we sense in us, into how many parts have they divided our soul?

44 Plato's meaning was rather that poetry is by nature enigmatic.
45 Microcosm.

How many seats have they assigned to it? Into how many orders and stages have they split this poor man, besides the natural and perceptible ones, and into how many functions and occupations? They make him an imaginary republic.

He is a subject that they hold and handle; they are allowed full power to take him apart, rearrange him, reassemble him, and stuff him, each according to his fancy; and yet they still do not have him. Not only in reality, but even in daydreams they cannot so regulate him that there will not be some cadence or some sound that escapes their architecture, prodigious as it is, and patched with a thousand false and fantastic bits.

^CAnd it is not right to excuse them. For with painters, when they paint the sky, the earth, the seas, the mountains, the remote islands, we condone it if they represent to us only some slight indication of them; and, as with things unknown, we content ourselves with any sort of approximation and fiction. But when they draw from nature for us in a subject that is familiar and known to us, we demand of them a perfect and exact representation of the lineaments and colors, and we despise them if they fail.

^AI feel grateful to the Milesian wench who, seeing the philosopher Thales continually spending his time in contemplation of the heavenly vault and always keeping his eyes raised upward, put something in his way to make him stumble, to warn him that it would be time to amuse his thoughts with things in the clouds when he had seen to those at his feet. Indeed she gave him good counsel, to look rather to himself than to the sky. ^CFor as Democritus says by the mouth of Cicero,

No one looks underfoot, but at the stars.

^ABut our condition makes the knowledge of what we have in our hands as remote from us and as far above the clouds as that of the stars. ^CAs Socrates says in Plato, whoever meddles with philosophy may have the same reproach made to him as that woman makes to Thales, that he sees nothing of what is in front of him. For every philosopher is ignorant of what his neighbor is doing, yes, and of what he himself is doing, and does not know what they both are, whether beasts or men.

^AThese people, who think Sebond's reasons too weak, who are ignorant of nothing, who govern the world, who know everything –

What causes rule the sea, and what the year;
Whether the stars are governed in their flight;
What makes the moon grow dark or spread her light;
What this concordant strife wills and can do;

<div align="right">HORACE</div>

– have they not sometimes sounded, amid their books, the difficulties that present themselves in knowing their own being? We
see indeed that the finger moves, and that the foot moves; that
some parts stir of themselves without our leave, and that others we
move by our command; that a certain apprehension engenders
a blush, a certain other, pallor. One imagination acts only on the
spleen, another on the brain; one makes us laugh, another weep.
Another paralyzes and stuns all our senses, and arrests the movement of our limbs. ᶜAt one object the stomach rises; at another,
a certain part lower down.

ᴬBut how a spiritual impression can cut such a swath in a massive
and solid object, and the nature of the relation and connection
between these wonderful springs of action, no man has ever
known. ᶜ*All those things are indeterminable by reason and concealed
in the majesty of nature*, says Pliny; and Saint Augustine: *The way in
which souls cling to bodies is completely wonderful, and cannot be understood by man; and this is man himself.* ᴬAnd yet we never doubt this,
for men's opinions are accepted in the train of ancient beliefs, by
authority and on credit, as if they were religion and law. They accept
as by rote what is commonly held about it. They accept this truth,
with all its structure and apparatus of arguments and proofs, as a firm
and solid body, no longer shakable, no longer to be judged. On the
contrary everyone competes in plastering up and confirming this
accepted belief, with all the power of their reason, which is a supple
tool, pliable, and adaptable to any form. Thus the world is filled and
soaked with twaddle and lies.

The reason why we doubt hardly anything is that we never test
our common impressions. We do not probe the base, where the fault
and weakness lies; we dispute only about the branches. We do
not ask whether this is true, but whether it has been understood
this way or that. We do not ask whether Galen said anything worth
saying, but whether he said thus or otherwise. Indeed it was very
right that that bridle and constraint on the liberty of our judgments,
and that tyranny over our beliefs, extended even to the schools and
the arts.

The god of scholastic knowledge is Aristotle; it is a religious matter to discuss any of his ordinances, as with those of Lycurgus at Sparta. His doctrine serves us as magisterial law, when it is peradventure as false as another. I do not know why I would not as readily accept either the Ideas of Plato, or the Atoms of Epicurus, or the Fullness and Void of Leucippus and Democritus, or the Water of Thales, or the Infinity of Nature of Anaximander, or the Air of Diogenes, or the Numbers and Symmetry of Pythagoras, or the Infinite of Parmenides, or the One of Musaeus, or the Water and Fire of Apollodorus, or the Similar Parts of Anaxagoras, or the Discord and Friendship of Empedocles, or the Fire of Heraclitus, or any other opinion out of that infinite confusion of theories and views which this fine human reason produces by its certainty and clear-sightedness in everything it meddles with – as I should Aristotle's opinion on this subject of the principles of natural things: which principles he constructs of three parts, matter, form, and privation. And what could be more inane than to make emptiness itself the cause of the production of things? Privation is a negative; by what notion can he have made it the cause and origin of the things that are? This, however, no one would dare to shake, except as an exercise in logic. Nothing in it is discussed to be placed in doubt, but only to defend the author of the school from foreign objections; his authority is the end beyond which it is not permitted to inquire.

It is very easy, upon accepted foundations, to build what you please; for according to the law and ordering of this beginning, the rest of the parts of the building are easily done, without contradictions. By this path we find our reason well founded, and we argue with great ease. For our masters occupy and win beforehand as much room in our belief as they need in order to conclude afterward whatever they wish, in the manner of the geometricians with their axioms; the consent and approval that we lend them giving them the wherewithal to drag us left or right, and to spin us around at their will. Whoever is believed in his presuppositions, he is our master and our God; he will plant his foundations so broad and easy that by them he will be able to raise us, if he wants, up to the clouds.

In this trade and business of knowledge, we have taken for ready money the statement of Pythagoras, that each expert is to be believed in his craft. The logician refers to the grammarian for the meaning of words; the rhetorician borrows from the logician the subjects of his arguments; the poet from the musician his measures; the geometrician from the arithmetician his proportions;

the metaphysicians take as their foundation the conjectures of physics. For each science has its presupposed principles, by which human judgment is bridled on all sides. If you happen to crash this barrier in which lies the principal error, immediately they have this maxim in their mouth, that there is no arguing against people who deny first principles.

Now there cannot be first principles for men, unless the Divinity has revealed them; all the rest – beginning, middle, and end – is nothing but dreams and smoke. To those who fight by presupposition, we must presuppose the opposite of the same axiom we are disputing about. For every human presupposition and every enunciation has as much authority as another, unless reason shows the difference between them. Thus they must all be put in the scales, and first of all the general ones, and those which tyrannize over us. ᶜThe impression of certainty is a certain token of folly and extreme uncertainty; and there are no people more foolish, or less philosophical, than the "philodoxes"[46] of Plato.

ᴬWe must know whether fire is hot, whether snow is white, whether there is anything hard or soft within our knowledge. And as for those answers about which ancient stories are made, as when the man who doubted heat was told to throw himself into the fire, and when the one who denied the cold of ice was told to put some into his bosom: they are most unworthy of the philosophical profession. If they had left us in our natural state, receiving external impressions as they present themselves to us through our senses, and had let us follow our simple appetites, regulated by the condition of our birth, they would be right to speak thus. But it is from them that we have learned to make ourselves judges of the world; it is from them that we get this fancy, that human reason is controller-general of all that is outside and inside the heavenly vault, embracing everything, capable of everything, by means of which everything is known and understood.

This answer would be good among the cannibals, who enjoy the happiness of a long, tranquil, and peaceable life without the precepts of Aristotle and without acquaintance with the name of physics. This answer might perhaps be better and stronger than all those that they will borrow from their reason and their invention. Not only we ourselves, but all the animals, and everything over which the

46 Plato gives this name to people who fill their minds with opinions of whose grounds they are ignorant.

domination of natural law is still pure and simple, would be capable of using this answer; but they have renounced it.

They must not tell me: "It is true, for you see it and feel it so." They must tell me whether what I think I feel, I therefore actually do feel; and if I feel it, let them next tell me why I feel it, and how, and what I feel. Let them tell me the name, the origin, the ins and outs of heat and cold, the qualities of him who acts and of him who suffers; or let them abandon their profession, which is to accept or approve nothing except by the way of reason. That is their touchstone for every kind of experiment; but indeed it is a touchstone full of falsity, error, weakness, and impotence.

How do we want to test reason better than by herself? If we are not to believe her speaking of herself, she will hardly be fit to judge of alien things; if she knows anything, at least it will be her being and her domicile. She is in the soul, and a part or effect of it. For true and essential reason, whose name we steal on false pretenses, dwells in the bosom of God; there is her lair and her retreat, it is from there that she issues when God is pleased to let us see some ray of her, as Pallas sallied from the head of her father to communicate herself to the world.

Now let us see what human reason has taught us of herself and the soul. ᶜNot of the soul in general, in which nearly all philosophy makes the heavenly bodies and the prime bodies participants; nor of the soul that Thales attributed even to the things that are thought inanimate, led on by consideration of the magnet; but of the soul that belongs to us, and which we should know better:

> ᴮFor the soul's nature is unknown on earth,
> Whether 'tis born, or enters in at birth,
> Whether, by death destroyed, with us it dies,
> Or 'mid vast caves and shades of Orcus flies,
> Or, by divine decree, slips into beasts.
>
> LUCRETIUS

ᴬReason taught Crates and Dicaearchus that there was no soul at all, but that the body stirred thus by a natural movement; Plato, that it was a substance moving by itself; Thales, a nature without rest; Asclepiades, an exercising of the senses; Hesiod and Anaximander, a thing composed of earth and water; Parmenides, of earth and fire; Empedocles, of blood:

> He vomits up his soul of blood;
>
> VIRGIL

Posidonius, Cleanthes, and Galen, a warmth or warm disposition:

> They have a fiery vigor and a heavenly source;
>
> VIRGIL

Hippocrates, a spirit spread throughout the body; Varro, an air received by the mouth, warmed in the lungs, moistened in the heart, and spread throughout the body; Zeno, the quintessence of the four elements; Heraclides Ponticus, the light; Xenocrates and the Egyptians, a mobile number; the Chaldeans, a power without determined form:

> ᴮA certain vital habit of the body
> Which the Greeks call a harmony.
>
> LUCRETIUS

ᴬLet us not forget Aristotle: what naturally makes the body move is something which he calls entelechy – by as frigid an invention as any other, for he speaks of neither the essence, nor the origin, nor the nature of the soul, but merely notes its effect. Lactantius, Seneca, and the better part of the dogmatists have confessed that it was a thing they did not understand.

ᶜAnd after all this enumeration of opinions – *Of these opinions let some god decide which is true*, says Cicero – ᴬ"I know by myself," says Saint Bernard, "how incomprehensible God is, since I cannot understand the parts of my own being." ᶜHeraclitus, who held that everything was full of souls and daemons, maintained nevertheless that one could not advance so far toward the understanding of the soul as to attain it, so profound was its essence.

ᴬThere is no less dissension and dispute about locating it. Hippocrates and Hierophilus place it in the ventricle of the brain; Democritus and Aristotle, throughout the body;

> ᴮAs in the body health is said to dwell,
> Though not a part of man, however well;
>
> LUCRETIUS

ᴬEpicurus, in the stomach:

> ᴮFor here terror and fear abound; near here
> Joys give us cheer.
>
> LUCRETIUS

ᴬThe Stoics, around and within the heart; Erasistratus, adjoining the membrane of the epicranium; Empedocles, in the blood; as also

494 ESSAYS

Moses, which was the reason he forbade eating the blood of animals, to which their soul is joined; Galen thought that each part of the body has its soul; Strato located it between the two eyebrows.

^C*What the form of the soul may be, or where it may dwell, must not even be inquired into*, says Cicero. I gladly leave this man his own words. Should I go changing the speech of eloquence? Besides, there is little profit in stealing the substance of his ideas: they are none too frequent, none too stout, and none too unknown.

^ABut the reason Chrysippus argues that it is around the heart, like the others of his sect, is not to be forgotten: "It is," he says, "because when we wish to assure someone of something, we put our hand on our stomach; and when we wish to pronounce ἐγώ, which means I, we drop the lower jaw toward the stomach." This bit should not be passed by without noting the inanity of so great a person. For besides the fact that these considerations are infinitely light in themselves, the latter one proves only to the Greeks that they have their soul in that place. There is no human judgment so alert but that sometimes it slumbers.

^CWhat are we afraid to say? Look at the Stoics, the fathers of human wisdom, who find that the soul of a man crushed under a ruin struggles and strains a long time to free itself, unable to get free of its burden, like a mouse caught in a trap.

Some hold that the world was made to give a body, as a punishment, to spirits fallen, by their own fault, from the purity in which they had been created, the first creation having been only incorporeal; and that according as they have come away more or less from their spirituality, they are more or less lightly or heavily incorporated. Thence comes the variety of so much created matter. But the spirit which, for its punishment, was invested with the body of the sun, must have had a most rare and particular measure of change.

The extremes of our investigations always fall finally into dazzlement; as Plutarch says of the beginning of histories, that as in maps, the farthest limits of known lands are occupied by swamps, deep forests, deserts, and uninhabitable places. That is why the grossest and most childish daydreams are most often found in those who treat higher things and treat them more deeply, becoming engulfed by their curiosity and presumption. The end and the beginning of knowledge are equal in stupidity.

See Plato soaring upward into his poetical clouds, see in his work the jargon of the gods. But what was he dreaming of when

^Ahe defined man as a two-legged animal without feathers, furnishing those who wanted to laugh at him with a comical opportunity? For having plucked a live capon, they went around calling it "Plato's man."

And what of the Epicureans? By what simplicity did they first go and imagine that their atoms, which they said were bodies having some weight and a natural movement downward, had built the world; until it was called to their attention by their adversaries that according to this description it was not possible for them to join and hold together, their fall being thus straight and perpendicular and producing parallel lines everywhere? Wherefore they were forced to add later a sideways, fortuitous movement, and also to furnish their atoms with curved and hooked tails, to make them capable of attaching themselves together and intertwining.

^CAnd even then, do not those who pursue them with this other consideration put them in trouble? If the atoms have, by chance, formed so many sorts of figures, why have they never happened to meet to make a house, or a shoe? Why do we not believe likewise that an infinite number of Greek letters scattered about the place would be capable of forming the web of the *Iliad*?

What is capable of reason, says Zeno, is better than what is not capable of it; there is nothing better than the world; therefore it is capable of reason. Cotta, by this same argument, makes the world a mathematician; and makes it a musician and organist by this other argument, also of Zeno: The whole is greater than the part; we are capable of wisdom, and parts of the world: therefore it is wise.

^AWe see innumerable similar examples of arguments not only false, but inept and inconsistent – arguments that accuse their authors not so much of ignorance as of witlessness – in the reproaches that the philosophers make to one another regarding the dissensions of their opinions and their schools. ^CAnyone who shrewdly gleaned an accumulation of the asininities of human wisdom would have wonders to tell.

I collect them with enjoyment as a display no less useful to consider, from a certain point of view, than sane and moderate opinions. ^ALet us judge from this what we are to think of man, his sense and his reason, since in these great men, who carried human capacity so high, are found such gross and apparent weak spots.

For myself, I prefer to believe that they treated knowledge casually, like a toy to play around with, and amused themselves

with reason as with a vain and frivolous instrument, putting forward all sorts of notions and fancies, sometimes more studied, sometimes more loose. This same Plato who defines man as he would a chicken, says elsewhere, after Socrates, that in truth he does not know what man is, and that he is one part of the world as difficult as any to know.

By this variety and instability of opinions they lead us as by the hand, tacitly, to this conclusion of their inconclusiveness. By profession they do not always present their opinion openly and apparently; they have hidden it now in the fabulous shades of poetry, now under some other mask. For our imperfection also provides this, that raw meat is not always fit for our stomach; it must be dried, altered, and corrupted. They do the same: they sometimes obscure their natural opinions and judgments and falsify them to accommodate themselves to public usage. They do not want openly to profess ignorance and the imbecility of human reason, ^cso as not to frighten the children; ^Abut they reveal it to us clearly enough under the guise of a muddled and inconsistent knowledge.

^BIn Italy I advised a man who was at pains to speak Italian, that provided he sought only to make himself understood, without wishing to excel at it otherwise, he should simply use the first words that came to his mouth, Latin, French, Spanish, or Gascon; and that by adding the Italian ending, he would never fail to hit some dialect of the country, either Tuscan, or Roman, or Venetian, or Piedmontese, or Neapolitan, and to meet some one out of so many forms.

I say the same thing about philosophy; it has so many faces and so much variety, and has said so much, that all our dreams or reveries are found in it. Human fancy cannot conceive anything good or evil that is not in it. ^c*Nothing so absurd can be said that it has not been said by some philosopher* [Cicero]. ^BAnd I let fly my caprices all the more freely in public, inasmuch as, although they are born with me and without a model, I know that they will find their relation to some ancient notion; and someone will not fail to say: "That is where he got it."

^cMy behavior is natural; I have not called in the help of any teaching to build it. But feeble as it is, when the desire to tell it seized me, and when, to make it appear in public a little more decently, I set myself to support it with reasons and examples, it was a marvel to myself to find it, simply by chance, in conformity with so many philosophical examples and reasons. What rule my life

belonged to, I did not learn until after it was completed and spent. A new figure: an unpremeditated and accidental philosopher!

^ATo return to our soul.[47] When Plato located reason in the brain, anger in the heart, and cupidity in the liver, it is probable that it was rather an interpretation of the movements of the soul that he wanted to make than a division and separation of it, as of a body into many members. And the most plausible of their opinions is that it is always a soul which, by its faculty, reasons, remembers, understands, judges, desires, and exercises all its other operations, by various instruments of the body: as the pilot steers his ship according to his experience of it, now tightening or slackening a rope, now hoisting the lateen yard or plying the oar; by one single power carrying out various actions. And that it is located in the brain, which is apparent from the fact that the wounds and accidents that affect this part immediately harm the faculties of the soul; from there it is not strange that it spreads through the rest of the body –

> ^CFrom heaven's highroad Phoebus never strays,
> But lights up all things with his golden rays;
>
> CLAUDIAN

– ^Aas the sun spreads from heaven outward its light and its powers, and fills the world with them:

> ^BThe soul's remainder, through the body spread,
> Obeys the mind, and by the mind is led.
>
> LUCRETIUS

^ASome have said that there was one general soul, like a great body, from which all the individual souls were extracted and to which they returned, always mingling again with this universal matter:

> For God, they say, in all is found:
> The land, the ocean vast, the sky profound;
> From him the flocks, the herds, wild beasts, and man,
> Each draw at birth their life's short tenuous span;
> To him all things return again, undone;
> Death there is none.
>
> VIRGIL

47 The editions published in Montaigne's lifetime add here: "(for I have chosen this single example as the most convenient to prove our weakness and vanity)."

Others, that they only rejoined it and reattached themselves to it; others, that they were produced from the divine substance; others, by angels, from fire and air. Some, that they exist from all antiquity; some, at the very time of need. Some make them descend from the moon's orbit and return to it. Most of the ancients, that they are engendered from father to son, in a similar manner of production to that of all other natural things; arguing this from the resemblance of children to fathers:

> Your father's virtue into you instilled;
> AUTHOR UNKNOWN

> The brave are of the brave and worthy born;
> HORACE

and from the fact that from fathers to children are seen to flow not only bodily marks, but also a resemblance in humors, in disposition, and in inclinations of the soul:

> Why, lastly, is the lions' race imbued
> With raging anger; why are foxes shrewd;
> Why do the deer inherit fear and speed;
> Unless some power of mind, sprung of its seed,
> Grows with the body at an equal pace?
> LUCRETIUS

that thereupon is founded divine justice, punishing in the children the fault of the fathers; inasmuch as the contagion of the paternal vices is to some extent imprinted on the soul of the children, and the unrulines of the fathers' will affects them.

Moreover, that if souls came from anything but a natural succession, and had been something else outside of the body, they would have a memory of their first existence, considering the natural faculties that are proper to them, of reflecting, reasoning, and remembering:

> [B]If then it slips into the body at its birth,
> Why do we not recall our bygone life on earth,
> And keep at least some traces of the things we did?
> LUCRETIUS

[A]For to value the condition of our souls as highly as we want to, we must presuppose them to be wholly knowing when they are in their natural simplicity and purity. Thus they would have been such, being free from the corporeal prison, as much before entering it as

we hope they will be after they have gone out of it. And this knowledge they would have to remember still while in the body, as Plato said that what we learned was only a recollection of what we had known; a thing which each man by experience can maintain to be false. In the first place, because we recollect only precisely what we are taught, and if memory were doing its job purely, it would at least suggest to us some point beyond what we have learned. Second, what it knew when it was in its purity was a real knowledge, by its divine intelligence understanding things as they are, whereas here it is made to receive falsehood and vice, if it is instructed about them. In this it cannot use its power of reminiscence, this idea and conception never having lodged in it.

To say that the corporeal prison stifles its natural faculties in such a way that they are wholly extinguished, is in the first place contrary to this other belief, that recognizes its powers to be so great, and the workings of it that men feel in this life so admirable, as to have concluded its divinity and eternity in the past, and immortality to come:

> [B]For if the power of mind has been so changed
> That all remembrance of the past has fled,
> That is not far, methinks, from being dead.
> LUCRETIUS

[A]Furthermore, it is here in us, and not elsewhere, that the powers and actions of the soul should be considered. All the rest of its perfections are vain and useless to it; it is for its present state that all its immortal life is to be paid and rewarded, and for man's life that it is solely accountable. It would be an injustice to have cut short its resource and powers; to have disarmed it, and to pass judgment and a sentence of infinite and perpetual duration upon it, for the time of its captivity and imprisonment, its weakness and illness, the time when it was forced and constrained; and to stop at the consideration of so short a time, perhaps one or two hours, or at worst a century, which is no more in proportion to infinity than an instant; in order, from this moment of interval, to decide and dispose definitively of its whole existence. It would be an inequitable disproportion to receive eternal compensation in consequence of so short a life.

[C]Plato, to escape this difficulty, wants future payments limited to the duration of a hundred years, corresponding to the duration of human life; and plenty of our contemporaries have given them temporal limits.

[A]Thus they judged that the generation of the soul followed the common condition of human things, as also its life, in the opinion of Epicurus and Democritus, which has been the most widely accepted, according to this fine evidence: that they saw that it was born at the moment the body was capable of receiving it; that its powers were seen to grow with those of the body; that they could recognize the weakness of its infancy, and, with time, its vigor and maturity, then its decline and old age, and finally its decrepitude:

> We feel the soul is with the body born,
> Grows up with it, and with it waxes old.
>
> LUCRETIUS

They perceived it to be capable of diverse passions and agitated by many painful emotions, through which it fell into lassitude and pain; capable of alteration and change, of blitheness, drowsiness, and languor; subject to its own sicknesses and to wounds, like the stomach or the foot:

> [B]Like the body, so the mind
> Is healed and cured by medicine, we find;
>
> LUCRETIUS

[A]dazed and muddled by the power of wine; displaced from its seat by the vapors of a hot fever; put to sleep by the application of certain medicaments, and aroused by others:

> [B]That mind must be corporeal is quite plain,
> Since darts and thrusts corporeal give it pain.
>
> LUCRETIUS

[A]They saw all its faculties stunned and overthrown by the mere bite of a sick dog, and that it had no such great stability of reason, no capacity, no virtue, no philosophical resolution, no tension of its powers, that could exempt it from subjection to these accidents. The saliva of a wretched mastiff, spilled on Socrates' hand, could shake all his wisdom and all his great and well-regulated ideas, and annihilate them in such a way that no trace would remain of his former knowledge:

> [B]The power of the soul
> Is troubled and, asunder cleft,
> Is all dispelled, by that same poison reft.
>
> LUCRETIUS

ᴬAnd this venom would find no more resistance in this soul than in that of a child of four; a venom capable of making all philosophy, if it were incarnate, raving mad. So that Cato, who twisted the neck of death itself and of fortune, could not have endured the sight of a mirror or of water, would have been crushed with terror and fright, if he had come down, by the contagion of a mad dog, with the disease that the doctors call hydrophobia:

> ᴮThe power of the disease, spread through the limbs,
> Troubles the soul, as on the salty ocean
> Waves foam and boil beneath the winds' commotion.
> LUCRETIUS

ᴬNow as for this point, philosophy has armed man well for suffering all other accidents, either with patience, or, if it costs too much to find, with an infallible riddance, that of escaping sensation completely. But these are means which are useful for a soul that is its own master and in its power, capable of reason and deliberation; not for that misfortune where, in a philosopher, a soul becomes the soul of a madman, troubled, overturned, and lost; which many occasions bring about, such as too vehement an agitation, which, by some strong passion, the soul can engender in itself, or a wound in a certain part of the person, or an exhalation from the stomach, casting us into bewilderment and dizziness:

> ᴮOft when the body ails, the mind will stray,
> Raving and ranting in a senseless way;
> Sometimes a lethargy will bear it deep,
> Eyes closed, head nodding, into endless sleep.
> LUCRETIUS

ᴬThe philosophers, it seems to me, have hardly touched this chord.
 ᶜNo more than another of like importance. They always have this dilemma in their mouths to console us for our mortal condition: "The soul is either mortal or immortal. If mortal, it will be without pain; if immortal, it will go on improving." They never touch the other branch: "What if it goes on getting worse?" And they leave to the poets the threats of future punishments. But by this they give themselves a good hand to play. These are two omissions which often strike me in their arguments. I return to the first.⁴⁸

48 The vulnerability of even the strongest soul.

^A^This soul loses the taste for the sovereign good of the Stoics, so constant and so firm. Our fine wisdom at this point must surrender and give up its arms. Moreover, through the vanity of human reason, they also considered that the mixture and association of two parts so different as the mortal and the immortal was unimaginable:

> For surely it is utter madness to combine
> A mortal thing with an eternal, and opine
> That both can feel and act as one. What more detached
> Can we imagine, more repugnant, more ill-matched,
> Than an immortal and a mortal thing, together,
> Trying to stay united through the fiercest weather?
>
> LUCRETIUS

Furthermore they felt that the soul was involved in death, like the body:

> ^B^It also sinks, weary with age;
>
> LUCRETIUS

^C^which, according to Zeno, the likeness of sleep shows us clearly enough; for he believes this is a fainting, and a fall of the soul as well as of the body: *He thinks that the soul is dragged down, and slips, as it were, and falls* [Cicero]. ^A^And the fact that in some its strength and vigor were seen to be maintained to the end of life, they attributed to the diversity of diseases; since men in this extremity are seen, one to retain one sense, one another, one his hearing, one his sense of smell, without alteration; and no such universal enfeeblement is seen but that some parts remain entire and vigorous:

> ^B^Just as a sick man's foot may well be racked
> With pain, while still his head remains intact.
>
> LUCRETIUS

The vision of our judgment is related to the truth as is the eye of the owl to the splendor of the sun, as Aristotle says. How could we convict it better than for such gross blindness in such a shining light?

^A^For the contrary belief, of the immortality of the soul, ^C^which Cicero says was first introduced, at least according to the testimony of books, by Pherecydes of Syros, in the time of King Tullus (others attribute the invention to Thales, others to others), ^A^is the part of human knowledge treated with most reservation and doubt. The

firmest dogmatists are constrained, principally on this point, to flee back to shelter in the shades of the Academy. No one knows what Aristotle has decided on this matter; ^cany more than all the ancients in general, who handle it with a wavering belief: *a most gratifying thing, which they promise rather than prove* [Seneca]. ^AHe hid beneath a cloud of difficult and unintelligible words and meanings, and left his adherents as much room for debate about his judgment as about the matter itself.

Two things made this opinion plausible to them: one, that without the immortality of the soul there would be no more basis for the vain hopes of glory, which is a consideration with marvelous credit in the world; the other, that, ^cas Plato says, ^Ait is a very useful impression that vices, even if they escape the dim and uncertain sight of human justice, will always remain a target for divine justice, which will pursue them even after the death of the guilty.

^cMan is possessed by an extreme concern with prolonging his existence; he has provided for it with all his faculties. For the preservation of the body there are sepulchers; for the preservation of the name, glory. Impatient with his fortune, he has used all his wits to rebuild himself and prop himself up with his inventions. The soul, through its confusion and weakness being unable to stand on its own feet, goes looking everywhere for consolations, hopes, and foundations in external circumstances where it clings and takes root; and, flimsy and fantastic as its imagination may create them, it rests more assured in them than in itself, and more gladly.

^ABut those most obstinate in this most just and clear persuasion of the immortality of our spirit, it is a marvel how they have fallen short and found themselves powerless to prove it by their human powers: ^c*They are dreams, not of a teacher, but of a wisher*, an ancient used to say.[49] ^AMan may recognize by this token that he owes to fortune and chance the truth that he discovers by himself; since even when it has fallen into his hand, he has not the ability to grasp it and keep it, and his reason has not the power to take advantage of it. All things produced by our own reason and ability, the true as well as the false, are subject to uncertainty and debate. It was for the chastisement of our pride and the instruction of our wretchedness and incapacity that God produced the disorder and confusion of the ancient tower of Babel.

49 Cicero.

All that we undertake without his assistance, all that we see without the lamp of his grace, is only vanity and folly. The very essence of truth, which is uniform and constant, we corrupt and adulterate by our weakness when fortune gives us possession of it. Whatever course man takes by himself, God allows him always to arrive at that same confusion, the picture of which he shows us so vividly by the just chastisement with which he beat down the arrogance of Nimrod and annihilated his vain enterprise in building his pyramid; *C I will destroy the wisdom of the wise, and will bring to nothing the understanding of the prudent* [I Corinthians].

A The diversity of idioms and languages with which he troubled that work, what else is it but that infinite and perpetual altercation and discordance of opinions and reasons, which accompanies and embroils the vain construction of human knowledge? *C* And embroils it usefully. What would hold us in, if we had one grain of knowledge?

This saint gave me great pleasure: *This very concealment of what is useful is either an exercise in humility or an attrition of pride* [Saint Augustine]. To what point of presumption and insolence do we not carry our blindness and our stupidity?

A But to resume my subject, it was really quite right that we should be beholden to God alone, and to the benefit of his grace, for the truth of so noble a belief, since from his liberality alone we receive the fruit of immortality, which consists in the enjoyment of eternal beatitude.

C Let us confess frankly that God alone has told us so, and faith; for a lesson of nature and of our reason it is not. And whoever will test his nature and his powers again and again, both inside and out, without this divine privilege; whoever will see man without flattering him, will see in him neither efficacy nor any faculty that savors of anything but death and earth. The more we give, and owe, and render to God, the more like Christians we act.

What this Stoic philosopher says he holds from the accidental consensus of the voice of the people, would it not have been better if he had held it from God? *When we discuss the eternity of souls, the agreement of men who either fear or honor the infernal powers is of no small moment to us. I adopt this public belief* [Seneca].

A Now the weakness of human arguments on this subject is particularly recognizable by the fabulous circumstances that they have added, consequent to this opinion, in order to discover what was the nature of our immortality. *C* Let us leave aside the Stoics –

they bestow on us a long life, as to the crows: our souls will last for a long time, they say; forever, they deny [Cicero] – who give souls a life beyond this one, but finite. ᴬThe most universal and accepted opinion, which remains to our day in various places, was the one of which they make Pythagoras the author; not that he was its first inventor, but because it received much weight and credit through the authority of his approbation. It is that our souls, on leaving us, did nothing but roll from one body to another, from a lion to a horse, from a horse to a king, thus strolling unceasingly from house to house. ᶜAnd he himself said that he remembered having been Aethalides, then Euphorbus, after that Hermotimus, finally having passed from Pyrrhus into Pythagoras; having a memory of himself for two hundred and six years.

Some added that these souls at times mount up to heaven again, and then come down again:

> O father, must we think some souls rise hence
> To heaven, then return to bodies dense?
> Poor souls, whence comes this baneful lust for light?
> VIRGIL

Origen makes them come and go eternally between the good and the bad state. The opinion that Varro reports is that in a cycle of four hundred and forty years they rejoin their first body; Chrysippus, that this must happen after a certain unlimited space of time. Plato, who says that he holds from Pindar and ancient poetry this belief in the infinite vicissitudes of change in which the soul is prepared – its punishments and its rewards in the other world being only temporary, as its life in this one is only temporary – concludes that it has a singular knowledge of the affairs of heaven, of hell, and of this world where it has passed to and fro and sojourned on many trips: matter for its recollection.

Here is its progress elsewhere: "He who has lived well rejoins the star to which he is assigned; he who has lived badly changes into a woman, and if even then he does not reform, he changes back into an animal of a kind suitable to his vicious ways, and he will see no end to his punishments until he has returned to his natural constitution, having rid himself by the power of reason of the gross, stupid, and elemental qualities that were in him."⁵⁰

50 From Plato's *Timaeus*.

^ABut I do not want to forget the objection that the Epicureans make to this transmigration from one body to another. It is amusing. They ask what order there would be if the throng of the dying came to be greater than that of those being born; for the souls dislodged from their abode would be trampling each other to get the first places in this new receptacle. And they also ask how they would spend their time while they were waiting for a lodging to be made ready for them. Or, on the other hand, if more animals were born than died, they say that the bodies would be in a bad way, awaiting the infusion of their soul; and it would come about that some of these would die before they had been alive:

> Lastly, it seems absurd that souls should stand
> Beside the marriage bed, ready at hand,
> And at the birth of beasts; that without end
> For mortal husks immortals should contend,
> As in a race, to beat the others in.

LUCRETIUS

Others have kept the soul in the body of the deceased, therewith to animate the serpents, worms, and other beasts that are said to be engendered of the corruption of our members, and even of our ashes. Others divide it into one mortal part and another immortal part. Others make it corporeal, and none the less immortal. Some make it immortal, without knowledge and without understanding.

There are also some who have thought that of the souls of the damned, devils are made – ^cand some of our religion have concluded thus – ^Aeven as Plutarch thinks that gods are made of those that are saved; for there are few things that that author asserts in such decisive words as he does this, maintaining everywhere else a doubting and ambiguous manner. "We must think," he says, "and firmly believe that the souls of men who are virtuous according to nature and divine justice change from men to saints, and from saints to demigods; and from demigods, after they are perfectly cleansed and purified, as in the sacrifices of purgation, being delivered from all capacity for suffering and from all mortality, they become, not by any civil ordinance, but in truth and in accordance with credible reason, entire and perfect gods, thereby receiving a very happy and very glorious end."

But if anyone wants to see him, who is nevertheless one of the most restrained and moderate of the lot, skirmishing with greater hardihood and telling us his miracles on the subject, I refer him to

his discourses "On the Moon" and "On the Daemon of Socrates," where it can be verified as clearly as anywhere else that the mysteries of philosophy have many strange things in common with those of poetry; the human understanding losing its way in trying to sound and examine all things to the utmost, just as we, tired and worn out by the long course of our life, fall back into childishness.

There are the fine and certain teachings that we derive from human knowledge on the subject of our soul.

There is no less rashness in what it teaches us about our bodily parts. Let us choose one or two examples, for otherwise we should lose ourselves in that vast and troubled sea of medical errors.

Let us learn whether they agree at least on this, from what matter men produce one another. ᶜFor as for their original production, it is no wonder if in a thing so lofty and ancient, the human understanding is troubled and dissipated. Archelaus the natural philosopher, of whom, according to Aristoxenus, Socrates was the disciple and darling, said that both men and animals were made from a milky slime squeezed out by the heat of the earth.

ᴬPythagoras says that our seed is the foam of our best blood. Plato, the flow from the marrow of the backbone, which he argues from the fact that this spot first feels the fatigue of the business. Alcmaeon, a part of the substance of the brain; and a sign that this is so, he says, is that the eyes grow dim in those who work immoderately at this exercise. Democritus, a substance extracted from the whole mass of the body; Epicurus, extracted from the soul and the body. Aristotle, an excrement derived from the nourishment of the blood, the last that spreads through our members. Others, blood cooked and digested by the heat of the genitals, which they judge from the fact that in extreme efforts men give out drops of pure blood; wherein there seems to be more probability, if any probability can be derived from such infinite confusion.

Now, to get results from this seed, how many contradictory opinions do they form! Aristotle and Democritus maintain that women have no sperm, and that it is only a sweat that they discharge in the heat of the pleasure and the movement, which contributes nothing toward generation; Galen and his followers, on the contrary, that without the meeting of seeds, generation cannot take place.

Here you see the doctors, the philosophers, the jurists, and the theologians at grips with our wives, pell-mell, in the dispute over how long women carry their fruit. And myself, I back up, with my

own example, those of them who maintain the possibility of an eleven months' pregnancy. The world is built of this experience; there is no little woman so simple that she may not have her say about all these contested matters; and still we cannot come to an agreement.

This is enough to prove that man is no more versed in the understanding of himself in the physical part than in the spiritual. We have set him up before himself, and his reason before his reason, to see what it would tell us about it. It seems to me that I have sufficiently demonstrated how little his reason understands about itself.

^CAnd he who understands nothing about himself, what can he understand? *As if he could really take the measure of anything, who knows not his own* [Pliny].

Truly Protagoras was telling us some good ones, making man the measure of all things, who never even knew his own. If it is not he, his dignity will not permit another creature to have this advantage. Now, he being in himself so contradictory, and one judgment incessantly subverting another, that favorable proposition was just a joke which led us necessarily to conclude the nullity of the compass and the compasser.

When Thales thinks that the knowledge of man is very difficult for man, he teaches him that the knowledge of any other thing is impossible for him.

[WARNING TO THE PRINCESS]

^AYou,⁵¹ for whom I have taken the pains to extend so long a work contrary to my custom, will not shrink from upholding your Sebond by the ordinary form of argument in which you are instructed every day, and in that you will exercise your mind and your learning. For this final fencer's trick must not be employed except as an extreme remedy. It is a desperate stroke, in which you must abandon your weapons to make your adversary lose his, and a secret trick that must be used rarely and reservedly. It is great rashness to ruin yourself in order to ruin another.

^BWe must not want to die in order to take revenge, as did Gobrias: for when he was at very close grips with a Persian lord,

51 This entire essay is addressed almost certainly to Margaret of Valois, daughter of Henry II and Catherine de' Medici and wife of Henry of Navarre, the future Henry IV of France.

and Darius came up sword in hand but feared to strike for fear of hitting Gobrias, he called to him to lay on boldly even if he should run them both through.

ᶜWeapons and conditions of combat so desperate that it is unbelievable that either party should escape, I have known to be condemned when offered. The Portuguese took fourteen Turks in the Indian Ocean, who, impatient of their captivity, resolved, and successfully, to reduce themselves and their captors and the vessel to ashes by rubbing some ship's nails together, until a spark fell on the barrels of gunpowder that were at hand.

ᴬHere we are shaking the barriers and last fences of knowledge, in which extremity is a vice, as in virtue. Stay on the highroad; it is no good to be so subtle and clever. Remember what the Tuscan proverb says: *He who grows too keen cuts himself* [Petrarch].

In your opinions and remarks, as well as in your conduct and everything else, I advise moderation and temperance, and avoidance of novelty and strangeness. All eccentric ways irritate me. You who, by the authority that your greatness brings you, and still more by the advantages which the qualities that are more your own give you, can by the flicker of an eye command whomever you please, should have given this assignment to some professional man of letters, who would have supported and enriched this theme for you in quite another way. However, here is enough for your needs.

Epicurus used to say of the laws that the worst were so necessary that without them men would devour one another. ᶜAnd Plato, very close, says that without laws we should live like brutish animals; and he tries to prove it.

ᴬOur mind is an erratic, dangerous, and heedless tool; it is hard to impose order and moderation upon it. And in my time those who have some rare excellence beyond the others, and some extraordinary quickness, are nearly all, we see, incontinent in the license of their opinions and conduct. It is a miracle if you find a sedate and sociable one.

People are right to give the tightest possible barriers to the human mind. In study, as in everything else, its steps must be counted and regulated for it; the limits of the chase must be artificially determined for it. They bridle and bind it with religions, laws, customs, science, precepts, mortal and immortal punishments and rewards; and still we see that by its whirling and its incohesiveness it escapes all these bonds. It is an empty body, with nothing

by which it can be seized and directed; a varying and formless body, which can be neither tied nor grasped.

[B]Indeed there are few souls so orderly, so strong and wellborn, that they can be trusted with their own guidance, and that can sail with moderation and without temerity, in the freedom of their judgments, beyond the common opinions. It is more expedient to place them in tutelage.

The mind is a dangerous blade, [c]even to its possessor, [A]for anyone who does not know how to wield it with order and discretion. [c]And there is no animal that must more rightly be given blinkers to hold its gaze, in subjection and constraint, in front of its feet, and to keep it from straying here or there outside the ruts that custom and the laws trace for it.

[A]Wherefore it will become you better to confine yourself to the accustomed routine, whatever it is, than to fly headlong into this unbridled license. But if one of these new doctors tries to show off his ingenuity in your presence, at the risk of his salvation and yours; to rid yourself of this dangerous pestilence that spreads day by day in your courts, this preservative, in case of extreme necessity, will keep the contagion of that poison from harming either you or the others present.

[MAN CAN HAVE NO KNOWLEDGE]

Thus the liberty and wantonness of these ancient minds produced, in philosophy and the knowledge of man, many schools of different opinions, each undertaking to decide and choose in order to take sides. But now [c]that men all go one pace – *who are addicted and devoted to certain set and fixed opinions, so that they are forced to defend even those things which they do not approve* [Cicero] – now [A]that we receive the arts by civil authority and ordinance, [c]so that the schools have only one pattern, similar teaching, and a circumscribed curriculum, [A]men no longer consider what the coins weigh and are worth, but each one in turn accepts them according to the value that common approbation and their currency give them. Men do not argue about the alloy, but about the rate of exchange: thus all things are accepted equally. They accept medicine as they do geometry; and sleight-of-hand, enchantments, ligatures,[52] communication with the spirits of the dead, prognostications, horoscopy,

52 Magic spells to cause impotence.

and even that ridiculous pursuit of the philosopher's stone, every-
thing is admitted without contradiction.

A man need only know that the seat of Mars is located in the
middle of the triangle of the hand, that of Venus on the thumb, that
of Mercury on the little finger; that when the heart line cuts the
tubercle of the index finger, it is a sign of cruelty; and that when it
comes to an end under the middle finger, and when the natural
median line forms an angle with the life line under the same spot, it
is a sign of a miserable death. That if, in a woman, the natural line is
open, and does not close the angle with the life line, it denotes that
she will be unchaste. I call you yourself to witness, whether with
this knowledge a man may not pass in any company with reputation
and favor.

Theophrastus said that human knowledge, forwarded by the
senses, could judge the causes of things to a certain extent; but
that having reached the ultimate and original causes, it had to stop
and be blunted, because of its weakness or the difficulty of things. It
is a moderate and pleasant opinion that our capacity can lead us to
the knowledge of some things, and that it has definite limits to its
power, beyond which it is temerity to employ it. This opinion is
plausible and presented by conciliatory people; but it is not easy to
set limits to our mind: it is curious and insatiable, and has no
occasion to stop at a thousand paces any more than at fifty.

Having found by experience that where one man had failed,
another has succeeded, and that what was unknown to one century
the following century has made clear, and that the sciences and arts
are not cast in a mold, but are formed and shaped little by little, by
repeated handling and polishing, as the bears lick their cubs into
shape at leisure, I do not leave off sounding and testing what my
powers cannot discover; and by handling again and kneading this
new material, stirring it and heating it, I open up to whoever follows
me some facility to enjoy it more at his ease, and make it more
supple and manageable for him:

> As Hymettian wax grows softer in the sun,
> Takes many shapes when molded by the thumb,
> And thus by usage useful does become.
>
> OVID

The second will do as much for the third; which is the reason why
difficulty should not make me despair, nor my impotence either, for
it is only my own.

Man is as capable of all things as he is of any. And if he confesses, as Theophrastus says, ignorance of first causes and principles, let him boldly give up all the rest of his knowledge. If his foundation is lacking, his argument is flat on the ground. Discussion and inquiry have no other aim and limit but principles; if this terminus does not stop their course, they fling themselves into infinite irresolution. ^C*One thing cannot be more or less understood than another, because there is only one definition of comprehension for everything* [Cicero].

^ANow it is likely that if the soul knew anything, it would first of all know itself; and if it knew anything outside of itself, that would be its body and shell before anything else. If we see even to this day the gods of medicine disputing about our anatomy,

> Vulcan against, Apollo for Troy stood,
>
> OVID

when do we expect them to agree? We are nearer to ourselves than the whiteness of snow or the weight of stone are to us. If man does not know himself, how does he know his functions and powers? Not that it is impossible that some true knowledge may dwell in us; but if it does, it does so by accident. And since by the same road, the same manner and process, errors are received into our soul, it has no way to distinguish them or to pick out truth from falsehood.

The Academics allowed some inclination of the judgment, and thought it too crude to say that it was no more likely that snow was white than black, and that we were no more assured of the movement of a stone that leaves our hand than of that of the eighth sphere. And to avoid this difficulty and strangeness, which in truth cannot lodge in our imagination at all easily; although they affirmed that we were not at all capable of knowing, and that truth is engulfed in deep abysses where human sight cannot penetrate, still they admitted that some things were more probable than others, and allowed their judgment the faculty of inclining rather to one probability than to another: they allowed it this leaning, though forbidding it any decision.

The position of the Pyrrhonians is bolder and at the same time more plausible. For that Academic inclination, and that leaning toward one proposition rather than another, what else is it but the recognition of some more apparent truth in this one than in that? If our understanding is capable of grasping the form, the lineaments, the carriage, and the face of truth, it would see it whole just as well as half there, nascent and imperfect. That appearance of likelihood

which makes them lean rather to the left than to the right – increase it; that ounce of likelihood that inclines the scales – multiply it by a hundred, by a thousand ounces: the final outcome will be that the scales will take sides completely, and settle on one choice and one entire truth.

But how can they let themselves be inclined toward the likeness of truth, if they know not the truth? How do they know the semblance of that whose essence they do not know? Either we can judge absolutely, or we absolutely cannot. If our intellectual and sensory faculties are without foundation and footing, if they do nothing but float and flutter, then to no purpose do we let our judgment be carried away by any part of their operation, whatever likelihood it may seem to offer us; and the surest attitude of our understanding, and the happiest, would be that in which it maintained itself poised, upright, inflexible, without motion and without agitation. *Between true or false appearances there is no difference that affects the mind's assent* [Cicero].

That things do not lodge in us in their own form and essence, or make their entry into us by their own power and authority, we see clearly enough. Because, if that were so, we should receive them in the same way: wine would be the same in the mouth of a sick man as in the mouth of a healthy man; he who has chapped or numb fingers would find the same hardness in the wood or iron he handles as does another. Thus external objects surrender to our mercy; they dwell in us as we please.

Now if for our part we received anything without alteration, if the human grip was capable and firm enough to grasp the truth by our own means; these means being common to all men, this truth would be bandied from hand to hand, from one man to another; and at least there would be one thing in the world, out of all there are, that would be believed by all men with universal consent. But this fact, that no proposition can be seen which is not debated and controverted among us, or which may not be, well shows that our natural judgment does not grasp very clearly what it grasps. For my judgment cannot make my companion's judgment accept it; which is a sign that I have grasped it by some other means than by a natural power that is in me and in all men.

Let us leave aside that infinite confusion of opinions that is seen among the philosophers themselves, and that perpetual and universal debate over the knowledge of things. For this is a very true presupposition: that men are in agreement about nothing, I mean

even the most gifted and ablest scholars, not even that the sky is over our head. For those who doubt everything also doubt that; and those who deny that we can understand anything say that we have not understood that the sky is over our head; and these two views are incomparably the strongest in number.

Besides this infinite diversity and division, it is easy to see by the confusion that our judgment gives to our own selves, and the uncertainty that each man feels within himself, that it has a very insecure seat. How diversely we judge things! How many times we change our notions! What I hold today and what I believe, I hold and believe it with all my belief; all my tools and all my springs of action grip this opinion and sponsor it for me in every way they can. I could not embrace or preserve any truth with more strength than this one. I belong to it entirely, I belong to it truly. But has it not happened to me, not once, but a hundred times, a thousand times, and every day, to have embraced with these same instruments, in this same condition, something else that I have since judged false?

At least we must become wise at our own expense. If I have often found myself betrayed under just these colors, if my touchstone is found to be ordinarily false, and my scales uneven and incorrect, what assurance can I have in them this time more than at other times? Is it not stupidity to let myself be fooled so many times by one guide?

Nevertheless, whether fortune moves us five hundred times from our position, whether it does nothing but empty and pour back incessantly into our belief, as into a vessel, more and more different opinions, always the present and the latest one is the certain and infallible one. For this one we must abandon possessions, honor, life and salvation, and everything:

> The latest find
> Kills prior things and spoils them in our mind.
> LUCRETIUS

[B]Whatever they preach to us, whatever we learn, we should always remember that it is man that gives and man that receives; it is a mortal hand that presents it to us, a mortal hand that accepts it. The things that come to us from heaven have alone the right and authority for persuasion, alone the stamp of truth; which also we do not see with our own eyes, or receive by our own means. This great and holy image could not be in so mean a domicile, unless God

prepares it for that purpose, unless God reforms and fortifies it by his particular and supernatural grace and favor.

^AAt least our faulty condition should make us behave more moderately and restrainedly in our changes. We should remember, whatever we receive into our understanding, that we often receive false things there, and by these same tools that are often contradictory and deceived.

Now it is no wonder if they are contradictory, being so easily inclined and twisted by very slight occurrences. It is certain that our apprehension, our judgment, and the faculties of our soul in general, suffer according to the movements and alterations of the body, which alterations are continual. Is not our mind more wide-awake, our memory more prompt, our reason more alert, in health than in sickness? Do not joy and gaiety make us receive the subjects that present themselves to our soul with a wholly different countenance than chagrin and melancholy? Do you think that the verses of Catullus or Sappho smile to an avaricious and crabbed old man as they do to a vigorous and ardent young man?

^BWhen Cleomenes, son of Anaxandridas, was sick, his friends reproached him for having new and unaccustomed humors and fancies: "I should think so," he said, "for I am not the same man that I am when in health. Since I am different, my opinions and fancies are also different."

^AAmong the pettifoggers of our palaces of justice this expression is current, and is used of criminals who strike their judges in a good mild and indulgent mood: *gaudeat de bona fortuna*, let him rejoice in this good fortune. For it is certain that judgments come sometimes more intent on condemnation, thornier and harsher, and sometimes more easygoing, indulgent, and inclined to pardon. As for a judge who brings with him from his home the pain of the gout, jealousy, or the pilfering of his valet, a judge whose whole soul is dyed and steeped in anger, there is no doubt that his judgment is biased in that direction.

^BThe venerable senate of the Areopagus judged by night, for fear that the sight of the plaintiffs might corrupt their justice. ^AThe very air and the serenity of the sky brings us some change, as this Greek verse in Cicero says:

Such are the minds of men as is the fertile light
That Father Jove himself sends down to make earth bright.
 HOMER

It is not only the fevers, the potions, and the great accidents that upset our judgment; the slightest things in the world whirl it around. And there is no doubt, even though we do not feel it, that if a continuous fever can prostrate our soul, tertian fever causes some alteration in it, according to its measure and proportion. If apoplexy completely deadens and extinguishes the sight of our intelligence, there is no doubt that a bad cold dazzles it. And consequently, we can hardly find a single hour in our life when our judgment is in its proper seat, our body being subject to so many continual changes, and filled with so many springs of action that I can well believe the doctors how unlikely it is that there will not always be one of them pulling crooked.

Moreover, this malady is not so easily discovered, unless it is wholly extreme and irremediable; inasmuch as reason always goes its way, even though crooked, lame, and broken-hipped, and with falsehood as with truth. Thus it is not easy to discover its miscalculation and irregularity. I always call reason that semblance of intellect that each man fabricates in himself. That reason, of which, by its condition, there can be a hundred contradictory ones about one and the same subject, is an instrument of lead and of wax, stretchable, pliable, and adaptable to all biases and all measures; all that is needed is the ability to mold it.

However good a judge's intentions are, unless he listens closely to himself, which few people amuse themselves in doing, his inclination to friendship, kinship, beauty, and vengeance, and not only things so weighty, but that fortuitous instinct that makes us favor one thing more than another and that assigns us, without leave of our reason, our choice between two like objects, or some shadow of equal emptiness, can insinuate insensibly into his judgment the favor or disfavor of a cause, and tip the scales.

I who spy on myself more closely, who have my eyes unceasingly intent on myself, as one who has not much business elsewhere –

> Quite without care
> What king, in frigid lands beneath the Bear,
> Is feared, or what makes Tiridates quake
>
> HORACE

– I would hardly dare tell of the vanity and weakness that I find in myself. My footing is so unsteady and so insecure, I find it so vacillating and ready to slip, and my sight is so unreliable, that on an empty stomach I feel myself another man than after a meal. If my

health smiles upon me, and the brightness of a beautiful day, I am a fine fellow; if I have a corn bothering my toe, I am surly, unpleasant, and unapproachable. [B]One and the same pace of a horse seems to me now rough, now easy, and the same road at one time shorter, another time longer, and one and the same shape now more, now less agreeable. [A]Now I am ready to do anything, now to do nothing; what is a pleasure to me at this moment will some time be a trouble. A thousand unconsidered and accidental impulses arise in me. Either the melancholic humor grips me, or the choleric; and at this moment sadness predominates in me by its own private authority, at that moment good cheer.

When I pick up books, I will have perceived in such-and-such a passage surpassing charms which will have struck my soul; let me come upon it another time, in vain I turn it over and over, in vain I twist it and manipulate it, to me it is a shapeless and unrecognizable mass.

[B]Even in my own writings I do not always find again the sense of my first thought; I do not know what I meant to say, and often I get burned by correcting and putting in a new meaning, because I have lost the first one, which was better.

I do nothing but come and go. My judgment does not always go forward; it floats, it strays,

> Like a tiny boat,
> Caught by a raging wind on the vast sea.
> CATULLUS

Many times (as I sometimes do deliberately), having undertaken as exercise and sport to maintain an opinion contrary to my own, my mind, applying itself and turning in that direction, attaches me to it so firmly that I can no longer find the reason for my former opinion, and I abandon it. I draw myself along in almost any direction I lean, whatever it may be, and carry myself away by my own weight.

Nearly every man would say as much of himself, if he considered himself as I do. Preachers know that the emotion that comes to them as they talk incites them toward belief; and that in anger we give ourselves up more completely to the defense of our proposition, imprint it on ourselves, and embrace it with more vehemence and approval than we do in our cool and sedate mood.

You recite a case simply to a lawyer, he answers you wavering and doubtful, you feel that it is a matter of indifference to him whether he undertakes to support one party or the other. Have you paid him

well to get his teeth into it and get excited about it, is he beginning to be involved in it, has he got his will warmed up about it? His reason and his knowledge are warmed up at the same time. Behold an evident and indubitable truth that appears to his intelligence. He discovers a wholly new light on your case, and believes it in all conscience, and persuades himself that it is so.

Indeed, I do not know if the ardor that is born of spite and obstinacy against the pressure and violence of authority, and of danger, ᶜor the concern for reputation, ᴮhas not sent some men all the way to the stake to maintain an opinion for which, among their friends and at liberty, they would not have been willing to burn the tip of their finger.

ᴬThe shocks and agitations that our soul receives through the bodily passions have great power over her; but even more do her own passions, which have so strong a grip on her that it is perhaps tenable that she has no other propulsion and motion except by the breath of her winds, and that without their agitation she would remain without action, like a ship on the open sea which the winds abandon without their aid. And whoever should maintain that view, ᶜfollowing the school of the Peripatetics, ᴬwould not do us much wrong, since it is known that most of the finest actions of the soul proceed from, and need, that impulsion of the passions. Valor, they say, cannot become perfect without the assistance of anger.

> ᶜEver was Ajax brave, but bravest in his madness.
>
> CICERO

Nor do we run to attack the wicked and the enemy vigorously enough, unless we are wrathful; and they want a lawyer to arouse anger in the judges to obtain justice from them.

Desires moved Themistocles, moved Demosthenes, and have impelled philosophers to toils, sleepless nights, and wanderings; they lead us to honor, learning, and health, useful ends. And that cowardice of the soul in enduring trouble and grief serves to nourish penitence and repentance in our conscience, and helps us to feel the scourges of God for our chastisement, and the scourges of the state's correction. ᴬCompassion serves as a spur to ᴮclemency, and the prudence to preserve and govern ourselves is aroused by our fear; and how many fine actions by ambition, how many by presumption! ᴬIn short, no eminent and lusty virtue is without some unruly agitation.

Might this not be one of the reasons that must have moved the Epicureans to relieve God of all care and solicitude about our affairs, inasmuch as the very effects of his goodness could not operate upon us without disturbing his repose by means of the passions, which are like pricks and incitements spurring the soul to virtuous actions? ᶜOr else did they believe otherwise, and take them as tempests that shamefully seduce the sould from its tranquillity? *As we think of the calm of the sea, when not the slightest breath of air stirs the waves; so we find a quiet and peaceful state of the soul, when there is no emotion that can move her* [Cicero].

ᴬWhat differences in sense and reason, what contradictions of ideas are offered us by the diversity of our passions! What assurance can we then take of a thing so unstable and mobile, subject by its condition to the mastery of disturbance, ᶜnever going except with a forced and borrowed pace? ᴬIf our judgment is in the hands even of sickness and perturbation; if it is from folly and heedlessness that it is bound to receive its impression of things, what certainty can we expect of it?

ᶜIs there not some rashness in philosophy to consider that men produce their greatest deeds and those most closely approaching divinity when they are out of their minds and frenzied and mad? We improve by the privation and deadening of our reason. The two natural ways to enter the cabinet of the gods and there foresee the course of destinies are madness and sleep. This is amusing to think about: by the dislocation that the passions bring about in our reason, we become virtuous; by the extirpation of reason that is brought about by madness or the semblance of death, we become prophets and soothsayers. I never was more willing to believe philosophy. It is a pure transport that the sacred truth inspired in the philosophical spirit, which wrests from it, against its intention, the admission that the tranquil state of our soul, the sedate state, the healthiest state that philosophy can acquire for her, is not her best state. Our waking is more asleep than sleep; our wisdom less wise than madness. Our dreams are worth more than our reasonings. The worst position we can take is in ourselves.

But does not philosophy think that we have enough sense to notice that the voice which makes the spirit when it is detached from man so clairvoyant, so great, so perfect, and while it is in man so earthly, ignorant, and shadowed, is a voice coming from the spirit which is a part of earthly, ignorant, and shadowed man, and for that reason a voice not to be trusted or believed?

^A^I have no great experience of these vehement agitations, being of an indolent and sluggish disposition, most of which suddenly surprise our soul without giving her time to know herself. But that passion which they say is produced by idleness in the hearts of young men, although it makes its way with leisure and a measured step, very evidently shows, to those who have tried to oppose its strength, the power of that conversion and alteration that our judgment suffers.

I attempted at one time to keep myself tensed to withstand it and beat it down: for I am so far from being one of those who invite vices, that I do not even follow them, unless they drag me away. I would feel it come to life, grow, and increase in spite of my resistance, and finally seize me, alive and watching, and possess me, to such an extent that, as from drunkenness, the picture of things began to seem to me other than usual. I would see the advantages of the object of my desire visibly expanding and growing, and increasing and swelling from the breath of my imagination; the difficulties of my undertaking growing easy and smooth, my reason and my conscience withdrawing. But, this fire having vanished all in an instant like a flash of lightning, I would see my soul regain another kind of sight, another state, and another judgment; the difficulties of the retreat would seem to me great and invincible, and the same things would appear in a light and aspect very different from that in which the heat of desire had presented them to me.

Which of these states is the more truthful, Pyrrho does not know. We are never without sickness. Fevers have their heat and their cold; from the effects of a burning passion we fall back into the effects of a shivering passion.

^B^As far as I had cast myself forward, so far I threw myself back again:

> As when the sea, with alternating flow,
> Now rushes forward foaming on the land,
> Covers the rocks, and bathes the farthest sand;
> Now, seething as it ebbs, retreats once more,
> And drags a shoal of pebbles from the shore.
>
> VIRGIL

^A^Now from the knowledge of this mobility of mine I have accidentally engendered in myself a certain constancy of opinions, and have scarcely altered my original and natural ones. For whatever

appearance of truth there may be in novelty, I do not change easily, for fear of losing in the change. And since I am not capable of choosing, I accept other people's choice and stay in the position where God put me. Otherwise I could not keep myself from rolling about incessantly. Thus I have, by the grace of God, kept myself intact, without agitation or disturbance of conscience, in the ancient beliefs of our religion, in the midst of so many sects and divisions that our century has produced.

The writings of the ancients, I mean the good writings, full and solid, tempt me and move me almost wherever they please; the one I am listening to always seems to me the strongest; I find each one right in his turn, although they contradict each other. The facility that good minds have of making whatever they like seem true, and the fact that there is nothing so strange but that they undertake to color it enough to deceive a simplicity like mine, shows evidently the weakness of their proof.

The sky and the stars have been moving for three thousand years; everybody had so believed, until it occurred to ^cCleanthes of Samos, or (according to Theophrastus) to Nicetas of Syracuse, ^Ato maintain that it was the earth that moved, ^cthrough the oblique circle of the Zodiac, turning about its axis; ^Aand in our day Copernicus has grounded this doctrine so well that he uses it very systematically for all astronomical deductions. What are we to get out of that, unless that we should not bother which of the two is so? And who knows whether a third opinion, a thousand years from now, will not overthrow the preceding two?

> Thus rolling age changes the times of things;
> What was of price, to disesteem it brings;
> Another follows, held in scorn of yore,
> And day by day is sought for more and more,
> And, found, flowers in men's esteem and praise.
> LUCRETIUS

Thus when some new doctrine is offered to us, we have great occasion to distrust it, and to consider that before it was produced its opposite was in vogue; and, as it was overthrown by this one, there may arise in the future a third invention that will likewise smash the second. Before the principles which Aristotle introduced were in credit, other principles satisfied human reason, as his satisfy us at this moment. What letters-patent have these, what special privilege, that the course of our invention stops at them, and that to them

belongs possession of our belief for all time to come? They are no more exempt from being thrown out than were their predecessors.

When I am pressed with a new argument, it is for me to think that what I cannot satisfy, another will satisfy; for to believe all likelihoods that we cannot shake off is great simplicity. The result of that would be that all the common herd – ^cand we are all of the common herd – ^Awould have its belief as easy to turn as a weathercock; for their soul, being soft and without resistance, would be forced to receive incessantly more and more different impressions, the last one always effacing the traces of the preceding one. He who finds himself weak should answer, following legal practice, that he will discuss it with his counsel, or refer to wiser men, from whom he received his teaching.

How long is it that medicine has been in the world? They say that a newcomer, whom they call Paracelsus, is changing and over-throwing the whole order of the ancient rules, and maintaining that up to this moment it has been good for nothing but killing men. I think he will easily prove that; but as for putting my life to the test of his new experience, I think that would not be great wisdom.

We must not believe every man, says the maxim, because any man may say anything.

A man of that profession of novelties and of reforms in physics was saying to me not long ago that all the ancients had evidently been mistaken about the nature and movements of the winds, which fact he would make so palpable that I could touch it, if I would hear him out. After I had taken some patience to listen to his arguments, which were full of likelihood: "What?" I said to him. "Then did those who navigated under the laws of Theophrastus go west when they headed east? Did they go sideways, or backward?" "That was luck," he replied; "at all events they miscalculated." I then replied to him that I would rather follow facts than reason.

Now these are things that often clash; and I have been told that in geometry (which thinks it has reached the high point of certainty among the sciences) there are irrefutable demonstrations that con-trovert the truth of experience. For instance, Jacques Peletier was telling me at my house that he had found two lines traveling toward each other so as to meet, which nevertheless he proved could never come to touch even at infinity. And the Pyrrhonians use their arguments and their reason only to ruin the apparent facts of experience; and it is marvelous how far the suppleness of our reason has followed them in this plan of combating the evidence of the

facts. For they demonstrate that we do not move, that we do not speak, that there is no weight or heat, with the same force of arguments with which we prove more likely things.

Ptolemy, who was a great man, had established the limits of our world; all the ancient philosophers thought they had its measure, except for a few remote islands that might escape their knowledge. It would have been Pyrrhonizing, a thousand years ago, to cast in doubt the science of cosmography, and the opinions that were accepted about it by one and all; ^Bit was heresy to admit the existence of the Antipodes. ^ABehold in our century an infinite extent of terra firma, not an island or one particular country, but a portion nearly equal in size to the one we know, which has just been discovered. The geographers of the present time do not fail to assure us that now all is discovered and all is seen,

> For what we have at hand always seems best of all.
>
> LUCRETIUS

The question is, if Ptolemy was once mistaken on the grounds of his reason, whether it would not be stupid for me now to trust to what these people say about it; ^Cand whether it is not more likely that this great body that we call the world is something quite different from what we judge.

Plato holds that it changes its aspect in all regards: that the sky, the stars, and the sun at times reverse the movement that we see in them, changing east to west. The Egyptian priests told Herodotus that since their first king, who lived eleven thousand and so many years before (and of all their kings they showed him effigies in the form of statues sculptured from life), the sun had four times changed its course; that the sea and the land change alternately into one another; that the birth of the world is undetermined. Aristotle, Cicero, say the same. And one of ours[53] says that it goes through an eternal and frequently recurring cycle of death and rebirth; calling to witness Solomon and Isaiah to avoid these objections: that at one time God was a creator without a creation; that he had been idle and then renounced his idleness and set about his work; and that in consequence he is subject to change.

In the most famous of the Greek schools, the world is held to be a god made by another, greater god, and is composed of a body and a soul that dwells in the center of it, spreading by musical numbers

53 Origen.

to its circumference; divine, very happy, very great, very wise, eternal. In it are other gods, the earth, the sea, the stars, which entertain each other with a perpetual harmonious agitation and divine dance, now meeting, now separating, hiding, appearing, changing order, now in front and now behind.

Heraclitus proved that the world was composed by fire; and that by order of destiny it must some day burst into flame and resolve itself in fire, and some day be reborn again. And of men Apuleius says: *Individually mortal, together perpetual.* Alexander wrote his mother the narrative of an Egyptian priest, drawn from their monuments, testifying to the antiquity of this timeless nation and including a true account of the birth and progress of the other countries. Cicero and Diodorus say in their day that the Chaldeans kept a record of four hundred thousand and so many years; Aristotle, Pliny, and others, that Zoroaster lived six thousand years before the age of Plato. Plato says that the people of the city of Saïs have written memories of eight thousand years, and that the city of Athens was built a thousand years before the aforesaid city of Saïs; [B]Epicurus, that while things here are as we see them, at the same time they are exactly alike and of the same fashion in many other worlds. Which he would have said with more assurance if he had seen the resemblances and parallels between this new world of the West Indies and our own, present and past, in such strange examples.

[C]In truth, considering what has come to our knowledge about the course of this terrestrial government, I have often marveled to see, at a very great distance in time and space, the coincidences between a great number of fabulous popular opinions and savage customs and beliefs, which do not seem from any angle to be connected with our natural reason. The human mind is a great worker of miracles; but this correspondence has something or other about it that is still queerer: it is found also in names, in incidents, and in a thousand other things.

[B]For nations were found there that never, so far as we know, had heard anything about us, where circumcision was in credit; where there were states and great governments maintained by women, without men; where our fasts and our Lent were represented, with the addition of abstinence from women. Where our crosses were in credit in various ways: here sepulchers were honored with them; there they applied them, and especially the Saint Andrew's cross, to defend themselves from nocturnal visions, and placed them on

children's beds against enchantments; elsewhere they found a wooden one, of great height, worshiped as the god of rain, and that very far inland.

There they found a very clear likeness of our shriving priests; the use of miters, the celibacy of the priests, the art of divining by the entrails of sacrificed animals; ^cabstinence from every kind of flesh and fish in their food; ^Bthe fashion among the priests of using a special language, and not the vulgar one, when officiating. And this fancy, that the first god was ousted by a second, his younger brother; that they were created with all comforts, and that since, because of their sin, these were cut off from them, their territory was changed, and their natural condition made worse. That they were once submerged by an inundation of waters from heaven; that only a few families escaped, which cast themselves into high mountain caves, which caves they stopped up, so that the water did not get in, having shut up many kinds of animals inside; that when they felt the rain stop, they put out some dogs, which having returned clean and wet, they judged that the water had not yet gone down much; later, having sent others out and seeing them come back muddy, they went out to repeople the world, which they found full of nothing but snakes.

In one place they came across the belief in the day of judgment, so that the people were strangely shocked by the Spaniards for scattering the bones of the dead while searching the tombs for riches, saying that these separated bones could not easily come together again; traffic by exchange, and none other; fairs and markets for that purpose; dwarfs and deformed persons to adorn the tables of princes; the practice of falconry according to the nature of their birds; tyrants' subsidies; refinement in gardening; dances, tumbling; instrumental music; coats of arms; tennis games, games of dice and of chance in which they grow so heated as to stake themselves and their liberty; no medicine other than that of charms; the system of writing in pictures; belief in a single first man, father of all nations; worship of a god who once lived as a man in perfect virginity, fasting, and penitence, preaching the law of nature and religious ceremonies, and who disappeared from the world without a natural death; the belief in giants; the custom of getting drunk on their beverages and of competition in drinking; religious ornaments painted with bones and death's-heads; surplices, holy water, sprinklers; women and servants competing in offering themselves to be burned or buried with the dead husband or master; a law that the

eldest succeed to all the property, and no portion is reserved for the younger but obedience; a custom, upon promotion to a certain office of great authority, that he who is promoted takes a new name and abandons his own; the custom of sprinkling lime on the knee of the newborn child, saying to him: "You have come from dust and will return to dust"; the art of augury.

These empty shadows of our religion that are seen in some of these examples testify to its dignity and divinity. It has insinuated itself to some extent not only into all the infidel nations on this side of the world by some sort of imitation, but also into these barbarous ones as by a common and supernatural inspiration.

For they also found there the belief in purgatory, but in a new form: what we ascribe to fire they ascribe to cold, and imagine the souls both purged and punished by the rigor of extreme cold.

And this example reminds me of another amusing difference: for whereas there were some nations who liked to uncover the end of their member, and cut off the skin in the Mohammedan and Jewish fashion, there were others who had such great scruples about uncovering it that with the help of little cords they wore their skin very carefully stretched and fastened above, for fear that this end might see the air. And this difference too, that, whereas we honor kings and festivals by dressing ourselves up in the finest clothes we have, in some regions, to show complete disparity and submission to their king, the subjects presented themselves before him in their vilest clothes, and on entering the palace put some old torn robe over their good one, so that all the brilliance and ornament should be the master's. But let us continue.

^If nature enfolds within the bounds of her ordinary progress, like all other things, also the beliefs, judgments, and opinions of men; if they have their rotation, their season, their birth, their death, like cabbages; if heaven moves and rolls them at its will, what magisterial and permanent authority are we attributing to them? ^BIf we feel palpably by experience that the form of our being depends on the air, the climate, and the soil where we are born – not only the complexion, the stature, the constitution and countenance, but also the faculties of the soul: ^Cthe climate affects not only the vigor of the body, but also that of the soul, says Vegetius – and if the goddess who founded the city of Athens chose for its situation a climate which made men prudent, as the priests of Egypt taught Solon: the air of Athens is thin, whereby the Atticans are reputed more acute; that of Thebes is thick, wherefore the Thebans are reputed gross

and solid [Cicero]; ^Bso that just as fruits are born different, and animals, men too are born more or less bellicose, just, temperate, and docile – here subject to wine, elsewhere to theft or lechery; here inclined to superstition, elsewhere to unbelief; ^Chere to freedom, here to servitude; ^Bcapable of one science or of one art, dull or ingenious, obedient or rebellious, good or bad, according to the influence of the place where they are situated – and take on a new disposition if you change their place, like trees; which was the reason why Cyrus would not allow the Persians to abandon their rugged and hilly country to move into another that was mild and flat, ^Csaying that fat, soft lands make men soft, and fertile lands infertile minds; ^Bif we see flourishing now one art, one opinion, now another, by some celestial influence; such-and-such a century produce such-and-such natures, and incline the human race to such-and-such a bent; the minds of men now lusty, now lean, like our fields; what becomes of all those fine prerogatives on which we flatter ourselves? Since a wise man can be mistaken, and a hundred men, and many nations, yes, and human nature according to us is mistaken for many centuries about this or that, what assurance have we that sometimes it stops being mistaken, ^Cand that in this century it is not making a mistake?

^AAmong other tokens of our imbecility, it seems to me that this does not deserve to be forgotten: that even through desire, man does not know how to find what he needs; that not by enjoyment, not even by imagination and wish, can we agree about what we need for our contentment. Let our thought cut out and sew at its pleasure, it will not even be able to desire what is fit for it, ^Cand satisfy itself:

> ^BFor what by reason do we want or fear?
> What plan so happily do you conceive
> But its successful trial makes you grieve?
>
> JUVENAL

^AThat is why ^CSocrates asked the gods only to give him what they knew to be salutary for him. And the prayer of the Lacedaemonians, public and private, was simply that good and beautiful things should be granted them, referring to the divine discernment the choice and selection of these:[54]

54 In the editions published in Montaigne's lifetime this passage, beginning "That is why Socrates," reads as follows: "That is why the Christian, humbler and wiser and recognizing better what he is, refers it to his creator to choose and ordain what he needs."

[B]We pray for wife and children; only he
Knows who the children, what the wife shall be.
JUVENAL

[A]And the Christian prays God that his will be done, so as not to fall into the mishap that the poets invent about King Midas. He prayed the gods that everything he touched should turn to gold. His prayer was granted: his wine was gold, his bread gold, and the feathers of his bed, and gold his shirt and clothes; so that he found himself overwhelmed beneath the enjoyment of his desire and endowed with an unendurable privilege. He had to unpray his prayers:

Stunned by this novel ailment, rich yet poor,
He loathes his wealth, hates what he craved before.
OVID

[B]Let us speak of myself. I asked of Fortune when I was young, as much as anything else, the order of Saint Michael; for it was then the utmost mark of honor of the French nobility, and very rare. She granted it to me ironically. Instead of raising and lifting me from my place to attain it, she treated me much more graciously: she debased it and lowered it to the level of my shoulders, and below.

[C]Cleobis and Bito, Trophonius and Agamedes, having prayed, the former their goddess, the latter their god, for a recompense worthy of their piety, got death for their present; so different are the celestial opinions of what we need from our own.

[A]God could grant us riches, honors, life, and health itself, to our prejudice sometimes; for not all that is pleasing to us is always salutary for us. If instead of a cure he sends us death or a worsening of our troubles – *thy rod and thy staff they comfort me* [Psalms] – he does so for the reasons of his providence, which considers what is due us much more surely than we can; and we must take it in good part, as from a very wise and very friendly hand:

[B]If my advice you'll hear,
Let the gods settle for us what is best,
And what is useful to our interest;
Man to them more than to himself is dear.
JUVENAL

For to ask them for honors, for high office, is to ask them to cast you into a battle, or a game of dice, or any other thing of which the outcome is unknown to you, and the profit doubtful.

^AThere is no combat so violent among the philosophers, and so bitter, as that which arises over the question of the sovereign good of man, ^Cout of which, by Varro's reckoning, two hundred and eighty-eight sects were born. *But he who disagrees about the supreme good, disagrees about the whole principle of philosophy* [Cicero].

> ^AThree guests of mine differ on what is good;
> Their various palates call for various food.
> What shall I serve? What not? What makes one glad,
> You don't enjoy; what you like, they find bad.
>
> HORACE

Nature should reply thus to their arguments and disputes.

Some say that our good lies in virtue, others in sensual pleasure, others in conforming to nature; one man in knowledge, ^Cone in having no pain, ^Aone in not letting ourselves be carried away by appearances. And this notion seems to resemble this other, ^Bof the ancient Pythagoras:

> ^AWonder at nothing: that is all I know
> To make men happy and to keep them so;
>
> HORACE

which is the goal of the Pyrrhonian school.

^CAristotle attributes wondering at nothing to greatness of soul. ^AAnd Arcesilaus used to say that to suspend the judgment and keep it upright and inflexible is a good thing, but to consent and incline it is a vice and a bad thing. It is true that by establishing this by a certain axiom, he was departing from Pyrrhonism. The Pyrrhonians, when they say that the sovereign good is Ataraxy, which is the immobility of the judgment, do not mean to say it in an affirmative way; but the same impulse of their soul that makes them avoid precipices and take cover in the cool of the evening, itself offers them this fancy and makes them refuse any other.

^BHow I wish that while I am alive, either some other man or Justus Lipsius,⁵⁵ the most learned man we have left, with a most polished and judicious mind, truly akin to my Turnebus, might have the will, and the health, and enough leisure, to compile into a register, according to their divisions and classes, as honestly and carefully as we can understand them, the opinions of ancient philosophy on the subject of our being and our conduct; their

55 A Belgian scholar (1547–1606) with whom Montaigne corresponded.

controversies, the credit and the sequence of the schools, the rela-
tions of the lives of the authors and followers to their precepts on
memorable and exemplary occasions. What a fine and useful work
that would be!

^AMoreover, if it is from ourselves that we derive the ruling of our
conduct, into what confusion do we cast ourselves! For the most
plausible advice that our reason gives us in the matter is generally for
each man to obey the laws of his country, ^Bwhich is the advice of
Socrates, inspired, he says, by divine counsel. ^AAnd what does
reason mean by that, unless that our duty has no rule but an
accidental one?

Truth must have one face, the same and universal. If man knew
any rectitude and justice that had body and real existence, he would
not tie it down to the condition of the customs of this country or
that. It would not be from the fancy of the Persians or the Indians
that virtue would take its form.

There is nothing subject to more continual agitation than the
laws. Since I was born I have seen those of our neighbors
the English change three or four times; not only in political matters,
in which people want to dispense with constancy, but in the most
important subject that can be, to wit, religion. At which I am
shamed and vexed, the more so because that is a nation with
which the people of my region formerly had such intimate acquain-
tance that there still remain in my house some traces of our
old cousinship.

^CAnd here at home I have seen things which were capital
offenses among us become legitimate; and we who consider other
things legitimate are liable, according to the uncertainty of the
fortunes of war, to be one day guilty of human and divine high
treason, when our justice falls into the mercy of injustice, and, after
a few years of captivity, assumes a contrary character.

How could that ancient god[56] more clearly accuse human knowl-
edge of ignorance of the divine being, and teach men that religion
was only a creature of their own invention, suitable to bind their
society together, than by declaring, as he did, to those who sought
instruction therein at his tripod, that the true cult for each man was
that which he found observed according to the practice of the place
he was in?

56 Apollo.

O God, what an obligation do we not have to the benignity of our sovereign creator for having freed our belief from the folly of those vagabond and arbitrary devotions, and having based it on the eternal foundation of his holy word?

^AWhat then will philosophy tell us in this our need? To follow the laws of our country – that is to say, the undulating sea of the opinions of a people or a prince, which will paint me justice in as many colors, and refashion it into as many faces, as there are changes of passion in those men? I cannot have my judgment so flexible.

What am I to make of a virtue that I saw in credit yesterday, that will be discredited tomorrow, ^cand that becomes a crime on the other side of the river? What of a truth that is bounded by these mountains and is falsehood to the world that lives beyond?

^ABut they are funny when, to give some certainty to the laws, they say that there are some which are firm, perpetual, and immutable, which they call natural, which are imprinted on the human race by the condition of their very being. And of those one man says the number is three, one man four, one more, one less: a sign that the mark of them is as doubtful as the rest. Now they are so unfortunate (for what else can I call it but misfortune, that out of such an infinite number of laws not even one is found that fortune ^cand the heedlessness of chance ^Ahave allowed to be universally accepted by the consent of all nations?), they are, I say, so wretched that of these three or four selected laws there is not a single one that is not contradicted and disavowed, not by one nation but by many. Now the only likely sign by which they can argue certain laws to be natural is universality of approval. For what nature had truly ordered for us we would without doubt follow by common consent. And not only every nation, but every individual, would resent the force and violence used on him by anyone who tried to impel him to oppose that law. Let them show me just one law of that sort – I'd like to see it.

Protagoras and Aristo assigned no other essence to the justice of the laws than the authority and judgment of the lawgiver; and said that apart from that, the good and the honest lost their qualities and remained empty names of indifferent things. Thrasymachus, in Plato, thinks that there is no other right than the advantage of the superior.

There is nothing in which the world is so varied as in customs and laws. A given thing is abominable here, which brings

commendation elsewhere: as in Lacedaemon cleverness in stealing. Marriages between close relatives are capital offenses among us, elsewhere they are in honor:

> There are some nations, it is said,
> Where mothers sons, and fathers daughters wed;
> And thus affection grows, doubled by love.
>
> OVID

The murder of infants, the murder of fathers, sharing of wives, traffic in robberies, license for all sorts of sensual pleasures, nothing in short is so extreme that it is not accepted by the usage of some nation.

^BIt is credible that there are natural laws, as may be seen in other creatures; but in us they are lost; that fine human reason butts in everywhere, domineering and commanding, muddling and confusing the face of things in accordance with its vanity and inconsistency. ^C*Nothing is ours any more; what I call ours is a product of art* [Cicero].

^AThings may be considered in various lights and from various viewpoints: it is principally from this that diversity of opinions arises. One nation looks at one side of a thing and stops there; another at another.

There is nothing so horrible to imagine as eating one's father. The nations which had this custom in ancient times, however, regarded it as testimony of piety and good affection, trying thereby to give their progenitors the most worthy and honorable sepulture, lodging in themselves and as it were in their marrow the bodies of their fathers and their remains, bringing them to life in a way and regenerating them by transmutation into their living flesh by means of digestion and nourishment. It is easy to imagine what a cruelty and abomination it would have been, to men saturated and imbued with this superstition, to abandon the mortal remains of their parents to the corruption of the earth and to let it become the food of beasts and worms.

Lycurgus considered in theft the quickness, diligence, boldness, and adroitness that there is in taking something from one's neighbor by surprise, and the useful return to the public in that every man looks more carefully to the conservation of what is his; and he thought that from this double training, in attack and defense, there resulted an increase in military efficiency (which was the principal science and virtue in which he wished to train this nation)

that more than offset the disorderliness and injustice of helping oneself to other people's property.

Dionysius the tyrant offered Plato a robe in the Persian style, long, damascened, and perfumed. Plato refused it, saying that having been born a man, he would not willingly wear a woman's robe; but Aristippus accepted it with this reply, that no accouterment could corrupt a chaste heart. ^CHis friends were scolding him for his cowardice in taking it so little to heart that Dionysius had spat in his face. "Fishermen," he said, "readily suffer being bathed by the waves of the sea from head to foot in order to catch a gudgeon." Diogenes was washing his cabbages, and said, seeing him pass: "If you knew how to live on cabbage, you would not pay court to a tyrant." To which Aristippus: "If you knew how to live among men, you would not be washing cabbages." ^ASee how reason provides plausibility to different actions. ^BIt is a two-handled pot, that can be grasped by the left or the right:

> You threaten war, O foreign ground;
> War must be brewing where armed steeds are found.
> Yet some day these same horses will submit
> In amity to bear the yoke and bit.
> Yes, there is hope for peace.
> VIRGIL

^CThey were preaching to Solon not to shed impotent and useless tears for the death of his son. "It is just for that," he said, "that I shed them the more rightly, because they are useless and impotent." Socrates' wife was exacerbating her grief by this circumstance: "O how unjustly these wicked judges are putting him to death!" "Would you rather that it was justly, then?" he replied.[57]

^AWe wear our ears pierced; the Greeks considered that a mark of slavery. We hide to enjoy our wives, the Indians do so publicly. The Scythians used to sacrifice strangers in their temples, elsewhere temples are a sanctuary.

> ^BFor this the vulgar rage, that every spot
> Detests its neighbor's gods, and questions not
> That those itself adores alone are gods.
> JUVENAL

57 Instead of this paragraph, in the editions published in Montaigne's lifetime, there appeared this sentence: "It follows from this diversity of aspects that judgments are diversely applied to the choice of things."

[A]I have heard tell of a judge who, when he came across a sharp conflict between Bartolus and Baldus,[58] or some matter debated with many contradictions, used to put in the margin of his book "Question for my friend."

The lawyers and judges of our time find enough angles for all cases to arrange them any way they please. In a field of knowledge so infinite, depending on the authority of so many opinions, and in so arbitrary a subject, it is impossible that there should not arise an extreme confusion of judgments. And so there is hardly a lawsuit so clear that opinions do not differ on it. The judgment one court has given is reversed by another, which reverses itself another time. Whereof we see common examples in the licentious practice, which is a monstrous stain on the ceremonious authority and luster of our justice, of not letting the decisions decide, and running from one judge to another to settle the same case.

As for the freedom of philosophical opinions concerning vice and virtue, it is a thing on which there is no need to expand, and on which there are several opinions which are better hushed up than published [C]to weak minds.

[B]Arcesilaus said that in lechery it was not a considerable matter on which side it was [C]and in what place. *And as for obscene pleasures, if nature requires them, we should not consider birth, or position, or rank, but beauty, age, and figure, Epicurus thinks* [Cicero]. *Nor do they think that virtuous loves are alien to the wise man* [Cicero]. *Let us ask up to what age young men are to be loved* [Seneca]. These last two passages from the Stoics, and on the same subject the reproach of Dicaearchus to Plato himself, show what excessive license, remote from common usage, even the soundest philosophy allows.

[A]The laws take their authority from possession and usage; it is dangerous to trace them back to their birth. They swell and are ennobled as they roll, like our rivers: follow them uphill to their source, it is just a little trickle of water, barely recognizable, which thus grows proud and strong as it grows old. Look at the ancient considerations that gave the first impetus to this famous torrent full of dignity, awe, and reverence; you will find them so trivial and frail that it is no wonder that these people who weigh everything and refer it to reason, and who accept nothing by authority and on credit, have judgments often far removed from popular judgments. Since they are men who take as their pattern the original image of

58 Italian legal authorities of the fourteenth century.

nature, it is no wonder if in most of their opinions they deviate from the common way.

As, for example: few of them would have approved the conditions and constraints of our marriages, ^cand most of them have wanted wives to be held in common and without obligation.

^AThey rejected our proprieties.[59] Chrysippus used to say that a philosopher will turn a dozen somersaults in public, even without breeches, for a dozen olives. ^cHe would hardly have advised Cleisthenes to refuse the beautiful Agarista, his daughter, to Hippocleides, for having seen him stand on his head on a table with his legs apart. Metrocles rather indiscreetly let a fart while debating in the presence of his school, and was staying in his house, hiding for shame, until Crates went to visit him and, adding to his consolations and reasons the example of his own freedom, started a farting contest with him, by which he rid him of this scruple, and furthermore drew him over to his own freer Stoical school from the more polite Peripatetic school of which he had hitherto been a follower.

What we call decency – not to dare to do openly what it is decent for us to do in private – they called stupidity; and to try to be clever by hushing up and disavowing what nature, custom, and our desire publish and proclaim about our actions, they considered a vice. And it seemed to them that it was profaning the mysteries of Venus to remove them from the secluded sanctuary of her temple and expose them to the sight of the people; and that to draw her sports from behind the curtain was to cheapen them (shame is a sort of weight; concealment, reservation, circumscription, are factors in esteem); that voluptuousness very ingeniously insisted, under the mask of virtue, on not being prostituted in the middle of the crossroads, trodden beneath the feet and eyes of the crowd, lacking the dignity and comfort of its accustomed cabinets. Hence ^Asome say that to abolish public brothels is not only to spread everywhere the lechery that was assigned to those places, but also to spur men on to that vice by making it difficult:

> You were Aufidia's spouse, now you are lovers;
> Now he that was your rival is her mate.
> Your wife you loved not; why love her as another's?
> Must you be insecure to copulate?
> MARTIAL

59 Here the editions published in Montaigne's lifetime add: "Everyone has heard of the shameless way of life of the Cynic philosophers."

This experience is diversified into a thousand examples:

> No one in all the city wished to touch
> Your wife, Cecilian, when they freely could.
> But now, guards posted, those who seek her couch
> Form a vast throng. Cecilian, you are shrewd.
> MARTIAL

A philosopher who was surprised in the act was asked what he was doing. He replied quite coolly: "I am planting a man"; not blushing at being discovered at that any more than if he had been found planting garlic.

^CIt is, in my opinion, through an overtender and respectful attitude, that a great and religious author[60] maintains that this action is so necessarily bound up with concealment and shame, that he cannot persuade himself that in the licentiousness of the Cynic embraces the business came to its conclusion. He believes that it stopped at merely representing lascivious movements, in order to maintain the shamelessness that their school professed; and that in order to eject what shame had restrained and withheld, they still needed later on to seek cover. He had not seen far enough into their debauchery. For Diogenes, practicing masturbation in public, expressed the wish in the presence of the bystanders that he could satisfy his stomach that way by rubbing it. To those who asked him why he did not seek a more comfortable place to eat than right out in the street, he answered: "Because I am hungry right out in the street."

The women philosophers who mingled with their school mingled also with their persons in all places without discrimination; and Hipparchia was received into the society of Crates only on condition of following in all things the practices and customs of his order.

These philosophers set an extreme price on virtue and rejected all other studies but morals; yet in all actions they attributed the sovereign authority to the decision of their sage, above the laws; and ordered no other bridle on sensual pleasures ^Athan moderation and the preservation of the liberty of others.

Heraclitus and Protagoras, from the fact that wine seems bitter to the sick man and pleasant to the healthy, the oar bent in the water

60 Saint Augustine.

and straight to those that see it outside, and from similar contrary appearances that are found in objects, argued that all objects had in themselves the causes of these appearances, and that there was some bitterness in wine that corresponded with the sick man's palate, a certain bent quality in the oar corresponding with the person who looks at it in the water; and so for all the rest. Which is to say that all is in all things, and consequently nothing in any; for where all is, there is nothing.

This theory reminds me of the experience we have that there is no sense or aspect, either straight or bitter, or sweet, or crooked, that the human mind does not find in the writings it undertakes to search. In the clearest, purest, and most perfect writing that can be, how much falsehood and lying has been brought to birth! What heresy has not found in it grounds and testimonies enough to make its start and to maintain itself? It is for that reason that the authors of such errors will never give up this form of proof, from the evidence of the interpretation of words.

A certain dignitary, trying to justify to me by authority that quest of the philosopher's stone in which he is completely immersed, lately alleged to me five or six passages from the Bible on which he said he had primarily relied for the discharge of his conscience (for he is an ecclesiastic by profession); and in truth, his discovery was not only amusing, but also very properly suited to the defense of that fine science.

In this way diviners' fables gain credit. There is no prognosticator, if he has enough authority for people to deign to leaf through him and study carefully all the implications and aspects of his words, who cannot be made to say whatever you want, like the Sibyls. For there are so many means of interpretation that, obliquely or directly, an ingenious mind can hardly fail to come across in any subject some sense that will serve his point.

ᶜIt is for this reason that a cloudy and doubtful style finds itself in such frequent and ancient usage. Let the author succeed in attracting and busying posterity with himself, which not only ability may do, but as much or more so the chance favor of the subject matter; let him for the rest express himself, through stupidity or shrewdness, a bit obscurely and contradictorily: he need not worry. Numerous minds, sifting him and shaking him, will squeeze out of him a quantity of meanings, either like his own, or beside it, or contrary to it, which will all do him honor. He will see himself

enriched with the means of his disciples, like tutors at the time
of the Lendit.[61]

^AThis is what has given value to many worthless things, what has
brought into credit many writings and loaded them with any kind of
matter that was wanted; one single thing receiving thousands
of different interpretations and points of view, and indeed as many
as we please.

^CIs it possible that Homer meant to say all they make him say,
and that he lent himself to so many and such different interpreta-
tions that the theologians, legislators, captains, philosophers, every
sort of people who treat of sciences, however differently and contra-
dictorily, lean on him and refer to him: the general master for all
offices, works, and artisans, the general counselor for all enterprises?
^AWhoever has needed oracles and predictions has found in him
enough for his purpose. It is a marvel what wonderful correspon-
dences a learned man, and a friend of mine, draws out of him in
support of our religion; and he cannot easily let go of this opinion,
that this was Homer's purpose (yet he is as well acquainted with this
poet as any man of our century). ^CAnd what he finds in favor of ours,
many of old had found in favor of theirs.

See how Plato is moved and tossed about. Every man, glorying
in applying him to himself, sets him on the side he wants. They trot
him out and insert him into all the new opinions that the world
accepts; and they make him differ from himself according to the
different course of things. They make his meaning disavow customs
that were licit in his century because they are illicit in ours. All this
vigorously and powerfully, in so far as the mind of the interpreter is
powerful and vigorous.

^AFrom the same foundation that Heraclitus had, and that maxim
of his that all things had in them the aspects that were found
in them, Democritus derived a wholly opposite conclusion,
that things had in them nothing at all of what we found in them;
and from the fact that honey was sweet to one and bitter to another,
he argued that it was neither sweet nor bitter. The Pyrrhonians
would say that they do not know whether it is sweet or bitter,
or neither, or both; for they always reach the extreme point of
doubt.

61 Tutors, especially in Paris, received yearly fees or presents from their pupils at
the time of the Lendit fair.

^CThe Cyrenaics maintained that nothing was perceptible from without, and that only that was perceptible which touched us by internal touch, like pain and pleasure; recognizing neither tone nor color, but only certain impressions that came to us from these; and that man had no other seat of his judgment. Protagoras thought that "what seemed to each man was true for each man." The Epicureans lodge all judgment in the senses, both in the knowledge of things and in pleasure. Plato decided that the judgment of truth, and truth itself, withdrawn from opinions and the senses, belonged to the mind and to reflection.

[THE SENSES ARE INADEQUATE]

^AThis subject has brought me to the consideration of the senses, in which lies the greatest foundation and proof of our ignorance. All that is known, is doubtless known through the faculty of the knower; for since judgment comes from the operation of him who judges, it stands to reason that he performs this operation by his means and will, not by the constraint of others, as would happen if we knew things through the power and according to the law of their own essence.

Now all knowledge makes its way into us through the senses; they are our masters:

> ^BNo shorter pathway can persuasion find
> Into the human heart and human mind.
> LUCRETIUS

^AKnowledge begins through them and is resolved into them.

After all, we would know no more than a stone, if we did not know that there is sound, smell, light, taste, measure, weight, softness, hardness, roughness, color, smoothness, breadth, depth. There are the base and the principles of the whole edifice of our knowledge. ^CAnd according to some, knowledge is nothing else but sensation. ^AWhoever can force me to contradict the senses has me by the throat; he could not make me retreat any further. The senses are the beginning and the end of human knowledge:

> Our senses, you will find, did first provide
> The idea of truth; they cannot be denied.
>
> In what then should we place a greater trust
> Than in the senses?
> LUCRETIUS

Attribute to them as little as you can, still you must grant them this, that by way of them and by their mediation proceeds all our instruction. Cicero says that Chrysippus, having tried to disparage the power and strength of the senses, presented himself with arguments to the contrary, and such violent objections, that he could not satisfy them. Whereupon Carneades, who was upholding the opposite side, boasted that he would use the very weapons and words of Chrysippus to combat him, and therefore exclaimed against him: "O wretched man, your strength has defeated you!"

We cannot conceive of an absurdity more extreme than to maintain that fire does not heat, that light does not illumine, that there is no weight or hardness in iron; these are items of knowledge brought to us by the senses; and man has no belief or knowledge that can compare with this sort for certainty.

The first consideration that I offer on the subject of the senses is that I have my doubts whether man is provided with all the senses of nature. I see many animals that live a complete and perfect life, some without sight, others without hearing; who knows whether we too do not still lack one, two, three, or many other senses? For if any one is lacking, our reason cannot discover its absence. It is the privilege of the senses to be the extreme limit of our perception. There is nothing beyond them that can help us to discover them; no, nor can one sense discover the other:

> [B]Can ears the errors of the eyes detect?
> Touch refute ears, or taste our touch correct?
> Nose confute touch, and eyes in turn prevail?
>
> LUCRETIUS

[A]Together they all form the farthest limit of our faculties:

> Its function is defined
> To each apart, to each its power assigned.
>
> LUCRETIUS

It is impossible to make a man who was born blind conceive that he does not see; impossible to make him desire sight and regret its absence. Wherefore we should take no assurance from the fact that our soul is content and satisfied with those senses we have, seeing that it has no means of feeling its malady and imperfection therein, if any there be. It is impossible to say anything to this blind man, by reason, argument, or comparison, that will place in his imagination any apprehension of light, color, and sight. There is nothing further

behind that can push that sense into evidence. When we see men blind from birth desire to see, it is not because they understand what they ask: they have learned from us that they lack something, that they have something to desire, which is in us; ^cwhich they name perfectly well, and its effects and consequences; ^Abut nevertheless they do not know what it is, nor do they have a close or distant apprehension of it.

I have seen a gentleman of a good house, born blind, or at least blind from such an age that he does not know what sight is. He understands so little what he lacks, that he uses and employs as we do words appropriate to sight, and applies them in a manner all private and his own. He was presented with a boy, whose godfather he was; taking him in his arms, he said: "My, what a handsome boy! How good it is to see him! What a gay face he has!" He will say like one of us: "This room has a fine view; it is a clear day, the sun is shining bright." There is more; for because hunting, tennis, and shooting are our sports, and he has heard this, he is fond of them and keenly interested in them, and thinks he has the same share in them that we do; he finds excitement and pleasure in them, and yet he takes them in only through his ears. They call to him that there goes a hare when they are in a bit of fine open country where he can spur his horse; and then they tell him later that there is a hare caught; and he is as proud of his catch as he hears the others say they are. The tennis ball he takes in his left hand and strokes with his racket; with the harquebus he shoots at random, and gets his fun by having his men tell him that he is either over or beside the mark.

What do we know about whether mankind is doing something equally foolish for lack of some sense, and whether by this lack the greater part of the face of things is hidden from us? What do we know about whether the difficulties we find in many works of nature come from that? And whether many actions of the animals that exceed our capacity are produced by the operation of some sense that we lack? And whether some of them have by this means a fuller and more complete life than ours?

We grasp an apple by almost all our senses; we find in it redness, smoothness, smell, and sweetness; besides these it may have other properties, like drying up or shrinking, to which we have no sense that corresponds. The properties that we call occult in many things, as that of the magnet to attract iron – is it not likely that there are sensory faculties in nature suitable to judge them and perceive them, and that the lack of such faculties causes our ignorance of the true

essence of such things? Perhaps it is some particular sense that reveals to cocks the hours of morning and midnight, and moves them to crow; ᶜthat teaches hens, before any practice and experience, to fear a sparrow hawk, and not a goose or a peacock, which are bigger creatures; which warns chickens of the quality in the cat that is hostile to them, and not to distrust the dog: to beware of mewing, a rather caressing sound, and not of barking, a harsh and quarrelsome sound; that teaches wasps, ants, and rats always to select the best cheese and the best pear, before having tasted them; ᴬand that guides the stag, ᶜthe elephant, the snake, ᴬto the knowledge of a certain herb suitable for their cure.

There is no sense that does not have great dominion, and bring us by its means to know an infinite number of things. If we lacked the understanding of sounds, of harmony and the voice, this lack would bring inconceivable confusion upon all the rest of our knowledge. For besides what is attached to the proper effect of each sense, how many arguments, consequences, and conclusions we draw in other things by the comparison of one sense with another! Let an intelligent man imagine human nature as produced originally without sight, and think how much ignorance and confusion such a lack would bring him, how much shadow and blindness in our soul: it will be seen from this how important to our knowledge of the truth is the privation of another such sense, or two, or three – if this privation is in us. We have formed a truth by the consultation and concurrence of our five senses; but perhaps we needed the agreement of eight or ten senses, and their contribution, to perceive it certainly and in its essence.

The schools that dispute man's knowledge dispute it principally because of the uncertainty and weakness of our senses; for since all knowledge comes to us by their means and mediation, if they err in the report they make to us, if they corrupt or alter what they carry to us from without, if the light that flows through them into our soul is obscured in passage, we have nothing left to go by. From this extreme difficulty have arisen all these fancies: that each object has in itself all that we find in it; that it has nothing of what we think we find in it; and this of the Epicureans, that the sun is no bigger than it looks to us:

> ᴮWhate'er it is, it has no greater size
> Than what it seems to be, seen by our eyes;
> LUCRETIUS

^Athat the appearances that show a body to be big to him who is near, and smaller to him who is far, are both true,

> ^BNor grant we therefore that our eyes are blind;
>
> Blame not on eyes the error of the mind;
>
> LUCRETIUS

^Aand, boldly, that there is no deception in the senses, that we must submit to their mercy, and seek elsewhere reasons to excuse the difference and contradiction that we find in them, in fact invent any other falsehood or reverie (they go as far as that) rather than accuse the senses.

^CTimagoras swore that however much he pressed or turned his eyes, he had never seen the light of a candle doubled; and that that appearance came from a defect of the mind, not of the organ.

^AOf all absurdities the most absurd ^Cto the Epicureans ^Ais to disavow the power and effect of the senses.

> Hence what the senses see is always true.
> And if our reason cannot well expound
> Why what from near was square, from far is round,
> Although we lack the cause, 'tis better still
> Either appearance to interpret ill,
> Than from our hands to let the obvious go,
> To spurn our primal trust and overthrow
> The bases on which life and safety stay.
> For not alone would reason fail; straightway
> Our very life would fall, unless we dare
> To trust our senses, shun great heights, beware
> Of other similar dangers.
>
> LUCRETIUS

^CThis desperate and most unphilosophical advice means nothing else than that human knowledge can maintain itself only by unreasonable, mad, and senseless reason; but that still it is better for man, in order to assert himself, to use it and any other remedy, however fantastic, than to admit his necessary stupidity: such a disadvantageous truth! He cannot escape the fact that the senses are the sovereign masters of his knowledge; but they are uncertain and deceivable in all circumstances. It is there that we must fight it out, and if just forces fail us, as they do, use stubbornness, heedlessness, impudence.

^BIn case what the Epicureans say is true, to wit, that we have no knowledge if the appearances of the senses are false; and if what the Stoics say is also true, that the appearances of the senses are so false that they can produce no knowledge for us; we shall conclude, at the expense of these two great dogmatic sects, that there is no knowledge.

^AAs for the error and uncertainty of the operation of the senses, each man can furnish himself with as many examples as he pleases, so ordinary are the mistakes and deceptions that they offer us. At the echo in a valley, the sound of a trumpet seems to come from in front of us, when it comes from a league behind:

> ^BTwo distant mountains like as one are seen,
> Though on the sea great distance lies between.
>
>
> Astern the hills and meadows seem to fly,
> Which our ship skirts near by...
>
>
> ...When in midstream our steed stops short,
> Some power seems to bear his body athwart
> And force him up against the rushing stream.
> LUCRETIUS

^AWhen rolling a harquebus bullet under the forefinger, the middle finger being entwined over it, we have to force ourselves hard to admit that there is only one, so strongly does our sense represent two to us. For that the senses are many a time masters of reason, and constrain it to receive impressions that it knows and judges to be false, is seen at every turn. I leave aside the sense of touch, whose operations are closer, more vivid and substantial, which, so many times, by the effect of the pain it brings to the body, overthrows all those beautiful Stoical resolutions, and compels the man to cry out at his stomach who has established with all resoluteness this doctrine in his soul, that the colic, like every other malady and pain, is an indifferent thing, not having the power to reduce at all the supreme happiness and felicity in which the sage is lodged by his virtue.

There is no heart so faint that the sound of our drums and trumpets will not warm it, or so hard that the sweetness of music will not awaken it and caress it; no soul so crabbed as not to feel touched by some reverence on contemplating the somber vastness of our churches, the diversity of ornaments, and the

order of our ceremonies, and on hearing the devotional sound of our organs and the harmony, so solemn and religious, of our voices. Even those who enter with disdain feel a certain shiver in their heart, and a certain awe, which makes them distrust their opinion.

^BAs for me, I do not consider myself strong enough to listen sedately to verses of Horace or Catullus sung by an adequate voice from a young and beautiful mouth. ^CAnd Zeno was right to say that the voice was the flower of beauty.

Someone tried to make me believe that a man whom all we Frenchmen know had overimpressed me by reciting to me some verses he had composed; that they were not the same on paper as in the air, and that my eyes would judge them contrary to my ears, so much influence utterance has in giving value and style to the works that come into its mercy. In which connection Philoxenus was not too choleric when, hearing someone giving a bad tone to some composition of his, he began to stamp on and break some tiles that belonged to the offender, saying: "I disrupt what is yours as you corrupt what is mine."

^AFor what reason did even those who had themselves put to death by their own sure resolve turn away their face in order not to see the stroke that they were having dealt them? And why cannot those who for their health desire and order someone to cut into them and cauterize them endure the sight of the preparations, instruments, and operations of the surgeon, since sight is to have no participation in this pain? Are these not fit examples to prove the authority that the senses have over the reason?

No matter if we are aware that these tresses are borrowed from a page or a lackey, that this rosy complexion is a product of Spain, and that this whiteness and smoothness comes from the ocean sea; still sight must compel us to find the object more lovely and agreeable for it, against all reason. For in this there is nothing of the lady's own:

> Jewels and gold hide flaws; we are tricked by art;
> The girl is of herself the smallest part.
> Oft in all this you ask where your love lies:
> By this Gorgon shield rich love deceives the eyes.
>
> OVID

How much power the poets ascribe to the senses, who make Narcissus madly in love with his own reflection –

All he admires for which he is admired;
Unwitting, loves himself; yearned for, he yearns;
Seeking, is sought; with flame self-kindled burns

OVID

– and Pygmalion's understanding so troubled by the impression of the sight of his ivory statue, that he loves and serves it as though it were alive:

Kisses he gives, and thinks they are returned;
Pursues and holds, and thinks the flesh gives way
Beneath his fingers, fears a mark will stay.

OVID

Put a philosopher in a cage of thin iron wire in large meshes, and hang it from the top of the towers of Notre Dame of Paris: he will see by evident reason that it is impossible for him to fall, and yet (unless he is used to the trade of the steeplejacks) he cannot keep the sight of this extreme height from terrifying and paralyzing him. For we have trouble enough feeling secure in the galleries that are in our steeples, if they are wrought with openwork, even though they are of stone. There are some who cannot even bear the thought of them. Lay a beam between these two towers of such width as we need to walk on: there is no philosophical wisdom of such great firmness that it can give us courage to walk on it as we should if it were on the ground.

I have often experienced this in our mountains on this side of the border (and yet I am one of those who are only moderately frightened at such things): that I could not endure the sight of that infinite depth without a shiver and a trembling of the back of my legs and thighs, even though I was fully my own length away from the actual edge, and could not have fallen unless I had conveyed myself purposely into danger. I have also noticed there that whatever the height might be, provided that in the side some tree or jutting rock is present to support our sight a little and break it up, this relieves us and gives us assurance, as if it were a thing from which in case of a fall we could get help; but that sheer and unbroken precipices we cannot even look at without vertigo: ^c*such that we cannot look down without dizziness both of eyes and of mind* [Livy]; ^Awhich is an evident imposture of our sight.

That fine philosopher put out his eyes[62] to relieve his soul of the

62 Democritus, according to Cicero, who, however, questions the story.

distractions that it received from them, and to be able to philoso-
phize in greater freedom.

But on that score he should also have had his ears stopped up,
[B]which Theophrastus says are the most dangerous instrument we
have for receiving violent impressions to disturb and alter us; [A]and
he should in short have deprived himself of all the other senses, that
is to say of his life and his being. For they all have this power to
command our reason and our soul. [C]*Again it often happens that our
mind is struck more vehemently by some sight, some depth of voice, some
songs; often again by care and fear* [Cicero].

[A]The doctors hold that there are certain temperaments that are
stirred even to fury by some sounds and instruments. I have seen
some who could not hear a bone gnawed under their table without
losing patience; and there is hardly a man who is not disturbed by
that harsh and piercing noise made by files scraping on iron; just as
many, on hearing someone chewing nearby, or someone talking who
has the passages of his nose or throat stopped up, are moved to the
point of anger and hatred. That piping prompter of Gracchus, who
softened, hardened, or directed his master's voice whenever he made
a harangue at Rome, what use was he, if the movement and quality
of the sound had not the power to move and alter the judgment of
the audience? Truly there is good reason to make so much of the
firmness of that fine faculty,[63] that lets itself be manipulated
and altered by the accidental movements of so light a wind!

This same deception that the senses convey to our understanding
they receive in their turn. Our soul at times takes a like revenge;
[C]they compete in lying and deceiving each other. [A]What we see and
hear when stirred with anger, we do not hear as it is:

A double sun appears, and twin cities of Thebes.
VIRGIL

The object that we love seems to us more beautiful than it is –

[B]Thus women oft we see, ugly and bent,
Receive men's love, and honors eminent
LUCRETIUS

– [A]and uglier the one that we loathe. To a man vexed and afflicted
the brightness of the day seems darkened and gloomy. Our senses
are not only altered, but often completely stupefied by the passions

63 The judgment.

of the soul. How many things we see which we do not notice if our mind is occupied elsewhere!

> Even in plain things you can plainly see,
> Unless you pay attention, they will be
> As though remote in time, or far away.
> LUCRETIUS

It seems as though the soul draws the powers of the senses inward and occupies them. Thus both the inside and the outside of man is full of weakness and falsehood.

ᴮThose who have compared our life to a dream were perhaps more right than they thought. When we dream, our soul lives, acts, exercises all her faculties, neither more nor less than when she is awake; but if more loosely and obscurely, still surely not so much so that the difference is as between night and bright daylight; rather as between night and shade. There she sleeps, here she slumbers: more and less. It is always darkness, and Cimmerian darkness.

ᶜSleeping we are awake, and waking asleep. I do not see so clearly in sleep; but my wakefulness I never find pure and cloudless enough. Moreover sleep in its depth sometimes puts dreams to sleep. But our wakefulness is never so awake as to purge and properly dissipate reveries, which are the dreams of the waking, and worse than dreams.

Since our reason and our soul accept the fancies and opinions which arise in it while sleeping, and authorize the actions of our dreams with the same approbation as they do those of the day, why do we not consider the possibility that our thinking, our acting, may be another sort of dreaming, and our waking another kind of sleep?

ᴬIf the senses are our first judges, it is not ours alone that must be consulted, for in this faculty the animals have as much right as we have, or more. It is certain that some have hearing keener than man's, others sight, others smell, others touch or taste. Democritus said that the gods and the animals had much more perfect sensitive faculties than man.

Now between the effects of their senses and ours, the difference is extreme. Our saliva cleans and dries up our wounds; it kills a snake:

> So great the distance and the difference here,
> That one man's food others as poison fear.
> By man's saliva touched, snakes oft decay,
> And bite themselves to death.
> LUCRETIUS

What property shall we attribute to saliva? According to us, or according to the snake? By which of the two points of view shall we prove its real essence, which we are seeking? Pliny says that there are in the Indies certain sea-hares which are poison to us and we to them, so that by a mere touch we kill them. Which is really poisonous, man or the fish? Which are we to believe, the fish about man, or man about the fish?

[B]A certain quality of air infects man, which does not harm the ox; another infects the ox, which does not harm man. Which of the two, in truth and in nature, is the pestilential quality?

[A]Those who have jaundice see all things as yellowish and paler than we do:

> [B]Moreover, all that jaundiced people see
> Becomes pale yellow. LUCRETIUS

[A]Those who have that malady that the doctors call hyposphagma, which is a suffusion of blood under the skin, see everything as red and bloody. These humors which thus change the operations of our sight, how do we know but that they predominate in animals and are the ordinary thing with them? For we see some that have yellow eyes like our sufferers from jaundice, others that have them red and bloodshot. It is probable that to them the color of objects appears different than to us. Which of the two is the true judgment? For it is not said that the essence of things is referred to man alone. Hardness, whiteness, depth, and bitterness concern the service and knowledge of the animals as well as ours; nature has given to them the use of these as well as to us.

When we press our eye, we perceive the bodies that we are looking at as longer and more extended. Many animals have an eye thus pressed. So this lengthiness is perhaps the real shape of this body, not that which our eyes assign to it in their ordinary position. [B]If we squeeze the eye from below, things seem double to us:

> Double the lights of lamps, flowering with flame,
> Double the face of man, his body twain.
> LUCRETIUS

[A]If our ears are stopped with anything, or our passages of hearing constricted, we receive the sound otherwise than we ordinarily do. The animals that have hairy ears, or that have only a very tiny hole in

place of an ear, consequently do not hear what we hear, and receive
the sound differently.

We see at festivals and in theaters that when we hold up a pane
tinted with some color against the light of the torches, everything in
the place appears to us green, or yellow, or violet:

> [B]In our great theaters this oft is done
> By veils of yellow, red, or rust, which run
> From poles and timbers, billowing but stretched tight.
> They dye the assembly with their tinted light,
> And on the stage, on statues row on row
> Of gods and parents, make their colors flow.
>
> LUCRETIUS

[A]It is likely that the eyes of animals, which we see are of different
colors, make bodies appear to them as matching their eyes.

To judge the action of the senses, then, we should first of all be in
agreement with the animals, and second, among ourselves. Which
we are not in the least; and we get into disputes at every turn because
one man hears, sees, or tastes something differently from someone
else; and we dispute about the diversity of the images that the senses
bring us as much as about anything else. By the ordinary rule of
nature, a child hears, sees, and tastes otherwise than a man of thirty,
and he otherwise than a sexagenarian.

The senses are in some people more obscure and dim, in others
more open and acute. We receive things in one way and another,
according to what we are and what they seem to us. Now since our
seeming is so uncertain and controversial, it is no longer a miracle
if we are told that we can admit that snow appears white to us, but
that we cannot be responsible for proving that it is so of its essence
and in truth; and, with this starting point shaken, all the knowledge
in the world necessarily goes by the board.

What of the fact that our senses interfere with each other?
A painting seems to the eye to be in relief, to the touch it seems
flat. Shall we say that musk is agreeable or not, which rejoices our
sense of smell and offends our taste? There are herbs and unguents
suitable for one part of the body which injure another. Honey
is pleasant to the taste, unpleasant to the sight. As for those rings
which are cut in the form of feathers and are called in heraldry
feathers without ends, there is no eye that can discern their width
and that can defend itself against this illusion, that on one side they
grow wider, and narrower and tapering on the other, even when you

roll them around your finger; however, to the touch they seem equal in width and everywhere alike.

[B]Those persons who, to enhance their voluptuousness, in ancient times used mirrors made to enlarge and magnify the object they reflect, so that the members which they were to put to work should please them the more by this ocular growth: to which of the two senses did they give the victory, to the sight which showed them these members stout and long as they liked, or to the touch which showed them small and contemptible?

[A]Is it our senses that lend the object these differing qualities, and do the objects nevertheless have only one? As we see in the bread we eat: it is only bread, but our use makes of it bones, blood, flesh, hair, and nails:

> [B]As food, dispersed through all our members, dies,
> And other substance of itself supplies.
> LUCRETIUS

[A]The moisture that the root of a tree sucks up becomes trunk, leaf, and fruit; and the air, being but one, by being applied to a trumpet is diversified into a thousand kinds of sounds. Is it our senses, I say, which likewise fashion these objects out of various qualities, or do they really have them so? And in the face of this doubt, what can we decide about their real essence?

Moreover, since the accidents of illnesses, madness, or sleep make things appear to us otherwise than they appear to healthy people, wise men, and waking people, is it not likely that our normal state and our natural disposition can also assign to things an essence corresponding to our condition, and accommodate them to us, as our disordered states do? And that our health is as capable of giving them its own appearance as sickness? [C]Why should the temperate man not have some vision of things related to himself, like the intemperate man, and likewise imprint his own character on them?

The jaded man assigns the insipidity to the wine; the healthy man, the savor; the thirsty man, the relish.

[A]Now, since our condition accommodates things to itself and transforms them according to itself, we no longer know what things are in truth; for nothing comes to us except falsified and altered by our senses. When the compass, the square, and the ruler are off, all the proportions drawn from them, all the buildings erected by their measure, are also necessarily imperfect and defective. The uncertainty of our senses makes everything they produce uncertain:

> As in a building, if the rule is false,
> If a bent square gives verticals untrue,
> And if the level is at all askew,
> Then all must be defective and at fault,
> Forward or backward leaning, lame and halt;
> Some part already seems about to fall;
> Then, from those first mistakes, down tumbles all.
> Thus any reasoning of yours on things
> Must needs be false, that from false senses springs.
>
> LUCRETIUS

Furthermore, who shall be fit to judge these differences? As we say in disputes about religion that we need a judge not attached to either party, free from preference and passion, which is impossible among Christians, so it is in this. For if he is old, he cannot judge the sense perception of old age, being himself a party in this dispute; if he is young, likewise; healthy, likewise; likewise sick, asleep, or awake. We would need someone exempt from all these qualities, so that with an unprejudiced judgment he might judge of these propositions as of things indifferent to him; and by that score we would need a judge that never was.

To judge the appearances that we receive of objects, we would need a judicatory instrument; to verify this instrument, we need a demonstration; to verify the demonstration, an instrument: there we are in a circle.

Since the senses cannot decide our dispute, being themselves full of uncertainty, it must be reason that does so. No reason can be established without another reason: there we go retreating back to infinity.

Our conception is not itself applied to foreign objects, but is conceived through the mediation of the senses; and the senses do not comprehend the foreign object, but only their own impressions. And thus the conception and semblance we form is not of the object, but only of the impression and effect made on the sense; which impression and the object are different things. Wherefore whoever judges by appearances judges by something other than the object.

And as for saying that the impressions of the senses convey to the soul the quality of the foreign objects by resemblance, how can the soul and understanding make sure of this resemblance, having of itself no communication with foreign objects? Just as a man who

does not know Socrates, seeing his portrait, cannot say that it resembles him.

Now if anyone should want to judge by appearances anyway, to judge by all appearances is impossible, for they clash with one another by their contradictions and discrepancies, as we see by experience. Shall some selected appearances rule the others? We shall have to verify this selection by another selection, the second by a third; and thus it will never be finished.

[CHANGING MAN CANNOT KNOW CHANGING THINGS]

Finally, there is no existence that is constant, either of our being or of that of objects. And we, and our judgment, and all mortal things go on flowing and rolling unceasingly. Thus nothing certain can be established about one thing by another, both the judging and the judged being in continual change and motion.

[CHANGING MAN CANNOT KNOW UNCHANGING GOD]

We have no communication with being,[64] because every human nature is always midway between birth and death, offering only a dim semblance and shadow of itself, and an uncertain and feeble opinion. And if by chance you fix your thought on trying to grasp its essence, it will be neither more nor less than if someone tried to grasp water: for the more he squeezes and presses what by its nature flows all over, the more he will lose what he was trying to hold and grasp. Thus, all things being subject to pass from one change to another, reason, seeking a real stability in them, is baffled, being unable to apprehend anything stable and permanent; because everything is either coming into being and not yet fully existent, or beginning to die before it is born.

Plato said that bodies never had existence, but did have birth; ^cthinking that Homer had made the Ocean father of the gods, and Thetis mother, to show us that all things are in perpetual flux, change, and variation – an opinion common to all the philosophers before his time, as he says, except Parmenides alone, who denied things movement, on whose power he sets great store. ^APythagoras thought that all matter is flowing and sliding. The Stoics, that there is no present time, and that what we call present is only the juncture

64 All the passage that follows, down to the fourth paragraph from the end of the essay, is copied almost word for word from Plutarch's *Moral Essays*, "On the Meaning of εἰ," in the French translation by Jacques Amyot.

and meeting of the future and the past. Heraclitus, that never had a man entered the same river twice.

ᴮEpicharmus, that he who once borrowed money does not owe it now; and that he who last night was invited to come to dine this morning, today comes uninvited, seeing that he and his hosts are no longer themselves: they have become others. ᴬAnd that no mortal substance can be found twice in the same state; for by the suddenness and nimbleness of its change, it is now dissipated, now reassembled; it comes, and then goes. So that what is beginning to be born never arrives at the perfection of being; forasmuch as this birth is never completed, and never stops as being at an end, but from the seed onward goes on ever changing and shifting from one thing into another. As from human seed is made first in the mother's womb a formless fruit, then a fully formed infant; then, outside the womb, an infant at the breast; afterward it becomes a boy; then in turn a youth; then a grown man; then an older man; finally a decrepit old man. So that the subsequent age and generation is always undoing and destroying the preceding one:

> ᴮTime alters all the nature of the world;
> From one state to another all must change;
> Nothing remains itself, but all things range;
> Nature modifies all and changes all.
> LUCRETIUS

ᴬAnd then we stupidly fear one kind of death, when we have already passed and are still passing through so many others. For not only, as Heraclitus used to say, is the death of fire the generation of air, and the death of air the generation of water; but even more obviously we can see it in ourselves. Our prime dies and passes when old age comes along, and youth ends in the prime of the grown man, childhood in youth, and infancy in childhood. And yesterday dies in today, and today will die in tomorrow; and there is nothing that abides and is always the same.

For, to prove that this is so, if we always remain one and the same, how is it that we rejoice now in one thing, and now in another? How is it that we love opposite things or hate them, praise them or blame them? How do we have different affections, no longer retaining the same feeling within the same thought? For it is not plausible that we take up different passions without changing; and what suffers change does not remain one and the same, and if it is not one and the

same, it also *is* not; but together with its *being the same*, it also changes its simple *being*, from one thing always becoming another. And consequently the senses of nature are mistaken and lie, taking what appears for what is, for want of really knowing what it is that *is*.

But then what really is? That which is eternal: that is to say, what never had birth, nor will ever have an end; to which time never brings any change. For time is a mobile thing, which appears as in a shadow, together with matter, which is ever running and flowing, without ever remaining stable or permanent. To which belong the words *before* and *after*, and *has been* or *will be*, which at the very first sight show very evidently that time is not a thing that *is*; for it would be a great stupidity and a perfectly apparent falsehood to say that that *is* which is not yet in being, or which already has ceased to be. And as for these words, *present, immediate, now*, on which it seems that we chiefly found and support our understanding of time, reason discovering this immediately destroys it; for she at once splits and divides it into future and past, as though wanting to see it necessarily divided in two.

The same thing happens to nature that is measured, as to time that measures it. For there is nothing in it either that abides or is stable; but all things in it are either born, or being born, or dying. For which reason it would be a sin to say of God, who is the only one that *is*, that he *was* or *will be*. For those terms represent declinings, transitions, or vicissitudes of what cannot endure or remain in being. Wherefore we must conclude that God alone *is* – not at all according to any measure of time, but according to an eternity immutable and immobile, not measured by time or subject to any decline; before whom there is nothing, nor will there be after, nor is there anything more new or more recent; but one who really is – who by one single *now* fills the *ever*; and there is nothing that really is but he alone – nor can we say "He has been," or "He will be" – without beginning and without end.

To this most religious conclusion of a pagan I want to add only this remark of a witness of the same condition,[65] for an ending to this long and boring discourse, which would give me material without end: "O what a vile and abject thing is man," he says, "if he does not raise himself above humanity!"

65 Seneca.

[CONCLUSION: MAN IS NOTHING WITHOUT GOD]

^CThat is a good statement and a useful desire, but equally absurd. For ^Ato make the handful bigger than the hand, the armful bigger than the arm, and to hope to straddle more than the reach of our legs, is impossible and unnatural. Nor can man raise himself above himself and humanity; for he can see only with his own eyes, and seize only with his own grasp.

He will rise, if God by exception lends him a hand; he will rise by abandoning and renouncing his own means, and letting himself be raised and uplifted by purely celestial means.

^CIt is for our Christian faith, not for his Stoical virtue, to aspire to that divine and miraculous metamorphosis.[66]

13
Of judging of the death of others

^AWhen we judge of the assurance of other men in dying, which is without doubt the most noteworthy action of human life, we must be mindful of one thing: that people do not easily believe that they have reached that point. Few men die convinced that it is their last hour; and there is no place where the deception of hope deludes us more. It never stops trumpeting into our ears: "Others have certainly been sicker without dying; the case is not as desperate as they think; and at worst, God has certainly worked other miracles."

And this comes about because we set too much importance on ourselves. It seems that the universe somehow suffers by our annihilation and that it has compassion for our state; because our vision, when altered, represents things to itself as being likewise altered, and we think they are failing it in proportion as it is failing them;

66 This conclusion (all that follows "raise himself above humanity!") replaced the following one, which appeared in all the editions published during Montaigne's lifetime: "There is no truer saying in all his Stoic school than that one. But to make the handful bigger than the hand, the armful bigger than the arm, and to hope to straddle more than the reach of our legs, is impossible and unnatural. Nor can man raise himself above himself and humanity; for he can see only with his own eyes, and seize only with his own grasp. He will rise, if God lends him his hand; he will rise by abandoning and renouncing his own means, and letting himself be raised and uplifted by divine grace; but not otherwise."

like travelers at sea, for whom mountains, countrysides, cities, heaven, and earth move right along with them and at the same pace:

> ᴮWe leave the port, and lands and towns retreat.
>
> VIRGIL

Who ever saw old age not praising times past and blaming the present, charging the world and the ways of men with its own misery and chagrin?

> The old man shakes his head and heaves a sigh,
> Compares the present day with days gone by,
> Praises his father's lot, and to satiety
> Prates of the dead, and of their piety.
>
> LUCRETIUS

We drag everything along with us.

ᴬWhence it follows that we consider our death a great thing, and one which does not pass so easily, nor without solemn consultation of the stars: ᶜ*so many gods in an uproar about one single head* [Seneca]. ᴬAnd we think so all the more, the more we prize ourselves. ᶜWhat? Should so much learning be lost, with so much damage, without the special concern of the destinies? Does a soul so rare and exemplary cost no more to kill than a plebeian and useless one? This life, which protects so many others, on which so many other lives depend, which employs so many people in its service, which fills so many places, is it displaced like one that holds only by its one single knot? Not one of us is convinced enough that he is only one.

ᴬHence come these words of Caesar to his pilot, more swollen than the sea that was threatening him:

> If under heaven's protection you decline
> To sail to Italy, then trust to mine.
> You fear because you know not who I am.
> Safe in my charge, break through the storms.
>
> LUCAN

And these:

> Caesar believed the risks to be
> Worthy now of his fate. "How great a task," said he,
> "The gods have to undo me, that they seek me out
> In a small skiff upon so great a sea!"
>
> LUCAN

^BAnd that public daydream that for a whole year the sun wore mourning on his face for Caesar's death:

> And likewise, mourning Rome, with Caesar dead,
> In dim rust-colored haze he veiled his head;
>
> VIRGIL

and a thousand similar ones by which the world lets itself be so easily tricked, believing that our losses affect heaven, ^Cand that its infinity is impassioned about our minute distinctions: *There is no such association between us and the heavens that at our death the splendor of the stars should also die* [Pliny].

^ANow it is not reasonable to form a judgment of the resolution and constancy of a man who does not yet recognize that he is in danger, even though he really is; nor is it enough for him to have died in this dangerous position, unless he placed himself in it precisely for that purpose. It happens to most men to stiffen their countenance and their words in order thereby to acquire a reputation that they still hope to enjoy alive. ^COf as many as I have seen die, fortune, not their design, has disposed their countenances. ^AAnd even among those who in ancient times did themselves to death, there is a big distinction as to whether it was a sudden death or a death that took time. That cruel Roman Emperor used to say of his prisoners that he wanted to make them feel death; and if anyone did away with himself in prison, he would say: "That one has escaped me." He wanted to extend death and make it felt by torments:

> ^BIn bodies, howsoever mangled, we have seen
> No boon of mortal wound, but the fierce cruelty
> Of keeping men alive even as we make them die.
>
> LUCAN

^AIn truth, it is not such a great thing, when one is all healthy and composed, to decide to kill oneself; it is quite easy to play tough before coming to grips. So that the most effeminate man in the world, Heliogabalus, amid his laxest sensualities, indeed made plans to kill himself ^Cdelicately ^Awhen the occasion should force him to. And so that his death should not belie the rest of his life, he expressly had a sumptuous tower built, the base and front of which were floored with planks enriched with gold and precious stones, to throw himself from; and he also had cords of gold and crimson silk made for strangling himself, and a gold sword forged for running himself through; and he kept venom in emerald and topaz vessels

for poisoning himself, according as the whim should seize him to choose from all these ways of dying:

[B]By a forced valor resolute and brave.

LUCAN

[A]Yet as for him, the luxuriousness of his preparations makes it more likely that he would have had a nosebleed from fear if he had been put to the test.

But even in those of stouter heart who have resolved on their execution, we must see, I say, whether it was by a blow that left them no time to feel its effect; for it is open to question whether, on seeing life flow away little by little, the body's feeling mingling with the soul's, keeping the means of repentance available, they would have had constancy and obstinacy in so dangerous an act of will.

In the civil wars of Caesar, Lucius Domitius, who upon being captured in the Abruzzi took poison, afterward repented. It has happened in our time that a man, having resolved to die and not having struck deep enough on his first attempt – the tenderness of the flesh repelling his arm – wounded himself again very hard two or three times afterward, but never could force himself to strike the blow home. [C]While Plautius Silvanus was on trial, Urgulania, his grandmother, sent him a dagger, with which, after trying without success to go through with killing himself, he had his servants cut his veins.

[B]Albucilla, in the time of Tiberius, struck herself too gently to kill herself, and gave her enemies the chance to imprison her and make her die in their own way. The general Demosthenes did the same thing after being routed in Sicily. [C]And C. Fimbria, having struck himself too feebly, got his valet to finish him off.

On the other hand, Ostorius, who was unable to use his arm, disdained to use that of his servant for anything but to hold the dagger straight and firm, and, taking a run, himself brought his throat against it and pierced it through.

[A]It is, in truth, a food that must be swallowed without chewing, unless a man has a leather-lined throat. And therefore the Emperor Hadrian had his doctor mark and encircle on his nipple precisely the mortal spot where the man was to aim whom he gave the charge of killing him. That is why Caesar, when they asked him what death he found most desirable, answered: "The least premeditated and the quickest."

[B]If Caesar dared say it, it is no longer cowardice for me to believe it.

ᴬ"A quick death," says Pliny, "is the supreme good fortune of human life." They do not like to recognize death. No one can say that he is resolved on it who fears to negotiate it, who cannot sustain it with open eyes. Those whom we see at executions running to meet their end, and hastening and urging the carrying out of the sentence, do not do so out of resolution; they want to deprive themselves of the time to consider it. Being dead does not trouble them, but dying does indeed:

> It is not death, but dying, that I fear.
>
> EPICHARMUS

That is a degree of firmness which I have learned by experience that I could reach, like those who plunge into dangers, as into the sea, with their eyes closed. ᶜThere is nothing, in my opinion, more illustrious in the life of Socrates than having had thirty whole days to ruminate his death sentence, having digested it all that time with a very certain expectation, without emotion, without alteration, and with a tenor of actions and words rather lowered and relaxed than strained and exalted by the weight of such a reflection.

ᴬPomponius Atticus, the one to whom Cicero wrote letters, being sick, sent for his son-in-law Agrippa and for two or three other friends of his and told them that having found by experience that he was gaining nothing by trying to cure himself, and that all he was doing to lengthen his life was also lengthening and increasing his pain, he was determined to put an end to both; he asked them to approve of his determination, or, at worst, not to waste their pains in trying to dissuade him. Now, he chose to kill himself by abstinence, and behold his disease accidentally cured: the remedy that he had employed to do away with himself restores him to health. The doctors and his friends, celebrating such a happy result and rejoicing with him over it, found themselves much mistaken; for it was impossible for them to make him change his mind for all that. He said that one way or another he would have to cross that line some day, and that being so far advanced, he wanted to save himself the trouble of beginning all over again another time. This man, having reconnoitered death quite at his leisure, was not only undismayed but even eager to meet it; for, being satisfied on the reason why he entered the combat, he made it a point of bravery to see it through to the end. It is very far beyond not fearing death, to want to taste it and relish it.

^CThe story of the philosopher Cleanthes is very similar. His gums were swollen and decayed; the doctors advised the strictest abstinence. After fasting for two days, he is so much better that they declare him cured and allow him to return to his accustomed way of life. He, on the contrary, already tasting some sweetness in this faintness, decides not to draw back again and crosses the line toward which he had advanced so far.

^ATullius Marcellinus, a young Roman, wanting to anticipate the hour of his destiny in order to rid himself of a malady that was treating him more roughly than he cared to be treated, although the doctors promised him a certain cure if not such a quick one, called together his friends to deliberate about it. Some, says Seneca, gave him the advice that through cowardice they would have taken for themselves; others, through flattery, that which they thought would be most agreeable to him. But a Stoic spoke to him thus: "Do not torment yourself, Marcellinus, as if you were deliberating about something important. It is no great thing to live – your valets and the animals live – but it is a great thing to die honorably, wisely, and with constancy. Think how long it has been that you have been doing the same thing: eating, drinking, sleeping; drinking, sleeping, and eating. We turn incessantly in this circle; not only evil and unendurable accidents, but the very satiety of living, makes us want to die."

Marcellinus did not need a man to advise him, but a man to help him. The servants feared to take a hand, but this philosopher made them understand that domestics are suspected only when it is doubtful whether the master's death was voluntary; that otherwise it would be as bad an example to hinder him as to kill him, inasmuch as

> To save a man against his will is just like killing.
> HORACE

After that, he observed to Marcellinus that, just as we give the attendants what is left on the tables when our meals are done, so it would not be unbecoming, now that his life was finished, to distribute something to those who had ministered to it. Now Marcellinus was of a free and liberal heart; he had a certain sum divided among his servants and comforted them. For the rest, there was no need of steel or blood; he undertook to leave this life, not run out of it; not to escape death, but to experience it. And to give himself

leisure to deal with it, having given up all nourishment, and, on the third day after, having had himself sprinkled with warm water, he fainted away little by little, and not without a certain voluptuousness, so he said. In truth, those who have had these failings of the heart that get their hold from our weakness say that they feel no pain in them, indeed rather a certain pleasure, as when we pass into sleep and rest.

Those are studied and digested deaths.

But in order that Cato alone might suffice for every example of virtue, it seems as if his good destiny gave him pain in the hand with which he gave himself the blow, that he might have leisure to confront death and collar it, strengthening his courage in the danger instead of softening it. And if it had been up to me to portray him in his proudest posture, this would have been all bloody, tearing out his own bowels, rather than sword in hand, as did the statuaries of his time. For this second murder was much more savage than the first.

14
How our mind hinders itself

[A]It is an amusing conception to imagine a mind exactly balanced between two equal desires. For it is indubitable that it will never decide, since inclination and choice imply inequality in value; and if we were placed between the bottle and the ham with an equal appetite for drinking and for eating, there would doubtless be no solution but to die of thirst and of hunger.

To provide against this difficulty, the Stoics, when they are asked whence comes the choice in our soul between two indifferent things, and what makes us take one rather than the other out of a large number of one-crown pieces when they are all alike and there is no reason which inclines us to a preference, answer that this movement of the soul is extraordinary and irregular, coming from an external, accidental, and fortuitous impulse in us.

It might rather be said, it seems to me, that nothing presents itself to us in which there is not some difference, however slight; and that either to the sight or to the touch, there is always something extra that attracts us, though it be imperceptibly. Likewise if we suppose a string equally strong throughout, it is impossible by all impossibility that it should break; for where do you want the break to begin? And to break everywhere at once is not in nature.

If anyone should further add to this the geometrical propositions which conclude by the certainty of their demonstrations that the thing contained is greater than the container, the center as great as the circumference; and which find two lines endlessly approaching each other and unable ever to meet, and the philosopher's stone, and the squaring of the circle, where reason and the fact are so opposite; he might perhaps derive from them some argument to support this bold saying of Pliny: *There is nothing certain but uncertainty, and nothing more miserable and arrogant than man.*[1]

15
That our desire is increased by difficulty

^AThere is no reason that does not have its opposite, says the wisest school of philosophers.[2] I was just now ruminating that fine saying that one of the ancients alleges as a reason for despising life: "No good can bring us pleasure, unless it is one for whose loss we are prepared: ^C*Grief for something lost and fear of losing it amount to the same thing*" [Seneca]; ^Ameaning to prove thereby that the enjoyment of life cannot be truly pleasant to us if we are in fear of losing it.

It might be said, however, on the contrary, that we clutch and embrace this good all the more tightly and with more affection because we see that it is less secure and fear that it may be taken from us. For we obviously sense that, just as fire is stirred up by the presence of cold, so our will is whetted by opposition:

> ^BHad Danae not been confined in a brazen tower,
> Never had Jove made Danae a mother;
>
> OVID

^Aand that there is nothing naturally so contrary to our enjoyment as the satiety that comes from facility, nor anything that whets it so much as rarity and difficulty. *In all things our pleasure is increased by the very danger which should make us avoid it* [Seneca].

> Galla, say no: love cloys, unless pain cuts the bliss.
>
> MARTIAL

1 This was one of the sentences inscribed on the ceiling of Montaigne's library. In the editions of the *Essays* published during his lifetime, he translates it after quoting it.
2 The Pyrrhonists.

To keep love in breath, Lycurgus ordained that the married people of Lacedaemon could have sexual relations only by stealth, and that it should be as great a shame to find them in bed together as with others. The difficulty of assignations, the danger of surprises, the shame of the next day,

> And listlessness, and silence,
> And, fetched up from the depths, a sigh,
>
> HORACE

that is what gives a tang to the sauce. ᶜHow many very lasciviously pleasant sports spring from the modest and shamefaced way of speaking about the works of love! ᴬEven sensual pleasure seeks stimulation from pain. It is much sweeter when it burns and stings. The courtesan Flora used to say that she had never lain with Pompey without making him carry away the marks of her bites:

> They hurt the longed-for body with their viselike grip,
> And with their teeth they lacerate the tender lip,
> Goaded by secret stings to hurt the very thing,
> Whate'er it be, from which these germs of madness spring.
>
> LUCRETIUS

It is the same way everywhere; difficulty gives value to things.

ᴮThe people of the March of Ancona prefer to make their vows to Saint James, and those of Galicia to Our Lady of Loreto.[3] At Liège they make much ado about the baths of Lucca, and in Tuscany about those of Spa. You see hardly a Roman in the fencing school at Rome, which is full of Frenchmen. That great man Cato found himself, just like the rest of us, weary of his wife as long as she was his, and desired her when she belonged to another man.

ᶜI have put out to stud an old horse who could not be controlled at the scent of mares. Facility presently sated him toward his own mares; but toward strange ones, and the first one that passes by his pasture, he returns to his importunate neighings and his furious heats, as before.

ᴬOur appetite scorns and passes over what is at hand, to run after what it has not:

> And flies over what's in the path, pursues what flees.
>
> HORACE

3 The Italians of Ancona go to Santiago de Compostela in Spain, the Spaniards of Galicia to Loreto in Italy.

To forbid us something is to make us want it:

> [B]Unless you start to guard your lass,
> She'll start to be no longer mine, alas.
>
> OVID

[A]To give it up to us completely is to breed in us contempt for it. Want and abundance fall into the same discomfort,

> The excess pains you, and the want pains me.
>
> ADAPTED FROM TERENCE

Desire and enjoyment make us equally dissatisfied.[4] Rigor in mistresses is annoying, but ease and facility, to tell the truth, is even more so; inasmuch as discontent and anger are born of the value in which we hold the thing desired, sharpen love, and warm it up; but satiety engenders distaste: it is a blunt, dull, weary, and drowsy feeling:

> [B]If she would reign long, let her scorn her lover.
>
> OVID

> Lovers, scorn away.
> Thus she who yesterday refused will come today.
>
> PROPERTIUS

[C]Why did Poppaea think of masking the beauties of her face, except to enhance them to her lovers? [A]Why have they veiled, even down to the heels, those beauties that every woman wants to show, that every man wants to see? Why do they cover with so many impediments, one on top of the other, the parts in which our desire and theirs principally dwells? And what is the use of those great bastions with which our women have just taken to arming their flanks, except to allure our appetite and to attract us to them by keeping us at a distance?

> She flees into the willows, and hopes first to be seen.
>
> VIRGIL

> [B]Sometimes her tunic, interposed, made a delay.
>
> PROPERTIUS

[A]What is the use of that art of virginal shame, that sedate coldness, that severe countenance, that profession of ignorance of

4 The A passages from here to "does not outweigh the harm" (four paragraphs later) first appeared in the 1582 edition.

things that they know better than we who instruct them in them, but to increase in us the desire to conquer, to overwhelm and subdue to our appetite all this ceremony and these obstacles? For there is not only pleasure but also glory in driving wild and seducing that soft sweetness and that childlike modesty, and in reducing a proud and commanding gravity to the mercy of our ardor. It is a glory, they say, to triumph over rigor, modesty, chastity, and temperance; and whoever dissuades the ladies from these attitudes betrays both them and himself. We must believe that their heart shudders with fright, that the sound of our words offends the purity of their ears, that they hate us for it and yield themselves to our importunity only with a forced constraint. Beauty, all-powerful as it is, has not the wherewithal to make itself relished without that interposition.

See how in Italy, where there is more beauty for sale, and of the most elegant, it must seek other extraneous means and other arts to make itself agreeable; and yet, in truth, do what it will, being venal and public, it remains weak and languishing. Just as, even in the case of valor, of two similar acts we still consider that one fairer and more worthy in which more obstacle and risk is offered.

It is an act of divine Providence to allow its holy Church to be agitated, as we see it is, by so many troubles and storms, in order to awaken pious souls by this opposition and bring them back from the idleness and sleepiness into which such long tranquillity had plunged them. If we weigh our loss against our gain, the number of those who have gone astray against the renewed vigor, zeal, and strength that have come to us in this struggle, I do not know that the benefit does not outweigh the harm.

We have thought to tie the knot of our marriages more firmly by taking away all means of dissolving them; but the knot of will and affection has become loosened and undone as much as that of constraint has tightened. And on the contrary, what kept marriages in Rome so long in honor and security was everyone's freedom to break them off at will. They loved their wives the better because they might lose them; and, with full liberty of divorce, five hundred years and more passed before anyone took advantage of it.

What is allowed, we scorn; what's not allowed, we burn for.

OVID

To this theme could be joined the opinion of an ancient, that punishments rather whet vices than dull their edge; [B]that they do

not engender a concern to do well – that is the work of reason and discipline – but only a concern not to be caught doing evil:

> Cut out the infected spot, and wider spreads contagion.
>
> RUTILIUS

^AI do not know if that is true, but this I know by experience, that never was any civil morale reformed in that way. The order and regulation of conduct depends on some other means.

^CThe Greek histories make mention of the Argippians, neighbors of Scythia, who live without rod or stick for offense. Not only does no one undertake to go and attack them, but whoever can escape to them is safe, because of their virtue and sanctity of life; and there is no one so bold as to touch them. People have recourse to them to settle the differences that arise between men of other countries.

^BThere is a nation where gardens and fields that people want to keep safe are closed off with a cotton thread, and it proves much surer and stronger than our ditches and hedges. ^C*Locked places invite the thief. The burglar passes by what is open* [Seneca].

Perhaps facility of access serves, among other means, to protect my house from the violence of our civil wars. Defense attracts enterprise; and mistrust, offense. I have weakened the intent of the soldiers by taking from their enterprise the elements of risk and military glory, which customarily served them as pretext and excuse. What is done courageously is always done honorably, in a time when justice is dead. I make the conquest of my house cowardly and treacherous for them. It is closed to no one who knocks. For all protection, there is only a porter of ancient custom and ceremony, who serves not so much to defend my door as to offer it with more decorum and grace. I have no guard or sentinel but that which the stars provide for me.

A gentleman is wrong to make a show of defending himself if he is not perfectly ready to do so. Whoever is open on one side is open on all. Our fathers did not think of building frontier garrisons. The means of assailing, I mean without battery and without army, and of surprising our houses, grow every day beyond the means of guarding ourselves. Generally wits grow sharper in that direction. Invasion concerns all; defense, only the rich.

My house was strong for the time when it was built. I have added nothing to it in that line, and would fear that its strength might be turned against myself. Besides, a peaceful time will require that we

defortify our houses. There is the danger of not being able to regain them. And it is difficult to be sure of them. For in the matter of intestine wars, your valet may be of the party that you fear. And where religion serves as a pretext, even kinship becomes untrustworthy, under the cloak of justice. The public finances will not maintain our private garrisons; they would be exhausted by the attempt. We do not have the means to maintain them without ruining ourselves, or, what is more harmful and unjust, without ruining the people. I would hardly be worse off if I lost my house.

Besides, if you are ruined, even your friends amuse themselves not so much in pitying you as in blaming your lack of vigilance and foresight, your ignorance or nonchalance in the duties of your profession.

The fact that so many guarded houses have been lost, whereas this one endures, makes me suspect that they were lost because they were guarded. That gives the assailant both the desire and a reason. Any defense bears the aspect of war. Let anyone thrust himself into my house, if God wills it; but at all events I shall not invite him. It is my retreat to rest myself from the wars. I try to withdraw this corner from the public tempest, as I do another corner in my soul. Our war may change forms all it will, and multiply and diversify itself into new factions; as for me, I do not budge. Amid so many fortified houses, I alone of my rank in France, as far as I know, have entrusted purely to heaven the protection of mine. And I have never removed a silver spoon or a title deed. I will neither fear, nor save myself, by halves. If the fullness of my gratitude earns me God's favor, it will last me to the end; if not, I have still lasted long enough to make my duration worthy of remark and of record. How so? It is a good thirty years.[5]

16
Of glory

^There is the name and the thing. The name is a sound which designates and signifies the thing; the name is not a part of the thing or of the substance, it is an extraneous piece attached to the thing, and outside of it.

5 Since the beginning of the civil wars of religion in 1562; or Montaigne may be counting from 1560.

God, who is himself all fullness and the acme of all perfection, cannot grow and increase within; but his name may grow and increase by the blessing and praise we give to his external works. Which praise, since we cannot incorporate it in him, inasmuch as he can have no accession of good, we attribute to his name, which is the part outside him that is nearest him. That is why it is to God alone that glory and honor belong. And there is nothing so remote from reason as for us to go in quest of it for ourselves; for since we are indigent and necessitous within, since our essence is imperfect and continually in need of betterment, it is this betterment that we should work for.

We are all hollow and empty. It is not with wind and sound that we have to fill ourselves; we need more solid substance to repair us. A starving man would be very foolish to try to provide himself with a fine garment rather than with a good meal: we must run to what is most urgent. As our ordinary prayers say, *Glory to God in the highest, and on earth peace toward men* [Saint Luke]. We are in want of beauty, health, wisdom, virtue, and suchlike essential qualities; external ornaments will be sought after we have provided for the necessary things. Theology treats this subject amply and more pertinently, but I am hardly versed in it.

Chrysippus and Diogenes were the first and the firmest exponents of the disdain for glory; and they said that of all pleasures there was none more dangerous or more to be avoided than what comes to us from the approbation of others. In truth, experience makes us aware of many harmful betrayals at its hands. There is nothing that poisons princes so much as flattery, and nothing by which the wicked more easily gain credit with them; nor is there any pandering so fitted and so common for corrupting the chastity of women as to feed and entertain them with their praises.

^BThe first enchantment that the Sirens employ to beguile Ulysses is of this nature:

> Most praiseworthy Ulysses, turn to us here, here,
> Greatest of heroes, whom the men of Greece hold dear.
> FROM A FRENCH TRANSLATION OF HOMER

^AThose philosophers said that all the glory in the world did not deserve that a man of understanding should so much as stretch out his finger to acquire it:

^BWhat's in the greatest glory, if it be but glory?
 JUVENAL

^AI mean for itself alone; for it often brings in its train many advantages for which it may become desirable. It gains us good will; it makes us less exposed to insults and injuries from others, and the like.

It was also one of the principal doctrines of Epicurus; for that precept of his school, CONCEAL YOUR LIFE, which forbids men to encumber themselves with public charges and negotiations, also necessarily presupposes our contempt for glory, which is an approbation that the world offers of the actions that we place in evidence. He who orders us to conceal ourselves and to be concerned only with ourselves, and who does not want us to be known to others, is even farther from wanting us to be honored and glorified. So he advises Idomeneus not to regulate his actions at all by common opinion or reputation, except to avoid the other accidental disadvantages that men's contempt might bring him.

Those arguments are infinitely true, in my opinion, and reasonable. But we are, I know not how, double within ourselves, with the result that we do not believe what we believe, and we cannot rid ourselves of what we condemn. Let us see the last words of Epicurus, which he spoke as he was dying. They are great and worthy of such a philosopher, and yet they bear a certain mark of commending his name and of that humor that in his precepts he had decried. Here is a letter that he dictated a little before his last gasp:

"EPICURUS TO HERMACHUS, GREETING.

"While I was passing the happy and the very last day of my life, I was writing this, afflicted all the while with such pain in the bladder and intestines that nothing could be added to its greatness. But it was compensated by the pleasure which the remembrance of my discoveries and my teachings brought to my soul. Now do you, as the affection that you have had since childhood for me and for philosophy requires, embrace the protection of the children of Metrodorus."

There is his letter. And what makes me infer that this pleasure, which he says he feels in his soul over his discoveries, somewhat concerns the reputation that he hoped to acquire from them after his death, is the provision in his will by which he wants his heirs Amynomachus and Timocrates to defray such costs as Hermachus should decree for the celebration of his birthday every January, and

also the expenditures that should be made on the twentieth day of each month for the entertainment of his intimate philosopher friends who should assemble in honor of the memory of himself and Metrodorus.

Carneades was the protagonist of the opposite opinion, and maintained that glory was desirable for itself; just as we embrace our posterity for itself, though we have no knowledge or enjoyment of it. This opinion has not failed to be more commonly followed, as those are apt to be which most suit our inclinations. ᶜAristotle gives glory the first rank among external goods: "Avoid, as two vicious extremes, immoderation both in seeking it and in fleeing it." ᴬI believe that if we had the books that Cicero had written on this subject, he would tell us some good ones; for that man was so frenzied with this passion that if he had dared, he would, I believe, have readily fallen into the excessive view into which others fell, that virtue itself was desirable only for the honor that always attended it:

> There is little difference 'twixt buried idleness
> And hidden virtue.
>
> <div align="right">HORACE</div>

Which is an opinion so false that I am vexed that it could ever have entered the head of a man who had the honor of bearing the name of philosopher.

If that were true, we should be virtuous only in public; and there would be no point in keeping under rule and order the operations of the soul, where lies the true seat of virtue, except in so far as they should come to the knowledge of others.

ᶜIs it only a question then of doing wrong slyly and subtly? "If you know," says Carneades, "that a snake is hiding in the place where, unsuspecting, a person by whose death you hope to profit is about to sit down, you act wickedly if you do not warn him; and the more so in case your action is to be known only to yourself." If we do not derive from ourselves the law of well-doing, if impunity to us is justice, to how many sorts of wickedness shall we not abandon ourselves every day!

What S. Peduceus did in faithfully returning the money that C. Plotius had entrusted to his sole knowledge, and what I have often done in the same way, I do not consider so laudable as I should consider it execrable for him to have failed to do it.

And I find it good and useful to recall in our days the example of P. Sextilius Rufus, whom Cicero accuses of having collected an

inheritance against his conscience, not only not contrary to the laws, but by the laws themselves. And M. Crassus and Q. Hortensius, who because of their authority and power had been called in by a foreigner to share in the succession of a forged will, so that by that means he might establish his own share, contented themselves with not being participants in the forgery, and did not refuse to make some profit out of it; feeling sufficiently covered if they kept themselves sheltered from accusers, witnesses, and laws. *Let them remember that they have God as witness, that is to say (as I believe), their own conscience* [Cicero].

^AVirtue is a very vain and frivolous thing if it derives its recommendation from glory. To no purpose should we undertake to have it keep its rank apart, and disjoin it from fortune: for what is there more fortuitous than reputation? ^C*Truly Fortune rules in all things; she illumines or obscures all things according to her pleasure rather than the truth* [Sallust]. ^ATo make actions be known and seen is purely the work of fortune.

^CIt is chance that attaches glory to us according to its caprice. I have very often seen it go ahead of merit, and often surpass merit by a long distance. He who first thought of the resemblance between a shadow and glory did better than he intended. They are always pre-eminently empty things. The shadow also sometimes goes ahead of its body, and sometimes much exceeds it in length.

^AThose who teach the nobility to seek only honor in valor – ^C*as if what is not noted were not honorable* [Cicero] – ^Awhat do they gain thereby but to instruct them never to hazard themselves unless they are seen, and to take good care that there are witnesses who can bring back news of their valor? Whereas a thousand occasions of well-doing present themselves without our being able to be noticed for it. How many fine individual actions are buried in the press of a battle! Whoever wastes his time checking others during such a melee is not very busy in it himself, and produces against himself the testimony he gives of his companions' behavior. ^C*True and wise greatness of soul judges goodness, which our nature mainly seeks, to lie in deeds, not in fame* [Cicero].

All the glory that I aspire to in my life is to have lived it tranquilly – tranquilly not according to Metrodorus or Arcesilaus or Aristippus, but according to me. Since philosophy has not been able to find a way to tranquillity that is suitable to all, let everyone seek it individually.

^ATo what but to fortune do Caesar and Alexander owe the infinite greatness of their renown? How many men has it extinguished at the beginning of their career, of whom we have no knowledge, who brought to their work the same courage as theirs, if the misfortune of their fate had not stopped them short at the birth of their enterprises! Through so many and such extreme dangers, I do not remember having read that Caesar was ever wounded. A thousand have died from lesser perils than ^cthe least of ^Athose he passed through.

An infinity of fine actions must be lost without a witness before one appears to advantage. A man is not always at the top of a breach or at the head of an army, in sight of his general, as on a stage. He is taken by surprise between the hedge and the ditch; he must tempt fortune against a hen roost; he must root out four paltry musketeers from a barn; he must go out alone from his company and do a job alone, as the need presents itself. And if you watch carefully, you will find by experience that the least brilliant occasions happen to be the most dangerous; and that in the wars that have taken place in our times, more good men have been lost on trivial and unimportant occasions and in fighting over some shack than in worthy and honorable places.

^cWhoever thinks his death ill employed unless it is on some signal occasion, instead of casting luster on his death, is likely to obscure his life, meanwhile allowing many just occasions for hazarding himself to escape him. And all the just ones are illustrious enough, since each man's conscience trumpets them sufficiently to himself. *Our glory is the testimony of our conscience* [II Corinthians].

^AWhoever is a good man only because people will know it, and because they will esteem him better for it after knowing it, whoever will do well only on condition that his virtue will come to the knowledge of men, that man is not one from whom one can derive much service.

> Orlando the remaining winter spent,
> I think, in doing deeds deserving fame;
> But they've been hid since then to such extent
> That if I tell them not, I'm not to blame:
> For ever was Orlando more intent
> A noble deed to do, than to proclaim.

> Nor ever would his exploits have been told
> Save when some witness was there to behold.
>
> ARIOSTO

We must go to war out of duty, and expect this reward, which cannot fail for all noble actions, however hidden they be, and even for virtuous thoughts: the contentment that a well-regulated conscience receives in itself from well-doing. We must be valiant for ourselves and for the advantage we derive from having our courage firmly grounded and secure against the assaults of fortune.

> ^BVirtue ignores the voice of the profane,
> And brightly shines with honors without stain;
> Nor takes, nor lays the fasces down
> For a plebeian cheer or frown.
>
> HORACE

^AIt is not for show that our soul must play its part, it is at home, within us, where no eyes penetrate but our own. There it protects us from the fear of death, of pain, and even of shame; there it makes us secure against the loss of our children, of our friends, and of our fortunes; and, when the opportunity presents itself, it also leads us on to the hazards of war. ^C*Not for any profit, but for the beauty of merit itself* [Cicero]. ^AThis profit is much greater, and more worthy of being coveted and hoped for, than honor and glory, which is nothing but a favorable judgment that people make of us.

^BWe have to pick a dozen men out of a whole nation to pass judgment about an acre of land; and the judgment of our inclinations and our actions, the most difficult and important matter there is, we refer to the voice of the common people and of the mob, the mother of ignorance, injustice, and inconsistency. ^CIs it reasonable to make the life of a sage depend on the judgment of fools? *Can anything be more foolish than to think that those whom we despise individually amount to something collectively?* [Cicero]. ^BWhoever aims to please them has never done; this is a shapeless and elusive target. ^C*Nothing is so unaccountable as the mind of the multitude* [Livy].

Demetrius used to say comically about the voice of the people that he set no more store by that which issued from above than by that which issued from below. This man goes still further: *My opinion is this, that though a thing is not shameful in itself, still it is not free from shame when it is praised by the multitude* [Cicero].

[B]No art, no suppleness of mind, could guide our steps in following so erratic and unregulated a guide. In that windy confusion of rumors, reports, and popular opinions that push us about, no worth-while road can be charted. Let us not set ourselves a goal so fluctuating and wavering: let us steadfastly follow reason. Let public approbation follow us there, if it will; and since it depends entirely on fortune, we have no reason to expect it rather by any other way than by that one. Even if I should not follow the straight road because of its straightness, I would follow it because I have found by experience that when all is said and done it is generally the happiest and the most useful. [C]*Providence has given this gift to man, that the honorable is the most profitable* [Quintilian]. [B]The ancient mariner spoke thus to Neptune in a great tempest: "O God, you may save me if you will; you may destroy me if you will; but I shall still hold my rudder straight."

I have seen in my time a thousand supple, two-faced, equivocating men, who no one doubted were more worldly-wise than I, ruin themselves where I saved myself:

> I laughed to see how wiles could fail.
> OVID

[C]Aemilius Paulus, setting out on his glorious expedition into Macedonia, warned the people of Rome above all to restrain their tongues concerning his actions during his absence. How great a disturber in great affairs is complete liberty of judgment! Inasmuch as not everyone has the firmness of Fabius in the face of universal, hostile, and abusive clamor; he preferred to let his authority be dismembered by the vain fancies of men, rather than earn a favorable reputation and popular approval by performing his charge less well.

[B]There is I know not what natural sweetness in hearing oneself praised, but we make much too much of it.

> I fear not praise, no heart of horn have I.
> But that the test of worth is in your cry
> "Bravo! Well done!" – this I deny.
> PERSIUS

[A]I do not care so much what I am to others as I care what I am to myself. I want to be rich by myself, not by borrowing. Strangers see only the results and outward appearances. Any man can put on

a good face outside, while full of fever and fright within. They do not see my heart, they see only my countenance.

People are right to decry the hypocrisy that is found in war; for what is easier for a practical man than to dodge the dangers and play tough, when his heart is full of flabbiness? There are so many ways to avoid occasions for risking our individual lives that we can deceive the world a thousand times before engaging ourselves in a dangerous situation; and even then, finding ourselves stuck, we can perfectly well hide our game for the moment with a good face and a confident word, though our soul trembles within us. ^CAnd if they had the use of the Platonic ring[1] which made whoever wore it invisible if it was given a turn toward the palm of the hand, plenty of people would often hide when they ought to show themselves the most, and would repent of being placed in so honorable a spot, where necessity makes them act assured.

> ^AWho craves false honor and fears calumny
> A liar and a hypocrite must be. HORACE

That is why all these judgments that are founded on external appearances are marvelously uncertain and doubtful; and there is no witness so sure as each man to himself.

On those occasions, how many servants do we not have associated in our glory? He who stands firm in an open trench, what does he do that fifty poor trench diggers have not done before him, who open the way for him and protect him with their bodies for five sous a day?

> ^BWhatever giddy Rome decide,
> Care not, nor struggle to correct or chide
> Her faulty scales. Seek not thyself outside.
> PERSIUS

^AWe call it making our name great to spread and sow it in many mouths; we want it to be received there in good part, and to profit by this growth: that is the most excusable element in this urge. But the excess of this malady goes so far that many seek to be talked about no matter how. Trogus Pompeius says of Herostratus, and Livy of Manlius Capitolinus, that they were more desirous of a big than of a good reputation. This vice is common. We care more that

1 The ring of Gyges, described in Plato's *Republic*, Book II.

people should speak of us than how they speak of us; and it is enough for us that our name should be current in men's mouths, no matter in what way it may be current. It seems that to be known is to have one's life and duration somehow in the keeping of others.

As for me, I hold that I exist only in myself; and as for that other life of mine that lies in the knowledge of my friends, ᶜconsidering it naked and simply in itself, ᴬI know very well that I feel no fruit or enjoyment from it except by the vanity of a fanciful opinion. And when I am dead, I shall feel it even less; ᶜand moreover I shall lose completely the use of the real benefits which sometimes accidentally come after it. ᴬI shall no longer have any grip by which to seize reputation, nor by which it can touch me or reach me.

Indeed as for expecting my name to receive it, in the first place I have no name that is sufficiently my own. Of two that I have, one is common to my whole race, and indeed to others also. There is a family in Paris and one in Montpellier named Montaigne, another in Brittany and in Saintonge called de la Montaigne. The change of a single syllable will tangle our threads so that I will share in their glory, and they, perhaps, in my shame. And moreover, mine were formerly surnamed Eyquem,[2] a name which still is attached to a well-known family in England.

As for my other name, it belongs to whoever wants to take it. Thus I shall perhaps honor a porter instead of myself. And then, even if I had a particular mark for myself, what can it mark when I am no longer there? Can it designate and benefit nothingness?

> ᴮNow does his tomb weigh lighter on his bones?
> Posterity applauds. Out of these stones,
> Out of his ashes, from his departed spirit,
> Do violets spring?
>
> PERSIUS

ᴬBut of this I have spoken elsewhere.[3]

Besides, in a whole battle in which ten thousand men are maimed or killed, there are not fifteen that are talked about. It must be some very eminent greatness, or some important consequence that fortune has attached to it, that gives prominence to an individual action, not only a musketeer's, but even a general's. For to

2 Actually Montaigne was the first of his family to drop the surname Eyquem.
3 In the chapter "Of Names" (I: 46).

kill a man, or two, or ten, to offer oneself courageously to death, that is indeed something for each one of us, for everything is at stake. But for the world these are things so ordinary, so many of them are seen every day, and so many of them are needed to produce one notable effect, that we cannot expect any particular commendation for them.

> [B]An incident well-known, trite, cheap,
> And taken from the midst of Fortune's heap.
> JUVENAL

[A]Of so many myriads of valiant men who have died sword in hand in the last fifteen hundred years in France, there are not a hundred who have come to our knowledge. The memory not only of the leaders, but of the battles and victories, is buried.

[C]The fortunes of more than half the world, for lack of a record, do not stir from their place, and vanish without duration. If I had in my possession all the unknown events, I should think I could very easily supplant those that are known, in every kind of examples.

[A]Why, even of the Romans and the Greeks, amid so many writers and witnesses of so many rare and noble exploits, how few have come down as far as our time!

> [B]The faint breath of its fame scarce reached our ears.
> VIRGIL

[A]It will be a lot if a hundred years from now people remember in a general way that in our time there were civil wars in France.

[B]The Lacedaemonians sacrificed to the Muses on going into battle, so that their deeds might be well and worthily written down, judging that it was a divine and uncommon favor that fine actions should find witnesses who could give them life and memory.

[A]Do we think that at every harquebus shot that touches us, and at every risk that we run, there is promptly a clerk to record it? And besides that, a hundred clerks may write it down, whose commentaries will last only three days and will come to no one's sight. We have not the thousandth part of the writings of the ancients: it is Fortune that gives them life, longer or shorter according to her favor; [C]and it is permissible to wonder whether what we have is not the worst, since we have not seen the rest. [A]People do not write histories about such petty things. A man must have been the leader in conquering an empire or a kingdom; he must have won fifty-two pitched battles, always with weaker numbers, like Caesar. Ten

thousand good comrades and many great captains died in his service, valiantly and courageously, whose names have endured only as long as their wives and children lived,

> [B]Whom dim rumor hides.
>
> VIRGIL

[A]Even of those whom we see doing bravely, three months or three years after they have been left on the field, you hear no more talk than if they had never been. Whoever will consider, with just measure and proportion, of what sort of men and what sort of deeds the glory is maintained in the memory of books, will find that in our time there are very few actions and very few persons who can claim any right to such remembrance. How many valiant men we have seen to survive their own reputation, who have seen and suffered the extinction in their presence of the honor and glory most justly acquired in their early years! And for three years of this fanciful and imaginary life shall we go and lose our real and essential life and engage ourselves in a perpetual death? The sages set themselves a fairer and juster end for so important an enterprise. [C]*The reward of a good deed is to have done it* [Seneca]. *The fruit of a service is the service itself* [Cicero].

[A]It might perhaps be excusable for a painter or another artisan, or even for a rhetorician or a grammarian, to toil to acquire a name by his works; but the actions of virtue are too noble in themselves to seek any other reward than from their own worth, and especially to seek it in the vanity of human judgments.

However, if this false opinion is of service to the public in keeping men within their duty; [B]if the people are thereby roused to virtue; if princes are touched by seeing the world bless the memory of Trajan and abominate that of Nero; if it moves them to see the name of that great gallows bird, once so frightful and so dreaded, so freely cursed and reviled by the first schoolboy who deals with it; [A]let it grow boldly and let it be fostered among us as much as possible.

[C]And Plato, employing every means to make his citizens virtuous, advises them also not to despise the good repute and esteem of the people. And he says that it happens by some divine inspiration that even the wicked, in words as well as in thought, often know how to distinguish correctly good men from bad. This person and his teacher are marvelous and bold workmen at bringing in divine operations and revelations everywhere that human power fails: *as the*

tragic poets have recourse to a god when they cannot unravel the end of their plot [Cicero]. Perhaps that is why Timon, by way of insult, called him "the great forger of miracles."

ᴬSince men, because of their inadequacy, cannot be sufficiently paid with good money, let false be employed too. This means has been practiced by all lawgivers, and there is no polity in which there is not some admixture either of empty ceremony or of lying opinion to serve as a curb to keep the people in their duty. That is why most of them have their fabulous origins and beginnings, enriched with supernatural mysteries. That is what has given credit to bastard religions and brought them into favor with men of understanding; and that is why Numa and Sertorius, to strengthen their peoples' belief, fed them with this stupid story, the one that the nymph Egeria, the other that his white hind, brought him from the gods all the decisions that he adopted.

ᶜAnd the authority that Numa gave to his laws by claiming the patronage of this goddess, Zoroaster, lawgiver of the Bactrians and the Persians, gave to his in the name of the god Oromazis; Trismegistus of the Egyptians, in the name of Mercury; Zamolxis of the Scythians, in the name of Vesta; Charondas of the Chalcidians, in the name of Saturn; Minos of the Candiots, in the name of Jupiter; Lycurgus of the Lacedaemonians, in the name of Apollo; Draco and Solon of the Athenians, in the name of Minerva. And every polity has a god at its head: falsely so the others, truly so the one that Moses set up for the people of Judea just out of Egypt.

ᴬThe religion of the Bedouins, as Sire de Joinville tells us, held among other things that the soul of any one of them who died for his prince departed into another body happier, handsomer, and stronger than the first; on account of which they risked their lives much more willingly:

> ᴮThey rush on weapons, death they seem to crave;
> The life they will regain they scorn to save.
>
> LUCAN

ᴬThat is a very salutary belief, however empty it may be. Every nation has many such examples of its own. But this subject would deserve a treatise in itself.

To say one more word on my first topic, neither do I advise the ladies to call their duty honor. ᶜ*In common parlance only that is called honorable which is glorious in popular opinion* [Cicero]. Their duty is the pith, their honor is only the rind. ᴬNor do I advise them to give

us this excuse for payment of their refusal. For I assume that their intentions, their desire, and their will, which are parts in which honor is not concerned, since nothing of them appears on the outside, are even better regulated than their acts:

> She who does not, because forbidden, really does.
>
> <div align="right">OVID</div>

The offense, both toward God and in the conscience, would be as great in the desiring as in the doing. And then these are actions of themselves hidden and secret; it would be very easy for women to conceal one of them from the knowledge of others, on which honor depends, if they had no other respect for their duty and for the affection they bear to chastity for its own sake.

ᶜAny person of honor chooses rather to lose his honor than to lose his conscience.

17
Of presumption

ᴬThere is another kind of vainglory, which is an over-good opinion we form of our own worth. It is an unreasoning affection, by which we cherish ourselves, which represents us to ourselves as other than we are; as the passion of love lends beauties and graces to the object it embraces, and makes its victims, with muddled and unsettled judgment, think that what they love is other and more perfect than it is.

However, I do not want a man to misjudge himself, for fear of erring in that direction, or to think himself less than he is. Judgment must maintain its rights in all matters; it is right that it should see, in this subject as elsewhere, what truth sets before it. If he is Caesar, let him boldly judge himself the greatest captain in the world.

We are nothing but ceremony; ceremony carries us away, and we leave the substance of things; we hang on to the branches and abandon the trunk and body. We have taught the ladies to blush at the mere mention of what they are not at all afraid to do; we dare not call our members by their right names, and we are not afraid to employ them in every kind of debauchery. Ceremony forbids our expressing in words things that are permissible and natural, and we obey it; reason forbids our doing things that are illicit and wicked, and no one obeys it. I find myself here entangled in the laws of

ceremony, for she does not allow a man either to speak well of himself, or to speak ill. We shall let her alone for the moment.

Those whom Fortune (whether we should call her good or bad) has caused to spend their lives in some eminent station, can testify to what they are by their public actions. But those whom she has employed only in a mass, ᶜand of whom no one will speak unless they do so themselves, ᴬmay be excused if they have the temerity to speak of themselves to those who have an interest in knowing them, after the example of Lucilius:

> He would confide, as unto trusted friends,
> His secrets to his notebooks; turn there still,
> Not elsewhere, whether faring well or ill.
> So that the old man's whole life lay revealed
> As on a votive tablet.
>
> HORACE

That man committed to his paper his actions and thoughts, and portrayed himself there as he felt he was. ᶜ*Nor did anyone doubt the honesty or disparage the motives of Rutilius or Scaurus for doing so* [Tacitus].

ᴬSo I remember that from my tenderest childhood people noticed in me some indefinable carriage of the body and certain gestures testifying to some vain and stupid pride. I want to say this first, that it is not unbecoming to have characteristics and propensities so much our own and so incorporated into us that we have no way of sensing and recognizing them. And of such natural inclinations the body is likely to retain a certain bent, without our knowledge or consent. It was a certain affectation in keeping with his beauty that made Alexander lean his head a little to one side, and Alcibiades speak softly and with a lisp. Julius Caesar used to scratch his head with one finger, which is the behavior of a man full of troublesome thoughts; and Cicero, it seems to me, was in the habit of wrinkling his nose, which is a sign of a mocking nature. Such gestures can arise in us unperceived.

There are others that are artificial, of which I do not speak, like bows and salutations, by which men gain credit, most often wrongfully, for being very humble and courteous; ᶜa man may be humble through vainglory. ᴮI am rather prodigal in taking off my hat, especially in summer, and I never receive this salute without returning it, from whatever class of man it may come, unless he is in my pay. I could wish that certain princes I know would be more sparing

and just in dispensing these salutes; for when they are thus strewn about indiscriminately, they have no more power. If they are given without consideration, they are given without effect.

Among the extraordinary mannerisms, let us not forget ᴬthe arrogance of the Emperor Constantius, who in public always held his head straight, without turning or bending it this way or that, not even to look at those who saluted him from the side; keeping his body fixed and motionless, without letting himself move with the swaying of his coach, without daring either to spit, or to blow his nose, or to wipe his face in front of people.

I do not know whether those gestures that people noticed in me were of the first kind, and whether I really had some occult propensity to this fault, as may well be; and I cannot answer for the movements of my body. But as for the movements of my soul, I want to confess here what I am aware of.

There are two parts in this vainglory, namely, to esteem ourselves too highly, and not to esteem others highly enough.

As for the first, ᶜit seems to me that first of all, these considerations should be taken into account: that I feel myself oppressed by an error of my soul which I dislike, both as unjust and, even more, as troublesome. I try to correct it, but uproot it I cannot. It is that I lower the value of the things I possess, because I possess them, and raise the value of things when they are foreign, absent, and not mine. This humor spreads very far. As the prerogative of authority makes husbands regard their own wives, and many fathers their children, with wicked disdain; so it is with me, and between two similar works I should always decide against my own. Not so much that zeal for my progress and improvement disturbs my judgment and keeps me from being satisfied with myself, as that dominion, of itself, breeds contempt of what we hold and control. Far-off governments, customs, and languages delight me; and I realize that Latin, by its dignity, beguiles me more than it should, as it does children and common people. The housekeeping, the house, the horse of my neighbor, if equal in value, seem better than my own, because they are not mine – the more so because I am very ignorant of my affairs. I wonder at the assurance and confidence each man has about himself, whereas there is virtually nothing that I know I know, or that I dare give my word that I can do. I do not have my means catalogued and arranged; and I know about them only after doing something: I am as doubtful of myself as of anything else. Whence it comes about that if I happen to do well in a task, I attribute it more

to my luck than to my ability; for I plan them all at random and in fear.

Likewise ᴬthis is generally true of me, that of all the opinions antiquity has held of man ꟲas a whole, ᴬthe ones I embrace most willingly and adhere to most firmly are those that despise, humiliate, and nullify us most. Philosophy seems to me never to have such an easy game as when she combats our presumption and vanity, when she honestly admits her uncertainty, weakness, and ignorance. It seems to me that the nursing mother of the falsest opinions, public and private, is the over-good opinion man has of himself.

These people who perch astride the epicycle of Mercury, ꟲwho see so far into the heavens, ᴬyank out my teeth. For in the study I am making, the subject of which is man, when I find such an extreme variety of judgments, so deep a labyrinth of difficulties one on top of the other, so much diversity and uncertainty in the very school of wisdom, you may well wonder – since these people have not been able to come to an agreement in the knowledge of themselves and their own state, which is ever present before their eyes, which is in them; since they do not know the motion of what they move themselves, or how to depict and decipher to us the springs that they hold and manage themselves – how I should believe them about the cause of the ebb and flow of the river Nile. The curiosity to know things was given to men as a scourge, says the Holy Scripture.

But to come to my own particular case, it would be very difficult, it seems to me, for anyone else to esteem himself less, or indeed for anyone else to esteem me less, than I esteem myself. ꟲI consider myself one of the common sort, except in that I consider myself so; guilty of the commoner and humbler faults, but not of faults disavowed or excused; and I value myself only for knowing my value.

If there is vainglory in me, it is infused in me superficially by the treachery of my nature, and has no body of its own to appear before my judgment. I am sprinkled with it, but not dyed.

ᴬFor in truth, as regards any kind of products of the mind, I have never brought forth anything that satisfied me; and the approbation of others does not repay me. My taste is delicate and hard to please, and especially regarding myself; ꟲI am incessantly disowning myself; and ᴬI feel myself, in every part, floating and bending with weakness. I have nothing of my own that satisfies my judgment. My sight is clear and controlled enough; but when I put it to work, it grows blurred, as I find most evidently in poetry. I love it infinitely;

I am a pretty good judge of other men's works; but in truth, I play the child when I try to set my hand to it; I cannot endure myself. A man may play the fool anywhere else, but not in poetry:

> For Gods and men and booksellers refuse
> To countenance a mediocre Muse.
>
> HORACE

Would God that maxim were written on the front of all our printers' shops, to deny entrance to so many versifiers:

> No man has more assurance than a bad poet.
>
> MARTIAL

ᶜWhy have we no such nations as these? Dionysius the Elder esteemed nothing of his own so highly as his poetry. At the time of the Olympic games, with chariots surpassing all others in magnificence, he also sent poets and musicians to present his verses, with royally gilded and tapestried tents and pavilions. When they came to deliver his verses, the grace and excellence of the pronunciation at first drew the attention of the people; but when later they came to ponder the ineptitude of the work, they first grew scornful, and, becoming more and more bitter in their judgment, they presently flew into a fury, and ran to all his pavilions and knocked them down and tore them to bits in resentment. And when his chariots did not make any kind of a showing in the races either, and the ship bringing his men back missed Sicily and was driven and shattered by the tempest against the coast of Tarentum, the people felt certain that it was the wrath of the gods, irritated, like themselves, against this bad poem. And even the sailors who escaped from the shipwreck seconded this opinion of the people.

The oracle that predicted his death also seemed to subscribe to this somewhat. It said that Dionysius would be near his end when he had vanquished men better than himself; which he took to mean the Carthaginians, who surpassed him in power. And in fighting them he often sidestepped victory and tempered it so as not to incur the fate predicted. But he misunderstood it; for the god was referring to the time he gained the award at Athens over better tragic poets than he, by favor and injustice, presenting in the competition his play entitled *The Leneians*; after which victory he suddenly died, partly of the excessive joy that he got from it.

ᴬWhat I find excusable in my own work I find so not in itself and in reality, but in comparison with other and worse things to which

I see people give credit. I am envious of the happiness of those who can rejoice and feel gratified in their work, for it is an easy way to give oneself pleasure, since the source of the pleasure is oneself. ^CEspecially so if there is a little firmness in their self-conceit. I know a poet to whom the strong and the weak, in the crowd and in the chamber, and heaven and earth, cry out that he does not know his business. For all that, he will not reduce one bit of the measure for which he has cut himself out; he is always beginning again, always reconsidering, and always persisting, all the stronger and more set in his opinion because it depends on him alone to maintain it. ^AMy works are so far from delighting me that as many times as I sample them again, so many times I am vexed with them:

> ^BWhen I reread I blush, for I see quite enough
> Fit to erase, though it was I who wrote the stuff.
>
> OVID

^AI have always an idea in my mind, ^Cand some blurred picture, ^Awhich offers me ^Cas if in a dream ^Aa better form than the one I have employed, but I cannot grasp it and exploit it. And that idea itself is on only a mediocre plane. From that I conclude that the productions of those great rich minds of the past are very far beyond the utmost stretch of my imagination and desire. Their writings not only satisfy and fill me, but astound me and transfix me with admiration. I judge their beauty; I see it, if not to the utmost, at least enough so that I cannot aspire to it myself.

Whatever I undertake, I owe a sacrifice to the Graces, as Plutarch says of someone, to curry their favor:

> If anything gives pleasure that I write,
> If it affects men's senses with delight,
> Unto the charming Graces it is due.
>
> AUTHOR UNKNOWN

They abandon me at every turn. Everything I write is crude; it lacks distinction and beauty. I do not know how to make things appear any more precious than they really are; my fashioning is no help to the matter. That is why I need my matter strong, with plenty of grip, and shining by its own light. ^CWhen I seize on popular and gayer matters, it is so as to go my own way, for I do not love a solemn and gloomy wisdom, as does the world, and to cheer up myself, not my style, which rather prefers grave and austere matters (at least if I should give the name of style to a formless and undisciplined

way of talking, a popular jargon, and a way of proceeding without definitions, without divisions, without conclusions, and confused, like that of Amafanius and Rabirius).

[A]I do not know how to please, or delight, or tickle: the best story in the world dries up in my hands and becomes dull. I do not know how to talk except in good earnest, and am wholly devoid of that facility, which I see in several of my acquaintances, of entertaining the first comer and holding the attention of a whole group, or tirelessly amusing the ear of a prince with all kinds of talk, matter never failing them, because of the gift they have of knowing how to use the first subject that comes to mind, and accommodating it to the humor and capacity of the people they are dealing with. [B]Princes are not very fond of serious talk, nor I of telling stories. [A]The first and easiest arguments, which are commonly the best received, I do not know how to use: [C]a bad popular preacher. On all matters I am apt to say the deepest things I know. Cicero thinks that in philosophical treatises the hardest part is the exordium. If that is so, I shall stick to the conclusion.

[A]Yet we must tune the string to all sorts of notes; and the sharpest is the one that least often comes into play. There is at least as great perfection in developing an empty theme as in sustaining a weighty one. Sometimes we must handle things superficially, sometimes go into them deeply. I well know that most people keep on that low plane, since they grasp things only by that outer bark; but I also know that the greatest masters, [C]both Xenophon [A]and Plato, are often seen relaxing into that humble and popular way of speaking and treating things, sustaining it with the graces that never fail them.

As for the rest, my language has no ease or polish; it is harsh [C]and disdainful, [A]with a free and unruly disposition. And I like it that way, [C]if not by judgment, then by inclination. [A]But I am quite conscious that sometimes I let myself go too far, and that in the effort to avoid art and affectation, I fall back into them in another direction:

> I strive to be concise,
> And grow obscure.
> HORACE

[C]Plato says that length and brevity are properties which neither decrease nor increase the worth of style.

^AIf I should attempt to follow that other style that is even, smooth, and orderly, I could not attain it. And even though the concision and cadences of Sallust are more to my humor, yet I consider Caesar both greater and less easy to imitate. And if my inclination leads me more to imitate Seneca's style, I nonetheless esteem Plutarch's more. As in action, so in speech I simply follow my natural bent; which is perhaps the reason why I can do better in speech than in writing. Movement and action animate words, notably in men who move about briskly, as I do, and become heated. Bearing, countenance, voice, robe and posture can give value to things which in themselves are nothing but babble. Messala complains, in Tacitus, of certain tight garments of his time, and of the form of the benches where the orators had to speak, which weakened their eloquence.

My French is corrupted, both in pronunciation and in other respects, by the barbarism of my home soil; I never saw a man from the south of France whose accent was not clearly marked and offending to pure French ears. Yet this is not because I am very expert in my Perigordian, for I have no more command of it than of German; and that does not worry me much. ^CIt is a language like others around me, on one side or another, those of Poitou, Saintonge, Angoumois, Limoges, and Auvergne: soft, drawling, loose-boweled. ^ATo be sure, there is above us, toward the mountains, a Gascon dialect that I find singularly beautiful, dry, brief, expressive, and indeed a more manly and military language than any that I understand; ^Cas sinewy, powerful, and pertinent as French is graceful, delicate, and abundant.

^AAs for Latin, which was given me for my mother tongue, I have lost through lack of practice the ability to use it quickly in speaking; ^Cyes, and in writing, in which they used to call me Master John. ^AThat is how little I am worth on that side.

Beauty is a great recommendation in dealings with men; it is the prime means of conciliation between them, and there is no man so barbarous and surly as not to be somewhat struck by its charm. The body has a great part in our being, it holds a high rank in it; so its structure and composition are well worth consideration. Those who want to split up our two principal parts and sequester them from each other are wrong. On the contrary, we must couple and join them together again. We must order the soul not to draw aside and entertain itself apart, not to scorn and abandon the body (nor can it do so except by some counterfeit monkey trick), but to rally to the

body, embrace it, cherish it, assist it, control it, advise it, set it right and bring it back when it goes astray; in short, to marry it and be a husband to it, so that their actions may appear not different and contrary, but harmonious and uniform.

Christians are particularly instructed about this bond; for they know that divine justice embraces this association and union of body and soul, even to making the body capable of eternal rewards, and that God watches the whole man in action and wills that he receive, in his entirety, punishment or reward, according to his merits.

^CThe Peripatetic sect, of all sects the most sociable, attributes to wisdom this sole care, to provide and procure the common good of these two associated parts. And they show that the other sects, for not having devoted themselves enough to the consideration of this mixture, have taken sides, one for the body, another for the soul, with equal error, and have put aside their subject, which is man, and their guide, which they generally avow is Nature.

^AThe first distinction that existed between men, and the first consideration that gave some men preeminence over others, was probably the advantage of beauty:

> ^BThey portioned out the fields, and gave
> To each after his beauty, strength, and intellect;
> For then beauty was prized, and strength enjoyed respect.
>
> LUCRETIUS

^ANow I am a little below medium height. This is not only an ugly defect, but also a disadvantage, especially for men in command or office; for the authority given by a fine presence and bodily majesty is lacking. ^CC. Marius was reluctant to accept soldiers who were not six feet in height. The Courtier[1] is quite right to prefer an average height to any other for the gentleman he is training, and to reject any peculiarity that will make people point him out. But as for choosing to have him shorter rather than taller if he fails to be of this medium height, I would not do so for a military man.

Little men, says Aristotle, may well be pretty, but not handsome; and in greatness is a great soul known, as is beauty in a great tall body. ^AThe Ethiopians and Indians, he says, in electing their kings and magistrates, considered the beauty and lofty stature of their persons. They were right; for it breeds respect in his followers and

1 *Il Libro del Cortegiano* (1528), by Baldassare Castiglione.

terror in the enemy to see marching at the head of a troop a leader of handsome and majestic stature:

> [B]Turnus himself moves with the foremost, arms in hand,
> Splendid in build, a full head taller than his band.
>
> VIRGIL

Our great, divine, and heavenly King, whose every particular should be carefully, religiously, and reverently noted, did not reject the recommendation of a handsome body: *fairer than the children of men* [Psalms]. [C]And Plato desires beauty, as well as temperance and courage, in the guardians of his Republic.

[A]It is a great annoyance to be addressed in the midst of your servants with the question: "Where is the master?" and to get only the tail end of the salute made to your barber or your secretary. As happened to poor Philopoemen. He was the first of his company to arrive at a house where he was expected, and his hostess, who did not know him and saw his rather unimpressive appearance, set him to work helping her maids draw water and stir up the fire in honor of Philopoemen. The gentlemen of his suite, having arrived and surprised him busy at this fine occupation (for he had not failed to obey the command given him), asked him what he was doing there. "I am paying," he answered them, "the penalty of my ugliness."

The other kinds of beauty are for women; the beauty of stature is the only beauty of men. Where smallness dwells, neither breadth and roundness of forehead, nor clarity and softness of eyes, nor the moderate form of the nose, nor small size of ears and mouth, nor regularity and whiteness of teeth, nor the smooth thickness of a beard brown as the husk of a chestnut, nor curly hair, nor proper roundness of head, nor freshness of color, nor a pleasant facial expression, nor an odorless body, nor just proportion of limbs, can make a handsome man.

For the rest, I have a strong, thick-set body, a face not fat but full, a temperament [B]between the jovial and the melancholy, moderately [A]sanguine and warm –

> My legs are stiff with bristles, my chest with shaggy hair
>
> MARTIAL

– sound and sprightly health, [B]rarely troubled by illnesses, [A]until I was well along in years. Such I was, for I am not considering myself at this moment, when I am well on the road to old age, having long since passed forty:

^BOld age shatters their powers, their ripened strength,
 And melts into decrepitude at length.

<div style="text-align:right">LUCRETIUS</div>

^AWhat I shall be from now on will be nothing but half a being, it will no longer be myself. I escape and steal away from myself every day:

 The passing years steal from us all things, one by one.

<div style="text-align:right">HORACE</div>

Adroitness and agility I have never had; and yet I am the son of a very nimble father whose sprightliness lasted him until his extreme old age. He scarcely ever found a man of his condition who was his equal in any bodily exercise; just as I have scarcely found any who did not surpass me, except in running, in which I was just fair. Of music, either vocal, for which my voice is very inept, or instrumental, they never succeeded in teaching me anything. At dancing, tennis, wrestling, I have never been able to acquire any but very slight and ordinary ability; at swimming, fencing, vaulting, and jumping, none at all. My hands are so clumsy that I cannot even write so I can read it; so that I would rather do over what I have scribbled than give myself the trouble of unscrambling it. ^CAnd I read hardly any better. I feel that I weigh upon my listeners. Otherwise, a good scholar.[2] ^AI cannot close a letter the right way, nor could I ever cut a pen, or carve at table worth a rap, ^Cor saddle a horse, or properly carry a bird and release it, or talk to dogs, birds, or horses.

^AMy bodily qualities, in short, are very well matched with those of my soul. There is no liveliness; there is only a full, firm vigor. I stand up well under hard work; but I do so only if I go to it of my own will, and as much as my desire leads me to it,

 When gently zest beguiles the rigors of the toil.

<div style="text-align:right">HORACE</div>

Otherwise, if I am not lured to it by some pleasure, and if I have any other guide than my own pure free will, I am good for nothing. For I have come to the point where except for health and life, there is nothing ^Cfor which I am willing to bite my nails, nothing ^Athat I am willing to buy at the price of mental torment and constraint:

2 A possible reminiscence of Clément Marot's well-known line, "Au demeurant, le meilleur fils du monde" ("For the rest, the best lad in the world"), which follows an impressive enumeration of the vices of his valet.

^BI would not buy at such a fee
All Tagus' sands, and all the gold it rolls to sea.
 JUVENAL

^CExtremely idle, extremely independent, both by nature and by art.
I would as soon lend my blood as my pains.

^AI have a soul all its own, accustomed to conducting itself in its
own way. Having had neither governor nor master forced on me to
this day, I have gone just so far as I pleased, and at my own pace. This
has made me soft and useless for serving others, and no good to
anyone but myself. And for my own sake there was no need to force
that heavy, lazy, and do-nothing nature. For having found myself
from birth in such a degree of fortune that I had reason to be content
with it, and having as much sense as I felt I had occasion for, I have
sought nothing, and have also acquired nothing:

I am not wafted by fair winds with swelling sails;
Yet neither do I steer my life through adverse gales.
In strength, wit, beauty, virtue, rank, and wealth, I'm cast
The last among the first, the first among the last.

 HORACE

The only ability I have needed is the ability to content myself with
my lot, ^Cwhich, however, if you take it rightly, requires a well-
ordered state of mind, equally difficult in every kind of fortune,
and which we see by experience is more readily found in want than
in abundance; perhaps because, as with our other passions, hunger
for riches is sharpened more by the use of them than by the lack
of them, and because the virtue of moderation is rarer than that of
patience. And all I needed was ^Ato enjoy pleasantly the good things
that God in his liberality had placed in my hands. I have never tasted
of any sort of tedious work. I have had hardly anything to manage
but my own affairs; ^Cor, if I have, it has been on condition of
managing them at my own times and in my own way, commissioned
by people who trusted me and knew me, and did not hustle me.
For experts get some service out of even a restive and broken-
winded horse.

^AEven my childhood was guided in a mild, free fashion, exempt
from rigorous subjection. All this has built up in me a delicate
disposition, unable to endure worry – to such a point that I like to
have the losses and disorders that concern me hidden from me; I put
under the heading of expenses what my nonchalance costs me for its
food and upkeep:

Things that the master ne'er perceives,
Superfluous, but a delight to thieves.

HORACE

I like to be ignorant of the count of what I have, so as to feel my loss less exactly. [B]I ask those who live with me, if they lack affection for me and for honest dealings, to cheat me and pay me with decent appearances. [A]Not having enough fortitude to endure the annoyance of the adverse accidents to which we are subject, and being unable to keep up the tension of regulating and ordering affairs, I foster as best I can this idea: to abandon myself completely to Fortune, expect the worst in everything, and resolve to bear that worst meekly and patiently. It is for that alone that I labor; that is the goal toward which I direct all my reflections.

[B]When in danger, I do not think so much how I shall escape, as how little it matters that I escape. Even if I should fall, what would it matter? Not being able to rule events, I rule myself, and adapt myself to them if they do not adapt themselves to me. I have hardly the skill to dodge Fortune and escape her or force her, and to direct and lead things foresightedly to serve my purpose. I have even less patience to stand the arduous and painful care that is needed for that. And the most painful situation for me is to be in suspense about urgent matters, and tossed between fear and hope. Deliberation, even about the slightest things, annoys me; and I feel my mind harder put to it to endure the various shocks and ups and downs of doubt and deliberation, than to settle down and accept any course whatever, after the die is cast. Few passions have troubled my sleep; but as for deliberations, the slightest one troubles it. Even as in roads I like to avoid the sloping and slippery sides, and cast myself into the beaten part, even the muddiest and boggiest, from which I cannot sink lower, and seek security there; just so I like pure misfortunes, which do not try me and worry me any more, once the uncertainty about mending them is over, and which drive me at a single bound directly into suffering:

[C]Uncertain ills torment us most.

SENECA

[B]When things happen, I bear myself like a man; in conducting them, like a child. The dread of falling gives me a greater fever than the fall. The game is not worth the candle. The miser is worse off for

his passion than the poor man, and the jealous man than the cuckold. And often it is not as bad to lose your vineyard as to go to court for it. The lowest step is the firmest. It is the seat of constancy. There you need nothing but yourself. Constancy is founded there and leans only upon itself.

Is there not a certain philosophical air about the case of a gentleman known to many? He married well along in years, having spent his youth in gay company, a great storyteller, a merry lad. Remembering how the subject of cuckoldry had given him material for talking and jesting about others, to take cover he married a woman whom he picked up in the place where each man can find one for his money, and made a compact with her that they would use these greetings: "Good morning, whore." "Good morning, cuckold." And there was nothing about which he talked more often and openly to visitors at his home than this arrangement of his; by which he checked the secret gossip of mockers, and blunted the point of this reproach.

[A]As for ambition, which is neighbor to presumption, or rather daughter, it would have been necessary, to advance me, for Fortune to come and take me by the hand. For as for taking pains for the sake of some uncertain hope, and submitting to all the difficulties that attend those who try to push themselves into favor at the beginning of their career, I could never have done it:

> [B]I do not purchase hope with ready cash.
>
> TERENCE

I cling to what I see and hold, and do not go far from port:

> Let one oar row in water, the other on the shore.
>
> PROPERTIUS

And then, a man seldom arrives at these advancements except by first risking what he has. And it is my opinion that if what a man has is enough to maintain the way of life to which he was born and brought up, it is folly to let go of it on the chance of increasing it. The man whom Fortune denies a foothold and the means of arranging a calm and restful life is excusable if he tosses what he has to chance, since in any case necessity sends him questing:

> [C]In evil we must take a risky path.
>
> SENECA

[B]And I sooner excuse a younger son for casting his inheritance to the winds than a man who has the honor of his house in his charge, and cannot become needy without being at fault.

[A]I have certainly found the road shorter and easier, with the advice of my good friends of past days, by getting rid of this desire and keeping quiet;

> Who would enjoy the prize without the dust;
>
> HORACE

also judging very sanely that my powers were not capable of great things, and remembering this saying of the late Chancellor Olivier, that the French are like monkeys who climb to the top of a tree, from branch to branch, and never stop moving until they have reached the highest branch, and show their rear ends when they get there.

> [B]'Tis shameful to take on a load that is too great,
> Then leave it when our knees buckle beneath its weight.
>
> PROPERTIUS

[A]Even the qualities that are not reproachable in me, I have found useless in this age. My easygoing ways would have been called cowardice and weakness; fidelity and conscience would have been thought squeamish and superstitious; frankness and independence, troublesome, thoughtless, and rash.

Misfortune has its uses. It is good to be born in a very depraved time; for by comparison with others, you are considered virtuous for a cheap price. Anyone who is only a parricide and sacrilegious in our days is a good and honorable man:

> [B]If now a friend denies not what was given him in trust,
> If he restores an ancient purse with all its coins and rust,
> This prodigy of honesty deserves to be enrolled
> In Tuscan books, and with a sacrificial lamb extolled.
>
> JUVENAL

And there was never time and place where a surer and greater reward was offered to princes for goodness and justice. The first man who thinks to push himself into favor and credit by that path, I am much mistaken if he will not outstrip his fellows without much effort. Force and violence can do something, but not always everything.

^CWe see merchants, village justices, and artisans keeping up with the nobility in valor and military knowledge. They do honorably in both private and public combats; they fight, they defend cities in our wars. A prince's distinction is smothered amid this crowd. Let him shine with humanity, truthfulness, loyalty, moderation, and especially justice, marks that are rare, unknown, and banished. It is only by the will of the people that he can do his job, and no other qualities can flatter their will as much as these, which are much more useful to them than the others. *Nothing is so popular as goodness* [Cicero].

^ABy such a comparison I would have thought myself ^Cgreat and rare, just as I think myself dwarfish and ordinary in comparison with certain past ages, in which it was a commonplace, if other, stronger qualities did not concur, to see a man ^Amoderate in his revenge, slow to resent offenses, religious in keeping his word, neither double-dealing nor shifty, nor accommodating his faith to the will of others or to the occasion. Rather would I let affairs break their necks than twist my faith for the sake of them. For as for this new-fangled virtue of hypocrisy and dissimulation, which is so highly honored at present, I mortally hate it; and of all vices, I know none that testifies to so much cowardice and baseness of heart. It is a craven and servile idea to disguise ourselves and hide under a mask, and not to dare to show ourselves as we are. In that way our men train for perfidy; ^Bbeing accustomed to speak false words, they have no scruples about breaking their word. ^AA generous heart should not belie its thoughts; it wants to reveal itself even to its inmost depths. ^CThere everything is good, or at least everything is human.

Aristotle considers it the function of magnanimity to hate and love openly, to judge, to speak with complete frankness, and to have no regard for the approbation or reprobation of others in comparison with truth. ^AApollonius said that it was for slaves to lie, and for free men to speak truth.

^CTruth is the first and fundamental part of virtue. We must love it for itself. He who tells the truth because he has some external obligation to do so and because it serves him, and who does not fear to tell a lie when it is not important to anybody, is not sufficiently truthful.

My soul by nature shuns lying and hates even to think a lie. I feel an inward shame and a stinging remorse if one escapes me, as sometimes it does, for occasions surprise me and move me unpremeditatedly.

^AWe must not always say everything, for that would be folly; but what we say must be what we think; otherwise it is wickedness. I do not know what people expect to gain by incessant feigning and dissimulating, unless it is not to be believed even when they speak truth. That may deceive people once or twice; but to make a profession of covering up, and to boast, as some of our princes have done, that they would throw their shirt in the fire if it were privy to their real intentions (which is a saying of the ancient Metellus of Macedon), and that a man who does not know how to dissemble does not know how to rule – this is warning those who have to deal with them that all they say is nothing but deceit and lies. ^C*The more artful and cunning a man is, the more he is hated and suspected when he loses his reputation for honesty* [Cicero]. ^AIt would be very naïve for a man to let himself be taken in by either the face or the words of one who takes pride in being always different outside and inside, as Tiberius did; and I do not know what part such people can have in human dealings, since they never offer anything that is accepted as good money. ^BHe who is disloyal to truth is also disloyal to falsehood.

^CThose who, in our time, in establishing the duties of a prince,[3] have considered only the good of his affairs, and have preferred that to caring for his fidelity and conscience, would have something to say to a prince whose affairs Fortune had so arranged that he could establish them once and for all by a single breach and betrayal of his word. But that is not the way it goes. You often fall into the same sort of bargain again; you make more than one peace, more than one treaty, in your life. The gain that lures them to the first breach of faith – and almost always there is gain in it, as in all other wicked deeds; sacrilege, murder, rebellion, treachery are always undertaken for some sort of profit – this first gain brings after it endless losses, casting this prince out of all relations and means of negotiation in consequence of this breach of faith.

When, during my childhood, Suleiman, of the Ottoman race, a race not overly careful about observing promises and pacts, landed his army at Otranto, he learned that Mercurino de' Gratinare and the inhabitants of Castro were held prisoners after having surrendered the place, contrary to the terms of capitulation, and sent word that they should be released; and he said that having other great enterprises at hand in that region, such a breach of faith, although it

3 Machiavelli and his disciples.

seemed somewhat useful at present, would bring upon him in the future a bad name and a distrust infinitely harmful.

[A]Now for my part I would rather be troublesome and indiscreet than flattering and dissembling. [B]I admit that a touch of pride and stubbornness may enter into keeping me sincere and outspoken without consideration for others; and it seems to me that I restrain myself a little less whenever it would be appropriate to restrain myself more, and that I react against the respect I owe by growing more heated. It may be, too, that I let myself follow my nature for lack of art. When I display to great men the same extreme freedom of tongue and bearing that I exercise in my own house, I feel how much it inclines toward indiscretion and incivility. But besides the fact that I am made that way, I have not a supple enough mind to sidestep a sudden question and escape it by some dodge, or to invent a truth, or a good enough memory to retain something thus invented, and certainly not enough assurance to maintain it; and I put on a bold face because of weakness. Therefore I give myself up to being candid and always saying what I think, by inclination and by reason, leaving it to Fortune to guide the outcome.

[C]Aristippus said that the chief fruit he had gathered from philosophy was that he spoke freely and openly to everyone.

[A]Memory is a wonderfully useful tool, and without it judgment does its work with difficulty; it is entirely lacking in me. What anyone wants to propound to me must be propounded piecemeal. For to answer a discourse in which there are several different headings is not in my power. I cannot receive a commission without my writing tablets. And when I have a speech of consequence to make, if it is of some length, I am reduced to the mean and miserable necessity of learning by heart, [C]word for word, [A]what I have to say; otherwise I would have neither manner nor assurance, being in fear that my memory would play me a bad trick. [C]But this way is no less difficult for me. To learn three lines of poetry I need three hours. And then, in a work of my own, the freedom and authority to change the order and alter a word, ever varying the material, makes it harder to keep in mind.

[A]Now, the more I distrust my memory, the more confused it becomes. It serves me better by chance encounter; I have to solicit it nonchalantly. For if I press it, it is stunned; and once it has begun to totter, the more I probe it, the more it gets mixed up and embarrassed. It serves me at its own time, not at mine.

This thing that I feel in my memory, I feel in several other parts. I flee command, obligation, and constraint. What I do easily and naturally, I can no longer do if I order myself to do it by strict and express command. Even as regards my body, the parts that have some particular freedom and jurisdiction over themselves sometimes refuse to obey me when I destine and bind them to a certain time and place for compulsory service. These forced and tyrannical advance orders repel them; they go limp from fear or spite and become paralyzed.

[B]Some time ago, being in a place where it is a barbarous discourtesy not to respond to those who invite you to drink, though I was treated with complete freedom, I tried to play the good fellow for the sake of the ladies who were in the party, according to the custom of the country. But then the fun began; for the threat and anticipation of having to force myself beyond my natural habit stopped up my gullet so that I could not swallow a single drop, and was deprived of drink, even as much as my meal required. I found myself brimful and my thirst quenched by all the drink that my imagination had anticipated.

[A]This effect is more apparent in those who have a more ardent and powerful imagination; but for all that, it is natural, and there is no one who does not feel it somewhat. An excellent archer, condemned to death, was offered his life if he would show some notable proof of his skill; he refused to try it, fearing that the excessive tension of his will would make his hand go astray, and that instead of saving his life, he would lose the reputation he had acquired for shooting with the bow.

A man whose thoughts are elsewhere will not fail, to the inch, to take always the same number and length of steps in the place where he walks; but if he goes at it attentively, measuring and counting them, he will find that what he did naturally and by chance, he will not do as exactly by design.

My library, which is a handsome one among country libraries, is situated at one corner of my house. If anything enters my fancy that I want to look up or write down there, for fear it may escape me even as I cross my courtyard, I have to give it into someone else's safekeeping. If in speaking I am emboldened to digress however little from my thread, I never fail to lose it; which is the reason I keep myself constrained, dry, and compressed in speaking. The people who serve me I have to call by the name of their job or their province, for it is very hard for me to remember names. [B]To be

sure, I will tell you that it has three syllables and a rough sound, that it begins or ends with such and such a letter. [A]And if I were to live a long time, I do not doubt that I would forget my own name, as others have done. [B]Messala Corvinus was two years without any trace of memory, [C]and this is also said of George of Trebizond. [B]And in my own interest I often ruminate about what sort of a life theirs was, and whether without this faculty I shall have enough left to support me with any comfort; and looking at it closely, I fear that this defect, if it is absolute, ruins all the functions of the mind. [C]*It is certain that the memory is the only receptacle, not only of philosophy, but of all that concerns the conduct of life, and of all the arts* [Cicero].

[A]I'm full of cracks, and leak out on all sides.
TERENCE

It has happened more than once that I have forgotten the watch-word that I had given [C]three hours before, [A]or received from another, [C]and forgotten where I had hidden my purse, in spite of what Cicero says about that. I help myself to lose what I lock up most carefully.

[A]Memory is the receptacle and container of knowledge; mine being so defective, I can hardly complain if I do not know much. I know in general the names of the arts and what they treat, but nothing beyond that. I leaf through books, I do not study them. What I retain of them is something I no longer recognize as anyone else's. It is only the material from which my judgment has profited, and the thoughts and ideas with which it has become imbued; the author, the place, the words, and other circumstances, I immediately forget.

[B]And I am so good at forgetting that I forget even my own writings and compositions no less than the rest. People are all the time quoting me to myself without my knowing it. Anyone who would like to know the sources of the verses and examples I have piled up here would put me to great trouble to tell him. And yet I have begged them only at well-known and famous doors, not content with their being rich unless they also came from rich and honorable hands; in them authority and reason concur. [C]It is no great wonder if my book follows the fate of other books, and if my memory lets go of what I write as of what I read, and of what I give as of what I receive.

[A]Besides the defect of my memory I have others which contribute greatly to my ignorance. My mind is slow and dull; it cannot

penetrate the slightest cloud, so that, for example, I could never offer it any enigma easy enough for it to unravel. There is no subtlety so empty that it will not stump me. Of games in which the mind has a part – chess, cards, draughts, and others – I understand nothing but the barest rudiments.

My apprehension is slow and muddled; but what it once grasps, it grasps well and embraces most entirely, closely, and deeply for such time as it does grasp it. My sight is long, sound, and whole, but it is easily tired by work and grows blurred; for that reason I cannot have long sessions with books except by the help of others. The younger Pliny will inform those who have not experienced it how important this delay is to those who devote themselves to this occupation.

There is no mind so puny or brutish as not to reveal some particular faculty shining out; there is none so buried but that some bit of it will burst forth. And how it happens that a mind that is blind and asleep to everything else is lively, clear, and excellent in some particular task, we must inquire of the masters. But the fine minds are the universal minds, open and ready for everything; ᶜif not well taught, at least teachable. ᴬAnd I say this to accuse my own; for whether by weakness or nonchalance (and to be nonchalant about what lies at our feet, what we have between our hands, what most concerns our use of life, is something far removed from my doctrine), there is no mind as inept as mine and none as ignorant of many such ordinary common things of which a man cannot be ignorant without disgrace. I must cite a few examples.

I was born and brought up in the country and in the midst of farming; I have had affairs and management in my hands ever since my predecessors in the possession of the property I enjoy left me their place. Now I cannot reckon, either with counters or with a pen; most of our coins I do not know; nor do I know the difference between one grain and another, either in the ground or in the barn, unless it is too obvious, and I can scarcely distinguish the difference between the cabbages and lettuces in my garden. I do not even understand the names of the chief household implements or the roughest principles of agriculture, which children know. ᴮI know still less of the mechanical arts, of trade and merchandise, of the diversity and nature of fruits, wines, and foods, and of how to train a bird, or doctor a horse or dog. ᴬAnd since I must make my shame quite complete, not a month ago I was caught ignorant that leaven was used to make bread, ᶜand what was meant by fermenting wine.

^AOnce in Athens people conjectured an aptitude for mathematics in a man who was seen ingeniously arranging a load of brushwood and making it into fagots. Truly they would draw the very opposite conclusion about me; for if you give me all the equipment of a kitchen, I shall starve.

From these lines of my confession you can imagine others at my expense. But whatever I make myself known to be, provided I make myself known such as I am, I am carrying out my plan. And so I make no excuse for daring to put into writing such mean and trivial remarks as these. The meanness of my subject forces me to do so. ^CBlame my project if you will, but not my procedure. ^AAt all events, I see well enough, without others telling me, how little value and weight all this has, and the folly of my plan. It is enough that my judgment is not unshod, of which these are the essays:

> Be nosy as you will, have such a nose
> That Atlas to support it would refuse;
> Latinus' self bewilder with your wit:
> Against my trifles you can say no whit
> More than I've said myself. Why use your teeth
> On teeth? If you'd be full, you must have meat.
> Save up your pains, your sting, for those who so
> Admire themselves; that this is naught, we know.
>
> MARTIAL

I am not obliged not to say stupid things, provided I do not fool myself and that I recognize them as such. And to slip up knowingly is so common for me that I scarcely ever slip up in any other way; I never slip up accidentally. It is a small matter to attribute my silly actions to the rashness of my disposition, since I cannot help commonly attributing my vicious actions to it.

One day at Bar-le-Duc I saw King Francis II presented, in remembrance of René, king of Sicily, with a portrait that this king had made of himself. Why is it not permissible in the same way for each man to portray himself with the pen, as he portrayed himself with a pencil?

So I do not want to forget this further scar, very unfit to produce in public: irresolution, a most harmful failing in negotiating worldly affairs. I do not know which side to take in doubtful enterprises:

> ^BNor yes nor no my inmost heart will say.
> PETRARCH

I can easily maintain an opinion, but not choose one.

^ABecause in human matters, whatever side we lean to, we find many probabilities to confirm us in it – ^Cand the philosopher Chrysippus said that he wanted to learn from Zeno and Cleanthes, his masters, nothing but their tenets, for when it came to proofs and reasons, he would furnish enough by himself – ^Aso in whatever direction I turn, I can always provide myself with enough causes and probabilities to keep me that way. So I keep within me doubt and freedom of choice until the occasion is urgent. And then, to confess the truth, I most often toss the feather to the wind, as they say, and abandon myself to the mercy of fortune; a very slight inclination or circumstance carries me away:

> When the mind doubts, a trifle pulls it to and fro.
>
> TERENCE

The uncertainty of my judgment is so evenly balanced in most occurrences that I would willingly submit to the decision of chance and of the dice. And I note, with much reflection on our human weakness, the examples that even sacred history has left us of this custom of entrusting to fortune and chance the determination of choice in doubtful cases: *The lot fell upon Matthias* [Acts].

^CHuman reason is a two-edged and dangerous sword. And even in the hand of Socrates, its most intimate and familiar friend, see what a many-ended stick it is.

^AThus I am fit only to follow, and I let myself be carried away easily by the crowd. I do not trust my own powers enough to undertake to command, or to guide; I am very glad to find my steps traced out by others. If I must run the risk of an uncertain choice, I would rather it should be under some man who is more sure of his opinions and wedded to them than I am to mine, ^Bwhose foundation and grounds I find slippery.

And yet I am not too easy to change, since I perceive a like weakness in the contrary opinions. ^C*The very habit of assenting seems to be dangerous and slippery* [Cicero]. ^ANotably in political matters, there is a fine field open for vacillation and dispute:

> As when an even scale with equal weights is pressed,
> Neither side rises, neither falls; it stays at rest.
>
> TIBULLUS

Machiavelli's arguments, for example, were solid enough for the subject, yet it was very easy to combat them; and those who

did so left it no less easy to combat theirs. In such an argument
there would always be matter for answers, rejoinders, replica-
tions, triplications, quadruplications, and that infinite web of
disputes that our pettifoggers have spun out as far as they could in
favor of lawsuits:

> We are hard hit, and hit out hard in turn.
>
> HORACE

For the reasons have little other foundation than experience, and
the diversity of human events offers us infinite examples in all sorts
of forms.

A learned person of our time says that where they say warm in
our almanacs, if someone wants to say cold, and wet where they say
dry, and always put down the opposite of what they forecast, and if
he had to lay a wager on one or the other coming true, he would not
care which side he took; except in cases that admit of no uncertainty,
such as promising extreme heat at Christmas and the rigors of
winter on Midsummer's Day. I have the same opinion about these
political arguments: whatever part they give you to play, you have as
good a chance as your opponent, provided you do not bump up
against principles that are too plain and obvious.

And therefore, to my mind, in public affairs there is no course so
bad, provided it is old and stable, that it is not better than change
and commotion. Our morals are extremely corrupt, and lean with
a remarkable inclination toward the worse; of our laws and customs,
many are barbarous and monstrous; however, because of the diffi-
culty of improving our condition and the danger of everything
crumbling into bits, if I could put a spoke in our wheel and stop it
at this point, I would do so with all my heart:

> ^BNever such shameful, foul examples do we find,
> But that still worse, untold, remain behind.
>
> JUVENAL

^AThe worst thing I find in our state is instability, and the fact that
our laws cannot, any more than our clothes, take any settled form. It
is very easy to accuse a government of imperfection, for all mortal
things are full of it. It is very easy to engender in a people contempt
for their ancient observances; never did a man undertake that with-
out succeeding. But as for establishing a better state in place of the
one they have ruined, many of those who have attempted it have
achieved nothing for their pains.

^CI give my prudence small share in my conduct; I readily let myself be led by the general way of the world. Happy the people who do what they are commanded better than those who command, without tormenting themselves about the reasons, who let themselves roll relaxedly with the rolling of the heavens. Obedience is not pure or tranquil in a man who reasons and argues.

^AAll in all, to return to myself, the only thing that makes me think something of myself is the thing in which no man ever thought himself deficient: my recommendation is vulgar, common, and popular, for who ever thought he lacked sense? That would be a proposition implying its own contradiction. ^CIt is a disease that is never where it is perceived; it is indeed tenacious and strong, but it is pierced and dispersed by the first glance from the patient's eye, like a dense fog by a glance from the sun. ^ATo accuse oneself would be to excuse oneself in that subject, and to condemn oneself would be to absolve oneself. There never was a porter or a silly woman who did not think they had enough sense to take care of themselves. We readily acknowledge in others an advantage in courage, in bodily strength, in experience, in agility, in beauty; but an advantage in judgment we yield to no one. And the arguments that come from simple natural reasoning in others, we think we would have found if we had merely glanced in that direction. As for knowledge, style, and such qualities that we see in the works of others, we sense very easily whether they surpass our own; but as for the simple products of the understanding, each man thinks he had it in him to hit upon the very same things, and does not easily perceive their weight and difficulty, ^Cunless – and hardly even then – they are at a great distance and beyond comparison. ^ASo this is a kind of exercise for which I must hope for very little commendation and praise, and a kind of composition offering little renown.

^CAnd then, for whom do you write? The learned men to whom it falls to pass judgment on books know no other value than that of learning, and admit no other procedure for our minds than that of erudition and art. If you have mistaken one of the Scipios for the other, what is there left for you to say that can be worth while? Anyone who does not know Aristotle, according to them, by the same token does not know himself. Common, ordinary minds do not see the grace and the weight of a lofty and subtle speech. Now, these two types fill the world. The third class into whose hands you come, that of minds regulated and strong in themselves, is so rare

that for this very reason it has neither name nor rank among us; it is time half wasted to aspire and strive to please this group.

^AIt is commonly said that the fairest division of her favors Nature has given us is that of sense; for there is no one who is not content with the share of it that she has allotted him. ^CIs that not reasonable? If anyone saw beyond, he would see beyond his sight.

^AI think my opinions are good and sound; but who does not think as much of his? One of the best proofs I have of mine is the little esteem I have for myself; for if these opinions had not been very firm, they would easily have let themselves be fooled by the singular affection I have for myself, being one who concentrates nearly all his affection upon himself and does not squander much of it elsewhere. All the affection that others distribute to an infinite multitude of friends and acquaintances, to their glory, to their greatness, I devote entirely to the repose of my mind and to myself. What escapes in other directions is not properly by command of my reason:

> Trained to live healthily and for myself.
>
> LUCRETIUS

Now I find my opinions infinitely bold and constant in condemning my inadequacy. In truth, this too is a subject on which I exercise my judgment as much as on any other. The world always looks straight ahead; as for me, I turn my gaze inward, I fix it there and keep it busy. Everyone looks in front of him; as for me, I look inside of me; I have no business but with myself; I continually observe myself, I take stock of myself, I taste myself. Others always go elsewhere, if they stop to think about it; they always go forward;

> No man tries to descend into himself;
>
> PERSIUS

as for me, I roll about in myself.

This capacity for sifting truth, whatever it may amount to in me, and this free will not to enslave my belief easily, I owe principally to myself. For the firmest and most general ideas I have are those which, in a manner of speaking, were born with me. They are natural and all mine. I produced them crude and simple, with a conception bold and strong, but a little confused and imperfect. Since then I have established and fortified them by the authority of others and the sound arguments of the ancients, with whom I found my judgment in agreement. These men have given me

a firmer grip on my ideas and a more complete enjoyment and possession of them.

[B]The recommendation everyone seeks for liveliness and promptness of wit, I aspire to for orderliness; what they seek for a brilliant and signal deed, or for some particular ability, I aspire to for order, consistency, and tranquillity of opinions and conduct. [C]*Certainly, if anything is becoming, it is uniformity in our whole lives and in our individual actions; which you cannot maintain if, imitating the nature of others, you eliminate your own* [Cicero].

[A]Here then you see to what extent I feel guilty of what I said was the first part of the vice of presumption. As for the second, which consists in not esteeming others highly enough, I do not know if I can excuse myself so well; for cost me what it may, I am determined to tell the facts about it.

Whether it may be that the continual association I have with the humors of the ancients, and the idea I have formed of those rich souls of the past, give me a distaste both for others and for myself; or whether we are indeed living in a time which produces only very mediocre things; at any rate, I know of nothing worthy of great admiration. Also, I know scarcely any men intimately enough to be able to judge them; and those I come in contact with most commonly through my situation are for the most part men who have little care for the culture of the soul, and to whom one can suggest no other blessing than honor, and no other perfection than valor.

What beauty I see in others I praise and esteem very gladly. Indeed, I often go farther than what I really think of it, and allow myself to lie to that extent. For I am incapable of inventing anything false. I am glad to testify for my friends to the praiseworthy qualities I find in them; and of one foot of value I am likely to make a foot and a half. But as for lending them qualities that are not there, I cannot, nor can I defend them openly for the imperfections they have.

[B]Even to my enemies I frankly render the testimony of honor that is due. [C]My feelings change; my judgment, no. [B]And I do not confuse my criticism with other circumstances that do not enter into it; and I am so jealous of the liberty of my judgment that I can hardly give it up for any passion whatsoever. [C]I do myself more harm by lying than I do to the person I lie about. This laudable and generous custom is observed of the Persian nation, that they speak of their mortal enemies, and wage war to the death against them, honorably and fairly, so far as their valor deserves it.

^AI know enough men who have various fine qualities, one wit, another courage, another skill, another conscience, another style, one one science, another another. But as for an all-round great man having all these fine parts together, or one part in such excellent degree as to cause amazement or comparison with the men of the past whom we honor, I have not had the good fortune to find any. And the greatest man I have known in person, I mean for natural qualities of the soul, and the best endowed, was Etienne de La Boétie. He was truly a full soul, handsome from every point of view; a soul of the old stamp, who would have achieved great results if fortune had willed it, for he had added much to this rich nature by learning and study.

But I do not know how it happens – ^cand yet beyond doubt it does happen – ^Athat there is as much vanity and weakness of under-standing in those who profess to have the greatest capacity, and who meddle with literary occupations and tasks that depend on books, as in any other sort of men; whether because people demand and expect more of them, and cannot excuse ordinary faults in them, or because the thought that they are learned emboldens them to show off and reveal too much of themselves, whereby they ruin and betray themselves. Just as an artisan shows his stupidity much better on some rich material he has in his hands, if he arranges and mixes it foolishly and contrary to the rules of his craft, than on some wretched stuff, and as people are more offended at a defect in a statue of gold than in one that is of plaster; so do these men when they display things that in themselves, and in their place, would be good; for they use them without discretion, doing honor to their memory at the expense of their intelligence: they do honor to Cicero, Galen, Ulpian, and Saint Jerome, and themselves they make ridiculous.

I gladly return to the subject of the ineptitude of our education. Its goal has been to make us not good or wise, but learned; it has attained this goal. It has not taught us to follow and embrace virtue and wisdom, but has imprinted in us their derivation and etymology. We know how to decline virtue, if we cannot love it. If we do not know what wisdom is by practice and experience, we know it by jargon and by rote. With our neighbors, we are not content to know their family, their kindred, and their connections; we want to have them as friends and form some association and understanding with them. Education has taught us the definitions,

divisions, and partitions of virtue, like the surnames and branches of a genealogy, without any further concern to form between us and virtue any familiar relationship and intimate acquaintance. It has chosen for our instruction not the books that have the soundest and truest opinions, but those that speak the best Greek and Latin; and amid its beautiful words, it has poured into our minds the most inane humors of antiquity.

A good education changes your judgment and conduct, as happened to Polemon, that dissipated young Greek, who, having gone by chance to hear a lecture by ᶜXenocrates, ᴬdid not notice merely the eloquence and mastery of the teacher, or bring back to his house merely the knowledge of some fine matter, but reaped a more perceptible and solid fruit, which was the sudden change and amendment of his former life. Who has ever felt such an effect from our education?

> Will you behave like Polemon,
> When he reformed, one bygone day? Will you lay down
> The badges of disease – wraps, anklets, pads – as he
> Tore from his drunken neck, they say, the wreath of glee,
> When the undinnered sage addressed him chidingly?
>
> HORACE

ᶜThe least contemptible class of people seems to me to be those who, through their simplicity, occupy the lowest rank; and they seem to show greater regularity in their relations. The morals and the talk of peasants I find commonly more obedient to the prescriptions of true philosophy than are those of our philosophers. *The common people are wiser, because they are as wise as they need be* [Lactantius].

ᴬThe most notable men that I have judged by outward appearances – for to judge them in my own way, I would need more light on them – were, in point of war and military ability, the duke of Guise, who died at Orléans, and the late Marshal Strozzi. As for able men of uncommon virtue, Olivier and L'Hôpital, chancellors of France. It seems to me that poetry too has flourished in our century. We have a wealth of good craftsmen in that trade: Daurat, Beza, Buchanan, L'Hôpital, Montdoré, Turnebus. As for those writing in French, I think they have raised its poetry to the highest point it will ever reach; and in the respects in which Ronsard and Du Bellay excel, I do not consider them far removed from the perfection of the

ancients. Adrianus Turnebus knew more, and knew better what he knew, than any man that lived in his time or for many years before.

^BThe lives of the duke of Alva, who died recently, and of our Constable de Montmorency were noble lives that had many rare similarities in fortune. But the beauty and glory of the latter's death, suddenly and in extreme old age, before the eyes of Paris and his king and in their service against his nearest kin, commanding an army victorious through his leadership, deserves, I think, to be placed among the notable events of my time. ^CSo do the constant goodness, the gentle conduct, and the conscientious affability of Monsieur de La Noue, amid such injustice of armed factions, true school of treachery, inhumanity, and brigandage, in which he was brought up – a great and very experienced warrior.

I have taken pleasure in making public in several places the hopes I have for Marie de Gournay le Jars, my covenant daughter, whom I love indeed more than a daughter of my own, and cherish in my retirement and solitude as one of the best parts of my own being. She is the only person I still think about in the world. If youthful promise means anything, her soul will some day be capable of the finest things, among others of perfection in that most sacred kind of friendship which, so we read, her sex has not yet been able to attain. The sincerity and firmness of her character are already sufficient, her affection for me more than superabundant, and such, in short, that it leaves nothing to be desired, unless that her apprehension about my end, in view of my fifty-five years when I met her, would not torment her so cruelly. The judgment she made of the first *Essays*, she a woman, and in this age, and so young, and alone in her district, and the remarkable eagerness with which she loved me and wanted my friendship for a long time, simply through the esteem she formed for me before she had seen me, is a phenomenon very worthy of consideration.[4]

^AThe other virtues are given little or no value nowadays; but valor has become common through our civil wars, and in this respect there are among us souls firm to the point of perfection, and in great numbers, so that a choice is impossible.

This is all the extraordinary and uncommon greatness that I have known up to this moment.

4 This paragraph, which does not appear in the Bordeaux Copy, is of doubtful authenticity.

18
Of giving the lie

[A]Yes, but someone will tell me that this plan of using oneself as a subject to write about would be excusable in rare and famous men who by their reputation had aroused some desire to know them. That is certain; I admit it; and I know full well that to see a man of the common sort, an artisan will hardly raise his eyes from his work, whereas to see a great and prominent personage arrive in a city, men leave workshops and stores empty. It ill befits anyone to make himself known save him who has qualities to be imitated, and whose life and opinions may serve as a model. In the greatness of their deeds Caesar and Xenophon had something to found and establish their narrative upon, as on a just and solid base. Desirable therefore would be the journals of Alexander the Great, and the commentaries that Augustus, [C]Cato, [A]Sulla, Brutus, and others left about their deeds. People love and study the figures of such men, even in bronze and stone.

This remonstrance is very true, but it concerns me only very little:

> Only to friends do I recite, and on request,
> Not to all men, or everywhere. Some will not rest,
> And keep reciting in the Forum or the baths.
>
> HORACE

I am not building here a statue to erect at the town crossroads, or in a church or a public square:

> [B]I do not aim to swell my page full-blown
> With windy trifles. . . .
> We two talk alone.
>
> PERSIUS

[A]This is for a nook in a library, and to amuse a neighbor, a relative, a friend, who may take pleasure in associating and conversing with me again in this image. Others have taken courage to speak of themselves because they found the subject worthy and rich; I, on the contrary, because I have found mine so barren and so meager that no suspicion of ostentation can fall upon my plan.

[C]I willingly judge the actions of others; I give little chance to

judge mine because of their nullity. ᴮI do not find so much good in myself that I cannot tell it without blushing.

ᴬWhat a satisfaction it would be to me to hear someone tell me, in this way, of the habits, the face, the expression, the favorite remarks, and the fortunes of my ancestors! How attentive I would be! Truly it would spring from a bad nature to be scornful of even the portraits of our friends and predecessors, ᶜthe form of their clothes and their armor. I keep their handwriting, their seal, the breviary and a peculiar sword that they used, and I have not banished from my study some long sticks that my father ordinarily carried in his hand. *A father's coat and his ring are the more dear to his children the more they loved him* [Saint Augustine].

ᴬHowever, if my descendants have other tastes, I shall have ample means for revenge: for they could not possibly have less concern about me than I shall have about them by that time.

All the contact I have with the public in this book is that I borrow their tools of printing, as being swifter and easier. In recompense, ᶜperhaps I shall keep some pat of butter from melting in the market place.

ᴬLest tunny-fish and olives lack a robe.

MARTIAL

ᴮTo mackerel I'll often give a shirt.

CATULLUS

ᶜAnd if no one reads me, have I wasted my time, entertaining myself for so many idle hours with such useful and agreeable thoughts? In modeling this figure upon myself, I have had to fashion and compose myself so often to bring myself out, that the model itself has to some extent grown firm and taken shape. Painting myself for others, I have painted my inward self with colors clearer than my original ones. I have no more made my book than my book has made me – a book consubstantial with its author, concerned with my own self, an integral part of my life; not concerned with some third-hand, extraneous purpose, like all other books. Have I wasted my time by taking stock of myself so continually, so carefully? For those who go over themselves only in their minds and occasionally in speech do not penetrate to essentials in their examination as does a man who makes that his study, his work, and his trade, who binds himself to keep an enduring account, with all his faith, with all his strength.

Indeed, the most delightful pleasures are digested inwardly, avoid leaving any traces, and avoid the sight not only of the public but of any other person.

How many times has this task diverted me from annoying cogitations! And all frivolous ones should be counted as annoying. Nature has made us a present of a broad capacity for entertaining ourselves apart, and often calls us to do so, to teach us that we owe ourselves in part to society, but in the best part to ourselves. In order to train my fancy even to dream with some order and purpose, and in order to keep it from losing its way and roving with the wind, there is nothing like embodying and registering all the little thoughts that come to it. I listen to my reveries because I have to record them. How many times, irritated by some action that civility and reason kept me from reproving openly, have I disgorged it here, not without ideas of instructing the public! And indeed, these poetic lashes –

> Bang in the eye, bang on the snout,
> Bang on the back of the apish lout!
>
> MAROT

– imprint themselves even better on paper than on living flesh. What if I lend a slightly more attentive ear to books, since I have been lying in wait to pilfer something from them to adorn or support my own?

I have not studied one bit to make a book; but I have studied a bit because I had made it, if it is studying a bit to skim over and pinch, by his head or his feet, now one author, now another; not at all to form my opinions, but certainly to assist, second, and serve those which I formed long ago.

ᴬBut whom shall we believe when he talks about himself, in so corrupt an age, seeing that there are few or none whom we can believe when they speak of others, where there is less incentive for lying? The first stage in the corruption of morals is the banishment of truth; for, as Pindar said, to be truthful is the beginning of a great virtue,ᶜand is the first article that Plato requires in the governor of his Republic. ᴬOur truth of nowadays is not what is, but what others can be convinced of; just as we call "money" not only that which is legal, but also any counterfeit that will pass. Our nation has long been reproached for this vice; for Salvianus of Massilia, who lived in the time of the Emperor Valentinian, says that to the French lying and perjury are not a vice but a manner of speaking. If a man wanted to go this testimony one better, he could say that it is now a virtue to

them. Men form and fashion themselves for it as for an honorable practice; for dissimulation is among the most notable qualities of this century.

Thus I have often considered what could be the source of that custom, which we observe so religiously, of feeling more bitterly offended when reproached with this vice, which is so common among us, than with any other; and that it should be the worst insult that can be given us in words, to reproach us with lying. On that, I find that it is natural to defend ourselves most for the defects with which we are most besmirched. It seems that in resenting the accusation and growing excited about it, we unburden ourselves to some extent of the guilt; if we have it in fact, at least we condemn it in appearance.

^BWould it not also be that this reproach seems to involve cowardice and lack of courage? Is there any more obvious cowardice than to deny our own word? Worse yet, to deny what we know?

^ALying is an ugly vice, which an ancient paints in most shameful colors when he says that it is giving evidence of contempt for God, and at the same time of fear of men. It is not possible to represent more vividly the horror, the vileness, and the profligacy of it. For what can you imagine uglier than being a coward toward men and bold toward God? Since mutual understanding is brought about solely by way of words, he who breaks his word betrays human society. It is the only instrument by means of which our wills and thoughts communicate, it is the interpreter of our soul. If it fails us, we have no more hold on each other, no more knowledge of each other. If it deceives us, it breaks up all our relations and dissolves all the bonds of our society.

^BCertain nations of the new Indies (there is no use mentioning their names, which are no more; for the desolation of their conquest – a monstrous and unheard-of case – has extended even to the entire abolition of the names and former knowledge of the places) offered to their gods human blood, but only such as was drawn from their tongue and ears, in expiation of the sin of falsehood, heard as well as uttered.

^AThat worthy fellow from Greece used to say that children play with knucklebones, men with words.

As for the varied etiquette of giving the lie, and our laws of honor in that matter, and the changes they have undergone, I shall put off till another time telling what I know about that, and shall meanwhile learn, if I can, at what time the custom began of weighing and

measuring words so exactly, and attaching our honor to them. For it is easy to see that it did not exist in olden times among the Romans and the Greeks. And it has often seemed to me novel and strange to see them giving each other the lie and insulting each other, without having a quarrel over it. The laws of their duty took some other path than ours. Caesar is called now a robber, now a drunkard, to his face. We see how free are the invectives they use against each other, I mean the greatest warlords of both nations, where words are avenged merely by words, and do not lead to other consequences.

19
Of freedom of conscience

^AIt is ordinary to see good intentions, if they are carried out without moderation, push men to very vicious acts. In this controversy on whose account France is at present agitated by civil wars, the best and soundest side is undoubtedly that which maintains both the old religion and the old government of the country. However, among the good men who follow that side (for I speak not of those who use it as a pretext either to wreak their private vengeances, or to supply their avarice, or to pursue the favor of princes; but of those who follow it out of true zeal toward their religion and a holy concern for maintaining the peace and the status of their fatherland) – of these, I say, we see many whom passion drives outside the bounds of reason, and makes them sometimes adopt unjust, violent, and even reckless courses.

It is certain that in those early times when our religion began to gain authority with the laws, zeal armed many believers against every sort of pagan books, thus causing men of letters to suffer an extraordinary loss. I consider that this excess did more harm to letters than all the bonfires of the barbarians. Of this Cornelius Tacitus is a good witness: for although the Emperor Tacitus, his kinsman, had by express ordinances populated all the libraries in the world with his works, nevertheless not one single complete copy was able to escape the careful search of those who wanted to abolish them because of five or six insignificant sentences contrary to our belief.

They also had this habit, of readily lending false praises to all the emperors who helped us and of universally condemning all the

actions of those who were hostile to us; as it is easy to see in the case of the Emperor Julian, surnamed the Apostate.[1]

He was, in truth, a very great and rare man, being one whose soul was deeply dyed with the arguments of philosophy, by which he professed to regulate all his actions; and indeed there is no sort of virtue of which he did not leave very notable examples. In point of chastity (of which the course of his life gives very clear testimony), we read of an action of his like those of Alexander and Scipio, that out of many very beautiful captive women he would not even look at one, and this in the flower of his age, for he was killed by the Parthians at the age of only thirty-one.

As for justice, he took the trouble to hear the disputants himself; and although out of curiosity he informed himself of the religion of those who appeared before him, at all events the enmity he bore to ours carried no weight in the scales. He himself made many good laws, and cut out a large part of the subsidies and taxes that his predecessors had levied.

We have two good historians who were eyewitnesses of his actions, one of whom, Marcellinus, sharply blames, in various parts of his history, that ordinance of his by which he barred the schools and forbade teaching to all Christian rhetoricians and grammarians; and he says that he could wish that action of his to be buried in silence. It is likely that if he had done anything harsher against us, Marcellinus would not have forgotten it, being very well affected to our side.

He was a harsh enemy to us, in truth, but not a cruel one. For even our own people tell of him this story, that as he was walking about the city of Chalcedon one day, Maris, the bishop of the place, actually dared to call him a wicked traitor to Christ, and that he did nothing about it except to answer: "Go, wretched man, and weep for the loss of your eyes." To which the bishop further replied: "I give thanks to Jesus Christ for having taken away my sight, so that I may not see your impudent face." In this, they say, Julian was affecting a philosophic patience. At all events, that action cannot be reconciled with the cruelties that they say he exercised against us. He was

1 Montaigne's defense of Julian was one of the items blamed by the papal censors when they examined his *Essays* during his stay in Rome in 1580–81. (See *Travel Journal*, pp. 1166, 1178.) The only changes he made on this account were insignificant.

(says Eutropius, my other witness) an enemy of Christianity, but without touching blood.[2]

And, to return to his justice, there is nothing in it that can be accused except the severities he practiced at the beginning of his reign against those who had followed the lead of Constantius, his predecessor.

As for his sobriety, he always lived a soldierly life; and in full peacetime he ate like a man who was preparing and inuring himself to the austerity of war.

The vigilance in him was such that he divided the night into three or four parts, of which the smallest was the one he gave to sleep; the rest he used to inspect in person the state of his army and his guard, or to study; for among other rare qualities of his, he was very outstanding in every kind of literature. They tell of Alexander the Great that when he was in bed, for fear that sleep should divert him from his thoughts and his studies, he had a basin placed next to his bed, and kept one of his hands out with a little copper ball in it, so that when sleep stole over him and relaxed the grasp of his fingers, this little ball should awaken him by the noise of its fall into the basin. But this man had his soul so intent on what he wanted, and so little muddled with fumes by virtue of his singular abstinence, that he easily dispensed with that artifice.

As for military ability, he was admirable in all the qualities of a great commander; and indeed he spent nearly all his life in the constant practice of war, for the most part with us in France against the Germans and Franks. We have hardly any memory of a man who faced more risks or who more often put his person to the test.

His death has something about it like that of Epaminondas; for he was struck by an arrow and tried to pull it out, and would have done so but that, the arrow being sharp, he cut and disabled his hand. He kept demanding incessantly to be carried back into the melee in this same state to encourage his soldiers, who contested this battle very courageously without him, until night separated the armies.

2 In the editions before 1588 Montaigne here gave his opinion of the falsity of the stories that Julian died with the words "Thou hast conquered, Nazarene," or "Be content, Nazarene," on his lips. Inasmuch as the 1588 edition was the first since 1580 that he worked over carefully, his suppression of it in 1588 may have been in response to the observations of the papal censor. At all events, after 1588 he restored these remarks, with very little change from their original form (next page, fourth paragraph).

He owed to philosophy the singular contempt in which he held his life and all human things. He had a firm belief in the eternity of souls.

In the matter of religion he was bad throughout. He was surnamed the Apostate for having abandoned ours; however, this theory seems to me more likely, that he had never had it at heart, but that, out of obedience to the laws, he had dissembled until he held the Empire in his hand. He was so superstitious in his own religion that even those who belonged to it in his time made fun of him; and they said that if he had won the victory over the Parthians, he would have exterminated the race of oxen from the world to satisfy his sacrifices. He was also infatuated with the knowledge of divination, and gave authority to all manner of prognostications.

He said among other things, as he was dying, that he was grateful to the gods and thanked them because they had not willed to kill him by surprise, having long before informed him of the place and time of his end; or by a soft or slack death, better suitable to idle and effeminate persons; or by a languishing, prolonged, and painful one; and that they had found him worthy to die in this noble fashion, in the course of his victories and in the flower of his glory. He had had a vision like that of Marcus Brutus, which first threatened him in Gaul and later reappeared to him in Persia just before his death.

ᶜThese words that they have him say when he felt himself struck, "Thou hast conquered, Nazarene," or, as others have it, "Be content, Nazarene," would not have been forgotten if they had been believed by my witnesses, who, being present in the army, noted even the slightest movements and words at his end, any more than certain other miracles that people attach to it.

ᴬAnd to come to the subject of my discussion, he had incubated paganism, says Marcellinus, for a long time in his heart; but because all his army was composed of Christians, he dared not reveal it. Finally, when he saw himself strong enough to dare to proclaim his will, he had the temples of the gods opened and tried in every way to set up idolatry. To attain his effect, having found the people in Constantinople at odds and the prelates of the Christian Church divided, he had them come to him at the palace and earnestly admonished them to lull these civic dissensions and urged that each man should serve his own religion without hindrance and without fear. This solicitation he made very urgently, in the hope that this complete freedom would augment the schisms and factions that divided them and would keep the people from uniting

and consequently strengthening themselves against him by their concord and unanimous understanding; for he had learned by experience, from the cruelty of some Christians, that there is no beast in the world so much to be feared by man as man.

Those are very nearly his words. Wherein this is worthy of consideration, that Emperor Julian uses, to kindle the trouble of civil dissension, that same recipe of freedom of conscience that our kings have just been employing to extinguish it. It may be said, on the one hand, that to give factions a loose rein to entertain their own opinions is to scatter and sow division; it is almost lending a hand to augment it, there being no barrier or coercion of the laws to check or hinder its course. But on the other hand, one could also say that to give factions a loose rein to entertain their own opinions is to soften and relax them through facility and ease, and to dull the point, which is sharpened by rarity, novelty, and difficulty. And yet I prefer to think, for the reputation of our kings' piety, that having been unable to do what they would, they have pretended to will what they could.

20
We taste nothing pure

^AThe weakness of our condition makes it impossible for things to come into our experience in their natural simplicity and purity. The elements that we enjoy are corrupted, and the metals likewise; and gold must be debased by some other material to fit it for our service.

^CNeither virtue thus in its simple form, which Aristo and Pyrrho and also the Stoics made the end of life, nor the sensual pleasure of the Cyrenaics and Aristippus could be serviceable to life without admixture.

^AOf the pleasures and good things that we have, there is not one exempt from some mixture of pain and discomfort:

> ^BRight from the fount of these delights of ours
> A bitter something rises, which chokes us 'mid the flowers.
> LUCRETIUS

Our utmost sensual pleasure has an air of groaning and lament about it. Wouldn't you say that it is dying of anguish? Indeed, when we forge a picture of it at its highest point, we deck it with sickly

and painful epithets and qualities: languor, softness, weakness, faintness, *morbidezza*: a great testimony to their consanguinity and consubstantiality.

^CProfound joy has more seriousness than gaiety about it; extreme and full contentment, more soberness than sprightliness. *Even felicity, unless it tempers itself, overwhelms* [Seneca]. Happiness racks us.

^AThat is what an old Greek verse says, in this sense: "The gods sell us all the good things they give us." That is to say, they give us none pure and perfect, none that we do not buy at the price of some evil.

^CToil and pleasure, very unlike in nature, are nevertheless joined by I know not what natural association. Socrates says that some god tried to lump together and confuse pain and pleasure, but that, not being able to come out successful, he decided to couple them, at least by the tail.

^BMetrodorus used to say that in sadness there is some alloy of pleasure. I do not know whether he meant something else, but for my part I indeed imagine that there is design, consent, and pleasure in feeding one's melancholy; I mean beyond the ambition that can also be involved. There is some shadow of daintiness and luxury that smiles on us and flatters us in the very lap of melancholy. Are there not some natures that feed on it?

> A certain kind of pleasure 'tis to weep.
>
> OVID

^CAnd one Attalus, in Seneca, says that the memory of our lost friends is agreeable to us like the bitterness in a wine that is too old –

> Boy, that serve old Falernian wine,
> Pour me a bitterer cup for mine
>
> CATULLUS

– and like apples sweetly tart.

^BNature reveals this confusion to us; painters hold that the movements and wrinkles of the face that serve for weeping serve also for laughing. In truth, before one or the other is completely expressed, watch the progress of the painting: you are in doubt toward which one it is going. And the extremity of laughter is mingled with tears. ^C*There is no evil without its compensation* [Seneca].

When I imagine man besieged by desirable delights – let us put the case that all his members should be forever seized with a pleasure like that of generation at its most excessive point – I feel him sink under the weight of his delight, and I see him wholly incapable of supporting a pleasure so pure, so constant, and so universal. In truth, he flees it when he is in it, and naturally hastens to escape it, as from a place where he cannot stand firm, where he is afraid of sinking.

[B]When I confess myself religiously to myself, I find that the best goodness I have has some tincture of vice. And I fear that Plato in his most verdant virtue (I who am as sincere and loyal an admirer of it, and of virtues of similar stamp, as a man can be), if he had listened to it closely – and he did listen to it closely – would have sensed in it some false note of human admixture, but an obscure note, perceptible only to himself. Man, in all things and throughout, is but patchwork and motley.

[A]The very laws of justice cannot subsist without some mixture of injustice. And Plato says that those men are undertaking to cut off the Hydra's head who aspire to remove all drawbacks and disadvantages from the laws. *Every exemplary punishment has in it some injustice against individuals, which is compensated by public utility,* says Tacitus.

[B]It is likewise true that for the uses of life and for the service of public business there may be excess in the purity and perspicacity of our minds. That penetrating clarity has too much subtlety and curiosity in it. These must be weighted and blunted to make them more obedient to example and practice, and thickened and obscured to relate them to this shadowy and earthy life. Therefore common and less high-strung minds are found to be more fit and more successful for conducting affairs. And the lofty and exquisite ideas of philosophy are found to be inept in practice. That acute vivacity of mind, that supple and restless versatility, disturbs our negotiations. Human enterprises must be handled more roughly and superficially, and a good and great part of them left for the rights of fortune. There is no need to light up affairs so deeply and so subtly. You get lost considering so many contrasting aspects and diverse shapes: [C]*in revolving mutually contradictory things, their minds had become stupefied* [Livy].

This is what the ancients say of Simonides: because his imagination presented him – on the question that King Hiero had put to

him,[1] to answer which he had had many days to meditate – with diverse acute and subtle considerations, being in doubt which was the most probable, he totally despaired of the truth.

[B]He who seeks and embraces all the circumstances and consequences impedes his choice. An average intelligence conducts equally well, and suffices to carry out, things of great or little weight. Note that the best managers are those who least know how to tell us how they are so, and that the self-satisfied storytellers most often do nothing worth while. I know one great talker and very excellent portrayer of every sort of managing, who has very pitifully let the revenue of a hundred thousand francs slip through his hands. I know another who speaks and gives advice better than any man in his council, and there is no better show of mind and competence in the world; however, in practice, his servants find him quite different; I mean without taking bad luck into account.

21
Against do-nothingness

[A]The Emperor Vespasian, though sick with the sickness of which he died, did not leave off wanting to know about the state of the Empire, and even in bed never stopped dispatching many affairs of consequence. And when his physician scolded him for it as a thing harmful to his health, he said: "An emperor must die standing." That is a fine statement, in my opinion, and worthy of a great prince.

The Emperor Hadrian used it later in this same connection. And kings ought often to be reminded of it, to make them feel that the great charge that is given them of commanding so many men is not an idle charge, and that there is nothing that can so justly spoil a subject's taste for putting himself at pains and in danger for the service of his prince as to see the prince himself meanwhile loafing about at paltry and frivolous occupations; and for being concerned for his preservation, when he sees his prince so careless of ours.[2]

[C]If anyone wants to maintain that it is better for the prince to conduct his wars through another than by himself, fortune will furnish him with enough examples of those for whom their

1 "What is God?"
2 This is probably intended as a hint for King Henry III.

lieutenants have achieved great enterprises, and furthermore of those whose presence would have done more harm than good. But no virtuous and courageous prince can endure anyone's addressing to him such shameful advice. Under color of preserving his head, like the statue of a saint, for the welfare of his state, they precisely degrade him from his office, which consists all in military action, and declare him incapable of it.

I know one who would much rather be beaten than sleep while people were fighting for him, who never without jealousy saw even his own men do anything great in his absence.[3]

And Selim I said with great reason, it seems to me, that the victories that are won without the master are not complete. How much more readily would he have said that that master ought to blush for shame to claim any share for his name, when he had employed in it only his voice and his thought – and not even that, seeing that in such tasks the plans and commands that bring honor are only those that are given on the spot and in the midst of the action. No pilot exercises his function on terra firma.

The princes of the Ottoman race, the first race in the world in the fortunes of war, have warmly embraced this opinion. And Bajazet II and his son, who departed from it, amusing themselves in the sciences and other stay-at-home occupations, thereby gave their empire some good slaps; and the one who rules at present, Amurath III, following their example, is making a pretty good start at coming out the same way. Was it not the king of England, Edward III, who made this remark about our Charles V, "There was never a king who put on armor less, and yet there never was a king who gave me so much to do"? He was right to find it strange, as an effect of chance more than of reason.

And let those find another adherent than me who want to number among the warlike and great-souled conquerors the kings of Castile and Portugal because, twelve hundred leagues from their idle abode, by the leadership of their agents, they made themselves masters of the East and West Indies – and one may wonder whether they would even have had the courage to go there and enjoy them in person.

ᴬThe Emperor Julian used to say even more, that a philosopher and a gallant man ought not even to breathe; that is to say, they should grant to bodily necessities only what cannot be refused them,

3 Henry IV.

ever keeping the soul and body busied in fair, great, and virtuous things. He was ashamed if he was seen to spit or sweat in public (which they also tell of the Lacedaemonian youth, and Xenophon of the Persian), because he considered that exercise, continual toil, and sobriety should have cooked and dried up all those superfluities. What Seneca says will not fit badly in this place, that the ancient Romans kept their youth standing: They taught their children nothing, he says, that they had to learn sitting.

ᶜIt is a noble craving to want even to die usefully and manfully; but the outcome lies not so much in our good resolution as in our good fortune. A thousand have proposed to conquer or die fighting, who have failed to do either, wounds and prison crossing this design and lending them a forced life. There are maladies that lay low even our desires and our consciousness.⁴

4 Here the 1595 edition adds:
"Fortune ought not to have seconded the vanity of the Roman legions who obliged themselves by oath to die or conquer. *I shall return victor from the battle, Marcus Fabius; if I fail, I invoke on myself the wrath of Father Jupiter, Mars Gradivus, and the other gods* [Livy].

"The Portuguese say that at a certain point in their conquest of the Indies they encountered soldiers who had condemned themselves with horrible execrations to come to no terms except to be killed or remain victorious; and as a mark of this vow they kept their heads and beards shaven. It is no use risking our lives and being obstinate; it seems that the blows flee from those who offer themselves to them too blithely, and are unwilling to reach the man who presents himself to them too willingly and spoils their purpose.

"Some men, unable to succeed in losing their life by the hand of the enemy, after having tried everything, have been constrained, in order to implement their resolve to return with honor or not return, to put themselves to death in the very heat of the combat. There are other examples of this; here is one. Philistus, head of the naval forces of Dionysius the Younger against the Syracusans, offered them battle, which was bitterly contested, the forces being equal. In this he had the better of it at the beginning, by his own process. But when the Syracusans closed in around his galley to board it, Philistus, after personally performing great deeds of valor to disengage himself, lost all hope of further resource, and with his own hand took away the life he had so freely and unsuccessfully abandoned to the hands of the enemy."

At this point in the Bordeaux Copy there is a sign for an insert, whence Strowski deduces that this passage might have been written on a separate slip and pasted onto the page. Against this, Zeitlin points out that the upper and right-hand margins are almost entirely empty. However, Montaigne would have found the space rather crowded for so long a passage. Strowski's view seems sound.

Moulay Moloch, king of Fez, who has just won against Sebastian, king of Portugal, that battle famous for the death of three kings and the transfer of that great kingdom to the crown of Castile, found himself gravely ill when the Portuguese entered his state by force of arms, and from then on kept getting worse, heading for death and foreseeing it. Never did a man use himself more vigorously and more gloriously. He found himself too weak to endure the ceremonial pomp of the entry into his camp, which according to their fashion is full of magnificence and brimful of action, and resigned that honor to his brother. But that was also the only function of a general that he resigned; all the others, the necessary and useful ones, he performed very strenuously and exactly; keeping his body reclining, but his understanding and his courage standing and firm to the last gasp, and somewhat beyond.

He could have undermined his enemies, who had advanced indiscreetly into his territory, and it grieved him terribly that for lack of a little life and because he had no one to substitute for himself in the conduct of this war and of the affairs of a troubled state, he had to seek a bloody and hazardous victory when he had another one pure[5] and clean in his hands. At all events, he husbanded the duration of his illness miraculously in exhausting his enemy and drawing them far from the navy and seaports they had on the coast of Africa, until the last day of his life, which, by design, he reserved and employed for this great day.

He drew up his army in a circle, besieging the camp of the Portuguese from all sides, and this circle, coming to bend and tighten, not only hindered them in the fighting, which was very bitter because of the valor of the young invading king, seeing that they had to face in all directions, but also hindered their flight after their rout. And finding all the outlets seized and closed, they were constrained to fall back upon themselves – *and they are heaped up not only by the slaughter, but by their flight* [Livy] – and pile up on one another, furnishing the victors with a very murderous and very complete victory.

Dying, he had himself carried and rushed wherever the need called him, and passing along the ranks he exhorted his captains and

5 Nearly all editions here read "sure" (*sur*); instead of "pure" (*pur*); but the Bordeaux Copy's reading looks more like *pur* to me. Marie de Gournay's 1635 edition gives *pur*.

soldiers one after another. But when one corner of his battle line let itself be broken through, they could not hold him back from mounting on horseback, sword in hand. He was struggling to get into the fray; when his men tried to stop him, one by the bridle, another by his robe and his stirrups, this effort finished off the little life he had left. They laid him down again. Recovering with a start from this swoon, and finding no other faculty left with which to warn them to keep silent about his death – which was the most necessary command he had then to make, in order not to engender some despair in his men by this news – he expired holding his finger against his closed mouth, the ordinary sign for keeping silence. Who ever lived so long and so far forward into death? Who ever died so much on his feet?

The extreme degree in treating death courageously, and the most natural, is to see it not only without being stunned, but without concern, continuing the course of life freely right into death. Like Cato, who spent his time sleeping and studying while having present in his head and heart a violent and bloody death, and holding it in his hand.

22
Of riding post

^BI have been not of the weakest in this exercise, which is suited to men of my build, solid and short. But I give up the business; it is too trying to keep it up for long.

^AI was just this moment reading that King Cyrus, the more easily to receive news from all parts of his empire, which was of very great extent, ascertained how much distance a horse could do at a stretch in one day; and at that distance he stationed men whose business it was to keep horses ready to equip those who should be coming toward him. ^CAnd some say that this speed of travel comes up to that of the flight of cranes.

^ACaesar says that Lucius Vibulus Rufus, being in haste to bring information to Pompey, traveled toward him day and night, changing horses to make speed. And he himself, from what Suetonius says, did a hundred miles a day in a hired coach. But he was a furious courier, for where rivers cut across his road he would cross them swimming; ^Cand would not turn from a direct route to go and look for a bridge or a ford. ^ATiberius Nero, going to see his brother

Drusus, who was sick in Germany, did two hundred miles in twenty-four hours with three coaches.

ᶜIn the war of the Romans against King Antiochus, T. Sempronius Gracchus, says Livy, *by relays of horses, with almost incredible speed, reached Pella from Amphissa on the third day*; and it appears, when you look at the location, that they were established posts, not freshly ordered for this ride.

ᴮCecinna's device for sending back news to his household was much swifter; he took swallows along with him, and released them toward their nests when he wanted to send back news of himself, marking them with some color to signify his meaning, according as he had prearranged with his people. At the theater in Rome the heads of families kept pigeons in their bosoms, to which they attached letters when they wanted to send instructions to their people at home; and these were trained to bring back an answer. D. Brutus used them when besieged in Mutina, and others elsewhere.

In Peru they rode post on men, who carried them on their shoulders in litters, with such agility that on a dead run the first carriers would toss their load to the second without losing a step.

ᶜI understand that the Wallachians, couriers of the Grand Sultan, make extraordinary speed, because they have the right to dismount the first passer-by they meet on their way, giving him their jaded horse; and that to guard against tiring, they bind themselves very tightly around the waist with a broad band.

23
Of evil means employed to a good end

ᴬThere is a wonderful relation and correspondence in this universal government of the works of nature, which well shows that it is neither accidental nor conducted by divers masters. The diseases and conditions of our bodies are seen also in states and governments: kingdoms and republics are born, flourish, and wither with age, as we do. We are subject to a useless and harmful surfeit of humors: either of good humors – for even this the doctors fear; and because there is nothing stable in us, they say that too blithe and vigorous a perfection of health must be artificially reduced and abated for us, for fear that our nature, unable to settle in any certain position and having no room for improvement, may retreat in disorder and too

suddenly; therefore they order purgings and bleedings for athletes to draw off this superabundance of health – or of evil humors, which is the ordinary cause of diseases.

States are often seen to be sick of a similar repletion, and it has been customary to use various sorts of purgation. Sometimes a great multitude of families are sent away to relieve the country of them, and these go to seek accommodations elsewhere at the expense of others. In this fashion our ancient Franks, starting from the depths of Germany, came and took possession of Gaul and drove out its first inhabitants. Thus was formed that infinite tide of men that poured into Italy under Brennus and others. Thus the Goths and Vandals, and also the people who are now in possession of Greece, abandoned their native country to go and settle elsewhere where they had more room. And there are scarcely two or three corners in the world which have not felt the effect of such movements.

By this means the Romans built their colonies; for, feeling their city growing immoderately, they would relieve it of the least necessary people and send them to inhabit and cultivate their conquered lands. Sometimes also they deliberately fostered wars with certain of their enemies, not only to keep their men in condition, for fear that idleness, mother of corruption, might bring them some worse mischief –

> [B]We bear the evils of long peace; fiercer than war,
> Luxury weighs us down
> JUVENAL

– [A]but also to serve as a bloodletting for their republic and to cool off a bit the too vehement heat of their young men, to prune and clear the branches of that too lustily proliferating stock. To this effect they once used their war against the Carthaginians.

In the treaty of Bretigny, Edward III, king of England, would not include, in the general peace that he made with our king, the question of the contested duchy of Brittany, in order that he might have a place to unload his soldiers, and that the crowd of Englishmen he had employed in his affairs on this side of the Channel might not rush back into England. This was one of the reasons why our King Philip consented to send his son John to the war overseas, so that he would take along with him a great number of hot-blooded young men who were in his armed forces.

There are many in our times who reason in like fashion, wishing that this heated passion that is among us might be deflected into

some war with our neighbors, for fear that these peccant humors which dominate our body at the moment, if they are not drained off elsewhere, may keep our fever still at its height and in the end bring on our total ruin. And indeed a foreign war is a much milder evil than a civil war. But I do not believe that God would favor so unjust an enterprise as to injure and pick a quarrel with others for our own convenience:

> ^BNothing, O Nemesis, may I so strongly covet
> That I would rob its rightful owner of it.
>
> CATULLUS

^AHowever, the weakness of our condition often pushes us to the necessity of using evil means to a good end. Lycurgus, the most virtuous and perfect lawmaker that ever was, hit upon this very unjust method of teaching his people temperance: to make the Helots, who were their slaves, forcibly drunk, so that the Spartans, seeing them thus lost and buried in wine, should hold the excess of this vice in horror.

Those were still more in the wrong who in ancient times allowed that criminals, whatever kind of death they were condemned to, should be cut up alive by the doctors, so that they might see our inner parts in their natural state and thereby establish more certainty in their art. For if we must go to excess, it is more excusable to do so for the health of the soul than for that of the body; as the Romans trained the people to valor and contempt for dangers and death by those furious spectacles of gladiators and fencers who fought to the death and cut up and killed each other in their presence:

> ^BWhat seeks this impious practice of a savage game,
> This death of youths, this blood-fed lust – what other aim?
>
> PRUDENTIUS

And this custom lasted until the Emperor Theodosius:

> Then seize this honor, Prince, delayed until your days;
> Take what your father left to take, heir to his praise.
> Let none be slain in Rome whose death serves as a thrill.
> Let the cruel arena be now content to spill
> The blood of beasts alone, not put on homicides.
>
> PRUDENTIUS

^AIt was in truth an admirable example, and very fruitful for the education of the people, to see every day before their eyes a hundred,

two hundred, even a thousand pairs of men, armed against one another, hack each other to pieces with such extreme firmness of courage that they were observed never to let slip a word of weakness or commiseration, never to turn their back or make even a cowardly movement to avoid their adversary's blow, but rather to extend their neck to his sword and offer themselves to the blow. Many of them, covered with mortal wounds, would send and ask the people if they were content with their performance of their duty, before lying down and giving up the ghost on the spot. They had to fight and die not only steadfastly, but even cheerfully, so that they were booed and cursed if they were seen to struggle against accepting death.

[B]Even the girls urged them on:

> Each blow makes the modest maiden leap;
> And every time the victor thrusts his weapon deep
> In the other's throat, she shrieks for joy, and gives command,
> Thumb down, to rip the bosom of the fallen man.
>
> PRUDENTIUS

[A]The early Romans used criminals for such examples; but later they used innocent slaves, and even freemen who sold themselves for this purpose; [B]finally Roman senators and knights, and even women:

> And now they sell their heads, to die upon the sand,
> And, with war quiet, each man seeks a foe at hand.
>
> MANILIUS

> Amid these novel sports and these alarms,
> The gentle sex takes part, unskilled in arms,
> And manly conflict shamelessly usurps.
>
> STATIUS

[A]This I should consider very strange and incredible if we were not accustomed to see every day in our wars many thousands of foreigners engaging their blood and their lives for money in quarrels in which they have no concern.

24
Of the greatness of Rome

[A]I want to say only a word about this infinite subject to show the simplicity of those who compare the pitiful grandeurs of this time

with those of Rome. In the seventh book of Cicero's *Familiar Letters* (and let the grammarians take away from them the epithet "familiar," if they will, for in truth it is not very appropriate; and those who instead of "familiar" have substituted *ad familiares*[1] can derive an argument in their favor from what Suetonius says in his *Life of Caesar*, that there was a volume of letters of his *ad familiares*), there is one addressed to Caesar, who was then in Gaul, in which Cicero repeats these words, which were at the end of another letter that Caesar had written to him: "As for Marcus Furius, whom you have recommended to me, I will make him king of Gaul; and if you want me to advance some other friend of yours, send him to me."

It was no novelty for a simple Roman citizen, as Caesar then was, to dispose of kingdoms, for indeed he deprived King Deiotarus of his to give it to a gentleman of the city of Pergamus, named Mithridates. And those who write his life record several other kingdoms sold by him; and Suetonius says that at one stroke he extracted from King Ptolemy three million six hundred thousand crowns, which was very close to selling him his kingdom:

> [B]For so much let Galatia go, for so much Pontus,
> So much Lydia.
> CLAUDIAN

Mark Antony said that the greatness of the Roman people showed itself not so much in what they took as in what they gave. [C]And yet, about a century before Antony, they had taken away one kingdom, among others, with such a wonderful show of authority that in all their history I know no mark that places the reputation of their prestige so high. Antiochus possessed all Egypt and was about to conquer Cyprus and other remnants of that empire. During the progress of his victories, C. Popilius came to him on behalf of the Senate, and immediately refused to take his hand until he had first read the letters he was bringing. When the king had read them and said he would think it over, Popilius drew a line with his stick around the place where he was, and said: "Give me an answer that I can take back to the Senate before you move out of this circle." Antiochus, astonished at the roughness of such a peremptory command, after thinking about it a little, said: "I will do what the Senate commands me." Then Popilius greeted him as a friend of the Roman people.

1 To his friends.

To have given up so great a monarchy and so fortunate and prosperous a career because of the impression made by three lines of writing! He was truly right to send word later to the Senate by his ambassadors, as he did, that he had received their orders with the same respect as if they had come from the immortal gods.

^BAll the kingdoms that Augustus won by right of war he restored to those who had lost them, or presented to strangers.

^AAnd in this connection Tacitus, speaking of Cogidunus, king of England, makes us feel that infinite power by a marvelous touch. The Romans, he says, were from all antiquity accustomed to leave the kings they had overcome in possession of their kingdoms, under their authority, *so that they might have even kings as instruments of slavery* [Tacitus].[2]

^CIt is probable that Suleiman, whom we have seen making a gift of the kingdom of Hungary and other states, had more regard for this consideration than for the one he was accustomed to allege: that he was glutted and overburdened with so many monarchies and so much power.

25
Not to counterfeit being sick

^AThere is an epigram in Martial that is one of the good ones (for there are all kinds in him), in which he humorously tells the story of Coelius, who pretended to have the gout to avoid paying court to some of the great in Rome, being present at their levee, and attending and following them; and, to make his excuse more plausible, had his legs anointed and swathed, and counterfeited completely the carriage and bearing of a gouty man. In the end fortune gave him the pleasure of making him so in fact:

> So much can skill and effort bring about:
> Coelius no longer feigns, but has, the gout.
> <div align="right">MARTIAL</div>

I have read, somewhere in Appian, ^CI think, ^Aa similar story of a man who, wishing to escape the proscriptions of the triumvirs of Rome, keeping himself hidden and disguised to avoid recognition by those who were after him, added also the device of pretending to

2 Montaigne translates this before quoting the Latin.

be blind in one eye. When he came to recover a little more liberty and wanted to take off the plaster he had long worn over his eye, he found that the sight of it had been effectually lost under this mask.

It is possible that the action of sight had become dulled through having been so long without exercise, and that the visual power had wholly transferred itself to the other eye. For we palpably feel that an eye which we keep covered up sends some part of its virtue to its fellow, so that the other one grows bigger and dilates. So also the inactivity, combined with the heat of the bindings and medicaments, might well have brought some gouty humor to Martial's man with the gout.

Reading in Froissart of the vow by a troop of young English gentlemen to wear their left eye bound up until they had crossed over into France and performed some exploit of arms against us, I have often been tickled by the idea that they might have been caught like those others and found themselves all one-eyed when they again saw the mistresses for whom they had undertaken this.

Mothers are right to scold their children when they imitate one-eyed, lame, and cross-eyed people, and other such personal defects. For not only can their body, still so tender, take on a bad twist, but it seems that fortune, I know not how, makes a game of taking us at our word; and I have heard of many examples of people who became sick after pretending to be so.

ᶜI have always had the habit, both on horseback and on foot, of carrying a rod or a stick in my hand, even to the point of trying to be elegant and resting on it in an affected manner. Many have threatened me that fortune would one day turn this foppery into a necessity. I base my confidence on the fact that I would then be the first of my family to have the gout.

ᴬBut let us lengthen this chapter and variegate it with another piece apropos of blindness. Pliny tells of a man who, dreaming in his sleep that he was blind, found himself so the next day, without any previous illness. The power of imagination can indeed contribute to such results, as I have said elsewhere,[1] and Pliny seems to be of this opinion. But it is more likely that the movements which the body felt within, of which the doctors may find out the cause, if they will, and which deprived him of his sight, were the occasion of the dream.

1 *Essays* I: 21, "Of the Power of the Imagination."

Let us add one more story close to this subject, which Seneca tells in one of his letters. "You know," he says, writing to Lucilius, "that Harpaste, my wife's fool, has stayed at my house as a hereditary charge, for my own taste sets me against these monsters; and if I have a mind to laugh at a fool, I do not have to look far for one, I laugh at myself. This fool has suddenly lost her sight. I am telling you something strange, but true. She does not realize that she is blind, and constantly urges her keeper to take her out, because she says my house is dark.

"What we laugh at in her, I pray you to believe happens to each one of us: no one knows that he is avaricious or covetous. The blind at least ask for a guide; we go astray of our own accord. I am not ambitious, we say, but in Rome you cannot live otherwise; I am not extravagant, but the city requires great expense; it is not my fault if I am choleric, if I have not yet set up any definite way of life – it is the fault of youth.

"Let us not look for our disease outside of ourselves; it is within us, it is planted in our entrails. And the very fact that we do not realize that we are sick makes our cure more difficult. If we do not soon begin to tend ourselves, when will we have provided for so many sores and so many maladies? Yet we have a very sweet medicine in philosophy. For of the others we feel the pleasure only after the cure; this one pleases and cures at the same time."

That is what Seneca says, which has carried me away from my subject; but there is profit in change.

26
Of thumbs

ᴬTacitus reports that among certain barbarian kings, to make an obligation binding, the custom was to clasp their right hands tightly together and interlock their thumbs; and when by dint of pressing them the blood had risen to the tips, they pricked them lightly and then sucked each other's blood.

The doctors say that the thumbs are the master fingers of the hand and that their etymology in Latin is from *pollere*.[1] The Greeks call it ἀντίχειρ, as though to say "another hand." And it seems that sometimes the Latins also take it in the sense of the entire hand:

1 To be powerful. The Latin word for *thumb* is *pollex*.

> But not excited by the gentle voice,
> Nor summoned by the soft thumb, does it rise.
> <div align="right">MARTIAL</div>

It was a sign of favor in Rome to close in and hold down the thumbs –

> Your partisan with both his thumbs will praise your game
> <div align="right">HORACE</div>

– and of disfavor to raise them and turn them outward:

> When the people's thumb turns up,
> They kill their man to please them.
> <div align="right">JUVENAL</div>

The Romans exempted from war those who were wounded in the thumb, as no longer having a firm enough grasp for weapons. Augustus confiscated the goods of a Roman knight who had maliciously cut off the thumbs of two young sons of his to excuse them from going into the army. And before his time the Senate, at the time of the Italian wars, condemned Caius Vatienus to prison for life and confiscated all his goods for having deliberately cut off the thumb of his left hand, to exempt himself from that expedition.

Someone, I don't remember who, having won a naval battle, had the thumbs of his vanquished enemies cut off, to deprive them of the means of fighting and pulling an oar. ^CThe Athenians had them cut off the Aeginetans to take away their superiority in naval skill.

^BIn Lacedaemon the schoolmaster chastised children by biting their thumbs.

<div align="center">27</div>

Cowardice, mother of cruelty

^AI have often heard it said that cowardice is the mother of cruelty. ^BAnd I have found by experience that the bitterness and hardness of a malicious and inhuman heart are usually accompanied by feminine weakness. I have observed that some of the most cruel are subject to weeping easily and for frivolous reasons. Alexander, tyrant of Pheres, could not bear to hear tragedies played in the theater for fear that his citizens might see him groaning at the misfortunes of Hecuba and Andromache, he who, without pity, had so many

people cruelly murdered every day. Could it be weakness of soul that made them so easily bent to every extreme?

[A]Valor, whose effect it is to act only against resistance –

> Nor is it joy to kill the bull unless he fights
>
> CLAUDIAN

– stops on seeing the enemy at its mercy. But pusillanimity, in order to say that it is also in the game, having been unable to take part in this first act, takes as its part the second, that of massacre and bloodshed. The murders in victories are usually done by the mob and the baggage officers. And what causes so many unheard-of cruelties in wars in which the people take part is that that beastly rabble tries to be warlike and brave by ripping up a body at their feet and bloodying themselves up to their elbows, having no sense of any other kind of valor:

> [B]The wolves and loathsome bears fall on a dying foe,
> And of the other beasts the lowest of the low,
>
> OVID

[A]like cowardly curs, that in the house tear and bite the skins of wild beasts that they did not dare attack in the fields.

What is it that makes our quarrels all mortal these days; and why, whereas our fathers recognized some degrees in revenge, do we nowadays begin with the ultimate, and from the outset speak of nothing but killing? What is it, if it is not cowardice?

Every man clearly feels that there is more defiance and disdain in beating his enemy than in finishing him off, and in making him lick the dust than in making him die. Moreover, the appetite for vengeance is thereby better assuaged and contented, for it aims only at making itself felt. That is why we do not attack an animal or a stone when they hurt us, because they are incapable of feeling our revenge. And to kill a man is to put him in shelter from our harm.

[B]And just as Bias called out to a wicked man, "I know that sooner or later you will be punished for it, but I am afraid I may not see it," and pitied the Orchomenians because the penalty Lyciscus paid for the treason committed against them came at a time when there was no one left of those who had been injured by it and who would take pleasure in this penalty; just so vengeance is to be pitied when its object loses the means of feeling it. For, as the avenger wants to be aware of it in order to derive pleasure from it, the one on whom

he takes revenge must be aware of it also in order to suffer pain and repentance.

^A "He will repent it," we say. And because we have given him a pistol shot in the head, do we think that he repents it? On the contrary, if we consider it, we will find that he makes a face at us as he falls. He does not even hold it against us, so far is he from repenting. ^C And we do him the greatest favor of life, which is to make him die suddenly and insensibly. ^A We are busy hiding like rabbits, trotting about and fleeing the officers of justice who are pursuing us; and he is at rest. Killing is good to avoid an injury to come, not to avenge one already done; ^C it is an act more of fear than of defiance, of precaution than of courage, of defense than of attack. ^A It is apparent that by it we abandon both the true end of vengeance and the care of our reputation. We fear that if he remains alive, he may renew the attack. ^C It is not against him, but for yourself, that you get rid of him.

In the kingdom of Narsinga this expedient would remain useless to us. There not only the men-at-arms but also the artisans settle their quarrels at sword's point. The king does not refuse the field to anyone who wants to fight, and looks on when they are persons of quality, rewarding the victor with a gold chain. But to conquer it, the first man who wants to can come to blows with the one who wears it; and he, for having disposed of one combat, has several on his hands.

^A If we thought that by valor we would always be masters of our enemy and triumph over him at our pleasure, we would be very sorry for him to escape us, as he does by dying. We want to conquer, but more safely than honorably; ^C and in our quarrel we seek an ending more than glory.

For an honorable man, Asinius Pollio represented a like error; having written some invectives against Plancus, he waited until he was dead to publish them. That was like thumbing one's nose at a blind man, or uttering filthy abuse at a deaf man, or wounding an insensible man, rather than run the risk of his resentment. And so it was said about him that it was only for ghosts to wrestle with the dead. He who waits to see the death of the author whose writings he wants to combat, what is he saying but that he is weak and quarrelsome? Aristotle was told that someone had spoken ill of him. "Let him do more," he said, "let him whip me, provided I am not there."

^A Our fathers contented themselves with avenging an insult by giving the lie, the lie by a blow, and so on in order. They were

valorous enough not to fear their enemy, living and outraged. We tremble with fear as long as we see him on his feet. And as proof that this is so, does not our fine practice of today involve pursuing to death the man we have insulted as well as the man who has insulted us?

^BIt is also a type of cowardice that has introduced into our single combats this custom of being accompanied by seconds, and thirds, and fourths. Formerly they were duels; nowadays they are encounters and battles. The first ones who hit upon it were afraid of being alone: ^c*since neither man had any confidence in himself* [Livy]. ^BFor naturally any company whatever brings comfort and relief in danger. Formerly they used third parties to guard against irregularity and foul play, ^cand to bear witness to the outcome of the combat. ^BBut since it has become the fashion for them to take part themselves, whoever is invited cannot honorably stand by as a spectator, for fear this may be attributed to lack of affection or of courage.

Besides the injustice and baseness of such an action, engaging another valor and strength than your own in the protection of your honor, I find it a disadvantage, for a good man who trusts fully in himself, to go and involve his fortune with that of a second. Each man runs enough risk for himself without running it also for another, and has enough to do to assure himself in his own valor for the defense of his life, without committing a thing so dear to the hands of a third party. For unless it has been expressly agreed to the contrary, it is a joint combat of the four. If your second is down, you have two on your hands, and rightly so. And if you say that it is unfair, it is indeed so, just like attacking, fully armed, a man who has only the stump of a sword, or, in full health, a man who is already badly wounded. But if these are advantages you have won in fighting, you may use them without reproach.

Disparity and inequality are weighed and considered only in regard to the state in which the fray begins; for the rest, take it up with fortune. And when you alone have three on you, your two companions having let themselves be killed, no one is wronging you, any more than I would do in war by striking with my sword, with a similar advantage, an enemy whom I saw engaged with one of our men. The nature of association has it that where there is troop against troop (as when our duke of Orléans challenged King Henry of England, a hundred against a hundred; ^cthree hundred against the same number, like the Argives against the Lacedaemonians; three to three, like the Horatii against the Curiatii), ^Bthe entire

number on either side is considered as only a single man. Wherever there is company the risk is confounded and mingled.

I have a family interest in this consideration; for my brother, the sieur de Mattecoulon, was called on in Rome to second a gentleman he hardly knew, who was the defender and challenged by another. In this combat he found himself by chance matched with one who was much closer and better known to him. (I would like to have someone justify by reason these laws of honor that so often clash with those of reason and confuse them.) After having disposed of his man, seeing the two principals still on their feet and intact, he went to the relief of his teammate. What less could he do? Should he have kept still and, if chance had so willed it, watched the man for whose defense he had come there being defeated? What he had done till then was of no help to the job: the quarrel was undecided.

The courtesy that you can and indeed should offer to your enemy when you have reduced him to bad terms and some great disadvantage, I do not see how you can offer it when the interest of another is at stake, where you are only an assistant, where the dispute is not your own.

He could be neither just nor courteous at the risk of the man to whom he had lent himself. Accordingly he was delivered from the prisons of Italy by a very prompt and solemn recommendation of our king.

Immoderate nation! We are not content with making our vices and follies known to the world by reputation, we go to foreign countries to display them in person. Put three Frenchmen in the deserts of Libya; they will not be together a month without harassing and scratching one another. You would think that this peregrination of ours is an affair specially arranged to give foreigners the pleasure of our tragedies, and most often to those who rejoice in our misfortunes and laugh at them.

We go and learn fencing in Italy, ᶜand practice it at the expense of our lives before we learn it. ᴮAnd yet by the rule of discipline we should put theory before practice. We betray ourselves as apprentices:

> Bitter your youth's first-fruits, harsh your apprenticeship
> Into the war to come.
>
> VIRGIL

I know very well that it is an art ᶜuseful for its purpose (in the duel between the two princes in Spain, cousins-german, the elder,

says Livy, by skill at arms and ruse easily overcame the reckless power of the younger), and an art, as I have learned by experience, ᴮthe knowledge of which has swelled the hearts of some beyond their natural measure. But this is not properly valor, since it draws its support from skill and has its basis in something other than itself.

The honor of the combat consists in the jealousy of courage, not of craft. And therefore I have observed a friend of mine, renowned as a grand master in this exercise, to choose in his quarrels weapons that deprived him of the means of this advantage, and which depended entirely on fortune and assurance, so that his victory should not be attributed to his fencing skill rather than his valor. And in my childhood the nobility avoided the reputation of good fencers as insulting, and learned it furtively, as a cunning trade, derogating from true and natural valor:

> To dodge, parry, withdraw, they do not seek;
> Nor does skill in their combat play a part;
> Their blows are not feints, now full, now oblique,
> Fury and rage forbid the use of art.
> Hear how their swords clash with a horrid shriek;
> Their feet stand fast, and never move apart.
> Their hands keep moving, though their feet remain,
> And not a thrust or slash is made in vain.
> TASSO

Shooting at the butts, tournaments, tiltings, practice at warlike combats, were the exercise of our fathers. This other exercise is all the less noble as it regards only a private end, which teaches us to destroy one another, contrary to the laws and justice, and in every way always produces harmful results. It is much more worthy and fitting to exercise at things that strengthen, not injure, our government, and that regard the public safety and the common glory.

Publius Rutilius, the consul, was the first who instructed the soldier in handling his weapons with skill and science, who joined art and valor, not for use in private quarrels, but for the wars and quarrels of the Roman people: ᶜfencing for the people and the civic good.

And besides the example of Caesar, who ordered his men to shoot principally at the faces of Pompey's soldiers in the battle of Pharsalia, a thousand other military leaders have thus bethought themselves of inventing new forms of weapons, new ways of striking and defending, according to the needs of the affair at hand.

[B]But just as Philopoemen condemned wrestling, in which he excelled, because the training for that exercise was different from that which pertained to military discipline, to which alone he considered that men of honor should apply themselves, so it seems to me that this adroitness to which we fashion our limbs, these dodges and movements to which young men are trained in this new school, are not only useless, but rather contrary and harmful to the practice of military combat.

[C]Moreover, our people commonly employ special weapons peculiarly planned for this purpose. And I have known the time when it was considered hardly the right thing for a gentleman, challenged to fight with sword and dagger, to present himself in military equipment. It is worthy of consideration that Laches, in Plato, speaking of an apprenticeship similar to ours in the handling of weapons, says he never saw any great warrior come out of this school, especially from its masters. As for these, our own experience tells us as much. Of the rest we can at least say that these are abilities that have no mutual relation or correspondence. And in the education of the children in his Republic, Plato forbids the arts of boxing, introduced by Amycus and Epeius, and of wrestling, by Antaeus and Cercyo, because they have another purpose than to make youths more fit for military service, and contribute nothing to it.

[B]But I am straying rather a bit from my theme.

[A]The Emperor Maurice, being warned by dreams and several prognostics that one Phocas, a soldier then unknown, was to kill him, was asking his son-in-law Philip who this Phocas was, his nature, his traits, and his habits; and when Philip told him among other things that he was cowardly and timorous, the Emperor immediately concluded from this that he was therefore murderous and cruel.

What makes tyrants so bloodthirsty? It is concern for their security, and the fact that their cowardly heart furnishes them with no other means of making themselves secure than by exterminating those who can injure them, even to the women, for fear of a scratch:

> [B]He strikes all things because he fears all things.
> CLAUDIAN

[C]The first cruelties are practiced for their own sake; thence arises the fear of a just revenge, which afterward produces a string of new cruelties, in order to stifle the first by the others.

Philip, king of Macedon, the one who had so many bones to pick with the Roman people, agitated by the horror of the murders committed by his orders, unable to make up his mind what to do against so many families injured by him at various times, decided to seize all the children of the people he had had killed, in order to destroy them one after the other, day by day, and thus make sure of his peace of mind.

Fine materials are always in place, wherever you sow them. I, who have more concern for the weight and utility of the arguments than for their order and sequence, should not fear to place here, a little out of the way, a very beautiful story. Among others condemned by Philip there had been one Herodicus, prince of the Thessalians. Later, Philip also had Herodicus' two sons-in-law put to death, each one leaving a very small son. Theoxena and Archo were the two widows. Theoxena could not be induced to remarry, though she was much sought after. Archo married Poris, the leading man among the Aenians, and had a number of children by him, all of whom she left very young when she died. Theoxena, spurred by a maternal love for her nephews, married Poris in order to have them under her own guidance and protection.

Then came the proclamation of the king's edict. This courageous mother, mistrustful both of Philip's cruelty and of the licentiousness of his satellites toward these fair and tender children, dared to state that she would rather kill them with her own hands than give them up. Poris, alarmed by this declaration, promised her to steal them away and take them to Athens into the safekeeping of some faithful guest-friends of his. They took the occasion of an annual feast that was celebrated at Aenia in honor of Aeneas, and they went to it. Having attended the ceremonies and the public banquet during the day, at night they slipped out in a vessel that was ready, to get away by sea.

The wind was against them; and finding themselves the next morning in sight of the land from which they had put to sea, they were pursued by the harbor guards. As these were catching up, while Poris was busy hurrying the sailors in their flight, Theoxena, frantic with love and vengeance, fell back on her first plan. She prepared weapons and poison, and, showing them to the boys, said: "Come, my children, death is henceforth the only means of your defense and freedom, and will give the gods matter for their sacred justice. These drawn swords, these cups, open the way to it. Courage! And you, my son, who are the eldest, grasp this blade and die the braver death."

Having this vigorous counselor on one side, the enemies at their throats on the other, they each ran in a frenzy to what was nearest at hand; and, half-dead, they were thrown into the sea. Theoxena, proud of having provided so gloriously for the safety of all her children, warmly embraced her husband and said: "Let us follow these boys, my dear, and enjoy the same grave with them." And holding each other in this embrace they plunged headlong into the sea; so that the ship was brought back to shore empty of its masters.

ᴬTyrants, in order to do both things together, both to kill and to make their anger felt, have used all their ingenuity to find a way to prolong death. They want their enemies to be gone, but not so fast that they may not have leisure to savor their vengeance. Thereupon they are in great perplexity; for if the tortures are violent, they are short; if they are long, they are not painful enough to suit them. So they go dispensing their instruments of torture. We see a thousand examples of it in antiquity, and I know not whether, without thinking about it, we do not retain some trace of this barbarity.

All that is beyond plain death seems to me pure cruelty.[1] Our justice cannot hope that the man who will not be deterred from doing wrong by the fear of dying on the block or the gallows will be prevented by the idea of a slow fire, or pincers, or the wheel. And I do not know but that we meanwhile drive them to despair. For what can be the state of a man's soul who is waiting twenty-four hours for death broken on a wheel, or, in the old fashion, nailed to a cross?

Josephus relates that during the wars of the Romans in Judaea, passing a place where they had crucified some Jews three days before, he recognized three of his friends and obtained leave to remove them from there. Two died, he says; the other lived on after.

ᶜChalcondylas, a trustworthy man, in the memoirs he left of things that happened in his time and in his vicinity, reports as an extreme punishment one that Emperor Mohammed II often practiced, of having men cut in two parts across the middle at the diaphragm with a single blow of a scimitar, whence it happened that they died as it were two deaths at once; and, he says, you saw both parts moving a long time after, full of life and writhing in torment.

1 This was one of the statements criticized by the papal censors in Rome when Montaigne was there in 1580–81. Montaigne neither changed nor suppressed it in later editions.

I do not believe there was much feeling in that movement. The most hideous tortures to see are not always the hardest to endure. And I find more atrocious what other historians report he inflicted on some lords of Epirus: that he had them flayed piecemeal with such a maliciously ordered arrangement that their life lasted two weeks in this anguish.

Also these two others. Croesus, having had a gentleman seized who was the favorite of his brother Pantaleon, took him into a fuller's shop, where he had him so scratched and carded with the cards and combs of this carder that he died of it.

When George Sechel, leader of those Polish peasants who, under pretext of a crusade, did so much harm, had been defeated in battle by the voivode of Transylvania and taken, he was for three days bound naked to a wooden horse, exposed to every kind of torture that anyone could devise against him; during which time the other prisoners were given neither food nor drink. In the end, while he still lived and could see, they gave his blood to drink to his dear brother Lucat, for whose safety he kept praying, drawing upon himself all the hatred for their misdeeds. And they had twenty of his most favored captains feed on him, tearing his flesh with their teeth and swallowing the morsels. The rest of his body and the inner parts, when he was dead, were boiled and given to others of his followers to eat.

28
All things have their season

^Those who compare Cato the Censor with the younger Cato, who was his own murderer,[1] ^compare two beautiful natures that are akin in form. The former displayed his in more aspects and excelled the other in military exploits and in the usefulness of his public services. But the virtue of the younger, besides the fact that it is blasphemy to compare any other with it in vigor, was much more spotless. For who can acquit the Censor of envy and ambition, when he dared to attack the honor of Scipio, a man in goodness and all excellent qualities far greater than he or any other man of his time?

1 In all editions through 1588 the sentence ended thus: "do great honor, in my opinion, to the former; for I find them separated by an extreme distance."

^AWhat they tell of him among other things, that in his extreme old age he set himself to learn Greek with an ardent appetite, as if to quench a long thirst, does not seem to me to be much in his honor. It is exactly what we call falling back into childhood.

All things have their season, good ones and all. And I may say my Lord's Prayer at the wrong time; ^Cas T. Quintius Flaminius, a general of the army, was denounced because he had been seen standing apart in the hour of conflict, spending his time praying God in a battle that he won.

^BThe sage sets bounds even to virtuous things.

JUVENAL

^AEudemonidas, seeing Xenocrates when he was very old busied about his school lessons, said: "When will this man know, if he is still learning?" ^BAnd Philopoemen said to those who were highly praising King Ptolemy for hardening his body every day in the exercise of arms: "It is not a praiseworthy thing in a king of his age to practice them; he should henceforth really employ them."

^AThe young man should make his preparations, the old man enjoy their fruits, say the sages. And the greatest defect they observe in our nature is that our desires incessantly renew their youth. We are always beginning to live over again. Our study and our desire should sometimes savor of old age. We have one foot in the grave, and our appetites and pursuits are just being born:

^BYou plan, right at the brink of doom,
On carving marbles; heedless of your tomb,
You play at building houses.

HORACE

^CThe longest of my plans has not a year in extent. Henceforth I think of nothing but making an end; I rid myself of all new hopes and enterprises; I take my last leave of every place I go away from, and dispossess myself every day of what I have: *For a long time I have had neither losses nor gains. I have more provisions for the road than I have road left* [Seneca].

I have lived, and run out the course that fortune gave.

VIRGIL

In short, this is all the comfort that I find in my old age, that it deadens in me many desires and cares by which life is troubled – care for how the world goes, care for riches, for greatness, for knowledge,

for health, for myself. ^AThat man² is learning to speak when he needs to learn to be silent forever.

^CWe may continue our studies at all times, but not our schooling: what a foolish thing is an old man learning his A B C!

> ^BDifferent men, different tastes; nor are all things
> Fit for all ages.
> <div align="right">MAXIMIANUS</div>

^AIf we must study, let us study something suitable to our condition, so that we may answer like the man who, when he was asked what was the purpose of these studies in his decrepitude, replied: "To depart a better man and more content."

Such a study was that of the younger Cato when, feeling his end approaching, he came upon Plato's discussion of the eternity of the soul. Not, obviously, that he had not been long furnished with every sort of equipment for such a departure. Of assurance, firm will, and learning, he had more than Plato has in his writings; his knowledge and his courage were in this regard above philosophy. It was not to ease his death that he took up this occupation; but like a man who would not even interrupt his sleep out of concern over such a resolve, he also continued, without choice and without change, his studies together with the other customary actions of his life.

^CThe night when he had just been rejected for the praetorship, he spent in play; the one in which he was to die, he spent reading. Loss of life and loss of office were equally indifferent to him.

<div align="center">

29

Of virtue

</div>

^AI find by experience that there is quite a difference between the erratic impulses of the soul and a habit of resolute steadfastness. And I see very well that nothing is beyond our power: we can even, says someone,³ surpass the deity itself – inasmuch as it is a greater thing to make oneself impassible by one's own efforts than to be so by one's natural condition – even combine with man's frailty a godlike resolution and assurance. But only by fits and starts. And in the lives of the heroes of times past there are sometimes

2 Cato the Censor, learning Greek in his old age.
3 Seneca.

miraculous moments that seem very far to surpass our natural powers; but they are indeed mere moments; and it is hard to believe that the soul can be dyed and imbued with such exalted qualities as these, so that they become ordinary and as it were natural to her.

It happens even to us, who are but abortions of men, sometimes to launch our soul, aroused by the ideas or examples of others, very far beyond her ordinary range; but it is a kind of passion that impels and drives her, and which to some extent tears her out of herself. For when this whirlwind is over, we see that without thinking about it she unbends and relaxes of herself, if not down to the lowest key, at least until she is no longer the same; so that then, for any occasion, for a lost bird or a broken glass, we let ourselves be moved just about like one of the vulgar.

ᶜExcept for order, moderation, and constancy, I believe that all things are achievable by a man who in general is very imperfect and defective.

ᴬFor this reason, say the sages, to judge a man really properly, we must chiefly examine his ordinary actions and surprise him in his everyday habit.

Pyrrho, the one who built such an amusing science out of ignorance, tried, like all the others who were truly philosophers, to make his life correspond to his doctrine. And because he maintained that the weakness of human judgment was so extreme as to be unable to take sides or lean either way, and would have it suspended in perpetual balance, considering and taking in all things as indifferent, they say that he always maintained the same manner and countenance. If he had begun to say something, he never failed to finish it, even though the man he was speaking to had gone away. If he was going somewhere, he would not change his course for any obstacle that he came on, and was saved from precipices, from being hit by carts, and from other accidents, by his friends. For to fear or avoid anything would have been to clash with his own propositions, which deprived even the senses of any choice or certainty. Sometimes he suffered being incised and cauterized with such constancy that he was not seen even to blink.

It is something to bring the soul to these ideas. It is more to put them into action, yet it is not impossible. But to put them into action with such perseverance and constancy as to establish them as our ordinary course of life, certainly, in these undertakings so remote from common usage, it is almost incredible that it can be done.

That is why he, being found once in his house quarreling very sharply with his sister and being reproached for thereby failing in his own theory of indifference, said: "What, must this silly woman also serve as testimony to my rules?" Another time when he was seen defending himself against a dog, he said: "It is very difficult entirely to strip off the man; and we must endeavor, and make it our duty, to combat things, first by actions, but if worst comes to worst, by reason and arguments."

About seven or eight years ago a villager two leagues from here, who is still living, having had his head long splitting from his wife's jealousy, came home one day from work, and when she welcomed him with her customary yelling, he went into such a fury that then and there, with the billhook that he was still holding in his hands, he reaped clean off the parts that put her in such a fever, and threw them in her face. And it is said that one of our young gentlemen, amorous and lusty, having by his perseverance finally softened the heart of a beautiful mistress, despairing at the fact that on the point of the attack he had found that he himself was soft and failing, and that

> Not in manly style
> Had his limp penis raised its senile head,
> TIBULLUS

he bereft himself of it as soon as he returned home and sent it, a cruel and bleeding victim, for the expiation of his offense. If this had been for reason and religion, like the priests of Cybele, what should we not say of so sublime an enterprise?

A few days ago, at Bergerac, five leagues from my house up the Dordogne River, a woman who had been tormented and beaten the night before by her husband, a surly and choleric man by nature, resolved to escape his roughness at the price of her life. When she got up, after chatting with her neighbors as usual, dropping a few words of recommendation to them about her affairs, she took a sister of hers by the hand, brought her onto the bridge, and, after taking leave of her as if in jest, without showing any other change or alteration, she threw herself down headlong into the river, where she perished. In this case, what is more is that this plan matured one whole night in her head.

It is quite another thing with the women of India. For, their custom being for the husbands to have several wives and for the dearest of these to kill herself right after her husband, each one aims,

by the intent of her whole life, to gain this point of advantage over the others; and the good offices that they render their husband look to no other reward than to be preferred to accompany him in death:

> [B]When on the deadly bed is thrown the final brand,
> The faithful group of wives with hair disheveled stand.
> Eager to join their spouse, living, for death they strive;
> The one disgrace for them is to be left alive.
> Ardent, the winners offer their bosoms to the flames,
> And each, pressing burned lips to his, her husband claims.
>
> PROPERTIUS

[C]A man still in our own days writes of having seen this custom in honor in these Oriental nations, that not only the wives bury themselves after their husband, but also the slave girls he has enjoyed. Which is done in this manner. The husband being dead, the widow may if she wants – but few want to – ask for two or three months' respite to arrange her affairs. The day being come, she mounts on horseback, arrayed as for a wedding, and with a gay countenance, as if going, as she says, to sleep with her husband, holding in her left hand a mirror, in the other an arrow. Having thus paraded in pomp, accompanied by her friends and relations and a crowd of holiday makers, she has soon arrived at the public place destined for such spectacles. It is a big square, in the middle of which there is a pit full of wood, and adjoining this a raised spot four or five steps high, onto which she is conducted, there to be served with a magnificent repast. After this she begins to dance and sing, and, when she sees fit, orders the fire to be lit. That done, she steps down and takes her husband's nearest of kin by the hand, and they go together to the river nearby, where she strips herself quite naked and distributes her jewels and garments to her friends, and plunges into the water, as if to wash away her sins. Leaving the water, she wraps herself in a yellow linen cloth fourteen fathoms long and again gives her hand to this kinsman of her husband; they go back onto the mound, where she makes a speech to the people and recommends to them her children, if she has any. Between the pit and the mound they are wont to draw a curtain, to keep from them the sight of this fiery furnace; which some wives forbid, to show the more courage. When she has finished speaking, a woman presents her with a vase full of oil to anoint her head and her whole body, which she throws in the fire when she has done with it, and at the same instant she leaps into it herself. At once the people throw over

her a quantity of fagots to keep her from lingering, and all their joy is changed to mourning and sadness.

If they are persons of lesser stuff, the body of the dead man is carried to the spot where they want to bury it and placed sitting up, with the widow on her knees before him embracing him tightly, and she remains in that posture while they build a wall around them. When this wall rises to the height of the woman's shoulders, one of her relations, taking hold of her head from behind, wrings her neck; and when she has given up the ghost, the wall is immediately raised and closed, and there they remain entombed.

ᴬIn this same country there was something similar in their Gymnosophists. For, not by the constraint of others, not by the impetuosity of a sudden impulse, but by the express profession of their order, their custom was, as soon as they had reached a certain age or saw themselves threatened by some disease, to have a funeral pile erected for themselves, and on it a richly adorned bed. And after having joyously feasted their friends and acquaintances, they set themselves on this bed with such resolution that when the fire was applied to it they were not seen to move either hands or feet. And thus died one of them, Calanus, in the presence of the whole army of Alexander the Great. ᴮAnd among them a man was esteemed neither holy nor blessed who had not killed himself thus, sending off his soul purged and purified by fire after everything mortal and terrestrial in him had been consumed.

ᴬThis constant premeditation through a whole life is what makes this a miracle.

Among our other disputes, that of *Fatum* has come in. And to attach things to come and even our will to a certain and inevitable necessity, people still use this argument of bygone days: "Since God foresees that all things are to happen thus, as undoubtedly he does, it is therefore necessary that they happen thus." To which our masters reply that to see something happen, as we do, and God likewise (for, all things being present to him, he sees rather than foresees), is not to force it to happen; indeed, we see because things happen, and things do not happen because we see. The event causes the knowledge, not the knowledge the event. What we see happen, happens; but it could have happened otherwise. And God, in the roll book of the causes of events which he has in his foreknowledge, has also those which are called fortuitous, and the voluntary ones, which depend on the freedom he has given to our will; and he knows that we shall err, because we shall have willed to err.

Now I have known a good many men to encourage their troops with this fatal necessity. For if our final hour is fixed at a certain point, neither enemy harquebus shots, nor our boldness, nor our flight and cowardice, can advance or retard it.

That is fine to say, but find a man who will act upon it. And if it is true that a strong live belief draws after it actions in kind, then surely this faith, of which our mouths are so full, is marvelously slight in our times, unless the contempt it has for works makes it disdain their company.

At all events, in this same connection Sire de Joinville, as credible a witness as any other, tells us of the Bedouins, a tribe mingled with the Saracens, whom King Louis the Saint had to deal with in the Holy Land, that in their religion they believed so firmly that from all eternity every man's days were predetermined and numbered by an inevitable preordination, that they went to war unarmed except for a Turkish-style sword, their body covered only with a white linen cloth. And as their strongest curse, when they got angry at their own men, they had this ever in their mouths: "Accursed be you like a man who arms himself for fear of death!" There is quite a different proof of belief and faith from ours.

And also of the same stamp is the proof given by two Florentine monks, in the time of our fathers. Being engaged in some learned controversy, they agreed both to enter the flames in the public square in the presence of all the people, each in order to verify his side. And all the preparations for this were already made, and the business just on the point of execution, when it was interrupted by an unforeseen accident.

^cA young Turkish lord, having performed a signal personal feat of arms in the sight of the two armies of Amurath and Hunyadi as they were ready to fight, and being asked by Amurath what had filled him, so young and inexperienced (for it was the first war that he had seen), with such noble vigor and courage, replied that his chief tutor in valor had been a hare. "Being out hunting one day," he said, "I found a hare in its lair, and although I had two excellent greyhounds at my side, still it seemed to me, in order not to miss it, that it was better to use my bow as well, for it offered me a very good target. I began to discharge my arrows, as many as forty that there were in my quiver, not only without hitting it, but without rousing it. After all this I slipped my dogs after it, who could do nothing either. By this I learned that it had been protected by its destiny; and that neither arrows nor swords avail except by the permission of our

fate, which it is not in us either to retard or advance." This story should serve to make us see, by the way, how pliable our reason is to all sorts of ideas.

A personage great in years, in name, in dignity, and in learning, boasted to me that he had been led to a certain very important change in his faith by an external impulsion that was just as bizarre, and moreover so inconclusive that I thought it a stronger argument in the opposite direction. He called it a miracle, and so did I, in a different sense.

Historians of the Turks say that the conviction of the fatal and inflexible prescription of their days, generally diffused among them, visibly helps give them assurance in danger.

And I know a great prince who nobly finds his profit in it, if fortune continues to give him a helping hand.[4]

ᴮThere has not yet occurred within our memory a more admirable act of resolution than that of those two who plotted the death of the prince of Orange.[5] It is a marvel how the second, who achieved it, could be keyed up to an enterprise in which his companion had come out so badly, although he had done everything he could; and, in his footsteps and with the same weapons, to go and attack a lord armed with so fresh a lesson of mistrust, powerful in his retinue of friends and in bodily strength, in his own hall, amid his guards, in a city wholly devoted to him. Certainly he employed a very determined hand and a courage moved by a vigorous passion. A dagger is surer for striking home; but since it needs more movement and strength of arm than a pistol, its blow is more subject to be turned aside or hindered. That that man ran to a certain death I have no great doubt; for the hopes with which he might have been beguiled could find no lodging in a sober understanding; and his conduct of his exploit shows that he had no lack of this, any more than of courage. The motives of so powerful a conviction may be various, for our fancy does whatever it pleases with itself and with us.

The asassination that was performed near Orléans[6] was not at all like this; there was more chance than vigor to it. The blow was not mortal, if fortune had not made it so; and the enterprise of shooting from horseback and from a distance at a man who was moving with

4 Quite possibly Henry IV.
5 Jehan de Jeaureguy, who wounded William the Silent in 1582, and Balthazar Gérard, who killed him in 1584, both using pistols.
6 That of François de Guise by Poltrot de Méré (1563).

the motion of his own horse, was the enterprise of a man who would rather fail in his attempt than fail to save himself. What followed afterward showed this. For he was so dazed and intoxicated at the thought of so exalted an execution that he lost his head and completely confused his wits in both managing his flight and managing his tongue when answering questions.

What did he have to do but to run back to his friends across a river? This is a means to which I have resorted in lesser dangers, and which I consider of little risk, however wide the crossing, provided your horse finds an easy place to go in and that you can count on an easy landing place on the other side in relation to the current. The other man, when his horrible sentence was pronounced to him, said: "I was prepared for this; I will astonish you by my endurance."

ᶜThe Assassins, a people dependent on Phoenicia, are considered among the Mohammedans as being of supreme devoutness and purity of morals. They hold that the most certain way to deserve Paradise is to kill someone of a different religion. Since they scorn all personal dangers in order to carry out so useful a mission, there have been many instances in which they presented themselves, singly or in pairs, to assassinate (we have borrowed that word from their name) their enemy in the midst of his forces. Thus was our Count Raymond of Tripoli killed in his city.

30
Of a monstrous child

ᴬThis story will go its way simply, for I leave it to the doctors to discuss it. The day before yesterday I saw a child that two men and a nurse, who said they were the father, uncle, and aunt, were leading about to get a penny or so from showing him, because of his strangeness. In all other respects he was of ordinary shape; he could stand on his feet, walk, and prattle, about like others of the same age. He had not yet been willing to take any other nourishment than from his nurse's breast; and what they tried to put in his mouth in my presence he chewed on a little and spat it out without swallowing. There seemed indeed to be something peculiar about his cries. He was just fourteen months old.

Below the breast he was fastened and stuck to another child, without a head, and with his spinal canal stopped up, the rest of his

body being entire. For indeed one arm was shorter, but it had been broken by accident at their birth. They were joined face to face, and as if a smaller child were trying to embrace a bigger one around the neck. The juncture and the space where they held together was only four fingers' breadth or thereabouts, so that if you turned the imperfect child over and up, you saw the other's navel below; thus the connection was in between the nipples and the navel. The navel of the imperfect child could not be seen, but all the rest of his belly could. In this way all of this imperfect child that was not attached, as the arms, buttocks, thighs, and legs, remained hanging and dangling on the other and might reach halfway down his legs. The nurse also told us that he urinated from both places. Moreover the limbs of this other were nourished and living and in the same condition as his own, except that they were smaller and thinner.

This double body and these several limbs, connected with a single head, might well furnish a favorable prognostic to the king that he will maintain under the union of his laws these various parts and factions of our state. But for fear the event should belie it, it is better to let it go its way, for there is nothing like divining about things past. *So that, when things have happened, by some interpretation they are found to have been prophesied* [Cicero]. As they said of Epimenides that he prophesied backward.

I have just seen a shepherd in Médoc, thirty years old or thereabouts, who has no sign of genital parts. He has three holes by which he continually makes water. He is bearded, has desire, and likes to touch women.

What we call monsters are not so to God, who sees in the immensity of his work the infinity of forms that he has comprised in it; and it is for us to believe that this figure that astonishes us is related and linked to some other figure of the same kind unknown to man. From his infinite wisdom there proceeds nothing but that is good and ordinary and regular; but we do not see its arrangement and relationship. *What he sees often, he does not wonder at, even if he does not know why it is. If something happens which he has not seen before, he thinks it is a prodigy* [Cicero].

We call contrary to nature what happens contrary to custom; nothing is anything but according to nature, whatever it may be. Let this universal and natural reason drive out of us the error and astonishment that novelty brings us.

31
Of anger

^APlutarch is admirable throughout, but especially where he judges human actions. We may see the fine things that he says in the comparison of Lycurgus and Numa, apropos of our great foolishness in abandoning children to the government and responsibility of their fathers.

^CMost of our states, as Aristotle says, leave to each man, in the manner of the Cyclopes, the guidance of their wives and children according to his own foolish and thoughtless fancy; and the Lacedaemonian and Cretan are almost the only ones which have committed the education of children to the laws. ^AWho does not see that in a state everything depends on their education and nurture? And yet, without any discernment, they are left to the mercy of the parents, however foolish and wicked these may be.

Among other things, how many times have I had a good mind, as I passed along our streets, to set up some trick to avenge little boys that I saw being flayed, knocked down, and bruised by some father or mother in a fury and frenzy of anger! You can see the fire and rage coming out of their eyes –

> ^BBurning with rage within, they're borne
> Down headlong, just like boulders from a mountain torn;
> The ground gives way beneath, the hanging slope falls in
>
> JUVENAL

(and according to Hippocrates, the most dangerous maladies are those which disfigure the face) – ^Awith a cutting, explosive voice, often against one who has just left its nurse's breast. And then see them, lamed and made stupid with blows; and our justice taking no account of it, as if these maimings and dislocations were not happening to members of our commonwealth:

> ^B'Tis good you've given to the people and the state
> A citizen, if for the state you make him fit,
> In farming, war, or peace, doing his useful bit.
>
> JUVENAL

^AThere is no passion that so shakes the clarity of our judgment as anger. No one would hesitate to punish with death a judge who had condemned his criminal through anger. Why is it any more

permissible for fathers and schoolmasters to whip and chastise children when they are in anger? It is no longer correction, it is vengeance. Chastisement takes the place of a medicine for children; and would we tolerate a doctor who was incensed and angry with his patient?

To behave rightly, we ourselves should never lay a hand on our servants as long as our anger lasts. While our pulse beats and we feel emotion, let us put off the business. Things will truly seem different to us when we have quieted and cooled down. It is passion that is in command at first, it is passion that speaks, it is not we ourselves.

^BSeen through it, faults appear greater to us, like bodies seen through a mist. Let a hungry man use meat; but a man who wants to use punishment should neither hunger nor thirst for it.

^AAnd then, the punishments that are inflicted with deliberation and discernment are better received and with more benefit by him who suffers them. Otherwise he thinks he has been condemned unjustly by a man agitated by wrath and fury, and alleges in his own justification the extraordinary movements of his master, his inflamed face, his unaccustomed oaths, his excitement, and his heedless precipitancy:

^BThe veins grow black with blood, the whole face swells with ire,
 More fiercely flash the eyes than with the Gorgon's fire.
 OVID

^ASuetonius relates that when Lucius Saturnius[1] had been condemned by Caesar, what helped him most with the people (to whom he appealed) and made him win his case was the animosity and bitterness that Caesar had brought to that judgment.

Saying is one thing and doing is another. We must consider the preaching apart from the preacher. Those men have given themselves an easy game who, in our time, have tried to attack the truth of our Church through the vices of her ministers; she draws her testimony from elsewhere. It is a stupid way of arguing, which would throw all things back into confusion. A man of good morals may have false opinions, and a wicked man may preach the truth, yes, even a man who does not believe it. No doubt it is a beautiful harmony when doing and saying go together, and I do not want to deny that words are of greater authority and efficacy when actions follow.

1 Corrected in the 1595 edition to "Caius Rabirius."

As Eudamidas said on hearing a philosopher discourse on war: "These remarks are fine, but the man who is speaking them is not to be believed, for he does not have ears accustomed to the sound of the trumpet." And Cleomenes, hearing a rhetorician haranguing about valor, burst into loud laughter; and, when the other took offense, he said to him: "I would do the same if it were a swallow that was talking about it; but if it were an eagle, I would gladly hear him."

I observe in the writings of the ancients, it seems to me, that the man who says what he thinks strikes home much more forcefully than the man who pretends. Listen to Cicero speaking of the love of liberty, and listen to Brutus on the subject. The writings themselves ring out to you that the latter was a man to buy it at the price of life. Let Cicero, the father of eloquence, treat of the contempt of death, and let Seneca treat of it too. The former drags it out languidly, and you feel that he wants to persuade you of something of which he is not persuaded; he gives you no heart, for he has none himself. The other animates and inflames you. I never read an author, especially of those who treat of virtue and duties, that I do not inquire curiously what kind of a man he was.

[B]For the ephors at Sparta, seeing a dissolute man propose a useful piece of advice to the people, commanded him to be silent and asked a good man to claim the idea and propose it.

[A]Plutarch's writings, if we savor them aright, reveal him to us well enough, and I think I know him even into his soul; yet I wish we had some memoirs of his life. And I have embarked on this digression apropos of the gratitude I feel toward Aulus Gellius for having left us in writing this story about his character, which concerns my subject of anger. A slave of his, a bad and vicious man, but one whose ears were pretty well filled with the lessons of philosophy, having for some fault of his been stripped by Plutarch's command, at first muttered, while he was being whipped, that he was punished without reason and that he had done nothing. But finally, starting to shout and to abuse his master in good earnest, he reproached him with not being a philosopher, as he boasted: for he had often heard him say that it was ugly to get angry – indeed, he had written a book about it – and the fact that right then, all plunged in anger, he was having him so cruelly beaten, completely belied his writings. To which Plutarch, all coldly and sedately, said: "How is this, clown, by what do you judge that I am angry at this moment? Does my face, my voice, my color, my speech, give you any evidence that I am excited? I do not think that my eyes are wild, my face agitated, my

voice terrifying. Am I red? Am I foaming at the mouth? Does any word escape me that I shall have to repent? Am I quivering? Am I trembling with rage? For I tell you, those are the true signs of anger." And then, turning to the man who was flogging him, he said: "Go right on with your job while this fellow and I are arguing." That is his story.

Archytas of Tarentum, coming back from a war in which he had been captain-general, found everything in a mess in his household, and his lands lying fallow through the bad management of his steward; and having sent for him, he said: "Go; if I were not angry I would thrash you properly!" Plato likewise, having grown hot against one of his slaves, gave Speusippus the job of chastising him, excusing himself from putting his hand to it himself on the grounds that he was angry. Charillus, a Lacedaemonian, said to a Helot who was behaving too insolently and boldly toward him: "By the gods, if I were not angry, I would have you put to death right now."

It is a passion that takes pleasure in itself and flatters itself. How many times, when we have got in stride for a wrong reason, if we are offered some good defense or excuse, we are vexed even at truth and innocence! In this connection I remember an amazing example from antiquity. Piso, a person of notable virtue in everything else, having become incensed at one of his soldiers because, returning alone from foraging, he could give him no account of where he had left a companion of his, took it for certain that he had killed him, and promptly condemned him to death. As he was at the gibbet, along comes this lost companion. The whole army made a great celebration about it, and after many hugs and embraces by the two comrades the executioner took them both into the presence of Piso, everyone present expecting confidently that it would be a great pleasure to him also. But it was quite the reverse. For through shame and vexation his fury, which was still in power, doubled; and by a subtle trick that his passion promptly suggested to him, he made the three of them guilty because he had found one of them to be innocent, and had all three dispatched: the first soldier because there was a sentence against him; the second, who had gotten lost, because he was the cause of his companion's death; and the executioner for not having obeyed the command that had been given him.

^BThose who have to deal with headstrong women may have experienced what a rage they are thrown into when we oppose silence and coldness to their agitation, and disdain to feed their

rage. The orator Celius was prodigiously choleric by nature. To one who was supping in his company, a man gentle and mild in conversation and who, in order not to excite him, took the course of approving and assenting to everything he said, he, unable to endure his spleen venting itself thus without nourishment, said: "By all the gods, contradict me in something, will you, so that we may be two." Likewise the women get angry only so that we may get angry in turn, in imitation of the laws of love. Phocion, to a man who was interrupting his talk by abusing him violently, did nothing but be silent and give him full opportunity to exhaust his anger; this done, with no mention of this disturbance, he resumed his talk at the place where he had left off. There is no retort so stinging as such contempt.

Of the most choleric man in France (and anger is always an imperfection, but more excusable in a military man, for in that profession there are certainly occasions that cannot do without it) I often say that he is the most patient man I know in curbing his anger: it agitates him with such violence and fury –

> So, when with crackling flames a caldron fries,
> The bubbling waters from the bottom rise;
> Above the brim they force their fiery way;
> Black vapors climb aloft, and cloud the day.
>
> VIRGIL

– that he has to constrain himself cruelly to moderate it. And for my part, I know of no passion that I could make such an effort to conceal and resist. I would not put wisdom at so high a price. I do not consider so much what he does as how much it costs him not to do worse.

Another was boasting to me of the self-control and mildness of his behavior, which is indeed singular. I said to him that it was indeed something, especially in people of eminent rank like himself, whom everyone watches, to present themselves always very even-tempered to the world; but that the main thing was to make provision for the inside and for oneself, and that to my taste it was not good management of one's affairs to eat one's heart out; which I was afraid he did in order to maintain this mask and this controlled appearance on the outside.

We incorporate anger by hiding it; as Diogenes said to Demosthenes, who, for fear of being seen in a tavern, was drawing back further inside it: "The further back you go, the deeper in you

go." I advise that we rather give our valet a slap on the cheek a little out of season than strain our inclination to represent this wise bearing. And I would rather produce my passions than brood over them at my expense; they grow languid when they have vent and expression. It is better that their point should operate outwardly than be turned against us. ^C*All vices are less weighty in the open, and most pernicious when they hide under an appearance of soundness* [Seneca].

^BI admonish those in my family who have the right to get angry, first, to husband their anger and not expend it at random, for that impedes its effect and its weight. Heedless and continual scolding becomes a habit and makes everyone discount it. The scolding you give a servant for stealing is not felt, because it is the very same that he has heard you use against him a hundred times for a glass badly rinsed or a stool badly placed. Second, not to get angry in the air, and to see to it that their reprimand reaches the person they are complaining about: for ordinarily they are yelling before he is in their presence and continue yelling for ages after he has left,

> And petulant madness with itself contends.
>
> CLAUDIAN

They go after their own shadow, and carry this tempest into a place where no one is punished or affected by it, except someone who has to put up with the racket of their voice. I likewise condemn in quarrels those who bluster and fume without an opponent; these rodomontades must be kept for where they will strike home:

> So roars the bull his challenge to the fight,
> And of his furious horns he tries the might
> Against a tree, and fiercely lashes out,
> And paws the sand in prelude to the bout.
>
> VIRGIL

When I get angry, it is as keenly, but also as briefly and privately, as I can. I do indeed lose my temper in haste and violence, but I do not lose my bearings to the point of hurling about all sorts of insulting words at random and without choice, heedless of whether I place my arrows pertinently where I think they will hurt the most (for I ordinarily use nothing but my tongue). My servants get off better on big occasions than small. The small ones take me by surprise, and bad luck will have it that once you are over the precipice it does not matter what gave you the push, you still go

all the way to the bottom: the fall provides its own rushing and excitement and acceleration. On big occasions I have this satisfaction, that they are so just that everyone expects to see a reasonable anger engendered; I glory in deceiving their expectation. I tense and prepare myself against them; they disturb my brain and threaten to carry me away very far if I followed them. Easily I keep from getting into this passion, and I am strong enough, if I am expecting it, to repel its onslaught, however violent its cause; but if it once occupies and seizes me, it carries me away, however inane its cause.

This is how I bargain with those who may argue with me: When you sense that I am the first one excited, let me go my way, right or wrong; I will do the same for you in my turn. The tempest is bred only of the competition of angers, which are prone to produce one another, and are not born at the same moment. Let us give each one its head, and we shall always be at peace. A useful prescription, but hard to carry out.

Sometimes it also happens that I play angry for the governing of my house, without any real emotion. As age makes my disposition sourer, I make an effort to oppose it, and will succeed, if I can, in being henceforth all the less peevish and hard to please as I shall have more excuse and inclination to be so, although hitherto I have been among those who are least so.

^AOne more word to close this chapter. Aristotle says that anger sometimes serves as a weapon for virtue and valor. That is quite likely; yet those who deny it answer humorously that it is a weapon whose use is novel. For we move other weapons, this one moves us; our hand does not guide it, it guides our hand; it holds us, we do not hold it.

32
Defense of Seneca and Plutarch

^AMy familiarity with these personages and the help they give to my old age ^cand my book, built up purely from their spoils, ^Aoblige me to espouse their honor.

As for Seneca, among a myriad of pamphlets which those of the so-called Reformed religion circulate in defense of their cause, and which sometimes come from good hands, so that it is a pity they are not busied on a better subject, I once saw one which, to enlarge and fill up the similarity he wants to find between the government of our

late poor King Charles IX and that of Nero, compares the late Cardinal of Lorraine with Seneca: their fortune, in having both been the first men in the government of their princes, and at the same time their character, their condition, and their conduct. In which, in my opinion, he does great honor to the said Lord Cardinal. For although I am one of those who have the highest esteem for his mind, his eloquence, his zeal for religion and the service of his king, and his good fortune to have been born in a century where it was so novel and so rare, and at the same time so necessary for the public good, to have an ecclesiastical personage of such nobility and dignity competent and capable of his charge, yet, to confess the truth, I do not consider his capacity nearly so great, nor his virtue so clear and entire and firm, as Seneca's.

Now this book I am speaking of, to attain its purpose, makes a very insulting description of Seneca, having borrowed its slurs from Dion the historian, whose testimony I do not at all believe. For not only is he inconsistent, in that after having called Seneca now very wise and now a mortal enemy of Nero's vices, he elsewhere makes him avaricious, usurious, ambitious, effeminate, voluptuous, and playing the philosopher on false pretenses; but besides, Seneca's virtue shows forth so live and vigorous in his writings, and the defense is so clear there against some of these imputations, as that of his wealth and excessive spending, that I would not believe any testimony to the contrary. And moreover it is much more reasonable in these matters to believe the Roman historians than the Greeks and foreigners. Now Tacitus and the others speak very honorably of both his life and his death, and depict him to us in all things as a very excellent and very virtuous person. And I will allege no other reproach against Dion's judgment than this one, which is unavoidable: that his sense of Roman affairs is so diseased that he dares to maintain Julius Caesar's cause against Pompey and Antony's against Cicero.

Let us come to Plutarch.

Jean Bodin is a good author of our day, equipped with much more judgment than the mob of scribblers of his time, and he deserves to be judged and considered. I find him a little bold in that passage of his *Method of History* in which he accuses Plutarch not only of ignorance (on which I would have let him have his say, for that is not my quarry), but also of often writing incredible and entirely fabulous things (those are his words). If he had simply said "things otherwise than they are," that would have been no great

reproach; for what we have not seen we take from the hands of others and on trust, and I see that he sometimes deliberately tells the same story in different ways, like Hannibal's judgment of the three best generals that ever lived: it is one way in the "Life of Flaminius," another way in that of Pyrrhus. But to charge him with having taken incredible and impossible things as genuine coin is to accuse the most judicious author in the world of lack of judgment.

And here is his example: "As," he says, "when he relates that a Lacedaemonian boy let his whole stomach be torn up by a young fox he had stolen, and kept it hidden under his robe until he died, rather than disclose his theft." In the first place, I find this example badly chosen, since it is very hard to assign bounds to the achievements of the faculties of the soul, whereas we have more chance to assign limits to physical powers and to know them. And for this reason, if it had been for me to do, I would have chosen rather an example of this second sort. And there are some of these that are less credible, as, among others, what he relates of Pyrrhus, that, all wounded as he was, he dealt so great a blow with his sword to a fully armed enemy of his that he clove him from the head down so that the body split into two parts.

In his example I find no great miracle, nor do I accept the excuse with which he shelters Plutarch, that he added the words "so they say," to warn us and hold our belief in check. For unless it is in things received on authority and reverence for antiquity or religion, he would not have been willing either to accept himself or to propose to our belief things incredible in themselves. And it is easy to see that he does not use this phrase "so they say" for that purpose here, because he himself tells us elsewhere, on this subject of the endurance of Lacedaemonian boys, some examples that happened in his time and that are harder to make anyone believe. Like the one to which Cicero also testified before him, having, so he says, been on the spot: that even down to their time there were children who, in the test of endurance by which they were tried before the altar of Diana, endured being whipped until the blood ran down all over them, not only without an outcry but even without a groan, and some till they voluntarily gave up their lives there. And the other one that Plutarch tells, along with a hundred other witnesses: that at a sacrifice, when a burning coal had slipped into the sleeve of a Lacedaemonian boy as he was serving incense, he let his whole arm be burned until the smell of the broiling flesh reached the bystanders.

There was nothing, according to their custom, in which their reputation was more concerned, or for which they had more blame and shame to suffer, than being caught stealing. I am so steeped in the greatness of those people that not only does Plutarch's story not seem incredible to me, as it does to Bodin, but I do not find it even rare and strange. ^CSpartan history is full of a thousand more cruel and uncommon examples: by this standard it is all miracle.

^AMarcellinus reports, on this subject of theft, that in his time they had not yet been able to find any kind of torture that could force Egyptians, when caught in this misdeed, which was very much practiced among them, to tell even their names.

^BA Spanish peasant, being put to the rack about his accomplices in the murder of the praetor Lucius Piso, cried out in the midst of the torments that his friends should not stir and should watch in all security, and that it was not in the power of pain to wring one word of confession from him. And they got nothing else out of him for the first day. The next day, as they were bringing him back to start his torture again, he shook himself free vigorously from the hands of his guards, and dashed his head against a wall and killed himself.

^CEpicharis glutted and wearied the cruelty of Nero's satellites and endured their fire, their beatings, and their instruments one whole day without a word to reveal her conspiracy. Upon being taken back to the torture the next day, her limbs all shattered, she slipped a lace of her dress around one arm of her chair with a running knot, and, thrusting her head into it, strangled herself by the weight of her body. Having the courage to die thus and escape more tortures like the first ones, does she not seem to have lent her life purposely to this test of her endurance in order to mock this tyrant and encourage others to a like attempt against him?

^AAnd if anyone will question our mounted musketeers on the experiences they have had in these civil wars, there will be found acts of endurance, obstinacy, and stubbornness in this miserable age of ours, and amid this rabble that is even more soft and effeminate than that of Egypt, worthy to be compared to those we have just related of Spartan virtue.

I know that there have been simple peasants who let the soles of their feet be grilled, the ends of their fingers be crushed with the cock of a pistol, their bleeding eyes be squeezed out of their heads by having a heavy cord pulled tight around their foreheads, before they would even put themselves to ransom. I have seen one, left for dead stark naked in a ditch, his neck all bruised and swollen from a halter

that was still hanging from it, by which he had been dragged along all night at a horse's tail, his body pierced in a hundred places with stabs from daggers, which had been dealt him not to kill him but to hurt and frighten him; who had endured all that, even to the point of losing speech and sentiment, resolved, so he told me, to die a thousand deaths (as in truth, so far as suffering goes, he had died one whole death) rather than promise anything; and yet he was one of the richest farm workers in the whole district. How many of them have been seen patiently letting themselves be burned and roasted for opinions borrowed from others, unknown, and not understood!

ᴮI have known hundreds of women – for they say that Gascon heads are somewhat harder than most – whom you would sooner have made to bite into hot iron than let go their bite of an opinion they had conceived in anger. Their obstinacy increases in the face of blows and constraint. And the man who made up the story of the woman whom neither threat of punishment nor cudgelings would stop from saying that her husband had lice, and who, when thrown into the water and drowning, still raised her hands above her head and made the sign of killing lice, made up a story, in truth, whose express image we see every day in the stubbornness of women. And stubbornness is the sister of constancy, at least in vigor and firmness.

ᴬWe must not judge what is possible and what is not, according to what is credible and incredible to our sense, as I have said elsewhere;[1] and it is a great error, and yet one into which most men fall ᶜ(which I am not saying for Bodin), ᴬto balk at believing about others what they themselves could not do – ᶜor would not. It seems to each man that the ruling pattern of nature is in him; to this he refers all other forms as to a touchstone. The ways that do not square with his are counterfeit and artificial. What brutish stupidity!

ᴬFor my part, I consider some men very far above me, especially among the ancients; and although I clearly recognize my inability to follow them with my steps, I do not fail to follow them with my eyes and judge the powers that raise them so high, ᶜof which I perceive in some degree the seeds in me, as I do also of the extreme baseness of some minds, which does not astonish me and which I do not disbelieve either. I well see the method which the great souls use to raise themselves, ᴬand I wonder at their greatness. And the flights

1 *Essays* I: 27, "It Is Folly to Measure the True and False by Our Own Capacity."

that I find very beautiful, I embrace; and if my powers do not reach them, at least my judgment applies itself to them very gladly.

The other example that Bodin alleges of incredible and entirely fabulous things said by Plutarch is that Agesilaus was fined by the ephors for having drawn to himself alone the heart and will of his citizens. I do not know what mark of falsity he finds in that; but at all events Plutarch is speaking there of things that must have been much better known to him than to us; and it was not new in Greece to see men punished and exiled for merely being too well liked by their fellow citizens, witness ostracism and petalism.[2]

There is also in the same place another accusation which annoys me for Plutarch, where Bodin says that Plutarch matched the Romans with the Romans and the Greeks among themselves without bias, but not the Romans with the Greeks: witness, he says, Demosthenes and Cicero, Cato and Aristides, Sulla and Lysander, Marcellus and Pelopidas, Pompey and Agesilaus; judging that he favored the Greeks by giving them such unequal companions. This is attacking precisely what is most excellent and praiseworthy in Plutarch. For in his parallels (which are the most admirable part of his work, and in which, in my opinion, he took particular satisfaction), the fidelity and sincerity of his judgments equals their depth and weight. He is a philosopher who teaches us virtue. Let us see if we can protect him against this reproach of prevarication and falsehood.

What I can think of as having given occasion to this judgment is the great and dazzling luster that the Roman names take on in our mind. It does not seem to us that Demosthenes can equal the glory of one who was consul, proconsul, and quaestor of that great republic. But if we will consider the truth of the thing and the men in themselves, which Plutarch most aimed to do, and will balance their characters, their natures, their abilities, rather than their fortunes, I think, in contrast to Bodin, that Cicero and the older Cato fall short of their parallels. For his purpose I would have chosen rather the example of the younger Cato compared to Phocion; for in this pair there would be found a more likely disparity to the advantage of the Roman.

As for Marcellus, Sulla, and Pompey, I see well that their exploits in war are more important, glorious, and pompous than those of the Greeks whom Plutarch compares with them; but the finest and

2 Forms of banishment in Athens and Syracuse, respectively.

most virtuous actions, either in war or elsewhere, are not always the most famous. I often see names of captains smothered under the splendor of other names of less merit; witness Labienus, Ventidius, Telesinus, and many others.

And to take it that way, if I had to complain on behalf of the Greeks, could I not say that Camillus is much less comparable to Themistocles, the Gracchi to Agis and Cleomenes, Numa to Lycurgus?

But it is folly to try to judge by one feature things with so many aspects. When Plutarch compares them, he does not make them equal for all that. Who could mark their differences more clearly and conscientiously? When he comes to parallel the victories, the exploits in arms, the power of the armies led by Pompey, and his triumphs, with those of Agesilaus, he says: "I do not believe that Xenophon himself, if he were alive, though he were allowed to write whatever he wanted to the advantage of Agesilaus, would dare place him in comparison." Does he speak of comparing Lysander with Sulla? "There is no comparison," he says, "either in the number of their victories or in the risks they ran in battle; for Lysander won only two naval battles," etc.

That is not taking anything away from the Romans; by having simply confronted them with the Greeks he cannot have done them any wrong, whatever disparity there may be between them. And Plutarch does not weigh them entire against each other; there is no overall preference; he compares the bits and the circumstances, one after the other, and judges them separately. Wherefore if someone wanted to convict him of partiality, he should have picked some particular judgment to pieces, or said in general that he had made a mistake in comparing a given Greek with a given Roman, since there were others that corresponded more for comparison and resembled each other better.

33
The story of Spurina

^APhilosophy does not think it has used its resources badly when it has given to reason the sovereign mastery of our soul and the authority to hold our appetites in check. They who judge that among the appetites there are none more violent than those which love engenders have this in favor of their opinion: that these affect

both body and soul, and the whole man is possessed by them, so that health itself depends on them, and medicine is sometimes constrained to pander to them.

But on the contrary, one might also say that the commingling of the body brings them some abatement and weakening; for such desires are subject to satiety and capable of material remedies. Many, having wished to deliver their soul from the continual alarms that this appetite gave them, have resorted to the incision and amputation of the parts that were stirred and altered. Others have quite beaten down the strength and ardor of these by frequent application of cold things like snow and vinegar. The haircloths of our ancestors were for this purpose; they are a fabric woven of horsehair, out of which some of them made shirts, others girdles to torture their loins.

A prince was telling me not long ago that in his youth, on a day of solemn festival at the court of King Francis I, where everybody was dressed up, a fancy took him to put on his father's hair shirt, which is still in his house. But for all his devoutness, he had not the endurance to wait for night to strip it off, and was very sick from it for a long time; adding that he thought there was no youthful heat so intense that the use of this recipe could not mortify it. However, he may never have felt the most burning heats, for experience shows us that such an urge often maintains itself under rough and wretched garments, and that sackcloth does not always have the power to make its wearer powerless.

Xenocrates went about it more rigorously; for when his disciples, to test his continence, smuggled into his bed the beautiful and famous courtesan Lais, quite naked save for the weapons of her beauty and wanton charms, her philters, he felt that in spite of his reasonings and his rules his recalcitrant body was beginning to rebel, and had those of his members burned that had lent an ear to this mutiny.

Whereas the passions that are all in the soul, such as ambition and avarice, give the reason much more to do, for it can find no help for them except in its own resources; nor are these appetites capable of satiety, but rather they grow sharper and increase by enjoyment.

The sole example of Julius Caesar may suffice to show us the disparity of these appetites, for never was a man more addicted to amorous pleasures. One evidence of this is the fastidious care he took of his person, even to using for that the most lascivious means then in vogue, such as having all the hairs plucked off his body and

covering himself with perfumes of exquisite choice. And he was naturally a handsome person, fair, with a tall and active figure, a full face, and dark, bright eyes, if we are to believe Suetonius, for the statues that are seen of him in Rome do not correspond in every respect with this picture.

Besides his wives, whom he changed four times, and without counting his youthful amours with Nicomedes, king of Bithynia, he had the maidenhead of the renowned queen of Egypt, Cleopatra; witness the little Caesarion who was born as a result. He also made love to Eunoe, queen of Mauritania, and in Rome to Post-humia, wife of Servius Sulpitius, to Lollia, wife of Gabinius, to Tertulla, wife of Crassus, and even to Mutia, wife of the great Pompey; which was the reason, say the Roman historians, why her husband repudiated her, a fact Plutarch confesses he did not know. And the Curios, father and son, later reproached Pompey, when he married Caesar's daughter, for becoming the son-in-law of a man who had made him a cuckold and whom he himself had been wont to call Aegisthus.

Besides all this number, he kept Servilia, sister of Cato and mother of Marcus Brutus, whence, everyone maintains, proceeded that great affection that he bore to Brutus, because Brutus was born at a time when there was a likelihood that he had been sired by him. So I have reason, it seems to me, to take him for a man extremely addicted to this form of debauch and of a very amorous constitution. But the other passion of ambition, with which he was also infinitely smitten, coming into conflict with this one, promptly made it give way.

'Remembering Mohammed II in this connection, the one who subjugated Constantinople and brought about the final extermination of the Greek name, I do not know when these two passions were found more evenly balanced: an equally indefatigable lecher and soldier. But when the two enter into competition with each other in his life, the quarrelsome ardor always dominates the amorous ardor. And the latter, although it was out of its natural season, fully regained sovereign authority only when he was in extreme old age, no longer capable of supporting the burden of war.

What is related as a contrary example of Ladislaus, king of Naples, is remarkable: that, a good captain, courageous and ambitious, he set himself as the principal aim of his ambition the satisfaction of his sensuality and the enjoyment of some rare beauty. His death was in keeping. Having by a well-prosecuted siege

reduced the city of Florence to such straits that the inhabitants were on the point of capitulating, he let them off provided they would deliver up to him a girl of their city of whom he had heard, of surpassing beauty. They were forced to grant her to him, and avert the public ruin by a private wrong.

She was the daughter of a doctor famous in his time, who, finding himself entangled in so foul a necessity, resolved on a lofty attempt. As all were arraying his daughter and bedecking her with ornaments and jewels to make her pleasing to this novel lover, he too gave her a handkerchief, exquisite in fragrance and workmanship, which she was to use in their first embraces – an article they rarely forget in those parts. This handkerchief, poisoned according to the full capacity of his craft, coming to rub against the aroused flesh and open pores of both, infused its venom so promptly that, their warm sweat suddenly changing to cold, they expired in each other's arms.

I return to Caesar.

[A]His pleasures never made him steal a single minute of time, or turn aside one step, from the occasions that presented themselves for his aggrandizement. This passion of ambition ruled all the others so sovereignly in him and possessed his soul with such full authority that it carried him away where it willed. Indeed it vexes me when I consider the greatness of this person in all other respects and the marvelous qualities that were in him: so much ability in every kind of learning that there is hardly a realm of knowledge on which he has not written. He was such an orator that many have preferred his eloquence to that of Cicero; and he himself, to my mind, did not think he owed him much in that particular; and his two "Anti-Catos" were written mainly to counterbalance the fine style that Cicero had employed in his "Cato."

As for the rest, was there ever a soul so vigilant, so active, and so enduring of labor as his? And without doubt it was also embellished with many rare seeds of virtue: I mean living, natural, and not counterfeit. He was singularly sober, and so little finicky in his eating that Oppius relates that one day at table, having been presented with medicated oil instead of plain oil in some sauce, he ate heartily of it so as not to shame his host. Another time he had his baker whipped for serving him other than ordinary bread.

Cato himself was wont to say of him that he was the first sober man who had set out to ruin his country. And as for the fact that the same Cato once called him "drunkard," that happened in this fashion. When both of them were in the Senate, where Catiline's

conspiracy was being discussed, in which Caesar was suspect, a sealed note was brought to him from outside. Cato, thinking that it was some warning from the conspirators, demanded that he give it to him, which Caesar was constrained to do to avoid a greater suspicion. It happened to be a love letter written to him by Servilia, Cato's sister. Cato, after reading it, threw it back to him, saying: "Take it, drunkard." This, I say, was rather a word of disdain and anger than an express accusation of that vice, just as we often insult those who anger us with the first insults that come to our lips, although they may not be at all deserved by those to whom we apply them. Besides, this vice with which Cato reproaches him is wonderfully akin to the one in which he had surprised Caesar; for Venus and Bacchus are prone to go together, according to the proverb. ᴮBut with me Venus is much more sprightly when accompanied by sobriety.

ᴬThe examples of his mildness and clemency toward those who had done him harm are infinite; I mean besides those he gave during the time when the Civil War was still in progress, which, as he himself makes palpable enough in his writings, he used in order to cajole his enemies and make them less afraid of his future victory and domination. But still it must be said that if those examples are not sufficient to prove his natural mildness, at least they show us a marvelous confidence and greatness of courage in this man. It often happened that he sent back to the enemy whole armies after having vanquished them, without even deigning to bind them by oath, if not to favor him, at least to hold back and not make war on him. He took certain captains of Pompey three or four times, and as many times set them at liberty again. Pompey used to declare all those his enemies who did not accompany him to war; Caesar had it proclaimed that he considered as his friends all those who did not stir and did not actually take arms against him. To those of his captains who deserted him to take service elsewhere, he still sent back their arms, horses, and equipment. The cities he had taken by force he left at liberty to follow which side they pleased, assigning them no other garrison than the memory of his mildness and clemency. On the day of his great battle of Pharsalia he forbade anyone to lay a hand on a Roman citizen except at the last extremity.

These are very hazardous traits, in my judgment; and it is no wonder if, in the civil wars by which we are afflicted, those who, like him, are combating the ancient order of their country, do not imitate his example. These are extraordinary methods, which it

befits only Caesar's fortune and his admirable foresight to employ successfully. When I consider the incomparable greatness of that soul, I excuse victory for being unable to shake free of him, even in that very unjust and very iniquitous cause.

To return to his clemency, we have many genuine examples of it in the time of his domination, when, all things being brought under his hand, he had no further need to dissemble. Caius Memmius had written some very biting orations against him, to which he had replied very sharply; yet that did not keep him soon after from helping to make him consul. When Caius Calvus, who had composed several insulting epigrams against him, employed some of his friends to reconcile them, Caesar took it upon himself to write him first. And when our good Catullus, who had handled him so roughly under the name of Mamurra, came to make his excuses to him, he had him sup at his own table that very day. Having been informed of some who were speaking ill of him, he did nothing about it but declare in one of his public speeches that he was informed of it. He feared his enemies even less than he hated them. When certain conspiracies and meetings organized against his life were revealed to him, he contented himself with publishing by edict that they were known to him, without otherwise prosecuting their authors.

As for the respect he had for his friends, when Caius Oppius was traveling with him and feeling bad, he left to him the only lodging that there was, and slept all night on the hard ground in the open.

As for his justice, he put to death a servant of his of whom he was particularly fond, for having slept with the wife of a Roman knight, although no one made any complaint. Never did a man bring more moderation to his victories or show more resolution in adverse fortune.

But all these fine tendencies were spoiled and stifled by the furious passion of ambition, by which he let himself be so forcibly carried away that one may easily maintain that it controlled the tiller by which all his actions were steered. Of a liberal man it made a public robber, to provide for his profusion and largesse, and it made him utter that ugly and very unjust saying, that if the most wicked and lost souls in the world had been faithful to him in the service of his aggrandizement, he would cherish and advance them by his power as well as the most worthy men. It intoxicated him with a vanity so extreme that he dared to boast in the presence of his fellow citizens that he had made the great Roman Republic a name

without form and without a body, and to say that his answers must henceforth serve as laws, and to remain seated while receiving the Senate when it came to call on him in a body, and to allow himself to be worshiped and have divine honors paid him in his presence.

To sum up, this single vice, in my opinion, ruined in him the finest and richest nature that ever was, and has made his memory abominable to all good men, because he willed to seek his glory in the ruin of his country and the subversion of the most powerful and flourishing republic that the world will ever see.

There might well, on the contrary, be found many examples of great personages whom voluptuousness made to forget the conduct of their affairs, as did Mark Antony and others; but where love and ambition were in equal balance and clashed together with equal forces, I make no doubt but that the latter would win the prize of mastery.

Now, to retrace my steps a bit, it is much to be able to curb our appetites by the arguments of reason, or to force our members by violence to stick to their duty. But to whip ourselves for the advantage of our neighbors; not only to rid ourselves of that sweet passion that tickles us, of the pleasure we feel in seeing that we are attractive to others and loved and sought after by all, but even to conceive a hatred and abhorrence of our charms which are the cause of their love, and to condemn our beauty because someone else is inflamed by it – of this I have encountered few examples. Here is one.

Spurina, a young man of Tuscany,

> [B]Just as a jewel sparkles, set in yellow gold,
> Adorning throat or head, or as, cunningly made,
> In boxwood or Orician terebinth inlaid,
> Ivory gleams,
>
> VIRGIL

[A]being endowed with a beauty so unique and excessive that the most continent eyes could not continently endure its brilliance, not content with leaving without relief so much fever and flame that he kindled everywhere, entered into furious spite against himself and against these rich presents that nature had made to him, as if these should be blamed for the fault of others, and deliberately slashed and disfigured with many wounds and scars the perfect proportion and symmetry that nature had so carefully observed in his face.

[C]To speak my mind about this, I wonder at such actions more than I honor them; these excesses are enemies to my rules. The

purpose was fine and conscientious, but, to my mind, a little lacking
in wisdom. What if his ugliness later served to cast others into the
sin of scorn and hatred or of envy for the glory of so rare a merit, or
of calumny, interpreting this impulse as a frantic ambition? Is there
any form from which vice may not, if it will, draw occasion for
exercising itself in some manner? It would have been more just and
also more glorious to have made of these gifts of God a subject for
exemplary virtue and regulated conduct.

Those who evade the common duties and that infinite number of
thorny and many-faceted rules that bind a man of precise probity in
civil life, achieve, in my opinion, a fine saving, whatever point of
especial rigor they may impose on themselves. It is in a sense dying
to escape the trouble of living well. They may have some other prize;
but the prize of difficulty it has never seemed to me they had, nor do
I think there is anything more arduous than keeping oneself straight
amid the waves and rush of the world, loyally responding to and
satisfying every part of one's charge.

It is perhaps easier to do without the whole sex than to behave
rightly in every respect in association with our wives; and a man
may live more carefree in poverty than in justly dispensed abun-
dance. Enjoyment conducted according to reason is more arduous
than abstinence. Moderation is a virtue that gives more trouble than
suffering does. The good life of the younger Scipio has a thousand
ways; the good life of Diogenes has only one. The latter surpasses
ordinary lives in innocence by as much as exquisite and accom-
plished lives surpass it in usefulness and power.caesar's

34
Observations on Julius Caesar's methods of making war

^It is reported of many leaders in war that they had certain books in
particular esteem, as the great Alexander did Homer; ^CScipio Afri-
canus, Xenophon; ^AMarcus Brutus, Polybius; Charles V, Philippe
de Commines. And it is said that in our day Machiavelli is still in
repute in other countries. But the late Marshal Strozzi, who took
Caesar as his choice, undoubtedly chose much better; for in truth
he should be the breviary of every warrior, as being the true and
sovereign model of the military art. And God knows, more-
over, with what grace and beauty he has embellished that rich
matter, with a manner of speaking so pure, so delicate, and so

perfect, that to my taste there are no writings in the world comparable to his in this respect.

I want to record here certain individual and unusual features, on the subject of his wars, that have remained in my memory.

When his army was in some fright at the rumor that was current of the great forces that King Juba was leading against him, he assembled them to reassure them and give them courage; and instead of abating the notion his soldiers had formed and minimizing his enemy's resources, he took a way quite opposite to the one we are accustomed to. For he told them not to trouble themselves any more to inquire about the forces that the enemy was leading, since he had very certain information about them. And then he gave them a number greatly surpassing both the truth and the report that was current in his army, following the advice of Cyrus in Xenophon; inasmuch as the deception is not so serious when we find the enemy in fact weaker than we had expected, as when, having judged them weak by report, we find them in truth very strong.

He accustomed his soldiers above all simply to obey, without meddling with criticizing or talking about their captain's plans, which he communicated to them only when he was about to put them into execution. And he took pleasure, if they had discovered anything about his intentions, in changing them on the spot to fool them. And often, for this purpose, having appointed a certain spot to camp, he would pass beyond it and lengthen the day's march, especially if it was bad and rainy weather.

The Swiss, at the beginning of his Gallic wars, sent to him to ask him to give them passage across Roman territory. Though he was determined to stop them by force, he nevertheless put on a favorable face and took a few days' delay in answering them, so as to use this leisure in assembling his army. Those poor people did not know how excellent a husbander of his time he was; for many a time he repeats that the most sovereign quality of a commander is the knowledge of how to seize occasions at the right point, and speed in execution, which in his exploits is truly unheard-of and incredible.

If he was scarcely scrupulous in that affair, in taking advantage of his enemy under color of a treaty of agreement, he was as little so in this, that he required no other virtue in his soldiers than valor, and scarcely punished any other vices than mutiny and disobedience. Often after his victories he would give them free rein for any sort of licentiousness, releasing them for a time from the rules of military discipline, adding withal that he had soldiers so well trained that,

even all perfumed and musked, they did not fail to go furiously into combat. Indeed, he liked them to be richly armed, and had them wear engraved, gilded, and silvered armor, so that care for saving it might make them fiercer in self-defense.

When he spoke to them, he called them comrades, an expression which we still use, but which his successor, Augustus, changed, believing that Caesar had used it for the necessity of his affairs and to flatter the heart of men who followed him only as volunteers –

> [B]My general when we crossed the Rhine,
> Here Caesar is my fellow; a leveler is crime
>
> LUCAN

– [A]but that this fashion was beneath the dignity of an emperor and general of an army; and he restored the fashion of calling them merely soldiers.

With this courtesy, however, Caesar combined great severity in keeping them in check. When the Ninth Legion mutinied near Placentia, he ignominiously cashiered it, although Pompey was then still afoot, and received it back into favor only after many supplications. He appeased them more by authority and audacity than by gentleness.

Where he speaks of his crossing of the river Rhine to Germany, he says that, considering it unworthy of the honor of the Roman people to take his army across in boats, he had a bridge built so as to cross firm-footed. It was there that he built that admirable bridge whose construction he describes in every particular. For in no place is he so prone to dwell on his exploits as in representing to us the subtlety of his inventions in this sort of manual works.

I have also noticed this, that he sets great store by his exhortations to the soldiers before combat. For where he wants to show that he was surprised or hard pressed, he always mentions the fact that he had not even the time to harangue his army. Before that great battle against the Turones, he says: "Caesar, having given orders for everything else, immediately ran where fortune carried him to exhort his men; and meeting the Tenth Legion, he had only time to tell them to remember their accustomed valor, not to be taken aback, and to sustain boldly the adversaries' attack. And because the enemy had already approached within a dart's throw, he gave the signal for battle; and from there having immediately passed on elsewhere to encourage others, he found that they were already at grips."

That is what he says in that place. In truth, his tongue did him very notable services in many places; and even in his own time, his military eloquence was in such high esteem that many in his army took down his harangues; and by that means there were volumes of them collected that lasted a long time after him. His speech had particular graces, so that his intimates, and among them Augustus, hearing anyone recite what had been collected of them, could recognize what was not his, even to phrases and words.

The first time he left Rome with a public command, he reached the river Rhone in a week, having in his coach in front of him one or two secretaries who were continually writing, and behind him the man who carried his sword. And certainly, even if a man were merely traveling, doing nothing else, he could hardly attain the speed with which, always victorious, having left Gaul and pursuing Pompey to Brundisium, Caesar subjugated Italy in eighteen days; returned from Brundisium to Rome; from Rome went right into the heart of Spain, where he overcame extreme difficulties in the war against Afranius and Petreius; and thence to the long siege of Marseilles. From there he returned into Macedonia, beat the Roman army at Pharsalia, and passed from there, pursuing Pompey, into Egypt, which he subjugated. From Egypt he went to Syria and the region of Pontus, where he fought Pharnaces, and from there into Africa, where he defeated Scipio and Juba; after which he retraced his steps through Italy into Spain, where he defeated Pompey's sons:

> [B]Swifter than lightning, or a tigress with her young.
>
> LUCAN

> As when a boulder from a mountain's side
> Is torn by wind or by the driving rain,
> Or sapped by time, and rolls toward the plain –
> Its impact shocks the earth, the mountains quake,
> Forests and herds and men are carried in its wake.
>
> VIRGIL

[A]Speaking of the siege of Avaricum, he says that it was his custom to stay night and day with the workmen that he was employing. In all undertakings of consequence, he always did the reconnoitering himself, and never brought his army into a place that he had not looked over first. And if we are to believe Suetonius, when he undertook to cross over into England, he was the first to test the landing place.

He was wont to say that he liked a victory obtained by intelligence better than one obtained by force. And in the war against Petreius and Afranius, when fortune presented him with a very apparent occasion and advantage, he refused it, hoping, he says, to get the better of his enemies with a little more time but less risk.

[B]In this, too, he did an amazing thing, when he commanded his whole army to swim across the river without any necessity:

> Rushing to the fight, the soldier swims
> The stream he would have feared in flight; his dampened limbs
> Grow warm in the armor; by running he restores
> His frozen joints.
>
> LUCAN

[A]I find him a little more restrained and deliberate in his enterprises than Alexander; for the latter seems to seek out dangers and run headlong to meet them, like an impetuous torrent that runs into and attacks everything it encounters, without discrimination or choice:

> [B]Thus surges bull-like Aufidus,
> Which flows through the Apulian Daunas' realm,
> When in a rage, with horrid flood,
> He aims the fruitful fields to overwhelm.
>
> HORACE

[A]Also he was occupied in war in the flower and first ardor of his youth, whereas Caesar took to it when he was already mature and well advanced in years. Besides, Alexander was of a more sanguine, choleric, and ardent temperament, and moreover he stimulated this humor further with wine, of which Caesar partook very sparingly. But where necessary occasions presented themselves and the matter required it, there was never a man who held his life more cheaply.

For my part, it seems to me I read in many of his exploits a determined resolve to lose his life, to avoid the shame of being vanquished. In that great battle that he had against the Turones, seeing the van of his army wavering, he ran to meet the front ranks of the enemy, without a buckler, just as he was; and this happened several other times. Hearing that his men were besieged, he passed in disguise through the enemy army to go and strengthen them by his presence. Having crossed over to Dyrrachium with very small forces, and seeing that the rest of his army, which he had left to Antony to lead, was slow to follow him, he undertook alone to cross

the sea again in a very heavy storm, and slipped away to go and himself take over the rest of his forces again, though the ports on the other side and the whole sea were held by Pompey.

And as for the undertakings he carried out with armed forces, there are many that in hazard surpass all the rules of military science; for with what feeble means did he undertake to subjugate the kingdom of Egypt, and afterward to go and attack the forces of Scipio and Juba, ten times greater than his own! People like him have had a mysterious and superhuman confidence in their fortune.

[B]And he used to say that a man must carry out, not deliberate about, high enterprises.

[A]After the battle of Pharsalia, having sent his army ahead into Asia, and crossing the strait of the Hellespont with a single vessel, he met Lucius Cassius at sea with ten great men-of-war; he had the courage not merely to await him, but to head straight toward him and summon him to surrender; and he got the better of him.

When he had undertaken that furious siege of Alésia, where there were eighty thousand defenders, and all Gaul had risen up to rush upon him and raise the siege with an army of one hundred and nine thousand[1] horse and two hundred and forty thousand foot, what boldness and maniacal confidence it was to refuse to abandon his enterprise for all that and to resolve to meet two such great difficulties at the same time! And yet he withstood them both; and after winning that great battle against those outside, he soon reduced to his mercy those whom he held besieged.

The same thing happened with Lucullus at the siege of Tigranocerta against King Tigranes, but under different conditions, in view of the softness of the enemy with whom Lucullus had to deal.

I want to note here two rare and extraordinary facts in connection with this siege of Alésia. One, that the Gauls, when they assembled the army that was to march on Caesar there, having numbered all their forces, resolved in their council to cut down a good part of that great multitude, for fear they might fall into confusion. This is a novel thing, to be afraid of being too many; but if you take it rightly, it is likely that an army corps should have a size moderated and ruled by certain limits, either because of the

1 This figure should be 8,000. Montaigne may well have miscopied "IIX milibus" (8,000) as "CIX milibus" (109,000) from his edition of Caesar's *De Bello Gallico*.

difficulty of feeding it, or because of the difficulty of leading it and keeping it in order. At least it would be very easy to prove by example that armies monstrous in number have hardly done anything worth while.

^CAccording to the saying of Cyrus in Xenophon, it is not the number of men, but the number of good men, that constitutes the advantage, the rest serving more as a hindrance than as a help. And Bajazet based his resolution to give battle to Tamerlane, against the advice of all his captains, mainly on the consideration that the numberless number of his enemy's men gave him assured hope of throwing them into confusion. Scanderbeg, a good judge and very expert, was wont to say that ten or twelve thousand faithful fighting men should be enough for a capable leader in war to guarantee his reputation in any sort of military emergency.

^AThe other point, which seems to be contrary to both usage and reason in warfare, is that Vercingetorix, who was named general-in-chief of all the parts of the revolted Gauls, decided to go and shut himself up in Alésia. For a man who is commanding a whole country should never tie himself down except in the extreme case, where his last position is at stake and there is nothing more to hope for except in defending it. Otherwise he must keep himself free in order to be able to provide in general for all parts of his government.

To return to Caesar, he became with time a little more slow and deliberate, as his close friend Oppius testifies; thinking that he should not lightly risk the honor of so many victories, which a single misfortune could make him lose. That is what the Italians say when they want to reprove that foolhardiness that is seen in young men, calling them "needy of honor," *bisognosi d'honore*; adding that they, being still in such great famine and dearth of reputation, are right to seek it at any price whatever, which men who have already acquired enough of it should not do. There may be some just moderation in this desire for glory, and some satiety in this appetite as in others. Plenty of people deal with it in this way.

He was far removed from the scrupulousness of the ancient Romans, who would avail themselves in their wars only of simple and natural valor; but still he brought to it more of a conscience than we would at this time, and did not approve every sort of means to gain victory. In the war against Ariovistus, when Caesar was in parley with him, there arose some commotion between the two armies, which began through the fault of Ariovistus' horsemen.

In this tumult Caesar found himself with a very great advantage over his enemy; however, he would not avail himself of it, for fear he might be reproached with having proceeded in bad faith.

He was wont to wear rich and brilliantly colored garments into battle, to make himself conspicuous.

He kept a tighter rein on his soldiers, and drew them up shorter, when they were near the enemy.

When the ancient Greeks wanted to accuse anyone of extreme incompetence, they said as a common proverb that he could neither read nor swim. Caesar had this same opinion, that the ability to swim was very useful for war, and he derived many advantages from it. If he had to make speed, he ordinarily crossed the rivers he encountered by swimming, for he liked to travel on foot like the great Alexander. In Egypt, when he was forced to get into a small boat in order to save himself, and so many people leaped in with him that he was in danger of going to the bottom, he chose rather to throw himself into the sea and reached his fleet, which was more than two hundred yards away, by swimming, holding his tablets above water in his left hand and dragging his armed tunic in his teeth, so that the enemy should not enjoy it; and he was already well advanced in years.

Never did a general inspire so much trust in his soldiers. At the beginning of his Civil Wars, his centurions offered each to pay one armed man out of his own purse, and the foot soldiers offered to serve him at their own expense, those who were better off undertaking further to defray the expenses of the needier.

The late Admiral de Chastillon recently showed us a similar case in our civil wars, for the Frenchmen in his army provided out of their own purses for the payment of the foreigners who accompanied him. There would hardly be found examples of such ardent and ready affection among those who follow the old order, under the old, established laws.[2]

^cPassion rules us much more tyrannically than reason. Nevertheless it happened in the war against Hannibal that, after the generous example of the Roman people in the city, the men-at-arms and captains refused their pay; and in the camp of Marcellus those who took any were called mercenaries.

2 Montaigne here refers to the loyalist Catholic army. The Admiral de Chastillon is the Protestant leader Gaspard de Coligny, killed in the Saint Bartholomew's Day Massacre.

ᴬHaving had the worst of it near Dyrrachium, Caesar's soldiers came of their own accord and offered themselves to be chastised and punished, so that he had rather to console them than to rebuke them. One single cohort of his withstood four of Pompey's legions for more than four hours, until it was almost completely wiped out with arrows; and they found a hundred and thirty thousand shafts in the trenches. A soldier named Scaeva, who commanded one of the approaches, maintained himself there invincible, with one eye shot out, a pierced shoulder and thigh, and his shield cut in two hundred and thirty places. It happened that many of his soldiers who were taken prisoner chose to accept death rather than promise to join the other side. When Granius Petronius had been captured by Scipio in Africa, Scipio, after putting his companions to death, sent word to him that he was giving him his life because he was a man of rank and a quaestor. Petronius replied that Caesar's soldiers were accustomed to give life to others, not to receive it; and immediately he killed himself with his own hand.

There are infinite examples of their fidelity. We must not forget the action of the men who were besieged at Salona, a city partisan to Caesar against Pompey, for a rare incident that occurred there. Marcus Octavius held them besieged, and those within were reduced to extreme necessity in all things, so that, to supply their shortage of men, most of them being killed or wounded, they freed all their slaves, and were constrained to cut off the hair of all the women to make ropes to work their machines, besides suffering an appalling dearth of victuals; nevertheless they were resolved never to surrender.

After the siege had dragged on at great length, so that Octavius had become more careless and less attentive to his enterprise, they chose one day about noon, and, after stationing the women and children on their walls to make a good appearance, sallied out with such fury against the besiegers that, having broken through the first, second, and third body of guards, and the fourth, and then the rest, and having made them completely abandon the trenches, they drove them right into the ships; and Octavius himself fled to Dyrrachium, where Pompey was. I have no memory for the moment of having come across any other example in which the besieged beat the whole body of the besiegers and won the mastery of the field, or in which a sortie resulted in a clear and complete victory in battle.

35
Of three good women

^AThey don't come by the dozen, as everyone knows, and especially in
the duties of marriage; for that is a bargain full of so many thorny
circumstances that it is hard for a woman's will to maintain itself
whole in it for long. Men, though they are in it on a little better
conditions, have a hard time to do so.

^BThe touchstone of a good marriage, and its real proof, is how
long the association lasts and whether it has been constantly plea-
sant, loyal, and agreeable. In our age women more commonly
reserve the display of their good offices and the vehemence of
their affection toward their husbands until they have lost them,
^Cand then at least seek to give evidence of their good will. Tardy
and unseasonable evidence! They prove by that rather that they love
them only dead.

^BLife is full of fireworks; death, of love and courtesy. As fathers
hide their affection from their children, likewise wives are prone
to hide theirs from their husbands, to maintain a decent respect.
This mystery is not to my taste. They may tear their hair and scratch
themselves in vain; I go straight to the ear of a chambermaid or
a secretary: "How did they get on? How did they live together?"

I am always reminded of that good remark: *They wail most
noticeably who mourn least* [Tacitus]. Their glum looks are odious
to the living and useless to the dead. We will willingly allow them to
smile afterward provided they smile on us during our life. ^CIs it not
enough to make me come back to life out of spite, to have someone
who spat in my face while I existed come and rub my feet when I am
beginning to exist no longer? ^BIf there is some honor in weeping for
husbands, it belongs only to those who have smiled upon theirs; let
those who have wept in his life smile in his death, outwardly as well
as inwardly.

So do not consider those moist eyes and that piteous voice;
consider that bearing, that coloring, and the plumpness of those
cheeks under those great veils: it is by those that she speaks plain
French. There are few who do not improve in health, a quality that
does not know how to lie. This ceremonious bearing looks not so
much backward as ahead; it is rather profit than payment. In my
childhood, a good and very beautiful lady, who is still living, the
widow of a prince, dressed with a little more adornment than is
permitted by our laws of widowhood. To those who reproached her

for it she said: "That is because I am no longer engaging in new loves, and have no desire to marry again."

Not to be completely out of tune with our usage, I have here chosen as examples three women who also employed the full power of their goodness and affection on the occasion of their husbands' deaths. However, they are slightly different examples, and so ardent that they entail a heroic sacrifice of life.

^APliny the Younger had a neighbor near one of his houses in Italy who was extremely tormented with some ulcers that had formed on his private parts. His wife, seeing him languish so long, entreated him to permit her to examine closely and at leisure the state of his malady, and said she would tell him more frankly than anyone else what he was to expect from it. After having obtained this of him and examined him carefully, she found that it was impossible that he could be cured, and that all he had to expect was to drag out for a very long time a painful and lingering life. So she advised him, as the most sure and sovereign remedy, to kill himself. And finding him a little soft for so stern a measure, she said to him: "Do not think, my dear, that the pains I see you suffer do not touch me as much as they do you, and that I am unwilling to use, in order to deliver myself from them, this medicine that I am prescribing for you. I want to accompany you in the cure as I have done in the disease. Put aside this fear, and believe that we shall have nothing but pleasure in this passage that is to deliver us from such torments; we will go away happily together."

This said, and having warmed up her husband's courage, she resolved that they should throw themselves into the sea out of a window in their house that opened on it. And to maintain to the end that loyal and vehement affection with which she had embraced him during his life, she also wanted him to die in her arms. But for fear that they should fail her, and that the grip of her embrace might be loosened by the fall and by fear, she had herself bound and attached very tightly to him around the waist, and thus abandoned her life for the repose of her husband's.

This woman was of low estate, and among people of such condition it is not so novel to see some trait of rare goodness:

> At the last
> Justice, leaving the earth, among them passed.
> VIRGIL

The other two are noble and rich, and among these examples of virtue rarely lodge.

Arria, the wife of Cecinna Paetus, a personage of consular rank, was the mother of another Arria, the wife of Thrasea Paetus, whose virtue was so renowned in Nero's time, and through this son-in-law the grandmother of Fannia; for the resemblance between the names and fortunes of these men and women has made many confuse them. This first Arria, when her husband Cecinna Paetus had been taken prisoner by the Emperor Claudius' men after the defeat of Scribonianus, whose party he had followed, entreated those who were taking him back a prisoner to Rome to take her into their ship, where she would be much less expense and trouble to them than the number of persons they would need to wait on her husband, and said that she alone would take care of his room, his cooking, and all other services. They refused, and she, jumping into a fishing boat that she hired on the spot, followed him in this fashion from Sclavonia.

One day when they were in Rome, in the presence of the Emperor, and Junia, widow of Scribonianus, accosted her familiarly on account of the similarity of their lots, she repulsed her rudely with these words: "What? I should speak to you or listen to you, in whose lap Scribonianus was killed, and you still live?" These words, together with many other signs, made her relations realize that, impatient of enduring her husband's lot, she was for doing away with herself. Thrasea, her son-in-law, at these words, besought her not to throw her life away and spoke to her thus: "What? If I incurred the same fortune as Cecinna, would you want my wife, your daughter, to do the same?" "How's that? Would I?" she replied. "Yes, yes, I would, if she had lived as long and in as good accord with you as I have with my husband." These answers increased the care they took of her and made them watch her behavior more closely.

One day she said to those who were guarding her: "Do what you will; you can perfectly well make me die a worse death, but keep me from dying you cannot"; and springing furiously from a chair in which she was sitting, she went and dashed her head with all her strength against the nearest wall, and from the blow fell full length in a swoon and badly hurt. After they had brought her to with great difficulty, she said: "I told you so, that if you refused me some easy way to kill myself, I would choose some other, however hard."

The end of so admirable a virtue was this: Since her husband Paetus had not a firm enough heart to put himself to death on his

own, as the Emperor's cruelty forced him to do, one day among others, after having first employed the arguments and exhortations appropriate to the advice she was giving him to do this, she took the dagger that her husband was wearing, and holding it drawn in her hand, for the conclusion of her exhortation she said to him: "Do this, Paetus." And at the same moment, having given herself a fatal blow in the stomach and then torn the dagger out of her wound, she presented it to him, at the same time ending her life with this noble, generous, and immortal saying: "*Paete, non dolet.*" She had time only to speak those three words of such beautiful substance: "See, Paetus, it did not hurt me."

> When chaste Arria passed the fatal sword,
> Drawn from her body, to Paetus, her lord,
> "My wound," she said, "believe me, gives no pain;
> The one that hurts, Paetus, you must sustain."
>
> MARTIAL

It is much more alive in its original form, and richer in meaning; for both the wound and the death of her husband, and her own, were so far from troubling her that indeed she had been the one to advise and promote them. But having done this high and courageous deed solely for her husband's benefit, in the last action of her life she is still thinking of him alone, and of taking away his fear of following her in death. Paetus immediately struck himself with this same blade; ashamed, in my opinion, to have needed so dear and precious a lesson.

Pompeia Paulina, a young and very noble Roman lady, had married Seneca in his extreme old age. Nero, his fine pupil, sent his satellites to him to announce the death sentence, which used to be carried out in this manner: When the Roman emperors of that time had condemned any man of rank, they sent word to him by their officers to select some death at his choice and to take his life within such or such a limit of time, which they prescribed to him, now shorter, now longer, according to the temper of their wrath; giving him leisure during that time to arrange his affairs, or sometimes depriving him of the means of doing so by the shortness of the time. And if the condemned man resisted their order, they brought special men to execute it, either cutting the veins of his arms and legs or forcibly making him swallow poison. But persons of honor did not wait for this necessity, and used their own doctors and surgeons to this effect.

Seneca heard their charge with a peaceful and steadfast countenance, and then asked for some paper to make his will; upon being refused this by the captain, he turned toward his friends and said to them: "Since I cannot leave you anything else in acknowledgment of what I owe you, I leave you at least the finest thing I have, to wit, the picture of my character and my life, which I beg you to keep in your memory, so that in so doing you may acquire the glory of true and sincere friends." And at the same time, now appeasing with gentle words the bitterness of the sorrow he saw them suffering, now hardening his voice to rebuke them for it, he said: "Where are those fine precepts of philosophy? What has become of the provisions against the accidents of fortune that we have been laying up for so many years? Was Nero's cruelty unknown to us? What could we expect of a man who had killed his mother and his brother, if not that he would also put to death his tutor, who educated him and brought him up?"

After having spoken these words to all, he turned to his wife and, embracing her tightly, since her heart and strength were giving way under the weight of her grief, asked her to bear this accident a little more patiently for the love of him, and said that the time had come when he had to show, no longer by arguments and discussions but by action, the profit that he had derived from his studies, and that he really embraced death not only without sorrow but cheerfully: "Wherefore, my dear," he said, "do not dishonor it with your tears, that it may not seem that you love yourself more than my reputation. Appease your sorrow and console yourself in the knowledge you have had of me and my actions, conducting the rest of your life by the honorable occupations to which you are devoted."

To this Paulina, having recovered her spirits a little and rekindled the magnanimity of her courage by a very noble affection, replied: "No, Seneca, I am not the woman to leave you without my company in such a need; I do not want you to think that the virtuous examples of your life have not yet taught me to be able to die well; and when could I do so either better or more honorably or more to my own desire, than with you? So be assured that I am going with you." Then Seneca, taking in good part such a fine and glorious resolution by his wife, and also to deliver himself from the fear of leaving her after his death at the mercy of the cruelty of his enemies, said: "I had advised you, Paulina, in what would serve you to lead your life more happily; so you prefer the honor of death. Truly I will not begrudge

it to you; let the constancy and resolution be equal in our common end, but let the beauty and the glory be greater on your part."

This done, they had the veins of their arms cut at the same time; but because Seneca's, being shrunk both by old age and by his abstinence, gave too long and slow a course to the blood, he ordered that the veins of his thighs be cut also. And for fear that the torment he was suffering from this might weaken his wife's heart, and also to deliver himself from the affliction he felt at seeing her in so piteous a condition, after having very lovingly taken leave of her, he begged her to allow herself to be carried into the next room; which was done.

But all these incisions being still insufficient to make him die, he commanded Statius Anneus, his doctor, to give him a draught of poison; which had hardly any more effect, for, because of the weakness and coldness of his limbs, it could not reach the heart. Therefore, besides that, they prepared a very hot bath for him; and then, feeling that his end was near, as long as he had breath he continued his most excellent discourses on the subject of the state that he was in, which his secretaries collected as long as they could hear his voice. And his last words remained long afterward in credit and honor among men (it is a very grievous loss to us that they have not come down to us). As he felt the last pangs of death, taking some of the bath water, all bloody as it was, he sprinkled his head with it, saying: "I dedicate this water to Jupiter the Deliverer."

Nero, informed of all this, fearing that the death of Paulina, who was one of the best-related ladies of Rome and toward whom he had no particular enmity, might be blamed on him, sent with all speed to have her wounds bound up, which her people did without her knowledge, she being already half-dead and unconscious. And the term of life she lived afterward, contrary to her intention, was lived very honorably and as befitted her virtue, the pale color of her face showing how much life had flowed out of her wounds.

These are my three very true stories, which I find as entertaining and as tragic as those that we make up at will in order to give pleasure to the public. And it astonishes me that those who engage in that business do not take it into their heads rather to choose ten thousand very beautiful stories that are found in books, which would give them less trouble and bring more pleasure and profit. And if anyone should wish to build up an entire and connected body of them, he would need to furnish only the connecting links of his own, like the solder of another metal; and by this means he could

amass a great many true events of all sorts, arranging and diversifying them as the beauty of the work should require, approximately as Ovid sewed and pieced together his *Metamorphoses* out of that great number of various fables.

In regard to this last couple, this too is worthy of consideration: that Paulina willingly offers to give up life for the love of her husband, and that her husband had once also given up death for the love of her. For us there is not a very even balance in this exchange; but from his Stoic attitude, I believe he thought he had done as much for her in prolonging his life for her sake as if he had died for her. In one of the letters he writes to Lucilius, after giving him to understand that since he had been seized by the fever in Rome, he promptly got into a coach to go off to a house of his in the country, against the advice of his wife, who wanted to stop him; and that he had replied to her that the fever he had was not a fever of the body but of the place, he goes on thus:

"She let me go, strongly recommending that I take care of my health. Now I, who know that her life is involved in mine, am beginning to look after myself in order to look after her. The privilege that my old age has given me, making me more firm and resolute in many things, I lose when I remember that in this old life there is a young one to which I am useful. Since I cannot bring her to love me more courageously, she is bringing me to love myself more solicitously; for we must allow something to honorable affections. And sometimes, even though occasions urge us to the contrary, we must call back life, even with torment; we must stop the soul from leaving between our teeth, since the law of living, for good men, is not as long as they please but as long as they ought.

"The man who does not value his wife or a friend of his so much as to prolong his life for them, and who stubbornly insists on dying, is too delicate and soft; the soul must command itself to do this when the benefit of those near and dear to us requires it; we must sometimes lend ourselves to our friends, and even when for our sake we would like to die, break off our plan for their sake. It is evidence of greatness of heart to return to life out of consideration for others, as many excellent persons have done. And it is a trait of singular goodness to preserve old age (whose greatest advantage is unconcern with its duration and a more courageous and disdainful use of life) if we feel that this service is sweet, agreeable, and profitable to someone who loves us. And we receive from it a very pleasant reward, for what is sweeter than to be so dear to our wife that out

of consideration for her we become dearer to ourself? Thus my Paulina has given me not only her fear to bear, but also my own. It was not enough for me to consider with how much resoluteness I could die, but I have also considered with how little resoluteness she could bear my death. I have constrained myself to live, and it is sometimes magnanimity to live."

Those are his words, ^cexcellent as is his wont.

36
Of the most outstanding men

^AIf I were asked my choice of all the men who have come to my knowledge, it seems to me I should find three outstanding above all the rest.

One is Homer. Not that Aristotle and Varro (for example) are not perhaps as learned as he, nor that possibly even in his art itself Virgil may not be compared with him. I leave it to those men to judge who know them both. I who know only the one can say only this according to my capacity, that I do not believe that the Muses themselves could surpass the Roman:

> ^BAs sweetly to his artful lyre he sings
> As when the Cynthian god fingers the strings.
> PROPERTIUS

^AHowever, in making this judgment, we still should not forget that it is principally from Homer that Virgil derives his ability; that he is his guide and his schoolmaster, and that one single detail of the *Iliad* furnished both body and matter for that great and divine *Aeneid*. That is not the way I reckon; I bring in several other circumstances that make this personage a source of wonder to me, almost above man's estate. And indeed I am often astonished that he, who by his authority created and brought into credit in the world many deities, has not himself gained the rank of a god. Being blind and poor, living before the sciences were reduced to rules and certain observations, he knew them so well that all those who since have taken it upon themselves to establish governments, to conduct wars, and to write about either religion or philosophy, ^cof whatever sect they might be, ^Aor about the arts, have used him as a master very perfect in the knowledge of all things, and his books as a nursery of every kind of ability:

Better than Crantor and Chrysippus, he points out –
And fuller too – what's fair, foul, useful, and what's not.

<div style="text-align: right">HORACE</div>

And as another says,

From whose perennial spring the poet sips,
And in Pierian waters wets his lips.

<div style="text-align: right">OVID</div>

And another:

To these add the companions of the Muse, of whom
Homer alone attained the stars.

<div style="text-align: right">LUCRETIUS</div>

And another:

From whose abundant mouth
All later poets draw their songs as from their source,
Draining into their rivulets his torrent's course,
Rich in the wealth of one.

<div style="text-align: right">MANILIUS</div>

It was against the order of nature that he created the most excellent production that can be. For things at birth are ordinarily imperfect; they gain in size and strength as they grow. He made the infancy of poetry and of several other sciences mature, perfect, and accomplished. For this reason he may be called the first and the last of poets, according to that beautiful testimony that antiquity has left to us about him: that having had no one he could imitate before him, he has had no one after him who could imitate him. His words, according to Aristotle, are the only words that have movement and action; they are the only substantial words.

Alexander the Great, having come upon a rich coffer among the spoils of Darius, commanded that it be reserved for him to keep his Homer in, saying that he was the best and most faithful counselor he had in his military affairs. For the same reason Cleomenes, son of Anaxandridas, used to say that he was the poet of the Lacedaemonians, because he was a very good master in the military art. This singular and particular tribute to him has also remained, that in Plutarch's judgment he is the only author in the world who has never sated or palled on men, appearing ever entirely different to his readers, and ever blooming in new grace. That madcap Alcibiades,

having asked one who professed to be a man of letters for a book of Homer, gave him a cuff because he had none; as if someone should find one of our priests without a breviary.

Xenophanes was complaining one day to Hiero, tyrant of Syracuse, that he was so poor he did not have enough to feed two servants. "What!" he replied. "Homer, who was much poorer than you, feeds well over ten thousand of them, dead as he is." ᶜWhat did Panaetius leave to be said when he called Plato the Homer of philosophers?

ᴬBesides this, what glory can be compared with his? There is nothing so alive in the mouths of men as his name and his works; nothing so well known and accepted as Troy, Helen, and his wars, which perhaps never existed. Our children are still called by the names he invented more than three thousand years ago. Who does not know Hector and Achilles? Not only certain private families but most nations seek their origin in his fictions. Mohammed, the second of that name, emperor of the Turks, writing to our Pope Pius II, says: "I am astonished how the Italians league themselves against me, seeing that we have our common origin in the Trojans, and that I, like them, have an interest in avenging the blood of Hector on the Greeks, whom they are favoring against me." Is it not a noble drama in which kings, commonwealths, and emperors keep playing their parts for so many ages, and for which this whole great universe serves as a theater? Seven Greek cities fell into dispute over his birthplace, so much honor did his very obscurity bring him:

Smyrna, Rhodos, Colophon, Salamis, Chios, Argos, and Athens.
AULUS GELLIUS

Another is Alexander the Great. Forⁱ if we will consider the age at which he began his enterprises, the small means with which he accomplished so glorious a design; the authority he gained even in his boyhood among the greatest and most experienced captains in the world, by whom he was followed; the extraordinary favor with which fortune embraced and furthered so many hazardous, and I might almost say rash, exploits of his:

1 The reader is now embarking on a non-stop sentence that includes many independent sentences within it and ends on p. 694 with the words: "I have been right to prefer him even to Caesar, who alone was able to make me doubtful of my choice."

^BThrough all that barred his way cutting a swath,
And glorying that ruin marked his path;

LUCAN

^A[and if we consider] his greatness in having, at the age of thirty-three, passed victoriously over all the habitable earth ^Band attained, in half a lifetime, the utmost achievement of human nature, so that you cannot imagine its lawful duration and the continuation of his growth in valor and fortune through a normal life span without imagining something superhuman, ^Aand in having caused so many royal lines to spring from his soldiers, leaving the world divided after his death among four successors, ordinary captains in his army, whose descendants remained for so long in control of those great possessions;

[If we consider] so many outstanding virtues that were in him – ^Bjustice, temperance, liberality, fidelity to his word, love for his people, humanity toward the vanquished –

(^AFor his character seems in truth not to incur any just reproach. ^BSome of his rare and extraordinary individual actions, yes. But it is impossible to conduct such great movements according to the rules of justice; such men require to be judged in gross, by the master purpose of their actions. The ruin of Thebes, the murder of Menander, of Hephaestion's doctor, of so many Persian prisoners of war at one stroke, of a troop of Indian soldiers not without prejudice to his word, and of the Cosseians even to their little children, are outbursts rather hard to excuse. For as for Clytus, amends were made for the fault beyond its weight; and this action bears witness, as much as any other, to the kindness of his nature, and that of itself it was a nature excellently formed for goodness; ^Cand it was said of him, ingeniously, that he had his virtues from nature, his vices from fortune. ^BAs for the fact that he was a bit boastful, a bit too impatient at hearing himself spoken ill of; and as for his mangers, weapons, and bridles, which he caused to be strewn about in India; all these things, it seems to me, may be condoned for his age and the remarkable prosperity of his fortune) –

If we consider withal so many military virtues – diligence, foresight, patience, discipline, subtlety, magnanimity, resolution, good fortune – wherein, even if the authority of Hannibal had not taught us so, he was the first of men; ^Aand the rare beauty and attributes of his person, truly miraculous; ^Band that carriage and that awe-inspiring bearing, in a face so young, ruddy, and radiant:

> Just like the morning star, Venus' delight,
> When he, who bathed in Ocean's waves by night,
> Raises his sacred head and melts the dark;

<div align="right">VIRGIL</div>

^Aand the excellence of his learning and capacity; and the duration and greatness of his glory – pure, clean, free from spot or envy; ^Band also the fact that long after his death it was a matter of religious belief to think that his medals brought good luck to those who wore them; and that more kings and princes have written his exploits than other historians have written the exploits of any other king or prince whatever; ^Cand that to this day the Mohammedans, who despise all other histories, accept and honor his alone by a special privilege:

^AIf anyone puts all this together, he will confess that I have been right to prefer him even to Caesar, who alone was able to make me doubtful of my choice. ^BAnd it cannot be denied that there is more of his own in Caesar's exploits, more of fortune in Alexander's. ^AThey had many equal qualities, and Caesar perhaps some greater ones.

^BThey were two fires or two torrents to ravage the world in divers places,

> As, spreading devastation in their flight,
> Torrents roar seaward from a mountain height,
> Or fires from opposing quarters rush
> Upon a forest thick with laurel brush.

<div align="right">VIRGIL</div>

But even if Caesar's ambition had more moderation in itself, it is so unfortunate in having for its abominable object the ruin of his country and the general detriment of the world, that ^Aall things put together and placed in the balance, I cannot help inclining to the side of Alexander.

The third, and the most outstanding, to my mind, is Epaminondas.

Of glory he has not anywhere near so much as others (nor is it a part of the substance of the thing). Of resolution and valor, not that which is sharpened by ambition, but that which wisdom and reason may implant in a well-ordered soul, he had all that can be imagined. As for proof of this virtue of his, he has given as much, in my opinion, as Alexander himself and as Caesar. For although his warlike exploits are not so frequent or so grand, they

are nevertheless, if you consider them well in all their circumstances, as important and vigorous, and bear as much evidence of military boldness and ability. The Greeks did him the honor of naming him, without contradiction, the first man among them; and to be the first man of Greece is easily to be the first in the world.

As for his knowledge and ability, this ancient judgment has come down to us, that never did a man know so much, and speak so little, as he. ^CFor he was a Pythagorean in sect. And what he did say, no man ever said better. An excellent orator and very persuasive.

^ABut as for his character and conscience, he very far surpassed all those who have ever undertaken to manage affairs. For in this respect, which must principally be considered, ^Cwhich alone truly marks what we are, and which I weigh alone against all the others together, ^Ahe yields to no philosopher, not even to Socrates.

^BIn this man innocence is a key quality, sovereign, constant, uniform, incorruptible. In comparison, it appears in Alexander as subordinate, uncertain, streaky, soft, and accidental.

^CAntiquity judged that if one examines minutely all the other great captains, there is found in each some special quality that makes him illustrious. In this man alone can be found a virtue and ability full and equal throughout, which, in all the functions of human life, leaves nothing to be desired, whether in public or private occupation, in peace or war, whether in living or in dying greatly and gloriously. I know no form or fortune of man that I regard with so much honor and love.

It is quite true that I consider his obstinacy in poverty, as described by his best friends, as somewhat overscrupulous. And that behavior alone, although lofty and very worthy of admiration, I feel is a little too bitter for me to want to imitate it, even in wish alone.

Only Scipio Aemilianus, if we could give him as proud and illustrious a death and as profound and universal a learning, could make me doubtful about my choice. Oh, what displeasure time has given me by withholding from our eyes precisely, out of the first lives, the noblest pair of lives there was in Plutarch, those of these two men, by the common agreement of the world, one the first of the Greeks, the other of the Romans! What a subject, what a workman!

For a man who was not a saint, but what they call a man of the world, of civil and common ways, of moderate eminence, the richest life that I know to have been lived among the living, as they say, and

the one composed of the most rich and desirable qualities, is, all things considered, in my opinion, that of Alcibiades.

But as for Epaminondas, [A]for an example of exceeding goodness, I want here to add some of his opinions.

[B]The sweetest contentment he had in all his life, he testified, was the pleasure he had given his father and mother by his victory at Leuctra. It says a lot that he preferred their pleasure to his own, so just and so full, for such a glorious action.

[A]He did not think it was permissible, even to recover the freedom of his country, to kill a man without full knowledge of the case. That is why he was so cool to the enterprise of his companion Pelopidas for the deliverance of Thebes. He also held that in battle a man should avoid encountering a friend who was on the opposite side, and spare him.

[C]And when his humanity, even toward the enemy, had made him suspect to the Boeotians – because after having miraculously forced the Lacedaemonians to open to him the pass that they had undertaken to guard at the entrance to the Morea, near Corinth, he had contented himself with walking over their bodies without pursuing them to the death – he was deposed from the rank of commander-in-chief: to be dismissed for such a cause did him much honor, and so did the shame they felt when necessity forced them to restore him soon after to his rank and to acknowledge how much their glory and safety depended on him; victory following him like his shadow wherever he led. The prosperity of his country died, as it was born, with him.

37
Of the resemblance of children to fathers

[A]This bundle of so many disparate pieces is being composed in this manner: I set my hand to it only when pressed by too unnerving an idleness, and nowhere but at home. Thus it has built itself up with diverse interruptions and intervals, as occasions sometimes detain me elsewhere for several months. Moreover, I do not correct my first imaginings by my second – [C]well, yes, perhaps a word or so, but only to vary, not to delete. [A]I want to represent the course of my humors, and I want people to see each part at its birth. It would give me pleasure to have begun earlier, and to be able to trace the course of my mutations. A valet who served me by writing at my dictation

thought he had made a rich booty by stealing from me several pieces chosen to his taste. It consoles me that he will gain no more by it than I have lost.

I have grown seven or eight years older since I began: not without some new acquisition. I have in that time become acquainted with the kidney stone through the liberality of the years. Familiarity and long acquaintance with them do not readily pass without some such fruit. I could wish that, out of many other presents that they reserve for those who frequent them long, they had chosen one that would have been more acceptable to me. For they could not have given me one that I had had in greater horror since my childhood. It was precisely, of all the accidents of old age, the one I feared the most. I had thought to myself many times that I was going forward too far, and that in making such a long journey I would not fail to get involved at last in some unpleasant encounter. I felt and protested enough that it was time to leave, that I should cut off life in the quick and in the breast, following the rule of the surgeons when they have to cut off some limb; ^cthat from the man who did not pay back on time, nature was accustomed to exact a very stiff usury. ^ABut those were vain propositions. I was so far from being ready to do that then, that in the eighteen months or thereabouts that I have been in this unpleasant state, I have already learned to adapt myself to it. I am already growing reconciled to this colicky life; I find in it food for consolation and hope. So bewitched are men by their wretched existence, that there is no condition so harsh that they will not accept it to keep alive.

^cListen to Maecenas:

> Make me lame in hand,
> Lame in foot and thigh,
> Shake out my loosened teeth:
> While life stays, so stay I.
> QUOTED BY SENECA

And Tamerlane cloaked with a foolish humanity the fantastic cruelty he exercised against lepers, putting to death all that came to his knowledge, in order, he said, to deliver them from the painful life they were living. For there was not one of them that would not rather have been a leper three times over than not be alive.

And when Antisthenes the Stoic was very sick and cried out, "What will deliver me from these evils?" Diogenes, who had come

to see him, offered him a knife and said, "This, if you want, very quickly." "I do not say from life," he replied, "I say from evils."

^AThe sufferings that affect us simply through the soul afflict me much less than they do most other men. Partly through judgment; for the world considers many things horrible or to be avoided at the cost of life, which are almost indifferent to me. Partly through a stupid and insensible disposition that I have toward accidents that do not come to me head-on – which disposition I consider one of the best parts of my natural condition. But the really essential and bodily sufferings I feel very keenly. And yet for all that, foreseeing them in other days with a feeble, delicate vision that was softened by the enjoyment of that long and happy health and repose that God lent me for the better part of my life, I had conceived them in imagination so unendurable that in truth I had more fear of them than I have found pain in them. Wherefore I continue to confirm this belief, that most of the faculties of our soul, ^cas we employ them, ^Atrouble the repose of life more than they serve it.

I am at grips with the worst of all maladies, the most sudden, the most painful, the most mortal, and the most irremediable. I have already experienced five or six very long and painful bouts of it. However, either I flatter myself or else there is even in this condition enough to bear up a man whose soul is unburdened of the fear of death and unburdened of the threats, sentences, and consequences which medicine dins into our ears. But the very impact of the pain has not such sharp and piercing bitterness as to drive a well-poised man to madness or despair. I have at least this profit from the stone, that it will complete what I have still not been able to accomplish in myself and reconcile and familiarize me completely with death: for the more my illness oppresses and bothers me, the less will death be something for me to fear. I had already accomplished this: to hold to life only by life alone. My illness will undo even this bond; and God grant that in the end, if its sharpness comes to surpass my powers, it may not throw me back to the other extreme, which is no less a vice, of loving and desiring to die.

> Fear not the final day, nor wish for it.
> MARTIAL

Those are two passions to fear, but one has its remedy much more ready than the other.

Moreover, I have always considered that precept formalistic which so rigorously and precisely orders us to maintain a good

countenance and a disdainful and composed bearing in the endurance of pain. Why does philosophy, which has regard only for real substance and actions, go playing around with these external appearances?[1] ^CLet her leave this care to the actors and the teachers of rhetoric who set so much store by our gestures. Let her boldly grant to pain this cowardice in the voice, provided it is neither in the heart nor in the stomach, and let her assign these voluntary complaints to the category of the sighs, sobs, palpitations, and pallors that nature has put out of our control. Provided the heart is without fear, the words without despair, let her be content! What matter if we twist our arms, provided we do not twist our thoughts? Philosophy trains us for ourselves, not for others; for being, not for seeming. ^ALet her confine herself to governing our understanding, which she has taken upon herself to instruct. In the attacks of the stone, let her preserve the soul's capacity for knowing itself, for following its accustomed course, combating the pain and enduring it, not prostrating itself shamefully at its feet; stirred and heated by the combat, not beaten down and overthrown; ^Ccapable of communication and conversation to a certain degree.

^AIn such extreme accidents it is cruelty to require of us so composed a bearing. If we play a good game, it is a small matter that we make a bad face. If the body finds relief in complaining, let it do so. If it likes agitation, let it tumble and toss at its pleasure. If it thinks that the pain evaporates somewhat (as some doctors say that it helps the delivery of women with child) for crying out more

1 The passage that follows, down to "not for seeming," appears only in the final edition, replacing this one:

"As if she were training men for acting in a comedy, or as if it were in her jurisdiction to prevent the movements and alterations which we by nature are forced to accept. Then let her prevent Socrates from blushing for affection or for shame, from blinking his eyes at the threat of a blow, from trembling and sweating in the fits of fever. The painting of poetry, which is free and works as it will, dares not deprive of tears even those persons it wishes to represent as accomplished and perfect:

> So heavy is his woe,
> It makes him bite his hands, and bite his lips,
> And down his cheeks the tears continuous flow.
> ARIOSTO

She should leave this responsibility to those who make a profession of regulating our bearing and expression."

violently, or if that distracts its torment, let it shout right out. ᶜLet us not command this voice to come out, but permit it to. Epicurus not only permits his sage to cry out in his torments but advises him to. *Even pugilists groan when, flourishing the cestus, they strike, because in throwing out the voice the whole body becomes tense, and the blow comes harder* [Cicero]. ᴬWe have enough labor with the pain without laboring over these superfluous rules.

I say this to excuse those whom we see ordinarily crying out and storming in the shocks and attacks of this sickness. As for me, I have passed through it until now with a little better countenance. Not that I give myself trouble, however, to maintain this external decorum; for I take little account of such an advantage. In this respect I lend the pain as much as it likes. But either my pains are not so excessive, or I bring to them more firmness than most people. I complain, I fret when the sharp pains afflict me, but I do not come to the point of letting go of myself, ᶜlike this man:

> With lamentation, wailing, sighs, and groans,
> He echoes back his plaint in grievous tones.
> ATTIUS, QUOTED BY CICERO

I test myself in the thickest of the pain, and have always found that I was capable of speaking, thinking, and answering as sanely as at any other time, but not as steadily, being troubled and distracted by the pain. When I am thought to be the most stricken and those present are sparing me, I often test my powers, and myself broach subjects as remote as possible from my condition. I can do anything by a sudden effort; but don't make it last long.

Oh, why have I not the faculty of that dreamer in Cicero who, dreaming he was embracing a wench, found that he had discharged his stone in the sheets! Mine extraordinarily diswench me.

ᴬIn the intervals of this excessive pain, ᶜwhen my ureters are languid without stinging me so much, ᴬI promptly return to my natural condition, since my soul takes no other alarm than that which comes from the senses and the body; which I certainly owe to the care I have taken to prepare myself by reason for such accidents:

> ᴮNow to me no kind
> Of toil comes new and unexpected. In my mind
> I have forecast them all and gone through them already.
> VIRGIL

[A]I am tested, however, pretty roughly for a beginner, and by a very sudden and very rough change, having fallen all at once from a very gentle and very happy condition of life to the most painful and grievous that can be imagined. For besides its being a disease very much to be feared in itself, it is making its beginnings in me much sharper and harder than is customary. The attacks seize me so often that I hardly feel perfect health any more. Yet I have kept my mind, up to now, in such a state that, provided I can hold fast, I find myself in a considerably better condition of life than a thousand others, who have no fever or illness but what they give themselves by the fault of their reasoning.

There is a certain type of subtle humility that is born of presumption, like this one: that we acknowledge our ignorance in many things, and are so courteous as to admit that there are in the works of nature certain qualities and conditions that are imperceptible to us and whose means and causes our capacity cannot discover. By this honest and conscientious declaration we hope to gain credence also about those things that we claim to understand. We have no need to go picking out miracles and remote difficulties; it seems to me that among the things we see ordinarily there are wonders so incomprehensible that they surpass even miracles in obscurity. What a prodigy it is that the drop of seed from which we are produced bears in itself the impressions not only of the bodily form but of the thoughts and inclinations of our fathers! Where does that drop of fluid lodge this infinite number of forms? [B]And how do they convey these resemblances with so heedless and irregular a course that the great-grandson will correspond to his great-grandfather, the nephew to the uncle?

In the family of Lepidus in Rome there were three, not in a row but at intervals, who were born with the same eye covered with cartilage. At Thebes there was a family that from their mother's womb bore the figure of a lance-head, and whoever did not bear it was considered illegitimate. Aristotle says that in a certain nation where the women were in common they assigned the children to their fathers by resemblance.

[A]It is probable that I owe this stony propensity to my father, for he died extraordinarily afflicted with a large stone he had in his bladder. He did not perceive his disease until his sixty-seventh year, and before that he had had no threat or symptom of it, in his loins, his sides, or elsewhere. And he had lived until then in a happy state of health, and very little subject to diseases; and he lasted seven years

more with this ailment, painfully dragging out the last years of his life. I was born twenty-five years and more before his illness, at a time when he enjoyed his best health, the third of his children in order of birth.

Where was the propensity to this infirmity hatching all this time? And when he was so far from the ailment, how did this slight bit of his substance, with which he made me, bear so great an impression of it for its share? And moreover, how did it remain so concealed that I began to feel it forty-five years later, the only one to this hour out of so many brothers and sisters, and all of the same mother? If anyone will enlighten me about this process, I will believe him about as many other miracles as he wants; provided he does not palm off on me some explanation much more difficult and fantastic than the thing itself.

Let the doctors excuse my liberty a bit, for by this same fatal infusion and insinuation I have received my hatred and contempt for their teachings. The antipathy I have for their art is hereditary with me. My father lived seventy-four years, my grandfather sixty-nine, my great-grandfather nearly eighty, without having tasted any sort of medicine; and as far as they were concerned, whatever was not in ordinary use passed as a drug. Medicine is based on examples and experience; so is my opinion. Isn't that a very clear-cut and very advantageous experience? I wonder if the doctors can find me three men in their records, born, bred, and dying at the same hearth, under the same roof, who lived as long under their rules. They must grant me this: that if not reason, at least fortune is on my side; now with doctors, fortune is much more valuable than reason. Let them not take me now at a disadvantage, let them not threaten me now that I am down; that would be unfair play. Besides, to tell the truth, I have gained enough advantage over them by my family examples, even though they should go no further. Human affairs do not have so much constancy. It is only eighteen years short of two hundred years that this test of ours has lasted, for the first of them was born in the year 1402.[2] It is truly quite normal that this experience should begin to fail us. Let them not reproach me with the infirmities that have me by the throat at this moment. Is it not enough for my part to have lived healthy for forty-seven years? Even if this is the end of my career, it is one of the longer ones.

2 Since this passage was published in 1580 and since 1402 + 200 − 18 = 1584, Montaigne's arithmetic is at fault here.

My ancestors had an aversion to medicine by some occult natural inclination; for the very sight of drugs filled my father with horror. When the seigneur de Gaviac, my paternal uncle, a churchman, sickly from his birth, and who for all that made that frail life last to sixty-seven years, once fell into a great and violent continued fever, it was ordained by the doctors that he should be told that if he would not help himself (they call help what most often is hindrance), he would infallibly be a dead man. The good man, terrified though he was by this horrible sentence, yet replied: "Then I am a dead man." But God soon made this prognosis vain.

[B]The last of the brothers – they were four – the sieur de Bussaguet, and the last by a long time, was the only one to submit to this art, by reason, so I believe, of the dealings he had with the other arts, for he was a counselor in the court of Parlement; and it turned out so badly for him that although he was apparently of a stronger constitution, he died long before the others, except for one, the sieur de Saint-Michel.

[A]It is possible that I received from them this natural antipathy to medicine; but had there been only this consideration, I would have tried to overcome it. For all those predispositions that are born in us without reason are bad; they are a kind of disease that we must combat. It may be that I had this propensity, but I have supported and fortified it by arguments which have confirmed me in my opinion. For I also hate the idea of refusing medicine because of the bitterness of its taste. That would hardly be like me, since I consider health worth purchasing by all the most painful cauteries and incisions that can be made.

[C]And, following Epicurus, it seems to me that sensual pleasures are to be avoided if they bring in their train greater pains, and that pains are to be sought which bring in their train greater pleasures.

[A]Health is a precious thing, and the only one, in truth, which deserves that we employ in its pursuit not only time, sweat, trouble, and worldly goods, but even life; inasmuch as without it life comes to be painful and oppressive to us. Pleasure, wisdom, knowledge, and virtue, without it, grow tarnished and vanish away; and to the strongest and most rigorous arguments that philosophy would impress on us to the contrary, we have only to oppose the picture of Plato being struck with a fit of epilepsy or apoplexy, and on this supposition defy him to call to his aid these noble and rich faculties of his soul. As far as I am concerned, no road that would lead us to health is either arduous or expensive. But I have certain other

notions that make me strangely mistrustful of all this merchandise. I do not say that there cannot be an art of it, that there are not, among so many works of nature, some things suited to the conservation of our health; that is certain.

[B]I quite understand that there is some simple that moistens, some other that dries; I know by experience both that horse-radish produces wind, and that senna leaves loosen the bowels. I know many such empirical facts, as I know that mutton nourishes me and wine warms me; and Solon used to say that eating, like other drugs, was a medicine against the disease of hunger. I do not deny the use we derive from the things of the world, or doubt the power and fertility of nature and its application to our need. I see full well that pikes and swallows are well off with her. I do distrust the inventions of our mind, of our science and art, in favor of which we have abandoned nature and her rules, and in which we know not how to maintain either moderation or bounds.

[C]As we call "justice" the hodgepodge of the first laws that fall into our hands, and their application and practice, often very inept and very iniquitous; and as those who ridicule it and accuse it do not thereby intend to malign that noble virtue, but only to condemn the abuse and profanation of that sacred title; so in medicine I do indeed honor that glorious name, its purpose, its promise, so useful to the human race; but what it designates among us I neither honor nor esteem.

[A]In the first place, experience makes me fear it; for as far as my knowledge goes, I see no group of people so soon sick and so late cured as those who are under the jurisdiction of medicine. Their very health is impaired and corrupted by the constraint of their regimens. The doctors are not content with having control over the sickness; they make health itself sick, in order to prevent people from being able at any time to escape their authority. From a constant and perfect health, do they not derive an argument for a great illness to come? I have been sick often enough; I have, without their help, found my sicknesses as easy to endure (and I have experienced almost every kind) and as short as anyone else's; and still I have not added to them the bitterness of their prescriptions. My health is free and entire, without rule or other discipline than that of my habit and my pleasure. Any place is good for me to stop at, for I need no other conveniences when sick than those I need when healthy. I am not upset at being without a doctor, without an apothecary, and without help; at which I see most people more

afflicted than by the disease. Why, do they themselves show us a happiness and a duration in their lives that bears witness to some evident effect of their craft?

There is no nation that has not been without medicine for many centuries, and those the first centuries, that is to say the best and happiest; and one-tenth of the world does not use it to this day. Countless nations are ignorant of it, where they live both more healthily and longer than we do here; and among us the common people get along happily without it. The Romans existed six hundred years before accepting it; and after trying it out, they drove it out of their city at the instance of Cato the Censor, who showed how easily he could do without it, having lived eighty-five years and kept his wife alive to an extreme old age, not without medicine, but without a doctor – for everything that is found to be salubrious for our life may be called medicine. He kept his family in health, says Plutarch, it seems to me, by eating rabbit; as the Arcadians, says Pliny, cure all illnesses with cow's milk. ^CAnd the Libyans, says Herodotus, universally enjoy uncommonly good health by the custom they have, after their children have reached the age of four, of cauterizing and burning the veins of their head and temples, whereby they block any defluxion of rheum for their whole lives. ^AAnd the village people of this part of the country, in any accident, use nothing but the strongest wine they can, mixed with a lot of saffron and spice, and all this with the same luck.

And to tell the truth, of all this diversity and confusion of prescriptions, what other purpose and effect is there after all than to empty the bowels, which a thousand domestic simples can do?

^BAnd yet I do not know whether this is as useful as they say, and whether our constitution does not, to a certain extent, need the presence of excrements, just as wine needs its lees for its preservation. You often see healthy men having attacks of vomiting or diarrhea from some accidental cause and evacuating vast quantities of excrements without any preceding need or any following benefit, indeed rather with impairment and damage. ^CIt was from the great Plato that I lately learned that of three sorts of movements that are natural to us the last and worst is that of purgations, which no sane man should undertake except in the most extreme necessity. We disturb and arouse a disease by attacking it head on. It is by our mode of life that we should weaken it, by gentle degrees, and bring it to its end. The violent struggles between the drug and the disease

are always at our expense, since the combat is fought out within us and the drug is an untrustworthy assistant, by its nature an enemy to our health, and having access to our constitution only through disturbance.

Let us let things take their course: the scheme of things that takes care of fleas and moles also takes care of men who have the same patience to let themselves be governed as fleas and moles. There is no use in our shouting "Giddap"; that will indeed make us hoarse, but not get us ahead. It is a proud and pitiless scheme. Our fear and our despair disgust it and delay it from coming to our aid, instead of inviting it to; it is obliged to let disease run its course, as well as health. As for letting itself be corrupted in favor of one to the prejudice of the other's rights, it will not do so; it would fall into disorder. Let us follow along, in God's name, let us follow! It leads those who follow; those who do not follow, it drags along, and their rage and their medicine too. Order a purge for your brain; it will be better employed there than on your stomach.

[A]A Lacedaemonian was asked what had made him live healthy so long. "Ignorance of medicine," he replied. And the Emperor Hadrian kept crying out as he was dying that the crowd of doctors had killed him. [B]A bad wrestler turned doctor. "Take heart," Diogenes said to him, "you are right; now you will bring down those who brought you down before."

[A]But they have this luck, [B]according to Nicocles, [A]that the sun shines on their successes, and the earth hides their failures. And besides, they have a very convenient way of making use of all kinds of results; for the good and the health that fortune, nature, or some other extraneous cause (of which the number is infinite) produces in us, it is the privilege of medicine to attribute to itself. All the happy results that happen to the patient who is under its care are due to it. The circumstances that have cured me and that cure a thousand others who do not call the doctors to their aid, they usurp in the case of their patients. And as for the mishaps, either they completely disavow them, by attributing the blame to the patient, for reasons so frivolous that they cannot possibly fail to find always a good enough number of them: he uncovered his arm; [B]he heard the noise of a coach,

> The wagons passing at the bends
> Of the narrow streets;
> JUVENAL

^Asomeone opened his window; he lay down on his left side; or some troublesome thought passed through his head – in short, a word, a dream, a look, seems to them sufficient excuse to put the blame off their own shoulders. Or, if they so please, they actually make use of our getting worse, and do their business by this other means that can never fail them, which is to reward us, when the disease has become hotter by their prescriptions, with the assurance they give us that it would have become even worse without their remedies. The man whom they have cast from a chill into a quotidian fever, without them would have had a continued fever. They need not worry about doing their job badly, since the damage turns to their profit. Truly they are right to require the full confidence of the patient; it must indeed be well-intentioned and very pliable to apply itself to notions so hard to believe.

^BPlato used to say very appropriately that it was for doctors alone to lie in all freedom, since our safety depends on the vanity and falsity of their promises.

^AAesop, an author of very rare excellence, although very few people have discovered his whole charm, is comic when he portrays the tyrannical authority that doctors usurp over these poor souls who are weakened and beaten down by sickness and fear. He tells how a sick man, asked by his doctor what effect he felt from the medicaments he had given him, answered: "I have sweated a lot." "That's good," said the doctor. Another time he asked him again how he had been getting on since then. "I have been very cold," he said, "and shivered a lot." "That's good," said the doctor. The third time he again asked him how he felt. "I feel myself swelling and puffing up," he said, "as if I had the dropsy." "Doing fine," said the doctor. When one of his close friends came afterward to inquire about his condition, he replied: "Truly, my friend, my health is so good that I'm dying."

There was a more just law in Egypt by which the doctor took charge of his patient for the first three days at the risk and peril of the patient, but after those three days at his own. For why, when their patron Aesculapius was struck by lightning for having brought back Helen[3] from death to life –

> ^BThen Jove grew wroth that mortals should return
> To light and living from the nether world,

3 The 1595 edition correctly changes "Helen" to "Hippolytus."

And with his bolt down to the Styx he hurled
The Phoebus-born inventor of such healing art
VIRGIL

— ^Ashould his followers be absolved, who send so many souls from life to death?

^BA doctor was boasting to Nicocles that his art was of great authority. "It certainly is," said Nicocles, "since it can with impunity kill so many people."

^AFor the rest, if I had been of their counsel, I would have made my discipline more sacred and mysterious. They began well enough, but they did not finish so. It was a good beginning to have made gods and demons the authors of their science, to have adopted a language apart, a writing apart, ^Cin spite of what philosophy feels, that it is madness to advise a man for his profit in an unintelligible manner: *As if some doctor should order his patient to take "something earth-born, bloodless, grass-crawling, carrying its house"*[4] [Cicero].

^AIt was a good rule in their art, and one that accompanies all fantastic, vain, and supernatural arts, that the patient's faith should by good hope and assurance anticipate their effective operation. And this rule they maintain to the point that they consider the most ignorant and incompetent doctor more suitable for a man who has faith in him than the most experienced stranger. Even the choice of most of their drugs is in some way mysterious and divine: the left foot of a tortoise, the urine of a lizard, the dung of an elephant, the liver of a mole, blood drawn from under the right wing of a white pigeon; and for us colicky folk (so disdainfully do they take advantage of our misery), pulverized rat turds, and other such monkey tricks that have more the appearance of a magical enchantment than of solid science. I leave aside their pills in uneven numbers, the appointment of certain days and festivals of the year, the distinguishing of certain hours for plucking the herbs of their ingredients, and that surly and solemn twist of their bearing and countenance, which even Pliny derides.

But they have made a mistake, I mean, by not adding to their fine beginning by making their assemblies and consultations more religious and secret. No profane person ought to have had access to them, any more than to the most secret ceremonies of Aesculapius. For the result of this mistake is that when their irresolution, the

4 Presumably a snail.

weakness of their arguments, divinations, and grounds, the bitterness of their contestations, full of hatred, jealousy, and self-consideration, come to be revealed to everyone, a man would have to be preternaturally blind not to feel that he runs a great risk in their hands.

Who ever saw a doctor use the prescription of his colleague without cutting out or adding something? Thereby they clearly enough betray their art and reveal to us that they consider their reputation, and consequently their profit, more than the interest of their patients. That doctor was wiser who prescribed to them of old that one single man should be involved in treating a sick person. For if he does nothing worth while, the reproach to the art of medicine will not be very great through the fault of one single man; and on the contrary, the glory will be great if he happens to hit it right. Whereas when doctors are many, at every turn they discredit the trade, inasmuch as they turn out to do harm more often than good. They should have been content with the perpetual disagreement that is found in the opinions of the principal ancient masters and authors of this science, which is known only to men well-versed in books, without revealing also to the public the controversies and inconsistencies of judgment which they foster and continue among themselves.

Do we want an example of the ancient controversy in medicine? Hierophilus lodges the original cause of diseases in the humors; Erasistratus, in the blood of the arteries; Asclepiades, in the invisible atoms flowing in our pores; Alcmaeon, in the exuberance or deficiency of our bodily powers; Diocles, in the inequality of the elements of the body and in the quality of the air we breathe; Strato, in the abundance, crudity, and corruption of the nourishment we take; Hippocrates lodges it in the spirits.

There is a friend of theirs,[5] whom they know better than I, who exclaims in this connection that the most important science in practice among us, being the one that is in charge of our preservation and health, is unfortunately the most uncertain, the most confused, and agitated by the most changes. There is no great danger in our miscalculating the height of the sun or the fraction of some astronomical computation; but here, where our whole being is at stake, it is not wisdom to abandon ourselves to the mercy and the agitation of so many conflicting winds.

5 Pliny.

Before the Peloponnesian War there was not much news of this science. Hippocrates brought it into repute. Everything he had established, Chrysippus overthrew. Later Erasistratus, grandson of Aristotle, overthrew everything that Chrysippus had written about it. After these came the Empirics, who adopted a wholly different method from the ancients in the handling of this art. When their credit began to age, Hierophilus put into practice another sort of medicine, which Asclepiades arrived to combat and annihilate in his turn. Then in their turn came into authority also the opinions of Themison, and later of Musa, and still later those of Vexius Valens, a doctor famous for his intimacy with Messalina. The empire of medicine fell in Nero's time to Thessalus, who abolished and condemned all that had been accepted until his time. His teaching was knocked down by Crinas of Marseilles, who again brought in the practice of regulating all medicinal operations by the ephemerides and movements of the stars, and eating, sleeping, and drinking at the hour that pleased the moon and Mercury. His authority was soon after supplanted by Charinus, a doctor of that same town of Marseilles. He combated not only the old medicine, but also the popular use of hot baths, customary for so many centuries before. He had people bathe in cold water, even in winter, and plunged sick men into the natural water of streams. Until Pliny's time no Roman had yet deigned to practice medicine; it was handled by foreigners and Greeks, as among us Frenchmen it is handled by Latinizers. For, as a very great doctor says, we do not readily accept the medicine that we understand any more than the drug that we ourselves gather. If the countries from which we get guaiacum, sarsaparilla, and chinaroot have doctors, how much, we may imagine, through this same recommendation of strangeness, rarity, and costliness, must they prize our cabbages and our parsley! For who would dare despise things sought out at such a distance, at the risk of such a long and perilous voyage?

Since those ancient mutations in medicine, there have been countless others down to our time, and for the most part complete and universal mutations, as are those that have been produced in our time by Paracelsus, Fioravanti, and Argenterius. For they change not merely one prescription, but, so they tell me, the whole contexture and order of the body of medicine, accusing of ignorance or deception all who have professed it before them. I leave you to judge where this puts the poor patient.

If we were even assured that when they make a mistake it would not harm us, even though it did not benefit us, it would be a very reasonable bargain to risk acquiring some gain without putting oneself in danger of loss.

[B]Aesop tells this story: that someone who had bought a Moorish slave, thinking that his color had come to him by accident and bad treatment from his former master, had him doctored with great care with many baths and beverages. The outcome was that the Moor did not at all improve his swarthy color, but he wholly lost his former health.

[A]How many times does it happen that we see doctors imputing the death of their patients to one another! I remember a very dangerous and mortal epidemic in the towns in my neighborhood a few years ago. When this storm, which had carried off an infinite number of people, had passed, one of the most famous doctors in the whole region published a pamphlet on the matter, in which he has second thoughts about their having used bloodletting and confesses that that was one of the principal causes of the damage that resulted. Moreover, medical authors hold that there is no medicine that has not something harmful in it; and if even those that serve us injure us somewhat, what must those do that are applied to us altogether inappropriately?

For my part, even if there were nothing else involved, I think that for those who hate the taste of medicine it is a dangerous and prejudicial effort to swallow it at such an inconvenient time and with so much aversion, and I believe it is a terrible trial for the patient at a time when he so much needs rest. Besides, considering the slight and tenuous grounds on which they usually diagnose our sicknesses, I argue that a very small error in the dispensing of their drugs can bring us much harm.

Now if the doctor's error is dangerous, we are in a very bad way, for it is most unlikely that he will not fall into it again often. He needs too many details, considerations, and circumstances to adjust his plan correctly: he must know his patient's constitution, his temperament, his humors, his inclinations, his actions, his very thoughts and fancies. He must be responsible for the external circumstances, the nature of the place, the condition of the air and weather, the position of the planets and their influences. He must know in the disease the causes, the symptoms, the effects, the critical days; in the drug the weight, the power, the country it comes from, the appearance, the age, the way of dispensing it; and

he must know how to proportion all these factors and relate them to one another in order to create a perfect symmetry. Wherein if he makes ever so slight an error, if among so many springs there is even a single one that pulls askew, that is enough to destroy us.

God knows how difficult is the knowledge of most of these details; for how, for example, shall he find the proper symptom of the disease, each disease being capable of an infinite number of symptoms? How many controversies and doubts they have among themselves over the interpretation of urines! Otherwise whence would come this continual altercation that we see among them over the diagnosis of the malady? How should we excuse this mistake into which they fall so often, of taking marten for fox? In the illnesses I have had, however little difficulty there was, I have never found three of them in agreement. I more readily note the examples that concern me.

Recently in Paris a gentleman was cut open by the doctors' orders, in whom they found no more of a stone in his bladder than in his hand. And there too a bishop who was a very good friend of mine had been insistently urged by most of the doctors whom he called into consultation to have himself cut; I myself, on the faith of others, helped to persuade him. When he was dead and was opened up, they found that his only trouble was in the kidneys. They are less excusable in this disease, since it is in some sort palpable. Hence surgery seems to me much more certain, because it sees and feels what it is doing. There is less conjecture and guesswork in it, whereas the doctors have no *speculum matricis* to reveal to them our brain, our lungs, and our liver.

The very promises of medicine are incredible. For, having to provide against different and contrary accidents, which often afflict us at the same time and have an almost necessary relation, like heat in the liver and cold in the stomach, they try to persuade us that of their ingredients this one will warm the stomach, that other one will cool the liver. One has its commission to go straight to the kidneys, indeed even to the bladder, without dispersing its operations elsewhere, and conserving its powers and its virtue in that long road full of disturbances, right to the spot to whose service it is destined by its occult property. Another will dry the brain, still another will moisten the lungs.

Once a potion has been concocted out of all this pile, is it not a sort of daydream to hope that these virtues will separate and sort themselves out of this mixture and confusion to go running on such

different errands? I would be infinitely afraid that they might lose or exchange their tags and get their quarters mixed up. And who could suppose that in this liquid confusion these faculties would not corrupt, confuse, and alter one another? What of the fact that the carrying out of this prescription depends on another practitioner, to whose good faith and mercy we again abandon our lives?

ᶜAs we have doublet makers and breeches makers to clothe us, and are served all the better by them because each one performs only his own specialty and needs a more restricted and limited skill than a tailor who undertakes everything; and as, in the matter of food, the great find it preferable to have separate functions for soup cooks and roasting cooks, which a cook who takes charge of everything cannot perform so exquisitely; so, for curing us, the Egyptians were right to reject the general practice of medicine and to subdivide this profession – to each disease, to each part of the body, its own workman, each being much more competently and less haphazardly treated by one who made it his specialty. Our physicians do not realize that he who takes care of everything takes care of nothing; that the policing of this microcosm in its entirety is more than they can digest. In their fear of arresting the course of a dysentery lest they produce a fever in the patient, they killed a friend[6] of mine who was worth more than the whole lot of them. They put their guesses in the scales against the present evils, and, so as not to cure the brain at the expense of the stomach, they injure the stomach and make the brain worse by their disorderly and dissentious drugs.

ᴬAs for contradictory and unsound reasoning, it is more apparent in this art than in any other. Aperients are useful for a man with the stone because by opening and dilating the passages, they move along that sticky matter of which the gravel and the stone are built and convey downward what is beginning to harden and accumulate in the kidneys. Aperients are dangerous for a man with the stone because by opening and dilating the passages, they move the matter of which the gravel is built along toward the kidneys, which, being apt to seize it by a natural propensity, will hardly fail to stop much of what has been carried to them. Moreover, if by chance there comes along some body a little too large to go through all those narrow passages that remain to be traversed in order to discharge it outside, this body, being set in motion by these aperients and cast into these

6 La Boétie.

narrow channels, will stop them up and bring on a certain and very painful death.

The same sort of solidity marks the advice they give us about our health habits. It is good to pass water often, for we see by experience that by letting it stagnate we give it an opportunity to discharge its excrements and lees, which will serve as matter to form the stone in the bladder. It is good not to pass water often, for the heavy excrements it draws along with it will not be carried away unless there is violence, as we see by experience that a stiffly rushing torrent sweeps the place through which it passes much cleaner than does the course of a gentle and sluggish stream. Likewise it is good to have frequent intercourse with women, for that opens the passages and moves the gravel and sand. Indeed it is also bad, for it heats the kidneys, tires them, and weakens them.[7]

7 Except for one B sentence, the next eight paragraphs, through "that is seen everywhere else in this art" (p. 717), are an addition of 1582 that replaces the following passage in the 1580 edition:

"In short, they have no argument that is not susceptible to such contradictions. As for their judgment concerning the operation of drugs, it is just as uncertain, or more so. I have twice been to drink the hot springs of our mountains, and I fell into line on that because it is a natural, simple, and unmixed potion, which at least is not dangerous, even if it is useless. And by chance it turned out to be in no way hostile to my taste (it is true that I take it according to my rules, not those of the doctors). Besides, the pleasure of the visits I have along the way with several relatives and friends, of the group of people who go there, and of the beautiful location, attracts me. These waters perform no miracle, no doubt, and I do not believe all the strange effects that are reported of them; for while I was there, many such rumors were spread which I discovered to be false on investigating them rather carefully. But people easily fool themselves about what they desire.

"You cannot take this away from them either, that these waters arouse the appetite, facilitate digestion, and lend us some new blitheness, if we do not go there completely beaten down in strength. But I have never been there or planned to go there except healthy and with pleasure.

"Now as for what I say about the difficulty involved in judging their effect, here is an example. I was first at Aigues-Caudes; from its waters I felt no effect, no apparent purgation; but after coming back I was a whole year without any twinge of the colic, on account of which I had gone there. Later I went to Bagnères; these made me evacuate a lot of sand and kept my bowels very loose for a long time after. But they preserved my health only two months; for after that I was very badly treated by my malady. I would ask, on the basis of this evidence, which ones my doctor thinks I should trust the most, having these various arguments and circumstances on either side.

It is good to bathe in the hot spring waters, since that relaxes and softens the places where the sand and stone settle; it is also bad, since this application of external heat helps the kidneys to cook, harden, and petrify the matter that is deposited there. For those who are at the baths it is more salubrious to eat little in the evening, so that the waters they are to drink the next morning may have more effect, finding the stomach empty and unobstructed; contrariwise, it is better to eat little at dinner[8] so as not to disturb the operation of the water, which is not yet completed, and not to burden the stomach so soon after this other work, and so as to leave the function of digesting to the night, which can do it better than the day, when body and mind are in perpetual motion and action.

That is how they go juggling and trifling at our expense in all their reasonings. [B]And they could not provide me with one proposition to which I could not construct a contrary one of equal force.

[A]So let people no longer cry out at those who, in this confusion, let themselves be gently led by their appetite and the advice of nature, and commit themselves to the common lot.

I have seen in the course of my travels almost all the famous baths of Christendom, and for a few years now have begun to make use of them; for in general I consider bathing healthful and believe that we incur no slight disadvantages to our health for having lost this custom, which was in times past generally observed in almost all nations and still is in many, of washing our body every day. And I cannot imagine that we are not much the worse for thus keeping our limbs encrusted and our pores stopped up with dirt.

And as for drinking the waters, first of all fortune has made this not at all hostile to my taste; second, it is natural and simple, and at least is not dangerous, even if it is useless. I take as warrant for this the infinite number of people of all sorts and constitutions who

"So let people no longer cry out at those who, in this uncertainty, let themselves be governed by their appetite and the simple advice of nature. Thus when they advise us one thing rather than another, when they prescribe aperients like hot spring waters, or when they forbid them, they do so with equal uncertainty, and doubtless commit to the mercy of fortune the result of their advice, since it is not in their power or that of their art to answer for the size of the sandy bodies that are being hatched in our kidneys, when a very slight difference in their size can produce opposite conclusions as to the effect on our health. By this example we may judge of the form of their reasonings. But to press them more sharply would require a man less ignorant of their art than I am."

8 The midday meal.

assemble there. And although I have perceived no extraordinary and miraculous effect there, but rather, on investigating a little more carefully than is usual, I have found false and ill-founded all the rumors of such effects that are spread in those places and believed (since people easily fool themselves about what they desire), yet at the same time I have hardly seen any people whom these waters made worse, and it cannot without malice be denied that they arouse the appetite, facilitate digestion, and lend us some new blitheness, if we do not go there too beaten down in strength, which I advise against doing. They are not able to restore a ponderous ruin; they can prop up a slight leaning or provide against the threat of some deterioration.

Anyone who does not bring to them enough cheerfulness to be able to enjoy the pleasure of the company that is found there, and the walks and exercises to which the beauty of the places where these baths are usually located invites us, will doubtless lose the best and surest part of their effect. For this reason I have up to now chosen to stay in and make use of those which are most pleasantly situated and which offer the most advantages in lodging, food, and company. Such are in France the baths of Bagnères; on the frontier of Germany and Lorraine, those of Plombières; in Switzerland, those of Baden; in Tuscany, those of Lucca, especially those of La Villa, which I have used most often and at different seasons.

Each nation has its own opinions concerning the use of waters, and wholly different rules and methods of taking advantage of them, although in my experience their effect practically never varies. Drinking them is not at all accepted in Germany; for all illnesses, they bathe and stay in the water like frogs almost from sun to sun. In Italy, when they drink nine days, they bathe at least thirty, and usually drink the water mixed with other drugs to assist its operation. Here they order us to walk to digest it; there they keep people in bed, where they have drunk the water, until they have voided it, continually warming their stomach and feet. As it is peculiar to most Germans to let themselves be cupped and bled by scarification in the bath, so the Italians have their *doccie*, which are certain trickles of this hot water that they lead through pipes, and for an hour in the morning and as much after dinner, for a month, they bathe the head, or the stomach, or any other part of the body that they are treating.

There are infinite other differences of customs between countries, or, to put it better, there is almost no resemblance between one country's customs and another's. Thus you see how

this part of medicine, to which alone I have abandoned myself, although it is the least artificial, still has its good share of the confusion and uncertainty that is seen everywhere else in this art.

The poets say everything they want with more emphasis and grace, witness these two epigrams:

Yesterday Alcon touched the statue of great Jove.
Though marble, soon to Jove the doctor's power was known.
Today out of his ancient shrine he has to move.
He's carried to his grave, although a god, and stone.

AUSONIUS

And the other:

Last night he bathed and dined and laughed with us;
Today we learn Andragoras is dead.
How came his sudden end, you wonder? Thus:
He dreamed his doctor sat beside his bed.

MARTIAL

In this connection I want to tell two stories.

The baron de Caupène in Chalosse and I hold in common the right of patronage to a benefice of great extent, at the foot of our mountains, called Lahontan. It is with the inhabitants of this region as it is said to be with those of the valley of Angrougne. They lived a life apart, with their own fashions, dress, and habits, ruled and governed by certain particular systems and customs, handed down from father to son, to which they bound themselves with no other constraint than that of reverence for their practice. This little state had continued from all antiquity in so happy a condition that no neighboring judge had been put to the trouble of inquiring into their doings, no lawyer retained to give them counsel, no foreigner ever called in to settle their quarrels; and no one of this district had ever been seen begging. They avoided marriages and dealings with the outer world, so as not to corrupt the purity of their government, until, so they tell, one of them, within the memory of their fathers, whose soul was spurred by noble ambition, took it into his head, in order to bring his name into credit and reputation, to make one of his sons Maître Pierre,[9] and having sent him to some neighboring town to learn how to write, finally made him into a fine village notary. This son, having become important, began to disdain

9 Lawyers in France are called *Maître* (Master).

their ancient customs and to put into their heads the notion of the
pomp of the regions on this side of the mountains. The first of his
cronies whose goat had a horn broken off he advised to demand
justice from the royal judges near by; and he went on from this one
to another until he had debased the whole place.

On the heels of this corruption, they say another of worse
consequence followed immediately, the work of a doctor who had
the notion of marrying one of their daughters and settling among
them. He first began to teach them the names of fevers, colds, and
abscesses, the situation of the heart, liver, and intestines, a science
until then very remote from their knowledge; and instead of the
garlic with which they had learned to drive out every sort of disease,
however violent and extreme, he accustomed them, for a cough or
a cold, to take strange mixtures, and began to make a traffic not only
of their health but also of their death. They swear that only since
then have they noticed that the night air made them heavy-headed,
that drinking when they were heated was harmful, and that autumn
winds were more unhealthy than those of spring; that since they
have used medicine they find themselves overwhelmed with a legion
of unaccustomed illnesses; and that they perceive a general decline
in their former vigor, and their lives cut short by half. That is the
first of my stories.

The other is that before the time of my gravelly subjection,
hearing many make much of billy-goat's blood as of a celestial
manna sent us in these latter ages for the protection and preserva-
tion of human life, and hearing it spoken of by men of under-
standing as an admirable and infallibly effective drug, I, who have
always thought myself a target for all the accidents that can strike
any other man, was pleased, in perfect health, to provide myself with
this miracle, and ordered that a billy-goat be fed on my place
according to the recipe; for he must be put aside during the hottest
months of summer and given only laxative herbs to eat and white
wine to drink.

I happened to come home on the day he was to be killed. They
came and told me that my cook had found in his paunch two or three
big balls that rattled against one another amid what he had eaten.
I was curious to have all his entrails brought into my presence, and
had that large, thick skin opened up. Out came three big lumps,
light as sponges, so that they appeared to be hollow, moreover hard
and firm on the outside, and spotted with several dull colors; one
perfectly round, of the size of an ordinary ball, the other two a little

smaller, imperfect in roundness but seeming to be progressing toward it. Upon having inquiries made of those who were accustomed to open up these animals, I found that this was a rare and unusual occurrence.

It is likely that these stones are cousins to our own; and if so, it is a very vain hope for people with the stone to derive their cure from the blood of an animal on its way to dying of a similar disease. For as for saying that the blood is not affected by this contagion and that its accustomed virtue is not impaired, it is rather to be believed that nothing is engendered in a body except by the connivance and communication of all the parts. The whole mass works together, although one part contributes more than the other according to the diversity of operations. Wherefore there is great likelihood that in every part of this goat there was some petrifying quality.

I was curious about this experiment, not so much for fear of the future and for myself, as because it happens that in my home, as in many others, the women accumulate such small drugs to aid the people, using the same recipe for fifty illnesses, and such a recipe as they will not take for themselves, and yet they are triumphant when things turn out well.

For the rest, I honor doctors, not, according to the precept,[10] out of necessity – for to this passage they oppose another of the prophet reproving King Asa for having had recourse to a doctor – but for love of themselves, having known many honest and lovable men among them. My quarrel is not with them but with their art, and I do not greatly blame them for making their profit of our stupidity, for most people do so. Many occupations, both less and more worthy than theirs, have no other foundation and support than in the folly of the public. I call them into my company when I am sick if they happen to be at hand, and I expect to be entertained by them, and I pay them as others do. I give them authority to order me to cover up warmly, if I like it better that way than another way; between leeks and lettuce they can choose what they want my broth to be made of, and prescribe for me either white wine or claret; and so with all other things that are indifferent to my appetite and habit.

10 *Honora medicum propter necessitatem* (Ecclesiasticus 38:1), which the Authorized Version renders: "Honour a physician with the honour due unto him for the uses which ye may have of him ..."

I quite understand that this is doing nothing for them, since bitterness and strangeness are qualities of the very essence of medicine. Lycurgus ordered wine for the sick Spartans. Why? Because healthy, they hated the use of it; just as a gentleman, a neighbor of mine, uses it as a very salutary drug for his fevers, because naturally he mortally hates the taste of it.

How many doctors we see who are of my disposition, disdaining medicine for their own use and adopting a liberal diet quite contrary to the one they prescribe for others! What is that if not quite shamelessly exploiting our simplicity? For they hold their own life and health no less dear than we do, and would accommodate their practice to their preaching if they themselves did not know its falsity.

It is the fear of death and pain, impatience of sickness, a frenzied and undiscerning thirst for a cure, that blinds us so; it is pure cowardice that makes our belief so soft and pliable. ᶜAnd yet most people do not so much believe as acquiesce. For I hear them complain and talk about it as we do, but in the end they decide: "What am I to do, then?" As if impatience were in itself a better remedy than patience. ᴬIs there any one among those who have abandoned themselves to this miserable subjection who does not surrender equally to every sort of imposture, who does not put himself at the mercy of whoever has the impudence to promise him his cure?

ᶜThe Babylonians carried their sick onto the public square. The doctor was the people; each passer-by, out of humanity and civility, was obliged to inquire into their condition and give them some salutary advice, according to his experience. We do hardly any differently. ᴬThere is not the simplest little woman whose mumblings and magic formulas we do not employ; and for my taste, if I had to take any, I would accept this medicine more willingly than any other, inasmuch as at least there is no harm to be feared from it.

ᶜWhat Homer and Plato said of the Egyptians, that they were all doctors, should be said of all peoples. There is no one who does not boast of some recipe and try it out on his neighbor if he will take his word for it.

ᴬThe other day I was in a company where some one or other of my fellow sufferers brought news of a kind of pill made up of a hundred-odd carefully counted ingredients. There was great rejoicing and singular consolation; for what rock could withstand

the impact from so numerous a battery? However, I understand from those who tried it that not the slightest particle of gravel deigned to be stirred by it.

I cannot tear myself away from this paper without saying this one word more about their giving us their experience as a warrant of the infallibility of their drugs. The greatest part, and, I believe, more than two-thirds of the medicinal virtues, consists in the quintessence or occult property of simples, concerning which we can have no other instruction than use; for quintessence is nothing else than a quality of which we cannot by our reason find out the cause. Among such proofs, I am content to accept those that they say they acquired by the inspiration of some daemon (for as for miracles, I never touch upon them); and also the proofs that are drawn from things that often fall into our use for some other consideration – for example, if in the wool which we are accustomed to wear there is found by accident some occult desiccative property that cures chilblains on our heels, or if in the radish that we eat for food there is found some aperient action. Galen reports that a leper happened to receive a cure by means of the wine he drank, since by chance a viper had slipped into the vessel. We find in this example the means and a likely method for this sort of experiment, as also in those to which the doctors say they were led by the example of certain animals. But in most of the other experiments to which they say they were led by fortune and had no other guide but chance, I find the progress of their investigation impossible to believe.

I imagine a man looking around him at the infinite number of things: plants, animals, metals.[11] I do not know where to have him begin his experiment; and even if his fancy lights first upon an elk's horn, which requires a very pliant and easy faith, he still finds himself just as perplexed about the next thing to do. He is faced with so many maladies and so many circumstances that before he has attained certainty about the point that the successful completion of his experiment should reach, human wit is wasting its ingenuity. And for him to find, among that infinite number of things, that the right one is this horn; among this infinite number of diseases, epilepsy; among so many constitutions, the melancholic; so many seasons, in winter; so many nations, the French; so many times of life, old age; so many celestial mutations, at the conjunction of

11 Montaigne is here setting up an imaginary case of a patient (an elderly Frenchmen of a melancholy temperament) looking for a cure for epilepsy.

Venus and Saturn; so many parts of the body, the finger – since he is guided in all this neither by theory, nor by conjecture, nor by example, nor by divine inspiration, but by the sole movement of fortune – he would have to be guided by a perfectly workmanlike, regular, and methodical fortune. And then, even if the cure should be performed, how can he be sure that this was not because the illness had reached its term, or a result of chance, or the effect of something else he had eaten or drunk or touched that day, or the merit of his grandmother's prayers? Moreover, even if this proof had been perfect, how many times was the experiment repeated? How many times was that long string of chances and coincidences strung again for a rule to be derived from it?

ᴮWhen the rule is derived, then by whom? Out of so many millions there are only three men who have undertaken to record their experiences. Will chance have lighted precisely on one of these? What if another man, and a hundred others, have had contrary experiences? Perhaps we would see some light if all the judgments and reasonings of men were known to us. But that three witnesses, and they three physicians, should lay down the law to mankind is not reasonable, unless human nature had deputed and chosen them and declared them to be our arbiters ᶜby express power of attorney.

ᴬTO MADAME DE DURAS¹²

Madame, you found me at this point when you recently came to see me. Because it may be that these absurdities will someday come into your hands, I want them also to bear witness that the author feels himself greatly honored by the favor that you will be doing them. You will recognize in them the same bearing and the same air that you have seen in his conversation. Even if I had been able to adopt some other style than my own ordinary one and some other better and more honorable form, I would not have done it; for I want to derive nothing from these writings except that they represent me to your memory as I naturally am. These same traits and faculties that you have been familiar with and have favored, Madame, with much more honor and courtesy than they deserve, I want to lodge (but without alteration or change) in a solid body that may last a few

12 Marguerite d'Aure de Gramont, widow of Jean de Durfort, seigneur de Duras; one of the favorite ladies in waiting to the queen, Margaret of Valois, and an accomplice in many of her escapades.

years, or a few days, after me, in which you will find them when you are pleased to refresh your memory of them, without otherwise taking the trouble to remember them, as indeed they are not worth it. I wish you may continue the favor of your friendship to me for the same qualities that produced it. I do not at all seek to be better loved and esteemed dead than alive.

^BRidiculous and yet common is the disposition of Tiberius, who was more concerned about extending his renown into the future than about making himself estimable and agreeable to the men of his own time. ^CIf I were one of those to whom the world may owe praise, I would ask for payment in advance and hold it quits. Let the praise make haste and pile up all around me, concentrated and massive rather than extended and durable, and let it vanish abruptly together with my consciousness of it, when its sweet sound will reach my ears no longer.

^AIt would be a stupid fancy, at this moment when I am ready to abandon dealings with men, to go and introduce myself to them by some new recommendation. I make no account of the goods that I have been unable to employ in the service of my life. Whatever I may be, I want to be elsewhere than on paper. My art and my industry have been employed in making myself good for something; my studies, in teaching me to do, not to write. I have put all my efforts into forming my life. That is my trade and my work. I am less a maker of books than of anything else. The capacity I have wished for was to serve my present and essential advantages, not to lay up a stock and reserve for my heirs.

^CIf a man has any good in him, let him show it in his conduct, in his ordinary talk, in the way he loves or quarrels, at play, in bed, at table, in the conduct of his affairs and the management of his household. Those whom I see composing good books in poor breeches should have tended to their breeches first, if they had asked me. Ask a Spartan if he would rather be a good rhetorician than a good soldier. As for me, I'd rather be a good cook, if I didn't have one to serve me.

^AGood Lord, Madame, how I would hate this sort of reputation, of being an able man in writing and a good-for-nothing and a fool elsewhere. I would even rather be a fool in all respects than have chosen so badly where to employ my ability. Consequently I am so far from expecting to do myself some new honor by these stupidities that I shall do well if I do not lose any of what little I have acquired. For this dead and mute portrait, besides what it takes away from my

natural being, does not represent me in my best state, but fallen far from my early vigor and cheerfulness, and beginning to grow withered and rancid. I am at the bottom of the barrel, which begins to taste of the lees.

Moreover, Madame, I would not have dared to stir up the mysteries of medicine so boldly, considering the credence that you and so many others give it, if I had not been led to it by its very own authors. I think they can claim only two of the ancient Latins, Pliny and Celsus. If you look at them some day, you will find that they speak far more roughly to their art than I do. I only pinch it, they slaughter it. Pliny, among other things, makes fun of the fact that when they are at the end of their rope, they have thought up the fine escape of sending the patients whom they have agitated and tormented for nothing with their drugs and diets, some to get help from vows and miracles, the others to the hot baths. (Don't be angry, Madame, he is not speaking of the baths on our side of the frontier which are under the protection of your house and all filled with the name of Gramont.) They have a third escape for getting rid of us and shaking off the reproaches that we may make to them for the small improvement in our ills, which they have had so long under their care that they have no device left to put us off with: that is to send us abroad for a change of air.

Madame, that is enough. Surely you give me leave to resume the thread of my argument, from which I had turned aside to talk with you.

It was Pericles, it seems to me, who, being asked how he was, said "You may judge by this," showing the amulets he wore attached to his neck and arm. He meant to imply that he was very sick, since he had come to the point of having recourse to such vain things and letting himself be equipped that way. I do not say that I may not be carried away someday by that ridiculous notion of committing my life and my health to the mercy and government of the doctors. I may fall into such a madness; I cannot answer for my future firmness. But then, too, if someone inquires of me how I am, I can say to him, like Pericles, "You may judge by this," showing my hand filled with six drams of opiate. It will be a very evident sign of a violent sickness. My judgment will be extraordinarily unhinged. If impatience and fear win this victory over me, people may infer from it a very fierce fever in my soul.

I have taken the trouble to plead this cause, which I understand rather poorly, to support a little and strengthen the natural aversion

to drugs and to the practice of our medicine which I have derived from my ancestors, so that it should not be merely a stupid and thoughtless inclination and should have a little more form; and also so that those who see me so firm against the exhortations and menaces that are made to me when my sickness afflicts me may not think that I am acting out of plain stubbornness; or in case there should be anyone so unpleasant as to judge that I am spurred by vainglory. That would be a well-aimed ambition, to want to derive honor from conduct that I have in common with my gardener and my muleteer! Surely my heart is not so inflated or windy that I would choose to exchange a solid, meaty, and marrowy pleasure like health for an imaginary, immaterial, and airy pleasure. Glory, even that of the four sons of Aymon,[13] is bought too dear by a man of my humor if it costs him three good attacks of colic. Health, in God's name!

Those who love our medicine may also have their own good, great, and strong considerations. I do not at all hate opinions contrary to mine. I am so far from being vexed to see discord between my judgments and others', and from making myself incompatible with the society of men because they are of a different sentiment and party from mine, that on the contrary, since variety is the most general fashion that nature has followed, ^cand more in minds than bodies, inasmuch as minds are of a substance suppler and susceptible of more forms, ^AI find it much rarer to see our humors and plans agree. And there were never in the world two opinions alike, any more than two hairs or two grains. Their most universal quality is diversity.

END OF BOOK TWO

13 The four sons of Aymon are the heroes of *Renaud de Montauban*, a twelfth-century *chanson de geste* named for one of the four.

BOOK THREE

Of the useful and the honorable

[B]No one is exempt from saying silly things. The misfortune is to say them with earnest effort.

Indeed this man will take great pains to say great trifles.

TERENCE

That does not concern me. Mine escape me as nonchalantly as they deserve. All the better for them. I would part with them promptly for the little they are worth. And I neither buy nor sell them except for what they weigh. I speak to my paper as I speak to the first man I meet. That this is true, here is proof.

To whom should perfidy not be detestable, since Tiberius refused it at such a sacrifice? They sent him word from Germany that if he saw fit they would rid him of Arminius by poison. He was the most powerful enemy the Romans had; he had treated them villainously under Varus, and was alone preventing them from extending their dominion over those countries. Tiberius made answer that the Roman people were accustomed to take vengeance on their enemies by open means, arms in hand, not by fraud and surreptitiously. He gave up the useful for the honorable.

He was, you will tell me, an impostor. I believe it; it is no great miracle in people of his profession. But the acknowledgment of virtue carries no less weight in the mouth of the man who hates it, inasmuch as truth wrests it from him by force, and if he will not receive it within, at least he covers himself with it as an ornament.

Our structure, both public and private, is full of imperfection. But there is nothing useless in nature, not even uselessness itself. Nothing has made its way into this universe that does not hold a proper place in it. Our being is cemented with sickly qualities: ambition, jealousy, envy, vengeance, superstition, despair, dwell in us with a possession so natural that we recognize their image also in the beasts – indeed even cruelty, so unnatural a vice. For in the midst of compassion we feel within us I know not what bittersweet pricking of malicious pleasure in seeing others suffer; even children feel it:

726

'Tis sweet, when the sea is high and winds are driving,
To watch from shore another's anguished striving.
 LUCRETIUS

Whoever should remove the seeds of these qualities from man
would destroy the fundamental conditions of our life. Likewise in
every government there are necessary offices which are not only
abject but also vicious. Vices find their place in it and are employed
for sewing our society together, as are poisons for the preservation of
our health. If they become excusable, inasmuch as we need them
and the common necessity effaces their true quality, we still must let
this part be played by the more vigorous and less fearful citizens,
who sacrifice their honor and their conscience, as those ancients
sacrificed their life, for the good of their country. We who are
weaker, let us take parts that are both easier and less hazardous.
The public welfare requires that a man betray and lie ^cand massacre;
^Blet us resign this commission to more obedient and suppler people.

Truly I have often been angry to see judges, by fraud and by false
hopes of favor or pardon, lure a criminal to confess his act, using
trickery and shamelessness in it. It would serve justice well, and
Plato himself, who favors this practice, to furnish me with other
means more suited to me. That is a malicious justice; and I consider
it no less harmed by itself than by others. I replied not long ago that
I would hardly betray the prince for a private person, since I would
be very unhappy to betray any private person for the prince. And not
only do I hate to deceive, but I hate to see anyone deceived in me.
I do not even want to furnish matter or occasion for deceiving.

In what little negotiating I have had to do between our princes,
in these divisions and subdivisions that tear our nation apart today,
I have studiously avoided letting them be mistaken about me and
deceived by my outward appearance. Professional negotiators make
every effort within their power to conceal their thoughts and to
feign a moderate and conciliatory attitude. As for me, I reveal myself
by my most vigorous opinions, presented in my most personal
manner – a tender and green negotiator, who would rather fail in
my mission than fail to be true to myself. However, up to this time it
has been with such good luck (for certainly fortune has the principal
share in it) that few men have passed between one party and another
with less suspicion and more favor and privacy.

I have an open way that easily insinuates itself and gains credit on
first acquaintance. Pure naturalness and truth, in whatever age, still

find their time and their place. And then few suspect or find odious the liberty of men who work without any self-interest, men who can truly use the answer of Hyperides to the Athenians when they complained of his harsh way of speaking: "Gentlemen, do not consider whether I speak freely, but whether I do so without accepting anything and thereby serving my private interests." My freedom has also easily freed me from any suspicion of dissimulation by its vigor – since I do not refrain from saying anything, however grave or burning, I could not have said worse behind their backs – and by its obvious simplicity and impartiality. I aspire to no other fruit in acting than to act, and do not attach to it long consequences and purposes. Each action plays its game individually: let it strike home if it can.

Moreover, I am not pressed by any passion either of hate or of love toward the great, nor is my will bound by personal injury or obligation. ᶜI look upon our kings simply with a loyal and civic affection, which is neither moved nor removed by private interest. For this I congratulate myself. ᴮI am attached to the general and just cause only with moderation and without feverishness. I am not subject to these penetrating, intimate mortgages and commitments. Anger and hatred are beyond the duty of justice, and are passions serving only those who do not hold to their duty enough by reason alone. All legitimate and equitable intentions are of themselves equable and temperate; otherwise they degenerate into the seditious and illegitimate. This is what makes me walk everywhere head high, face and heart open.

In truth, and I am not afraid to confess it, I would easily carry, in case of need, one candle to Saint Michael and one to the dragon, according to the old woman's plan.[1] I will follow the good side right to the fire, but not into it if I can help it.[2] Let Montaigne be engulfed in the public ruin, if need be; but if not, I shall be grateful to fortune if it is saved; and as much rope as my duty gives me, I use for its preservation. Was it not Atticus who, holding to the just side and the losing side, escaped by his moderation in that universal shipwreck of the world amid so many revolutions and divisions?

1 This story is found earlier in Calvin and later in Aubigné.
2 Rabelais gave great popularity to this phrase, "jusqu'au feu exclusivement," which he used several times. The "Montaigne" in the next sentence is the château.

For private men like him it is easier; and in this sort of task I think one may be justified in lacking the ambition to put oneself forward without being asked. To keep oneself wavering and half-and-half, to keep one's allegiance motionless and without inclination in one's country's troubles and in civil dissensions, I consider neither handsome nor honorable. ^c*That is not a middle way, but no way at all, like that of people awaiting the event so as to adapt their plans to fortune* [Livy].

That may be permitted in regard to the affairs of our neighbors. And Gelo, tyrant of Syracuse, thus suspended his inclination in the wars of the barbarians against the Greeks, keeping an ambassador at Delphi with presents to be on the lookout to see which way fortune would fall and to take the right moment to win over the victor. It would be a sort of treason to do this in our own domestic affairs, in which ^Bone must ^cnecessarily ^Btake sides by deliberate plan. But not to involve oneself, for a man who has neither responsibility nor express command that presses him, I find that more excusable (and nevertheless I am not using this excuse for myself) than to keep out of foreign wars, even though, according to our laws, no one need be involved in them who does not want to be. Nevertheless, even those who espouse a cause completely can do so with such order and moderation that the storm will be bound to pass over their heads without harm. Did we not have reason to hope for this in the case of the late bishop of Orléans, the sieur de Morvilliers? And I know some, among those who are fighting valiantly at this moment, whose conduct is either so equable or so mild that they are likely to remain on their feet, whatever harmful dislocation and fall heaven may be preparing for us.

I hold that it properly belongs to kings to quarrel with kings, and I laugh at these souls who wantonly expose themselves to such disproportionate conflicts. For a man is not picking a private quarrel with a prince in marching against him openly and courageously for the sake of his honor and according to his duty. If he does not love such a person, he does better, he esteems him. And notably the cause of the laws and the defense of the old-time order always has this in its favor, that even those who are troubling it for their private purposes excuse its defenders, if they do not honor them.

But we must not call "duty," as we do every day, an inner bitterness and asperity that is born of private interest and passion; nor "courage," a treacherous and malicious conduct. Their propensity to malignity and violence they call zeal. It is not the cause that inflames

them, it is their self-interest. They kindle war not because it is just, but because it is war.

Nothing keeps us from getting along comfortably and in good faith between two hostile parties. Conduct yourself in this case with an affection, if not equal (for it may allow of different measures), at least temperate, and which will not engage you so much to either one that he can demand everything of you. And also content yourself with a modest measure of their favor, and with swimming in troubled waters, without wanting to fish in them.

The other way, of offering yourself with all your power to one side and to the other, bears even less resemblance to prudence than to conscience. The man to whom you betray another by whom you are equally well received, does he not know that you will do the same to him in turn? He considers you a wicked man; meanwhile he listens to you, pumps you, and makes his profit of your disloyalty; for double-dealing men are useful in what they bring, but we must take care that they carry away as little as possible.

I say nothing to one that I cannot say to the other, at his own time, with only the accent a little changed; and I report only the things that are indifferent or known, or which serve both in common. There is no reason of utility for which I would permit myself to lie to them. What has been entrusted to my silence, I conceal religiously; but I take as little to conceal as I can. They are a troublesome charge, the secrets of princes, to one who has no use for them. I like to offer this bargain: that they trust little to me, but boldly trust what I bring them. I have always known more about these matters than I wanted.

ᶜAn open way of speaking opens up another man's speech and draws it out, as do wine and love.

ᴮTo King Lysimachus, who asked him "What do you want me to pass on to you of my possessions?" Philippides wisely answered, "What you will, provided it is none of your secrets." I notice that people bridle if they are kept in the dark about the nature of the business on which they are employed, or if some ulterior intent is concealed from them. As for me, I am glad not to be told any more than they want me to put into practice, and I do not want my knowledge to exceed and constrain my words. If I am to serve as an instrument of deceit, at least let it be with a clear conscience. I do not want to be considered either so affectionate or so loyal a servant as to be found fit to betray anyone. He who is unfaithful to himself is excusably so to his master.

But these are princes who do not accept men halfway and scorn limited and conditional services. There is no remedy. I frankly tell them my limits. For a slave I must be only to reason, and even that I can scarcely manage. ^cAnd they too are wrong to demand of a free man the same subjection and obligation to their service as they demand of a man whom they have made and bought, or whose fortune is particularly and expressly attached to theirs. ^BThe laws have freed me from great anxiety; they have chosen me my party and given me a master. Any other superiority and obligation must be relative to that one, and restricted. Yet this is not to say that if my affection bore me in another direction, I would put my hand to it at once. Will and desires are a law unto themselves; actions must receive their law from public regulation.

This whole procedure of mine is just a bit dissonant from our ways. It would not be fit to produce great results or to endure. Innocence itself could neither negotiate among us without dissimulation nor bargain without lying. And so public occupations are by no means my quarry; what my profession requires, I perform in the most private manner that I can. As a boy I was plunged into them up to the ears, and it worked; yet I disengaged myself in good time. Since then I have often avoided becoming involved in them, rarely accepted them, never asked for them, keeping my back turned on ambition; but, if not like rowers who thus advance backward, yet in such a way that I am less obliged to my resolution than to my good fortune for not having embarked in them. For there are ways less hostile to my taste and more suited to my capacity, by which, if fortune had formerly called me to public service and to my advancement toward worldly prestige, I know I would have passed over the arguments of my reason to follow it.

Those who commonly contradict what I profess, saying that what I call frankness, simplicity, and naturalness in my conduct is art and subtlety, and rather prudence than goodness, artifice than nature, good sense than good luck, do me more honor than they take away from me. But surely they make my subtlety too subtle. And if anyone follows and watches me closely, I will concede him the victory if he does not confess that there is no rule in their school that could reproduce this natural movement and maintain a picture of liberty and license so constant and inflexible on such tortuous and varied paths, and that all their attention and ingenuity could not bring them to it.

The way of truth is one and simple; that of private profit and the advantage of one's personal business is double, uneven, and random. I have often seen this counterfeit and artificial liberty in practice, but most often without success. It is apt to smack of Aesop's ass, who, in emulation of the dog, came and threw himself gaily with both feet on his master's shoulders; but for all the petting that the dog received for the same show of affection, the poor ass received twice as many cudgelings. *What most becomes a man is what is most a part of him* [Cicero]. *I do not want to deprive deceit of its proper place; that would be misunderstanding the world. I know that it has often served profitably and that it maintains and feeds most of men's occupations. There are lawful vices, as there are many either good or excusable actions that are unlawful.

Justice in itself, natural and universal, is regulated otherwise and more nobly than that other, *special, national* justice, constrained to the need of our governments. *We have no solid and exact image of true law and genuine justice; we use the shadow and reflections of it* [Cicero]. *So that the sage Dandamis,³ hearing tell of the lives of Socrates, Pythagoras, and Diogenes, judged them to be great men in every other respect, but too enslaved to reverence for the laws, to authorize and support which true virtue has to give up much of its original vigor. And not only by their permission, but even by their persuasion, many vicious actions take place. *There are crimes committed as a result of decrees of the Senate and of popular votes* [Seneca]. *I follow common usage in language, which distinguishes between things useful and honorable, so that it calls dishonorable and foul some natural actions that are not only useful but necessary.

But let us continue our examples of treachery. Two pretenders to the kingdom of Thrace had fallen into dispute over their rights. The Emperor prevented them from coming to blows; but one of them, under color of leading to a friendly accord by an interview, having invited his competitor to an entertainment in his own house, had him imprisoned and killed. Justice required that the Romans obtain satisfaction for this crime; difficulty blocked the ordinary ways. What they could not do lawfully without war and hazard, they undertook to do by treachery. What they could not do honorably they did expediently. For this, one Pomponius Flaccus was found fit. This man, after drawing the other into his nets by deceitful words

3 A Hindu sage of the time of Alexander the Great. The story comes from Plutarch.

and assurances, instead of the honor and favor he had promised him, sent him bound hand and foot to Rome. There one traitor betrayed the other, contrary to common usage; for they are full of mistrust, and it is hard to surprise them with their own craft: witness the grievous experience we have just had.

Let him who will be a Pomponius Flaccus, and there are enough who will. As for me, both my word and my honor are, like the rest, parts of this common body. Their best operation is public service; I take that for granted. But just as, if I were ordered to take charge of the Palace of Justice and its lawsuits, I would reply, "I don't understand anything about it"; or to take charge of leading some military pioneers, I would say, "I am called to a more worthy role"; so if anyone wanted to employ me to lie, to betray, and to perjure myself for some notable service, even if not to assassinate or poison, I would say, "If I have robbed or stolen from any man, send me rather to the galleys." For it is lawful for a man of honor to speak as did the Lacedaemonians, when defeated by Antipater, on the matter of terms of accord: "You can impose as many heavy and ruinous burdens on us as you please, but if you command us to do shameful and dishonorable things, you will waste your time." Every man should have sworn to himself what the kings of Egypt had their judges solemnly swear: that they would not deviate from their conscience for any command, even that they themselves gave them.

In such commissions there is an evident mark of ignominy and condemnation; and whoever gives you one accuses you, and gives it to you, if you understand it rightly, as a burden and a punishment. As much as public affairs are bettered by your deed, so much your own are worsened; the better you do, the worse you do. And it will be nothing new, nor perhaps will it be without some air of justice, if the same man punishes you for it who put you to work. ᶜPerfidy may in a given case be excusable; it is so only when it is employed to punish and betray perfidy.

ᴮAs it happens, there have been many instances in which treachery was not only refused but punished by those for whom it was undertaken. Who does not know the denunciation by Fabricius of Pyrrhus' doctor? But this also happens, that the man who has ordered it has avenged it rigorously on the man he had employed, refusing such an unbridled authority and power and disowning such an abandoned and cowardly servitude and obedience.

Jaropelc, a Russian duke, suborned a Hungarian nobleman to betray Boleslaus, king of Poland, by either killing him or giving the

Russians opportunity to do him some notable damage. This man went about it smoothly, devoted himself more than before to the service of this king, and succeeded in becoming one of his council and one of his most trusted men. With these advantages, and adroitly seizing the opportunity offered by his master's absence, he betrayed to the Russians Wieliczka, a great and rich city, which was entirely sacked and burned by them, with the total slaughter not only of its inhabitants of all ages and both sexes, but also of a great number of neighboring nobles whom he had assembled there for that purpose. When Jaropelc, sated with his vengeance and wrath – which, however, was not without reason (for Boleslaus had done him great harm and by similar conduct) – and glutted with the fruit of this treachery, came to consider its ugliness naked and by itself, and to look at it with a sane vision no longer troubled by his passion, he began to feel such remorse and revulsion that he had his agent's eyes put out and his tongue and private parts cut off.

Antigonus persuaded the Argyraspides to betray to him Eumenes, their general, his adversary; but after they had delivered him up and he had had him killed, he desired to be himself the agent of divine justice for the punishment of so detestable a crime, and consigned them into the hands of the governor of the province, giving him an express command to destroy them and bring them to a bad end by any means whatever. So that out of their great number not one ever again saw the air of Macedonia. The better he had been served by them, the more wicked and punishable he judged their service.

The slave who betrayed the hiding place of his master P. Sulpicius was set free, according to the promise of Sulla's proscription; but according to the promise of public justice, free as he was, he was thrown headlong from the Tarpeian rock. They have them hanged with the purse of their payment around their neck. Having satisfied their second and special promise, they satisfy the general and primary one.

Mohammed II, wanting, according to the tradition of his dynasty, to get rid of his brother in order to exercise his power without rival, employed for this purpose one of his officers, who choked him by pouring a quantity of water too fast down his throat. This done, in expiation of this murder Mohammed delivered the murderer into the hands of the dead man's mother (for they were brothers only through the father). She, in his presence, opened up the murderer's stomach, and while it was still warm, reaching with

her hands for his heart and tearing it out, she threw it to the dogs to eat.

And our King Clovis had the three servants of Cannacre hanged after they had betrayed their master to him, to which act he had suborned them.

[B]And even to worthless men, when they have profited from a vicious action, it is very sweet to be able thenceforth in all security to attach to it some act of goodness and justice, as if by conscientious compensation and correction. [C]Besides, they look upon the ministers of such horrible crimes as people who reproach them with them, and they seek by their death to stifle the knowledge and evidence of such proceedings.

[B]Now if by good fortune you are rewarded for a base act (so that public necessity may not be deprived of such extreme and desperate remedies), he who rewards you will without fail consider you an accursed and execrable man, unless he is one himself; and he will think you a worse traitor than did the man whom you have betrayed. For it is with your own hands, undenying and unprotesting, that you prove to him the malignity of your heart. But he employs you on your business just as one employs the scum of society as "executioners of high justice" – an office as useful as it is dishonorable. Besides being low, such functions also prostitute one's conscience. Since Sejanus' daughter could not be punished with death in a certain type of judgment at Rome because she was a virgin, she was, to give way to the laws, violated by the executioner before he strangled her. Not only his hand but his soul is slave to the public convenience.

[C]When the first Amurath, to sharpen the punishment of his subjects who had given support to the parricidal rebellion of his son against him, ordered that their nearest of kin should lend a hand to the execution, I find it very honorable in some of them to have chosen rather to be very unjustly held guilty of another man's parricide than to serve justice by a parricide of their own. And where, in the capture of some hovels in my time, I have seen rascals, in order to save their own lives, consent to hang their friends and comrades, I have held them to be worse off than the hanged. They say that Vitold, prince of the Lithuanians, once made this law, that condemned criminals had to execute with their own hands the capital sentence given against them; finding it strange that a third person, innocent of the fault, should be employed in a homicide and burdened with it.

^BThe prince, when some urgent circumstance or sudden and unexpected accident of state necessity makes him deviate from his word and his faith or otherwise forces him from his ordinary duty, should attribute this necessity to a blow from the divine rod. Vice it is not, for he has abandoned his own reason to a more universal and powerful reason; but it is certainly misfortune. So that to someone who asked me "What remedy?" I replied: "No remedy. If he was really racked between these two extremes ^C(*but let him beware that he is not seeking a pretext for perjury* [Cicero]), ^Bit had to be done. But if he did it without regret, if it did not grieve him to do it, it is a sign that his conscience is in a bad way."

^CIf there should be a prince with so tender a conscience that no cure seemed to him worth so onerous a remedy, I would not esteem him the less. He could not ruin himself more excusably or becomingly. We cannot do everything. Do what we will, we must often commit the protection of our vessel, as to a sheet anchor, to the guidance of Heaven. For what juster necessity is he reserving himself? What is less possible for him to do than what he cannot do except at the expense of his faith and his honor, things which perhaps should be dearer to him than his own safety, yes, and even than the safety of his people? When with folded arms he simply calls God to his aid, may he not hope that the divine goodness is not such as to refuse the favor of its extraordinary hand to a hand pure and just?

^CThose are dangerous examples, rare and sickly exceptions to our natural rules. We must yield to them, but with great moderation and circumspection. No private utility is worthy of our doing this violence to our conscience; the public utility yes, when it is very apparent and very important.

^BTimoleon protected himself appropriately against the unnaturalness of his deed by the tears he shed, remembering that it was with a brother's hand that he had killed the tyrant; and it justly pricked his conscience that it had been necessary to purchase the public advantage at such a price in honorable conduct. Even the Senate, delivered from slavery by his means, did not dare to decide roundly about a deed so lofty and so sharply split into two weighty and contrary aspects. But when the Syracusans most opportunely at that very moment sent to ask the Corinthians for their protection and a leader fit to restore their city to its former dignity and clear Sicily of several petty tyrants who were oppressing it, the Senators chose Timoleon for this task, with this new evasion and declaration: that

according as he bore himself well or ill in his charge, their verdict would take sides in favor of the liberator of his country or against the murderer of his brother. This fantastic decision has, however, some excuse in the danger of the example and the importance of so unusual a deed. And they did well to discharge their own judgment of it or support it elsewhere with extraneous considerations. Now Timoleon's deportment on this expedition soon made his cause clearer, so worthily and virtuously did he bear himself in every way; and the good fortune that accompanied him in the difficulties he had to overcome in this noble task seemed to be sent to him by the gods conspiring in favor of his justification.

This man's purpose is excusable if any could be so. But the utility of augmenting the public revenue, which served as pretext to the Roman Senate for the foul decision that I am about to relate, is not strong enough to warrant any such injustice. Certain cities had redeemed themselves by a payment of money and regained their liberty, with the orders and permission of the Senate, from the hands of L. Sulla. The matter having come up for reconsideration, the Senate condemns them to be taxable as before, and declares that the money they have used to redeem themselves shall remain lost to them. Civil wars often produce these ugly examples: we punish private individuals for having believed in us when we were different, and the selfsame magistrate inflicts the penalty of his own change[4] on someone who cannot do anything about it. The master whips his pupil for his docility, and the guide his blind man. Horrible image of justice!

There are rules both false and lax in philosophy. The example that is proposed to us for making private utility prevail over our pledged word does not receive enough weight from the circumstance that they introduce into it. Robbers have seized you; they have set you free again after extracting from you an oath to pay a certain sum. People are wrong to say that an honest man will be quit of his word without paying, once he is out of their hands. Nothing of the sort. What fear has once made me will, I am bound still to will when without fear. And even if it has forced only my tongue without my will, I am still bound to make good my word to the last penny. As for me, when my tongue has sometimes

4 All modern French texts I have seen read *jugement* (judgment); but the word in Montaigne's hand on the Bordeaux Copy (plate 726 of the 1912 phototypic edition) seems to be *changement* (change).

thoughtlessly run ahead of my thoughts, I have scrupled to disavow it for all that. Otherwise we shall come by degrees to overthrow all the rights that a third person obtains from our promises and oaths. *As if force could be brought to bear on a brave man* [Cicero]. In this alone does private interest have the right to excuse us for failing our promise, if we have promised something wicked and unjust in itself; for the rights of virtue must prevail over the rights of our obligation.

^BI once placed Epaminondas in the first rank of outstanding men,[5] and I do not take this back. To what a height did he raise consideration for his private duty, he who never killed a man he had vanquished, who even for the inestimable good of restoring liberty to his country scrupled to kill a tyrant or his accomplices without due form of justice, and who judged anyone a wicked man, however good a citizen he was, who among his enemies and in battle did not spare his friend and his host. There is a soul of rich composition. To the roughest and most violent of human actions he wedded good-ness and humanity, indeed the most delicate that can be found in the school of philosophy. That heart, so great, full, and obstinate against pain, death, and poverty – was it nature or art that had made it tender to the point of such an extreme gentleness and goodness in disposition? Terrible with blood and iron, he goes breaking and shattering a nation invincible against anyone but himself, and turns aside in the middle of such a melee on meeting his host and his friend. Truly that man was in command of war itself, who made it endure the curb of benignity at the point of its greatest heat, all inflamed as it was and foaming with frenzy and slaughter. It is a miracle to be able to mingle some semblance of justice with such actions; but it belongs only to the strength of Epaminondas to be able to mingle with them the sweetness and ease of the gentlest ways, and pure innocence.

And whereas one man said to the Mamertines that statutes had no application toward armed men; another, to the Tribune of the People, that the times for justice and for war were two; a third,[6] that the noise of weapons kept him from hearing the voice of the laws; this man was not even kept from hearing the voices of civility and pure courtesy. Had he not borrowed from his enemies the practice of sacrificing to the Muses when going to war, in order by their sweetness and gaiety to soften that martial fury and fierceness?

5 *Essays*, II: 36, "Of the Most Outstanding Men," pp. 694–6.
6 The three men, in order, are Pompey, Caesar, and Marius.

Let us not fear, after so great a preceptor, to consider ^cthat there are some things illicit even against the enemy; ^Bthat the common interest must not require all things of all men against the private interest – ^c*the memory of private rights remaining even in the disruption of public ties* [Livy]:

> ^BNo power can defend
> Or sanction treachery against a friend;
>
> OVID

– and that not all things are permissible for an honorable man in the service ^cof his king, or ^Bof the common cause, or of the laws. ^c*For our country does not come before all other duties; and it is good for it to have citizens who are dutiful to their parents* [Cicero]. ^BIt is a lesson proper for the times. We have no need to harden our hearts with these plates of steel, it is enough to harden our shoulders; it is enough to dip our pens in ink without dipping them in blood. If it is greatness of heart and the effect of rare and singular virtue to despise friendship, private obligations, our word, and kinship, for the common good and obedience to the magistrate, truly it is enough to excuse us from this that it is a greatness that cannot lodge in the greatness of Epaminondas' heart.

I abominate the rabid exhortations of that uncontrolled soul:[7]

> When weapons flash, no pious sentiments,
> Though you confront your fathers, you must feel;
> No, slash their venerable faces with the steel.
>
> LUCAN

Let us take away from wicked, bloody, and treacherous natures this pretext of reason. Let us abandon this monstrous and deranged justice and stick to more human imitations. How much time and example can do! In an encounter in the civil war against Cinna one of Pompey's soldiers, having unwittingly killed his brother, who was on the opposite side, for shame and regret killed himself on the spot. And some years after, in another civil war of the same people, a soldier asked his captains for a reward for having killed his brother.

We poorly argue the honor and beauty of an action from its utility, and we commit a fallacy in thinking that everyone is obliged to perform – ^cand that it is honorable for everyone to perform – ^Ban action merely because it is useful:

7 Caesar, the speaker in the verses that follow.

^CNot everything is fit for every man alike.
 PROPERTIUS

^BLet us choose the most necessary and useful action of human
society; that will be marriage. Yet the council of saints finds the
contrary way more honorable, and excludes from marriage the most
venerable vocation of men, as we assign to stud those horses which
are of least value.

2
Of repentance

^BOthers form man; I tell of him, and portray a particular one, very
ill-formed, whom I should really make very different from what he
is if I had to fashion him over again. But now it is done.

Now the lines of my painting do not go astray, though
they change and vary. The world is but a perennial movement. All
things in it are in constant motion – the earth, the rocks of the
Caucasus, the pyramids of Egypt – both with the common motion
and with their own. Stability itself is nothing but a more languid
motion.

I cannot keep my subject still. It goes along befuddled and
staggering, with a natural drunkenness. I take it in this condition,
just as it is at the moment I give my attention to it. I do not portray
being: I portray passing. Not the passing from one age to another,
or, as the people say, from seven years to seven years, but from day to
day, from minute to minute. My history needs to be adapted to the
moment. I may presently change, not only by chance, but also by
intention. This is a record of various and changeable occurrences,
and of irresolute and, when it so befalls, contradictory ideas:
whether I am different myself, or whether I take hold of my subjects
in different circumstances and aspects. So, all in all, I may indeed
contradict myself now and then; but truth, as Demades said, I do
not contradict. If my mind could gain a firm footing, I would not
make essays, I would make decisions; but it is always in apprentice-
ship and on trial.

I set forth a humble and inglorious life; that does not matter. You
can tie up all moral philosophy with a common and private life just
as well as with a life of richer stuff. Each man bears the entire form
of man's estate.

^CAuthors communicate with the people by some special extrinsic mark; I am the first to do so by my entire being, as Michel de Montaigne, not as a grammarian or a poet or a jurist. If the world complains that I speak too much of myself, I complain that it does not even think of itself.

^BBut is it reasonable that I, so fond of privacy in actual life, should aspire to publicity in the knowledge of me? Is it reasonable too that I should set forth to the world, where fashioning and art have so much credit and authority, some crude and simple products of nature, and of a very feeble nature at that? Is it not making a wall without stone, or something like that, to construct books without knowledge and without art? Musical fancies are guided by art, mine by chance.

At least I have one thing according to the rules: that no man ever treated a subject he knew and understood better than I do the subject I have undertaken; and that in this I am the most learned man alive. Secondly, that no man ever ^Cpenetrated more deeply into his material, or plucked its limbs and consequences cleaner, or ^Breached more accurately and fully the goal he had set for his work. To accomplish it, I need only bring it to fidelity; and that is in it, as sincere and pure as can be found. I speak the truth, not my fill of it, but as much as I dare speak; and I dare to do so a little more as I grow old, for it seems that custom allows old age more freedom to prate and more indiscretion in talking about oneself. It cannot happen here as I see it happening often, that the craftsman and his work contradict each other: "Has a man whose conversation is so good written such a stupid book?" or "Have such learned writings come from a man whose conversation is so feeble?"

^CIf a man is commonplace in conversation and rare in writing, that means that his capacity is in the place from which he borrows it, and not in himself. A learned man is not learned in all matters; but the capable man is capable in all matters, even in ignorance.

^BIn this case we go hand in hand and at the same pace, my book and I. In other cases one may commend or blame the work apart from the workman; not so here; he who touches the one, touches the other. He who judges it without knowing it will injure himself more than me; he who has known it will completely satisfy me. Happy beyond my deserts if I have just this share of public approval, that I make men of understanding feel that I was capable of profiting by knowledge, if I had had any, and that I deserved better assistance from my memory.

Let me here excuse what I often say, that I rarely repent [c]and that my conscience is content with itself – not as the conscience of an angel or a horse, but as the conscience of a man; [B]always adding this refrain, not perfunctorily but in sincere and complete submission: that I speak as an ignorant inquirer, referring the decision purely and simply to the common and authorized beliefs. I do not teach, I tell.

There is no vice truly a vice which is not offensive, and which a sound judgment does not condemn; for its ugliness and painfulness is so apparent that perhaps the people are right who say it is chiefly produced by stupidity and ignorance. So hard it is to imagine anyone knowing it without hating it.

[c]Malice sucks up the greater part of its own venom, and poisons itself with it. [B]Vice leaves repentance in the soul, like an ulcer in the flesh, which is always scratching itself and drawing blood. For reason effaces other griefs and sorrows; but it engenders that of repentance, which is all the more grievous because it springs from within, as the cold and heat of fevers is sharper than that which comes from outside. I consider as vices (but each one according to its measure) not only those that reason and nature condemn, but also those that man's opinion has created, even false and erroneous opinion, if it is authorized by laws and customs.

There is likewise no good deed that does not rejoice a wellborn nature. Indeed there is a sort of gratification in doing good which makes us rejoice in ourselves, and a generous pride that accompanies a good conscience. A boldly vicious soul may perhaps arm itself with security, but with this complacency and satisfaction it cannot provide itself. It is no slight pleasure to feel oneself preserved from the contagion of so depraved an age, and to say to oneself: "If anyone should see right into my soul, still he would not find me guilty either of anyone's affliction or ruin, or of vengeance or envy, or of public offense against the laws, or of innovation and disturbance, or of failing in my word; and in spite of what the license of the times allows and teaches each man, still I have not put my hand either upon the property or into the purse of any Frenchman, and have lived only on my own, both in war and in peace; nor have I used any man's work without paying his wages." These testimonies of conscience give us pleasure; and this natural rejoicing is a great boon to us, and the only payment that never fails us.

To found the reward for virtuous actions on the approval of others is to choose too uncertain and shaky a foundation. [c]Especially in an age as corrupt and ignorant as this, the good opinion of

the people is a dishonor. Whom can you trust to see what is praiseworthy? God keep me from being a worthy man according to the descriptions I see people every day giving of themselves in their own honor. *What were vices now are moral acts* [Seneca].

Certain of my friends have sometimes undertaken to call me on the carpet and lecture me unreservedly, either of their own accord or at my invitation, as a service which, to a well-formed soul, surpasses all the services of friendship, not only in usefulness, but also in pleasantness. I have always welcomed it with the wide-open arms of courtesy and gratitude. But to speak of it now in all conscience, I have often found in their reproach or praise such false measure that I would hardly have erred to err rather than to do good in their fashion.

^BThose of us especially who live a private life that is on display only to ourselves must have a pattern established within us by which to test our actions, and, according to this pattern, now pat ourselves on the back, now punish ourselves. I have my own laws and court to judge me, and I address myself to them more than anywhere else. To be sure, I restrain my actions according to others, but I extend them only according to myself. There is no one but yourself who knows whether you are cowardly and cruel, or loyal and devout. Others do not see you, they guess at you by uncertain conjectures; they see not so much your nature as your art. Therefore do not cling to their judgment; cling to your own. ^C*You must use your own judgment. . . . With regard to virtues and vices, your own conscience has great weight: take that away, and everything falls* [Cicero].

^BBut the saying that repentance follows close upon sin does not seem to consider the sin that is in robes of state, that dwells in us as in its own home. We can disown and retract the vices that take us by surprise, and toward which we are swept by passion; but those which by long habit are rooted and anchored in a strong and vigorous will cannot be denied. Repentance is nothing but a disavowal of our will and an opposition to our fancies, which leads us about in all directions. It makes this man disown his past virtue and his continence:

> Why had I not in youth the mind I have today?
> Or why, with old desires, have red cheeks flown away?
>
> HORACE

It is a rare life that remains well ordered even in private. Any man can play his part in the side show and represent a worthy man on the

boards; but to be disciplined within, in his own bosom, where all is permissible, where all is concealed – that's the point. The next step to that is to be so in our own house, in our ordinary actions, for which we need render account to no one, where nothing is studied or artificial. And therefore Bias, depicting an excellent state of family life, says it is one in which the master is the same within, by his own volition, as he is outside for fear of the law and of what people will say. And it was a worthy remark of Julius Drusus to the workmen who offered, for three thousand crowns, to arrange his house so that his neighbors would no longer be able to look into it as they could before. "I will give you six thousand," he said; "make it so that everyone can see in from all sides." The practice of Agesilaus is noted with honor, of taking lodging in the churches when traveling, so that the people and the gods themselves might see into his private actions. Men have seemed miraculous to the world, in whom their wives and valets have never seen anything even worth noticing. Few men have been admired by their own households.

ᶜNo man has been a prophet, not merely in his own house, but in his own country, says the experience of history. Likewise in things of no importance. And in this humble example you may see an image of greater ones. In my region of Gascony they think it a joke to see me in print. The farther from my lair the knowledge of me spreads, the more I am valued. I buy printers in Guienne, elsewhere they buy me. On this phenomenon those people base their hopes who hide themselves while alive and present, to gain favor when dead and gone. I would rather have less of it. And I cast myself on the world only for the share of favor I get now. When I leave it, I shall hold it quits.

ᴮThe people escort this man back to his door, with awe, from a public function. He drops his part with his gown; the higher he has hoisted himself, the lower he falls back; inside, in his home, everything is tumultuous and vile. Even if there is order there, it takes a keen and select judgment to perceive it in these humble private actions. Besides, order is a dull and somber virtue. To win through a breach, to conduct an embassy, to govern a people, these are dazzling actions. To scold, to laugh, to sell, to pay, to love, to hate, and to deal pleasantly and justly with our household and ourselves, not to let ourselves go, not to be false to ourselves, that is a rarer matter, more difficult and less noticeable.

Therefore retired lives, whatever people may say, accomplish duties as harsh and strenuous as other lives, or more so. ^CAnd private persons, says Aristotle, render higher and more difficult service to virtue than those who are in authority. ^BWe prepare ourselves for eminent occasions more for glory than for conscience. ^CThe shortest way to attain glory would be to do for conscience what we do for glory. ^BAnd Alexander's virtue seems to me to represent much less vigor in his theater than does that of Socrates in his lowly and obscure activity. I can easily imagine Socrates in Alexander's place; Alexander in that of Socrates, I cannot. If you ask the former what he knows how to do, he will answer, "Subdue the world"; if you ask the latter, he will say, "Lead the life of man in conformity with its natural condition"; a knowledge much more general, more weighty, and more legitimate.

The value of the soul consists not in flying high, but in an orderly pace. ^CIts greatness is exercised not in greatness, but in mediocrity. As those who judge and touch us inwardly make little account of the brilliance of our public acts, and see that these are only thin streams and jets of water spurting from a bottom otherwise muddy and thick; so likewise those who judge us by this brave outward appearance draw similar conclusions about our inner constitution, and cannot associate common faculties, just like their own, with these other faculties that astonish them and are so far beyond their scope. So we give demons wild shapes. And who does not give Tamerlane raised eyebrows, open nostrils, a dreadful face, and immense size, like the size of the imaginary picture of him we have formed from the renown of his name? If I had been able to see Erasmus in other days, it would have been hard for me not to take for adages and apophthegms everything he said to his valet and his hostess. We imagine much more appropriately an artisan on the toilet seat or on his wife than a great president, venerable by his demeanor and his ability. It seems to us that they do not stoop from their lofty thrones even to live.

^BAs vicious souls are often incited to do good by some extraneous impulse, so are virtuous souls to do evil. Thus we must judge them by their settled state, when they are at home, if ever they are; or at least when they are closest to repose and their natural position.

Natural inclinations gain assistance and strength from education; but they are scarcely to be changed and overcome. A thousand

natures, in my time, have escaped toward virtue or toward vice through the lines of a contrary training:

> As when wild beasts grow tame, shut in a cage,
> Forget the woods, and lose their look of rage,
> And learn to suffer man; but if they taste
> Hot blood, their rage and fury is replaced,
> Their reminiscent jaws distend, they burn,
> And for their trembling keeper's blood they yearn.
>
> LUCAN

We do not root out these original qualities, we cover them up, we conceal them. Latin is like a native tongue to me; I understand it better than French; but for forty years I have not used it at all for speaking or writing. Yet in sudden and extreme emotions, into which I have fallen two or three times in my life – one of them when I saw my father, in perfect health, fall back into my arms in a faint – I have always poured out my first words from the depths of my entrails in Latin; ^CNature surging forth and expressing herself by force, in the face of long habit. ^BAnd this experience is told of many others.

Those who in my time have tried to correct the world's morals by new ideas, reform the superficial vices; the essential ones they leave as they were, if they do not increase them; and increase is to be feared. People are likely to rest from all other well-doing on the strength of these external, arbitrary reforms, which cost us less and bring greater acclaim; and thereby they satisfy at little expense the other natural, consubstantial, and internal vices.

Just consider the evidence of this in our own experience. There is no one who, if he listens to himself, does not discover in himself a pattern all his own, a ruling pattern, which struggles against education and against the tempest of the passions that oppose it. For my part, I do not feel much sudden agitation; I am nearly always in place, like heavy and inert bodies. If I am not at home, I am always very near it. My excesses do not carry me very far away. There is nothing extreme or strange about them. And besides I have periods of vigorous and healthy reaction.

The real condemnation, which applies to the common run of men of today, is that even their retirement is full of corruption and filth; their idea of reformation, blurred; their penitence, diseased and guilty, almost as much as their sin. Some, either from being glued to vice by a natural attachment, or from long habit, no longer

recognize its ugliness. On others (in whose regiment I belong) vice weighs heavily, but they counterbalance it with pleasure or some other consideration, and endure it and lend themselves to it for a certain price; viciously, however, and basely. Yet it might be possible to imagine a disproportion so extreme that the pleasure might justly excuse the sin, as we say utility does; not only if the pleasure was incidental and not a part of the sin, as in theft, but if it was in the very exercise of the sin, as in intercourse with women, where the impulse is violent, and, they say, sometimes invincible.

The other day when I was at Armagnac, on the estate of a kinsman of mine, I saw a country fellow whom everyone nicknames the Thief. He gave this account of his life: that born a beggar, and finding that by earning his bread by the toil of his hands he would never protect himself enough against want, he had decided to become a thief; and he had spent all his youth at this trade in security, by virtue of his bodily strength. For he reaped his harvest and vintage from other people's lands, but so far away and in such great loads that it was inconceivable that one man could have carried off so much on his shoulders in one night. And he was careful besides to equalize and spread out the damage he did, so that the loss was less insupportable for each individual. He is now, in his old age, rich for a man in his station, thanks to this traffic, which he openly confesses. And to make his peace with God for his acquisitions, he says that he spends his days compensating, by good deeds, the successors of the people he robbed; and that if he does not finish this task (for he cannot do it all at once), he will charge his heirs with it, according to the knowledge, which he alone has, of the amount of wrong he did to each. Judging by this description, whether it is true or false, this man regards theft as a dishonorable action and hates it, but hates it less than poverty; he indeed repents of it in itself, but in so far as it was thus counterbalanced and compensated, he does not repent of it. This is not that habit that incorporates us with vice and brings even our understanding into conformity with it; nor is it that impetuous wind that comes in gusts to confuse and blind our soul, and hurls us for the moment headlong, judgment and all, into the power of vice.

I customarily do wholeheartedly whatever I do, and go my way all in one piece. I scarcely make a motion that is hidden and out of sight of my reason, and that is not guided by the consent of nearly all parts of me, without division, without internal sedition. My judgment takes all the blame or all the praise for it; and the blame it once

takes, it always keeps, for virtually since its birth it has been one; the same inclinations, the same road, the same strength. And in the matter of general opinions, in childhood I established myself in the position where I was to remain.

There are some impetuous, prompt, and sudden sins: let us leave them aside. But as for these other sins so many times repeated, planned, and premeditated, constitutional sins, ^cor even professional or vocational sins, ^BI cannot imagine that they can be implanted so long in one and the same heart, without the reason and conscience of their possessor constantly willing and intending it to be so. And the repentance which he claims comes to him at a certain prescribed moment is a little hard for me to imagine and conceive.

^cI do not follow the belief of the sect of Pythagoras, that men take on a new soul when they approach the images of the gods to receive their oracles. Unless he meant just this, that the soul must indeed be foreign, new, and loaned for the occasion, since their own showed so little sign of any purification and cleanness worthy of this office.

^BThey do just the opposite of the Stoic precepts, which indeed order us to correct the imperfections and vices that we recognize in us, but forbid us to be repentant and glum about them. These men make us believe that they feel great regret and remorse within; but of amendment and correction, ^cor interruption, ^Bthey show us no sign. Yet it is no cure if the disease is not thrown off. If repentance were weighing in the scale of the balance, it would outweigh the sin. I know of no quality so easy to counterfeit as piety, if conduct and life are not made to conform with it. Its essence is abstruse and occult; its semblance, easy and showy.

As for me, I may desire in a general way to be different; I may condemn and dislike my nature as a whole, and implore God to reform me completely and to pardon my natural weakness. But this I ought not to call repentance, it seems to me, any more than my displeasure at being neither an angel nor Cato. My actions are in order and conformity with what I am and with my condition. I can do no better. And repentance does not properly apply to the things that are not in our power; rather does regret. I imagine numberless natures loftier and better regulated than mine, but for all that, I do not amend my faculties; just as neither my arm nor my mind becomes more vigorous by imagining another that is so. If imagining and desiring a nobler conduct than ours produced repentance of

our own, we should have to repent of our most innocent actions, inasmuch as we rightly judge that in a more excellent nature they would have been performed with greater perfection and dignity, and we should wish to do likewise.

When I consider the behavior of my youth in comparison with that of my old age, I find that I have generally conducted myself in orderly fashion, according to my lights; that is all my resistance can accomplish. I do not flatter myself; in similar circumstances I should always be the same. It is not a spot, it is rather a tincture with which I am stained all over. I know no superficial, halfway, and perfunctory repentance. It must affect me in every part before I will call it so, and must grip me by the vitals and afflict them as deeply and as completely as God sees into me.

In business matters, several good opportunities have escaped me for want of successful management. However, my counsels have been good, according to the circumstances they were faced with; their way is always to take the easiest and surest course. I find that in my past deliberations, according to my rule, I have proceeded wisely, considering the state of the matter proposed to me, and I should do the same a thousand years from now in similar situations. I am not considering what it is at this moment, but what it was when I was deliberating about it.

ᶜThe soundness of any plan depends on the time; circumstances and things roll about and change incessantly. I have fallen into some serious and important mistakes in my life, not for lack of good counsel but for lack of good luck. There are secret parts in the matters we handle which cannot be guessed, especially in human nature – mute factors that do not show, factors sometimes unknown to their possessor himself, which are brought forth and aroused by unexpected occasions. If my prudence has been unable to see into them and predict them, I bear it no ill will; its responsibility is restricted within its limitations. It is the outcome that beats me; and ᴮif it favors the course I have refused, there is no help for it; I do not blame myself; I accuse my luck, not my work. That is not to be called repentance.

Phocion had given the Athenians some advice that was not followed. When however the affair came out prosperously against his opinion, someone said to him: "Well, Phocion, are you glad that the thing is going so well?" "Indeed I am glad," he said, "that it has turned out this way, but I do not repent of having advised that way."

When my friends apply to me for advice, I give it freely and clearly, and without hesitating as nearly everyone else does because, the affair being hazardous, it may come out contrary to my expectations, wherefore they may have cause to reproach me for my advice; that does not worry me. For they will be wrong, and I should not have refused them this service.

^CI have scarcely any occasion to blame my mistakes or mishaps on anyone but myself. For in practice I rarely ask other people's advice, unless as a compliment and out of politeness, except when I need scientific information or knowledge of the facts. But in things where I have only my judgment to employ, other people's reasons can serve to support me, but seldom to change my course. I listen to them all favorably and decently; but so far as I can remember, I have never up to this moment followed any but my own. If you ask me, they are nothing but flies and atoms that distract my will. I set little value on my own opinions, but I set just as little on those of others. Fortune pays me properly. If I do not take advice, I give still less. Mine is seldom asked, but it is followed even less; and I know of no public or private enterprise that my advice restored to its feet and to the right path. Even the people whom fortune has made somewhat dependent on it have let themselves be managed more readily by anyone else's brains. Being a man who is quite as jealous of the rights of my repose as of the rights of my authority, I prefer it so; by leaving me alone, they treat me according to my professed principle, which is to be wholly contained and established within myself. To me it is a pleasure not to be concerned in other people's affairs and to be free of responsibility for them.

^BIn all affairs, when they are past, however they have turned out, I have little regret. For this idea takes away the pain: that they were bound to happen thus, and now they are in the great stream of the universe and in the chain of Stoical causes. Your fancy, by wish or imagination, cannot change a single point without overturning the whole order of things, and the past and the future.

For the rest, I hate that accidental repentance that age brings. The man who said of old that he was obliged to the years for having rid him of sensuality had a different viewpoint from mine; I shall never be grateful to impotence for any good it may do me. ^C*Nor will Providence ever be so hostile to her own work that debility should be ranked among the best things* [Quintilian]. ^BOur appetites are few in old age; a profound satiety seizes us after the act. In that I see nothing of conscience; sourness and weakness imprint on us

a sluggish and rheumatic virtue. We must not let ourselves be so carried away by natural changes as to let our judgment degenerate. Youth and pleasure in other days did not make me fail to recognize the face of vice in voluptuousness; nor does the distaste that the years bring me make me fail to recognize the face of voluptuousness in vice. Now that I am no longer in that state, I judge it as though I were in it.

^CI who shake up my reason sharply and attentively, find that ^Bit is the very same I had in my more licentious years, except perhaps in so far as it has grown weaker and worse as it has grown old. ^CAnd I find that even if it refuses, out of consideration for the interests of my bodily health, to put me in the furnace of this pleasure, it would not refuse to do so, any more than formerly, for my spiritual health. ^BI do not consider it any more valiant for seeing it *hors de combat*. My temptations are so broken and mortified that they are not worth its opposition. By merely stretching out my hands to them, I exorcise them. If my reason were confronted with my former lust, I fear that it would have less strength to resist than it used to have. I do not see that of itself it judges anything differently than it did then, nor that it has gained any new light. Wherefore, if there is any convalescence, it is a deformed convalescence.

^CMiserable sort of remedy, to owe our health to disease! It is not for our misfortune to do us this service, it is for the good fortune of our judgment. You cannot make me do anything by ills and afflictions except curse them. They are for people who are only awakened by whipping. My reason runs a much freer course in prosperity. It is much more distracted and busy digesting pains than pleasures. I see much more clearly in fair weather. Health admonishes me more cheerfully and so more usefully than sickness. I advanced as far as I could toward reform and a regulated life when I had health to enjoy. I should be ashamed and resentful if the misery and misfortune of my decrepitude were to be thought better than my good, healthy, lively, vigorous years, and if people were to esteem me not for what I have been, but for ceasing to be that.

In my opinion it is living happily, not, as Antisthenes said, dying happily, that constitutes human felicity. I have made no effort to attach, monstrously, the tail of a philosopher to the head and body of a dissipated man; or that this sickly remainder of my life should disavow and belie its fairest, longest, and most complete part. I want to present and show myself uniformly throughout. If I had to live

over again, I would live as I have lived. I have neither tears for the past nor fears for the future. And unless I am fooling myself, it has gone about the same way within me as without. It is one of the chief obligations I have to my fortune that my bodily state has run its course with each thing in due season. I have seen the grass, the flower, and the fruit; now I see the dryness – happily, since it is naturally. I bear the ills I have much more easily because they are properly timed, and also because they make me remember more pleasantly the long felicity of my past life.

Likewise my wisdom may well have been of the same proportions in one age as in the other; but it was much more potent and graceful when green, gay, and natural, than it is now, being broken down, peevish, and labored. Therefore I renounce these casual and painful reformations.

^BGod must touch our hearts. Our conscience must reform by itself through the strengthening of our reason, not through the weakening of our appetites. Sensual pleasure is neither pale nor colorless in itself for being seen through dim and bleary eyes. We should love temperance for itself and out of reverence toward God, who has commanded it, and also chastity; what catarrh lends us, and what I owe to the favor of my colic, is neither chastity nor temperance. We cannot boast of despising and fighting sensual pleasure, if we do not see or know it, and its charms, its powers, and its most alluring beauty.

I know them both; I have a right to speak; but it seems to me that in old age our souls are subject to more troublesome ailments and imperfections than in our youth. I used to say so when I was young; then they taunted me with my beardless chin. I still say so now that my ^Cgray ^Bhair gives me authority to speak. We call "wisdom" the difficulty of our humors, our distaste for present things. But in truth we do not so much abandon our vices as change them, and, in my opinion, for the worse. Besides a silly and decrepit pride, a tedious prattle, prickly and unsociable humors, superstition, and a ridiculous concern for riches when we have lost the use of them, I find there more envy, injustice, and malice. Old age puts more wrinkles in our minds than on our faces; and we never, or rarely, see a soul that in growing old does not come to smell sour and musty. Man grows and dwindles in his entirety.

^CSeeing the wisdom of Socrates and several circumstances of his condemnation, I should venture to believe that he lent himself to it to some extent, purposely, by prevarication, being seventy, and

having so soon to suffer an increasing torpor of the rich activity of his mind, and the dimming of its accustomed brightness.

[B]What metamorphoses I see old age producing every day in many of my acquaintances! It is a powerful malady, and it creeps up on us naturally and imperceptibly. We need a great provision of study, and great precaution, to avoid the imperfections it loads upon us, or at least to slow up their progress. I feel that, notwithstanding all my retrenchments, it gains on me foot by foot. I stand fast as well as I can. But I do not know where it will lead even me in the end. In any event, I am glad to have people know whence I shall have fallen.

3

Of three kinds of association

[B]We must not nail ourselves down so firmly to our humors and dispositions. Our principal talent is the ability to apply ourselves to various practices. It is existing, but not living, to keep ourselves bound and obliged by necessity to a single course. The fairest souls are those that have the most variety and adaptability. [C]Here is an honorable testimony to the elder Cato: *He had a mind so equally versatile for all things that whatever he was doing, you would say that he was born for that one thing alone* [Livy].

[B]If it were up to me to train myself in my own fashion, there is no way so good that I should want to be fixed in it and unable to break loose. Life is an uneven, irregular, and multiform movement. We are not friends to ourselves, and still less masters, we are slaves, if we follow ourselves incessantly and are so caught in our inclinations that we cannot depart from them or twist them about. I say this now because I cannot easily shake off the importunity of my soul, which cannot ordinarily apply itself unless it becomes wrapped up in a thing, or be employed unless with tension and with its whole being. However trivial a subject you give it, it is prone to enlarge and stretch it to the point where it must work on it with all its strength. For that reason its idleness is a painful occupation for me, and bad for my health. Most minds need foreign matter to arouse and exercise them; mine needs it rather to settle down and rest – *the vices of idleness must be shaken off by occupation* [Seneca]; for its principal and most laborious study is studying itself.

[C]Books are for my mind one of the kinds of occupations which entice it away from its study. [B]At the first thoughts that come to it, it

stirs about and shows signs of vigor in all directions, practices its touch now for power, now for order and grace, ^Carranges, moderates, and fortifies itself. ^BIt has the power to awaken its faculties by itself. Nature has given to it as to all minds enough material of its own for its use, and enough subjects of its own for invention and judgment.

^CMeditation is a powerful and full study for anyone who knows how to examine and exercise himself vigorously: I would rather fashion my mind than furnish it. There is no occupation that is either weaker or stronger, according to the mind involved, than entertaining one's own thoughts. The greatest minds make it their profession, *to whom living is thinking* [Cicero]. Thus nature has favored it with this privilege, that there is nothing we can do so long, and no action to which we can devote ourselves more commonly and easily. It is the occupation of the gods, says Aristotle, from which springs their happiness and ours.

Reading serves me particularly to arouse my reason by offering it various subjects to set my judgment to work, not my memory.

^BTherefore few conversations hold my interest if devoid of vigor and effort. It is true that pleasantness and beauty satisfy and occupy me as much as weight and depth, or more. And inasmuch as I grow sleepy in any other sort of conversation, and lend it only the rind of my attention, it often happens in such abject and feeble sort of talk, small talk, that I make silly and stupid remarks and replies, ridiculous and unworthy of a child, or, still more awkwardly and impolitely, maintain an obstinate silence. I have a dreamy way of withdrawing into myself, and, besides, a dull and childish ignorance of many common things. By these two qualities I have earned the honor that five or six stories can be truthfully told about me, as silly as can be told about any man whatever.

Now to go on with my subject, this fastidious disposition makes me hard to please in dealings with men – I have to cull them out on the sorting tray – and makes me ill-fitted for ordinary actions. We live and deal with plain people. If association with them is a burden to us, if we disdain to adjust ourselves to humble and vulgar souls – and the humble and vulgar ones are often as well-regulated as the subtler ones ^C(all wisdom is foolish that does not adapt itself to the common folly) – ^Bwe should no longer meddle with either our own affairs or those of others: both private and public affairs are worked out with these people.

The least strained and most natural ways of the soul are the most beautiful; the best occupations are the least forced. Lord,

what a favor wisdom does for those whose desires she adjusts to their power! There is no more useful knowledge. "According to one's power," that was the refrain and favorite saying of Socrates,[1] a saying of great substance. We must direct and fix our desires on the easiest and nearest things. Is it not a stupid humor of mine to be out of tune with a thousand to whom I am joined by fortune, whom I cannot do without, only to cling to one or two, who are not associated with me, or rather to a fantastic desire for something I cannot recapture? My easygoing ways, opposed to all bitterness and asperity, may very well have relieved me of envy and hostility; to be loved I will not say, but no man ever gave more occasion not to be hated. But the coolness of my dealings has rightly robbed me of the good will of many, who are to be excused for interpreting it in another and worse sense.

I am very capable of forming and maintaining rare and exquisite friendships, inasmuch as I grasp so hungrily at any acquaintances that suit my taste, I make advances and I throw myself at them so avidly, that I hardly fail to attach myself and to make an impression wherever I land. I have often made happy proof of this. In ordinary friendships I am somewhat barren and cool, for my pace is not natural if it is not under full sail. Besides, my fortune, having trained me from my youth for a single perfect friendship and given me a taste for it, has in truth given me a certain distaste for the others; and has imprinted too deeply on my fancy that friendship is an animal made for company, not for the herd, as that ancient[2] said. And furthermore, by nature I find it hard to communicate myself by halves and moderately, and with that servile and suspicious prudence that is prescribed to us for association in these numerous and imperfect friendships; and it is prescribed to us especially in these times when we cannot talk about the world except with danger, or falsely.

Yet I see clearly that whoever, like myself, has as his goal the comforts of life (I mean the essential comforts), should shun like the plague these fastidious and squeamish humors. I would admire a soul with different levels, which could both be tense and relax, which would be well off wherever fortune might take it, which could chat with a neighbor about his building, his hunting, and his

1 According to Xenophon, *Memorabilia*, I, iii, 3. Montaigne wrote an Italian version of this ("Mentre si puo") on the first page of several volumes in his library.
2 Plutarch.

lawsuit, and keep up an enjoyable conversation with a carpenter and a gardener. I envy those who know how to be familiar with the humblest of their retinue and carry on a conversation with their own servants.

^CAnd I do not like Plato's advice, always to talk to our servants, whether male or female, in masterful terms, without playfulness and without familiarity. For besides the reason I have given, it is inhuman and unjust to make so much of this accidental privilege of fortune. And the administrations which admit the least disparity between servants and masters seem to me the most equitable.

^BOthers study how to elevate their minds and hoist them up tight; I, how to humble mine and lay it to rest. It is defective only when it reaches out:

> You tell of Aeacus' line
> And wars men waged by sacred Troy.
> How much a cask of Chian wine
> Will cost us, or what servant boy
> Will heat my bath, or when whose bed
> Will keep out cold, you leave unsaid.
>
> <div align="right">HORACE</div>

Thus, as the Lacedaemonian valor needed moderation and the soft and gracious notes of the flute to soothe it in war, for fear it should fling itself into recklessness and fury, whereas all other nations ordinarily use shrill and powerful sounds and voices that arouse and inflame the courage of the soldiers to the utmost; similarly it seems to me, contrary to the usual opinion, that in using our minds, we have more need, for the most part, of lead than of wings, of coolness and repose than of ardor and agitation. Above all, in my opinion, it is thoroughly playing the fool to act knowing among those who are not, to speak always formally, *favellar in punta di forchetta*.[3] You must stoop to the level of the people you are with, and sometimes affect ignorance. Lay aside your strength and subtlety; in common usage it is enough to retain order. For the rest, crawl along the ground, if they want.

Learned men are prone to stumble over this stone. They are always parading their mastery and scattering their book learning on all sides. In these days they have poured it so hard into the boudoirs and ears of the ladies, that if they have not retained its

3 "To talk on the point of a fork" (Italian idiom).

substance, at least they have the appearance of it. For every sort of subject and matter, however humble and commonplace, they use a novel and learned manner of speaking and writing:

> Thus they express their fears, thus they outpour
> Anger, joys, secrets of the soul; what more?
> They copulate in learned style.
> <div align="right">JUVENAL</div>

They quote Plato and Saint Thomas in matters where the first comer would make as good a witness. The learning that could not reach their mind remains on their tongue.

If the wellborn ladies will take my advice, they will content themselves with displaying their own natural riches. They conceal and cover up their own beauties under foreign beauties. It is very simple-minded to put out your own light so as to shine by a borrowed light. They are buried and entombed under art. *Right out of a bandbox* [Seneca]. ᴮThe reason is that they do not know themselves well enough. The world has nothing more beautiful; it is for them to do honor to the arts and to decorate decoration. What do they need but to live beloved and honored? They possess and know only too much for this; they need only arouse a little and rekindle the faculties that are in them. When I see them intent on rhetoric, astrology, logic, and similar drugs, so vain and useless for their needs, I begin to fear that the men who advise them to do this, do so as a means of gaining authority over them under this pretext. For what other excuse could I find for them? Enough that without our help they can adjust the charm of their eyes to gaiety, severity, or sweetness, season a "no" with harshness, uncertainty, or encouragement, and that they need no interpreter for the speeches we make in courting them. With this knowledge they hold the whip hand and master the schoolmasters and the school.

If, however, it vexes them to yield to us in any matter whatever, and if they want, out of curiosity, to have a share in book learning, poetry is an amusement suited to their needs; it is a wanton and subtle art, in fancy dress, wordy, all pleasure, all show, like themselves. They will also derive various benefits from history. In philosophy, from the part that is useful for life, they will take the lessons that will train them to judge our humors and characteristics, to defend themselves against our treacheries, to control the impetuosity of their own desires, to husband their freedom, to prolong the pleasures of life, and to bear humanly the inconstancy of a lover,

the rudeness of a husband, and the annoyance of years and wrinkles; and things of that sort. That is the most I should assign to them in the matter of learning.

There are private, retiring, and inward natures. My essential pattern is suited to communication and revelation. I am all in the open and in full view, born for company and friendship. The solitude that I love and preach is primarily nothing but leading my feelings and thoughts back to myself, restraining and shortening not my steps, but my desires and my cares, abandoning solicitude for outside things, and mortally avoiding servitude and obligation, ^cand not so much the press of people as the press of business. ^BSolitude of place, to tell the truth, rather makes me stretch and expand outward; I throw myself into affairs of state and into the world more readily when I am alone. At the Louvre and in the crowd I withdraw and contract into my skin; the crowd drives me back to myself, and I never entertain myself so madly, licentiously, and privately as in places full of respect and ceremonious prudence. Our follies do not make me laugh, our wisdom does.

By nature I am not an enemy to the bustle of courts; I have spent part of my life in them, and I am built to get along cheerfully in large companies, provided it is at intervals and at my own times. But that indolence of taste that I have been speaking of attaches me forcibly to solitude, even at home, in the midst of a numerous household and as many visitors as anywhere. I see enough people there, but rarely those with whom I like to converse; and I there reserve, both for myself and for others, an unusual freedom. There we have a truce on ceremony, on waiting on people and escorting them here and away, and other such troublesome prescriptions of our code of manners (oh, what a servile and bothersome practice!); everyone there behaves as he pleases; anyone who wants to, communes with his own thoughts; I remain mute, dreamy, and locked up in my thoughts, without my guests' taking offense.

The men whose society and intimacy I seek are those who are called talented gentlemen; the idea of them spoils my taste for the others. It is, if you take it rightly, the rarest type among us, and a type that is chiefly due to nature. The object of this association is simply intimacy, fellowship, and conversation: exercise of minds, without any other fruit. In our talks all subjects are alike to me. I do not care if there is neither weight nor depth in them; charm and pertinency are always there; everything is imbued with mature and constant good sense, and mingled with kindliness, frankness, gaiety,

and friendliness. It is not only on the subject of lineal substitutions or the affairs of kings that our mind shows its beauty and strength; it shows it as much in private confabulations. I know my men even by their silence and their smiles, and perhaps find out more about them at table than in the council chamber. Hippomachus used to say shrewdly that he knew good wrestlers by seeing them just walk in the street.

If learning is pleased to enter our conversation, she will not be turned out; she will not be magisterial, overbearing, and troublesome, as she usually is, but subordinate and docile. We seek only to pass the time; when it is time to be instructed and preached at, we will go and find her on her throne. Let her stoop to our level just for once, if she will; for, useful and desirable as she is, even so I suppose that in a pinch we could perfectly well get along without her completely, and do our business without her. A wellborn mind that is practiced in dealing with men makes itself thoroughly agreeable by itself. Art is nothing else but the list and record of the productions of such minds.

Another pleasant association for me is that of ^Cbeautiful and ^Bwell-bred women: ^C*For we too have practiced eyes* [Cicero]. ^BIf the soul has not so much to enjoy here as in the first association, the bodily senses, which conversely take a greater part in this one, bring it to a proportion close to the other, though in my opinion not equal. But it is an association in which we must keep a bit on guard, especially those in whom the body has much power, as in my case. I burned myself at it in my youth, and suffered all the furies that the poets say come upon all those who let themselves go after women without restraint and without judgment. It is true that this whiplash has since been a lesson to me:

> A Greek who from Capharean rocks sailed safe away
> Never again into Euboean seas will stray.
>
> OVID

It is madness to fasten all our thoughts upon it and to become involved in a furious and reckless passion. But on the other hand, to go into it without love and without binding our will, like actors, to play the standard role of our age and customs and put into it nothing of our own but the words, that is indeed providing for our safety, but in cowardly fashion, like a man who would abandon his honor, his profit, or his pleasure for fear of danger. For it is certain that from such a relationship those who form it can hope for no fruit

that will please or satisfy a noble soul. We must have really desired what we expect to get real pleasure from enjoying. I say this even though fortune may unjustly reward a passionate mask, as happens often because there is not a woman, however ill-favored she may be, who does not think herself quite attractive, ^cand who does not think well of her youth or her laugh, or her graceful movements. For there are no absolutely ugly women, any more than there are absolutely beautiful ones. And the Brahman girls who have nothing else to recommend them go to the market place, when the people have been assembled by the public crier for this purpose, and display their matrimonial parts, to see if in this respect at least they are not good enough to get a husband.

^BConsequently there is not one who does not let herself be easily persuaded by the first vow a man takes to be true to her. Now the necessary outcome of this common and ordinary treachery of the men of today is what experience is already showing us, that they rally and fall back upon themselves or each other to escape us; or else that they too, for their part, fall in line with this example that we give them, play their part in the farce, and lend themselves to this negotiation, without passion, without interest, and without love: ^c*Unsusceptible to passion, whether their own or another's* [Tacitus]. They think, following the argument of Lysias in Plato, that they can give themselves up to us more profitably and conveniently the less we love them. ^BIt will turn out as it does in plays: the public will have as much pleasure in it as the comedians, or more.

For my part, I no more recognize Venus without Cupid than maternity without offspring: they are things that lend and owe their essence to each other. Thus this cheating recoils on the man who does it. It does not cost him much, but he gets nothing worth while out of it either. Those who made Venus a goddess regarded her chief beauty as incorporeal and spiritual; but the beauty that these people seek is not so much as human, or even brutish. The animals do not want it so gross and so earthy. We see that imagination and desire often heat them and excite them before the body does; we see in both sexes that among the crowd they pick and choose for their affections, and that they have bonds of enduring fondness for each other. Even those to whom old age denies bodily vigor still tremble, neigh, and quiver with love. We see them, before the act, full of hope and ardor, and when the body has played its game, still reveling in the sweetness of this memory; and we see some who swell with pride when they have finished and who, weary and sated, give out

songs of glee and triumph at their deed. Anyone who has only to relieve his body of a natural necessity has no reason for troubling others with such elaborate preparations; that is no meat for a gross and coarse hunger.

Being one who does not ask to be thought better than I am, I will say this about the errors of my youth. Not only because of the danger [c]to health (and yet I did not manage well enough to escape having two touches of it, slight, however, and incipient), [B]but also out of scorn I did not addict myself much to venal and public intimacies. I wanted to make the pleasure keener by difficulty, by desire, and by a certain glory; and I liked the way of Emperor Tiberius, who in his love affairs was won by modesty and noble birth as much as by any other quality, and the whim of the courtesan Flora, who lent herself to no one less than a dictator or a consul or a censor, and took her pleasure in the dignity of her lovers. Certainly pearls and brocade add to the pleasure, and titles and retinue.

Moreover, I used to set great store by the mind, but only provided the body was not deficient. For, to answer in all conscience, if beauty of one or the other had necessarily to be lacking, I would have chosen sooner to give up the mental. It has its use in better things; but in the matter of love, a matter which is chiefly concerned with sight and touch, you can do something without the graces of the mind, nothing without the graces of the body.

Beauty is the real advantage of the ladies. [c]It is so much their own that ours, though it demands somewhat different characteristics, is at its best only when indistinguishable from theirs, boyish and beardless. They say that at the court of the Grand Turk the youths that serve him on account of their beauty, whose number is infinite, are dismissed, at the latest, at twenty-two. [B]Reason, wisdom, and the offices of friendship are oftener found among men; therefore they govern the affairs of the world.

These two kinds of association are accidental and dependent on others. One is annoying by its rarity, the other withers with age; thus they would not have provided well enough for the needs of my life. Association with books, which is the third kind, is much more certain and more our own. It yields the other advantages to the first two, but it has for its share the constancy and ease of its service. It is at my side throughout my course, and accompanies me everywhere. It consoles me in old age and in solitude. It relieves me of the weight of a tedious idleness, and releases me at any time from disagreeable company. It dulls the pangs of sorrow, unless they are extreme and

overpowering. To be diverted from a troublesome idea, I need only have recourse to books: they easily turn my thoughts to themselves and steal away the others. And yet they do not rebel at seeing that I seek them out only for want of those other pleasures, that are more real, lively, and natural; they always receive me with the same expression.

He may well go on foot, they say, who leads his horse by the bridle. And our James, king of Naples and Sicily, who, handsome, young, and healthy, had himself carried around the country on a stretcher, lying on a wretched feather pillow, dressed in a gown of gray cloth with a cap to match, meanwhile followed by great regal pomp, litters, hand-led horses of all sorts, gentlemen and officers, showed an austerity still weak and wavering. The sick man is not to be pitied who has a cure up his sleeve. In the practice and application of this maxim, which is very true, lies all the fruit I reap from books. Actually I use them scarcely any more than those who do not know them at all. I enjoy them, as misers enjoy treasures, because I know that I can enjoy them when I please; my soul takes its fill of contentment from this right of possession.

I do not travel without books, either in peace or in war. However, many days will pass, and even some months, without my using them. I'll do it soon, I say, or tomorrow, or when I please. Time flies and is gone, meanwhile, without hurting me. For I cannot tell you what ease and repose I find when I reflect that they are at my side to give me pleasure at my own time, and when I recognize how much assistance they bring to my life. It is the best provision I have found for this human journey, and I am extremely sorry for men of understanding who do not have it. I sooner accept any other kind of amusement, however trivial, because this one cannot fail me.

When at home, I turn aside a little more often to my library, from which at one sweep I command a view of my household. I am over the entrance, and see below me my garden, my farmyard, my courtyard, and into most of the parts of my house. There I leaf through now one book, now another, without order and without plan, by disconnected fragments. One moment I muse, another moment I set down or dictate, walking back and forth, these fancies of mine that you see here.

ᶜIt is on the third floor of a tower; the first is my chapel, the second a bedroom and dressing room, where I often sleep in order to be alone. Above it is a great wardrobe. In the past it was the most useless place in my house. In my library I spend most of the days of

my life, and most of the hours of the day. I am never there at night. Adjoining it is a rather elegant little room, in which a fire may be laid in winter, very pleasantly lighted by a window. And if I feared the trouble no more than the expense, the trouble that drives me from all business, I could easily add on to each side a gallery a hundred paces long and twelve wide, on the same level, having found all the walls raised, for another purpose, to the necessary height. Every place of retirement requires a place to walk. My thoughts fall asleep if I make them sit down. My mind will not budge unless my legs move it. Those who study without a book are all in the same boat.

The shape of my library is round, the only flat side being the part needed for my table and chair; and curving round me it presents at a glance all my books, arranged in five rows of shelves on all sides. It offers rich and free views in three directions, and sixteen paces of free space in diameter.

In winter I am not there so continually; for my house is perched on a little hill, as its name indicates, and contains no room more exposed to the winds than this one, which I like for being a little hard to reach and out of the way, for the benefit of the exercise as much as to keep the crowd away. There is my throne. I try to make my authority over it absolute, and to withdraw this one corner from all society, conjugal, filial, and civil. Everywhere else I have only a verbal authority, essentially divided. Sorry the man, to my mind, who has not in his own home a place to be all by himself, to pay his court privately to himself, to hide! Ambition pays its servants well by keeping them ever on display, like a statue in a market place. *Great fortune is great slavery* [Seneca]. Even their privy is not private. I have found nothing so harsh in the austere life that our monks practice as this that I observe in the orders of these men, a rule to be perpetually in company, and to have numbers of others present for any action whatsoever. I find it measurably more endurable to be always alone than never to be able to be alone.

[B]If anyone tells me that it is degrading the Muses to use them only as a plaything and a pastime, he does not know, as I do, the value of pleasure, play, and pastime. I would almost say that any other aim is ridiculous. I live from day to day, and, without wishing to be disrespectful, I live only for myself; my purposes go no further.

In my youth I studied for ostentation; later, a little to gain wisdom; now, for recreation; never for gain. As for the vain and

spendthrift fancy I had for that sort of furniture,[4] ^cnot just to supply my needs, but to go three steps beyond, ^Bfor the purpose of lining and decorating my walls, I have given it up long ago.

Books have many charming qualities for those who know how to choose them. But no blessing without a drawback: it is a pleasure that is no clearer or purer than the others; it has its disadvantages, and very weighty ones. The mind is exercised in books, but the body, whose care I have not forgotten either, remains meanwhile inactive, droops and grieves. I know of no excess more harmful to me, or more to be avoided in my declining years.

Those are my three favorite and particular occupations. I will not speak of those that I owe the world out of civic duty.

4
Of diversion

^BI was once employed to console a lady who was truly afflicted (for most of their mourning is put on and perfunctory):

> Ever ready in her are copious tears,
> Ever at hand and waiting on her word
> To flow as she decrees. JUVENAL

It is bad procedure to oppose this passion, for opposition pricks the aggrieved and drives them further into sadness. We exasperate the trouble by the heat of the argument. We see in ordinary conversation that if I have said something casually and someone disputes it, I passionately espouse it; and much more so anything I am interested in.

And then, by so doing you make a rough approach to your operation; whereas the first greetings of the doctor to his patient should be gracious, gay, and agreeable, and an ugly and churlish doctor never did any good. So on the contrary, you must from the first encourage and humor their grief and show some signs of approving and excusing it. By this understanding you gain authority to proceed further, and by an easy and imperceptible slope you slip into arguments more solid and suited to their cure.

4 Books.

Since my chief wish was to delude the people present who had their eyes on me, I decided to cover up the trouble. Moreover, I find by experience that I am a poor and unprofitable hand at persuading. I present my reasons either too pointed and dry, or too brusquely, or too carelessly. After I had gone along with her suffering for a time, I did not attempt to cure it by strong, live reasons, because I lack them, or because I thought I could effect my purpose better otherwise. ^CNor did I choose any of the various sayings that philosophy prescribes for consolation: that what we lament is no evil, like Cleanthes; that it is a slight evil, like the Peripatetics; that this lamenting is an action neither just nor laudable, like Chrysippus; or this one of Epicurus, closer to my style, that we should transfer our thoughts from unpleasant to pleasant things; nor did I, like Cicero, arm myself with this whole pile of cures, dispensing it according to the occasion. ^BBut, very gently deflecting our talk and diverting it bit by bit to subjects nearby, then a little more remote, as she gave me more of her attention, I imperceptibly stole away from her this painful thought and kept her in good spirits and entirely soothed for as long as I was there. I made use of diversion. Those who followed me in the same service found no improvement in her, for I had not laid the axe to the roots.

^CPerhaps I have touched elsewhere[1] on a certain sort of public diversion. And the military practice that Pericles used in the Peloponnesian War, and a thousand others have used elsewhere, to draw out enemy forces from their countries, is only too frequent in the histories.

^BIt was an ingenious shift by which the sieur de Himbercourt saved both himself and others in the city of Liège, which the duke of Burgundy, who was laying siege to it, had bid him enter to carry out the terms of the surrender agreed on. These townspeople, assembled by night to provide for this, broke into mutiny against the accepted agreements, and many of them decided to fall upon the negotiators, whom they had in their power. He, getting wind of the first wave of these people who were coming to burst into his lodgings, promptly released in their direction two of the inhabitants of the town (for there were some with him), charged with new and milder offers to be proposed in their council, which he had made up on the spot for his need. These two stopped the first tempest, bringing this excited

1 *Essays* II: 23, "Of Evil Means Employed to a Good End," pp. 628–9. The "public diversion" there consists of trying to cure civil war by foreign war.

mob back into the town hall to hear their message and deliberate on it. The deliberation was short: behold a second storm bursts out, as violent as the first; and he dispatches four new similar mediators to meet them, protesting that this time they have even fatter terms to offer them, which will be entirely to their contentment and satisfaction. Whereby these people were again turned back to their conclave. In short, by thus dispensing pastimes, diverting their fury, and dissipating it in empty discussions, he finally put it to sleep and got through until daylight, which was his principal task.

This other story is also of this category. Atalanta, a girl of outstanding beauty and marvelous agility, to rid herself of the throng of a thousand suitors who sought her in marriage, gave them these terms, that she would accept the man who could match her in running, with the proviso that those who failed should lose their lives. There were enough who considered this prize worth such a risk and who incurred the penalty of that cruel bargain.

Hippomenes, whose turn came after the others, addressed the tutelary goddess of this amorous ardor, calling her to his aid; and she, granting his prayer, supplied him with three golden apples and a plan to use them. When the race was under way, as Hippomenes sensed his mistress pressing close on his heels, he let slip, as if inadvertently, one of these apples. The girl, distracted by its beauty, did not fail to turn aside to pick it up:

> The startled girl, craving the shining apple,
> Turns from her course, picks up the rolling gold.
>
> OVID

He did the same at the proper points with the second and third, until, by thus turning her out of her course and diverting her, he won the race.

When the doctors cannot purge a catarrh, they divert it and lead it off into some other less dangerous part. I observe that this is also the most ordinary remedy for ailments of the soul. *Also sometimes the mind must be diverted to other interests, preoccupations, cares, business; finally, it is often to be cured by a change of place, as with sick people who are slow in convalescing* [Cicero]. We rarely make the soul meet the troubles head on. We do not make it withstand or beat down their attack, we have it avoid and sidestep them.

This other lesson is too high and too difficult. It is only for first-class men to dwell purely on the thing itself, consider it, and judge it. It belongs to the one and only Socrates to become

acquainted with death with an ordinary countenance, to become familiar with it and play with it. He seeks no consolation outside the thing itself; dying seems to him a natural and indifferent incident. He fixes his gaze precisely on it, and makes up his mind to it, without looking elsewhere.

The disciples of Hegesias, who, inflamed by the fine arguments of his lectures, starve themselves to death, ^cand so thick and fast that King Ptolemy forbade him to entertain his school any more with these homicidal doctrines, ^Bdo not consider death in itself; they do not judge it. It is not there that they fix their thoughts; the goal to which they run is a new existence.

These poor people whom we see on the scaffold, full of burning devotion, busying all their senses with it as much as they can, their ears intent on the instructions that are given them, their eyes and hands on heaven, their voice on praying aloud, with a violent and continual excitement, are certainly doing something laudable and suitable to such an extremity. They are to be praised for piety, but not properly for constancy. They avoid the struggle; they turn their consideration away from death, as we amuse children while they are being lanced. I have seen some who, if by chance their eye fell on those horrible preparations for death that were going on around them, stiffened with fear and frenziedly cast their thoughts elsewhere. Those who are passing a fearful abyss are ordered to close or turn away their eyes.

^cSubrius Flavius had to be put to death at Nero's command, and that at the hands of Niger (both of them were generals); when he was led to the place for the execution, seeing that the hole that Niger had had dug to put him in was uneven and badly made, he said, turning to the soldiers who were present: "Not even that is according to military discipline." And to Niger, who was exhorting him to hold his head firm: "If only you would strike as firmly!" And he guessed right. Niger, his arm trembling, took several blows to cut his head off. That man certainly seems to have had his thoughts directly fixed on the object.

^BThe man who dies in the melee, arms in hand, does not then study death; he neither feels it nor considers it; he is carried away by the heat of the battle. A gentleman I know, who fell while fighting in the lists and felt himself stabbed with a dagger nine or ten times by his enemy, while everyone present was calling to him to think of his conscience, told me afterward that although these voices had come to his ears, they had not touched him at all, and that he

had never had a thought except for disengaging and avenging himself. He killed his man in that same combat.

^CThe man who brought L. Silanus his death sentence did much for him, for after hearing him reply that he was indeed prepared to die, but not by criminal hands, he rushed on him with his soldiers to overpower him – while Silanus, all unarmed, defended himself obstinately with fists and feet – and killed him in the struggle, thus dissipating in a prompt and tumultuous anger the painful anticipation of a lingering and elaborate death to which he was destined.

^BOur thoughts are always elsewhere; the hope of a better life stays and supports us, or the hope of our children's worth, or the future glory of our name, or flight from the ills of this life, or the vengeance that threatens those who cause our death:

> On ocean rocks, I hope, if the just gods
> Have power left, you'll drain your cup of pains,
> And often cry out Dido's name . . .
> I'll hear: the news shall reach me 'mongst the shades.
>
> VIRGIL

^CXenophon was sacrificing, crowned with a garland, when they came and announced to him the death of his son Gryllus in the battle of Mantinea. At the first impact of this news he threw his garland on the ground; but when, from the rest of the account, he learned how valiantly his son had died, he picked the garland up and put it back on his head.

^BEven Epicurus consoles himself at the end with the eternity and utility of his writings. ^C*All labors that lead to glory and distinction are endurable* [Cicero]. And the same wound, the same hardship, says Xenophon, does not weigh on an army general as on a common soldier. Epaminondas took his death much more cheerfully when he was informed that victory had remained with his side. *These are the consolations, these the salves for the greatest sorrows* [Cicero]. ^BAnd other such circumstances occupy, divert, and distract us from consideration of the thing in itself.

^CIndeed the arguments of philosophy are all the time running alongside the matter and sidestepping it, and barely brushing the crust of it. The first man of the first and most authoritative school of philosophy, the great Zeno, speaking against death, says: "No evil is honorable; death is honorable; hence it is no evil." Against drunkenness: "No one entrusts his secret to the drunkard; everyone

entrusts it to the sage; hence the sage will not be a drunkard." Is that hitting the bull's-eye? I love to see these leading souls unable to shake off our common lot. Perfect men as they are, still they are men, and most heavily so.

ᴮVengeance is a sweet passion, whose impact is great and natural: I see this well enough, though I have no experience of it in myself. Recently, in order to lead a young prince away from it,[2] I did not tell him that we must turn our cheek to the man who has just struck the other one, for charity's sake, nor did I represent to him the tragic results that poetry attributes to this passion. I let the passion alone and applied myself to making him relish the beauty of a contrary picture, the honor, favor, and good will he would acquire by clemency and kindness. I diverted him to ambition. That is how it is done.

If your passion in love is too powerful, disperse it, they say; and they say true, for I have often tried it with profit. Break it up into various desires, of which one may be ruler and master, if you will; but for fear it may dominate and tyrannize you, weaken it, check it, by dividing and diverting it:

> When the capricious vein throbs in the restless member,
> <div align="right">PERSIUS</div>

> Eject the gathered sperm in anything at all.
> <div align="right">LUCRETIUS</div>

And see to it in good time, for fear it may be troublesome to you if once it has seized you:

> Unless by vagrant loves, a roving, vagrant boy,
> You cure your wounds when fresh, and old by new destroy.
> <div align="right">LUCRETIUS</div>

I was once afflicted with an overpowering grief, for one of my nature, and even more justified than powerful. I might well have been destroyed by it if I had trusted simply to my own powers. Needing some violent diversion to distract me from it, by art and study I made myself fall in love, in which my youth helped me. Love solaced me and withdrew me from the affliction caused by friendship.

2 This might well be Henry of Navarre, who visited Montaigne right after the victory of Coutras in 1587.

Everywhere else it is the same. A painful notion takes hold of me; I find it quicker to change it than to subdue it. I substitute a contrary one for it, or, if I cannot, at all events a different one. Variation always solaces, dissolves, and dissipates. If I cannot combat it, I escape it; and in fleeing I dodge, I am tricky. By changing place, occupation, and company, I escape into the throng of other occupations and thoughts, where it loses my trace and so loses me.

Nature proceeds thus by the benefit of our inconstancy. For time, which she has given us as the sovereign physician of our passions, gains its effect principally in this way: furnishing our imagination with other and ever other business, it dissolves and breaks up that first sensation, however strong it may be.

A wise man sees his dying friend hardly less vividly after twenty-five years[3] than in the first year; [C]and according to Epicurus, no less vividly; for he attributed no alleviation of afflictions either to their anticipation or to their old age. [B]But so many other thoughts traverse this one that in the end it languishes and tires.

To deflect the bent of popular rumor, Alcibiades cut off the ears and tail of his handsome dog and drove him out into the public square, so that the people, given this subject to babble about, might leave his other actions in peace. I have also known women, for this purpose of diverting people's opinions and conjectures and putting the gossips off the track, to cover their true affections with counterfeit ones. But I knew one who, in counterfeiting, let herself be caught in good earnest, and abandoned the true original affection for the pretended one. And I learned from her that men who are well lodged in women's graces are fools to consent to this masquerade. Since the public greetings and conversations are reserved for this planted suitor, believe me when I say he is not very able if he does not at last take your place and send you to his. [C]That really is cutting out and sewing a shoe for someone else to put on.

[B]It takes little to divert and distract us, for it takes little to hold us. We scarcely look at things in gross and alone; it is the minute and superficial circumstances and notions that strike us, and the empty husks that peel off from the things:

> As now in summer the cicadas leave behind
> Their filmy shells.
> LUCRETIUS

3 Montaigne wrote this about twenty-five years after the death of his friend La Boétie.

Even Plutarch regrets his daughter for the monkey tricks of her childhood. The remembrance of a farewell, an action, a particular grace, a last recommendation, afflicts us. Caesar's robe troubled all Rome, as his death had not done. The very sound of the names, which rings in our ears – "My poor master!" or "My great friend!" "Alas, my dear father!" or "My sweet daughter!" – when these refrains pain me and I look at them closely, I find that they are only grammatical and vocal complaints. The word and the sound hurt me, just as the exclamations of preachers move their auditors more than their reasons, and as we are struck by the piteous voice of the animal that is being killed for our use; so that I do not weigh or penetrate meanwhile the true and solid essence of my subject:

> 'Tis with these stimuli that grief provokes itself.
>
> LUCAN

These are the foundations of our mourning.

ᶜThe obstinacy of my kidney stones, especially in the penis, has sometimes cast me into long retentions of urine, for three, even four days, and so far forward into death that it would have been madness to hope, or even to wish, to avoid it, in view of the cruel attacks that this condition brings. Oh what a grand master in the art of torture was that good Emperor[4] who had his criminals' penises tied so they would die from not being able to piss! Finding myself in this plight, I considered by what slight causes and objects my imagination fostered in me the regret for life; out of what atoms the gravity and difficulty of this dislodgment from life built itself up in my soul; for what frivolous thoughts we made room in so great an affair: a dog, a horse, a book, a glass, and what not, counted for something in my loss. With others it is their ambitious hopes, their purse, their learning – no less foolishly, in my opinion. I saw death nonchalantly when I saw it universally, as the end of life. I dominate it in the mass; in detail it harasses me. The tears of a lackey, the distribution of my old clothes, the touch of a well-known hand, a commonplace phrase of consolation, make me disconsolate and sorry for myself.

ᴮThus the laments in fiction trouble our souls, and in Virgil and Catullus the regrets of Dido and Ariadne impassion even those who do not believe in them. ᶜIt is a sign of a hard and obstinate nature to feel no emotion about them; it is reported as a miracle about Polemon that he was of this stamp, but then, too, he did not even

4 Tiberius.

turn pale at the bite of a mad dog, who took away the calf of his leg.
^BAnd no matter how great a man's wisdom, he can never grasp, through his judgment alone, the cause of another's grief in all its intensity; his understanding is always enhanced by actual presence, when the eyes and ears have a share in it, organs that cannot be stirred except by incidental details.

Is it reasonable for the arts themselves to make their use and profit of our natural feeble-mindedness and stupidity? The orator, rhetoric says, in that farce that is his plea, will be moved by the sound of his own voice and his own feigned emotions, and will let himself be tricked into the passion he is portraying. He will imprint on himself a real and essential sorrow by means of this mummery that he enacts, in order to transmit it to the judges, whom it concerns even less; like those persons who are hired at funerals to assist in the ceremony of mourning and sell their tears by weight and measure, and also their sadness. For even though they go through borrowed emotions, nevertheless it is certain that in the process of adjusting themselves to their rearranged facial expression they are often entirely carried away and inwardly affected with a genuine melancholy.

I was one of the several friends of Monsieur de Gramont who escorted his body from the siege of La Fère, where he was killed, to Soissons. I observed that everywhere we passed, the people were moved to tears and lamentation by the mere solemn pomp of our convoy; for even the name of the deceased was unknown to them.

^CQuintilian says he has seen actors so deeply engaged in a mournful role that they were still weeping from it after they returned home; and that he himself, having undertaken to arouse some passion in others, espoused it himself to the point of being overcome not only by tears but by the pallor of countenance and the bearing of a man really overwhelmed with grief.

^BIn a region near our mountains the women play the part of Prester Martin;[5] for even as they magnify their grief for their lost husband by remembering the good and agreeable qualities he had, at the same time they also assemble and proclaim his imperfections, as if to bring themselves to some sort of balance and to turn themselves aside from pity to disdain; ^Cwith much better grace, at that, than we who, at the loss of a casual acquaintance, pride

5 A legendary priest who at Mass took both parts, giving the responses as well as the questions.

ourselves on lending him new and undeserved praises and making him quite another man, when we have lost sight of him, than he seemed to us when we were seeing him. As if regret were an instructive thing, or tears enlightened our understanding by washing it. From this moment I renounce any favorable testimonials that anyone may want to give me not because I shall deserve them but because I shall be dead.

[B]If you ask that man "What interest have you in this siege?" he will say: "The interest of example and of common obedience to the prince. I aspire to no profit whatever from it, and as for glory, I know how small a share of it can concern a private person like myself. I have no passion or quarrel in this." Yet see him on the next day, all changed, all boiling and red with anger at his post in the line of attack: it is the gleam of so much steel, and the fire and racket of our cannon and drums, that have injected this new rigor and hatred into his veins.

A frivolous cause, you will tell me. What do you mean, a cause? None is needed to agitate our soul: a daydream without body or subject dominates and agitates it. If I take to building castles in Spain, my imagination fabricates comforts and pleasures there by which my soul is really tickled and rejoiced. How many times we trouble our mind with anger or sadness by such shadows, and involve ourselves in fanciful passions which transform both our soul and our body. [C]What astonished, laughing, and confused grimaces daydreams produce on our faces! What starts and agitations of our limbs and our voice! Does it not seem that this man, alone as he is, has false visions of a throng of other men with whom he is dealing, or of some inner demon that is persecuting him?

[B]Inquire of yourself where is the object of this change. Is there anything besides ourselves in nature that feeds on inanity and is subject to its power?

Cambyses, because in his sleep he had dreamed that his brother was to become king of Persia, had put him to death – a brother whom he loved and had always trusted. Aristodemus, king of the Messenians, killed himself because he fancied there was a bad omen in some howling of his dogs. And King Midas did as much, disturbed and upset by some unpleasant dream he had dreamed. It is pricing our life exactly as it really is to abandon it for a dream.

And yet hear our soul triumph over the misery of the body, over its weakness, over the fact that it is a target for all kinds of injury and alterations. Truly it has a fine right to talk!

Poor clay, to which Prometheus did first impart
 Its shape! He played a thoughtless role.
Body he planned, but mind he saw not in his art;
 His first concern should have been soul.

<div align="right">PROPERTIUS</div>

5
On some verses of Virgil

^BTo the extent that useful thoughts are fuller and more solid, they are also more absorbing and more burdensome. Vice, death, poverty, disease, are grave subjects and grieve us. We should have our soul instructed in the means to sustain and combat evils, and in the rules for right living and right belief, and should often arouse it and exercise it in this fine study. But for a soul of the common sort this must be done with some respite and with moderation; it goes mad if it is too continually tense.

In my youth I needed to warn and urge myself to stick to my duty: blitheness and health do not go so well, they say, with these wise and serious reflections. At present I am in another state. The conditions of old age warn me, sober me, and preach to me only too much. From an excess of gaiety I have fallen into an excess of severity, which is more disagreeable. Wherefore at this point I deliberately let myself go a bit to license and sometimes occupy my soul with youthful wanton thoughts to give it a rest. Henceforth I shall be only too sedate, too heavy, and too mature. The years lecture me every day in coldness and temperance. This body of mine flees disorder and fears it. It is my body's turn to guide my mind toward reform. It dominates in turn, and more roughly and imperiously. It does not leave me a single hour, sleeping or waking, unoccupied with instruction about death, patience, and penitence. I defend myself against temperance as I once did against sensual pleasure; for it pulls me too far back, even to the point of insensibility.

Now I want to be master of myself in every direction. Wisdom has its excesses, and has no less need of moderation than does folly. Thus, for fear I may dry up, wither, and grow heavy with prudence, in the intervals that my ills grant me –

Lest my mind dwell too much upon its ills

<div align="right">OVID</div>

– I very gently sidestep and avert my gaze from this stormy and cloudy sky that I have in front of me, which, thank God, I do indeed consider without fright, but not without effort and study, and I amuse myself in the remembrance of my past youth:

> The soul craves what it has lost,
> And wholly throws itself into the past.
>
> PETRONIUS

Let childhood look ahead, old age backward: was not this the meaning of the double face of Janus? Let the years drag me along if they will, but backward. As long as my eyes can discern that lovely season now expired, I turn them in that direction at intervals. If youth is escaping from my blood and my veins, at least I want not to uproot the picture of it from my memory:

> Our lives are two
> If we can relish our past life anew.
>
> MARTIAL

^CPlato orders men to attend the exercises, dances, and games of youth, in order to rejoice in others at the suppleness and beauty of body that is no longer in themselves, and to call to mind the grace and charm of that flowering age; and he wants them to attribute the honor of victory in these sports to the young man who has most exhilarated and delighted the greatest number of them.

^BOnce I used to mark the burdensome and gloomy days as extraordinary. Those are now my ordinary ones; the extraordinary are the fine serene ones. I am on my way to the point where I will leap for joy as at a novel favor when nothing pains me. Though I tickle myself, I can scarcely wring a poor laugh out of this wretched body any more. I am merry only in fancy and in dreams, to divert by trickery the gloom of old age. But indeed it would require another remedy than a dream: a feeble struggle, that of art against nature. It is great simplicity to lengthen and anticipate human discomforts, as everyone does. I would rather be old less long than be old before I am old. Even the slightest occasions of pleasure that I can come upon, I seize. I know indeed by hearsay several kinds of pleasures that are prudent, strong, and glorious; but opinion has not enough power over me to give me an appetite for them. ^CI do not so much want them noble, magnificent, and ostentatious, as sweet, easy, and ready at hand. *We depart from nature; we give ourselves up to the people, who are not a good guide in anything* [Seneca].

^BMy philosophy is in action, in natural and present practice, little in fancy. Would I might take pleasure in playing at cobnut or with a top!

He set not people's shouts before the public safety.

ENNIUS, QUOTED BY CICERO

Pleasure is a rather unambitious quality. It thinks itself rich enough in itself without adding the prize of reputation, and prefers to be in the shade. We should take the whip to a young man who spent his time discriminating between the taste of wines and sauces. There is nothing I ever knew less or valued less than this. At present I am learning it. I am much ashamed of it, but what should I do? I am still more ashamed and vexed at the circumstances that drive me to it. It is for us to trifle and play the fool, and for the young to stand on their reputation and in the best place. They are going toward the world, toward reputation; we are coming from it. ^C*Let them have to themselves weapons, horses, spears, clubs, ball games, swimming, and races; let them leave to us old men, out of many sports, dice and knuckle-bones* [Cicero].

^BThe laws themselves send us home. I can do no less, on behalf of this puny condition into which my age pushes me, than furnish it with toys and pastimes, like childhood: and into that indeed we are falling back. Both wisdom and folly will have all they can do to support me and help me by their alternate services in this calamity of old age:

Mingle a dash of folly with your wisdom.

HORACE

Likewise I flee the slightest pains; and those that formerly would not even have scratched me, now pierce me through and through: so easily is my habit of body beginning to apply itself to illness. ^C*To a frail body every pain is intolerable* [Cicero].

^BAnd nothing that is hard can a sick mind endure.

OVID

I have always been sensitive and susceptible to pain; now I am still more tender, and exposed on all sides:

Anything cracked will shatter at a touch.

OVID

My judgment keeps me indeed from kicking and grumbling

against the discomforts that nature orders me to suffer, but not from feeling them. I, who have no other aim but to live and be merry, would run from one end of the world to the other to seek out one good year of pleasant and cheerful tranquillity. A somber, dull tranquillity is easy enough to find for me, but it puts me to sleep and stupefies me; I am not content with it. If there are any persons, any good company, in country or city, in France or elsewhere, residing or traveling, who like my humors and whose humors I like, they have only to whistle in their palm and I will go furnish them with essays in flesh and bone.

Since it is the privilege of the mind to rescue itself from old age, I advise mine to do so as strongly as I can. Let it grow green, let it flourish meanwhile, if it can, like mistletoe on a dead tree. But I fear it is a traitor. It has such a tight brotherly bond with the body that it abandons me at every turn to follow the body in its need. I take it aside and flatter it, I work on it, all for nothing. In vain I try to turn it aside from this bond, I offer it Seneca and Catullus, and the ladies and the royal dances; if its companion has the colic, it seems to have it too. Even the activities that are peculiarly its own cannot then be aroused; they evidently smack of a cold in the head. There is no sprightliness in its productions if there is none in the body at the same time.

ᶜOur masters are wrong in that, seeking the causes of the extraordinary flights of our soul, they have attributed some to a divine ecstasy, to love, to warlike fierceness, to poetry, to wine, but have not assigned a proper share to health – an ebullient, vigorous, full, lazy health, such as in the past my green years and security supplied me with now and then. The blaze of gaiety kindles in the mind vivid, bright flashes beyond our natural capacity, and some of the lustiest, if not the most extravagant, enthusiasms.

Now then, it is no wonder if a contrary state weighs down my spirits, nails them down, and produces a contrary effect.

ᴮDrooping with the body, it rises to no task.
MAXIMIANUS

Moreover, my mind wants me to be grateful to it because, so it says, it concedes much less to this bond than is usual with most men. At least, while we have a truce, let us banish troubles and difficulties from our relations:

So while we may, let's banish wrinkle-fronted age;
HORACE

gloomy things should be lightened with pleasantries [Sidonius Apollinaris].

I love a gay and sociable wisdom, and shun harshness and austerity in behavior, holding every surly countenance suspect:

^CThe sullen arrogance of a gloomy face.
BUCHANAN

^BThat sad group also has its sodomites.
MARTIAL

^CI heartily agree with Plato when he says that an easy or a difficult humor is of great importance to the goodness or badness of the soul. Socrates had a settled expression, but serene and smiling, not settled like that of old Crassus, who was never seen to laugh. ^BVirtue is a pleasant and gay quality.

^CI know well that very few people will frown at the license of my writings who do not have more to frown at in the license of their thoughts. I conform well to their hearts, but I offend their eyes. It is a well-ordered humor that criticizes Plato's writings and glides over his supposed relations with Phaedo, Dion, Stella, and Archeanassa. *Let us not be ashamed to say what we are not ashamed to think* [author unknown].

^BI hate a surly and gloomy spirit that slides over the pleasures of life and seizes and feeds upon its misfortunes: like flies, which cannot cling to a smooth and well-polished body, and attach themselves to and rest on rough and uneven places, and like leeches that suck and crave only bad blood.

Furthermore, I have ordered myself to dare to say all that I dare to do, and I dislike even thoughts that are unpublishable. The worst of my actions and conditions does not seem to me so ugly as the cowardice of not daring to avow it. Everyone is discreet in confession; people should be so in action. Boldness in sinning is somewhat compensated and bridled by boldness in confessing. ^CWhoever would oblige himself to tell all, would oblige himself not to do anything about which we are constrained to keep silent. God grant that this excessive license of mine may encourage our men to attain freedom, rising above these cowardly and hypocritical virtues born of our imperfections; that at the expense of my immoderation I may draw them on to the point of reason. A man must see his vice and study it to tell about it. Those who hide it from others ordinarily hide it from themselves. And they do not consider it covered up

enough if they themselves see it; they withdraw and disguise it from their own conscience. *Why does no one confess his vices? Because he is still in their grip now; it is only for a waking man to tell his dream* [Seneca].

The diseases of the body become clearer as they increase. We find that what we were calling a cold or a sprain is the gout. The diseases of the soul grow more obscure as they grow stronger; the sickest man is least sensible of them. That is why they must be handled often in the light of day, with a pitiless hand, be opened up and torn from the hollow of our breast. As in the matter of good deeds, so in the matter of evil deeds, mere confession is sometimes reparation. Is there any ugliness in doing wrong that can dispense us from the duty of confessing it?

ᴮIt is painful for me to dissemble, so much so that I avoid taking others' secrets into my keeping, not really having the heart to disavow what I know. I can keep silent about it, but deny it I cannot without effort and displeasure. To be really secret a man must be so by nature, not by obligation. In the service of princes it is a small thing to be secret if one is not a liar to boot. If the man who was asking Thales the Milesian whether he should solemnly deny having committed adultery had asked me, I would have answered him that he should not do it, for lying seems to me even worse than adultery. Thales advised him quite differently: to swear to his innocence, so as to shield the greater fault by the lesser. However, this advice was not so much a choice as a multiplication of vices.

Whereupon let us say this word in passing, that we offer a good bargain to a man of conscience when we propose to him some difficulty as a counterpoise to vice. But when we shut him up between two vices, we put him to a rough choice, as they did to Origen: that he should either worship an idol or endure being carnally enjoyed by a big ugly Ethiopian who was brought before him. He submitted to the first condition, and sinfully, it is said. On this basis those women would not be wrong who protest to us these days, according to their error,¹ that they would rather burden their conscience with ten men than with one Mass.

If it is indiscretion to publish one's errors thus, there is no great danger that it will pass into an example and custom. For Aristo used to say that the words men fear most are those that uncover them. We

1 Protestantism.

must tuck up this stupid rag that covers our conduct. They send their conscience to the brothel and keep their countenance in good order. Even those who are traitors and assassins espouse the laws of ceremony and fix their duty there. Yet it is not for injustice to complain of indecorum, ᶜor malice of indiscretion. It is a pity that a wicked man is not also a fool, and that outward decency should palliate his vice. These decorative incrustations belong only to a good, healthy wall that deserves to be preserved or whitened.

ᴮIn honor of the Huguenots, who condemn our private and auricular confession, I confess myself in public, religiously and purely. Saint Augustine, Origen, and Hippocrates have published the errors of their opinions; I, besides, those of my conduct.[2] I am hungry to make myself known, and I care not to how many, provided it be truly. Or to put it better, I am hungry for nothing, but I have a mortal fear of being taken to be other than I am by those who come to know my name.

A man who does everything for honor and glory, what does he think to gain by presenting himself to the world in a mask, concealing his true being from public knowledge? Praise a hunchback for his handsome figure, and he is bound to take it as an insult. If you are a coward and people honor you as a valiant man, is it you they are talking about? They take you for another. I would just as soon have such a man find gratification in having people doff their hat to him, thinking that he is master of the troop, when he is one of the meanest of the retinue.

As Archelaus, king of Macedonia, was passing in the street, someone poured some water on him. Those with him said he should punish the man. "Yes," he said, "but he did not pour water on me, but on the man he thought I was." ᶜSocrates said to the man who informed him that people were speaking ill of him: "Not at all; there is nothing in me of what they say."

ᴮAs for me, if someone praised me for being a good pilot, for being very modest, or for being very chaste, I would owe him no thanks. And similarly if someone called me traitor, robber, or drunkard, I would consider myself offended just as little. Those who have a false opinion of themselves can feed on false approbations; not I, who see myself and search myself to my very entrails,

2 Montaigne seems not to have known Saint Augustine's *Confessions*, though he much admired *The City of God*.

who know well what belongs to me. I am pleased to be less praised, provided I am better known. ^CI might be considered wise with the kind of wisdom I consider folly.

^BI am annoyed that my essays serve the ladies only as a public article of furniture, an article for the parlor. This chapter will put me in the boudoir. I like their society when it is somewhat private; when public, it is without favor or savor.

In farewells we exaggerate the warmth of our affection toward the things we are leaving. I am taking my last leave of the world's pastimes; here are our last embraces. But let us come to my theme.

What has the sexual act, so natural, so necessary, and so just, done to mankind, for us not to dare talk about it without shame and for us to exclude it from serious and decent conversation? We boldly pronounce the words "kill," "rob," "betray"; and this one we do not dare pronounce, except between our teeth. Does this mean that the less we breathe of it in words, the more we have the right to swell our thoughts with it?

^CFor it is a good one that the words least in use, least written and most hushed up, are the best known and most generally familiar. No age, no type of character, is ignorant of them, any more than of the word "bread." They impress themselves on everyone without being expressed, without voice and without form. It is also a good one that this is an action that we have placed in the sanctuary of silence, from which it is a crime to drag it out even to accuse and judge it. Nor do we dare to chastise it except roundaboutly and figuratively. A great favor for a criminal, to be so execrable that justice deems it unjust to touch and see him: free and saved by virtue of the severity of his condemnation.

Is it not the same as in the matter of books, which become all the more marketable and public by being suppressed? For my part I am going to take Aristotle at his word when he says that bashfulness serves as an ornament to youth but a reproach to old age.

^BThese verses are preached in the ancient school, a school I adhere to much more than to the modern; ^Cits virtues seem to me greater, its vices less:

> ^BThose who flee Venus too much sin no less
> Than those who do pursue her to excess.
> <div align="right">AMYOT'S PLUTARCH</div>

> Thou, goddess, thou alone rul'st over everything;
> Without thee nothing rises to the light of day;
> Nothing becomes, without thee, lovable or gay.
>
> LUCRETIUS

I do not know who can have put Pallas and the Muses on bad terms with Venus and made them cold toward Love; but I know no deities better suited or more indebted to one another. Whoever takes away from the Muses their amorous fancies will rob them of the best subject they have and the noblest matter of their work. And whoever makes Love lose the communication and service of poetry will disarm him of his best weapons. In this way they charge the god of intimacy and affection, and the patron goddesses of humanity and justice, with the vice of ingratitude and lack of appreciation.

I have not been so long cashiered from the roll and retinue of this god as not to have a memory informed of his powers and merits:

> I know the traces of the ancient flame.
>
> VIRGIL

There is still some remnant of heat and emotion after the fever:

> In wintry years, let me not lack this heat.
>
> JOHANNES SECUNDUS

Dried out and weighed down as I am, I still feel some tepid remains of that past ardor:

> As the Aegean, when those winds have died
> Which only lately made it churn and leap,
> Does not at once grow calm, or put aside
> The roar and violence of the raging deep.
>
> TASSO

But from what I understand of it, the powers and worth of this god are more alive and animated in the painting of poetry than in their own reality,

> And verses have their fingers to excite.
>
> JUVENAL

Poetry reproduces an indefinable mood that is more amorous than love itself. Venus is not so beautiful all naked, alive, and panting, as she is here in Virgil:

The goddess ceased to speak, and snowy arms outflung
Around him faltering, soft fondling as she clung.
He quickly caught the wonted flame; the heat well-known
Entered his marrow, ran through every trembling bone.
Often a brilliant lightning flash, not otherwise,
Split by a thunderclap, runs through the cloudy skies.

 He spoke,
Gave the embraces that she craved; then on her breast,
Outpoured at last, gave himself up to sleep and rest.
 VIRGIL

What I find worth considering here is that he portrays her as a little too passionate for a marital Venus. In this sober contract the appetites are not so wanton; they are dull and more blunted. Love hates people to be attached to each other except by himself, and takes a laggard part in relations that are set up and maintained under another title, as marriage is. Connections and means have, with reason, as much weight in it as graces and beauty, or more. We do not marry for ourselves, whatever we say; we marry just as much or more for our posterity, for our family. The practice and benefit of marriage concerns our race very far beyond us. Therefore I like this fashion of arranging it rather by a third hand than by our own, and by the sense of others rather than by our own. How opposite is all this to the conventions of love! And so it is a kind of incest to employ in this venerable and sacred alliance the efforts and extravagances of amorous license, as it seems to me I have said elsewhere.[3] A man, says Aristotle, should touch his wife prudently and soberly, lest if he caresses her too lasciviously the pleasure should transport her outside the bounds of reason. What he says on account of conscience, the doctors say on account of health: that an excessively hot, voluptuous, and assiduous pleasure spoils the seed and hinders conception. They say, on the other hand, that for a languid encounter, as this one is by its nature, we should present ourselves rarely and at considerable intervals, to fill it with a just and fertile heat:

Athirst to take the member in and hide it deep.
 VIRGIL

I see no marriages that sooner are troubled and fail than those that progress by means of beauty and amorous desires. It needs more

3 *Essays* I: 30, "Of Moderation."

solid and stable foundations, and we need to go at it circumspectly; this ebullient ardor is no good for it.

Those who think to honor marriage by joining love to it act, it seems to me, the same as those who, to favor virtue, hold that nobility is nothing else but virtue. These are things that have a certain relationship, but there is a great difference between them. There is no point in mixing up their names and titles; we wrong one or the other by confusing them. Nobility is a fine quality, and introduced with reason. But inasmuch as it is a quality dependent on others, and which can fall to a vicious and worthless man, it is well below virtue in esteem. It is a virtue, if indeed it is one, that is artificial and visible, dependent upon time and fortune, varying in form according to countries, living and mortal, with no more source than the river Nile, genealogical and common to many, a matter of succession and resemblance, derived by inference, and a very weak inference at that. Knowledge, strength, goodness, beauty, riches, all other qualities, fall into the range of communication and association; this one is self-consuming, of no use in the service of others.

One of our kings was proposed the choice between two competitors for the same office, one of whom was a nobleman, the other was not. He ordered that they choose, without regard to this quality, the one who had the more merit; but that if the worth should be entirely equal, they should then take nobility into account. That was giving it exactly its proper place. Antigonus said to a young stranger who was asking him for the post of his father, a man of valor who had just died: "My friend, in such benefits I do not consider so much the nobility of my soldiers as I do their prowess." ^cIn truth, it should not go as it did with the functionaries of the kings of Sparta, trumpeters, minstrels, cooks, whose duties were inherited by their children, no matter how ignorant they were, in preference to the most experienced men in the trade.

The people of Calicut make of their nobles a superhuman species. Marriage is forbidden them, and every other occupation but war. Of concubines they may have their fill, and the women as many lovers, without jealousy toward one another; but it is a capital and unpardonable crime to mate with a person of another condition than their own. And they consider themselves polluted if they are so much as touched by them in passing, and, as their nobility is marvelously injured and damaged by this, they kill those who have merely approached a little too close to them; so that the ignoble

are obliged to cry out as they walk, like the gondoliers in Venice at the street corners, to avoid collisions; and the nobles command them to move aside in the direction they want. Thereby the nobles avoid an ignominy that they consider perpetual; and the others, a certain death. No length of time, no princely favor, no office or virtue or riches can make a commoner become a noble. In which this custom helps, that marriages are forbidden between one trade and another. A girl from a shoemaker's family cannot marry a carpenter. And the parents are obliged to train their children exactly for the father's calling and not for any other; whereby the distinction and continuity of their fortune is maintained.

ᴮA good marriage, if such there be, rejects the company and conditions of love. It tries to reproduce those of friendship. It is a sweet association in life, full of constancy, trust, and an infinite number of useful and solid services and mutual obligations. No woman who savors the taste of it,

> Whom the nuptial torch with welcome light has joined,
>
> CATULLUS

would want to have the place of a mistress or paramour to her husband. If she is lodged in his affection as a wife, she is lodged there much more honorably and securely. When he dances ardent and eager attention elsewhere, still let anyone ask him then on whom he would rather have some shame fall, on his wife or his mistress; whose misfortune would afflict him more; for whom he wishes more honor. These questions admit of no doubt in a sound marriage.

The fact that we see so few good marriages is a sign of its price and its value. If you form it well and take it rightly, there is no finer relationship in our society. We cannot do without it, and yet we go about debasing it. The result is what is observed about cages: the birds outside despair of getting in, and those inside are equally anxious to get out. ᶜSocrates, when asked which was preferable, to take or not to take a wife, said: "Whichever a man does, he will repent it." ᴮIt is a compact to which the saying is applied most appropriately, *man* is *to man* either *a god* or *a wolf* [Cecilius, quoted by Symmachus; and Plautus]. Many qualities must come together to construct it. It is found nowadays better suited to simple plebeian souls, in which luxury, curiosity, and idleness do not disturb it so much. Men with unruly humors like me, who hate any sort of bond or obligation, are not so fit for it:

> Sweeter it is to me to live with neck unyoked.
> MAXIMIANUS

Of my own choice, I would have avoided marrying Wisdom herself, if she had wanted me. But say what we will, the custom and practice of ordinary life bears us along. Most of my actions are conducted by example, not by choice. At all events, I did not really bid myself to it, I was led to it, and borne by extraneous circumstances. For not only inconvenient things, but anything at all, however ugly and vicious and repulsive, can become acceptable through some condition or circumstance: so inane is our human posture. And I was borne to it certainly more ill-prepared and contrary than I am now after having tried it. And, licentious as I am thought to be, I have in truth observed the laws of marriage more strictly than I had either promised or expected. It is no longer time to kick when we have let ourselves be hobbled. A man must husband his freedom prudently; but once he has submitted to an obligation, he must keep to it under the laws of common duty, at least make an effort to. Those who make this bargain only to behave with hatred and contempt act unjustly and harmfully. And that fine rule that I see passing from hand to hand among the women like a sacred oracle,

> Serve your husband as your master
> And guard against him as a traitor,
> FRENCH; SOURCE UNKNOWN

which is to say "Behave toward him with a constrained, hostile, and distrustful reverence," a war cry and a challenge, is equally unjust and hard. I am too soft for such thorny plans. To tell the truth, I have not yet attained such perfection of cleverness and refinement of wit as to confound reason with injustice and cast into derision any order and rule that does not accord with my appetite. Because I hate superstition, I do not promptly throw myself into irreligion. If a man does not always do his duty, at least he must always love and acknowledge it. ^CIt is treachery to get married without getting wedded. ^BLet us pass on.

Our poet represents a marriage full of harmony and well matched, in which, nevertheless, there is not much loyalty. Did he mean that it is not impossible to give in to the impact of love and nonetheless reserve some duty toward marriage, and that one may injure marriage without breaking it up completely? ^CA servant

may shoe his master's mule[4] without hating him for all that.
[B]Beauty, opportunity, destiny (for destiny has a hand in it too) –

> There is a destiny that rules
> The parts our clothes conceal; for if the stars abhor you,
> Unheard-of length of member will do nothing for you
>
> JUVENAL

– have attached her to a stranger; not so wholly, perhaps, that she
may not have some tie left by which she still holds to her husband.
Love and marriage are two intentions that go by separate and
distinct roads. A woman may give herself to a man whom she
would not at all want to have married; I do not mean because of
the state of his fortune, but because of his personal qualities. Few
men have married their mistresses who have not repented it – [C]even
in the other world: what a bad match Jupiter made with his wife,
whom he had first frequented and enjoyed in love affairs! It is the
old saying: "Shit in your hat and then put it on your head."

[B]I have seen in my time, in high place, love shamefully and
dishonorably cured by marriage: the considerations are too differ-
ent. We love, without conflict, two diverse and contrary things.
Isocrates used to say that people liked Athens the way men like
the ladies they serve for love. Everyone loved to come and wander
around and pass his time there; no one loved it enough to marry it,
that is to say, to reside and settle there. I have been vexed to see
husbands hate their wives for the mere fact that they themselves are
doing them wrong. At least we should not love them less for our
own fault. Through repentance and compassion, at least, they
should be dearer to us.

They are different ends, Isocrates says, and yet in some sort
compatible. Marriage has for its share utility, justice, honor, and
constancy: a flat pleasure, but more universal. Love is founded on
pleasure alone, and in truth its pleasure is more stimulating, lively,
and keen: a pleasure inflamed by difficulty. There must be a sting and
a smart in it. It is no longer love if it is without arrows and without
fire. The liberality of the ladies is too profuse in marriage, and blunts
the point of affection and desire. [C]Just see the pains that Lycurgus
and Plato take in their laws to avoid this disadvantage.

[B]Women are not wrong at all when they reject the rules of life
that have been introduced into the world, inasmuch as it is the men

4 Presumably, steal from him.

who have made these without them. There is naturally strife and wrangling between them and us: the closest communion we have with them is still tumultuous and tempestuous.

In our author's opinion we treat them inconsiderately in the following way. We have discovered, he says, that they are incomparably more capable and ardent than we in the acts of love – and that priest[5] of antiquity so testified, who had been once a man and then a woman,

> To him in both aspects was Venus known.
>
> OVID

– and besides, we have learned from their own mouth the proof that was once given in different centuries by an emperor and an empress[6] of Rome, master workmen and famous in this task: he indeed deflowered in one night ten captive Sarmatian virgins; but she actually in one night was good for twenty-five encounters, changing company according to her need and liking,

> Her secret parts burning and tense with lust,
> And, tired by men, but far from sated, she withdrew.
>
> JUVENAL

We know about the dispute that occurred in Catalonia from a woman complaining of the too assiduous efforts of her husband: not so much, in my opinion, that she was bothered by them (for I believe in miracles only in matters of faith), as by way of a pretext to curtail and curb, in the very thing that is the fundamental act of marriage, the authority of husbands over their wives, and to show that the peevishness and malignity of wives extends beyond the nuptial bed and treads underfoot the very graces and sweets of Venus; to which complaint the husband, a truly brutish and perverted man, answered that even on fast days he could not do with less than ten. There intervened that notable sentence of the queen of Aragon, by which, after mature deliberation with her council, this good queen, to give for all time a rule and example of the moderation and modesty required in a just marriage, ordained as the legitimate and necessary limit the number of six a day, relinquishing and giving up much of the need and desire of her sex, in order, she said, to establish an easy and consequently permanent and

5 Tiresias.
6 Proculus and Messalina.

immutable formula. At which the doctors cry out: "What must the feminine appetite and concupiscence be when their reason, their reformation, and their virtue are set at this rate?" ^CConsider these varying judgments about our sexual needs, and then the fact that Solon, chief of the lawgiving school, assesses conjugal intercourse, in order to keep from failing, at only three times a month. ^BAfter believing and preaching all this, we have gone and given women continence as their particular share, and upon utmost and extreme penalties.

There is no passion more pressing than this, which we want them alone to resist, not simply as a vice of its own size, but as an abomination and execration, more to be resisted than irreligion and parricide; and meanwhile we give in to it without blame or reproach. Even those of us who have tried to get the better of it have sufficiently admitted what difficulty, or rather impossibility, there was in subduing, weakening, and cooling off the body by material remedies. We, on the contrary, want them to be healthy, vigorous, plump, well-nourished, and chaste at the same time: that is to say, both hot and cold. For marriage, which we say has the function of keeping them from burning, brings them but little cooling off, according to our ways. If they take a husband in whom the vigor of youth is still boiling, he will pride himself on expending it elsewhere:

> Bassus, for shame, or we must go to law:
> I bought your penis at a heavy price;
> You've sold it, Bassus, it is yours no more.
>
> MARTIAL

^CThe philosopher Polemon was justly brought to justice by his wife, for sowing in a sterile field the fruit that was due to the genital field. ^BIf they take one of those broken-down ones, there they are in full wedlock worse off than virgins or widows. We consider them well provided for because they have a man beside them, as the Romans considered Clodia Laeta, a Vestal, violated because Caligula had approached her, even though it was attested that he had only approached her. But on the contrary, their need is only increased thereby, inasmuch as the contact and company of any male whatever awakens their heat, which would remain quieter in solitude. And for the purpose, it is likely, of rendering their chastity more meritorious by this circumstance and consideration, Boleslaus and Kinge, his wife, the king and queen of Poland, by mutual agreement

consecrated it by a vow, while lying together on their very wedding night, and maintained it in the face of marital opportunities.

We train them from childhood to the ways of love. Their grace, their dressing up, their knowledge, their language, all their instruction, has only this end in view. Their governesses imprint in them nothing else but the idea of love, if only by continually depicting it to them in order to disgust them with it. My daughter (she is the only child I have) is at the age at which the laws allow the most ardent of them to marry. She is of a backward constitution, slight and soft, and has been brought up by her mother accordingly, in a retired and private manner: so that she is now only just beginning to grow out of the naïveté of childhood.

She was reading a French book in my presence. The word *fouteau* occurred, the name of a familiar tree.[7] The woman she has to train her stopped her short somewhat roughly and made her skip over that perilous passage. I let her go ahead in order not to disturb their rules, for I do not involve myself at all in directing her: the government of women has a mysterious way of proceeding; we must leave it to them. But if I am not mistaken, the company of twenty lackeys could not have imprinted in her imagination in six months the understanding and use and all the consequences of the sound of those wicked syllables as did this good old woman by her reprimand and interdict:

> The ripened maid delights to learn
> In wanton Ionic dance to turn,
> And fondly dreams, when still a child,
> Of loves incestuous and wild.
>
> HORACE

Let them dispense with ceremony a bit, let them speak freely; we are but children compared with them in this knowledge. Hear them describe our wooings and our conversations, and you will realize full well that we bring them nothing that they have not known and digested without us. ᶜCould it be as Plato says, that they were once dissipated boys? ᴮMy ear one day happened to be in a place where without suspicion it could snatch some of the talk they were having among themselves. If only I might repeat it! By Our Lady, I said, we make fine use of our time by going off to study the phrases of Amadis and the stories of Boccaccio and Aretino so as to seem

7 Beech.

worldly-wise! There is not a word, not an example, not a trick that they do not know better than our books: it is a teaching that is born in their veins,

And Venus herself inspired them,
VIRGIL

which those good schoolmasters, nature, youth, and health, continually breathe into their souls. They have no need to learn it, they breed it:

Nor any more delighted is a snow-white dove,
Or if there be another thing more hot for love,
To keep on plucking kisses with a biting bill,
Than is a woman with her many-fancied will.
CATULLUS

If this natural violence of their desire were not somewhat held in check by the fear and honor with which they have been provided, we would be shamed. The whole movement of the world resolves itself into and leads to this coupling. It is a matter infused throughout, it is a center to which all things look. We still see some of the ordinances of wise old Rome drawn up for the service of love, and the precepts of Socrates for the instruction of courtesans:

Nor do the Stoics' little volumes hate
On silken cushions to lie in state.
HORACE

Zeno, among his laws, also made rules for the splitting and battering operations required to deflower virgins. What was the point of the philosopher Strato's book "Of Carnal Conjunction"? And what did Theophrastus treat of in those he entitled, one "The Lover," the other "Of Love"? And Aristippus in his, "Of Ancient Delights"? What is the purpose of Plato's so extensive and vivid descriptions of the boldest amours of his time? And "The Book of the Lover" by Demetrius Phalerius? And "Clinias, or the Ravished Lover," by Heraclides Ponticus? And Antisthenes' book "Of Begetting Children, or of Weddings," and the other, "Of the Master or the Lover"? And Aristo's "On Amorous Exercises"? And Cleanthes', one "Of Love," the other "On the Art of Loving"? The "Dialogues on Love" of Sphaerus? And Chrysippus' fable of Jupiter and Juno, shameless beyond all endurance, and his fifty very

lascivious Epistles? For I must leave aside the writings of the philosophers who followed the Epicurean sect.

^BFifty deities were in times past assigned to this office, and there were nations where, to assuage the lust of those who came to their devotions, they kept girls and boys in the churches to be enjoyed, and it was a ceremonious act to use them before coming to service. ^C*Doubtless incontinence is necessary for the sake of continence; a conflagration is extinguished by fire* [Tertullian].

^BIn most parts of the world this part of our body was deified. In one and the same province some flayed off the skin in order to offer and consecrate a piece of it, the others offered and consecrated their seed. In another, the young men publicly pierced and opened it in various places between the flesh and the skin, and put skewers through these openings, the longest and thickest that they could endure; and of these skewers they afterward made a fire as an offering to their gods. They were considered deficient in vigor and chastity if they were upset by the power of this cruel pain. Elsewhere the most sacred magistrate was revered and recognized by those parts of him; and in many ceremonies an effigy of it was carried in pomp in honor of various divinities.

The Egyptian ladies, at the festival of the Bacchanals, wore a wooden one around their neck, exquisitely fashioned, big and heavy, according to each one's capacity; besides which the statue of their god displayed one which surpassed in size the rest of the body.

The married women hereabouts form a figure of one with their kerchiefs over their forehead to glory in the enjoyment they have of it; and when they come to be widows they put it down in back and hide it beneath their coifs.

The most modest matrons in Rome were honored to offer flowers and garlands to the god Priapus; and the virgins at the time of their nuptials were made to sit on his least seemly parts. And I know not but that I have seen some semblance of a like devotion in my time. What was the meaning of that ridiculous part of the breeches worn by our fathers, which is still seen on our Swiss? What is the point of the show we make even now of the shape of our pieces under our galligaskins, and what is worse, often by falsehood and imposture beyond their natural size?

^CI am tempted to believe that this sort of garment was invented in better and more conscientious ages so as not to deceive people, so that each man alike might publicly and gallantly render an account of his capacity. The simpler nations still have it somewhat

corresponding to the real size. In those days the workman was taught the art, as is done in measuring the arm or the foot.

[B]That good man who, when I was young, castrated so many beautiful ancient statues in his great city, so that the eye might not be corrupted, [C]following the advice of that other ancient worthy –

> Nude bodies shown in public lead to shameful acts
> ENNIUS, QUOTED BY CICERO

– [B]should have called to mind that nothing was gained unless he also had horses and asses castrated, and finally all nature, just as in the mysteries of the Bona Dea[8] all semblance whatever of masculinity was excluded.

> Yes, everything on earth, the race of man and beast,
> Fish of the sea, and flocks, and gaily painted birds,
> Rush into passionate flame.
> VIRGIL

[C]The gods, says Plato, have furnished us with a disobedient and tyrannical member, which, like a furious animal, undertakes by the violence of its appetite to subject everything to itself. To women likewise they have given a gluttonous and voracious animal which, if denied its food in due season, goes mad, impatient of delay, and, breathing its rage into their bodies, stops up the passages, arrests the breathing, causing a thousand kinds of ills, until it has sucked in the fruit of the common thirst and therewith plentifully irrigated and fertilized the depth of the womb.

[B]Now my legislator should also have called to mind that it is perhaps a more chaste and fruitful practice to let them know the living reality early than to leave them to guess it according to the freedom and heat of their imagination. In place of the real parts, through desire and hope, they substitute others three times life-size. [C]And a certain man of my acquaintance ruined his chances by exposing his in a place where he was not yet in a position to put them to their more serious use.

[B]What mischief is not done by those enormous pictures that boys spread about the passages and staircases of palaces! From these, women acquire a cruel contempt for our natural capacity.

[C]How do we know that Plato did not have this in mind when,

8 Originally a Roman goddess of chastity.

imitating other well-constituted states, he ordained that men and women, young and old, should appear in one another's sight stark naked in gymnastics?

[B]The Indian women, who see the men in the raw, have at least cooled their sense of sight. [C]And although the women of the great kingdom of Pegu, who have nothing to cover them below the waist but a cloth slit in front and so narrow that whatever ceremonious modesty they seek to preserve, at each step they can be seen whole, may say that this is a device thought up in order to attract the men to them and divert them from their fondness for other males, to which that nation is altogether addicted, it might be said that they lose by it more than they gain and that a complete hunger is sharper than one that has been satisfied at least by the eyes.

[B]Moreover, Livia used to say that to a good woman a naked man is no more than a statue.

[C]The Lacedaemonian women, more virginal as wives than our women are as maidens, saw the young men of their city every day stripped at their exercises, and were not too careful themselves to cover their thighs in walking, considering themselves, as Plato says, sufficiently covered by their virtue without a farthingale.[9]

But those men of whom Saint Augustine tells us attributed to nudity a wonderful power of temptation by doubting whether at the universal judgment women will rise again in their own sex and not rather in ours, lest they tempt us still in that holy state.

[B]In short, we allure and flesh them by every means; we incessantly heat and excite their imagination; and then we bellyache. Let us confess the truth: there is hardly one of us who is not more afraid of the shame that comes to him for his wife's vices than for his own; who does not take better care (wonderful charity) of his good wife's conscience than of his own; who would not rather be a thief and sacrilegious and have his wife be a murderess and a heretic, than not to have her be more chaste than her husband.

And the women will gladly offer to go to the law courts to seek gain, and to war to seek a reputation, rather than be obliged to keep so difficult a guard in the midst of idleness and pleasures. Don't they see that there is not a merchant, or a lawyer, or a soldier who will not leave his business to run after this other – and the porter and the cobbler, all harassed and worn out as they are with work and hunger?

9 In French, "de leur vertu sans vertugade."

Would you give, for all Mygdonian Phrygia's gold,
Or all the wealth Achaemenes possesses,
Or what Arabia's full coffers hold,
 One of Licinia's tresses,

While to your kisses sweet her neck so white
She bends, or, cruel, tenderly denies
Those in which more than you she takes delight,
 And soon she'll snatch by surprise?
 HORACE

^CIniquitous appraisal of vices! Both we and they are capable of a thousand corruptions more harmful and unnatural than lasciviousness. But we create and weigh vices not according to nature but according to our interest, whereby they assume so many unequal shapes. The severity of our decrees makes women's addiction to this vice more exacerbated and vicious than its nature calls for, and involves it in consequences that are worse than their cause.

^BI do not know whether the exploits of Caesar and Alexander surpass in hardship the resoluteness of a beautiful young woman brought up in our fashion, in full view of and contact with the world, assailed by so many contrary examples, keeping herself entire in the midst of a thousand continual and powerful solicitations. There is no action more thorny, or more active, than this inaction. I find it much easier to bear a suit of armor all one's life than a virginity; and the vow of virginity is the most noble of all vows, as being the hardest: ^C*The power of the Devil is in the loins*, says Saint Jerome.

^BCertainly we have resigned to the ladies the most arduous and vigorous of human duties, and we leave them the glory of it. That should serve them as a singular spur to persevere in it. This is a fine occasion for them to defy us and to trample underfoot that vain preeminence in valor and virtue that we claim over them. They will find, if they take note, that they will be not only very esteemed for this but also more loved. A gallant man does not abandon his pursuit for being refused, provided the refusal is dictated by chastity rather than choice. We can swear, threaten, and complain all we like: we lie, we love them the better for it. There is no allurement like a modesty that is not heartless and surly. It is stupidity and baseness to persevere against hatred and contempt, but against a virtuous and constant resolution mingled with a grateful good will, it is the exercise of a noble and generous soul. They may recognize our

services up to a certain degree, and honorably make us feel that they do not disdain us.

ᶜFor that law that commands them to abominate us because we adore them and to hate us because we love them is indeed cruel, if only for its difficulty. Why shall they not hear our offers and requests so long as they keep within the duty of modesty? Why do we go surmising that they have some more licentious idea within? A queen of our time used to say shrewdly that to refuse to hear these advances was a testimony of weakness and an accusation of one's own facility; and that a lady who had not been tempted could not boast of her chastity.

ᴮThe limits of honor are by no means so curtailed. It has room to relax, it can allow itself some freedom without transgressing. At its frontier there is some space that is free, indifferent, and neutral. If a man has been able to hunt it down and bring it to bay by force right in its corner and stronghold, he is a fool if he is not satisfied with his fortune. The prize of victory is estimated by its difficulty. Do you want to know what impression your service and your merit have made on her heart? Measure it by her character. Some may grant more who do not grant so much. The obligation for the benefit is entirely relative to the will of the person who grants it. The other circumstances that enter into a benefit are dumb, dead, and fortuitous. It costs her more to give that little than it costs her companion to give her all. If in anything rarity is a value, it must be in this. Do not consider how little it is, but how few have it. The value of money changes according to the coinage and the place where it is minted.

Whatever the spite and indiscretion of some men may make them say in the excess of their discontent, virtue and truth always regain their advantage. I have known women whose reputation was long unjustly damaged to restore themselves to the universal esteem of men by their constancy alone, without any effort or artifice. Everyone repents and takes back what he had believed of them; after being slightly suspect girls, they hold the first rank among ladies of virtue and honor. Someone said to Plato: "Everyone is speaking ill of you." "Let them talk," he said, "I will live in such a fashion as to make them change their tune."

Besides the fear of God and the prize of so rare a glory, which should incite women to preserve themselves, the corruption of our time forces them to; and if I were in their place, there is nothing I would not do rather than entrust my reputation to such dangerous

hands. In my time the pleasure of telling about it (a pleasure which yields little in sweetness to that of the thing itself) was permitted only to those who had some faithful and unique friend. Nowadays the ordinary conversation at gatherings and at table consists of boasts of the favors received and the secret liberality of the ladies. Truly one must be abject and base in heart beyond measure to allow these tender charms to be so cruelly persecuted, pawed over, and ransacked by such ungrateful, indiscreet, and fickle persons.

This immoderate and illegitimate exasperation of ours against this vice is born of the most vain and tempestuous malady that afflicts human souls, which is jealousy.

> Who forbids taking a light from a flaming torch?
>
> OVID

> Give all they will, yet thereby nothing's lost.
>
> PRIAPEIA

Jealousy and her sister envy seem to me among the most foolish of the troop. Of the latter I can scarcely speak: this passion, which is painted as being so strong and powerful, has, by its good grace, no access to me. As for the other, I know it, at least by sight. The animals have a sense of it: when the shepherd Crastis fell in love with a goat, her mate out of jealousy came and butted his head as he was asleep and crushed it. We have raised this fever to an excessive pitch, after the example of same barbarian nations. The better disciplined ones have been touched by it, which is reasonable, but not carried away:

> Never adulterer, by sword of husband slain,
> Did with his purple blood the Stygian waters stain.
>
> JOHANNES SECUNDUS

Lucullus, Caesar, Pompey, Antony, Cato, and other brave men were cuckolds and knew it without stirring up a tumult about it. In those days there was only one fool of a Lepidus who died in anguish over it.

> Then you will suffer the adulterer's fate:
> They'll spread your legs, and cram your open gate
> With radishes and mullets.
>
> CATULLUS

And the god of our poet, when he surprised one of his companions with his wife, contented himself with putting them to shame:

> And one merry wag among the gods,
> Wished that thus he might be disgraced;
>
> <div align="right">OVID</div>

and, for all that, he allows himself to be warmed by the sweet caresses she offers him, complaining that it was on this account she had come to mistrust his affection:

> Why go seek causes from afar? Whither has gone,
> Goddess, your faith in me?
>
> <div align="right">VIRGIL</div>

In fact she asks a favor of him for a bastard of hers –

> I ask for arms, a mother for her son
>
> <div align="right">VIRGIL</div>

– which is liberally granted her; and Vulcan speaks honorably of Aeneas,

> Arms for a warrior must be made,
>
> <div align="right">VIRGIL</div>

with a humanity truly more than human. And I will consent that this excess of goodness be left to the gods:

> Nor is it fair to equal men with gods.
>
> <div align="right">CATULLUS</div>

As for the confusion of children, ^cnot only do the most serious legislators ordain and favor it in their republics, but furthermore ^Bit does not concern the women, in whom this passion of jealousy is, I know not how, still more firmly seated:

> For often Juno, mistress of the gods,
> Burns at her husband's daily escapades.
>
> <div align="right">CATULLUS</div>

When jealousy seizes these poor, weak, and unresisting souls, it is pitiful how cruelly it drags them about and tyrannizes over them. It insinuates itself into them under the title of friendship, but once it possesses them, the same causes that served as the foundation of good will serve as the foundation of mortal hatred. ^cOf all the diseases of the mind it is the one which the most things serve to feed and the fewest things to remedy. ^BThe virtue, the health, the merit, the reputation, of the husband are the firebrands of the wives' ill will and fury:

No hatreds are so keen as those of love.

PROPERTIUS

This fever disfigures and corrupts all that is otherwise beautiful and good in them; and in a jealous woman, however chaste she may be and however good a housewife, there is no action that does not smack of bitterness and unpleasantness. It is a frenzied agitation, which tosses them to an extreme completely contrary to its cause. A good example was one Octavius in Rome. After he had slept with Pontia Posthumia, his affection was increased by the enjoyment, and he sought most urgently to marry her. When he was unable to persuade her, his extreme love threw him into the reactions of the most cruel and mortal hatred: he killed her. Likewise the ordinary symptoms of that other love malady are intestine hatreds, plots, conspiracies,

'Tis known what woman in a rage can do,

VIRGIL

and a rage which is all the more fretful for being constrained to justify itself under the pretext of good will.

Now the duty of chastity is very extensive. Is it their will that we want our women to curb? That is a very supple and active faculty; it has a lot of agility if we try to immobilize it. What if dreams sometimes involve them so far that they cannot deny them? It is not in them, nor perhaps in Chastity herself, since she is a female, to keep themselves from lust and desire. If their will alone concerns us, where are we? Imagine the great rush if a man had the privilege of being borne swift as a bird, without eyes to see or tongue to tell, into the arms of each woman who would accept him.

^CThe Scythian women put out the eyes of all their slaves and prisoners of war to make use of them more freely and secretly.

^BOh, what a terrific advantage is opportuneness! If someone asked me the first thing in love, I would answer that it is knowing how to seize the right time; the second likewise, and the third too; it is a point that can accomplish anything.

I have often lacked luck, but also sometimes enterprise: God keep from harm the man who can laugh at this. These days love calls for more temerity, which our young men excuse on the pretext of ardor; but if the women considered the matter closely, they would find that temerity comes rather from contempt. I used to be scrupulously afraid of giving offense, and I am inclined to respect what

I love. Besides, in these negotiations, if you take away respect you rub out the glamor. In this I like to have a man somewhat play the child and the timid slave. If not altogether in this, in other situations I have something of the stupid bashfulness that Plutarch speaks of, and the course of my life has been harmed and blemished by it in various ways: a quality very ill-suited to my nature in general – and indeed what are we but sedition and discrepancy? My eyes are tender for enduring a refusal, as they are for refusing; and it troubles me so much to be troublesome to others that on the occasions when duty forces me to test out someone's will in a doubtful matter which may cost him some trouble, I do it halfheartedly and against the grain. But if the matter affects my personal interest, ᶜthough Homer truly says that bashfulness is a stupid virtue in a needy man, ᴮI ordinarily commission a third person to blush in my place. And with the same difficulty I dismiss people who want to use me; so that it has happened to me sometimes to have the wish to refuse but not the strength.

Thus it is folly to try to bridle in women a desire that is so ᶜburning and so ᴮnatural to them. And when I hear them boast of having such a virginal and cold disposition, I laugh at them: they are leaning over too far backward. If it is a toothless and decrepit old woman or a dry and consumptive young one, though it is not altogether credible, at least they have some semblance of truth in saying it. But those who still move and breathe make their position worse in this way, since ill-considered excuses serve as accusation. Like a gentleman, one of my neighbors, who was suspected of impotence,

> Whose member, feebler than a tender beet,
> Never rose even up to middle height,
>
> CATULLUS

who, three or four days after his wedding, to justify himself, went around boldly swearing that he had ridden twenty stages the night before; which was afterward used to convict him of pure ignorance and to annul his marriage. Besides, what these women say has no value, for there is neither continence nor virtue unless there is an urge to the contrary. "It is true," they should say, "but I am not ready to give myself up." The saints themselves talk that way. I mean those women who boast in good earnest of their coldness and insensibility and who, with a straight face, want to be believed. For when it is with an affected countenance, in which the eyes belie their words, and with the jargon of their profession which has its effect in

reverse, I think that's fine. I am a great admirer of naturalness and freedom, but there is no help for it: unless it is completely simple and childlike, it is unbecoming to ladies and out of place in these dealings: it promptly slides into shamelessness. Their disguises and their faces deceive only fools. Lying holds an honorable place in love; it is a detour that leads us to truth by the back door.

If we cannot hold back their imagination, what do we expect of them? Deeds? There are enough of these that escape all outside communication, by which chastity may be corrupted:

> That which he does unwitnessed, he does often.
>
> MARTIAL

And the deeds that we fear the least are perhaps the most to be feared; silent sins are the worst:

> A simpler prostitute offends me less.
>
> MARTIAL

ᶜThere are acts by which they can lose their chastity without unchastity, and, what is more, without their knowledge. *A midwife, for instance, making a manual examination of some virgin's integrity, whether through malice, unskilfulness, or accident, by inspecting it has destroyed it* [Saint Augustine]. Some have lost their maidenhead for having looked for it; some have destroyed it in sport.

ᴮWe could not possibly circumscribe precisely for them the actions that we forbid them. We must formulate our rules in general and uncertain terms. The very idea that we form of their chastity is ridiculous; for among the extreme examples I know of is Fatua, wife of Faunus, who never let herself be seen by any man whatever after her wedding; and Hiero's wife, who never noticed her husband's stinking breath, thinking that this was a quality common to all men. They must become insensible and invisible in order to satisfy us.

Now let us confess that the crux in judging this duty lies principally in the will. There have been husbands who have suffered cuckoldry not only without reproach or sense of offense toward their wives but with singular obligation to and recommendation of their virtue. Some women, who loved their honor better than their life, have prostituted it to the frenzied appetite of a mortal enemy to save their husband's life, and done for him what they would not at all have done for themselves. This is not the place to extend these examples; they are too lofty and too rich to be displayed in this light; let us keep them for a nobler setting.

^CBut for examples of more commonplace luster, are there not women every day who lend themselves for the mere profit of their husbands and by their express order and mediation? And in ancient times Phaulius of Argos offered his wife to King Philip out of ambition; just as out of civility a certain Galba, who had Maecenas to supper, seeing that his wife and his guest were beginning to conspire by glances and signs, let himself sink down on his cushion, acting like a man weighed down with sleep, to lend a hand to their understanding. And he admitted it with rather good grace; for when at this point a servant made bold to lay hands on the wine that was on the table, he shouted at him: "Don't you see, you rogue, that I am asleep only for Maecenas?"

^BOne woman may be of loose conduct, and yet have a more reformed disposition than another who conducts herself in a more regular manner. As we see some who complain of having been vowed to chastity before the age of discretion, so I have seen some complain truthfully of having been vowed to debauchery before the age of discretion. The vice of the parents can be the cause of this, or the force of necessity, which is a rough counselor. In the East Indies, where chastity was in singular repute, nevertheless custom allowed a married woman to abandon herself to any man who presented her with an elephant, and that with some glory for having been valued at so high a price.

^CPhaedo the philosopher, a man of good family, after the capture of his country, Elis, made it his trade to prostitute the beauty of his youth as long as it lasted to anyone that wanted it for the price in money, so as to make a living. And Solon was the first in Greece, they say, who, by his laws, gave women the liberty to provide for the necessities of their life at the expense of their chastity, a custom which Herodotus says was accepted in many governments before his time.

^BAnd then what is the fruit of this painful anxiety? For whatever justice there may be in jealousy, it still remains to be seen whether its agitation is really useful. Is there someone who thinks to shackle women by his ingenuity?

> Put on a lock, confine her. But then who will guard
> The guards themselves? Your wife is shrewd; with them
> she'll start.
> JUVENAL

What occasion will not be enough for them in so knowing an age?

Curiosity is vicious in all things, but here it is pernicious. It is folly to want to be enlightened about a disease for which there is no medicine that does not make it worse and aggravate it; the shame of which is increased and made public principally by jealousy; revenge for which wounds our children more than it cures us. You dry up and die in quest of a proof so obscure.

How pitifully have those men reached their goal who in my time have succeeded in this quest! If the informer does not present at the same time the remedy and relief, the information he gives is injurious and he deserves a dagger-thrust more than does a man who gives you the lie. People make no less fun of the man who takes pains to do something about it than of the man who is unaware of it. The mark of cuckoldry is indelible; once a man is stamped with it he is stamped forever; the punishment makes it public more than the fault. It is a fine thing to see our private misfortunes torn out of the shadows and doubt to be trumpeted on the tragic stage, and especially misfortunes that pinch us only by the telling. For "a good wife" and "a good marriage" are said not about those that are so, but about those that are not talked about. We have to be ingenious to avoid this annoying and useless knowledge. And the Romans had the custom, when returning from a trip, of sending someone ahead to the house to make their arrival known to their wives, in order not to surprise them. And therefore a certain nation introduced the custom that the priest open the way to the bride on the wedding day, to rid the husband of doubt and of the curiosity of investigating in this first trial whether she comes to him a virgin or damaged by another's love.

"But people talk about it." I know a hundred honorable men who are cuckolded, honorably and not very discreditably. A gallant man is pitied for it, not disesteemed. Make your virtue stifle your misfortune, make good people curse the occasion of it, make the man who wrongs you tremble at the very thought of it. And then, who is not talked about in this sense, from the smallest to the greatest?

> Who many legions did command, and was
> A better man than you, poor wretch, in many ways.
> LUCRETIUS

See how many honorable men are involved in this reproach in your presence? Don't think that you are spared any more elsewhere. "But even the ladies will laugh at it." And what are they fonder of laughing at these days than a peaceful and well-settled marriage?

^CEach one of you has made someone a cuckold: now nature is all in similarities, in compensation and tit for tat. ^BThe frequency of this accident should by this time have moderated its bitterness; it will soon have become a custom.

Miserable passion, which has also this about it, that it is incommunicable,

> E'en Fortune would not lend an ear to our laments.
> CATULLUS

For to what friend do you dare entrust your griefs, who, even if he does not laugh at them, will not use them as an approach and an instruction to get a share in the quarry himself? ^CThe bitternesses of marriage, like the sweets, are kept secret by the wise. And among the other annoying conditions that are found in it, this, for a talkative man like myself, is one of the main ones: that custom makes it improper and prejudicial to communicate to anyone all that we know and feel about it.

^BTo give women the same advice in order to disgust them with jealousy would be a waste of time. Their very essence is so steeped in suspicion, vanity, and curiosity, that one should not expect to cure them by any legitimate way. They often recover from this ailment by a form of health much more to be feared than the disease itself. For as there are enchantments that can take away the evil only by unloading it onto another, so they are apt to transfer this fever to their husbands when they lose it.

However, to tell the truth, I do not know if a man can suffer anything worse from them than jealousy. It is the most dangerous of their conditions, as the head is of their members. Pittacus used to say that everyone had his weakness, and that his was his wife's bad temper: except for that, he would consider himself happy in every respect. It is a very grievous misfortune where a man so just, so wise, so valiant, feels the whole state of his life altered by it; what are we small fry to do?

^CThe senate of Marseilles was right to grant the request of the man who asked permission to kill himself to deliver himself from his tempestuous wife; for this is a disease which never goes away without taking everything with it, and which has no effective solution but flight or endurance, though both are very hard.

^BThat man knew what it was all about, it seems to me, who said that a good marriage was one made between a blind wife and a deaf husband.

Let us also see to it that the great and violent rigor of this obligation that we enjoin on them does not produce two effects contrary to our purpose: that is, that it does not make the pursuers keener and the wives more ready to surrender easily. For as for the first point, by increasing the value of the place, we increase the value and desire of the conquest. May it not have been Venus herself who thus shrewdly raised the price of her merchandise by making panders of the laws, knowing how insipid a pleasure it is unless it is given value by imagination and a high cost? In short, it is all hog's flesh that is given variety by the sauce, as Flamininus' host said.[10] Cupid is a treacherous god; he makes it his sport to wrestle with piety and justice; he glories in the fact that his power clashes with every other power and that all other rules yield to his.

> He seeks out matter for his sin.
> OVID

And as for the second point, would we not be less cuckolded if we were less afraid to be, according to the nature of women? For prohibition incites and invites them:

> You would, they won't; and when you won't, they will.
> TERENCE

> They are ashamed to go by the permitted way.
> LUCAN

What better interpretation could we find for Messalina's behavior? In the beginning she made her husband a cuckold in secret, as people do; but carrying on her affairs too easily, through his stupidity, she soon disdained that practice. Now behold her making love openly, acknowledging her lovers, entertaining them and favoring them in the sight of one and all. She wanted him to feel it. When that animal could not be awakened for all that, and made her pleasures flat and insipid by the over-lax facility with which he seemed to authorize and legitimize them, what did she do? Wife of a healthy, live emperor, and in Rome, the theater of the world, at high noon, in a public festival and ceremony, and with Silius, whom

10 Plutarch twice reports ("Sayings of Kings" and "Life of Flamininus") the story told by Flamininus to the ambassadors of Antiochus when they tried to impress him with the variety of their master's army. The name of the host who served such varied dishes to Flamininus is not given.

she had been enjoying a long time beforehand, she got married one day when her husband was out of town.

Does it not seem as if she was on her way to becoming chaste through her husband's nonchalance, or seeking another husband who would whet her appetite by his jealousy, ^cand who by opposing her would arouse her? ^BBut the first difficulty she encountered was also the last. The animal awoke with a start. One is often worse off with these deaf and unconscious people. I have found by experience that this extreme tolerance, when it comes apart, produces some of the harshest acts of vengeance; for the anger and fury, heaped up together, catching fire all of a sudden, explodes all its energy at the first attack,

> And looses all the reins of wrath.
>
> VIRGIL

He put her to death and also a great number of those who were intimate with her, even to some who could not help it and whom she had invited to her bed with scourges.

What Virgil says of Venus and Vulcan, Lucretius had said more appropriately of a stolen enjoyment between her and Mars:

> He who rules the savage things
> Of war, the mighty Mars, oft on thy bosom flings
> Himself; the eternal wound of love drains all his powers;
> Wide-mouthed, with greedy eyes thy person he devours,
> Head back, his very soul upon thy lips suspended:
> Take him in thy embrace, goddess, let him be blended
> With thy holy body as he lies; let sweet words pour
> Out of thy mouth.
>
> LUCRETIUS

When I ruminate that *rejicit* (flings), *pascit* (devours), *inhians* (wide-mouthed), *molli* (soft), *fovet* (fondles), *medullas* (marrow), *labefacta* (trembling), *pendet* (suspended), *percurrit* (runs through), and that noble *circumfusa* (blended), mother of the pretty *infusus* (outpoured),[11] I despise those petty conceits and verbal tricks that have sprung up since. These good people needed no sharp and subtle play on words; their language is all full and copious with a natural and constant vigor. They are all epigram, not only the tail

11 Some of these words are taken from the Virgil quotation (p. 783) that gives this chapter its title.

but the head, stomach, and feet. There is nothing forced, nothing dragging; the whole thing moves at the same pace. *Their whole contexture is manly; they are not concerned with pretty little flowers* [Seneca]. *This is not a soft and merely inoffensive eloquence; it is sinewy and solid, and does not so much please as fill and ravish; and it ravishes the strongest minds most. When I see these brave forms of expression, so alive, so profound, I do not say "This is well said," I say "This is well thought." It is the sprightliness of the imagination that elevates and swells the words. *It is the heart that makes a man eloquent* [Quintilian]. *Our people call judgment language and fine words full conceptions.

This painting is the result not so much of manual dexterity as of having the object more vividly imprinted in the soul. Gallus[12] speaks simply, because he conceives simply. Horace is not content with a superficial expression; it would betray him. He sees more clearly and deeply into the thing. His mind unlocks and ransacks the whole storehouse of words and figures in order to express itself; and he needs them to be beyond the commonplace, as his conception is beyond the commonplace. Plutarch says that he saw the Latin language through things. It is the same here: the sense illuminates and brings out the words, which are no longer wind, but flesh and bone. *The words mean more than they say. *Even the weak-minded feel some notion of this; for when I was in Italy I said whatever I pleased in ordinary talk, but for serious discourse I would not have dared trust myself to an idiom that I could neither bend nor turn out of its ordinary course. I want to be able to do something of my own with it.

Handling and use by able minds give value to a language, not so much by innovating as by filling it out with more vigorous and varied services, by stretching and bending it. They do not bring to it new words, but they enrich their own, give more weight and depth to their meaning and use; they teach the language unaccustomed movements, but prudently and shrewdly. And how little this gift is given to all is seen in so many French writers of our time. They are bold and disdainful enough not to follow the common road, but want of invention and of discretion ruins them. There is nothing to be seen in them but a wretched affectation of originality, cold and absurd disguises, which instead of elevating the substance bring it

12 The poems that Montaigne knew, and occasionally quoted, as those of Gallus, are now attributed to Maximianus.

down. Provided they can strut gorgeously in their novelty, they care nothing about effectiveness. To seize a new word they abandon the ordinary one, which is often stronger and more sinewy.

In our language I find plenty of stuff but a little lack of fashioning. For there is nothing that might not be done with our jargon of hunting and war, which is a generous soil to borrow from. And forms of speech, like plants, improve and grow stronger by being transplanted. I find it sufficiently abundant, but not sufficiently ^Cpliable and ^Bvigorous. It ordinarily succumbs under a powerful conception. If your pace is tense, you often feel it growing limp and giving way under you, and that when it fails you Latin comes to your aid, and Greek to others.

Of some of those words that I have just picked out it is harder for us to perceive the energy, because the frequent use of them has somewhat debased and vulgarized their grace for us; as in our vernacular we encounter excellent phrases and metaphors whose beauty is withering with age and whose color has been tarnished by too common handling. But that takes away nothing of their savor to those who have a good nose, nor does it detract from the glory of those ancient authors who, as is likely, first brought these words into this luster.

Learning treats of things too subtly, in a mode too artificial and different from the common and natural one. My page makes love and understands it. Read him Leon Hebreo and Ficino:[13] they talk about him, his thoughts and his actions, and yet he does not understand a thing in it. I do not recognize in Aristotle most of my ordinary actions: they have been covered and dressed up in another robe for the use of the school. God grant these men may be doing the right thing! If I were of the trade, I ^Cwould naturalize art as much as they artify nature. ^BLet us leave Bembo and Equicola[14] alone.

When I write, I prefer to do without the company and remembrance of books, for fear they may interfere with my style. Also because, in truth, the good authors humble me and dishearten me too much. I am inclined to do the trick of that painter who, after

13 Leon Hebreo, or Jehudah Abarbanel, a Portuguese-born Jewish scholar, published his *Dialoghi d'Amore* in Italian in 1535. Marsilio Ficino of Florence (1433–99), who sought to reconcile Platonism with Christianity and in whose Latin translation Montaigne read Plato, was noted in sixteenth-century France for his version of the theory of love set forth in Plato's *Symposium*.

14 Italian authors of philosophical treatises on love which appeared not long before Montaigne's time.

painting a miserable picture of some cocks, forbade his boys to let any real cock come into his shop. ^CAnd to give myself a little luster I would rather need the device of the musician Antinonides,[15] who, when he had to make music, arranged that either before or after him the audience should be steeped in some other bad singers.

^BBut it is harder for me to do without Plutarch. He is so universal and so full that on all occasions, and however eccentric the subject you have taken up, he makes his way into your work and offers you a liberal hand, inexhaustible in riches and embellishments. It vexes me that I am so greatly exposed to pillage by those who frequent him.[16] ^CI cannot be with him even a little without taking out a drumstick or a wing.

^BFor this purpose of mine it is also appropriate for me to write at home, in a backward region, where no one helps me or corrects me, where I usually have no contact with any man who understands the Latin of his Paternoster and who does not know even less French.[17] I would have done it better elsewhere, but the work would have been less my own; and its principal end and perfection is to be precisely my own. I would indeed correct an accidental error, and I am full of them, since I run on carelessly. But the imperfections that are ordinary and constant in me it would be treachery to remove.

When I have been told, or have told myself: "You are too thick in figures of speech. Here is a word of Gascon vintage. Here is a dangerous phrase." (I do not avoid any of those that are used in the streets of France; those who would combat usage with grammar make fools of themselves.) "This is ignorant reasoning. This is paradoxical reasoning. This one is too mad. ^CYou are often playful: people will think you are speaking in earnest when you are making believe." ^B"Yes," I say, "but I correct the faults of inadvertence, not those of habit. Isn't this the way I speak everywhere? Don't I represent myself to the life? Enough, then. I have done what I wanted. Everyone recognizes me in my book, and my book in me."

15 Mentioned by Plutarch in his "Life of Demetrius." The name should be Antigenidas or Antigenides.

16 In other words, people who borrow from Plutarch may also unconsciously be borrowing from Montaigne, since Montaigne has borrowed so much from Plutarch.

17 Montaigne presumably means the French of Paris and the Ile-de-France.

Now I have an aping and imitative nature. When I used to dabble in composing verse (and I never did any but Latin), it clearly revealed the poet I had last been reading. And of my first essays, some smell a bit foreign. ᶜIn Paris I speak a language somewhat different than at Montaigne. ᴮAnyone I regard with attention easily imprints on me something of himself. What I consider, I usurp: a foolish countenance, an unpleasant grimace, a ridiculous way of speaking. Vices even more: once they prick me, they stick to me and will not go away without shaking. I have been observed to swear more often by imitation than by nature.

ᶜA murderous imitation, like that of the horribly big and strong apes that King Alexander encountered in a certain region of the Indies. Otherwise it would have been hard to get the better of them, but they lent him the means of doing so by that inclination of theirs to imitate everything they saw done. For from this the hunters got the idea of putting on shoes in their sight with many knots in the laces, of rigging themselves out in headgear with running nooses, and of seeming to anoint their eyes with glue. Thus their apish nature brought these poor imprudent beasts to harm. They glued up their own eyes, hobbled their own feet, and strangled themselves.

That other faculty of ingeniously mimicking the gestures and words of another on purpose, which often brings pleasure and wonder, is not in me any more than in a stump.

When I swear in my own way, it is only "by God,"[18] which is the most straightforward of all oaths. They say that Socrates swore by the dog, Zeno by the same interjection that Italians use now, *cappari*,[19] and Pythagoras by water and air.

ᴮI so easily receive these superficial impressions without thinking of them that when I have had "Sire" or "Highness" in my mouth for three days in a row, a week later they will slip out instead of "Excellency" or "Lordship." And what I have begun to say in sport and in jest I will say seriously the next day. Wherefore in writing I am the more unwilling to accept the well-worn topics, for fear I may treat them at someone else's expense.

Any topic is equally fertile for me. A fly will serve my purpose; and God grant that this topic I have in hand now was not taken up at the command of so flightly a will! Let me begin with whatever subject I please, for all subjects are linked with one another.

18 *Par Dieu* is much milder in French than its English equivalent.

19 Montaigne means that Zeno swore "by the goats," not that he swore in Italian. He first wrote "les capres," then changed this to "cappari."

But I am displeased with my mind for ordinarily producing its most profound and maddest fancies, and those I like the best, unexpectedly and when I am least looking for them; which suddenly vanish, having nothing to attach themselves to on the spot: on horseback, at table, in bed, but mostly on horseback, where my thoughts range most widely. In speech I am rather sensitively jealous of attention and silence if I am speaking in earnest: whoever interrupts me stops me. When I travel, the very necessity of the road cuts conversation short; besides, I most often travel without company fit for these protracted discussions, whereby I get full leisure to commune with myself.

It turns out as with my dreams. While dreaming I recommend them to my memory (for I am apt to dream that I am dreaming); but the next day I may well call to mind their coloring just as it was, whether gay, or sad, or strange; but as to what they were besides, the more I strain to find out, the more I plunge it into oblivion. So of these chance thoughts that drop into my mind there remains in my memory only a vain notion, only as much as I need to make me rack my brains and fret in quest of them to no purpose.

Now then, leaving books aside and speaking more materially and simply, I find after all that love is nothing else but the thirst for sexual enjoyment ᶜin a desired object, and Venus nothing else but the pleasure of discharging our vessels – a pleasure which becomes vicious either by immoderation or by indiscretion. For Socrates love is the appetite for generation by the mediation of beauty. ᴮAnd considering often the ridiculous titillation of this pleasure, the absurd, witless, and giddy motions with which it stirs up Zeno and Cratippus, that reckless frenzy, that face inflamed with fury and cruelty in the sweetest act of love, and then that grave, severe, and ecstatic countenance in so silly an action; ᶜand that our delights and our excrements have been lodged together pell-mell, ᴮand that the supreme sensual pleasure is attended, like pain, with faintness and moaning; I believe that ᶜwhat Plato says is true, that ᴮman is the plaything of the gods:

> What savage jest is this!
> CLAUDIAN

and that it was in mockery that nature left us the most confused of our actions to be the most common, in order thereby to make us all equal and to put on the same level the fools and the wise, and us and the beasts. The most contemplative and wisest of men, when

I imagine him in that position, seems to me an impostor to put on wise and contemplative airs; here are the peacock's feet that humble his pride:

> Against truth said in laughing
> Is there a law?
> HORACE

^CThose who will not allow serious ideas in the midst of games act, as someone says, like a man who is afraid to worship the statue of a saint if it is undraped.

^BWe eat and drink as the animals do, but these are not actions that hinder the operations of our mind. In these we keep our advantage over them. But this other puts every other thought beneath its yoke and by its imperious authority brutifies and bestializes all the theology and philosophy there is in Plato; and yet he does not complain of it. In everything else you can keep some decorum; all other operations come under the rules of decency. This one cannot even be imagined other than vicious or ridiculous. Just to see this, try to find a wise and discreet way of doing it. Alexander used to say that he knew himself to be mortal chiefly by this action and by sleep. Sleep suffocates and suppresses the faculties of our mind; the sexual act likewise absorbs and dissipates them. Truly it is a mark not only of our original corruption but also of our inanity and deformity.

On the one hand Nature pushes us on to it, having attached to this desire the most noble, useful, and pleasant of all her operations; and on the other hand she lets us accuse and shun it as shameless and indecent, blush at it, and recommend abstinence. ^CAre we not brutes to call brutish the operation that makes us?

^BThe various nations in their religions have many conventions in common, such as sacrifices, lamps, burning incense, fasts, offerings, and, among other things, the condemnation of this action. All opinions come to this, besides the very widespread practice of cutting off the foreskin, ^Cwhich is a punishment of the act. ^BPerhaps we are right to blame ourselves for making such a stupid production as man, to call the action shameful, and shameful the parts that are used for it. ^C(At present mine are truly shameful and pitiful.)

The Essenes, of whom Pliny speaks, maintained their numbers for several centuries without nurses and without baby clothes, by the influx of foreigners who, following this fine humor, continually joined them: a whole nation risked exterminating itself rather

than involve themselves in a woman's embrace, and forfeiting the continuation of mankind rather than create a man. They say that Zeno had to do with a woman only once in his life, and then out of civility, so as not to seem too obstinately to disdain the sex.

[B]Everyone shuns to see a man born, everyone runs to see him die. [C]For his destruction we seek a spacious field in broad daylight; for his construction we hide in a dark little corner. [B]It is a duty to hide and blush in order to make him; and it is a glory and a source of many virtues to be able to unmake him. One is an offense, the other an act of grace; for Aristotle says that to benefit someone, in a certain phrase of his country, is to kill him. [C]The Athenians, to put the disgrace of these two actions on the same level, when they had to purify the island of Delos and justify themselves to Apollo, forbade both any burial and any birth within its territory. [B]*We are ashamed of our very selves* [Terence]. [C]We regard our being as vice.

[B]There are nations that cover themselves when eating. I know a lady, and one of the greatest, who has this same opinion, that chewing is a disagreeable grimace which takes away much of women's grace and beauty; and she does not like to appear in public with an appetite. And I know a man who cannot bear to see anyone eat or to be seen eating, and who avoids any company even more when he is filling than when he is emptying himself.

[C]In the empire of the Turk are found a great number of men who, to outdo others, never let themselves be seen when they have their meals; who have only one a week; who cut and mangle their face and limbs; who never speak to anyone: all of them people[20] who think they honor their nature by denaturing themselves, who prize themselves for their contempt, and think to improve themselves by their impairment. [B]What a monstrous animal to be a horror to himself, [C]to be burdened by his pleasures, to regard himself as a misfortune!

[B]There are some who conceal their lives –

> They change for exile their sweet homes and hearths
>
> VIRGIL

– and hide them from the sight of other men; who avoid health and cheerfulness as hostile and harmful qualities. Not only many sects

20 Most modern French editions read "toutes gens fanatiques" ("all of them fanatical people"); but "fanatiques" does not appear in the Bordeaux Copy.

but many nations curse their birth and bless their death. ^CThere are some nations in which the sun is abominated and the darkness adored.

^BWe are ingenious only in maltreating ourselves; that is the true quarry of the power of our mind – ^Ca dangerous tool when out of control.

^BO wretched men, who hold their joys as crimes!
 MAXIMIANUS

Alas, poor man! You have enough necessary ills without increasing them by your invention, and you are miserable enough by nature without being so by art. You have real and essential deformities enough without forging imaginary ones. ^CDo you find that you are too much at your ease unless your ease strikes you as unpleasantness? ^BDo you think you have fulfilled all the necessary duties to which nature obligates you, and that she is wanting and idle in you unless you take on new duties? You are not afraid to offend the universal and indubitable laws, and are proudly intent on your own laws, which are partial and fanciful; and the more particular, uncertain, and contradicted they are, the more you devote your effort to them. ^CThe positive rules of your own invention possess and bind you, and the rules of your parish; those of God and the world leave you untouched. ^BJust run through a few examples that would illustrate this idea; your life is all made up of them.

The verses of these two poets, treating of lasciviousness as reservedly and discreetly as they do, seem to me to reveal it and illuminate it more closely. The ladies cover their bosoms with a veil, the priests many sacred things; painters put shadows in their work to bring out the light more; and it is said that the sun and wind strike harder by reflection than direct. An Egyptian made a wise answer to the man who asked him: "What are you carrying there hidden under your cloak?" "It is hidden under my cloak so that you won't know what it is." But there are certain other things that people hide only to show them.

Listen to this man, who is more open:

And pressed her naked body unto mine.
 OVID

I feel that he is caponizing me. Let Martial turn up Venus' skirts as high as he pleases, he will not succeed in revealing her so completely. He who says everything satiates and disgusts us; he who is afraid to

express himself leads us on to think more than there is. There is treachery in this sort of modesty, and especially in half opening to us, as these do, so fair a road to the imagination. Both the action and the picture of it should smack of theft.

I like the love-making of the Spaniards and Italians, more respectful and timid, more mannered and veiled. I don't know who it was in ancient times who wanted his throat as long as a crane's neck so as to relish longer what he swallowed. That wish is more appropriate in this quick and precipitate pleasure, especially for such natures as mine, for I have the failing of being too sudden. In order to arrest its flight and prolong it in preambles, everything among them serves as a favor and a recompense: a glance, a bow, a word, a sign. If a man could dine off the steam of a roast, wouldn't that be a fine saving? This is a passion that with very little solid essence mixes in much more vanity and feverish dreams: it should be satisfied and served accordingly. Let us teach the ladies to make the most of themselves, to respect themselves, to beguile and fool us. We make our ultimate attack the first one; the French impetuosity is always there. If the ladies spin out and spread out their favors in small amounts, each man, even to miserable old age, will find there some little scrap of pleasure, according to his worth and merit.

He who has no enjoyment except in enjoyment, who must win all or nothing, who loves the chase only in the capture, has no business mixing with our school. The more steps and degrees there are, the more height and honor there is in the topmost seat. We should take pleasure in being led there, as is done in magnificent palaces, by divers porticoes and passages, long and pleasant galleries, and many windings. This arrangement would redound to our advantage; we would stay there longer and love there longer. Without hope and without desire we no longer go at any worth-while gait.

Our mastery and entire possession is something for them to fear infinitely. Once they have wholly surrendered to the mercy of our fidelity and constancy, they are in a very hazardous position. Those are rare and difficult virtues. As soon as the ladies are ours, we are no longer theirs:

> The lust of greedy mind once satisfied,
> We fear nor care for oaths once sworn, but now denied.
>
> CATULLUS

ᶜAnd Thrasonides, a young Greek, was so much in love with his love that having won his mistress' heart he refused to enjoy her, so as

not to deaden, satiate, and weaken by enjoyment that restless ardor
on which he prided and fed himself.

BDearness gives relish to the meat. See how much the form of
salutation which is peculiar to our nation debases by its facility the
charm of kisses, which Socrates says are so powerful and dangerous
for stealing our hearts. It is a disagreeable custom, and unfair to the
ladies, to have to lend their lips to any man who has three footmen at
his heels, however unattractive he may be:

> A bluish ice, from nostrils like a dog's,
> Comes hanging down, his beard stiffens and clogs...
> A hundred times I'd rather kiss his ass.
>
> MARTIAL

And we ourselves do not gain much by it; for as the world is divided,
for three beautiful women we have to kiss fifty ugly ones. And for
a tender stomach, as men of my age have, one bad kiss is too high
a price for one good one.

In Italy they play the part of timid suitors even with the women
who are for sale, and they defend the practice thus: that there are
degrees in enjoyment, and that by courting they want to obtain for
themselves that which is most complete. These women sell only
their bodies; the will cannot be put on sale, it is too free and too
much its own master. Thus these men say that they are wooing their
will; and they are right. It is the will that must be courted and
solicited. I abhor the idea of a body void of affection being mine.
And it seems to me that such frenzy is close to that of the boy who
went and defiled out of love the beautiful statue of Venus that
Praxiteles had made, or that of the frantic Egyptian hot after the
carcass of a dead woman he was embalming and shrouding; which
gave rise to the law that was made since then in Egypt, that the
bodies of beautiful young women and of those of good family
should be kept three days before being put in the hands of the
undertakers. Periander behaved more monstrously when he
extended his conjugal affection (more regular and legitimate) to
the enjoyment of Melissa, his dead wife.

CDoesn't it seem a lunatic humor in Luna, unable otherwise
to enjoy her darling Endymion, to put him to sleep for several
months, and take her satisfaction in enjoying a boy who stirred
only in his dreams?

BI say likewise that we love a body without soul or sentiment,
when we love a body without its consent and desire. Not all

enjoyments are alike. Some are meager and languid. A thousand causes other than good will may win us this concession from the ladies. It is not sufficient evidence of affection; there may be treachery in it as elsewhere; sometimes they go to it with only one buttock:

> As cool as if preparing frankincense and wine...
> You'd think her absent or of marble.
> MARTIAL

I know some who would rather lend that than their coach, and who communicate only in that way. You must observe whether they like your company for yet some other purpose or for this alone, as they might that of some husky stable-boy; in what rank and at what value you are lodged there,

> If to you alone
> She gives herself, and marks that day with a whiter stone.
> CATULLUS

What if she eats your bread with the sauce of a more agreeable imagination?

> 'Tis you she holds, but sighs for other, absent loves.
> TIBULLUS

What! have we not seen someone in our own time use this act for the purpose of a horrible vengeance, thereby to poison and kill, as he did, an honorable woman?

Those who know Italy will never find it strange if for this subject I do not seek examples elsewhere; for that nation may be called the teacher of the world in this. They have generally more beautiful women and fewer ugly ones than we; but in rare and outstanding beauties I think we are on a par. And I judge as much of their intellects. Of the ordinary sort they have many more, and obviously brutishness is incomparably rarer there; in unusual minds and minds of the highest stature, we concede them nothing. If I had to extend this comparison, it would seem to me I could say that on the contrary valor is more common and natural among us than among them; but in them we sometimes see it so full and vigorous that it surpasses the sturdiest examples that we have.

The marriages of that country are lame in this: their custom commonly imposes so harsh and so slavish a law on the wives that the most distant contact with a stranger is as capital an offense to them as the most intimate. The result of this law is that all

approaches necessarily become substantial; and since it all comes to the same for them, they have a very easy choice. ^CAnd once they have broken through these partitions, believe me, they are on fire: *Lust, like a wild beast, irritated by its chains, is then let loose* [Livy]. ^BWe must give them a little more rein:

> Lately I saw, rebellious to the bit, a colt
> With stubborn mouth run like a thunderbolt.
>
> OVID

The desire for company is weakened by giving it a little liberty.

We run about the same chance. They are too extreme in constraint, we in license. It is a fine practice of our nation that our sons are received into good families to be brought up and trained as pages, as in a school of nobility. And it is considered a discourtesy and an affront to refuse one of noble birth. I have perceived – for so many houses, so many different styles and forms – that the ladies who have tried to give the maidens in their retinue the most austere rules have not come out any better. Moderation is needed: a good part of their conduct must be left to their own discretion; for one way or another, there is no discipline that can curb them in all directions. But it is quite true that a girl who has escaped safe, bag and baggage, from a free schooling, inspires much more confidence than one who comes out safely from a severe, prison-like school.

Our fathers trained their daughters' faces to bashfulness and timidity (hearts and desires were the same); we, to self-assurance: we don't know what we're doing. ^CThat is for the Sarmatian women, who may not lie with a man until with their own hands they have killed another in war.

^BFor me, who have no rights in this except through the ears, it is enough that they retain me as counsel, according to the privilege of my age. So I counsel them abstinence, ^Cas I do to us; ^Bbut if this generation is too hostile to it, at least discretion and modesty. ^CFor as the story tells about Aristippus, speaking to some young men who blushed to see him enter the house of a courtesan, "The vice is in not coming out, not in entering." ^BIf she will not keep her conscience clear, let her keep her name clear; if the substance is not worth much, let the appearance be preserved.

I commend gradation and delay in the dispensation of their favors. ^CPlato shows that in every kind of love the defenders are forbidden to yield easily and promptly. ^BIt is a trait of greediness, which they must cover up with all their art, to surrender so

heedlessly, completely, and impetuously. By conducting themselves with order and measure in granting their favors, they beguile our desire much better and conceal their own. Let them always flee before us, I mean even those who intend to let themselves be caught; they conquer us better in flight, like the Scythians. Indeed, according to the law that Nature gives them, it is not properly for them to will and desire; their role is to suffer, obey, consent. That is why Nature has given them a perpetual capacity, to us a rare and uncertain one. They have their hour always, so that they may be ready for ours: *^cborn to be passive* [Seneca]. ^BAnd whereas Nature has willed that our appetites should show and declare themselves prominently, she has made theirs occult and internal, and has furnished them with parts ^cunsuitable for show and ^Bsimply for the defensive.

^cWe must leave to Amazonian license actions like this one. When Alexander was passing through Hyrcania, Thalestris, queen of the Amazons, came to find him with three hundred warriors of her own sex, well mounted and well armed, having left the remainder of a large army that was following her beyond the neighboring mountains; and said to him, right out loud and in public, that the fame of his victories and valor had brought her there to see him, to offer him her resources and power in support of his enterprises; and that finding him so handsome, young, and vigorous, she, who was perfect in all his qualities, advised him that they should lie together, so that of the most valiant woman in the world and the most valiant man who was then alive there should be born something great and rare for the future. Alexander thanked her just the same for the rest; but to allow enough time for the accomplishment of her last request, he stopped in that place thirteen days, which he celebrated as lustily as he could in honor of so courageous a princess.

^BWe are in almost all things unjust judges of their actions, as they are of ours. I admit the truth when it hurts me, just as when it serves me. It is an ugly aberration that pushes them so often to change and keeps them from fixing their affection on any object whatever, as we see of that goddess[21] to whom are attributed so many changes and lovers. Yet the truth is that it is contrary to the nature of love if it is not violent, and contrary to the nature of violence if it is constant. And those who are astonished at this and exclaim against it and seek out the causes of this malady in women as if it were unnatural and

21 Venus.

incredible, why don't they see how often they accept it in themselves without being appalled and calling it a miracle? It would perhaps be more strange to see any stability in it. It is not simply a bodily passion. If there is no end to avarice and ambition, neither is there any to lechery. It still lives after satiety; no constant satisfaction or end can be prescribed to it, for it always goes beyond its possession.

And furthermore, inconstancy is perhaps somewhat more pardonable in them than in us. They can allege, as we can, the inclination to variety and novelty which is common to us both; and allege secondly, as we cannot, that they buy a cat in a bag (^CJoanna, queen of Naples, had Andreasso, her first husband, strangled at the bars of her window with a gold and silk cord woven by her own hand, when in matrimonial duties she found that neither his parts nor his efforts corresponded well enough with the expectations she had formed of them on seeing his build, his beauty, his youth and agility, whereby she had been caught and deceived); ^Bthat action involves more effort than submission; and that consequently they are always able to satisfy our needs, whereas it may be otherwise when it is up to us to satisfy theirs.

^CPlato for this reason wisely established in his laws that in order to decide on the suitability of a marriage the judges should see the young men who aspire to it stark naked, and the girls naked down to the girdle only. ^BWhen they come to try us, they may not find us worthy of their choice:

> Having explored his body, found his member limp
> As a wet thong, impossible by hand to primp,
> She leaves the dastard bed.
> MARTIAL

It is not enough that a man's will should carry straight. Weakness and incapacity legitimately break up a marriage:

> A stronger lover elsewhere must be found
> By whom her virgin zone may be unbound.
> CATULLUS

Why not? And according to her standard, a more licentious and active amorous relationship,

> If he cannot last out the pleasant task.
> VIRGIL

But is it not a great impudence to bring our imperfections and

weaknesses where we desire to please and leave a good opinion and recommendation of ourselves? For the little that I need nowadays,

> Even for one
> Encounter, limp,
> > HORACE

I would not want to trouble a person whom I have to reverence and fear:

> Nor ever fear
> A man whose life, alas, has tottered past
> His fiftieth year.
> > HORACE

Nature should have contented herself with making this age miserable, without making it also ridiculous. I hate to see it, for one inch of wretched vigor that heats it up three times a week, bustle about and swagger with the same fierceness as if it had some great and proper day's work in its belly: a real flash in the pan. ᶜAnd I marvel to see such a lively and frisky flame so sluggishly congealed and put out in a moment. This appetite should belong only to the flower of beauty and youth. ᴮJust rely on age, if you want to find out, to second that indefatigable, full, constant, and great-souled ardor that is in you: it will leave you nicely in the lurch! Rather pass it on boldly to some tender, dazed, and ignorant boy, still trembling under the rod and blushing at it,

> Even as Indian ivory, stained with red,
> Or lilies mingled in the flower bed
> With roses.
> > VIRGIL

He who can await, the morning after, without dying of shame, the disdain of those fair eyes that have witnessed his limpness and impertinence,

> Her silent looks made eloquent reproach,
> > OVID

has never felt the satisfaction and pride of having conquered them and put circles around them by the vigorous exercise of a busy and active night. When I have seen one of them grow weary of me, I have

not promptly blamed her fickleness; I have wondered whether I did not have reason rather to blame Nature. Certainly she has treated me unfairly and unkindly –

> But if the penis be not long or stout enough...
> Even the matrons – all too well they know –
> Look dimly on a man whose member's small.
>
> PRIAPEA

– ^cand done me the most enormous damage.

Each one of my parts makes me myself just as much as every other one. And no other makes me more properly a man than this one.

I owe a complete portrait of myself to the public. The wisdom of my lesson is wholly in truth, in freedom, in reality; disdaining, in the list of its real duties, those petty, feigned, customary, provincial rules; altogether natural, constant, and universal; of which propriety and ceremony are daughters, but bastard daughters.

We will readily take care of the vices of appearance when we have taken care of those of reality. When we have done with the latter, we will attack the others, if we find we need to attack them. For there is danger that we dream up new duties to excuse our negligence toward our natural duties and mix them up. As proof of this: we see that in places where faults are crimes, crimes are only faults; that in nations where the laws of propriety are rarer and looser, the primitive and common laws are better observed; for the innumerable multitude of so many duties smothers, weakens, and dissipates our concern. Application to trivial things draws us away from urgent ones. Oh what an easy and applauded route those superficial men take, compared with ours! These are shadows with which we comfort ourselves and pay one another off; but we do not really pay, we rather add to our debt to that great Judge who tucks up our rags and tatters from around our shameful parts and does not merely pretend to see us throughout, even to our inmost and most secret filth. Our virginal modesty would be a useful propriety if it could keep him from making this discovery.

In short, whoever would wean man of the folly of such a scrupulous verbal superstition would do the world no great harm. Our life is part folly, part wisdom. Whoever writes about it only reverently and according to the rules leaves out more than half

of it.[22] I am not making excuses to myself, and if I did, I would make excuses rather for my excuses than for any other part of me. I am making excuses to certain humors which I believe to be stronger in number than those that are on my side. In consideration of them I will further say this – for I wish to satisfy everyone, though it is a very difficult thing *for one single man to accommodate himself to so great a variety of ways, discourses, and wills* [Cicero] – that they should not properly blame me for what I quote from authorities accepted and approved for many centuries; and that it is not right that they should refuse me, because I lack rhyme, the dispensation that even churchmen, and some of the most proudly crested at that, enjoy in our time. Here are two of them:

> May I die if your crack is more than a faint line.
> BEZA

> A friendly tool contents and treats her well.
> SAINT-GELAIS

And what about the many others?

I like modesty, and it is not by judgment that I have chosen this scandalous way of speaking; it is nature that has chosen it for me. I do not commend it, any more than I do any forms that are contrary to accepted practice; but I excuse it, and by particular and general circumstances I make the accusation lighter. Let's get on.

Likewise [B]whence can come that usurpation of sovereign authority that you assume over those women who grant you favors at their own expense –

> If she gave you furtive favors in the black of night
> CATULLUS

– so that you immediately put on the rights, the coldness, and the authority of a husband? It is a free compact; why do you not keep to it as you want to hold them to it? [C]There is no power of prescription in voluntary things.

22 Here, in the handwritten marginal additions to the Bordeaux Copy, Montaigne added and then crossed out approximately this (some of it is blotted and undecipherable): "My initial preface shows that I was not hoping for so much. The wisest and soundest writings of authors and the reception given to my plan have made me bolder, so that I have spurred myself to break the ice and show our. . ." (The rest of this is torn off.)

[B]It is contrary to form, but still it is true that in my time I have handled this business, as far as the nature of it would permit, as conscientiously as any other business and with some air of justice; and that I swore to them only what I felt about my affection, and represented to them candidly its decadence, its vigor, and its birth, its fits and its lapses. One does not always go about it at the same pace. I have been so sparing in promising that I think I have carried out more than I promised or owed. They have found me faithful even to the point of serving their inconstancy – I mean an avowed and sometimes multiplied inconstancy. I have never broken with them as long as I held to them even by a bit of thread; and whatever occasions for it they have given me, I have never broken with them to the point of scorn or hatred. For such intimacies, even when acquired on the most shameful terms, still oblige me to some good will. Anger and somewhat heedless impatience I have sometimes shown them on the occasion of their ruses and evasions and our quarrels; for by my nature I am subject to sudden outbursts which, though slight and brief, often harm my affairs. If they wanted to test the freedom of my judgment, I did not shirk giving them sharp paternal advice and pinching them where they smarted. If I have left them with any reason to complain of me, it is rather for having found in me a love which, compared with modern usage, was stupidly conscientious. I have kept my word in things in which I might easily have been excused. In those days they sometimes surrendered with honor and on conditions that they readily suffered the conqueror to break. I have more than once, in the interest of their honor, made pleasure yield in its greatest stress; and when reason urged me, I have armed them against myself, so that they conducted themselves more safely and severely by my rules, when they freely relied on them, than they would have done by their own.

[C]As much as I could, I have taken upon myself alone the risk of our assignations, to free them of it, and I have always arranged our meetings in the hardest and most unexpected ways, so that they might be less under suspicion and besides, in my opinion, more accessible. Meetings are chiefly exposed in the places people think are automatically enclosed. Things least feared are least guarded against and observed. You can more easily dare what no one thinks you will dare, which becomes easy by its difficulty.

[B]Never was a man more impertinently genital in his approaches. This way of loving is more according to the rules; but who knows better than I how ridiculous it is to people nowadays, and how

ineffectual? Yet I shall not repent of it; I have nothing more to lose there:

> A votive tablet shows
> I hung my dedicated clothes,
> Dripping with brine,
> Here in the sea-god's shrine.
>
> HORACE

It is time now to speak of it openly. But just as I might peradventure say to another: "My friend, you are dreaming; love in your time has little to do with faith and probity" –

> If under reason's certain rule
> You seek to bring this, all you do is add
> This to your tasks: with reason to go mad
>
> TERENCE

– so, on the contrary, if I were to begin over again, it would certainly be by the same method and the same procedure, however fruitless it might be for me. ^CIneptitude and stupidity are praiseworthy in a blameworthy action. ^BThe further I depart from their attitude in this, the nearer I approach my own.

For the rest, in this business I did not let myself go entirely; I took pleasure in it, but I did not forget myself; I preserved entire the little sense and discretion that nature has given me, for their service and mine: a little excitement, but no folly. My conscience was also involved in it to the point of licentiousness and dissoluteness; but to the point of ingratitude, treachery, malignity, and cruelty, no. I did not purchase the pleasure of this vice at all costs, but contented myself with its proper and simple cost: ^C*No vice is self-contained* [Seneca].

^BI hate almost equally a stagnant and sleepy idleness and a thorny and painful busyness. The one pinches me, the other puts me to sleep. I like wounds as much as bruises, and cutting blows as much as dry ones. I found in this business, when I was more fit for it, a just moderation between these two extremes. Love is a sprightly, lively, and gay agitation; I was neither troubled nor afflicted by it, but I was heated and moreover made thirsty by it. A man should stop there; it is hurtful only to fools.

A young man asked the philosopher Panaetius whether it would be becoming to a wise man to be in love. "Let us leave aside the wise man," he replied, "but you and I, who are not, let us not get

involved in a thing so excited and violent, which enslaves us to others and makes us contemptible to ourselves." He spoke truly, that we should not entrust a thing so precipitous in itself to a soul that has not the wherewithal to withstand its assaults and to disprove in practice the saying of Agesilaus, that wisdom and love cannot live together. It is a vain occupation, it is true, unbecoming, shameful, and illegitimate; but carried on in this fashion, I consider it healthy, proper to enliven a heavy body and soul; and as a physician, I would prescribe it to a man of my temperament and condition as readily as any other recipe to rouse him and keep him in vigor till he is well on in years, and to keep him from the clutches of old age. While we are only in its outskirts and the pulse still beats,

> While hair is freshly gray, old age hale and erect,
> While Lachesis has thread to spin, and while I stand
> And walk on my own feet, no staff in my right hand,
>
> JUVENAL

we need to be stimulated and tickled by some biting agitation such as this. See how much youth, vigor, and gaiety it gave back to the wise Anacreon. And Socrates, when older than I am, speaking of an object of his love, said: "When I had leaned my shoulder against his and brought my head close to his, as we were looking into a book together, I suddenly felt, without prevarication, a stinging in my shoulder like some animal's bite, and I was more than five days with it prickling, and a continual itching flowed into my heart." A touch, and an accidental one, and by a shoulder, to inflame and alter a soul cooled and enervated by age, and the first of all human souls in reformation! ^CIndeed, why not? Socrates was a man, and wanted neither to be nor to seem anything else.

^BPhilosophy does not strive against natural pleasures, provided that measure goes with them; ^Cshe preaches moderation in them, not flight. ^BThe power of her resistance is employed against alien and bastard pleasures. She says that the appetites of the body are not to be augmented by the mind, and warns us ingeniously ^Cnot to try to arouse our hunger by satiety, not to stuff instead of filling the belly, ^Bto avoid ^Call enjoyment that brings us want and ^Ball meat and drink that makes us thirsty and hungry; as, in the service of love, she orders us to take an object that simply satisfies the body's need, that does not stir the soul, which should not make this its business but simply follow and assist the body.

But am I not right to consider that these precepts, which by the way are in my opinion still a bit rigorous, concern a body that performs its function, and that for a run-down body, as for a broken-down stomach, it is excusable to warm it up and support it by art, and by the mediation of fancy to restore appetite and blitheness to it, since by itself it has lost them?

May we not say that there is nothing in us during this earthly imprisonment that is purely either corporeal or spiritual, and that we do wrong to tear apart a living man, and that it seems somewhat reasonable that we should behave as favorably at least toward the use of pleasure as we do toward pain? Pain, for example, was vehement even to perfection in the souls of the saints, through penitence; the body naturally had a share in it by virtue of their union, and yet could have little share in the cause. Yet they were not content that it should simply follow and assist the afflicted soul; they afflicted the body itself with atrocious and appropriate torments, in order that, vying with each other, the soul and the body should plunge man into pain, the more salutary for its harshness.

^CIn a similar case, that of bodily pleasures, is it not unjust to cool the soul toward them and say that she should be dragged to them as to some constrained and servile obligation and necessity? It is rather for her to hatch them and foment them, to offer and invite herself to them, since the authority of ruling belongs to her; as it is also for her, in my opinion, in the pleasures that are her own, to inspire and infuse into the body all the feeling their nature allows, and to strive to make them sweet and salutary to it. For it is indeed reasonable, as they say, that the body should not follow its appetites to the disadvantage of the mind; but why is it not also reasonable that the mind should not pursue its appetites to the disadvantage of the body?

^BI have no other passion to keep me in breath. What avarice, ambition, quarrels, lawsuits, do for others who, like me, have no assigned occupation, love would do more agreeably. It would restore to me vigilance, sobriety, grace, care for my person; would secure my countenance, so that the grimaces of old age, those deformed and pitiable grimaces, should not come to disfigure it; ^Cwould take me back to sane and wise studies, whereby I might make myself more esteemed and more loved, ridding my mind of despair of itself and its employment, and reacquainting it with itself; ^Bwould divert me from a thousand troublesome thoughts, ^Ca thousand melancholy moods, ^Bthat idleness ^Cand the bad state of our health ^Bloads us with

at such an age; would warm up again, at least in dreams, this blood that nature is abandoning; would hold up the chin and stretch out a little the muscles ^cand the soul's vigor and blitheness ^Bfor this poor man who is going full speed toward his ruin.

But I quite understand that love is a very hard commodity to recover. By weakness and long experience our taste has become more delicate and exquisite. We demand more when we bring less; we most want to choose when we least deserve to be accepted. Knowing ourselves for what we are, we are less bold and more distrustful; nothing can assure us of being loved, knowing our condition and theirs. I am ashamed to find myself amid this green and ardent youth,

> Whose member firmer stands, in its undaunted pride,
> > Than a young tree upon a mountainside.

<div align="right">HORACE</div>

Why should we go offering our wretchedness amid this sprightliness?

> That ardent youngsters may stand round and watch,
> > Not without mocking shout,
> As into ashes our weak torch burns out?

<div align="right">HORACE</div>

They have strength and right on their side; let us make way for them, we have no hold left.

^cAnd this bud of nascent beauty does not let itself be handled by such stiff hands or be won over by purely material means. For as that ancient philosopher replied to one who mocked him for having been unable to win the good graces of a tender youth he was pursuing: "My friend, the hook will not bite into such fresh cheese."

^BNow this is a relationship that needs mutuality and reciprocity. The other pleasures that we receive may be acknowledged by recompenses of a different nature; but this one can be paid for only in the same kind of coin. ^cIn truth, in this delight the pleasure I give tickles my imagination more sweetly than that which I feel. ^BNow there is no nobility in a man who can receive pleasure where he gives none; it is a mean soul that is willing to owe everything and takes pleasure in fostering relations with persons to whom he is a burden. There is neither beauty, nor grace, nor intimacy so exquisite that a gallant man should desire it at this price. If they can be kind to us only out of pity, I had much rather not live at all than live

on alms. I would like to have the right to ask it of them in the style I have seen beggars use in Italy: "*Do good for your own sake*"; ^cor in the manner in which Cyrus exhorted his soldiers: "Who loves himself, let him follow me."

^BRally, someone will tell me, round women of your own condition, whom company in like fortune will make easier for you. Oh what a stupid and insipid compromise!

> I will
> Not pluck at a dead lion's beard.
>
> MARTIAL

^cXenophon uses it as an objection and an accusation against Meno that in his love affairs he made use of persons who had passed their flower. I find more sensual pleasure in merely seeing the just and sweet union of two young beauties, or in merely considering it in imagination, than in myself making the second in a sad and ill-formed union. ^BI resign that fantastic appetite to the Emperor Galba, who was addicted only to tough old meat, and to this poor wretch:

> Would God that as I dream of you I might behold you,
> And press sweet kisses on your altered locks,
> Take your worn body in my arms and thus enfold you!
>
> OVID

^cAnd among the leading forms of ugliness I count artificial and forced beauties. Hemon, a young boy of Chios, thinking by fine attire to acquire the beauty that nature denied him, presented himself to the philosopher Arcesilaus and asked him whether a wise man could fall in love. "Yes indeed," he replied, "provided it is not with a bedecked and sophisticated beauty like yours." An avowed ugliness and old age is less old and less ugly to my taste than another that is painted and glossed over.

^BShall I say it, provided no one takes me by the throat for it? Love does not seem to me properly and naturally in its season except in the age next to childhood:

> If you should place him in a troop of girls,
> With his ambiguous face and flowing curls,
> A thousand sharp onlookers could be wrong
> And fail to pick him out amid the throng.
>
> HORACE

^CNor beauty either. For when Homer makes beauty last until the chin begins to show a shadow, Plato himself remarks that such a flower is rare. And it is well known why the sophist Dion so humorously called the downy hairs of adolescence Aristogeitons and Harmodiuses.[23] ^BIn manhood I find it already out of place; not to speak of old age:

> For pitiless past the withered oaks
> Love flies.
> HORACE

^CAnd Margaret, queen of Navarre, like a woman, prolongs the advantage of women very far, ordaining that at thirty it is time for them to change the title of "beautiful" to "good."

^BThe shorter the possession we give Love over our life, the better we are. Look at his bearing: he is a beardless boy. Who does not know how in his school they proceed contrary to all order? Study, exercise, practice, are ways leading to incapacity; the novices there give the lessons: ^C*Love knows no rule* [Saint Jerome]. ^BCertainly Love's conduct has much more style when it is mingled with heedlessness and confusion; mistakes and misadventures give it point and grace. Provided it is sharp and hungry, it matters little whether it is prudent. See how he goes reeling, tripping, and wantonly playing; you put him in the stocks when you guide him by art and wisdom, and you constrain his divine freedom when you subject him to those hairy and callous hands.

Moreover, I often hear women portray this relationship as wholly spiritual and disdain to place in consideration the interest that the senses have in it. Everything contributes to it. But I may say that I have often seen us excuse the weakness of their minds in favor of their bodily beauties; but I have never yet seen that for the sake of our beauty of mind, however wise and mature that mind may be, they were willing to grant favors to a body that was slipping the least little bit into decline. Why is not one of them seized with desire for that noble ^CSocratic ^Bexchange of body for soul, ^Cbuying a philosophical and spiritual intelligence and generation at the price of her thighs, the highest price to which she can raise them? Plato ordains in his *Laws* that whoever has performed some signal and useful exploit in war, regardless of his ugliness or old age, may

23 Because these hairs deliver lovers of the boys who grow them from the tyranny of love, as Harmodius and Aristogeiton delivered Athens from tyranny.

not for the war's duration be refused a kiss or other amorous favor from whomever he wants. What he finds so just in recommendation of military worth, may it not also be so in recommendation of some other kind of worth? And why is not one of them seized with desire [B]to gain before her sisters the glory of this chaste love? And I do mean chaste,

> For if it comes to love's encounter,
> Like fire in straw, mighty in size, with little power,
> They spend their rage in vain.
>
> VIRGIL

The vices that are stifled in thought are not the worst.

To conclude this notable commentary, which has escaped from me in a flow of babble, a flow sometimes impetuous and harmful –

> And as an apple, secret present from her love,
> Falls out from the chaste bosom of the maid,
> Where she has quite forgot it, hid beneath her robe,
> When at her mother's step she starts, afraid;
> As she rises it falls, rolls off at a swift pace;
> A guilty blush spreads o'er her downcast face
>
> CATULLUS

– I say that males and females are cast in the same mold; except for education and custom, the difference is not great. [C]Plato invites both without discrimination to the fellowship of all studies, exercises, functions, warlike and peaceful occupations, in his commonwealth. And the philosopher Antisthenes eliminated any distinction between their virtue and ours. [B]It is much easier to accuse one sex than to excuse the other. It is the old saying: The pot calls the kettle black.

6
Of coaches

[B]It is very easy to demonstrate that great authors, when they write about causes, adduce not only those they think are true but also those they do not believe in, provided they have some originality and beauty. They speak truly and usefully enough if they speak ingeniously. We cannot make sure of the master cause; we pile up several of them, to see if by chance it will be found among them,

For one cause will not do;
We must state many, one of which is true.

LUCRETIUS

Do you ask me whence comes this custom of blessing those who sneeze? We produce three sorts of wind. That which issues from below is too foul; that which issues from the mouth carries some reproach of gluttony; the third is sneezing. And because it comes from the head and is blameless, we give it this civil reception. Do not laugh at this piece of subtlety; it is, they say, from Aristotle.

It seems to me I have read in Plutarch (who, of all the authors I know, is the one who best combined art with nature and judgment with knowledge) that he gives the reason for the heaving of the stomach that afflicts those who travel by sea, as fear, having found some reason by which he proves that fear can produce such an effect. I, who am very subject to seasickness, know very well that this cause does not affect me, and I know it, not by reasoning, but by necessary experience. Not to mention what I have been told, that the same thing often happens to animals, and especially to pigs, without any apprehension of danger; and what an acquaintance of mine has told me about himself, that though he was very subject to it, the desire to vomit had left him two or three times when he found himself oppressed with fright in a big storm. [C]And hear this ancient: *I was too sick to think about the danger* [Seneca]. [B]I was never afraid on the water, nor indeed anywhere else (and I have often enough had just occasions, if death is one), at least not to the point of being confused or bewildered.

Fear sometimes arises from want of judgment as well as from want of courage. All the dangers I have seen, I have seen with open eyes, with my sight free, sound, and entire; besides, it takes courage to be afraid. It once served me in good stead, compared with others, so to conduct my flight and keep it orderly, that it was carried out, [C]if not without fear, at all events [B]without terror and without dismay; it was excited, but not dazed or distracted.

Great souls go much further yet and offer us examples of flights not merely composed and healthy, but proud. Let us tell of the one that Alcibiades reports of Socrates, his comrade in arms: "I found him," he says, "after the rout of our army, him and Laches, among the last of the fugitives; and I observed him at my leisure and in safety, for I was on a good horse and he on foot, and we had fought that way. I noticed first how much presence of mind and resolution

he showed compared with Laches; and then the boldness of his walk, no different from his ordinary one, his firm and steady gaze, considering and judging what was going on around him, looking now at one side, now the other, friends and enemies, in a way that encouraged the former and signified to the latter that he was a man to sell his blood and his life very dear to anyone who should try to take them away. And thus they made their escape; for people are not inclined to attack such men; they run after the frightened ones." That is the testimony of that great captain, which teaches us what we experience every day, that there is nothing that throws us so much into dangers as an unthinking eagerness to get clear of them. ^c*Where there is less fear, there is generally less danger* [Livy].

^BOur common people are wrong to say that such-and-such a man fears death, when they mean to say that he thinks about it and foresees it. Foresight is equally suitable in whatever concerns us, whether for good or ill. To consider and judge the danger is in a way the opposite of being stunned by it.

I do not feel myself strong enough to sustain the impact and impetuosity of this passion of fear, or of any other vehement passion. If I were once conquered and thrown by it, I would never get up again quite intact. If anything made my soul lose its footing, it would never set it back upright in its place; it probes and searches itself too keenly and deeply, and therefore would never let the wound that had pierced it close up and heal. It has been well for me that no illness has yet laid it low. Each attack made on me I meet and fight off in my full armor; thus the first one that swept me off my feet would leave me without resources. I have no secondary defense: no matter where the torrent should break my dike, I would be helpless and be drowned for good.

^cEpicurus says that the wise man can never pass into a contrary state. I have an opinion about the converse of this saying: that anyone who has once been very foolish will never at any other time be very wise.

^BGod tempers the cold according to the cloak, and gives me passions according to my means of withstanding them. Nature, having uncovered me on one side, has covered me up on the other; having disarmed me of strength, she has armed me with insensibility and a controlled, or dull, apprehensiveness.

Now I cannot long endure (and I could endure them less easily in my youth) either coach, or litter, or boat; and I hate any other transportation than horseback, both in town and in the country.

But I can endure a litter less than a coach, and for the same reason I can more easily bear a rough tossing on the water, whereby fear is produced, than the movement felt in calm weather. By that slight jolt given by the oars, stealing the vessel from under us, I somehow feel my head and stomach troubled, as I cannot bear a shaky seat under me. When the sail or the current carries us along evenly or when we are towed, this uniform movement does not bother me at all. It is an interrupted motion that annoys me, and most of all when it is languid. I cannot otherwise describe its nature. The doctors have ordered me to bind and swathe my abdomen with a towel to remedy this trouble; which I have not tried, being accustomed to wrestle with the weaknesses that are in me and overcome them by myself.

^cIf my memory were sufficiently stored with them, I should not begrudge my time to tell here the infinite variety of examples that histories offer us of the use of coaches in the service of war, varying according to the nations and according to the age; of great effect, it seems to me, and very necessary, so that it is a wonder that we have lost all knowledge of them. I will say only this, that quite recently, in our fathers' time, the Hungarians put coaches very usefully to work against the Turks, there being in each one a targeteer and a musketeer and a number of harquebuses lined up, loaded and ready, the whole thing covered with a wall of shields, like a galiot. They formed their battlefront of three thousand such coaches, and after the cannon had played, had them advance and made the enemy swallow this salvo before tasting the rest; which was no slight advantage. Or they launched them into the enemy squadrons to break them and open them up; not to mention the advantage they could derive from them by flanking enemy troops on their march through open country where they were vulnerable, or by covering a camp in haste and fortifying it.

In my time a gentleman on one of our frontiers, who was unwieldy of person and found no horse capable of bearing his weight, having a feud on his hands, went about the country in a coach of this very description, and made out very well. But let us leave these war coaches. The kings of our first dynasty went about the country in a chariot drawn by four oxen.

^BMark Antony was the first who had himself drawn in Rome – and a minstrel girl beside him – by lions harnessed to a chariot. Heliogabalus did as much later, calling himself Cybele, the mother of the gods; and also by tigers, imitating the god Bacchus; he also

sometimes harnessed two stags to his coach, and another time four dogs, and yet again four naked wenches, having himself, stark naked too, drawn by them in pomp. The Emperor Firmus had his chariot drawn by ostriches of marvelous size, so that it seemed rather to fly than to roll.

The strangeness of these inventions puts into my head this other notion: that it is a sort of pusillanimity in monarchs, and evidence of not sufficiently feeling what they are, to labor at showing off and making a display by excessive expense. It would be excusable in a foreign country; but among his own subjects, where he is all-powerful, he derives from his dignity the highest degree of honor he can attain. Just as, it seems to me, for a gentleman it is superfluous to dress with studied care at home: his house, his retinue, his cuisine, answer for him sufficiently.

ᶜThe advice that Isocrates gives his king seems to me not without reason: that he be splendid in furniture and plate, since that is a lasting investment which passes on to his successors; and that he avoid all magnificences that flow away immediately out of use and memory.

ᴮI liked to adorn myself when I was a youth, for lack of other adornments, and it was becoming to me; there are those on whom fine clothes weep. We have marvelous stories of the frugality of our kings about their own persons and in their gifts – kings great in prestige, in valor, and in fortune. Demosthenes fights tooth and nail against the law of his city that allotted public monies to lavish games and feasts; he wants the greatness of the city to be manifest in its quantity of well-equipped ships and of good, well-supplied armies.

ᶜAnd Theophrastus is rightly blamed for setting forth a contrary opinion in his book on riches, and maintaining that lavish expenditure was the true fruit of opulence. These are pleasures, says Aristotle, that touch only the lowest of the people, that vanish from memory as soon as people are sated with them, and that no judicious and serious man can esteem. The outlay would seem to me much more royal as well as more useful, just, and durable, if it were spent on ports, harbors, fortifications, and walls, on sumptuous buildings, churches, hospitals, colleges, and the improvement of streets and roads, for which Pope Gregory XIII is gratefully remembered in my time, and in which our Queen Catherine would leave evidence for many years of her natural liberality and munificence, if her means were equal to her wish. Fortune has given me great displeasure by interrupting the construction of the handsome new

bridge[1] of our great city, and depriving me of the hope of seeing it in full use before I die.

[B]Besides, it seems to the subjects, spectators of these triumphs, that they are given a display of their own riches, and entertained at their own expense. For peoples are apt to assume about kings, as we do about our servants, that they should take care to prepare for us in abundance all we need, but that they should not touch it at all for their own part. And therefore the Emperor Galba, having taken pleasure in a musician's playing during his supper, sent for his money box and gave into his hand a handful of crowns that he fished out of it, with these words: "This is not the public money, this is my own." At all events, it most often happens that the people are right, and that their eyes are feasted with what should go to feed their bellies.

Liberality itself is not in its proper light in the hands of a sovereign; private people have more right to exercise it. For, to be precise about it, a king has nothing that is properly his own; he owes his very self to others.

[C]The authority to judge is not given for the sake of the judge, but for the sake of the person judged. A superior is never appointed for his own benefit, but for the benefit of the inferior, and a doctor for the sick, not for himself. All authority, like all art, has its end outside of itself: *no art is directed to itself* [Cicero].

[B]Wherefore the tutors of young princes who make it a point to impress on them this virtue of liberality and preach to them not to know how to refuse anything, and to think nothing so well spent as what they give away (a lesson that I have seen in great favor in my time), either look more to their own profit than to their master's, or do not well understand to whom they speak. It is all too easy to impress liberality on a man who has the means to practice it all he wants at the expense of others. [C]And since its value is reckoned not by the measure of the gift, but by the measure of the giver's means, it amounts to nothing in such powerful hands. They find themselves prodigal before they are liberal. [B]Therefore liberality is little to be commended compared with other royal virtues, and it is the only one, as the tyrant Dionysius said, that goes with tyranny itself. I would rather teach him this verse of the ancient farmer:[2] that whoever wants to reap a good crop must sow with the hand, not

1 The Pont Neuf, as it is still called, was completed in 1604.
2 Montaigne translates the Greek verse of Corinna after quoting it.

pour out of the sack; [c]he must scatter the seed, not spill it; [B]and that since he has to give, or, to put it better, pay and restore to so many people according to their deserts, he should be a fair and wise distributor. If the liberality of a prince is without discretion and without measure, I would rather he were a miser.

Royal virtue seems to consist most of all in justice; and of all the parts of justice, that one best marks kings which accompanies liberality; for they have particularly reserved it as their function, whereas they are prone to exercise all other justice through the intermediary of others. Immoderate largesse is a feeble means for them to acquire good will; for it alienates more people than it wins over: [c]*The more you have already practiced it on, the fewer you will be able to practice it on. What is more foolish than to take pains so that you can no longer do what you enjoy doing?* [Cicero.] [B]And if it is exercised without regard to merit, it puts to shame him who receives it, and is received ungraciously. Tyrants have been sacrificed to the hatred of the people by the hands of the very ones whom they have unjustly advanced; for such men think to assure their possession of unde-served goods by showing contempt and hatred for the man from whom they received them, and rallying to the judgment and opinion of the people in that respect.

The subjects of a prince who is excessive in gifts become exces-sive in requests; they adjust themselves not to reason but to example. Surely we often have reason to blush for our impudence; we are overpaid according to justice when the recompense equals our service; for do we owe no service to our prince by natural obligation? If he bears our expenses, he does too much; it is enough that he helps out. The surplus is called benefit, and it cannot be exacted, for the very name of liberality rings of liberty. By our method, it is never done; the receipts are no longer taken into account; people love only the future liberality. Wherefore the more a prince exhausts himself in giving, the poorer he makes himself in friends. [c]How could he assuage desires that grow the more they are fulfilled? He who has his mind on taking, no longer has it on what he has taken. Covetous-ness has nothing so characteristic about it as ingratitude.

The example of Cyrus will not be amiss here to serve the kings of our time as a touchstone for ascertaining whether their gifts are well or ill bestowed, and to make them see how much more happily that emperor dealt them out than they do. Whereby they are reduced to doing their borrowing from unknown subjects, and rather from those they have wronged than from those they have benefited; and

from them they receive no aid that is gratuitous in anything but the name.

Croesus reproached Cyrus for his extravagance and calculated how much his treasure would amount to if he had been more close-fisted. Cyrus, wanting to justify his liberality, sent dispatches in all directions to the grandees of his state whose career he had particularly advanced, and asked each one to help him out with as much money as he could for an urgent need of his, and to send him a declaration of the amount. When all these statements were brought to him, since each of his friends, thinking it was not enough to offer him merely as much as he had received from his munificence, added much that was more properly his own, it turned out that the total amounted to much more than the savings estimated by Croesus. Whereupon Cyrus said to him: "I am no less in love with riches than other princes, and am rather a more careful manager of them. You see at how small a cost I have acquired the inestimable treasure of so many friends, and how much more faithful treasurers they are to me than mercenary men without obligation, without affection, would be; and how much better my wealth is lodged than in coffers, where it would call down upon me the hatred, envy, and contempt of other princes."

[B]The emperors derived an excuse for the superfluity of their public games and spectacles from the fact that their authority depended somewhat (at least in appearance) on the will of the Roman people, who from time immemorial had been accustomed to being flattered by that sort of spectacle and extravagance. But it was private citizens who had nourished this custom of gratifying their fellow citizens and companions, chiefly out of their own purse, by such profusion and magnificence; this had an altogether different flavor when it was the masters who came to imitate it. [C]*The transfer of money from its rightful owners to strangers should not be regarded as liberality* [Cicero].

Philip, because his son was trying to win the good will of the Macedonians by presents, scolded him for it in a letter in this manner: "What, do you want your subjects to regard you as their purser, not as their king? Do you want to win them over? Win them over with the benefits of your virtue, not the benefits of your coffers."

[B]It was, however, a fine thing to bring and plant in the amphitheater a great quantity of big trees, all branching and green, representing a great shady forest, arranged in beautiful

symmetry, and on the first day to cast into it a thousand ostriches, a thousand stags, a thousand wild boars, and a thousand fallow deer, leaving them to be hunted down by the people; on the next day to have a hundred big lions, a hundred leopards, and three hundred bears slaughtered in their presence; and for the third day, to have three hundred pairs of gladiators fight it out to the death, as the Emperor Probus did.

It was also a fine thing to see those great amphitheaters faced with marble on the outside, wrought with ornaments and statues, the inside sparkling with many rare enrichments –

> Here is the diamond circle, the golden portico
> CALPURNIUS

– all the sides of this vast space filled and surrounded from top to bottom with three or four score tiers of seats, also of marble, covered with cushions –

> "Let him begone," he says,
> "And leave the cushioned seats of knights, seeing he pays
> None of the lawful tax"
> JUVENAL

– where a hundred thousand men could sit at their ease. Also, first of all, to have the place at the bottom, where the games were played, open artificially and split into crevasses representing caverns that vomited forth the beasts destined for the spectacle; and then, second, to flood it with a deep sea, full of sea monsters and laden with armed vessels to represent a naval battle; and third, to level it and dry it off again for the combat of the gladiators; and for the fourth show to strew it with vermilion and storax instead of sand, in order to set up a stately banquet there for all that huge number of people – the final act of a single day:

> How often have we seen
> Part of the sandy floor sink down, wild beasts emerge
> Out of the open chasm, and from its depths upsurge
> Forests of golden growing trees with yellow bark.
> Not only forest monsters were for us to mark,
> But I saw sea-calves mingled in with fighting bears,
> And hippopotami, the shapeless herd that wears
> The name of river-horse.
> CALPURNIUS

Sometimes they created a high mountain there, full of fruit trees and other trees in leaf, spouting a stream of water from its top as from the mouth of a living spring. Sometimes they brought in a great ship which opened and came apart of itself and, after having spewed forth from its belly four or five hundred fighting beasts, closed up again and vanished without assistance. At other times, from the floor of the place, they made spouts and jets of water spring forth which shot upward to an infinite height, then sprinkled and perfumed that infinite multitude. To protect themselves against damage from the weather, they had that immense space hung with awnings, sometimes made of purple worked with the needle, sometimes of silk of one color or another, and they drew them forward or back in a moment, as they had a mind to:

> The awnings, though the sun scorches the skin,
> Are, when Hermogenes appears, drawn in.
>
> <div align="right">MARTIAL</div>

The nets, too, which they put in front of the people to protect them from the violence of the loosened beasts, were woven of gold:

> Even the woven nets
> Glitter with gold.
>
> <div align="right">CALPURNIUS</div>

If there is anything excusable in such extravagances, it is when the inventiveness and the novelty of them, not the expense, provide amazement.

Even in these vanities we discover how fertile those ages were in minds different from ours. It is with this sort of fertility as with all other productions of Nature. This is not to say that she then put forth her utmost effort. We do not go in a straight line; we rather ramble, and turn this way and that. We retrace our steps. I fear that our knowledge is weak in every direction; we do not see very far ahead or very far behind. It embraces little and has a short life, short in both extent of time and extent of matter:

> Ere Agamemnon, heroes were the same;
> Many there were, but no one knows their name;
> They all are hurried on unwept
> Into unending night.
>
> <div align="right">HORACE</div>

Before the Trojan War, before Troy fell,
Were other bards with other tales to tell.
LUCRETIUS

^cAnd Solon's story of what he had heard from the priests of
Egypt about the long life of their state, and their manner of learning
and preserving the histories of other countries, does not seem to me
a testimony to be rejected in this consideration. *If we could view
that expanse of countries and ages, boundless in every direction, into
which the mind, plunging and spreading itself, travels so far and wide
that it can find no limit where it can stop, there would appear in that
immensity an infinite capacity to produce innumerable forms* [adapted
from Cicero].

^BEven if all that has come down to us by report from the past
should be true and known by someone, it would be less than nothing
compared with what is unknown. And of this very image of the
world which glides along while we live on it, how puny and limited
is the knowledge of even the most curious! Not only of particular
events which fortune often renders exemplary and weighty, but of
the state of great governments and nations, there escapes us
a hundred times more than comes to our knowledge. We exclaim
at the miracle of the invention of our artillery, of our printing; other
men in another corner of the world, in China, enjoyed these
a thousand years earlier. If we saw as much of the world as we do
not see, we would perceive, it is likely, a perpetual multiplication and
vicissitude of forms.

There is nothing unique and rare as regards nature, but there
certainly is as regards our knowledge, which is a miserable founda-
tion for our rules and which is apt to represent to us a very false
picture of things. As vainly as we today infer the decline and
decrepitude of the world from the arguments we draw from our
own weakness and decay –

This age is broken down, and broken down the earth
LUCRETIUS

– so vainly did this poet infer the world's birth and youth from the
vigor he saw in the minds of his time, abounding in novelties and
inventions in various arts:

The universe, I think, is very new,
The world is young, its birth not far behind;

> Hence certain arts grow more and more refined
> Even today; the naval art is one.
> LUCRETIUS

Our world has just discovered another world (and who will guarantee us that it is the last of its brothers, since the daemons, the sibyls, and we ourselves have up to now been ignorant of this one?) no less great, full, and well-limbed than itself, yet so new and so infantile that it is still being taught its A B C; not fifty years ago it knew neither letters, nor weights and measures, nor clothes, nor wheat, nor vines. It was still quite naked at the breast, and lived only on what its nursing mother provided. If we are right to infer the end of our world, and that poet is right about the youth of his own age, this other world will only be coming into the light when ours is leaving it. The universe will fall into paralysis; one member will be crippled, the other in full vigor.

I am much afraid that we shall have very greatly hastened the decline and ruin of this new world by our contagion, and that we will have sold it our opinions and our arts very dear. It was an infant world; yet we have not whipped it and subjected it to our discipline by the advantage of our natural valor and strength, nor won it over by our justice and goodness, nor subjugated it by our magnanimity. Most of the responses of these people and most of our dealings with them show that they were not at all behind us in natural brightness of mind and pertinence.

The awesome magnificence of the cities of Cuzco and Mexico (and, among many similar things, the garden of that king in which all the trees, the fruits, and all the herbs were excellently fashioned in gold, and of such size and so arranged as they might be in an ordinary garden; and in his curio room were gold replicas of all the living creatures native to his country and its waters), and the beauty of their workmanship in jewelry, feathers, cotton, and painting, show that they were not behind us in industry either. But as for devoutness, observance of the laws, goodness, liberality, loyalty, and frankness, it served us well not to have as much as they: by their advantage in this they lost, sold, and betrayed themselves.

As for boldness and courage, as for firmness, constancy, resoluteness against pains and hunger and death, I would not fear to oppose the examples I could find among them to the most famous ancient examples that we have in the memories of our world on this side of the ocean. For as regards the men who subjugated them, take

away the ruses and tricks that they used to deceive them, and the people's natural astonishment at seeing the unexpected arrival of bearded men, different in language, religion, shape, and countenance, from a part of the world so remote, where they had never imagined there was any sort of human habitation, mounted on great unknown monsters, opposed to men who had never seen not only a horse, but any sort of animal trained to carry and endure a man or any other burden; men equipped with a hard and shiny skin and a sharp and glittering weapon, against men who, for the miracle of a mirror or a knife, would exchange a great treasure in gold and pearls, and who had neither the knowledge nor the material by which, even in full leisure, they could pierce our steel; add to this the lightning and thunder of our cannon and harquebuses – capable of disturbing Caesar himself, if he had been surprised by them with as little experience and in his time – against people who were naked (except in some regions where the invention of some cotton fabric had reached them), without other arms at the most than bows, stones, sticks, ᶜand wooden bucklers; ᴮpeople taken by surprise, under color of friendship and good faith, by curiosity to see strange and unknown things: eliminate this disparity, I say, and you take from the conquerors the whole basis of so many victories.

When I consider that indomitable ardor with which so many thousands of men, women, and children came forth and hurled themselves so many times into inevitable dangers for the defense of their gods and of their liberty, and that noble, stubborn readiness to suffer all extremities and hardships, even death, rather than submit to the domination of those by whom they had been so shamefully deceived (for some of them when captured chose rather to let themselves perish of hunger and fasting than to accept food from the hands of such basely victorious enemies), I conclude that if anyone had attacked them on equal terms, with equal arms, experience, and numbers, it would have been just as dangerous for him as in any other war we know of, and more so.

Why did not such a noble conquest fall to Alexander or to those ancient Greeks and Romans? Why did not such a great change and alteration of so many empires and peoples fall into hands that would have gently polished and cleared away whatever was barbarous in them, and would have strengthened and fostered the good seeds that nature had produced in them, not only adding to the cultivation of the earth and the adornment of cities the arts of our side of the ocean, in so far as they would have been necessary, but also adding

the Greek and Roman virtues to those originally in that region? What an improvement that would have been, and what an ameli- oration for the entire globe, if the first examples of our conduct that were offered over there had called those peoples to the admira- tion and imitation of virtue and had set up between them and us a brotherly fellowship and understanding! How easy it would have been to make good use of souls so fresh, so famished to learn, and having, for the most part, such fine natural beginnings! On the contrary, we took advantage of their ignorance and inexperience to incline them the more easily toward treachery, lewdness, avarice, and every sort of inhumanity and cruelty, after the example and pattern of our ways. Who ever set the utility of commerce and trading at such a price? So many cities razed, so many nations exterminated, so many millions of people put to the sword, and the richest and most beautiful part of the world turned upside down, for the traffic in pearls and pepper! Base and mechanical victories! Never did ambition, never did public enmities, drive men against one another to such horrible hostilities and such miserable calamities.

Coasting the sea in quest of their mines, certain Spaniards landed in a fertile, pleasant, well-populated country, and made their usual declarations to its people: that they were peaceable men, coming from distant voyages, sent on behalf of the king of Castile, the greatest prince of the habitable world, to whom the Pope, representing God on earth, had given the principality of all the Indies; that if these people would be tributaries to him, they would be very kindly treated. They demanded of them food to eat and gold to be used in a certain medicine, and expounded to them the belief in one single God and the truth of our religion, which they advised them to accept, adding a few threats.

The answer was this: As for being peaceable, they did not look like it, if they were. As for their king, since he was begging, he must be indigent and needy; and he who had awarded their country to him must be a man fond of dissension, to go and give another person something that was not his and thus set him at strife with its ancient possessors. As for food, they would supply them. Gold they had little of, and it was a thing they held in no esteem, since it was useless to the service of their life, their sole concern being with passing life happily and pleasantly; however, they might boldly take any they could find, except what was employed in the service of their gods. As for one single God, the account had pleased them, but they did

not want to change their religion, having followed it so advanta-geously for so long, and they were not accustomed to take counsel except of their friends and acquaintances. As for the threats, it was a sign of lack of judgment to threaten people whose nature and means were unknown to them. Thus they should promptly hurry up and vacate their land, for they were not accustomed to take in good part the civilities and declarations of armed strangers; otherwise they would do to them as they had done to these others – showing them the heads of some executed men around their city.

There we have an example of the babbling of this infancy. But at all events, neither in that place nor in several others where the Spaniards did not find the merchandise they were looking for, did they make any stay or any attack, whatever other advantages there might be; witness my Cannibals.[3]

Of the two most powerful monarchs of that world, and perhaps of this as well, kings of so many kings, the last two that they drove out, one, the king of Peru, was taken in a battle and put to so excessive a ransom that it surpasses all belief; and when this had been faithfully paid, and the king in his dealings had given signs of a frank, liberal, and steadfast spirit and a clear and well-ordered understanding, the conquerors, after having extracted from him one million three hundred and twenty-five thousand five hundred ounces of gold, besides silver and other things that amounted to no less, so that their horses thenceforth went shod with solid gold, were seized with the desire to see also, at the price of whatever treachery, what could be the remainder of this king's treasures, [c]and to enjoy freely what he had reserved. [B]They trumped up against him a false accusation and false evidence that he was planning to rouse his provinces in order to regain his freedom. Whereupon, in a beautiful sentence pronounced by those very men who had set afoot this treachery against him, he was condemned to be publicly hanged and strangled, after being permitted to buy his way out of the torment of being burned alive by submitting to baptism at the moment of the execution. A horrible and unheard-of calamity, which nevertheless he bore without belying himself either by look or word, with a truly royal bearing and gravity. And then, to lull the people, stunned and dazed by such a strange thing, they counter-feited great mourning over his death and ordered a sumptuous funeral for him.

3 Described in *Essays* I: 31.

The other one, the king of Mexico, had long defended his besieged city and shown in this siege all that endurance and perseverance can do, if ever prince and people did so, when his bad fortune put him in his enemies' hands alive, on their promise that they would treat him as a king; nor did he in his captivity show anything unworthy of this title. After this victory, his enemies, not finding all the gold they had promised themselves, first ransacked and searched everything, and then set about seeking information by inflicting the cruelest tortures they could think up on the prisoners they held. But having gained nothing by this, and finding their prisoners' courage stronger than their torments, they finally flew into such a rage that, against their word and against all law of nations, they condemned the king himself and one of the principal lords of his court to the torture in each other's presence. This lord, finding himself overcome with the pain, surrounded with burning braziers, in the end turned his gaze piteously toward his master, as if to ask his pardon because he could hold out no longer. The king, fixing his eyes proudly and severely on him in reproach for his cowardice and pusillanimity, said to him only these words, in a stern, firm voice: "And I, am I in a bath? Am I more comfortable than you?" The other immediately after succumbed to the pain and died on the spot. The king, half roasted, was carried away from there, not so much out of pity (for what pity ever touched souls who, for dubious information about some gold vase to pillage, had a man grilled before their eyes, and what is more, a king so great in fortune and merit?), but because his fortitude made their cruelty more and more shameful. They hanged him later for having courageously attempted to deliver himself by arms from such a long captivity and subjection, and he made an end worthy of a great-souled prince.

Another time they burned alive, all at once and in the same fire, four hundred and sixty men, the four hundred being of the common people, the sixty from among the chief lords of a province, all merely prisoners of war.

We have these narrations from themselves, for they not only admit them but boast of them and preach them. Would it be as a testimonial to their justice or their zeal for religion? Truly, those are ways too contrary and hostile to so holy an end. If they had proposed to extend our faith, they would have reflected that faith is not spread by possession of territory but by possession of men, and they would have been more than satisfied with the murders brought about by the necessity of war, without adding to these an

indiscriminate butchery, as of wild animals, as universal as fire and sword could make it, after purposely sparing only as many as they wanted to make into miserable slaves for the working and service of their mines: with the result that many of the leaders were punished with death by order of the kings of Castile, who were justly shocked by the horror of their conduct; and almost all were disesteemed and loathed. God deservedly allowed this great plunder to be swallowed up by the sea in transit, or by the intestine wars in which they devoured one another; and most of them were buried on the spot without any profit from their victory.

As for the fact that the revenue from this, even in the hands of a thrifty and prudent prince,[4] corresponds so little to the expectation of it given to his predecessors and to the abundance of riches that was first encountered in these new lands (for although much is being gotten out, we see that it is nothing compared with what was to be expected), the reason is that the use of money was entirely unknown, and that consequently their gold was found all collected together, being of no other use than for show and parade, like a chattel preserved from father to son by many powerful kings who were constantly exhausting their mines to make that great heap of vases and statues for the adornment of their palaces and their temples; whereas our gold is all in circulation and in trade. We cut it up small and change it into a thousand forms; we scatter and disperse it. Imagine it if our kings thus accumulated all the gold they could find for many centuries and kept it idle.

The people of the kingdom of Mexico were somewhat more civilized and skilled in the arts than the other nations over there. Thus they judged, as we do, that the universe was near its end, and they took as a sign of this the desolation that we brought upon them. They believed that the existence of the world was divided into five ages and into the life of five successive suns, of which four had already run their time, and that the one which gave them light was the fifth. The first perished with all other creatures by a universal flood of water. The second, by the heavens falling on us, which suffocated every living thing; to which age they assign the giants, and they showed the Spaniards some of their bones, judging by the size of which these men must have stood twenty hands high. The third, by fire, which burned and consumed everything. The fourth, by a turbulence of air and wind which beat down even many

4 King Philip II of Spain.

mountains; the men did not die, but they were changed into baboons (to what notions will the laxness of human credulity not submit!). After the death of this fourth sun, the world was twenty-five years in perpetual darkness, in the fifteenth of which a man and a woman were created who remade the human race; ten years later, on a certain day of their calendar, the sun appeared newly created, and since then they reckon their years from that day. The third day after its creation the old gods died; the new ones have been born since little by little. What they think about the manner in which this last sun will perish, my author[5] did not learn. But their calculation of this fourth change coincides with that great conjunction of stars which produced, some eight hundred years ago, according to the reckoning of the astrologers, many great alterations and innovations in the world.

As for pomp and magnificence, whereby I entered upon this subject, neither Greece nor Rome nor Egypt can compare any of its works, whether in utility or difficulty or nobility, with the road which is seen in Peru, laid out by the kings of the country, from the city of Quito as far as Cuzco (a distance of three hundred leagues), straight, even, twenty-five paces wide, paved, lined on both sides with fine high walls, and along these, on the inside, two ever-flowing streams, bordered by beautiful trees, which they call *molly*. Wherever they encountered mountains and rocks, they cut through and leveled them, and filled the hollows with stone and lime. At the end of each day's journey there are fine places furnished with provisions, clothes, and arms, for travelers as well as for the armies that have to pass that way.

In my estimate of this work I have counted the difficulty, which is particularly considerable in that place. They did not build with any stones less than ten feet square; they had no other means of carrying than by strength of arm, dragging their load along; and they had not even the art of scaffolding, knowing no other device than to raise an equal height of earth against their building as it rose, and remove it afterward.

Let us fall back to our coaches. Instead of these or any other form of transport, they had themselves carried by men, and on their shoulders. That last king of Peru, the day that he was taken, was thus carried on shafts of gold, seated in a chair of gold, in the midst

5 Lopez de Gomara, a Spanish contemporary of Montaigne, whose histories of Cortez and of the West Indies Montaigne read in translation.

of his army. As many of these carriers as they killed to make him fall – for they wanted to take him alive – so many others vied to take the place of the dead ones, so that they never could bring him down, however great a slaughter they made of those people, until a horseman seized him around the body and pulled him to the ground.

7

Of the disadvantage of greatness

[B]Since we cannot attain it, let us take our revenge by speaking ill of it. Yet it is not absolutely speaking ill of something to find some defects in it; there are some in all things, however beautiful and desirable they may be. In general greatness has this evident advantage, that it can step down whenever it pleases, and that it almost has the choice of both conditions. For one does not fall from every height; there are more from which one can descend without falling.

It does indeed seem to me that we overvalue it, and overvalue too the resolution of people we have either seen or heard of who despised it or laid it down of their own accord. Its essence is not so obviously advantageous that it cannot be refused except by a miracle.

I find the effort to bear ills a very hard one; but as for being content with a mediocre measure of fortune, and eschewing greatness, I find very little difficulty in that. To eschew greatness is a virtue, it seems to me, which I, who am only a gosling, could attain without great striving. What may not be done by those who would also put in consideration the glory that goes with this refusal, in which there may lurk more ambition than in the very desire and enjoyment of greatness, inasmuch as ambition never follows its own bent better than by some out-of-the-way and unused path?

I sharpen my courage toward endurance, I weaken it toward desire. I have as much to wish for as another, and I allow my wishes and inclinations as much freedom and indiscretion; yet it has never occurred to me to wish for empire or royalty, or for the eminence of those high and commanding fortunes. I do not aim in that direction, I love myself too well. When I think of growing, it is in a lowly way, with a constrained and cowardly growth, strictly for myself: in resolution, wisdom, health, beauty, and even riches. But that

prestige, all that powerful authority, oppresses my imagination. And quite in contrast to that other,[1] I would perhaps prefer to be second or third in Périgueux rather than first in Paris; at least, without prevarication, rather the third in Paris than the first in responsibility. I want neither to be a wretched unknown, wrangling with a doorkeeper, nor to make the crowds where I pass split in adoration. I am trained to a middle station, by my taste as well as by my lot. [C]And I have shown, in the conduct of my life and of my enterprises, that I have rather avoided than otherwise stepping above the degree of fortune in which God placed me at birth. Every natural arrangement is equally just and easy.

[B]My soul is so craven that I do not measure good fortune by its height; I measure it by its facility.

[C]But if my heart is not great enough, it is compensatingly open, and it orders me boldly to publish its weakness. If I were asked to compare the life of L. Thorius Balbus, a gentleman, handsome, learned, healthy, intelligent, abounding in all sorts of advantages and pleasures, leading a tranquil life all his own, his soul well prepared against death, superstition, pain, and the other encumbrances of human necessity, at last dying in battle, arms in hand, for the defense of his country, on the one hand; and on the other hand the life of M. Regulus, great and lofty as every man knows it to be, and his admirable end; the one without a name, without distinction, the other marvelously exemplary and glorious: I would certainly say what Cicero says, if I could speak as well as he.[2] But if I had to apply their lives to mine, I would also say that the first is as much according to my reach – and according to my desire, which I accommodate to my reach – as the second is far beyond it; that I can attain the latter only by veneration, but that I could readily attain the other in practice. Let us return to our temporal greatness, from which we started.

[B]I have a distaste for mastery, both active and passive. [C]Otanes, one of the seven who had some right to aspire to the throne of Persia, took a course that I would gladly have taken. He abandoned to his competitors his chance of attaining it either by election or by lot, provided that he and his family might live in that empire free of all subjection and mastery save that of the ancient laws, and have

1 Caesar, whom Plutarch represents as saying of a tiny village that he would rather be the first man there than the second in Rome.
2 Cicero (*De Finibus* II. xx) sets Regulus far above Balbus.

every freedom that would not be prejudicial to these; balking at either commanding or being commanded.

[B]The toughest and most difficult occupation in the world, in my opinion, is to play the part of a king worthily. I excuse more of their faults than people commonly do, in consideration of the dreadful weight of their burden, which dazes me. It is difficult for a power so immoderate to observe moderation. And yet even for men of a less excellent nature, it is a singular incitement to virtue to be lodged in a place where you can do no good that is not put in the record and account, where the slightest good action affects so many people, and where your ability, like that of preachers, is principally addressed to the populace, an inexact judge, easy to dupe, easy to satisfy.

There are few things on which we can give a sincere judgment, because there are few in which we have not in some way a private interest. Superiority and inferiority of position, mastery and subjection, are forced into a natural envy and contention; they must pillage one another perpetually. I do not believe either one about the rights of the other; let us give the floor to reason, which is inflexible and impassive, when we can dispose of it.

Less than a month ago I was leafing through two Scottish books debating this subject. The democrat makes the king's situation worse than a carter's; the monarchist lodges him a few fathoms above God in power and sovereignty.

Now the disadvantage of greatness, which I have chosen to comment on here because of an occasion that has just called my attention to it, is this. There is perhaps nothing more pleasant in association with men than the trials of strength we have with one another, in rivalry of honor and worth, whether in exercises of the body or of the mind; and in these sovereigns have no real share. In truth, it has often seemed to me that by force of respect princes are treated disdainfully and insultingly in these matters. For what used to offend me immeasurably in my childhood, that those who exercised with me would not take it seriously, considering me unworthy of their making an effort, is what we see happen to princes every day, since everyone considers himself too base to make an effort against them. If people recognize that princes have the slightest desire for victory, there is no one who will not labor to give it to them and who will not rather betray his own glory than offend theirs; everyone exerts only as much effort as is needed to serve their honor.

What share do they have in the melee in which everyone is on their side? I seem to see those paladins of times past going into jousts and combats with enchanted bodies and weapons.

Brisson, in a race against Alexander, only pretended to run his best; Alexander scolded him for it, but he should have had him whipped.

In consideration of this, Carneades used to say that the sons of princes learned nothing rightly but how to manage horses, since in every other exercise everyone gives way to them and lets them win; but a horse, who is neither a flatterer nor a courtier, will throw the son of a king just as he would the son of a porter.

Homer was constrained to consent that Venus, so sweet and delicate a saint, should be wounded in the battle of Troy, so as to endow her with courage and boldness, qualities not found in those who are exempt from danger. The gods are made to be angry, to fear, to flee, to be jealous, sorrowful, and passionate, in order to honor them with virtues which among us are built of these imperfections. He who does not share the risk and difficulty can claim no involvement in the honor and pleasure that follow hazardous actions. It is a pity to have so much power that everything gives way to you. Your fortune repels society and companionship too far from you; it plants you too far apart. That ease and slack facility of making everything bow beneath you is the enemy of every kind of pleasure. That is sliding, not walking; sleeping, not living. Imagine man accompanied by omnipotence: he is sunk; he must ask you for hindrance and resistance, as an alms; his being and his welfare are in indigence.[3]

Their good qualities are dead and wasted, for these are felt only by comparison, and they are out of comparison. They have little knowledge of true praise, being battered with such continual and uniform approbation. Are they dealing with the stupidest of their subjects? They have no way of getting the advantage over him. If he says: "It is because he is my king," it seems to him he has said clearly enough that he lent a hand to his own defeat.

3 Here Montaigne added in the margin of the Bordeaux Copy: "Evil is in its turn a good to man, and good an evil. Neither is pain something for him always to flee, nor pleasure for him always to follow." He later scratched this out here, but added it about a third of the way through the "Apology for Raymond Sebond" (*Essays* II: 12, p. 442), deleting "and good an evil."

Their royal status stifles and consumes their other real and essential qualities; these are sunk in royalty; and it leaves them nothing to recommend themselves by but those actions that directly concern and serve it, the duties of their office. It takes so much to be a king that he exists only as such. That extraneous glare that surrounds him hides him and conceals him from us; our sight breaks and is dissipated by it, being filled and arrested by this strong light. The Senate decreed the prize for eloquence to Tiberius; he refused it, thinking that from a judgment so far from free, even if it had been honest, he could have no satisfaction.

As we yield to them all the advantages of honor, so we confirm and authorize the defects and vices they have, not only by approbation but also by imitation. Every one of the followers of Alexander carried his head on one side, as he did; and the flatterers of Dionysius bumped into one another in his presence, stumbled upon and knocked over what was at their feet, to signify that they were as shortsighted as he. Even hernias have sometimes served as a recommendation and favor. I have seen men affect deafness. And because the master hated his wife, Plutarch saw courtiers repudiate theirs, whom they loved.

What is more, lechery has been seen in fashion among them, and every sort of dissoluteness; as also disloyalty, blasphemy, cruelty; as also heresy; also superstition, irreligion, laxity, and worse, if worse there be: an example even more dangerous than that of the flatterers of Mithridates, who, because their master was envious of the honor of being a good doctor, brought him their limbs to be incised and cauterized. For those others allow their soul to be cauterized, a nobler and more delicate part.

But, to end where I began, when the Emperor Hadrian was arguing with the philosopher Favorinus about the interpretation of some word, Favorinus soon yielded him the victory. When his friends complained to him, he said: "You are jesting; would you want him to be less learned than I, he who commands thirty legions?" Augustus wrote some verses against Asinius Pollio. "And I," said Pollio, "am keeping quiet; it is not wise to be a scribe against a man who can proscribe." And they were right. For Dionysius, because he could not match Philoxenus in poetry, and Plato in prose, condemned the one to the quarries and sent the other to be sold as a slave on the island of Aegina.

8
Of the art of discussion

^BIt is a practice of our justice to condemn some as a warning to others. ^CTo condemn them because they have done wrong would be stupidity, as Plato says; for what is done cannot be undone. But they are condemned so that they may not do the same wrong again, or so that others may avoid the example of their wrongdoing.

^BWe do not correct the man we hang; we correct others through him. I do the same. My errors are by now natural and incorrigible; but the good that worthy men do the public by making themselves imitable, I shall perhaps do by making myself evitable:

> See Bassus' squalor, see how Albius' son
> Lives poorly: lessons these to everyone
> Not to squander his estate.
> HORACE

By my publishing and accusing my imperfections, someone will learn to fear them. The parts that I most esteem in myself derive more honor from self-accusation than from self-commendation. That is why I fall back into the former and dwell on it more often. But when all is said and done, you never speak about yourself without loss. Your self-condemnation is always accredited, your self-praise discredited.

There may be some people of my temperament, I who learn better by contrast than by example, and by flight than by pursuit. This was the sort of teaching that Cato the Elder had in view when he said that the wise have more to learn from the fools than the fools from the wise; and also that ancient lyre player who, Pausanias tells us, was accustomed to force his pupils to go hear a bad musician who lived across the way, where they might learn to hate his discords and false measures.

The horror I feel for cruelty throws me back more deeply into clemency than any model of clemency could attract me to it. A good horseman does not correct my seat as does an attorney or a Venetian on horseback; and a bad way of speaking reforms mine better than a good one. Every day the stupid bearing of another warns and admonishes me. What stings, touches and arouses us better than what pleases. These times are fit for improving us only backward, by disagreement more than by agreement, by difference more than by similarity. Being little taught by good examples, I make use of

the bad ones, whose lessons are common. ᶜI have tried to make myself as agreeable as I saw others unpleasant, as firm as I saw others lax, as mild as I saw others violent. But I was setting myself unattainable standards.

ᴮThe most fruitful and natural exercise of our mind, in my opinion, is discussion. I find it sweeter than any other action of our life; and that is the reason why, if I were right now forced to choose, I believe I would rather consent to lose my sight than my hearing or speech. The Athenians, and the Romans too, preserved this practice in great honor in their academies. In our time, the Italians retain some vestiges of it, to their great advantage, as is seen by a comparison of our intelligence with theirs.

The study of books is a languishing and feeble activity that gives no heat, whereas discussion teaches and exercises us at the same time. If I discuss with a strong mind and a stiff jouster, he presses on my flanks, prods me right and left; his ideas launch mine. Rivalry, glory, competition, push me and lift me above myself. And unison is an altogether boring quality in discussion.

As our mind is strengthened by communication with vigorous and orderly minds, so it is impossible to say how much it loses and degenerates by our continual association and frequentation with mean and sickly minds. There is no contagion that spreads like that one. I know by enough experience how much it is worth per yard. I love to argue and discuss, but in a small group and for my own sake. For to serve as a spectacle to the great and make a competitive parade of one's wit and chatter is an occupation that I find very unbecoming to a man of honor.

Stupidity is a bad quality; but to be unable to endure it, to be irritated and chafed by it, as happens to me, is another sort of malady which is scarcely less troublesome than stupidity; and that is what I now wish to accuse in myself.

I enter into discussion and argument with great freedom and ease, inasmuch as opinion finds in me a bad soil to penetrate and take deep roots in. No propositions astonish me, no belief offends me, whatever contrast it offers with my own. There is no fancy so frivolous and so extravagant that it does not seem to me quite suitable to the production of the human mind. We who deprive our judgment of the right to make decisions look mildly on opinions different from ours; and if we do not lend them our judgment, we easily lend them our ears. Where one scale of the balance is totally empty, I let the other vacillate under an old woman's dreams. And it

seems to me excusable if I take rather the odd number than the even, Thursday rather than Friday; if I am happier to be twelfth or four-teenth than thirteenth at table; if I would rather see a hare skirting my path when I travel than crossing it, and rather give my left foot than my right to be booted first. All such idle fancies, which are in credit around us, deserve at least to be listened to. For me they outweigh only emptiness, but they do outweigh that. Popular and chance opinions count in weight for something, and not nothing, in nature. And he who does not let himself go that far may perhaps fall into the vice of obstinacy to avoid that of superstition.

So contradictions of opinions neither offend nor affect me; they merely arouse and exercise me. We flee from correction; we should face it and go to meet it, especially when it comes in the form of discussion, not *ex cathedra*. At every opposition we do not consider whether it is just, but, right or wrong, how we can get rid of it. Instead of stretching out our arms to it, we stretch out our claws.

I could stand to be rudely jarred by my friends: "You're a fool, you're dreaming." I like to see people speak up bravely among gallant men, and to see the words go where the thought goes. We should strengthen and toughen our ears against this tenderness toward the ceremonious sound of words. I like a strong, manly fellowship and familiarity, a friendship that delights in the sharp-ness and vigor of its intercourse, as does love in bites and scratches that draw blood. ᶜIt is not vigorous and generous enough if it is not quarrelsome, if it is civilized and artful, if it fears knocks and moves with constraint. *For there can be no discussion without contradiction* [Cicero].

ᴮWhen someone opposes me, he arouses my attention, not my anger. I go to meet a man who contradicts me, who instructs me. The cause of truth should be the common cause for both. What will he answer? The passion of wrath has already smitten his judgment. Confusion has seized it before reason. It would be useful if we decided our disputes by a wager, if there was a material mark of our losses, so that we might keep an account of them, and my valet could say to me: "It cost you a hundred crowns twenty times last year to be ignorant and stubborn."

I give a warm welcome to truth in whatever hand I find it, and cheerfully surrender to it and extend my conquered arms, from as far off as I see it approach. ᶜAnd provided they do not go about it with too imperious and magisterial a frown, I lend a hand to the criticism people make of my writings, and have often changed them more out

of civility than to improve them, loving to gratify and foster my critics' freedom to admonish me by the ease with which I yield – yes, even at my own expense. However, it is certainly hard to induce the men of my time to do this. They have not the courage to correct because they have not the courage to suffer being corrected, and they always speak with dissimulation in one another's presence. I take such great pleasure in being judged and known that it is virtually indifferent to me in which of the two forms I am so. My thinking so often contradicts and condemns itself that it is all one to me if another does the job, especially seeing that I give to his criticism only as much authority as I wish. But I break off with a man who bears himself as high-handedly as one man I know, who regrets having given advice if it is not accepted, and is affronted if you balk at following it.

That Socrates always smilingly welcomed the contradictions offered to his arguments might be said to be due to his strength and to the fact that, since the advantage was certain to fall on his side, he accepted them as matter for new glory. But we see on the contrary that there is nothing which makes us so sensitive to contradictions as the idea of our superiority and the disdain for our adversary, and that in reason it is rather for the weaker to accept with good grace the criticisms that correct him and set him right.

[B]In truth, I seek more the company of people who treat me roughly than that of those who fear me. It is an insipid and harmful pleasure to have to do with people who admire us and give way to us. Antisthenes ordered his children never to thank or be grateful to a man who praised them. I feel much prouder of the victory I win over myself when, in the very heat of the battle, I make myself bow beneath the force of my adversary's reason, than I feel gratified by the victory I win over him through his weakness.

In fine, I receive and acknowledge any sort of blows that are straightforward, however weak they may be, but I am only too intolerant of those that are out of order. I care little about the subject matter, opinions are all one to me, and I am almost indifferent about which opinion wins. I will argue peaceably a whole day if the debate is conducted with order. [C]It is not so much strength and subtlety that I ask for as order: the order that we see every day in the altercations of shepherds and shop boys, never among us. If they get off the track, it is by way of incivility; so indeed do we. But their turbulence and impatience never sidetrack them from their theme; their argument follows its course. If they get ahead of one another, if

they do not wait for one another, at least they understand one another. For me any answer is only too good if it is to the point. [B]But when the argument is confused and disorderly, I give up the substance and attach myself angrily and indiscriminately to the form, and throw myself into a headstrong, malicious, and imperious way of arguing, which I have to blush for afterward. [C]It is impossible to discuss things in good faith with a fool.

Not only is my judgment corrupted in the hands of so impetuous a master, but my conscience is also. Our disputes ought to be forbidden and punished like other verbal crimes. What vice do they not stir and heap up, being always governed and commanded by anger? We feel hostility first against the reasons, and then against the men. We learn to argue only in order to contradict; and with each man contradicting and being contradicted, it turns out that the fruit of the argument is to ruin and annihilate the truth. Thus Plato, in his Republic, prohibits this exercise to inept and ill-born minds.

[B]What is the use of your setting out in quest of that which is, with a man whose pace and gait are no good? We do no wrong to the subject when we leave it in order to see about the way to treat it. I do not mean a scholastic and artificial way; I mean a natural way, that of a sound understanding. What will come of it in the end? One goes east, the other west; they lose the main point and mislay it in the throng of incidentals. After an hour of stormy argument, they do not know what they are looking for; one is low, another high, another wide of the mark. One man catches at a word or a smile. One is no longer aware of his opponent's points, so involved is he in the course of his argument; and he is thinking about following himself, not you. One man, finding his back too weak, fears everything, denies everything, mixes up and confuses the point from the outset, [C]or, at the height of the debate, rebels and is flatly silent,[1] through spiteful ignorance affecting a haughty contempt or a stupidly modest avoidance of contention. [B]One man, provided he can strike, does not care how much he lays himself open. Another counts his words, and weighs them as reasons. This one uses only the advantage of his voice and lungs. Here is one who concludes against himself. And this one, who deafens you with useless preambles and digressions. [C]This other arms himself with sheer insults

1 Or, "flattens out." All the best editions give the reading "se mutine à se faire tout plat"; but on the Bordeaux Copy Montaigne's word looks to me more like "taire" than "faire."

and seeks a German quarrel[2] to get rid of the company and con-versation of a mind that presses his own hard. [B]This last fellow sees nothing in reason, but holds you besieged within the dialectical enclosure of his clauses and with the formulas of his art.

Now who will not begin to distrust learning and to doubt whether any solid fruit can be derived from it for the needs of life, considering the use we make of it: [C]*studies that cure nothing* [Seneca]? [B]Who has acquired understanding from logic? Where are her fine promises? [C]*Neither for living better nor for reasoning more fitly* [Cicero]. [B]Do we witness more of a jumble in the chatter of fishwives than in the public disputations of the professional logi-cians? I would rather have my son learn to speak in the taverns than in the schools of talk.

Take a Master of Arts, converse with him: Why does he not make us feel this artificial excellence and captivate the women and the ignoramuses like ourselves with admiration for the strength of his reasons and the beauty of his order? Why does he not dominate and persuade us at will? Why does a man with such advantages in matter and method mix insults, recklessness, and fury with his fencing? Let him strip off his hood, his gown, and his Latin; let him not beat our ears with pure and undigested Aristotle; and you will take him for one of us, or worse. It seems to me that with this complication and interlacing of language with which they beset us it turns out as with sleight-of-hand performers: their dexterity attacks and overpowers our senses, but it does not shake our belief at all. Aside from this legerdemain, they do nothing that is not common-place and mean. For being more learned they are none the less inept.

I love and honor learning as much as those who have it; and in its true use it is man's most noble and powerful acquisition. But in those (and their number is infinite) who base their fundamental capacity and worth on it, who appeal from their understanding to their memory, [C]*hiding under the shadow of others* [Seneca], [B]and can do nothing except by the book, I hate it, if I dare say so, a little more than stupidity. In my country and in my time learning often enough mends purses, rarely minds. If it encounters dull minds, it weighs them down and suffocates them, like a crude and undigested mass; if sharp ones, it is apt to purify, clarify, and subtilize them to the point of inanition. It is a thing of almost indifferent quality: a very useful accessory to a wellborn mind, pernicious and harmful to another. Or

2 A quarrel without any reason.

rather it is a thing of very precious use, which will not let itself be possessed at a low price: in one hand it is a scepter, in another a fool's bauble. But let us get on.

What greater victory do you expect than to teach your enemy that he is no match for you? When you win the advantage for your proposition, it is truth that wins; when you win the advantage for order and method, it is you who win. ᶜIt is my opinion that in Plato and Xenophon Socrates argues more for the sake of the arguers than for the sake of the argument, and to instruct Euthydemus and Protagoras rather in their own impertinence than in the impertinence of their art. He takes hold of the first subject that comes along like a man who has a more useful aim than to illuminate it: to wit, to illuminate the minds that he undertakes to manage and exercise.

ᴮAgitation and the chase are properly our quarry; we are not excusable if we conduct it badly and irrelevantly; to fail in the catch is another thing. For we are born to quest after truth; to possess it belongs to a greater power. It is not, as Democritus said, hidden in the bottom of abysses, but rather elevated to an infinite height in the divine knowledge. ᶜThe world is but a school of inquiry. ᴮThe question is not who will hit the ring, but who will make the best runs at it. He who speaks true can speak as foolishly as he who speaks false; for we are concerned with the manner, not the matter, of speaking. My humor is to consider the form as much as the substance, the advocate as much as the cause, as Alcibiades ordered we should do.

ᶜAnd every day I amuse myself reading authors without any care for their learning, looking for their style, not their subject. Just as I seek the company of some famous mind, not to have him teach me, but to come to know him.

ᴮAny man may speak truly; but to speak with order, wisely, and competently, of that few men are capable. Thus it is not the falsity that comes from ignorance that offends me, but the ineptitude. I have broken off many dealings that would have been useful to me because of the irrelevant bickering of those with whom I was dealing. I do not get excited once in a year over the mistakes of those over whom I have authority; but over the stupidity and obstinacy of their brutish and asinine assertions, excuses, and defenses, we are at each other's throats every day. They understand neither what is said nor why, and answer accordingly; it is enough to drive a man to despair. I never feel my head roughly jarred except by another head, and I put up with the vices of my servants sooner than with their

heedlessness, importunity, and stupidity. Let them do less, provided they are capable of doing something. You live in hope of kindling their will; but from a stump there is nothing worth while to be hoped for or enjoyed.

But supposing I take things otherwise than as they are? Perhaps I do; and this is why I blame my impatience, and hold, in the first place, that it is equally a fault in one who is right and in one who is wrong, for it is always a tyrannical ill humor to be unable to endure a way of thinking different from your own; and then in truth there is no greater, more constant, or more uncouth absurdity, than to become worked up and stung by the absurdities of the world. For it irritates us chiefly with ourselves; and that philosopher[3] of times past would never have lacked occasion for his tears as long as he considered himself. ᶜMyso, one of the Seven Sages, of a Timonian and Democritic humor, when he was asked what he was laughing at to himself, answered: "At the fact that I am laughing to myself."

ᴮHow many stupid things I say and reply every day, in my own judgment; and so assuredly how many more in the judgment of others! ᶜIf I bite my lips over them, what must the others do? In short, we must live among the living, and let the river flow under the bridge, without caring, or, at the very least, without being upset by it. ᴮAfter all, why can we encounter someone with a crooked and malformed body without being moved, when we cannot bear encountering an ill-ordered mind without getting angry? This vicious violence has more to do with the judge than with the fault. Let us always have this saying of Plato in our mouths: ᶜ"If I find a thing unsound, is it not because I myself am unsound? ᴮAm I not myself at fault? May not my admonition be turned around against me?" A wise and divine refrain, which scourges the most universal and common error of mankind. ᶜNot only the reproaches that we make to one another, but also our reasons and arguments in controversial matters can ordinarily be turned against ourselves; and we run ourselves through with our own weapons. Whereof antiquity has left me weighty examples enough. ᴮThis was ingeniously well said, and much to the point, by the man who thought it up:

Every man likes the smell of his own dung.
ADAPTED FROM ERASMUS

3 Heraclitus. Cf. *Essays* I: 50, "Of Democritus and Heraclitus."

^COur eyes see nothing behind us. A hundred times a day we make fun of ourselves in the person of our neighbor and detest in others the defects that are more clearly in ourselves, and wonder at them with prodigious impudence and heedlessness.

Only yesterday I had occasion to see a man of understanding and good birth making fun, as comically as justly, of the silly habit of another man who splits everybody's head with his genealogies and family connections, more than half of them false (those people are most prone to pounce on such silly subjects whose quality is most doubtful and least sure); and he himself, if he had turned back upon himself, would have found himself scarcely less intemperate and boring in spreading abroad and extolling the distinctions of his wife's family. Oh importunate presumption, whereby the wife sees herself armed by the hands of her very husband! If they understood Latin, we ought to say to them:

> Come now, if of herself she is not mad enough,
> Encourage her.
> TERENCE

I do not mean that no man should criticize another unless he is clean himself, for then no one would criticize; nor indeed that he must be clean of the same sort of fault. But I mean that our judgment, laying upon another the blame which is then in question, should not spare us from judging ourselves. It is a charitable service in one who cannot remove a vice from within himself to try to remove it nevertheless from within another, where it may have a less malignant and stubborn root.

Nor does it seem to me an appropriate reply to someone who warns me of my fault, to say that it is also in him. What of it? The warning is still true and useful. If we had a good nose, our excrement ought to stink worse to us inasmuch as it is our own. And Socrates is of the opinion that a man who found himself and his son and a stranger guilty of some violence and wrongdoing should begin by presenting himself to be sentenced according to the law and by imploring the help of the executioner's hand to purge himself; and do so second for his son and last for the stranger. If this precept takes a little too high a tone, at least he should present himself first for punishment by his own conscience.

^BThe senses act as the proper and primary judges for us, and they perceive things only by their external accidents; thus it is no wonder that in all the functions that serve the welfare of society there is

always such a universal admixture of ceremony and outward show that the best and most effective part of a government consists in these externals. It is still man we are dealing with, and it is a wonder how physical his nature is.

As for those[4] who, in recent years, tried to construct for us a system of religious practice that is all contemplative and spiritual, they should not be astounded if there are some who think that religion would have melted away and slipped through their fingers if it did not hold fast among us as a mark, title, and instrument of division and faction rather than by itself.

As in conversation: the gravity, the gown, and the fortune of the speaker often give authority to vain and inept remarks. No one would presume that a personage so redoubtable and with such a following does not have within him some more than vulgar capacity, and that a man to whom so many commissions and offices are given, a man so disdainful and so supercilious, is not abler than this other man who bows to him at such a distance and whom no one employs. Not only the words, but also the grimaces, of these people are considered and taken into account, everyone applying himself to put some fine and solid interpretation on them. If they stoop to common discussion and you offer them anything but approbation and reverence, they beat you down with the authority of their experience: they have heard, they have seen, they have done – you are overwhelmed with examples. I would fain tell them that the fruit of a surgeon's experience is not the history of his practice and his remembering that he has cured four people of the plague and three of the gout, unless he can derive from that experience the means of forming his judgment and can make us aware that he has become wiser in the practice of his art.

^CSo in a concert of instruments we do not hear a lute, a spinet, and the flute; we hear a rounded harmony, the effect of the various elements joined into a whole.

^BIf travels and offices have improved them, this ought to show in their increased understanding. It is not enough to count experiences, we must weigh and sort them; and we must have digested and distilled them, to extract from them the reasons and conclusions they contain.

There never were so many historians. It is always good and useful to listen to them, for they furnish us with an abundance of fair and

4 The Protestants.

laudable instructions from the storehouse of their memory, a great help, surely, in the service of our life. But we are not looking for that at the moment; we are looking to see whether these narrators and collectors are themselves laudable.

I hate every sort of tyranny, both in words and in acts. I am inclined to resist with all my mind these vain externals that delude our judgment through the senses; and keeping a close watch on men of extraordinary eminence, I have found that they are for the most part men like the rest:

> For solid common sense is rare in that estate.
>
> JUVENAL

Perhaps we esteem them and see them as less than they really are because they undertake more and show themselves more: they do not correspond to the burden they have taken on. There must be more vigor and power in the bearer than in the load. A man who has not exerted his full strength leaves you to guess whether he has any strength left over, whether he has been tested to the breaking point; a man who succumbs under his load reveals his measure and the weakness of his shoulders. That is why we see so many inept souls among the learned, and more than of the other kind. They would have made good husbandmen, good tradesmen, good artisans; their natural vigor was cut to that proportion. Learning is a thing of great weight; they collapse under it. Their mind has neither enough vigor nor enough skill to spread out and distribute that noble and powerful matter, to make use of it and derive help from it. It can do nothing except in a strong nature, and these are very rare. ᶜAnd the weak ones, says Socrates, corrupt the dignity of philosophy in handling it. It appears both useless and harmful when it is badly encased. ᴮThis is how they spoil themselves and make fools of themselves,

> Just like an ape, man's mimic, whom in jest
> A prankish boy in silken clothes has dressed,
> And left his buttocks and his backside bare,
> To give the guests a laugh.
>
> CLAUDIAN

Likewise for those who rule and command us, who hold the world in their hands, it is not enough to have an ordinary understanding, to be able to do what we are able to do; they are far below us if they are not far above us. As they promise more, so they owe

more; and therefore silence is for them a bearing not only decorous and grave, but often also profitable and economical. For Megabysus, having gone to see Apelles in his studio, remained a long time without saying a word, and then began to discuss the painter's works, for which he received this rough reprimand: "As long as you kept silence, you seemed to be quite something because of your chains and your pomp; but now that we have heard you speak, there is no one, even to the boys in my shop, who does not despise you." Those magnificent trappings, that grand state, did not permit him to be ignorant with a common ignorance and to speak without pertinence about painting. He should have maintained in silence that external and presumptive competence. To how many stupid souls in my time has a cold and taciturn mien served as a title to wisdom and capacity!

Dignities and offices are necessarily given more by fortune than by merit; and people are often wrong to blame kings for this. On the contrary, it is a marvel that they have such good luck, having so little information:

> ^CTo know his people is a prince's greatest virtue.
>
> MARTIAL

^BFor nature has not given them a vision that can scrutinize a whole populace in order to discern preeminence and to penetrate our bosoms, where dwells the knowledge of our wills and of our best worth. They must sift us by conjecture and gropingly, by family, wealth, learning, the voice of the people – very feeble evidence. If anyone could find a way in which men could be judged by justice and chosen by reason, with that single stroke he would establish a perfect form of government.

"Yes, but he successfully carried out that great affair." That is saying something, but it is not saying enough; for this maxim is justly accepted, that we must not judge plans by results. ^CThe Carthaginians punished the bad plans of their commanders even when they were corrected by a fortunate outcome. And the Roman people often refused a triumph for great and very profitable victories because the conduct of the leader did not correspond to his good luck. ^BWe commonly perceive in the actions of this world that Fortune, to teach us how much power she has in all things, and because she takes pleasure in beating down our presumption, having been unable to make the incompetent wise, makes them lucky, as if to vie with virtue. And she likes to take a hand in favoring those

operations in which the web is most purely her own. Whence it is observed every day that the simplest among us brings to a successful conclusion very big tasks, both public and private. And as Siramnes the Persian replied to those who were astounded how his affairs turned out so badly seeing that his plans were so wise, that he was sole master of his plans, but of the outcome of his affairs Fortune was mistress; so these people can answer in the same way, but with an opposite twist.

Most of the things of this world are done by themselves:

> The fates find out a way.
> VIRGIL

The outcome often justifies very inept management. Our intervention is little more than a routine, and more commonly a calculation of usage and example than of reason. Astonished at the greatness of an affair, I once learned, from those who had carried it through, their motives and their procedure; I found nothing but commonplace ideas; and the most commonplace and most used are also perhaps the surest and the most desirable for practice, if not for show.

What if the flattest reasons are the best founded, if the lowest, loosest, and most threadbare are the best adapted to affairs? To preserve the authority of the King's Council there is no need to have the profane take part in it or see into it from closer than the first barrier. It must be revered on trust and as a whole if we want to foster its reputation.

In my deliberations I outline the matter a little and consider it sketchily in its first aspects; the heart and core of the matter I am accustomed to entrust to heaven:

> The rest leave to the gods.
> HORACE

Good and bad luck are in my opinion two sovereign powers. It is unwise to think that human wisdom can fill the role of Fortune. And vain is the undertaking of him who presumes to embrace both causes and consequences and to lead by the hand the progress of his affair – vain especially in the deliberations of war. There was never more military circumspection and prudence than is sometimes seen among us. Could it be that they are afraid of losing themselves on the way, and are reserving themselves for the denouement of the drama?

I will say more, that even our wisdom and deliberation for the most part follow the lead of chance. My will and my reasoning are moved now in one way, now in another, and there are many of these movements that are directed without me. My reason has accidental impulsions that change from day to day:

> The phases of their minds are changed; their breasts conceive
> Other emotions than before, when a stormy wind
> Drove the clouds on.
> VIRGIL

Just observe who are the most powerful in the cities and who do their jobs best: you will ordinarily find that they are the least able. It has happened to women, children, and madmen to rule great states just as well as the ablest princes. ^cAnd the gross-witted, says Thucydides, succeed as rulers more commonly than the subtle. ^BWe attribute the effects of their good fortune to their wisdom.

> ^cAs each man his own fortune plies,
> So he excels, and we all call him wise.
> PLAUTUS

^BWherefore I do indeed say that in every way, events are meager evidence of our worth and capacity.

Now I was just on this point, that we need only see a man elevated in dignity: even if we had known him three days before as an insignificant person, there glides imperceptibly into our minds a picture of greatness and ability, and we persuade ourselves that, growing in status and authority, he has grown in merit. We judge him not by his worth, but, as we do with counters, by the rights conferred upon him by his rank. Let chance turn again, let him fall back and be mixed up in the crowd again, and everyone will inquire with wonder about the cause that had raised him so high. "Is this he?" they say. "Didn't he know anything more about it when he was there? Are princes content with so little? Truly, we were in good hands!" This is a thing that I have often seen in my time. Yes, even the mask of greatness put on in our plays affects and deludes us somewhat. What I myself adore in kings is the crowd of their adorers. All deference and submission is due to them, except that of our understanding. My reason is not trained to bend and bow, it is my knees.

Melanthius, being asked what he thought of Dionysius' tragedy, said: "I did not see it, it is so obfuscated by words." So most of those

who judge the speeches of the great ought to say: "I did not under-
stand his meaning, it was so obfuscated by gravity, greatness,
and majesty."

Antisthenes was trying to persuade the Athenians one day to
order their asses to be used in tilling the fields as well as the horses;
whereupon he was answered that that animal was not born for such
a service. "That is all one," he replied, "it just depends on your giving
the order; for the most ignorant and incapable men whom you
employ in command in your wars do not fail to become immediately
very worthy of their charge, because you employ them in it."

To this is related the custom of so many peoples who canonize
the king they have created from among themselves, and are not
content to honor him if they do not adore him. Those of Mexico,
after the ceremonies of his coronation are completed, no longer dare
look him in the face; but as if they had deified him by his royalty,
they have him swear not only to maintain their religion, their laws,
their liberties, and to be valiant, just, and kind, but also to make the
sun move with its customary light, the clouds shed rain in due
season, the rivers run their courses, and the earth bear all things
necessary for his people.

I differ from this common fashion and am more distrustful of
ability when I see it accompanied by greatness of fortune and public
esteem. We must take note how much of an advantage it is for a man
to speak at his own time, to choose his own point, to break off the
discussion or change it with magisterial authority, to defend himself
against the objections of others with a nod, a smile, or a silence, in
the presence of a company that trembles with reverence and respect.

A man of prodigious fortune, coming to add his opinion to some
light discussion that was going on casually at his table, began
precisely thus: "It can only be a liar or an ignoramus who will say
otherwise than," and so on. Pursue that philosophical point, dagger
in hand.

Here is another observation from which I derive much use: that
in arguments and discussions not all the remarks that seem good to
us should be accepted immediately. Most men are rich with bor-
rowed capacity. It may happen to a given man to make a fine point,
a good answer and maxim, and put it forward without recognizing
its force. ^CThat we do not possess all we borrow may perhaps be
verified in myself. ^BWe must not always yield to it, whatever truth or
beauty it may have. We must either deliberately oppose it, or draw
back under color of not understanding it, in order to feel out on all

sides how it is lodged in its author. It may happen that we run on the point of his sword and help his blow to carry beyond its reach.

I have sometimes employed, in the necessity and pressure of combat, ripostes that penetrated beyond my intent and my hope. I gave them only for their number; they were received for their weight. Just as when I debate with a vigorous man I take pleasure in anticipating his conclusions, I save him the trouble of explaining himself, I try to foretell his idea while it is still nascent and imperfect (the order and pertinence of his understanding warn and threaten me from afar), so with these others I do just the opposite: we must understand nothing except what they express, and presuppose nothing. If they judge in general terms, "This is good, that is not," and hit it right, see whether it is fortune that hits it for them. ^CLet them circumscribe and limit their statement a little: why it is so, how it is so.

These universal judgments that I find so common signify nothing. They are like men who salute a whole people in a crowd and in a body. Those who have a real acquaintance with them salute them and notice them by name and individually. But that is a hazardous undertaking. Hence I have seen it happen more than once a day that minds with a weak foundation, trying to play clever by pointing out the beauties of some book they are reading, fix their admiration with so bad a choice that instead of teaching us the excellence of the author they teach us their own ignorance.

It is safe to exclaim "That is beautiful!" after hearing an entire page of Virgil. In that way the shrewd ones save themselves. But to undertake to follow him step by step and to try to note with a specific and selective judgment where a good author surpasses himself, where he rises high, weighing the words, the phrases, the ideas, one after the other – get away from there. *We must see not only what each one says, but also what he thinks, and also why he thinks it* [Cicero].

Every day I hear stupid people say things that are not stupid. ^BThey say something good; let us find out how far they understand it, let us see where they got it. We help them to use that fine remark or that fine reason, which they do not possess; they only have it in keeping. They have probably brought it forth by accident and gropingly; we give it authority and value for them. You lend them a hand. What for? They are not grateful to you for it and become all the more inept for it. Do not second them, let them go; they will handle the matter like men who are afraid of getting scalded; they

do not dare change its setting or its lighting, or go into it deeply. Shake it ever so little and it escapes them; they abandon it to you, strong and fine as it may be. They are fine weapons, but they are badly shafted. How many times I have seen this by experience!

Now if you happen to enlighten and confirm them, they promptly seize and steal from you the advantage of your interpretation. "That is what I meant to say; that is just my idea; if I did not express it so, it was only for lack of words." Empty wind! We must use even malice to correct this arrogant stupidity. ᶜThe doctrine of Hegesias that we must neither hate nor blame but instruct is right elsewhere; but here ᴮit is injustice and inhumanity to aid and set right a man who has no use for your help and is the worse for it. I like to let them get mired and stuck even more than they are, and so deep that, if it is possible, they may recognize themselves at last.

Stupidity and senselessness are not curable by a bit of admonition. ᶜAnd we may properly say of this sort of repair work what Cyrus replied to the man who urged him to harangue his army on the point of a battle: that men do not become courageous and warlike on the spot by a good harangue any more than someone suddenly becomes a good musician by listening to a good song. These are apprenticeships that have to be served beforehand by long and constant education.

ᴮWe owe this care to our families, this assiduity in correction and instruction; but to go and preach at the first passer-by and play schoolmasters to the ignorance or ineptitude of the first man we meet is a practice I greatly dislike. I rarely do so, even in discussions that I am in on, and rather give up the whole thing than come down to these misplaced and pedantic lessons. ᶜMy nature is unsuited, either in speaking or in writing, for beginners. ᴮBut as for things that are said in company or among others, however false or absurd I may judge them to be, I never cut across by either word or sign.

Moreover, nothing vexes me so much in stupidity as the fact that it is better pleased with itself than any reason can reasonably be. It is unfortunate that wisdom forbids you to be satisfied with yourself and trust yourself, and always sends you away discontented and diffident, whereas opinionativeness and heedlessness fill their hosts with rejoicing and assurance. It is for the most incompetent to look at other men over their shoulders, always returning from the combat full of glory and cheer. And besides, this arrogance of language and gaiety of countenance usually give them the victory in the eyes of the audience, which is generally weak and incapable of

judging and discerning clearly where the real advantages lie. ᶜObstinacy and heat of opinion is the surest proof of stupidity. Is there anything so certain, resolute, disdainful, contemplative, grave, and serious as an ass?

ᴮMay we not include under the title of discussion and communication the sharp, abrupt repartee which good spirits and familiarity introduce among friends, bantering and joking wittily and keenly with one another? An exercise for which my natural gaiety makes me rather fit; and if it is not so high-pitched and serious as that other exercise I have just been speaking of, it is no less keen and ingenious, ᶜand no less profitable, as Lycurgus thought. ᴮFor my part, I bring to it more freedom than wit, and have more luck at it than inventiveness. But I am perfect in forbearance, for I endure retaliation, not only sharp but even indiscreet, without being disturbed. And when a sally is made against me, if I have no brisk retort to make on the spot, I do not go wasting my time pursuing the point with a boring and lax argumentativeness bordering on obstinacy; I let it pass, and, cheerfully lowering my ears, put off getting my revenge until a better time. There is no merchant who always gains.

Most men change their countenance and their voice when strength fails them and, by an ill-timed anger, instead of getting revenge, reveal their weakness and their impatience at the same time. In this gay mood we sometimes pluck the secret strings of each other's imperfections, which, when we are calm, we cannot touch without offense, and we profitably give one another a hint of each other's defects.

There are other games, played by hand, thoughtless and violent, French style, which I mortally hate: I have a tender and sensitive skin. As a result of them I have in my lifetime seen two princes of our royal blood brought to their graves.[5] ᶜIt is ugly to fight in play.

ᴮFor the rest, when I want to judge someone, I ask him how satisfied he is with himself, to what extent he is pleased with his words or his work. I want to get away from those fine excuses: "I did it in play:

5 Presumably King Henry II, killed in a jousting accident in 1559, and Henri, marquis de Beaupréau, of the Bourbon-Montpensier family, who died in 1560 of wounds received in a tournament. Since Montaigne frequently uses "seen" for "known," he may have known of these deaths without having witnessed them, and may be referring to the count d'Enghien, killed in a game in 1546, rather than to Beaupréau.

This work unfinished from the anvil came;

OVID

I was not an hour at it; I have not looked at it since." Well, then, I say, let us put these pieces aside, give me something that represents you fully, by which you would like to be measured. And then, what do you think is finest in your work? Is it this part or that? Is it the charm, or the matter, or the originality, or the judgment, or the knowledge? For I notice generally that people are as mistaken in judging their own work as that of others, not only because of the affection that is involved, but also because they have not the capacity to know and distinguish it for what it is. The work, by its own power and fortune, may second the workman beyond his inventiveness and knowledge and outstrip him. For my part, I do not judge the value of any other work less clearly than my own; and I place the *Essays* now low, now high, very inconsistently and uncertainly.

There are many books that are useful by reason of their subjects, from which the author derives no commendation; and there are good books, like good works, which shame the workman. I may write of the fashion of our banquets and our clothes, and write with bad grace; I may publish the edicts of my time and the letters of princes that pass into the hands of the public; I may make an abridgment of a good book (and every abridgment of a good book is a stupid abridgment), and that book may come to be lost, and things like that. Posterity will derive singular utility from such compositions; but what honor shall I get, unless for my good fortune? A good part of the famous books are of this sort.

When some years ago I read Philippe de Commines, certainly a very good author, I noted this remark as uncommon: That we must be very careful not to serve our master so well that we keep him from finding a fair reward for our service. I should have praised the idea, not him; I came across it in Tacitus not long ago: *Benefits are agreeable as long as they seem returnable; but if they go much beyond that, they are repaid with hatred instead of gratitude.* ^cAnd Seneca says vigorously: *For he who thinks it is shameful not to repay does not want the man to live whom he ought to repay.* Q. Cicero, in a weaker vein: *He who thinks he cannot repay you can by no means be your friend.*

^BThe subject, according to what it is, may give a man a reputation for learning and a good memory; but in order to judge the qualities that are most his own and most worthy, the strength and beauty of his mind, we must know what is his and what is not; and in what is

not his, how much is due him in consideration of the choice, arrangement, embellishment, and style that he has supplied. What if he has borrowed the matter and made the form worse, as often happens? We who have little contact with books are in this strait, that when we see some fine piece of inventiveness in a new poet, some strong argument in a preacher, we dare not praise them for it until we have found out from some learned man whether this element is their own or someone else's. Until then I always stand on my guard.

I have just run through Tacitus' *History* at one reading (which rarely happens to me; it has been twenty years since I put one whole hour at a time on a book), and I did it at the persuasion of a gentleman[6] whom France esteems highly, both for his own worth and for a constant pattern of capacity and goodness that is seen in him and his several brothers. I know of no author who introduces into a register of public events so much consideration of private behavior and inclinations. ^CAnd it seems to me, in contrast to how it seems to him, that having especially to trace the lives of the emperors of his time, so strange and extreme in every way, and the many notable actions that their cruelty in particular produced in their subjects, he had a stronger and more attractive matter to treat and narrate than if he had had to tell of battles and universal commotions. So that I often find him sterile, skimming over these noble deaths as if he were afraid to bore us with their number and length.

^BThis form of history is by far the most useful. Public movements depend more upon the guidance of fortune, private ones on our own. This is rather a judgment of history than a recital of it; there are more precepts than stories. It is not a book to read, it is a book to study and learn; it is so full of maxims that you find every sort, both right and wrong; it is a nursery of ethical and political reflections for the provision and adornment of those who hold a place in the management of the world. He always pleads with solid and vigorous arguments, in a pointed and subtle fashion, following the affected style of his time. They were so fond of an inflated manner that when they did not find any point and subtlety in the things, they borrowed it from the words. He rather takes after Seneca's writing; he seems to

6 Villey believes that this is probably Louis de Foix, comte de Gurson, an old friend to whose wife Montaigne had dedicated his chapter "Of the Education of Children" (I: 26).

me more meaty, Seneca more pointed. His service is more suited to
a disturbed and sick state, as ours is at present; you would often say
that it is us he is describing and decrying.

Those who doubt his good faith clearly accuse themselves of
wishing him ill for some other reason. He has sound opinions and
leans to the good side in Roman affairs. I have a small complaint,
however, in that he judged Pompey more harshly than is consistent
with the opinion of the good men who lived and dealt with him, and
considered him quite on a par with Marius and Sulla, except in so far
as he was more covert. Pompey's intent in the government of affairs
has not been acquitted of ambition or vengefulness, and even his
friends feared that victory might have carried him away beyond the
bounds of reason; but not to such an unbridled measure as it did
those two. There is nothing in his life that threatened such delib-
erate cruelty and tyranny. Besides, we ought not to balance suspicion
against evidence; so I do not believe Tacitus on this point.

That his narratives are sincere and straightforward might per-
haps be argued from the very fact that they do not always exactly
warrant the conclusions of his judgment, which he follows accord-
ing to the bias he has taken, often going beyond the matter he is
presenting to us, which he has not deigned to slant one little bit. He
needs no excuse for having approved of the religion of his time, in
accordance with the laws that ordered him to, and for not having
known the true religion. That was his misfortune, not his fault.

I have chiefly considered his judgment, and I am not very clear
about it in every instance. For example, these words in the letter
which Tiberius, when old and sick, sent to the Senate: "What
shall I write to you, gentlemen, or how shall I write to you, or
what shall I not write to you at this time? May the gods and god-
desses destroy me in worse manner than I feel myself perish every
day, if I know." I do not perceive why he ascribes them so surely to
a poignant remorse tormenting the conscience of Tiberius; at least
when I was reading that passage, I did not see it.

This also seemed to me a little mean-spirited, that when he had
to say that he had held a certain honorable office at Rome, he should
apologize by adding that he did not say so out of ostentation. This
touch seems shabby to me for a soul of his kind. For not to dare to
speak roundly of oneself shows some lack of heart. A stout and lofty
judgment which judges sanely and surely uses its own examples on
all occasions as well as those of others, and testifies frankly about

itself as about a third party. We must pass over these common rules of civility in favor of truth and liberty.

^CI dare not only to speak of myself, but to speak only of myself; I go astray when I write of anything else, and get away from my subject. I do not love myself so indiscriminately, nor am I so attached and wedded to myself, that I cannot distinguish and consider myself apart, as I do a neighbor or a tree. It is as great a fault not to see how far our worth extends, as to say more about it than we see. We owe more love to God than to ourselves and we know him less, and yet we speak our fill of him.

^BIf his writings tell us anything about his qualities, Tacitus was a great man, upright and courageous, not of a superstitious but of a philosophical and high-minded virtue. We may find him bold in his testimony, as when he maintains of a soldier who was carrying a load of wood that his hands became stiff with cold and stuck to his burden, so that they remained there attached and dead, having separated from his arms.

When he says that Vespasian, by the favor of the god Serapis, cured a blind woman in Alexandria by anointing her eyes with his saliva, and I know not what other miracle, he conforms to the example and duty of all good historians. They keep a record of important events; among public incidents are also popular rumors and opinions. It is their part to relate common beliefs, not to regulate them. That part concerns the theologians and philosophers, directors of consciences. Therefore his fellow historian, a great man like himself, said very wisely: *Indeed, I set down more things than I believe; for I can neither affirm things that I doubt, nor suppress what I have heard* [Quintus Curtius]. ^CAnd this other: *These are things that it is not worth while either to affirm or to refute; we must abide by report* [Livy]. And, writing in an age in which belief in prodigies was beginning to diminish, he says he does not want for all that to fail to insert in his *Annals*, and give a footing to, things accepted by so many good people with such reverence for antiquity. ^BThat is very well said. Let them deliver history to us more as they receive it than as they see fit.

I who am king of the matter I treat, and who owe an accounting for it to no one, do not for all that believe myself in all I write. I often hazard sallies of my mind which I mistrust, ^Cand certain verbal subtleties at which I shake my ears; ^Bbut I let them run at a venture. ^CI see that some gain honor by such things. It is not for

me alone to judge them. I present myself standing and lying down, front and rear, on the right and the left, and in all my natural postures. ᴮMinds, even those alike in strength, are not always alike in application and taste.

That is what my memory of Tacitus offers me in gross, and rather uncertainly. All judgments in gross are loose and imperfect.

9
Of vanity

ᴮThere is perhaps no more obvious vanity than to write of it so vainly. What the Divinity has so divinely told us about it[1] ought to be carefully and continually meditated by people of understanding.

Who does not see that I have taken a road along which I shall go, without stopping and without effort, as long as there is ink and paper in the world? I cannot keep a record of my life by my actions; fortune places them too low. I keep it by my thoughts. Thus I knew a gentleman who gave knowledge of his life only by the workings of his belly; you would see on display at his home a row of chamber pots, seven or eight days' worth. That was his study, his conversation; all other talk stank in his nostrils.

Here you have, a little more decently, some excrements of an aged mind, now hard, now loose, and always undigested. And when shall I make an end of describing the continual agitation and changes of my thoughts, whatever subject they light on, since Diomedes filled six thousand books with the sole subject of grammar? What must prattle produce, when the stammering and loosening of the tongue smothered the world with such a horrible load of volumes? So many words for the sake of words alone! O Pythagoras, why did you not conjure away this tempest?[2]

One Galba was blamed in the past for living idly. He replied that each man should give account of his actions, not of his leisure. He was wrong; for justice has cognizance and corrective power also over those who are on a holiday.

1 "Vanity of vanities, saith the Preacher, vanity of vanities; all is vanity." Ecclesiastes 1:2.
2 Pythagoras is said to have imposed on his disciples a silence of two to five years.

But there should be some legal restraint aimed against inept and useless writers, as there is against vagabonds and idlers. Both I and a hundred others would be banished from the hands of our people. This is no jest. Scribbling seems to be a sort of symptom of an unruly age. When did we write so much as since our dissensions began? When did the Romans write so much as in the time of their downfall? Besides the fact that mental refinement does not mean wiser conduct in a society, this idle occupation arises from the fact that everyone goes about the duties of his office laxly, and takes time off.

The corruption of the age is produced by the individual contribution of each one of us; some contribute treachery, others injustice, irreligion, tyranny, avarice, cruelty, in accordance with their greater power; the weaker ones bring stupidity, vanity, idleness, and I am one of them. It seems to be the season for empty things, when harmful ones weigh upon us. In a time when it is so common to do evil, it is practically praiseworthy to do what is merely useless. I console myself by thinking that I shall be one of the last on whom they will have to lay hands. While they are attending to the more urgent cases, I shall have leisure to reform. For it seems to me that it would be contrary to reason to prosecute petty offenses when we are infested with great ones. And the physician Philotimus said to a man who gave him his finger to dress, and from whose complexion and breath he recognized an ulcer of the lungs: "My friend, this is not the moment to waste time on your fingernails."

However, in this connection, I saw some years ago that an important person whose memory I hold in unusual esteem, in the midst of our great disorders when there was neither law, nor justice, nor any magistrate doing his duty, any more than now, publicly suggested some puny reforms or other in dress, cookery, and legal procedure. These are amusements with which they feed a maltreated people, to tell them that they have not been completely forgotten. Those others do likewise, who confine themselves to insistently prohibiting certain ways of speaking, and dancing, and games, to a people ruined by all sorts of execrable vices. It is no time to wash and clean up when we are seized with a violent fever. ᶜIt is for the Spartans alone to start combing and arranging their hair when they are on the point of flinging themselves into some extreme danger to their lives.

ᴮAs for me, I have this other worse habit, that if I have one shoe on wrong, I also leave my shirt and my cloak on wrong; I scorn to reform halfway. When I am in a bad way, I grow bent on misfortune;

I abandon myself in despair, and let myself slip toward the precipice, ^cand, as they say, throw the handle after the ax. ^BI persist in growing worse, and think myself no longer worth my care: either entirely well or entirely ill.

It is a favor for me that the desolation of this state coincides with the desolation of my age; I suffer the times to increase my ills more willingly than I would have suffered them to disturb my well-being. The words I utter in misfortune are words of anger; my courage bristles up instead of lying down. And, in contrast to others, I find myself more devout in good fortune than in bad, following the precept of Xenophon, if not his reason for it; and I am more apt to turn loving eyes to Heaven in thanks than in request. I take more pains to improve my health when it smiles on me than I do to get it back when I have parted from it. Prosperity is discipline and education to me, as are adversities and rods to others. ^cAs if good fortune were incompatible with a good conscience, men never become good except in bad fortune. ^BGood fortune to me is a singular spur to moderation and modesty. Prayer wins me, threats repel me; ^cfavor makes me bend, fear makes me stiffen.

^BAmong human characteristics, this one is rather common: to be better pleased with other people's things than with our own, and to love movement and change.

> We only heed the daylight's pleasant course
> Because each hour proceeds on a fresh horse.
> PETRONIUS

I have my share of that. Those who go to the other extreme, of taking delight in themselves, of valuing what they have above other things and recognizing nothing as more beautiful than what they see, if they are not wiser than we, are in truth happier. I do not envy their wisdom, but I do their good fortune.

This greedy appetite for new and unknown things indeed helps to foster in me the desire to travel, but enough other circumstances contribute to it. I gladly turn aside from governing my house. There is a certain satisfaction in being in command, were it only of a barn, and in being obeyed by one's people; but it is too monotonous and languid a pleasure. And then it is necessarily mingled with many bothersome thoughts. Now the poverty and oppression of your tenants afflicts you, now a quarrel between your neighbors, now their encroachments upon you:

It may be vineyards beaten down with hail,
Deceitful soil that makes the harvest fail,
Or trees that blame the rains, the skies that grill
The fields, or winter's devastating chill;

<div align="right">HORACE</div>

and the fact that hardly once in six months will God send a spell of
weather with which your steward is fully satisfied, and which, if it is
good for the vines, does not harm the meadows:

The sun burns down with too extreme a heat,
Or sudden rains and icy frosts lay low,
And windstorms harass as they whirl and blow.

<div align="right">LUCRETIUS</div>

Add to that the new and well-shaped shoe of the man of days gone
by, which hurts your foot;[3] and the fact that a stranger does not
understand how much it costs you and how much you sacrifice to
keep up that appearance of order which people see in your family,
and that perhaps you buy it too dear.

I was late in taking up the management of a household. Those
whom nature had sent into the world before me relieved me of
that burden for a long time. I had already contracted a different
bent, more suitable to my disposition. At all events, from what I have
seen of it, it is an occupation more bothersome than difficult;
whoever is capable of anything else will very easily be capable
of this. If I sought to get rich, this way would seem too long to
me; I would have served kings, a more productive traffic than any
other. Since ^cthe only thing I aspire to acquire is the reputation of
having acquired nothing, just as I have squandered nothing, in
conformity with the rest of my life, unsuited for doing good or
doing evil, and since ^BI seek only to pass by, I can do that, thank
God, without much attention.

3 Plutarch, in his "Life of Aemilius Paulus," tells this story of a Roman who had
divorced his wife. "This person being highly blamed by his friends, who
demanded, Was she not chaste? was she not fair? was she not fruitful? holding
out his shoe, asked them, Whether it was not new? and well made? Yet, added
he, none of you can tell where it pinches me. Certain it is, that great and open
faults have often led to no separation; while mere petty repeated annoyances,
arising from unpleasantness or incongruity of character, have been the occasion
of such estrangement as to make it impossible for man and wife to live together
with any content."

If worst comes to worst, meet poverty halfway by retrenching expenses. That is what I am striving to do, that and to reform before poverty forces me to. Furthermore, I have established enough levels in my soul where I can get along with less than I have; get along contentedly, I mean. ^C*Not by the calculation of your income, but by your manner of living and your culture, is your wealth really to be reckoned* [Cicero]. ^BMy real need does not so wholly take up all I have that Fortune does not have something of mine to bite on without biting into the flesh.

My presence, ignorant and uninterested as I am, is very helpful in my domestic affairs. I take part in them, but grudgingly. Besides, there is this about my household, that while I burn the candle privately at my end, the other end is not spared in the least.

^CTraveling hurts me only by its expense, which is great and beyond my means. Being accustomed to travel not only with the necessary retinue, but with a decent one, I have to make my trips that much shorter and less frequent; and I use on them only skimmings and reserves, temporizing and postponing until these come to hand. I will not have the pleasure of wandering spoil the pleasure of my repose; on the contrary, I intend that they shall feed and favor each other.

Fortune has helped me in this, that since my principal profession in this life was to live it comfortably, and rather relaxedly than busily, it rid me of the need to multiply my riches to provide for a multitude of heirs. As for the one I have, if she does not have enough with what has been so plentifully enough for me, too bad for her; if she is improvident, she will not deserve that I should wish her any more. And each man, according to the example of Phocion, provides adequately for his children who provides for them in so far as they are not unlike himself. I certainly should not concur with the action of Crates. He left his money with a banker, with this condition: that if his children were fools, he should give it to them; if they were clever, he should distribute it to the most simple-minded of the people. As if fools, for being less capable of doing without riches, were more capable of using them.

^BAt all events, the damage resulting from my absence does not seem to warrant, as long as I can afford it, my refusing to accept the chances that come up to gain diversion from the vexation of being present. There is always something that goes wrong. The affairs, now of one house, now of another, pester you. You pry into everything too closely; your perspicacity hurts you here, as indeed it does

often enough elsewhere. I avoid occasions for vexation, and turn away from the knowledge of things that are going badly; and yet I cannot contrive well enough not to be constantly bumping into something at home that I do not like. ^CAnd the knaveries that they most hide from me are the ones I know best. There are some that we must ourselves help to conceal, so that they will hurt less. ^BTrivial pinpricks: ^Csometimes trivial, ^Bbut always pinpricks. The pettiest and slightest nuisances are the most acute; and as small letters hurt and tire the eyes most, so do small matters sting us most. ^CThe throng of petty troubles pains us more than the violence of a single one, however great it may be. ^BThe more crowded and sharp these domestic thorns are, the more sharply and without warning they prick us, easily catching us unawares.

^CI am no philosopher. Evils crush me according to their weight; and their weight depends on their form as much as on their matter, and often more. I have more experience of them than the common people; so I have more patience. In short, if they do not wound me, they hurt me.

^BLife is a tender thing and easy to disturb. From the moment I am inclined to bad humor – ^C*for no one resists after yielding to the first impulse* [Seneca] – ^Bhowever stupid the cause that so impelled me, I irritate my humor in that direction, and it then feeds and exasperates itself by its own movement, attracting and accumulating matter upon matter to feed on.

> Small drops of water hollow out a stone.
>
> LUCRETIUS

These regular drippings wear me down. ^CRegular annoyances are never slight. They are continual and irreparable, especially when they arise from details of household management, which are continual and unavoidable.

^BWhen I consider my affairs from a distance and as a whole, I find, possibly because my memory of them is scarcely exact, that they have gotten along until now, and prospered beyond my expectations and calculations. It seems to me that I get more out of them than is in them; their success fools me. But when I am in the midst of the job, and see all these parts in operation,

> Then is our soul distraught with countless cares,
>
> VIRGIL

a thousand things give me reason to desire and fear. To give them up

completely is very easy for me; to become involved in them without worrying, very difficult. It is pitiful to be in a place where everything you see involves and concerns you. And I seem to enjoy more gaily the pleasures of someone else's house, and to approach them with a purer relish. ^CDiogenes answered in my vein the man who asked him what sort of wine he liked best. "Other people's," he said.

BMy father loved to build up Montaigne, where he was born; and in all this administration of domestic affairs, I love to follow his example and his rules, and shall bind my successors to them as much as I can. If I could do better for him, I would. I glory in the fact that his will still operates and acts through me. God forbid that I should allow to fail in my hands any semblance of life that I could restore to so good a father. Whenever I have taken a hand in completing some old bit of wall and repairing some badly constructed building, it has certainly been out of regard more to his intentions than to my own satisfaction. CAnd I blame my indolence that I have not gone further toward completing the things he began so handsomely in his house; all the more because I have a good chance of being the last of my race to possess it, and the last to put a hand to it. BFor as regards my own personal inclination, neither the pleasure of building, which is said to be so alluring, nor hunting, nor gardens, nor the other pleasures of a retired life, can amuse me very much. That is a thing for which I am annoyed with myself, as I am for all other notions that are a nuisance to me. I do not care so much that ideas be vigorous and learned, as I care that they be easy and suitable for life; Cthey are true and sound enough if they are useful and pleasing.

BThose people are the death of me who, hearing me declare my incompetence in household occupations, go and whisper in my ears that it is disdain, and that I neglect to learn the implements of farming, its seasons, its order, how my wines are made, how grafting is done, the names and shapes of herbs and fruits, the way to prepare the food I live on, Cand the names and prices of the materials I wear, Bbecause my heart is set on some higher knowledge. That kind of thing is foolishness, and rather stupidity than vanity. I would rather be a good horseman than a good logician:

> Why not make something that will meet a need,
> By plaiting wicker and the pliant reed? VIRGIL

CWe entangle our thoughts in generalities, and the causes and conduct of the universe, which conduct themselves very well

without us, and we leave behind our own affairs and Michel, who concerns us even more closely than man in general.

^BNow I do indeed stay at home most of the time, but I should like to enjoy myself there more than elsewhere:

> For my old age a haven may it be,
> An end of weary trips by land and sea,
> And soldiery.
>
> HORACE

I don't know whether I shall accomplish this. I wish that instead of some other part of his estate, my father had handed down to me that passionate love that he had in his old age for his household. He was very happy in being able to keep his desires down to his means, and to be pleased with what he had. Political philosophy may condemn, for all I care, the meanness and sterility of my occupation, if I can once acquire a taste for it, as he did. I am of the opinion that the most honorable occupation is to serve the public and to be useful to many. ^C*The fruits of genius, virtue, and all excellence are most reward-ing when they benefit some neighbor* [Cicero]. ^BFor my part, I stay out of it; partly out of conscience (for in the same way that I see the weight attached to such employments, I see also what little qualifi-cation I have for them; ^Cand Plato, a master workman in all political government, nevertheless abstained from it); ^Bpartly out of laziness. I am content to enjoy the world without being all wrapped up in it, to live a merely excusable life, which will merely be no burden to myself or others.

Never did a man abandon himself more fully and relaxedly to the care and rule of a stranger than I would, if I had someone. One of my wishes at this moment would be to find a son-in-law who could spoonfeed my old age comfortably and put it to sleep, in whose hands I could deposit full sovereignty over the management and use of my possessions, that he might do with them as I do, and enjoy my present profits in my place, provided he brought to it a truly grateful and friendly heart. But then, we live in a world where loyalty in our own children is unknown.

Whoever has charge of my purse in my travels, has it absolutely and without having to render an account. He could cheat me just as well if I kept accounts; and, unless he is a devil, I oblige him to be honest by such abandoned trust. ^C*Many, by their fear of being cheated, have taught how to cheat, and by their suspicions have justified other men in doing wrong* [Seneca]. ^BThe commonest security I take from

my people is ignorance. I assume the existence of vices only after having seen them, and I trust the younger ones farther, whom I regard as less corrupted by bad examples. I would rather be told at the end of two months that I have spent four hundred crowns than have my ears drummed every evening with three, five, seven. Yet I have been robbed as little as the next man by this sort of larceny. It is true that I lend a hand to my ignorance; I purposely keep my knowledge of my money somewhat hazy and uncertain; up to a certain point I am glad to be able to be in doubt about it. You have to leave a little room for the dishonesty or improvidence of your servant. If we have enough left altogether to play our part, let that surplus of fortune's liberality run a little more at her mercy: ^Cthe gleaner's share. After all, I do not prize the fidelity of my people as much as I despise the damage they do me. ^BOh, what a vile and stupid study it is to study one's money, to take pleasure in handling it, weighing it, and counting it over and over! That is the way avarice makes its approach.

In the eighteen years that I have been managing an estate, I have not succeeded in prevailing upon myself really to study a title deed or my principal affairs, which necessarily have to pass within my knowledge and attention. This is not a philosophical scorn for transitory and mundane things; my taste is not so refined, and I value them at least at their worth; but it certainly is inexcusable and childish laziness and negligence. ^CWhat would I not do rather than read a contract, rather than go and disturb those dusty masses of papers, a slave to my affairs, or still worse, to those of others, as so many people are for the sake of money? Nothing costs me dear except care and trouble, and I seek only to grow indifferent and relaxed.

^BI was, I think, better fitted to live on another man's fortune, if that could be done without obligation and servitude. And at that I do not know, when I look at it closely, whether, given my disposition and my lot, there is not more abjection, trouble, and bitterness in what I have to endure from business and servants and household, than there would be in serving a man born greater than myself, who would lead me in some sort of comfort. ^C*Servitude is the obedience of a broken and abject mind, lacking free will* [Cicero]. ^BCrates did worse, when he cast himself into the freedom of poverty to get rid of the indignities and cares of a household. That I would not do – I hate poverty as much as pain – but I certainly would change this sort of life for another less brilliant and less busy.

Absent from home, I strip off all such thoughts; and I should then feel less the ruin of a tower than I feel, when present, the fall of a tile. My soul easily achieves detachment from a distance, but on the spot it suffers like a winegrower's. ^CA rein fixed badly on my horse, a stirrup leather slapping against my leg, will keep me in a bad humor a whole day. ^BI raise my courage enough to meet annoyances, my eyes I cannot.

The senses, ye gods, the senses!
AUTHOR UNKNOWN

At home I am responsible for all that goes wrong. Few masters – I am speaking of those of medium condition like me, and if there are any, they are more fortunate – can rely so much on another that a good part of the load does not remain on their shoulders. That ^Ctends to make me less gracious in entertaining visitors – and I may perhaps have kept one or another of them here more by my kitchen than by my graciousness, as bores do – and ^Btakes away much of the pleasure I should derive at home from the visits and gatherings of my friends. A gentleman never looks so stupid in his own house as when we see him caught up in the business of housekeeping, whispering in the ear of one servant, threatening another with his eyes; it should flow imperceptibly and seem like a normal process. And I think it ugly to talk to your guests about the way you are treating them, whether to excuse it or boast of it.

I love order and cleanliness –

The plates and glasses
Reflect my face
HORACE

– as much as abundance; and in my house I give careful attention to what is needful, little to ostentation.

If a footman starts fighting at another man's house, if a dish is tipped over, you only laugh at it; you sleep, while the master arranges with his butler for your next day's entertainment.

^CI speak of these things as I see them, generally not failing to appreciate what a pleasant occupation for certain natures is a peaceful, prosperous household, conducted in a determined order; and not wishing to fasten my own errors and shortcomings to the matter, or to give the lie to Plato, who thinks the happiest occupation for each man is to carry on his own affairs without injustice.

^BWhen I travel, I have only myself and the use of my money to think about; that is disposed of with a single precept. For amassing it too many qualities are required; about that I know nothing. About spending, I know something, and making a show of what I spend, which is really its principal use. But I apply myself to it too ambitiously, which makes it uneven and shapeless, and immoderate besides, in both directions. If it makes a show and is useful, I let myself go injudiciously; and I tighten up just as injudiciously if it does not shine and does not please me.

Whatever it is, whether art or nature, that imprints in us this disposition to live with reference to others, it does us much more harm than good. We defraud ourselves of our own advantages to make appearances conform with public opinion. We do not care so much what we are in ourselves and in reality as what we are in the public mind. Even the joys of the mind, and wisdom, appear fruitless to us, if they are enjoyed by ourselves alone, if they do not shine forth to the sight and approbation of others.

There are men whose gold flows in great streams through underground places, imperceptibly; others beat it all out into sheets and leaf; so that for some, farthings are worth crowns, for the others the reverse, since the world judges expense and means according to the show. All anxious care about riches smells of avarice, as does even spending and liberality, when it is too systematic and artificial. They are not worth painful watchfulness and care. He who tries to make his spending exact makes it pinched and constrained. Saving and spending are in themselves indifferent things, and take on the color of good or bad only according to the intention we apply to them.

The other thing that invites me to these excursions is that the present moral state of our country does not suit me. I could easily console myself for this corruption as regards the public interest –

> Worse than the Iron Age, times for whose shame
> Nature herself in vain would find a name,
> Or metal symbolizing their ill fame
>
> JUVENAL

– but with regard to my own, no. I in particular suffer from it too much. For in my neighborhood we have now grown old, through the long license of these civil wars, in so riotous a form of government,

> Where right and wrong are interchanged,
>
> VIRGIL

that in truth it is a marvel that it can subsist.

> In arms they till the soil, and ever their delight
> Is to amass new loot, and live by lawless might.
>
> VIRGIL

In fine, I see from our example that human society holds and is knit together at any cost whatever. Whatever position you set men in, they pile up and arrange themselves by moving and crowding together, just as ill-matched objects, put in a bag without order, find of themselves a way to unite and fall into place together, often better than they could have been arranged by art. King Philip collected the most wicked and incorrigible men he could find, and settled them all in a city he had built for them, which bore their name.[4] I judge that from their very vices they set up a political system among themselves and a workable and regular society.

I see not one action, or three, or a hundred, but morals in common and accepted practice, so monstrous, especially in inhumanity and treachery, that I have not the heart to think of them without horror; and I marvel at them almost as much as I detest them. The practice of these arrant villainies bears the mark of vigor and strength of soul as much as of error and disorder.

Necessity reconciles men and brings them together. This accidental link afterward takes the form of laws; for there have been some as savage as any human opinion can produce, which have nevertheless maintained their bodily health and long life as well as those of Plato and Aristotle could do.

And indeed all those imaginary, artificial descriptions of a government prove ridiculous and unfit to put into practice. These great, lengthy altercations about the best form of society and the rules most suitable to bind us, are altercations fit only for the exercise of our minds; as in the liberal arts there are several subjects whose essence is controversy and dispute, and which have no life apart from that. Such a description of a government would be applicable in a new world, but we take men already bound and formed to certain customs; we do not create them, like Pyrrha or Cadmus. By whatever means we may have power to correct and reform them, we can hardly twist them out of their accustomed bent without breaking up everything. Solon was asked whether he had

4 Poneropolis, which in Greek means "City of the Wicked."

established the best laws he could for the Athenians. "Yes indeed," he answered, "the best they would have accepted."

^CVarro excuses himself in the same way, saying that if he had to write about religion as something new, he would say what he thinks of it; but since it is already formed and accepted, he will speak of it more according to custom than according to nature.

^BNot in theory, but in truth, the best and most excellent government for each nation is the one under which it has preserved its existence. Its form and essential fitness depend on habit. We are prone to be discontented with the present state of things. But I maintain, nevertheless, that to wish for the government of a few in a democratic state, or another type of government in a monarchy, is foolish and wrong.

> Love your own state, and be it what it will.
> If it is royal, then love royalty;
> If oligarchy or democracy,
> God brought you into it, so love it still.
> PIBRAC[5]

Good Monsieur de Pibrac, whom we have just lost, such a noble mind, such sound opinions, such a gentle character! This loss, and that of Monsieur de Foix,[6] which we suffered at the same time, are important losses to our crown. I do not know if France has another pair left, comparable in sincerity and ability, to substitute for these two Gascons in the councils of our kings. They were souls beautiful in different ways, and certainly rare and beautiful by the standards of our times, each in his own way. But who placed them in this age, they who were so out of tune and proportion with our corruption and tempests?

Nothing presses a state hard except innovation; change alone lends shape to injustice and tyranny. When some part is dislocated, we can prop it up; we can fight against letting the alteration and corruption natural to all things carry us too far from our beginnings and principles. But to undertake to recast so great a mass, to change the foundations of so great a structure, that is a job for those ^Cwho

5 Guy du Faur de Pibrac (1529–84), distinguished moderate magistrate and man of letters, was the author of a book of *Quatrains* of which Montaigne here quotes one.
6 Paul de Foix (1528–84), counselor and ambassador, was the addressee of one of Montaigne's dedicatory letters (No. 8).

wipe out a picture in order to clean it, [B]who want to reform defects of detail by universal confusion and cure illnesses by death, [C]*who desire not so much to change as to overthrow everything* [Cicero]. [B]The world is ill fitted to cure itself; it is so impatient of its affliction that it aims only at getting rid of it, without considering the cost. We see by a thousand examples that it usually cures itself to its own disadvantage. Riddance from a present evil is not cure, unless there is an all-round improvement in condition.

[C]The surgeon's aim is not to kill the diseased flesh; that is only the road to his cure. He looks beyond, to make the natural flesh grow again, and restore the part to its proper condition. Whoever proposes merely to remove what is biting him falls short, for good does not necessarily succeed evil; another evil may succeed it, and a worse one, as happened to Caesar's slayers, who cast the Republic into such a state that they had reason to repent of having meddled with it. To many others since, right down to our own times, the same thing has happened. The French, my contemporaries, could tell you a thing or two about it. All great changes shake the state and throw it into disorder.

Anyone who would aim straight at a cure and would reflect on it before taking any action, would be likely to cool off about setting his hand to it. Pacuvius Calavius corrected the error of this procedure by a signal example. His fellow citizens were in revolt against their magistrates. He, a person of great authority in the city of Capua, one day found means to lock up the Senate in the palace, and, calling the people together in the market place, told them that the day had come when in full liberty they could take vengeance on the tyrants who had so long oppressed them, and whom he held alone and disarmed at his mercy. He advised them that these men should be brought out one by one, by lot, and that they should decide about each one individually, and have their sentence executed on the spot; with this provision also, that at the same time they should decide to appoint some honorable man in the place of the condemned man, so that the office should not remain vacant. They had no sooner heard the name of one senator than there arose a cry of general dissatisfaction against him. "I see very well," said Pacuvius, "that we must dismiss this one; he is a wicked man; let us have a good one in exchange." There was a prompt silence, everyone being much at a loss whom to choose. The first man bold enough to name his choice met a still greater unanimity of voices to refuse him, citing a hundred imperfections and just causes for rejecting him. These

contradictory humors having grown heated, it fared still worse with
the second senator, and the third: as much disagreement about
election as agreement about dismissal. Having tired themselves
out uselessly in this dispute, they began bit by bit, one this way,
one that, to steal away from the assembly, each one bearing away this
conclusion in his mind, that the oldest and best-known evil is always
more bearable than an evil that is new and untried.

^BBecause I see us pitifully agitated (for what have we not done?) –

> Alas, by scars and sins our souls are stained,
> And brothers' blood. From what have we refrained
> In this hard age? What evil have we fled
> Or left undone? When has our youth, in dread
> Of irritated Gods, its hands restrained?
> What altar not profaned?
> HORACE

– I do not immediately jump to the conclusion that

> Though even Safety would
> Preserve this family, henceforth she never could.
> TERENCE

Perhaps we are not on our last legs, for all that. The preservation of
states is a thing that probably surpasses our understanding. ^CAs
Plato says, a civil government is a powerful thing and hard to
dissolve. It often holds out against mortal internal diseases, against
the mischief of unjust laws, against tyranny, against the excesses
and ignorance of the magistrates and the license and sedition of
the people.

^BIn all our fortunes we compare ourselves with what is above us
and look toward those who are better off; let us measure ourselves
with what is below: there is no one so ill-starred that he may not find
a thousand examples to console him. ^CIt is our weakness that we are
more unhappy to see people ahead of us than happy to see people
behind us. ^BHowever, Solon used to say that if someone made
a pile of all the ills together, there is no one who would not choose
rather to take back with him the ills he has than to come to a
legitimate division with all other men, and take his rightful share.
Our government is in bad health; yet some have been sicker without
dying. The gods play pelota with us and drive us about in every way:

> Truly the Gods play with us as with balls.
> PLAUTUS

The stars fatally destined the state of Rome for an example of what they can do in this way. In it are comprised all the forms and vicissitudes that affect a state: all that order can do, and disorder, and good fortune, and misfortune. What state ought to despair of its condition, seeing the shocks and commotions by which Rome was disturbed, and which it withstood? If extent of dominion is the health of a state (which I do not at all believe, ᶜand I like Isocrates when he instructs Nicocles not to envy princes who have broad dominions, but rather those who know how to keep in good condition the ones that have been handed down to them), ᴮthe Roman state was never so healthy as when it was sickest. The worst of its forms was the most fortunate.

One can hardly distinguish the features of any kind of government under the first emperors; it was the thickest and most horrible confusion imaginable. Nevertheless Rome endured it and continued in it, preserving not a monarchy confined within its own bounds, but all those nations, so unlike, so remote, so ill-disposed, ruled with so little order and conquered so unjustly:

> Fortune gives no right
> To any nation, to indulge her spite
> Against the state that rules o'er land and sea.
>
> LUCAN

All that totters does not fall. The fabric of so great a body holds together by more than a single nail. It holds together even by its antiquity, like old buildings whose foundations have been worn away by age, without cement or mortar, which yet live and support themselves by their own weight:

> The day it clung to healthy roots is past,
> Its weight now holds it up. LUCAN

Furthermore, it is not a good procedure to reconnoiter only the flank and the moat; to judge the security of a place, we must see from what direction it can be approached, and what is the condition of the attacker. Few vessels sink of their own weight and without external violence. Now let us turn our eyes in all directions: everything is crumbling about us; in all the great states that we know, whether in Christendom or elsewhere, take a look: you will find an evident threat of change and ruin:

> They have their own misfortunes, and have all
> Been through the storm.
>
> ADAPTED FROM VIRGIL

The astrologers have an easy game when they warn us, as they do, of great and imminent alterations and mutations; their prophecies are present and palpable; we do not need to go to the heavens for that.

We may derive not only consolation from this universal company of evils and menaces, but even some hope for the duration of our state, inasmuch as naturally nothing falls where everything falls. Universal sickness is individual health; conformity is a quality hostile to dissolution. For my part, I do not despair about it, and in it I seem to see ways of saving ourselves:

> Perhaps a god will yet restore,
> By happy change, our bliss of yore.
>
> HORACE

Who knows but that God wills it to happen as with bodies that purge themselves and are restored to better condition by long and grievous maladies, which give them back a clearer and more complete health than they took away from them?

What most weighs me down is that when I count up the symptoms of our trouble, I see as many that are natural and that Heaven sends us from its own stock, as of those that our disorder and human imprudence contribute. ᶜIt seems as if the very stars have ordained that we have lasted long enough beyond the ordinary term. And this also weighs me down, that the evil that most nearly threatens us is not an alteration in the entire and solid mass, but its dissipation and disintegration, the worst of our fears.

ᴮAlso in these ramblings of mine I fear the treachery of my memory, lest inadvertently it may have made me record something twice. I hate to reexamine myself, and never reread, if I can help it, what has once escaped me. Now I am bringing in here nothing newly learned. These are common ideas; having perhaps thought of them a hundred times, I am afraid I have already set them down. Repetition is boring anywhere, even in Homer; but it is ruinous in things that attract only superficial and passing attention. I dislike inculcation, even of useful things, as in Seneca; ᶜand I dislike the practice of his Stoical school of repeating, in connection with every subject, in full length and breadth, the principles and premises for general use, and restating ever anew their common and universal arguments and reasons.

[B]My memory grows cruelly worse every day,

As though with thirsty throat I'd quaffed
Some soporific Lethean draught.

HORACE

Henceforth – for thank God, up to now, no serious blunder has resulted – whereas others seek time and opportunity to think over what they have to say, I shall have to avoid any preparation, for fear of binding myself to some obligation on which I should be dependent. To be held and bound puts me off my track, and likewise to depend on so feeble an instrument as my memory.

I never read the following story without indignation, and natural and personal resentment. Lyncestes, accused of conspiracy against Alexander, on the day when he was brought before the army, according to custom, to be heard in his own defense, had in his head a studied oration, of which, all hesitating and stammering, he pronounced a few words. As he was growing more and more confused, struggling with his memory and searching it, the soldiers nearest him charged him and killed him with their pikes, considering him convicted. His confusion and his silence was to them as good as a confession. Since he had had so much leisure to prepare himself in prison, it was not, in their opinion, his memory that failed him: it was his conscience that tied his tongue and took away his strength. That certainly was good reasoning! The place, the audience, the anticipation, daze a man even when nothing is at stake but the ambition to speak well. What can a man do when it is a speech on which his life depends?

For my part, the very fact of being bound to what I have to say is enough to break my grip on it. When I have committed and entrusted myself entirely to my memory, I lean so heavily on it that I overburden it: it takes fright at its load. As long as I rely on it, I place myself outside myself, till I risk losing countenance; and some days I have found myself hard pressed to conceal the slavery in which I was bound, whereas my plan in speaking is to display extreme carelessness and unstudied and unpremeditated gestures, as if they arose from the immediate occasion. For I would as soon say nothing worth while as show I had come prepared to be eloquent, an unbecoming thing, especially for people of my profession, [c]and too binding a thing for a man who cannot live up to much: the preparation gives more hope than it fulfills. Often a man stupidly strips to his doublet only to jump no better than he would in a cloak. *There is*

nothing so unfavorable to those who wish to please as the expectation they arouse [Cicero].

[B]It is recorded of the orator Curio that when he stated first the division of his oration into three or four parts, or the number of his arguments and reasons, it often happened that he either forgot one, or added one or two extra. I have always carefully guarded against falling into this predicament, having always hated these promises and prescriptions, not only out of distrust of my memory, but also because this method owes too much to artificiality. [C]*A simpler style becomes a soldier* [Quintilian]. [B]Enough that I have promised myself henceforth never again to take up the task of speaking on formal occasions. For, as for reading one's speech, besides being unnatural, it is a great disadvantage for those who naturally have some power of gesture. And as for throwing myself on the mercy of my improvisation, that is even less desirable; mine is sluggish and confused, and could not meet sudden and important emergencies.

Reader, let this essay of myself run on, and this third extension of the other parts of my painting. I add, but I do not correct. First, because when a man has mortgaged his work to the world, it seems to me that he has no further right to it. Let him speak better elsewhere, if he can, and not adulterate the work he has sold. From such people nothing should be bought until after their death. Let them think carefully before publishing. Who is hurrying them?

[C]My book is always one. Except that at each new edition, so that the buyer may not come off completely empty-handed, I allow myself to add, since it is only an ill-fitted patchwork, some extra ornaments. These are only overweights, which do not condemn the original form, but give some special value to each of the subsequent ones, by a bit of ambitious subtlety. Thence, however, it will easily happen that some transposition of chronology may slip in, for my stories take their place according to their timeliness, not always according to their age.

[B]Second, because, as far as I am concerned, I fear to lose by the change: my understanding does not always go forward, it goes backward too. I distrust my thoughts hardly any less for being second or third than for being first, or for being present than for being past. We often correct ourselves as stupidly as we correct others. [C]My first edition was in the year 1580. Since then I have grown older by a long stretch of time; but certainly I have not grown

an inch wiser. Myself now and myself a while ago are indeed two; but when better, I simply cannot say. It would be fine to be old if we traveled only toward improvement. It is a drunkard's motion, staggering, dizzy, wobbling, or that of reeds that the wind stirs haphazardly as it pleases.

Antiochus had written vigorously in favor of the Academy; in his old age he took a different stand. Whichever of the two I followed, should I not still be following Antiochus? After having established the doubtfulness of human opinions, to try to establish their certainty, was that not establishing doubt, not certainty, and promising that if he had been given another age to live he would still be ready for some new change, not so much better as different?

ᴮThe favor of the public has given me a little more boldness than I expected; but what I fear most is to surfeit my readers: I would rather irritate them than weary them, as a learned man of my time has done. Praise is always pleasing, from whomever and for whatever reason it may come; yet to enjoy it properly, we must be informed of the cause of it. Even imperfections have a way of recommending themselves. Vulgar and popular esteem is seldom happy in its choice; and in my time I am much mistaken if the worst writings are not those which have gotten the best share of the wind of public favor. Certainly I give thanks to those good people who deign to take my feeble efforts in good part.

There is no place where the faults of workmanship are so apparent as in material which has nothing in itself to recommend it. Do not blame me, reader, for those that slip in here through the caprice or inadvertency of others: each hand, each workman, contributes his own. I do not concern myself with spelling, and simply order them to follow the old style; or with punctuation; I am inexpert in both. When they wholly shatter the sense, I am not much troubled about it, for at least they relieve me of responsibility; but when they substitute a false meaning, as they do so often, and twist me to their view, they ruin me. However, when the thought is not up to my strength, a fair-minded man should reject it as not mine. Anyone who knows how little I like to work, how much I am formed in my own way, will easily believe that I would rather write as many more essays again than subject myself to going over these again for such childish correction.

So I was saying a while ago that being planted in the deepest mine of this new metal,[7] not only am I deprived of any great familiarity with people of different morals and opinions from mine, by which they hold together with a bond that shuns all other bonds;[8] but also I am not free from danger among people to whom everything is equally permissible, and most of whom cannot make their account with the law worse – from which arises the extreme degree of licentiousness. Counting up all the particular circumstances concerning myself, I find no man of our country to whom the defense of the laws costs more, both in gains ceasing and in damages ensuing, as the lawyers say, than myself. ᶜAnd certain people make much of their zeal and eagerness who, weighing things justly, do much less than I.

ᴮAs a house that has always been free, very accessible, and at anyone's service (for I have never let myself be induced to make it an instrument of war, in which I take part most willingly when it is most distant from my neighborhood), my house has deserved considerable popular affection, and it would be very hard to scold me on my own dunghill. And I think it is a wonderful and exemplary masterpiece that it is still virgin of blood and pillage, under so long a storm, with so many changes and disturbances in the neighborhood. For, to tell the truth, it was possible for a man of my disposition to escape any one constant and continued form of danger, whatever it might be; but the conflicting invasions and incursions and the alternations and vicissitudes of fortune around me have up to now more exasperated than mollified the temper of the country, and burden me again and again with insuperable dangers and difficulties. I escape; but I dislike the fact that it is more by good luck, and even by my prudence, than because of justice; and I dislike being outside the protection of the laws and under another safeguard than theirs. As things stand, I live more than half by others' favor, which is a harsh obligation. I do not want to owe my safety either to the kindness and benignity of the great, who approve of my obedience to the laws and my

7 An allusion to the Juvenal quotation on p. 886 which itself alludes to the legend of four ages (gold, silver, bronze, and iron), and suggests that a new metal is needed to represent the new depths to which man has sunk.

8 Montaigne's meaning is probably that he, a Catholic, lives surrounded by Protestants. It may also be that the injustice and wickedness of his neighbors unites them.

independence, or to the affable ways of my predecessors and myself. For what if I were different? If my conduct and the frankness of my dealings obligate my neighbors or my kinsmen, it is cruel that they can acquit themselves by letting me live, and say: "We grant him ^cleave to continue to hold the divine service freely in the chapel of his house, all the churches around having been emptied and ruined by us; and we grant him ^Bthe use of his property, and his life, since he shelters our wives and our cattle in time of need." For a long time we in my house have had a share in the praise given to Lycurgus, the Athenian, who was the general depositary and guardian of his fellow citizens' purses.

Now I hold that we should live by right and authority, not by ^creward or ^Bfavor. How many gallant men have chosen rather to lose their lives than to owe them! I avoid subjecting myself to any sort of obligation, but especially any that binds me by a debt of honor. I find nothing so expensive as that which is given me and for which my will remains mortgaged by the claim of gratitude, and I more willingly accept services that are for sale. Rightly so, I think: for the latter I give only money, for the others I give myself. The tie that binds me by the law of honesty seems to me much tighter and more oppressive than is that of legal constraint. A notary ties me down more gently than I do myself. Is it not reasonable that my conscience should be much more firmly bound in matters in which someone relies on it alone? In other cases my fidelity owes nothing, for nothing has been lent it; let them use the trust and security they have taken outside of me. I would much rather break the imprisonment of a wall and of the laws than that of my word. ^cI am scrupulous to the point of superstition in keeping my promises, and I like to make them uncertain and conditional in all matters. To those of no weight I give weight by jealous regard for my rule: it torments me and burdens me with its own interest. Yes, even in undertakings in which I am alone concerned and wholly free, if I say what I plan to do, it seems to me that I prescribe it for myself, and that to give knowledge of it to another is to impose it upon myself. It seems to me that I promise it when I mention it. Thus I seldom air my plans.

^BThe sentence I pass upon myself is sharper and stiffer than that of the judges, who only consider me with respect to common obligation; the grip of my conscience is tighter and more severe. I am lax in following duties to which I should be dragged if I did

not go to them. ^c*Even a just action is just only in so far as it is voluntary* [Cicero]. ^BIf the action does not have something of the splendor of freedom, it has neither grace nor honor.

When I am forced by law, my will gives scant assent.
TERENCE

When necessity tugs me, I like to relax my will, *because whatever is exacted by power is ascribed rather to him who commands than to him who executes* [Valerius Maximus]. I know some who follow this vein to the point of injustice: who give rather than give back, lend rather than pay, and do good most stingily to the person they are obliged to. I do not go that far, but I come close to it.

I am so fond of throwing off burdens and obligations that I have sometimes counted as profit the ingratitude, affronts, and indignities that I had received from those to whom, either by nature or by accident, I owed some duty of friendship, taking the occasion of their offense as that much acquittance and discharge of my debt. Although I continue to pay them the external civilities that public interest prescribes, I find it a great saving, all the same, ^cto do for the sake of justice what I used to do for the sake of affection, and ^Bto relieve myself a little of the inner tension and solicitude of my will – ^c*It is the part of a wise man to restrain, as he would a chariot, the first impulse of good will* [Cicero] – ^Bwhich is a little too urgent and pressing when I put my heart into it, at least for a man who has no wish to be under pressure. And this economy serves me as some consolation for the imperfections of those with whom I am concerned. To be sure, I am sorry that they are worth less for it, but the fact remains that I am also spared in this way something of my diligence and obligation toward them.

I approve of a man who loves his son less for being mangy or hunchbacked, and not only when he is malicious, but also when he is ill-favored and ill-born – God himself has taken off that much from his natural value and estimation – provided he bears himself in his coolness toward him with moderation and exact justice. With me, nearness of kin does not alleviate defects, it rather aggravates them.

After all, as far as I understand the science of benefaction and gratitude, which is a subtle science and of great utility, I see no one freer and less indebted than I am up to this point. What I owe, I owe to the ordinary and natural obligations. There is no one who is more absolutely clear of any others:

The gifts of princes are to me unknown.
ADAPTED FROM VIRGIL

Princes ᶜgive me much if they take nothing from me, and ᴮdo me enough good when they do me no harm; that is all I ask of them. Oh, how much I am obliged to God that it was his pleasure that I should receive all I have directly from his grace, and that he has kept all my indebtedness for himself privately! ᶜHow earnestly I beseech his holy mercy that I may never owe thanks for essential things to anyone! Blessed liberty, which has guided me so far! May it continue to the end!

ᴮI try to have no express need of anyone. ᶜ*All my hope is in myself* [imitated from Terence]. ᴮThis is a thing that each man can arrange for himself, but more easily those whom God has sheltered from natural and urgent necessities. It is very pitiful and hazardous to be dependent on another. We ourselves, who are our most proper and certain resource, have not made ourselves secure enough. I have nothing of my own but myself, and even there my possession is partly defective and borrowed. I cultivate ᶜboth my courage, which is the stronger, and also my fortune, ᴮto find in them enough to satisfy me if everything else should forsake me.

ᶜHippias of Elis furnished himself not merely with learning, that in the lap of the Muses he might, in case of need, dispense cheerfully with any other company; and not merely with the knowledge of philosophy, to teach his soul to be contented with itself and manfully to do without the comforts that come to it from outside, when fate so ordains. He was so careful as to learn also to cook, to shave, and to make his clothes, his shoes, and his rings, so as to be as self-sufficient as he could, and escape from dependence on outside help.

ᴮWe enjoy borrowed goods much more freely and gaily when our enjoyment is not forced and constrained by need, and when we have, both in our will and in our fortune, the strength and the means to do without them.

ᶜI know myself well; but it is hard for me to imagine anyone's liberality so pure, any hospitality so free and genuine, that it would not seem to me ill-favored, tyrannical, and tainted with reproach, if necessity had entangled me in it. As giving is an ambitious quality and a prerogative, so is accepting a quality of submission: witness Bajazet's insulting and quarrelsome refusal of the presents that Tamerlane sent him. And those offered on behalf of Emperor

Suleiman to the emperor of Calicut made him so angry that not only did he refuse them rudely, saying that neither he nor his predecessors were accustomed to take, and that it was their part to give; but besides, he had the ambassadors sent for this purpose thrown into a dungeon.

When Thetis, says Aristotle, flatters Jupiter, when the Lacedaemonians flatter the Athenians, they do not keep refreshing their memory of the good they have done them, which is always odious, but their memory of the benefits they have received from them. A man whom I see so freely making use of one and all and putting himself under obligation to them, would not do so if he weighed the bond of an obligation as carefully as a wise man should: perhaps sometimes it is paid, but it is never dissolved. Cruel fetters for a man who likes to give his freedom elbowroom in all directions.

Those who know me, both above and below me, know whether they have ever seen a man less demanding of others. If I surpass all modern examples in this respect, it is no great wonder, for so many parts of my character contribute to it: a little natural pride, inability to endure refusal, limitation of my desires and designs, incapacity for any kind of business, and my very favorite qualities, idleness and freedom. Through all these I have conceived a mortal hatred of being obliged either to another or by another than myself. I employ every power to the utmost to do without, before I employ the kindness of another, however slight or weighty the occasion. My friends annoy me greatly when they ask me to ask a favor of a third person. And it seems to me hardly less expensive to release a man who is indebted to me by using him, than to bind myself for my friends' sake to a man who owes me nothing. Excepting that condition, and this other, that they desire of me nothing involving trouble and care, for I have declared war to the death against all care, I am accommodating and approachable for any man's need.

ᴮBut I have avoided receiving still more than I have sought to give; ᶜand indeed this is much the easier choice, according to Aristotle. ᴮMy fortune has allowed me to do but little good to others, and what little it has allowed me it has assigned to rather meager quarters. If it had brought me into the world to hold some rank among men, I should have been ambitious to make myself loved, not to make myself feared or admired. Shall I express this more insolently? I should have thought as much of giving pleasure as of gaining profit. ᶜCyrus, very wisely, and through the mouth of

a very good captain and still better philosopher,[9] esteems his kindness and his good deeds far beyond his valor and his warlike conquests. And Scipio the Elder, whenever he wants to put his best foot forward, gives more weight to his affability and humanity than to his hardihood and his victories; and he has ever in his mouth this proud saying: that he left his enemies as good reason to love him as his friends.

[B]I mean to say, then, that if we must thus owe something, it should be by a more legitimate title than the one I am speaking of, to which the law of this miserable war binds me; and not with so great a debt as that of my total preservation: that overwhelms me. I have gone to bed a thousand times in my own home, imagining that someone would betray me and slaughter me that very night, arranging with fortune that it should be without fright and not lingering. And after my Paternoster I have cried out:

> Shall a godless soldier possess these well-tilled fields?
> VIRGIL

What remedy is there? It is my birthplace and that of most of my ancestors; they set on it their affection and their name.[10] We become hardened to whatever we are accustomed to. And for a wretched condition such as ours, a very favorable gift of nature is habit, which benumbs our senses to the suffering of many ills. Civil wars are worse in this respect than other wars, that they make us all sentinels in our own houses.

> How sad to guard our life with gate and wall,
> And scarcely trust the strength of our own hall.
> OVID

It is a great extremity to be beset even in our household and domestic repose. The region where I live is always the first and the last in the battles of our troubled times, and peace never shows her full face there:

> Even in time of peace, they quake for fear of war.
> OVID

9 Xenophon.
10 Montaigne, appropriately for this chapter, shows here his vanity over his nobility, which is probably intensified by awareness that it is recent. Actually his only ancestor born at Montaigne was his father; and the name came from the estate, not from the family.

> Whenever Fortune stirs unrest,
> Then war is rife. I would be better blessed
> If placed beneath the sun of Orient,
> Or in the frozen North, under a nomad's tent.
>
> LUCAN

I sometimes derive from nonchalance and laxity a way of strengthening myself against these considerations; they too, to some extent, lead us toward fortitude. It often happens that I imagine and await mortal dangers with some pleasure: I plunge head down, stupidly, into death, without looking at it and recognizing it, as into a silent and dark abyss which swallows me up at one leap and overwhelms me in an instant with a heavy sleep free from feeling and pain. And in these quick and violent deaths, the consequence that I foresee gives me more comfort than the occurrence gives me fear. ^CThey say that as life is not better for being long, so death is better for not being long. ^BIt is not so much that I keep aloof from the thought of being dead as that I enter into familiar terms with dying. I wrap myself up and nestle in this storm, so that it must blind me and sweep me away furiously with a sudden and numbing attack.

Even so, if it happened to be true, as some gardeners say, that roses and violets spring up more fragrant near garlic and onions, because these draw in and suck up whatever there is that smells bad in the ground, and if likewise these depraved natures absorbed all the venom of my air and climate and made me all the better and purer for their vicinity, I would not be wholly a loser. That is not the case; but there may be something in this, that goodness is more beautiful and attractive when it is rare; and that contrariety and diversity strengthen well-doing and compress it within itself, and inflame it by jealousy of opposition and love of glory.

^CRobbers are gracious enough to have no particular grudge against me. Have I any against them? I should have to hate too many people. Like consciences, under different kinds of fortune, harbor like cruelty, disloyalty, and robbery; and it is all the worse when it is more cowardly, more secure and dark, in the shadow of the laws. I hate open injustice less than treacherous injustice, warlike less than peaceful. Our fever has come upon a body that is hardly the worse for it. The fire was there, it has caught flame; the noise is greater, the evil little greater.

[B]I ordinarily reply to those who ask me the reason for my travels, that I know well what I am fleeing from, but not what I am looking for. If they tell me that among foreigners there may be just as little health, and that their ways are no better than ours, I reply, first, that that is not easy,

So many are the shapes of crime![II]

VIRGIL

Second, that it is always a gain to change a bad state for an uncertain one, and that the troubles of others should not sting us like our own.

I do not want to forget this, that I never rebel so much against France as not to regard Paris with a friendly eye; she has had my heart since my childhood. And it has happened to me in this as happens with excellent things: the more other beautiful cities I have seen since, the more the beauty of Paris has power over me and wins my affection. I love her for herself, and more in her own essence than overloaded with foreign pomp. I love her tenderly, even to her warts and her spots. I am a Frenchman only by this great city: great in population, great in the felicity of her situation, but above all great and incomparable in variety and diversity of the good things of life; the glory of France, and one of the noblest ornaments of the world. May God drive our discords far from her! Entire and united, I think she is protected against any other violence. I warn her that of all parties the worst will be the one that throws her into discord. And for her I fear only herself. And I fear certainly as much for her as for any other part of this state. As long as she endures, I shall not lack a retreat in which to give up the ghost, sufficient to make me lose my regret for any other retreat.

Not because Socrates said it, but because it is really my feeling, and perhaps excessively so, I consider all men my compatriots, and embrace a Pole as I do a Frenchman, setting this national bond after the universal and common one. I am scarcely infatuated with the sweetness of my native air. Brand-new acquaintances that are wholly of my own choice seem to me to be well worth those other common chance acquaintances of the neighborhood. Friendships purely of our own acquisition usually surpass those to which community of climate or of blood binds us. Nature has put us into the world free and unfettered; we imprison ourselves in certain narrow

II Presumably, since Virgil is speaking of crime in wartime, the point is that war-torn France will be richer in crime than relatively peaceful Italy.

districts, like the kings of Persia, who bound themselves never to drink any other water than that of the river Choaspes, stupidly gave up their right to use any other waters, and dried up all the rest of the world as far as they were concerned.

ᶜWhat Socrates did near the end of his life, in considering a sentence of exile against him worse than a sentence of death, I shall never, I think, be so broken or so strictly attached to my own country as to do. These divine lives have quite a few aspects that I embrace more by esteem than by affection. And there are also some so lofty and extraordinary that I cannot embrace them even by esteem, inasmuch as I cannot understand them. That was a very fastidious attitude for a man who considered the world his city. It is true that he disdained peregrination and had scarcely set foot outside the territory of Attica. What are we to say of his grudging his friends' money to save his life, and refusing to get out of prison by the intervention of others, so as not to disobey the laws, and that at a time when they were so thoroughly corrupt? These examples are of the first type for me. Of the second type are others that I could find in this same person. Many of these rare examples exceed my power of performing, but some even exceed my power of judging.

ᴮBesides these reasons, travel seems to me a profitable exercise. The mind is continually exercised in observing new and unknown things; and I know no better school, as I have often said, for forming one's life, than to set before it constantly the diversity of so many other lives, ᶜideas, and customs, ᴮand to make it taste such a perpetual variety of forms of our nature. In it the body is neither idle nor overworked, and this moderate movement puts it in good condition. I stay on horseback, though I have the colic, without dismounting and without pain, for eight or ten hours,

> Beyond the strength and lot of age.
> VIRGIL

No season is hostile to me except the fierce heat of a burning sun; for umbrellas, which Italy has used since the ancient Romans, burden the arm more than they relieve the head. ᶜI should like to know what device the Persians had so long ago, in the infancy of luxury, to make themselves a fresh breeze and shade at their pleasure, as Xenophon relates. ᴮI love rain and mud like a duck. Change of air and climate has no effect on me; all skies are alike to me. Only the inward troubles that I produce in myself get the better of me, and they attack me less when I travel.

I am hard to set in motion; but once under way, I go as far as anyone wants. I balk as much at little undertakings as at great ones, and at getting equipped for a day's trip and a visit to a neighbor as for a real journey. I have learned to make my day's journeys Spanish fashion, at a single stage: long and sensible stages; and in extreme heat I make them by night, from sunset to sunrise. The other way, of eating your dinner on the way in haste and confusion, is inconvenient, especially on short days. My horses are the better for it. Never has a horse failed me that could make the first day's trip with me. I water them everywhere, and only see to it that they have enough road left to settle their water. My laziness in getting up gives my attendants time to dine at their ease before starting. As for me, it is never too late for me to eat; appetite comes to me as I eat, and not otherwise; I am never at all hungry except at table.

Some people complain of my taking pleasure in continuing this exercise, married and old as I am. They are wrong. It is a better time to leave your family when you have set it on the way to go on without you, when you have left it in an order that will not belie its past arrangement. It is a much greater imprudence to go away leaving in your house a less faithful guardian, who will have less care to provide for your needs.

The most useful and honorable science and occupation for a woman is the science of housekeeping. I know some that are miserly, very few that are good managers. This is her ruling quality, which a man should seek out before any other, as the sole dowry on which the ruin or salvation of our households depends. ᶜDon't tell me! From what experience has taught me, I require of a married woman, above all other virtues, the virtues of a good housewife. ᴮI place my wife in a position to show these, leaving the entire government of my affairs in her hands by my absence. It irritates me to see in many households Monsieur coming home around noon, harassed and dirty from the mill of business, when Madame is still busy doing her hair and fixing herself up in her boudoir. That is for queens to do; and I'm not even sure about that. It is ridiculous and unfair that the idleness of our wives should be supported by our sweat and toil. ᶜNo one, if I can help it, shall have readier, quieter, and freer enjoyment of my property than myself. ᴮIf the husband provides the matter, Nature herself wills that the wife provide the form.

As for the duties of marital love that some people consider injured by absence, I do not believe it. On the contrary, it is

a relationship that is readily cooled by too continual association, and harmed by assiduity. Every strange woman seems to us an attractive woman. And every man feels by experience that seeing one another continually cannot match the pleasure of parting and being together again at intervals. ^CThese interruptions fill me with a fresh love for my family and give me back a sweeter enjoyment of my home. Alternation warms my appetite now for the one choice, now for the other.

^BI know that friendship has arms long enough to hold and join from one end of the world to the other; and especially this kind, in which there is a continual interchange of services that reawaken the bond and memory of it. The Stoics indeed say that there is so great a tie and fellowship between the sages that the one who dines in France feeds his comrade in Egypt; and that if one merely extends his finger, wherever he is, all the sages on the habitable earth feel help from it.

Enjoyment and possession are principally a matter of imagination. ^CIt embraces more warmly what it is in quest of than what we have at hand, and more continually. Count up your daily musings, and you will find that you are most absent from your friend when he is in your company; his presence relaxes your attention and gives your thoughts liberty to absent themselves at any time and for any reason.

^BFrom the distance of Rome I keep and control my house and the goods I have left behind there; I see my walls, my trees, and my revenue grow and decrease, within two inches, just as when I am there:

My house appears before my eyes, and forms of places loved.
 OVID

If we enjoy only what we touch, farewell to our crowns when they are in our coffers, and our children if they are off hunting. We want them nearer. In the garden – is that far? Half a day away? What about ten leagues – is that far or near? If it is near, what about eleven, twelve, thirteen, and so on, step by step? Truly, if there is a woman who will prescribe to her husband after how many steps ends the near, and with how many steps begins the far, I would advise her to stop him in between:

Let's set an end, and with debate have done . . .
I use my freedom, and subtract your units, one by one,

As bit by bit I might pluck out hairs from a horse's tail,
Until the pile has dwindled and my arguments prevail.

<div align="right">HORACE</div>

And let them boldly call philosophy to their aid, which someone might accuse – since it sees neither one end nor the other of the joint between too much and too little, long and short, light and heavy, near and far, since it cannot recognize either the beginning or the end of it – of being a very uncertain judge of the middle. ᶜ*Nature has given us no knowledge of the limits of things* [Cicero].

ᴮAre they not still wives and mistresses of the deceased, who are not at the end of this world, but in the other world? We embrace both those who have been and those who are not yet, not merely the absent. We have not made a bargain, in getting married, to keep continually tied to each other by the tail, like some little animals or other that we see, ᶜor like the bewitched people of Karenty, in doglike fashion. And a wife should not have her eyes so greedily fixed on the front of her husband that she cannot see the back of him, if need be.

ᴮBut may not this remark of that most excellent painter of their humors be applicable here, to show the cause of their complaints?

If you are late, your wife assumes you're having an affair
With someone, or someone with you, drinking, banishing care;
That you alone have all the fun, she all the ills to bear.

<div align="right">TERENCE</div>

Or might it not be that opposition and contradiction are in themselves meat and drink to them, and that they are comfortable enough provided they make you uncomfortable?

In true friendship, in which I am expert, I give myself to my friend more than I draw him to me. I not only like doing him good better than having him do me good, but also would rather have him do good to himself than to me; he does me most good when he does himself good. And if absence is pleasant or useful to him, it is much sweeter to me than his presence; and it is not really absence when we have means of communication. In other days I made use and advantage of our separation. We filled and extended our possession of life better by separating: he lived, he enjoyed, he saw for me, and I for him, as fully as if he had been there. One part of us remained idle when we were together; we were fused into one. Separation in space made the conjunction of our wills richer. This insatiable

hunger for bodily presence betrays a certain weakness in the enjoyment of souls.

As for my old age, which they bring up against me, it is, on the contrary, for youth to be enslaved to public opinion and to constrain itself for the sake of others. It can give satisfaction to both, to the public and to itself; we have only too much to do to satisfy ourselves alone. As natural comforts fail us, let us sustain ourselves with artificial ones. It is unjust to excuse youth for following its pleasures and to forbid old age to seek any. ᶜYoung, I covered up my blithe passions with prudence; old, I disperse my sad ones by dissipation. Besides, the Platonic laws prohibit traveling before the age of forty or fifty, to make the travel more useful and instructive. I should more willingly agree to the second article of the same laws, which forbids it after sixty.

ᴮ"But at such an age you will never return from so long a journey." What do I care? I undertake it neither to return from it nor to complete it; I undertake only to move about while I like moving. ᶜAnd I walk for the sake of walking. Those who run after a benefice or a hare do not run; they only run who run at prisoner's base and to practice running.

ᴮMy plan is everywhere divisible; it is not based on great hopes; each day's journey forms an end. And the journey of my life is conducted in the same way. However, I have seen enough distant places where I should have liked to be detained. Why not, if Chrysippus, Cleanthes, Diogenes, Zeno, Antipater, so many sages of the surliest sect, left their country indeed with no cause for complaint about it, and solely for the enjoyment of a different atmosphere? Truly the greatest trouble with my peregrinations is that I cannot bring to them a resolution to fix my abode wherever I please, and that I must always be thinking of coming back, to conform to popular feelings.

If I were afraid to die in any other place than that of my birth, if I thought I would die less comfortably away from my family, I should scarcely go out of France; I should not go out of my parish without terror. I feel death continually clutching me by the throat or the loins. But I am made differently: death is the same to me anywhere. However, if I had the choice, it would be, I think, rather on horseback than in a bed, and out of my house, away from my people.

There is more heartbreak than consolation in taking leave of our friends. I willingly forget that duty of our courtesy, for of all the

duties of friendship that is the only unpleasant one; and I would forget just as willingly to bid that great eternal farewell. If some advantage is derived from this audience, there are a hundred disadvantages. I have seen many dying men pitifully besieged by all this throng: the crowd stifles them. It is contrary to duty, and testimony of scant affection and scant concern, to let you die in peace: one torments your eyes, another your ears, another your tongue; there is not a sense or a part of you that they do not shatter. Your heart is wrung with pity to hear the laments of your friends, and perhaps with anger to hear other laments that are feigned and counterfeit. A man who has always had fastidious tastes finds them more so when he is in a weakened condition. In such great need he must have a gentle hand, suited to his feelings, to scratch him just where he itches; otherwise he should not be touched at all. If we need a wise woman[12] to bring us into the world, we certainly need a still wiser man to help us out of it. Such a man, and a friend to boot, should be purchased at any price to assist us on such an occasion.

I have not attained that disdainful vigor which finds fortitude in itself, which nothing can either aid or disturb; I am a peg lower. I try to burrow and hide from this passing, not through fear, but through design. It is not my idea to prove or display my fortitude in this act of dying. For whom? Then will end all my right to reputation and my interest in it. I am content with a collected, calm, and solitary death, all my own, in keeping with my retired and private life. In contrast with the Roman superstition, which considered a man unfortunate who died without speaking and who did not have his nearest relatives to close his eyes, I have enough to do to console myself without having to console others, enough thoughts in my head without having circumstances bring me new ones, and enough matter for reflection without borrowing it. Dying is not a role for society; it is an act for one single character. Let us live and laugh among our friends, let us go die and look sour among strangers. You will find, if you pay, someone who will turn your head, rub your feet, who will not trouble you any more than you want, showing you an indifferent face, letting you reflect and lament as you like.

Day by day I rid myself by reflection of that childish and inhuman humor that makes us want to arouse compassion and mourning in our friends by our misfortunes. We make more of our troubles

12 *Sage femme*, literally "wise woman," means midwife.

than they are worth, to draw their tears. And the firmness in supporting misfortune that we praise in all men, we blame and reproach in our friends when the misfortune is our own. We are not content that they should be aware of our woes, unless they are also afflicted by them.

We should spread joy, but cut down sadness as much as we can. ᶜHe who asks for pity without reason is a man not to be pitied when there is reason. To be always lamenting for ourselves is the way never to be lamented; by continually putting on a pitiful act, we become pitiable to no one. He who acts dead when still alive is subject to be thought alive when dying. I have seen it get some people's goat to be told that their color was good and their pulse even; I have seen them restrain their laughter because it betrayed their recovery, and hate health because it was not pitiable. What is more, they were not women.

ᴮI represent my ailments, at most, just as they are, and avoid words of foreboding and deliberate exclamations. If not cheerfulness, at least a composed countenance is appropriate in people attending a sick sage. Just because he sees himself in the opposite condition, he does not pick a quarrel with health; he likes to contemplate it strong and entire in others, and enjoy it at least by association. Just because he feels himself slipping, he does not utterly reject the thoughts of life, or avoid ordinary conversation. I want to study sickness when I am healthy; when it is on me, it makes its impression real enough, without the help of my imagination. We prepare ourselves beforehand for the journeys we undertake, and are resolved on them; the time when we are to take horse we leave to our companions and put it off for them.

I feel this unexpected profit from the publication of my behavior, that to some extent it serves me as a rule. Sometimes there comes to me a feeling that I should not betray the story of my life. This public declaration obliges me to keep on my path, and not to give the lie to the picture of my qualities, which are normally less disfigured and distorted than might be expected from the malice and sickness of the judgments of today. The uniformity and simplicity of my behavior indeed produces an appearance easy to interpret, but, because the manner of it is a bit new and unusual, it gives too fine a chance to calumny. Yet the fact is, it seems to me, that to anyone who wants to abuse me fairly I give plenty to bite on in my known and avowed imperfections, and enough to gorge on, without skirmishing with the wind. If it seems to him that by beating him to the

accusation and revelation myself I am drawing the teeth of his mordancy, it is reasonable that he should exercise his right of amplification and extension (attack has rights beyond justice), that he should magnify into trees the vices whose roots I show him in myself, and that he should use for this not only those that possess me, but also those that merely threaten me. Harmful vices, in both quality and number; let him beat me with them.

^CI would frankly follow the example of the philosopher Bion. Antigonus was trying to taunt him on the subject of his origin; he cut him short. "I am," he said, "the son of a slave, a butcher, branded, and of a whore whom my father married because of the baseness of his fortune. Both were punished for some misdeed. An orator bought me when I was a child, finding me attractive, and when he died, left me all his possessions. Having transported them to this city of Athens, I devoted myself to philosophy. Let not historians be at a loss in seeking information about me; I will tell them what's what about it." Free and generous confession weakens reproach and disarms slander.

^BYet the fact remains that all in all, it seems to me that I am as often praised as dispraised beyond reason. Even as it seems to me also that from my youth, in rank and degree of honor, I have been given a place rather above than below what I am entitled to.

^CI should be more at home in a country where these orders of precedence were either regulated or despised. Among men, as soon as an altercation over precedence in walking or sitting goes beyond three replies, it is uncivil. I have no fear of ceding or preceding unfairly to avoid such a bothersome argument, and never did a man covet my right to go first but that I yielded it to him.

^BBesides this profit that I derive from writing about myself, I hope for this other advantage, that if my humors happen to please and suit some worthy man before I die, he will try to meet me. I give him a big advantage in ground covered; for all that long acquaintance and familiarity could have gained for him in several years, he can see in three days in this record, and more surely and exactly.

^CAmusing notion: many things that I would not want to tell anyone, I tell the public; and for my most secret knowledge and thoughts I send my most faithful friends to a bookseller's shop.

> We bare our hearts to scrutiny.
> PERSIUS

^BIf by such good signs I knew of a man who was suited to me,

truly I would go very far to find him; for the sweetness of harmonious and agreeable company cannot be bought too dearly, in my opinion. Oh, a friend! How true is that old saying, that the enjoyment of one is sweeter and more necessary than that of the elements of water and fire!

To return to my story, there is thus no great evil in dying far off and alone. ᶜIndeed we think it a duty to retire for natural actions less unsightly and less hideous than this. ᴮBut besides, those who are reduced to dragging out a long, lingering life ought perhaps not to wish to involve a large family in their misery. ᶜTherefore the Indians in a certain province thought it just to kill a man who had fallen into such straits; and in another province they abandoned him alone to keep alive however he could.

ᴮTo whom do the dying not finally make themselves annoying and unbearable? Ordinary duties do not go so far. You teach your best friends perforce to be cruel, hardening both wife and children by long habit not to feel and pity your woes any more. The groans of my colic no longer cause emotion in anyone. And even if we derived some pleasure from their company (which does not always happen, because of the disparity of conditions which easily produces contempt or envy of anyone whatever), is it not too much to take advantage of this for a long period of time? The more I saw them cheerfully restraining themselves for my sake, the more I should be sorry for their pains. We have a right to lean, but not to lie down so heavily, on others, or to find our support in their ruin, like the man who had little children's throats cut to use their blood to cure a disease of his own. Or that other, who was furnished with tender young girls to keep his old limbs warm at night, and mingle the sweetness of their breath with the sourness and oppressiveness of his. I should be prone to recommend Venice to myself for retirement in such a feeble condition of life.

ᶜDecrepitude is a solitary quality. I am sociable to excess. Yet it seems reasonable to me that henceforth I should withdraw my troublesome self from the sight of the world and brood on it by myself, that I should shrink back and retire into my shell like a tortoise. I am learning to see men without clinging to them; that would be an outrage in so steep a pass. It is time to turn my back on company.

ᴮ"But on such a long journey you will be forced to stop miserably in some hovel where you will lack everything." Most of the

necessary things I carry around with me. And then, we cannot escape Fortune if she undertakes to attack us. I need nothing extraordinary when I am sick; what nature cannot do for me, I do not want to have done by a pill. At the very beginning of my fevers and the maladies that lay me low, while still whole and in the neighborhood of health, I reconcile myself with God by the last Christian offices, and find myself thereby more free and unburdened, feeling all the more triumphant over the sickness. Of notary and counsel I have less need than of physicians. What affairs of mine I shall not have settled when quite well, let no one expect me to settle when sick. What I mean to do for the service of death is always done; I should not dare delay it a single day. And if there is nothing done, that will mean either that doubt has put off my choice – for sometimes not to choose is to choose well – or that I have quite decided to do nothing.

I write my book for few men and for few years. If it had been durable matter, it would have had to be committed to a more stable language.[13] In view of the continual variation that has prevailed in ours up to now, who can hope that its present form will be in use fifty years from now? ᶜIt slips out of our hands every day, and has halfway changed since I have been alive. We say that at this moment it is perfected. Every century says as much of its own. I have no mind to think that of it as long as it flees and changes form as it does. It is for the good and useful writings to nail it to themselves, and its credit will go as go the fortunes of our state.

ᴮTherefore I do not fear to insert a number of personal items, whose usefulness will not extend beyond this generation, and which touch on things particularly known to some who will see further into them than those of ordinary understanding. After all this I do not want people to go on debating, as I often see them troubling the memory of the dead: "He thought thus, he lived thus; he wanted this; if he had spoken as he was dying, he would have said, he would have given. . . . I knew him better than anyone else." Now, as far as decency permits me, I here make known my inclinations and feelings; but I do so more freely and willingly by word of mouth to anyone who wishes to be informed of them. At all events, in these memoirs, if you look around, you will find that I have said everything or suggested everything. What I cannot express I point to with my finger:

13 Latin.

> But if you have a penetrating mind,
> These little tracks will serve the rest to find.
> LUCRETIUS

I leave nothing about me to be desired or guessed. If people are to talk about me, I want it to be truly and justly. I would willingly come back from the other world to give the lie to any man who portrayed me other than I was, even if it were to honor me. Even the living, I perceive, are spoken of otherwise than they really are. And if I had not supported with all my strength a friend that I lost, they would have torn him into a thousand contrasting appearances.[14]

To finish telling my feeble humors, I confess that in my travels I hardly ever come to my lodgings without the question passing through my mind whether I could be sick and dying there in comfort. I want to be lodged in a place that I will have all to myself, not noisy, or dirty, or smoky, or stuffy. I try to humor death by these frivolous circumstances, or rather to relieve myself of any other encumbrance, so that I can give my attention exclusively to it, which will easily weigh me down enough without any other load. I want death to have a share in the ease and comfort of my life. It is a great and important part of it, and I hope that from this day forth it will not belie the past.

Death has some shapes that are easier than others, and assumes different qualities according to each man's fancy. Among natural deaths, that which comes from enfeeblement and stupor seems to me gentle and pleasant. Among violent ones, I picture less comfortably falling from a precipice than being crushed by a falling building, and a piercing sword thrust than a harquebus shot; and I would rather have drunk the potion of Socrates than stabbed myself like Cato. And, though it is all one, yet my imagination feels as great a difference between throwing myself into a fiery furnace and into

14 Montaigne is speaking about La Boétie. Here the 1588 edition added: "I know well that I will leave behind no sponsor anywhere near as affectionate and understanding about me as I was about him. There is no one to whom I would be willing to entrust myself fully for a portrait; he alone enjoyed my true image, and carried it away. That is why I myself decipher myself so painstakingly." In the Bordeaux Copy, after "portrait," Montaigne added and then crossed out: "and if there should be any, I repudiate them, for I know them to be excessively prejudiced in my favor." All this was deleted presumably out of consideration for Montaigne's "covenant daughter" and literary executrix, Marie de Gournay.

the channel of a shallow river, as between death and life. ᶜSo foolishly does our fear consider the means more than the result! ᴮIt is only an instant; but it is of such gravity that I would willingly give several days of my life to go through it in my own way.

Since each man in his imagination finds it more or less bitter, since each man has some choice between forms of dying, let us try a little further to find one that is free from all unpleasantness. Might we not make it even voluptuous, as did the "partners in death" of Antony and Cleopatra? I leave aside the harsh and exemplary achievements of philosophy and religion. But among men of little account there have been some, such as a Petronius and a Tigillinus in Rome, who, pledged to kill themselves, put death as it were to sleep by the comfort of their preparations. They made it flow and glide past amid the laxity of their customary pastimes, among wenches and gay companions: no talk of consolation, no mention of a will, no ambitious affectation of constancy, no discourse about their future state, but amidst games, feasting, jests, common and ordinary conversation, music, and amorous verse. Could we not imitate this resoluteness with more decent behavior? Since there are deaths good for fools, deaths good for wise men, let us find some that are good for people in between.

ᶜIn my imagination I can conceive of an easy and – since die we must – comparatively desirable form of death. The Roman tyrants thought they were giving his life to a criminal when they gave him the choice of his death. But was not Theophrastus, a philosopher so delicate, modest, and wise, forced by reason to dare to speak this line, Latinized by Cicero:

> Fortune, not wisdom, rules the life of man.

How easy fortune makes it for me to trade in my life, having placed it in such a position that henceforth it is neither necessary nor a hindrance to anyone! It is a condition that I would have accepted at any season of my life, but now that it is time to pack up my odds and ends and strap my bags, I take most particular pleasure in giving scarcely any pleasure or displeasure to anyone by dying. Fortune has contrived, by an artful compensation, that those who can hope for some material profit from my death will receive at the same time a material loss from it. Death often weighs heavier on us by its weight on others, and pains us by their pain almost as much as by our own, and sometimes even more.

[B]Among the comforts I seek in lodgings I do not include pomp or large size – rather, I hate them – but a certain simple cleanliness which is more often met with in places where there is less art, and which Nature honors with a certain grace that is all her own. *A meal where not abundance but neatness prevails* [Lipsius]. *More wit than expense* [C. Nepos].

And then, the people who are likely to be surprised by death on the road are those whom business forces to go through the Grisons in midwinter. I, who travel most often for my pleasure, do not direct myself so badly. If it looks ugly on the right, I take the left; if I find myself unfit to ride my horse, I stop. And in so doing I truly see nothing that is not as pleasant and comfortable as my own house. It is true that I find superfluity always superfluous, and feel uneasy even amid delicacy and abundance. Have I left something unseen behind me? I go back; it is still on my road. I trace no fixed line, either straight or crooked. Do I fail to find what I have been told about, in the place I go? As it often happens that the judgments of others do not agree with mine – and I have found them more often wrong – I do not regret my trouble; I have learned that what they told me about was not there.

I have as adaptable a constitution and as ordinary tastes as any man in the world. The diversity in fashions from one nation to another affects me only with the pleasure of variety. Each custom has its reason. Let there be plates of tin, wood, or earthenware, boiled meat or roast, butter or nut oil or olive oil, hot or cold food, it is all the same to me – so much the same that, as I grow older, I blame this liberal capacity and shall need to be fastidious and choosy to check my indiscriminate appetite and to give a rest to my stomach now and then.

[C]When I have been outside of France and people have asked me, out of courtesy, if I wanted to be served in French fashion, I have laughed at the idea and made straight for the tables thickest with foreigners. [B]I am ashamed to see my countrymen besotted with that stupid disposition to shy away from ways contrary to their own; they think they are out of their element when they are out of their village. Wherever they go, they stick to their ways and abominate foreign ones. Do they find a compatriot in Hungary, they celebrate this adventure: see them rally round and join forces, and condemn all the barbarous customs that they see. Why not barbarous, since they are not French? Still, these are the ablest ones, who have noticed them enough to abuse them. Most of them take the trip only for the

return. They travel covered and wrapped in a taciturn and incommunicative prudence, defending themselves from the contagion of an unknown atmosphere.

What I am saying about these men reminds me of what I have sometimes observed, in a similar situation, in some of our young courtiers. They stick exclusively with men of their own sort, and look upon us as people from the other world, with contempt or pity. Take away from them their talk of the mysteries of court, and they are out of their field, as green and clumsy to us as we are to them. It is very truly said that a well-bred man is an all-round man.

On the contrary, I travel very fed up with our own ways, not to look for Gascons in Sicily – I have enough of them at home; I rather look for Greeks and Persians; these men I talk to, I study; it is to them I attune and apply myself. And what is more, it seems to me that I have encountered hardly any customs that are not as good as ours. I am not risking much, for I have hardly been out of sight of my weathervanes.

For the rest, most of the chance company you meet on the road is more of a nuisance than a pleasure. I do not attach myself to it, especially now that old age sets me somewhat alone and apart from the common ways. You suffer for others, or others for you; both discomforts are painful, but the latter seems to me even harsher. It is rare good fortune, but inestimably comforting, to have a worthy man, of sound understanding and ways that conform with yours, who likes to go with you. I have missed such a man extremely on all my travels. But such company must have been chosen and acquired before you leave home.

No pleasure has any savor for me without communication. Not even a merry thought comes to my mind without my being vexed at having produced it alone without anyone to offer it to. *If wisdom were given me on this condition, that I keep it hidden and unuttered, I should reject it* [Seneca]. The other raised it a tone higher: *If such a life were granted a wise man that, with an abundance of all things pouring in, he could have full leisure to consider and contemplate everything worth knowing, still, if his solitude were such that he could never see a human being, he would abandon life* [Cicero]. I like the idea of Archytas, that it would be unpleasant to be even in heaven and to wander among those great and divine celestial bodies, without the presence of a companion.

But still it is better to be alone than in boring and foolish company. Aristippus liked to live as a stranger everywhere.

If fate permitted me my life to guide
As I myself decide,
 VIRGIL

I should choose to spend it with my rear in the saddle:

Eager to see
Where the sun's fires hold revelry,
Where clouds and rains sport humidly.
 HORACE

"Have you no more comfortable pastimes? What do you lack? Is not your house open to fine healthy air, sufficiently furnished, and more than sufficiently capacious? ^CRoyal majesty with all its pomp has put up there more than once.[15] ^BAre there not more families below yours in orderliness than there are above it in eminence? Is some extraordinary and indigestible domestic worry festering in you?

Which, planted in your breast, burns and torments you?
 ENNIUS

Where do you think you can exist without constraint and without disturbance? *Fortune never grants unmixed favors* [Q. Curtius]. Then realize that you are the only one who constrains you, and that you will follow yourself everywhere, and be sorry for yourself everywhere. For there is no satisfaction here below except for souls either brutish or divine. If a man has no contentment with such just occasion for it, where does he expect to find it? For how many thousands of men does such a condition as yours set the limit of their desires? Reform yourself alone, for in that your power is complete, whereas your only right toward fortune is patience. ^C*There is no peace and quiet except that which reason has contrived* [Seneca]."

^BI see the reasonableness of this admonition, and see it perfectly well; but it would have been quicker and more to the point to tell me in a word: "Be wise." This resolution is beyond wisdom; it is wisdom's work and product. The physician does thus who keeps shouting at a poor languishing patient to be cheerful; he would be advising him a little less ineptly if he told him: "Be well." For my part, I am but a man of the lower sort. A salutary precept, definite, and easy to understand, is: "Be content with what is yours; that is to

15 Henry of Navarre spent the night at Montaigne once in 1584 and once in 1587.

say, with reason." Yet the execution of it is no more in the power of the wisest men than in mine. It is a popular saying, but terribly far-reaching; what does it not comprehend? All things are subject to distinction and modification.

I know well that if you take it literally, this pleasure in traveling is a testimony of restlessness and irresolution. And indeed these are our ruling and predominant qualities. Yes, I confess, I see nothing, even in a dream or a wish, that I could hold myself to; variety alone satisfies me, and the enjoyment of diversity, at least if anything satisfies me. In traveling, I am encouraged by the very fact that I can stop without loss, and that I have a place where I can turn aside from it comfortably.

I love a private life because it is by my own choice that I love it, not because of unfitness for public life, which is perhaps just as well suited to my nature. I serve my prince the more gaily because I do so by the free choice of my judgment and my reason, ^cwithout personal obligation, ^Band because I am not thrown back on his service and constrained to it by being unacceptable and unwelcome to every other party. So with the rest. I hate the morsels that necessity carves for me. Any advantage on which I had to depend exclusively would have me by the throat.

> Let one oar row in water, the other on the shore.
> PROPERTIS

A single cord never keeps me in place. "There is vanity," you say, "in this amusement." But where is there not? And these fine precepts are vanity, and all wisdom is vanity. ^c*The Lord knoweth the thoughts of the wise, that they are vain* [Psalms; and Corinthians]. ^BThese exquisite subtleties are only fit for preaching; they are arguments that would send us all saddled into the other world. Life is a material and corporeal movement, an action which by its very essence is imperfect and irregular; I apply myself to serving it in its own way:

> We suffer each a self-made fate.
> VIRGIL

^c*We must so act as not to oppose the universal laws of nature; but, these being safeguarded, let us follow our own nature* [Cicero].
^BWhat is the use of these lofty points of philosophy on which no human being can settle, and these rules that exceed our use and our strength? I often see people propose to us patterns of life which

neither the proposer nor his hearers have any hope of following, or, what is more, any desire to follow. From this same sheet of paper on which he has just written the sentence against an adulterer, the judge steals a scrap for a billet-doux to his colleague's wife. ^CThe lady you have just been rubbing against in illicit intercourse will presently, in your very presence, cry out more bitterly against the same fault in her friend than would Portia.[16] ^BAnd some condemn men to die for crimes that they do not even regard as faults. In my youth I have seen a gentleman offer the public with one hand verses excelling both in beauty and in licentiousness, and with the other at the same moment the most contentious work on theological reform that the world has feasted on for a long time.

This is the way men behave. We let laws and precepts go their own way, we take another; not only because our character is dissolute, but often also because our opinion and judgment oppose them. Listen to a philosophical lecture: the inventiveness, the eloquence, the pertinence immediately strike your mind and stir you; there is nothing that tickles or pricks your conscience; they are not speaking to her, are they? Yet Aristo used to say that neither a bath nor a lesson is any use unless it cleans and scours. You can linger on the bark, but only after you have extracted the pith; just as after swallowing the good wine out of a beautiful cup we examine its engraving and workmanship.

In all the barracks of ancient philosophy you will find this, that the same workman publishes rules of temperance, and publishes at the same time amorous and licentious writings. ^CAnd Xenophon, in the bosom of Clinias, wrote against Aristippic sensuality. ^BIt is not that there is any miraculous conversion stirring them by fits and starts. Rather it is this: that Solon represents himself now as himself, now in the shape of a lawgiver; now he speaks for the crowd, now for himself; and for himself he takes the free and natural rules, feeling sure of firm and entire health.

> Let great physicians cure the dangerous ills.
> JUVENAL

^CAntisthenes permits the sage to love, and to do in his own way whatever he finds opportune, without attention to the laws, inasmuch as he is better advised than they, and has more knowledge

16 Portia, daughter of Cato, who killed herself on learning of the death of her husband Brutus at Philippi.

of virtue. His disciple Diogenes said to oppose reason to perturbations, confidence to fortune, nature to laws.

[B]For delicate stomachs we need strict and artificial diets. [C]Good stomachs simply follow the prescriptions of their natural appetite. [B]So do our doctors, who eat the melon and drink the new wine while they keep their patient tied down to syrups and slops.

"I do not know about their books," said the courtesan Lais, "or their wisdom, or their philosophy, but those men knock at my door as often as any others." Since our licentiousness always carries us beyond what is lawful and permitted, men have often made the precepts and laws of our life strict beyond universal reason.

> None thinks he sins enough unless he sins
> A little further than the laws permit.
> JUVENAL

It would be desirable that there should be more proportion between the command and the obedience; and a goal that we cannot reach seems unjust. There is no man so good that if he placed all his actions and thoughts under the scrutiny of the laws, he would not deserve hanging ten times in his life – even such a man that it would be a very great loss and very unjust to punish and destroy him.

> Olus, what is it to thee
> What he does with his skin, or she?
> MARTIAL

And one man might not offend the laws at all, who would not for all that deserve in any degree to be praised as a virtuous man, [C]and whom philosophy would very justly cause to be whipped: [B]so confused and uneven is this relationship.

We have no wish to be good men according to God; we cannot be so according to ourselves. Human wisdom has never yet come up to the duties that she has prescribed for herself; and if she ever did come up to them, she would prescribe herself others beyond, to which she would ever aim and aspire, so hostile to consistency is our condition. [C]Man ordains that he himself shall be necessarily at fault. He is not very clever to cut out his own duty by the pattern of a different nature than his own. To whom does he prescribe what he expects no one to do? Is it wrong of him not to do what it is impossible for him to do? The laws which condemn us not to be able, themselves accuse us for not being able.

[B]At worst, this deformed liberty to present ourselves in two aspects, the actions in one fashion and the speeches in another, may be permissible for those who tell of things; but it cannot be so for those who tell of themselves, as I do; I must go the same way with my pen as with my feet. Life in society should have some relation to other lives. The virtue of Cato was vigorous beyond the measure of his time; and for a man who took a hand in governing others, a man dedicated to the public service, it might be said that his was a righteousness, if not unrighteous, at least vain and out of season. [C]Even my own conduct, which deviates by hardly an inch from the usual, nevertheless makes me somewhat unapproachable and unsociable to my generation. I do not know if I am disgusted without reason with the world I frequent, but I do know well that it would be without reason if I complained that it was more disgusted with me than I am with it.

[B]The virtue assigned to the affairs of the world is a virtue with many bends, angles, and elbows, so as to join and adapt itself to human weakness; mixed and artificial, not straight, clean, constant, or purely innocent. The annals to this day reproach one of our kings for having given in too simply to the conscientious persuasions of his confessor. Affairs of state have bolder precepts:

> Let him who would be pure from courts retire.
>
> LUCAN

I once tried to employ in the service of public dealings ideas and rules for living as crude, green, unpolished – or unpolluted – as they were born in me or derived from my education, and which I use, [C]if not [B]conveniently, [C]at least surely, [B]in private matters: a scholastic and novice virtue. I found them inept and dangerous for such matters. He who walks in the crowd must step aside, keep his elbows in, step back or advance, even leave the straight way, according to what he encounters. He must live not so much according to himself as according to others, not according to what he proposes to himself but according to what others propose to him, according to the time, according to the men, according to the business.

[C]Plato says that whoever escapes with clean breeches from handling the affairs of the world, escapes by a miracle. And he also says that when he ordains that his philosopher shall be head of a government, he does not mean a corrupted government like that of Athens, much less one like ours, on which wisdom herself would

waste her Latin. Just as an herb transplanted to a soil very ill-suited to its nature will much rather conform to it than reform it to suit itself.

[B]I feel that if I had to train myself thoroughly for such occupations, I should need a great deal of change and reclothing for it. Even if I had enough power over myself to do that (and why couldn't I, with time and pains?), I wouldn't want to. By the little experience I have had in that profession, I am just that much disgusted with it. I sometimes feel rising in my soul the fumes of certain temptations toward ambition; but I stiffen and hold firm against them:

> But thou, Catullus, persevere, persist.
> CATULLUS

I am seldom summoned to public affairs, and I offer myself to them just as little. [C]Freedom and laziness, which are my ruling qualities, are qualities diametrically opposite to that trade.

[B]We cannot distinguish the faculties of men; they have divisions and boundaries that are delicate and hard to determine. To conclude from the competence of a man's private life some competence for public service is to conclude badly. One man guides himself well who does not guide others well, [C]and produces Essays, who cannot produce results; another [B]directs a siege well who would direct a battle badly, and talks well in private who would be bad at addressing a crowd or a prince. In fact, to be able to do one is perhaps rather evidence of inability to do the other than otherwise. [C]I find that lofty minds are hardly less adaptable to humble things than are humble minds to lofty things. Is it credible that Socrates should have given the Athenians cause to laugh at his expense because he never could count up the votes of his tribe and make a report on them to the council? Truly, the veneration I have for the perfections of that great man deserves that his fortune should furnish such a magnificent example in excuse of my principal imperfections.

[B]Our ability is cut up into little pieces. Mine has no breadth, and its pieces are wretchedly few. Saturninus said to those who had conferred on him full command: "Comrades, you have lost a good captain to make a bad general."

Whoever boasts, in a sick age like this, that he employs a pure and sincere virtue in the service of the world, either does not know what virtue is, since our ideas grow corrupt with our conduct (indeed, hear them portray it, hear most of them glorying in their behavior and making their rules; instead of portraying virtue, they

portray injustice pure and simple, and vice, and present it thus falsified for the education of princes), or, if he does know, he boasts wrongly, and, say what he will, does a thousand things of which his conscience accuses him. I would willingly take Seneca's word about the experience he had in such circumstances, provided he was willing to tell me about it openheartedly. The most honorable mark of goodness in such a predicament is to acknowledge freely our fault and that of others, to resist and hold back with all our power the inclination toward evil, to go down that slope unwillingly, to hope for the better and desire the better.

I perceive that in the strife that is tearing France to pieces and dividing us into factions, each man labors to defend his cause – but even the best of them resort to dissimulation and lying. Whoever would write about them roundly would write about them rashly and harmfully. The justest party is still a member of a worm-eaten and maggoty body. But in such a body the least diseased member is called healthy; and quite rightly, since our qualities have no titles except by comparison. Civic innocence is measured according to the places and the times.

I should like very much to see in Xenophon a eulogy of Agesilaus such as this: that Agesilaus, asked by a neighboring prince with whom he had once been at war to let him pass across his territories, granted the request, giving him passage across the Peloponnesus, and not only did not imprison him or poison him, having him at his mercy, but welcomed him courteously, without doing him any harm. To natures like Xenophon's, that would not be saying anything; elsewhere and in other times men will take account of the honesty and magnanimity of such an action. The wretched monkeys in our schools would have laughed at it, so little does Spartan innocence resemble French.

We are not without virtuous men, but only by our standards. Whoever has morals established and regulated above his time, either let him twist or blunt his rules, or, what I rather advise him, let him withdraw apart and have nothing to do with us. What would he gain by it?

If I discern a man in holiness and virtue rare,
To a two-headed child this freak of nature I compare,
Or to a pregnant mule, or fish found 'neath the plowman's share.
 JUVENAL

We may regret better times, but not escape the present; we may

wish for different magistrates, but we must nevertheless obey those that are here. And perhaps there is more merit in obeying the bad than the good. As long as the image of the ancient and accepted laws of this monarchy shines in some corner, there will I be planted. If by bad fortune they come to contradict and interfere with each other, and produce two sides dubious and difficult to choose between, my choice is likely to be to steal away and escape from that tempest; in the meantime nature may lend me a hand, or the hazards of war. Between Caesar and Pompey I should have declared myself openly. But among those three robbers[17] who came after, I should have had either to hide, or to follow with the wind, which I consider permissible when reason no longer guides.

> Whither do you leave the course?
>
> VIRGIL

This stuffing is a little out of my subject. I go out of my way, but rather by license than carelessness. My ideas follow one another, but sometimes it is from a distance, and look at each other, but with a sidelong glance. ^cI have run my eyes over a certain dialogue of Plato,[18] a fantastic motley in two parts, the beginning part about love, all the rest about rhetoric. The ancients do not fear these changes, and with wonderful grace they let themselves thus be tossed in the wind, or seem to. ^BThe titles of my chapters do not always embrace their matter; often they only denote it by some sign, like those other ^ctitles, *The Maid of Andros*, *The Eunuch*,[19] or those other ^Bnames, Sulla, Cicero, Torquatus. I love the poetic gait, by leaps and gambols. ^cIt is an art, as Plato says, light, flighty, daemonic. There are works of Plutarch's in which he forgets his theme, in which the treatment of his subject is found only incidentally, quite smothered in foreign matter. See his movements in "The Daemon of Socrates." Lord, what beauty there is in these lusty sallies and this variation, and more so the more casual and accidental they seem.

It is the inattentive reader who loses my subject, not I. Some word about it will always be found off in a corner, which will not fail to be sufficient, though it takes little room. ^BI seek out change indiscriminately and tumultuously. ^cMy style and my mind alike go roaming. ^B"A man must be a little mad if he does not want to be

17 Antony, Octavius, Lepidus.
18 The *Phaedrus*.
19 Two comedies of Terence.

even more stupid," ^csay the precepts of our masters, and even more so their examples.

^BA thousand poets drag and languish prosaically; but the best ancient prose – ^cand I scatter it here indiscriminately as verse – ^Bshines throughout with the vigor and boldness of poetry, and gives the effect of its frenzy. To poetry we must certainly concede mastery and preeminence in speech. ^CThe poet, says Plato, seated on the tripod of the Muses, pours out in a frenzy whatever comes into his mouth, like the spout of a fountain, without ruminating and weighing it; and from him escape things of different colors and contradictory substance in an intermittent flow. He himself is utterly poetic, and the old theology is poetry, the scholars say, and the first philosophy. It is the original language of the Gods.

^BI want the matter to make its own divisions. It shows well enough where it changes, where it concludes, where it begins, where it resumes, without my interlacing it with words, with links and seams introduced for the benefit of weak or heedless ears, and without writing glosses on myself. Who is there that would not rather not be read than be read sleepily or in passing? ^c*Nothing is so useful that it can be of value when taken on the run* [Seneca]. If to take up books were to take them in, and if to see them were to consider them, and to run through them were to grasp them, I should be wrong to make myself out quite as ignorant as I say I am.

^BSince I cannot arrest the attention of the reader by weight, it is all to the good if I chance to arrest it by my embroilment. "True, but he will afterward repent of having wasted his time over it." That may be, but still he will have wasted his time over it. And then there are natures like that, in whom understanding breeds disdain, who will think the better of me because they will not know what I mean. They will conclude that my meaning is profound from its obscurity, which, to speak in all earnest, I hate very strongly, and I would avoid it if I could avoid myself. Aristotle somewhere boasts of affecting it: blameworthy affectation!

^CBecause such frequent breaks into chapters as I used at the beginning seemed to me to disrupt and dissolve attention before it was aroused, making it disdain to settle and collect for so little, I have begun making them longer, requiring fixed purpose and assigned leisure. In such an occupation, if you will not give a man a single hour, you will not give him anything. And you do nothing for a man for whom you do nothing except while

doing something else. Besides, perhaps I have some personal obligation to speak only by halves, to speak confusedly, to speak discordantly.

[B]I was about to say that I am ill-disposed toward that kill-joy reason; and that if those extravagant projects that torment our lives, and those wondrously subtle ideas, have any truth in them, I consider it too expensive and inconvenient. On the contrary, I apply myself to make use of vanity itself, and asininity, if it brings me any pleasure, and let myself follow my natural inclinations without examining them too closely.

I have seen elsewhere[20] ruined houses, and statues both divine and human: it is always man we are dealing with. All that is true; and yet I could not revisit the tomb of that great and mighty city so often that I would not marvel at it and revere it. The care of the dead is recommended to us. Now, I have been brought up from childhood with these dead. I was familiar with the affairs of Rome long before I was with those of my own house. I knew the Capitol and its location before I knew the Louvre, and the Tiber before the Seine. I have had the abilities and fortunes of Lucullus, Metellus, and Scipio more in my head than those of any of our men. They are dead. So indeed is my father, as completely as they; and he has moved as far from me and from life in eighteen years as they have in sixteen hundred. Nevertheless I do not cease to embrace and cherish his memory, his friendship, and his society, in a union that is perfect and very much alive.

Indeed, by inclination I pay greater service to the dead. They can no longer help themselves; therefore they need my help all the more, it seems to me. It is here that gratitude shows in its proper luster. A benefit is less richly bestowed when there is reciprocity and return. Arcesilaus, visiting [C]Ctesibius, [B]who was sick, and finding him poorly off, very quietly slipped under his pillow some money he was giving him; and by concealing it from him, gave him also release from gratitude. Those who have deserved friendship and gratitude from me have never lost it through being no longer there; I have paid them better and more carefully in their absence and ignorance. I speak more affectionately of my friends when there is no way left for them to know of it.

20 Elsewhere than in Rome. Montaigne's mind is already so full of Rome as he starts this paragraph that he seems to forget he has not yet mentioned it in this connection.

Now, I have started a hundred quarrels in defense of Pompey and for the cause of Brutus. This friendship still endures between us; even present things we hold only by imagination. Finding myself useless for this age, I throw myself back upon that other, and am so bewitched by it that the state of that ancient Rome, free, just, and flourishing (for I love neither her birth nor her old age), interests me passionately. Therefore I cannot revisit so often the site of their streets and houses and those ruins stretching deep down to the Antipodes, that I do not muse over them. ^CIs it by nature or by an error of the imagination that the sight of the places we know were frequented and inhabited by people whose memory is held in honor, somehow stirs us more than hearing the story of their deeds or reading their writings? *Such is the power of places to call up memories. And in this city this is infinite; for wherever we walk we set our foot on history* [Cicero]. ^BI like to reflect on their faces, their bearing, and their clothes. I chew over those great names between my teeth and make them resound in my ears. ^C*I venerate them and always rise to honor such great names* [Seneca]. ^BOf things that are in some part great and admirable, I admire even the common parts. I would enjoy seeing them talk, walk, and sup. It would be ingratitude to despise the remains and images of so many worthy and most valiant men, whom I have seen live and die, and who give us so many good instructions by their example, if we only knew how to follow them.

And then, this very Rome that we behold deserves our love, allied for so long and by so many claims to our crown: the only common and universal city. The sovereign magistrate who commands there is acknowledged equally elsewhere. It is the metropolitan city of all Christian nations; the Spaniard and the Frenchman, every man is at home there. To be one of the princes of that state one need only be of Christendom, wherever it may be. There is no place here below that heaven has embraced with such favorable influence and such constancy. Her very ruin is glorious and stately:

^CMore precious for her memorable ruins.
 SIDONIUS APOLLINARIS

^BEven in the tomb she retains some marks and the picture of empire. ^C*That it may be manifest that in one place Nature rejoiced in her work* [Pliny].

^BSome might blame themselves and rebel inwardly at being tickled by so vain a pleasure. Our humors are not too vain if they are pleasant; whatever they may be, if they give constant

contentment to a man capable of common sense, I would not have the heart to pity him.

I owe much to Fortune in that up to this point she has done nothing hostile to me, at least nothing beyond my endurance. Might it not be her way to leave in peace those who do not trouble her?

> The more a man himself denies,
> The more to that man Heaven supplies.
> Since I am naked, I aspire
> To join the men who nought desire...
> For they lack much who much require.
>
> HORACE

If she continues, she will send me hence well contented and satisfied:

> For nothing more do I annoy the gods.
>
> HORACE

But beware the crash. There are thousands who are wrecked in port.

I easily console myself for what will happen here when I am here no longer; present things keep me busy enough,

> The rest I leave to Fortune.
>
> OVID

Besides, I do not have that strong bond that they say attaches men to the future by the children who bear their name and their honor;[21] and perhaps I ought to desire them all the less, if they are so desirable. I am only too much attached to the world and to this life by myself. I am content to be in Fortune's grip by the circumstances strictly necessary to my existence, without extending her jurisdiction over me in other directions; and I have never thought that to be without children was a want that should make life less complete and less contented. The sterile profession has its advantages too. Children are numbered among the things that we have no great reason to desire, especially at this time when it would be so hard to make them good. *Nothing good can be produced now, so corrupted are the seeds* [Tertullian]. And yet, once acquired, they give one good reason to regret their loss.

He who left me in charge of my house predicted that I was due to ruin it, considering how little I was inclined toward domesticity. He

21 Montaigne had one daughter, but no sons.

was mistaken; here I am as when I first came into it, if not a little better off; yet without public office and without benefice.

For the rest, if Fortune has done me no violent or extraordinary injury, neither has she done me any great favor. All her gifts that my house enjoys were there more than a hundred years before me. For my own part I possess no essential and solid benefit that I owe to her liberality. She has done me some windy favors, honorary and titular, without substance, and, in truth, did not merely grant them, but offered them to me unasked, Lord knows; to me who am wholly material, whom only reality satisfies, and a very massive reality, and who, if I dared confess it, should not judge avarice much less excusable than ambition, or pain less to be avoided than shame, or health less desirable than learning, or riches than nobility.

Among her empty favors there is none that so pleases that silly humor in me which feeds upon it, as an authentic bull of Roman citizenship, which was granted to me lately when I was there, pompous in seals and gilt letters, and granted with all gracious liberality. And because these bulls are given in various styles, more or less favorable, and because before I had seen one I would have been very glad to have been shown their formula, I will, to satisfy some person, if anyone is sick with the same curiosity as mine, transcribe it here in due form:

ON THE REPORT MADE TO THE SENATE BY ORAZIO MAS-SIMI, MARZO CECIO, ALESSANDRO MUTI, CONSERVATORS OF OUR FAIR CITY, CONCERNING THE RIGHT OF ROMAN CITIZENSHIP TO BE GRANTED TO THE MOST ILLUSTRI-OUS MICHEL DE MONTAIGNE, KNIGHT OF THE ORDER OF SAINT MICHAEL AND GENTLEMAN OF THE CHAMBER IN ORDINARY TO THE MOST CHRISTIAN KING, THE SENATE AND PEOPLE OF ROME HAVE DECREED:

Considering that, by ancient custom and practice, those men have ever been adopted among us with ardor and eagerness, who, distinguished in virtue and nobility, have been greatly useful and ornamental to our Republic, or might be so in the future; We, deeply moved by the example and authority of our ancestors, resolve that we should imitate and follow this noble custom. Wherefore, since the most illustrious Michel de Montaigne, Knight of the Order of Saint Michael, and Gentleman of the Chamber in ordinary to the Most Christian King, is most zealous for the Roman name, and, by the honor and distinction of his family and his own virtuous merits, most worthy to be admitted to Roman citizenship by the supreme judgment and will of the Senate and People of Rome: it has pleased the Senate and People of Rome that

the most illustrious Michel de Montaigne, adorned with all qualities and
very dear to this noble people, should be inscribed as a Roman citizen, himself
and his posterity, and invested with all the advantages and honors enjoyed by
those who were born Citizens and Patricians of Rome, or who have been
made such by the best of rights. Wherein the Senate and People of Rome
consider that they do not so much confer the Rights of Citizenship on him as
a gift, as pay them as a debt, nor do him more benefit than they receive from
him, who, in accepting this Citizenship, gives a singular ornament and honor
to the City itself. Which Senatus-Consultus these Conservators have caused to
be transcribed by the secretaries of the Roman Senate and People and
deposited in the archives of the Capitol, and have had this act drawn up
and sealed with the common seal of the City. In the year 2331 since the
foundation of Rome, A.D. 1581, 13th of March.

ORAZIO FOSCO
Secretary of the Sacred Senate
and of the People of Rome

VINCENTE MARTOLI
Secretary of the Sacred Senate
and of the People of Rome[22]

Being a citizen of no city, I am very pleased to be one of the
noblest city that ever was or ever will be. If others examined
themselves attentively, as I do, they would find themselves, as I do,
full of inanity and nonsense. Get rid of it I cannot without getting
rid of myself. We are all steeped in it, one as much as another; but
those who are aware of it are a little better off – though I don't know.

This common attitude and habit of looking elsewhere than at
ourselves has been very useful for our own business. We are an object
that fills us with discontent; we see nothing in us but misery and
vanity. In order not to dishearten us, Nature has very appropriately
thrown the action of our vision outward. We go forward with the
current, but to turn our course back toward ourselves is a painful
movement: thus the sea grows troubled and turbulent when it is
tossed back on itself. Look, says everyone, at the movement of the
heavens, look at the public, look at that man's quarrel, at this man's
pulse, at another man's will; in short, always look high or low, or to
one side, or in front, or behind you.

It was a paradoxical command that was given us of old by that
god at Delphi: "Look into yourself, know yourself, keep to yourself;

22 Montaigne quotes the entire document in the original Latin. For the trouble
it took him to get it, see *Travel Journal*, p. 1174.

bring back your mind and your will, which are spending themselves elsewhere, into themselves; you are running out, you are scattering yourself; concentrate yourself, resist yourself; you are being betrayed, dispersed, and stolen away from yourself. Do you not see that this world keeps its sight all concentrated inward and its eyes open to contemplate itself? It is always vanity for you, within and without; but it is less vanity when it is less extensive. Except for you, O man," said that god, "each thing studies itself first, and, according to its needs, has limits to its labors and desires. There is not a single thing as empty and needy as you, who embrace the universe: you are the investigator without knowledge, the magistrate without jurisdiction, and all in all, the fool of the farce."

10
Of husbanding your will

ᴮIn comparison with most men, few things touch me, or, to put it better, hold me; for it is right that things should touch us, provided they do not possess us. I take great care to augment by study and reasoning this privilege of insensibility, which is naturally well advanced in me. I espouse, and in consequence grow passionate about, few things. My sight is clear, but I fix it on few objects; my sensitivity is delicate and tender. But my perception and application are hard and deaf: I do not engage myself easily. As much as I can, I employ myself entirely upon myself; and even in that subject I would still fain bridle my affection and keep it from plunging in too entirely, since this is a subject that I possess at the mercy of others, and over which fortune has more right than I have. So that even in regard to health, which I so esteem, I ought not to desire it and give myself to it so frantically as to find illnesses therefore unbearable. ᶜOne must moderate oneself between hatred of pain and love of pleasure; and Plato prescribes a middle way of life between the two.

ᴮBut the passions that distract me from myself and attach me elsewhere, those in truth I oppose with all my strength. My opinion is that we must lend ourselves to others and give ourselves only to ourselves. If my will happened to be prone to mortgage and attach itself, I would not last: I am too tender, both by nature and by practice,

Fleeing affairs, and born in idle ease.
OVID

To engage in contested disputes only to see my opponent get the better of me, or to have to turn back red-faced after giving hot pursuit, might well vex me cruelly. If I were to bite off as much as others do, my soul would never have the strength to bear the alarms and emotions that afflict those who embrace so much; it would be put out of joint from the start by this inner agitation.

If people have sometimes pushed me into the management of other men's affairs, I have promised to take them in hand, not in lungs and liver; to take them on my shoulders, not incorporate them into me; to be concerned over them, yes; to be impassioned over them, never. I look to them, but I do not brood over them. I have enough to do to order and arrange the domestic pressures that oppress my entrails and veins, without giving myself the trouble of adding extraneous pressures to them; I am enough involved in my essential, proper, and natural affairs, without inviting in foreign ones.

Those who know how much they owe to themselves, and for how many duties they are obligated to themselves, find that nature has given them in this a commission full enough and not at all idle. You have quite enough to do at home; don't go away.

Men give themselves for hire. Their faculties are not for them, they are for those to whom they enslave themselves; their tenants are at home inside, not they. This common humor I do not like. We must husband the freedom of our soul and mortgage it only on the right occasions; which are in very small number, if we judge sanely. See the people who have been taught to let themselves be seized and carried away: they do so everywhere, in little things as in big, in what does not touch them as in what does; they push in indiscriminately wherever there is business ᶜand involvement, ᴮand are without life when they are without tumultuous agitation. ᶜ*They are in business for business' sake* [Seneca]. They seek business only for busyness.

It is not that they want to be on the go, so much as that they cannot keep still; no more nor less than a stone that has started falling, and that does not stop until it comes to rest. Occupation is to a certain manner of people a mark of ability and dignity. ᴮTheir mind seeks its repose in movement, like children in the cradle. They may be said to be as serviceable to their friends as they are importunate to themselves. No one distributes his money to others, everyone distributes his time and his life on them. There is nothing of which we are so prodigal as of the only things in which avarice would be useful to us and laudable.

I take a wholly different attitude. I keep myself to myself, and commonly desire mildly what I desire, and desire little; occupy and busy myself likewise: rarely and tranquilly. Whatever they desire and take in hand, they do with all their will and vehemence. There are so many bad spots that, for greatest safety, we must slide over this world a bit lightly and on the surface. ᶜWe must glide over it, not break through into it. ᴮEven sensual pleasure is painful in its depth:

> Treacherous ashes hide
> The fires through which you stride.
>
> HORACE

Messieurs of Bordeaux[1] elected me mayor of their city when I was far from France and still farther from such a thought. I excused myself, but I was informed that I was wrong, since the king's command also figured in the matter. It is an office that must appear all the handsomer for this, that it has no remuneration or gain other than the honor of its execution. The term is two years; but it can be extended by a second election, which happens very rarely. This was done in my case, and had been done only twice before: some years earlier to Monsieur de Lansac, and recently to Monsieur de Biron, Marshal of France, to whose place I succeeded; and I left mine to Monsieur de Matignon, also Marshal of France, proud of such noble company,

> ᶜEach a good minister in peace and war.
>
> VIRGIL

ᴮFortune willed to have a hand in my promotion by this particular circumstance that she put in of her own. Not wholly vain: for Alexander disdained the Corinthian ambassadors who were offering him citizenship in their city; but when they came to tell him that Bacchus and Hercules were also on that list, he thanked them graciously for their offer.

On my arrival I deciphered myself to them faithfully and conscientiously, exactly such as I feel myself to be: without memory, without vigilance, without experience, and without vigor; also without hate, without ambition, without avarice, and without violence; so that they should be informed and instructed about what they were to expect of my service. And because their knowledge of my

1 The jurats, who formed a sort of municipal council.

late father had alone incited them to this, and their honor for his memory,[2] I added very clearly that I should be very sorry if anything whatsoever were to weigh so heavily on my will as their affairs and their city had formerly done on his, while he was administering it in this same spot to which they had called me.

I remembered in my boyhood having seen him old, his soul cruelly agitated by this public turmoil, forgetting the sweet air of his home, to which the weakness of years had attached him long since, and his household and his health; and, truly heedless of his life, which he nearly lost in this, engaged for them in long and painful journeys. He was like that; and this disposition in him sprang from a great goodness of nature: there was never a more kindly and public-spirited soul.

This course, which I commend in others, I do not love to follow, and I am not without excuse. He had heard it said that we must forget ourselves for our neighbor, that the individual was not to be considered at all in comparison with the general.

Most of the rules and precepts of the world take this course of pushing us out of ourselves and driving us into the market place, for the benefit of public society. They thought to achieve a fine result by diverting and distracting us from ourselves, assuming that we were attached to ourselves only too much and by too natural a bond; and they have spared no words to that end. For it is not new for the sages to preach things as they serve, not as they are. ᶜTruth has its inconveniences, disadvantages, and incompatibilities with us. We must often be deceived that we may not deceive ourselves, and our eyes sealed, our understanding stunned, in order to redress and amend them. *For it is the ignorant who judge, and they must frequently be deceived, lest they err* [Quintilian]. ᴮWhen they order us to love three, four, fifty degrees of things before ourselves, they imitate the technique of the archers who, to hit the mark, take aim a great distance above the target. To straighten a bent stick you bend it back the other way.

I think that in the temple of Pallas, as we see in all other religions, there were apparent mysteries to be shown to the people, and other mysteries, more secret and high, to be shown only to those

2 Probably Montaigne sincerely believed this; but it now seems more likely that he was elected because he was the man most acceptable to all four royal personages concerned with the election: Henry III, Catherine de' Medici, Henry of Navarre, and Margaret of Valois. See Alexandre Nicolaï, *Les Belles Amies de Montaigne* (1950), pp. 135–45.

who were initiated. It is likely that among the latter is to be found the true point of the friendship that each man owes to himself. Not ᶜa false friendship, that makes us embrace glory, learning, riches, and such things with paramount and immoderate affection, as members of our being; nor ᴮan overindulgent and undiscriminating friendship, in which it happens as we see with ivy, that it decays and ruins the wall it clings to; but a salutary and well-regulated friendship, useful and pleasant alike. He who knows its duties and practices them, he is truly of the cabinet of the Muses; he has attained the summit of human wisdom and of our happiness. This man, knowing exactly what he owes to himself, finds it in his part that he is to apply to himself his experience of other men and of the world, and, in order to do so, contribute to public society the duties and services within his province. ᶜHe who lives not at all unto others, hardly lives unto himself. *He who is a friend to himself, know that that man is a friend to all* [Seneca].

ᴮThe main responsibility of each of us is his own conduct; ᶜand that is what we are here for. ᴮJust as anyone who should forget to live a good and saintly life, and think he was quit of his duty by guiding and training others to do so, would be a fool; even so he who abandons healthy and gay living of his own to serve others thereby, takes, to my taste, a bad and unnatural course.

I do not want a man to refuse, to the charges he takes on, attention, steps, words, and sweat and blood if need be:

> To die for what is dear,
> Country or friends, I do not fear.
> HORACE

But this is by way of loan and accidentally, the mind holding itself ever in repose and in health, not without action, but without vexation, without passion. Simply to act costs it so little that it is acting even in sleep. But it must be set in motion with discretion. For the body receives the loads that are placed on it exactly according as they are; the mind often extends them and makes them heavier to its cost, giving them the measurements it sees fit. We do like things with different degrees of effort and tension of the will. The one goes very well without the other.[3] For how many people risk themselves every day in the wars, which are no concern to them, and press forward to the dangers of battles, the loss of which will not trouble their next

3 Action without passion.

night's sleep! This man in his own house, outside of this danger which he would not have dared to face, is more passionate about the outcome of this war, and more worked up in his soul about it, than the soldier who is spending his blood and his life in it.

I have been able to take part in public office without departing one nail's breadth from myself, ᶜand to give myself to others without taking myself from myself. ᴮThis fierceness and violence of desire hinders more than it serves the performance of what we undertake, fills us with impatience toward things that come out contrary or late, and with bitterness and suspicion toward the people we deal with. We never conduct well the thing that possesses and conducts us:

> ᶜPassion handles all things ill.
> STATIUS

ᴮHe who employs in it only his judgment and skill proceeds more gaily. He feints, he bends, he postpones entirely at his ease according to the need of the occasions; he misses the target without torment or affliction, and remains intact and ready for a new undertaking; he always walks bridle in hand. In the man who is intoxicated with a violent and tyrannical intensity of purpose we see of necessity much imprudence and injustice; the impetuosity of his desire carries him away. These are reckless movements, and, unless fortune lends them a great hand, of little fruit.

Philosophy wills that in chastising injuries received we keep anger out of it, not so that the vengeance may be less, but on the contrary so that it may be all the better dealt out and heavier; which purposes, so philosophy thinks, this impetuosity hinders. ᶜNot only does anger confuse, but of itself it also tires, the arms of those who chastise. That fire benumbs and consumes their strength. ᴮAs in precipitancy – *more haste, less speed* [Quintus Curtius] – haste trips itself up, hobbles and stops itself. ᶜ*Speed gets itself tangled up* [Seneca]. ᴮFor example, according to what I see by ordinary experience, avarice has no greater impediment than itself: the more tense and vigorous it is, the less fertile it is. Commonly it catches riches more promptly when masked with an image of liberality.

A friend of mine, a gentleman and a very fine man, nearly drove himself out of his mind by too passionate an attention and devotion to the affairs of a prince, his master. And that master[4] thus portrayed himself to me: that he sees the gravity of accidents like anyone else,

4 Henry of Navarre.

but in those that have no remedy he at once makes up his mind to bear them; in the others, after making the necessary provisions, which he can do promptly thanks to his quick-wittedness, he composedly awaits what may ensue. In truth, I have seen him at work, maintaining a great nonchalance and freedom in his actions and countenance throughout very great and thorny affairs. I find him greater and more capable in bad fortune than in good; ᶜhis losses are more glorious to him than his victories, and his grief than his triumph.

ᴮConsider that even in actions which are vain and frivolous, in chess, tennis, and the like, this fierce and ardent involvement of an impetuous desire instantly casts the mind and limbs into thoughtlessness and disorder: we daze and hamper ourselves. He who bears himself more moderately toward winning and losing is always self-possessed. The less he becomes excited and impassioned about the game, the more advantageously and surely he plays it.

Moreover, we impede the mind's grasp and grip by giving it so many things to seize. Some must be simply presented to it, others attached to it, others incorporated into it. It can see and feel all things, but it should feed only on itself, and should be instructed about what properly concerns it and what is properly of its own possession and its own substance. The laws of Nature teach us what we rightly need. When the sages tell us that according to Nature no one is indigent and that everyone is so according to opinion, they distinguish subtly between the desires that come from her and those that come from the disorder of our imagination; in this way: those whose limits we can see are hers, those that flee before us and whose end we cannot reach are ours. Poverty of goods is easy to cure, poverty of soul impossible.

> ᶜFor if what is enough for man could be enough,
> It were enough; but since it is not, how can I
> Suppose that any wealth my soul could satisfy?
> LUCILIUS, QUOTED BY NONIUS MARCELLUS

Socrates, seeing a great quantity of riches, jewels, and costly articles carried in pomp through his city, said: "How many things I do not desire!" ᴮMetrodorus lived on twelve ounces a day, Epicurus on less; Metrocles slept in winter with the sheep, in summer in the cloisters of the churches. ᶜ*Nature supplies what it demands* [Seneca]. Cleanthes lived by his hands and boasted that Cleanthes, if he wanted, could feed still another Cleanthes.

[B]If what Nature flatly and originally demands of us for the preservation of our being is too little – as indeed, there is no better way of expressing how little that is and how cheaply our life can be maintained than by this consideration, that it is so little as to escape the grasp and shock of fortune by its very littleness – then let us grant ourselves something further: let us also call the habits and condition of each of us *nature*; let us rate and treat ourselves according to this measure, let us stretch our appurtenances and our accounts that far. For in going thus far we certainly seem to me to have some justification. Habit is a second nature, and no less powerful. [C]What my habit lacks, I hold that I lack. [B]And I would almost as soon be deprived of life as have it reduced and cut down very far from the state in which I have lived it for so long.

I am no longer headed for any great change or inclined to plunge into a new and untried way of life, not even a better one. It is too late to become other than I am. And as I would be sorry about any great good fortune that might now fall into my hands, because it would not come at a time when I could enjoy it –

What good are Fortune's gifts if I'm denied their use?
HORACE

– [C]so likewise I[5] would complain of any inward acquisition. It is almost better never to become a good man than so late, or an expert in living when one has no more life. I, who am on my way out, would readily resign to anyone who came along what wisdom I am learning for dealing with the world. Mustard after dinner. I have no use for a good thing of which I can make no use. What good is knowledge to a man who no longer has a head? It is an insult and unkindness of fortune to offer us presents which fill us with a just resentment that they failed us in their season. Guide me no more, I can go no more. Of all the parts that ability has, patience is enough for us. Give the

5 The remainder of this paragraph and the three paragraphs that follow replace the following much shorter passage that appeared in the 1588 edition: "Likewise I achieve little reform in wisdom for the use and society of the world without regret that this improvement has come to me so late, and that I have no more leisure to use it: henceforth I need no other ability than endurance against death and old age. What is the use of a new knowledge of life in such a decline, and new skill to lead me in this path in which I have only three steps left to walk? Just to see, go and teach rhetoric to a man relegated to the deserts of Arabia. We need no art for a fall."

capacity of an excellent treble to a singer who has rotten lungs, and eloquence to a hermit relegated to the deserts of Arabia!

^BWe need no art for a fall; ^cthe end is found of itself at the conclusion of every task. My world is done for, my form is emptied; I belong entirely to the past, and I am bound to recognize it and conform my departure to it.

I want to mention this as an example: that the recent eclipsing of ten days by the Pope[6] has so taken me aback that I cannot feel comfortable with it. I belong to the years in which we reckoned differently. Such an ancient and long practice claims me and calls me back to it. I am constrained to be a bit of a heretic on that point, incapable of innovation, even when it is corrective. My imagination, in spite of me, is always casting itself ten days forward or back and muttering in my ears: "This rule concerns those who are yet to be."

If health itself, sweet as it is, happens to revisit me by fits and starts, it is rather in order to make me regret it than to return into my possession; I no longer have anywhere to harbor it. Time is forsaking me; without it nothing can be possessed. Oh, what little account I should make of those great elective dignities I see in the world which are given only to men ready to depart; in which people do not consider so much how well the duties will be discharged as how briefly they will be discharged. Right from their entry people look to their exit.

^BIn short, here I am in the act of finishing up this man, not of making another out of him. By long usage this form of mine has turned into substance, and fortune into nature.

So I say that every one of us feeble creatures is excusable for considering as his own what is comprised under this measure.[7] But it is also true that beyond these limits there is nothing left but confusion. This is the broadest extent that we can grant to our claims. The more we amplify our need and our possession, the more we involve ourselves in the blows of fortune and adversity. The range of our desires should be circumscribed and restrained to a narrow limit of the nearest and most contiguous good things; and moreover their course should be directed not in a straight line that ends up elsewhere, but in a circle whose two extremities by a short sweep meet and terminate in ourselves. Actions that are performed without this

6 The reform of the calendar by Gregory XIII, adopted in France in 1582.
7 The measure mentioned six paragraphs earlier, by which habitual needs are counted as natural.

reflexive movement, I mean a searching and genuine reflexive movement – the actions, for example, of the avaricious, the ambitious, and so many others who run in a straight line, whose course carries them ever forward – are erroneous and diseased actions.

Most of our occupations are low comedy. *The whole world plays a part* [Petronius]. We must play our part duly, but as the part of a borrowed character. Of the mask and appearance we must not make a real essence, nor of what is foreign what is our very own. We cannot distinguish the skin from the shirt. ᶜIt is enough to make up our face, without making up our heart. ᴮI see some who transform and transubstantiate themselves into as many new shapes and new beings as they undertake jobs, who are prelates to their very liver and intestines, and drag their position with them even into their privy. I cannot teach them to distinguish the tips of the hat that are for them from those that are for their office, or their retinue, or their mule. *They give themselves up so much to their fortune that they even unlearn their natures* [Quintus Curtius]. They swell and inflate their soul and their natural speech to the height of their magisterial seat.

The mayor and Montaigne have always been two, with a very clear separation. For all of being a lawyer or a financier, we must not ignore the knavery there is in such callings. An honest man is not accountable for the vice or stupidity of his trade, and should not therefore refuse to practice it: it is the custom of his country, and there is profit in it. We must live in the world and make the most of it such as we find it. But the judgment of an emperor should be above his imperial power, and see and consider it as an extraneous accident; and he should know how to find pleasure in himself apart, and to reveal himself like any Jack or Peter, at least to himself.

I do not know how to involve myself so deeply and so entirely. When my will gives me over to one party, it is not with so violent an obligation that my understanding is infected by it. In the present broils of this state, my own interest has not made me blind to either the laudable qualities in our adversaries or those that are reproachable in the men I have followed. ᶜPeople adore everything that is on their side; as for me, I do not even excuse most of the things that I see on mine. A good work does not lose its grace for pleading against my cause.

ᴮExcept for the knot of the controversy I have maintained my equanimity and pure indifference. ᶜ*And beyond the necessities of war I bear no special hatred* [adapted from Livy]. ᴮFor which I am pleased with myself, inasmuch as I see men commonly fail in the opposite

direction. ^C*Let him make use of passion who cannot make use of reason* [Cicero]. ^BThose who prolong their anger and hatred beyond the affairs in question, as most men do, show that it comes from another part of them and from a personal cause; just as a man who, cured of an ulcer, still has his fever, shows that it had another, more hidden origin. ^CThe fact is that they have no hatred for the cause in general and in so far as it hurts the interest of all and of the state; they resent it only in that it galls them in private. That is why they are stung by it with a personal passion and beyond justice and public reason. *For they did not all blame the terms as a whole so much as they each blamed those that affected them individually* [Livy].

^BI want the advantage to be for us, but I do not fly into a frenzy if it is not. ^CI adhere firmly to the healthiest of the parties, but I do not seek to be noted as especially hostile to the others and beyond the bounds of the general reason. I condemn extraordinarily this bad form of arguing: "He is of the League, for he admires the grace of Monsieur de Guise." "The activity of the king of Navarre amazes him: he is a Huguenot." "He finds this to criticize in the king's morals: he is seditious in his heart." And I did not concede even to the magistrate[8] that he was right to condemn a book for having placed a heretic among the best poets of this century. Should we not dare say of a thief that he has a fine leg? And if she is a whore, must she also necessarily have bad breath?

In wiser ages, did they revoke the proud title of Capitolinus, which they had previously given to Marcus Manlius as the preserver of public religion and liberty? Did they smother the memory of his liberality and his feats of arms and the military rewards accorded to his valor, because he afterward aspired to kingship, to the prejudice of his country's laws?

If they have formed a hatred for an advocate, the next day in their view he becomes ineloquent. I have elsewhere[9] touched on the zeal that impels good men into similar faults. For my part, I can perfectly well say: "He does this wickedly and that virtuously." Likewise in predictions or in the unfavorable outcome of affairs, they want everyone to be blind and stupid in his own cause, and our conviction and judgment to serve, not the truth, but the aim of our desire.

8 The papal censor who examined the *Essays* when Montaigne was in Rome in 1580–81. See *Travel Journal*, pp. 1166, 1178.
9 *Essays* 1: 32, "We Should Meddle Soberly with Judging Divine Ordinances."

I should rather err toward the other extreme, so much do I fear being suborned by my desire. Besides, I am somewhat tenderly distrustful of the things I wish for.

I have in my time seen wonders in the undiscerning and prodigious ease with which peoples let their belief and hope be led and manipulated in whatever way has pleased and served their leaders, passing over a hundred mistakes one on top of the other, passing over phantasms and dreams. I am no longer amazed at those who are hoodwinked by the monkey tricks of Apollonius and Mahomet. Their sense and understanding is entirely smothered in their passion. Their discernment is left no other choice than the one that smiles upon them and comforts their cause.

I had observed this to a supreme degree in the first of our feverish factions.[10] This other,[11] which has been born since, in imitating it surpasses it. Wherefore I am led to believe that this is a characteristic inseparable from popular errors. After the first one that starts out, the others push each other forward, following the wind like waves. A man is not a part of the body if he can renounce it, if he does not wander along with the common movement. But truly we wrong the just sides when we want to assist them with fraud. I have always opposed that practice. It has effect only with sickly heads; with sane ones, there are ways that are surer, as well as more honest, for keeping up their courage and accounting for adverse events.

[B]Heaven has not seen, and will never again see, so grave a discord as that between Caesar and Pompey. However, I seem to recognize in those noble souls a great moderation toward one another. It was a rivalry in honor and authority, which did not carry them away into furious and undiscerning hatred, a rivalry without malignity and without detraction. In their bitterest exploits I discover some remnant of respect and good will; and thus I judge that if it had been possible, each of them would have wished to do his business without the ruin of his fellow rather than with his ruin. How differently it goes with Marius and Sulla! Make a note of it.

We must not rush so frantically after our passions and interests. Just as when I was young I opposed the progress of love, which I felt advancing too far upon me, and took care that it should not be so pleasing to me as in the end to overpower me and hold me completely at its mercy, so I do the same on all other occasions

10 The Protestants.
11 The League.

where my will is seized with too strong an appetite. I lean in the opposite direction from its inclination, as I see it plunging in and getting drunk with its own wine. I avoid feeding its pleasure to such an extent that I can no longer regain control of it without cruel loss.

The souls that through stupidity see things only by half enjoy this good fortune, that harmful things hurt them less. It is a spiritual leprosy that has some appearance of health, and such health as philosophy does not scorn at all. But yet it is not right to call it wisdom, as we often do. And in this manner someone in antiquity made fun of Diogenes, who, in the depth of winter, stark naked, was embracing a snow figure as a test of his endurance. Coming upon him in that posture, this man said to him: "Are you very cold now?" "Not at all," answered Diogenes. "Then," the other went on, "what difficult and exemplary thing do you think you are doing by remaining there?" To measure the fortitude we must necessarily know the suffering.

But the souls that will have to see adversities and the injuries of fortune in all their depth and sharpness, that will have to weigh them and taste them according to their natural bitterness and their gravity, let them employ their art to keep from entering into their causes and let them turn aside from the approaches that lead to them. What did King Cotys do? He paid liberally for the beautiful rich vessel that had been offered to him; but because it was singularly fragile, he immediately broke it himself, to remove early such an easy occasion for anger against his servants. ᶜIn like manner I have deliberately avoided having my affairs mixed up with others', and have not sought to have my property contiguous with that of my relations and of those with whom I am to be joined by close friendship: whence ordinarily arise grounds for estrangement and dissension.

ᴮI used to be fond of games of chance with cards and dice. I gave them up long ago for this reason only, that however good a face I put on my losses, I did not fail to feel stung by them within.

A man of honor, who must take the giving of the lie or an affront to heart, ᶜwho is not one to take a silly excuse as payment and consolation for his loss, ᴮshould avoid letting doubtful affairs and contentious altercations run their course.

I shun gloomy dispositions and surly men like those with the plague, and in subjects that I cannot discuss disinterestedly and dispassionately I do not meddle unless duty forces me to. ᶜ*It is better*

for them not to begin than to desist [Seneca]. ^BThe safest way, then, is to be prepared before the occasions.

I know well that some wise men have taken another way, and have not feared to grapple, and engage themselves to the quick, with many subjects. Those men are sure of their strength, under which they take cover in all kinds of adverse events, making their power of endurance wrestle with the misfortunes:

> As a great rock that juts out into the vast ocean,
> Open to the wild winds, exposed to the sea's commotion,
> Endures the entire power and threats of sky and deep,
> Standing unmoved.
>
> <div align="right">VIRGIL</div>

Let us not tackle these examples; we would not come up to them. These men obstinately determine to see resolutely and without perturbation the ruin of their country, which possessed and commanded their entire will. For our common souls there is too much effort and harshness in that. Cato therefore abandoned the noblest life that ever was. We little men must flee the storm from further away; we must try to avoid feeling it, not try to endure it, and dodge the blows we cannot parry.

^CZeno, seeing Chremonides, a young man he loved, come over to sit beside him, promptly got up. And when Cleanthes asked him the reason, he said: "I understand that the doctors principally prescribe rest and forbid excitement for all kinds of tumors."

^BSocrates does not say: "Do not surrender to the charms of beauty, withstand it, make an effort to oppose it." "Flee from it," he says, "run from the sight of it and from meeting it, as from a potent poison that darts and strikes from afar." ^CAnd his good disciple,[12] imagining or recounting (but in my opinion recounting rather than imagining) the rare perfections of the great Cyrus, makes him mistrustful of his powers to withstand the charms of the divine beauty of the illustrious Panthea, his captive, and has him commit the visiting and guarding of her to another who had less liberty than he.

^BAnd the Holy Ghost in like manner: *Lead us not into temptation.* We do not pray that our reason may not be combated and overcome by concupiscence, but that it may not even be tested by it, that we may not be brought into a state where we even have to suffer the

12 Xenophon.

approaches, solicitations, and temptations of sin; and we supplicate our Lord to keep our conscience tranquil, fully and perfectly delivered from dealing with evil.

^CThose who say they have got the better of their vindictive passion or of some other kind of painful passion often tell the truth as things are, but not as they were. They speak to us when the causes of their error have been fostered and developed by themselves. But go back further, call these causes back to their beginning; there you will take them unprovided. Do they expect their fault to be lesser for being older, and the sequel of an unjust beginning to be just?

^BHe who desires the good of his country as I do, without getting ulcers and growing thin over it, will be unhappy, but not stunned, to see it threatened either with ruin or with conditions of survival no less ruinous. Poor vessel, which the waves, the winds, and the pilot pull about with such contrary purposes:

> In such diverse ways,
> Do pilot, winds, and waves impel.
>
> BUCHANAN

He who does not gape after the favor of princes as a thing he cannot do without is not much stung by the coolness of their reception and countenance or by the inconstancy of their will. He who does not brood over his children or his honors with a slavish fondness manages to live comfortably after their loss. He who does good chiefly for his own satisfaction is not much upset by seeing men judge his actions contrary to his merit. A quarter of an ounce of patience is remedy enough against such annoyances. I find myself well off with this recipe, buying myself off at the beginning as cheaply as I can, and I feel that by means of it I have escaped much travail and many difficulties. With very little effort I arrest this first movement of my emotions, and abandon the subject that is beginning to weigh on me before it carries me away. ^CHe who does not arrest the start has no chance to arrest the course. He who cannot close the door to emotions will not drive them out once they are in. He who cannot get the better of the beginning will not get the better of the end. Nor will he withstand their fall who has been unable to withstand their first stirring. *For they drive themselves on by themselves when once reason is abandoned; and weakness is self-indulgent and is carried out to sea without knowing it, and finds no place to stand still* [Cicero]. ^BI feel in time the little winds that come to test

me out and murmur within me, forerunners of the storm: ^C*the mind is shaken long before it is overpowered* [Seneca]:

^BAs when
The rising winds murmur, caught in some wooded glen,
Then roll roaring along, forecasting gales for sailors.
VIRGIL

How many times have I done myself a very evident injustice to avert the hazard of receiving an even worse one from the judges, after an age of vexations, of vile and dirty practices, more hostile to my nature than the rack and the flames! ^C*It is proper to shun lawsuits as much as is permissible, and perhaps even a little more than is permissible. For it is not only generous, but sometimes even profitable, to come down a little from our rights* [Cicero]. If we were really wise, we should rejoice and boast, like the young man of a great family whom I heard one day informing everyone with naïve delight that his mother had just lost her lawsuit, as if it were her cough, her fever, or something else troublesome to keep. Even the favors that fortune might have given me by my kinship or acquaintance with those who have sovereign authority in those things, I have very conscientiously and insistently avoided using to the prejudice of others or to raise my rights above their right value.

In short, ^BI have managed so well by my daily efforts – fortunately, may I say – that here I am still virgin of lawsuits, which have not failed to offer themselves to my service many times with a very just title, if I had wanted to listen to them, and virgin of quarrels. I shall soon have spent a long life without serious offense received or given, and without having heard anything worse than my name: a rare favor of Heaven.

Our greatest agitations have ridiculous springs and causes. What a disaster our last duke of Burgundy incurred because of a quarrel about a cartload of sheepskins! And was not the engraving of a seal the first and principal cause of the most horrible upheaval that this machine has ever suffered?[13] For Pompey and Caesar are only the offshoots and the sequel of the other two. And I have seen in my time the wisest heads in this kingdom assembled, with great ceremony and public expense, for treaties and accords of which the real

13 The rivalry of Marius and Sulla, caused by a seal that Sulla had engraved to commemorate his victories over Jugurtha. "This machine" is of course the earth.

decision meanwhile depended in all sovereignty on the talk in the ladies' boudoir and the inclination of some little woman. ^CThe poets understood this well who put Greece and Asia to fire and sword for an apple. ^BSee why that man goes off to risk his honor and his life with his sword and dagger; let him tell you whence comes the source of this quarrel; he cannot do so without blushing, so frivolous is the occasion of it.

At the beginning only a little reflection is needed; but once you are embarked, all the ropes start pulling. Then you need great resources, much more difficult and important. ^CHow much easier it is not to go into it than to get out of it! ^BNow we should proceed in the opposite way from the reed, which on first shooting up produces a long, straight stem, but afterward, as if it had grown languid and out of breath, comes to form frequent thick knots, like so many pauses, which show that it no longer has this first vigor and constancy. We must rather begin gently and coolly, and save our breath and our vigorous efforts for the thick and culmination of the business. We guide affairs at their beginnings and hold them at our mercy; but afterward, when they are under way, it is they that guide us and carry us away, and we have to follow them.

^CYet this is not to say that this plan has relieved me of all difficulty, and that I have not often had trouble curbing and bridling my passions. They are not always to be governed according to the importance of the occasion, and even their beginnings are often sharp and violent. At all events, a fine saving and some profit may be derived from this plan, except for those who in well-doing are not content with any profit if no reputation is involved. For in truth, such an action is valued only by each man in himself. You are happier for it, but not more esteemed, if you have reformed before joining in the dance and before the matter was in view. At the same time, however, not only in this but in all other duties of life, the road of those who aim at honor is very different from the one followed by those whose goal is order and reason.

^BI find some who enter the lists heedlessly and furiously, and slow up in the charge. Plutarch says that those who through the vice of false shame are soft and easy in granting whatever they are asked, are afterward easy in failing their word and recanting; by the same token, he who enters a quarrel lightly is apt to get out of it just as lightly. This same difficulty that keeps me from cutting into it would spur me on when I was once stirred up and heated. It is a bad habit: once you are in it, you must go through with it or burst.

ᶜ"Undertake softly," said Bias, "but pursue hotly." ᴮFor want of prudence men fall back into want of courage, which is still less tolerable.

Most of the settlements of our quarrels nowadays are shameful and dishonest: we seek only to save appearances, and meanwhile betray and disavow our true intentions. We plaster over the fact: we know how we have said it and in what sense, and those present know it, and our friends, whom we wanted to have feel our advantage. It is at the expense of our frankness and of the honor of our courage that we disown our thought, and seek rabbit-holes in falsehood in order to come to an agreement. We give ourselves the lie to save the lie we have given to someone else.

You must not consider whether your action or your word may have another interpretation; it is your true and sincere interpretation that you must henceforth maintain, whatever it costs you. Your virtue and your conscience are addressed; these are not parts to put behind a mask. Let us leave these vile means and expedients to the chicanery of the Palace of Justice.

The excuses and reparations that I see made every day to purge our indiscretion seem to me uglier than indiscretion itself. It would be better to offend your adversary once more than to offend yourself by making such amends to him. You have defied him when you were moved with anger, and you are going to appease and flatter him when you are in a more sober and affable mood; thus you are giving way further than you have advanced. I do not consider anything a gentleman can say as vicious as the unsaying of it seems to me shameful, when it is an unsaying that is wrenched from him by authority; inasmuch as stubbornness is more excusable in him than pusillanimity.

Passions are as easy for me to avoid as they are hard for me to moderate. ᶜ*They are more easily torn from the mind than checked* [Seneca]. ᴮHe who cannot attain that noble impassibility of the Stoics, let him take refuge in the bosom of this plebeian stupidity of mine. What those men did by virtue, I train myself to do by disposition. The middle region harbors the tempests; the two extremes, philosophers and rustics, concur in tranquillity and happiness:

> Happy who knows the origin of things,
> And who can scorn inexorable fate
> And fear, and greedy Acheron's howls of hate.

Happy also is he who knows the woodland clan,
The nymphs, and old Sylvanus, and the great god Pan.
 VIRGIL

All things are weak and tender at birth. Therefore we must have
our eyes open to the beginnings; for as then, when a thing is little,
we do not discover its danger, so when it is grown we no longer
discover the remedy for it. I would have found it harder to digest the
million frustrations that I would have encountered every day in an
ambitious career, than I have found it to arrest the natural inclina-
tion that bore me to it:

I shrank with rightful dread
From raising my conspicuous head.
 HORACE

All public actions are subject to uncertain and diverse interpreta-
tions, for too many heads judge them. Some say about this muni-
cipal service of mine (and I am glad to say a word about it, not that it
is worth it, but to serve as an example of my conduct in such things)
that I went about it like a man who exerts himself too weakly and
with a languishing zeal; and they are not at all far from having a case.
I try to keep my soul and my thoughts in repose. ^C*Always calm by
nature, now even more so with age* [Q. Cicero]. ^B And if they some-
times veer under some rough and penetrating attack, it is in truth
without my consent. From this natural languor, however, one ought
not to derive any proof of impotence (for lack of assiduity and lack of
sense are two different things), and still less of insensibility and
ingratitude toward the people of Bordeaux, who did everything in
their power to gratify me, both before they knew me and after, and
did much more for me by giving me my office again than by giving it
to me in the first place. I wish them all possible good, and certainly,
had an occasion arisen, there is nothing I would have spared for
their service. I bestirred myself for them just as I do for myself.
They are a good people, warlike and idealistic, yet capable of
obedience and discipline and of serving some good purpose if they
are well guided.

People also say that my administration passed without a mark or
a trace. That's a good one! They accuse me of inactivity in a time
when almost everyone was convicted of doing too much.

I have a lively way of acting, wherever my will carries me along.
But this eagerness is an enemy to perseverance. If anyone wants to

use me according to my nature, let him give me tasks in which vigor and freedom are needed, tasks that require direct, brief, and even hazardous conduct; in those I can do something. If it has to be long, subtle, laborious, artificial, and tortuous, he will do better to apply to someone else.

Not all important offices are difficult. I was prepared to work myself a bit more roughly if there had been any great need of it. For it is in my power to do something more than I do or than I like to do. I did not leave undone, as far as I know, any action that duty genuinely required of me. I easily forgot those that ambition mixes up with duty and covers with its name. Those are the ones that most often fill the eyes and ears, and satisfy men. Not the thing but the appearance pays them. If they hear no noise, it seems to them that we are asleep.

My humors are the opposite of noisy humors. I could easily check a disturbance without being disturbed, and punish a disorder without losing my temper. Do I need anger and inflammation? I borrow it and wear it as a mask. My behavior is mild, rather tame than fierce. I do not condemn a magistrate who sleeps, provided that those who are under his care are also asleep; the laws sleep too. For my part I commend a gliding, obscure, and quiet life, ^c*neither groveling and abject nor overbearing* [Cicero]. ^BMy fortune so wills it. I was born of a family that from way back has flowed along without glamor and without tumult, a family ambitious above all for integrity.

Men of our time are so formed for agitation and ostentation that goodness, moderation, equability, constancy, and such quiet and obscure qualities are no longer felt. Rough bodies are felt, smooth ones are handled imperceptibly. Sickness is felt, health little or not at all; nor do we feel the things that charm us compared with those that harm us. It is acting for our private reputation and profit, not for the good, to put off and do in the public square what we can do in the council chamber, and at high noon what we could have done the night before, and to be jealous to do ourselves what our colleague does as well. Thus some surgeons of Greece used to perform the operations of their art on platforms in the sight of the passers-by in order to acquire a greater practice and clientele. They think that good rules can be heard only to the sound of trumpets.

Ambition is not a vice for little fellows and for undertakings such as ours. Someone said to Alexander: "Your father will leave you a great dominion, easy and peaceful." That boy was envious of his

father's victories and of the justice of his government. He would not have wanted to enjoy the empire of the world softly and peacefully. ^CAlcibiades, in Plato, prefers to die supremely young, handsome, rich, noble, learned, rather than to stand still in that condition.

^BThis malady is perhaps excusable in so strong and full a soul. When these dwarfish and puny soullets behave like vain baboons and think to spread their name for having rightly judged an affair or continued the order of the guards at a city gate, the more they hope to raise their head, the more they show their tail. These minute good works have neither body nor life: they vanish at the first telling and travel only from one street corner to the next. Entertain your son and your valet with them boldly, like that ancient[14] who, having no other auditor of his praises or witness of his valor, boasted to his chambermaid, exclaiming: "Oh, Perrette, what a gallant and capable man you have for a master!" Entertain yourself with them, if worst comes to worst, like a councillor of my acquaintance who, after disgorging a boatload of paragraphs with extreme effort and equal ineptitude, retired from the council chamber to the Palace urinal, where he was heard muttering very conscientiously between his teeth: "*Not unto us, O Lord, not unto us, but unto thy name give glory*" [Psalms]. If he cannot get it from anyone else, let him pay himself out of his own purse.

Renown does not prostitute itself at so cheap a rate. The rare and exemplary actions to which it is due would not endure the company of that innumerable crowd of petty everyday actions. Marble will exalt your titles as much as you please for having had a piece of wall patched up or a public gutter cleaned out; but men who have sense will not. Reputation does not follow every good deed if difficulty and strangeness are not joined to it. Nor indeed is even esteem due to every action that is born of virtue, according to the Stoics, and they do not want even recognition accorded to a man who through temperance abstains from a blear-eyed old woman. ^CThose who have acknowledged the admirable qualities of Scipio Africanus refuse him the glory that Panaetius accords him for having abstained from taking gifts, as a glory belonging not so much to him as to his whole age.

^BWe have the pleasures suitable to our lot; let us not usurp those of greatness. Ours are more natural and all the more solid and sure

14 Plutarch tells about this man ("Of Progress in Virtue") but does not name him.

for being humbler. Since we will not do so out of conscience, at least out of ambition let us reject ambition. Let us disdain this base and beggarly hunger for renown and honor which makes us grovel for it before all sorts of people – ᶜ*What is that praise that may be sought in the market place?* [Cicero] – ᴮabjectly and at no matter how vile a price. It is dishonor to be so honored. Let us learn to be no more avid of glory than we are capable of it. To be puffed up at every useful and harmless action is for people with whom these are extraordinary and rare; they want to put them at the price they cost them. In proportion as a good deed is more brilliant, I deduct from its goodness the suspicion I have that it was performed more to be brilliant than to be good: put on display, it is half sold. Those actions have much more grace which escape from the hand of the workman nonchalantly and noiselessly, and which some worthy man later picks out and lifts back out of obscurity to push them into the light for their own sake. ᶜ*To me indeed all things seem more praiseworthy which are done without ostentation and without public witness* [Cicero], says the most vainglorious man in the world.

ᴮI had nothing to do but conserve and endure, which are noiseless and imperceptible acts. Innovation has great luster, but it is forbidden in these times, when we are hard pressed and have to defend ourselves mainly against innovations. ᶜAbstention from doing is often as noble as doing, but it is less open to the light; and the little that I am worth is almost all on that side.

ᴮIn short, the occasions in my term of office were suited to my disposition, for which I am very grateful to them. Is there anyone who wants to be sick in order to see his doctor at work, and shouldn't we whip any doctor who would wish us the plague in order to put his art into practice? I have not had that iniquitous and rather common disposition of wanting the trouble and sickness of the affairs of this city to exalt and honor my government; I heartily lent a shoulder to make them easy and light. Anyone who will not be grateful to me for the order, the gentle and mute tranquillity, that accompanied my administration, at least cannot deprive me of the share of it that belongs to me by right of my good fortune. And I am so made that I like as well to be lucky as wise, and to owe my successes purely to the grace of God as to the effect of my own action.

I had published elaborately enough to the world my inadequacy in such public management. I have something still worse than inadequacy: that I hardly mind it, and hardly try to cure it, in view

of the course of life that I have designed for myself. I did not satisfy myself either in this undertaking, but I accomplished about what I had promised myself, and far surpassed what I had promised those whom I had to deal with. For I am apt to promise a little less than what I can do and what I hope to deliver. I am sure I left no cause for offense or hatred. As for leaving regret and desire, at the very least I know this well, that I did not greatly care about that:

> My trust in such a monster place?
> Ignore the meaning of the sea's smooth face,
> The quiet waves?
>
> VIRGIL

II
Of cripples

ᴮIt is two or three years since they shortened the year by ten days in France. How many changes were supposed to follow this reform! It was literally moving heaven and earth at the same time. Nevertheless there is nothing budging from its place: my neighbors find the hour for sowing and reaping, the opportune moment for their business, the harmful and the propitious days, exactly at the same point to which they had always assigned them. Neither was the error felt in our habits, nor is the improvement felt. So much uncertainty there is in all things; so gross, ᶜobscure, and obtuse ᴮis our perception!

They say that this regularization could have been carried out in a less inconvenient fashion, after the example of Augustus, by subtracting for a few years the bissextile day, which in any event is an awkward and confusing day, until they had managed to satisfy this debt exactly; which has not been done even by this correction, and we still remain a few days in arrears. And also by this same means we could have provided for the future by ordaining that after the revolution of such-and-such a number of years this irregular day would be eclipsed forever, so that our miscalculation thenceforth could not exceed twenty-four hours.

We have no other way of computing time but by years. The world has been using this measure for many centuries; and yet it is a measure that we have still not succeeded in fixing, and such that we are every day in doubt what form other nations have variously

given it and in what sense they used it. What if, as some say, the heavens contract in on us as they grow older and throw us into uncertainty even about the hours and days; and about the months, since Plutarch says that even in his time astrology[1] had not been able to determine the motion of the moon? Here we are in fine condition to keep a record of past events!

I was just now musing, as I often do, on how free and vague an instrument human reason is. I see ordinarily that men, when facts are put before them, are more ready to amuse themselves by inquiring into their reasons than by inquiring into their truth. They leave aside the cases and amuse themselves treating the causes. ^CComical prattlers![2]

The knowledge of causes belongs only to Him who has the guidance of things, not to us who have only the enduring of them, and who have the perfectly full use of them according to our nature, without penetrating to their origin and essence. Nor is wine pleasanter to the man who knows its primary properties. On the contrary, both the body and the soul disturb and alter the right they have to the enjoyment of the world by mixing into it the pretension to learning. Determining and knowing, like giving, appertains to rule and mastery; to inferiority, subjection, and apprenticeship appertains enjoyment and acceptance. Let us return to this habit of ours.

^BThey pass over the facts, but they assiduously examine their consequences. They ordinarily begin thus: "How does this happen?" What they should say is: "But does it happen?" Our reason is capable of filling out a hundred other worlds and finding their principles and contexture. It needs neither matter nor basis; let it run on; it builds as well on emptiness as on fullness, and with inanity as with matter:

> Suited to give solidity to smoke.
> PERSIUS

I find that in almost every case we ought to say: "That is not so at all." And I would often use that reply, but I dare not, for they cry out that it is an evasion produced by feeblemindedness and ignorance. And I am ordinarily obliged to play the fool for company's sake and discuss frivolous subjects and stories which I entirely disbelieve.

1 By "astrology" Montaigne means both astrology and astronomy.
2 Montaigne's play on words, *Plaisans causeurs*, is beyond my power to render.

Besides, it is truly a little rude and quarrelsome flatly to deny a statement of fact. And few people fail, especially in things of which it is hard to persuade others, to affirm that they have seen the thing or to cite witnesses whose authority stops us from contradicting. Following this custom, we know the foundations and causes of a thousand things that never were; and the world skirmishes amid a thousand questions of which both the pro and the con are false. ^C*The false is so close to the true that the wise man should not trust himself in so dangerous a spot* [Cicero].

^BTruth and falsehood are alike in face, similar in bearing, taste, and movement; we look upon them with the same eye. I find not only that we are lax in defending ourselves against deception, but that we seek and hasten to run ourselves through on it. We love to embroil ourselves in vanity, as something in conformity with our being.

I have seen the birth of many miracles in my time. Even when they are smothered at birth, we do not fail to foresee the course they would have taken if they had lived out their full age. For it is only a matter of finding the end of the string, and we can unwind as much as we want. And there is more distance between nothing and the smallest thing in the world than there is between this and the biggest.

Now the first persons who are convinced of a strange initial fact, as they spread their story, feel from the opposition they meet where the difficulty of persuasion lies, and go and call that place with some false patch. ^CBesides, *by the innate desire in men to foster rumors diligently* [Livy], we naturally scruple to return what has been lent us without some interest and addition from our own stock. The private error first creates the public error, and afterward in turn the public error creates the private error. ^BThus this whole structure goes on building itself up and shaping itself from hand to hand; so that the remotest witness is better instructed about it than the nearest, and the last informed more convinced of it than the first. It is a natural progression. For whoever believes anything esteems that it is a work of charity to persuade another of it, and in order to do so does not fear to add out of his own invention as much as he sees to be necessary in his story to take care of the resistance and the defect he thinks there is in the other person's comprehension.

I myself, who am singularly scrupulous about lying and who scarcely concern myself with giving credence and authority to what I say, perceive nevertheless that when I am excited over

a matter I have in hand, ^ceither by another man's resistance or by the intrinsic heat of the narration, ^BI magnify and inflate my subject by voice, movements, vigor and power of words, and further by extension and amplification, not without prejudice to the simple truth. But I do so, however, on this condition, that for the first man who catches me up and asks me for the naked and unvarnished truth, I promptly abandon my straining and give it to him without exaggeration, without overemphasis or padding. ^cA lively and noisy way of speaking, such as mine ordinarily is, is apt to be carried away into hyperbole.

^BThere is nothing on which men are commonly more intent than on making a way for their opinions. Where the ordinary means fail us, we add command, force, fire, and the sword. It is unfortunate to be in such a pass that the best touchstone of truth is the multitude of believers, in a crowd in which the fools so far surpass the wise in number. ^c*As if anything were so common as lack of sense!* [Cicero.] *A fine evidence of sanity is the multitude of the insane!* [Saint Augustine.] ^BIt is a difficult thing to set one's judgment against accepted opinions. The first conviction, taken from the subject itself, seizes the simple; from them it spreads to the able, under the authority of the number and antiquity of the testimonies. For my part, in a matter on which I would not believe one, I would not believe a hundred ones. And I do not judge opinions by their years.

A little while ago one of our princes,[3] in whom the gout had ruined a fine constitution and a blithe disposition, let himself be so strongly persuaded by a report of the marvelous operations of a priest who by means of words and gestures cured all illnesses, that he made a long journey to go and find him, and by the power of his imagination persuaded his legs and put them to sleep for a few hours, so that he derived from them a service that they had long since forgotten how to do for him. If fortune had allowed five or six such incidents to accumulate, they could have made this miracle a part of nature. People later found so much simplicity and so little artfulness in the architect of these works that he was judged not even worthy of any punishment. So indeed we would judge of most such things if we tracked them into their lair. ^c*We wonder at things that deceive us by their distance* [Seneca]. ^BThus our sight often represents strange

3 According to Florimond de Raemond, this was Monsieur de Nemours, nephew of Louise of Savoy.

images at a distance, which vanish as they approach. *Rumor never stops at evidence* [Quintus Curtius].

It is a marvel from what empty beginnings and frivolous causes such famous impressions ordinarily spring. That in itself hampers investigation. For while we are looking for powerful and weighty causes and ends, worthy of such great renown, we lose the true ones; they escape our view by their littleness. And in truth, in such researches a very prudent, attentive, and subtle inquirer is needed, impartial and unprejudiced.

To this moment all these miracles and strange events have eluded me. I have seen no more evident monstrosity and miracle in the world than myself. We become habituated to anything strange by use and time; but the more I frequent myself and know myself, the more my deformity astonishes me, and the less I understand myself.

The privilege of bringing such accidents into public knowledge and credit is reserved mainly to fortune. Passing day before yesterday through a village two leagues from my house, I found the place still stirred up about a miracle that had just failed to come off, by which the neighborhood had been entertained for months; and folk from the adjoining provinces were beginning to get excited about it and to come running up, people of all classes, in great crowds. A young man of the place had amused himself in his house one night by counterfeiting the voice of a spirit, with no more trickery in mind than enjoying a momentary joke. When this succeeded a little better than he expected, in order to extend the scope of the farce he took as an associate a throughly stupid and silly village girl; and in the end there were three of them, of the same age and similar ability. And from preaching at home they went on to preaching in public, hiding under the altar of the church, speaking only at night, and forbidding anyone to bring any light. From words tending to the conversion of the world and the threat of judgment day (for these are subjects under whose authority and reverence imposture most easily hides), they proceeded to some visions and actions so silly and ridiculous that there is hardly anything so crude in children's play. Yet if fortune had seen fit to favor them a little, who knows to what point this buffoonery would have grown? These poor devils are at this moment in prison and will probably pay the penalty for the common folly; and who knows but some judge will avenge himself on them for his own stupidity? We see clearly in this case, which is exposed; but in many things of similar quality, surpassing our

knowledge, it is my opinion that we should suspend our judgment just as much in the direction of rejecting as of accepting.

Many abuses are engendered in the world, ᶜor, to put it more boldly, all the abuses in the world are engendered, ᴮby our being taught to be afraid of professing our ignorance ᶜand our being bound to accept everything that we cannot refute. ᴮWe talk about everything didactically and dogmatically. The style in Rome was that even what a witness deposed to having seen with his own eyes, and what a judge decided with his most certain knowledge, was drawn up in this form of speech: "It seems to me." It makes me hate probable things when they are planted on me as infallible. I like these words, which soften and moderate the rashness of our propositions: "perhaps," "to some extent," "some," "they say," "I think," and the like. And if I had had to train children, I would have filled their mouths so much with this way of answering, ᶜinquiring, not decisive – ᴮ"What does that mean? I do not understand it. That might be. Is it true?" – that they would be more likely to have kept the manner of learners at sixty than to represent learned doctors at ten, as they do. Anyone who wants to be cured of ignorance must confess it. ᶜIris is the daughter of Thaumas.[4] Wonder is the foundation of all philosophy, inquiry its progress, ignorance its end. ᴮI'll go further: There is a certain strong and generous ignorance that concedes nothing to knowledge in honor and courage, ᶜan ignorance that requires no less knowledge to conceive it than does knowledge.

ᴮIn my youth, I read about the trial of a strange case, which Corras, a counselor of Toulouse, had printed, about two men who impersonated one another. I remember (and I remember nothing else) that he seemed to me, in describing the imposture of the man he judged guilty, to make it so marvelous and so far surpassing our knowledge and his own, who was judge, that I found much rashness in the sentence that had condemned the man to be hanged. Let us accept some form of sentence which says "The court understands nothing of the matter," more freely and ingenuously than did the Areopagites, who, finding themselves hard pressed by a case that they could not unravel, ordered the parties to come back in a hundred years.

The witches of my neighborhood are in mortal danger every time some new author comes along and attests to the reality of their

4 Iris: the rainbow, messenger of the gods to men. Thaumas: wonder.

visions. To apply the examples that the Holy Writ offers us of such things, very certain and irrefragable examples, and bring them to bear on our modern events, requires greater ingenuity than ours, since we see neither their causes nor their means. It belongs perhaps only to that most powerful testimony[5] to say to us: "This is a miracle, and that, and not this other." God must be believed in these things, that is truly most reasonable; but not, by the some token, one of us, who is astonished at his own narrative (and he is necessarily astonished unless he is out of his senses), whether he tells it about someone else or against himself.

I am sluggish and tend to hold to the solid and the probable, avoiding the ancient reproaches: *Men put greater faith in those things that they do not understand* [author unknown]. *By a twist of the human mind, obscure things are more readily believed* [Tacitus]. I see indeed that people get angry, and I am forbidden to doubt on pain of execrable insults. A new way of persuading! Thank God, my belief is not controlled by anyone's fists. Let them bully those who accuse them of holding a false opinion; I accuse them only of holding a difficult and rash one, and condemn the opposite affirmation, just as they do, if not so imperiously. [c]*Let them appear as probable, not be affirmed positively* [Cicero].

[B]He who imposes his argument by bravado and command shows that it is weak in reason. In a verbal and scholastic altercation these people may have as good an apparent case as their contradictors; but in the effective consequences they draw from them, the latter have much advantage.

To kill men, we should have sharp and luminous evidence; and our life is too real and essential to vouch for these supernatural and fantastic accidents. As for druggings and poisonings, I put them out of my reckoning; those are homicides, and of the worst sort. However, even in such matters they say that we must not always be satisfied with confessions, for such persons have sometimes been known to accuse themselves of having killed people who were found to be alive and healthy.

In those other extravagant accusations, I should be inclined to say that it is quite enough that a man, whatever recommendation he may have, should be believed about what is human; about what is beyond his conception and of supernatural effect, he should be believed only when some supernatural approbation has sanctioned

5 The testimony of God in the Bible.

him. This privilege that it has pleased God to give to some of our testimonies must not be cheapened and communicated lightly.

My ears are battered by a thousand stories like this: "Three people saw him on such-and-such a day in the east; three saw him the next day in the west, at such-and-such a time, in such-and-such a place, dressed thus." Truly, I would not believe my own self about this. How much more natural and likely it seems to me that two men are lying than that one man should pass with the winds in twelve hours from the east to the west! How much more natural that our understanding should be carried away from its base by the volatility of our untracked mind than that one of us, in flesh and bone, should be wafted up a chimney on a broomstick by a strange spirit!

Let us not look for outside and unknown illusions, we who are perpetually agitated by our own home-grown illusions. It seems to me that we may be pardoned for disbelieving a marvel, at least as long as we can turn aside and avoid the supernatural explanation by nonmarvelous means. And I follow Saint Augustine's opinion, that it is better to lean toward doubt than toward assurance in things difficult to prove and dangerous to believe.

A few years ago I passed through the territory of a sovereign prince, who, as a favor to me and to beat down my incredulity, did me the kindness of letting me see, in his own presence and in a private place, ten or twelve prisoners of this nature,[6] and among others one old woman, indeed a real witch in ugliness and deformity, long very famous in that profession. I saw both proofs and free confessions, and some barely perceptible mark or other on this wretched old woman, and I talked and asked questions all I wanted, bringing to the matter the soundest attention I could; and I am not the man to let my judgment be throttled much by preconceptions. In the end, and in all conscience, I would have prescribed them rather hellebore[7] than hemlock. *It seemed to be a matter rather of madness than of crime* [Livy]. Justice has its own corrections proper for such maladies.

As for the objections and arguments that worthy men have brought up against me, both on this subject and often on others, I have not felt any that are binding and that do not admit of a solution more likely than their conclusions. It is true indeed that the proofs and reasons that are founded on experience and fact I do

6 Prisoners accused of witchcraft.
7 An herb supposed to cure insanity.

not attempt to disentangle; moreover they have no end to take hold of; I often cut them, as Alexander did his knot. After all, it is putting a very high price on one's conjectures to have a man roasted alive because of them.

ᶜThey relate various examples, and Praestantius tells one about his father, that having fallen into a sleep much deeper than any ordinary sound sleep, he imagined he was a mare and served some soldiers as a packhorse; and what he imagined, he really was. If sorcerers thus dream materially, if dreams can thus sometimes incorporate themselves in reality, still I do not believe that our will should be accountable to justice for them.

ᴮThis I say as one who is neither a judge nor a counselor to kings, and who considers himself nowhere near worthy of such eminence, but a man of the common sort, born and pledged to obedience to the public reason both in his deeds and in his words. If anyone should put my musings into account to the prejudice of the pettiest law, or opinion, or custom of his village, he would do himself a great wrong, and as great a one to me. ᶜFor in what I say I guarantee no certainty except that it is what I had at the time in my mind, a tumultuous and vacillating mind.

I talk about everything by way of conversation, and about nothing by way of advice. *Nor am I ashamed, as those men are, to admit that I do not know what I do not know* [Cicero]. ᴮI would not speak so boldly if it were my right to be believed; and this was what I replied to a great personage who complained of the violence and vehemence of my exhortations: "Feeling you tensed and prepared in one direction, I propose the other to you with all the care I can, to enlighten your judgment, not to compel it. God holds your heart and will provide you with your choice. I am not so presumptuous as even to desire that my opinions should tip the scale in a thing of such importance; my fortune has not trained them for such powerful and exalted decisions." Truly, I have not only a great number of propensities but also plenty of opinions which I would be glad to make my son dislike, if I had one. What if the truest opinions are not always the most suitable to man, so wild is his composition!

Apropos or malapropos, no matter, they say in Italy as a common proverb that he does not know Venus in her perfect sweetness who has not lain with a cripple. Fortune, or some particular incident, long ago put this saying into the mouth of the people; and it is said of males as well as of females. For the queen of the Amazons replied

to the Scythian who was inviting her to make love: *"The lame man does it best!"*[8] In that feminine commonwealth, to escape the domination of the males, they crippled them from childhood – arms, legs, and other parts that gave men an advantage over them – and made use of them only for the purpose for which we make use of women over here.

I would have said that the irregular movement of the lame woman brought some new pleasure to the business and a spice of sweetness to those who try it. But I have just learned that ancient philosophy, no less, has decided the question. It says that since the legs and thighs of lame women, because of their imperfection, do not receive the food that is their due, the result is that the genital parts, which are above, are fuller, better nourished, and more vigorous. Or else that, since this defect prevents exercise, those who are tainted by it dissipate their strength less and come more entire to the sports of Venus. Which is also the reason why the Greeks decried women weavers as being hotter than other women: because of the sedentary trade they perform, without much bodily exercise. What can we not reason about at this rate? Of these last I might also say that the joggling that their work gives them as they are thus seated arouses and solicits them, as the shaking and trembling of their coaches does the ladies.

Do not these examples confirm what I was saying at the beginning: that our reasons often anticipate the fact, and extend their jurisdiction so infinitely that they exercise their judgment even in inanity and nonbeing? Not only is our invention flexible in forging reasons for all sorts of dreams, but our imagination is equally prone to receive impressions from the very unreliable appearances given by falsehood. For by the sole authority of the ancient and public use of that proverb, I once made myself believe that I had received more pleasure from a woman because she was not straight, and credited that to the account of her charms.

Torquato Tasso, in the comparison he makes between France and Italy, says he has observed that we have thinner legs than the Italian gentlemen, and attributes the cause of this to the fact that we are continually on horseback; which is the same cause from which Suetonius draws a wholly opposite conclusion, for he says, on the contrary, that Germanicus had made his legs stouter by continuing this same exercise.

8 Greek proverb, which Montaigne quotes, then translates.

There is nothing so supple and erratic as our understanding: it is the shoe of Theramenes, good for either foot. And it is double and diverse, and matters are double and diverse. "Give me a silver drachma," said a Cynic philosopher to Antigonus. "That is not a king's present," he replied. "Then give me a talent." "That is not a present for a Cynic."

> Whether this heat opens up secret pores and routes
> Whereby the sap can penetrate the tender shoots,
> Or rather hardens and constricts the gaping veins,
> And thus protects the plants against the searching rains,
> The scorching of the sun, the north wind's piercing blast.
>
> VIRGIL

Every medal has its reverse [Italian proverb]. That is why Clitomachus said of old that Carneades had surpassed the labors of Hercules, in having torn away from man the habit of assent – that is to say, opinion and rashness in judging. This very vigorous idea of Carneades sprang up in antiquity, in my opinion, from the impudence of those who profess to know and from their immoderate arrogance.

Aesop was put up for sale with two other slaves. The buyer asked the first what he could do; he, to put a high value on himself, promised mountains and marvels, and that he could do this and that. The second answered as much and more about himself. When it came to Aesop, and he had also been asked what he could do, he said: "Nothing, for these men have taken everything already; they can do everything."

That is what has happened in the school of philosophy. The pride of those who attributed to the human mind a capacity for all things produced in others, through spite and emulation, the opinion that it is capable of nothing. These men maintain the same extreme in ignorance that the others maintain in knowledge; so that it cannot be denied that man is immoderate in all things, and cannot be stopped except by necessity and inability to go further.

12
Of physiognomy

ᴮAlmost all the opinions we have are taken on authority and on credit. There is no harm in this: we could not make a worse choice

than our own in so feeble an age. The version of the sayings of
Socrates that his friends have left us we approve only out of respect
for the universal approval these sayings enjoy, not by our own
knowledge. They are beyond our experience. If anything of the
kind were brought forth at this time, there are few men who
would prize it.

We perceive no charms that are not sharpened, puffed out, and
inflated by artifice. Those which glide along naturally and simply
easily escape a sight so gross as ours. They have a delicate and
hidden beauty; we need a clear and well-purged sight to discover
their secret light. Is not naturalness, according to us, akin to stu-
pidity and a matter for reproach?

Socrates makes his soul move with a natural and common
motion. So says a peasant, so says a woman. ^CHis mouth is full of
nothing but carters, joiners, cobblers, and masons. ^BHis are induc-
tions and similes drawn from the commonest and best-known
actions of men; everyone understands him. Under so mean a form
we should never have picked out the nobility and splendor of his
admirable ideas, we ^Cwho consider flat and low all ideas that are not
raised up by learning, and ^Bwho perceive richness only in pomp and
show. Our world is formed only for ostentation; men inflate them-
selves only with wind, and go bouncing around like balls. This man
did not propose to himself any idle fancies: his aim was to furnish us
with things and precepts that serve life really and more closely:

> To keep the mean, to hold our aim in view,
> And follow nature.
> LUCAN

He was also always one and the same, and raised himself, not by
sallies but by disposition, to the utmost point of vigor. Or, to speak
more exactly, he raised nothing, but rather brought vigor, hardships,
and difficulties down and back to his own natural and original
level, and subjected them to it. For in Cato we see very clearly that
his is a pace strained far above the ordinary; in the brave exploits
of his life and in his death we feel that he is always mounted on his
high horse. The other walks close to the ground, and at a gentle and
ordinary pace treats the most useful subjects; and behaves, both in
the face of death and in the thorniest trials that can confront us,
in the ordinary way of human life.

It happened fortunately that the man most worthy to be known
and to be presented to the world as an example should be the one of

whom we have most certain knowledge. We have light on him from the most clear-sighted men who ever lived; the witnesses we have of him are wonderful in fidelity and competence.

It is a great thing to have been able to impart such order to the pure and simple notions of a child that, without altering or stretching them, he produced from them the most beautiful achievements of our soul. He shows it as neither elevated nor rich; he shows it only as healthy, but assuredly with a very blithe and clear health. By these vulgar and natural motives, by these ordinary and common ideas, without excitement or fuss, he constructed not only the best regulated but the loftiest and most vigorous beliefs, actions, and morals that ever were. ᶜIt is he who brought human wisdom back down from heaven, where she was wasting her time, and restored her to man, with whom lies her most proper and laborious and useful business. ᴮSee him plead before his judges, see by what reasonings he rouses his courage in the hazards of war, what arguments fortify his patience against calumny, tyranny, death, and his wife's bad temper. There is nothing borrowed from art and the sciences; even the simplest can recognize in him their means and their strength; it is impossible to go back further and lower. He did a great favor to human nature by showing how much it can do by itself.

We are each richer than we think, but we are trained to borrow and beg; we are taught to use the resources of others more than our own. In nothing does man know how to stop at the limit of his need; of pleasure, riches, power, he embraces more than he can hold; his greed is incapable of moderation. I find that it is the same with the curiosity for knowledge. Man cuts out for himself much more work than he can do or has any reason to do, ᶜtrying to stretch the usefulness of knowledge as wide as its matter. *In learning, as in all other things, we suffer from intemperance* [Seneca]. And Tacitus is right to praise Agricola's mother for having curbed in her son too boiling an appetite for learning. Looked at steadily, it is like men's other goods; it has in it much intrinsic and natural vanity and weakness, and it costs dear.

It is far more hazardous to acquire than any other food or drink. For with other things, what we have bought we carry home in some vessel, and there we have a chance to examine its value and how much we shall take of it and when. But learning we can at the outset put into no other vessel than our mind; we swallow it as we buy it, and leave the market place already either infected or

improved. There is some of it that only hampers and burdens us instead of feeding us, and also some which, under color of curing us, poisons us.

[B]I once took pleasure in seeing men in some place, through piety, take a vow of ignorance, as one might of chastity, poverty, penitence. It is also castrating our disorderly appetites, to blunt that cupidity that pricks us on to the study of books, and to deprive the soul of that voluptuous complacency which tickles us with the notion of being learned. [C]And it is accomplishing richly the vow of poverty to add to it also that of the mind.

[B]We need hardly any learning to live at ease. And Socrates teaches us that it is in us, and the way to find it and help ourselves with it. All this ability of ours that is beyond the natural is as good as vain and superfluous. It is a lot if it does not load us down and bother us more than it serves us. [C]*Little learning is needed for a good mind* [Seneca]. [B]These are feverish excesses of our mind, a meddlesome and restless instrument.

Collect yourself: you will find in yourself Nature's arguments against death, true ones, and the fittest to serve you in case of necessity; they are the ones that make a peasant, and whole nations, die as steadfastly as a philosopher.

[C]Should I have died less cheerfully before having read the *Tusculans*?[1] I think not. And now that I find myself close to death, I feel that my tongue has grown richer, my courage not at all. This is as Nature made it for me, and arms itself for the conflict in a common and ordinary way. Books have served me not so much for instruction as for exercise.

What if [B]knowledge, trying to arm us with new defenses against natural mishaps, has imprinted in our fancy their magnitude and weight, more than her reasons and subtleties to protect us from them? [C]They are subtleties indeed, with which she often alarms us very idly. Authors, even the most compact and the wisest – around one good argument see how many others they strew, trivial ones, and if you look at them closely, bodiless. These are nothing but verbal quibbles, to deceive us. But inasmuch as this may be done usefully, I do not want to expose them any further. There are enough of that sort in this book in various places, either from borrowing or from imitation. Yet we should take a little care not to call strength

1 Cicero's *Tusculan Disputations*, of which the first book deals with contempt of death.

what is only nicety, or solid what is only acute, or good what is only beautiful: *which delight more tasted than drunk* [Cicero]. Not all that entertains us sustains us, *when it is a question not of the wit but of the soul* [Seneca].

^BTo see the trouble to which Seneca puts himself to be prepared for death, to see him sweat from the exertion of steeling and reassuring himself, and writhe about interminably on his perch, would have shaken his reputation with me if he had not very valiantly maintained it in dying. His agitation, so burning, so frequent, ^cshows that he was hot and impetuous himself. *A great soul speaks more relaxedly and assuredly. . . . There is not one color for the mind, another for the soul* [Seneca]. We have to convince him at his own expense.[2] And it ^Bshows perceptibly that he was hard pressed by his adversary.

Plutarch's manner, inasmuch as it is more disdainful and less tense, is, to my mind, all the more virile and persuasive; I would easily believe that the movements of his soul were more assured and more regulated. The one, sharper, pricks us and startles us, touches our mind more. The other, more sedate, forms us, settles and fortifies us constantly, touches our understanding more. ^cThe former ravishes our judgment, the latter wins it.

I have likewise seen other writings, still more revered, which, in portraying the conflict their authors sustain against the goads of the flesh, show these so stinging, so powerful and invincible that we, who are of the refuse of the people, have as much to wonder at in the strangeness and unheard-of vigor of their temptation as in their resistance.

^BTo what end do we keep forcing our nature with these efforts of learning? Let us look on the earth at the poor people we see scattered there, heads bowed over their toil, who know neither Aristotle nor Cato, neither example nor precept. From them Nature every day draws deeds of constancy and endurance purer and harder than those that we study with such care in school. How many of them I see all the time who ignore poverty! How many who desire death, or who meet it without alarm and without affliction! This man who is digging up my garden, this morning he buried his father or his son. The very names by which they call diseases relieve and soften their harshness: phthisis is the cough to them; dysentery, looseness of the bowels; pleurisy, a cold; and according as they name

2 In other words, by his own arguments, which Montaigne has just quoted.

them mildly, so also they endure them. A disease must be very grave to interrupt their ordinary work; they take to their beds only to die. ^C*That simple and open virtue has been converted into obscure and subtle knowledge* [Seneca].

^BI was writing this about the time when a mighty load of our disturbances settled down for several months with all its weight right on me. I had on the one hand the enemy at my door, on the other hand the freebooters, worse enemies: ^C*they fight not with arms but with vices* [Livy]; ^Band I was sampling every kind of military mischief all at once.

> To right and left appears the dreaded foe,
> On either side the threat of instant woe.
>
> OVID

Monstrous war! Other wars act outward; this one acts also against itself, eats and destroys itself by its own venom. It is by nature so malignant and ruinous that it ruins itself together with all the rest, and tears and dismembers itself with rage. We see it more often dissolving of itself than for lack of any necessary thing or through the power of the enemy. All discipline flies from it. It comes to cure sedition and is full of it, would chastise disobedience and sets the example of it; and employed in defense of the laws, plays the part of a rebel against its own laws. What have we come to? Our medicine carries infection:

> Poison to our disease
> Are all these remedies.
>
> AUTHOR UNKNOWN

> Grows all the stronger, all the sicker, with the cure.
>
> VIRGIL

> Our mad confounding of all good and ill
> Has made the gods avert their righteous will.
>
> CATULLUS

In these epidemics one can distinguish at the beginning the well from the sick; but when they come to last, like ours, the whole body is affected, head and heels alike; no part is free from corruption. For there is no air that is inhaled so greedily, that so spreads and penetrates, as does license. Our armies are no longer bound and held together except by foreign cement; of Frenchmen one can no longer form a steadfast and disciplined army corps. How shameful!

There is only so much discipline as borrowed soldiers show us; as for ourselves, we follow our own lead and not our leader's, every man his own way. The leader has more trouble within than without. It is for the commander to follow, court, and bend, for him alone to obey; all the rest is free and dissolute. It pleases me to see how much baseness and pusillanimity there is in ambition, by how much abjection and servility it must attain its goal. But this displeases me, to see decent natures, capable of justice, grow corrupt every day in managing and commanding this confusion. Long sufferance begets custom, custom consent and imitation. We had enough ill-born souls without spoiling the good and generous ones. So that, if we keep this up, there will hardly be anyone left to whom to entrust the health of this state, in case fortune restores it to us.

> At least do not prevent this youth from bringing aid
> To a disordered world.[3]
>
> VIRGIL

ᶜWhat has become of that ancient precept, that soldiers should fear their leader more than the enemy? And that wonderful example of the apple tree that happened to be enclosed within the precincts of a Roman army camp, and was found the next day when they broke camp, leaving the owner the entire count of his delicious ripe apples? I wish our youth, instead of the time they spend on less useful peregrinations and less honorable apprenticeships, would put half of it into witnessing naval warfare under some good captain-commander of Rhodes, and half into observing the discipline of the Turkish armies; for theirs has many differences from ours and advantages over ours. This is one: that our soldiers become more licentious on expeditions, theirs more restrained and timid; for offenses or thefts committed against humble people, which are punished with the bastinado in peacetime, are capital offenses in war. For an egg taken without paying, the predetermined penalty is fifty blows with a stick; for anything not suitable for food, however trivial, they are impaled or decapitated without delay. I was amazed to see in the history of Selim, the most cruel conqueror that ever was, that when he subjugated Egypt, the wonderful gardens around

3 Montaigne is applying to Henry of Navarre, heir presumptive since 1584, Virgil's appeal on behalf of Augustus.

the city of Damascus, abounding in delicate fruits, and all open and unenclosed, remained undespoiled by the hands of his soldiers.

ᴮBut is there any disease in a government so bad that it is worth combating with so deadly a drug?⁴ Not even, said Favonius, the usurpation of tyrannical authority over a state.

ᶜPlato likewise does not consent to have the repose of his country violated in order to cure it, and does not accept an improvement that costs the blood and ruin of the citizens, ruling that it is the duty of a good man in that case to let everything alone and merely to pray God to lend extraordinary aid. And he seems offended with his great friend Dion for having proceeded a little bit differently.

I was a Platonist on that score before I knew there had been a Plato in the world. And if this personage [Plato] must be completely excluded from our [Christian] fellowship – he who, by the sincerity of his conscience, had enough merit with the divine favor to penetrate so deeply into the light of Christianity through the general darkness of the world of his time – I do not think it becomes us well to let ourselves be taught by a pagan how great an impiety it is to expect no help from God that is simply his own and without our cooperation.

I often doubt whether among so many men who meddle in such a business a single one has been found of so feeble an understanding as to have been genuinely persuaded that he was moving toward reformation by the worst of deformations; that he was heading for his salvation by the most express ways that we have of very certain damnation; that by overthrowing the government, the authorities, and the laws under whose tutelage God has placed him, by dismembering his mother and giving the pieces to her ancient enemies to gnaw on, by filling the hearts of brothers with parricidal hatreds, by calling the devils and the furies to his aid, he could bring help to the sacrosanct sweetness and justice of the divine word.

ᴮAmbition, avarice, cruelty, vengeance, do not have enough natural impetuosity of their own; let us spark them and fan their flames by the glorious title of justice and piety. No worse state of things can be imagined than where wickedness comes to be legitimate and, with the leave of the authorities, assumes the cloak of virtue. ᶜ*Nothing is more deceptive in appearance than a depraved religion, in which the will of the gods is offered as a pretext for crimes*

4 As civil war.

[Livy]. The extreme of injustice, according to Plato, is when what is unjust is held to be just.

^BThe people suffered very greatly at that time,⁵ not only present losses –

> In all the fields
> Reigns such confusion
> VIRGIL

– but future also. The living had to suffer; so did those who were not yet born. They pillaged them, and consequently me too, even of hope, snatching from them all they had to provide for their living for many years.

> The brutal horde destroys whate'er they can't impound,
> And burns innocent hovels to the ground.
> OVID

> In walls there is no trust; the ravaged fields are bare.
> CLAUDIAN

Besides this shock I suffered others. I incurred the disadvantages that moderation brings in such maladies. I was belabored from every quarter; to the Ghibelline I was a Guelph, to the Guelph a Ghibelline. One of my poets says this well, but I do not know where it is. The situation of my house, and my acquaintance with men in my neighborhood, presented me in one aspect, my life and my actions in another. There were no formal accusations, for there was nothing they could sink their teeth into; I never transgress the laws, and if anyone had proceeded against me, he would have been found guiltier than I. It was mute suspicions that were current secretly, for which there is never a lack of apparent grounds in such a mixed-up confusion, any more than there is of envious or inept minds.

^CI ordinarily assist the unfair presumptions against me that fortune sows about by a way I have always had of avoiding justifying, excusing, and interpreting myself, thinking that it is compromising my conscience to plead for it. *For clarity is lessened by argument* [Cicero]. And as if everyone saw into me as clearly as I do myself,

5 At the time mentioned on p. 969 when Montaigne found himself buffeted on all sides by enemies and freebooters. The occasion was the siege of the Protestant-held town of Castillon, about five miles from Montaigne, by a League army under Mayenne in the summer of 1586.

instead of retreating from the accusation, I advance to meet it and rather enhance it by an ironic and mocking confession, if I do not flatly keep silent about it as about something unworthy of an answer. But those who attribute this to an over-haughty confidence show me hardly less ill will than those who attribute it to the weakness of an indefensible cause – especially the great, toward whom lack of submission is the ultimate offense, and who are rough on any righteousness that is aware of itself and does not feel itself to be abject, humble, and suppliant. I have often bumped myself on that pillar.

At all events, over what happened to me then [B]an ambitious man would have hanged himself, and so would an avaricious man.

I have no sort of concern with acquiring.

> Let me keep what I have, or even less, and live
> Just for myself, whatever life the gods may give.
>
> HORACE

But the losses that befall me through others' wrongdoing, whether by theft or violence, hurt me about as much as they do a man who is sick and tormented with avarice. The injury has immeasurably more bitterness than the loss.

A thousand different kinds of troubles assailed me in single file; I would have suffered them more cheerfully in a single pile. I already considered to whom among my friends I could commit a needy and unfortunate old age; after letting my eyes wander all over, I found myself stripped to my shirt. To let oneself fall plumb down and from such a height, it must be into the arms of an affection solid, vigorous, and favored by fortune. These are rare, if there are any. In the end I recognized that the surest thing was to entrust myself and my need to myself; and that if it happened that I was lodged only coolly in fortune's favors I should recommend myself all the more strongly to my own favor, and attach myself, and look all the more closely, to myself. [C]In all things men cast themselves on the resources of others to spare their own, which alone are sure and alone powerful, if we know how to arm ourselves with them. Every man rushes elsewhere and into the future, because no man has arrived at himself.

[B]And I resolved that these were useful troubles. First, because bad students must be instructed with the rod when reason cannot do the job, [C]as by fire and by the force of wedges we restore a warped piece of wood to straightness. [B]I have long been preaching to myself

to stick to myself and break away from outside things; nevertheless I still keep turning my eyes to one side. Inclination, a favorable word from a great man, a pleasant countenance, tempt me. God knows if there is any scarcity of those in these times, and how little they mean! I still listen without frowning to the seductions that are held out to me to draw me into the market place, and I defend myself so softly that it looks as if I would prefer to succumb to them. Now a spirit so indocile needs some beatings; and we need to knock together and tighten the hoops, with good mallet strokes, on this cask that is splitting its seams, cracking up, and falling completely to pieces.

Second, because this misfortune served me as practice to prepare myself for worse, just in case I, who through the generosity of fortune and the nature of my character hoped to be one of the last, came to be one of the first to be caught by this storm; teaching me in good time to restrict my way of life and arrange it for a new state of things. True freedom is to have power over oneself for everything. ᶜ*He is most powerful who has power over himself* [Seneca].

ᴮIn an ordinary, tranquil time a man prepares for moderate and common accidents, but in this confusion that we have been in for thirty years every Frenchman, whether as an individual or as a member of the community, sees himself at every moment on the verge of the total overthrow of his fortune. Therefore we must keep our courage supplied with stronger and more vigorous provisions. Let us be grateful to destiny for having made us live in an age that is not soft, languid, and idle. Many a man who could never have been famous by any other means will make himself famous by his misfortune.

ᶜAs I seldom read in histories of such commotions in other states without regretting that I could not be present to consider them better, so my curiosity makes me feel some satisfaction at seeing with my own eyes this notable spectacle of our public death, its symptoms and its form. And since I cannot retard it, I am glad to be destined to watch it and learn from it.

Thus do we eagerly seek to recognize, even in shadow and in the fiction of the theaters, the representation of the tragic play of human fortune. Not that we lack compassion for what we hear; but the exceptional nature of these pathetic events arouses a pain that gives us pleasure. Nothing tickles that does not pain. And good historians avoid peaceful narratives as if they were stagnant water and dead sea,

in order to get back to the seditions and wars to which they know that we summon them.

I doubt if I can decently admit at what little cost to the repose and tranquillity of my life I have passed more than half of it amid the ruin of my country. The patience with which I bear misfortunes that do not affect me personally is rather too small a price to pay; and before complaining to myself I consider not so much what is taken away from me as what I still keep safe, both within and without. There is consolation in dodging now one, now another of the evils that aim at us successively, and strike elsewhere around us. Also, in the matter of public calamities, the more universally my sympathy is dispersed, the weaker it is. Besides, almost certainly, *we feel public calamities only so far as they concern our private affairs* [Livy]; and the state of health from which we started was such that it is itself a solace for the regret that we should have for it. It was health, but only in comparison with the sickness that followed it.

We have not fallen from very high. The corruption and brigandage that enjoy dignity and established status seem to me the least endurable. We are robbed less wickedly in a forest than in a place of safety. There was a universal conjunction of members, each individually vying in rottenness with the others, and most of them afflicted with age-old ulcers which no longer admitted of cure or asked for it.

^BSo this collapse truly stimulated rather than crushed me, with the help of my conscience, which bore itself not only peaceably but proudly; and I found no reason to complain of myself. Also, since God never sends men evils any more than goods entirely unmixed, my health for that time was unusually good; and just as without health I can do nothing, so with it there are few things I cannot do. It gave me the means to rouse all my resources and to put out my hand to ward off the blow that would otherwise easily have made a deeper wound. And I found that with my endurance I had some foothold against Fortune, and that I would need a great shock to throw me out of my saddle.

I do not say this to irritate her into making a more vigorous attack on me. I am her servant, I hold out my hands to her; in God's name let her be satisfied. Do I feel her assaults? Indeed I do. As those whom grief overwhelms and possesses yet let themselves at intervals be caressed by some pleasure, and a smile escapes them, so I too have enough power over myself to make my ordinary condition

peaceable and unburdened of painful imaginings; but once in a while I fail to keep my guard up against the stings of these unpleasant thoughts, which overcome me even as I am arming myself to drive them away or to wrestle with them.

Now a further increase of trouble came upon me following the others. Both outside and inside my house I was greeted by a plague of the utmost virulence. For as healthy bodies are subject to graver illnesses because they can be overcome only by these, so the very salubrious air of my place, where in the memory of man no contagion, even though in the neighborhood, had been able to get a foothold, became poisoned and produced strange results:

> Young men and old commingled crowd the tomb; no head
> Escapes ruthless Proserpina.
>
> HORACE

I had an absurd situation to put up with: the sight of my house was frightful to me. All that was in it was unguarded and abandoned to anyone who wanted it. I, who am so hospitable, had a great deal of trouble finding a retreat for my family: a family astray, a source of fear to their friends and themselves, and of horror wherever they sought to settle, having to shift their abode as soon as one of the group began to feel pain in the end of his finger. All illnesses are taken for the plague; people do not give themselves the time to recognize them. And the best part of all is that according to the rules of the profession, after any approach to danger you have to be forty days in a trance of anxiety over that illness, with your imagination meanwhile working you up in its own way and turning even your health into a fever.

All this would have affected me much less if I had not had to feel for the sufferings of others and serve for six months of misery as guide to this caravan. For I carry my own preservatives within me, which are resolution and patience. Apprehension, which is particularly feared in this disease, does not oppress me much. And if I had been alone and wished to take flight, it would have been a much more cheerful and distant one. It is a kind of death that does not seem to me one of the worst: it is generally quick, numbed, painless, consoled by the public situation, without ceremony, without mourning, without a crowd around.

But as for the people round about, not the hundredth part could save themselves:

> You may see the shepherds' realms
> Deserted, and the fields vacated far and wide.
> VIRGIL

In this place the best part of my revenue is from manual labor; the land that a hundred men worked for me has lain idle for a long time.

Now, what example of resoluteness did we not see then in the simplicity of this whole people? Each man universally gave up caring for his life. The grapes remained hanging on the vines, the principal produce of the country, as all prepared themselves indifferently, and awaited death that evening or the next day with face and voice so little frightened that it seemed that they had made their peace with this necessity and that they were under a universal and inevitable sentence of death. Death is always that. But on how little depends our resoluteness in the face of death! A few hours' difference in our distance from it, the mere consideration of having company, makes our apprehension of it different. See these people: because they are dying in the same month, children, young people, old people, they are no longer stunned, they no longer bewail one another. I saw some who feared to remain behind, as in a horrible solitude; and found them generally to be concerned only about their burial. It pained them to see the bodies scattered amid the fields, at the mercy of the animals that promptly appeared in swarms.

^cHow divergent human fancies are! The Neorites, a nation which Alexander subjugated, throw the bodies of the dead into the deepest parts of their forests to be devoured, the only sepulture considered happy among them.

^BHere a man, healthy, was already digging his grave; others lay down in them while still alive. And one of my laborers, with his hands and feet, pulled the earth over him as he was dying. Was that not taking shelter so as to go to sleep more comfortably? ^cAn undertaking rather comparable in loftiness with that of the Roman soldiers who were found after the battle of Cannae with their heads thrust into holes that they had made and filled up with their hands, suffocating themselves. ^BIn short, a whole nation was suddenly, by habit alone, placed on a level that concedes nothing in firmness to any studied and premeditated fortitude.

Most of the instructions that learning uses to encourage us are more showy than powerful and more ornamental than effective. We have abandoned Nature and we want to teach her her lesson, she

who used to guide us so happily and so surely. And yet the traces of her teaching and the little that remains of her image – imprinted, by the benefit of ignorance, on the life of that rustic, unpolished mob – learning is constrained every day to go and borrow, to give its disciples models of constancy, innocence, and tranquillity. It is fine to see these disciples, full of so much beautiful knowledge, obliged to imitate that stupid simplicity, and imitate it in the primary actions of virtue; and a fine thing that our sapience learns from the very animals the most useful teachings for the greatest and most necessary parts of our life: how we should live and die, husband our possessions, love and bring up our children, maintain justice – a singular testimony of human infirmity; and that this reason of ours that we handle as we will, always finding some diversity and novelty, leaves in us no apparent trace of Nature. And men have done with Nature as perfumers do with oil: they have sophisticated her with so many arguments and farfetched reasonings that she has become variable and particular for each man, and has lost her own constant and universal countenance; and we must seek in the animals evidence of her that is not subject to favor, corruption, or diversity of opinion.

For it is indeed true that they themselves do not always go exactly in Nature's road; but they deviate from it so little that you can always perceive the ruts. Just so, horses that are led by hand do indeed leap and prance about, but not beyond the length of their halters, and nonetheless they still follow the steps of the man who leads them; and so the hawk takes its flight, but under the restraint of the leash.

[c]*Meditate upon exile, torture, wars, diseases, shipwreck, so that you may not be a novice to any misfortune* [Seneca]. [B]Of what use to us is this curiosity to anticipate all the ills of human nature, and prepare ourselves with so much trouble to encounter even those which are perhaps never to touch us? [c]*The possibility of suffering makes us as unhappy as the suffering* [Seneca]. We are struck not only by the blow, but by the wind and the noise of it. Or [B]why go right now, like the most feverish, for it certainly is a fever, and have yourself whipped because it may happen some day that fortune will have you whipped, [c]and put on your furred gown on Midsummer Day because you will need it at Christmas? [B]"Hurry up and experience the evils that may befall you, especially the most extreme. Test yourself in them," they say, "make sure." On the contrary, the easiest and most natural thing would be to unburden even our thoughts of them. Apparently they will not come soon enough, their true being

does not last us long enough; our mind must extend and prolong them, incorporate them into itself and dwell on them beforehand, as if they did not weigh reasonably upon our senses. ᶜ"They will weigh heavily enough when they are there," says one of the masters, not of some tender sect, but of the hardest.⁶ "Meanwhile favor yourself; believe what you like best. What good does it do you to welcome and anticipate your bad fortune, to lose the present through fear of the future, and to be miserable now because you are to be so in time?" Those are his words.

ᴮLearning doubtless does us a good service by instructing us very exactly about the dimensions of evils,

> Whetting with cares the minds of mortal men.
> VIRGIL

It would be a pity if part of their greatness escaped our feeling and knowledge.

It is certain that to most people preparation for death has given more torment than the dying. ᶜIt was once said truly and by a very judicious author: *the senses are less affected by the suffering than by the thought of it* [Quintilian].

Sometimes the very feeling that death is at hand animates us with a prompt resolve no longer to avoid a thing that is completely unavoidable. Many gladiators in times past have been seen, after fighting like cowards, to swallow death courageously, offering their throat to the enemy's sword and inviting it. The prospect of a more distant death needs a courage that is steady, and consequently difficult to come by.

ᴮIf you don't know how to die, don't worry; Nature will tell you what to do on the spot, fully and adequately. She will do this job perfectly for you; don't bother your head about it.

> To know the hour of death in vain you strive,
> Mortals, and by what road it will arrive.
> PROPERTIUS

> It gives less pain to bear a certain, sudden blow;
> Long to endure a life of fear is greater woe.
> MAXIMIANUS

We trouble our life by concern about death, and death by concern about life. ᶜOne torments us, the other frightens us. ᴮIt is not

6 Seneca, a Stoic.

against death that we prepare ourselves; that is too momentary a thing. ^CA quarter hour of suffering, without consequence, without harm, does not deserve any particular precepts. ^BTo tell the truth, we prepare ourselves against the preparations for death.

Philosophy orders us to have death ever before our eyes, to foresee and consider it before the time comes, and afterward gives us the rules and precautions to provide against our being wounded by this foresight and this thought. That is what those doctors do who make us ill so that they may have something on which to employ their drugs and their art. ^CIf we have not known how to live, it is wrong to teach us how to die, and make the end inconsistent with the whole. If we have known how to live steadfastly and tranquilly, we shall know how to die in the same way.

They may boast about it all they please. *The whole life of a philosopher is a meditation on death* [Cicero]. But it seems to me that death is indeed the end, but not therefore the goal, of life; it is its finish, its extremity, but not therefore its object. Life should be an aim unto itself, a purpose unto itself; its rightful study is to regulate, conduct, and suffer itself. Among the many other duties comprised in this general and principal chapter on knowing how to live is this article on knowing how to die; and it is one of the lightest, if our fear did not give it weight.

^BTo judge by utility and natural truth, the lessons of simplicity yield little to those which learning preaches to us to the contrary. Men are diverse in inclination and strength; they must be led to their own good according to their nature and by diverse routes. ^C*Wherever the tempest drives me, there I land* [Horace].

^BI never saw one of my peasant neighbors cogitating over the countenance and assurance with which he would pass this last hour. Nature teaches him not to think about death except when he is dying. And then he has better grace about it than Aristotle, whom death oppresses doubly, both by itself and by such a long foreknowledge. Therefore it was Caesar's opinion that the least premeditated death was the happiest and the least oppressive. ^C*He suffers more than is necessary who suffers before it is necessary* [Seneca].

The bitterness of this imagination springs from our curiosity. We are always impeding ourselves in this way, by trying to anticipate and overrule the prescriptions of nature. It is only for the learned to dine the worse for the idea of death when in perfect health, and to knit their brows at it. The common people need neither remedy nor consolation except when the blow falls, and consider only

precisely as much of it as they feel. ^BIsn't that what we say, that the stupidity and lack of apprehension of the vulgar gives them this endurance of present troubles and this profound nonchalance about sinister accidents to come, ^Cthat their souls, because they are thick and obtuse, are less penetrable and unstable? ^BFor Heaven's sake, if that is so, let us henceforth hold a school of stupidity. Learning promises us no greater boon than this, to which stupidity so gently leads its disciples.

We shall have no lack of good teachers, interpreters of the simplicity of nature. Socrates will be one. For as far as I can remember, he speaks in about this sense to the judges who are deliberating over his life:

"I am afraid, gentlemen, that if I entreat you not to put me to death, I shall involve myself in the charge of my accusers, which is that I claim to be wiser than others, as having some more hidden knowledge of the things that are above and below us. I know that I have had no association or acquaintance with death, nor have I known anyone who has had experience of its qualities to inform me about it. Those who fear it presuppose that they know it. As for me, I know neither what death is like nor what it is like in the other world. Perhaps death is something indifferent, perhaps desirable.

^C"It is likely, however, that if it is a transmigration from one place to another, it is an improvement to go and live with so many great persons who have passed on and to be exempt from having any more to do with unjust and corrupt judges. If it is an annihilation of our being, it is still an improvement to enter upon a long and peaceful night. We feel nothing sweeter in life than a deep and tranquil rest and sleep, without dreams.

^B"The things that I know to be bad, like wronging our neighbor and disobeying our superior, whether God or man, I carefully avoid. Those which I do not know to be either good or bad, I cannot fear.

^C"If I am going off to die and leave you alive, the gods alone can see with whom it will go better, you or me. Wherefore, as far as I am concerned, you will decide as you please. But according to my habit of advising just and profitable things, I do indeed say that for the sake of your conscience you will do better to set me free, unless you see further into my case than I do. And if you judge according to my past actions, both public and private, according to my intentions, and according to the profit that so many of our citizens, young and old, derive every day from my conversation, and the good that I do you all, you cannot duly discharge your obligation to my merit

except by ordering that in view of my poverty I be maintained in the Prytaneum at the public expense; which I have often known you to grant to others with less reason.

"Do not take it as obstinacy or disdain that I do not follow the custom and supplicate you and try to move you to commiseration. I have friends and relatives – not being, as Homer says, born of wood or stone any more than others – capable of presenting themselves in tears and mourning, and I have three weeping children to move you to pity. But I would bring shame on my city, at my age and with such a reputation for wisdom as here I am accused of, to stoop to such cowardly behavior. What would people say of the other Athenians?

"I have always admonished those who have listened to me not to redeem their life by a dishonorable action. And in my country's wars, at Amphipolis, at Potidaea, at Delium, and others that I have been in, I have shown in action how far I was from guaranteeing my safety by my shame. Moreover, I would be trying to harm your sense of duty and inviting you to do ugly things; for you should not be persuaded by my prayers, but by the pure and solid reasons of justice.

"You have sworn to the gods to abide by the laws; it would seem that I wanted to suspect you and countercharge you with not believing that there are any gods. And I would actually be testifying against myself that I did not believe in them as I should, distrusting their guidance and not committing my affair purely into their hands. I trust in them for everything and hold it for certain that in this they will do what is best for you and for me. Good men, living or dead, have nothing to fear from the gods."

BIs that not a Csober, sane Bplea, Cbut at the same time natural and lowly, Binconceivably lofty, Ctruthful, frank, and just beyond all example – Band employed in what a critical need! CTruly he was right to prefer it to the one that the great orator Lysias had put in writing for him, excellently fashioned in the forensic style, but unworthy of so noble a criminal. Should people have heard a supplicating voice from the mouth of Socrates? Should that proud virtue have quit at the height of its display? And should his rich and powerful nature have committed his defense to art, and, in its loftiest test, renounced truth and sincerity, the ornaments of his speech, to bedeck itself with the make-up of the figures and fictions of a memorized oration? He did very wisely, and like himself, not to corrupt an incorruptible tenor of life and such a saintly model of human nature in order to prolong his decrepitude by a year and betray the immortal memory of that glorious end. He owed his life

not to himself but to the world as an example. Would it not be a public loss if he had finished it in an idle and obscure fashion?

ᴮAssuredly, such a nonchalant and mild way of considering his death deserved to have posterity consider it all the more on his behalf; which it did. And there is nothing in justice so just as what fortune ordained for his glory. For the Athenians held those who had been the cause of his death in such abomination that they shunned them like excommunicated persons; they considered everything they had touched as polluted; no one would wash with them at the baths; no one greeted them or said hello to them. So that finally, no longer able to bear this public hatred, they hanged themselves.

If anyone thinks that among the many examples of the sayings of Socrates that I might have chosen to serve my purpose I selected this one badly, and if he judges that this speech is elevated above common ideas – I chose it deliberately. For I judge otherwise, and hold that it is a speech which in its naturalness ranks far behind and below common opinions. ᶜIn an unstudied and artless boldness and a childlike assurance ᴮit represents the pure and primary impression ᶜand ignorance ᴮof Nature. For it may be believed that we are naturally afraid of pain, but not of death for its own sake: it is a part of our being no less essential than life. To what purpose would Nature have engendered in us a hatred and horror of death, seeing that it holds a rank of very high utility with her in fostering the succession and vicissitude of her works, and that in this universal commonwealth it promotes birth and increase more than loss or ruin?

> Thus is the universe renewed.
> LUCRETIUS

ᶜFrom one death come a thousand lives.
> OVID

ᴮThe failing of one life is the passage to a thousand other lives.

ᶜNature has implanted in the animals an instinct for taking care of themselves and for their preservation. They go so far as to be afraid of being injured, of knocks and wounds, of our fettering and beating them: accidents subject to their sense and experience. But they cannot fear our killing them, nor have they the faculty of imagining or inferring death. So it is further said that ᴮthey are seen not only to suffer it gaily – most horses neigh at their death,

swans greet it with song – but moreover to seek it out in their need, as many examples of elephants show.

Besides, isn't the method of arguing that Socrates uses here equally admirable in its simplicity and its vigor? Truly it is much easier to talk like Aristotle and live like Caesar than it is to talk and live like Socrates. There lies the extreme degree of perfection and difficulty; art cannot reach it.

Now our faculties are not so trained. We neither essay them nor know them. We invest ourselves with those of others, and let our own lie idle.

Even so someone might say of me that I have here only made a bunch of other people's flowers, having furnished nothing of my own but the thread to tie them. Indeed I have yielded to public opinion in carrying these borrowed ornaments about on me. But I do not intend that they should cover and hide me; that is the opposite of my design, I who wish to make a show only of what is my own, and of what is naturally my own; and if I had taken my own advice I would at all hazards have spoken absolutely all alone. ᶜI load myself with these borrowings more and more heavily every day beyond my intention and my original form, following the fancy of the age and the exhortation of others. If it is unbecoming to me, as I believe it is, no matter; it may be useful to someone else.

ᴮSome people quote Plato and Homer who have never looked at them. And I myself have taken enough passages elsewhere than at their source. Without trouble and without competence, having a library of a thousand volumes around me in this place where I write, I will presently borrow, if I please, from a dozen such patch-makers, people whom I do not often leaf through, enough to bedeck this treatise on physiognomy. I need only the preliminary epistle of some German to stuff me with quotations. This is the way we go begging an appetizing glory, to cheat the fools of this world.

ᶜThese concoctions of commonplaces, by means of which so many men husband their study, are hardly useful except for commonplace subjects, and they serve to show us off, not to guide us: a ridiculous fruit of learning, which Socrates belabors so comically against Euthydemus. I have known books to be made out of things never either studied or understood, the author entrusting to various of his learned friends the search for this and that material to build it, contenting himself for his part with having planned the project and piled up by his industry this stack of unfamiliar provisions; at least the ink and the paper are his. That, in all conscience, is buying or

borrowing a book, not making one. It is teaching men, not that you can make a book, but, what they might have been in doubt about, that you cannot make one.

^BA magistrate was boasting in my presence of having heaped up two hundred-odd quotations from others in a single decision he had written as a presiding judge. ^CBy proclaiming this to everybody he seemed to me to efface the glory that people were giving him for it. ^BA petty and absurd boast, in my opinion, for such a subject and such a person.

^CI, among so many borrowings of mine, am very glad to be able to hide one now and then, disguising and altering it for a new service. At the risk of letting it be said that I do so through failure to understand its original use, I give it some particular application with my own hand, so that it may be less purely someone else's. ^BThese others put their thefts on parade and into account; and so they have better credit with the laws than I.[7] ^CWe naturalists judge that the honor of invention is greatly and incomparably preferable to the honor of quotation.

^BIf I had wanted to speak from knowledge, I would have spoken earlier. I would have written at a time nearer to my studies, when I had more wit and memory, and would have trusted myself more to the vigor of that age than of this one, if I had wanted to make a profession of writing. ^CMoreover, one gracious favor that fortune perhaps offered me by the mediation of this work would then have come in a more propitious season.[8] ^BTwo of my acquaintances, great men in this ability, have in my opinion lost by half for having refused to publish at forty in order to wait until sixty. Maturity, like youth, has its defects, and worse ones. And old age is as unsuited to this sort of work as to all others. Whoever puts his decrepitude into print plays the fool, if he hopes to squeeze out of it humors that do not smell of ungraciousness, dreaminess, and drowsiness. Our mind grows constipated and sluggish as it grows old.

I speak ignorance pompously and opulently, and speak knowledge meagerly and piteously, ^Cthe latter secondarily and

7 Here the 1588 edition added: "Like those who steal horses, I paint their mane and tail, and sometimes blind them in one eye; if the first owner used them as amblers I set them to trotting, and put them to carrying the pack if they served for the saddle." After a large number of revisions, Montaigne cut the passage out.

8 Presumably an allusion to Montaigne's friendship with Marie de Gournay, whom he first met in 1588, four years before he died.

accidentally, the former expressly and principally. And there is nothing I treat specifically except nothing, and no knowledge except that of the lack of knowledge. [B]I have chosen the time when my life, which I have to portray, lies all before my eyes; what is left is more related to death. And even of my death, if I should find it garrulous, as others do, I would willingly give an account to the public on my way out.

About Socrates, who was a perfect model in all great qualities, it vexes me that he hit on a body and face so ugly as they say he had, and so incongruous with the beauty of his soul, [C]he who was so madly in love with beauty. Nature did him an injustice. [B]There is nothing more likely than the conformity and relation of the body to the spirit. [C]*It matters a great deal in what sort of body the soul is lodged; for there are many things about the body that sharpen the mind, many that blunt it* [Cicero]. This man is speaking of an unnatural ugliness and deformity of limbs. But we also call ugliness an unattractiveness at first glance, which resides chiefly in the face, and often arouses our distaste for very slight causes: the complexion, a spot, a rugged expression, or some inexplicable cause, when the limbs are symmetrical and perfect.

The ugliness which clothed a very beautiful soul in La Boétie was in this category. This superficial ugliness, which is very imperious for all that, is less prejudicial to the state of the spirit and not very certain in its effect on men's opinion. The other, which is more properly called deformity, is more substantial and more apt to strike home inwardly. Not every shoe of smooth leather but every well-formed shoe shows the form of the foot within.

[B]So Socrates said of his ugliness that it betrayed what would have been just as much ugliness in his soul, if he had not corrected it by training. [C]But in saying this I hold that he was jesting according to his wont. So excellent a soul was never self-made.

[B]I cannot say often enough how much I consider beauty a powerful and advantageous quality. Socrates called it "a short tyranny," [C]and Plato, "the privilege of nature." [B]We have no quality that surpasses it in credit. It holds the first place in human relations; it presents itself before the rest, seduces and prepossesses our judgment with great authority and a wondrous impression. [C]Phryne would have lost her case even in the hands of an excellent attorney, if, opening her robe, she had not corrupted her judges by her dazzling beauty. And I find that Cyrus, Alexander, Caesar, those

three masters of the world, did not forget beauty in carrying out their great affairs; nor did Scipio the Elder.

One and the same word in Greek embraces the beautiful and the good. And the Holy Ghost often calls good those whom it means to call beautiful. I would readily uphold the ranking of good things found in a song, taken from some ancient poet, which Plato says was widely known: health, beauty, riches.

Aristotle says that to the beautiful belongs the right to command, and that when there are any whose beauty approaches that of the images of the gods, veneration is likewise their due. To one who asked him why people frequented beautiful persons longer and more often, he said: "That question is proper only for a blind man." Most philosophers, and the greatest, paid for their schooling, and acquired wisdom, by the mediation and favor of their beauty.

[B]Not only in the men who serve me, but also in animals, I consider it as within two fingers' breath of goodness. Yet it seems to me that the cast and formation of the face and those lineaments from which people infer certain inward dispositions and our fortunes to come, are things that do not fall very directly and simply under the heading of beauty and ugliness; any more than every good odor and clear air promises health, or every closeness and stench promises infection, in time of pestilence. Those who accuse the ladies of belying their beauty by their character do not always hit the mark. For in a not too well formed face there may dwell an air of probity and trustworthiness; as, on the contrary, I have sometimes read between two beautiful eyes threats of a malignant and dangerous nature. There are favorable physiognomies; and in a crowd of victorious enemies you will instantly choose, among men unknown to you, one rather than another to whom to surrender and entrust your life; and beauty has no real part in the choice.

The face is a weak guarantee; yet it deserves some consideration. And if I had to whip the wicked, I would do so more severely to those who belied and betrayed the promises that nature had implanted on their brows; I would punish malice more harshly when it was hidden under a kindly appearance. It seems as if some faces are lucky, others unlucky. And I think there is some art to distinguishing the kindly faces from the simple, the severe from the rough, the malicious from the gloomy, the disdainful from the melancholy, and other such adjacent qualities. There are beauties not only proud but bitter; others are sweet, and even beyond

that, insipid. As for prognosticating future events from them, those are matters that I leave undecided.

As I have said elsewhere, I have very simply and crudely adopted for my own sake this ancient precept: that we cannot go wrong by following Nature, that the sovereign precept is to conform to her. I have not, like Socrates, corrected my natural disposition by force of reason, and have not troubled my inclination at all by art. I let myself go as I have come. I combat nothing. My two ruling parts, of their own volition, live in peace and good accord. But my nurse's milk, thank God, was moderately healthy and temperate.

^CShall I say this in passing: that I see held in greater price than it is worth a certain idea of scholastic probity, almost the only one practiced among us, a slave to precepts, held down beneath fear and hope? What I like is the virtue that laws and religions do not make but perfect and authorize, that feels in itself enough to sustain itself without help, born in us from its own roots, from the seed of universal reason that is implanted in every man who is not dena- tured. This reason, which straightens Socrates from his inclination to vice, makes him obedient to the men and gods who command in his city, courageous in death not because his soul is immortal but because he is mortal. It is a ruinous teaching for any society, and much more harmful than ingenious and subtle, which persuades the people that religious belief is enough, by itself and without morals, to satisfy divine justice. Practice makes us see an enormous distinc- tion between devoutness and conscience.

^BI have a favorable bearing, both in itself and in others' inter- pretation –

> What did I say, *I have?* Chremes, I mean I had!
> TERENCE

> You see, alas, only the bones of this worn body
> MAXIMIANUS

– one very unlike that of Socrates. It has often happened that on the mere credit of my presence and manner, persons who had no knowl- edge of me have placed great trust in me, both for their own affairs and for mine; and in foreign countries I have derived singular and rare favors from this. But the following two experiences are perhaps worth my telling in detail.

A certain person made a plan to take my house and myself by surprise. His scheme was to arrive alone at my door and press rather

insistently for entry. I knew him by name and had reason to trust him as a neighbor, and to some extent a relative of mine. I opened to him, ᶜas I do to everyone. ᴮHere he was completely terrified, his horse out of breath and all worn out. He entertained me with this bit of fiction: that he had just been set upon a half a league away by an enemy of his, whom I also knew, and I had heard of their feud; that this enemy had been wonderfully hot on his heels, and that, having been surprised in disarray and weaker in number, he had sought safety at my door; that he was greatly troubled about his men, whom he said he supposed to be dead or captured.

I tried quite naïvely to comfort, reassure, and refresh him. Soon after, up came four or five of his soldiers, with the same bearing and the same fright, wanting to come in; and then others and still others after them, well equipped and well armed, until there were twenty-five or thirty, pretending to have the enemy at their heels. ᶜThis mystery was beginning to arouse my suspicion. ᴮI was not unaware in what sort of an age I was living, how much my house might be envied; and I had several examples of others of my acquaintance to whom similar misadventures had happened. However, feeling that there was nothing to be gained by having begun to be pleasant if I did not go through with it, and being unable to get rid of them without ruining everything, I abandoned myself to the most natural and simple course, as I always do, and gave orders for them to come in.

Besides, the truth is that I am by nature little given to distrust and suspicion. I am apt to lean toward the milder excuse and interpretation. I take men according to the common order, and do not believe in these perverted and unnatural inclinations unless I am forced to by strong evidence, any more than in monsters and miracles. And besides, I am the sort of man who readily commits himself to Fortune and abandons himself bodily into her arms. For which I have up to now had more occasion to applaud myself than to complain; and I have found her both wiser ᶜand more friendly to my affairs ᴮthan I am.

There have been some actions in my life the conduct of which might justly be called difficult, or, if you wish, prudent. Even of those, put it that one-third was my doing, truly two-thirds were richly her doing. ᶜWe err, it seems to me, in that we do not trust ourselves enough to heaven, and we expect more from our own conduct than belongs to us. That is why our plans so often go astray. Heaven is jealous of the extent we attribute to the claims of human

wisdom, to the prejudice of its own; and the more we amplify them, the more it cuts them down.

^BThese men remained on horseback in my courtyard, the leader with me in my main room; he had not wanted to have his horse stabled, saying that he had to withdraw as soon as he had news of his men. He saw himself master of his undertaking, and nothing now remained but its execution. He has often said since, for he was not afraid to tell this story, that my face and my frankness had disarmed him of his treachery. He remounted his horse, his men constantly keeping their eyes on him to see what signal he would give them, very astonished to see him go away and abandon his advantage.

Another time, trusting in some truce or other that had just been proclaimed between our armies, I started on a journey through an extraordinarily ticklish part of the country. They had no sooner got wind of me than up rode three or four groups of horsemen from different places to catch me. One of them reached me on the third day, when I was attacked by fifteen or twenty masked gentlemen followed by a wave of mounted archers. There I was, seized and made prisoner, withdrawn into the thick of a neighboring forest, unhorsed, my valises seized, my coffers searched, my money box taken, horses and equipment divided among new masters. We were a long time in that thicket disputing over the matter of my ransom, which they set so high that it was quite apparent that I was scarcely known to them. They started a big dispute over my life. In truth, there were many threatening circumstances that showed the danger I was in.

> ^CNow you need all your courage, now a steadfast heart,
> Aeneas.
>
> VIRGIL

^BI kept standing on my rights under the truce, which were to give up to them only the gain they had made in despoiling me, which was not to be despised, without promise of any other ransom. After we had been there two or three hours, and they had mounted me on a horse that was not likely to escape them, and had committed me to the particular care of fifteen or twenty musketeers and scattered my men among some others with orders that we should be led as prisoners by different routes, and after I had already been taken a distance of two or three harquebus shots away,

Having prayed for help to Castor and to Pollux,

CATULLUS

behold, a sudden and very unexpected change came over them. I saw the leader return to me with gentler words, taking pains to search for my belongings scattered among the troop, and having them returned to me as far as they could be recovered, even including my money box. The best present they made me was finally my freedom; the rest did not concern me much ^cat that time.

^BThe true cause of so unusual an about-face and change of mind, without any apparent motivation, and of such a miraculous repentance, at such a time, in a premeditated and deliberate enterprise which had been made lawful by custom (for from the outset I openly confessed to them what party I belonged to and what road I was taking), I truly do not even now well know. The most conspicuous among them, who took off his mask and let me know his name,[9] repeated to me then several times that I owed my deliverance to my face and the freedom and firmness of my speech, which made me undeserving of such a misadventure; and he asked me to assure him of similar treatment should the occasion arise. It is possible that the divine goodness willed to make use of this vain instrument for my preservation. It also protected me the next day from other, worse ambushes, of which these very men had warned me.

The second of these men is still on his feet to tell the tale; the first was killed not long ago.[10]

If my face did not answer for me, if people did not read in my eyes and my voice the innocence of my intentions, I would not have lasted so long without quarrel and without harm, considering my indiscreet freedom in saying, right or wrong, whatever comes into my head, and in judging things rashly. This habit may with reason appear uncivil and ill adapted to our usage, but I have not known anyone who judged it to be injurious or malicious, or who took offense at my freedom if he had it from my own lips. Words when reported have a different sense, as they have a different sound.

9 Here the 1588 edition included this additional remark: "(I would like to find out in my turn what kind of countenance he would have in a similar accident)." Montaigne does not tell the man's name anywhere, and it is not known. He was the victim of a similar hold-up on his way to Paris in 1588 (see Letter 34).
10 The man who started to seize Montaigne's château and then changed his mind, and the leader of the marauders who made him a prisoner on the road.

Moreover, I hate no one; and I am so squeamish about hurting that for the service of reason itself I cannot do it. And when occasions have summoned me to sentencing criminals, I have tended to fall short of justice. *I wish there were no more crimes committed than I have the heart to punish when they have been committed* [Livy].

They say that Aristotle was reproached for having been too merciful to a wicked man. "In truth," he said, "I was merciful to the man, not to the wickedness."

Ordinary judgments are exasperated to vengeance by the horror of the misdeed. That very thing cools mine: horror at the first murder makes me fear a second, and hatred of the first cruelty makes me hate any imitation of it. To me, who am only a jack of clubs,[II] may apply what they said about Charillus, king of Sparta: "He could not possibly be good, since he is not bad to the wicked." Or else thus, for Plutarch presents it in these two ways, as he does a thousand other things, variously and contrastingly: "He must certainly be good, since he is good even to the wicked." As I do not like to take a hand in legitimate actions against people who resent them, so, to tell the truth, I am not scrupulous enough to refrain from taking a hand in illegitimate actions against people who consent to them.

13
Of experience

There is no desire more natural than the desire for knowledge. We try all the ways that can lead us to it. When reason fails us, we use experience –

> Experience, by example led,
> By varied trials art has bred
> MANILIUS

– which is a weaker and less dignified means. But truth is so great a thing that we must not disdain any medium that will lead us to it. Reason has so many shapes that we know not which to lay hold of; experience has no fewer. The inference that we try to draw from the resemblance of events is uncertain, because they are always

II A person of no importance.

dissimilar: there is no quality so universal in this aspect of things as diversity and variety.

Both the Greeks and the Latins, and we ourselves, use eggs for the most express example of similarity. However, there have been men, and notably one at Delphi, who recognized marks of difference between eggs, so that he never took one for another; ^cand although there were many hens, he could tell which one the egg came from.

^BDissimilarity necessarily intrudes into our works; no art can attain similarity. Neither Perrozet nor any other can smooth and whiten the backs of his cards so carefully that some gamesters will not distinguish them simply by seeing them slip through another man's hands. Resemblance does not make things so much alike as difference makes them unlike. ^cNature has committed herself to make nothing separate that was not different.

^BTherefore I do not much like the opinion of the man who thought by a multiplicity of laws to bridle the authority of judges, cutting up their meat for them. He did not realize that there is as much freedom and latitude in the interpretation of laws as in their creation. And those people must be jesting who think they can diminish and stop our disputes by recalling us to the express words of the Bible. For our mind finds the field no less spacious in registering the meaning of others than in presenting its own. As if there were less animosity and bitterness in commenting than in inventing!

We see how mistaken he was. For we have in France more laws than all the rest of the world together, and more than would be needed to rule all the worlds of Epicurus: ^c*As formerly we suffered from crimes, so now we suffer from laws* [Tacitus]. ^BAnd yet we have left so much room for opinion and decision to our judges, that there never was such a powerful and licentious freedom. What have our legislators gained by selecting a hundred thousand particular cases and actions, and applying a hundred thousand laws to them? This number bears no proportion to the infinite diversity of human actions. Multiplication of our imaginary cases will never equal the variety of the real examples. Add to them a hundred times as many more: and still no future event will be found to correspond so exactly to any one of all the many, many thousands of selected and recorded events that there will not remain some circumstance, some difference, that will require separate consideration in forming a judgment. There is little relation between our actions, which are in perpetual

mutation, and fixed and immutable laws. The most desirable laws
are those that are rarest, simplest, and most general; and I even think
that it would be better to have none at all than to have them in such
numbers as we have.

Nature always gives us happier laws than those we give ourselves.
Witness the picture of the Golden Age of the poets, and the state
in which we see nations live which have no other laws. Here are
some who employ, as the only judge in their quarrels, the first
traveler passing through their mountains. And these others on
market day elect one of themselves who decides all their suits
on the spot. What would be the danger in having our wisest men
settle ours in this way, according to the circumstances and at sight,
without being bound to precedents, past or future? For every foot its
own shoe. King Ferdinand, when he sent colonists to the Indies,
wisely provided that no students of jurisprudence should accompany
them, for fear that lawsuits might breed in this new world,
this being by nature a science generating altercation and division;
judging, with Plato, that lawyers and doctors are a bad provision for
a country.

Why is it that our common language, so easy for any other use,
becomes obscure and unintelligible in contracts and wills, and that
a man who expresses himself so clearly, whatever he says or writes,
finds in this field no way of speaking his mind that does not fall into
doubt and contradiction? Unless it is that the princes of this art,
applying themselves with particular attention to picking out solemn
words and contriving artificial phrases, have so weighed every
syllable, so minutely examined every sort of combination, that
here they are at last entangled and embroiled in the endless number
of figures and in such minute partitions that they can no longer fall
under any rule or prescription or any certain interpretation. ^c*What is
broken up into dust becomes confused* [Seneca].

^BWho has seen children trying to divide a mass of quicksilver
into a certain number of parts? The more they press it and knead it
and try to constrain it to their will, the more they provoke the
independence of this spirited metal; it escapes their skill and keeps
dividing and scattering in little particles beyond all reckoning. This
is the same; for by subdividing these subtleties they teach men to
increase their doubts; they start us extending and diversifying the
difficulties, they lengthen them, they scatter them. By sowing
questions and cutting them up, they make the world fructify and
teem with uncertainty and quarrels, ^cas the earth is made more

fertile the more it is crumbled and deeply plowed. *Learning makes difficulties* [Quintilian].

[B]We were perplexed over Ulpian, we are still perplexed over Bartolus and Baldus. We should have wiped out the traces of this innumerable diversity of opinions, instead of wearing them as decoration and cramming the heads of posterity with them.

I do not know what to say about it, but it is evident from experience that so many interpretations disperse the truth and shatter it. Aristotle wrote to be understood; if he did not succeed, still less will another man, less able, and not treating his own ideas. By diluting the substance we allow it to escape and spill it all over the place; of one subject we make a thousand, and, multiplying and subdividing, fall back into Epicurus' infinity of atoms. Never did two men judge alike about the same thing, and it is impossible to find two opinions exactly alike, not only in different men, but in the same man at different times. Ordinarily I find subject for doubt in what the commentary has not deigned to touch on. I am more apt to trip on flat ground, like certain horses I know which stumble more often on a smooth road.

Who would not say that glosses increase doubts and ignorance, since there is no book to be found, whether human or divine, with which the world busies itself, whose difficulties are cleared up by interpretation? The hundredth commentator hands it on to his successor thornier and rougher than the first one had found it. When do we agree and say, "There has been enough about this book; henceforth there is nothing more to say about it"?

This is best seen in law practice. We give legal authority to numberless doctors, numberless decisions, and as many interpretations. Do we therefore find any end to the need of interpreting? Do we see any progress and advance toward tranquillity? Do we need fewer lawyers and judges than when this mass of law was still in its infancy? On the contrary, we obscure and bury the meaning; we no longer find it except hidden by so many enclosures and barriers.

Men do not know the natural infirmity of their mind: it does nothing but ferret and quest, and keeps incessantly whirling around, building up and becoming entangled in its own work, like our silkworms, and is suffocated in it. *A mouse in a pitch barrel* [Erasmus]. It thinks it notices from a distance some sort of glimmer of imaginary light and truth; but while running toward it, it is crossed by so many difficulties and obstacles, and diverted by so many new quests, that it strays from the road, bewildered. Not very different

from what happened to Aesop's dogs, who, discovering something that looked like a dead body floating in the sea, and being unable to approach it, attempted to drink up the water and dry up the passage, and choked in the attempt. ᶜTo which may be joined what a certain Crates said of the writings of Heraclitus, that they needed a good swimmer for a reader, so that the depth and weight of Heraclitus' learning should not sink him and drown him.

ᴮIt is only personal weakness that makes us content with what others or we ourselves have found out in this hunt for knowledge. An abler man will not rest content with it. There is always room for a successor, ᶜyes, and for ourselves, ᴮand a road in another direction. There is no end to our researches; our end is in the other world. ᶜIt is a sign of contraction of the mind when it is content, or of weariness. A spirited mind never stops within itself; it is always aspiring and going beyond its strength; it has impulses beyond its powers of achievement. If it does not advance and press forward and stand at bay and clash, it is only half alive. ᴮIts pursuits are boundless and without form; its food is ᶜwonder, the chase, ᴮambiguity. Apollo revealed this clearly enough, always speaking to us equivocally, obscurely, and obliquely, not satisfying us, but keeping our minds interested and busy. It is an irregular, perpetual motion, without model and without aim. Its inventions excite, pursue, and produce one another.

> So in a running stream one wave we see
> After another roll incessantly,
> And line by line, each does eternally
> Pursue the other, each the other flee.
> By this one, that one ever on is sped,
> And this one by the other ever led;
> The water still does into water go,
> Still the same brook, but different waters flow.
> LA BOÉTIE

It is more of a job to interpret the interpretations than to interpret the things, and there are more books about books than about any other subject: we do nothing but write glosses about each other. ᶜThe world is swarming with commentaries; of authors there is a great scarcity.

Is it not the chief and most reputed learning of our times to learn to understand the learned? Is that not the common and ultimate end of all studies?

Our opinions are grafted upon one another. The first serves as a stock for the second, the second for the third. Thus we scale the ladder, step by step. And thence it happens that he who has mounted highest has often more honor than merit; for he has only mounted one speck higher on the shoulders of the next last.

[B]How often and perhaps how stupidly have I extended my book to make it speak of itself! [C]Stupidly, if only for this reason, that I should have remembered what I say of others who do the same: that these frequent sheep's eyes at their own work testify that their heart thrills with love for it, and that even the rough, disdainful blows with which they beat it are only the love taps and affectations of maternal fondness; in keeping with Aristotle, to whom self-appreciation and self-depreciation often spring from the same sort of arrogance. For as for my excuse, that I ought to have more liberty in this than others, precisely because I write of myself and my writings as of my other actions, because my theme turns in upon itself – I do not know whether everyone will accept it.

[B]I have observed in Germany that Luther has left as many divisions and altercations over the uncertainty of his opinions, and more, as he raised about the Holy Scriptures.

Our disputes are purely verbal. I ask what is "nature," "pleasure," "circle," "substitution." The question is one of words, and is answered in the same way. "A stone is a body." But if you pressed on: "And what is a body?" – "Substance." – "And what is substance?" and so on, you would finally drive the respondent to the end of his lexicon. We exchange one word for another word, often more unknown. I know better what is man than I know what is animal, or mortal, or rational. To satisfy one doubt, they give me three; it is the Hydra's head.

Socrates asked Meno what virtue was. "There is," said Meno, "the virtue of a man and of a woman, of a magistrate and of a private individual, of a child and of an old man." "That's fine," exclaimed Socrates; "we were in search of one virtue, and here is a whole swarm of them."

We put one question, they give us back a hive of them. As no event and no shape is entirely like another, so none is entirely different from another. [C]An ingenious mixture on the part of nature. If our faces were not similar, we could not distinguish man from beast; if they were not dissimilar, we could not distinguish man from man. [B]All things hold together by some similarity; every example is lame, and the comparison that is drawn from experience

is always faulty and imperfect; however, we fasten together our comparisons by some corner. Thus the laws serve, and thus adapt themselves to each of our affairs, by some roundabout, forced, and biased interpretation.

Since the ethical laws, which concern the individual duty of each man in himself, are so hard to frame, as we see they are, it is no wonder if those that govern so many individuals are more so. Consider the form of this justice that governs us: it is a true testimony of human imbecility, so full it is of contradiction and error. What we find to be leniency and severity in justice – and we find so much of them that I do not know whether the mean between them is met with as often – are sickly parts and unjust members of the very body and essence of justice.

Some peasants have just informed me hastily that a moment ago they left in a wood that belongs to me a man stabbed in a hundred places, who is still breathing, and who begged them for pity's sake to bring him some water and help him to get up. They say that they did not dare go near him, and ran away, for fear that the officers of the law would catch them there and hold them accountable for the accident – as is done with those who are found near a murdered man – to their total ruin, since they had neither ability nor money to defend their innocence. What could I say to them? It is certain that this act of humanity would have got them into trouble.

How many innocent people we have found to have been punished – I mean by no fault of their judges – and how many there have been that we have not found out about! Here is something that happened in my time. Certain men are condemned to death for a murder, the sentence being, if not pronounced, at least decided and determined. At this point the judges are informed by the officers of an inferior court nearby that they have some prisoners who confess outright to this murder and throw a decisive light on the whole business. They deliberate whether because of this they should interrupt and defer the execution of the sentence passed upon the first accused. They consider the novelty of the case and the precedent it would set in suspending the execution of sentences; that the sentence has been passed according to law, and that the judges have no right to change their minds. In short, these poor devils are sacrificed to the forms of justice.

Philip, or some other, took care of a similar problem in this manner. He had sentenced a man, by a definitive judgment, to pay a heavy fine to another. The truth came to light some time after, and

it turned out that he had decided unfairly. On one side were the rights of the case, on the other side the rights of judicial forms. He gave some satisfaction to both, letting the sentence stand and compensating the loss of the convicted man out of his own purse. But he was dealing with a reparable accident; my men were irreparably hanged. ᶜHow many condemnations I have seen more criminal than the crime!

ᴮAll this reminds me of these ancient notions: that a man is forced to do wrong in detail if he wants to do right in gross, and injustice in little things if he wants to achieve justice in great ones; that human justice is formed on the model of medicine, according to which all that is useful is also just and honest; and what the Stoics hold, that Nature herself goes against justice in most of her works; ᶜand what the Cyrenaics hold, that there is nothing just in itself, that customs and laws shape justice; and the Theodorians, who consider theft, sacrilege, and every sort of lechery just for a wise man, if he knows that it is profitable for him.

ᴮThere is no remedy. My position, like that of Alcibiades, is this: I shall never turn myself over, if I can help it, to a man who can dispose of my head, where my honor and my life depend on the skill and diligence of my attorney more than on my innocence. I would risk a kind of justice that would take into account my good deeds as well as my bad, from which I would have as much to hope as to fear. Lack of punishment is not sufficient pay for a man who does better than not doing wrong. Our justice offers us only one of her hands, and the left at that. Whoever he is, he comes out of it with a loss.

ᶜIn China – a kingdom whose government and arts, without dealings with and knowledge of ours, surpass our examples in many branches of excellence, and whose history teaches me how much ampler and more varied the world is than either the ancients or we ourselves understand – the officers deputed by the prince to inspect the state of his provinces, even as they punish those who are corrupt in their office, also reward, from pure liberality, those who have conducted themselves better than the average and better than the requirements of their duty. People come before them not merely to defend themselves, but to gain by it, and not simply to be paid, but also to receive presents.

ᴮNo judge has yet, thank God, spoken to me as a judge in any cause whatever, my own or another man's, criminal or civil. No prison has received me, not even for a visit. Imagination makes the sight of one, even from the outside, unpleasant to me. I am so

sick for freedom, that if anyone should forbid me access to some corner of the Indies, I should live distinctly less comfortably. And as long as I find earth or air open elsewhere, I shall not lurk in any place where I have to hide. Lord, how ill could I endure the condition in which I see so many people, nailed down to one section of this kingdom, deprived of the right to enter the principal towns and the courts and to use the public roads, for having quarreled with our laws! If those that I serve threatened even the tip of my finger, I should instantly go and find others, wherever it might be. All my little prudence in these civil wars in which we are now involved is employed to keep them from interrupting my freedom of coming and going.

Now laws remain in credit not because they are just, but because they are laws. That is the mystic foundation of their authority; they have no other. ^CAnd that is a good thing for them. They are often made by fools, more often by people who, in their hatred of equality, are wanting in equity; but always by men, vain and irresolute authors.

There is nothing so grossly and widely and ordinarily faulty as the laws. ^BWhoever obeys them because they are just, does not obey them for just the reason he should. Our French laws, by their irregularity and lack of form, rather lend a hand to the disorder and corruption that is seen in their administration and execution. Their commands are so confused and inconsistent that they are some excuse for both disobedience and faulty interpretation, administration, and observance.

Then whatever may be the fruit we can reap from experience, what we derive from foreign examples will hardly be much use for our education, if we make such little profit from the experience we have of ourselves, which is more familiar to us, and certainly sufficient to inform us of what we need.

I study myself more than any other subject. That is my metaphysics, that is my physics.

> By what art God our home, the world, controls;
> Whence the moon rises, where she sets, how rolls
> Her horns together monthly, and again
> Grows full; whence come the winds that rule the main;
> Where Eurus' blast holds sway; whence springs the rain
> That ever fills the clouds; ^Cwhether some day
> The citadels of the world will pass away.
>
> PROPERTIUS

ᴮInquire, you who the laboring world survey.

LUCAN

ᶜIn this universe of things I ignorantly and negligently let myself be guided by the general law of the world. I shall know it well enough when I feel it. My knowledge could not make it change its path; it will not modify itself for me. It is folly to hope it, and greater folly to be troubled about it, since it is necessarily uniform, public, and common. The goodness and capacity of the governor should free us absolutely and fully from worrying about his government.

Philosophical inquiries and meditations serve only as food for our curiosity. The philosophers with much reason refer us to the rules of Nature; but these have no concern with such sublime knowledge. The philosophers falsify them and show us the face of Nature painted in too high a color, and too sophisticated, whence spring so many varied portraits of so uniform a subject. As she has furnished us with feet to walk with, so she has given us wisdom to guide us in life: a wisdom not so ingenious, robust, and pompous as that of their invention, but correspondingly easy and salutary, performing very well what the other talks about, in a man who has the good fortune to know how to occupy himself simply and in an orderly way, that is to say naturally. The more simply we trust to Nature, the more wisely we trust to her. Oh, what a sweet and soft and healthy pillow is ignorance and incuriosity, to rest a well-made head!

ᴮI would rather be an authority on myself than on ᶜCicero.[1] ᴮIn the experience I have of myself I find enough to make me wise, if I were a good scholar. He who calls back to mind the excess of his past anger, and how far this fever carried him away, sees the ugliness of this passion better than in Aristotle, and conceives a more justi-fied hatred for it. He who remembers the evils he has undergone, and those that have threatened him, and the slight causes that have changed him from one state to another, prepares himself in that way for future changes and for recognizing his condition. The life of Caesar has no more to show us than our own; an emperor's or an ordinary man's, it is still a life subject to all human accidents. Let us only listen: we tell ourselves all we most need.

He who remembers having been mistaken so many, many times in his own judgment, is he not a fool if he does not distrust it forever after? When I find myself convicted of a false opinion by another

1 The 1588 edition read: "than on Plato."

man's reasoning, I do not so much learn what new thing he has told me and this particular bit of ignorance – that would be small gain – as I learn my weakness in general, and the treachery of my understanding; whence I derive the reformation of the whole mass. With all my other errors I do the same, and I feel that this rule is very useful for my life. I do not regard the species and the individual, like a stone I have stumbled on; I learn to mistrust my gait throughout, and I strive to regulate it. ᶜTo learn that we have said or done a foolish thing, that is nothing; we must learn that we are nothing but fools, a far broader and more important lesson.

ᴮThe slips that my memory has made so often, even when it reassures me most about itself, are not vainly lost on me; there is no use in her swearing to me now and assuring me, I shake my ears. The first opposition offered to her testimony puts me in suspense, and I would not dare trust her in any weighty matter, or guarantee her in another person's affairs. And were it not that what I do for lack of memory, others do still more often for lack of good faith, I should always accept the truth in matters of fact from another man's mouth rather than from my own.

If each man watched closely the effects and circumstances of the passions that dominate him, as I have done with the ones I have fallen prey to, he would see them coming and would check their impetuosity and course a bit. They do not always leap at our throats at a single bound; there are threats and degrees.

> As when a rising wind makes white waves fly,
> The sea heaves slowly, raises billows high,
> And surges from the depths to meet the sky.
> VIRGIL

Judgment holds in me a magisterial seat, at least it carefully tries to. It lets my feelings go their way, both hatred and friendship, even the friendship I bear myself, without being changed and corrupted by them. If it cannot reform the other parts according to itself, at least it does not let itself be deformed to match them; it plays its game apart.

The advice to everyone to know himself must have an important effect, since the god of learning and light had it planted on the front of his temple, as comprising all the counsel he had to give us. ᶜPlato also says that wisdom is nothing else but the execution of this command, and Socrates, in Xenophon, verifies it in detail.

ᴮThe difficulties and obscurity in any science are perceived only by those who have access to it. For a man needs at least some degree of intelligence to be able to notice that he does not know; and we must push against a door to know that it is closed to us. ᶜWhence arises this Platonic subtlety, that neither those who know need inquire, since they know, nor those who do not know, since in order to inquire they must know what they are inquiring about. ᴮThus in this matter of knowing oneself, the fact that everyone is seen to be so cocksure and self-satisfied, that everyone thinks he understands enough about himself, signifies that everyone understands nothing about it, ᶜas Socrates teaches Euthydemus in Xenophon.

ᴮI, who make no other profession, find in me such infinite depth and variety, that what I have learned bears no other fruit than to make me realize how much I still have to learn. To my weakness, so often recognized, I owe the inclination I have to modesty, obedience to the beliefs that are prescribed me, a constant coolness and moderation in my opinions, and my hatred for that aggressive and quarrelsome arrogance that believes and trusts wholly in itself, a mortal enemy of discipline and truth. Hear them laying down the law: the first stupidities that they advance are in the style in which men establish religions and laws. ᶜ*Nothing is more discreditable than to have assertion and proof precede knowledge and perception* [Cicero].

ᴮAristarchus used to say that in former times there were scarcely seven wise men in the world, and that in his time there were scarcely seven ignorant men. Would we not have more reason than he to say that in our time? Affirmation and opinionativeness are express signs of stupidity. This man must have fallen on his nose a hundred times in one day; there he stands on his "ergos,"² as positive and unshaken as before. You would think that someone had since infused in him some sort of new soul and intellectual vigor, and that he was like that ancient son of the earth, who renewed his courage and strength by his fall:

> Whose limbs, however tired,
> By touching Mother Earth, with energy were fired.
> LUCAN

2 Montaigne's word, *ergots*, means the spurs or hackles of a gamecock. But it also may mean *ergos* or *ergotisms*, the quibbling use of Latin *ergo* (therefore) by a choplogic (see Rabelais, *Pantagruel*, chap. 10).

Does not this headstrong incorrigible think that he picks up a new mind by picking up a new argument?

It is from my experience that I affirm human ignorance, which is, in my opinion, the most certain fact in the school of the world. Those who will not conclude their own ignorance from so vain an example as mine, or as theirs, let them recognize it through Socrates, ᶜthe master of masters. For the philosopher Antisthenes used to say to his pupils: "Let us go, you and I, to hear Socrates; there I shall be a pupil with you." And, maintaining this doctrine of his Stoic sect, that virtue was enough to make a life fully happy and free from need of anything whatever, he would add: "Excepting the strength of Socrates."

ᴮThis long attention that I devote to studying myself trains me also to judge passably of others, and there are few things of which I speak more felicitously and excusably. It often happens that I see and distinguish the characters of my friends more exactly than they do themselves. I have astonished at least one by the pertinence of my description, and have given him information about himself. By training myself from my youth to see my own life mirrored in that of others, I have acquired a studious bent in that subject, and when I am thinking about it, I let few things around me which are useful for that purpose escape my notice: countenances, humors, statements. I study everything: what I must flee, what I must follow. So I reveal to my friends, by their outward manifestations, their inward inclinations. I do not attempt to arrange this infinite variety of actions, so diverse and so disconnected, into certain types and categories, and distribute my lots and divisions distinctly into recognized classes and sections:

> How many kinds there are, their titles manifold,
> We are not told.
> VIRGIL

ᶜThe scholars distinguish and mark off their ideas more specifically and in detail. I, who cannot see beyond what I have learned from experience, without any system, present my ideas in a general way, and tentatively. As in this: ᴮI speak my meaning in disjointed parts, as something that cannot be said all at once and in a lump. Relatedness and conformity are not found in low and common minds such as ours. Wisdom is a solid and integral structure, each part of which holds its place and bears its mark. ᶜ*Wisdom alone is wholly directed toward itself* [Cicero]. ᴮI leave it to artists, and I do

not know if they will achieve it in a matter so complex, minute, and accidental, to arrange into bands this infinite diversity of aspects, to check our inconsistency and set it down in order. Not only do I find it hard to link our actions with one another, but each one separately I find hard to designate properly by some principal characteristic, so two-sided and motley do they seem in different lights.

ᶜWhat is remarked as rare in Perseus, king of Macedonia, that his mind, sticking to no one condition, kept wandering through every type of life and portraying such a flighty and erratic character that neither he nor anyone else knew what kind of a man he was, seems to me to fit nearly everybody. And above all men, I have known another of his stature[3] to whom this conclusion would apply still more properly, I think: no middle position, always being carried away from one extreme to the other by causes impossible to guess; no kind of course without tacking and changing direction amazingly; no quality unmixed; so that the most likely portrait of him that men will be able to make some day, will be that he affected and studied to make himself known by being unknowable.

ᴮWe need very strong ears to hear ourselves judged frankly; and because there are few who can endure frank criticism without being stung by it, those who venture to criticize us perform a remarkable act of friendship; for to undertake to wound and offend a man for his own good is to have a healthy love for him. I find it a rough task to judge a man in whom the bad qualities exceed the good. ᶜPlato prescribes three qualities in a man who wants to examine another man's soul: knowledge, good will, boldness.

ᴮSometimes people used to ask me what I would have thought myself good for, if anyone had thought of using me while I was young enough:

> While better blood gave strength, before the snows
> Of envious age were sprinkled on my brows.
>
> VIRGIL

"For nothing," I said. And I readily excuse myself for not knowing how to do anything that would enslave me to others. But I would have told my master home truths, and watched over his conduct, if he had been willing. Not in general, by schoolmasterly lessons, which I do not know – and I see no true reform spring from them

3 Presumably Henry IV of France. Instead of "another of his stature," Montaigne first wrote "another king since."

in those who know them – but by observing his conduct step by step, at every opportunity, judging it with my own eyes, piece by piece, simply and naturally, making him see how he stands in public opinion, and opposing his flatterers.

There is not one of us who would not be worse than the kings if he were as continually spoiled as they are by that rabble. How could it be otherwise, if Alexander, that great man both as king and as philosopher, could not defend himself against them?

I should have had enough fidelity, judgment, and independence for that. It would be a nameless office; otherwise it would lose its effect and its grace. And it is a part that cannot be played indiscriminately by all. For truth itself does not have the privilege to be employed at any time and in any way; its use, noble as it is, has its circumscriptions and limits. It often happens, as the world goes, that people blurt it out into a prince's ear not only fruitlessly, but harmfully, and even unjustly. And no one will make me believe that a righteous remonstrance cannot be applied wrongfully, and that the interest of the substance must not often yield to the interest of the form.

For this occupation I should want a man who is content with his fortune,

Who would be what he is, and nothing else prefers,

MARTIAL

and born to a middle rank; because on the one hand he would not fear to touch his master's heart deeply and to the quick, at the risk of losing his preferment thereby; and on the other hand, being of middle station, he would have easier communication with all sorts of people. ᶜI would have this an office for one man alone, for to spread the privilege of this freedom and intimacy among several would engender a harmful irreverence. And certainly I should require of that man, above all, the fidelity of silence.

ᴮA king is not to be believed when he boasts of his constancy in awaiting the shock of the enemy for the sake of his glory, if, for his own good and improvement, he cannot endure the freedom of a friend's words, which have no other power than to sting his ears, the rest of their effect being in his own hands. Now, there is no class of men that has as great need as they of true and frank admonitions. They endure a public life, and have to suit the opinions of so many spectators, that, since people have formed the habit of concealing from them anything that disturbs their plans,

they find themselves, without realizing it, the object of the hatred and detestation of their people, often for reasons that they could have avoided at no sacrifice, even of their pleasures, if they had been advised and set right in time. Ordinarily their favorites look out for themselves more than for their master; and this serves them well, since in truth most of the duties of true friendship are hard and dangerous to attempt toward a sovereign; so that there is need, not only of much affection and frankness, but of much courage as well.

In fine, all this fricassee that I am scribbling here is nothing but a record of the essays of my life, which, for spiritual health, is exemplary enough if you take its instruction in reverse. But as for bodily health, no one can furnish more useful experience than I, who present it pure, not at all corrupted or altered by art or theorizing. Experience is really on its own dunghill in the subject of medicine, where reason yields it the whole field. Tiberius used to say that whoever had lived twenty years should be responsible to himself for the things that were harmful or beneficial to him, and know how to take care of himself without medical aid. ᶜAnd he might have learned this from Socrates, who, advising his disciples, carefully and as a principal study, the study of their health, used to add that it was difficult for an intelligent man who was careful about his exercise, his drinking, and his eating not to know better than any doctor what was good or bad for him.

ᴮAnd indeed, medicine professes always to have experience as the touchstone for its workings. So Plato was right in saying that to become a true doctor, the candidate must have passed through all the illnesses that he wants to cure and all the accidents and circumstances that he is to diagnose. It is reasonable that he should catch the pox if he wants to know how to treat it. Truly I should trust such a man. For the others guide us like the man who paints seas, reefs, and ports while sitting at his table, and sails the model of a ship there in complete safety. Throw him into the real thing, and he does not know how to go at it. They make a description of our diseases like that of a town crier proclaiming a lost horse or dog: such-and-such a coat, such-and-such a height, such-and-such ears; but present it to him, and he does not know it for all that.

For heaven's sake, let medicine some day give me some good and perceptible relief, and you will see how I shall cry out in good earnest:

At last I yield to an efficient science.

HORACE

The arts that promise to keep our body in health and our soul in health promise us much; but at the same time there are none that keep their promise less. And in our time those who profess these arts among us show the results of them less than any other men. The most you can say for them is that they sell medicinal drugs; but that they are doctors you cannot say.

I have lived long enough to give an account of the practice that has guided me so far. For anyone who wants to try it I have tasted it like his cupbearer. Here are a few items, as memory supplies me with them. ^cI have no habit that has not varied according to circumstances, but I record those that I have seen most frequently in action, which have had most hold on me up to this moment.

^BMy way of life is the same in sickness as in health; the same bed, the same hours, the same food serve me, and the same drink. I make no adjustments at all, save for moderating the amount according to my strength and appetite. Health for me is maintaining my accustomed state without disturbance. Do I see that sickness dislodges me in one direction? If I trust the doctors, they will turn me aside in another. And both by fortune and by art, there I am off my road. I believe nothing with more certainty than this: that I cannot be hurt by the use of things that I have been so long accustomed to.

It is for habit to give form to our life, just as it pleases; it is all-powerful in that; it is Circe's drink, which varies our nature as it sees fit. How many nations, and three steps from us, regard as ridiculous the fear of the night dew, which appears so hurtful to us; and our boatmen and peasants laugh at it. You make a German sick if you put him to bed on a mattress, like an Italian on a feather bed, and a Frenchman without curtains and a fire. A Spaniard's stomach cannot stand our way of eating, nor can ours stand to drink Swiss fashion.

A German pleased me at Augsburg by attacking the disadvantages of our fireplaces by the same argument we ordinarily use to condemn their stoves. For in truth, that stifling heat, and the smell of that material they are made of when it gets hot, give most of those who are not used to them a headache; not me. But after all, since this heat is even, constant, and general, without flame, without smoke, without the wind that the opening of our chimneys brings us, it has good grounds in other respects for comparison with ours.

Why do we not imitate the Roman architecture? For they say that in ancient times the fire was made only outside their houses, and at the foot of them; whence the heat was breathed into the entire dwelling by pipes, contrived in the thickness of the walls that surrounded the rooms that were to be warmed. This I have seen clearly indicated, I don't know where, in Seneca.

This German, hearing me praise the comforts and beauties of his city, which certainly deserves it, began to sympathize with me because I had to leave it; and one of the first discomforts he mentioned to me was the heavy-headedness that the fireplaces elsewhere would cause me. He had heard someone make this complaint, and associated it with us, being disabled by habit from noticing it at home.

All heat that comes from fire makes me feel weak and heavy. Yet Evenus said that the best condiment of life was fire. I prefer any other way of escaping from the cold.

We are afraid of the wine at the bottom of the cask; in Portugal its flavor is considered delicious, and it is the drink of princes.

In short, each nation has many customs and usages that are not only unknown, but savage and miraculous, to some other nation.

What shall we do with this people that admits none but printed evidence, that does not believe men unless they are in a book, or truth unless it is of competent age? ᶜWe dignify our stupidities when we put them in print. ᴮIt carries very different weight with this people if you say "I have read it" than if you say "I have heard it." But I, who do not disbelieve men's mouths any more than their hands, and who know that people write just as injudiciously as they speak, and who esteem this age just as if it were another that is past, I quote a friend of mine as readily as Aulus Gellius or Macrobius, and what I have seen as what they have written. ᶜAnd, as they hold that virtue is no greater for being of longer standing, so I consider that truth is no wiser for being older. ᴮI often say that it is pure stupidity that makes us run after foreign and scholarly examples. There is as great an abundance of them in this age as in that of Homer and Plato. But is it not true that we seek rather the honor of quoting than the truth of the statement? As if it were greater to borrow our proofs from the shop of Vascosan or Plantin[4] than from what may be seen in our own village. Or rather, indeed, that we have not the wit to pick out and put to use what happens

4 Two famous printers of Montaigne's day.

before our eyes, and to judge it keenly enough to make it an example? For if we say we lack authority to gain credence for our testimony, we say so without reason. By the same token, in my opinion, from the most ordinary, commonplace, familiar things, if we could put them in their proper light, can be formed the greatest miracles of nature and the most wondrous examples, especially on the subject of human actions.

Now, on my subject, leaving aside the examples that I know from books, ᶜand what Aristotle says about Andro of Argos, that he crossed the arid sands of Libya without drinking, ᴮa gentleman who has acquitted himself worthily in several charges said in my presence that he had gone from Madrid to Lisbon in midsummer without drinking. He is in vigorous health for his age, and has nothing extraordinary in his way of living except this, that he will go two or three months, even a year, so he told me, without drinking. He feels some thirst, but he lets it pass, and maintains that it is an appetite that easily grows languid by itself; and he drinks more out of caprice than from need or for pleasure.

Here is another. It was not long ago that I found one of the most learned men in France, and a man of no mean fortune, studying in the corner of a hall, which had been partitioned off for him with hangings; and around him an unrestrained hubbub of his servants. He told me, ᶜand Seneca said much the same thing of himself, ᴮthat he derived profit from this racket, as if, battered by this noise, he withdrew and concentrated in himself better for contemplation, and that this storm of voices drove his thoughts inward. While a student at Padua, he had for so long a time a study exposed to the rattle of coaches and the tumult of the square that he trained himself not only to disregard the noise but to use it for the benefit of his studies. ᶜSocrates replied to Alcibiades, who wondered how he could endure the perpetual din of his wife's scolding: "Like those who are accustomed to the ordinary sound of wheels drawing water." ᴮI am quite the opposite; my mind is sensitive and ready to take flight; when it is absorbed in itself, the slightest buzz of a fly is the death of it.

ᶜSeneca, in his youth, having bitten hard on Sextius' example of eating nothing that had been killed, got along without it for a year with pleasure, as he says. And he left off only so as not to be suspected of borrowing this rule from certain new religions that were disseminating it. At the same time, from the precepts of Attalus he adopted this one, not to sleep any more on yielding

mattresses; and continued to use, even in his old age, the kind that does not give way under the body. What the practice of his time makes him reckon as austerity, ours makes us consider effeminacy.

^BLook at the difference between the life of my manual laborers and my own. The Scythians and Indians are in no respect more remote from my powers and ways. I know I have taken boys out of begging into my service, who soon after have left me, my kitchen, and their livery, just to return to their former life. And I found one of them afterward picking up mussels in the dump heap for his dinner, and neither by entreaties nor by threats could I tear him away from the savor and sweetness he found in indigence. Beggars have their splendors and their sensual pleasures as well as rich men, and, it is said, their political dignities and orders.

These are results of habit. It can shape us not only into whatever form it pleases (therefore, say the sages, we must choose the best form, which habit will promptly make easy for us), but also shape us for change and variation, which is the noblest and most useful of its teachings. The best of my bodily qualities is that I am flexible and not very stubborn. I have inclinations that are more personal and customary, and more agreeable to me, than others; but with very little effort I turn away from them, and easily slip into the opposite habit. A young man should violate his own rules to arouse his vigor and keep it from growing moldy and lax. And there is no way of life so stupid and feeble as that which is conducted by rules and discipline.

> If he would drive a mile, he looks to bookish lore
> To designate the time; and if his eye is sore,
> He scans his stars, and gets the salve then, not before.
>
> JUVENAL

He will even plunge often into excess, if he will take my advice; otherwise the slightest dissipation will ruin him, and he will become awkward and disagreeable in company. The most unsuitable quality for a gentleman is overfastidiousness and bondage to certain particular ways; and they are particular if they are not pliable and supple. It is shameful for a man to keep from doing what he sees his companions do, because he cannot or dare not. Let such men stick to their kitchens. In anyone else it is unbecoming, but in a military man it is bad and intolerable; he, as Philopoemen said, should get accustomed to every change and vicissitude of life.

Although I was trained as much as possible for freedom and adaptability, yet it is a fact that through carelessness, and because I have lingered more in certain ways as I grow old (my age is past training and henceforth has nothing to consider except holding its own), habit, imperceptibly, has already so imprinted its character upon me in certain things that I call it excess to depart from it. And I cannot, without an effort, sleep by day, or eat between meals, or breakfast, or go to bed without a long interval, ^cof about three full hours, ^Bafter supper, or make a child except before going to sleep, or make one standing up, or endure my sweat, or quench my thirst with pure water or pure wine, or remain bareheaded for long, or have my hair cut after dinner; and I would feel as uncomfortable without my gloves as without my shirt, or without washing when I leave the table or get up in the morning, or without canopy and curtains for my bed, as I would be without really necessary things. I could dine without a tablecloth; but very uncomfortably without a clean napkin, German fashion; I soil napkins more than they or the Italians do, and make little use of spoon or fork. I am sorry that people have not carried on a fashion that I saw begun, after the example of kings, of changing napkins, like plates, with each course. We are told of that tough soldier Marius that as he grew old he grew fastidious in his drinking, and drank only out of one particular cup of his. I too indulge my preference for a glass of a certain shape and do not willingly drink from a common glass, any more than I like to be served by a common hand. I dislike all metal compared with a clear and transparent material. ^cLet my eyes also taste, according to their capacity.

^BI owe many such weaknesses to habit. Nature too, for her part, has brought me her share: such as no longer being able to stand two full meals a day without overloading my stomach, or complete abstinence from one of those meals without filling myself with wind, drying up my mouth, and numbing my appetite; and suffering from too long exposure to the night air. For in the last few years, being in the military service, when whole nights are spent on duty, as often happens, after five or six hours I begin to be troubled by my stomach, as well as by a violent headache, and I do not last until daytime without vomiting. As the others are going off to breakfast I go off to sleep, and after that I am as gay as before.

I had always understood that the evening dew fell only at nightfall, but being long and familiarly associated these past years with a lord who was imbued with the belief that the dew is sharper and

more dangerous when the sun begins to set, an hour or two before sundown, when he carefully avoids it, although he does not fear the night dew, he nearly imprinted in me not so much his opinion as his feeling.

What shall we say of the fact that even doubt and inquiry strikes our imagination and changes us? Those who yield suddenly to these propensities bring total ruin upon themselves. And I am sorry for several gentlemen who, by the stupidity of their doctors, have made prisoners of themselves, though still young and sound in health. It would still be better to endure a cold than to lose the enjoyment of social life forever through disuse by giving up so general a practice.[5] ᶜIt is a troublesome science which decries the pleasantest hours of the day. ᴮLet us extend our possession to our utmost means. Most often we toughen ourselves if we persist, and correct our constitutions, as Caesar did his epilepsy, by despising it and fighting it. We should conform to the best rules, but not enslave ourselves to them, unless to those, if any there are, to which bondage and slavery is useful.

Both kings and philosophers defecate, and ladies too. Public lives are owed to ceremony; mine, obscure and private, enjoys every natural dispensation; soldier and Gascon are also qualities a bit subject to indiscretion. Wherefore I will say this about that action: that we should relegate it to certain prescribed nocturnal hours, and force and subject ourselves to them by habit, as I have done; but not subject ourselves, as I have done as I grew old, to any concern for a particularly comfortable place and seat for this function, and make it a nuisance by slowness and fastidiousness.

And yet in the dirtiest functions is it not somewhat excusable to require more care and cleanliness? ᶜ*Man is by nature a clean and dainty animal* [Seneca]. Of all natural functions that is the one that I can least willingly endure to have interrupted. ᴮI have seen many soldiers inconvenienced by the irregularity of their bowels; mine and I never fail the moment of our assignation, which is when I jump out of bed, unless some violent occupation or illness disturbs us.

I have no idea then, as I was saying, where sick men can better place themselves in safety than in keeping quietly to the way of life in which they have been brought up and trained. Change of any sort is disturbing and hurtful. Go ahead and believe that chestnuts hurt a native of Périgord or of Lucca, or milk and cheese the

5 As that of going out at night.

mountaineers. They keep prescribing for sick men a way of life not only new, but contrary: a change that a healthy man could not endure. Prescribe water to a Breton of seventy, shut up a seaman in an overheated room, forbid a Basque footman to take walks. You deprive them of movement, and in the end, of air and light.

> Is it so great a thing to be alive?[6]
>
> AUTHOR UNKNOWN

> Obliged to wean our souls from things on which they thrive,
> We give up living, just to keep alive.
> Should they be said to live who cannot breathe free air
> Or see the light, without oppressive care?
>
> MAXIMIANUS

If they do no other good, they do at least this, that they prepare their patients early for death, undermining little by little and cutting off their enjoyment of life.

Both in health and in sickness I have readily let myself follow my urgent appetites. I give great authority to my desires and inclinations. I do not like to cure trouble by trouble; I hate remedies that are more nuisance than the disease. To be subjected to the stone and subjected to abstaining from the pleasure of eating oysters, those are two troubles for one. The disease pinches us on one side, the rule on the other. Since there is a risk of making a mistake, let us risk it rather in pursuit of pleasure. The world does the opposite, and thinks nothing beneficial that is not painful; it is suspicious of ease.

My appetite in many things has of its own accord suited and adapted itself rather happily to the health of my stomach. Sharpness and pungency in sauces were pleasant to me when I was young; later, when my stomach grew irritated by them, my taste promptly followed suit. ᶜWine hurts sick people; it is the first thing that my mouth finds distasteful, and with an invincible distaste. ᴮWhatever I accept with dislike hurts me, and nothing hurts me that I do with hunger and zest; I have never received harm from any action that was really pleasant to me. And yet I have made all the conclusions of medicine give way very extensively to my pleasure. And in my youth,

> When Cupid, flitting round me to and fro
> In yellow tunic, shed his radiant glow,
>
> CATULLUS

6 According to Montaigne, La Boétie had said this during his fatal illness. See Letter 2, p. 1287.

I lent myself as licentiously and thoughtlessly as any other man to the desire that held me in its grip,

> And fought my battles not without distinction;
>
> HORACE

more, however, in continuation and endurance than in violence:

> I scarce remember lasting up to six.
>
> OVID

It is certainly distressing and miraculous to confess at what a tender age I first chanced to fall under its subjection. It was indeed by chance, for it was long before the age of choice and knowledge. I do not remember about myself so far back. And my lot may be coupled with that of Quartilla, who had no memory of her maidenhood.

> Hence goatish smells, precocious hair,
> A beard to make my mother stare.
>
> MARTIAL

The doctors ordinarily adjust their rules beneficially to the violence of the sharp cravings that come upon sick people; no great desire can be imagined that is so strange and vicious that nature is not involved in it. And then how much it is to satisfy the imagination! In my opinion that faculty is all-important, at least more important than any other. The most grievous and ordinary troubles are those that fancy loads upon us. I like this Spanish saying from several points of view: *God defend me from myself.* I am sorry, when I am sick, that I do not have some desire that would give me the pleasure of satisfying it; medicine would hardly deter me from it. It is the same when I am well; I see scarcely anything more to hope and wish for. It is pitiful to be languid and enfeebled even in our desires.

The art of medicine is not so fixed that we are without authority, no matter what we do; it changes according to the climates and according to the moons, according to Fernel and according to L'Escale. If your doctor does not think it good for you to sleep, to drink wine, or to eat such-and-such a food, don't worry: I'll find you another who will not agree with him. The variety of medical arguments and opinions embraces all kinds of forms. I saw a wretched patient fainting and dying with thirst in order to be cured, and being laughed at later by another doctor who condemned

that advice as harmful. Had he not put his pain to good use? A man of that trade died recently of the stone, who had practiced extreme abstinence to combat his illness; his colleagues say that on the contrary this fasting dried him up and baked the gravel in his kidneys.

I have noticed that when I am wounded or sick, talking excites me and hurts me as much as any irregularity I may commit. It is costly and tiring for me to use my voice, for it is loud and strained; so that when I have come to hold the ear of the great with affairs of weight, I have often put them to the trouble of asking me to moderate my voice.

This story deserves a digression: Someone in a certain Greek school was speaking loudly, as I do; the master of ceremonies sent him word to speak lower. "Let him send me," he said, "the tone in which he wants me to speak." The other replied that he should take his tone from the ears of the person he was speaking to. That was well said, provided it is understood to mean: "Speak according to the business you have with your hearer." For if it means "Enough that he hear you," or "Be guided by him," I do not think it is right. The tone and movement of my voice express and signify my meaning; it is for me to guide it to make myself understood.

There is a voice for instructing, a voice for flattering, a voice for scolding. I want my voice not only to reach my listener, but perhaps to strike him and pierce him. When I berate my footman in a sharp and bitter tone, it would be fine if he should say to me: "Master, speak lower, I can hear you very well." ^C*There is a kind of voice adapted to the hearing, not by its volume, but by its quality* [Quintilian]. ^BSpeech belongs half to the speaker, half to the listener. The latter must prepare to receive it according to the motion it takes. As among tennis players, the receiver moves and makes ready according to the motion of the striker and the nature of the stroke.

Experience has further taught me this, that we ruin ourselves by impatience. Troubles have their life and their limits, ^Ctheir illnesses and their health.

The constitution of diseases is patterned after the constitution of animals. They have their destiny, limited from their birth, and their days. He who tries to cut them short imperiously by force, in the midst of their course, prolongs and multiplies them, and stimulates them instead of appeasing them. I agree with Crantor, that we must neither obstinately and heedlessly oppose evils nor weakly succumb to them, but give way to them naturally, according to their condition

and our own. ᴮWe should give free passage to diseases; and I find that they do not stay so long with me, who let them go ahead; and some of those that are considered most stubborn and tenacious, I have shaken off by their own decadence, without help and without art, and against the rules of medicine. Let us give Nature a chance; she knows her business better than we do. "But so-and-so died of it." So will you, if not of that disease, of some other. And how many have not failed to die of it, with three doctors at their backsides? Example is a hazy mirror, reflecting all things in all ways. If it is a pleasant medicine, take it; it is always that much present gain. ᶜI shall never balk at the name or the color, if it is delicious and appetizing. Pleasure is one of the principal kinds of profit.

ᴮI have allowed colds, gouty discharges, looseness, palpitations of the heart, migraines, and other ailments to grow old and die a natural death within me; I lost them when I had half trained myself to harbor them. They are conjured better by courtesy than by defiance. We must meekly suffer the laws of our condition. We are born to grow old, to grow weak, to be sick, in spite of all medicine. That is the first lesson that the Mexicans give their children, when, as soon as they come out of their mother's womb, they greet them thus: "Child, you have come into the world to endure; endure, suffer, and keep quiet."

It is unjust to complain that what may happen to anyone has happened to someone. ᶜ*Complain if anything has been unjustly decreed against you alone* [Seneca]. ᴮLook at an old man praying God to keep him in entire and vigorous health, that is to say, to restore his youth.

> Fool, why aspire in vain with childish prayers?
> OVID

Is it not madness? His condition does not allow it. ᶜThe gout, the stone, indigestion, are symptoms of length of years, as are heat, rains, and winds of long journeys. Plato does not believe that Aesculapius was at any pains to attempt by treatment to prolong life in a wasted and feeble body, useless to its country, useless to its calling and for producing healthy, robust children; and he does not consider such concern consistent with divine justice and forethought, which should guide all things toward utility. ᴮMy good man, it is all over. No one can put you on your feet again; at most they will plaster and prop you up a bit, ᶜand prolong your misery an hour or so:

^BLike one who, wishing to support a while
A tottering building, props the creaking pile,
Until one day the house, the props, and all
Together with a dreadful havoc fall.

MAXIMIANUS

We must learn to endure what we cannot avoid. Our life is composed, like the harmony of the world, of contrary things, also of different tones, sweet and harsh, sharp and flat, soft and loud. If a musician liked only one kind, what would he have to say? He must know how to use them together and blend them. And so must we do with good and evil, which are consubstantial with our life. Our existence is impossible without this mixture, and one element is no less necessary for it than the other. To try to kick against natural necessity is to imitate the folly of Ctesiphon, who undertook a kicking match with his mule.

I do little consulting about the ailments I feel, for these doctors are domineering when they have you at their mercy. They scold at your ears with their forebodings. And once, catching me weakened by illness, they treated me insultingly with their dogmas and magisterial frowns, threatening me now with great pains, now with approaching death. I was not floored by them or dislodged from my position, but I was bumped and jostled. If my judgment was neither changed nor confused by them, it was at least bothered. It is still agitation and struggle.

Now I treat my imagination as gently as I can, and would relieve it, if I could, of all trouble and conflict. We must help it and flatter it, and fool it if we can. My mind is suited to this service; it has no lack of plausible reasons for all things. If it could persuade as well as it preaches, it would help me out very happily.

Would you like an example? It tells me that it is for my own good that I have the stone; that buildings of my age must naturally suffer some leakage. It is time for them to begin to grow loose and give way. It is a common necessity – otherwise would it not have been a new miracle performed for me? Thereby I pay the tribute due to old age, and I could not get a better bargain. – That the company should console me, since I have fallen into the commonest ailment of men of my time of life. On all sides I see them afflicted with the same type of disease, and their society is honorable for me, since it preferably attacks the great; it is essentially noble and dignified. – That of the men who are stricken by it there are few that get off

more cheaply; and at that, they pay the penalty of an unpleasant diet and daily doses of loathsome medicinal drugs, whereas I am indebted solely to my good fortune. For a few ordinary broths of eryngo and rupturewort that I have swallowed two or three times to please the ladies, who, with kindness greater than the sharpness of my pain, offered me half of theirs, seemed to me as easy to take as they were useless in their effect. The others have to pay a thousand vows to Aesculapius, and as many crowns to their doctor, for the easy and abundant outflow of gravel which I often get through the kindness of nature. ᶜEven the propriety of my behavior in ordinary company is not disturbed by it, and I can hold my water ten hours and as long as anyone.

ᴮ"Fear of this disease," says my mind, "used to terrify you, when it was unknown to you; the cries and despair of those who make it worse by their lack of fortitude engendered in you a horror of it. It is an affliction that punishes those of your members by which you have most sinned. You are a man of conscience:

> Punishment undeserved gives pain.
>
> OVID

Consider this chastisement; it is very gentle in comparison with others, and paternally tender. Consider its lateness; it bothers and occupies only the season of your life which in any case is henceforth wasted and barren, having given way, as if by agreement, to the licentiousness and pleasures of your youth.

"The fear and pity that people feel for this illness is a subject of vainglory for you; a quality of which, even if you have purged your judgment and cured your reason of it, your friends still recognize some tincture in your makeup. There is pleasure in hearing people say about you: There indeed is strength, there indeed is fortitude! They see you sweat in agony, turn pale, turn red, tremble, vomit your very blood, suffer strange contractions and convulsions, sometimes shed great tears from your eyes, discharge thick, black, and frightful urine, or have it stopped up by some sharp rough stone that cruelly pricks and flays the neck of your penis; meanwhile keeping up conversation with your company with a normal countenance, jesting in the intervals with your servants, holding up your end in a sustained discussion, making excuses for your pain and minimizing your suffering.

"Do you remember those men of past times who sought out troubles with such great hunger, to keep their virtue in breath and in

practice? Put the case this way, that nature is bearing and pushing you into that glorious school, which you would never have entered of your own free will. If you tell me that it is a dangerous and mortal disease, what others are not? For it is a doctor's trick to except some, which they say do not lead in a straight line to death. What does it matter if they go there by accident and slip and deviate easily toward the road that leads us there?

C"But you do not die of being sick, you die of being alive. Death kills you well enough without the help of illness. And illnesses have put off death for some, who have lived longer for thinking that they were on their way out and dying. Furthermore, there are diseases, as there are wounds, that are medicinal and salutary.

B"The stone is often no less fond of life than you. We see men in whom it has continued from their childhood up to their extreme old age; and if they had not deserted it, it was ready to accompany them still further. You kill it more often than it kills you; and even if it set before you the picture of imminent death, would it not be a kind service for a man of that age to bring him home to meditations upon his end?

C"And what is worse, you have no reason left for being cured. In any case, the common fate will call you any day. BConsider how artfully and gently the stone weans you from life and detaches you from the world; not forcing you with tyrannical subjections, like so many other afflictions that you see in old people, which keep them continually hobbled and without relief from infirmities and pains, but by warnings and instructions repeated at intervals, intermingled with long pauses for rest, as if to give you a chance to meditate and repeat its lesson at your leisure. To give you a chance to form a sound judgment and make up your mind to it like a brave man, it sets before you the lot that is your condition, the good and also the bad, and a life that on the same day is now very joyous, now unbearable. If you do not embrace death, at least you shake hands with it once a month. CWhereby you have the further hope that it will catch you some day without a threat, and that, being so often led to the port, confident that you are still within the accustomed limits, some morning you and your confidence will have crossed the water unawares. BWe have no cause for complaint about illnesses that divide the time fairly with health."

I am obliged to Fortune for assailing me so often with the same kind of weapons. She fashions and trains me against them by use,

hardens and accustoms me. Henceforth I know just about at what cost I shall be quit of them.

^CFor lack of a natural memory I make one of paper, and as some new symptom occurs in my disease, I write it down. Whence it comes that at the present moment, when I have passed through virtually every sort of experience, if some grave stroke threatens me, by glancing through these little notes, disconnected like the Sibyl's leaves, I never fail to find grounds for comfort in some favorable prognostic from my past experience.

^BFamiliarity also serves to give me better hopes for the future. For now that this process of evacuation has continued so long, it is probable that nature will not change this course and that no worse will come of it than what I already feel. Besides, the nature of this disease is not ill-suited to my hasty and impetuous disposition. When it assails me mildly it frightens me, for that means for long. But by nature it has vigorous and violent spurts; it shakes me to pieces, for a day or two.

My kidneys lasted an age without weakening; it will soon be another age since their condition changed. Evils have their period like good things; perhaps this ailment is coming to an end. Age weakens the heat of my stomach; its digestion being thereby less perfect, it sends on this crude matter to my kidneys. Why cannot the heat of my kidneys be likewise weakened, at some other turn, so that they can no longer petrify my phlegm, and nature may take steps to find some other way of purgation? The years have evidently made some of my rheums dry up. Why not these excrements that provide material for the gravel?

But is there anything so sweet as that sudden change, when from extreme pain, by the voiding of my stone, I come to recover as if by lightning the beautiful light of health, so free and so full, as happens in our sudden and sharpest attacks of colic? Is there anything in this pain we suffer that can be said to counterbalance the pleasure of such sudden improvement? How much more beautiful health seems to me after the illness, when they are so near and contiguous that I can recognize them in each other's presence in their proudest array, when they vie with each other, as if to oppose each other squarely! Just as the Stoics say that vices are brought into the world usefully to give value to virtue and assist it, we can say, with better reason and less bold conjecture, that nature has lent us pain for the honor and service of pleasure and painlessness. When Socrates, after being relieved of his irons, felt the relish of the itching that their

weight had caused in his legs, he rejoiced to consider the close alliance between pain and pleasure, how they are associated by a necessary link, so that they follow and engender each other in turn. And he called out that goodly Aesop should have taken from this consideration a subject fit for a fine fable.

The worst thing I see in other maladies is that they are not as serious in their immediate effect as in their consequences. You are a whole year recovering, always full of weakness and fear. There is so much risk and so many steps in returning to safety that it is never done. Before they have unmuffled you of a kerchief, and then of a cap, before they have given you back the enjoyment of fresh air, and wine, and your wife, and melons, it is great good luck if you have not relapsed into some new misery. My sickness has this privilege, that it carries itself clean off, whereas the others always leave some imprint and change for the worse that makes the body susceptible to a new disease, and they lend a hand to one another. Those illnesses are excusable that content themselves with their own possession of us, without extending it and without bringing on their sequels; but courteous and gracious are those whose passage brings us some useful consequence. Since I have had the stone, I have found myself rid of other ailments, more so, it seems to me, than I was before; and I have had no fever since. I argue that the extreme and frequent vomitings that I endure purge me; and, on the other hand, my loss of appetite and the unusual fasts I undergo digest my morbid humors, and nature voids in these stones its superfluous and harmful matter.

Do not tell me that it is a medicine too dearly bought. For what about all the stinking potions, cauteries, incisions, sweatings, setons, diets, and all the methods of cure that often bring us death because we cannot endure their violence and relentlessness? So when I have an attack, I take it as medicine; when I am exempt, I take it as lasting and complete deliverance.

Here is another benefit of my illness, peculiar to it: that it almost plays its game by itself and lets me play mine, unless I lack courage; in its greatest throes I have held out for ten hours on horseback. Just bear it, you need no other regimen. Play, dine, run, do this and do that too, if you can; your dissipation will do more good than harm. Say as much to a man with the pox, the gout, or a hernia! Other maladies have more inclusive bonds, hamper our actions far more, disturb our whole order, and involve the entire state of life in consideration of them. Mine only pinches the skin; it leaves

your understanding and will at your disposal, and your tongue, and your feet, and your hands; it rather awakens you than puts you to sleep. The soul is smitten by the burning of a fever, and floored by an epileptic fit, and dislocated by a violent migraine, and in short stunned by all the ailments that hurt the whole body and the noblest parts. Here, it is not attacked. If it fares badly, it is its own fault; it betrays, abandons, and unhorses itself.

It is only fools that let themselves be persuaded that this hard, solid body that is baked in our kidneys can be dissolved by potions. Therefore, once it is in motion, there is nothing to do but give it passage; it will take it anyway.

I notice also this particular convenience, that it is a disease in which we have little to guess about. We are freed from the worry into which other diseases cast us by the uncertainty of their causes and conditions and progress – an infinitely painful worry. We have no concern with doctoral consultations and interpretations; the senses reveal to us what it is, and where it is.

By such arguments, both strong and weak, I try to lull and beguile my imagination and salve its wounds, as Cicero did his disease of old age. If they get worse tomorrow, tomorrow we shall provide other ways of escape.

^CHere is proof. Now it has happened again that the slightest movements force the pure blood out of my kidneys. What of it? I do not, just for that, give up moving about as before and pricking after my hounds with youthful and insolent ardor. And I think I come off well from such an important accident when it costs me nothing but a dull heaviness and uneasiness in that region. It is some big stone that is crushing and consuming the substance of my kidneys, and my life that I am letting out little by little, not without some natural pleasure, as an excrement that is henceforth superfluous and a nuisance. ^BDo I feel something crumbling? Do not expect me to go and amuse myself testing my pulse and my urine so as to take some bothersome precaution; I shall be in plenty of time when I feel the pain, without prolonging it by the pain of fear. ^CHe who fears he will suffer, already suffers from his fear.

Besides, the uncertainty and ignorance of those who presume to explain the workings of Nature and her inner processes, and all the false prognostications of their art, should make us know that she has utterly unknown ways of her own. There is great uncertainty, variety, and obscurity about what she promises us or threatens us with. Except for old age, which is an indubitable sign of the

approach of death, in all other ailments I see few signs of the future on which to base our divination.

[B]I judge myself only by actual sensation, not by reasoning. What would be the use, since I intend to apply only waiting and endurance? Do you want to know how much I gain by this? Look at those who do otherwise, and who depend on so many different persuasions and counsels: how often imagination oppresses them, without the help of the body! Many a time, when safe and free from these dangerous attacks, I have taken pleasure in communicating their symptoms to the doctors as if they were just beginning inside me. I suffered the doom of their horrible conclusions most comfortably, and remained that much more obliged to God for his grace and better informed of the vanity of this art.

There is nothing that should be recommended so much to youth as activity and vigilance. Our life is nothing but movement. I have trouble getting under way, and am late in everything: getting up, going to bed, at meals. Seven o'clock is early for me, and where I am in charge I do not dine before eleven or sup till after six. In other days I attributed the fevers and illnesses into which I fell to the sluggishness and drowsiness that long sleep had brought on me, and I have always repented going back to sleep in the morning. [C]Plato is more set against excess in sleep than excess in drinking.

[B]I like to sleep hard and alone, even without a woman, in the royal style, rather well covered up. My bed is never warmed, but since I have grown old they give me, when I need them, cloths to warm my feet and stomach. They used to criticize the great Scipio for being such a sleeper, in my opinion for no other reason than that it annoyed men that in him alone there was nothing to criticize. If I am particular about anything in my way of life, it is rather about sleeping than anything else; but generally I yield and adapt myself to necessity as much as anyone. Sleeping has occupied a large part of my life, and even at this age I continue to sleep eight or nine hours at a stretch. I am weaning myself profitably from this lazy propensity, and am obviously the better for it. I feel the impact of the change a little, but in three days it is done. And I hardly know anyone who can live with less sleep when necessary, or who stands up better under exercise, or who is bothered less by military duties.

My body is capable of steady but not of vehement or sudden exertion. These days I shun violent exercises which put me into a sweat; my limbs grow tired before they grow warm. I can stay on my feet a whole day, and I do not weary of walking; but on

pavement, ^csince my early youth, ^BI have not liked to go except on horseback. On foot I get muddy right up to my buttocks; and in our streets small men are subject to being jostled ^cand elbowed, ^Bfor want of presence. And I have always liked to rest, whether lying or sitting, with my legs as high as my seat or higher.

There is no occupation so pleasant as the military one, an occupation both noble in execution (for the strongest, most generous, and proudest of all virtues is valor) and noble in its cause: there is no more just and universal service than the protection of the peace and greatness of your country. You enjoy the company of so many noble, young, active men, the regular sight of so many tragic spectacles, the freedom of that artless relationship, a manly and unceremonious way of life, the variety of a thousand diverse actions, the brave harmony of martial music which delights your ears and arouses your soul, the honor of this exercise, even its severity and hardship, ^cwhich Plato esteems so lightly that in his Republic he makes women and children share them. A volunteer, ^Byou assign yourself specific roles and risks according to your judgment of their brilliance and importance, and you see when life itself may be justifiably devoted to them:

> I thought how beautiful to die in arms.
> VIRGIL

To fear the common risks that affect so great a throng, not to dare what so many kinds of souls dare, that is for a heart immeasurably weak and base. Company reassures even children. If others surpass you in knowledge, in grace, in strength, in fortune, you have external causes to blame; but if you yield to them in firmness of soul, you have only yourself to blame. Death is more abject, more lingering and distressing, in bed than in battle; fevers and catarrhs are as painful and fatal as a harquebus shot. Whoever is prepared to bear valiantly the accidents of everyday life would not have to swell his courage to become a soldier. ^c*To live, my Lucilius, is to fight* [Seneca].

I do not remember ever having had the itch; yet scratching is one of the sweetest gratifications of nature, and as ready at hand as any. But repentance follows too annoyingly close at its heels. I mostly scratch my ears, which are sometimes itchy on the inside.

^BI was born with all my senses sound almost to perfection. My stomach is comfortably good, as is my head and also my wind, and they usually keep up through my fevers. I have recently turned

fifty-six, six years beyond the age[7] which some nations, not without cause, had prescribed as such a just limit of life that they allowed no one to exceed it. Yet I still have flashes of recovery so clear, though inconstant and brief, that they fall little short of my youthful health and freedom from pain. I am not speaking of vigor and sprightliness; it is not reasonable that they should follow me beyond their limits:

> I can endure no longer to remain
> Upon a doorstep in the rain.
>
> HORACE

My face immediately betrays me, and ᶜand my eyes; ᴮall my changes begin there, and seem a little worse than they really are. I often move my friends to pity before I feel the reason for it. My mirror does not alarm me, for even in my youth I have more than once found myself thus wearing a muddy complexion and an ill-omened look, without any serious consequences; so that the doctors, finding inside me no cause responsible for this outward change, attributed it to the spirit and to some secret passion gnawing me within. They were wrong. If my body obeyed my orders as well as my soul, we should get along a little more comfortably. My soul was then not only free from disturbance, but also full of satisfaction and gaiety – as it usually is, half by nature, half by design:

> Nor does the sickness of my mind infect my limbs.
>
> OVID

I hold that this temperateness of my soul has many a time lifted up my body from its falls. My body is often depressed; whereas if my soul is not jolly, it is at least tranquil and at rest. I had a quartan fever for four or five months, which quite disfigured me; my mind still kept going not only peacefully but cheerfully. If the pain is outside of me, the weakness and languor do not distress me much. I know several bodily infirmities that inspire horror if you merely name them, which I should fear less than a thousand passions and agitations of the spirit that I see prevalent. I have made up my mind to my inability to run any more; it is enough that I crawl. Nor do I complain of the natural decay that has hold of me –

7 In 1588 Montaigne had written simply: "I have recently passed the age which..."

Who marvels at a goiter in the Alps?
 JUVENAL

– any more than I regret that my term of life is not as long and sound as that of an oak.

I have no cause to complain of my imagination. I have had few thoughts in my life that have even interrupted the course of my sleep, unless they have been those of desire, which awakened me without afflicting me. I seldom dream, and then it is about fantastic things and chimeras usually produced by amusing thoughts, more ridiculous than sad. And I hold that it is true that dreams are faithful interpreters of our inclinations; but there is an art to sorting and understanding them.

> ᶜThat dreams repeat whate'er holds men in sway –
> The thoughts, the sights, deeds, worries of the day –
> Is not surprising.
> ACCIUS, QUOTED BY CICERO

Plato says, moreover, that it is the function of wisdom to draw from them instructions for divining the future. I see nothing in that, except for the marvelous experiences related by Socrates, Xenophon, and Aristotle, personages of irreproachable authority. Historians say that the Atlantes never dream, and also that they eat nothing that has been killed; which I add because that is perhaps the reason they do not dream. For Pythagoras prescribed a certain preparation of food to induce appropriate dreams. Mine are gentle and bring on no bodily agitation or vocal utterance. I have known many people of my time to be amazingly agitated by them. Theon, the philosopher, walked in his sleep, and so did the servant of Pericles, on the very tiles and roof of the house.

ᴮI make little choice at table, and attack the first and nearest thing, and I change reluctantly from one flavor to another. I dislike a crowd of dishes and courses as much as any other crowd. I am easily satisfied with few dishes, and I hate the notion of Favorinus that at a feast your food should be stolen from you just as you are gaining appetite, and a new dish always substituted, and that it is a wretched supper if the guests have not been glutted with various birds' rumps, and that the beccafico alone deserves to be eaten whole.

I often eat salt meats; however, I prefer bread without salt, and my baker at home serves no other at my table, contrary to the

custom of the country. When I was a child, I was corrected mainly for refusing things that people ordinarily like best at that age: sugar candies, preserves, pastry. My tutor fought this hatred of dainty foods as being a sort of daintiness. And indeed it is nothing else but fastidious taste, whatever it applies to. Whoever rids a child of some particular and obstinate fondness for brown bread, bacon, or garlic, rids him of finical taste. There are some who act like patient sufferers if they do without beef and ham amid partridges. They have a good time; that is the daintiness of the dainty; it is the taste of a soft existence that is cloyed with the ordinary and accustomed things, ^c*by which luxury beguiles the tedium of wealth* [Seneca]. ^BNot to make good cheer with what another savors, to take particular care of what you eat and drink, is the essence of this vice:

> If you fear a meal of greens upon a modest plate.
>
> HORACE

True enough, there is this difference, that it is better to enslave your desire to the things easiest to obtain; but it is always a vice to enslave yourself. I once called a relative of mine fastidious, who in our galleys had lost the ability to use our beds and to get undressed for sleep.

If I had any male children, I should cordially wish them my own fortune. The good father that God gave me, who has no return from me except gratitude for his goodness, but certainly a very hearty gratitude, sent me from the cradle to be brought up in a poor village of his, and kept me there as long as I was nursing, and even longer, training me to the humblest and commonest way of life. ^c*A well-behaved stomach is a great part of liberty* [Seneca]. ^BNever take on, and still less give to your wives, the charge of their upbringing. Let them be formed by fortune under the laws of the common people and of nature; leave it to custom to train them to frugality and austerity, so that they may have rather to come down from rigorousness than climb toward it. His notion aimed at still another goal, to ally me with the people and that class of men that needs our help; and he considered that I was duty bound to look rather to the man who extends his arms to me than to the one who turns his back on me. And this was the reason why he also had me held over the baptismal font by people of the lowliest class, to bind and attach me to them.

His plan has succeeded not at all badly. I am prone to devote myself to the little people, whether because there is more vainglory in it, or through natural compassion, which has infinite power over

me. The side I condemn in our wars I will condemn more harshly when it is flourishing and prosperous; I will be somewhat reconciled to it when I see it miserable and crushed.[8] How I enjoy contemplating the fine spirit of Chelonis, daughter and wife of kings of Sparta! While her husband Cleombrotus had the advantage over her father Leonidas in the conflicts within her city, she was the good daughter and rallied to her father in his exile, in his misery, opposing the victor. Did fortune chance to turn? There she is, her will changed with fortune's, courageously taking the side of her husband, whom she followed everywhere his ruin led him, having apparently no choice but to rush to the side where she was most needed and where she could best show her compassion. I am more naturally inclined to follow the example of Flaminius, who lent himself to those who needed him more than to those who could benefit him, than that of Pyrrhus, who was prone to truckle to the great and be arrogant with the weak.

Long sessions at table [c]annoy me and [B]disagree with me; for, perhaps because I formed the habit as a boy, for lack of better self-control, I eat as long as I am there. Therefore at home, [c]though the meals are on the short side, [B]I like to sit down a little after the others, in the manner of Augustus; but I do not imitate him in also leaving the table before the others. On the contrary, I like to rest a long time after and listen to stories, provided I do not take part, for it tires me and disagrees with me to talk on a full stomach, whereas I find it a very healthy and pleasant exercise to shout and argue before a meal. [c]The ancient Greeks and Romans had more sense than we, to assign to eating, which is one of the principal actions of life, several hours and the best part of the night, if some other unusual occupation did not interfere; eating and drinking less hastily than we, who perform all our actions on the run, and prolonging this natural pleasure with greater leisure and enjoyment, interspersing with it various useful and agreeable duties of society.

[B]Those who must take care of me could easily deprive me of what they think harmful to me; for in such matters I never desire or find wanting what I do not see. But likewise they waste their time

8 This statement is slightly altered from the 1588 edition, where it was more specific: "In our troubles I condemn the cause of one of the parties, but more when it flourishes and prospers; I have at times been somewhat reconciled to it, to see it miserable and crushed."

preaching me abstinence from the things that are set before me. So that when I want to fast, I have to be set apart from the supper table, and to be served just so much as is necessary for the prescribed collation; for if I sit down to table I forget my resolution. When I order a change in the preparation of some meat, my servants know that it means that my appetite is weakened and that I will not touch it.

All meats that can be eaten rare, I like that way, and I like them well-hung, even, in many cases, to the point of smelling high. Toughness is the only thing that annoys me as a rule (toward any other quality I am as indifferent and tolerant as any man I have known), so that, contrary to the common humor, even among fish I sometimes find some too fresh and too firm. It is not the fault of my teeth, which have always been good, even excellent, and which only just now are beginning to be threatened by old age. I learned from childhood to rub them with my napkin both in the morning and before and after meals.

God is merciful to those whose life he takes away bit by bit; that is the only benefit of old age. The last death will be all the less complete and painful; by then it will kill only a half or a quarter of a man. Here is a tooth that has just fallen out, without pain, without effort; that was the natural term of its duration. Both that part of my being and several others are already dead, others half dead, even some of the most active, which held the highest rank in my vigorous prime. Thus do I melt and slip away from myself. How stupid it would be of my mind if it were to feel the last leap of this decline, which is already so far advanced, as acutely as if it were the whole fall. I hope this will not happen.

ᶜIn truth, I gain one principal consolation in thinking about my death, that it will be normal and natural, and that henceforth in this matter I cannot demand or hope for any but illegitimate favor from destiny. Men enjoy a fond belief that in other days their lives were longer, as their stature was greater. But Solon, who belongs to those old days, nevertheless limits the extreme duration of life to seventy years. Shall I, who in all matters have so worshiped that *golden mean* of the past, and have taken the moderate measure as the most perfect, aspire to an immoderate and prodigious old age? Whatever happens contrary to the course of Nature may be disagreeable, but what happens according to her should always be pleasant. *Everything that happens according to Nature should be considered good* [Cicero]. Thus, says Plato, the death that is brought on by wounds

or maladies may be called violent, but that which takes us by surprise as old age guides us to it is the easiest of all and in a way delightful. *Young men lose their lives by violence, old men by ripeness* [Cicero].

[B]Death mingles and fuses with our life throughout. Decline anticipates death's hour and intrudes even into the course of our progress. I have portraits of myself at twenty-five and thirty-five; I compare them with one of the present: how irrevocably it is no longer myself! How much farther is my present picture from them than from that of my death! We abuse Nature too much by pestering her so far that she is constrained to leave us and abandon our guidance – our eyes, our teeth, our legs, and the rest – to the mercy of foreign assistance that we have begged, and to resign us to the hands of art, weary of following us.

I am not excessively fond of either salads or fruits, except melons. My father hated all kinds of sauces; I love them all. Eating too much bothers me; but I have as yet no really certain knowledge that any kind of food intrinsically disagrees with me; even as I do not notice whether the moon is full or waning, or whether it is spring or autumn. There are changes that take place in us, irregular and unknown. Radishes, for example, I first found to agree with me, then to disagree, now to agree again. In several respects I feel my stomach and appetite vary that way: I have changed back from white wine to claret, and then from claret to white. I am very fond of fish, and have my fat days on the lean days, and my feasts on the fast days. I believe what some say, that it is easier to digest than meat. As it goes against my conscience to eat meat on fish days, so it goes against my taste to mix fish with meat; the difference between them seems to me too great.

Ever since my youth I have occasionally skipped a meal; either to sharpen my appetite for the next day, for, as Epicurus used to fast and make lean meals to accustom his appetite to do without abundance, I do so, on the contrary, to train my appetite to profit better from abundance and use it more joyfully; or to conserve my vigor for the sake of some action of body or mind, for in me both of these grow cruelly lazy through repletion, and I hate above all things the stupid coupling of so healthy and sprightly a goddess with that little belching god of indigestion, all bloated with the fumes of his liquor;[9] or to cure my sick stomach; or for want of proper company, for I say, like that same Epicurus, that we should not so much

9 Venus and Bacchus.

consider what we eat as with whom we eat, and I commend Chilo because he would not promise to be at Periander's feast until he was informed who were the other guests. There is no preparation so sweet to me, no sauce so appetizing, as that which is derived from society.

I think it is healthier to eat more slowly and less, and to eat more often. But I want to make the most of appetite and hunger; I would take no pleasure in dragging out three or four puny meals a day, regulated as if I were taking medicine. ᶜWho would assure me that I would find again at supper the gaping appetite I had in the morning? Let us take – old men especially – let us take advantage of the first opportunity that comes our way. Let us leave the daily diets to the almanac-makers and the doctors.

ᴮThe greatest benefit that good health gives me is sensual pleasure; let us stick to the first pleasure that is present and known. I avoid consistency in these laws of fasting. He who wants to make the most of a habit, let him avoid continuing it; we grow hardened to it, our powers go to sleep in it; six months later you will have so perverted your stomach by your habit that your only profit will be to have lost the freedom to treat it otherwise without damage.

I do not keep my legs and thighs any more covered in winter than in summer: silk hose, nothing else. For the relief of my colds I have allowed myself to keep my head warmer, and my stomach because of my stone; my ailments became accustomed to this in a few days and disdained my ordinary precautions. I thus had graduated from a cap to a kerchief, and from a bonnet to a lined hat. The padding of my doublet serves now only for ornament; it is no good unless I add a rabbit's skin or a vulture's, and a skullcap for my head. Follow these steps and you will go at a fine pace. I will do nothing of the sort, and would gladly disown the start I have made, if I dared. Are you falling into some new ailment? This reform is of no more use to you; you are accustomed to it; look for another. Thus men ruin themselves by letting themselves become entangled in restricting regimens, and by superstitiously tying themselves down to them. They still need more, and still more after that; it is never done.

For the sake of our occupations and pleasure, it is much more convenient to skip our dinner, as the ancients did, and put off making good cheer till the hour of retirement and rest, without breaking up the day; thus I formerly used to do. For the sake of health, on the contrary, I have since found by experience that it is better to dine, and that digestion is better performed awake.

I am not much subject to thirst, either in health or in sickness. To be sure, in the latter case I am apt to have a dry mouth, but no thirst. Normally I drink only when I develop a thirst in eating, and far along into the meal. I drink pretty well for a man of ordinary build; in summer and at an appetizing meal, I not only exceed the limits of Augustus, who drank precisely three times and no more, but, so as not to violate the rule of Democritus, who forbade stopping at four as an unlucky number, I slip on at a pinch to five, about three half-pints; for the little glasses are my favorites, and I enjoy emptying them, which others avoid as unbecoming. I mix my wine most often with as much water, sometimes with half as much. And when I am at home, by an ancient practice that my father's doctor prescribed for him and for himself, they mix what I need in the wine cellar two or three hours before serving it. ᶜThey say that Cranaus, king of the Athenians, was the inventor of this practice of mixing wine with water; whether for better or for worse, I have heard it argued. I think it more fitting and healthy for children not to drink wine until they are sixteen or eighteen. ᴮThe most usual and common way of living is the best; all peculiarities seem to me things to be avoided; and I should hate as much to see a German putting water in his wine as a Frenchman drinking it pure. Public usage lays down the law in such things.

I fear a stuffy atmosphere and avoid smoke like the plague; the first repairs I hurried to make in my house were in the chimneys and the privies, which as a rule are unbearably defective in old buildings; and among the hardships of war I reckon those thick clouds of dust in which we are kept buried in the hot season for a whole day's journey. My breathing is free and easy, and my colds most often pass off without a cough and without damage to my lungs.

The rigor of summer is more of an enemy to me than that of winter; for besides the discomfort of heat, less easily remedied than that of cold, and besides the beating of the sun's rays on my head, my eyes are hurt by any dazzling light. Right now I could not eat dinner seated opposite a blazing, bright fire. To deaden the whiteness of paper, in the time when I was more in the habit of reading, I used to lay a piece of glass on my book, and found much relief in it. To this moment I am ignorant of the use of spectacles, and I see just as far as I ever did, and as any man. It is true that at the decline of day I begin to feel blurring and weakness in reading, an exercise that has always tired my eyes, but especially at night. ᶜHere is a step backward, just barely perceptible. I shall draw back another step, from the second

to the third, from the third to the fourth, so quietly that I shall have to be a confirmed blind man before I feel the decadence and old age of my sight. So artfully do the Fates untwist the thread of our life. And so I doubt that my hearing is on the verge of growing dull, and you will see that when I have half lost it I shall still be blaming the voices of those who are speaking to me. We must really strain our soul to make it feel how it is ebbing away.

[B]My walk is quick and firm; and I know not which of the two, my mind or my body, I have had more difficulty in keeping in one place. That preacher is indeed a friend of mine who holds my attention through a whole sermon. In solemn places, where everyone has such a strained expression, where I have seen the ladies keep even their eyes so steady, I have never succeeded in keeping some part of me from always wandering; even though I may be seated there, I am hardly settled there. [C]As the chambermaid of the philosopher Chrysippus said of her master that he was only drunk in his legs – for he had the habit of moving them about, whatever position he was in, and she would say it when wine befuddled the others and he felt no effect from it – so people might have said of me from my childhood that I was crazy in the feet, or had quicksilver in them, so fidgety and restless are they, wherever I place them.

[B]It is bad manners, besides being harmful to health and even to pleasure, to eat greedily, as I do. I often bite my tongue and sometimes my fingers, in my haste. Diogenes, coming upon a boy who was eating that way, gave his tutor a box on the ear for it. [C]There were men at Rome who taught people to chew, as well as to walk, gracefully. [B]By this I lose the leisure for talking, which is such a sweet seasoning for the dinner table, provided the remarks are appropriate, pleasant, and brief.

There is jealousy and envy between our pleasures; they clash and interfere with each other. Alcibiades, a connoisseur in making good cheer, banished even music from the table, so that it should not disturb the pleasure of conversation, [C]for the reason that Plato ascribes to him, that it is a practice of vulgar men to call in instrumentalists and singers to their feasts, for lack of the good talk and enjoyable remarks with which intelligent men know how to entertain each other. [B]Varro asks this of a banquet: a gathering of people of handsome presence and agreeable conversation, who are neither mute nor garrulous; cleanliness and delicacy in the food and the place; and fair weather. [C]A well-planned dinner takes more than a little art and gives more than a little pleasure; neither the great

generals nor the great philosophers have spurned the practice and science of it. My imagination has entrusted three dinners to the keeping of my memory, which fortune rendered outstandingly pleasant to me at different times in my more flourishing days. For each of the guests himself brings the principal charm, according to the good temper of body and soul in which he happens to be. My present condition excludes me from this.

BI, who operate only close to the ground, hate that inhuman wisdom that would make us disdainful enemies of the cultivation of the body. I consider it equal injustice to set our heart against natural pleasures and to set our heart too much on them. CXerxes was a fool, who, wrapped in all human pleasures, went and offered a prize to anyone who would find him others. But hardly less of a fool is the man who cuts off those that nature has found for him. BWe should neither pursue them nor flee them, we should accept them. I accept them with more gusto and with better grace than most, and more willingly let myself follow a natural inclination. CWe have no need to exaggerate their inanity; it makes itself felt enough and evident enough. Much thanks to our sickly, kill-joy mind, which disgusts us with them as well as with itself. It treats both itself and all that it takes in, whether future or past, according to its insatiable, erratic, and versatile nature.

> Unless the vessel's pure, all you pour in turns sour.
>
> HORACE

I, who boast of embracing the pleasures of life so assiduously and so particularly, find in them, when I look at them thus minutely, virtually nothing but wind. But what of it? We are all wind. And even the wind, more wisely than we, loves to make a noise and move about, and is content with its own functions, without wishing for stability and solidity, qualities that do not belong to it.

The pure pleasures of imagination, as well as the pains, some say, are the greatest, as the scales of Critolaus expressed it. No wonder; it composes them to its liking and cuts them out of whole cloth. I see signal, and perhaps desirable, examples of this every day. But I, being of a mixed constitution, and coarse, am unable to cling so completely to this single and simple object as to keep myself from grossly pursuing the present pleasures of the general human law – intellectually sensual, sensually intellectual. The Cyrenaic philosophers hold that the bodily pleasures, like the pains, are the more powerful, as being both twofold and more equitable.

^BThere are some who ^Cfrom savage stupidity, as Aristotle says, ^Bare disgusted with them; I know some who are that way from ambition. Why do they not also give up breathing? Why do they not live on their own air, ^Cand refuse light, because it is free and costs them neither invention nor vigor? ^BLet Mars, or Pallas, or Mercury give them sustenance, instead of Venus, Ceres, and Bacchus, just to see what happens. ^CWon't they try to square the circle while perched on their wives! ^BI hate to have people order us to keep our minds in the clouds while our bodies are at table. I would not have the mind nailed down to it nor wallowing at it, but attending to it; ^Csitting at it, not lying down at it.

Aristippus defended the body alone, as if we had no soul; Zeno embraced only the soul, as if we had no body. Both were wrong. Pythagoras, they say, followed a philosophy that was all contemplation, Socrates one that was all conduct and action; Plato found the balance between the two. But they say so to make a good story, and the true balance is found in Socrates, and Plato is much more Socratic than Pythagorean, and it becomes him better.

^BWhen I dance, I dance; when I sleep, I sleep; yes, and when I walk alone in a beautiful orchard, if my thoughts have been dwelling on extraneous incidents for some part of the time, for some other part I bring them back to the walk, to the orchard, to the sweetness of this solitude, and to me. Nature has observed this principle like a mother, that the actions she has enjoined on us for our need should also give us pleasure; and she invites us to them not only through reason, but also through appetite. It is unjust to infringe her laws.

When I see both Caesar and Alexander, in the thick of their great tasks, so fully enjoying ^Cnatural and therefore necessary and just ^Bpleasures, I do not say that that is relaxing their souls, I say that it is toughening them, subordinating these violent occupations and laborious thoughts, by the vigor of their spirits, to the practice of everyday life: ^Cwise men, had they believed that this was their ordinary occupation, the other the extraordinary.

We are great fools. "He has spent his life in idleness," we say; "I have done nothing today." What, have you not lived? That is not only the fundamental but the most illustrious of your occupations. "If I had been placed in a position to manage great affairs, I would have shown what I could do." Have you been able to think out and manage your own life? You have done the greatest task of all. To show and exploit her resources Nature has no need of fortune; she

shows herself equally on all levels and behind a curtain as well as without one. To compose our character is our duty, not to compose books, and to win, not battles and provinces, but order and tranquillity in our conduct. Our great and glorious masterpiece is to live appropriately. All other things, ruling, hoarding, building, are only little appendages and props, at most.

[B]I take pleasure in seeing an army general, at the foot of a breach that he means to attack presently, lending himself wholly and freely to his dinner and his conversation, among his friends; [c]and Brutus, with heaven and earth conspiring against him and Roman liberty, stealing some hour of night from his rounds to read and annotate Polybius with complete assurance. [B]It is for little souls, buried under the weight of business, to be unable to detach themselves cleanly from it or to leave it and pick it up again:

> Brave men, who have endured with me
> Worse things, now banish cares with revelry;
> Tomorrow we shall sail the mighty sea.
>
> HORACE

Whether it is in jest or in earnest that the Sorbonne acquired its proverbial reputation for theological drinking and feasting, I think it right that the faculty should dine all the more comfortably and pleasantly for having used the morning profitably and seriously in the work of their school. The consciousness of having spent the other hours well is a proper and savory sauce for the dinner table. Thus did the sages live. And that inimitable straining for virtue that astounds us in both Catos, that disposition, severe to the point of being troublesome, submitted thus meekly and contentedly to the laws of human nature, and of Venus and Bacchus, [c]in accordance with the precepts of their sect, which require the perfect sage to be as expert and versed in the enjoyment of the natural pleasures as in any other duty of life. *A wise palate should go with a wise heart* [Cicero].

[B]Relaxation and affability, it seems to me, are marvelously honorable and most becoming to a strong and generous soul. Epaminondas did not think that to mingle with the dance of the boys of his city, [c]to sing, to play music, [B]and to concentrate attentively on these things, was at all derogatory to the honor of his glorious victories and the perfect purity of character that was his. And among so many admirable actions of Scipio, [c]the grandfather, a personage worthy of the reputation of celestial

descent,[10] [B]there is nothing that lends him more charm than to see him playing nonchalantly and childishly at picking up and selecting shells and running potato races by the sea with Laelius, and in bad weather amusing and tickling his fancy by writing comedies portraying the meanest and most vulgar actions of men; [c]and, his head full of that wonderful campaign against Hannibal and Africa, visiting the schools in Sicily, and attending lectures on philosophy until he armed to the teeth the blind envy of his enemies in Rome. [B]Nor is there anything more remarkable in Socrates than the fact that in his old age he finds time to take lessons in dancing and playing instruments, and considers it well spent.

This same man was once seen standing in a trance, an entire day and night, in the presence of the whole Greek army, overtaken and enraptured by some deep thought. He was seen, [c]the first among so many valiant men of the army, to run to the aid of Alcibiades, who was overwhelmed by enemies, to cover him with his body, and to extricate him from the melee by sheer force of arms; and the first among the people of Athens, all outraged like him at such a shameful spectacle, to come forward to rescue Theramenes, whom the Thirty Tyrants were having led to his death by their satellites; and he desisted from this bold undertaking only at the remonstrance of Theramenes himself, though he was followed by only two men in all. He was seen, when courted by a beauty with whom he was in love, to maintain strict chastity when necessary. He was seen, in the battle of Delium, to pick up and save Xenophon, who had been thrown from his horse. He was [B]constantly [c]seen [B]to march to war [c]and walk the ice [B]barefoot, to wear the same gown in winter and in summer, to surpass all his companions in enduring toil, to eat no differently at a feast than ordinarily.

[c]He was seen for twenty-seven years to endure with the same countenance hunger, poverty, the indocility of his children, the claws of his wife; and in the end calumny, tyranny, prison, irons, and poison. [B]But if that man was summoned to a drinking bout by the duty of civility, he was also the one who did the best in the whole army. And he never refused to play at cobnut with children, or to ride a hobbyhorse with them, and he did so gracefully; for all actions, says philosophy, are equally becoming and honorable in

10 Instead of this phrase, Montaigne had written in 1588: "Scipio the Younger (everything considered, the first man of the Romans)." His first attribution was the correct one.

a wise man. We have material enough, and we should never tire of presenting the picture of this man as a pattern and ideal of all sorts of perfection. ᶜThere are very few full and pure examples of life, and those who educate us are unfair when they set before us every day feeble and defective models, hardly good in a single vein, which rather pull us backward, corrupters rather than correctors.

ᴮPopular opinion is wrong: it is much easier to go along the sides, where the outer edge serves as a limit and a guide, than by the middle way, wide and open, and to go by art than by nature; but it is also much less noble and less commendable. ᶜGreatness of soul is not so much pressing upward and forward as knowing how to set oneself in order and circumscribe oneself. It regards as great whatever is adequate, and shows its elevation by liking moderate things better than eminent ones. ᴮThere is nothing so beautiful and legitimate as to play the man well and properly, no knowledge so hard to acquire as the knowledge of how to live this life well ᶜand naturally; ᴮand the most barbarous of our maladies is to despise our being.

He who wants to detach his soul, let him do it boldly, if he can, when his body is ill, to free it from the contagion; at other times, on the contrary, let the soul assist and favor the body and not refuse to take part in its natural pleasures and enjoy them conjugally, bringing to them moderation, if it is the wiser of the two, for fear that through lack of discretion they may merge into pain. ᶜIntemperance is the plague of sensual pleasure; and temperance is not its scourage, it is its seasoning. Eudoxus, who made pleasure the supreme good, and his fellows, who raised it to such high value, savored it in its most charming sweetness by means of temperance, which they possessed in singular and exemplary degree.

ᴮI order my soul to look upon both pain and pleasure with a gaze equally ᶜself-controlled – *for it is as wrong for the soul to overflow from joy as to contract in sorrow* [Cicero] – and equally ᴮfirm, but gaily at the one, at the other severely, and, according to its ability, as anxious to extinguish the one as to extend the other. ᶜViewing good things sanely implies viewing bad things sanely. And pain has something not to be avoided in its mild beginning, and pleasure something to be avoided in its excessive ending. Plato couples them together and claims that it is equally the function of fortitude to fight against pain and against the immoderate and bewitching blandishments of plea-sure. They are two fountains: whoever draws the right amount from the right one at the right time, whether city, man, or beast, is very fortunate. The first we must take as a necessary medicine, but more

sparingly; the other for thirst, but not to the point of drunkenness. Pain, pleasure, love, hatred, are the first things a child feels; if when reason comes they cling to her, that is virtue.

^BI have a vocabulary all my own. I "pass the time," when it is rainy and disagreeable; when it is good, I do not want to pass it; I savor it, I cling to it. We must run through the bad and settle on the good. This ordinary expression "pastime" or "pass the time" represents the habit of those wise folk who think they can make no better use of their life than to let it slip by and escape it, pass it by, sidestep it, and, as far as in them lies, ignore it and run away from it, as something irksome and contemptible. But I know it to be otherwise and find it both agreeable and worth prizing, even in its last decline, in which I now possess it; and nature has placed it in our hands adorned with such favorable conditions that we have only ourselves to blame if it weighs on us and if it escapes us unprofitably. ^C*The life of the fool is joyless, full of trepidation, given over wholly to the future* [Seneca]. ^BHowever, I am reconciling myself to the thought of losing it, without regret, but as something that by its nature must be lost; not as something annoying and troublesome. ^CThen too, not to dislike dying is properly becoming only to those who like living. ^BIt takes management to enjoy life. I enjoy it twice as much as others, for the measure of enjoyment depends on the greater or lesser attention that we lend it. Especially at this moment, when I perceive that mine is so brief in time, I try to increase it in weight; I try to arrest the speed of its flight by the speed with which I grasp it, and to compensate for the haste of its ebb by my vigor in using it. The shorter my possession of life, the deeper and fuller I must make it.

Others feel the sweetness of some satisfaction and of prosperity; I feel it as they do, but it is not in passing and slipping by. Instead we must study it, savor it, and ruminate it, to give proper thanks for it to him who grants it to us. They enjoy the other pleasures as they do that of sleep, without being conscious of them. To the end that sleep itself should not escape me thus stupidly, at one time I saw fit to have mine disturbed, so that I might gain a glimpse of it. I meditate on any satisfaction; I do not skim over it, I sound it, and bend my reason, now grown peevish and hard to please, to welcome it. Do I find myself in some tranquil state? Is there some voluptuous pleasure that tickles me? I do not let my senses pilfer it, I bring my soul into it, not to implicate herself, but to enjoy herself, not to lose herself but to find herself. And I set her, for her part, to admire

herself in this prosperous estate, to weigh and appreciate and amplify the happiness of it. She measures the extent of her debt to God for being at peace with her conscience and free from other inner passions, for having her body in its natural condition, enjoying controlledly and adequately the agreeable and pleasant functions with which he is pleased to compensate by his grace for the pains with which his justice chastises us in its turn; how much it is worth to her to be lodged at such a point that wherever she casts her eyes, the sky is calm around her: no desire, no fear or doubt to disturb the air for her, no difficulty, ^cpast, present, or future, ^Bover which her imagination may not pass without hurt.

This consideration gains great luster by comparison between my condition and that of others. Thus I set before me in a thousand forms those who are carried away and tossed about by fortune or their own error, and also those, closer to my way, who accept their good fortune so languidly and indifferently. They are the people who really "pass their time"; they pass over the present and what they possess, to be the slaves of hope, and for shadows and vain images that fancy dangles before them –

> Like ghosts that after death are said to flit,
> Or visions that delude the slumbering wit
> VIRGIL

– which hasten and prolong their flight the more they are pursued. The fruit and goal of their pursuit is to pursue, as Alexander said that the purpose of his work was to work,

> Believing nothing done while aught was left to do.
> LUCAN

As for me, then, I love life and cultivate it just as God has been pleased to grant it to us. I do not go about wishing that it should lack the need to eat and drink, ^cand it would seem to me no less excusable a failing to wish that need to be doubled. *The wise man is the keenest searcher for natural treasures* [Seneca]. Nor do I wish ^Bthat we should sustain ourselves by merely putting into our mouths a little of that drug by which Epimenides took away his appetite and kept himself alive; nor that we should beget children insensibly with our fingers or our heels, ^cbut rather, with due respect, that we could also beget them voluptuously with our fingers and heels; nor ^Bthat the body should be without desire and without titillation.

Those are ungrateful ^Cand unfair ^Bcomplaints. I accept with all my heart ^Cand with gratitude ^Bwhat nature has done for me, and I am pleased with myself and proud of myself that I do. We wrong that great and all-powerful Giver by refusing his gift, nullifying it, and disfiguring it. ^CHimself all good, he has made all things good. *All things that are according to nature are worthy of esteem* [Cicero].

^BOf the opinions of philosophy I most gladly embrace those that are most solid, that is to say, most human and most our own; my opinions, in conformity with my conduct, are low and humble. ^CPhilosophy is very childish, to my mind, when she gets up on her hind legs and preaches to us that it is a barbarous alliance to marry the divine with the earthly, the reasonable with the unreasonable, the severe with the indulgent, the honorable with the dishonorable; that sensual pleasure is a brutish thing unworthy of being enjoyed by the wise man; that the only pleasure he derives from the enjoyment of a beautiful young wife is the pleasure of his consciousness of doing the right thing, like putting on his boots for a useful ride. May her followers have no more right and sinews and sap in deflowering their wives than her lessons have!

That is not what Socrates says, her tutor and ours. He prizes bodily pleasure as he should, but he prefers that of the mind, as having more power, constancy, ease, variety, and dignity. The latter by no means goes alone, according to him – he is not so fanciful – but only comes first. For him temperance is the moderator, not the adversary, of pleasures.

^BNature is a gentle guide, but no more gentle than wise and just. ^C*We must penetrate into the nature of things and clearly see exactly what it demands* [Cicero]. ^BI seek her footprints everywhere. We have confused them with artificial tracks, ^Band for that reason the sovereign good of the Academics and the Peripatetics, which is "to live according to nature," becomes hard to limit and express; also that of the Stoics, a neighbor to the other, which is "to consent to nature."

^BIs it not an error to consider some actions less worthy because they are necessary? No, they will not knock it out of my head that the marriage of pleasure with necessity, ^Cwith whom, says an ancient, the gods always conspire, ^Bis a very suitable one. To what purpose do we dismember by divorce a structure made up of such close and brotherly correspondence? On the contrary, let us bind it together again by mutual services. Let the mind arouse and quicken

the heaviness of the body, and the body check and make fast the lightness of the mind. *He who praises the nature of the soul as the sovereign good and condemns the nature of the flesh as evil, truly both carnally desires the soul and carnally shuns the flesh; for his feeling is inspired by human vanity, not by divine truth* [Saint Augustine].

There is no part unworthy of our care in this gift that God has given us; we are accountable for it even to a single hair. And it is not a perfunctory charge to man to guide man according to his nature; it is express, simple, and of prime importance, and the creator has given it to us seriously and sternly. Authority alone has power over common intelligences, and has more weight in a foreign language. Let us renew the charge here. *Who would not say that it is the essence of folly to do lazily and rebelliously what has to be done, to impel the body one way and the soul another, to be split between the most conflicting motions?* [Seneca.]

Come on now, just to see, some day get some man to tell you the absorbing thoughts and fancies that he takes into his head, and for the sake of which he turns his mind from a good meal and laments the time he spends on feeding himself. You will find there is nothing so insipid in all the dishes on your table as this fine entertainment of his mind (most of the time we should do better to go to sleep completely than to stay awake for what we do stay awake for); and you will find that his ideas and aspirations are not worth your stew. Even if they were the transports of Archimedes himself, what of it? I am not here touching on, or mixing up with that brattish rabble of men that we are, or with the vanity of the desires and musings that distract us, those venerable souls, exalted by ardent piety and religion to constant and conscientious meditation on divine things, who, anticipating, by dint of keen and vehement hope, the enjoyment of eternal food, final goal and ultimate limit of Christian desires, sole constant and incorruptible pleasure, scorn to give their attention to our beggarly, watery, and ambiguous comforts, and readily resign to the body the concern and enjoyment of sensual and temporal fodder. That is a privileged study. Between ourselves, these are two things that I have always observed to be in singular accord: supercelestial thoughts and subterranean conduct.

Aesop, that great man, saw his master pissing as he walked. "What next?" he said. "Shall we have to shit as we run?" Let us manage our time; we shall still have a lot left idle and ill spent. Our

mind likes to think it has not enough leisure hours to do its own business unless it dissociates itself from the body for the little time that the body really needs it.

They want to get out of themselves and escape from the man. That is madness: instead of changing into angels, they change into beasts; instead of raising themselves, they lower themselves. ^CThese transcendental humors frighten me, like lofty and inaccessible places; and nothing is so hard for me to stomach in the life of Socrates as his ecstasies and possessions by his daemon, nothing is so human in Plato as the qualities for which they say he is called divine. ^BAnd of our sciences, those seem to me most terrestrial and low which have risen the highest. And I find nothing so humble and so mortal in the life of Alexander as his fancies about his immortalization. Philotas stung him wittily by his answer. He congratulated him by letter on the oracle of Jupiter Ammon which had lodged him among the gods: "As far as you are concerned, I am very glad of it; but there is reason to pity the men who will have to live with and obey a man who exceeds ^Cand is not content with ^Ba man's proportions."

^CSince you obey the gods, you rule the world.
HORACE

^BThe nice inscription with which the Athenians honored the entry of Pompey into their city is in accord with my meaning.

You are as much a god as you will own
That you are nothing but a man alone.
AMYOT'S PLUTARCH

It is an absolute perfection and virtually divine to know how to enjoy our being rightfully. We seek other conditions because we do not understand the use of our own, and go outside of ourselves because we do not know what it is like inside. ^CYet there is no use our mounting on stilts, for on stilts we must still walk on our own legs. And on the loftiest throne in the world we are still sitting only on our own rump.

^BThe most beautiful lives, to my mind, are those that conform to the common ^Chuman ^Bpattern, ^Cwith order, but ^Bwithout miracle and without eccentricity. Now old age needs to be treated a little more tenderly. Let us commend it to that god who is the protector of health and wisdom, but gay and sociable wisdom:

Grant me but health, Latona's son,
And to enjoy the wealth I've won,
And honored age, with mind entire
And not unsolaced by the lyre.

HORACE

END OF BOOK THREE

TRAVEL JOURNAL

Note on the travel journal

The *Essays* are the only book of his own that Montaigne published or intended for publication. However, he left one other extensive piece of writing, a journal of his trip to Germany, Switzerland, and Italy from June 22, 1580, to November 30, 1581 – between the first publication of the *Essays* (Books I and II) in 1580 and Montaigne's return home to take up his duties as mayor of Bordeaux.

He made the trip for pleasure and for health.[1] He wanted very much to see Rome, his cultural homeland, as well as Florence, Venice, and other cities of renown. Perhaps most of all he simply wanted to see the world. From what his secretary writes, Montaigne would rather have gone to Cracow and to Greece than make the Italian tour that was familiar to so many;[2] but he had friends with him who wanted to reach Rome, and he gave way. He had one specific purpose: to try the effect of mineral baths on the kidney stone that had been afflicting him for two years when he set out. Much of the *Travel Journal* is a clinical case history of the spas he visited, the baths he took, the waters he drank, the stones and urine that he passed.

Besides this, the *Journal* is a sightseer's record of the places and people that Montaigne saw. The reader finds some surprises. Montaigne shows a lively interest in all sorts of details of everyday living – prices, foods, lodgings, as well as manners and customs in the larger sense – nearly always, to be sure, with the hope of coming to know people of other nations better through their way of life. He loves gadgets and tells about them at some length. Faithful in the practice of his religion, he is eager to study other religions as well, by observation and by discussion. Wherever he goes, he tries to live as the natives do. In order to "live Italian" he even writes a large part of his *Journal* in that language; and in Augsburg he is chagrined to learn that he has attracted notice as a foreigner. He is a good mixer, and his cheerfulness is contagious.

1 Conjectures have been made about more serious purposes – a mission for the king, the hope of the ambassadorship to Venice, and others – but they remain conjectures. For Montaigne's love of travel, see *Essays* III: 9, "Of Vanity."

2 See *Travel Journal*, p. 1115. The party included Montaigne, four other noblemen – his youngest brother, Bertrand de Mattecoulon; his brother-in-law, Bernard de Cazalis; young Charles d'Estissac; and a Monsieur du Hautoy – and a number of servants.

The main interest of the *Journal* is in the light it sheds on Montaigne and the *Essays*. Hard as he tries to be completely candid in all he writes, his published work reveals the effect of forces that often limit his candor: his concern for the public welfare, his sense of the urbane tone that will please his reader, and the like. In the *Travel Journal* we can watch him without his knowing. This work changes little in the portrait that emerges from the *Essays*, but it adds some touches and confirms our sense of Montaigne's sincerity.

About half of the *Travel Journal* was written – presumably in large part at Montaigne's dictation – by a secretary about whom we know nothing. Montaigne wrote the remaining half, partly in French and about half in Italian, a language he handled fluently but not always surely. These divisions, which are marked in our text, are the following:

> The Journal by the Secretary, in French, pp. 1056–1156.
> The Journal by Montaigne in French, pp. 1156–1208.
> The Journal by Montaigne in Italian, pp. 1208–1266.
> The Journal by Montaigne in French, pp. 1266–1270.

The *Journal* has a curious history. For almost two hundred years the manuscript remained buried in a chest at Montaigne, where in 1770 it was discovered by Canon Prunis, a historian of the region in quest of materials. The first two pages were missing and have never been found. Four years later it was published by Meunier de Querlon. Three simultaneous editions appeared first, then another in the same year (1774), finally a fifth in the year following. All five were edited by Querlon. No other French edition appeared until 1837. Meanwhile the manuscript disappeared in the Revolution and has never been found again.

As a result, of course, all subsequent editors, translators, and other students of the *Journal* are dependent on the five Querlon editions, which offer not only many variants but also a good many apparent misplacements and misreadings. Two relatively recent editions give much additional help: that of Alessandro d'Ancona (in Italian, Città di Castello, 1889), with its wealth of information and corrections concerning persons and places named in the *Journal*; and that of Louis Lautrey (Hachette, 1906), with its bold and generally impressive conjectural emendations. The most valuable and accessible modern editions are those by Arthur Armaingaud (Conard, 1928–29; Volumes VII–VIII of Montaigne's

Œuvres complètes), Maurice Rat (Garnier, 1942), Charles Dédéyan (Les Belles Lettres, 1946), and Silvestre de Sacy (Club Français du Livre, 1954).

There are no good studies of the *Travel Journal* in English. Three of the best are in French: Sainte-Beuve's fine article in the *Nouveaux Lundis*, "Montaigne en voyage" (1862); Dédéyan's useful *Essai sur le Journal de voyage de Montaigne* (Boivin, 1946), and Imbrie Buffum's excellent *L'Influence du voyage de Montaigne sur les Essais* (Princeton, 1946).

The *Journal* has been translated three times into English: by the younger William Hazlitt (1842), W. G. Waters (1903), and E. J. Trechmann (Hogarth, 1929). The first two translations are very weak, the third very good. Trechmann is very faithful to Montaigne – more so, it seems to me, than in his translation of the *Essays* – and has scrupulously reproduced the style of the *Journal* with its many verbless sentences, repetitions, and awkward constructions. I have been a little freer, though not very much, on the ground that Montaigne probably never even reread the *Journal* as he reread and revised the *Essays*, and that he would have wished to make it clear and readable if he had intended to publish it. I remain greatly indebted, however, to Trechmann, as well as to d'Ancona, Lautrey, Buffum, and others mentioned above.

Since the reader has an even harder time finding a particular passage in the *Journal* than in the *Essays*, I have introduced into the text the divisions shown in the following table. Montaigne bears no responsibility for any of these.

ANALYTICAL TABLE OF THE TRIP

ACROSS FRANCE TOWARD SWITZERLAND (1580)

SWITZERLAND (1580)

GERMANY, AUSTRIA, AND THE ALPS (1580)

ITALY: THE ROAD TO ROME (1580)

ITALY: ROME (1580–1581)

ITALY: FROM ROME TO LORETO AND LA VILLA (1581)

ITALY: FIRST STAY AT LA VILLA (1581)

ITALY: FLORENCE – PISA – LUCCA (1581)

ITALY: SECOND STAY AT LA VILLA (1581)

ITALY: RETURN TO ROME (1581)

ITALY AND FRANCE: THE RETURN HOME (1581)

TABLE OF MONEY VALUES

FRENCH MONEY OF ACCOUNT

12 deniers = 1 sou 20 sous = 1 livre

The values of the money of account are not related to any metallic equivalents. There are two systems, that of Tours (tournois) and that of Paris (parisis). Parisis money is worth 125 per cent of tournois at each level: 4 parisis (deniers, sous, livres) = 5 tournois (deniers, sous, livres). The reckoning here is in tournois, which was internationally current, as the parisis system was not.

OTHER COINS MENTIONED IN THE JOURNAL

baiocco (Roman) = about 6 deniers or 0.5 sou
batz, batzen (German) = about 2.3 sous
carolus (French) = 10 deniers or 0.83 sou
crown (écu) (French) = 3 livres or a little more
crown (scudo) (Italian) = 50 sous or 2.5 livres
gold crown, sun-crown (French) = 1 French crown
florin (German) = about 2 livres
franc (French) = 1 livre
giulio (Roman) = about 5 sous, 10 baiocchi
lira (Italian) = about 8.5 sous
pistolet or demi-pistole (Spanish) = about 1.1 crowns
quattrino (Roman) = 1.2 deniers or 0.1 sou
real (Spanish) = about 4 or 5 sous
teston (French and Roman) = about 14.5 sous
thaler (German and other) = about 9 sous

Across France toward Switzerland
(September 5–28, 1580)

[THE JOURNAL BY THE SECRETARY, IN FRENCH]

Monsieur de Montaigne dispatched Monsieur de Mattecoulon[1] post-haste with the said groom to visit the said count,[2] and found that his wounds were not mortal. At the said BEAUMONT,[3] Monsieur d'Estissac[4] joined the group to make the same trip, accompanied by a gentleman, a valet, a mule, and on foot a muleteer and two lackeys. He was returning to our party to go halves on the expense.

On Monday, September 5th, 1580, we left the said Beaumont after dinner and came without stopping to sup at

MEAUX, which is a small town, beautiful, situated on the river Marne. It is in three parts; the town and the suburb are on this side of the river, toward Paris.

Across the bridges there is another big place called the Market, surrounded on all sides by the river and a very handsome moat, where there is a great multitude of inhabitants and houses. This place was formerly very well fortified with great strong walls and towers; but in our second Huguenot troubles, because most of the inhabitants of this place were of that party, all those fortifications were demolished. This part of the town withstood the attack of the English[5] when all the rest was lost; and as a reward, all the inhabitants of the said locality are still exempt from the taille and other taxes. They show on the river Marne an island two or three hundred paces long, which they say was an earthwork erected in the water by the English to batter the said Market with their engines and which with time has taken this permanent shape.

1 Bertrand-Charles de Montaigne, sieur de Mattecoulon, Montaigne's youngest brother, then aged twenty.
2 Unidentified. The first two manuscript pages of the *Journal* were missing when the rest of it was found.
3 Beaumont-sur-Oise.
4 Charles d'Estissac (c. 1563–86), son of Louise d'Estissac, to whom Montaigne dedicated Chapter 8 of Book II of the *Essays*, "Of the Affection of Fathers for Their Children."
5 Under Henry V in 1421.

In the suburb we saw the Abbey of Saint-Faron, a very old building where they show the dwelling of Ogier the Dane and his hall. There is an ancient refectory, with great long stone tables of unusual size, in the middle of which, before our civil wars, there welled up a spring of fresh water which served for their meals. Most of the monks still are noblemen. Among other things there is a very old and honorable tomb, on which there are the stone figures of two outstretched knights, of extraordinary size. They maintain that these are the bodies of Ogier the Dane and some other one of those paladins. There is neither an inscription nor any coat of arms; there are only these words in Latin, which an abbot had placed there about a hundred years ago, that "these are two unknown heroes who are buried here." Among their treasures they show some bones of these knights. The arm bone, from the shoulder to the elbow, is about the length of the whole arm of an ordinary-sized man of our time, and a little longer than that of Monsieur de Montaigne. They also show two of their swords, which are about the length of one of our two-handed swords, and are very much hacked by blows on the edge.

At the said place of Meaux Monsieur de Montaigne went to visit the treasurer of the Church of Saint Stephen, a man named Juste Terrelle, known among the savants of France; a little man, sixty years old, who has traveled to Egypt and Jerusalem and spent seven years in Constantinople, and who showed him his library and the curiosities of his garden. The most curious thing we saw there was a box-tree spreading its branches in a circle, so thick and so artfully clipped that it seems to be a very polished and very massive ball, of the height of a man.

From Meaux, where we dined on Tuesday, we came to sleep at

CHARLY, seven leagues. On Wednesday after dinner we came to sleep at

DORMANS, seven leagues. The next day, which was Thursday morning, we came to dine at

ÉPERNAY, five leagues. On arriving there, Messieurs d'Estissac and de Montaigne went off to Mass, as was their custom, in the Church of Our Lady. And because the said seigneur de Montaigne had once read that when Marshal Strozzi was killed at the siege of Thionville his body was brought to the said church, he inquired about his sepulture and found that he was buried there, without any indication in the form of a stone, or coat of arms, or epitaph,

opposite the high altar. And we were told that the queen had had
him buried thus without pomp or ceremony because that was the
will of the said marshal. The bishop of Rennes, of the Hennequin
family in Paris, was then officiating in the said church, of which he is
abbot; for it was also the day of the Festival of Our Lady of
September.

In the said church after Mass, Monsieur de Montaigne spoke to
Monsieur Maldonado,[6] a Jesuit whose name is very famous because
of his erudition in theology and philosophy, and they had several
talks together on learned matters, both then and after dinner, at the
said Monsieur de Montaigne's lodgings, where the said Maldonado
came to see him. And among other things, because Maldonado had
just come from the baths of Spa, which are at Liège, where he had
been with Monsieur de Nevers, he told him that those were ex-
tremely cold waters and that the people there maintained that the
colder you could take them, the better. They are so cold that some
who drink them start to shiver and shudder; but soon after one feels
a great warmth in the stomach. For his part he used to take a
hundred ounces; for there are people who furnish glasses that hold
their measure, according to what each person wants. The waters are
drunk not only on an empty stomach but also after meals. Their
operation, which he told us about, is like that of the waters of
Gascony. As for himself, he said that he had noted their power by
the harm that they had not done him, for he had drunk of them
several times while all sweating and stirred up. He has observed by
experience that frogs and other little animals that are thrown into
these waters die immediately; and he said that a handkerchief placed
over a glass full of the said water will turn yellow immediately. They
drink it for at least two or three weeks. That is a place where one is
very well accommodated and lodged, and it is recommended for any
kind of obstruction and gravel. However, neither Monsieur de
Nevers nor he had got much healthier for his stay.

He had with him a steward of Monsieur de Nevers, and they
gave Monsieur de Montaigne a printed paper on the subject of the
dispute between the dukes of Montpensier and of Nevers, so that
he might be informed about it and be able to inform gentlemen who
might inquire about it.

We left there Friday morning and came to

6 Juan Maldonado (1533–84), eminent Spanish professor of philosophy and
theology, especially exegesis. Montaigne was to see him again in Rome.

CHÂLONS, seven leagues. We stayed there at the Crown, a handsome lodging; and they serve you on silver plate, and most of the bedding and coverlets are of silk. The common buildings of this whole part of the country are of chalkstone, cut into little square pieces of half a foot or thereabouts; and others of turf of the same shape. The next day we left there after dinner and came to sleep at

VITRY-LE-FRANÇOIS, seven leagues. This is a small town situated on the river Marne, built thirty-five or forty years ago in place of the other Vitry, which was burned.[7] It still has its original form, well-proportioned and pleasant, and the center of it is a large square, one of the handsomest in France.

Here we learned three memorable stories. One, that the dowager duchess of Guise de Bourbon, eighty-seven years old, was still alive, and still could do a quarter of a league on foot.

The second, that a few days before there had been a hanging at a place called Montier-en-Der, near here, upon this occasion: Seven or eight girls around Chaumont-en-Bassigni plotted together a few years ago to dress up as males and thus continue their life in the world. One of them came to this place under the name Mary, earning her living as a weaver, a well-disposed young man who made friends with everybody. At the said Vitry he became engaged to a woman who is still alive, but because of some disagreement that arose between them, their compact went no further. Later he went to the said Montier-en-Der, still earning his living at the said trade, and fell in love with a woman, whom he married and with whom he lived for four or five months, to her satisfaction, so they say. But she was recognized by someone from the said Chaumont, the matter was brought before justice, and she was condemned to be hanged, which she said she would rather undergo than return to a girl's status; and she was hanged for using illicit devices to supply her defect in sex.

The other story is of a man still alive named Germain, of low condition, without any trade or position, who was a girl up to the age of twenty-two, seen and known by all the inhabitants of the town, and noticed because she had a little more hair about her chin than the other girls; and they called her Bearded Mary.[8] One day when

7 In 1545, a year after Charles V had burned Vitry-en-Perthois, Francis I founded Vitry-le-François on the same spot.
8 Montaigne tells this story in the *Essays*, I: 21.

she made an effort in jumping, her virile instruments came out, and Cardinal de Lenoncourt, then bishop of Châlons, gave her the name Germain. Germain has not married, however; he has a big, very thick beard. We were not able to see him because he was in the village. In this town there is still a song commonly in the girls' mouths, in which they warn one another not to stretch their legs too wide for fear of becoming males, like Marie Germain. They say that Ambroise Paré has put this story into his book on surgery. The story is very certain, and was attested to Monsieur de Montaigne by the most eminent officials of the town.

From here we set out Sunday morning after breakfast and came without stopping to

BAR-LE-DUC, nine leagues, where Monsieur de Montaigne had been before.[9] He now found nothing remarkable and new but the extraordinary expense that a private priest, dean of the place, had put into public works, and continues to put in every day. His name is Gilles de Trèves. He has built the most sumptuous chapel, in regard to marble, paintings, and decorations, that there is in France; and has also built and almost finished furnishing the most beautiful town house that there is in France, of the most beautiful construction, the best proportioned and upholstered, the most elaborately and richly decorated, and the best to live in. He wants to make a college of it, and is in the process of endowing it and setting it in operation at his own expense.

From Bar-le-Duc, where we dined Monday morning, we came to sleep at

MAUVAGES, four leagues, a little village where Monsieur de Montaigne was stopped by reason of his colic, which was also the reason why he abandoned the plan he had made to see Toul, Metz, Nancy, Joinville, and Saint-Dizier, which are towns scattered around this route, as he had intended, in order to reach the baths of Plombières in all haste.

From Mauvages we set out Tuesday in the morning and came to dine at

VAUCOULEURS, one league from there; and we passed along the river Meuse to a village called

DOMRÉMY, on the Meuse, three leagues from the said Vaucouleurs, the native village of the famous Maid of Orleans, whose name was Jeanne Darc or Dallis. Her descendants were ennobled by

9 With the court in 1559. See *Essays* II: 17, p. 602.

the favor of the king, and they showed us the arms that the king gave them, which are azure, a straight sword crowned and with a hilt of gold, and two gold fleurs-de-lys at the side of the said sword. A receiver of Vaucouleurs gave an escutcheon thus painted to Monsieur de Cazalis.[10] The front of the little house where she was born is all painted with her exploits; but age has greatly damaged the painting. There is also a tree beside a vineyard which they call the Maid's Tree, which has nothing else remarkable about it.

We came this evening to sleep at

NEUFCHÂTEAU, five leagues. Here, in the church of the Cordeliers, there are many tombs, three or four hundred years old, of the nobility of the region, on which all the inscriptions are in this form: *Here lies So-and-so, who was dead when time was passing through the year twelve hundred, etc.* Monsieur de Montaigne saw their library, in which there are many books, but nothing rare, and a well from which water is drawn in very big buckets by working with the feet a wooden pedal, supported on a pivot, to which is connected a round piece of wood to which the rope of the well is attached. He had seen others like it elsewhere. Next to the well is a big stone vessel raised five or six feet above the brim, up to which the bucket mounts; and without anyone touching it, the water is poured into the said vessel, and the bucket goes down again when it is empty. This vessel is of such a height that from it, by means of lead pipes, the well water is led to their refectory and kitchen and bakery, and spouts out of raised stone outlets in the form of natural springs.

From Neufchâteau, where we breakfasted in the morning, we came to sup at

MIRECOURT, six leagues, a beautiful little town where Monsieur de Montaigne heard news of Monsieur and Madame de Bourbonne, who live in the near vicinity.

The next day after breakfast he went a quarter of a league from here, out of his way, to see the "nuns of Poussay." These are religious houses, of which there are several in these parts, established for the education of girls of good family. Each girl has a benefice, for her maintenance, of a hundred, two hundred, or three hundred crowns,[11] some worse, some better, and a private habitation in

10 This member of Montaigne's party is presumably Bernard de Cazalis, who a year before had married Montaigne's youngest sister, Marie; or it may be a brother of Bernard.

11 A French crown (écu) is about three livres. See Table of Money Values, p. 1055.

which she lives apart. Girls at nurse are received. There is no obligation of virginity, except for the officers, such as the abbess, prioress, and others. They are dressed in all freedom, like other young ladies, except for a white veil on their head, and in church, during the service, a great cloak, which they leave in their seat in the choir. Company is received in all freedom in the rooms of the individual girls, whom people go to see, whether to pay suit to them for marriage or for other reasons. Those who leave may resign and sell their benefice to anyone they choose, provided she is of the requisite rank; for there are lords of the region who are formally responsible (and they affirm their responsibility by oath) for testifying to the lineage of the girls who are presented. It is not improper for one single nun to have three or four benefices. Moreover, they perform the divine service, as elsewhere. Most of them end their days here and do not want to change their condition.

From here we came to sup at

EPINAL, five leagues. This is a beautiful little town on the river Moselle, where we were refused entry because we had passed through Neufchâteau, where the plague had been not long before.

The next morning we came to dine at

PLOMBIÈRES, four leagues. From Bar-le-Duc on, the leagues resume the standard of Gascony, and grow longer as you come toward Germany, until they are finally doubled or tripled.

We entered on Friday, September 16th, 1580, at two in the afternoon. This place is situated on the confines of Lorraine and Germany in a deep valley between several high, steep hills which close it in on all sides. At the bottom of this valley there issue several springs, some naturally cold, some hot. The hot water has no smell or taste, and is as hot as one can stand it for drinking, so that Monsieur de Montaigne was forced to pour it from one glass to another. There are only two springs from which people drink. The one that issues from the eastern slopes and produces the bath which they call the Queen's Bath leaves a sort of sweet taste in the mouth like licorice, without aftertaste; but it seemed to Monsieur de Montaigne that if you paid special attention to it, you could detect a faint taste of iron. The other, which springs from the foot of the mountain opposite, of which Monsieur de Montaigne drank for only one day, is a little more bitter, and one may detect in it the flavor of alum.

The custom of the place is only to bathe, and to bathe two or three times a day. Some take their meals in the bath, where they commonly have themselves cupped and scarified; and they use it only after being purged. If they drink, it is a glass or two in the bath. The people here considered Monsieur de Montaigne's practice strange, for without previous medicine he would drink nine glasses of the water, which came to about one pot, every morning at seven, and dine at noon; and on the days when he bathed, which was every other day, he did so about four o'clock, staying in the bath only about an hour. And those days he was apt to go without supper.

Here we saw men who had been cured of ulcers, and others of red spots on the body. The custom is to be here for at least a month. They recommend much more highly the spring season, in May. They hardly use the baths after the month of August, because of the coldness of the climate; but we still found company here, because the dryness and the heat had been greater and lasted longer than usual.

Among other friendships, Monsieur de Montaigne formed an intimate one with the seigneur d'Andelot, of Franche-Comté, whose father was grand equerry to the Emperor Charles V. He himself was first field marshal in the army of Don John of Austria, and was the man who remained as governor of Saint-Quentin when we lost it. One part of his beard was all white, and part of one eyebrow; and he told Monsieur de Montaigne that this change had come upon him in an instant, one day when he was at home full of grief for the loss of a brother of his whom the duke of Alva had put to death as an accomplice of the counts of Egmont and Horn; and that this part of his face had been resting on his hand, so that those present thought it was some flour that by chance had fallen on him just there. He has remained like that ever since.

This bath was formerly frequented by the Germans only; but for a few years now people of Franche-Comté and many Frenchmen have been arriving here in great crowds. There are several baths, but one great and principal one, built in an oval shape, of ancient construction. It is thirty-five paces long and fifteen wide. The hot water issues from underneath in several springs, and cold water is made to flow in from above to temper the bath according to the wish of those who are using it. The places are divided off on the sides by bars, suspended like those in our stables; and they throw boards

over the top to keep out the sun and rain. All around the baths there are three or four rows of stone steps in the manner of a theater, on which those who are bathing can sit or lean. Singular modesty is observed here; and yet it is indecent for the men to go in otherwise than quite naked except for a little pair of drawers, and the women except for a shift.

We lodged at the Angel, which is the best inn, since it communicates with both baths. Our whole lodgings, in which there were several rooms, cost only fifteen sous a day. The landlords in all the places supply wood into the bargain; but the country round about is so full of it that it costs them only the price of cutting. The landladies are very good cooks. In the very crowded season these lodgings would have cost a crown a day, which is cheap. The feed for the horses was seven sous; all other kinds of expense equally reasonable. The quarters here are not sumptuous, but very convenient; for by the use of many galleries they make each room independent of the others. The wine and bread are bad.

They are a good people, free, sensible, considerate. All the laws of the country are religiously observed. Every year they renew on a tablet, in front of the great bath, in the German and French languages, the laws written below:

"Claude de Rynach, Knight, Lord of Saint-Balesmont, Montureulz en Ferrette, Lendacourt, etc., Councillor and Chamberlain to His Sovereign Lordship the Duke, etc., and his Bailiff for the Vosges:

"Be it known that in order to secure the repose and tranquillity of sundry ladies and other notable personages assembling from various regions and countries at these baths of Plombières, we have, pursuant to the intention of His Highness, instituted and ordained, and do institute and ordain, as follows:

"To wit, that the ancient corrective discipline for minor offenses will remain in the hands of the Germans, as of old; to whom it is enjoined that they see to the observance of the ceremonies, statutes, and rules which they have used to maintain the decorum of the said baths and to punish the offenses that shall be committed by the people of their nation, without exception of persons, by form of ransom, and without using any blasphemy or other irreverent language against the Catholic Church and the traditions thereof.

"All persons, of whatever quality, condition, region, and province they may be, are forbidden to provoke one another by insulting

language tending to pick a quarrel, to bear arms in the said baths, to give the lie, or to lay hand to weapons, on pain of being severely punished as disturbers of the peace, rebels, and disobedient to His Highness.

"Also all prostitutes and shameless girls are forbidden to enter the said baths or to approach within five hundred paces of them, on pain of being whipped at the four corners of the said baths; and on pain, for the hosts who shall have received or harbored them, of imprisonment of their persons and arbitrary fine.

"Under the same penalty all persons are forbidden to use toward the ladies, gentlewomen, and other women and girls who are at the said baths, any lascivious or shameless language, to touch them dishonorably, or to enter or leave the said baths disrespectfully, contrary to public decency.

"And because, by the benefit of the said baths, God and nature procure us many cures and reliefs, and a decent cleanliness and purity is required to obviate many contagions and infections that might be engendered here; the Master of the said baths is expressly ordered to take pains to examine the persons of those who shall enter the baths, by day as well as by night, and to make them preserve modesty and silence during the night, without noise, scandal, or mockery. And if any person is not obedient to him in this matter, the Master shall promptly bring information against him to the magistrate, to have exemplary punishment inflicted on him.

"Moreover, it is prohibited and forbidden to all persons coming from infected places to enter or approach this place of Plombières, on pain of death; it is very expressly enjoined upon the mayors and officers of justice to take careful heed of this, and upon all the inhabitants of the said place to give us billets containing the names and surnames and residence of the persons whom they have received and lodged, on pain of imprisonment of their persons.

"All which ordinances above declared have this day been made public before the Great Bath of the said Plombières, and copies of them have been posted, in both the French and German languages, in the nearest and most conspicuous place to the Great Bath, and signed by us, Bailiff for the Vosges. Given at the said Plombières, the fourth day of the month of May in the year of grace of Our Lord, one thousand five hundred . . ."

<div align="right">(The name of the Bailiff)</div>

We stopped at the said place from the said day, the 16th,[12] until the 27th of September. Monsieur de Montaigne drank of the said water eleven mornings, nine glasses each for eight days and seven glasses each for three days, and bathed five times. He found the water easy to drink and always passed it before dinner. He experienced no other effect from it than to urinate. His appetite was good. His sleep, his bowels, nothing of his ordinary condition was made worse by this drinking. On the sixth day he had a very violent attack of colic, worse than his ordinary ones, and had it in his right side, where he had never felt any pain except a very slight one at Arsac, without aftereffect. This one lasted him four hours, and he clearly felt the effect of it and the passage of the stone through the ureters and the lower abdomen. The first two days he passed two little stones that were in the bladder, and afterward at times some gravel. But he left the said baths judging that he still had in the bladder both the stone of the aforesaid colic and some other small ones whose descent he thought he had felt. He considers the effect of these waters and their quality, as regards himself, very like that of the high spring at Bagnères, where the bath is. As for the bath, he finds it very mild in temperature; and in truth children six months or a year old are ordinarily seen playing in it like frogs. He sweated abundantly and gently. He ordered me, as a favor to his hostess, according to the humor of the nation, to leave a wooden escutcheon of his arms,[13] which a painter of the said place made for a crown, and the hostess had it carefully attached to the wall on the outside.

On the said day, September 27th, after dinner, we left and passed through a mountainous country, which everywhere resounded under our horses' feet as if we were riding over a vault, and it seemed as though drums were drumming all around us; and we came to sleep at

REMIREMONT, two leagues, a beautiful little town, and a good lodging at the Unicorn; for all the towns of Lorraine (this is the last) have hostelries as comfortable and entertainment as good as any place in France.

12 The text reads "18th."
13 Montaigne describes his coat of arms (*Essays* I: 46, p. 246) as follows: "I bear azure powdered with trefoils or, with a lion's paw of the same, armed gules in fesse."

Here is that most famous abbey of nuns, of the same kind as those I spoke of at Poussay. They claim, against the duke of Lorraine, the sovereignty and principality of this town. Messieurs d'Estissac and de Montaigne went to see them immediately after arriving, and visited several private lodgings that are very handsome and very well furnished. Their abbess, of the house of Dinteville, had died, and they were occupied in choosing another; one candidate was the sister of the count of Salm. They went to see the deaconess, a member of the house of Ludre, who had done Monsieur de Montaigne the honor of sending someone to visit him at the baths of Plombières and bring him artichokes, partridges, and a barrel of wine. They learned here that certain neighboring villages owe the nuns as rent two basins of snow every Pentecost day, or in default of that a wagon harnessed with four white oxen. It is said that they never have failed to receive this rental of snow, yet in the season when we passed there the heat was as great as it is in any season in Gascony. They wear only a white veil on their head, and above it a wisp of crape. They wear black robes of whatever material and fashion they please while they are on the premises, elsewhere colored ones; petticoats as they please, and shoes and pattens; coifs over their veils. Like the others, they must be descended from at least four noble houses on the father's side and as many on the mother's. Our party took leave of them when evening came.

The next day at daybreak we left. Just as we had mounted, the deaconess sent a gentleman to Monsieur de Montaigne, requesting him to go to her, which he did. This delayed us an hour. This society of ladies gave him powers of attorney to handle their affairs at Rome. On leaving here, for a long time we followed a very beautiful and very pleasant valley, skirting the Moselle river; and we came to dine at

BUSSANG, four leagues, a wretched little village, the last French-speaking one, where Messieurs d'Estissac and de Montaigne, dressed in linen smocks which were lent them, went to see some silver mines that the duke of Lorraine has here, a good two thousand paces into the hollow of a mountain. After dinner we followed along the mountains, where we were shown, among other things, on inaccessible rocks, the eyries where they catch goshawks (and these cost only three testons of the money of the country), and the source of the Moselle; and we came to sup at

THANN, four leagues, our first town in Germany, subject to the Emperor, very beautiful.

Switzerland
(September 29–October 7, 1580)

The next morning we found a very beautiful big plain, flanked on the left hand by hillsides covered with vineyards of the most beautiful and best cultivated sort and of such extent that the Gascons who were there said they had never seen so many in succession. The vintage was in progress. We came to dine at

MULHOUSE, two leagues, a beautiful little town of Switzerland,[1] in the canton of Basel. Monsieur de Montaigne went to see the church; for they are not Catholics here. He found it, like the churches throughout the country, in good condition; for there is almost nothing changed, except for the altars and images, whose absence was not found disfiguring. He took infinite pleasure in seeing the freedom and good government of this nation, and in seeing his host of the Sign of the Grapes return from a meeting of the Council of the said town, held in a very magnificent gilded palace, where he had been presiding, to serve his guests at table. And a man without retinue or authority, who served them with drink, had led four companies of foot into France against the king under Casimir, and had been a pensioner of the king at three hundred crowns a year for more than twenty years. This gentleman related to him at table, without ambition or affectation, his condition and his life; and told him among other things that they have no scruples on account of their religion about serving the king against the Huguenots themselves – which several others also told us as we went along; that at our siege of La Fère there were more than fifty from their town; and that they indiscriminately marry women of our religion before the priest, and do not force them to change.

From there, after dinner, we went through a beautiful, flat, very fertile country, adorned with many beautiful villages and hostelries, and came to sleep at

BASEL, three leagues, a beautiful city of the size of Blois or thereabouts, in two parts; for the Rhine goes through in the middle under a big and very wide wooden bridge.

The municipality did Messieurs d'Estissac and de Montaigne the honor of sending them, by one of their officers, some of their

1 Mulhouse, now in Alsace, was not then in the canton of Basel or in Switzerland. It was a free Imperial city allied with the Swiss Confederation.

wine, with a long welcoming speech which was delivered to them while they were at table and to which Monsieur de Montaigne made a long reply, both parties being uncovered, in the presence of several Germans and Frenchmen who were in the common room with them. The host served them as interpreter. The wines here are very good.

A remarkable thing we saw here was the house of a doctor named Felix Platerus, the most painted and enriched with dainty adornments in the French style that it is possible to see; which the said doctor built very large, ample, and sumptuous. Among other things, he is preparing a book of simples, which is already well advanced; and whereas the others have the herbs painted according to their colors, he has discovered the art of pasting them in their natural state on the paper so perfectly that the tiniest leaves and fibers appear there just as in nature, and he turns the leaves of his book without anything dropping out; and he showed some simples that had been pasted there for more than twenty years. We also saw, both at his house and in the public school, some entire skeletons of men that stand up by themselves.

There is this, that their town clock, not the one in the *faubourg*,[2] always strikes the hours one hour ahead of time. If it strikes ten o'clock, that means it is only nine; because once, they say, just such an accidental error of their clock saved their town from an attack that had been planned against it.

Basilee is so called, not from the Greek word, but because *Base* means "passage" in German.

We saw a great many men of learning, such as Grynaeus, and the man who wrote the *Theatrum*, and the said doctor (Platerus) and François Hotman.[3] These last two came to sup with our party on the day after our arrival. Monsieur de Montaigne judged that they were not in agreement over their religion, from the answers he received: some calling themselves Zwinglians, others Calvinists, others

2 That is, the part of town across the river.

3 The Grynaeus in question is variously identified as Samuel, professor of eloquence and jurisprudence, or Simon, author of an *Encomion medicinae*. The author of the *Theatrum vitae humanae* is Theodor Zwinger. Felix Plater is best known for a treatise on the parts of the human body. François Hotman, the famous French-born Protestant jurist who wrote the *Franco-Gallia*, took refuge in Switzerland after the Massacre of Saint Bartholomew's Day in 1572 and stayed on there.

Martinists;[4] and indeed he was informed that many still fostered the Roman religion in their heart. The form of giving the sacrament is generally into the mouth; however, anyone who wants may put out his hand for it, and the ministers do not dare to touch this chord in these differences in religion.

Their churches have inside the appearance I have told of elsewhere. On the outside they are covered with images, and the ancient tombs are still intact, on which there are prayers for the souls of the departed. The organs, the bells, the crosses of the belfries, and every sort of image in the stained-glass windows are intact, also the benches and seats in the choir. They put the baptismal fonts in the former place of the high altar, and they have another altar built at the head of the nave for the Lord's Supper; the one in Basel is on a very fine plan.

The church of the Carthusians, which is a very handsome building, is carefully preserved and kept up: even the ornaments and the furniture are there, which the Protestants allege as evidence of their fidelity, being obliged to this by the faith they pledged at the time of their agreement. The bishop of the place, who is very hostile to them, resides outside the town within his diocese, and keeps most of the country people in the old religion; he enjoys a good 50,000 livres of income from the city, and the election of the bishop continues.

Several people complained to Monsieur de Montaigne about the dissoluteness of the women and the drunkenness of the inhabitants.

Here we saw a poor man's little boy cut open for rupture and treated very roughly by the surgeon. Here we saw a very handsome public library on the river and in a very beautiful site. We stayed all the next day, and the following day after dinner we took the road along the Rhine for two leagues or thereabouts; and then we left it on our left hand, going through a very fertile and rather flat country.

They have an infinite abundance of fountains in all this country; there is no village or crossroad where there are not very beautiful ones. They say there are more than three hundred in Basel by actual count.

They are so accustomed to balconies, even near Lorraine, that in all the houses, between the windows of the upstairs rooms, they leave doorways overlooking the street, looking forward to making

4 Lutherans.

balconies there some day. In all this part of the country, from Epinal on, there is no village house so small as not to have glass windows; and the good dwellings are greatly ornamented by being well equipped, both inside and out, with these and with panes of glass worked in many fashions. They also have plenty of iron, and good workmen in this material; they surpass us by far; and moreover, there is no church so small as not to have a magnificent clock and sundial. They are also excellent in making tiles, so that the house-tops are greatly embellished with motley forms of tile, soldered with lead and variously worked, and also the floors of their rooms; and there is nothing more delicate than their stoves, which are of earthenware. They use a lot of pine, and have very good craftsmen in carpentry; for their casks are all carved and mostly varnished and painted.

Their *poêles*, that is to say common rooms for taking meals, are sumptuous. In each common room, which moreover is very well furnished, there are likely to be five or six tables equipped with benches, where all the guests dine together, each party at its own table. The smallest inns have two or three such rooms, very handsome; they are well lit by windows richly glazed. But it is very apparent that they have more care for their dinners than for anything else; for the bedrooms are just as wretched as the common rooms are fine. There are never any curtains for the beds, and always three or four beds in a room, right next to one another; no fireplace, and you get warm only in the common rooms and the dining rooms; for to have a fire anywhere else is unheard of, and they think it very bad if you go into their kitchens. They are not at all clean in their bedroom service; for lucky is the man who gets a white sheet, and it is their style never to cover the pillow with a case; and they rarely offer any other covering than that of a feather quilt, and that very dirty. However, they are excellent cooks, especially of fish. They have no protection from the night damp or the wind but the window alone, which is not protected by shutters; and their houses are full of windows and very light, both in the common rooms and in the bedrooms; and they hardly ever close the windows even at night.

Their service at table is very different from ours. They never mix water with their wine, and are almost right not to; for their wines are so small that our gentlemen found them even weaker than those of Gascony when these are well baptized; and yet for all that they are very delicate.

They have the menservants dine at the masters' table or at another nearby at the same time with them; for it takes only one servant to wait on a big table, inasmuch as, everyone having his silver goblet or cup in front of his place, the man who serves takes care to fill this goblet as soon as it is empty, without moving it from its place, pouring wine into it from a distance with a pewter or wooden vessel with a long beak; and as for the meat, they serve only two or three dishes at each course. They mix together several well-prepared meats in combinations very different from ours, and serve them sometimes one on top of the other, using certain iron implements with long legs. On top of this implement there is one dish, and underneath another. Their tables are very wide, and either round or square, so that it is hard to place the serving dishes on them. The servant easily takes away all these dishes at once and serves two more, and there are up to six or seven such changes; for one dish is never served until the other is off. And as for the plates, when they want to serve the fruit, after the meat is taken away they put in the middle of the table a wicker basket or a big tray of painted wood, into which basket the most eminent person tosses his plate first, and then the others; for in this they observe a strict precedence of rank. This basket the servant easily takes off and then serves the fruit in two dishes like the rest, pell-mell; and they usually include radishes, just as they serve cooked pears with the roast.

Among other things they hold crayfish in great honor, and serve up a dish of them, always with a cover, as a privilege; and they offer them to one another, as they hardly do with any other viand. However, all this country is full of them, and they serve them every day, though they consider them delicacies. They do not give you water to wash with on sitting down and getting up; everyone goes to get some at a little water jug set in a corner of the room, as in our monasteries.

Most of them use wooden plates, yes, and wooden pots and chamber pots, and these as clean and white as possible. Others in addition place pewter plates on the wooden ones until the last course, the fruit, when there are never any but of wood. They use wood only out of custom; for even where they use it they give you silver goblets to drink from, and have an infinite quantity of them.

They clean and polish their wooden furniture scrupulously, even to the bedroom floors. Their beds are raised so high that commonly you climb into them by steps; and almost everywhere they have little beds under the big ones.

Since they are excellent workers in iron, almost all their spits are turned by springs or by means of weights, like clocks, or else by certain broad, light sails of pine that they place in the funnels of their chimneys, which turn with great speed in the draft caused by the smoke and steam of the fire; and they turn the roast slowly for a long time; for they dry out their meat a little too much. These windmills are used only in the large inns where there is a big fire, as at Baden. Their motion is very uniform and constant. Most of the chimneys between Lorraine and here are not in our style; they build up the hearth in the middle or the corner of a kitchen and use almost the whole width of this kitchen for the chimney flue. This is a great opening seven or eight paces square, which narrows as it goes up to the top of the house. This gives them room to place in one spot their big sail, which with us would occupy so much space in our flues that the passage of the smoke would be blocked.

The slightest meals last three or four hours because of the length of these servings; and in truth they also eat much less hastily and more healthily than we do. They have a great abundance of all sorts of food, both meat and fish, and they cover their tables very sump- tuously – at least ours. On Friday they did not serve meat to anyone, and they say that on that day they generally do not eat any. The prices are like those in France around Paris. The horses ordinarily get more oats than they can eat.

We came to sleep at

HORN, four leagues, a little village belonging to the duke of Austria.

The next day, which was Sunday, we heard Mass here, and I noticed that the women all keep on the left side of the church and the men on the right, without mixing. They have several rows of cross-benches, one behind the other, of the right height for sitting down. The women kneel on these and not on the ground, and consequently look as though they were standing; the men have, besides these, wooden crossrails to lean on, and they too kneel only on the seats in front of them. Whereas we join our hands in prayer to God at the elevation of the host, they stretch them apart wide open, and hold them thus raised until the priest exhibits the pax. They gave Messieurs d'Estissac and de Montaigne the third bench of the men, and the other benches ahead of them were afterward taken by men of inferior appearance; as also on the women's side. It seemed to us that the most honored women were not in the first rows. The interpreter and guide we had taken at Basel, a sworn

messenger of the town, came to Mass with us, and showed by his manner that he attended with great devoutness and zeal.

After dinner we passed over the river Aar at Brügg, a beautiful little town belonging to Their Excellencies of Bern, and on the other side came to see an abbey[5] which Queen Catherine of Hungary gave to their lordships of Bern in the year 1524, where are buried Leopold, archduke of Austria, and a great number of gentlemen who were killed with him by the Swiss in the year 1386.[6] Their arms and names are still inscribed here, and their spoils are carefully preserved. Monsieur de Montaigne here spoke to a gentleman of Bern who is in command, and he had them shown everything. In this abbey there are loaves of bread all ready, and soup, for travelers who ask for some; and, by the constitution of the abbey, no one is ever refused.

From here we crossed in a ferryboat which is worked by an iron pulley attached to a high cord that goes across the river Reuss, which flows from Lake Lucerne, and we came to

BADEN, four leagues, a small town, with a separate borough where the baths are. It is a Catholic town under the protection of the eight cantons of Switzerland, in which several great assemblies of princes have been held. We did not lodge in the town, but in the said borough, which is right at the foot of the mountain along a river, or rather torrent, called the the Limmat, which comes from the Lake of Zurich. There are two or three uncovered public baths, which only the poor people use. The others, in very great number, are enclosed in the houses, and are divided and separated into several little private cells, closed in and covered, which they rent with the rooms; the cells are as dainty and well-equipped as possible, and veins of hot water are drawn to them for each bath.

The inns are very magnificent. In the one where we lodged there have been as many as three hundred mouths to feed in one day. There was still much company when we were there, and fully a hundred and seventy beds serving the guests that were there. There are seventeen common rooms and eleven kitchens, and an inn next to ours has fifty furnished bedrooms. The walls of the inns are all covered with the escutcheons of the gentlemen who have lodged there.

5 Königsfelden.
6 At Sempach.

The town is up above on the ridge, small and very beautiful, as they almost all are in this region. For besides the fact that they make their streets wider and more open than ours and their squares larger, and have so many windows everywhere richly glazed, they have the custom of painting nearly all the houses on the outside and loading them with mottoes, which make a very pleasant sight; and besides, there is no town in which there are not several fountains, flowing with streams of water, which have been erected sumptuously at the street corners, either of wood or of stone. This makes their towns appear much more beautiful than those of France.

The water of the baths gives off a smell of sulphur, like those of Aigues-Caudes and others. Its warmth is moderate, like that of Barbotan or Aigues-Caudes, and for this reason the baths are very mild and pleasant. If anyone has to escort ladies who want to bathe respectably and with delicacy, he may bring them here, for they are alone in the bath, which seems like a very rich cabinet, bright, with glazed windows, covered all around with painted wainscoting, and very neatly floored, with chairs and little tables to read or play on while in the bath if you want. The bather can empty and let in as much water as he pleases; and each bedroom is next to its bath. The walks along the river are fine, as well as the artificial walks of certain galleries.

These baths are situated in a valley commanded by the sides of mountains that are high but nevertheless for the most part fertile and cultivated. For drinking, the water is a little insipid and flat, as if it had been poured back and forth a lot; and as for the taste, it smacks of sulphur and has a sort of salty tang to it. The people of the region use it principally for bathing, during which they have themselves cupped and bled so heavily that I have sometimes seen the two public baths look like pure blood. Those who customarily drink take a glass or two at the most. People ordinarily stop here five or six weeks, and the baths are occupied almost all summer long. No other nation uses them, or very few, except the Germans; but they come here in very great crowds.

The use of them is very ancient, and Tacitus mentions it. Monsieur de Montaigne tried his best to find the main source, but could not learn anything about it; from all appearances, the sources are all very low and virtually on a level with the river. It is less clear than the other waters that we have seen elsewhere, and when you draw it, it carries certain very fine little filaments. It does not have those little

sparkles that you see shining in other sulphurous waters when you take them into the glass, including, as the seigneur Maldonado said, those of Spa.

The day after we arrived, which was Monday, Monsieur de Montaigne drank seven little glasses of it, which amounted to one big chopin of his house; the next day five big glasses, which amounted to ten of the little ones and might make a pint. This same Tuesday morning at nine o'clock, while the others were dining, he got into the bath and after coming out sweated very hard in bed. He stayed in the bath only a half hour; for the people of the country who are in it all day long playing and drinking are in the water only up to the loins; he stayed in up to the neck, stretched out the full length of his bath.

This day there left the bath a Swiss lord, a very good servant of our crown, who had had a long talk with Monsieur de Montaigne all the preceding day about the affairs of the country of Switzerland, and showed him a letter which the French ambassador, son of the President de Harlay, had written him from Soleure, where he is staying, advising him to serve the king during his absence, for he had been summoned by the queen to meet her at Lyons, and to oppose the designs of Spain and Savoy. The duke of Savoy, who had just died, had made an alliance a year or two ago with certain cantons; which the king had openly resisted, alleging that they, being already allied with him, could not accept any new bonds without prejudice to him; some of the cantons had realized this, thanks especially to the mediation of the said Swiss lord, and had refused this alliance. In truth, in all these parts they receive the name of the king with reverence and friendship, and offer us all possible courtesies. The Spaniards are in bad odor.

This Swiss had a train of four horses: his son, who is already in the service of the king like his father, on one; a valet on another; a tall, beautiful daughter on another, with a cloth saddle cover and a woman's stirrup in the French fashion, a portmanteau behind her and a bonnet box at the saddlebow, without any woman with her (and yet they were two full days' journey from their home, which is a town where the said lord is governor); the goodman himself on the fourth.

The ordinary dress of the women seems to me as neat as our own, even the head-dress, which is a bonnet *à la coquarde*, turning up behind and with a slight projection in front, over the forehead; this is trimmed all around with tufts of silk or fur borders; the

natural hair hangs down behind, all braided. If you take off this bonnet of theirs in play (for it does not stay on any better than ours), they are not offended, and you see their head quite bare. The younger ones, instead of a bonnet, wear merely a garland on their head. They do not have much difference in dress to distinguish their ranks. You salute them by kissing your hand to them and offering to touch theirs. Otherwise, if in passing you take off your hat and make them a bow, most of them stand still without any movement, and that is their ancient fashion. Some nod their head a little to return your salute. They are generally handsome women, tall and fair.

They are a very good nation, especially to those who conform to them. Monsieur de Montaigne, to essay completely the diversity of manners and customs, let himself be served everywhere in the mode of each country, no matter what difficulty this caused him. At all events, in Switzerland he said he suffered no inconvenience, except for having at table only a little cloth half a foot square for a napkin; and the same cloth the Swiss do not even unfold at their dinner, and yet they have plenty of sauces and many varieties of soups; but they always serve as many wooden spoons, with silver handles, as there are people. And never is a Swiss without a knife, with which they pick up everything; and they hardly ever put their hands into the dish.

Almost all their towns bear, above the particular arms of the town, those of the Emperor and the house of Austria; and indeed most of them have been dismembered from the said archduchy only by the bad management of that house. They say here that all the members of this house of Austria, except the Catholic King, are reduced to great poverty, especially the Emperor, who is held in small esteem in Germany.

The water that Monsieur de Montaigne drank on Tuesday caused him three stools and was all voided before noon. Wednesday morning he took the same amount as the day before. He finds that when he makes himself sweat in the bath, the next day he makes much less urine and does not pass the water he has drunk; which he experienced also at Plombières. For the water that he takes the next day comes out colored and very scanty, whereby he judges that it promptly changes into nourishment, whether this happens by the evacuation of the preceding sweat or by the fasting; for when he bathed he took only one meal; this was the reason why he bathed only once.

On Wednesday his landlord bought a lot of fish; the said lord asked him why that was. He was told in reply that most people of the said place of Baden ate fish on Wednesdays for religious reasons; which confirmed what he had heard, that those here who hold to the Catholic religion are much more strict and devout because they are surrounded by the contrary faith. He argued thus, that when confusion and mixture occurs in the same town and spreads in one and the same government, this relaxes the affections of men, for the mingling reaches down to individuals, as happens at Augsburg and in the Imperial towns; but when a town has only one system of government (for the towns of Switzerland have each their separate laws and government, apart from one another, and do not depend on one another in the matter of their administration; they are united as a league only in certain general respects), the towns that each form a separate state and a separate civil body with all its members have the wherewithal to fortify and maintain themselves; they are undoubtedly strengthened and further joined and united by the impact of the neighboring contagion.

We quickly adapted ourselves to the warmth of their stoves, and not one of us felt any discomfort from it. For once you have swallowed a certain smell in the air that strikes you as you come in, all that remains is a gentle and even warmth. Monsieur de Montaigne, who slept in a room with a stove in it, was very pleased with it and with feeling all night a pleasant and moderate warmth of air. At least you do not burn either your face or your boots, and you are free from the smoke you get in France. Also, whereas we put on our warm furred dressing gowns when we enter the house, they on the contrary stay in their doublets and go bareheaded in the heated room, and get dressed warmly to go back into the open air.

On Thursday he drank the same amount; the water operated both in front and behind, and he voided gravel, not in any great quantity; and he found the waters even more active than others he had tried, whether by the strength of the water or because his body was so disposed; and yet he drank less of them than he had of any others, and passed them not as undigested as the others.

On this Thursday he spoke to a minister of Zurich, a native of this place, who arrived here, and found that the Zurichers' first religion had been Zwinglian; from which this minister told him they had come closer to the Calvinist, which was a little milder. And questioned about predestination, the minister replied that they held a mean between Geneva and Augsburg, but that they did not bother

their people with this dispute. Of his own private judgment he inclined more to the extreme of Zwingli, and praised it highly as the creed that came closest to primitive Christianity.

On Friday, the 7th of October, after breakfast, at seven o'clock in the morning, we left Baden; and before leaving, Monsieur de Montaigne again drank his measure of the said waters; thus he drank here five times. On the doubtful question of their operation, in which he sees as much occasion for good hope as in any others, both for the drinking and for the bathing, he would recommend these baths as gladly as any others he had seen until then; inasmuch as the lodgings are so conveniently located, so clean, so well distributed, each person having the share he wants, without dependence or difficulty of access from one room to another, so that there are quarters for private persons of low condition and others for the great; separate baths, galleries, kitchens, cabinets, chapels, for separate parties. And in the inn next to ours, which is called the Town Court, ours being the Rear Court (they are public houses belonging to the co-ruling cantons, and are kept by tenants) – in the said inn next to ours they also have some fireplaces, French style. The master bedrooms all have stoves.

The payment exacted of foreigners is a bit tyrannical, as in all countries and especially our own. Four rooms furnished with nine beds, two of which had stoves and a bath, cost us a crown a day for each of the masters; and for the servants, four batzen each, that is to say nine sous and a little over; the horses six batzen, which is about fourteen sous a day; but besides that they added several thievish charges, contrary to their custom.

The Swiss keep guard in their towns and even in the borough where the baths are, which is only a village. Every night there are two sentinels who do the rounds of the houses, not so much to guard against enemies as for fear of fire or other disturbance. When the hours strike, one of them is obliged to shout out aloud at the top of his voice to the other and ask him what time it is; to which the other in the same voice answers with news of the time, and adds that he should keep good watch.

The women here do their washing in the open and in the public laundry, setting up near the waters a little wood fire over which they heat their water; and they do it better, and also scour their pots and pans much better, than in our hostelries in France. In the hostelries each chambermaid has her own particular job, also each manservant.

It is a misfortune for a stranger that, however diligently you try, it is impossible to get information about the notable sights of each place from the people of the country, unless you come across some who are abler than the ordinary; and they do not know what you are asking them. I say this apropos of the fact that, after staying here for five days and showing all possible curiosity, we had not heard about what we found on the way out of town: a stone of the height of a man, which seemed to be a part of some pillar, without ornament or carving on it, planted at the corner of a house to be visible to those passing on the highroad, on which there is a Latin inscription that I had no means of transcribing; but it is simply a dedication to the emperors Nerva and Trajan.

We came and crossed the Rhine at the town of Kaiserstuhl, which is one of the allies of the Swiss, and Catholic; and beyond it we followed the said river through a very beautiful flat country until we came upon some waterfalls where it breaks against the rocks, and which they call the cataracts, like those of the Nile. The reason is that below Schaffhausen the Rhine encounters a bed full of big rocks, where it is broken up; and below, in these same rocks, it comes to a fall about two pikes high where it makes a great drop, foaming and making an amazing noise. This stops the course of boats and interrupts navigation on the said river. We came on without a stop and had supper at

SCHAFFHAUSEN, four leagues, the capital town of one of the cantons of the Swiss, of the religion I have mentioned above, that of the people of Zurich. On leaving Baden we left Zurich on the right, where Monsieur de Montaigne had planned to go, being only two leagues away; but it was reported to him that the plague was there.

At Schaffhausen we saw nothing rare. They are building a citadel that will be rather handsome. There is a butt for crossbow shooting and a place for this practice, as beautiful, large, and well provided with shade, seats, galleries, and rooms, as can be; and there is a similar place for harquebus shooting. There are water mills for sawing wood, of which we had seen several elsewhere, and for pounding flax and shelling millet.

There is also a tree, fashioned like others we had seen, especially at Baden, but not of comparable size. The first and lowest branches they use to form the floor of a round gallery twenty paces in diameter; these branches they then bend upward and make them embrace this gallery all around and rise up as high as they can.

Afterward they clip the tree, and keep it from throwing out branches up to the height that they want to give this gallery, which is about ten feet. There they take the other branches that come from the tree, which they lay over certain wicker mats to form the roof of the chamber, and then bend them down to make them join those that are climbing up, and they fill all the gaps with verdure. After this they again clip the tree up to the top, where they let the branches spread freely. This makes a very beautiful appearance and a very handsome tree. Besides this, at the foot of the tree they have made a fountain spring up, which spouts up above the floor of this gallery.

Monsieur de Montaigne paid a visit to the burgomasters of the town, who, to do him honor, came with other public officers to sup at our inn, and there presented some wine to Monsieur d'Estissac and him. This was not without several ceremonious speeches on both sides. The principal burgomaster was a gentleman, brought up as a page with the late duke of Orléans, but he had already forgotten all his French.

The canton professes to be strongly on our side, and has given recent evidence of it by refusing, in our favor, the confederation that the late duke of Savoy sought with the cantons, of which I have made mention above.

On Saturday, the 8th of October, at eight o'clock in the morning, after breakfast, we left Schaffhausen, where the Crown offers very good lodgings. A learned man of the country had a talk with Monsieur de Montaigne and told him among other things that the inhabitants of this town are not in reality very well disposed toward our court; so that in all the deliberations he had attended concerning the alliance with the king, most of the people were always in favor of breaking it off; but owing to the intrigues of certain rich men this turned out differently.

As we were leaving we saw an iron machine, such as we had also seen elsewhere, by which they raise large stones to load the wagons without using manpower.

We passed along the Rhine, which we had on our right hand, as far as Stein, a little town allied to the cantons, of the same religion as Schaffhausen (and yet along the road there were lots of stone crosses), where we recrossed the Rhine over another wooden bridge; and skirting the river bank, having it on our left hand, we passed by another little town, also one of the allies of the Catholic cantons. There the Rhine expands to a marvelous width, as does our Garonne at Blaye, and then it narrows again as far as Constance.

Germany, Austria, and the Alps
(October 8–27, 1580)

CONSTANCE, four leagues, where we arrived around four o'clock. This is a town of the size of Châlons, belonging to the archduke of Austria, and Catholic. Because it was once, and in the last thirty years, held by the Lutherans, whom the Emperor Charles V forcibly dislodged from it, the churches still show this in the absence of images. The bishop, who is a nobleman of this country and a cardinal, living at Rome, draws a good forty thousand crowns of revenue from it. There are canonries in the Church of Our Lady which are worth fifteen hundred florins a year and are held by noblemen. We saw one of these on horseback, coming from outside, licentiously dressed as a warrior; and indeed they say there are many Lutherans in the town.

We climbed the bell tower, which is very high, and found there a man posted as a sentinel, who never leaves there, whatever the occasion, and is confined there.

They are erecting on the bank of the Rhine a big covered building fifty paces long and forty wide, or thereabouts; they will put in it twelve or fifteen great wheels, by means of which they will continually raise a great quantity of water to a floor which will be one story higher, and other, iron wheels in like number (for the lower ones are of wood); and they will raise the water in the same way from this floor to another above. This water, having been raised to this height, which is about fifty feet, will flow out through a big wide artificial canal and be led into their town to set several mills grinding. The artisan who was supervising this construction had five thousand seven hundred florins for his labor alone, and was furnished with wine besides. At the very bottom of the water they are making a platform, closed all around, to break the course of the water, they say, and so that it may come to rest in this box and thus be drawn up more easily. They are also erecting some machines by means of which they can raise or lower all this wheelwork according as the river happens to be high or low.

The Rhine does not have that name here; for at the head of the town it spreads out into the form of a lake, which is fully four German leagues wide and five or six long. They have a beautiful terrace overlooking the pointed end of this big lake, where they unload the merchandise; and fifty paces from the lake a handsome

little house where they keep a sentinel continually; and they have attached to it a chain by which they close the entrance to the port, having driven many piles which enclose on two sides the part of the lake in which boats are docked and loaded. At the Church of Our Lady there is a conduit which proceeds above the Rhine into the suburbs of the town.

We recognized that we were leaving the country of Switzerland by the fact that a little before we arrived in the town we saw several noblemen's manors; for you hardly see any in Switzerland. But as for private houses, both in the towns and in the country along the route we followed, they are incomparably more handsome than in France, and lack nothing but slate roofs; and especially in the hostelries, where the treatment is better, for what they lack for our service is due not to indigence – this is readily recognizable from the rest of their equipment; and there is not an inn but where everyone drinks out of large silver vessels, most of them gilded and chased – but to custom. It is a very fertile country, notably in wines.

To come back to Constance: we were badly lodged at the Eagle, and received from the landlord a sample of the barbaric German unruliness and pride, over the quarrel of one of our footmen with our guide from Basel. And because the thing even came before the judges, to whom Monsieur de Montaigne went to complain, the provost of the place – an Italian gentleman who has settled and married here and has long had the right of citizenship – answered Monsieur de Montaigne, when he asked whether his servants would be believed in their testimony on our behalf, that yes, they would be believed, provided Monsieur de Montaigne discharged them; but that immediately afterward he could take them back into his service. This was a remarkable piece of subtlety.

The next day, which was Sunday, we remained until after dinner because of this disturbance, and changed our lodging to the Pike, where we were very well off. The son of the commandant of the town, who was brought up as a page with Monsieur de Méru,[1] always attended the gentlemen of our party at their meals and elsewhere; yet he knew not a word of French.

The courses at their tables are changed frequently. Here, and often since, after the cloth was removed, they were given other new

1 Charles de Montmorency, seigneur de Méru, third son of the Constable Anne de Montmorency.

courses with the wine: the first, *canaules*,[2] as the Gascons call them; then gingerbread; and for the third a soft white bread cut into slices but still holding together; between the slices they toss a lot of spices and salt, and also on top of the crust of the loaf.

This country is extremely full of leper hospitals, and the roads are all full of lepers.

The village people serve their laborers for breakfast very flat *fouaces*[3] in which there is fennel, and on top of the *fouaces* little bits of bacon cut up very small, and cloves of garlic.

Among the Germans, to pay honor to a man, they always go to his left side, in whatever position he may be, and consider it an offense to place themselves on his right, saying that in order to show deference to a man you must leave him free on his right side to put his hand to his weapons.

Sunday after dinner we left Constance, and after crossing the lake one league away from the town, we came to sleep at

MARKDORF, two leagues, which is a little Catholic town, and we stayed at the Cologne, the posthouse which is situated here for the Emperor for the trip from Italy into Germany. Here, as in several other places, they fill the mattresses with leaves from a certain tree, which serve the purpose better than straw and last longer. It is a town surrounded by a vast region of vineyards, where very good wines are produced.

On Monday, October 10th, we left after breakfast; for Monsieur de Montaigne was lured by the fine day to change his plan of going to Ravensburg that day, and turned aside a day's journey to go to Lindau. Monsieur de Montaigne never ate breakfast; but they would bring him a piece of dry bread that he ate on the way, and this was sometimes helped down by the grapes he found; for the vintage was still under way in that region and the country was full of vines, especially around Lindau. They raise them from the ground on trellises and thus leave a quantity of fine roads surrounded by verdure, which are very beautiful. We passed a town named Buchhorn,[4] which is Imperial and Catholic, on the shore of the Lake of Constance, into which town all the merchandise from Ulm, Nuremberg, and elsewhere is brought in wagons, and beyond there they

2 A cake shaped like a crown.
3 A thick cake cooked fast in coals, the occasion for the war in Rabelais' *Gargantua*.
4 Now Friedrichshafen.

take the Rhine route across the lake. We arrived about three o'clock in the afternoon at

LINDAU, three leagues, a small town situated a hundred paces into the lake, which hundred paces you pass over a stone bridge; there is only this entrance, all the rest of the town being surrounded by this lake. The lake is a good league wide, and beyond it rise the mountains of the Grisons. This lake and all the rivers hereabouts are low in winter and swollen in summer, because of the melted snows.

In all this country the women cover their head with a fur hat or bonnet like our calotte; the outside is of some better sort of fur such as squirrel, and the inside of lambskin; and such a bonnet costs only three testons. The window that is in the front of our calottes they wear behind, and through it appears all their braided hair. They are usually shod with boots, either red or white, which are not unbecoming to them.

Both religions are practiced. We went to see the Catholic church, built in the year 866 and preserved in its entirety; and we also saw the church used by the [Protestant] ministers. All the Imperial towns are free to choose their religion, Catholic or Lutheran, according to the wish of the inhabitants. They attach themselves more or less to the one they favor. At Lindau there are only two or three Catholics, from what the priest told Monsieur de Montaigne. The priests do not fail for all that to receive their revenues freely and to perform their service, as do also some nuns who are here. The said sieur de Montaigne also spoke to the minister, from whom he did not learn much of anything except that they feel the usual hatred of Zwingli and Calvin. They say that in truth there are few towns that do not have something particular in their belief; and under the authority of Martin, whom they accept as their chief, they get up many disputes over the interpretation of the meaning of Martin's writings.[5]

We lodged at the Crown, which is a handsome inn. On the paneled wall of the dining room there was a sort of cage, of the same length as the wall, to lodge a great number of birds; it had alleyways hung and fitted with brass wire, which gave the birds room to move about from one end of the room to the other.

5 In his chapter "Of Experience" (*Essays* III: 13, p. 997) Montaigne wrote later: "I have observed in Germany that Luther has left as many divisions and altercations over the uncertainty of his opinions, and more, as he raised about the Holy Scriptures."

Their furniture and woodwork is all of pine only, which is the most common tree in their forests; but they paint, varnish, and scour it with care, and even have brushes of hair with which they dust their benches and tables.

They have a great abundance of cabbage, which they chop up small with a special instrument, and they put a great quantity of it thus chopped up into vats with salt and make soups out of it all winter.

Here Monsieur de Montaigne tried covering himself in bed with a feather quilt, as is their custom; and he was greatly pleased with this practice, finding that it was a covering both warm and light. In his opinion there is nothing to complain of, except, for delicate souls, the bedding; but if anyone brought a mattress, which is unknown here, and a curtain, in his baggage, he would find nothing lacking. For as to table fare, they are so abundant in provisions, and diversify their courses with so many sorts of soups, sauces, salads – for example, besides the dishes that we are accustomed to, some of them offered us soups made of quinces; others, baked apples cut into slices on the soup, and cabbage salads; they also make broths without bread, of various sorts, as with rice, into which everyone fishes together, for there is no individual serving – and all this of such good flavor in the good inns, that the cuisines of the French nobility hardly seemed comparable; and there are few French noblemen that have dining rooms so well adorned.

They have a great abundance of good fish, which they serve in with the meat course; they disdain trout, and eat only the roe; they have lots of game, woodcocks, young hares, which they dress in a manner very different from ours, but at least as good. We never saw victuals so tender as they ordinarily serve them. They mix stewed plums and pear and apple tarts with the meat course, and sometimes serve the roast first and the soup at the end, sometimes the other way around. Their fruit for dessert is only pears and apples, which are very good, nuts, and cheese. Together with the meat they bring out a tray of silver or pewter with four compartments, in which they put various sorts of powdered spices; and they mix caraway, or some similar seed, which is tangy and hot, with their bread; and their bread is mostly made with fennel. After the meal they put full glasses back on the table and serve two or three courses of various things that provoke thirst.

Monsieur de Montaigne found three things lacking in his travels: one, that he had not brought along a cook to instruct in

their ways so that some day the cook could try them at home; another, that he had not brought along a German valet or sought the company of some gentleman of the country – for to live at the mercy of some poor blockhead of a guide he found to be a great inconvenience; the third, that before making the trip he had not looked into the books that might have informed him about the rare and remarkable things in each place, or that he did not have a Münster[6] or some other such book in his coffers.

In truth there entered into his judgment a bit of passion, a certain scorn for his country, which he regarded with hatred and indignation for other considerations; but at all events, he preferred the conveniences of this country to the French, beyond comparison, and conformed to them even to drinking wine without water. As for drinking bouts, he was never invited to any except out of courtesy, and never attempted any.

The cost of living in Southern Germany is higher than in France; for by our reckoning a man and horse cost at least a sun-crown a day. The landlords reckon, in the first place, the meal at four, five, or six batzen each for table d'hôte. They make another item of all you drink before and after these two meals, and even the smallest collations; so that Germans commonly set out in the morning from their inn without drinking. The courses that are served after the meal and the wine that is drunk with these, which constitutes the principal expense of them, are put on the account with the collations. In truth, to see the profusion of their services, and notably of wine, especially where it is extremely dear and brought from distant parts, I find their dearness excusable.

They themselves invite the servants to drink with them and keep them at table for two or three hours. Their wine is served in vessels like big pitchers, and it is a crime to see an empty goblet and not fill it immediately; and never any water, not even for those who ask for some, unless they are held in great respect.

Afterward they reckon the oats for the horses, and then the stable, which also includes the hay. There is this good thing about them, that they tell you almost with their first words what they charge; and you do not gain much by haggling. They are vainglorious, choleric, and heavy drinkers; but, said Monsieur de Montaigne, they are neither traitors nor thieves.

6 Sebastian Münster. Montaigne owned a copy of his *Cosmographie universelle*.

We left Lindau after breakfast, and around two o'clock in the afternoon came to

WANGEN, two leagues, where an accident to our baggage mule, which was injured, forced us to stop, and we were constrained to hire a wagon for the next day at three crowns a day; the wagoner, who had four horses, paid his own expenses out of that. This is a little Imperial town that has never been willing to harbor a congregation of any other religion than the Catholic; in which scythes are made, so famous that they send them to be sold even as far as Lorraine.

Monsieur de Montaigne left the next day, which was Wednesday, October 12th, in the morning, and turned off short toward Trent by the most direct and usual route, and we came to dine at

ISNY, two leagues, a little Imperial town, very pleasantly laid out.

Monsieur de Montaigne, as was his custom, promptly went and found a doctor of theology of this town, to pick up information, and this doctor dined with our party. He found that all the people were Lutherans, and saw the Lutheran church, which, like the others that they hold in the Imperial towns, has been usurped from the Catholic churches. Amid other talk that they had together about the sacrament, Monsieur de Montaigne noted that some Calvinists had informed him along the way that the Lutherans mingled in with the original opinions of Martin several strange errors, such as Ubiquitism, maintaining that the body of Jesus Christ is everywhere, as in the host; whereby they fall into the same difficulty as Zwingli, though by a different path, the one by being too sparing of the presence of the body, the other by being too prodigal of it (for by this reckoning the sacrament has no privilege over the body of the Church or the assembly of three good men). And that their principal arguments were that the divinity was inseparable from the body, wherefore, the divinity being everywhere, the body was everywhere also; and second, that since Jesus Christ had always to be at the right hand of the Father, he was everywhere, inasmuch as the right hand of God, which is the power, is everywhere. This good doctor loudly denied this imputation, and defended himself against it as against a calumny; but in fact it seems to Monsieur de Montaigne that he did not defend himself very well.

He kept Monsieur de Montaigne company in going to visit a very beautiful and sumptuous monastery, where Mass was being said; and he entered and watched without taking off his bonnet until Messieurs d'Estissac and de Montaigne had finished their prayers. In a cellar of the abbey they went to see a long, cylindrical stone,

without any other workmanship, taken, so it seems, from a column, on which is this inscription in very legible Latin letters: "that the emperors Pertinax and Antonius Verus have repaired the roads and bridges at a distance of eleven thousand paces from Campidonum," which is Kempten, where we went for the night. This stone might have been there because the road was under repair; for the said town of Isny is not thought to be very ancient. However, having reconnoitered the approaches to the said Kempten in both directions, not only did we find that there is no bridge, but we could not recognize any repair work worthy of such workmen. There are indeed some mountains cut through, but no handiwork on a grand scale.

KEMPTEN, three leagues, a town of the size of Sainte-Foy, very beautiful and populous and abounding in good lodgings. We were at the Bear, which is a very handsome inn. They served us silver cups of more different kinds (which are used only for ornament, very elaborately worked and covered with the coats of arms of various lords) than you will find in any but a few noblemen's houses. Here there was evidence of what Monsieur de Montaigne was saying elsewhere, that they omit what they do of our usage because they despise it; for though they had a great abundance of pewter plate, scoured just as at Montaigne, they served only on wooden plates, well polished indeed and very handsome.

The seats in all this country are supplied with cushions to sit on, and most of their wainscoted ceilings are vaulted in a half-moon shape, which gives them a lovely grace. As for the linen, of which we were complaining at the beginning, we have never since had any lack of it; and for my master I have never failed to get some to make him curtains for his bed. And if one napkin was not enough for him, they changed it for him several times.

In this town there is a certain merchant who does a business of a hundred thousand florins a year in linen. Monsieur de Montaigne, on leaving Constance, would have gone to that canton in Switzerland[7] from which linens come for all Christendom, except that to return to Lindau, he would have had a four or five hour crossing of the lake.

This town is Lutheran; and what is strange is that here too, as at Isny, the Catholic church holds very solemn services; for the next day, which was Thursday morning, a working day, Mass was said in the abbey outside the town as it is at Notre Dame de Paris on Easter

7 Appenzell.

Day, with music and organ, and there were only monks present. The people outside these Imperial towns have not had this freedom to change their religion. Those here go to this service on holidays. It is a very beautiful abbey. The abbot holds it by right of principality, and it is worth fifty thousand florins of income to him. He is of the house of Stein. All the monks are of necessity gentlemen. Hildegarde, wife of Charlemagne, founded it in the year 783, and is buried here and held to be a saint; her bones have been disinterred from a vault where they used to be and placed in a shrine.

The same Thursday morning Monsieur de Montaigne went to the church of the Lutherans, which was like the others of their sect and of the Huguenots, except that at the place of the altar, which is at the head of the nave, there are some wooden benches that have elbow rests on them, so that those who take their Lord's Supper may kneel as they normally do. Here he met two old ministers, one of whom was preaching in German to a not very large congregation. When he had finished, they sang a psalm in German in a chant somewhat remote from ours. After each verse the very fine organ, recently installed, gave a musical response. As often as the preacher named Jesus Christ, both he and the people took off their bonnets. After the sermon the other minister went over and stood by the altar with his face turned toward the people and a book in his hand; and a young woman came before him, head bare and hair loose, and there made a slight curtsy in the mode of the country, and remained standing there alone. Shortly afterward a young man, who was an artisan, with a sword at his side, also came forward and took his place by the side of this woman. The minister said a few words to both in their ear, then ordered each to say the paternoster, and afterward began to read out of a book. He read certain rules for people who marry; and he had them touch each other's hands, without kissing. This done, he went away, and Monsieur de Montaigne caught up with him. They had a long talk together; he took the said lord to his house and study, which was handsome and well fitted out. His name is Johannes Tilianus, of Augsburg. The said lord asked about a new confession which the Lutherans have drawn up and which all the doctors and princes who support it have signed; but it is not in Latin.

As they were leaving the church, the violins and drums attending the newlyweds were leaving by the other side. Asked whether they permitted dancing, the minister answered, "Why not?" Asked why they had Jesus Christ and many images painted on the windows and

on the new organ, he replied that they did not prohibit images intended to instruct people, provided people did not worship them. Then why had they removed the old images from the churches? It was not they that had done this, he replied; it was their good disciples the Zwinglians, incited by the evil spirit, who had passed there before them and committed these ravages, as well as many others. This is the same reply that others of the Lutheran confession had made to the said lord, particularly the doctor at Isny, who, when asked whether he hated the figure and effigy of the cross, immediately exclaimed, "How could I be such an atheist as to hate this figure, so blessed and glorious for Christians?" and that those were diabolical opinions. That same man said quite brazenly at dinner that he would rather hear a hundred Masses than participate in the Calvinist communion.

At this place they served us the meat of white hares. The town is situated on the river Iller. We dined here on the said Thursday, and came away by a hilly and sterile road to sleep at

PFRONTEN, four leagues, a little village, Catholic like all the rest of this country, which belongs to the archduke of Austria.

I had forgotten to say on the subject of Lindau that at the entrance to the town there is a large wall which gives evidence of great antiquity, on which I did not perceive anything written. I understand that its name in German means Old Wall, which they told me comes from that wall.

On Friday morning, although our inn was very wretched, we found no lack of victuals.

It is their custom never to warm either their sheets for sleeping or their clothes for when they get up; and they are offended if you light a fire in their kitchen for this purpose or use the one that is there; and this is one of the biggest quarrels we had in all the inns. Even here, in the midst of mountains and forests where ten thousand feet of pine do not cost fifty sous, they would not allow us to make a fire, any more than elsewhere.

Friday morning we left here and again took the easier road to the left, leaving the mountain path which goes straight to Trent; for Monsieur de Montaigne was minded to make a few days' detour to see certain beautiful towns of Germany, and repented that at Wangen he had abandoned his original plan of going there and had taken this other route. On the way, as we had done elsewhere in several places, we came across some water mills which receive water only through a wooden flume that takes the water at the foot of some

rise, and then, raising and supporting it high above the ground, sends it down a very steep slope at the end of this flume. We came to dine at

FÜSSEN, one league. This is a little Catholic town belonging to the bishop of Augsburg. Here we found a lot of people of the retinue of the archduke of Austria, who was at a castle near by with the duke of Bavaria.

Here we placed our baggage on a float, as they call it – some pieces of wood joined together, which are taken apart when you are in port – to be taken to Augsburg on the river Lech, and I[8] and several others went along with it.

There is an abbey here where they showed our gentlemen a chalice and a stole, kept in a reliquary, which had belonged to a saint whom they call Magnus, who they say was a son of a king of Scotland and a disciple of Columbanus. Pepin founded this monastery for the said Magnus and made him its first abbot; and at the top of the nave these words are inscribed, and above these words some notes of music for a tune: *Having heard by fame of the virtue of the blessed Magnus, King Pepin has endowed, with royal liberality, the place where the saint lived.* Charlemagne afterward enriched it, as is also written in the said monastery. After dinner, both parties of us came to sleep at

SCHONGAU, four leagues, a little town of the duke of Bavaria, and consequently strictly Catholic; for this prince, more than any other in Germany, has kept his jurisdiction pure of contagion, and is very stubborn about it.

There are good lodgings at the Star, and with a new ceremonial form: they ranged the saltcellars on a square table from corner to corner, and the candlesticks at the other corners, and made a Saint Andrew's cross of them. They never serve eggs, at least up to now, except hard-boiled, cut into quarters in salads, which are very good and made with fresh herbs; they serve new wine, ordinarily right after it is made; they thresh the wheat in the barns as they need it, and thresh it with the big end of the flail. On Saturday we went on to dine at

LANDSBERG, four leagues, a little town of the said duke of Bavaria, situated on the said river Lech, very handsome for its size: walled inner town, outer town, and castle. We arrived here on a market day, when there was a great number of people. In the

8 The secretary.

middle of a very big square is a fountain which spouts water out of a hundred pipes to the height of a pike and scatters it in a very artful way, the pipes being pointed in whatever direction is wanted. There is a very beautiful church in the town and another in the outer town, which are both on the rise of a steep hill, as is the castle also.

Monsieur de Montaigne here went to see a college of Jesuits, who are very comfortably settled there in a brand new building and are engaged in building a beautiful church. Monsieur de Montaigne had as long a talk with them as his time allowed. Count von Helffenstein is in command at the castle. If anyone even dreams of any other religion than the Roman, he must keep quiet about it.

On the gate that separates the inner from the outer town there is a great Latin inscription of the year 1552, where they say in these words that "the *Senate and the People* of this town have built this monument to the memory of William and Louis, brothers, dukes *of both Bavarias*."[9] There are lots of other mottoes in this same place, like this one, *It befits a soldier to be rough, not adorned with gold but relying on his courage and his sword*, and at the head, *The world is a cage of fools*. And in another very conspicuous place are certain words extracted from some Latin historian about the battle that the consul Marcellus lost against a king of this nation: *The battle in which Carloman, king of the Bavarians, fought with Marcellus the consul and defeated him*, etc. There are many other good Latin mottoes at the doors of private houses. They often repaint their towns and their churches, which gives them a very flourishing appearance. And, as if precisely in honor of our passage, during the last three or four years these had almost all been renovated where we were; for they put down the dates of their work.

The clock of this town, like many others of this country, strikes all the quarter-hours; and they say that the one in Nuremberg strikes the minutes.

We left here after dinner, through a long plain of very level pasture land, like the plain of Beauce, and came to

AUGSBURG, four leagues, which is considered the most beautiful town in Germany, as Strasbourg is considered the strongest.

The first thing we noticed on our arrival was a strange arrangement, and one that shows their cleanliness: the steps of the staircase of our inn all covered with linen, on which we had to walk, so as not to dirty the steps, which they had just washed and scoured, as they

9 Here and below the italicized passages are quoted in Latin.

do every Saturday. We have never noticed any cobwebs or mud in their inns. In some there are curtains for those who want to draw them over the windows.

There are hardly any tables in the bedrooms, except those that they attach to the foot of each bed, which hang there by hinges and may be raised or lowered as you wish. The footboards of the beds rise two or three feet above the frames, and often to the level of the headboard; the wood in them is very handsome and elaborately carved; but our walnut much surpasses their pine. Also they served here very shiny pewter plates underneath the wooden ones, out of disdain. They often hang against the wall, beside the beds, linen and curtains, so that people may not dirty their wall by spitting.

The Germans are much in love with coats of arms; for in all the inns there are thousands that the gentlemen of the country passing through leave on the walls, and all their windows are furnished with them.

The order of the courses is often changed. Here crayfish were served up first – which everywhere else are served just before the end – and of unusual size. In many hostelries, big ones, they serve everything covered. What makes their panes shine so much is that they have no windows fixed in our style, and that their frames can be taken out when they want, and they furbish their glasswork very often.

The next morning, which was Sunday, Monsieur de Montaigne went to see several churches; and in the Catholic ones, which are in great number, he found the service everywhere very well done. There are six Lutheran churches and sixteen ministers; two of the six are usurped from the Catholic churches, the other four they have built. He saw one this morning which resembles a great college hall: neither images, nor organs, nor crosses. The wall loaded with lots of writings in German, passages from the Bible; two pulpits, one for the minister – and there was one preaching then – and another below where the man is who leads the singing of the psalms. At each verse they wait for him to give the pitch for the following one; they sing pell-mell, whoever wishes, and whoever wishes remains covered. After that a minister who was in the crowd went up to the altar, where he read a lot of prayers out of a book; and at certain prayers the people rose and clasped their hands, and at the name of Jesus Christ made a low bow. After he had finished reading, uncovered, he turned to the altar, on which there was a napkin, a ewer, and

a saucer with water in it; a woman, followed by ten or twelve other women, presented to him a child in swaddling clothes, its face uncovered. Three times the minister took water from this saucer with his fingers and sprinkled it over the child's face, saying certain words. This done, two men approached, and each of them put two fingers of his right hand on this child; the minister spoke to them, and it was done. Monsieur de Montaigne spoke to this minister on his way out. They receive no revenue from the churches; the Senate pays them publicly. There was much more of a crowd in this church alone than in two or three of the Catholic churches together.

We did not see one beautiful woman. Their clothes are very different from one another's. Among the men it is hard to distinguish the nobles, for their velvet bonnets are worn by all kinds of people, and everyone wears a sword at his side.

We were lodged at the sign of a tree called *Linden* in this country, next to the palace of the Fuggers.[10] One of this family, dying a few years ago, left two solid millions of French crowns to his heirs; and these heirs, to pray for his soul, gave the Jesuits here thirty thousand florins in ready money, with which they have set themselves up very well. The said house of the Fuggers is roofed with copper. In general the houses are much more beautiful, big, and tall than in any city of France, the streets much wider. Monsieur de Montaigne estimates the city to be of the size of Orléans.

After dinner we went to see some fencing in a public hall where there was a big crowd. You pay on entrance, as you do to see the mountebanks, and extra for seats on the benches. They fought with the poniard, the two-handed sword, the double-ended staff, and the cutlass; afterward we saw some prize contests with the crossbow and the longbow, in a place even more magnificent than at Schaffhausen.

We saw a big channel of water flowing from there to the town gate by which we had entered; this water is conveyed from outside the town by a wooden aqueduct, which runs under the footbridge over which we had passed and above the river that flows through the town moat. This channel of water sets in motion certain very numerous wheels which work several pumps, and by two lead channels these raise the water of a spring, which at this spot is very low, to the top of a tower at least fifty feet high. Here the

10 The fabulously wealthy banking family, probably the richest in Europe, established in Augsburg since 1368.

water pours into a big stone vessel, and from this vessel it comes down through many conduits, and from these is distributed throughout the town, which by this means alone is all crowded with fountains. Individuals who want a rivulet for themselves are allowed it on payment to the town of ten florins of rent a year, or two hundred florins paid up for good. It is now forty years since the town has been adorned with this rich work.

Marriages between Catholics and Lutherans are common, and the more eager party submits to the laws of the other. There are a thousand such marriages; our landlord was Catholic, his wife Lutheran.

They dust their glassware with a hair-duster attached to the end of a stick.

They say that there are very fine horses for forty or fifty crowns.

The corporation of the town did Messieurs d'Estissac and de Montaigne the honor of sending them as a present at their supper fourteen big vessels full of their wine, which were offered them by seven sergeants dressed in livery and an eminent officer of the town, whom they invited to supper; for that is the custom, and you have something given to the porters; they gave them a crown. The officer who supped with them told Monsieur de Montaigne that there were three such officers in the town who were responsible for thus honoring strangers of some quality, and that for this reason they took pains to learn their visitors' rank, in order to observe accordingly the ceremonies that were their due: they give more wines to some than to others. To a duke, one of the burgomasters comes to make the present; they took us for barons and knights. Monsieur de Montaigne, for some reason, wanted our party to dissemble and not tell their ranks; and he walked unattended all day long through the town; he thinks that this served to have them even more highly honored. This was an honor that was paid them in all the towns in Germany.

When he passed through the Church of Our Lady, being extremely cold (for the cold began to prick them on leaving Kempten, and until then they had had the most fortunate weather possible), he had, without thinking about it, his handkerchief to his nose, thinking that since he was thus alone and very plainly dressed, no one would pay attention to him. When they were better acquainted with him, they told him that the church people had found this bearing strange. At last he had fallen into the fault that he most avoided, that of making himself noticeable by some mannerism at variance

with the taste of those who saw him; for as far as in him lies, he conforms and falls into line with the ways of the place where he happens to be, and in Augsburg he wore a fur cap around the town.

They say in Augsburg that they are free, not from mice, but from the big rats with which the rest of Germany is infested; and on that subject they relate many miracles, attributing this privilege to one of their bishops who is buried here; and with the earth from his grave, which they sell in little lumps the size of hazelnuts, they say you can drive away this vermin in whatever country you take it to.

On Monday we went to see, in the Church of Our Lady, the marriage ceremony of a rich and ugly girl of the town with an agent of the Fuggers, a Venetian; we saw not one beautiful woman there. The Fuggers, who are many and all very rich, hold the principal positions in the town. We also saw two rooms in their house, the one high, large, paved with marble, the other low, rich in medals ancient and modern, with a little chamber at the end. They are among the most sumptuous rooms I have ever seen. We also saw the dancing of this company; it was nothing but *allemandes*.[11] They break them off at the end of each number, and return the ladies to their seats, which are benches ranged along the sides of the room in two rows, covered with red cloth; the men do not mingle with the women. After a short pause, they go and get them again; the man kisses his hand to the lady; the lady receives him without kissing hers, and then, putting his hand under her armpit, she embraces him cheek to cheek and puts his right hand on her shoulder. The men dance and converse with them uncovered and not very richly dressed.

We saw other houses of these Fuggers in other parts of the town, which is beholden to them for all the expense that they employ in embellishing it; these are pleasure houses for the summer. In one we saw a clock that is worked by the motion of water, which serves as a counterpoise. In the same place were two big covered fish ponds, twenty paces square, full of fish. On all four sides of each pond there are many little pipes, some straight, the others bent upward; through all these pipes the water pours very charmingly into these ponds, some sending the water in straight, the others spurting it upward to the height of a pike. Between these two ponds there is a space ten paces wide floored with planks; through these planks go lots of little brass jets which cannot be seen. While the ladies are busy watching the fish play, you have only to release some spring:

11 A dance somewhat like the waltz.

immediately all these jets spurt out thin, hard streams of water to the height of a man's head, and fill the petticoats and thighs of the ladies with this coolness. In another place where there is an amusing fountain-pipe, while you are looking at it anyone who wants to can open the passage to little imperceptible tubes, which from a hundred places cast water into your face in tiny spurts; and in that place is this Latin sentence: *You were looking for trifling amusements; here they are; enjoy them.*

There is also an aviary twenty paces square, twelve or fifteen feet high, enclosed on all sides with well-knotted and interlaced brass wire; inside, ten or twelve pine trees and a fountain; this is all full of birds. Here we saw some Polish pigeons, which they call Indian, and which I have seen elsewhere; they are large, and have a beak like a partridge.

We also saw the handiwork of a gardener, who, foreseeing the storms and cold, had transported into a little covered shed lots of artichokes, cabbages, lettuce, spinach, endive, and other plants that he had picked, as if to eat them on the spot; and by putting their roots into a certain sort of earth, he hoped to keep them good and fresh for two or three months; and indeed he then had a hundred artichokes, not at all withered, and yet he had picked them more than six weeks before.

We also saw a bent instrument of lead, open on both sides, and hollow. Having once filled it with water, holding both holes up, you suddenly and dexterously turn it upside down, so that one end drinks out of a vessel full of water, and the other discharges it outside; when you have started this flow, the result is that, to avoid the vacuum, the water always keeps filling the tube and running out without stopping.[12]

The arms of the Fuggers are a shield divided in the middle: on the left, a fleur-de-lys azure on a field or; on the right, a fleur-de-lys or on a field azure; which the Emperor Charles V gave them when he ennobled them.

We went to see some people who were taking two ostriches from Venice to the duke of Saxony. The male was blacker and had a red neck; the female was more grayish, and laid lots of eggs. They were leading them on foot, and they say that the beasts got less tired than they, and were all the time escaping from them; but they keep them attached by a collar that girds them around the loins over the thighs,

12 The instrument described is a siphon.

and another over the shoulders; these go around their whole body; and they have long leashes by which they stop them or turn them as they please.

On Tuesday, by a singular courtesy of the lords of the town, we went to see a postern which is in the said town, by which they admit at all hours of the night anyone who wants to enter, whether on foot or on horseback, provided he tells his name and the person with whom he will stay in town or the name of the hostelry he is seeking. Two trusty men, paid by the town, preside over this entrance. People on horseback pay two batzen to enter, people on foot one. The corresponding outside door is sheathed with iron; at the side, there is a piece of iron attached to a chain, which piece of iron you pull. This chain, by a very long route with many turns, leads to the bedroom of one of the porters, which is very high up, and rings a bell. The porter, from his bed and in his shirt, by a certain machine that he moves back and forth, opens this first door, more than a hundred paces from his room. The man who has entered finds himself on a bridge forty paces long or thereabouts, all covered over, which crosses the town moat; along the bridge is a wooden channel, and along this the machinery moves which opens this first door, which is immediately closed again on those who have entered. When this bridge is passed, you find yourself in a little place where you speak to this first porter and tell him your name and address. Having heard it, he rings a bell to notify his mate, who is lodged one story below in this gateway, where there is a big lodging; he, by working a spring in a gallery adjoining his room, in the first place opens a little iron barrier, and then, by turning a big wheel, raises the drawbridge, without the visitor's being able to perceive any of these movements, which are concealed by the thickness of the walls and doors; and everything is promptly closed again with a great racket. Beyond the bridge a big door opens, very thick, which is of wood and reinforced with many big sheets of iron. The stranger finds himself in a room, and all the way along sees no one to speak to. After he is shut up there, they open another, similar door to him; he enters a second room in which there is a light; there he finds a brass vessel hanging down by a chain; there he puts the money he owes for his passage. This money is pulled up by the porter; if he is not satisfied, he lets the man stew there till morning; if he is satisfied, as he customarily is, he opens for him in the same way still another big door like the others, which closes as soon as he has passed, and there he is in the town.

It is one of the most ingenious things that can be seen. The queen of England sent an ambassador expressly to ask the city government to reveal the working of these machines; it is said that they refused. Under this gateway is a great vault that will lodge five hundred horse under cover, either to be used for help, or to be sent to war without the knowledge of the townspeople.

On leaving there we went to see the Church of the Holy Cross, which is very beautiful. They make a great celebration there about a miracle that occurred nearly a hundred years ago. A woman would not swallow the body of Our Lord. Having taken it out of her mouth and put it, wrapped in wax, into a box, she confessed; and they found the whole thing changed into flesh. For this they cite plenty of attestations, and this miracle is written down in many places in Latin and in German. They show under crystal that wax, and then a little morsel having the redness of flesh. This church is roofed with copper, like the house of the Fuggers, and that is not very rare here.

The church of the Lutherans is right next to this one; here, as elsewhere, the construction and lodgings are like the cloisters of the Catholic churches. At the door of this church they have placed the image of Our Lady holding Jesus Christ, with other saints and some children, and these words: *Suffer the little children to come unto me*, etc.

In our inn there was a machine consisting of two iron pistons which plunged to the bottom of a very deep well. With a boy at the top working a certain mechanism and making these iron pistons go up and down two or three feet, the pistons, one after the other, beat and pressed the water at the bottom of this well and, pushing it with their plungers, forced it to gush through a leaden pipe which delivers it to the kitchens and wherever it is needed.

They have a whitewasher on their payroll who immediately goes over any part of their walls that has been blackened.

They served us pasties, both large and small, in earthenware vessels of the color and exact shape of a pie crust. Few meals pass at which they do not offer you sugar candies and boxes of sweet-meats. The bread is the most excellent possible; the wines are good, and in this region these are more often white; none is grown around Augsburg, and they bring them from five or six days' journey away. For every hundred florins that the landlords spend on wine, the republic demands sixty, and half that amount from other private persons who buy it only for their own use.

They also have in many places the custom of putting perfumes in the bedrooms and dining rooms.

The town was originally entirely Zwinglian. Later, when the Catholics were recalled, the Lutherans took the place of the Zwinglians; at present there are more Catholics in positions of authority, although they are greatly outnumbered. Monsieur de Montaigne also visited the Jesuits here and found some very learned ones.

Wednesday morning, October 19th, we breakfasted here. Monsieur de Montaigne was very sorry, being only a day's journey from the Danube, to leave without seeing it or the town of Ulm, which lies on its course, and a bath half a day's journey beyond which is called Sauerbrunnen. It is a bath in flat country, of cold water, which they heat up to use it for drinking or bathing. It has something stinging in its taste that makes it pleasant to drink, and it is good for maladies of the head and stomach; a famous bath, where you are very magnificently lodged in very well-appointed inns, as at Baden, from what we were told; but wintertime was advancing fast, and then this road was quite in the opposite direction from ours, and we would have had to retrace our steps back to Augsburg; and Monsieur de Montaigne strenuously avoided passing over the same road twice.

I left an escutcheon of the arms of Monsieur de Montaigne in front of the door of the dining room at his lodging; it was very well painted, and cost me two crowns to the painter and twenty sous to the carpenter.

The town is bathed by the river Lech, Lycus. We passed through a very beautiful countryside, fertile in wheat, and came to sleep at

BRUCK, five leagues, a big village in a very handsome setting in the duchy of Bavaria, Catholic. We left there the next day, which was Thursday, October 20th, and after continuing through a great plain of wheat (for this region has no wines) and then a prairie as far as the eye could reach, we came to dine at

MUNICH, four leagues, a city about as big as Bordeaux, chief city of the duchy of Bavaria, where they[13] have their principal residence on the river Isar, Ister. It has a handsome castle and finer stables than I have ever seen in France or Italy, vaulted, to lodge two hundred horses. It is a town strongly Catholic, populous, handsome, and mercantile.

13 The dukes of Bavaria.

From a day's journey above Augsburg you can plan on spending four livres a day for man and horse, and forty sous per footman, at the least.

Here we found curtains in our bedrooms and no testers, and moreover everything very clean; they clean their floors with saw-dust, which they boil.

Everywhere in this country they cut up two varieties of turnip, applying the same care and diligence as in threshing wheat. Seven or eight men, with large knives in each hand, slash them, with a rhythmic beat, in vessels resembling our wine presses; this makes it possible for them to put them up and salt them for the winter, like their cabbages. With those two vegetables they fill, not their gardens, but their lands in the country, and they have harvests of them.

The duke, who is here now, married the sister of the duke of Lorraine, and has by her two rather big boys and a girl. The duke and his brother are both in town; they had gone hunting, ladies and all, the day we were there.

On Friday morning we left here, and, through the forests of the said duke, saw countless numbers of reddish animals[14] in flocks, like sheep; and we came without stopping to

ICKING, six leagues, a wretched little village in the same duchy. The Jesuits, who govern in this region, have caused a great commotion, which makes them hated by the people, by forcing the priests to get rid of their concubines, under great penalties; and to see the priests complain of it, it seems that formerly this was so tolerated that they practiced it as if it were something legitimate; and they are still busy making remonstrances about it to the duke.

Here we had the first eggs that we had been served in Germany on a fish day, or otherwise than cut up into quarters in salads. Also they served us in wooden goblets with staves and hoops like barrels, among many of silver. The lady of a noble house who was in this village sent some of her wine to Monsieur de Montaigne.

Early on Saturday morning we left here; and after coming upon the river Isar on our right and a large lake at the foot of the Bavarian mountains, and climbing for an hour's ride a little mountain on top of which there is an inscription saying that a duke of Bavaria had had the rock cut through a hundred years ago or thereabouts, we plunged right into the heart of the Alps by an easy, comfortable, and delightfully well-kept road, the beautiful, serene weather favoring

14 Fallow deer.

us. On descending this little mountain we came upon a very beautiful lake, a Gascon league in length and as much in breadth, wholly surrounded by very high and inaccessible mountains; and still following this route at the foot of the mountains, from time to time we came upon level patches of very pleasant meadowland, on which there are houses; and without stopping we came on to sleep at

MITTENWALD, a little village belonging to the duke of Bavaria, rather well situated along the river Isar. Here they served us the first chestnuts we had been served in Germany, and quite raw. There is a steam bath in the hostelry where travelers are accustomed to be sweated, for a batz and a half. I went there while the gentlemen were having supper. There were lots of Germans who were being cupped and bled.

The next morning, Sunday, October 23rd, we continued along this path between the mountains, and on it came upon a gate and a house that shuts off the passage. This is the entrance to the district of Tyrol, which belongs to the archduke of Austria. We came to dine at

SEEFELD, a little village and abbey, three leagues, pleasant site. The church is rather fine, famous for the following miracle. In 1384 a certain man, whose name is given in the particulars, not willing to be content on Easter Day with the common host, asked for the great one. When he had it in his mouth, the earth opened under him and swallowed him up to his neck, and he held on to the corner of the altar. The priest took the host out of his mouth. They still show the hole, covered with an iron grill, and the altar that received the imprint of this man's fingers, and the host, which is all reddish, as with drops of blood. We also found here a recent writing, in Latin, about a Tyrolean who, having a few days before tried to swallow a piece of meat which stuck in his throat, and being unable either to swallow it or throw it up for three days, made a vow and came to this church, where he was instantly cured.

On leaving here we found, in the highlands we were crossing, some beautiful villages; and then, having come down a half hour's descent, at the foot of it we came upon a beautiful town, well located; above, on a precipitous hill which seems inaccessible, a handsome castle[15] commands the road of this descent, which is narrow and cut out of the rock. It is not quite wide enough for an

15 Fragenstein.

ordinary wagon, as indeed is the case in many places in these mountains; so that the carters who venture up here are accustomed to cut down the ordinary wagons by at least a foot.

Beyond we found a valley of great length, through which passes the river Inn, which flows into the Danube at Vienna. In Latin it is called *Aenus*. It is five or six days by water from Innsbruck to Vienna. This valley seemed to Monsieur de Montaigne to present the most agreeable landscape he had ever seen: now contracting as the mountains pressed close, then widening, now on the side we were on, which was the left side of the river, and creating new land for plowing and cultivating on the very slopes of the less steep mountains; now on the other side; and then revealing plains on two or three levels, one above the other; and all full of beautiful noblemen's houses and of churches; and all this closed and walled in on all sides by mountains of measureless height.

On a rocky hill on our side we discovered a crucifix in a place where it is impossible for any man to have gone without the artificial aid of ropes, by which a man could let himself down from above. They say that the Emperor Maximilian, grandfather of Charles V, while hunting, lost his way on this mountain, and in testimony to the danger he had escaped had this image erected. This story is also painted in the town of Augsburg in the hall that serves the crossbowmen. In the evening we went to

INNSBRUCK, three leagues, chief town of the county of Tyrol, *Aenopontum* in Latin. Here dwells Ferdinand, archduke of Austria. A very beautiful little town and very well built in the depth of this valley, full of fountains and streams, which are a very ordinary attraction in the towns we have seen in Germany and Switzerland. The houses are almost all built in terraces along the hillside.

We lodged at the Rose, a very good inn; they served us in pewter plates. As for napkins in the French fashion, we had already had some a few days before. Around some of the beds there were curtains; and to show the character of the nation, they were beautiful and rich, of a certain kind of linen, cut and open-worked, for the rest short and narrow, in short of no use for what we use them for; and a little tester three fingers wide with lots of tassels. They gave me some sheets for Monsieur de Montaigne which had four fingers' width of rich white lacework all around.

As in most of the other towns of Germany, there are men here all night in the streets who call out the hours that have struck.

Everywhere we have been they have this custom of serving fish in with the meat; but on fish days, however, they do not serve meat with the fish, at least not to us.

On the Monday we left here, skirting the said river Inn on our left hand, along that beautiful plain; we went to dine at

HALL, two leagues; and we made this trip just to see it. It is a little town like Innsbruck, the size of Libourne or thereabouts, on the said river, which we crossed again over a bridge. It is from here that they extract the salt that supplies all Germany, and every week nine hundred loaves are made, at a crown apiece. These loaves are of the thickness of a half a hogshead and of about that shape; for the vessel that serves them as a mold is of that kind. This belongs to the archduke; but the expense is very great. For the preparation of the salt I saw more wood here in one place than I ever saw anywhere else; for in several great caldrons made of iron plates, thirty good paces around, they boil this salt water from which they make their salt, which comes from more than two long leagues away, from one of the neighboring mountains.

There are several fine churches, notably that of the Jesuits, which Monsieur de Montaigne visited; and at Innsbruck he visited others, which are magnificently situated and accommodated.

After dinner we again saw that side of the river, for there is a beautiful house in that place where Archduke Ferdinand of Austria is staying, whose hands Monsieur de Montaigne wanted to kiss; and he had stopped by there in the morning, but had found that the archduke was busy in his council, from what a certain count had told him. After dinner we stopped by again and found him in a garden, or least we thought we had caught a glimpse of him. However, those who went to tell him that our gentlemen were there and why, reported that he begged them to excuse him, but that on the next day he would be more at leisure; that at all events if they had any need of his favor they should make this known to a certain Milanese count. This coolness, added to the fact that they were not even allowed to see the castle, offended Monsieur de Montaigne a little; and as he was complaining about it that same day to an officer of the house, he was answered that the said prince had replied that he did not like to see Frenchmen and that the house of France was hostile to his. We returned to

INNSBRUCK, two leagues. Here we saw in a church eighteen very handsome bronze effigies of the princes and princesses of the house of Austria.

We also went to attend a supper party given by the Cardinal of Austria and the margrave of Burgau, sons of the said archduke by a concubine from the town of Augsburg, a merchant's daughter,[16] whom, having had these two sons by her and no others, he married to legitimize them; and in that same year the said woman passed away. The whole court still wears mourning for her.

Their service was about like that of our princes. The hall was hung with black cloth, also the dais and chairs. The cardinal is the elder, and I think he is not yet twenty. The margrave drinks only bottled wine, and the cardinal very diluted wine. They have no special container for their place settings, but these are uncovered; and the service of the courses is in our style. When they come to sit down, it is a bit away from the table, and this is moved close to them, all loaded with food, the cardinal at the head; for the head with them is always the right side.

We saw in this palace some tennis courts and a rather handsome garden. The archduke is a great builder and deviser of such luxuries. We saw at his place ten or twelve field pieces, carrying a ball the size of a large goose egg, mounted on wheels as gilded and enriched as possible, and even the pieces are all gilded. They are only of wood, but the muzzle is sheathed with an iron plate, and the bore is entirely lined with the same kind of plate. One single man can carry one on his back, and fire it not as often, but with almost as big a charge, as those cast in metal.

At his castle in the fields we saw two oxen of unusual size, all gray, with white heads, which the duke of Ferrara had given him; for the said duke had married one of his sisters, the duke of Florence another, the duke of Mantua a third. He had three of his sisters at Hall, whom they called the three queens; for the daughters of the Emperor are given these titles, as others are called countesses or duchesses because of their lands; and they give them the surname of the kingdoms possessed by the Emperor. Of the three, two are dead; the third is still there, but Monsieur de Montaigne could not see her; she is shut up like a nun, and has welcomed and established the Jesuits there.

Here they hold that the said archduke cannot leave his estates to his children and that they revert to the successors to the Empire; but they were unable to give us an intelligible reason for this,

16 Philippine Welser (1527–80), member of one of the big business families of Augsburg.

and what they say about his wife – that she was not of suitable lineage – does not appear plausible, since he married her, and everyone holds that she was legitimate, and also the children. At all events, he is amassing a big pile of money in order to have enough to give them.

On Tuesday we left in the morning and resumed our road, crossing that plain and following the mountain path. At one league from the inn we climbed a little mountain an hour's ride high, by an easy road. On our left hand we had a view of several other mountains, which, having a more extended and gentler incline, are covered with villages and churches, and for the most part cultivated right to the top, very pleasant to see for the diversity and variety of the sites. The mountains on our right hand were a little wilder, and there were only rare spots where there was any habitation. We crossed several streams or torrents with various courses; and on our way, both on the heights and at the foot of our mountains, we found many little towns and big villages and many handsome hostelries, and among other things two castles and gentlemen's houses on our left hand.

About four leagues from Innsbruck, on our right hand, on a very narrow road, we came upon a richly worked bronze tablet, attached to a rock, with this Latin inscription: "The Emperor Charles V, returning from Spain and Italy from receiving the imperial crown, and Ferdinand, king of Hungary and Bohemia, his brother, coming from Pannonia, seeking each other after being eight years without seeing each other, met on this spot in the year 1530, and Ferdinand here ordered this memorial to be made." They are represented embracing each other.[17] A little later, passing through a gateway set up across the road, we found on it some Latin verses making mention of the passage of the said Emperor, and of his lodging in this place, after he had captured the king of France, and Rome.[18]

Monsieur de Montaigne said that he liked this mountain pass very much because of the diversity of the objects to be seen, and we found no discomfort except from the thickest and most unendurable dust that we had ever felt, which accompanied us across this whole pass between the mountains.[19] Ten hours later (Monsieur de Montaigne said that this stretch represented one stage, or post, for

17 This memorial still exists, on the Lueg Pass.
18 In 1525 (at Pavia) and 1527 respectively.
19 The Brenner Pass.

him; it is true that his custom, whether or not he is to stop on the road, is to feed his horses oats before leaving the inn in the morning) we arrived, with him still fasting, late at night at

STERZING, seven leagues, a little town of the said county of Tyrol, rather pretty, above which, a quarter of a league away, there is a beautiful new castle.

On the table here they served us rolls, quite round, joined together. In all Germany the mustard is served liquid and is of the taste of French white mustard. The vinegar everywhere is white. Wine is not grown on these mountains, but wheat grows in almost sufficient abundance for the inhabitants. They drink very good white wines.

There is the greatest security in all these passes, and they are heavily traveled by merchants, carriers, and carters. Instead of the cold for which this pass is decried, we had an almost unendurable heat.

The women in this region wear cloth bonnets just like our toques, and their hair hanging in braids, as elsewhere. Monsieur de Montaigne, coming across a pretty young girl in a church, asked her if she could speak Latin, taking her for a schoolboy.

There were curtains for the beds here, of coarse linen dyed red, divided into alternating strips of four fingers' width, one part being of a close weave, the other of a loose weave. We have found no bedroom or public room in all our travel in Germany that was not wainscoted, the ceilings being very low.

Monsieur de Montaigne had the colic this night for two or three hours and was very hard pressed, from what he said in the morning; and in the morning on rising he passed a stone of medium size, which broke easily. It was yellowish on the outside, and, when broken, more whitish on the inside. He had caught a cold the day before and felt bad. He had not had an attack of the colic since the one at Plombières. This one partly removed the suspicion he had that he had taken into his bladder at the said Plombières more sand that he had got rid of, and he feared that some matter had stopped there and become caught and stuck; but seeing that he had got rid of this one, he finds it reasonable to believe that it would have attached itself to the others if there had been any. As soon as he was on the road he complained of pain in his loins, which was the reason, he said, why he lengthened this day's journey, thinking he was more relieved on horseback than he would have been elsewhere.

In this town he sent for the schoolmaster, to talk with him about his Latin; but the man was a fool from whom he was unable to derive any information about the things of this country.

The next day, which was Wednesday, October 26th, after breakfast, we left here through a plain half a quarter-league wide, having the river Isarco [Eisack] on our right side. This plain lasted us for about two leagues; and on the neighboring mountains were many cultivated and inhabited spots, often in locations whose approaches we could not even guess at. There are four or five castles on this road. Afterward we crossed the river over a wooden bridge and followed it on the other side. We found many workers repairing the roads merely because they were stony, about as much so as those in Périgord. Afterward, through a stone gateway, we climbed to a height where we found a plain a league wide or thereabouts, and from it discovered on the other side of the river another at an equal height, but both of them barren and stony. The rest of the country, along the river below us, consisted of very handsome meadows. We came, without stopping, to sup at

BRESSANONE, four leagues, a very beautiful little town through which the river passes under a wooden bridge; it is a bishopric. We saw here two very beautiful churches, and were lodged at the Eagle, a handsome inn. The surrounding plain is not very wide; but the mountains round about, especially on our left hand, stretch out so gently that they allow themselves to be combed and primped right up to the ears. Everything seems to be filled with steeples and villages well up into the mountainside, and near the town are many beautiful houses very pleasantly built and situated.

Monsieur de Montaigne said that all his life he had distrusted other people's judgment on the matter of the conveniences of foreign countries, since every man's taste is governed by the ordering of his habit and the usage of his village; and he had taken very little account of the information that travelers gave him; but in this spot he wondered even more at their stupidity, for he had heard, and especially on this trip, that the passes of the Alps in this region were full of difficulties, the manners of the people uncouth, roads inaccessible, lodgings primitive, the air insufferable. As for the air, he thanked God that he had found it so mild, for it inclined rather toward too much heat than too much cold; and in all this trip up to that time we had had only three days of cold and about an hour of rain. But that for the rest, if he had to take his daughter, who is only eight, for a walk, he would as soon do so on this road as on any path

in his garden. And as for the inns, he had never seen a country where they were so plentifully distributed and so handsome, for he had always lodged in handsome towns well furnished with victuals and wine, and more reasonably than elsewhere.

There was a way of turning a spit here which was by a machine with several wheels, by which a cord was tightly wound around a big iron vessel. When this began to unwind, they slowed down its unwinding, so that this movement lasted about an hour, and then it had to be wound up again. As for smokejacks, we had seen several already.

They have so great an abundance of iron that besides all the windows being grated, and in various ways, their doors, even the shutters, are covered with iron plates.

Here we found vineyards again, which we had lost sight of since before Augsburg.

Hereabouts most of the houses are vaulted on every floor; and what they do not know how to do in France, to use pantiles to cover very narrow slopes, they do in Germany, even on the steeples. Their tile is smaller and hollower, and in some places plastered over the joints.

We left Bressanone the next morning and came upon that same very open valley, and the hillsides along most of the road were adorned with many beautiful houses. Having the river Isarco on our left hand, we passed through a little town where there are many artisans of all sorts, called Klausen; from there we came to dine at

KOLMANN, three leagues, a little village where the archduke has a pleasure house. Here they served us goblets of painted earthenware among those of silver, and they washed the glasses with white sand; and the first course was served in a very neat little frying pan, which they put on the table with a little iron instrument to support it and raise its handle. In this frying pan were eggs poached in butter.

As we left there the road narrowed on us a bit and some rocks pressed in on us, so that, since the defile was narrow for both us and the river together, we would have been in danger of colliding, if they had not placed between it and the travelers a wall as a barrier, which in various places extends for more than a German league. Although most of the mountains close to us here are wild rocks, some massive, others split and broken up by the flow of the torrents, and others scaly and sending down pieces of astounding size (I believe it must be dangerous here in very stormy weather), just as elsewhere, we

have also seen whole forests of pines torn up from their footing and carrying down in their fall little mountains of earth clinging to their roots; yet the fact remains that the country is so populous that above these first mountains we saw others higher up, cultivated and inhabited, and we learned that on top of them there are big, beautiful fields which furnish wheat to the towns below, and very rich farmers and beautiful houses.

We crossed the river over a wooden bridge, of which there were several, and put it on our left. We discovered, among other things, a castle on the most eminent and inaccessible mountain height that presented itself to our sight, which they say belongs to a baron of the district, who lives in it and has a fine estate and fine hunting grounds up there. Above all these mountains there is still a top fringe of the Alps; these the people leave alone, for they block the outlet from this valley, so that you continually have to return to our channel and come out again by one of the two ends.

The archduke draws from this country of Tyrol, whose whole revenue derives from these mountains, three hundred thousand florins a year; and he has more from here than from all the rest of his domain. We crossed the river once more over a stone bridge and came early to

BOLZANO, four leagues, a town of the size of Libourne, on the said river, rather unattractive compared with the others in Germany, so that Monsieur de Montaigne exclaimed that he clearly recognized that he was beginning to leave Germany: the streets narrower, and no handsome public square. There still remained fountains, streams, painted houses, and glass windows.

There is so great an abundance of wines here that they supply all Germany with them. The best bread in the world is eaten all along these mountains. Here we saw the church, which is one of the most beautiful. Among other things there is a wooden organ; it is high up, near the crucifix, before the high altar; and yet the person who plays it sits more than twelve feet below, at the foot of the pillar to which it is attached; and the bellows are outside the wall of the church, more than fifteen paces behind the organist, supplying him with their wind from underground.

The open space in which this town lies is scarcely bigger than is needed to contain it; but the mountains, especially on our right hand, stretch out their flanks a little and enlarge it.

From this place Monsieur de Montaigne wrote to François Hotman, whom he had seen at Basel, that he had taken such great

pleasure in visiting Germany that he left it with great regret, although it was Italy he was going to; that foreigners had to suffer here as elsewhere from the exactions of innkeepers; but that he thought this might be corrected if a man was not at the mercy of guides and interpreters, who sell accommodations and participate in this profit. All the rest seemed to him full of comfort and courtesy, and especially of justice and security.

We left Bolzano on the Friday morning early and came, to give a measure of oats to the horses and have breakfast ourselves, to

BRONZOLO, two leagues, a little village above which the river Isarco, which had led us thus far, comes to mingle with the river Adige, which runs on to the Adriatic Sea, and runs on wide and peaceful, no longer in the manner of those we had come upon among these mountains above, noisy and furious. So this plain, as far as Trent, begins to widen a bit, and the mountains to lower their horns a bit in some places; however, they are less fertile on their flanks than the preceding ones. There are some marshes in this valley which hug the road; the rest is very easy and level and almost always in the bottom of the valley.

Two leagues beyond Bronzolo we came to a big town in which there was a great gathering of people because of a fair. Beyond this, another village, well built, named Salorno, where the archduke has a small castle, on our left hand, in a strange location, on the top of a crag.

Italy: The Road to Rome
(October 28–November 29, 1580)

From there we came to sleep at

TRENT, five leagues, a town a little larger than Agen, not very pleasant, and having completely lost the graces of the German towns; the streets mostly narrow and tortuous.

About two leagues above Trent, the Italian language begins. This town is divided in half between these two languages, and there is a quarter in the town and a church which they call that of the Germans, and a preacher of their language. As for the new religions, there has been no talk of them since Augsburg. It is situated on this river Adige. We saw the cathedral, which seems to be a very ancient building, and right near it is a square tower which gives evidence of great antiquity. We saw the new

church, of Our Lady, where our Council[1] was held. In this church there is an organ, given by a private person, of surpassing beauty, raised up within a marble structure, elaborately carved with many excellent statues, notably those of certain little singing boys. This church was built, as it tells us, in 1520, by *"Bernardus Clesius, cardinal,"* who was bishop of this town and a native of this same place.

This used to be a free town and under the charge and rule of the bishop. Later, when pressed by war against the Venetians, they called the count of Tyrol to their aid, in return for which he has retained a certain authority and right over their city. The bishop and he are in dispute, but the bishop, who is at present Cardinal Madruccio, has possession.

Monsieur de Montaigne said he had taken note along the way of the citizens who have benefited the towns of their birth: the Fuggers at Augsburg, to whom is due most of the embellishment of that city, for they have filled all the street corners with their palaces, and the churches with many works; and this Cardinal Clesius, for besides this church and several streets that he restored at his own expense, he had some very fine building done in the castle of the town. It is not much on the outside, but inside it is the best furnished and painted and decorated and the most livable to be seen anywhere. All the panels on the ground floor have many rich paintings and mottoes; the raised work is elaborately gilded and carved; the floor, of a certain earth hardened and painted like marble, partly arranged in our style, partly in German style, with stoves. One of these is of earthenware, burnished like brass, and made in the form of several large human figures, which receive the fire into their limbs; and one or two others, near a wall, give out water that comes from the fountain in the court very far below: it is a fine piece of work. Here we also saw, among the other paintings on the ceiling, a nocturnal triumph by torchlight,[2] which Monsieur de Montaigne greatly admired. There are two or three round chambers; in one there is an inscription saying that this Clesius, in the year 1530, had been sent to the coronation of the Emperor Charles V, which was performed by Pope Clement VII on Saint Matthew's Day, as ambassador from Ferdinand, king of Hungary

1 The Council of Trent, held in the Church of Santa Maria Maggiore from 1545 to 1563.
2 The Triumph of Caesar.

and Bohemia, count of Tyrol, and brother of the said Emperor; and that there, from being bishop of Trent, he was made a cardinal. And around the chamber he has had placed and hung on the wall the arms and names of the gentlemen who accompanied him on this trip, about fifty, all vassals of this bishopric and counts or barons. There is also a trap door in one of the said chambers by which he could slip into town without using his doors. There are also two rich fireplaces.

He was a good cardinal. The Fuggers built, but for the service of their descendants; this man built for the public; for he has left this castle furnished with better than a hundred thousand crowns' worth of furniture, which is still there, for the bishops his successors; and in the public purse of the succeeding bishops a hundred and fifty thousand thalers in ready money, which they enjoy without damage to the capital; and yet they have left his Church of Our Lady unfinished, and him rather meanly buried. Among other things there are several paintings from the life and a lot of maps. The bishops that succeeded him have added no furniture to this castle – and there is some for both seasons, winter and summer – and it cannot be alienated.

We are now going by the Italian miles, five of which come to one German mile; and they count up to twenty-four hours a day without dividing them in the middle.[3] We lodged at the Rose, a good inn.

We left Trent Saturday after dinner and followed a similar road in that valley, now widened and flanked by high uninhabited mountains, having the said river Adige on our right hand. Here we passed a castle of the archduke which commands the road, as elsewhere we have found many similar obstacles that close off the roads and hold them subject; and when it was already very late (and until then we had not yet had any taste of evening damps, so regularly did we schedule our travel), we arrived at

ROVERETO, fifteen miles, a town belonging to the said archduke. Here we found our own style of lodging again, and found lacking not only the cleanliness of the bedrooms and furniture of Germany, and their windowpanes, but also their stoves, in which Monsieur de Montaigne found much more comfort than in fireplaces.

3 Most subsequent references to the time of day in the *Journal* follow this pattern. Since they also reckon by starting the day at sunset, this translation simply gives the equivalents in our system of counting the time.

As for food, the crayfish here failed us; in which connection Monsieur de Montaigne remarked as a great wonder that they had been served us at every meal since Plombières, and for nearly two hundred leagues of country. Here, and along these mountains, they very commonly eat snails, much larger and fatter than in France, and not so good in taste. They also eat truffles, which they peel and put, in very fine slices, into oil and vinegar; these are not bad. At Trent they served some that had been kept a year. Here again, and to Monsieur de Montaigne's taste, we found lots of oranges, lemons, and olives.

On the beds are slit curtains of linen or a kind of rough serge, in broad bands, and fastened at intervals. Monsieur de Montaigne also regretted those featherbeds that are used as a covering in Germany. They are not beds such as ours, but of very fine down, enclosed in very white fustian at the good inns. The underbedding even in Germany is not of this sort, and you cannot use it as a cover without discomfort.

I truly believe that if Monsieur de Montaigne had been alone with his own attendants he would rather have gone to Cracow or toward Greece by land than make the turn toward Italy; but the pleasure he took in visiting unknown countries, which he found so sweet as to make him forget the weakness of his age and of his health, he could not impress on any of his party, and everyone asked only to return home. Whereas he was accustomed to say that after spending a restless night, he would get up with desire and alacrity in the morning when he remembered that he had a new town or region to see. I never saw him less tired or complaining less of his pains; for his mind was so intent on what he encountered, both on the road and at his lodgings, and he was so eager on all occasions to talk to strangers, that I think this took his mind off his ailment.

If someone complained to him that he often led his party, by various roads and regions, back very close to where he had started (which he was likely to do, either because he had been told about something worth seeing, or because he had changed his mind according to the occasions), he would answer that as for him, he was not going anywhere except where he happened to be, and that he could not miss or go off his path, since he had no plan but to travel in unknown places; and that provided he did not fall back upon the same route or see the same place twice, he was not failing to carry out his plan. And as for Rome, which was the goal of the

others, he desired less to see it than the other places, since it was known to every man, and there was not a lackey who could not tell them news of Florence and Ferrara. He also said that he seemed to be rather like people who are reading some very pleasing story and therefore begin to be afraid that soon it will come to an end, or any fine book; so he took such pleasure in traveling that he hated to be nearing each place where he was to rest, and toyed with several plans for traveling as he pleased, if he could get away alone.

On Sunday morning, wishing to reconnoiter Lake Garda, which is famous in that country, and from which comes very excellent fish, he hired three horses for himself and the seigneurs de Cazalis and de Mattecoulon, at twenty batzen each; and Monsieur d'Estissac hired two others for himself and the sieur du Hautoy, and without any servant, leaving their own horses at this inn (at Rovereto) for that day, they went to dine at

TORBOLE, eight miles, a little village within the jurisdiction of Tyrol. It is situated at the head of this great lake. At the other side of this head there is a little town and a castle, called La Riva, to which they were taken on the lake, which is five miles going and as much coming back; and they made the trip with five rowers in three hours or thereabouts. They saw nothing at the said La Riva but a tower which seems to be very old, and, by chance, the lord of the place, who is Signor Fortunato Madruccio, brother of the cardinal who is at present bishop of Trent. The view down the lake is boundless, for it is thirty-five miles long. The width, all they could discover of it, was only the said five miles. This head of the lake belongs to the county of Tyrol, but all the lower part, on both sides, is under Venetian rule; here there are lots of beautiful churches, and plenty of beautiful parks of olive and orange trees, and other such fruit trees. This lake becomes furiously agitated when there is a storm. The surroundings of the lake are mountains more forbidding and arid than any others that we had seen on our road, from what the said lords reported; adding that on leaving Rovereto they had crossed the river Adige and left the road to Verona on their left hand, and had entered a low valley where they had found a very long village and a little town; that it was the roughest road they had seen, and the wildest view, because of these mountains which obstructed their way. Leaving Torbole, they returned for supper to

ROVERETO, eight miles. Here they put their baggage on some of those rafts which they call floats in Germany, to be taken to

Verona on the said river Adige for a florin, and the next day I had charge of taking it there. At supper they served us poached eggs for the first course, and a pike, amid great plenty of every kind of flesh.

The next day, which was Monday, they left here early in the morning; and following this valley, rather populous but hardly fertile, and flanked by high scaly and arid mountains, they came to dine at

BORGHETTO, fifteen miles, which is still in the county of Tyrol; this county is very large. In this connection, Monsieur de Montaigne, asking whether it consisted of anything but this valley through which we had passed and the mountaintops that had been offered to our sight, was given this answer: that there were many such mountain valleys, just as big and fertile, and other handsome towns, and that it was like a dress which we see only pleated, but that if it were spread out the Tyrol would be a very big country.

We[4] still had the river on our right hand. Leaving here after dinner, we followed the same sort of road as far as Chiusa, which is a little fort that the Venetians have won, in the hollow of a rock on this river Adige; we descended along this river by a steep slope of massive rock, where horses have a hard time getting secure footing, and went through the said fort, where the state of Venice, whose jurisdiction we had entered one or two miles after leaving Bor-ghetto, maintains twenty-five soldiers. They came to sleep at

VOLARGNE, twelve miles, a little village and a miserable inn, as are all those on this road as far as Verona. Here, from the castle of the place, a maiden lady, sister of the absent lord, sent some wine to Monsieur de Montaigne.

The next morning they completely lost the mountains on their right hand, and left far on one side on their left hand a chain of hills. For a long time they followed a barren plain, which then, approach-ing the said river, became a little better, and fertile in vines trained on trees, as they are in this country; and on All Saints' Day, before Mass, they arrived at

VERONA, twelve miles, a city of the size of Poitiers, and like it having a vast quay, on the said river Adige, which goes through it and over which there are three bridges. I also arrived here with my baggage. Without the health certificates that they had gotten at Trent and had confirmed at Rovereto, they could not have entered

4 The "we" does not include the secretary, who usually refers to the rest of the party as "they." The same discrepancy occurs occasionally later.

the city; and yet there was no rumor of danger from the plague; but it is out of custom, or in order to filch some quattrino or so that they cost.

We went to see the cathedral, where Monsieur de Montaigne found the behavior of the men strange on such a day, at High Mass: they were talking right in the choir of the church, covered, standing, their backs turned toward the altar, and looking as if they were not thinking of the service except at the elevation. There was an organ, and some violins which accompanied it during Mass. We also saw some other churches, in which there was nothing singular – nothing in the adornment or beauty of the women, among other things.

They went to the Church of Saint George, among other places; the Germans have left plenty of evidence of having been there, and many escutcheons. There is one inscription, among others, stating that certain German noblemen, having accompanied the Emperor Maximilian in taking Verona from the Venetians, placed some work or other on an altar here. He thought it remarkable that the Signory preserves in its city the evidence of its losses, as also it preserves in their entirety the proud tombs of the poor lords of La Scala.[5] It is true that our host of the Little Horse, which is a very good inn where we were treated to a superfluity of food at a cost of one-fourth more than in France, enjoys possession of one of these tombs for his family. We saw the castle here, and the party was shown through by the lieutenant of the governor of the castle. The Signory maintains sixty soldiers there: rather, from what they told Monsieur de Montaigne at the castle itself, against the townspeople than against foreigners.

We also saw a convent of monks who are called the Jesuates of Saint Jerome. They are not priests, and neither say Mass nor preach, and are mostly ignorant; and they pride themselves on being excellent distillers of orange-flower liqueurs and similar waters, both here and elsewhere. They are dressed in white, and wear dark brown robes and little white birettas; many are handsome young men. Their church is very well accommodated, as is their refectory, where their table was already laid for supper. Our gentlemen saw here certain old ruins, very ancient, of the time of the Romans, which these men say were an amphitheater, and they patch them up with other fragments that are discovered underneath. On our return

5 More commonly known as the Scaligers.

from there we found that they had perfumed their cloisters for us, and they had us enter a cabinet full of phials and earthenware vessels, and there they perfumed us.

The finest thing we saw here, and what Monsieur de Montaigne said was the handsomest building he had seen in his life, was a place they call the Arena. This is an oval amphitheater, which seems almost entire – all the seats, all the arches and outer structure – except the extreme end of the outer part: in short, there is enough left to reveal the shape and use of these buildings as they were. The Signory is employing some criminals' fines on it, and has repaired some bit; but what they are doing is very far from what would be needed to restore it entirely; and he strongly doubts whether the whole city is up to this restoration. It is oval in shape; there are forty-three tiers of steps, each a foot or more high, and it is about six hundred paces around at the top. The noblemen of the country still use it for jousting and other public pleasures.

We also saw the Jews, and Monsieur de Montaigne was in their synagogue and had quite a talk with them about their ceremonies.

There are some very beautiful squares and beautiful market places. From the castle, which is up high, we could make out Mantua in the plain, twenty miles away on the right of our road. They have no lack of inscriptions; for they never even repair some little gutter, either in town or on the roads, without inscribing on it the name of the podestà and that of the workman. They have this in common with the Germans, that they all have coats of arms, the merchants as well as others; and in Germany not only the big towns but most of the small ones have some sort of coat of arms of their own.

We left Verona and saw on our way out the Church of Our Lady of the Miracles, which is famous for several strange incidents, in consideration of which they are rebuilding it anew, of a very handsome round shape. The steeples here are covered in many places with bricks laid crosswise. We passed over a long plain of varied nature, now fertile, now otherwise, having the mountains very far off on our left hand and some on our right, and, without stopping, came to sup at

VICENZA, thirty miles. This is a big city, a little smaller than Verona, where there are plenty of noblemen's palaces.

The next day we saw several churches, and the fair that was being held here: in a big square, many booths that are built of wood on the spot for this purpose.

We also saw some Jesuates, who have a handsome monastery here; and we saw their shop for waters, which they sell to the public; and we got two bottles of perfume for a crown;[6] for they also make medicinal waters for all maladies. Their founder is P. Urb.[7] Saint Giovanni Colombini, a Sienese gentleman, who founded the order in the year 1367. Cardinal di Pelveo is for the present their protector. They have no monasteries except in Italy, and there they have thirty. They have a very handsome habitation. They flagellate themselves every day, they say; each of them has his little chains at his place in their oratory, where they pray God without singing, and are there together at certain hours.

The old wines were then already beginning to fail us, and it troubled me because of his colic that he should drink those muddy wines – which were otherwise good, however. We regretted leaving those of Germany, although they are for the most part spiced and have various scents which the Germans find delicious, especially sage; and they call that sage wine, which is not bad when you get used to it, for otherwise their wine is good and generous.

We left here Thursday after dinner; and by a very level, wide, straight road, with ditches on both sides, and a little raised, having on all sides a very fertile terrain, with the mountains, as usual, visible a long way off, we came to sleep at

PADUA, eighteen miles. The hostelries cannot be compared for any sort of treatment with those of Germany. It is true that they are a third less expensive and very near the same as in France.

The city is indeed very vast, and in my opinion its enclosed area is at least the size of Bordeaux. The streets are narrow and ugly; very sparsely populated, few beautiful houses; the situation very pleasant, with an open plain extending very far all around.

We were here all the next day, and saw the fencing, dancing, and riding schools, where there were more than a hundred French gentlemen; which Monsieur de Montaigne reckoned as a great disadvantage for the young men of our country who go there,

6 The Italian crown (scudo) was worth 10 giulii, 100 baiocchi, or in French money 50 sous or .833 crown (écu). It is not always clear, however, in the Italian part of the *Travel Journal*, whether Montaigne is speaking in terms of French or Italian crowns.

7 In the papacy of Urban V. This is an addition made by Montaigne, according to Querlon.

inasmuch as this society accustoms them to the ways and language of their own nation and deprives them of the means of acquiring foreign acquaintances.

The Church of Saint Anthony seems to him beautiful; the roof is not in one piece, but in several domelike projections. There are many rare sculptures in marble and bronze. He looked with a kindly eye at the bust of Cardinal Bembo, which shows the sweetness of his character and something indefinable of the elegance of his mind.

There is a hall, the biggest I ever saw without pillars, where their justice is dispensed; and at one end is the head of Livy, thin, showing him as a studious and melancholy man: an ancient work that lacks only speech. His epitaph is there also; when they found it they erected it thus to do themselves honor, and with reason. Paulus, the jurisconsult, is also there, over the door of this place; but Monsieur de Montaigne thinks this is a recent work. The house which is on the site of the ancient Arena is worth seeing, and so is its garden. The students live here very reasonably at seven crowns a month for the master and six for the valet, in the most decent pensions.

We left there Saturday morning early by a very fine causeway along the river, having on either side very fertile plains of wheat, very well shaded with trees sown in orderly rows in the fields where they have their vines, and the road furnished with plenty of beautiful pleasure houses, and among others a house of the Contarini family, at the gate of which an inscription states that the king[8] lodged there on his way back from Poland. We came to

FUSINA, twenty miles, where we dined. This is only a hostelry, from which one embarks for Venice. Here all the boats along this river land, by means of machines and pulleys turned by two horses in the manner of those that turn oil mills. They transport these boats, with wheels that they put underneath, over a wooden flooring, and launch them into the canal which goes on into the sea, in which Venice is situated. We dined here, and having got into a gondola, we came to sup at

VENICE, five miles. Next day, which was Sunday morning, Monsieur de Montaigne saw Monsieur du Ferrier, ambassador of the king, who gave him a very cordial welcome, took him to Mass,

8 Henry III of France, who was king of Poland for about five months before becoming king of France in 1574.

and kept him to dinner with him.[9] On the Monday Monsieur d'Estissac and he dined there again. Among other remarks of the said ambassador, this one seemed strange to him: that he had no dealings with any man of the city, and that they were such a suspicious sort of people that if one of their gentlemen spoke to him twice, they would hold him suspect; and also this, that the city of Venice was worth fifteen hundred thousand crowns in revenue to the Signory.

For the rest, the rarities of this town are well enough known. Monsieur de Montaigne said he had found it different from what he had imagined, and a little less wonderful. He reconnoitered it and all its particulars with extreme diligence. The government, the situation, the arsenal, the Square of Saint Mark, and the crowds of foreign people seemed to him the most remarkable things.

On Monday, November 7th, at supper, Signora Veronica Franca,[10] a Venetian gentlewoman, sent a man to present him with a little book of letters that she had composed; he had the said man given two crowns.

On the Tuesday after dinner he had the colic, which lasted him two or three hours – not one of the most extreme, to look at him – and before supper he passed two big stones, one after the other.

He did not find here that famous beauty that they attribute to the ladies of Venice, and yet he saw the noblest of those who make a traffic of it; but it seemed to him as wonderful as anything else to see such a number of them as a hundred and fifty or thereabouts spending like princesses on furniture and clothes, having no other funds to live on except from this traffic; and many of the nobles of the place even keeping courtesans at their expense in the sight and knowledge of all.

For his own service he hired a gondola for day and night at two lire, which is about seventeen sous, without any expense for the boatman. Food is as expensive as in Paris, but still this is the city where you live at the cheapest rate in the world, inasmuch as a train of valets is of no use to us at all here, for everyone goes around by

9 A note on the manuscript in Montaigne's hand reads (according to Quer-lon): "This old man, who has passed seventy-five, from what he says, enjoys a healthy and cheerful old age. His manners and his talk have something scholastic about them; little vivacity or incisiveness. His opinions very evidently lean, in the matter of our affairs, toward the Calvinistic innovations."

10 One of the many distinguished Venetian courtesans.

himself; and the expense for clothes likewise; and then there is no need of a horse.

On Saturday, November 12th, we left here in the morning and came to

FUSINA , five miles, where we took a boat, men and baggage, for two crowns. Monsieur de Montaigne has customarily been afraid of the water; but in the belief that it is the motion alone which upsets his stomach, and wanting to test whether the movement of this river, which is even and uniform, since the boat is drawn by horses, would upset it, he tried it and found that he had no trouble from it. You have to pass two or three locks on this river, which close and open for travelers. We came by water to sleep at

PADUA, twenty miles. Here Monsieur de Cazalis left the party and stayed on here as a boarder for seven crowns a month, well lodged and treated. He could have kept a lackey for five crowns; and yet these are pensions of the highest class, where there was good company, and especially the sieur de Millac, son of Monsieur de Salagnac. They usually have no valets and only a houseboy or some women who wait on them; each one has a very clean bedroom; the fire for their rooms, and candles, they furnish for themselves. They treat you well, as we saw. You live here very reasonably; which is in my opinion the reason why many foreigners, even those who are no longer students, reside here. It is not the custom to go about the town on horseback or with many attendants. In Germany I noticed that everyone wears a sword at his side, even the workmen; in the territories of this Signory, quite to the contrary, no one wears one.

Sunday, November 13th, after dinner we left here to see some baths which were on our right hand. Monsieur de Montaigne headed straight for Abano. This is a little village near the foot of the mountains, three or four hundred paces above which there is a somewhat elevated stony place. This height, which is very spacious, has many springs of boiling hot water spouting from the rock. Around the source it is too hot to bathe in, let alone to drink. It leaves a trace around its course that is quite gray, like burned ash, and a lot of sediment that is in the form of hard sponges. The taste is a bit salty and sulphurous. The whole countryside is full of steam; for the streams that flow here and there in the plain carry this heat and the smell very far.

There are two or three little houses here, rather poorly accommodated for sick people, into which they turn aside canals of these waters to make them into baths for the houses. Not only is there

steam where the water is, but the rock itself steams through all its crevices and joints and gives out heat all over, so that they have pierced holes in some places where a man can lie down and get hot and sweaty from this exhalation; which happens instantly. Monsieur de Montaigne put some of this water into his mouth after it had stood a long time and lost its excessive heat; he found its taste more salty than anything else.

Further along, on our right hand, we discovered the abbey of Praglia, which is very famous for its beauty, its wealth, and its courtesy in receiving and entertaining strangers. He would not go there, considering that he was to revisit all this region, notably Venice, at his leisure,[II] and thought nothing of this visit; and what had made him undertake it was his extreme hunger to see that city. He said that he could not have stayed peacefully in Rome or anywhere else in Italy without having had a look at Venice; and for that purpose he had turned out of his way. In this hope he left at Padua, with one Master François Bourges, a Frenchman, the works of Cardinal Cusanus, which he had bought in Venice.

From Abano we passed on to a place called San Pietro Basso, and we still had the mountains on our right very near. It is a countryside of meadows and pastures which is likewise all steaming in various places from these waters, some boiling, others tepid, others cold; the taste a little more dead and insipid than the others'; less smell of sulphur, indeed virtually none at all; a little saltiness.

We found here some traces of ancient buildings. There are two or three wretched little houses round about to lodge the sick; but in truth this is all very primitive, and I would not be minded to send my friends here. They say it is the Signory that takes little care of the place and fears the influx of foreign lords. These last baths, he said, reminded him of those of Préchacq, near Dax. The trace of these waters is all reddish, and left some of the mud on his tongue; he found no taste in it; he thinks the waters contain more iron.

From here we passed by a very beautiful house belonging to a gentleman of Padua, where the Cardinal d'Este, ill with the gout, had been staying for more than two months, to enjoy the comfort of the baths and, even more, the proximity of the ladies of Venice; and right near there we stopped to sleep at

II He never did return. Presumably this is one of the plans interrupted by his recall to France as mayor of Bordeaux.

BATTAGLIA, eight miles, a little village on the Frassine canal, which, having no depth, sometimes only two or three feet, nevertheless conveys surprisingly big boats. Here we were served on earthenware dishes and wooden plates for lack of pewter; otherwise passably enough.

Monday morning I went on ahead with the mule. They went to see some baths which are five hundred paces from here, by the levee along this canal. There is, so Monsieur de Montaigne reported, only one house over the bath, with ten or twelve rooms. In April and May they say that plenty of people go there, but most of them lodge in the said village or in this château of the Signor Pic, in which the Cardinal d'Este was dwelling. The water of the baths comes down from a little mountain ridge, and flows through channels into the said house and on below; they do not drink it at all, and rather drink that of San Pietro, which they send for. It comes down from this same ridge by channels right near the good sweet water; according as it takes a shorter or longer course, it is more or less hot. He went to the top of the hill to see the source; they could not show it to him, and put him off by saying that it came from underground. He finds little taste to it in the mouth, like that of San Pietro, little smell of sulphur, little saltiness; he thinks that if anyone drank it he would get the same effect as from that of San Pietro. The trace it leaves in its conduits is red.

In this house there are baths and other places where the water only trickles down, and you place the sick member under it; they told him that it is usually the forehead for head ailments. They have also, in some places in these channels, made little stone cells in which you shut yourself up, and then, when you open the airhole to the channel, the steam and heat immediately make you sweat hard; these are dry vapor-baths, of which they have several kinds.

The principal use made is of the mud bath. They fetch the mud from a big basin that is below the house, in the open, by means of an instrument with which they draw it to take it to the house, which is quite near. There they have several wooden instruments fit for legs, arms, thighs, and other parts, to lay and enclose the said limbs in after filling this wooden vessel full of this mud, which they renew according to the need. This mud is black like that of Barbotan, but not so granulated, and greasier, warm with a moderate warmth, and with virtually no smell. All these baths have no great advantage unless it is the proximity to Venice; everything about them is crude and unattractive.

They left Battaglia after breakfast and followed that canal, which they call the Two-Road Canal, from the causeways on either side. Very near there they came upon the bridge of the canal.[12] In this place they have made highways on the outside of the canal walls, at the height of the said causeways, on which travelers pass; the highways on the inside go down to the level of the bottom of the canal. At that point there is a stone bridge which joins these two highways, over which bridge flows the canal from one arch of a viaduct to the other. Over this canal there is a very high bridge; the boats which follow the canal pass under it and above those which want to cross this canal. There is another big stream right at the bottom of the plain which comes from the mountains and whose course crosses this canal. In order to conduct it without interrupting this canal, this stone bridge has been made across which the canal flows and under which flows this stream, cutting across the canal, over a planking dressed with wood on the sides, so that this stream is capable of carrying boats: there would be enough room both in width and in height. And then with other boats continually passing on the canal and coaches on the arch of the highest bridge, there were three roads, one above the other.

From there, still keeping this canal on our right hand, we skirted a little town called Monselice, low-lying, but whose confining wall goes up to the top of a mountain and encloses an old castle which used to belong to the lords of this town; now it is nothing but ruins. And leaving the mountains on our right, we followed the road to the left, raised, handsome, level, and which in the hot season must be well shaded; on either side of us there were very fertile plains that have, according to the custom of the country, amid their wheat fields many trees arranged in rows, from which hang their vines. Very big gray oxen are so common here that I no longer found strange what I had noted about those of the Archduke Ferdinand. We came onto a raised causeway, and on both sides were marshes more than fifteen miles wide stretching as far as the eye could reach.

12 The original of the following passage is even more confusing than this translation of it and may well include many misreadings of the manuscript. Modern editors offer a variety of conjectures, none of them very comprehensible. This much at least should be clear: a mountain stream flows between artificial banks across and beneath the canal. The canal at this point flows over a viaduct. A bridge crosses it above.

These were formerly great ponds, but the Signory attempted to dry them up to get farmland; they have succeeded in some places, but very few. At present it is a huge extent of muddy land, sterile and full of reeds. They lost more than they gained by trying to change its nature.

We crossed the river Adige on our right, on a ferry: a deck resting on two little boats, with a capacity of fifteen or twenty horses, which slides along a rope attached on the other side of the water, more than five hundred paces away; and to keep the rope in the air there are several little boats in between, which support this long rope with forked sticks.

From there we came to sleep at

ROVIGO, twenty-five miles, a very small town still in the territory of the said Signory. We lodged outside the town. They began to serve us salt in blocks, from which you take some like sugar. There is no less abundance of food than in France, whatever people are accustomed to say; and the fact that they do not lard their roast takes away hardly any of its savor. Their bedrooms, for lack of glass and proper closing of the windows, are less clean than in France; the beds better made, smoother, with lots of mattresses; but they have hardly any but badly woven little canopies, and are very parsimonious of white sheets. Anyone who went alone or with a small retinue would get none. The cost as in France, or a little more.

This is the birthplace of the excellent Celius, who took from it the surname Rhodiginus.[13] It is very pretty, and there is a very handsome square; the river Adige passes through the middle.

Tuesday morning, November 15th, we left here, and after doing a long stretch on the causeway, like that at Blois, and crossing the river Adige, which we came upon on our right, and then the Po, which we found on the left, over a ferry like that of the day before (except that on this platform there is a permanent cabin in which you pay the toll while crossing, according to the printed regulations they have posted there; and in the middle of the crossing they stop their boat short to settle accounts and get their pay before landing), and after getting off in a low plain, where it seems as though in very rainy weather the road would be impassable, we came in one stage, in the evening, to

13 Author of a popular compilation which Montaigne owned and borrowed from once or twice, the *Lectionum antiquarum libri triginta*.

FERRARA, twenty miles. Here for their passports and health certificates they stopped us for a long time at the gate, and everyone else likewise. The city is of the size of Tours, situated in very flat country: many palaces, most of the streets wide and straight, not very populous.

On the Wednesday morning Messieurs d'Estissac and de Montaigne went to kiss the duke's hands. He was informed of their intention; he sent a lord of his court to welcome them and bring them to his cabinet, where he was with two or three others, waiting for them. We passed through several closed chambers where there were several well-dressed gentlemen. They had us all come in. We found him standing at a table waiting for them. He put his hand to his bonnet when they came in, and remained uncovered as long as Monsieur de Montaigne spoke to him, which was rather a long time. He asked him first if he understood the language, and having been answered yes, he told them in very eloquent Italian that he was very glad to see gentlemen of that nation, being at the service of, and under much obligation to, the Most Christian King. They had some other conversation together and then they withdrew, the lord duke never having covered himself.

We saw in a church the effigy of Ariosto, a little fuller in face than he appears in his books; he died at the age of fifty-nine, on the 6th of June, 1533.

They serve fruit here on plates.

The streets are all paved with bricks. The colonnades, which are continuous at Padua and serve as a great convenience for walking about in all weather under cover without getting muddy, are lacking here. At Venice the streets are paved with the same material, and so sloping that there is never any mud.

I had forgotten to say about Venice that the day we left there we found on our path several boats with their holds filled entirely with fresh water; the boatload is worth a crown delivered at Venice and the water is used to drink or to dye cloth. While we were at Fusina we saw how with horses incessantly turning a wheel, water is drawn from a stream and poured into a channel, from which channel the said boats receive it, lining up below.

We were all that day at Ferrara, and there saw many beautiful churches, gardens, private houses, and everything that they told us was remarkable: among other things, at the Jesuates, a rose tree that bears flowers every month of the year; and even then there was one, which was given to Monsieur de Montaigne. We also saw the

Bucentaur,[14] which the duke, to emulate the one at Venice, had had made for his new wife, who is beautiful and too young for him, to take her around on the river Po. We also saw the duke's arsenal, in which there is a piece of ordnance thirty-five spans long which carries a shot one foot in diameter.

The cloudy new wines that we were drinking, and the water, just as muddy as when it comes out of the river, alarmed him about his colic.

On all the bedroom doors in the hostelry is written: Remember your health certificate. As soon as you have arrived you must send your name to the authorities, and the number of your men. Then they send word to give them lodging; otherwise they do not do so.

On Thursday morning we left here[15] and went through a level and very fertile country, difficult for pedestrians in muddy weather, inasmuch as the soil of Lombardy is very rich; and then, the roads being closed in by ditches on either side, they have no space in which to step aside to avoid the mud, so that many people of the country walk with little stilts half a foot high. We went in the evening, without stopping, to

BOLOGNA, thirty miles, a large and beautiful city, much bigger and more populous than Ferrara. At the inn where we lodged, the young seigneur de Monluc[16] had arrived an hour before, coming from France; he had stopped in the said city to attend the schools of fencing and horsemanship.

On Friday we saw the fencing of the Venetian who boasts of having invented new techniques in that art which prevail over all others; and in truth his style of fencing is in many respects different from the usual ones. The best of his students was a young man from Bordeaux named Binet.

Here we saw a square tower,[17] ancient, so constructed that it leans all to one side and seems to threaten its own downfall. We also saw the academy of the sciences, which is the handsomest building I have ever seen for this purpose.

14 The state barge.
15 It is curious that the secretary's account says nothing of Montaigne's visit to the poet Tasso, then insane, about which Montaigne speaks bitterly in the *Essays* (II: 12, p. 441).
16 Blaise de Monluc, grandson of his famous namesake.
17 Presumably the Torre Garisenda, which has the greater lean of the two leaning towers of Bologna.

On the Saturday after dinner we saw some comedians, with whom Monsieur de Montaigne was very pleased; and there, or from some other cause, he got a headache, which he had not had for several years; and yet at the same time he said he had a lack of pain in his kidneys more pure than he had been accustomed to for a long time, and enjoyed a comfortable feeling in his stomach such as he had had on returning from Bagnères. His headache passed away during the night.

This is a city all enriched with handsome wide colonnades and a very great number of beautiful palaces. You live as at Padua, or just about, and very reasonably; but the city is a little less peaceable because of the old feuds that exist between factions of certain families in the city, one of which has always had the French on their side, the other the Spaniards, who are here in very great numbers. In the square there is a very handsome fountain.

On Sunday Monsieur de Montaigne had planned to take the road to the left toward Imola, the March of Ancona, and Loreto, to get to Rome; but a German told him that he had been robbed by bandits in the duchy of Spoleto. So he turned right, toward Florence. We immediately plunged into a rugged road and mountainous country, and came to sleep at

Loiano, sixteen miles, a rather uncomfortable little village. There are only two hostelries in this village, which are famous among all those in Italy for the treachery that is practiced on travelers in feeding them with fine promises of every sort of comfort before they set foot to the ground, and laughing at them when they have them at their mercy: about which there are popular proverbs.

We left here early the next morning and until evening followed a road which in truth is the first on our trip that can be called uncomfortable and wild, and in the midst of mountains more difficult than in any other part of this trip; we came to sleep at

scarperia, twenty-four miles, a very small town of Tuscany, where they sell quantities of little cases, scissors, and similar merchandise.

Monsieur de Montaigne took all possible pleasure in the rivalry among the landlords. They have the custom of sending seven or eight leagues to meet strangers and conjuring them to choose their inn. You will often find the landlord himself on horseback, and in various places many well-dressed men in wait for you; and all along the road, Monsieur de Montaigne, who wanted to draw them out, had himself amusingly entertained with the various offers that each

one made him; and there is nothing that they will not promise.[18] There was one who offered him a hare purely as a gift if he was willing just to visit his house. Their disputes and competition stop at the gates of the town, and they do not dare say one more word. They have this in common, that they offer you a guide on horseback at their expense to guide you and carry part of your baggage to the inn you are going to; which they always do, and pay their expense. I do not know whether or not they are obliged to by some ordinance because of the danger of the roads.

We had made our bargain as early as Bologna for what we were to pay and get at Loiano. Urged as we were by the people of the inn where we stayed and elsewhere, Monsieur de Montaigne had sent one of us to inspect all the inns, the food, and the wines, and to learn the conditions before we all dismounted; and he chose the best. But it is impossible to make such careful terms that you escape their trickery; for they will make you lack the wood, the candles, the linen, or the hay that you have forgotten to specify.

This route is full of travelers, for it is the ordinary highroad to Rome.

I was here informed[19] of a stupid thing I had done in forgetting to visit a mountaintop ten miles this side of Loiano and two miles off the road, from which, in rainy or stormy weather and by night, you can see flames coming out to a very great height; and my informant told me that in the big upheavals there are sometimes disgorged little pieces of money with some figure or other. We should have seen what all this was.

We left Scarperia the next morning with our landlord as guide and went along a fine road between many populated and cultivated hills. We turned out of our way to the right for about two miles to see a palace that the duke of Florence[20] built here twelve years ago, which he exercises all his five natural senses to embellish. It seems as though he purposely chose an inconvenient, sterile, and mountainous site, yes, and even without springs, so as to have the honor of sending to get water five miles from there, and his sand and lime another five miles. It is a place that has nothing level about it. You

18 A note in the original edition, possibly by Querlon but more probably by Montaigne, here adds: "Anche ragazze et ragazzi" – "Even young girls and young boys."
19 This paragraph seems to have been written by Montaigne.
20 Francis I de' Medici, grand duke of Tuscany.

have a view of many hills, which is the general shape of the country. The house is called Pratolino. The building is contemptible to see it from far off, but from near it is very beautiful, though not up to the most beautiful in France. They say that there are six score furnished rooms; we saw ten or twelve of the finest. The furniture is pretty, but not magnificent.

There is one miraculous thing, a grotto with several cells and rooms; this part surpasses all that we have ever seen elsewhere. It is encrusted and formed all over of a certain material which they say is brought from certain mountains, and they have joined it invisibly with nails. There is not only music and harmony made by the movement of the water, but also a movement of several statues and doors with various actions, caused by the water; several animals that plunge in to drink; and things like that. At one single movement the whole grotto is full of water, and all the seats squirt water on your buttocks; and if you flee from the grotto and climb the castle stairs and anyone takes pleasure in this sport, there come out of every other step of the stairs, right up to the top of the house, a thousand jets of water that give you a bath.

The beauty and richness of this place cannot be described in detail. Among other things, below the castle there is a walk fifty feet wide and five hundred paces long or thereabouts, which has been made almost level, at great expense. On both sides there are long and very handsome railings of freestone; every five or ten paces along these railings there are springing fountains in the wall, so that there are nothing but fountain jets all along the walk. At the bottom there is a beautiful fountain that pours into a big basin through a conduit set in a marble statue of a woman doing her washing. She is wringing out a tablecloth of white marble, from the dripping of which this water comes out; and underneath there is another vessel where it seems as if there is water boiling for washing. There is also a marble table in a hall of the castle around which there are six seats, at each of which you raise a lid of this marble by a ring, and under the lid there is a vessel attached to the said table. In each of the said six vessels there springs up a fountain of fresh water in which each man may cool his glass, and in the middle is a big one to put the bottle in.

We also saw some very wide holes in the ground where they keep a large quantity of snow all year round; and it is placed on a litter of broom, and then all this is covered, up to a great height, in the form of a pyramid, with thatch, like a little barn. There are a thousand

reservoirs. And they are building the body of a giant, which is three cubits wide at a rough estimate, and the rest in the same proportion; from this will pour a fountain in great abundance. There are a thousand reservoirs and ponds, and all this drawn from two springs by an infinity of earthen pipes. In a very handsome big aviary we saw some little birds like goldfinches, which have two long feathers in their tail like those of a big capon. There is also a singular stove. We stayed here two or three hours and then resumed our journey and went over the top of certain hills to

FLORENCE, seventeen miles, a city smaller in size than Ferrara, situated in a plain, surrounded by a thousand highly cultivated hills. The river Arno passes through and is crossed by bridges. We found no moats around the walls.

That day Monsieur de Montaigne passed two stones and a lot of gravel, without having had any other feeling of it than a slight pain in the lower abdomen.

On the same day we saw the grand duke's stable, very large, vaulted, in which there were not many valuable horses; indeed, he was not there that day. There we saw a sheep of a very strange shape; also a camel, some lions, some bears, and an animal the size of a very big mastiff and the shape of a cat, all marked in black and white, which they call a tiger.

We saw the Church of San Lorenzo, where still hang the flags that we lost under Marshal Strozzi in Tuscany. There are in this church several pieces of flat painting, and very beautiful and excellent statues by Michelangelo. We saw the cathedral, which is a very big church with the bell tower all faced with black and white marble; it is one of the most beautiful and sumptuous things in the world.

Monsieur de Montaigne said that he had never until then seen a nation where there were so few beautiful women as the Italian.

The lodgings he found much less comfortable than in France and Germany; for the food is not half so abundant as in Germany, nor so well prepared. They serve the food without larding in both places; but in Germany it is much better seasoned, and varied with sauces and soups. The lodgings in Italy are much worse: no common rooms; the windows large and wide open, except for a big wooden shutter that keeps out the light if you want to keep out the sun or the wind; which he found much more intolerable and irremediable than the lack of curtains in Germany. Besides, they have only little cots with wretched canopies, one at the most in each bedroom, with

a truckle bed underneath; and anyone who hated to lie hard would find himself up against it. An equal or greater lack of linen. The wines generally worse, and for those who hate a sickly sweetness, unbearable in this season. The expense, it is true, is a little less. They say that Florence is the most expensive city in Italy. I had made our bargain, before my master arrived at the hostelry, the Angel, at seven reals a day for man and horse, and four reals for a man on foot.

The same day we saw a palace of the duke, where he himself takes pleasure in working at counterfeiting oriental stones and cutting crystal; for he is a prince somewhat interested in alchemy and the mechanical arts, and above all a great architect.

The next day Monsieur de Montaigne led the way up to the top of the cathedral, where there is a globe of gilt brass which from below seems of the size of a ball, and when you are there proves capable of holding four people.[21] There he saw that the marble with which this church is encrusted, even the black (for this work is all variegated and carved), is already beginning to give way in many places and is cracking from the frost and the sun; which made him fear that this marble was not very genuine.

He wanted to see the houses of the Strozzi and the Gondi, where some of their kin still reside. We also saw the palace of the duke, where Cosimo, the duke's father, has had a painting made of the capture of Siena and the battle we lost. Yet in various places in this city, and especially in the said palace on the old walls, the fleurs-de-lys hold the first rank of honor.

Messieurs d'Estissac and de Montaigne were at a dinner of the grand duke; for so they call him here. His wife was seated in the place of honor; the duke below; below the duke, the duchess's sister-in-law; below her, her husband, the brother of the duchess. This duchess[22] is beautiful by Italian notions, an agreeable and imperious face, big bust, and breasts the way they like them. To Monsieur de Montaigne she seemed certainly clever enough to have bewitched this prince and to keep him devoted to her for a long time. The duke is a stout, dark man of my height, large limbs, face and bearing full of courtesy, passing always uncovered through the throng of his courtiers, who are a handsome group. He has a healthy bearing, that of a man of forty. On the other side of the

21 The text says "forty," but "four" is probably intended.
22 Bianca Capello of Venice, who had been the grand duke's mistress during his first marriage.

table were the duke's two brothers, the cardinal and another young man of eighteen.

They bring drink to this duke and his wife in a basin, in which there is an uncovered glass full of wine and a glass bottle full of water; they take the glass of wine, pour as much as they do not want into the basin, fill it with water themselves, and then put the glass back in the basin, which the cupbearer holds for them. The duke put in a good deal of water; she, almost none. The fault of the Germans is to use immoderately big glasses; here it is the opposite, to have them so extraordinarily small.

I do not know why this city should be privileged to be surnamed "the beautiful"; it is so, but without any advantage over Bologna, and little over Ferrara, and it is incomparably inferior to Venice. True, it is fine to discover from this bell tower the infinite multitude of houses that cover the hills all around for a good two or three leagues, and this plain where the city is situated, which seems to extend to a length of two leagues; for the houses seem to touch each other, so thickly are they sown. The city is paved with slabs of flat stone, without method or order.

After dinner the four gentlemen and a guide took post horses to go and see a place of the duke's called Castello. The house has nothing worth while about it; but there are various things about the gardens. The whole estate is situated on the slope of a hill, so that the straight walks are all on a slope, but a soft and easy one; the cross walks are straight and level. One sees there many arbors, very thickly interwoven and covered with all kinds of odoriferous trees such as cedars, cypresses, orange trees, lemon trees, and olive trees, the branches so joined and interlaced that it is easy to see that the sun at its greatest strength could not get in; and copses of cypress and of those other trees disposed in order so close to each other that there is room for only three or four people to pass abreast. There is a big reservoir, among other things, in the middle of which you see a natural-looking artificial rock, and it seems all frozen over, by means of that material with which the duke has covered his grottoes at Pratolino; and above the rock is a large bronze statue of a very old hoary man seated on his rear with his arms crossed, from all over whose beard, forehead, and hair water flows incessantly, drop by drop, representing sweat and tears; and the fountain has no other conduit than that.

Elsewhere they had the very amusing experience of seeing what I have noted above; for as they were walking about the garden and

looking at its curiosities, the gardener left their company for this purpose; and as they were in a certain spot contemplating certain marble statues, there spurted up under their feet and between their legs, through an infinite number of tiny holes, jets of water so minute that they were almost invisible, imitating supremely well the trickle of fine rain, with which they were completely sprinkled by the operation of some underground spring which thegardener was working more than two hundred paces from there, with such artifice that from there on the outside he made these spurts of water rise and fall as he pleased, turning and moving them just as he wanted. This same game is found here in several places.

They also saw the master fountain, which issues from a conduit in two very big bronze effigies, of which the lower holds the other in his arms and is squeezing him with all his might;[23] the other half fainting, his head thrown back, seems to spurt this water forcibly out of his mouth; and it shoots out with such power that the stream of water rises thirty-seven fathoms above the height of these figures, which are at least twenty feet high. There is also a chamber among the branches of an evergreen tree, but much richer than any other that they had seen; for it is all filled out with the live green branches of the tree, and on all sides this chamber is so closed in by this verdure that there is no view out except through a few apertures that must be opened up by pushing aside the branches here and there; and in the center, through a concealed pipe, a jet of water rises right in this chamber through the center of a small marble table. Water music is also made here, but they could not hear it, for it was late for people who had to get back to town. They also saw the duke's escutcheon here high over a gateway, very well formed of some branches of trees fostered and maintained in their natural strength by fibers that one can barely discern. They were here in the most unpropitious season for gardens, and were all the more amazed. There is also a handsome grotto, where you see all sorts of animals represented to the life, spouting the water of these fountains, some by the beak, some by the wing, some by the claw or the ear or the nostril.

I forgot to say that in the palace of this prince, in one of the big rooms, is seen the figure of a four-footed animal in bronze relief on a pillar, represented to the life, of a strange shape, the front all scaly,

23 Hercules squeezing Antaeus, figures by Bartolommeo Ammannati.

and on the backbone something that looked like horns. They say that it was found in a mountain cavern of this country and brought here alive a few years ago.[24] We also saw the palace where the Queen Mother was born.[25]

In order to try out all the comforts of this city, as he had of others, Monsieur de Montaigne wanted to see the rooms to let and the conditions of the boarding houses; he found nothing worth while. You find rooms to let only in the hostelries, so they told him; and those that he saw were dirty and much more expensive than in Paris or even in Venice; and the board wretched, at more than twelve crowns a month for the master.

Also there is no worth-while practice either of arms, or of horsemanship, or of letters.

Pewter is rare in all this region, and food is served only in vessels of painted earthenware, rather dirty.

Thursday morning, November 24th, we left here and found a country moderately fertile, very thickly populated and cultivated everywhere, the road bumpy and stony; and in one stretch, which was very long, we came very late to

SIENA, thirty-two miles, four stages; they make them of eight miles, longer than ours ordinarily are.

On Friday Monsieur de Montaigne examined the town with curiosity, notably in respect to our wars.[26] It is an irregular town, planted on the ridge of a hill, on which the better part of the streets are situated; its two slopes are covered with various streets in tiers, and some of these go climbing to still greater heights. It is numbered among the beautiful towns of Italy, but not of the first rank, nor of the size of Florence. Its appearance testifies to its great antiquity. It has a great abundance of fountains, from which most of the private persons drain off small streams for their particular service. They have good, cool cellars here.

The cathedral, which scarcely yields to that of Florence, is coated almost all over, inside and out, with this same marble: square pieces of marble, some a foot thick, others less, which they apply like

24 This seems to be a sculptured Etruscan chimaera, discovered around 1558. The travelers either misunderstood their informant or were misinformed, perhaps deliberately.
25 Catherine de' Medici was born in the Pitti Palace.
26 Siena was captured by the French under Lansac in 1552; though heroically defended under Monluc in 1554–55, it was finally lost.

wainscoting to these buildings made of brick, the ordinary building material of this country.

The handsomest part of the town is the round plaza,[27] very beautiful and grand, curving in from all directions toward the palace that forms one of the fronts of this circle and is less curved than the rest. Opposite the palace, at the upper end of the place, there is a very beautiful fountain, which, through several conduits, fills a great basin where everyone can draw very fine water. Several streets converge in this circle by graded stone steps. There are plenty of very ancient streets and dwellings: the principal ones are those of the Piccolomini, the Ciaia, the Tolomei, and the Colombini, and that of the Cerretani. We saw evidences of three or four hundred years of age. The arms of the city, which you see on many pillars, are the she-wolf with Romulus and Remus hanging at her teats.

The duke of Florence treats the noblemen who favored our side courteously, and has near his person Silvio Piccolomini, the most able nobleman of our time in every kind of knowledge and exercise of arms. As one who has to guard himself principally against his own subjects, he lets his towns take care of fortifying themselves, and concentrates on citadels, which are supplied with arms and guarded with all possible expense and diligence, and with such suspicion that very few people are permitted to approach them.

The women mostly wear hats on their heads. We saw some who took them off out of reverence, like the men, at the point of the elevation during Mass.

We were lodged at the Crown, fairly well, but still without windowpanes or frames.

Monsieur de Montaigne, asked by the gatekeeper at Pratolino whether he was amazed at the beauty of the place, after praising it, strongly condemned the ugliness of the doors and windows – big pine planks, without shape or workmanship, and clumsy and awkward locks like those in our villages – and then the roofing of hollow tiles; and he said that if there was no means of getting slate or lead or brass, they should at least have hidden these tiles by the shape of the building, which the gatekeeper said he would repeat to his master.

The duke still allows the ancient mottoes and emblems of this town to exist, and everywhere these ring of liberty; yet they have taken from their places and hidden in a certain spot in the

27 The Piazza del Campo.

town the tombs and epitaphs of the Frenchmen who died,[28] under color of some improvement in the building and shape of their church.

On Saturday the 26th after dinner we continued the journey through a countryside of similar aspect and came to sup at

BUONCONVENTO, twelve miles, a *castello* of Tuscany: so they call walled villages which, because of their smallness, do not deserve the name of towns.

Sunday morning very early we left here, and since Monsieur de Montaigne wanted to see Montalcino because of the associations the French have had with it, he turned out of his way to the right, and with Messieurs d'Estissac, de Mattecoulon, and du Hautoy, went to the said Montalcino, which they say is a badly built town of the size of Saint-Emilion, situated on one of the highest mountains in the whole region, but accessible. They happened to arrive there as High Mass was being said, and they heard it. At one end there is a castle where the duke keeps his garrisons; but in Monsieur de Montaigne's opinion, all this is not very strong, for the place is commanded on one side by another higher mountain within a hundred paces of it.

In this duke's territories the memory of the French is maintained in such great affection that you can scarcely remind the people of the French without tears coming to their eyes; for even war seems sweeter to them, if accompanied by some form of liberty, than the peace they enjoy under tyranny. When Monsieur de Montaigne inquired there whether there were not some tombs of the Frenchmen, he was answered that there had been several in the Church of Saint Augustine, but that they had been covered up by the duke's command.

The road of this day's journey was mountainous and stony, and brought us in the evening to

LA PAGLIA, twenty-three miles, a tiny village of five or six houses at the foot of several barren and forbidding mountains.

The next morning early we resumed our trip along a very stony bottom, where we crossed and recrossed a hundred times a torrent which runs all the length of it. We came to a big bridge built by the present Pope Gregory, where the territories of the duke of Florence end, and entered those of the Church. We came upon Acquapendente, which is a little town; and it is so named, I believe, because of

28 Those who died in the capture or in the defense of Siena.

a torrent which right next to it hurtles over some rocks into the plain. From there we passed San Lorenzo, which is a walled village, and through Bolseno, which is another, turning about the lake that is named Bolseno, thirty miles long and ten miles wide, in the middle of which are seen two rocks like islands, on which they say there are monasteries. We continued without a halt, by this mountainous and barren road, to

MONTEFIASCONE, twenty-six miles, a little town situated on the top of one of the highest mountains in all the district. It is small, and shows signs of considerable age.

We left here in the morning and crossed a beautiful fertile plain in which we came upon Viterbo, which is in part situated on the crest of a hill. It is a beautiful town, of the size of Senlis. We noticed here many beautiful houses, a great abundance of workmen, beautiful and pleasant streets; in three parts of town, three very beautiful fountains. Monsieur de Montaigne would have stopped here because of the beauty of the place, but his mule, which went ahead of him, had already passed on. Here we began to climb a high mountainside, at the nearer foot of which is a little lake which they call Vico. From there, through a very pleasant valley surrounded by low hills on which there is lots of timber (a somewhat rare commodity in these parts), and by this lake, we came in good time to

RONCIGLIONE, nineteen miles, a little town and castle belonging to the duke of Parma,[29] as there are also on these roads many houses and lands belonging to the house of Farnese.

The inns on this road are of the best, since it is the ordinary post highway. They take five giulii per day to rent a horse, or two giulii per post; and the rate is the same if you want them for two or three posts or for several days, your horse being cared for at no expense to you: for from place to place the landlords take charge of the horses of their fellow landlords; indeed, if your hired one fails you, they stipulate that you can take another instead somewhere else on your road. At Siena, we had the experience of seeing a Fleming who was in our company – unknown, a foreigner, all alone – being trusted with a hired horse which was to take him to Rome. There is this exception, that you pay the hire before starting out; but for the rest, the horse is at your mercy, subject to your word that you will leave him where you promise to.

29 Ottavio Farnese.

Monsieur de Montaigne rejoiced in their custom of dining and supping late, in accordance with his humor; for here they do not dine in the good houses before two in the afternoon or sup before nine; so that in places where we found actors, the play begins only at six o'clock, by torchlight, and lasts two or three hours, and then you go to supper. He said that it was a good country for lazy people, for you get up very late.

We left here the next day three hours before daylight, so eager was he to see the pavement of Rome. He found that the night damp gave his stomach as much trouble morning as evening, or very little less, and felt bad because of it until daylight, although the night was clear. At a distance of fifteen miles we caught sight of the city of Rome, and then lost it again for a long time. There are some villages on the road, and hostelries. We came across some districts with roads raised and paved with very big paving stones, which, to look at them, seemed something ancient; and nearer the city some evidently very ancient ruins, and some stones which the popes have reerected in honor of their antiquity. Most of the ruins are of brick, witness the Baths of Diocletian – a small, simple brick like ours, not of the size and thickness that is seen in the antiquities and old ruins in France and elsewhere.

Rome did not make a great show to see it from this road. We had far on our left the Apennines; the country is unpleasant, full of humps and deep clefts, incapable of allowing the passage of troops in battle formation; the land bare, treeless, to a large extent barren; the country very open for more than ten miles around; and almost all of this sort, with very few houses.

Italy: Rome
(November 30, 1580–April 19, 1581)

Through this sort of country we arrived at about eight in the evening on the last day of November, the feast of Saint Andrew, at the Porta del Popolo, in

ROME, thirty miles. Here they made some difficulties for us, as elsewhere, because of the plague at Genoa.

We took lodgings at the Bear, where we also stayed the next day; and on the second day of December we took rented rooms in the house of a Spaniard, opposite Santa Lucia della Tinta. Here we were well accommodated with three handsome bedrooms, dining room,

larder, stable, and kitchen, at twenty crowns a mouth, out of which the host provided a cook and fire for the kitchen.

The inns are generally furnished a little better than in Paris, since they have a great deal of gilt leather, with which the lodgings of a certain class are upholstered. We could have had lodging at the same price as our own at the Gold Vase, rather near there, upholstered with cloth of gold and silk, like that of kings. But besides that the bedrooms were not separate, Monsieur de Montaigne thought that this magnificence was not only useless but also troublesome on account of the care required by this furniture, for each bed was worth four or five hundred crowns. At our inn we had made a bargain to be supplied with linen about the same as in France; the custom of the country is to be a little more sparing.

Monsieur de Montaigne was annoyed to find so great a number of Frenchmen here that he met almost no one in the street who did not greet him in his own language. New to him was the sight of so great a court, so thronged with prelates and churchmen, and it seemed to him more populous in rich men, and coaches, and horses, by far, than any other that he had ever seen. He said that the appearance of the streets in many respects, and especially in the multitude of people, reminded him more of Paris than any other city he had ever been in.

The modern city is built all along the river Tiber, on both sides. The hilly quarter, which was the site of the old city, where he went every day and took a thousand walks, is occupied by a few churches and some remarkable houses and gardens of the cardinals. He judged by very clear appearances and by the height of the ruins that the shape of these mountains and of the slopes was completely changed from the old shape; and he held it as certain that in many places we were walking on the tops of entire houses. It is easy to judge, by the Arch of Severus, that we are more than two pikes' length above the ancient street level; and in truth, almost everywhere, you walk on the top of old walls which the rain and the coach ruts uncover.

He disagreed with those who compared the freedom of Rome to that of Venice, principally on these grounds: that even the houses were so unsafe that those who brought rather ample means were ordinarily advised to give their purse in keeping to the bankers of the city, so as not to find their strongbox broken open, as had happened to many. *Item*, that going about at night was hardly very safe. *Item*, that in this month of December, our first month here, the general of

the Franciscans was suddenly dismissed from his office and locked up for having condemned in his sermon, at which the Pope and the cardinals were present, the idleness and pomp of the prelates of the Church, without going into any particulars, and merely using, with some asperity in his voice, some ordinary commonplaces on this subject. *Item*, that his [Montaigne's] baggage had been inspected by the customs on his entry into the city, and examined right down to the smallest articles, whereas in most of the other cities of Italy these officers were content when you merely offered your baggage for inspection; and that besides this, they had taken from him all the books they had found in order to examine them, which took so long that a man who had anything else to do might well consider them lost; besides, the rules were so extraordinary here that the book of hours of Our Lady, because it was of Paris, not of Rome, was suspect to them, and also the books of certain German doctors of theology against the heretics, because in combating them they made mention of their errors. In this connection he was grateful for his good luck because, though he had not been warned at all that this was to happen to him, and though he had passed through Germany and was of an inquiring nature, he had no forbidden book in the lot. However, some lords of the city told him that even if some had been found, he would have got off with the loss of the books.

Twelve or fifteen days after our arrival he felt ill; and because of an unusual defluxion of his kidneys which threatened him with some kind of ulcer, by the prescription of a French doctor of the Cardinal de Rambouillet, aided by the dexterity of his apothecary, he overcame his scruples one day and took some cassia in big doses on the end of a knife first lightly dipped in water, which he swallowed very easily, and had two or three stools from it. The next day he took some Venetian turpentine, which they say comes from the mountains of Tyrol, two large doses done up in a wafer on a silver spoon, sprinkled with one or two drops of some good-tasting syrup; he observed no other effect from it than a smell of March violets in his urine. After that he took three times, but not in quick succession, a certain sort of drink that had precisely the taste and color of almond milk, and indeed his doctor told him it was just that; however, he thinks there were some *quatre-semences-froides*[1] in it.

1 A combination of the four "cold" seeds: cucumber, gourd, melon, and pumpkin.

There was nothing difficult or extraordinary in the taking of this last except the hour of the morning: all that, three hours before the meal. Nor did he feel what good that almond milk did him, for the same indisposition still lasted afterward; and later, on the twenty-third of December, he had a very severe colic, for which he took to his bed around noon and was there until evening, when he ejected a lot of gravel, and after that a big hard stone, long and smooth, which stopped five or six hours in passing through the penis. All this time, since his baths, his bowels had been in good order, and he thought that this protected him against many worse accidents. At this time he skipped several meals, now dinner, now supper.

On Christmas Day we went to hear the Pope's Mass at Saint Peter's, where Monsieur de Montaigne had a convenient place for seeing all the ceremonies at his ease. There are several particular forms: the Gospel and the Epistle are said first in Latin and then in Greek, as is also done on Easter Day and Saint Peter's Day. The Pope gave Communion to several others, and with him at this service there officiated the cardinals Farnese, Medici, Caraffa, and Gonzaga. There is a certain instrument for drinking from the chalice, in order to provide safety from poison. It seemed novel to him, both at this Mass and others, that the Pope and cardinals and other prelates are seated, and, almost all through the Mass, covered, chatting and talking together. These ceremonies seem to be more magnificent than devout.

For the rest, it seemed to him that there was nothing special about the beauty of the women worthy of that preeminence that reputation gives to this city over all the others in the world; and moreover that, as in Paris, the most singular beauty was found among those who put it on sale.

On December 29th Monsieur d'Elbène, who was then ambassador, a studious gentleman and long a good friend of Monsieur de Montaigne, recommended that he kiss the Pope's feet. Monsieur d'Estissac and he got into the said ambassador's coach. When the ambassador was admitted to audience, he had them called by the Pope's chamberlain. They found the Pope and with him the ambassador alone, which is the fashion; he has beside him a little bell that he rings when he wants someone to come to him. The ambassador was seated at his left hand, uncovered; for the Pope never takes off his cap for anyone whatever, nor is any ambassador with him with his head covered. Monsieur d'Estissac entered first, and after him Monsieur de Montaigne, and then Messieurs de

Mattecoulon and du Hautoy. After one or two steps into the chamber, in the corner of which the said Pope is seated, those who enter, whoever they may be, put one knee on the ground and wait for the Pope to give them his benediction, which he does; after that they get up again and proceed until about the middle of the room. It is true that most people do not go straight to him, cutting across the room, but sidle along the wall in order, after turning, to make straight for him. At this halfway point they once more get down on one knee and receive the second benediction. This done, they go toward him as far as a velvet carpet spread out at his feet seven or eight feet farther forward. At the edge of this carpet they go down on both knees. There the ambassador, who was presenting them, knelt on one knee and pulled back the Pope's robe from his right foot, on which there is a red slipper with a white cross on it. Those who are on their knees drag themselves in this position up to his foot and lean down to the ground to kiss it. Monsieur de Montaigne said he had raised the end of his foot a bit. They made way for one another to kiss, then withdrew to one side, still in this posture. This done, the ambassador covered the Pope's foot again, and, rising from his seat, told him what seemed proper for the recommendation of Monsieur d'Estissac and Monsieur de Montaigne. The Pope, with a courteous countenance, admonished Monsieur d'Estissac to pursue study and virtue, and Monsieur de Montaigne to continue in the devotion he had always borne to the Church and the service of the Most Christian King, and said that he would gladly be of service to them whenever he could: those are Italian phrases of service. They for their part said not a word to him; but having there received another benediction before the Pope rose, which is the sign of dismissal, went back the same way. This is done according to each person's notion; however, the commonest way is to move away backward, or at least to withdraw to the side, in such a way that one always looks the Pope in the face. At the halfway point, as in coming, they again went down on one knee and had another benediction; and at the door, again on one knee, the final benediction.

The language of the Pope is Italian, smacking of the Bolognese patois, which is the worst idiom in Italy; and then by nature his speech is halting.[2] For the rest, he is a very handsome old man, of middle height, erect, his face full of majesty, a long white beard,

2 This is Pope Gregory XIII (Ugo Buoncompagno of Bologna, 1502–1585), Pope from 1572 until his death, a strong fighter against Protestantism, who

more than eighty years old, as healthy and vigorous for his age as anyone can wish, without gout, without colic, without stomach trouble, and not subject to any ailment: of a gentle nature, not very passionate about the affairs of the world; a great builder, and in that respect he will leave in Rome and elsewhere exceptional honor to his memory; a great almoner, I should say beyond all measure. Among other evidences of this, there is not a girl about to marry whom he does not aid in setting up house, if she is of low estate; and in this respect they count his liberality as ready money. Besides that,[3] he has built colleges for the Greeks, and for the English, Scots, French, Germans, and Poles, and has endowed each one with more than ten thousand crowns a year in perpetuity, besides the huge expense of the buildings. He has done this to call to the Church the children of those nations, corrupted by evil opinions against the Church; and there the boys are lodged, fed, dressed, instructed, and provided with everything, without one quattrino of their own going into it for anything whatever. The troublesome public charges he readily casts off on the shoulders of others and avoids giving himself trouble.

He gives as many audiences as one wants. His replies are short and decided, and you waste your time if you combat his reply with new arguments. In what he judges to be just, he trusts himself; and even for his son, whom he loves with a frenzy, he will not stir a bit against this justice of his. He gives advancement to his relations, but[4] without any prejudice to the rights of the Church, which he preserves inviolable. He is very lavish in public buildings and the improvement of the city's streets; and in truth, his life and his conduct have nothing very extraordinary about them one way or the other, but incline much more to the good.

On the last day of December the two of them [Montaigne and d'Estissac] dined at the house of the cardinal of Sens, who observes more of the Roman ceremonies than any other Frenchman. The very long benedicites and graces were said by two

publicly celebrated the Massacre of Saint Bartholomew's Day. Most of the details given here, except for his age, are confirmed by other witnesses.

3 These few lines, from "there is not" to "Besides that," are an addition to the manuscript in Montaigne's hand.

4 The following passage, from "but without" to "the city's streets," and the shorter one a few lines later, "but incline much more to the good," are additions to the manuscript in Montaigne's hand.

chaplains in response to each other in the fashion of the church service. During his dinner a paraphrase of the Gospel of the day was read in Italian. They washed with him both before and after the meal. Everyone is served with a napkin to wipe his mouth and hands with; and in front of those to whom they want to do particular honor, who are seated beside or opposite the master, they place big silver squares on which their saltcellar stands, of the same sort as those they put before the great in France. On top of this there is a napkin folded in four, and on this napkin the bread, knife, fork, and spoon. On top of all this there is another napkin, which you are to use, and leave the rest in the state it is in; for after you are at table, they give you, beside this square, a silver or earthenware plate which you use. Of all that is served at table the carver gives portions on plates to those who are seated, in the order of seating, and they do not put their hand to the dish, least of all to the master's dish.

They also served Monsieur de Montaigne with drink, as they ordinarily did at the ambassador's when he ate there, in this way: they presented to him a silver basin on which there was a glass with wine and a little bottle, of the size of those you put ink in, full of water. He takes this glass with his right hand and this bottle with the left, and pours as much water as he likes into his glass, and then puts this bottle back into the basin. When he drinks, the man who serves him offers the said basin under his chin, and he himself then replaces his glass in the said basin. This ceremony is performed only for one or two persons at most below the master.

The table was removed immediately after grace, and the chairs promptly arranged along one side of the room, on which the cardinal had them sit, after him. Then there appeared two churchmen, well dressed, with I know not what instruments in their hands, who knelt before the cardinal and informed him of I know not what service that was being performed in some church. He said nothing at all to them, but as they rose after speaking and were going away, he raised his cap to them a little.

A little later he took them in his coach to the Hall of the Consistory, where the cardinals assembled to go to vespers. The Pope arrived and dressed to go to vespers too. The cardinals did not kneel at his benediction, as the people do, but received it with a deep inclination of the head.

On the third day of January, 1581, the Pope passed in front of our window. In front of him walked about two hundred horses bearing

persons of his court of one or the other robe.[5] Beside him was the Cardinal de' Medici, who was conversing with him covered and was taking him to dine with him. The Pope had on a red hat, his white apparel and red velvet hood, as usual, and was mounted on a white hackney harnessed with red velvet with gold fringes and lace. He mounts on horseback without the help of a groom, and yet is in his eighty-first year. Every fifteen steps he gave his benediction. After him came three cardinals, and then about a hundred men-at-arms, lance on thigh, in full armor except for the head. There was also another hackney with the same trappings, a mule, a handsome white charger, and a litter following him, and two robe bearers who carried valises at their saddlebow.

That same day Monsieur de Montaigne took some turpentine, without any reason except that he had a cold, and afterward he passed a lot of gravel.

On January 11th, in the morning, as Monsieur de Montaigne was leaving the house on horseback to go to the bankers', it happened that they were taking out of prison Catena, a famous robber and bandit captain who had kept all Italy in fear and to whom some monstrous murders were ascribed, especially those of two Capuchins whom he had made to deny God, promising on that condition to save their lives, and then massacred without any reason either of advantage or of vengeance. Monsieur de Montaigne stopped to see this spectacle. Besides the formalities used in France, they carry in front of the criminal a big crucifix covered with a black curtain, and on foot go a large number of men dressed and masked in linen, who, they say, are gentlemen and other prominent people of Rome who devote themselves to this service of accompanying criminals led to execution and the bodies of the dead; and there is a brotherhood of them. There are two of these, or monks dressed and masked in the same way, who attend the criminal on the cart and preach to him; and one of them continually holds before his face a picture on which is the portrait of Our Lord, and has him kiss it incessantly; this makes it impossible to see the criminal's face from the street. At the gallows, which is a beam between two supports, they still kept this picture against his face until he was launched. He made an ordinary death, without movement or word; he was a dark man of thirty or thereabouts.

After he was strangled, they cut him into four quarters. They

5 Churchmen or laymen.

hardly ever kill men except by a simple death, and exercise their severity after death. Monsieur de Montaigne here remarked what he has said elsewhere,[6] how much the people are frightened by the rigors exercised on dead bodies; for these people, who had appeared to feel nothing at seeing him strangled, at every blow that was given to cut him up cried out in a piteous voice. As soon as a criminal is dead, one or several Jesuits or others get up on some high spot and shout to the people, one in this direction, the other in that, and preach to them to make them take in this example.

We remarked in Italy, and especially in Rome, that there are almost no bells at all for the service of the Church, and less in Rome than in the smallest village in France; also that there are no images, unless they have been made very recently. Many old churches have not a one.

On January 14th he again took turpentine without any apparent effect.

On this same day I saw two brothers executed, former servants of the Castellano's secretary, who had killed him a few days before in the city by night, in the very palace of the said Signor Giacomo Buoncompagno, the Pope's son. They tore them with red-hot pincers, then cut off their fist in front of the said palace, and having cut it off they put on the wound capons that they had killed and immediately opened up. They were executed on a scaffold: first they were clubbed with a big wooden mace, and then their throats were cut immediately. This is a punishment they say is sometimes used in Rome, though others maintained that it had been adapted to the misdeed, since they had killed their master in that way.

As for the size of Rome, Monsieur de Montaigne said that the space enclosed by the walls, which is more than two-thirds empty, including ancient and modern Rome, might equal the enclosure you would make around Paris if you walled in all the *faubourgs* that surround it. But if you count the size by the number and crowding of houses and habitations, he thinks that Rome does not come within a third of the size of Paris. In the number and size of public squares, and beauty of streets and houses, Rome wins by far.

He also found the cold of winter very nearly approaching that of Gascony. There were heavy frosts around Christmas, and some unbearably cold winds. It is true that even then there is very often thunder, hail, and lightning.

6 *Essays* II: 11, p. 382.

The palaces are divided into numerous apartments, one leading to another; you thread your way through three or four rooms before you are in the principal one. In certain places where Monsieur de Montaigne dined in ceremony, the buffets are not where you dine but in another room through which you pass first, and they go there to get you a drink when you ask for it; and the silver plate is on display there.

Thursday, January 26th, Monsieur de Montaigne – after going to see Mount Janiculum, beyond the Tiber, and to look at the sights of that place (among others a large piece of old wall that had fallen in ruins two days before), and to contemplate the configuration of all the parts of Rome, which may not be seen so clearly from any other place; and from there having gone down to the Vatican to see the statues enclosed in the niches of the Belvedere and the beautiful gallery that the Pope is erecting for paintings from all parts of Italy, which is very nearly finished – lost his purse and what was in it; and he thought what had happened was that in giving alms two or three times, the weather being very rainy and unpleasant, instead of putting his purse back into his pocket he had slipped it through the slashings of his breeches.

All these days he spent his time only in studying Rome. At the beginning he had taken a French guide; but when this man quit because of some fancy or other, he made it a point of pride to learn all about Rome by his own study, aided by various maps and books that he had read to him in the evening; and in the daytime he would go on the spot to put his apprenticeship into practice; so that in a few days he could easily have guided his guide.

He said that one saw nothing of Rome but the sky under which it had stood and the plan of its site; that this knowledge that he had of it was an abstract and contemplative knowledge of which there was nothing perceptible to the senses; that those who said that one at least saw the ruins of Rome said too much, for the ruins of so awesome a machine would bring more honor and reverence to its memory: this was nothing but its sepulcher. The world, hostile to its long domination, had first broken and shattered all the parts of this wonderful body; and because, even though quite dead, over-thrown, and disfigured, it still terrified the world, the world had buried its very ruin. These little signs of its ruin that still appear above the bier had been preserved by fortune as testimony to that infinite greatness which so many centuries, so many conflagrations, and all the many conspiracies of the world to ruin it had not been

able to extinguish completely. But it was likely that these disfigured limbs which remained were the least worthy, and that the fury of the enemies of that immortal glory had impelled them to destroy first of all what was most beautiful and most worthy; and the buildings of this bastard Rome which they were now attaching to these ancient ruins, although fully adequate to carry away the present age with admiration, reminded him precisely of the nests which sparrows and crows in France suspend from the arches and walls of the churches that the Huguenots have recently demolished.

He feared further, seeing the space that this tomb occupies, that we were not aware of all of it, and that the sepulcher itself was for the most part buried; and that judging from the fact that such paltry rubble as pieces of tile and broken pots had built up in ancient times to a pile of such excessive size that it equals in height and breadth several natural mountains (for he compared it in height to the hill of Gurson and estimated it to be twice as broad),[7] this must have been an express ordinance of the Fates, to make the world feel that they had conspired for the glory and preeminence of this city by so novel and extraordinary a testimonial to its greatness.

He said he could not easily make people agree, seeing the small space occupied by some of these seven hills, and notably the most famous ones, like the Capitoline and the Palatine, that so great a number of buildings had been arrayed there. Merely to see what remains of the Temple of Peace, beside the Forum Romanum, of whose quite recent fall you still see evidence, as of a great mountain broken up into many horrible rocks, it does not seem that two such buildings could fit into the whole space of the Capitoline Hill, where there were fully twenty-five or thirty temples, besides many private houses.

But in truth, many conjectures that we make from the description of this ancient city have hardly any verisimilitude, since even its site has infinitely changed in form, some of the valleys having been filled up, even in the lowest places that were there; as for example, in the place of the Velabrum, which because of its lowness received the sewage of the city and had a lake, hills have arisen of the height of the other, natural hills that are round about, as a result of the piling and heaping up of the ruins of these great buildings; and Mount Savello is nothing but the ruin of a part of the Theater of Marcellus.

7 The short passage in parentheses is an addition to the manuscript in Montaigne's hand.

He thought that an ancient Roman could not recognize the site of his city even if he saw it. It has often happened that after digging deep down into the ground people would come merely down to the head of a very high column which was still standing down below. They do not seek any other foundations for their houses than old ruined buildings or vaults, such as are seen at the bottom of all the cellars, nor the support of the ancient foundation or of a wall which is in its place; but on the very broken pieces of the old buildings, however fortune has located them, they have planted the feet of their new palaces, as on great chunks of rocks, firm and assured. It is easy to see that many streets are more than thirty feet below those of today.

On January 28th Monsieur de Montaigne had the colic, which did not keep him from any of his ordinary actions, and passed a rather biggish stone and other smaller ones.

On the 30th he went to see the most ancient religious ceremony there is among men, and watched it very attentively and with great profit: that is, the circumcision of the Jews.

He had already seen their synagogue at another time, one Saturday morning, and their prayers, in which they sing without order, as in the Calvinist churches, certain lessons from the Bible in Hebrew, that are suited to the occasion. They sing the same songs, but with extreme discord, because they do not keep time and because of the confusion of so many voices of every sort of age; for the children, even the very youngest, take part, and all without exception understand Hebrew. They pay no more attention to their prayers than we do to ours, talking of other affairs in the midst of them and not bringing much reverence to their mysteries. They wash their hands on coming in, and in that place it is an execrable thing to doff one's hat; but they bow the head and knees where their devotions ordain it. They wear over their shoulders or on their head a sort of cloth with fringes attached: the whole thing would be too long to describe. After dinner their doctors each in turn give a lesson on the Bible passage for that day, doing it in Italian. After the lesson some other doctor present selects some one of the hearers, and sometimes two or three in succession, to argue with the reader about what he had said. The one we heard seemed to him to argue with great eloquence and wit.

But as for the circumcision, it is done in private houses, in the most convenient and lightest room in the boy's house. Where he was, because the house was inconvenient, the ceremony was

performed at the entrance door. They give the boys a godfather and a godmother, as we do; the father names the child. They circumcise them on the eighth day from their birth. The godfather sits down on a table and puts a pillow on his lap; the godmother brings him the infant there and then goes away. The child is wrapped in our style; the godfather unwraps him below, and then those present and the man who is to do the operation all begin to sing, and accompany with songs all this action, which lasts a short quarter of an hour. The minister may be other than a rabbi, and whatever he may be among them, everyone wishes to be called to this office, for they hold that it is a great blessing to be employed at it often: indeed, they pay to be invited to do it, offering, one a garment, another some other commodity for the child; and they hold that he who has circumcised up to a certain number, which they know, when he is dead has this privilege, that the parts of his mouth are never eaten by worms.

On the table where this godfather is seated there is also a great preparation of all the instruments necessary for this operation. Besides that, a man holds in his hands a phial full of wine and a glass. There is also a brazier on the ground, at which brazier this minister first warms his hands, and then, finding this child all stripped, as the godfather holds him on his lap with his head toward him, he takes his member and with one hand pulls back toward himself the skin that is over it, with the other pushing the glans and the member within. To the end of this skin which he holds toward the said glans he applies a silver instrument which stops the said skin there and keeps the cutting edge from injuring the glans and the flesh. After that, with a knife he cuts off this skin, which they immediately bury in some earth which is there in a basin among the other preparations for this mystery. After that the minister with his bare nails plucks up also some other particle of skin which is on this glans and tears it off by force and pushes the skin back beyond the glans.

It seems there is much effort and pain in this; however, they find no danger in it, and the wound is always cured in four or five days. The boy's outcry is like that of ours when they are baptized. As soon as this glans is thus uncovered, they hastily offer some wine to the minister, who puts a little in his mouth and then goes and sucks the glans of this child, all bloody, and spits out the blood he has drawn from it, and immediately takes as much wine again, up to three times. This done, they offer him, in a little paper cup, some red

powder which they say is dragon's blood,[8] with which he salts and covers the whole wound; and then he very tidily wraps this boy's member with cloths cut specially for this. That done, they give him a glass full of wine, which wine they say he blesses by some prayers that he says. He takes a swallow of it, and then dipping his finger in it he three times takes a drop of it with his finger to the boy's mouth to be sucked; and afterward they send this glass, in the same state, to the mother and the women, who are in some other part of the house, to drink what wine is left. Besides that, another person takes a silver instrument, round as a tennis ball, held by a long handle (which instrument is pierced with little holes, like our cassolettes), and carries it to the nose, first of the minister, and then of the child, and then of the godfather: they suppose that these are odors to confirm and enlighten minds for devotion. He meanwhile still has his mouth all bloody.

On the 8th, and then again on the 12th, he had a touch of colic and passed some stones without great pain.

The Shrovetide that took place in Rome that year was more licentious, by permission of the Pope, than it had been for several years before: we found, however, that it was not much of a thing. Along the Corso, which is a long street in Rome that gets its name from this very thing, they race, now four or five boys, now some Jews, now some old men stark naked, from one end of the street to the other. You have no pleasure in it except in seeing them pass in front of the place where you are. They do the same with horses, on which are little boys who drive them with whips, and with donkeys and buffaloes driven with goads by men on horseback. For each race there is a prize offered which they call *il palio*: pieces of velvet or cloth. The gentlemen, in a certain part of the street where the ladies have a better view, run at the quintain on fine horses, and have good grace at it; for there is nothing that this nobility so commonly knows how to do well as exercises on horseback. The stand which Monsieur de Montaigne had made cost them three crowns. It was indeed situated in a very fine place in the street.

On those days all the beautiful gentlewomen of Rome were seen at leisure: for in Italy they do not mask themselves as in France, and show themselves with faces quite uncovered. As for perfect and rare beauty, there is no more of it, he said, than in France, and except in three or four he found no excellence; but commonly they are more

8 A red resin used as an astringent.

attractive, and you do not see so many ugly ones as in France. Their heads are without comparison more advantageously dressed, and the lower part below the girdle. The body is better in France: for here they are too loose around the girdle and carry that part like our pregnant women. Their countenance has more majesty, softness, and sweetness. There is no comparison between the richness of their apparel and of ours: all is full of pearls and precious stones. Wherever they let themselves be seen in public, whether in a coach, at a festival, or in the theater, they are apart from the men; however, at dances they intermingle freely enough, where there are occasions for talking and touching hands.

The men are very simply dressed, for all occasions, in black and Florentine serge; and because they are a little darker than we are, they somehow do not look like dukes, counts, and marquises, which they are, but have a rather mean appearance; for the rest, they are as courteous and gracious as possible, whatever the common run of Frenchmen say, who cannot call people gracious who find it hard to endure their excesses and their ordinary insolence. In every way we do all we can to get a bad reputation here. However, they have an ancient affection or reverence for France which makes those people very respected and welcome who deserve the least bit to be, and who merely control themselves without offending them.

On Thursday before Lent he went to the feast of the Castellano. A good deal of preparation had been made, notably an amphitheater very artfully and richly disposed for combat in the lists, which combat took place at night, before supper, in a square barn with an oval-shaped entrenchment in the middle. Among other singularities, the pavement was painted in an instant with various designs in red: having first coated the pavement with some sort of plaster or lime, they laid over it a piece of parchment or leather cut into a stencil of the devices they wanted; and then they passed a brush dipped in red over this piece and printed through the openings what they wanted on the pavement, and so quickly that in two hours the whole nave of a church would be painted so.

At supper the ladies are served by their husbands, who stand about them and give them drink and what they ask for. They served a great deal of roast fowl dressed in its natural feathers as if alive; capons cooked entire in glass bottles; quantities of hares, rabbits, and live birds in pasties; admirably folded linen. The ladies' table, which was of four dishes, could be taken off in pieces, and underneath there was another all served and covered with sweetmeats.

The men do not wear masks when they go visiting. They do wear inexpensive masks when they walk about town in public or set up teams for tilting at the ring. There were two fine rich companies got up in this fashion on Shrove Monday to run at the quintain; they surpass us above all in abundance of very handsome horses.

[THE JOURNAL BY MONTAIGNE IN FRENCH]

Having dismissed the one of my men who was doing this fine job, and seeing it so far advanced, whatever trouble it may be to me, I must continue it myself.

On February 16th, returning from the station,[9] I came across a priest in vestments in a little chapel busy curing a possessed man: he was a melancholy man and as if half dead. They were holding him on his knees before the altar, with some kind of cloth around his neck by which they held him fast. The priest read in his presence lots of prayers and exorcisms, commanding the devil to leave this body, and he read them from his breviary. After this he turned his remarks to the patient, now speaking to him, now speaking to the devil in his person, and then insulting him, beating him with great blows of his fist, spitting in his face. The patient replied to his questions with a few inept replies: now for himself, saying how he felt the movements of his malady; now for the devil, how much he feared God and how much these exorcisms acted against him. After that, which lasted a long time, the priest, for his last effort, retired to the altar and took the pyx, in which was the *Corpus Domini*, in his left hand, in the other hand holding a lighted taper upside down so that he made it melt and be consumed, meanwhile uttering prayers, and at the end harsh and threatening words against the devil, in the loudest and most magisterial voice he could. As the first candle went out close to his fingers, he took another, and then a second and third additional one. This done, he replaced the pyx, that is to say the transparent vessel containing the *Corpus Domini*, and came and joined the patient again, speaking to him now as to a man, had him untied, and returned him to his people to take him back home.

He told us that this devil was of the worst type, obstinate, and would cost a lot of effort to cast out. And to ten or twelve of us gentlemen who were there he told several stories about this science and his ordinary experience of it, notably that the day before he had

9 A church where a procession goes for a service.

rid a woman of a big devil who, in coming out, had pushed nails, pins, and a tuft of his hair out of this woman through her mouth. And because someone answered him that she was not yet completely recovered, he said that this was another sort of spirit, lighter and less harmful, who had returned into her that morning; but that this sort (for he knows their names, their divisions, and their most particular distinctions) was easy to conjure. That is all I saw. My man made no other face than to gnash his teeth and twist his mouth when they presented the *Corpus Domini* to him, and he sometimes mouthed these words, *si fata volent*;[10] for he was a notary, and knew a little Latin.

On the first day of March I went to the station of Saint Sixtus.[11] At the high altar the priest who was saying Mass was beyond the altar, his face turned toward the people; behind him there was no one. The Pope went there that same day; a few days before he had had removed from this church the nuns who were there, because that place was a little too far out of the way, and had accommodated there all the poor who were begging throughout the city – a very fine arrangement. The cardinals gave twenty crowns each to start this movement off, and extremely generous alms were given by other private persons. The Pope endowed this hospital with five hundred crowns a month.

In Rome there are a great many private devotions and brotherhoods in which many great evidences of piety are seen. The people as a whole seem to me less devout than in the good towns in France, though indeed more ceremonious, for in that respect they are extreme. I am writing here in freedom of conscience. Here are two examples.

While a certain man was in bed with a courtesan, amid the license of that relationship, behold at midnight the Ave Maria rang; she immediately jumped out of bed onto the floor and got on her knees to say her prayer. When a man was with another courtesan, behold the good mother (for the young ones especially have old governesses, whom they treat as mothers or aunts) comes banging at the door, and with anger and fury tears from this young one's neck a ribbon from which hung a little Madonna, so as not to contaminate it with the filth of her sin.

10 "If the Fates will."
11 The Sistine Chapel. The nuns were removed (and replaced by the poor) not from the chapel itself but from a neighboring convent.

The young one felt extreme contrition for having forgotten to take it from her neck as she was accustomed to do.

The ambassador from the tsar of Muscovy also came that day to this station, dressed in a scarlet mantle and a cassock of cloth of gold, with a hat in the form of a nightcap, of cloth of gold, furred, and beneath it a skullcap of cloth of silver. He is the second ambassador who has come from Muscovy to the Pope. The other was in the time of Pope Paul III. There they maintained that his mission was to move the Pope to interpose in the war that the king of Poland was making on his master, alleging that it was up to his master to sustain the first attack of the Turk, and that if his neighbor weakened him he would remain incapable of the other war, which would be a great window opened to the Turk to come at us; offering besides to give ground on certain differences in religion that he had with the Roman Church. He was lodged with the Castellano, as the other one had been in the time of Pope Paul, and was entertained at the Pope's expense. He strongly insisted on not kissing the Pope's feet but only his right hand, and would not give in until it was attested to him that the Emperor himself was subject to that ceremony: for the example of kings was not enough for him. He did not know how to speak any language but his own, and had come without an interpreter. He had only three or four men in his retinue, and said that he had passed through great danger in crossing Poland in disguise. His nation is so ignorant of the affairs of this part of the world that he brought to Venice letters from his master addressed to the Grand Governor of the Signory of Venice. Questioned about the meaning of this inscription, he said that they thought Venice was under the dominion of the Pope and that he sent governors there as he did to Bologna and elsewhere. God knows with what relish these magnificos received this piece of ignorance! He made presents, both there and to the Pope, of sables and black fox, which is a still rarer and richer fur.

On March 6th I went to see the Vatican Library, which is in five or six large rooms all in a row. There are a large number of books attached onto several rows of desks; there are also some in coffers, which were all opened to me; lots of books written by hand, and especially a Seneca and the *Moral Essays* of Plutarch. Among the remarkable things I saw there were the statue of the good Aristides with a handsome bald head, a thick beard, a big forehead, a look full of gentleness and majesty: his name is written on the very ancient pedestal; a book from China, in strange characters, the leaves made

of some material much softer and more pellucid than our paper; and because this cannot endure the stain of ink, the writing is on only one side of the sheet, and the sheets are all double and folded at the outside edges, by which they hold together. They think it is the membrane of some tree. I also saw a bit of the ancient papyrus, on which there were unknown characters: it is the bark of a tree. I saw the breviary of Saint Gregory, written by hand; it bears no evidence of the year, but they hold that it has come down from him from hand to hand. It is a missal about like ours, and was brought to the last Council of Trent to serve as a testimony of our ceremonies. I saw a book by Saint Thomas Aquinas in which there are corrections in the hand of the author himself, who wrote badly, a small lettering worse than mine. *Item*, a Bible printed on parchment, one of those that Plantin has just done in four languages, which King Philip sent to the present Pope, as is stated in the inscription on the binding; the original of the book that the king of England[12] composed against Luther, which he sent about fifty years ago to Pope Leo X, inscribed with his own hand, with this most elegant Latin distich, also in his own hand:

> To Leo Ten, Henry, king of the English, sends
> This work, a pledge of loyalty between two friends.

I read the prefaces, the one to the Pope, the other to the reader: he excuses himself because of his military occupations and lack of ability; for scholastic Latin, it is good.

I saw the library without any difficulty; anyone can see it thus, and can make whatever extracts he wants; and it is open almost every morning. I was guided all through it and invited by a gentleman to use it whenever I wanted. Our ambassador was leaving Rome at that time without having seen it, and complained that they wanted him to pay court to Cardinal Sirleto, master of this library, for this permission: and, he said, he had never been able to see that handwritten Seneca, as he hugely desired to do. Fortune brought me to it, since on this testimony of his I considered the thing hopeless. All things are easy in this way from certain angles, and inaccessible from others. Opportunity and opportuneness have their privileges, and often offer to the common people what they refuse to kings. Curiosity often gets in its own way, as also do greatness and power.

12 Henry VIII.

I also saw here a handwritten Virgil in extremely large lettering and those long, narrow characters that we see here in the inscriptions of the time of the emperors, as for example around the age of Constantine, which have a sort of Gothic fashion and have lost that square proportion that is in the old Latin writings. This Virgil confirmed me in what I have always judged, that the first four lines that they put in the *Aeneid*[13] are borrowed: this book does not have them. There is an Acts of the Apostles written in very beautiful gold Greek lettering, as fresh and recent as if it were of today. This lettering is massive and has a solid body raised on the paper, so that if you pass your hand over it you feel the thickness. I think we have lost the use of this kind of writing.

On March 13th an old patriarch of Antioch, an Arab, very well versed in five or six languages of that part of the world, and having no knowledge of Greek or any other of our tongues, with whom I had become quite intimate, made me a present of a certain mixture to help my stone, and prescribed the use of it for me in writing. He enclosed it for me in a little earthenware pot, and told me that I could keep it ten or twenty years, and hoped for such results from it that from the first taking I should be completely cured of my malady. In order that, if I should lose his writing, I may find it here: "You must take this drug as you are going to bed after a light supper, in a dose the size of two peas, and mix it with lukewarm water after crumbling it with your fingers, and take it five times, leaving out every other day."

Dining one day in Rome with our ambassador, with Muret[14] and other learned men present, I got on the subject of the French translation of Plutarch;[15] and against those who esteemed it much less highly than I do, I maintained at least this: that where the translator missed the real meaning of Plutarch, he has substituted

13 These lines are not included in the text in modern editions.
14 Marc-Antoine Muret (1526–85), one of the leading Latinists of his time, a teacher of Montaigne at the Collège de Guyenne in Bordeaux, author of a Latin play *Julius Caesar*, commentator of Ronsard's first *Amours*. He fled from France to Italy in 1554 because of a morals charge, and from 1563 on taught at the University of Rome. Montaigne praises him in the *Essays* (I: 26, pp. 156–7) as the best orator of his time.
15 The famous Amyot translation of the *Lives* (1559) and *Moral Essays* (1572), which were Montaigne's favorite books. See *Essays* II: 4, p. 318, and *passim*.

another that is probable and well in keeping with what precedes and what follows. In order to show me that even in this I was granting him too much, two passages were produced. One, the critique of which they attribute to the son of Monsieur Mangot, advocate in the Parlement of Paris, who had just left Rome, is in the "Life of Solon," at about the middle, where he says that Solon boasted of having freed Attica and removed the boundaries that separated inherited plots of land. He was wrong, for the Greek word signifies certain marks which were placed on lands that were mortgaged or alienated, so that purchasers should be warned of this mortgage. What he substituted about "limits" has no recognizable sense, for that would be making the lands not free but common. Estienne's Latin[16] comes closer to the truth. The second passage, right at the end of the treatise "On the Education of Children": "The observation of these rules," he says, "may rather be wished than advised." The Greek, they say, suggests "is more to be desired than hoped for," a sort of proverb that is found elsewhere. Instead of this clear and easy meaning, the one the translator has substituted is weak and strange. Wherefore, accepting their assumptions about the proper meaning of the words, I admitted their conclusion in good faith.

The churches in Rome are less beautiful than in most of the good towns of Italy, and likewise in Italy and Germany in general they are ordinarily less beautiful than in France. At Saint Peter's one sees, at the entrance of the new church, banners hanging as trophies: their inscription states that they are banners won by the king [of France] from the Huguenots; it does not specify where and when. Beside the Gregorian chapel, in which you see an infinite number of votive tablets attached to the wall, there is among others a little square picture, rather wretched and badly painted, of the battle of Mont-contour. In the room next to the Sistine Chapel (where, on the wall, there are several paintings of memorable incidents concerning the Holy See, such as the naval battle of John of Austria),[17] there is a picture representing that Pope treading underfoot the head of that Emperor[18] who came to ask his pardon and kiss his feet; but not the

16 The Latin translation by Henri Estienne (Stephanus) in 1572.

17 The great victory of the Spaniards and Venetians over the Turks at Lepanto in 1571.

18 Pope Alexander III and Frederick Barbarossa, in Venice, in 1177. The Emperor acknowledged Saint Peter's right to tread enemies underfoot, and the Pope then claimed it equally for himself.

words spoken by both men according to history. There are also two places where the wounding and the death of Admiral de Châtillon[19] are painted very authentically.

On March 15th Monsieur de Monluc[20] came to get me at day-break to carry out the plan we had made the day before of going to see Ostia. We crossed the Tiber by the Bridge of Our Lady and went out by the Porta del Porto, which in ancient times they called Port-uensis; from there we followed an uneven road, through country moderately fertile in wines and wheat; and after about eight miles, returning to the Tiber, we descended into a large plain covered with meadows and pasture land, at the end of which was once situated a large town, many great and handsome ruins of which may be seen on the shores of the Lake of Trajan, which is an overflow of the Tyrrhenian Sea and into which ships used to come; but now the sea comes into it only very little, and still less into another lake a little above this place, which they call the Port of Claudius. We might have dined here with the cardinal of Perugia, who was there; and in truth there is nothing so courteous as these lords and their servants. And the said lord cardinal sent me word by one of my men who promptly went to convey my respects that he had reason to complain of me; and this same valet was taken for a drink to the wine cellar of the said cardinal, who had no friendship or acquaintance with me, and in this was practicing only an ordinary hospitality toward all strangers who have some breeding. However, I was afraid that the daylight might fail us for making the tour I wanted to make, since I had greatly lengthened my trip in order to see these two banks of the Tiber.

Here we crossed by boat a little branch of the Tiber and entered the Sacred Isle, about the length of a good Gascon league, covered with pasture land. There are some ruins and marble columns, as there are many in this place Porto, where the old city of Trajan used to be; and the Pope has some of them dug up every day and taken to Rome. When we had crossed this island we came upon the Tiber, and since we had no suitable means of getting the horses across, we were about to retrace our steps; but by chance, behold there arrived

19 Châtillon, better known as Coligny, the Protestant leader, was killed in the Massacre of Saint Bartholomew's Day in 1572. Pope Gregory XIII hailed the news of the massacre with great joy.
20 Blaise de Monluc, grandson of the marshal, whom Montaigne had already seen in Bologna. See *Travel Journal*, p. 1129.

on the other bank several gentlemen – the sieur du Bellai, the baron
de Chasai, the sieur de Marivau, and others. Whereupon I crossed
the river and made a deal with these gentlemen that they should
take our horses and we theirs. Thus they returned to Rome by the
road on which we had come, and we by theirs, which was the one
straight to Ostia.

Ostia, fifteen miles, is situated along the old bed of the Tiber;
for the river has changed its course a little and moves farther from
the old course every day. We had a snack for breakfast at a little
tavern. Beyond we saw La Rocca, a small, rather strongly fortified
castle; no guard is mounted there. The popes, especially the present
one, have erected on this seacoast big towers or lookouts, about
every mile, to provide against the raids that the Turks often used to
make, especially at vintage time, taking cattle and men. From these
towers, by means of a cannon shot, they warn one another with such
great speed that immediately the alarm is flying to Rome. Around
Ostia are the salt marshes, which supply all the territories of the
Church: there is a large marshy plain into which the sea flows.

All along this road from Ostia to Rome, which is the Via
Ostensis, there are great marks of its ancient beauty: a great many
causeways, many ruins of aqueducts, and almost the entire length of
it sown with great ruins, and more than two-thirds of the said road
still paved with those big square black slabs with which they used to
pave their highways. Seeing this bank of the Tiber, you easily accept
as true the opinion that on both sides this road was lined with
residences all the way from Rome to Ostia. Among other ruins,
about halfway to Rome we came across on our left hand a very
beautiful sepulcher of a Roman praetor, the inscription of which is
still seen entire. The ruins of Rome are discernible for the most part
only by the solidity and thickness of the construction. They used to
make stout brick walls and then encrust them with slabs either of
marble or of some other white stone, or a certain cement, or big tiles
coated on the outside. This crust, on which the inscriptions were,
has almost everywhere been ruined by the years; whereby we have
lost most of our knowledge of such things. Inscriptions are seen
wherever the building has walls of thick and massive stone.

The approaches to Rome, almost everywhere, look uncultivated
and barren, either for want of soil, or, what I consider more likely,
because this city has hardly any laborers and men who live by the
work of their hands. When I came here I found on the way many
groups of villagers who came from the Grisons and Savoy to earn

something in the season by laboring in the vineyards and the gardens; and they told me that every year this was their source of income.

The city is all court and all nobility: every man shares in the ecclesiastical idleness. There are no shop-lined streets, or fewer than in a small town: it is nothing but palaces and gardens. You see no Rue de la Harpe or Rue de Saint-Denis; it seems to me that I am always on the Rue de Seine or on the Quai des Augustins in Paris. The city hardly changes its appearance from a working day to a holiday. All through Lent they do the rounds of the stations; there is no less of a crowd on a working day than on any other. At this time there are nothing but coaches, prelates, and ladies. We returned to sleep at

ROME, fifteen miles. On March 16th I wanted to go and try the Roman steam baths, and went to those of Saint Mark, which are considered among the noblest. Though I was unattended, I was treated there moderately well and with all possible respect. The custom is to bring lady friends if you want, who are rubbed down with you by the attendants. There I learned that quicklime and orpiment mixed with lye, two parts of lime and the third of orpiment, go to make that drug and unguent with which they make the body hair fall out, after applying it for a short half of a quarter hour.

On the 17th I had my colic for five or six hours, endurable, and some time after passed a stone as big as a big pine nut, and of that shape.

At this time we had roses in Rome, and artichokes; but as for me, I found the heat nothing extraordinary, keeping dressed and covered as at home.

Fish are less abundant than in France; their pike especially is no good at all, and they leave it for the people. They rarely have soles and trout; very good barbel, much bigger than in Bordeaux, but expensive. Dorados are highly prized, and the mullets bigger than ours and a little firmer. The oil here is so excellent that the pricking which remains in my throat in France when I have eaten much of it, I do not have at all here. They eat fresh grapes here all year long, and even as late as this time of year there are very good ones hanging from the trellises. Their mutton is no good and is held in scant esteem.

On the 18th the ambassador of Portugal made obeisance to the Pope for the kingdom of Portugal on behalf of King Philip

– the same ambassador who was here to represent the deceased king and the Cortes opposed to King Philip.

On my return from Saint Peter's I met a man who informed me humorously of two things: that the Portuguese made their obeisance in Passion week;[21] and then, that on this same day the station was at San Giovanni Porta Latina, in which church a few years before certain Portuguese had entered into a strange brotherhood. They married one another, male to male, at Mass, with the same ceremonies with which we perform our marriages, read the same marriage gospel service, and then went to bed and lived together. The Roman wits said that because in the other conjunction, of male and female, this circumstance of marriage alone makes it legitimate, it had seemed to these sharp folk that this other action would become equally legitimate if they authorized it with ceremonies and mysteries of the Church. Eight or nine Portuguese of this fine sect were burned.

I saw the Spanish ceremony. They fired a salvo of cannon from the Castle of Sant' Angelo, and the ambassador was conducted to the palace by the Pope's trumpeters and drummers and archers. I did not go in to watch the harangue and the ceremony. The ambassador from the tsar of Muscovy, who was at a decorated window to see this ceremony, said that he had been invited to see a great assemblage, but that in his country, when they speak of troops of horse, it is always twenty-five or thirty thousand; and he laughed at all this ado, from what I was told by the very man who was commissioned to talk to him through an interpreter.

On Palm Sunday I found in a church at vespers a boy sitting beside the altar on a chair, dressed in a great new robe of blue taffeta, head bare, with a crown of olive branches, holding in his hand a lighted torch of white wax. He was a boy of fifteen or thereabouts, who, by order of the Pope, had been delivered from prison that day; he had killed another boy.

At Saint John Lateran some transparent marble is to be seen.

The next day the Pope did the seven churches. He had on boots with the hairy side in, and on each foot a cross of whiter leather. He always takes a Spanish horse, a hackney and a mule, and a litter, all decked out in the same way; that day the horse was missing. His groom had two or three pairs of gilt spurs in his hand and was waiting for him at the foot of Saint Peter's stairs; he refused them

21 The point being that they suffered in making it.

and asked for his litter, in which there were two red hats of almost the same fashion hanging on nails.

On this day in the evening my *Essays* were returned to me, corrected according to the opinion of the learned monks. The Master of the Sacred Palace[22] had been able to judge them only by the report of some French friar, since he did not understand our language at all; and he was so content with the excuses I offered on each objection that this Frenchman had left him that he referred it to my conscience to redress what I should see was in bad taste. I begged him on the contrary to follow the opinion of the man who had made the judgment, admitting in certain things – such as having used the word "fortune," having named heretic poets, having excused Julian, and the objection to the idea that anyone who was praying should be free from evil impulses at the time; *item*, esteeming as cruelty whatever goes beyond plain death; *item*, that a child should be brought up to do anything;[23] and other things of that sort – that this was my opinion, and that they were things I had put in, not thinking they were errors; in other matters denying that the corrector had understood my thought. The said Master, who is an able man, was full of excuses for me, and wanted me to realize that he was not very sympathetic to these revisions; and he pleaded very ingeniously for me, in my presence, against another man, also an Italian, who was opposing me.

They did not return to me the book on the histories of the Swiss, translated into French, solely because the translator – whose name, however, is not given – is a heretic; but it is a marvel how well they know the men of our countries. And the best part was that they told me that the preface was condemned.

That same day, in the Church of Saint John Lateran, in place of the ordinary penitents who are seen performing this office in

22 The Master of the Sacred Palace at this time was Sisto Fabri (1541–94), professor of theology at the University of Rome, soon (1583) to be made general of the Dominican Order.

23 The passages criticized in the *Essays*, in order of mention, are these, or others like them: Fortune: II: 4, p. 320, and *passim*. Heretic poets (Beza and Buchanan): II: 17, p. 609. Julian: II: 19, *passim*. Praying: I: 56, *passim*. Torture: I: 31, p. 189; II: 11, p. 381. Training a child: I: 26, p. 150.

Montaigne made no changes because of the criticisms, probably in part at least in order not to alter his self-portrait. In the *Essays* later he once alludes to his use of the word "fortune" (I: 56, p. 284), and once defends himself for praising heretics as poets (III: 10, p. 942).

most of the churches, Monsignor the Cardinal San Sisto was seated in a corner, tapping on the head, with a long wand that he had in his hand, the passers-by, including the ladies, but with a smiling face, and with greater courtesy according to their rank and beauty.

On the Wednesday of Holy Week I did the seven churches with Monsieur de Foix[24] before dinner, and we put in about five hours at it. I do not know why some people are scandalized to see the vice of some particular prelate freely accused, when it is known and public; for that day, both at Saint John Lateran and at the Church of the Holy-Cross-in-Jerusalem, I saw the history, written at full length in a very conspicuous place, of Pope Sylvester II, which is the most damaging that can be imagined.

The tour around the city, which I have made several times on the city side from the Porta del Popolo to the Porta San Paolo, can be made in a good three hours or four, traveling light and at a walk; the tour of the part on the other side of the river is made in an hour and a half at the most.

Among other pleasures that Rome furnished me in Lent were the sermons. There were excellent preachers, such as that renegade rabbi who preaches to the Jews on Saturday after dinner in the Church of the Trinity. There are always sixty Jews there; this number is compelled to attend. He was a very famous doctor among them, and by their very arguments, by their rabbis, and by the text of the Bible, he combats their belief. In that science and in the languages used in it he is admirable.

There was another preacher who preached to the Pope and the cardinals, named Padre Toledo (in depth of learning, in pertinence, and in readiness, he is a very rare man); another, very eloquent and popular, who was preaching to the Jesuits, with much ability, besides his excellent language; the last two are Jesuits. It is a marvel how much of a place this College holds in Christendom; and I believe there never was a brotherhood and body among us that held such a rank, or, to sum up, that produced such results as these men will, if their plans continue. They will soon possess all Christendom: it is a nursery of great men in every sort of greatness. It is the one limb of our Church that most threatens the heretics of our time.

24 Paul de Foix (1528–84), to whom Montaigne dedicated La Boétie's French verses. After the death of Foix, Montaigne praised him highly in the *Essays* (III: 9, p. 888).

One preacher's joke was that we turned our coaches into astro-
labes. The commonest exercise of the Romans is to promenade
through the streets; and ordinarily the enterprise of leaving the
house is undertaken solely to go from street to street, without
having any place in mind to stop at; and some streets are particularly
affected to that use. To tell the truth, the greatest profit that is
derived from this is to see the ladies at the windows, and notably the
courtesans, who show themselves at their Venetian blinds with such
treacherous artfulness that I have often marveled how they tantalize
our eyes as they do; and often, having got off my horse immediately
and obtained admission, I wondered at how much more beautiful
they appeared to be than they really were. They know how to
present themselves by their most agreeable feature; they will show
you only the upper part of the face, or the lower, or the side, and
cover themselves or show themselves in such a way that not one
single ugly one is seen at the window. All the men are there taking
off their hats and making deep bows, and receiving an ogling glance
or two as they pass. The gain from having spent the night there for
a crown, or for four, is to pay court to them the next day in public.
Some ladies of quality are also seen at the windows, but of a different
style, and with a bearing very easy to discern. On horseback you see
better; but that is a matter either for unimportant folk like me or for
the young men mounted on hired horses, which they show off. The
people of rank go only in coaches; and the more licentious, in order
to have more of a view upward, have the top of the coach open with
skylights. That is what the preacher meant about astrolabes.

On Maundy Thursday in the morning, the Pope, in full ponti-
ficals, takes his stand on the first portico of Saint Peter's, on the
second story, attended by the cardinals, himself holding a torch in
his hand. There, on one side, a canon of Saint Peter's reads aloud
a Latin bull by which are excommunicated an infinite variety of
people, among others the Huguenots, under that very name, and all
the princes who have appropriated some part of the territories of the
Church; at which articles the cardinals de' Medici and Caraffa, who
were next to the Pope, laughed very hard. This reading lasts a good
hour and a half; for at each article that this canon reads in Latin,
Cardinal Gonzaga on the other side, also uncovered, reads as much
in Italian. After that the Pope threw this lighted torch down to the
people, and, for sport or otherwise, Cardinal Gonzaga threw
another; for there were three of them lighted. This falls on the
people; down below the greatest scramble in the world ensues to see

who will get a bit of this torch, and they fight very roughly with fists and sticks. While this condemnation is being read, there is also a big piece of black taffeta which hangs over the parapet of the said balcony in front of the Pope. The excommunication done, they turn up this black drape, disclosing another of a different color; the Pope then gives public blessings.

On these days they show the Veronica, which is a disfigured face, of a dark and somber color, in a square frame like a big mirror.[25] It is shown with great ceremony from the height of a pulpit five or six paces wide. The hands of the priest who holds it are clad in red gloves, and there are two or three other priests who support him. There is nothing viewed with such great reverence as this, the people prostrate on the ground, most of them with tears in their eyes, with cries of commiseration. A woman who they said was possessed of a spirit became frantic on seeing this face, screamed, stretched out and twisted her arms. These priests, walking around this pulpit, display the image to the people, now this way, now that; and at every movement the people to whom it is presented cry out.

They also show at the same time and with the same ceremony the lance-head in a crystal bottle. Several times on this day this exhibition takes place, with an assemblage of people so huge that even very far outside the church, as far as this pulpit can be seen, there is a tremendous crush of men and women.

It is a true papal court: the pomp of Rome, and its principal grandeur, lies in displays of devotion. It is fine to see the ardor for religion of so innumerable a people on these days.

They have a hundred brotherhoods and more, and there is hardly a man of quality who is not attached to some one of these; there are some for foreigners. Our kings belong to that of the Gonfalon. These private societies perform many acts of religious fellowship, which are principally practiced in Lent; but on this day they walk in companies, dressed in linen; each company has its fashion, white, red, blue, green, or black; most of them have their faces covered.

The noblest and most magnificent thing I have seen here or elsewhere is the incredible number of people scattered throughout the city on this day at their devotions, and especially in these companies. For besides a large number of others that we had seen by day and who had come to Saint Peter's, as night began this city

25 This is the cloth with which it is said Saint Veronica wiped the face of Jesus on the cross, and which retained his image in his blood.

seemed to be all on fire: these companies marching in order toward Saint Peter's, each man carrying a torch, and almost all these of white wax. I think there passed before me twelve thousand torches at the least; for from eight in the evening until midnight the street was always full of this procession, conducted in such good and measured order that although there were various companies and parties, starting from various places, there was never a breach or interruption to be seen; each body having a large choir of music, always singing as they went, and in the center of the ranks a file of Penitents, who scourge themselves with ropes; there were five hundred of them at least, their backs all flayed and bleeding in a piteous fashion.

This is an enigma that I do not yet well understand. They are all torn and cruelly wounded, and torment and beat themselves without stopping. Yet to see their bearing, the steadiness of their steps, the firmness of their speech (for I heard several speak), and their faces (for many were uncovered in the street), it did not appear that they were even in the midst of a painful or indeed a serious action, and yet there were some as young as twelve or thirteen. Right in front of me there was a very young one who had a pleasant face; a young woman lamented to see him wound himself so. He turned toward us and said to her, laughing: "That's enough. Tell her that I'm doing this for her sins, not for mine." Not only do they show no distress or constraint in this action, but they do it cheerfully, or at least with such nonchalance that you see them talk with one another about other matters, laugh, yell in the street, run, and jump, as people do in a crowd so great that the ranks are broken.

There are men among them who carry wine, which they offer the Penitents to drink; some of them take a swallow. They also give them sugar candy; and very often those who carry this wine put some in their mouth and then blow it out and with it wet the end of the scourges, which are made of cord and become so clotted and glued together with blood that they have to be wet to separate the thongs; for some they blow this same wine on their wounds.

To see their shoes and hose, it is quite apparent that they are people of very little means who sell themselves for this service, at least most of them. I was told indeed that they greased their shoulders with something; but I have seen their wounds so raw and the beating so lengthy that there is no medicament that could

take away the feeling of it; and then what do those who hire them do it for, if it is only a counterfeit?[26]

This ceremony has many other particularities. When they arrived at Saint Peter's they did nothing, except that they were shown the *Holy Face*, and then they went out again and made room for others.

On that day the ladies have great freedom; for all night the streets are full of them, and they almost all go on foot. However, in truth, the city seems to be very well-behaved, especially in this sort of debauchery. All oglings and amorous manifestations cease.

The handsomest sepulcher is that of the Santa Rotonda, because of the illuminations. Among other things, there are a great number of lights, from top to bottom, incessantly rolling and turning.

On the eve of Easter I saw at Saint John Lateran the heads of Saint Paul and Saint Peter that are shown there, which still have their flesh, color, and beard, as if they were alive: Saint Peter, a white and slightly longish face, his color ruddy and inclined to the sanguine, a forked gray beard, his head covered with a papal miter; Saint Paul, dark, his face broad and stouter, the head bigger, the beard gray, thick. They are up high in a special place. The way of showing them is that they call the people by the sound of bells, and by fits and starts lower a curtain behind which are these heads, side by side. They let them be seen for the time it takes to say an Ave Maria, and immediately raise the curtain again; after that they lower it again in the same way, and this up to three times. They repeat this exhibition four or five times during the day. The place is about as high as a pike, and then there is a heavy iron grill through which you look. They light several tapers around it on the outside; but it is hard to discern very clearly all the details. I saw them two or three times. The polish of these faces had some resemblance to our masks.

On the Wednesday after Easter, when Monsieur Maldonado, who was then in Rome, asked me what opinion I had of the mores of this city, and especially in the matter of religion, he found his judgment entirely in conformity with mine: that the common people were incomparably more devout in France than here; but the rich, and especially the courtiers, a little less. He told me further that to those who alleged that France was totally lost in heresy, and especially to Spaniards, of whom there are a great

26 Montaigne speaks of this scene also in the *Essays* (I: 14, p. 49).

number in his College, he maintained that there were more men who were truly religious in the city of Paris alone than in all Spain put together.

They have their boats towed upstream on the river Tiber with ropes by three or four pairs of buffaloes.

I do not know how others feel about the air of Rome; for myself, I found it very pleasant and healthy. The sieur de Vialard said that he had lost his subjection to migraines here; which went to support the opinion of the people, that it is very bad for the feet and good for the head. There is nothing so hostile to my health as boredom and idleness; here I had always some occupation, if not as pleasant as I could have desired, at least sufficient to overcome boredom: like visiting the antiquities and the vineyards, which are gardens and pleasure spots of singular beauty, and where I learned how aptly art can make use of a rugged, hilly, and uneven spot; for here they derive from them charms that cannot be duplicated in our level places, and very artfully take advantage of this diversity. Among the most beautiful vineyards are those of the cardinals d'Este at Monte Cavallo, Farnese on the Palatine, Orsini, Sforza, Medici; that of Pope Julius, that of Madama;[27] the gardens of Farnese and of Cardinal Riario at Trastevere, and of Cesio outside the Porta del Popolo. These are beauties open to anyone who wants to enjoy them, and for whatever purpose, even to sleep there, even in company if the masters are not there, and they do not like to go there much. Or I could go to hear sermons, which they have at all times, or theological disputations; or else sometimes visit some woman of the public sort, in which I found this disadvantage: that they sell their mere conversation as dear (which was what I was looking for, to hear them talk and be in on their subtleties), and are as sparing of it, as the whole business.

All these amusements kept me busy enough; for melancholy, which is the death of me, and irritability, I had no occasion, either inside or outside my house. Thus Rome is a pleasant place to live in; and I can argue from that how much I would have enjoyed it if I could have tasted it more privately; for in truth, despite my craft and the trouble I have taken, I have known it only by its public visage, which it offers to the meanest stranger.

On the last of March I had an attack of colic which lasted me all night but was bearable enough; it disturbed my belly with gripings

27 The duchess of Parma, daughter of Charles V.

and gave a sting to my urine beyond the usual. I passed some large gravel and two stones.

On Low Sunday I saw the ceremony of alms for maidens. The Pope has, besides his ordinary equipage, twenty-five horses that are led ahead of him with caparisons and saddlecloths of cloth of gold, very richly decked out, and ten or twelve mules with saddlecloths of crimson velvet, all this led by his armed lackeys on foot; his litter covered with crimson velvet. In front of him four men on horseback carried, on the end of certain staffs covered with red velvet and gilded at the handle and the ends, four red hats. He himself was on his mule. The cardinals who followed him were also on their mules, decked in their pontifical vestments; the tails of their gowns were attached with a cord to their mules' headstalls. The maidens were a hundred and seven in number, each accompanied by an old female relative. After Mass they came out of the church and formed a long procession. On their return from there, one after the other, passing through the choir of the Church of Santa Maria sopra Minerva, where this ceremony is performed, they kissed the Pope's feet; and he, after giving them the benediction, gave each one with his own hand a white damask purse containing a promissory note. It is understood that when they have found a husband they collect their alms, which is thirty-five crowns a head, besides a white dress which they each get for the wedding and which is worth five crowns. Their faces are covered with a linen veil, with only a place open for seeing.

I used to say about the advantages of Rome, among other things, that it is the most universal city in the world, a place where strangeness and differences of nationality are considered least; for by its nature it is a city pieced together out of foreigners; everyone is as if at home. Its ruler embraces all Christendom with his authority; his princely jurisdiction is binding on foreigners in their own homes just as here. At his own election and that of all the princes and grandees of his court the consideration of their origin has no weight. The freedom of the government of Venice, and the advantages of its trade, people it with foreigners; but they are nevertheless as if at someone else's house. Here they hold their own offices, property, and responsibilities; for it is the seat of ecclesiastics. You see as many or more foreigners in Venice (for the influx of foreigners you see in France, in Germany, or elsewhere, does not come into comparison with the number here), but of resident, domiciled foreigners, far fewer. The common people are no more dismayed at our fashion in

dress, or the Spanish or German fashion, than at their own; and you hardly see a beggar who does not ask alms of us in our own language.

I therefore sought, and employed all my five natural senses, to obtain the title of Roman citizen, were it only for the ancient honor and the religious memory of its authority. I found some difficulty in this; however, I surmounted it without any Frenchman's favor or even knowledge. The authority of the Pope was employed in it through the medium of Filippo Musotti,[28] his majordomo, who had taken a singular liking to me and went to great pains for this. And letters-patent were dispatched to me on "the 3rd day before the Ides of March, 1581," which were delivered to me on the 5th of April, very authentic, in the same form and favorable terms as were used for the lord Giacomo Buoncompagno, duke of Sora, son of the Pope. It is a vain title; but at all events I received much pleasure in having obtained it.[29]

On April 3rd I left Rome early in the morning by the Porta San Lorenzo Tiburtina. I went along a rather level road, through a country for the most part fertile in wheat, and, like all the approaches to Rome, little inhabited. I crossed the river Teverone, which is the ancient Anio, first by the bridge of Mammolo, and second by the Lucano bridge, which still retains its ancient name. On this bridge there are some ancient inscriptions, and the principal one is very legible. There are also two or three Roman tombs along this road; there are no other traces of antiquity and very little of that big ancient paving, and yet this is the Via Tiburtina. I came to dine at

TIVOLI, fifteen miles. This is the ancient Tiburtum, lying at the roots of the mountains, the town extending along the first rather steep slope, which makes its situation and view very rich, for it commands an immense plain in all directions, and great Rome itself. Its view is toward the sea, and it has the mountains behind it. This river Teverone bathes it, and near there takes a marvelous leap, coming down from the mountains and disappearing through a hole in the rock five or six hundred paces below, and then coming into the plain, where it meanders along playfully and joins the Tiber a little above the city.

28 Alessandro (not Filippo) Musotti, prefect of the apostolic palace, later to be papal nuncio at Venice.
29 Near the end of the chapter "Of Vanity" (*Essays* II: 9, p. 930), Montaigne quotes this document in full.

Here are to be seen that famous palace and garden of the cardinal of Ferrara:[30] it is a very beautiful thing, but incomplete in many parts, and the work is not being continued by the present cardinal. Here I examined everything most particularly. I would try to describe it here, but there are published books and pictures on the subject. The gushing of an infinity of jets of water checked and launched by a single spring that can be worked from far off, I had seen elsewhere on my trip, both at Florence and at Augsburg, as has been stated above. The music of the organ, which is real music and a natural organ, though always playing the same thing, is effected by means of the water, which falls with great violence into a round arched cave and agitates the air that is in there and forces it, in order to get out, to go through the pipes of the organ and supply it with wind. Another stream of water, driving a wheel with certain teeth on it, causes the organ keyboard to be struck in a certain order; so you hear an imitation of the sound of trumpets. In another place you hear the song of birds, which are little bronze flutes that you see at regals; they give a sound like those little earthenware pots full of water that little children blow into by the spout, this by an artifice like that of the organ; and then by other springs they set in motion an owl, which, appearing at the top of the rock, makes this harmony cease instantly, for the birds are frightened by his presence; and then he leaves the place to them again. This goes on alternately as long as you want.

Elsewhere there issues a noise as of cannon shots; elsewhere a more frequent smaller noise, as of harquebus shots. This is done by a sudden fall of water into channels; and the air, laboring at the same time to get out, engenders this noise. All these inventions, or similar ones, produced by these same natural causes, I have seen elsewhere.

There are ponds or reservoirs, with a stone margin all around and many tall freestone pillars above this parapet, about four paces apart from each other. From the head of these pillars water comes out with great force, not upward, but toward the pond. The mouths, being thus turned inward and facing one another, cast and scatter the water into this pond with such force that these shafts of water come to meet and clash in the air, and produce a thick and continual rain falling into the pond. The sun, falling upon it, engenders, both at the bottom of this pond and in the air and all around this place,

30 Cardinal d'Este. The palace is the Villa d'Este.

a rainbow so natural and vivid that it lacks nothing of the one we see in the sky. This I had not seen elsewhere.

Under the palace there are great hollows, artificially made, and air holes which give out a cold vapor and cool off all the lower part of this house enormously; this part, however, is not completed.

I also saw many excellent statues there, and notably one sleeping nymph, one dead one, a celestial Pallas, the Adonis[31] in the home of the bishop of Aquino; the bronze she-wolf and the boy taking out a thorn, in the Capitol; the Laocoön and the Antinous of the Belvedere; the Comedy in the Capitol, the Satyr in the vineyard of Cardinal Sforza; and of modern workmanship, the Moses[32] in the sepulcher of San Pietro in Vinculis, the beautiful woman at the feet of Pope Paul III in the new Church of Saint Peter – these are the statues I have liked best in Rome.

It was to rival this place that Pratolino was built. As to the richness and beauty of the grottoes, Florence is infinitely superior; as to abundance of water, Ferrara;[33] in variety of sports and amusing mechanisms derived from water, they are equal, unless the Florentine has a little more elegance in the arrangement and order of the whole body of the place; Ferrara excels in ancient statues, and in the palace, Florence.[34] In situation and beauty of prospect Ferrara is infinitely superior; and I should say the same in all nature's favors, if it did not have this extreme misfortune, that all its waters, except the fountain that is in the little garden all the way at the top, and which is seen in one of the palace rooms, is only water from the Teverone, a branch of which the cardinal has taken over and diverted to a separate channel for his service. If this water were as clear and good to drink as on the contrary it is muddy and ugly, this place

31 The passage that follows, from "the Adonis" to "in Rome," at the end of the paragraph, seems to be a later addition referring to original statues in Rome, not, as one might suppose, to copies at Tivoli.

32 By Michelangelo.

33 Throughout this paragraph Montaigne uses "Ferrara" to refer to the Villa d'Este at Tivoli, "Florence" to refer to Pratolino (see pp. 1132–3).

34 The punctuation of the text of this passage is confusing and contradictory. Some editors take it to mean this: "Ferrara excels in ancient statues and in the palace. Florence infinitely surpasses Ferrara in situation of place and beauty of prospect; and I should say in all nature's favors..." The part about the Teverone that follows, however, seems to me compatible only with the reading given in our text above, and thus decisive.

would be incomparable, especially its great fountain, which is of the finest workmanship, and more beautiful to see with its adjuncts than anything else either in this garden or elsewhere. At Pratolino, on the contrary, what water there is is spring water and drawn from far away. Because the Teverone comes down from much higher mountains, the inhabitants of this place use it as they will, and the example of several private individuals makes this work of the cardinal's less marvelous.

I left here the next day after dinner, and passed by a great ruin on the right-hand side of the road as we came back, which they say comprises six miles and is a villa. They say it is the *Praedium* of the Emperor Hadrian.

On this road from Tivoli to Rome there is a stream of sulphurous water that cuts across the road. The edges of the channel are all whitened with sulphur, and it gives off a smell for more than half a league away. They do not use it for medicine. In this stream there are small bodies formed of the scum of the water, so closely resembling our sugar-coated candies that there are few people that would not be fooled; and the inhabitants of Tivoli make all sorts of things of this same material, of which I bought two boxes for 7 sous 6 deniers.

There are some antiquities in the town of Tivoli, such as two baths of a very ancient shape, and the remains of a temple in which there are still several pillars entire; which temple they say was that of their ancient Sibyl. However, on the cornices of this church you still see five or six large letters which were not continued; for the following part of the wall is still entire. I do not know if there were any letters before these, for that part is broken; but in what can be seen, there is only CE... ELLIUS L. F.[35] I do not know what that can be. We returned in the evening to

ROME, fifteen miles; and I made all this trip back by coach without any discomfort, contrary to my wont. They have an observance here much more careful than elsewhere, for they make a distinction between the streets, the quarters of the town, even the apartments of their houses, in respect to health, and set so much store by this that they change their habitation with the seasons; and even of those who rent them, some keep two or three rented palaces

35 The inscription may have read CURANTE L. CELLIO. L. F., "Supervised by L. Cellius, son of Lucius." This Cellius was at one time in charge of many public works in Rome.

at very great expense, so as to move with the seasons in accordance with their doctors' orders.

On April 15th I went to say good-by to the Master of the Sacred Palace[36] and his colleague, who urged me not to make use of the censorship of my book, in which censorship some other Frenchmen had informed them there were many stupid things; saying that they honored both my intention and affection for the Church and my ability, and thought so well of my frankness and conscience that they left it to myself to cut out of my book, when I wanted to republish it, whatever I found too licentious in it, and among other things the uses of the word "fortune." It seemed to me that I left them well pleased with me; and to excuse themselves for having scrutinized my book so attentively and condemned it in certain details, they cited me many books of our time by cardinals and churchmen of very good reputation, censured for a few such imperfections which did not affect in the least the reputation of the author or of the work as a whole. They urged me to help the Church by my eloquence (those are their courteous formulas) and to make my abode in this city, at peace and without interference from them. These are persons of great authority and potential cardinals.

We were eating artichokes, beans, and peas around mid-March. In April it is daylight at their ten o'clock, and I think on the longest days at nine.[37]

At this time I made the acquaintance, among others, of a Pole, the most intimate friend of the late Cardinal Hosyusz, who presented me with two copies of the booklet he had written on the cardinal's death and corrected with his own hand.

The pleasures of residence in this city increased by more than half with acquaintance. I never tasted air more temperate for me or more suited to my constitution.

On April 18th I went to see the inside of the palace of Signor Giovanni Giorgio Cesarini, where there are numberless rare antiquities, and notably the authentic busts of Zeno, Posidonius, Euripides, and Carneades, as their very ancient Greek inscriptions tell. He has also the portraits of the most beautiful living Roman ladies and of the Signora Clelia-Fascia Farnese, his wife, who is, if not the

36 See above, p. 1166.
37 Around 5 A.M. and 4 A.M. respectively, counting from sundown the day before.

most comely, beyond comparison the most lovable woman then in Rome, or, as far as I know, anywhere else. This man says he is of the race of the Caesars, and as such bears by his own right the banner of the Roman nobility; he is rich, and has on his coat of arms the column with the bear fastened to it, and above the column an eagle with wings spread.

A great beauty of Rome is the vineyards and gardens, and the season for them is well on in the summer.

Italy: From Rome to Loreto and La Villa
(April 19–May 7, 1581)

On Wednesday, the 19th of April, I left Rome after dinner, and we were escorted as far as the Ponte Molle by Messieurs de Noirmoutier, de la Trémouille, and du Bellai, and other gentlemen. Having crossed this bridge, we turned to the right, leaving on our left hand the main road to Viterbo, by which we had come to Rome, and on our right hand the Tiber and the hills. We followed an open and uneven road, through country not very fertile and uninhabited, and passed the place they call Prima Porta, which is the first gate, seven miles from Rome; and some say that the ancient walls of Rome went as far as this, which I do not consider at all likely. Along this road, which is the ancient Via Flaminia, there are some unknown and rare antiquities. We came to sleep at

CASTELNUOVO, sixteen miles, a little walled village belonging to the house of Colonna, buried among hills in a site that strongly reminded me of the fertile approaches to our Pyrenees on the Aigues–Caudes road. The next day, April 20th, we continued through the same country, hilly but very pleasant, fertile and thickly inhabited, and arrived, in a low valley along the Tiber, at

BORGHETTO, a little walled village belonging to Duke Ottavio Farnese. We left here after dinner, and after following a very pleasant valley between these hills, we crossed the Tiber at Orte, where big piles of stone are still to be seen, relics of the bridge that Augustus had built there to connect the country of the Sabines, the one toward which we were heading, with that of the Falisci, which is on the other side. Afterward we came upon Otricoli, a tiny little town belonging to the cardinal of Perugia. In front of this town you see, in a beautiful site, some great and important ruins; the hilly

and extremely pleasant country offers a very humpy aspect, but very fertile all over and thickly populated.

On this road one comes across an inscription in which the Pope says that he made and leveled this road, which he calls Via Buoncompagna, after his name. This custom of thus putting in writing and leaving a testimony of such works, which is seen in Italy and Germany, is a very good spur; and a man who does not care about the public will be motivated to do something good by this hope of reputation. In truth, most of this road used to be difficult going, but it has now been made passable even for coaches for as far as Loreto. We came to sleep at

NARNI, ten miles, Narnia in Latin, a little town belonging to the Church, situated on the top of a rock, at the foot of which rolls the river Nera, Nar in Latin. On one side the said town looks out over a very pleasant plain in which the said river plays and winds around itself curiously. In the square there is a very beautiful fountain. I saw the cathedral and noticed this, that the tapestry in it has French inscriptions and rhymes in our ancient language. I was unable to learn how that came about; but I did learn from the people that from time immemorial they have had a great inclination in our favor. The said tapestry bears a picture of the Passion and occupies one whole side of the nave.

Because Pliny says that in this place is found a certain kind of earth that is softened by heat and dried by rains, I asked the inhabitants about it; they knew nothing about it. A mile from there they have some cold springs which have the same effect as our hot ones; sick people use them, but they are not well known. The inn, according to Italian standards, is one of the good ones; yet we had no candle, but oil light everywhere.

On the 21st, early in the morning, we descended into a very pleasant valley in which the said river Nera runs, which river we crossed over a bridge at the gates of Terni, which we passed through; and in the square we saw a very ancient column that is still standing. I perceived no inscription on it, but it has beside it the statue of a lion in relief, beneath which in old letters there is a dedication to Neptune, and also the said Neptunus carved in relief in marble with his train. In this same square there is an inscription that they have set up in a prominent place: to one "A. Pompeius A. F., the inhabitants of this town, which is called Interamna, because of the river Nera that hems it in on one side, and another stream on the other, have erected a statue for the services he has rendered

to this people." The statue is not there, but I could judge the age of this inscription by the form of writing with a diphthong *periculeis*[1] and similar words.

This is a beautiful town in a singularly pleasant site. To the rear, from where we came, it has the very fertile plain of this valley, and beyond, the most highly cultivated inhabited hillsides; and among other things, so many olive trees that there is nothing more beautiful to see, since among these hillsides there are sometimes very high mountains which are seen to be cultivated and bearing all sorts of fruits even to the summit. I had my colic very badly, and it had gripped me for twenty-four hours and was then in its last effort; however, I did not fail for all that to enjoy the beauty of that place.

Beyond there we penetrated a little further into the Apennines, and found that this new road that the Pope has constructed there is in truth a beautiful, great, and noble work of improvement, great in expense and convenience. The people of the neighborhood were constrained to build it; but they do not complain so much about this as that without any compensation, even where there happened to be tillable fields, orchards, and the like, nothing was spared for this highway. We saw on our right hand a pleasant hilltop occupied by a tiny little town. The people call it Colle Scipoli: they say that in ancient times it was Castrum Scipionis. The other mountains are higher, arid, and stony. Between these and the bed of a winter torrent, we came to

SPOLETO, eighteen miles, a famous and commodious town, situated among these mountains and at their foot. Here we were compelled to show our health certificate, not because of the plague, which was not then in any part of Italy, but for the fear they are in of one Petrino, their fellow townsman, who is the most notorious robber outlaw in Italy and the most famous for his exploits, by whom they and the towns round about are afraid of being surprised.

This region is dotted with many taverns; and where there are no buildings, they have arbors, where there are tables spread with boiled eggs and cheese and wine. They have no butter here, and serve everything fricasseed in oil.

On leaving there, this same day after dinner, we found ourselves in the valley of Spoleto, which is the most beautiful plain between the mountains that it is possible to see, two big Gascon leagues wide. We descried many houses on the nearby crests. The road in

1 Instead of the classical form *periculis*.

this plain is a continuation of that road of the Pope's that I have just spoken of, in a deliberate straight line like a racecourse. We left many towns on either side, among others, on the right hand, the town of Trevi. Servius says, speaking of Virgil, that this is the "olive-bearing Mutusca" that he speaks of in Book Seven.[2] Others deny it and argue to the contrary. At all events, it is a town perched on a high mountain, and in one place extending halfway down all along its slope. This mountain, covered all over with olive trees, is a very pleasant location. By this new road, restored three years ago, which is the finest that can be seen, we came in the evening to

FOLIGNO, twelve miles, a handsome town situated on this plain, which on arrival reminded me of the plan of Sainte-Foy-la-Grande, although it is much richer, and the town beyond comparison much more beautiful and populous. There is a little river or stream that is called Topino. In ancient times this town was called Fulignium, others say Fulcinia; it was built on the site of the Forum Flaminium.

The hostelries on this route, or most of them, are comparable to the French, except that the horses get hardly anything but hay to eat. They serve fish marinated, and have little of it fresh. Throughout Italy they serve beans raw, and also peas and green almonds, and they seldom cook the artichokes. Their floors are paved with tiles. They attach their oxen by the muzzle with a piece of iron that pierces the part between the nostrils, like buffaloes. The baggage mules, of which they have plenty, and very handsome ones, have their forefeet shod not in our way but with a round shoe going all around the hoof and bigger than the hoof. In various places here you come upon monks who give holy water to passers-by and expect alms from them, and many children asking for alms, promising to say their full ten paternosters, which they show in their hands, for whoever gives them money. The wines here are not much good.

The next morning, after leaving this beautiful plain, we again headed along the mountain road, where we again came across many beautiful level spots, sometimes high up, sometimes at the foot of the mountains. But toward the beginning of this morning we had for some time a very handsome view of a thousand varied hills, clad on all sides with all kinds of beautifully shady fruit trees and the finest wheat fields possible, often in a place so steep and precipitous that it was a miracle that even horses could get to them; the most beautiful valleys, an infinite number of streams, so many houses and

2 *Aeneid* VII. 711: "oliviferaeque Mutuscae."

villages here and there, that I was reminded of the approaches to Florence, except that there is no palace or house of any distinction here; and there the terrain is dry and barren for the most part, whereas in these hills there is not an inch of useless ground. It is true that the spring season brought out the best in them. Often, very far above our heads, we would see a beautiful village, and below our feet, as if at the Antipodes, another, each one having many and various attractions. This fact itself gives them no mean luster, that among such fertile mountains as these the Apennines show their frowning and inaccessible peaks, from which you see many torrents rolling down, which, having lost their first fury, soon after, in these valleys, turn into very pleasant and very gentle streams. Among these summits you discover, both on the heights and down below, many fertile plateaus, sometimes so large as to extend out of sight when looked at from a certain angle. It does not seem to me that any painting can represent so rich a landscape.

From here on the appearance of our road varied, now one way, now another; but the going was always very easy; and we came for dinner to

LA MUCCIA, twenty miles, a tiny little town situated on the river Chienti.

From here we followed a low and easy road through these mountains, and because I had given a box on the ear to our driver, which is a great outrage according to the usage of the country – witness the driver who killed the prince of Tresignano – seeing myself no longer followed by the said driver, and being privately a little concerned that he might lodge a complaint against me or cause some other trouble, I stopped, contrary to my plan (which was to go to Tolentino), for supper at

VALCHIMARA, eight miles, a little village and relay station, on the said river Chienti.

The next day, Sunday, we still followed this valley between cultivated and fertile mountains as far as Tolentino, a tiny little town through which we passed, and afterward found the country getting flatter, and we now had on our flanks only very accessible low hills; this country reminding me very much of the Agenais where it is prettiest, along the Garonne, except that here, as in Switzerland, you see no castles or gentlemen's houses, but there are many villages or towns on the hillsides. This was all a very pretty road, following the Chienti, and paved with bricks toward the end, by which we came to dine at

MACERATA, eighteen miles, a beautiful town of the size of Libourne, situated on a height approximately round in shape, and rising equally on all sides toward its center. There are not many handsome buildings. I noticed here a freestone palace, all cut on the outside into square diamond points, like the palace of the Cardinal d'Este in Ferrara; this form of structure is pleasing to the sight. The entry to this town is a new gate, on which is inscribed "Porta Buoncompagna," in letters of gold; it is part of the series of roads that this Pope has rebuilt. Here is the seat of the legate for the country of the Marches.

On these roads they give you the boilings of the local wine, when it is their own wines that they offer: for they boil and cook it until half of it is gone, to make it better.

We could tell indeed that we were on the highway to Loreto, so full were the roads of people going and coming: many not only private individuals but companies of rich people making the journey on foot, dressed as pilgrims; and some with a banner and then a crucifix going on ahead – and these dressed in livery.

After dinner we went through ordinary country, now cutting across plains and a few rivers, and then a few easy hills; but the whole very fertile, and the road for the most part paved with bricks laid edgewise. We passed the town of Recanati, a long town situated on a height and stretched out following the folds and contours of its hill, and came in the evening to

LORETO, fifteen miles. This is a little village enclosed in walls and fortified against the incursion of the Turks, standing on a slightly raised site, looking over a very beautiful plain and, from very near, the Adriatic Sea or Gulf of Venice; so that they say that when the weather is good, they can make out beyond the gulf the mountains of Sclavonia. In short, it is a very beautiful site.

There are hardly any other inhabitants than those in the service of this cult, such as many landlords – and yet the inns are rather dirty – and many tradesmen, to wit, sellers of wax, of images, beads, Agnus Dei, *Salvators*,[3] and such wares, for which there are a large number of handsome and richly furnished shops. I left nearly fifty good crowns there, for my part.

The priests, churchmen, and College of Jesuits are all gathered in one big palace which is not old, where there also resides

3 Medals or images of the Lamb of God and of the Savior.

a governor – a churchman, to whom one applies for all things – under the authority of the legate and the Pope.

The place of devotion is a very small house, very old and mean-looking, built of brick, longer than it is wide. Across the head they have built a partition, which has an iron door on each side; in between the two doors an iron grating; all this crude, old, and without any show of richness. This grill occupies the width between one door and the other; through it you can see right to the end of this little building; and this end, which is about the fifth part of the size of the building, is the location of the principal shrine. Here you see high up on the wall the image of Our Lady, made, they say, of wood; all the rest is so heavily adorned with rich votive tablets from so many places and princes, that all the way to the ground there is not an inch of space empty and not covered with some plate of silver or gold.

I was able to find room there only with the greatest difficulty, and as a great favor, to place a tablet on which there are four silver figures attached: that of Our Lady, my own, that of my wife, that of my daughter. At the foot of mine there is engraved on the silver: "Michel de Montaigne, Gascon Frenchman, Knight of the Order of the King, 1581"; at that of my wife's, "Françoise de La Chassaigne, his wife"; at that of my daughter's, "Léonor de Montaigne, his only daughter."[4] All are in a row on their knees on the tablet, and Our Lady above them in the foreground.

There is an entry into this chapel other than by the two doors I have spoken of, which entry leads to the outside. So as you enter the chapel by that door, my tablet is located on the left hand, opposite the door that is in this corner; and I left it very carefully fixed and nailed there. I had had a little silver chain and ring made with which to hang it on some nail; but they preferred to attach it completely. In this little place is the fireplace of the building, which you see by turning up some old curtains that cover it. Few are permitted to enter; indeed, by the sign on the front of the door, which is of very richly worked metal (and furthermore, there is an iron grill in front of this door), the restriction is that without the governor's permission no one shall enter.

Among other things, for its rarity, they had left with the other, rich presents the candle that a Turk had recently sent here after making a vow to Our Lady of Loreto when he was in some extreme

4 These inscriptions are all in Latin.

necessity and wanting to catch hold of any sort of rope to help himself.

The other and larger part of this little hut serves as a chapel. It has no daylight, and its altar is beneath the grill against this partition that I have spoken of. In this chapel there is not an ornament, no bench, no railing, no painting or tapestry on the wall: for of itself it serves as a reliquary. One may not wear any sword or weapon here, and there is neither precedence nor regard to high rank.

We received our Easter Sacrament in this chapel, which not all are permitted to do, since there is another place reserved for this purpose because of the great crowd of people who ordinarily come to receive Communion. There are so many people who come to this chapel at all hours that you have to see to it early to get a place there. A German Jesuit said Mass for me and administered the Communion to me.

People are forbidden to scratch anything from this wall; and if it were permitted to take anything away, there would not be enough to last three days. This place is full of innumerable miracles, for which I refer to the books; but there are several, and very recent ones, involving mishaps that have befallen those who out of devotion have carried away something from this building, even with the Pope's permission; and a small fragment of brick which had been removed at the time of the Council of Trent has been brought back.

The four walls of this hut are covered and reinforced on the outside by an extremely rich and elaborately carved screen, made of the finest marble that can be had anywhere; few pieces of workmanship are to be seen more exquisite and excellent than this. All around and above this square structure is a beautiful big church; many handsome chapels all around; tombs, and among others that of Cardinal d'Amboise, which Cardinal d'Armagnac has had erected there. This little square structure is like the choir of other churches; there is a choir, but it is in a corner. All this great church is covered with tablets, paintings, and stories. We saw there many rich ornaments, and I was astonished that there were not even more to be seen, in view of the renown of this church, which has been famous for so long. I believe they melt down the old things and use them for other purposes. They estimate the alms in coined money at ten thousand crowns.

There is more show of religion here than in any place I have seen.

What is lost – I mean of money or anything else not merely worth picking up, but worth stealing for people of that profession –

the person who finds it puts into a certain public place set aside for this purpose; and whoever wants to get it back gets it back there with no questions asked. When I was there, there were many such things – beads, handkerchiefs, unclaimed purses – that were there for the first comer to take.

In what you buy for the service of the church and to leave there, no artisan wants anything for his labor, in order, they say, to have a share in the grace. You pay only for the silver or the wood. Alms or liberality are permitted, but in fact they refuse it. The church people are as obliging as possible in everything: for confession, for Communion, or for anything else, they take nothing. It is usual to give money to some priest of your choice to distribute to the poor in your name when you have left.

As I was in that sanctuary, along comes a man who offers the first priest he meets a silver cup, saying that he had made a vow to do so; and because he had vowed to spend twelve crowns, which the cup did not amount to, he promptly paid the surplus to the said priest, who argued for the payment of the money as for a thing very exactly due, in order to help in the complete and conscientious execution of his promise; that done, he had this man enter this sanctuary, offer this chalice himself to Our Lady, and say a short prayer there; and the money he threw into the common alms box. These examples they see every day, and they are pretty nonchalant about them. Not everyone who wants to is readily allowed to give; at least it is a favor to be accepted.

I stayed here Monday, Tuesday, and Wednesday morning; after Mass we left. But, to say a word about my experience of this place, which I liked very much: there at the same time was Michel Marteau, seigneur de la Chapelle, a Parisian, a very rich young man with a big retinue. I had him and some of his attendants give me a very particular and careful account of the facts of the cure, which he said he had derived from this place, of one leg of his; it is not possible to represent better or more exactly the effect of a miracle. All the surgeons of Paris and Italy had failed at it. He had spent more than three thousand crowns on it: his knee, swollen, useless, and very painful for more than three years, by this time worse, more red and inflamed, and swollen to the point of giving him a fever; at that point, after abandoning all other medicaments and aids for several days, while sleeping, suddenly he dreams that he is cured and he seems to see a flash of lightning; he wakes up, cries out that he is cured, calls his men, gets up, walks around, which he

had never done since his malady; the swelling in his knee goes down, the withered and virtually dead skin all around his knee continues to mend ever since, without any other sort of aid. Now completely cured, he has returned to Loreto; for it was on another trip a month or two before that he had been cured, and he had meanwhile been in Rome with us. From his own mouth and from all his men that is all you can get for certain.

The miracle of the transporting of that little house, which they hold to be the very one in which Jesus Christ was born in Nazareth – its removal first to Sclavonia, and then near here, and finally here – is represented on large marble tablets in the church, attached all along the pillars, in Italian, Sclavonian, French, German, and Spanish. In the choir there hangs an ensign of our kings, and no arms of any other king.

They say that they often see the Sclavonians come to this devotion in large groups, with shouts as soon as they discover the church from the sea, and then on the spot so many protestations and promises to Our Lady to have her return to them, and so many regrets for having given her occasion to abandon them, that it is a wonder.

I found out that from Loreto it is possible to go along the seashore to Naples in eight days, by easy stages, a trip I would like to make. You have to pass by way of Pescara and the city of Chieti, where there is a mail carrier that leaves every Sunday for Naples.

I offered money to a number of priests; most of them were obstinate in refusing it, and those that did accept some did so with all the difficulties in the world.

They store and keep their grain here in cellars underneath the street.

It was on April 25th that I offered my ex-voto.

The trip from Rome to Loreto, which took us four days and a half, cost me six crowns in coin, which are fifty sous apiece, per horse, and the man who rented us the horses fed them and us. The bargain is disadvantageous, inasmuch as they hurry your daily journeys because of the expense they have, and then have you treated as stingily as they can.

On the 26th I went to see the port three miles beyond, which is handsome; and there is a fort that belongs to the community of Recanati.

Don Luca Giovanni, the beneficiary, and Giovanni Gregorio da Cagli, custodian of the sacristy, gave me their names, so that if

I had business with them either for myself or for others, I might write to them; these men did many courteous things for me. The former is in charge of this little chapel, and would not take anything from me. I am obliged to them for what they did for me and for their courteous words.

On the said Wednesday after dinner I followed along a road through fertile, open, and varied countryside, and came for supper to

ANCONA, fifteen miles. This is the chief town of the Marches; to the Latins the Marches were Picoenum. It is thickly populated, especially with Greeks, Turks, and Sclavonians; very mercantile, well built, flanked by two big headlands that run down into the sea, on one of which there is a large fort, by way of which we arrived. On the other, which is very near, there is a church. Between these two headlands and on their slopes, on either side, this city is set; but the main part is situated at the bottom of the valley and along the sea, where there is a very fine port in which there is still to be seen a great arch in honor of the Emperor Trajan, his wife, and his sister.

They say that one may often cross to Sclavonia in eight, ten, or twelve hours. I believe that for six crowns or a little more I could have found a bark that would have taken me to Venice. I gave thirty-three demi-pistoles for the hire of eight horses as far as Lucca, which is about eight days' journey. The driver has to feed the horses, and in case I am on the road four or five days more than the eight, I have the horses free for that time, and need only pay the expenses of the horses and the boys.

This country is full of excellent setters, and for six crowns there would be found some for sale. There were never so many quails to eat, but very lean.

I stayed on the 27th until after dinner, to see the beauty and the configuration of this town. At San Ciriaco, which is the church on one of the two headlands, there are more famous relics than in any other church in the world, and they were shown to us.

We verified the fact that the quails come over here from Sclavonia in great abundance, and that every night people stretch the nets on the shore on this side, and call them with a counterfeit call of theirs; and they call them back down from way up in the air, where they are in passage; and they say that around the month of September they go back across the sea to Sclavonia.

In the night I heard a cannon shot. From the Abruzzi on, in the kingdom of Naples and beyond the city, at every league there is

a tower; the first one that discovers a corsair galley makes a signal with fire to the second watchtower, the second to the third, with such rapidity that they have found that in an hour the warning runs from the end of Italy as far as Venice.

Ancona was so called in ancient times from the Greek word, because of the angle that the sea forms in this place;[5] for its two horns advance and make a deep cove, where the town is protected in front by these two headlands and the sea, and also behind by a high rise, where formerly there used to be a fortress. There is also a Greek church, and over the door, on an old stone, some letters that I think are Sclavonian. The women here are generally beautiful, and there are many fine men and good artisans.

After dinner we followed the seacoast, which is gentler and more accessible than our ocean coast, and cultivated all the way to the water, and came to sleep at

SINIGAGLIA, twenty miles, a beautiful little town situated in a very beautiful plain right next to the sea, and it makes a fine port; for a river coming down from the mountains washes it on one side. They are making it into a channel studded and lined with large wooden piles on either side, where boats take shelter; and the entry to it is closed. I saw no antiquities here; besides, we stayed outside of town in a handsome hostelry which is the only one in this place. They formerly called it Senogallia, from our ancestors who settled here after Camillus had beaten them; it is in the jurisdiction of the duke of Urbino.

I did not feel very well. The day I left Rome, as Monsieur d'Ossat was walking with me, I tried to salute another gentleman, with such heedlessness that with my right thumb I wounded the corner of my right eye so that the blood immediately came out, and it has been very red for a long time. Then it got better; and "then there was pain in that sinister thumbnail."[6]

I was forgetting to say that at Ancona, in the Church of San Ciriaco, there is a low tombstone of one "Antonia, a Rocamoro on her father's side, a Valletta on her mother's, a Frenchwoman from Guienne, married to Paciotto of Urbino, a Portuguese,"[7] who has been buried ten or twelve years.

5 Ἀγχών, elbow, or bend. It was founded by Doric Greeks from Syracuse.
6 This remark in Latin, seemingly a quotation, plays on the two meanings of *sinistrum*: left (hand), and sinister. Thus his right nail became left (sinister).
7 Montaigne quotes the inscription in Latin.

We left here early in the morning and followed the seashore by a very pleasant road. Near our dinnertime we crossed the river Metro, Metaurus, over a large wooden bridge, and dined at

FANO, fifteen miles, a little town in a beautiful and very fertile plain next to the sea, rather badly built, heavily walled. We were very well treated here as for bread, wine, and fish; the lodging is not worth much. It has this advantage over the other towns on this coast, like Sinigaglia, Pesaro, and others, that it has an abundance of fresh water, many public fountains and private wells, whereas the others have to go as far as the mountains to fetch their water. Here we saw a big ancient arch on which there is an inscription under the name of Augustus, "who had given walls to the city." The town used to be called Fanum, and was Fanum Fortunae.[8]

Almost everywhere in Italy they sift their flour with wheels, whereby a baker does more work in an hour than we do in four.

You find rhymers at almost all the hostelries who make rhymes on the spot, suitable for the persons present. There are instruments in all the shops, even those of the clothes menders at the street corners.

This town is famous above all those in Italy for beautiful women; we saw none but very ugly ones; and when I inquired of a good man of the town, he told me that that time had passed.

On this route you pay about ten sous per meal, twenty sous a day per man; the horse, for hire and expenses, about thirty sous; which makes fifty sous.

This town belongs to the Church.

We abandoned the idea of going a little farther on this same road to see Pesaro, a beautiful town and worth seeing, and then Rimini, and then ancient Ravenna; and especially, at Pesaro, a handsome building, strangely situated, which the duke of Urbino is having built, so I was told. That is the road down to Venice.

We left the coast and took our left, following a broad plain through which the Metaurus passes. You discover everywhere, on either hand, very beautiful hillsides, and the aspect of this country-side is not unlike the plain of Blaignac at Castillon. In this plain, on the other side of this river, the battle took place which Salinator and Claudius Nero fought against Hasdrubal, in which Hasdrubal was killed. At the entrance to the mountains which you encounter at the end of this plain, right at the entrance, is

8 The Temple of Fortune.

FOSSOMBRONE, fifteen miles, belonging to the duke of Urbino, a town lying against the slope of a mountain, having at the base one or two beautiful streets, very straight, level, and well located; however, they say that the people of Fano are much richer than themselves. Here in the square is a large marble pedestal with a very long inscription, which is of the time of Trajan, in honor of a private inhabitant of this place, and another inscription against the wall which bears no indication of the time. This was in ancient times the Forum Sempronii; but they hold that their first town was farther over toward the plain and that the ruins are still there in a much more beautiful site. This town has a stone bridge to cross the Metaurus, toward Rome, by the Via Flaminia.

Because I arrived here early (for the miles are short and our days' journeys were of only seven or eight hours' riding), I talked to several worthy men who told me what they knew about their town and the environs. Here we saw a garden of the cardinal of Urbino, and lots of vines grafted onto other stocks. I talked with a good man who makes books, named Vincentius Castellani, who is from here.

I left here the next morning, and after riding three miles I turned off to the left and crossed a bridge over the Candigliano, the river that flows into the Metaurus, and went three miles along some wild mountains and rocks, by a narrow and rather difficult road, at the end of which we saw a passage a good fifty paces long which has been cut through one of these high rocks. And because this is a big job, to which Augustus first set his hand, there was an inscription in his name, which time has effaced; and another is to be seen at the other end in honor of Vespasian.[9]

Around here you see plenty of big walls rising from the bed of the river, which is extremely deep; below the road, cut and leveled rocks of tremendous thickness; and all along this road, which is the Via Flaminia, by which you go to Rome, traces of their big paving blocks, which are for the most part buried; and their road, which was forty feet wide, is now not even four.

I had turned out of my way to see this, and I retraced my steps to my road, which I followed along the base of some accessible and fertile mountains. Toward the end of our stage, we began to go up and down hill, and came to

9 The Furlo Pass, where the Via Flaminia passes through a tunnel about forty yards long.

URBINO, sixteen miles, a town of little distinction, on the top of a mountain of medium height, but lying in all directions according to the slopes of the place, so that there is nothing level about it, and everywhere you have to go up and down. The market was being held, for it was Saturday.

Here we saw the palace, which is very famous for its beauty. It is a great mass, for it stretches right to the foot of the mountain. The view extends to a thousand other neighboring mountains and has not much charm, nor is there anything very attractive about this whole building either inside or around it, and it has only a tiny little garden of twenty-five paces or thereabouts. They boast that it has as many bedrooms as there are days in the year. In truth, there are a very great number of them, and, in the manner of Tivoli and other palaces of Italy, through one door you often see twenty other doors in succession in one direction and as many or more in the other direction. There is something ancient about it, but the main part of it was built in 1476 by Federigo Maria della Rovere,[10] who inscribed inside many of his titles and his great offices and exploits in war, with which his walls are thickly covered, as well as an inscription saying that this is the most beautiful house in the world. It is of brick, and all built with arches, without any wooden flooring, like most of the buildings in Italy.

The present duke is his grandnephew. He descends from a line of good princes, who are loved by their subjects. They are all men of letters, from father to son, and have a fine library in this palace, but the key was not to be found. They incline to Spain. The arms of the king of Spain are seen in rank and favor, and the Order of England and that of the Golden Fleece, and nothing of ours.

They themselves show a painting of the first duke of Urbino, a young man who was killed by his subjects for his injustice; he was not of this line. The present one married the sister of the duke of Ferrara, ten years older than he. They are on bad terms, and separated, purely because of her jealousy, so they say. What with this and her age, which is forty-five, they have little hope of children, the lack of which they say will cause this duchy to revert to the Church, and they are unhappy about it.

I saw here a portrait from life of Pico della Mirandola: a pale, very handsome face, beardless, seeming about seventeen or eighteen,

10 This should be Federigo da Montefeltro.

a longish nose, gentle eyes, rather thin face, blond hair falling down to his shoulders, and a strange costume.

In many places in Italy they have a fashion of making winding staircases, even very steep and narrow ones, so that you can mount to the top of them on horseback; this is also the fashion here, with tiles set on a slant. It is a cold place, they say, and the duke makes it a habit to be here only in summer. To provide against this cold, in two of their bedrooms there are to be seen other square rooms in a corner, closed in on all sides except for a window or so which lets in light from the room; within these shelters is the master's bed.

After dinner I turned out of my way another five miles to see a place that the people from time immemorial have called Hasdrubal's Tomb, on a very high and steep hill which they call Monte d'Elce. Here there are four or five wretched little houses and a little church, and you see also a building of large bricks or tiles, twenty-five paces round or thereabouts, and twenty-five feet high. All around it there are supports of the same brick at every three paces. I do not know what the masons call these pieces, which they make for support like beaks.[11] We climbed up it, for there is no entry from below. We found a vault there, nothing inside, no cut stone, nothing inscribed. The inhabitants say that there used to be a piece of marble on which there were a few marks, but that it has been taken away in our time. Why this name was given it I do not know, and I scarcely believe that it is really what they say. To be sure, it is certain that he was defeated and killed rather near here.

Afterward we followed a very mountainous road, which became muddy merely because it had rained for an hour, and we crossed the Metaurus again – by a ford, since it is nothing but a torrent that will not bear a boat – which we had crossed another time since dinner; and toward the end of the day we came by a low and easy road to

CASTEL-DURANTE,[12] fifteen miles, a little town situated in the plain along the Metaurus, belonging to the duke of Urbino. The people here were making a bonfire and celebrating the birth of a male child to the princess of Bisignano, sister of their duke.

Our drivers unsaddle their horses whenever they unbridle them, whatever state they are in, and have them drink anyway. Here and at Urbino we drank wines that had been sophisticated to make them milder.

11 Presumably flying buttresses.
12 Modern Urbania.

On Sunday morning we came along a rather fertile plain surrounded by hills, and passed first through a beautiful little town, Sant' Angelo, belonging to the said duke, along the Metaurus, with very beautiful approaches. We found in the town some little girls dressed up for May Day like queens of mid-Lent, for it was the eve of the first of May. From here, following this plain, we went through still another little town in the same jurisdiction, named Marcatello, and, by a road that already was beginning to smack of the Apennine mountains, we came to dine at

BORGO-PACE, ten miles, a little village and a wretched inn for a meager meal, in a corner of the mountains.

After dinner, we followed first a narrow, wild, and stony road, and then had to climb a high mountain, two miles up and four miles downward slope; the road shaly and annoying, but not frightening or dangerous, the precipices not being so steeply cut that the eye does not have something to rest on. We followed the Metaurus right to its lair, which is in this mountain; thus we have seen its birth and its end, having seen it fall into the sea at Sinigaglia. On descending this mountain we perceived a very beautiful and large plain, in which runs the Tiber, only eight miles or so from its source, and other mountains beyond: a prospect rather resembling that which is offered in the Limagne of Auvergne to those who descend the Puy de Dôme to Clermont-Ferrand. On the top of our mountain ends the jurisdiction of the duke of Urbino, and that of the duke of Florence begins, with that of the Pope on the left hand. We came to sup at

BORGO SAN SEPOLCRO, thirteen miles, a little town in this plain, belonging to the said duke of Florence, having nothing singular about it; we left it on the first day of May.

A mile from this town we crossed a stone bridge over the river Tiber, which still has its clear, beautiful waters – a sign that that dirty reddish color, *flavum Tiberim*,[13] which you see in it at Rome, comes from the admixture of some other river. We crossed this four-mile plain, and at the first hill found a little town on top. Several girls, both here and elsewhere on the road, came to meet us and seized our horses' bridles, and there asked for some liberality for the day's festival, singing a certain song to that effect.

From this hill we went back down into a very stony bottom, which we followed a long time along the bed of a torrent, and then

13 "The yellow Tiber." An expression used by Horace in his *Odes*.

we had a barren and very stony mountain to climb, three miles for the ascent and descent, from which we descried another large plain, in which we crossed the river Chiassa over a stone bridge, and afterward the river Arno over a very big, handsome stone bridge, on the hither side of which we lodged at

PONTE BORIANO, a tiny little house, eighteen miles. A bad inn, like the three preceding ones and most of those on this route. It would be great folly to bring good horses this way, for there is no hay.

After dinner we followed a long plain all split by horrible crevices which the waters make in a strange fashion, and I believe it must be very ugly in winter; but then, they are repairing the road. On our left, very soon after dinner, we passed the town of Arezzo in this same plain, two miles or so away. Its site, however, seems to be a little raised. We crossed the river Ambra on a handsome stone bridge of great height, and came for supper to

LEVANELLA, ten miles. The hostelry is a mile or so short of the said village, and is famous; indeed it is held to be the best in Tuscany, and with reason; for by the standard of the hostelries of Italy it is one of the best. It is so highly thought of that they say the nobility of the region often gather there, as at Le More's in Paris or Guillot's in Amiens. They serve on pewter plates there, which is a great rarity. It is a house by itself, very beautifully situated in a plain, and has a spring at its service.

We left there in the morning and followed a very fine straight road across this plain, and on it passed through four little towns or walled villages, Montevarchi, San Giovanni, Figline, and Ancisa, and came to dine at

PIAN DELLA FONTE, twelve miles, a pretty poor inn, where there is also a spring, a little above the said village of Ancisa, which is situated in the valley of the Arno. They maintain that Petrarch, who speaks of it, was born at the said Ancisa, at least in a nearby house a mile from there, of which you no longer find anything but very unimpressive ruins; however, they do point out the place. They were then sowing melons there among the others that were already sown, and they expected to gather them in August.

This morning I had a heaviness in the head and trouble with my vision, as from my old migraines, which I had not felt for ten years.

This valley through which we passed was once all marshes, and Livy maintains that Hannibal was forced to cross them on an

elephant, and lost an eye there because of the bad weather. It is in truth a very flat, low area, and subject to floods from the Arno.

I would not eat any dinner there, and was sorry for it, for that would have helped me to vomit, which is my promptest cure; otherwise I carry about this heavy-headedness for a day or two, as happened to me then. We found this road full of people of the region, bringing various kinds of foods to Florence. We arrived at

FLORENCE, twelve miles, by one of the four stone bridges which are there over the Arno.

The next day, after having heard Mass, we left there, and turning a bit off the straight road, went to see Castello, of which I have spoken elsewhere;[14] but because the duke's daughters were there, and at this very hour were going through the garden to hear Mass, we were asked to be good enough to wait, which I did not wish to do.

On the road we met many processions. The banner goes ahead, the women after, most of them very beautiful, with straw hats, which they make better in this region than anywhere else in the world, and well dressed for village women, their slippers and pumps white. After the women walks the curate, and after him come the men. The day before, we had seen a procession of monks, almost all wearing these straw hats.

We followed a very beautiful, very wide plain, and to tell the truth I was virtually forced to confess that neither Orléans, nor Tours, nor Paris itself, is surrounded by so great a number of houses and villages, and so far out, as Florence; as for beautiful houses and palaces, that is beyond doubt. Along this route we came to dine at

PRATO, ten miles, a little town belonging to the said duke, situated on the river Bisenzio, which we crossed by a stone bridge at the gate of the said town.

There is no other region so well supplied, among other things, with bridges, and such solid ones; and indeed along the roads everywhere you come across big cut stones on which is written what piece of road each district has to keep up and be responsible for. In the palace of the said place we saw the arms and name of the legate da Prato, who they say was a native of here. Over the door of this palace is a large crowned statue, holding the world in its hand, and at its feet, *Rex Robertus*.[15] Here they say that this town was

14 *Travel Journal*, p. 1135.
15 Robert of Anjou, king of Naples, to whom the town surrendered in 1313.

formerly ours; the fleurs-de-lys are everywhere; but the town's own arms bear gules powdered with fleurs-de-lys or. The cathedral here is beautiful and enriched with much black and white marble.

On leaving here we took another side road, a detour of a good four miles, to go to the Poggio, a house about which they make much ado, belonging to the duke, situated on the river Ombrone; the form of this building is the model of Pratolino. It is a marvel that in such a small mass there can be contained a hundred very beautiful rooms. Here I saw among other things a great number of beds of very beautiful stuff that is not expensive: they are some of those light varicolored materials which are nothing but very fine wool, and they line it with four-thread taffeta of the same color as the material. Here we saw the duke's distillery and his workroom fitted with a lathe and other instruments; for he is a great mechanic.

From here, by a very straight road through extremely fertile country, the road enclosed by trees with vines attached which form a hedge, a thing of great beauty, we came for supper to

PISTOIA, fourteen miles, a big town on the river Ombrone; the streets very wide, paved, like Florence, Prato, Lucca, and others, with big and very wide stone slabs. I was forgetting to say that from the table in the rooms at Poggio you see Florence, Prato, and Pistoia. In the said Pistoia there are very few people; the churches are beautiful, and there are many beautiful houses. I inquired about the sale of straw hats, which they made for fifteen sous. It seems to me that they would be worth quite as many francs[16] in France. Near this town and in its territory Catiline was defeated long ago.

At Poggio there are some tapestries representing every kind of hunting; among others, I noticed one hanging that showed the hunting of ostriches, which they show being pursued by men on horseback, and speared with javelins.

The Latins called Pistoia Pistorium; it belongs to the duke of Florence. The say that the ancient feuds of the houses of the Cancellieri and the Panciatici, which existed formerly, made it as it is now, as it were uninhabited, so that it numbers only eight thousand souls in all; and Lucca, which is no bigger, has twenty-five thousand inhabitants and more.

Messer Taddeo Rospigliosi, who had had a letter of recommendation from Rome on my behalf from Giovanni Franchini, invited me to dinner the next day, with all the others who were in our

16 The franc was worth one livre, or twenty sous.

company. The palace is very ornate, the service a little strange in the order of dishes; little meat, few servants; the wine served again after the meal, as in Germany.

We saw the churches: at the elevation in the principal church they blew trumpets. Among the choirboys there were some priests in their vestments who played on sackbuts.

This poor town compensates for its lost liberty by a vain image of its ancient constitution. They have nine Priors and a Gonfalonier, whom they elect every two months. These have charge of keeping order, and are maintained by the duke, as they formerly were by the public; they are lodged in the palace, and hardly ever leave it except all together, being perpetually confined there. The Gonfalonier marches in front of the podestà whom the duke sends there, which podestà has in fact all the power; and the said Gonfalonier salutes no one, imitating the petty royalty they imagine themselves to be. I felt pity to see them feed on this monkey business; and meanwhile the grand duke has increased the taxes by ten times over what they formerly were.

In most of the big gardens in Italy they grow grass in the principal walks, and mow it.

About this time the cherries were beginning to ripen; and on the road from Pistoia to Lucca we found village people who offered us bunches of strawberries for sale.

We left here on Thursday, Ascension Day, after dinner, and first followed that plain for a while, and then a slightly hilly road, and afterward a very beautiful wide plain. In the wheat fields they have many trees, well arranged, and covered and linked to one another by vines: these fields seem like gardens. The mountains that are seen on this route are heavily covered with trees, chiefly olive and chestnut trees and mulberry trees for their silkworms. In this plain you come upon

LUCCA, twenty miles, a city one-third smaller than Bordeaux, free, except that because of its weakness it has cast itself under the protection of the Emperor and the house of Austria. It is well enclosed and flanked; the moats not deep, with a little channel of water flowing in them, and full of green plants; flat and broad at the bottom. All around the wall, on the raised walk on the inside, two or three rows of trees are planted which serve for shade, and, they say, for faggots in case of need. From the outside you see only a wood that hides the houses. They always have a guard of three hundred foreign soldiers.

The city is thickly populated, notably with silk workers; the streets narrow but handsome, and almost everywhere beautiful big houses. They are running a little channel through it from the river Serchio; they are building a palace at an expense of a hundred and thirty thousand crowns, and it is well advanced.

They say they have six-score thousand souls as subjects, not counting the city. They have a few small fortified places, but no town under their subjection. Their gentlemen and men-at-arms all make a profession of trade. The Buonvisi are the richest here. Strangers enter only by one gate, where there is a heavy guard.

It is one of the most pleasant sites for a town that I ever saw, surrounded by two full leagues of plain, of superlative beauty at the narrowest point, and then beautiful mountains and hills, where most of them have country lodgings.

The wines here are moderately good; the cost of living twenty sous a day; the hostelries in the manner of this country, pretty unimpressive. I received many courtesies from several private persons, and wines and fruits and offers of money.

I was here Friday and Saturday, and left on Sunday after dinner – dinner for the others, not for me, since I was fasting. The hills nearest the city are studded with plenty of pleasant houses very close together. Most of the trip was by a low road, rather easy, between the mountains, almost all very shady and inhabitable, all the way along the river Serchio. We passed several ordinary villages and two very large walled villages, Decimo and Borgo, on this side of the said river, which we had on our right hand, and then crossed over a bridge of unusual height, with one arch embracing a great width of the said river; and we saw three or four bridges of this kind.

Italy: First Stay at La Villa
(May 7–June 21, 1581)

We came about two o'clock in the afternoon to the

BATH OF LA VILLA, sixteen miles. It is a thoroughly hilly country. In front of the bath, along the river, there is a plain of three or four hundred paces, above which the bath is on the side of a medium-sized mountain, part way up, about as high up as the spring of Bagnères, where they drink near the town.

The site of the bath is fairly level, and there are thirty or forty houses very well fitted for this purpose; the rooms pretty, quite private, and as free as you like, each with a toilet, and each with a door to an adjacent room and another for private use. I inspected almost all the houses before making a bargain, and settled on the finest, especially for the view, which overlooks (at least the room I chose) all this little valley, and the river Lima, and the mountains that shelter the said valley, all well cultivated and green all the way to the summit, full of chestnut and olive trees, and elsewhere of vines, which they plant around the mountains, girding the mountains with terraces. The edge of the terrace toward the outside, a little raised, is vine; the hollow of the terrace is wheat. All night from my room I heard, very soft, the sound of the river.

Between these houses is a place to walk, open on one side in the form of a terrace, from which you look down on that small plain below the walk through a public trellis, and you see along the river in that small plain, two hundred paces below you, a handsome little village which also serves for these baths when there is a crowd. Most of the houses new; a fine road to go there; and a handsome square in the said village. Most of the inhabitants of this place stay here in the winter and have their shops here, especially apothecaries' shops; for almost all are apothecaries.

My landlord is named Captain Paulino, and he is an apothecary. He gave me a dining room, three bedrooms, a kitchen, and also a garret for our men, and in them eight beds, for two of which there was a canopy; furnished salt, a napkin every day, a tablecloth every third day, all the iron utensils for the kitchen, and candlesticks, for eleven crowns, a few sous more than ten pistolets, for a fortnight. The pots, dishes, and plates, which are of earthenware, we bought, as well as the glasses and knives; they have meat, as much as you want, veal and kid; not much else. At each inn they offer to do your marketing for you, and I think you could have it done for twenty sous a man per day; and if you want to do it yourself, you find in every inn some man or woman capable of doing your cooking. The wine is not very good; but anyone who wants can have it brought from either Pescia or Lucca.

I was the first to arrive here, except for two Bolognese gentlemen who did not have any big retinue. Thus I had a choice and, from what they say, a better bargain than I would have had in the crowd, which they say is very great here. But their practice is not to begin to come until June, and to stay here until September; for by

October they are gone; and they very often have gatherings here solely for recreation. Any visiting that they do earlier – as we found some who were returning home after being here a month already – or in October, is extraordinary.

In this place there is a house belonging to the lords of Buonvisi, much more magnificent than the others, and assuredly very handsome; they call it the Palace. It has a beautiful live spring in the dining room, and many other conveniences. It was offered to me, at least a four-room apartment that I wanted, and the whole thing if I needed it. The four rooms, furnished as above, they would have let me have for twenty crowns of the country[1] for a fortnight; I was willing to give a crown a day. In consideration of the season and the price, which changes, my landlord is bound to our bargain only for the month of May; we will have to make a new one if I want to stay longer.

There is water to drink here and also to bathe in; a covered bath, vaulted and rather dark, half as wide as my dining room at Montaigne. There is also a certain dripping apparatus that they call *la doccia*:[2] this consists of pipes by which you receive hot water on various parts of the body, and especially on the head, the water coming down on you in steady streams and warming the part of your body that they are beating down on; and then the water is received in a wooden trough, like that of washerwomen, along which it flows away. There is another bath, vaulted in the same way, and dark, for the women; the whole thing coming from a spring from which one drinks, rather unattractively situated, in a hollow to which one has to go down several steps.

On Monday morning, May 8th, with great difficulty, I took some cassia which my landlord offered me, not with the grace of the man in Rome, and I took it with my own hands. I dined two hours later and could not finish my dinner; the operation of the cassia made me throw up what I had taken, and vomit again later. I had three or four stools from it, with great pain in the belly because of the flatulence, which tormented me for almost twenty-four hours, and I have promised myself not to take any more of it. I would rather have a fit of colic than have my belly thus upset, my taste altered, and my health disturbed by this cassia; for I had come here in good condition; so that on Sunday after supper, which

1 Italian scudi, not French écus. One écu was worth about 1.2 scudi.
2 The shower.

was the only meal I had that day, I went very blithely to see the bath of Corsena, which is a good half mile from here, on the other side of this same mountain; you have to go up and then come down again to about the same height as the baths on this side. This other bath is more famous for the bathing and *la doccia*; for ours has no generally accepted use, either according to the doctors or by usage, except for drinking; and they say that the other has a more ancient reputation. However, for all this age, which goes back to the times of the Romans, there is no trace of antiquity at either bath.

There are three or four large baths there, vaulted except for a hole in the middle of the vault like a vent hole; they are dark and unattractive. There is another hot spring two or three hundred paces from there, a little higher up on this same mountain, called Monte San Giovanni; and there they have made a hut with three baths, also covered; no house nearby, but room to place a mattress to rest on for an hour or so in the day. At Corsena they do not drink at all. Moreover, they diversify the operation of its waters: one cools, one warms, one for this malady, one for another; and on this subject a thousand miracles; but in short, there is no sort of malady that does not find its cure there.

There is one handsome inn with many rooms, and about a score of others not very handsome. In the matter of convenience they cannot compare with ours, nor in the beauty of the view, although they have our river at their feet and their view extends farther into a valley; and yet they are much more expensive. Many drink here, and then go to bathe there. For the moment Corsena has the reputation.

On Tuesday, May 9th, 1581, early in the morning before sunrise, I went to drink right from the spout of our hot spring, and drank seven glasses right in a row, which hold three pounds and a half: that is the way they measure.[3] I think that would be about twelve glasses, or our quart. It is a very moderately hot water, like that of Aigues-Caudes or Barbotan, having less taste and savor than any other I have ever drunk. I could perceive nothing of it but its tepidness and a little sweetness. For that day it had no effect on me, and yet I was five hours from drinking it until dinner, and I did not pass a single drop of it. Some said I had taken too little, for here they order a *flask*, that is, two *jars*, which is eight pounds, or sixteen or

3 The Italian pound was only twelve ounces; see below, p. 1210.

seventeen of my glasses. I myself think that it found me so empty because of my medicine that it found room to serve me for food.

This same day I had a visit from a Bolognese gentleman, a colonel of twelve hundred foot, in the pay of the signory of Lucca, who is staying four miles from the baths; and he came and did me many civilities, and was with me about two hours; he ordered my landlord and others in the place to favor me to the extent of their power.

This signory has a rule to use foreign officers, and distributes its men in the villages by number and according to the country, and gives them a colonel to command them: one has a larger, another a smaller command. The colonels are paid; the captains, who are inhabitants of the country, are paid only in wartime, and command the individual companies when there is need. My colonel had sixteen crowns a month in wages, and has no responsibility but to keep himself ready.

They live more by rule in these baths than in ours, and especially keep strict fast as regards drinking. I found myself better lodged here than at any other baths, even at Bagnères. The situation of the country is quite as beautiful at Bagnères, but not at any other bath; the places for bathing at Baden surpass all others by far in magnificence and convenience; the inn at Baden bears comparison with any other, except for the view from here.

Wednesday morning early I again drank of this water; and being pretty disturbed over the little effect I had felt from it the day before (for I had indeed had a stool immediately after taking it, but I attributed that to the medicine of the preceding day, not having passed one drop of water that resembled that of the bath), I took on Wednesday seven glasses measured by the pound, which was at least double what I had taken the other day, and I believe I have never taken so much at one time. I felt from it a great desire to sweat, which I would not indulge at all, having often heard that this was not the effect I needed; and, as on the first day, I kept to my room, now walking around, now at rest. The water proceeded mostly through the rear, and made me have several loose, light stools, without any effort.

I hold that it did me harm to take this purge of cassia, for the water, finding nature moving to the rear and provoked, followed that course; whereas, because of my kidneys, I would have liked it better to the front; and I am thinking, at the first baths I take, of preparing only by some fasting the day before. Also I believe this water is very weak and of little effect, and consequently safe and

without risk: apprentices and delicate people would be well off with it. They take it to cool the liver and get rid of red pimples on the face, a fact I carefully note as a service I owe to a very virtuous lady in France.[4]

The water of San Giovanni they use a lot for cosmetics, for it is extremely oily. I saw that they exported it in barrelfuls to foreign countries, and still more of that which I was drinking, on many donkeys and mules, to Reggio, Modena, Lombardy, to drink. Some take it here in bed, and their principal instructions are to keep their stomach and feet warm, and not to move around much. The people in the neighborhood have it brought three or four miles to their houses. To show that it is not very aperient, they have the custom of having water brought here from a bath near Pistoia, which has an acrid taste and is very hot at its source; and the apothecaries here keep it to drink before the water from here, one glassful, and hold that it helps it along, being active and aperient.

The second day I passed some water that was clear, but not without some alteration of color, as elsewhere, and voided a lot of gravel; but it was helped along by the cassia, for I passed a lot of it on the day I took the cassia.

Here I learned of a memorable incident. An inhabitant of this place, a soldier named Giuseppe, who is still alive and commands [the oarsmen on] one of the galleys of the Genoese as a convict, and several of whose near relations I saw, was captured by the Turks in a battle at sea. To regain his liberty he became a Turk (and there are many of this condition, and especially in the mountains near this place, still alive), was circumcised, and married in their territory. Coming to pillage this coast, he went so far from his base that there he was, with a few other Turks, caught by the people, who had risen up. He had the presence of mind to say that he had come to surrender deliberately, that he was a Christian. He was set at liberty a few days later, came to this place, and to the house opposite the one I am lodging in; he entered and encountered his mother. She asked him roughly who he was and what he wanted; for he still had on his sailor's clothes, and it was strange to see him there. Finally he made himself known, for he had been lost for ten or twelve years, and embraced his mother. She uttered one cry and fell quite distracted; until the next day they did not see much sign of life in her, and the doctors were entirely without hope. She finally came back to herself

4 Quite possibly Montaigne's wife.

but she did not live long afterward, and everyone judged that this shock shortened her life. Our Giuseppe was feted by one and all, was received into the Church to abjure his error, and received the Sacrament from the bishop of Lucca, with several other ceremonies. It was just humbug: he was a Turk at heart. To return to the Turks he steals away from here, goes to Venice, and mixes with them again. Resuming his travels, here he falls into our hands again; and because he is a man of unusual strength and a soldier well versed in naval matters, the Genoese still keep him and use him, well bound and fettered.

This nation has many soldiers, inhabitants of the country, who are all registered for the service of the signory. The colonels have no other responsibility than to drill them often in marksmanship, skirmishing, and such things. The men receive no pay, but they may bear arms, chain mail, harquebuses, and whatever they please; and then they cannot be seized in person for any debt, and in war they receive pay. Among them are the captains, ensigns, sergeants. Only the colonel must necessarily be a foreigner and be paid. The colonel from the Borgo, the one who had come to visit me the day before, sent me from the said place (which is four miles from the bath) a man with sixteen lemons and sixteen artichokes.

The mildness and weakness of this water is further argued by the fact that it turns so easily into food; for it is immediately colored and digested, and does not stimulate the desire to urinate the way the others do, as I observed by my own experience and that of others at the same time.

Although I was pleasantly and very comfortably lodged, in such a way as to rival my lodging in Rome, still I had neither window frame nor fireplace, and still less windowpanes, in my room. This shows that in Italy they do not have as frequent storms as we do; for if they did, it would be an intolerable discomfort to have no other than wooden windows in nearly all the houses. Except for that, I was very well bedded.

Their beds are wretched little trestles on which they throw planks, according to the length and width of the bed; on top of these a straw mattress and a regular mattress, and there you are very well lodged, if you have a canopy. And to keep your trestles and planks from showing, three remedies: one, to have strips of the same stuff as the canopy, as I had in Rome; another, to have your canopy long enough to hang down to the ground and cover everything, which is the best way; the third, for the covering, which is fastened

at the corners with buttons, to hang down to the ground; it should be of some light stuff, such as white fustian, with another covering underneath for warmth. At least I am learning this economy for my retinue, and for general use at home, and I have no need for bedsteads. One is very comfortable, and then it is a recipe against bedbugs.

The same day after dinner I bathed, contrary to the rules of this region, where they say that one operation impedes the other, and want to keep them distinct: drink for one spell, and then bathe for another. They drink eight days and bathe thirty: drink in this bath, and bathe in the other. The bath is very mild and pleasant. I was in it for half an hour, and it made me sweat only a little; it was about suppertime. I went to bed on leaving there, and supped on a salad of sugared lemon, without anything to drink; for that day I did not drink a pound, and I think that if the whole count had been kept until the next day, it would be clear that I had voided by this means almost all the water I had taken.

It is a stupid habit to keep count of what you piss.

I did not feel bad, but lively, as at the other baths; and yet I was greatly concerned to see that my water did not pass. Perhaps the same had happened to me elsewhere; but here they make a tragedy of this, and from the first day, if you fail to void at least two-thirds, they advise you to give up drinking or to take medicine.

For my part, if I judge rightly about these waters, they are not such as to do either much harm or much good; there is nothing but mildness and weakness in them, and it is to be feared that they warm up the kidneys more than they purge them; and I think I need hotter and more aperient waters.

On Thursday morning I again drank five pounds, fearing to be ill served by them and not to void them. They made me have one stool and urinate very little.

This same morning, writing to Monsieur d'Ossat, I was overcome by such painful thoughts about Monsieur de La Boétie,[5] and I was in this mood so long, without recovering, that it did me much harm.

The bottom of this bath is all red and rusty, as is the channel through which it passes: this, added to its insipidity, makes me believe that it contains much iron, and that it is binding. On

5 Montaigne's dear friend, who died eighteen years earlier. See, for example, *Essays* I: 28; *Letters*, No. 2.

Thursday, in five hours that I waited to dine, I voided only the fifth part of what I had drunk.

What a vain thing medicine is! I chanced to say that I repented of having purged myself so much, and that this made the water, finding me empty, serve as food and stay in me. I have just seen a doctor named Donati in print speaking of these waters, who says he advises dining little and supping better. I think my conjecture backs him up. His colleague Franciotti is of the contrary view, as in many other things.

That day I had some feelings of heaviness in the kidneys which I feared that the waters themselves caused me, and I was afraid that they were stagnating there; yet on counting up everything I passed in twenty-four hours, I came about up to my point, seeing how little I drank at meals.

Friday I did not drink, and instead of drinking went to bathe in the morning and wash my head, contrary to the common practice of the place.

It is a custom of the country to help along one's water by some drug mixed in, such as sugar candy, or manna, or still stronger medicine, which they mix with the first glass of their water; and most ordinarily they use the water of the Tettuccio, which I tasted; it is salty. I have some suspicion that the apothecaries, instead of sending to get it near Pistoia, where they say it is, sophisticate some natural water; for I found its taste extraordinary, besides the saltiness. They have it heated up and start by drinking one, two, or three glasses. I have seen it drunk in my presence without any effect. Some put salt in the water for the first and second glasses or more. They consider sweating virtually fatal, and also sleeping after drinking. I felt that the operation of this water strongly inclined me to sweat.

[THE JOURNAL BY MONTAIGNE IN ITALIAN]

Let us try to speak this other language[6] a little, especially since I am in this region where I seem to hear the most perfect Tuscan speech, particularly among those natives who have not corrupted and altered it with that of their neighbors.

On Saturday morning early I went to take the water of Bernabò. This is one spring among all the others on this mountain; and it is a marvel how many there are, both hot and cold. The mountain is not very high. It is perhaps three miles around. People drink only

6 Tuscan. For Montaigne's comment on this experience, see *Essays* III: 5, p. 807.

from this one principal spring, and from one other that has been used for a few years. One Bernabò, a leper, had tried both waters and baths from all the other springs, and, giving up, resolved on this one; here he was cured. Thereby it came into repute.

There are no houses around, and only a small covered shed and stone seats around the duct, which, although it is of iron and has not been there long, is mostly eaten away underneath. They say it is the strength of the water that consumes it, and this is very likely. This water is a little hotter than the other, and in the general opinion heavier and more violent. It has a little more odor of sulphur, but only a little; and where it falls, it whitens the spot with an ashen color, like ours, but less. It is a little less than a mile from my lodging around the foot of the mountain; its site is a good deal lower than all the other hot springs. It is about a pike's length or two from the river.

I took five pounds of this water, with some discomfort, because I was none too well that morning. The day before, I had taken a long walk of three miles after dinner in the heat; and after supper I felt the effect of this water somewhat more; I began to get rid of it in half an hour. I took a big detour of about two miles to return to my house. I do not know whether this unusual exercise did me good, because on the other days I returned immediately to my room so as not to be chilled by the morning air; and the houses are not thirty paces from the spring. The first water that I voided was natural and pretty gravelly, the rest white and undigested. Broke wind endlessly. About the third pound that I got rid of began to recover a sort of reddish color. I had discharged more than half of it before dinner.

Going around this mountain in all directions I found many hot springs. And furthermore, the peasants say that in certain places in winter the mountain smokes: a proof that there are still others. They seem to me of about the same heat, without smell, without taste, without fumes, compared with ours.

I saw another place at Corsena much lower than the baths, where there are a large number of shower baths, more comfortable than the others. They say there are still more springs that feed these pipes, some eight or ten; and they have different names inscribed over each tap, indicating their effects: the Savory, the Gentle, the Enamored, the Crown, the Desperate, etc. In truth, some of the channels are hotter than others.

The mountains around are almost all fertile in wheat and grapes, whereas fifty years ago they were covered with woods and chestnuts. You see a few bare mountains with snow on top, but very distant.

The people eat "wooden bread": so they proverbially call the bread made of chestnuts, which is their principal crop; and it is prepared like what they call *pain d'épice*[7] in France. I never saw so many toads and snakes. And for fear of the snakes the boys often do not dare to pick the strawberries, of which there is a very great abundance on the mountains and in the hedges.

Some people take three or four grains of candied coriander with each glass of water to get rid of the wind.

On Whitsunday, May 14th, I took five pounds and more of the water of Bernabò, because my glass held more than one pound. The four principal holidays of the year they call *Pasqua*.[8] I voided a lot of gravel the first time, and in less than two hours I had got rid of more than two-thirds of the water, having taken it with a desire to urinate and with my usual appetite as at the other baths. It made my bowels loose and purged me thoroughly in that respect. The Italian pound is only twelve ounces.

You live here very cheaply. A pound of meat, veal, very good and very tender, is about three French sous. Plenty of trout, but small. There are good workmen at making parasols, which in these parts they carry everywhere. The country is hilly, and there are few level roads. However, there are some very pleasant ones, and even the approaches to the mountains are mostly paved.

After dinner I gave a dance for the peasant girls, and danced in it myself so as not to appear too reserved. In certain parts of Italy, including all of Tuscany and Urbino, the women curtsy French style, at the knees.

Near the channel of the spring at La Villa there is a square marble that was put there just 110 years ago, on these Calends of May, on which are inscribed the virtues of this spring. I omit it, because it is found in many printed books which deal with the baths of Lucca. At all the baths you find a good many small clocks[9] for public use. I always had two on my table, which were lent to me.

This evening I ate nothing but three slices of bread, toasted, with butter and sugar, without drinking.

7 Gingerbread.
8 In this neighborhood these would seem to be Easter (*Pasqua d'uove*, of eggs), Whitsunday (*Pasqua di rose*, of roses), Christmas (*Pasqua di ceppo*, of the log), and Ascension Day (with no special name).
9 Presumably hourglasses.

On Monday, judging that this water had sufficiently opened the way, I went back to drinking that of the ordinary spring, and took five pounds of it. It did not induce me to sweat, as it used to do. The first time I passed some of the water I discharged some gravel, which seemed in fact to be broken up stones. This water seemed to me almost cold in comparison with that of Bernabò, although that of Bernabò had a very moderate warmth; it is very far from coming up to that of Plombières and the ordinary water of Bagnères. It had a good effect in both directions; and so it was lucky that I did not believe those doctors who ordered me to give up drinking if it did not succeed on the first day.

On Tuesday, May 16th, as is the custom in these parts (and I like it), I discontinued drinking, and stayed in the bath an hour and more, under the spout, because the water everywhere else seems cold to me. Since I still felt that wind remaining in the lower bowels and intestines, without pain, and a little in the stomach, I was afraid that the water was the particular cause of this; wherefore I discontinued it. I enjoyed the bath so much that I would gladly have gone to sleep in it. It did not make me sweat, but it moved my bowels. I dried myself well and stayed in bed for a while.

Every month they hold a review of the soldiers of each vicariate. The colonel, our man, from whom I had received a world of courtesies, held his. There were two hundred soldiers, pikesmen and musketeers. He had them fight. They are extremely well trained for peasants. But this is his principal responsibility, to keep them in order and teach them military discipline.

The people are all divided among themselves into the French faction and the Spanish faction; and in this strife serious quarrels are always arising. They make public demonstrations of their feelings. The women and men of our side wear over their right ear bunches of flowers, a biretta, locks of hair, and all that kind of thing; the Spaniards wear them on the other side.

These peasants and their wives are dressed like gentlefolk. You never see a peasant woman who does not wear white shoes, fine thread stockings, a colored apron of light silk taffeta; and they dance, capriole, and pirouette very well.

When they speak of the "Prince" in this signory, they mean the Council of One Hundred and Twenty. The colonel cannot take a wife without the permission of the "Prince," and he has great difficulty in obtaining it, because they do not want him to acquire friends and family relationships in the region; and moreover he

cannot buy any property. No soldier leaves the country without permission; and there are many who through poverty go begging through these mountains, and buy their arms with what they gain.

On Wednesday I was at the bath and stayed there more than an hour, sweated a little, and bathed my head.

We see here that the German custom of warming clothes and everything else in winter by their stoves is convenient; for our bath attendant, by holding a little charcoal under a *focone*, and raising the mouth of it with a brick, so that it gets air to feed the fire, warms the clothes very well and quickly, and indeed more conveniently than do our fires. A *focone* is one of our warming pans.

Here they call unmarried girls and girls of marriageable age *bambe*; and boys, until they have a beard, *putti*.

On Thursday I was a little more prompt and took my bath earlier. I sweated a little in the bath and bathed my head under the spout. I felt my strength a little weakened by the bath, and a little heaviness in the kidneys; I was still discharging gravel as I did from drinking, and a lot of phlegm. Indeed it seemed to me that this had the same effect on me as drinking. I continued on Friday.

Every day they sold unlimited quantities of water from this spring and from the other at Corsena, for various parts of Italy. It seemed to me that these baths cleared up my complexion. I was still bothered by that wind around the groin, without pain, which made me discharge in my urine a lot of foam, and bubbles that did not burst for some time. Sometimes there were also black hairs, but not many. I had noticed at other times that I discharged many of them. My urine was usually cloudy and charged with matter. The urine had something greasy on its surface.

This nation is not in the habit of eating as much meat as we do. Only ordinary meat is sold. They hardly know the price of it. A very fine young hare was sold me in this season at the very first word, so to speak, for six of our sous. They do not hunt them, they do not breed them, because no one buys them.

On Saturday, because the weather was cloudy and there was such a wind as made you feel the lack of shutters and windows, I stayed quiet without bathing or drinking. I perceived one great effect of these waters: that my brother,[10] who had never noticed voiding any

10 Presumably Bertrand de Mattecoulon, whom the party had left in Rome but who had rejoined them here.

gravel by himself or at the other baths where he had drunk with me, yet discharged an infinite amount of it here.

On the Sunday morning I bathed, but not my head; and after dinner I gave a dance with public prizes, as is the custom at these baths; and I wanted to give the first one of this year. First, five or six days beforehand, I had the party announced in all the neighboring places. The day before, I sent special invitations to all the gentlemen and ladies who were staying at the two baths. I invited them to the ball and to supper afterward.

I sent to Lucca for the prizes. The custom is to give several of these, so as not to appear to select just one woman out of them all, and so as to avoid jealousy and suspicion. There are always eight or ten for the women; for the men, two or three. I was asked by many women not to forget themselves, or a niece, or a daughter. On the day before, Messer Giovanni da Vincenzo Saminiati, a great friend of mine, sent me from Lucca a leather belt and a biretta of black cloth for the men, as I had written asking him to do. For the women, two taffeta aprons, one green, the other violet (for it must be noted that there is always some more honorable prize for the one or two you want to favor), two aprons of coarse muslin, four papers of pins, four pairs of pumps (but I gave one of these to a pretty girl, not at the dance); a pair of slippers (to which I added a pair of pumps, and made a single prize of the two); three crystal nets and three tresses of hair, which made three prizes; four little necklaces. There were nineteen prizes for the women. It all came to six crowns, little more. I had five fife players. I gave them food for the whole day and a crown for the lot; which was my good luck, for they do not normally do it for that price. These prizes are hung from a sort of hoop, heavily decorated all over, and are displayed for everyone to see.

We began the dance in the square with the women of the neighborhood, and at first I was afraid that we would be left alone. Soon there came much company from all directions, and particularly a good many gentlemen and ladies of this signory, whom I received and entertained to the best of my ability. At all events, it seemed to me that they were satisfied. Since it was a bit warm, we went to the hall of the Buonvisi palace, which was very suitable.

As day was beginning to fall, a little after five in the afternoon, I addressed myself to the most important ladies, saying that since I lacked sufficient skill and boldness to judge such beauties and

graces and nice manners as I saw in these girls, I begged them to assume this charge of judging and to distribute the prizes to the company according to their merits. We were held up on ceremony for a bit because they refused to assume this charge, which they took to be too much courtesy to them. Finally I added this condition, that if they would be good enough to take me into their counsel, I would give my opinion. And this was the result, that I picked out with my eyes now this one, now that; wherein I did not fail to have some regard for beauty and grace, pointing out that the charm of the dance depended not only on the movement of the feet, but also on the carriage and grace and charm and elegance of the whole person. Thus the presents were distributed, more to one, less to another, according to their merit, this lady offering them to the dancers on my behalf, and I on the contrary referring all the obligation to her. The thing went off in a very orderly and regular manner, except that one of the girls refused the prize. She sent to beg me that for her sake I should give it to another girl; which I did not consent to do. The other was not one of the most attractive.

They were called up one by one from their places, and came before that lady and me, who were seated side by side. I would give the present that seemed right to me to the lady, kissing it, and she, taking it, would give it to the girl, saying graciously: "Here is this lord knight who is giving you this fine present: thank him." "On the contrary, you are obliged to her ladyship, who out of so many others has judged you worthy to receive a prize. I am very sorry that the present is not more worthy of such-and-such a quality of yours" – and I named these according to what they were. The same thing was promptly done with the men. The gentlemen and ladies are not included in this competition, although they take part in the dancing.

In truth it is a beautiful thing, and a rare one to us French, to see these peasant girls, so elegant, and dressed like ladies, dance so well: they are a match for the rarest of our ladies in that ability, but they dance differently.

I invited them all to supper, for the banquets in Italy are nothing but a very light meal by French standards – a few cuts of veal and one or two brace of chicken is all. There stayed to supper Signor Francesco Gambarini, the colonel of this vicariate, a gentleman of Bologna who is like a brother to me; one French gentleman; and no others; except that I had Divizia sit at the table. She is a poor peasant woman of the neighborhood, living about two miles from the baths,

who, like her husband, has no other way of earning a living except by the work of her own hands; ugly, thirty-seven years old, with a swollen neck. She can neither write nor read. But in her tender youth there was an uncle in her father's house who was always reading Ariosto and other poets in her presence, and her mind was found to be so born to poetry that she not only composes verses with the most wonderful readiness possible, but also brings into them ancient fables, names of the gods, countries, sciences, famous men, as if she had been brought up to study. She delivered a number of verses in my honor. To tell the truth, they are nothing but verses and rhymes. Her delivery is elegant and very rapid.

The company at the ball amounted to a hundred visitors and more, although the season was unfavorable; for at that time the great and most important harvest of the whole year takes place, that of silk; and these days they tire themselves out with work, without regard for any holiday, morning and evening, collecting the mulberry leaves for their silkworms; and all these girls are employed in this labor.

On Monday morning I went to the bath a little later, because I got a shave and a haircut. I bathed my head and gave it a shower for more than a quarter of an hour under the main tap.

Among others at my dance was the Lord Vicar, who administers justice. Thus they call a magistrate appointed for six months, whom the signory sends to each vicariate to judge civil cases in the first instance, and he decides them up to a certain small sum. There is another officer for criminal cases. I gave him to understand that it seemed reasonable to me that the signory should make some rule (which would be very easy; and I suggested to him the ways that seemed most appropriate to me) obliging the innumerable dealers who come here to take these waters and carry them all over Italy to show a certificate of the amount of water they carry, so as to deprive them of the opportunity of perpetrating a fraud. Whereof I gave him an experience of my own, which was this: One of these muleteers came to my landlord, a private person, and begged him to give him a statement in writing that he was taking away twenty-four loads of this water; and he had only four. The landlord at first refused, for that reason; but the other added that in four to six days he would be returning to get the twenty loads. I said that this muleteer had not returned. The Lord Vicar received this advice of mine very well; but he did all he could to find out

who that witness was and who was that muleteer, what he looked like, what horses he had. I never would tell him either one, never.

I also told him that I wanted to initiate the custom observed in all the famous baths of Europe, that persons above a certain rank leave their coat of arms there as a token of the obligation they have to those waters; for which he thanked me very much on behalf of the signory.

In these days they were beginning to mow the hay in some places.

On Tuesday I stayed two hours in the bath and gave my head a shower for a little more than a quarter of an hour.

There came to the baths in these days a merchant from Cremona, living in Rome. He was suffering from many extraordinary infirmities. Nevertheless he talked and walked, and led quite a jolly life, as far as I could see. His principal failing, he said, was a weak head: he had lost his memory so completely that when eating he never remembered what had been put before him at table. If he left the house to go on some business of his, he had to go back to the house ten times to ask where he was to go. He could hardly finish the paternoster: from the end he went a hundred times to the beginning, never noticing at the end that he had begun, or, on beginning again, that he had ended. He had been deaf and blind, and had suffered from toothache. He felt so much heat in the kidneys that he always had to have a strip of lead around them. He had been living under doctors' orders for many years, and observing them most religiously.

It was an amusing thing to see the various prescriptions of the doctors from various parts of Italy, so contradictory, and particularly on the matter of these baths and showers, that out of twenty consulted there were not two in agreement; on the contrary, they almost all condemned one another and accused one another of homicide.

This man was subject to an amazing accident because of the flatulence: the wind rushed out of his ears with such fury that many times it would not let him sleep. Instead, whenever he yawned he immediately felt great winds coming out of his ears. He said that for getting the bowels moving the best remedy he had was to put four big candied coriander seeds in his mouth for a bit, and after moistening and smoothing them a little, to put them up the anus; which had a very apparent and prompt effect.

On him I first saw one of those big hats made of peacock feathers, covered with light taffeta, the crown a good hand's-breadth high, and big; and inside it a coarse muslin cap of the size of the head to keep out the sun; and around it wings a foot and a half wide, in place of our parasols, which in truth are a nuisance to carry on horseback.

Since at other times I have repented of not having written more in detail on the subject of the other baths, so that I could derive rules and examples for those I used later, this time I want to expatiate.

On Wednesday I went to the bath. I felt a heat in my body, more sweat than usual, a little weakness, dryness and bitterness in my mouth, and an indescribable dizziness on getting out of the bath, as happened to me on account of the heat of the waters at all the other baths: Plombières, Bagnères, Préchacq. At that of Barbotan and at this one never, except this Wednesday; whether because I had gone there much earlier than on the other days, and before discharging my bowels, or because I found the water much hotter than usual. I was there for an hour and a half, and showered my head for about a quarter of an hour.

I did many things contrary to the common rule: taking a shower in the bath, for the custom is to do one separately, and then the other; taking a shower with this water, whereas there are few who do not go to the other bath for a shower, and take it from this tap or that, some at the first, some at the second, some at the third, according to the doctor's prescription; drinking and then bathing and then drinking, thus mixing up the days for one or the other, whereas the others drink for certain days and then use the baths for a stretch; not observing the appropriate periods, for the others drink for ten days at the most, and bathe at least twenty-five days in succession; bathing only once a day, whereas they always bathe twice; taking such a short shower, whereas they always stay in it at least an hour in the morning and the same in the evening. As for getting tonsured, as they all do, and then putting on the bald place a little piece of satin with a sort of net to keep it on the head, my polished head had no need of it.

This same day, in the morning, the Lord Vicar came to visit me – one of the principal gentlemen of this signory, coming specially from the other baths, where he was staying. Among other things he told me an amazing story about himself, that the bite of a beetle on the fleshy tip of his thumb a few years ago had brought him to such an extremity that he nearly died of exceeding faintness; and from

that he fell into such misery that he was five months in bed without moving, lying constantly on his loins, thus heating them so immoderately that they engendered the renal calculus, from which he suffered a great deal for over a year, as well as from colic. Finally his father, governor of Velletri, sent him a certain green stone which had come into his hands through a monk who had been in India. As long as he had this stone against his back he never felt either pain or flow of gravel. And he had been in this state for two years. As for the sting, his thumb and almost his whole hand had remained useless, and even his arm so weakened that every year he comes to the baths of Corsena to shower that arm and hand, as he was doing then.

The common people here are very poor. At this time they were eating green mulberries, which they picked from the trees as they stripped them of their leaves for the silkworms.

Since our terms for renting the house for the month of June had been left undecided, I wanted to clear this up with my landlord, who, realizing how much I was in demand with all his neighbors, and particularly with the steward of the Buonvisi palace, who had offered it to me for a gold crown a day, made up his mind to let me have my rooms for as long as I liked at the rate of twenty-five gold crowns a month; this agreement beginning on the first of June, and the first bargain being in force until then.

The inhabitants of this place are very full of envy and of secret deadly enmities, although they are all related.

A woman here told me this proverb:

> To make your wife conceive, the surest way
> Is: send her to the bath, and stay away.

Among other very pleasant things in my house was this, that I could go from the bath to bed by a level path only thirty paces long.

I did not like to see these mulberry trees stripped of their leaves, looking like winter in the middle of summer.

The gravel I was continually voiding seemed to me much rougher than usual, and left me with an indescribable stinging in my prick.

Every day you could see being brought to this place from all sides samples of various wines in tiny little bottles, so that the visitors there who liked them might order some; and there were very few good wines. There were light, rather bitter, and raw whites, or really coarse, rough reds, unless you sent to Lucca or Pescia for the white Trebbiano, very mature, though not too delicate for all that.

On Thursday, the feast of Corpus Christi, I took a temperate bath for an hour or more; I sweated very little, and came out of it without any alteration. I showered my head for half of a quarter hour, and on going back to bed went to sleep for a while. I found this bathing and showering pleasurable rather than otherwise. I felt on my hands and other parts of the body a rash, and moreover I noticed that many of the peasants around here had the itch, and many children suffered from milk crust.

It happens here as elsewhere, that what we seek with so much difficulty is held in contempt by the people of the country: and I saw many of them who had never tasted these waters and had a low opinion of them. Withal there are few old people.

With the phlegm that I voided in my urine (which happens to me continually) there was gravel enveloped and suspended. I seemed to feel this effect from the bath when I put my groin under the spout, that it drove the winds out of me. And certainly I have felt my right testicle suddenly and clearly be reduced in size at times, if it had chanced to swell up, as happens to me fairly often. From this I almost conclude that this swelling is caused by the effect of the wind enclosed inside it.

On Friday I bathed as usual and showered my head a bit more. The extraordinary quantity of gravel that I continually voided made me suppose that it had not been enclosed in the kidneys, because you could have made a big ball of it by squeezing it; and that what the water did was rather to make it conceive and gradually give birth.

On Saturday I bathed for two hours and took a shower for more than a quarter of an hour. On Sunday I kept quiet. On this day a gentleman from Bologna treated us to another ball.

The lack of clocks in this place and in most of Italy seemed to me very inconvenient.

In the bathhouse there is a Madonna, and these verses:

> Pray grant to all who enter, Goddess kind,
> To leave here sound in body and in mind.

One cannot praise too highly, both for beauty and for utility, this way of cultivating the mountains right up to the summit, forming terraces in a circle around them, and supporting the tops of these terraces now with stones, now with other ramparts, if the ground does not hold them of itself; filling with wheat the flat part of the terrace, wider or narrower as it happens to be; bordering with vines the outside of the flat part toward the valley, that is to say the

circumference and edge; and where they cannot find or form a flat surface, as for example near the summit, putting vines all over.

At this ball[11] a woman began to dance with a pitcher full of water on her head, keeping it steady and firm, with no lack of lively movements.

The doctors were stupefied to see most of our Frenchmen drink in the morning and then bathe on the same day.

Monday morning I stayed in the bath two hours. I did not give myself a shower because I took three pounds of water on a whim, which made my bowels move. I used to bathe my eyes every morning, holding them open in the water. I felt no effect from it, either good or bad. I believe that I got rid of those three pounds of water in the bath – where I urinated a good many times and then sweated a little more than usual – and in my stool. Having felt more constipated than usual for the last few days, I used the aforementioned three grains of candied coriander, which drove out a lot of wind, of which I was very full, but little matter. Although I purged my kidneys wonderfully, I did not stop feeling some pricking there; and I judged that it was due rather to wind than to anything else.

Tuesday I stayed two hours in the bath, showered myself for half an hour, and did not drink. Wednesday I stayed in the bath an hour and a half and showered myself about half an hour.

Up to now, to tell the truth, from the little dealing and familiarity I have had with the people of this country, I have not noted those miracles of wit and reason with which rumor credits them. I have seen no extraordinary ability: indeed they have marveled at and made too much of that little power of ours.[12] Thus today certain doctors who had to hold an important consultation for a young lord, Signor Paolo Cesi (nephew of Cardinal Cesi), who was at these baths, came to ask me, at his behest, to be good enough to hear their opinions and arguments, because he was resolved to rely wholly on my judgment. I laughed about this to myself. Many other similar things have happened to me, both here and in Rome.

My eyes still sometimes felt dazzled when I had grown tired either from reading or from fixing them steadily on some bright and brilliant object; and I have been very worried to feel this weakness continuing ever since the day I had a migraine recently

11 The one referred to four paragraphs earlier, given by the gentleman from Bologna.
12 Presumably in the sense of *mine*.

near Florence: that is to say, a heaviness in the head around the forehead, without pain, a certain clouding of the eyes that did not shorten my sight but somehow troubled it at times. After this the migraine came upon me again two or three times; and on those occasions it lasted longer, without, however, interfering with my activities. But since this showering of my head it has attacked me again every day, and my eyes have begun to run, as before, without pain or redness; and it has been more than ten years from the time I last had this headache until I got this migraine.

Fearing also that this water might weaken my head, on Thursday I would not take a shower, but bathed for an hour. During Friday, Saturday, and Sunday I discontinued the cure in every form, for that reason and because I felt a good deal less cheerful, since I was still discharging gravel furiously; but my head, still the same, was not restored to its former good condition. At certain times I felt this alteration, which was increased by the working of the imagination.

On Monday morning I drank, in thirteen glasses, six pounds and a half of water from the ordinary spring. I passed about three pounds of this, white and undigested, before dinner; the rest little by little. This headache, although it was not continuous or very troublesome, made my complexion much worse. I did not feel any failing or weakness in my head, as sometimes formerly, but only a weight on the eyes accompanied by rather cloudy vision.

On this day they began to cut the rye on our plain.

On Tuesday at daybreak I went to the Bernabò spring and there drank six pounds, one at a time. It was raining a bit. I sweated a little. It gave me a movement and washed out my bowels lustily. For that reason I could not judge how much I had given out. I did not urinate much, but in two hours my urine had taken on some color.

They take boarders here for six gold crowns a month, or a little more, for lodging in a private room, as comfortable as you please; with a valet, as much again. If you have no valet, you will still be furnished by the landlord with many provisions for eating suitably.

Before the natural day was over I had passed all the water, and more than I had drunk of all kinds of drink. I had only one little drink at dinner, half a pound. I ate little supper.

On Wednesday, a rainy day, I took seven pounds, one at a time, from the ordinary spring, and passed them, as well as what I had drunk besides.

On Thursday I took nine pounds: seven in a row at first, and then, when I had begun to discharge it, I sent for two more pounds.

I discharged it in both ways. I drank very little at dinner. On Friday and Saturday I did the same. On Sunday I stayed quiet.

On Monday I took seven glasses, seven pounds. I was still voiding gravel, but a little less than after a bath; I saw examples of this effect of the baths in a good many other people at the same time. On this day I felt a pain in my groin as from the descent of stones, and I passed a small one.

On Tuesday, another. And I can say, and almost affirm, that I have observed that this water has the power to break them up, because I could feel the large size of some of them as they were coming down, and then I discharged them in smaller pieces. This Tuesday I drank eight pounds in eight times.

If Calvin had known that the Preaching Friars hereabouts call themselves Ministers, he would no doubt have given another name to his.

Wednesday I took eight pounds, eight glasses. I almost always passed the first half of it, undigested and natural, in three hours; then about a half a pound, reddish and colored; the rest after dinner and at night.

In this season people were gathering at the bath. And from those examples that I saw, and from the opinion of the doctors, especially of Donati, who has written about these waters, I had made no great mistake in bathing my head in this bath; for they too have the custom, when they are in the bath, of giving their stomach a shower with a long pipe, attaching one end to the tap and the other to their body in the bath; and since ordinarily they took their head shower with this same water, they bathed on the same day that they took the shower. So I cannot have made a great mistake in mixing the two together, or in having taken the water from the channel of the spring itself instead of the pipe. And perhaps I was wrong not to continue. And the feeling I have about it up to now seems to be that I have stirred up the humors which in time would have been driven out and purged.

This Donati permitted drinking and bathing on the same day. And I am sorry I did not have the boldness, as I had the desire, and with some reason, to drink in the bath in the morning. He greatly praised Bernabò, but with those reasons and arguments that the medicos use.

The effect of these waters on the gravel, which continued in me all the time, was not to be seen in a number of others who

were free from this infirmity. Which I say because I cannot make up my mind to believe that they produced the gravel that I discharged.

Thursday morning I was in the bath for an hour without bathing my head, and before daybreak, in order to have the first place. For that reason, I believe, and because I slept afterward in bed, I felt bad: my mouth, dry and thirsty, and so hot that in the evening, on going to bed, I drank two big glasses of that water, cooled; from which I felt no other change.

On Friday I stayed quiet. The Minister Friar of Saint Francis (so they call the provincials),[13] a worthy man and courteous and learned, who was at the bath with many other friars of various orders, sent me a handsome present of very good wine, marzipan, and other things to eat.

On Saturday I did not take the cure, and went to dine at Menabbio, a handsome large village at the top of one of these mountains. I took some fish along, and was received into the house of a rich soldier who has traveled much in France and other places, and took a wife and got rich in Flanders. He is called Signor Santo. There are vast numbers of peasant soldiers here, a beautiful church, and few who have not traveled much; everyone is strongly divided into these Spanish and French factions. Without thinking about it I put a flower at my left ear. The French faction took it as an insult.

After dinner I climbed up to the fort, which is a place protected by high walls right at the top of the hill, very steep, but thoroughly cultivated everywhere. And here among the ever-present crags, among the rocky precipices and steep places and rugged hills, you find not only vines and wheat, but also meadows; and in the plain they have no grass. I then came straight down by another side of the mountain.

On Sunday morning I went to the bath with several other gentlemen. I stayed there half an hour. There came to me from Signor Ludovico Pinitesi a beautiful present of a horse laden with very beautiful fruit, and among other things some early figs, of which none had yet been seen at the bath, and twelve bottles of very sweet wine. And at the same time the aforesaid friar sent

13 A provincial is the superior of all the Franciscan monasteries in one province.

me other kinds of fruit in great quantity; so that I too was able to exercise liberality to the country people.

After dinner was the ball, where a number of gentlewomen gathered, well dressed, but of ordinary beauty, although they were among the most beautiful of Lucca.

In the evening Signor Ludovico di Ferrari, of Cremona, whom I knew very well, sent me a present of some boxes of very good quince jelly, scented, and some lemons, and some oranges of extraordinary size.

At night, a little before daybreak, I was seized by a cramp in the calf of the right leg, with very great pain, not continuous but intermittent. I remained in that discomfort for half an hour. I had felt one not long before, but it passed in a flash.

On Monday I went to the bath and was there for an hour with my stomach under the tap. That vein in my leg still pricked me a little.

Just at this time we began to feel the heat and to hear the grasshoppers, though no more than in France; until then the seasons had seemed cooler to me than at home.

Free nations do not have the same distinction between people's ranks as do the others; and even those of the lowest class have something lordly in their manner. When they ask for alms they always mix in some authoritative word: "Give me alms, will you?" or "Give me alms, understand!" As they say in Rome: "Do good for your own sake."[14]

On Tuesday I stayed in the bath for an hour.

Italy: Florence – Pisa – Lucca
(June 21–August 13, 1581)

On Wednesday, June 21st, early, I left La Villa, after receiving, when I took leave of the company of men and women who were there, all the indications of friendliness that I could desire. I came through steep, but pleasant and wooded mountains, to

Pescia, twelve miles, a little walled village on the river Pescia, in Florentine territory. Handsome houses, open streets, the famous wines of Trebbiano; situated among very thick olive trees; the

14 Montaigne quotes this again in the *Essays* (III: 5, p. 829).

people most affectionate toward France: and for this reason, they say, the city bears a dolphin as its arms.[1]

After dinner we came upon a beautiful plain, heavily populated with châteaux and houses. And through absent-mindedness, despite my intention and settled plans, I forgot to see Montecatini, where they have the hot salt water of the Tettuccio, which I left a mile off my road on the right, about seven miles from Pescia; and I did not realize this until I had nearly reached

PISTOIA, eleven miles. I was lodged outside the city, where the son of Rospigliosi[2] came to see me.

Anyone who goes through Italy with other than hired horses does not know what he is doing. And it seems to me more convenient to change them from place to place than to put yourself in the hands of the drivers for a long trip. From Pistoia to Florence, which is twenty miles, the horses cost only four giulii.

From here, passing through the town of Prato, I came to dine at

CASTELLO, in a hostelry opposite the grand duke's palace, where we went after dinner to examine the garden more minutely. And it happened to me here as in many other things: imagination transcended the reality. I had seen it in the winter bare and stripped. I had thought more of its future beauty in the milder season than appeared to me in actuality. Castello, seventeen miles. After dinner I came to

FLORENCE, three miles.

On Friday I saw the public procession, and the grand duke in his coach. Among other displays one saw a car in the form of a theater, gilt on top, in which there were four little boys and a friar dressed up to represent Saint Francis, standing up, holding his hands as you see them in the pictures, with a crown on his cowl – either a friar or a man dressed as a friar, with a false beard. There were some armed boys of the city, and among them one as Saint George. There came to meet him in the square a big dragon, supported pretty clumsily and carried by men, spouting fire noisily from his mouth. The boy gave him one with the lance and the sword, and cut his throat.

1 The French for dolphin, *dauphin*, also means the eldest son of the king. The Pescian dolphin appears to owe its place on their coat of arms to another pun, on *pesce* (fish).
2 Taddeo Rospigliosi had entertained Montaigne at Pistoia before. See *Travel Journal*, p. 1198.

I was warmly entertained by a Gondi who lives at Lyons and who sent me some excellent wines, that is to say, Trebbiano.

It was so hot as to astonish even the natives.

This morning at daybreak I had the colic in my right side. It afflicted me for about three hours. Then I ate my first melon. Cucumbers and almonds are eaten in Florence from the beginning of June.

About the 23rd they had the chariot race in a beautiful large square,[3] rectangular, longer than it is wide, surrounded on all sides by beautiful houses. At each end was placed a square wooden obelisk, and a long rope was attached from one to the other, so that people could not cross the square; and some men placed themselves across to reinforce the said rope. All the balconies crowded with ladies, and in one palace the grand duke, his wife, and his court. The populace along the square, and on a kind of grandstand, as I was too.

Five empty coaches raced. They were assigned their places by lot at one side of one pyramid. And some said that the outside one had the advantage, because it could make the turns more easily. They started at the sound of trumpets. The third turn around the pyramid they started from is the one that gives the victory. The grand duke's coach was ahead all the way until the third lap. Here Strozzi's coach, which had been second all the way, with the horses given free rein, putting on greater speed than before and closing in, placed the victory in doubt. I noticed that the silence of the people was broken when they saw Strozzi coming close, and with shouts and applause they gave him all the encouragement possible under the eyes of the prince. And then, when this dispute and altercation came to be judged by certain gentlemen, and those favoring Strozzi referred it to the opinion of the populace present, there immediately arose from the people a universal shout and a public consensus in favor of Strozzi, who finally had it – contrary to justice, in my opinion. The prize would be worth a hundred crowns. I enjoyed this spectacle more than any other I had seen in Italy for its resemblance to the ancient type of race.

Because today was Saint John's Eve, certain little fires were placed at the top of the cathedral in a circle in two or three rows, from which rockets were launched into the air. They say that it is not the custom in Italy, as in France, to make Saint John's fires.

3 The Piazza di Santa Maria Novella.

Saturday, Saint John's Day, which is the principal holiday in Florence, and the one they celebrate most; so that at this feast even the young girls are seen in public; however, I saw no great beauty. In the morning, in the palace square, the grand duke appeared on a stand (under a canopy, along the walls of his palace) decked with very rich tapestry, having on his left side the Pope's nuncio, and much further away the ambassador of Ferrara. There passed before him all his villages and fortified places, as they were called by a herald. So, for Siena, a young man came forward dressed in black and white velvet, carrying in his hand a kind of large silver vessel and the figure of the she-wolf of Siena. Thus dressed and laden, this man made an offering to the grand duke and a little speech. When he had finished, there came forward as they were called some badly dressed boys on very wretched horses and mules, carrying one a silver cup, another a torn and dilapidated banner. These in great numbers passed along their way without saying a word, without respect and without ceremony, more as if for a joke than otherwise; and they were the fortified places depending on the State of Siena. Every year this is repeated as a matter of form.

There also passed by there a car carrying a large square wooden pyramid, and on certain steps around it some little boys dressed some in one way, some in another, as angels or saints; and at the top, at the height of the tallest houses, a Saint John, a man dressed up in his guise, bound to an iron bar. The officials, and particularly those of the mint, followed this car.

At the end came another car, on which were certain young men bearing three prizes for the different races, having at their side the Barbary horses that were to race that day, and the boys who were to ride them, with the colors of their masters, who are among the highest lords. The horses are small and handsome.

The heat did not seem to me more violent than in France. However, to escape it in these hotel rooms, I was forced to sleep at night on the dining room table, putting mattresses and sheets on it; not having found here any comfortable lodging to rent, for this city is not a good one for strangers; also to escape the bugs, with which the beds are most thickly infested.

There is not much fish, and no trout or other fish is eaten except what comes from elsewhere and is marinated. I saw that the grand duke sent to Giovanni Marliani, a Milanese lodging in the same hotel where I was, a present of wine, bread, fruit, and fish; but the fish alive, small, in earthenware coolers.

I had a dry and arid mouth all day and felt parched not from thirst, but from an internal heat which I have experienced at other times in our hot spells. I ate nothing but fruit and salad with sugar. In short, I was not well.

Those open-air recreations that are practiced in France after supper here come before it. And on the longest days they often sup at night. Day breaks in the morning between seven and eight.

After dinner the Barbary horses ran for the prize. The Cardinal de' Medici's horse won it. This prize was worth two hundred crowns. It is not a very entertaining sight, because, being in the street, you see nothing but these horses going furiously past.

On Sunday I saw the Pitti Palace, and among other things a marble mule representing an actual mule that is still alive, because of its long service carrying materials for building this palace. So the Latin verses say.[4]

At this palace we saw the chimaera, which has between the shoulders a nascent head with horns and ears, and a body in the form of a little lion.

On the Saturday the grand duke's palace was open and full of country people, to whom everything was open, and the great hall was full of groups of dancers, some here, some there. To these people I believe this is a kind of symbol of their lost liberty, which is refreshed at this main festival of the city.

On Monday I went to dine at the house of Signor Silvio Piccolomini, well known for his valor and in particular for his mastery in fencing. Many topics were brought up, for there was a good company of other gentlemen. He utterly despises the fencing technique of the Italian masters, the Venetian, the Bolognese, that of Patinostrato, and others. And in this respect he praises only a pupil of his own who is at Brescia, where he teaches this art to certain gentlemen. He says that there is no rule or art in the usual teaching; and he particularly condemns the practice of thrusting the sword forward and putting it at the power of the enemy, and then the *botta passada*[5] to make another assault and stop; for he says that this is completely different from what is actually seen among combatants. He was about to publish a book on this subject. As for matters of war, he has great contempt for artillery; and I was very pleased with him on

4 The bedding, stones, wood, columns, all that store
 It carried hither, brought, conveyed, and bore.
5 Thrust in which one foot crosses over the other.

this account.[6] He praises Machiavelli's book *On the Art of War* and follows his opinions. He says that of the sort of men who plan fortifications the most outstanding is now in Florence in the service of the most serene grand duke.[7]

It is customary here to put snow into the wine glasses. I put only a little in, not being too well in body, having pain in the sides many times, and all the time ejecting an incredible amount of gravel; besides this, I could not restore my head to its original condition. Dizziness and a kind of heaviness on the eyes, the forehead, the cheeks, teeth, nose, and face. It came into my mind that it was the sweet, heady white wines, because at the time the migraine first seized me again I had drunk a great quantity of Trebbiano, when heated by traveling and by the season, and when its sweetness did not quench my thirst.

I finally confessed that Florence is rightly called "the beautiful."

On this day I went alone for fun to see the women who let themselves be seen by anyone who wants. I saw the most famous: nothing exceptional. The lodgings are gathered in one particular part of town, and are therefore contemptible, and wretched besides, and they do not approach in any way those of the Roman or Venetian prostitutes; nor do they themselves in beauty or grace or dignity. If one of them wants to live outside these limits, she must be of little account and must perform some other trade for concealment.

I saw the shops of the silk spinners; they have certain machines, by turning which one single woman can twist and turn five hundred spindles at once.

Tuesday morning I ejected a little red stone.

Wednesday I saw the grand duke's casino. What seemed most important to me was a rocky structure in the form of a pyramid, composed and fabricated of all kinds of natural minerals, one piece of each, joined together. This structure later spouted water, by which many objects inside it were seen to be set in motion, water mills and windmills, little church bells, soldiers of the guard, animals, hunts, and a thousand such things.

Thursday I would not wait to see another horse race. I went after dinner to Pratolino, which I studied again very minutely. And being asked by the caretaker of the palace to give my opinion

6 For Montaigne's similar views see *Essays* I: 48, p. 256.
7 Francesco Pacciotto of Urbino.

of these beauties and of those of Tivoli, I talked about this, not comparing these places in general, but part by part, with the various advantages of the one and the other, each one alternately being the victor.

Friday at the Giunti's shop I bought a number of comedies, eleven of them, and certain other little books. And here I saw Boccaccio's will printed together with certain treatises on the *Decameron*. This will shows an amazing poverty and lowliness of fortune in that great man. He leaves some sheets and then certain parts of beds to his female relatives and his sisters; the books to a certain friar, whom he orders to communicate them to anyone who asks for them. He takes account even of vessels and the meanest pieces of furniture. He gives orders for Masses and for his burial. It is printed as it was recovered, on a very tattered and ruined sheet of parchment.

As the Roman and Venetian prostitutes come to the windows for their lovers, so these come to the doors of their houses, where they stand in the public view at the convenient hours; and there you see them in groups, some with more company, some with less, chatting and singing in the street.

On Sunday, July 2nd, I left Florence after dinner, and after crossing the Arno on the bridge, we left it on our right hand but followed its course. We passed some beautiful fertile plains in which are the most famous melon beds in Tuscany. The good melons are not ripe until the 15th of July. The place in particular where the most excellent ones are grown is called Legnaia, three miles this side of Florence.

We went along a road through country mostly level and fertile, and very thickly built up throughout – almost without a break – with houses, small walled towns, and villages. We passed through, among others, one pretty town named Empoli. The sound of this name has something ancient about it. A most pleasant site. I did not discover here any vestige of antiquity except a ruined bridge on the road nearby, which has something old about the look of it.

I noted three things worth considering: to see the people of these parts working, some in threshing wheat or stacking it, some at sewing or spinning, on the Sunday holiday. The second, to see these country people lute in hand, and even the shepherd girls with Ariosto in their mouth; this is to be seen throughout Italy. The third is to see how they leave the reaped wheat on the fields for ten or fifteen days or more, without fear of their neighbor.

Toward dark we arrived at

LA SCALA, twenty miles: one single lodging house, pretty good. I did not eat supper, and slept little, troubled by a toothache on the right side, which I felt many times with my headache. It bothered me most when eating, and I was not able to touch a thing without very great pain.

On Monday morning, July 3rd, we followed the level road along the Arno, and, toward the end, a plain abounding with wheat. We arrived about noon at

PISA, twenty miles, a city belonging to the duke of Florence, situated in this plain on the Arno, which passes through the middle of it and six miles from here pours into the sea, and brings to this city a good many kinds of craft.

At this time the school[8] was closing, as is the custom, for three months of the great heat.

Here we came across the excellent company of the Desiosi, actors.

Because I was not satisfied with the hostelry, I rented a house with four bedrooms and a dining room. The landlord was to do the cooking and supply the furniture. A fine house. The whole thing for eight crowns a month. Because what he had promised by way of tablecloths and napkins was too skimpy (seeing that in Italy the custom is to change the napkins very little except when they change the tablecloths, and the tablecloths twice a week), we left the servants to board themselves, and we ate at the hostelry at four giulii a day.

The house was in a most beautiful location, with a pleasant view, overlooking the channel through which the Arno passes and crosses the city. This bed is very wide and more than five hundred paces long, bending and curving a bit, making a pleasant sight, revealing more easily by its curve both ends of this channel, with three bridges which there cross the Arno, full of vessels and merchandise. Both banks of this channel are built up with handsome walls with parapets at the top, like the Quai des Augustins in Paris. And then broad streets on both sides, and on the edge of the streets a row of houses. Ours was located there.

On Wednesday, July 5th, I saw the cathedral, where the palace of the Emperor Hadrian used to be. There are countless numbers of marble columns, varied in workmanship and form; very

8 The University.

handsome metal doors. It is decorated with various spoils from Greece and Egypt, and built of ancient ruins, so that you see inscriptions upside down, others half cut off, and in certain places unknown characters, which they say are ancient Etruscan.

I saw the bell tower, of extraordinary appearance, leaning by seven arm's-lengths, like that other one at Bologna, and others; surrounded on all sides by pilasters and open galleries.

I saw the neighboring Church of Saint John,[9] itself also very rich in famous works of sculpture and painting – among others, a marble pulpit with thickly crowded figures, so rare that the Lorenzo who killed Duke Alessandro is said to have taken off the heads of some of these statuettes and made a present of them to the queen.[10] The shape of the church resembles that of the Rotunda in Rome.

The natural son of the duke lives here, and I saw him, an old man. He lives comfortably on the liberality of the duke, and nothing else matters to him. There is wonderful hunting and fishing here. He makes this his business.

Of holy relics, rare works, and marbles and stones wonderful for their rarity, size, and workmanship, you find as many here as in any other city of Italy.

I took inordinate pleasure in the cemetery building that is called the Campo Santo, of unusual size, rectangular, three hundred paces long and one hundred wide. An inner corridor goes all around, forty paces wide, roofed with lead, paved with marble. The walls are covered with ancient paintings.

The nobles of this city have their tombs indoors under this corridor. There are the names and arms of the families to the number of four hundred – among others that of Gondi of Florence, founder of that house – of whom there are now barely four that have survived the wars and the ruin of this most ancient city; of the people just as few: it is inhabited and possessed by foreigners. Of these noble families there are several marquises, counts, and grandees in other parts of Christendom to which they have moved.

In the middle of this building there is an uncovered place where they are continually performing burials. It is stated positively by all that the bodies which are put here swell in eight hours so much that you can see the ground rise; in the following eight it goes down and subsides; in the final eight the flesh is so utterly consumed that

9 The Battisterio or Baptistery.
10 Catherine de' Medici.

before twenty-four hours are up there is nothing left but the bare bones. This miracle is similar to that other at the cemetery in Rome, where if you put in the body of a Roman, the earth promptly ejects it. This place is paved beneath with marble like the corridor, and earth is laid over it to the height of one or two yards. They say that this earth was brought from Jerusalem, because the Pisans took part in that enterprise with a large army.[11] With the bishop's permission, a little of this earth is taken away and sprinkled on other graves, with the idea that the bodies will be promptly consumed. This seems likely, because for a cemetery of a city of this size you see very few bones, almost none, and no place where they are gathered together and enclosed, as in other cities.

The neighboring mountains produce very beautiful marble, for which this city has many renowned workmen. At this time they were working on a very richly worked theater for the king of Fez, in Barbary, which he plans to build with fifty very high marble columns.

In this city our arms may be seen in countless places, and also a column that King Charles VIII gave to the cathedral. And in one house, on the wall toward the street, the said king is represented life-size, on his knees before the Madonna, who appears to be giving him counsel. The inscription says that when the said king was supping in this house it came into his mind to give the Pisans their ancient freedom, whereby he surpassed the greatness of Alexander. The titles of the said king are there: king of Jerusalem, of Sicily, etc. The words concerning that matter of the granting of freedom have been purposely disfigured and half effaced. Other private houses still have these arms as a decoration, to show the nobility that this king gave them.

There are not many vestiges of ancient buildings here. There is a handsome brick ruin where the palace of Nero was, and it retains his name; and the Church of Saint Michael, which used to be a temple of Mars.

Thursday, which was the feast of Saint Peter, I was told that formerly it was the custom for the bishop to go in procession to the Church of Saint Peter, four miles outside the city, and from there to the sea, where he threw in a ring and "married" the sea; for this city

11 On the order of Archbishop Ubaldo (1188–1200), fifty-three Pisan ships in Frederick Barbarossa's crusade brought back loads of earth for this cemetery from the Mount of Calvary.

used to have a very powerful navy. Now only a schoolmaster goes there. But the priests in procession go to the church, where there is a great granting of indulgences. The Pope's bull of a little less than four hundred years ago (if I take as authority a book that dates it after 1200)[12] says that this church was built by Saint Peter, and that as Saint Clement was performing the service at a marble table, three little drops of blood fell on it from the nose of the said saint. These three drops seem as though they had been imprinted there for only three days. The Genoese broke this table and carried away one of these drops. Therefore the Pisans removed the rest of the said table from the said church and carried it into their city. But every year they carry it back in procession to its place on the said Saint Peter's Day. The people go there all night in boats.

On Friday, the 7th of July, I went early to see the dairy farms of Don Pietro de' Medici, two miles distant from the town. He has a world of possessions there which he holds in his own name; every five years he rents to new tenants; and he takes half of the produce. A soil most abundant with wheat; pastures where he keeps all sorts of animals. I dismounted to see the particularities of the house. There are a great number of people working at making curds, butter, and cheeses, and divers implements for that work.

From there, following the plain, I arrived at the shore of the Tyrrhenian Sea, where I saw Lerici on the right hand; on the other, Leghorn; nearer, a fortified town standing in the sea. From there when it is clear you can make out the island of Gorgona, and beyond that Capraia, and beyond that Corsica. I turned to the left along the shore until we reached the mouth of the Arno, which is difficult to enter for ships, seeing that from various little streams which flow together into the Arno come earth and mud, which accumulate there and raise the bottom of the said mouth.

I bought some fish there, which I then sent to the actresses.[13]

Along this river you see many tamarisk thickets.

On Saturday I bought a barrel for six giulii, which I have had hooped with silver. It cost three crowns at the artificer's. I bought, besides, a bamboo cane to lean on, six giulii; a little vase and a cup of Indian nut, which has the same effect on the spleen and on the gravel as the tamarisk, eight giulii. The artisan, an able man and famous for making fine mathematical instruments, taught me that

12 The bull is actually of Innocent VI and dated 1354 in Avignon.
13 Of the Desiosi troupe. See above, p. 1231.

all trees bear as many circles and rings as they have lasted years; and showed this to me in all the woods he had in his shop; for he is a cabinet maker. And the part that faces north is narrower and has its rings closer and denser than the other. Therefore he boasts that whatever wood is brought him, he can judge how old the tree was, and in what position it stood.

At this time the trouble in my head was still with me, always remaining the same; together with such constipation that my bowels would not move without artificial help in the form of sweetmeats — a feeble help. The kidneys in good condition, considering.

This city was not long ago blamed for its bad air; but since Duke Cosimo has drained the marshes that are all around, it is good. And it was so bad that when people wanted to confine someone and get him out of the way, they confined him in Pisa, where in a few months it finished him.

This place produces no partridges, for all the trouble the princes have gone to.

Girolamo Borro,[14] a physician, doctor of the University of Rome, came to see me several times at my house. And when I went to visit him on the 14th of July he made me a present of his book on the ebb and flow of the sea, in the vulgar tongue; and he showed me another book he had written, in Latin, on the diseases of the body.

This same day, near my house, twenty-one Turkish slaves escaped from the arsenal, having found a frigate fully equipped, which Signor Alessandro di Piombino had left while he went fishing.

Except for the Arno and the beautiful way in which it flows through the town, these churches and vestiges of antiquity, and its private works, Pisa has little distinction and charm. It seems deserted. And in this respect, in the shape of its buildings, its size, and the width of its streets, it is a lot like Pistoia. It is extremely short of water, and the water is bad, for it all has a marshy taste.

The men are very poor, and no less haughty, hostile, and discourteous toward foreigners, especially toward the French since the death of a bishop of theirs, Pietro Paolo Bourbon,[15] who said he was of the house of our princes; and there is a family of that name here.

14 Borro is the man whom Montaigne describes (*Essays* I: 26, pp. 134–5) as having got in trouble with the Inquisition in Rome for being too perfect an Aristotelian.

15 Pietro Jacopo Bourbon del Monte, archbishop of Pisa from 1574 to 1575.

He was so affectionate toward our nation and so liberal that he had given orders that every Frenchman arriving here should immediately be brought to his house. He has left to the Pisans a most honored memory of his good life and liberality. It is only five or six years since he died.

On July 17th I joined twenty-five others in playing raffle at a crown apiece, for some belongings of Fargnocolo, one of the comedians. First they drew lots to see who should play first, second, and so on to the last. They follow this order. Then, there being various things to play for, they made two equal parts of them. The man who made the most points won the one, he who made the least the other. It fell to my lot to come out second.

On the 18th, at the Church of Saint Francis, there arose a great squabble between the priests of the cathedral and the friars. A Pisan gentleman had been buried at the aforementioned church the day before, and the priests wanted to say Mass. They came there with their equipment and paraphernalia. They alleged their ancient custom and privilege. The friars, on the contrary, alleged that it was their business and no one else's to say Mass in their own church. One priest, approaching the high altar, tried to seize the marble table. A friar attempted to drag him away. The vicar, patron of this church of priests, slapped this friar. One thing leading to another, gradually the matter came to fighting with fists, sticks, candlesticks, torches, and the like; they used everything. The end of it was that Mass was said by neither party. This angry combat caused a great scandal. As soon as the news of it spread, I went there; and the whole thing was related to me.

On the 22nd at dawn three galleys of Turkish corsairs landed on the coast nearby and carried off fifteen or twenty fishermen and poor shepherds as prisoners.

On the 25th I went to visit Cornacchini, a famous doctor and lecturer of Pisa. He lives in his own way, which is very different from the rules of his art. He sleeps immediately after dining, drinks a hundred times a day, and so on. He recited to me some of his verse, pleasant and in rustic patois. He does not set much store by the baths in the near vicinity of Pisa, but thinks well of those at Bagno-Acqua,[16] sixteen miles from Pisa. He says they are wonderful for getting rid of liver ailments (and he told me a great many miracles about them) as well as for the stone and the colic; but his

16 Now Casciana.

advice is, before using them, to drink the waters of La Villa. He has become convinced that except for bloodletting, medicine is nothing compared to the baths, for a man who knows how to use them and avail himself of them well. He said further that at these baths of Bagno-Acqua there are good lodgings, and that you are comfortable and at your ease there.

On the 26th in the morning I passed some turbid and black urine, more so than I had ever seen it before, with one small stone; and this did not stop the pain which I had already suffered for about twenty hours, below the navel and in the member; it was easy to bear, however, and caused no alteration in the loins and the side. A little later I passed another little stone, and my pain subsided.

On Thursday, July 27th, we left Pisa early, I feeling very satisfied with the courtesy and kindness I had received from Signor Vinta-vinti, from Lorenzo Conti, from San Miniato (in whose house lives the knight Camillo Gatani; he offered to have his brother come to France with me), from Borro and other artisans and tradesmen with whom I had dealt. And I hold for certain that I would not have lacked even money if I had needed it, although this city is consid-ered very uncivil and the inhabitants haughty. But at any rate a man who is courteous makes others so.

Among other things, this town is most abundant in pigeons, hazelnuts, and mushrooms.

For a while we crossed the plain, and at the foot of a hill we came upon the so-called "Baths of Pisa." There are several of them, and an inscription on marble which I could not quite decipher. It consists of Latin verses in rhyme, which testify to the virtues of these waters; and the inscription was dated 1300, as far as I could make out.

The largest and most respectable of these baths is square, and, except for one side, very well arranged, with a marble staircase. Each side is thirty paces long. In one corner you see the tap of the spring. I drank some water to judge it. It seemed to me tasteless and without any odor. I felt only a little sharpness on the tongue. Very moderate heat; very easy to drink. I noticed at this tap that in this water there were again those white corpuscles or atoms that I cursed in the baths of Baden, and judged to be filth and dirt coming from outside. Now I think rather that it comes from some quality of the mines; the more so because these particles appear thicker at the tap and where the water springs from, and where in reason it should be purer and cleaner, as I experienced more clearly at Baden. A solitary place; wretched lodgings. These waters are almost abandoned, and those

who use them go there in the morning from Pisa, four miles, and return home. This big bath is uncovered, and it alone bears any sign of antiquity: they call it Nero's Bath. Public rumor says that this emperor conducted this water by means of aqueducts into his palace in Pisa.

There is another covered bath of common workmanship, which the common people use, with clear and very pure water. They say it is good for the liver and for the itch produced by the heat of the liver. They take the same quantity of the drink as at the other baths, and they walk around after drinking, and they follow Nature, whether she makes you sweat or operates in other ways.

As soon as I had climbed this hill,[17] there appeared a most beautiful view looking over that great plain, the sea, the islands, Leghorn, Pisa. When I had come down, we entered the plain on this side, in which stands

Lucca, ten miles. This morning I ejected another much bigger stone, which clearly seemed to be detached from a larger body. God knows! His will be done!

We were at the hostelry on the same terms as at Pisa, at four giulii per master and three per servant, per day. On the 28th, being almost forced to it by the most courteous offers of Signor Ludovico Pinitesi, I took a ground-floor apartment in his house, very cool and nobly furnished, with five bedrooms, a dining room, and a kitchen; and I was provided with all sorts of furniture, most honorably and delicately, according to Italian custom, which in many matters not only compares with but surpasses the French.

A very great ornament indeed to the buildings in Italy is the very high, beautiful, and broad vaults. They make the entrances to the houses pleasant and dignified, because all the lower part is built with that construction, with wide and high doors. In summer the gentlemen of Lucca eat in public under these entryways, in sight of anyone passing along the street.

To tell the truth, wherever I have stayed in Italy, except Florence (because there I did not leave the hotel, in spite of the discomforts you find in that sort of house, especially when it is hot) and Venice (where we put up in a house too public, and in bad condition, since we were to stay there only a short time), I have always had not only good but even delightful lodgings. My room was secluded; I lacked

17 The Monte San Giuliano, which keeps the Pisans from seeing Lucca, as Dante noted (*Inferno* XXXIII. 30).

nothing; there was no hindrance or disturbance at all. Since courtesies are sometimes tiresome and annoying, it very seldom happened that I was visited by the local people. I slept and studied as I pleased, and when I wanted to go out I could talk anywhere with women or men, with whom I could pleasantly pass an hour or two of the day; and then shops, churches, squares. And, continually changing the scene, I did not lack matter to feed my curiosity. In the meantime I enjoyed a tranquil mind, as far as my infirmities and old age allow; for very few occasions came along from outside to disturb it. I felt only one lack, that of company that I liked, being forced to enjoy these good things alone and without communication.

The Lucchesi play *pallone*[18] very well, and you often see some beautiful games. It is not their custom for the men to go along the street on horseback, or very little; and still less in coaches. The ladies, yes, but on mules; and they go with a servant on foot. Houses to let are very hard to find for foreigners, for very few come here, and this city in itself is well populated. For an ordinary house with four furnished bedrooms and one dining room and kitchen, I was asked seventy crowns a month rent.

You cannot enjoy the company of the Lucchesi because they are all, even the children, continually occupied at their business and in acquiring goods by means of trade. Therefore the city is somewhat tiresome and disagreeable for strangers.

On the 10th of August we went outside the town for a pleasure trip with some other gentlemen of Lucca, from whom I had borrowed horses. I saw some very pleasant villas around the town at three or four miles' distance, with porticoes and loggias, which are a great ornament to them. Among others, a big loggia, all vaulted inside, covered with branches and tendrils of vines planted all around it, and supported on some props: a living and natural arbor.

My headache at times left me for five or six days or more, but I could not quite get rid of it.

I had an impulse to learn the Florentine language by methodical study. I put a lot of time and concentration into it, but got very little benefit out of it.

In this season we felt a much greater heat than is commonly felt.

On the 12th I also went outside of Lucca to visit the villa of Signor Benedetto Buonvisi: moderately attractive. Among other

18 A game somewhat like court tennis, but played with a wooden armlet instead of a racket.

things I saw there formations of certain little thickets that they make in steep places. In an area of about fifty paces they plant various trees, of those that stay green all year round. This place they encircle with little ditches, and inside it they construct certain little covered alleys. In the middle is a place for the fowler, who, with a silver whistle and a number of thrushes caught for the purpose and tied down, having arranged on all sides a number of birdlime snares, at a certain season of the year, say about November, will in one morning make a catch of two hundred thrushes; and this is done only in a certain area on a certain side of the city.

On Sunday the 13th I left Lucca, having ordered that the said Messer Ludovico Pinitesi be offered fifteen crowns for the use of his house. This reckoning came to one crown a day, with which he was very satisfied.

We went on this day to visit a great many of the villas of gentlemen of Lucca, which are clean, nice, and handsome. They have lots of water, but artificial – that is to say, not running, not natural or continuous. It is a marvel to see so great a rarity of springs in so hilly a place. They draw certain waters from streams, and for the sake of beauty they arrange them in the manner of fountains with vases, grottoes, and other works of similar service.

We came to supper this evening in a villa of the said Messer Ludovico, having still in our company his son Messer Orazio, who received us very comfortably in this villa and gave us a very good supper, by night, under a large portico, very cool, and open on all sides, and then had us sleep in good separate rooms, with very white clean linen sheets, such as we had enjoyed in Lucca at the father's house.

Italy: Second Stay at La Villa
(August 14–September 12, 1581)

Monday early we left there. And along the road, without dismounting, after stopping a while to visit the villa of the bishop, who was there (and we were made much of by his men, and invited to stay there to dinner), we came to dine at

THE BATHS OF LA VILLA, fifteen miles. I received a warm welcome and greetings from all those people. In truth it seemed that I had come back to my own home. I went back to the same

room I had the first time, at the price of twenty crowns a month, and on the same conditions.

Tuesday August 15th I went to the bath early and stayed there a little less than an hour. I again found it rather cold than otherwise. It did not start me sweating at all. I arrived at these baths not only healthy, but I may further say in all-round good spirits. After bathing, I passed some cloudy urine; and in the evening, after walking a good bit over alpine and not at all easy roads, I passed some that was quite bloody; and in bed I felt something indefinably wrong with the kidneys.

On the 16th I continued the bathing, and I went to the women's bath, where I had not yet been, in order to be separate and alone. I found it too hot, either because it was really so or indeed because my pores, being opened from the bathing of the day before, had made me get hot easily. At all events I stayed there an hour at most and sweated moderately. My urine was natural; no gravel at all. After dinner my urine again came turbid and red, and at sunset it was bloody.

On the 17th I found this same bath more temperate. I sweated very little. The urine rather turbid, with a little gravel; my color a sort of yellow pallor.

On the 18th I stayed two hours in the aforesaid bath. I felt I know not what heaviness in the kidneys. My bowels were reasonably loose. From the very first day I felt full of wind, and my bowels rumbling. I can easily believe that this effect is characteristic of these waters, because the other time I bathed I clearly perceived that they brought on the flatulence in this way.

On the 19th I went to the bath a little later to give way to a lady of Lucca who wanted to bathe, and did bathe, before me; for this rule is observed, and reasonably so, that the ladies may enjoy their own bath when they please. I again stayed there two hours. There came over me a little heaviness in my head, which had been in the best of condition for several days. My urine was still turbid, but in different ways, and it carried off a lot of gravel. I also noticed some sort of commotion in the kidneys. And if my feelings are correct, these baths can do much in that particular; and not only do they dilate and open up the passages and conduits, but furthermore they drive out the matter, dissipate and scatter it. I voided gravel that seemed really to be stones broken up into pieces.

In the night I felt in the left side the beginning of a very violent and painful colic, which tore me for a good while and yet did not run

its ordinary course: it did not reach the belly and the groin, and ended in a way that made me believe it was wind.

On the 20th I was two hours in the bath. The wind in my lower intestines gave me much annoyance and discomfort all day. I continually voided very turbid, red, thick urine with some little gravel. I felt bad in my head. My bowels were rather livelier than usual.

Feast days are not observed here as religiously as we observe them, especially Sunday. The women do most of their work after dinner.

On the 21st I continued my bathing. After taking my bath I had a lot of pain in my kidneys. My urine was very turbid. I voided gravel, but not much. The pain I suffered then in the kidneys, as far as I could judge, was caused by wind, which was stirring all over. From the turbidity of the urine I guessed that some large stone was about to descend. I guessed only too well.

After writing this up in the morning, I came to be greatly afflicted with colicky pains immediately after dinner. And in order not to leave me too relaxed, one of these spasms attacked me together with a very acute toothache in the left jaw, which I had not felt before. Not being able to endure this discomfort, after two or three hours I went to bed, where in a short time this pain in the jaw left me.

Since the colic still tormented me, and I finally sensed (from feeling it move from place to place and occupy different parts of my body) that it was rather wind than a stone, I was forced to ask for an enema, which was administered to me at nightfall very comfortably, made of oil, camomile, and anise, and nothing else, by the prescription of the apothecary alone. Captain Paulino served me with it with such skill that, feeling the wind rushing out against it, he stopped and drew back; and then continued very gently, so that I took in the whole thing without trouble. He did not need to remind me to retain it as long as I could, for it did not give me any desire to move my bowels. I stayed this way for as long as three hours, and then I tried to void it by myself. Being out of bed, I took a mouthful of marzipan with great difficulty, and four drops of wine. After going back to bed and sleeping a bit, I felt an inclination to go to the toilet; and by daybreak I had gone four times, though still keeping some part of the said enema that was not voided.

In the morning I felt much relieved, having got rid of an infinite amount of wind. I was left very tired, but with no pain. I ate a little

dinner, without appetite; I drank without relish, although I felt very thirsty. After dinner that pain in my left jaw attacked me once again, from which I suffered very much from dinner to supper time. Considering it certain that this flatulence was caused by the bath, I let the bath alone. I got through the night with a good sleep.

In the morning on waking I found myself again weary and short of breath, my mouth dry, with a sharp bad taste, and my breath as if I had a fever. I did not feel any pain, but I continued passing this extraordinary and very turbid urine, which all the time carried with it sand and reddish gravel, but not in great quantity.

On the 24th, in the morning, I pushed down a stone that stopped in the passage. I remained from that moment until dinnertime without urinating, in order to increase my desire to do so. Then I got my stone out, not without pain and bleeding, both before and after: as big and long as a pine nut, but as thick as a bean at one end, and having, to tell the truth, exactly the shape of a prick. It was a very fortunate thing for me to be able to get it out. I have never ejected one comparable in size to this one. I had guessed only too truly from the quality of my urines that this would be the result. I shall see what is to follow.

There would be too much weakness and cowardice on my part if, finding myself every day in a position to die in this manner, and with every hour bringing death nearer, I did not make every effort toward being able to bear death lightly as soon as it surprises me. And in the meantime it will be wise to accept joyously the good that it pleases God to send us. There is no other medicine, no other rule or science, for avoiding the ills, whatever they may be and however great, that besiege men from all sides and at every hour, than to make up our minds to suffer them humanly, or to end them courageously and promptly.

On August 25th my urine regained its usual color, and I found my body in the same condition as before; except that many times, both day and night, I suffered in my left cheek; but it was a sort of pain that did not last at all. I remember that this pain bothered me at other times in my home.

On Saturday the 26th I was in the bath for an hour in the morning.

On the 27th after dinner I was cruelly tormented by a very acute toothache, so that I sent for the doctor, who, when he had come and considered everything, and especially that my pain had left me in his presence, judged that this defluxion had no body unless a very subtle

one, and that it was wind and flatulence that mounted from the stomach to the head and, mingling with a little humor, gave me that discomfort. This indeed seemed to me very likely, considering that I had suffered similar accidents in other parts of the body.

On Monday, August 28th, at dawn, I went to drink at Bernabò's spring, and drank seven pounds four ounces of the water, at twelve ounces to the pound. It made my bowels move once. I voided a little less than half of it before dinner. I clearly felt that it sent vapors to my head and made it heavy.

On Tuesday the 29th I drank at the ordinary spring nine glasses, which each contained one ounce less than a pound. Immediately my head felt bad. To tell the truth, my head was of itself in bad condition, and it had never fully recovered from the bad state it had fallen into in my first season of bathing. I was troubled by it more rarely and in a little different way than a month before, because my eyes were not weakened or dazzled. I suffered more in the back, and never in the head without the pain passing immediately to the left cheek, affecting the whole of it, the teeth, even the lower ones, the ear, part of the nose. The pain was brief, but most of the time very acute, and seized me very many times, day and night. Such was the condition of my head this season.

I do believe that the fumes of this water, from drinking and also from bathing (though more so in the former case than in the latter), are very bad for the head, and, I can say with assurance, even worse for the stomach. And therefore their custom is generally to take medicine to provide against this.

During that whole day and night I passed all but a pound of the water, counting what I drank at table, which was very little, and less than a pound. After dinner, toward sunset, I went to the bath and stayed there three-quarters of an hour. I sweated a little.

On Wednesday, August 30th, I drank nine glasses, eighty-one ounces. I passed half of it before dinner.

On Thursday I discontinued the drinking, and in the morning went on horseback to see Controne, a very populous municipality in these mountains. There are many beautiful fertile plains, and pastures at the top of the mountains. This municipality has many little villas, comfortable stone lodgings, their roofs covered with stone. I made a long tour around these hills before returning home.

I did not like the way I had got rid of the water I had taken lately. Therefore I thought of giving up drinking it. I was displeased

because I did not pass it all, and the count of what I urinated did not match with what I had drunk. More than three glasses of the water of the bath must have remained inside me. Besides, I had an attack of constipation, in contrast with my ordinary state.

Friday, September 1st, 1581, I bathed for an hour in the morning. I sweated some in the bath, and voided with the urine a large quantity of red gravel. When drinking, I had voided none, or little. My head remained still in the same state, that is to say bad.

I began to find these baths unpleasant. And if news had come from France, which I was expecting, having been four months without receiving any, I would have been ready to leave at the first opportunity, and do my autumn cure at any other baths whatever. If I went toward Rome, I would come across at a short distance from the main road the baths of Bagno-Acqua, and those of Siena and Viterbo; if I went toward Venice, those of Bologna, and then those of Padua.

I had my coat of arms made in Pisa, gilt, and in handsome vivid colors, for a French crown and a half, and then pasted on a board (for it was on canvas) at the bath, and this board I had very carefully nailed up on the wall of the room I stayed in, with this condition: that it was to be considered as given to the room, not to Captain Paulino the landlord, and that on no account was it to be removed, whatever might happen to the house in the future. And this he promised and swore.

On Sunday, September 3rd, I went to bathe and stayed there an hour and a little more. I felt a quantity of wind, but without pain.

That night and the morning of Monday the 4th, I was cruelly tormented by a toothache, and I continued to suspect that it was some decayed tooth. I chewed mastic in the morning without any relief. From the change that this very acute pain brought me there also followed constipation, because of which I did not dare to resume drinking at the bath; and thus I did very little by way of a cure. Toward dinnertime and for three or four hours after dinner it gave me some peace. Toward two in the afternoon it attacked me with such fury in the head and both jaws that I could not stay on my feet. The sharpness of the pain made me want to vomit. Now I was all in a sweat, now chilled. This pain that attacked me on every side led me to believe that the trouble was not caused by a bad tooth. For although the left side was in much greater torment, nevertheless in both temples, and the chin, and even in the shoulders and the throat, in every part, I felt at times the greatest pain; so that

I passed the cruelest night that I remember ever having passed. It was really rage and fury.

In the night I sent for an apothecary, who gave me some brandy to put on the side of my mouth that tormented me most. I received wonderful help from it, for at the very instant that I put it into my mouth, all my pain subsided. But as soon as I had spat it out, the pain seized me again as before; so that I had the glass continually to my mouth. I could not keep the brandy in my mouth, because as soon as the pain left me, weariness sent me fast asleep, and as soon as I was asleep a drop of this brandy would go down my throat, and so I had to spray it again. At daybreak my pain passed.

I was visited Tuesday morning in bed by all the gentlemen who were at the baths. I had a small mastic plaster applied to my left temple over the pulse. On this day I felt little pain. At night they put hot tow on my cheek and on the left side of my head. I slept without pain, but a troubled sleep.

On Wednesday I still felt the pain in the teeth and the left eye. I voided some gravel with my urine, but not in the great quantity that I voided it the first time I was here. I passed certain solid grains of it, like millet, and red.

On Thursday, September 7th, in the morning I was an hour in the big bath.

This same morning they delivered into my hands, by way of Rome, letters from Monsieur de Tausin, written in Bordeaux on August 2nd, by which he advised me that the day before, by general consent, I had been made mayor of that city; and he urged me to accept this charge for the love of my country.[19]

On Sunday, September 10th, I bathed for an hour in the morning in the women's bath; and since it was a bit warm, I sweated some.

After dinner I went alone on horseback to see some other places in the neighborhood, and a little villa called Granajolo, which stands on the top of one of the highest mountains in these parts. As I passed over these heights, they seemed to me the most beautiful, fertile, and pleasant inhabited slopes that could possibly be seen.

Talking with the natives, I asked one very elderly man whether they used our baths, and he replied that it worked out with them as it did with the people who live near Our Lady of Loreto: that those people rarely go there on a pilgrimage, and that there is little use of

19 For Montaigne's mayoralty, see especially *Essays* III: 10, "Of Husbanding Your Will."

the baths except for the benefit of foreigners and those who live far away.[20] He said he was very sorry about one thing, that for a number of years he had observed that the baths did more harm than good to those who used them. He said that the cause of it was this: that whereas in times past there was not a single apothecary in these parts, and you never saw a doctor except rarely, now you see the contrary; for those people who consider their own profit have spread the notion that the baths are of no value unless you take medicine, not only after and before the bath, but even mixing it with the operation of the waters; and they would not readily consent to your taking the waters pure. From this, he said, there followed this very evident result, that more people died from these baths than were cured by them. And he held it for certain that in a little while they would fall into universal disrepute and be abandoned.

Monday, September 11th, in the morning, I voided a good quantity of gravel, most of it looking like millet, solid, red on the surface and gray inside.

Italy: Return to Rome
(September 12–October 15, 1581)

On September 12th, 1581, we left the baths of La Villa early in the morning and came to dine at

LUCCA, fourteen miles. These days they were beginning to gather the grapes.

The Feast of the Holy Cross is one of the principal ones in this city; and for a week around it freedom is given to anyone who wants it and who has been banished on account of a civil debt, to return in security to his house, to give him opportunity to attend to his devotions.

I have not found in Italy a single good barber to shave my beard and cut my hair.

20 Compare *Essays* II: 15, p. 564: "The people of the March of Ancona prefer to make their vows to Saint James [of Compostela in Galicia], and those of Galicia to Our Lady of Loreto [in the March of Ancona]. At Liège they make much ado about the baths of Lucca, and in Tuscany about those of Spa."

On Wednesday evening we went to hear vespers in the cathedral, where there was a gathering of the whole city, and processions. The relic of the Holy Face[1] was to be seen uncovered; it is held in great veneration by them, inasmuch as it is very ancient and famous for several miracles. For its service the cathedral was built; thus the little chapel in which this relic is kept still stands in the middle of this great church, in an undesirable place, and against every rule of architecture. When vespers were over, the whole procession moved to another church, which in times past was the cathedral.

Thursday I heard Mass in the choir of the said cathedral, along with all the officials of the signory. In Lucca they take great delight in music, and they all join in the singing. It is apparent, however, that they have very few good voices. This Mass was sung with all possible effort, and yet it was not much. They had built for the occasion a big, very high altar of wood and cardboard, covered with images and big silver candlesticks and many silver vessels placed in this order, a basin in the middle and four plates around it; and, adorned in this manner from top to bottom, it produced a notable and beautiful effect.

Every time the bishop says Mass, as he said it today, at the point where he says the *Gloria in excelsis* they set fire to a certain bundle of tow fixed to an iron grating that hangs in the middle of the church for this purpose.

In this region the weather was already much colder and humid.

On Friday the 15th of September I had almost a flux of urine – that is to say, I passed nearly twice as much water as I had drunk. If some part of the water from the bath had remained in my body, I believe I voided it.

On Sunday morning I passed a rough little stone, without any difficulty. I had felt it slightly during the night in the groin and the base of the penis.

On Sunday, September 17th, the ceremony of the changing of the city's Gonfalonier took place. I went to see it at the palace.

They work here almost without regard to Sundays, and there are many shops open.

On Wednesday, September 20th, after dinner, I left Lucca, having first had two bales of stuff made up to send to France. We followed a fast and level road. The country is barren like the Landes

1 A cedar crucifix supposedly carved by Saint Nicomedes and brought miraculously from the Orient in 782. The chapel for it was built in 1484.

of Gascony. We crossed a big stream over a bridge built by Duke Cosimo. In this place are mills for making iron, belonging to the grand duke, and a handsome lodging. There are also three fish-ponds, or places separated like enclosed ponds, and paved with bricks on the bottom, in which are kept an infinite number of eels, which are easy to see, there being little water. Then we crossed the Arno at Fucecchio and arrived at dusk at

LA SCALA, twenty miles. I left La Scala at sunrise and passed along a fine and almost level road. The country was hilly, with small and very fertile hills like the hills of France. We passed through the middle of Castel-Fiorentino, a little walled-in place, and then passed by the foot of and near Certaldo, Boccaccio's native place, a pretty country seat on a hill. We came to dine at

POGGIBONSI, eighteen miles, a little village. From there to supper at

SIENA, twelve miles. It seems to me that the weather was colder at this season in Italy than in France.

The square in Siena is the most beautiful that is to be seen in any city. Mass is said there every day in public, at an altar in view of all the houses and shops round about, so that the artisans and all these people can hear it without leaving their place and abandoning their work. And when the elevation takes place a trumpet sounds to give notice to all.

On Sunday, September 24th, after dinner, we left Siena, and after following a fast though slightly uneven road (this country being hilly with fertile hills and mountains unlike the Alps), we reached

SAN CHIRICO, twenty miles, a little stronghold. We lodged outside the walls. Since the pack horse had lain down in a little stream that we crossed at a ford, all my things, and particularly my books, were ruined, and it took time to dry them. On the neighboring hills to the left stood Montepulciano, Montichiello, and Castiglioncello.

Early on Monday I went to see a bath two miles away, which is called Vignone, from the name of a little château that is near it. The bath is situated in a rather high place, at the foot of which passes the river Orcia. In this place there are a dozen little houses, or thereabouts, uncomfortable and disgusting, located around it. It looks verminous and wretched. A large pond surrounded by walls and steps, in the middle of which you see bubbling up several springs of that hot water, which, having no odor of sulphur, little vapor, and

a reddish sediment, seems to be rather ferruginous than anything else. It is not drunk. The length of this pond is sixty paces, the width thirty-five. In certain places around this pond there are four or five spots set apart and covered, where it is usual to bathe. This bath is rather well-known.

They do not drink this water, but they do drink that of San Cassiano, which has a bigger reputation, near the said San Chirico, eighteen miles toward Rome, on the left-hand side of the main road.

Considering the cleanliness of these earthenware vessels, which are so white and neat that they seem like porcelain, and are so cheap, they really seemed to me more pleasant for eating than the pewter of France, especially when it is dirty, as you find it in the hostelries.

These days I felt a little headache, from which I had thought I was fully freed. And, as before, there came around the eyes, the forehead, and other parts of the front of the head, a heaviness, weakness, and disturbance, which greatly troubled my mind. Tuesday we came to dine at

LA PAGLIA, thirteen miles, and to sleep at

SAN LORENZO, sixteen miles: wretched inns. The vintage was beginning in these parts.

On Wednesday morning there arose a dispute between our men and the drivers from Siena: considering that we had been longer on this journey than usual and that they had to meet the expenses for the horses, they said they would not pay this expense for that evening. The thing went so far that it was necessary to speak to the mayor, who, after hearing me, ruled in my favor, and put one of the drivers in prison. I stated that the horse's falling into the water, which had ruined most of my things, had been the cause of our delay.

Near the main road six miles from Montefiascone, or thereabouts, a few paces away on the right, is a bath named [Naviso],[2] situated in a very large plain, and three or four miles from the nearest mountain. It consists of a little lake, at one end of which you see a big spring bubbling lustily and spouting scalding water. It stinks strongly of sulphur, and forms a white scum and sediment. From this spring on one side a conduit branches off, which leads the water to two baths that are in a nearby house; which house stands

2 Montaigne left the name blank.

alone, with a good many little rooms, but wretched ones. I do not believe that much of a crowd comes here. They drink for seven days, ten pounds each time; but they have to let the water cool a little first to take away that great heat, as is done at the baths of Préchacq. They take their baths the same number of days. This house and the baths are in the domain of a certain church.[3] It rents for fifty crowns. But besides this profit from the sick people who go there in the spring, the man who leases the house sells a certain mud which is drawn from the said lake; and this mud is good for humans when dissolved in warm oil to soothe the itch, or indeed for scabby sheep and dogs, when dissolved in water. This mud sells in its crude form for two giulii a load, in dried balls for seven quattrini apiece. Here we came across a large number of Cardinal Farnese's dogs, which were brought here to be bathed. About three miles from here we reached

VITERBO, sixteen miles. It was so late that we had to make one meal of dinner and supper. I was then very hoarse and chilled, and had slept fully dressed on a table at San Lorenzo because of the bugs; which I had not had to do except there and in Florence. At Viterbo I ate some sort of acorn called *gensole*. These are found in many places in Italy. They are tasty. There are still so many starlings here that you can get one for one baiocco.[4]

On Thursday, September 28th, in the morning, I went to see some other baths near this town, situated in the plain a good way off, and far from the mountain. First you see buildings in two different places where not long ago there used to be baths, which have been ruined by neglect.[5] The ground, however, gives off a great stench. There is also a wretched little hovel in which a tiny little spring of hot water makes a little lake to bathe in.[6] This water has no smell and an insipid taste; it is moderately hot. I judged that it had a lot of iron in it. This water is drunk. Farther on is the palace that is called the Pope's, because it is believed that Pope Nicholas[7] built it or rebuilt it. At the foot of this palace and in the ground, in a very low spot, there are three different springs of hot water. One of these serves for drinking. It is of moderate and temperate heat; no stink,

3 The Church of Sant' Angelo in Spata, in Viterbo.
4 About a half a sou.
5 The baths of San Paolo and Almadiani.
6 The bath of the Madonna.
7 Nicholas V.

no odor. In taste, it has a little tang and sharpness. I think it contains much niter. I had gone with the intention of drinking for three days. It is drunk as in other places in regard to quantity. You take a walk afterward, and it is a good thing to sweat.

This water has a very great reputation, and is carried in loads all over Italy. And this is the water which the doctor[8] who has written about baths in general says is the best for drinking of all the waters of Italy. In particular they attribute to it great virtue for kidney troubles. It is drunk most commonly in May. It was a bad omen for me to read an inscription on the wall by one who cursed the doctors for having sent him there, and who had got much worse; and besides, the bathkeeper said the season was too far advanced, and was cool in encouraging me to drink.

There is only one lodging, though it is large and respectably comfortable, a mile and a half from Viterbo. I went there on foot. There are three or four baths, varying in their effect, and also a place for showers. These waters form a very white scum, which readily hardens and becomes solid as ice, making a hard crust on the water. The whole place appears whitened and encrusted in this way. Put a piece of linen on it, and immediately you see it loaded with this scum, and as solid as if it were frozen. This stuff[9] is useful for cleaning your teeth, and is exported and sold. When you chew it, the only taste you get is of earth or sand. It is said to be the same substance as marble. Who knows whether it might not also become petrified in the kidneys? They say, however, that this water, which is carried in bottles, forms no sediment and keeps clear and very pure. I believe it may be drunk with pleasure, and that it gets some taste from its sharpness that makes it easy to drink.

Returning from there, in this same plain, which is very long and eight miles wide, I went to see the place where the inhabitants of Viterbo (among whom there is not a single gentleman; they are all laborers and merchants) collect the flax and hemp, which is a great industry of theirs. The men do this work; there are no women among them. There was a great quantity of it and many laborers around a certain lake of water which is equally hot and boiling at every season.[10] They say that this lake has no bottom. From it they

8 Andrea Bacci, author of *De Thermis* (Venice, 1571).
9 Calcium carbonate.
10 The Bulicame, which Dante mentions in the *Inferno* (XIV. 79–80).

draw off water to form other little tepid lakes, in which they put the hemp and flax to steep.

Back at the house, having made this trip going on foot and returning on horseback, I ejected a small, red, solid stone, as big as a big grain of wheat. I had felt its descent a little around the groin the day before. It stopped in the passage. In order to ease it out it is good to hold the urine from passing and squeeze the prick a little, so that it may come out more vigorously. The seigneur de Langon showed me this remedy at Arsac.

On Saturday, the Feast of Saint Michael, after dinner, I went to the Madonna della Quercia, a mile out of the town. You go by a very fine big road, level and straight, bordered with trees from one end to the other, built with great care by Pope Farnese [Paul III]. The church is beautiful, most religious, and full of innumerable votive tablets. The Latin inscription states that a hundred years ago or thereabouts a man, attacked by robbers and half dead, took refuge by an oak on which was this image of the Madonna, and after praying to her became miraculously invisible to the robbers and thus escaped a most certain danger. This miracle gave rise to this local cult of the Madonna. Around this oak was built this very beautiful church. The trunk of the oak is now seen cut at the base, and the part where the image is placed is attached to the wall, and the branches around it are cut away.

On Saturday, the last day of September, in the morning, I left Viterbo and took the road to Bagnaia, a place belonging to Cardinal Gambara, very ornate, and provided among other things with fountains. And in this respect it seems not only to equal but to surpass both Pratolino and Tivoli. In the first place it has running spring water, which Tivoli has not; and this is so abundant (as it is not at Pratolino) that it suffices for an infinite number of purposes. The same Messer Tomaso da Siena who directed the work at Tivoli, or most of it, is also in charge of this, which is not finished; and thus, always adding new inventions to the old, he has put into this, his latest work, much more art, beauty, and grace. Among a thousand other members of this excellent body you see a high pyramid which spouts water in many different ways: one jet rises, another falls. Around this pyramid are four beautiful little lakes, clear, clean, full of water. In the middle of each is a little stone ship with two musketeers which draw water and shoot it against the pyramid, and in each a trumpeter which also draws water. You go around these lakes and the pyramid by very beautiful alleys with balustrades

of fine stone, most artfully carved. The others liked other parts more. The palace is small but clean and pretty. Certainly, if I know anything about it, this place easily takes the prize for the use and service of water. The cardinal was not there. But since he is French at heart, his men showed us all the courtesy and friendliness that could be desired.

From here, following the straight road, we came upon Caprarola, a palace of Cardinal Farnese, which is very greatly renowned in Italy. I have seen none in Italy that may be compared with it. It has a great moat around it, cut out of the tufa. The building is above, in the manner of a terrace; you do not see the tiles. The form is pentagonal, but to the eye it appears distinctly square. Inside, however, it is perfectly round, with wide corridors going around it, all vaulted and painted on all sides. The rooms are all square; the building, very large; very beautiful public rooms. One of these is wonderful: on its vaulted ceiling (for the building is vaulted throughout) you see the celestial sphere, with all the constellations; around it on the walls, the terrestrial globe, the regions and the whole world, everything painted very richly directly on the wall itself.

In various other places you see depicted the noblest actions of Pope Paul III and of the house of Farnese. The persons are portrayed so true to life that where you see portrayed our Constable, or the Queen Mother, or her sons Charles, Henry, and the duke of Alençon, and the queen of Navarre,[11] they are immediately recognized by those who have seen them; likewise King Francis, Henry II, Pietro Strozzi, and others. In one and the same room, you see the effigy of King Henry II at one end and in the place of honor, under which the inscription says "Preserver of the House of Farnese," and at the other end King Philip,[12] whose inscription says "For the many benefits received from him."

Outside there are also many noteworthy and beautiful things, among others a grotto, which, spraying water artfully into a little lake, gives the appearance to the eye and the ear of the most natural rainfall. The location is barren and alpine. And the cardinal has to draw the water for his fountain all the way from Viterbo, eight miles away.

11 These personages are respectively the Constable Anne de Montmorency, Catherine de' Medici, Charles IX, Henry III, Duke Francis of Alençon, and Margaret of Valois, queen of Navarre.
12 Philip II of Spain.

From here, following a level road and a large plain, we came upon some very big meadows, in the middle of which, in certain dry and grassless spots, you see springs bubbling up of pure cold water, but stinking so much of sulphur that the odor of it is perceived from a great distance.[13] We came to sleep at

MONTEROSSI, twenty-three miles. On Sunday, October 1st, to

ROME, twenty-two miles. We felt at this season an extreme cold and an icy north wind from the mountains.

On Monday and for some days after, I had indigestion in my stomach. And for this reason I took some meals apart in order to eat less; and my bowels were loose, so that I felt physically pretty sprightly, except for my head, which has never completely recovered.

On the day I arrived in Rome I received the letters from the jurats of Bordeaux,[14] who wrote me very courteously about the fact that they had elected me mayor of their city, and urgently requested me to join them.

On Sunday, October 8th, 1581, I went to the Baths of Diocletian on Monte Cavallo to see an Italian who had been for a long time a slave of the Turks, and had learned a thousand rare tricks in riding.[15] For example, while riding at full speed he would stand up straight on the saddle, hurl a javelin with all his might, and then suddenly drop back into the saddle. Galloping furiously and hold-ing the saddlebow with one hand, he would get off his horse and touch the ground with his right foot while the left remained in the stirrup; and many times in this way he dismounted and jumped into the saddle again. He would turn his body around in the saddle several times, galloping all the while. He shot a Turkish bow forward and backward with great ease. Leaning his head and shoulders on the horse's neck and holding his feet straight up in the air, he let the horse go at full speed. He took a club and threw it in the air and caught it again on the run. Standing up on the saddle, he aimed a lance at a glove and pierced it, as people tilt at the ring. On foot he made a pike revolve around his neck, in front and behind, having first given it a hard push with his hand.

On October 10th, after dinner, the French ambassador sent a footman to tell me that if I wished, he was coming to pick me

13 La Solfatara, near Ronciglione.
14 The municipal council.
15 Compare *Essays* I: 48, p. 261.

up in his coach to take me to see the furniture of Cardinal Orsini, which was being sold, since he had died this summer in Naples and had left as heir to all his vast property a niece of his, a little girl. Among other rare things was a taffeta coverlet lined with swans' feathers. In Siena you see a good many of these swans' skins complete with feathers, and I was asked no more than a crown and a half for one, all prepared. They are the size of a sheepskin, and a few of them would be enough to make a coverlet of this sort. I also saw an ostrich egg, decorated all over and painted with pretty pictures. Also a square box to put jewels in, which contained a certain quantity of them; but since the box was most artfully arranged with mirrors all around, when it was opened it appeared much wider and deeper in every direction, and seemed to hold ten times as many jewels as were in it, since one and the same thing was seen many times by the reflection of the mirrors, and the mirrors were not easy to detect.

On Thursday, October 12th, the cardinal of Sens took me alone with him in his coach to see the Church of Saints John and Paul, of which he is the patron, as he is of those friars who make the waters and perfumes I spoke of above;[16] it is situated on Mount Celio. And this lofty site seems to be made artificially, since underneath it is all vaulted, with great corridors and underground rooms. It is said that the Forum Hostilium[17] was there. The gardens and vineyards of these friars are so placed as to give a beautiful view of Rome, old and new, from a place set apart by its steep and precipitous height, and almost inaccessible on every side.

This same day I gave a well-filled wooden case to a carrier to send to Milan. The muleteers ordinarily take twenty days on the road there. The whole thing weighed 150 pounds, and you pay four baiocchi, which comes to two French sous, per pound. There were many things of value in it, above all a very handsome Agnus Dei necklace, which had not its like in Rome, having been made especially for the Empress's ambassador, who had it blessed by the Pope; and also a *cavalliere*.[18]

16 The Jesuates. See above, pp. 1118–20.
17 Montaigne presumably has in mind the Cura Hostilia, where at one time the Senate met. It was located on the Forum, some distance away.
18 A kind of chaplet.

Italy and France: The Return Home
(October 15–November 30, 1581)

On Sunday morning, October 15th, I started out from Rome and left my brother[1] there with forty-three gold crowns, with which, he had decided, he could stay there and learn fencing for five months. Before I left he had rented a nice little room for twenty giulii a month. Messieurs d'Estissac, de Monluc, de Chasai, Morens, and several others accompanied me for the first stage. And if I had not started early in order to save these gentlemen the trouble, there would have been a good many others ready to come, who had already hired horses, Messieurs du Bellai, d'Ambres, d'Alègre, and others. I came to sleep at

RONCIGLIONE, thirty miles, having hired the horses for as far as Lucca at twenty giulii each, the driver paying the expenses of the said horses.

On Monday morning I was astonished to feel such a piercing cold that it seemed to me I had never experienced such a cold winter, and to see the vintage and vine harvest not yet finished in these parts. I came to dine at

VITERBO, where I put on my furs and all my winter trappings; and from there to sup at

SAN LORENZO, twenty-nine miles. From there I came to sleep at

SAN CHIRICO, thirty-two miles. All these roads have been repaired this year by order of the duke of Tuscany; which work is very fine and serves the public to great advantage. May God reward him for it! For the most difficult roads have by this means become as fast and comfortable as the streets of a city.

It was an astounding thing to see the great multitude of people who were going to Rome. On this account it was to be observed that horses for hire to go to Rome were beyond all price for their scarcity, and to return from Rome they let you have them for nothing. Near Siena, as in innumerable other places, there is a double bridge, that is to say a bridge above which another stream crosses over an aqueduct. We arrived in the evening at

SIENA, twenty miles. Tonight I felt some colic for about two hours, and it seemed to me I felt the stone descending.

1 Bertrand de Mattecoulon, who was later to be involved in a duel in Rome (see *Essays* II: 27, p. 639).

Early on Thursday Guglielmo Felice, a Hebrew doctor, came to see me and gave me a long lecture on the regimen I should follow for my kidneys and gravel. In this condition I left Siena; and the colic seized me again, and lasted three or four hours. At the end of this time I clearly perceived, from an extreme pain in the groin, the prick, and the ass, that the stone had descended. I came for supper to

PONTE A ELSA, twenty-eight miles. Here I voided a stone bigger than a grain of millet, with some red gravel, without pain or difficulty in the passage. I left here Friday morning and stopped on the road at

ALTO PASCIO, sixteen miles. I stayed here an hour to have the animals fed. Here, without much pain, I passed with a good deal of gravel a long stone, partly solid and partly soft, of the size of a big grain, and bigger. On the road we came upon a number of country people who were picking the vine leaves, which they keep as fodder for the animals in the winter; others were gathering ferns to make their litter. We came to sleep at

LUCCA, eight miles. Here a number of gentlemen and artisans came to visit me.

On Saturday morning, October 21st, I ejected another stone, which stopped a while in the passage but nevertheless came out without pain or difficulty. This one was rather round than otherwise, hard and massive, but harsh and rough, white inside and red outside, much bigger than a grain. Meanwhile I voided gravel all the time. From this we see that nature sometimes purges itself, and you feel a sort of flux of this stuff. God be thanked that it comes out without serious pain and does not disturb my actions!

As soon as I had eaten a grape (for on this trip I ate very little or nothing in the morning), I left Lucca without waiting for certain gentlemen who were getting ready to come and accompany me. I had a fine road, mostly level, with the hills covered with number-less olive trees on my right, on my left some marshes, and the sea not far off.

In one place in the state of Lucca I came across a machine that is half ruined owing to the negligence of the said lords; and this lack does great harm to the surrounding country. This machine was made for the purpose of draining the soil in these marshes and making them fertile. A great ditch had been dug, at the end of which three wheels were kept continually in motion by means of a stream of running water which came falling down from the

mountain onto them. These wheels, with certain vessels attached to them, drew the water from one side of this ditch, and on the other side poured it into another, higher ditch and channel; which ditch, made for this purpose and provided with walls on each side, carried this water into the sea. Thus the whole country around was drained.

I passed through the middle of Pietrasanta, a fairly large fortress town of the duke of Florence, with many houses but empty of people, because, from what they say, the air is so bad that you cannot live there, and most of them die or barely exist. We came for supper to

MASSA DI CARRARA, twenty-two miles, a town belonging to the prince of Massa, of the house of Cibo. You see a fine castle on the top of a hill. About midway up this hill, around the said castle and below it, are the streets and houses, surrounded by good walls. And further down, outside the said walls, is a large suburb in the plain, surrounded by other new walls. The place is handsome: handsome streets, handsome painted houses.

I was forced to drink new wines – they drink no others in these parts – which, with a certain kind of wood and the whites of eggs, are made so clear that they lack none of the color of the old wines; but they have an indefinable unnatural taste.

On Sunday, October 22nd, I first followed a very level road, having the Tyrrhenian Sea still on my left, a harquebus-shot away. And on this road, between us and the sea, we saw some ruins, not very big, which the people of the country say used to be a great city called Luna.[2]

Then we came to Sarzana, a town belonging to the Republic of Genoa; and you see their coat of arms there, a Saint George on horseback. They keep a guard of Swiss soldiers, since the town once belonged to the duke of Florence. And if the prince of Massa were not in between them, there is no doubt that Pietrasanta and Sarzana, the frontier towns of the two states, would be continually at grips.

We passed Sarzana, where we were forced to pay four giulii per horse for one stage, and where a great artillery celebration was being held for the passage of Don Giovanni de' Medici, natural brother of the duke of Florence, who was returning from

2 An ancient Etruscan town, already decayed in Roman times, and demolished by the Arabs in 1016.

Genoa from seeing the Empress,[3] on whom many other princes of Italy had also gone to call, on behalf of his said brother. And among other things there was much ado about the sumptuosity of the duke of Ferrara, who had come to meet her at Padua with four hundred carriages. He had asked permission of the Signory of Venice to pass through their territory with six hundred horse, and upon their replying to his request that they would allow him to come with a certain somewhat smaller number, he put all his people into carriages and thus brought them all, but diminished the number of horses. I came across this prince Don Giovanni on the way, a young man very handsome in person, accompanied by twenty men in good harness but on hired horses; a way of traveling which is not considered unbecoming in Italy, even for a prince. After passing Sarzana, we left the road to Genoa on our left.

To get to Milan it makes little difference whether you go by way of Genoa or by the other way; it comes to the same thing. I wanted to see that city, and the Empress, who was there. What bothered me was that there are two routes to go there, one three days' journey from Sarzana, which has forty miles of very bad and very alpine road, of rocks and precipices and bad inns; this road is little frequented. The other is through Lerici, three miles from Sarzana, where you embark on the sea and in twelve hours cross over to Genoa. Since I cannot endure the water because of the weakness of my stomach, and feared the discomfort of this route even less than the difficulty of getting lodgings, because of the great crowd of people in Genoa; and moreover, since it was said that the road from Genoa to Milan was none too safe from robbers; and since I had nothing but my return home on my mind; I decided to pass up Genoa, and followed the road on the right through many mountains, always keeping to the bottoms and the valley along the river Magra. And having this river on our left, we passed now through the state of Genoa, now through that of the duke of Florence, now that of the lords of the house of Malespina. Finally, by a road that was reasonably good, except for a few steep and precipitous spots, we came to sleep at

PONTREMOLI, thirty miles, a very long town, full of ancient buildings which are not very attractive. There are a few ruins, and

3 Maria, widow of Maximilian II.

they say that the town was called Appua[4] by the ancients. It now belongs to the state of Milan, and recently the Fieschi family held it.

At table the first thing they gave me was cheese, as they do around Milan and in the country around Piacenza. Following the Genoese practice, they gave me olives without pits, prepared with oil and vinegar like a salad – very good.

The site of this town is among the mountains and at the foot of them.

To wash your hands they furnished a basin full of water placed on a stool. Everyone had to wash his hands in the same water.

I left here Monday morning, the 23rd, and on leaving the house climbed the Apennines – very high, but the road not at all hard or dangerous. All day we were climbing and coming down mountains, mostly alpine and barren. In the evening we came to sleep at

FORNOVO, in the state of the count of San Secondo, thirty miles. It was a pleasure to find myself out of the hands of those scoundrels of the mountains, who practice every sort of cruelty imaginable on travelers in charging for food and horses.

They put on the table for me an assortment of condiments in the form of excellent relishes of various kinds. One of these was made with quinces.

In these parts you find that horses for hire are extremely scarce. You are in the hands of people who have no rules and who do not keep their word to foreigners. Others paid two giulii per horse for each stage; they demanded of me three, four, and five giulii for each stage, so that every day it came to more than a crown to hire one horse, because they also counted two stages where there was only one.

Here I was two stages away from Parma; and to Piacenza from Parma it was the same distance as from Fornovo, so that by going to Parma I would have lengthened the trip by only two stages. I decided not to go there so as not to upset my trip home, having put aside all other plans. This place is a tiny village of six or seven little houses, situated on a plain along the flooded river Taro – I think that is the name of it – which we followed for a time on Tuesday morning, coming to dine at

BORGO SAN DONNINO, twelve miles, a little stronghold which the duke of Parma is beginning to surround with fine walls, well-flanked. Here they put on the table a mustard-like relish made

4 In ancient times there was a people of Liguria called the Appuans, but no town of Appua is believed to have existed.

with apples and oranges cut in pieces, like half-cooked quince marmalade.

From here, leaving on our right Cremona at the same distance as Piacenza, we followed a very fine level road in a countryside where as far as the horizon you see no mountains or unevenness, with very fertile soil; changing horses at every stage. I took these two stages at a gallop to test the strength of my loins, and felt neither pain nor fatigue from it; my urine was natural.

Near Piacenza there are two big columns, one on either side of the road, with about forty paces between them. At the foot of these columns are Latin inscriptions which forbid building or planting trees or vines between them. I do not know whether they merely wanted to preserve the width of the road, or indeed to keep the esplanade open, as we see it to be, from these columns to the town, which is half a mile away. We came to sleep at

PIACENZA, twenty miles, a very big city. Having arrived very early, I went all around in it for three hours. Muddy, unpaved streets, small houses. And in the square, which is its most beautiful spot, is the Palace of Justice, and the prisons, surrounded by shops of no account and the crowd of citizens from all around.

I saw the castle, which is in the hands of King Philip, who keeps here a guard of three hundred Spaniards, badly paid, so I understood from them. The dian[5] is sounded morning and evening with the instruments that we call oboes and they call *pifferi*; and it is sounded for an hour. There are many people in the castle, and handsome pieces of artillery. The duke of Parma never goes there. He for his part (and he was in the city at that time) is lodged in the citadel, which is a castle in another place; and he never goes to the castle that King Philip holds.

In short, I saw nothing here worth seeing except the new Monastery of Saint Augustine, built with money that King Philip has used here, in exchange for another Church of Saint Augustine, from the materials of which he has made this castle; for he holds part of the revenue of the church itself. The church remains to be built, and is well begun. But the lodgings of the friars, who are seventy in number, and the double cloisters, are finished. In corridors, dormitories, wine cellars, and other facilities, this building seems to me the most sumptuous and magnificent that I have seen anywhere, if I remember rightly, for the service of the Church.

5 Normally, the reveille.

At table here they put on the salt in a lump, the cheese in a big piece without a dish.

The duke of Parma was expecting the arrival in Piacenza of the first-born son of the archduke of Austria, which son I saw at Innsbruck; and now it was said that he was going to Rome to be crowned king of the Romans.

They offer water for the hands, and for mixing with the wine, with a big brass spoon. The cheese they eat here is exactly like the Piacentini cheeses that are sold all over.

Piacenza is exactly halfway between Rome and Lyons. In order to go more directly to Milan I would have had to go and sleep at Marignano, thirty miles, and from there to Milan it is ten miles. I lengthened my trip by ten miles in order to see Pavia. I left early on Wednesday, October 25th, following a fine road, in which I urinated one soft little stone and a lot of gravel.

We passed through the middle of a walled village of Count Santafiore. Toward the end of the trip we crossed the Po on a ferry made of scaffolding placed on two boats and surmounted by a little cabin, with a long rope resting in various places on some small boats arranged in order on the river. Near this place the Ticino joins the Po. We came early to

PAVIA, thirty short miles. Immediately I set about seeing the principal sights of the city: the bridge over the Ticino, the cathedral, the churches of the Carmelites, Saint Thomas, Saint Augustine, in which is the shrine of Saint Augustine, a rich sepulcher of white marble with many statues.

In a certain square in the city may be seen a brick column, on top of which is a statue which seems to be a copy of the one of Antoninus Pius[6] on horseback in front of the Capitol. This one is smaller and not at all comparable in beauty. But what makes me more doubtful is that this statue has two stirrups and a saddle with saddlebows in front and behind, whereas the other does not have these; and this is all the more in agreement with the opinion of the learned, that stirrups, and saddles of this kind, were invented later. Perhaps some ignorant sculptor thought that these were lacking. I also saw the beginning of Cardinal Borromeo's building for the use of the students.

The city is large and rather beautiful, comfortably populated, and there is no lack of artisans of many kinds. There are few

6 Not Antoninus Pius, but Marcus Aurelius.

beautiful houses; and the one in which the Empress stayed these past days is not much. I saw the arms of France, but the lilies had been effaced. In short, there is nothing rare here.

In these parts horses are hired for two giulii per stage. The best hostelry, or, to be more precise, the best hotel in which I have stayed from Rome to here was the Post at Piacenza; and I believe it is the best in Italy, after that of Verona. The worst on this journey was the Falcon in Pavia. Here and in Milan you pay extra for firewood, and the beds lack mattresses.

I left Pavia on Thursday, October 26th. I took the road to the right, half a mile off the direct route, to see the spot where they say the shattering of King Francis' army occurred,[7] which is a level place; and also to see the Charterhouse, which with good reason has the reputation of being a very beautiful church. The façade of the entrance, all of marble, with numberless carvings, is really something stupendous. There is also an altar decoration in ivory, on which are carved the Old and the New Testament. Besides this there is the marble tomb of Gian Galeazzo Visconti, founder of the church; and then the choir, and the decorations of the high altar, and the cloisters, very beautiful and of unusual size. These are the finest things. The house is very large in area and gives the impression – not only in the size and number of its different buildings, but even more in the number of people, servants, horses, coaches, laborers, and artisans – of being the court of a very great prince. They are continually working on it at incredible expense, which the Fathers pay out of their revenues. The site is in the middle of a very beautiful meadow. From here we came to

MILAN, twenty miles. This city is the most populous in Italy, large, and full of all sorts of artisans and merchandise. It is not too much unlike Paris, and has much the appearance of a French city. It lacks the palaces of Rome, Naples, Genoa, Florence; but in size it beats them all, and in its crowds of people it comes up to Venice.

On Friday, October 27th, I went to see the castle from the outside, and went almost all around it. It is a very big building and wonderfully strong. The garrison in it consists of at least seven hundred Spaniards, excellently supplied with artillery; and they were adding more defenses all around. This day I stopped there

7 The battle of Pavia, in which Francis I was defeated and taken prisoner by Charles V in 1525.

because of the very heavy rain that suddenly caught us. Until then the weather and the roads had treated us very kindly.

On Saturday, October 28th, I left Milan in the morning. I set out on a fine level road, and although it rained continuously and the road was full of water, there was no mud, for the country is sandy. I came for dinner to

BUFFALORA, eighteen miles. Here we crossed the bridge over the river Naviglio, which is narrow, but deep enough to carry big boats to Milan. And a little farther on we crossed the Ticino by boat and came to sleep at

NOVARA, twelve miles, a little town, not very attractive, standing in a plain, with vineyards and groves and fertile land around it. We left there in the morning and came and stopped a bit to feed our animals at

VERCELLI, ten miles, a town belonging to the duke of Savoy, also in a plain and along the river Sesia, which we crossed by boat. The said duke has built in this place, in a great hurry and with a world of people, a fortress – a handsome one, as far as I could see from outside – and has thereby aroused the suspicion of the Spaniards near these parts.

From here we passed through the middle of San German and then Santhià, two little walled villages. And, always following a beautiful plain, fertile mainly in walnuts (for in this region there are no olives, and no oil except from walnuts), we came to sleep at

LIVORNO, twenty miles, a little village with a good many houses. We left Monday early, and following a level road came to dine at

CHIVASSO, ten miles; and from here, crossing a lot of rivers and streams by boat and at fords, we came to

TURIN, ten miles. We could easily have arrived here in time to dine. A small city in a very watery location, not very well built or attractive, although a little stream runs through the middle of the streets to clean away the dirt. In Turin I paid five and a half crowns per horse for my use as far as Lyons, six days, their expenses to be paid by the drivers.

Here they ordinarily speak French, and they all appear very devoted to France. The language of the people is a language that has almost nothing Italian about it but the pronunciation; the rest of it is French words.

We left here on Tuesday, the last of October, and came along a level road to dine at

SAN AMBROGIO, two stages. From there, following a narrow plain between the mountains, to sleep at

SUSA, two stages, a little walled place with a good many houses. Here I felt a great pain in my right knee, which pain had already bothered me a good many days, but kept increasing all the time. The hostelries are better here than in other parts of Italy – good wines, bad bread, much to eat, courteous innkeepers – and throughout Savoy. On All Saints' Day, after hearing Mass, I came to

NOVALESA, one stage. Here I hired eight *marroni*[8] to carry me in a chair to the top of Mont Cenis and take me down in a sledge on the other side.

[THE JOURNAL BY MONTAIGNE IN FRENCH]

Here they speak French; so I quit this foreign language, which I use easily but with very little sureness, not having had the time to learn it at all well, since I was always in the company of Frenchmen.

I made the ascent of Mont Cenis halfway on horseback, halfway on a litter carried by four men, with another four who relieved them. They carried me on their shoulders. The ascent takes two hours, stony and difficult for horses that are not accustomed to it, but otherwise without danger or difficulty; for since the mountain is broad and rises steadily, you find no precipices, and no danger except of a stumble.

From the top of the mountain you see beneath you a plain two leagues wide, many little houses, lakes, and fountains, and the posthouse; no trees, but a lot of grass and meadows that are useful in the mild season. At that time everything was covered with snow. The descent is one league, steep and straight, and I was taken on a sledge by the same *marrons*. And for all their service, for the eight of them, I paid two crowns. The sledging alone costs only one teston. It is a pleasant sport, but without any risk.

We dined, without much appetite, at

LANSLEBOURG, two stages, which is a village at the foot of the mountain, where Savoy begins; and we came on to sleep in a little village[9] two leagues away. There are lots of trout all around here and excellent old and new wines. From here we came, by a hilly and stony road, to dine at

8 French *marrons*: litter-carriers.
9 Possibly Termignon.

SAINT-MICHEL, five leagues, a village where the posthouse is. From here we came to rest, very late and very wet, at

LA CHAMBRE, five leagues, a little town from which the marquises de La Chambre take their title. On Friday, November 3rd, we came to dine at

AIGUEBELLE, four leagues, a little enclosed town, and to sleep at

MONTMÉLIAN, four leagues, a town with a fort which occupies the top of a low ridge that rises out of the middle of the plain between these high mountains. The said town is situated below the said fort on the river Isère, which goes on to Grenoble, seven leagues from the said place. Here I clearly felt the excellence of the Italian oils, for those over here began to give me a stomach-ache, whereas the others never gave me an aftertaste. We came to dine at

CHAMBÉRY, two leagues, the principal town of Savoy, small, handsome, and mercantile, set among the mountains, but in a place where they recede a long way and form a very big plain. From here we passed over the Mont du Chat, high, steep, and rocky, but not at all dangerous or hard, at the foot of which lies a big lake, and along this a castle called Bourdeau, where they make very renowned swords; and to rest at

YENNE, four leagues, a small town.

On Sunday morning we crossed the Rhone, which we had on our right, after passing a little fort on the river which the duke of Savoy has built between some rocks that are very close together; and along one of these rocks there is a little narrow path at the end of which is the said fort, not very unlike Chiusa, which the Venetians set at the end of the mountains of Tyrol. From here, still going along the low ground between the mountains, we came without a stop to

SAINT-RAMBERT, seven leagues, a tiny little town in the said valley. Most of the towns in Savoy have a stream in the middle that washes them; and the streets on both sides, as far as the said stream, are covered with big porch roofs, so that you are under cover and dry in all weather. It is true that the shops are the darker for it.

On Monday morning, November 6th, we left Saint-Rambert, where Monsieur Francesco Cenami, a banker from Lyons who had retired here because of the plague, sent his nephew to me with some of his wine and many very nice compliments. I left here Monday morning early, and after at last coming completely out of the mountains, I began to enter upon the really French plains. Here I crossed the river Ain in a boat at the harbor of Chazey, and came on without stopping to

MONTLUEL, six leagues, a small town on a much-traveled road, belonging to the duke of Savoy, and the last of his. On Tuesday after dinner I took the post and came to sleep at

LYONS, two stages, three leagues. I liked the sight of the city very much. On Friday I bought from Joseph de La Sone three unused little cropped horses to go in file, for two hundred crowns; and the day before I had bought from Malesieu one pacing horse for fifty crowns and another cropped one for thirty-three.

On Saturday, Saint Martin's Day, in the morning I had a bad stomach-ache, and stayed in bed until afternoon, when I had diarrhea; I ate no dinner and very little supper.

On Sunday, November 12th, Monsieur Alberto Giachinotti of Florence, who showed me many other courtesies, had me to dinner at his house, and offered to lend me money, though he had no knowledge of me until then.

On Wednesday, November 15th, I left Lyons after dinner, and by a hilly road came to sleep at

LA BOURDELLIÈRE, five leagues, a village in which there are only two houses. From here on Thursday morning we took a fine level road, and around the middle of it, near Feurs, a little village, we crossed the river Loire by boat and came on without stopping to

L'HÔPITAL, eight leagues, a little walled place. From here Friday morning we followed a hilly road in bitter, snowy weather with a cruel wind against us, and came on to

THIERS, six leagues, a small town on the river Allier, very mercantile, well-built, and populous. Their principal traffic is in paper, and they are renowned for carved knives and playing cards. It is equidistant from Lyons, Saint-Flour, Moulins, and Le Puy.

The closer I came to home, the more the length of the road seemed annoying; and indeed, counting the days, I was not halfway from Rome to my house until Chambéry at the earliest. This town is part of the appanages of the house of [Bourbon][10] belonging to the duke of Montpensier.

I went to Palmier's to see the cards made. There are as many workmen and as much to do in this as in any other worthy business. The common cards are sold at only one sou, and the fine ones at two caroli.

On Saturday we followed the rich plain of the Limagne, and, after crossing the Dore and then the Allier by boat, came to sleep at

10 Montaigne leaves the name blank.

PONT-DU-CHÂTEAU, four leagues. The plague has ravaged this place badly, and I heard many remarkable stories about it. The manor house, which is the ancestral home of Viscount de Canillac, was burned down as they were trying to purify it with fire. The said lord sent one of his men to me with many offers by word of mouth, and to ask me to write to Monsieur de Foix to recommend his son, whom he had just sent to Rome.

On Sunday, November 19th, I came to dine at

CLERMONT, two leagues, and stopped here for the sake of my young horses.

On Monday the 20th I left in the morning, and, at the top of the Puy de Dôme, I passed a rather large stone, broad and flat in shape, which had been in the passage since morning, and I had felt it the day before, only at the base of the penis; and at the time when it was about to descend into the bladder, I also felt it a bit in the kidneys. It was neither soft nor hard. I passed through

PONTGIBAUD, where I went to greet Madame de La Fayette in passing, and I was half an hour in her parlor. This house has less beauty than reputation; the site of it is rather ugly than otherwise, the garden small, square, and the alleys in it raised a good four or five feet; the beds are at the bottom, with many fruit trees and few herbs in them, and the sides of these sunken beds are lined with freestone.

It was snowing so hard, and the weather was so bitter, with a cold wind, that you saw nothing of the country. I came to sleep at

PONTAUMUR, seven leagues, a little village. Monsieur and Madame du Lude were two leagues from there. The next day I came to sleep at

PONTCHARRAUD, a little village, six leagues. This road is studded with wretched hostelries as far as Limoges; they do not lack passable wines, however. No one passes but muleteers and messengers bound for Lyons.

My head was not in good shape; and if storms and cold winds and rain are bad for it, I gave it its fill of them on these roads, where they say the winter is more severe than anywhere else in France.

On Wednesday, November 22nd, in very bad weather, I left here, and having passed through Felletin, a little town that seems to be well built, situated in a valley bottom all surrounded by high slopes, and which was still half deserted because of the recent plague, I came to sleep at

CHATAIN, five leagues, a wretched little village. Here I drank some new and unpurified wine, for lack of old wine. On Thursday

the 23rd, with my head still in the same condition, in rough weather, I came to sleep at

SAUVIAT, five leagues, a little village that belongs to Monsieur de Lauzun. From here I came the next day to sleep at

LIMOGES, six leagues, where I stayed all day Saturday, and bought a mule for ninety sun-crowns, and paid five crowns for a mule-load from Lyons to here, having been cheated in this of four livres; for all the other loads cost only three and two-thirds crowns. From Limoges to Bordeaux we paid one crown per hundredweight.

On Sunday, November 26th, I left Limoges after dinner and came to sleep at

LES CARS, five leagues, where there was no one but Madame des Cars. On Monday I came to sleep at

THIVIERS, six leagues. Tuesday to sleep at

PÉRIGUEUX, five leagues. Wednesday to sleep at

MAURIAC, five leagues. On Thursday, Saint Andrew's Day, the last of November, to sleep at

MONTAIGNE, seven leagues, which I had left on June 22nd, 1580, to go to La Fère. Thus my travels had lasted seventeen months and eight days.[11]

11 On his copy of Beuther's *Ephemeris historica*, under the date November 30, Montaigne wrote this note: "1581, I arrived in my house, back from a trip I had made in Germany and Italy from June 22, 1579 [read 1580] until the said day; on which day the year before I had arrived in Rome."

LETTERS

Note on the Letters

Not many of Montaigne's letters have been found. The best French edition includes thirty-nine that are well authenticated. Of these, seven are dedicatory letters and one a preface (mostly introducing posthumous works of La Boétie published by Montaigne in 1570), one is an inscription to a friend on a copy of the *Essays*, two are joint letters of remonstrance from the mayor and jurats of Bordeaux; the other twenty-eight are regular letters. Nearly all the regular letters were written in the last ten years of Montaigne's life. Most of them concern public affairs and date from Montaigne's mayoralty (1581–85); more than half of them are addressed to his able loyalist collaborator in keeping the peace, Marshal de Matignon, the king's lieutenant-general in Guienne. Two of the finest are to Henry IV.

Like most letters, these vary in their interest. Many are full of details of persons and places of minor import to any but the specialist. Yet even these, like most of the rest, clearly show Montaigne's vigilance as mayor and his activity as a public-spirited citizen. Trusted and consulted by important persons of both parties, he played a much larger and busier part in the affairs of his time than he ever revealed in the *Essays*.

Most of the regular letters were discovered around the middle of the nineteenth century, but the only complete edition is that of Arthur Armaingaud in 1939 (*Œuvres complètes*, XI, 159–266). Most of them have been put into English by W. C. Hazlitt, whose translation, though generally good, is often very erratic.

This is the first publication of all thirty-nine letters in English. They are annotated, and arranged in chronological order.

1. *To Antoine Duprat*

[August 24, 1562(?)]

To Messire Antoine Duprat,[1] Provost of Paris

In my last letter, sir, I told you about the troubles that ravaged Agenais and Périgord, where our mutual friend Memy,[2] taken prisoner, was brought to Bordeaux and had his head cut off. Today I want to tell you that the people of Nérac,[3] having, through the indiscretion of a young captain of their town, lost between a hundred and six-score men in a skirmish against some troops of Monluc,[4] withdrew into Béarn with their ministers, not without great danger to their lives, about the fifteenth day of July, at which time the people of Casteljaloux surrendered, and the minister of that place was put to death. The people of Marmande, Saint-Macaire, and Bazas[5] also fled, but not without cruel loss, for immediately the château of Duras was pillaged and that of Monségur was forced, a little stronghold where there were two ensigns and a great number of people of the religion.[6]

There every kind of cruelty and violence was practiced, on the first day of August, without regard for quality, sex, or age. Monluc violated the daughter of the minister, who was killed with the others. I have the extreme sorrow to tell you that involved in this

1 The authenticity of this letter has been questioned but seems very likely. Antoine Duprat, seigneur de Nantouillet et de Précy, baron de Thiers et de Thoucy, grandson of the chancellor of the same name, had become provost of Paris in 1553.

2 Captain Memy or Mesny was governor of Castillon and on the Protestant side.

3 Protestant town about seventy miles southeast of Bordeaux, seat of the court of Navarre.

4 Blaise de Monluc (c.1500–1577), author of the *Commentaires*, a great but cruel Catholic general, at this time lieutenant-general of the king in Guienne. Montaigne knew him fairly well, wrote of him in the *Essays* (II: 8, p. 348), and saw his grandson and namesake twice in Italy (*Travel Journal*, pp. 1129, 1162). At the time of this episode Monluc was about sixty.

5 Casteljaloux, Marmande, Saint-Macaire, and Bazas: Protestant towns located in the area between Nérac and Bordeaux. Duras and Monségur are in the same area.

6 The Protestants. Montaigne here, like most Catholics of his time, speaks of Protestantism simply as "the religion."

massacre was your relative, the wife[7] of Gaspard Duprat, and two of her children. She was a noble woman, whom I have been in a position to see often when I went into those parts, and at whose house I was always assured of finding good hospitality. In fine, I say no more to you about it today, for this account gives me pain and sorrow.

> Whereupon I pray God to have you in his holy care.
> August 24th.
> Your servant and good friend,

MONTAIGNE

2. *To His Father:* ON THE DEATH OF LA BOÉTIE

EXTRACT FROM A LETTER THAT MONSIEUR DE MONTAIGNE THE COUN-SELOR WROTE TO MONSEIGNEUR DE MONTAIGNE HIS FATHER CONCERNING CERTAIN DETAILS THAT HE NOTED IN THE ILLNESS AND DEATH OF THE LATE MONSIEUR DE LA BOÉTIE[8]

[1563(?)]

As for his last words, if any man is to give a good account of them, no doubt it is I: partly because all through his illness he was as glad to talk to me as to any other; and also because, owing to the unique and brotherly friendship that we had borne each other, I had a very certain knowledge of what he had intended, judged, and willed during his life, no doubt as great as one man can have of another. And because I knew this to be lofty, virtuous, full of very certain resolution, and in short admirable, I readily foresaw that if illness left him the power to express himself, nothing would escape him in such a necessity but what was great and full of good example. Thus I was as attentive as I could be.

It is true, sir, that since my memory is very short and was further disturbed by the confusion that my mind was to suffer from so heavy and important a loss, it is impossible that I have not forgotten many

7 Born Marguerite de Lupé, often known as Marguerite de Torrebreu.
8 This account was published by Montaigne at the end of the volume of La Boétie's *Œuvres* late in 1570. By this time Montaigne's father was dead. It seems very likely that this is substantially a letter written by Montaigne to his father soon after La Boétie died, in August 1563.

things that I would like to be known. But those I have remembered I shall report to you as truthfully as I can.

For to portray him thus proudly steadfast in his brave demeanor, to make you see that invincible courage in a body struck down and battered by the furious attacks of death and pain, would require, I confess, a far better style than mine. Because although whenever he spoke about weighty and important matters during his life, he spoke about them in such a way that it would have been hard to write them so well, yet at this point it seemed that his mind and tongue were vying in their effort, as if to do him their ultimate service. For without a doubt I never saw him so full of such beautiful ideas or of such eloquence as he was all through this illness. Moreover, sir, if you find that I have tried to place in account his slightest and most ordinary remarks, I have done so on purpose. For, being said at that time, and in the thick of so great a task, they are a remarkable testimony to a soul full of repose, tranquillity, and assurance.

As I was returning from the Parlement on Monday, August 9, 1563, I sent to invite him to dine at my house. He sent word back that he thanked me but that he was feeling a bit poorly, and that I would give him pleasure if I would come and spend an hour with him before he left for Médoc. I went to see him soon after dinner. He was lying down fully dressed, and already showed an indefinable change in his face. He told me that it was an attack of diarrhea with stomach pains, which he had contracted the day before in a game with Monsieur d'Escars when wearing his doublet under a silk gown, and that the cold often brought him such ailments.

I thought he was right to go ahead with the plan he had already made to go away, but that he should go no farther that evening than Germignan, which is only two leagues from town. I thought so because the place where he was staying had houses all around it infected with the plague, of which he was somewhat apprehensive, since he had recently returned from Périgord and Agenais, which had been all full of the plague when he left; and then, for an ailment like his, I had sometimes been much better off for a horseback ride. So he left, and with him his wife Madame de La Boétie and his uncle Monsieur de Bouilhonnas.

The next day, very early in the morning, one of his servants came to me on behalf of Madame de La Boétie, who informed me that he had felt very bad in the night from a violent dysentery. She was

sending for a doctor and an apothecary, and asked me to come, as I did after dinner.

On my arrival, he seemed delighted to see me; and as I wanted to take leave of him and go back, and promised to see him again the next day, he asked me, with more affection and insistence than ever about anything else, to be with him as much as I could. This touched me considerably. Nevertheless I was leaving when Madame de La Boétie, who already had a vague premonition of some mishap, asked me, with tears in her eyes, not to go that evening. So she stopped me, and he rejoiced with me over this. The next day I went home, and on Thursday I went to see him again. His trouble was getting worse: his flow of blood and his stomach pains, which weakened him even more, were increasing from hour to hour.

On Friday I again left him, and on Saturday went to see him again and found him already very worn down. He told me then that his illness was a bit contagious and moreover unpleasant and melancholic; that he knew my nature very well and asked me to be with him only for short periods but as often as I could. I did not leave him again.

Until Sunday he had not talked with me at all of what he thought about himself, and we talked only about particular occurrences in his illness and what the ancient doctors had said about them; about public affairs very little, for I found him completely disgusted with them from the first day.[9] But on Sunday he had a spell of great weakness; and when he had recovered consciousness, he said that he had seemed to be in some great confusion of all things and had seen nothing but a thick cloud and a dense fog in which everything was pell-mell and without order. However, he was not painfully affected by this accident. "Death has nothing worse about it than that, my brother," I said to him then. "Why," he replied to me, "it has nothing as bad about it."

From then on – because, from the beginning of his illness, he had had no sleep, and in spite of all the remedies he kept always getting worse, so that they had already tried certain potions on him which they use only in the last extremities – he began to lose all hope of cure, and told me so.

9 La Boétie died in the second year of the French religious civil wars. His "Memoir on the Edict of January 1562" shows his deep concern with the problem and his sense of the necessity of religious unity.

This same day, because it was judged suitable to do so, I said to him that because of the extreme friendship I bore him, it would be unbecoming to me if I did not take care that, as all his actions in health had been seen to be as full of wisdom and good counsel as those of anyone else in the world, he should continue them still in his sickness; and that if God willed that he get worse, I would be very sorry if for lack of advice he should leave any of his domestic affairs at loose ends, both because of the damage that his relatives might suffer from this and for the sake of his reputation. He accepted this from me very graciously, and after making up his mind about the difficulties that had kept him undecided in this matter, he asked me to call his uncle and his wife, and no others, to have them hear what he had planned about his will. I told him that he would alarm them. "No, no," he said to me, "I will console them, and give them much better hope for my health than I have myself."

And then he asked me whether the faint spells he had undergone had not alarmed us a little: "That is nothing, my brother," I said; "these are accidents common in such illnesses." "Indeed it is nothing, my brother," he replied, "even if what you feared the most were to happen." "It would be nothing but happiness for you," I answered, "but the loss would be mine, for I would lose the company of so great, so wise, and so sure a friend, such a friend that I would be certain never to find another like him."

"That might well be, my brother," he said; "and I assure you that what makes me take such care as I do for my cure, and not hurry so much to complete the passage that I have already half completed, is the consideration of your loss and of that of this poor man and this poor woman (speaking of his uncle and his wife), both of whom I love with all my heart, and who will find it very hard, I am certain, to bear the loss they will suffer in me, which in truth is very great both for you and for them. I am considering also the unhappiness that will be felt by many good people who have loved and esteemed me during my life, whose society indeed, I confess, if I had my choice, I would still be happy not to lose. And if I am going away, my brother, I beg you, who know them, to bear witness to them of the good will I have borne them even to this last limit of my life. And then, my brother, perhaps I was not born so useless as not to have the means of doing some service to the commonwealth. But however that may be, I am ready to leave when it shall please God, being fully assured that I shall enjoy the bliss that you predict for me.

And as for you, my friend, I know you to be so wise that whatever your loss, you will still adapt yourself willingly and patiently to whatever His Holy Majesty shall be pleased to decree about me; and I beg you to see to it that grief over losing me does not drive this good man and that good woman beyond the bounds of reason."

Then he asked me how they were behaving now. Well enough, I told him, in view of the importance of the matter. "Yes," he went on, "now, when they still have a little hope. But if once I have taken it all away from them, my brother, you will have a very hard time restraining them." For this reason, as long as he lived thereafter, he always concealed from them his opinion that his death was certain, and entreated me very urgently to do the same. Whenever he saw them around him, he put on the most cheerful manner and fed them with fine hopes.

At this point I left him to go and call them. They composed their faces as well as they could for a time. And when we had all sat down around the bed and the four of us were alone, he spoke thus, his face calm and as if delighted:

"My uncle, my wife, I assure you on my word that no new stroke of my illness or bad opinion I have of my cure has put it into my head to have you called in order to tell you what I plan. For, thank God, I feel very well and am full of good hope. But having learned long ago, both by long experience and by long study, what little security there is in the instability and inconstancy of human affairs and especially in our life, which we hold so dear, and yet which is but smoke and a mere nothing; and considering also that since I am sick I have come that much closer to the danger of death, I have decided to put some order into my domestic affairs, after first getting your opinion about them."

And then, addressing his remarks to his uncle, he said: "My good uncle, if at this time I had to give you an account of the great obligations I have to you, I would not have done for some time. It is enough for me that to this day, wherever I have been and no matter to whom I have spoken about it, I have always said that everything a very wise, very good, and very liberal father could have done for his son, you have done all that for me, both in the care that was needed to instruct me in humane letters, and when you were pleased to push me into public employment; so that the whole course of my life has been full of great and commendable friendly services from you. In short, whatever I have, I hold from you, I so acknowledge it, I am indebted to you for it; you are my true father.

Thus, as the son of the family, I have no right to dispose of anything unless you are pleased to give me leave to do so."

Then he was silent, and waited until sighs and sobs gave his uncle a chance to answer him that he would always regard as very good whatever his nephew pleased. Then, in order to make his uncle his heir, he begged him to take from him the property that belonged to him.

And then, turning his words to his wife, he said: "My likeness (so he often called her because of some ancient affinity between them), having been joined to you by the holy bond of marriage, which is one of the most respectable and inviolable that God has ordained for us here below for the maintenance of human society, I have loved, cherished, and esteemed you as much as I possibly could, and I am quite certain that you have rendered me reciprocal affection, which I cannot sufficiently acknowledge. I beg you to take what I give you of my goods and be content with it, even though I well know that it is little in comparison with your merits."

And then, turning his words to me, he said: "My brother, whom I love so dearly and whom I chose out of so many men in order to renew with you that virtuous and sincere friendship, the practice of which has for so long been driven from among us by our vices that there remain of it only a few old traces in the memory of antiquity, I entreat you to accept as a legacy my library and my books, which I give you as a sign of my affection toward you: a very small present, but one which comes from a willing heart and which is appropriate for you because of your fondness for letters. It will be μνημόσυνον *tui sodalis*."[10]

And then, speaking to all three of us in general, he praised God that in such extreme need he found himself in the company of all the dearest persons he had in this world, and said that it seemed to him very beautiful to see a gathering of four persons so in accord and so united by friendship, for he was assured that we loved one another unanimously for each other's sake. And having recommended us to one another, he went on thus: "Having set my estate in order, now I must think of my conscience. I am a Christian, I am a Catholic; as such have I lived, as such do I intend to end my life. Let a priest be sent for, for I will not fail in this last duty of a Christian."

At this point he finished his speech, which he had carried through with such assurance on his face and such strength in word

10 "A remembrance of your friend" (adapted from Catullus).

and voice, that whereas I had found him, when I came into his room, weak, dragging out his words slowly one after the other, his pulse very low as with a slow fever, and drawing toward death, his face pale and all subdued, it now seemed that, as if by a miracle, he had just gained some new vigor: his color ruddier, his pulse stronger, so that I had him feel mine to compare them. At that moment my heart was so sad that I could not answer him.

But two or three hours later, both to keep up his great courage, and because I wished, in the zeal I have had all my life for his glory and honor, that there should be more people in his room to witness so many fine proofs of greatness of soul, I told him that I had blushed for shame that my courage had failed on hearing what he, who was suffering this illness, had had the courage to tell me. That up to then I had thought that God gave us no such great power against human calamities, and I had had difficulty believing what I had come across on this subject in the histories; but that having felt such a proof of it, I praised God that this had been in a person by whom I was so loved and whom I loved so dearly; and that this would serve me as an example, to play this same part in my turn.

He interrupted me to beg me to use it in this way, and to show in action that the talks we had had together during our health had been not merely borne in our mouths but deeply engraved on heart and in soul, in such a way as to be put into execution on the first occasions that offered; adding that this was the true object of our studies, and of philosophy. And, taking me by the hand, he said: "My brother, my friend, I assure you that I have done many things in my life, it seems to me, with as much pain and difficulty as I do this. And when all is said, I had been prepared for it for a very long time and had known my lesson all by heart. But have I not lived enough up to my present age? I was soon to be thirty-three. God granted me this grace, that all my life up to now has been full of health and happiness. In view of the inconstancy of things human, that could hardly last any longer. Henceforth it would have been time to get down to business and to see a thousand unpleasant things, like the disadvantages of old age, of which by this means I am quit. And then it is likely that up to this time I have lived with more simplicity and less malice than I would perhaps have done if God had let me live until the concern with getting rich and improving my affairs came into my head. As for me, I am certain that I am going away to find God and the abode of the blessed." And because I showed, especially in my face, that I could hardly bear to hear him, he said to me: "What,

my brother, do you want to put fear into me? If I felt fear, who but you should take it away from me?"

In the evening, when the notary arrived who had been sent for to receive his will, I had him put it in writing, and then asked Monsieur de La Boétie whether he did not want to sign it. "Not sign it," said he, "I want to make it myself. But, my brother, I would like to be given a little leisure, for I find myself extremely weary and so weak that I can hardly do a thing more." I started to change the subject, but he recovered himself suddenly and said to me that it did not take much leisure to die, and asked me to find out whether the notary had a good swift hand, for he would not make many stops in dictating. I called the notary, and on the spot he dictated his will so fast that it was very hard for the man to follow him. And when he had finished he asked me to read it to him, and, speaking to me, he said: "That's a fine thing we care for, our riches! *Sunt haec quae hominibus vocantur bona.*"[11] After the will had been signed, since his room was full of people, he asked me if it would do him any harm to talk. I told him no, but that he should speak very softly.

Then he sent for Mademoiselle de Saint-Quentin, his niece, and spoke to her thus: "My niece, my dear, since I have known you[12] I have always thought I could see shining in you some traits of a very fine nature; but these last services that you perform with such kind affection and such diligence in my present hour of need show me great promise in you; and truly I am obliged to you for this and thank you for it most affectionately. For the rest, for the discharge of my conscience, I admonish you to be first of all devout toward God. For without a doubt that is the main part of our duty, without which no other action can be either good or fine; and if that part is really sincere, it draws after it necessarily all other virtuous actions. After God, you must love and honor your father and mother, especially your mother, my sister, whom I esteem one of the best and most sensible women in the world; and I beg you to take from her the example of your life. Do not let yourself be carried away by pleasures. Flee like the plague those mad intimacies in which you sometimes see women indulge with men. For even though at the beginning these may have nothing bad about them, yet little by little

11 "Those are the things that by men are called good" (author unknown).
12 La Boétie addresses his niece, a young girl, as *tu*. He uses *vous* to all the others, and they to him.

they corrupt the mind and lead it to idleness, and beyond, into the ugly mire of vice. Believe me, the surest guardian of a girl's chastity is austerity. I pray you and want you to remember me because you often had before your eyes the affection I have borne you, but not to complain and grieve over my loss; and this I forbid to all my friends as much as I can, since it would seem that they were envious of the good which, thanks to my death, I shall soon find myself enjoying. And I assure you, my dear girl, that if at this moment God gave me a choice either to return and live on or to finish the journey I have begun, I would have a very hard time choosing. Farewell, my dear niece."

After that he sent for Mademoiselle d'Arsac, his stepdaughter, and said to her: "My daughter, you have no great need of my advice, having such a mother, whom I have found so wise and so well suited to my nature and my wishes, and who has never failed me in anything. You will be very well instructed by such a schoolmistress. And do not think it strange if I, who am not at all related to you by blood, care and am concerned about you. For since you are the daughter of a person who is so close to me, it is impossible that whatever concerns you should not concern me too. And therefore I have always shown fully as much concern for the affairs of Monsieur d'Arsac, your brother, as for my own. And perhaps it will not hurt your advancement that you have been my stepdaughter. You have wealth and beauty enough, you are a gentlewoman of good family. All you need is to add to these the riches of the mind, which I beg you to be willing to do. I do not forbid you the vice that is so detestable in women, for I refuse even to think that it can come into your mind – indeed I believe the very name of it is horrible to you. Farewell, my stepdaughter."

The whole room was full of wails and tears, which nevertheless did not interrupt the train of his speeches, which were a little long. But after all this he ordered everyone to leave except his "garrison," as he called the girls who served him. And then, calling my brother Beauregard,[13] he said to him: "Monsieur de Beauregard, I thank you very much for the trouble you are taking for me. Allow

13 Thomas de Montaigne, seigneur de Beauregard, second in age in his generation to Michel, born on May 17, 1534. Soon after the death of La Boétie he was married, for the second time, to La Boétie's stepdaughter, Jacquette d'Arsac, whom we have just met. He thus became lord of Arsac, Lilhan, Loirac, and Castera.

me to reveal something I have in my heart to tell you." When my brother had encouraged him, he went on thus: "I swear to you that of all those who have set about the reformation of the Church, I have never thought there was a single one who went about it with better zeal and more complete, sincere, and simple affection than you. And I certainly believe that it was only the vices of our prelates, which without a doubt need great correction, and certain imperfections that the course of time has brought into our Church, that incited you to this. I do not want to dissuade you from it now; for I do not readily ask anyone to do anything whatever against his conscience. But I do want to advise you, out of respect for the good reputation that the family you belong to has acquired by continual concord – a family that is as dear to me as any family in the world: Lord, what a family! from which there never has come any act other than that of a worthy man – out of respect for the will of your father, that good father to whom you owe so much, the will of your good uncle, and your brothers, to avoid these extremes. Do not be so sharp and so violent; accommodate yourself to them. Do not form a band and body apart; unite with them. You see how many ruins these dissensions have brought into this kingdom, and I warrant you they will bring much greater ones yet. And since you are wise and good, keep from bringing these disturbances into the midst of your family, for fear of making it lose the glory and the happiness that it has enjoyed until this hour. Take what I say to you about this in good part, Monsieur de Beauregard, and as a sure testimony of the friendship I bear you. For that is the reason I have held back until now from saying this to you. And perhaps because I say it to you in the state in which you see me, you will give more authority and weight to my words." My brother thanked him very heartily.

On Monday morning he was so ill that he had lost all hope of life, so that as soon as he saw me, he called me very piteously and said to me: "My brother, have you no compassion for all the torments I suffer? Don't you see that from now on all the help you give me serves only to prolong my pain?" Soon after this he fainted, so that they nearly gave him up for lost. Finally they revived him with vinegar and wine. But he could not see for a long time after, and, hearing us lament around him, he said to us: "My Lord, who is tormenting me so? Why do they take me out of that great pleasant rest that I am in? Leave me alone, I beg you." And then, hearing my voice, he said to me: "So you too, my brother, do not want me to be cured. Oh, what bliss you are making me lose!" Finally, having

recovered still further, he asked for a little wine. And then, feeling better for it, he said to me that it was the best drink in the world. "Surely no," said I to get him talking, "water is that." "You're quite right," he replied, "ὕδωρ ἄριστον."[14] All his extremities, even his face, were already icy with cold, with a death sweat that ran down all along his body; and hardly any sign of a pulse could be detected any longer.

That morning he made confession to his priest; but the priest, because he had not brought everything he needed, could not say Mass to him. But on Tuesday morning Monsieur de La Boétie asked for him, to help him, he said, to perform his last duty as a Christian. Thus he heard Mass and received the Sacrament. And as the priest was taking leave of him, he said to him: "My spiritual father, I humbly entreat you all, both you and those who are under your charge, pray God for me – if it is ordered by the most sacred rolls of God's plans that I am now to end my days – that he have pity on my soul, and forgive me my sins, which are infinite, since it is not possible that so vile and base a creature as I can have carried out the commands of so lofty and powerful a master. Or, if it seems to him that there is still need of me here below, and he wants to reserve me for some other time, beg him to put a quick end to the anguish I suffer, and to grant me the grace to guide my steps henceforth according to his will, and to make me better than I have been."

At this point he stopped a bit to catch his breath; and seeing that the priest was going away, he called him back and said to him: "I want to say this also in your presence: I protest that as I have been baptized, as I have lived, so I want to die in the faith and religion which Moses first planted in Egypt, which the patriarchs then received in Judea, and which, from hand to hand, in the progress of time, has been brought into France." To look at him, it seemed that he would have talked even longer if he could have; but he stopped, begging his uncle and me to pray God for him. "For these," he said, "are the best services that Christians can do for one another." In speaking, he had uncovered one shoulder, and he asked his uncle to cover it up again, although he had a servant nearer to him. And then, looking at me, he said: "*Ingenui est cui multum debeas, ei plurimum velle debere.*"[15]

14 "Water is the best" (Pindar).
15 "It is the part of a noble mind to want to owe more to the man to whom we owe much" (Cicero).

Monsieur de Belot[16] came to see him after noon. Giving him his hand, he said to him: "My good friend, I was here on the point of paying my debt, but I have found a good creditor who has remitted it for me." A little later, as he woke with a start: "All right! All right! Let it come when it will, I'm waiting for it, strong and firm of foot" – words that he repeated two or three times during his illness. And then, as they were forcibly opening his mouth to make him swallow, he said, turning to Monsieur de Belot: "*An vivere tanti est?*"[17]

In the evening he began really to look like death; and as I was supping he had me called, having nothing left but the likeness and shadow of a man, and, as he said about himself, *non homo, sed species hominis*.[18] And he said to me, with great difficulty: "My brother, my friend, please God I may see in reality what I have just seen in imagination!"

After waiting for a time while he no longer spoke but uttered piercing sighs in trying to speak (for from then on his tongue was beginning stubbornly to refuse to do its work), I said: "What are these visions, my brother?" "Great, great," he replied. "It never happened," I went on, "that I did not have the honor of sharing in all the ideas that came into your mind. Don't you want me to enjoy this honor still?" "Certainly I do," he replied, "but, my brother, I cannot express them: they are marvelous, infinite, and ineffable." We left it at that, for he could go no further. Thus a little earlier he had wanted to speak to his wife, and had told her, with the gayest face that he could put on, that he had a story to tell her. And he seemed to try to speak, but, his strength failing him, he asked for a little wine to restore it. It was to no avail, for he suddenly fainted, and for a long time could not see.

Being already very close to his death, and hearing the lamentations of Madame de La Boétie, he called her and spoke to her thus: "My likeness, you are tormenting yourself before it is time; won't you have pity on me? Take courage. Surely more than half

16 Jean de Belot, also a counselor in the Parlement of Bordeaux and a mutual friend. La Boétie had addressed one Latin satire to him and Montaigne (as against two to Montaigne alone) expressing the wish to flee the evil Old World for the New. In December 1567, Montaigne wrote him a letter to warn the Parlement of Protestant movements near Montaigne.

17 "Is it so great a thing to be alive?" The source of this quotation has not been found. Montaigne later quotes it in the *Essays* (III: 13, p. 1014).

18 "Not a man, but the semblance of a man" (author unknown).

the pain I bear is for the evil I see you suffer, not for my own; and with reason; for it is not properly we ourselves who feel the ills that we feel within us, but certain senses that God has placed in us; whereas what we feel for others we feel by certain judgment and the faculty of reason. But I am going off." This he said because his heart was failing him. Then, fearing that he had alarmed his wife, he recovered himself and said: "I am going off to sleep. Good night, my wife, go now." That was the last leave he took of her.

After she had gone, he said to me: "My brother, stay close to me, please." And then, feeling either the pangs of death sharper and more pressing, or the force of some hot medicine that they had made him swallow, he spoke in a louder and stronger voice, and tossed in his bed with the greatest violence; so that all the company began to have some hope, for until then it was weakness alone that had made us fear to lose him. Then, among other things, he began to entreat me again and again with extreme affection to give him a place; so that I was afraid that his judgment was shaken. Even when I had remonstrated with him very gently that he was letting the illness carry him away and that these were not the words of a man in his sound mind, he did not give in at first and repeated even more strongly: "My brother, my brother, do *you* refuse me a place?" This until he forced me to convince him by reason and tell him that since he was breathing and speaking and had a body, consequently he had his place. "True, true," he answered me then, "I have one, but it is not the one I need; and then when all is said, I have no being left." "God will give you a better one very soon," said I. "Would that I were there already," he replied. "For three days now I have been straining to leave."

In this distress he often called me simply to know whether I was near him. Finally he began to rest a little, which confirmed us still more in our good hope; so that on leaving his room, I rejoiced at this with Madame de La Boétie. But an hour later, or thereabouts, speaking my name once or twice and then heaving a great sigh to himself, he gave up the ghost, at about three o'clock on the Wednesday morning, August 18th, 1563, after living 32 years, 9 months, and 17 days . . .

3. *To His Father:* DEDICATION OF
MONTAIGNE'S TRANSLATION OF SEBOND

[June 18, 1568]

To Monseigneur de Montaigne[19]

Sir, in carrying out the task you set me last year at your home at Montaigne, I have cut out and trimmed with my own hand for Raymond Sebond, that great Spanish theologian and philosopher, a costume in the French style, and have stripped him, as well as I could, of that wild bearing and barbaric demeanor that you saw in him at first; so that in my opinion he has enough style and *savoir-faire* to present himself in any good company. It may well be that delicate and fastidious persons will note here some Gascon trait and habit; but it will be the more to their shame for having by their carelessness let a man get ahead of them in this who is a complete novice and apprentice at such a task.

Now, sir, it is right that he should come to the light of day, and progress in favor, under your name, since to you he owes all the improvement and correction he has here. However, I clearly see that if you are pleased to have a reckoning with him, it will be you that will owe him much in the end. For in exchange for his excellent and very religious arguments, his lofty and as it were divine conceptions, it will turn out that you for your part have brought to him only words and language: a merchandise so vulgar and so vile that the more of it a man has, the less, peradventure, he is worth.

Sir, I pray God to give you a very long and very happy life.
Your very humble and very obedient son.
From Paris, June 18th, 1568.

MICHEL DE MONTAIGNE

19 Montaigne had translated Sebond's *Liber Creaturarum, sive Theologia Naturalis*, as *Théologie naturelle*, at his father's request. In the early pages of his "Apology for Raymond Sebond" (*Essays* II: 12, pp. 387–9) he speaks in a very deprecatory way of the work and suggests that he did the thousand-page translation in a few days. The letter above is dated from Paris on the very day his father died.

4. *To Henri de Mesmes:* DEDICATORY
EPISTLE TO LA BOÉTIE'S TRANSLATION
OF PLUTARCH'S "RULES OF MARRIAGE"

[April 30, 1570]

To Monsieur de Mesmes, Lord of Roissi and Malassise, Councillor to the King in his Privy Council[20]

Sir, one of the most notable follies that men commit is to employ the strength of their understanding to smash and ruin common and accepted opinions which bring us satisfaction and contentment. For whereas everything under heaven employs the means and instruments that nature has placed in its hands for their proper use, the profit and advantage of its own being, these people – in order to seem to have a livelier and more alert mind, one that receives and lodges in it nothing that is not tested and weighed a thousand times by the subtlest powers of reason – stir up their soul out of a peaceful and restful posture in order in the end to fill it, after a long quest, with doubt, uneasiness, and feverishness. It is not without reason that childlikeness and simplicity have been so recommended by truth itself.[21] For my part I prefer to be more at ease and less able, more happy and less understanding.

That is why, sir, although the clever ones make fun of our concern for what will happen here after us, since our soul will be lodged elsewhere and no longer affected by things here below, yet I think it is a great consolation to the frailty and brevity of this life to believe that it can be strengthened and prolonged by reputation and renown, and I very willingly embrace an opinion so pleasant and favorable, which is inborn in us, without anxiously inquiring how or why this can be.

So that, having loved above all else the late Monsieur de La Boétie, the greatest man of our time, in my opinion, I would think I was grossly failing in my duty if I wittingly let a name as rich as his and a memory so worthy of commendation vanish and be lost, and if I did not try, by those same parts of him, to revive him and

20 Henri de Mesmes (1532–96), seigneur de Roissi et de Malassise, chancellor of the kingdom of Navarre, eminent jurist, public servant, and patron of letters.
21 That is, by the Bible. Montaigne's anti-Protestant argument here anticipates those in the "Apology for Raymond Sebond" (*Essays* II: 12).

bring him back to life. I do believe that he has some sense of this and that these services of mine affect him and give him joy. In truth, he is still lodged in me so entire and so alive that I cannot believe he is either so irrevocably buried or so totally removed from our communication.

Now, sir, because each new revelation I give of him and of his name is just that much of a multiplication of this second life of his, and, moreover, because his name is ennobled and honored by the place that receives it, it is up to me not only to spread it as much as I possibly can, but also to entrust it to the keeping of honorable and virtuous persons. Among these persons you hold such a rank that in order to give you an occasion to take in this new guest and give him a warm welcome, I have decided to present you with this little work, not for any service that you might derive from it, for I know well that you have no need of an interpreter in order to frequent Plutarch and his companions; but it is possible that Madame de Roissi,[22] seeing the order of her household and of your fine concord represented here to the life, will be very pleased to learn that the goodness of her natural inclination has not only attained but surpassed all that the wisest philosophers have been able to conceive about the duty and laws of marriage. And, at all events, it will always be an honor to me to be able to do anything that proves a pleasure to you or yours, because of the obligation I have to render you service.

> Sir, I pray God to give you a long and very happy life.
> From Montaigne, April 30th, 1570.
> Your humble servant,

MICHEL DE MONTAIGNE

22 Jeanne Hennequin, third cousin of her husband, married to him since 1552.

5. *To Michel de L'Hôpital:* DEDICATORY
EPISTLE TO LA BOÉTIE'S LATIN "POEMS"

[April 30, 1570]

To Monseigneur de L'Hôpital, Chancellor of France[23]

Sir, it is my opinion that you men into whose hands both fortune and reason have placed the government of the world's affairs seek nothing more assiduously than a way to attain a knowledge of the men in the public offices under you. For there is hardly any community so sickly as not to have plenty of men in it to supply each of its offices adequately, provided that the selection and apportionment could be justly made. And if that point were gained, nothing further would have to be done to attain the perfect composition of a state.

Now, the more desirable this is, the more difficult it is also, since your eyes can neither reach so far as to pick and choose among a multitude so great and so spread out, nor penetrate to the depths of men's hearts to see their intentions and their conscience, the main parts to be considered; so that there has never been a commonwealth so well established that we did not often observe in it a weakness in this choice and this apportionment. And in those in which ignorance and malice, disguise, favors, intrigues, and violence are in command, if some selection is made according to order and merit, we doubtless owe this to fortune, which, by the inconstancy of its varied movement, has for once found itself in the path of reason.[24]

Sir, this consideration has often consoled me, for I know that Monsieur Etienne de La Boétie, one of the men most fit and needed for the highest offices in France, lived all his life, stagnating and underrated, by the ashes of his hearth at home, to the great detriment of our commonwealth; for as regards himself, I tell you, sir, that he was so abundantly furnished with the goods and treasures which defy fortune that never did a man live more satisfied or more content. To be sure, I know that he rose to those local dignities that are considered great; and I also know that never did a man bring to them more ability, and that at the age of thirty-two, when he died, he had acquired more true reputation on that level than any man

23 Michel de L'Hôpital (1503–73), a great moderate statesman, chancellor of France since 1560, had resigned in 1568 in protest at the prevalence of violence and corruption. He was a fine Latin poet and patron of poetry.
24 This last clause is virtually the title of one of the *Essays* (I: 34).

before him. But the fact remains that it is unreasonable to leave a worthy captain in the status of common soldier, and to employ in modest positions those who would also do well in the highest. In truth, his powers were put to poor and insufficient use; so that, beyond the needs of his office, he had many great talents left over, idle and useless, from which the commonwealth could have derived service, and he himself glory.

Now, sir, since he was so careless about pushing himself into the public eye (for unfortunately virtue and ambition rarely dwell together), and since he belonged to an age so thick-witted or so full of envy that he could not be aided at all by the testimony of others, I am prodigiously eager that at least his memory after him, to which alone from now on I owe the good offices of our friendship, should receive the reward of his merit and be well lodged in the good opinion of honorable and virtuous persons.

For this reason I have wanted to place him in the public eye and to present him to you, sir, by these few Latin verses that he left us; in the opposite way from the mason, who places the handsomest part of his building toward the street, and the merchant, who makes a show and display of the richest sample of his wares. What was most commendable in him, the true juice and marrow of his worth, has followed him, and all we have left is the bark and the leaves. The man who could bring out the disciplined movements of his soul, his piety, his virtue, his justice, the liveliness of his mind, the weight and soundness of his judgment, the loftiness of his conceptions, so far elevated above those of the vulgar, his learning, the graces that were ordinary companions of his actions, the tender love he bore to his wretched country, and his mortal and sworn hatred of every vice, but especially of that ugly traffic that is hatched under the honorable name of justice – that man would certainly engender in all good men a singular affection for him, mingled with a prodigious regret for his loss. But, sir, this is far beyond my powers, and moreover he never thought of leaving any evidence to posterity even of the fruit of his studies; and all we have left is what he wrote upon occasion by way of pastime.

Be that as it may, I beg you, sir, to give him a friendly reception, and – as our judgment often infers something very great from something trivial, and as the very sports of great personages reveal to the clear-sighted some honorable mark of the rank from which they come – to rise through this work of his to the knowledge of him, and consequently to love and embrace his name and his

memory. In so doing, sir, you will only be making return in kind for the very decided opinion he had of your virtue, and thus you will be accomplishing what he infinitely desired during his life. For there was not a man in the world in whose acquaintance and friendship he would rather have been lodged than in yours.

But if anyone is scandalized at my making such bold use of another's property, I tell him that no spoken or written statement in the schools of philosophy ever represented the rights and duties of sacred friendship as exactly as did the practice that my friend and I formed together.

For the rest, sir, this slight present, to kill two birds with one stone, will also serve, if you please, as testimony of the honor and reverence that I have for your ability and for the unique qualities that are within you. As for those that are external and fortuitous, it is not my way to place them in account.

> Sir, I pray God to give you a long and very happy life.
> From Montaigne, April 30th, 1570.
> Your humble and obedient servant,
>
> MICHEL DE MONTAIGNE

6. *Notice to the Reader of La Boétie's Translations*

[August 10, 1570]

NOTICE TO THE READER[25]

Reader, you owe to me all that you enjoy of the late Monsieur Etienne de La Boétie; for I tell you that for his own part, there is nothing here that he would ever have hoped to show you, or indeed that he considered worthy of bearing his name in public. But I, who am not so high-handed, finding nothing else in his library, which he left me in his will, still did not want this to be lost. And from what little judgment I have, I am hopeful that you will find that the very ablest men of our time very often make much ado about slighter things than this. I understand from those who knew him younger than I did, for our acquaintance began only about six years[26] before

25 Because the undated letter to Lansac (No. 7) preceded this in the volume in which they were published, Armaingaud infers that it was composed later.
26 In his chapter "Of Friendship" (I: 28, p. 174) Montaigne speaks of the friendship as lasting four years; he had earlier written "four or five years."

his death, that he had written many other Latin and French verses, as for example under the name of Gironde, and I have heard him recite some rich bits of these. Indeed, the man who wrote "The Antiquities of Bourges"[27] quotes some which I recognize. But I do not know what has happened to them all, or to his Greek poems. And in truth, as each sally came into his head, he discharged it on the first piece of paper that came to hand, with no further care for preserving it.

Be assured that I have done what I could, and that in the seven years since we lost him I have been able to recover only what you see here, except for a "Discourse on Voluntary Servitude" and some Memoirs concerning our troubles over the Edict of January 1562.[28] But as for these last two pieces, I find their fashion too delicate and elegant to abandon them to the gross and heavy air of so unpleasant a season. Farewell.

From Paris, August 10th, 1570.

7. *To Louis de Lansac:* DEDICATORY EPISTLE TO LA BOÉTIE'S TRANSLATION OF XENOPHON'S "OECONOMICUS"

[1570(?)]

To Monsieur de Lansac, Knight of the Order of the King, Councillor in his Privy Council, Superintendent of his Finances, and Captain of a hundred gentlemen of his household[29]

Sir, I send you the "Oeconomicus"[30] of Xenophon, put into French by the late Monsieur de La Boétie: a present that has seemed

27 Jean Chaumeau, who quotes some of La Boétie's verses in his "History of Berry" (Lyons, 1566).
28 Montaigne had intended to publish the "Discourse on Voluntary Servitude" in his chapter "Of Friendship," but changed his mind presumably when it appeared in a Protestant publication. See *Essays* I: 28, p. 175 and note 2.
The "Memoir on the Edict of January 1562" was a judicious but firm criticism of the government's policy of tolerance and compromise, which Montaigne presumably did not publish in order not to add fuel to the fires of civil hatred. It was published in book form by Paul Bonnefon in 1922.
29 Louis de Saint-Gelais, seigneur de Lansac or Lanssac (1512–89), eminent adviser and tutor to royalty, ambassador, and financial administrator. He had many dealings with the Parlement of Bordeaux while Montaigne was a member of that body. For his son Guy, see note 113 (Letter 29).
30 Treatise on household management.

to me well suited to you, both because it sprang originally, as you know, from the hand of a notable gentleman, a very great man in both war and peace, and because it received its second form from this person, whom I know you loved and esteemed while he lived. This will always serve you as a spur to continue your good opinion and good will toward his name and his memory. And to speak boldly, sir, do not be afraid to find your good feeling for him somewhat increased; for since your taste of him has been only from the public evidence he gave of himself, it is my duty to assure you that he had so many degrees of ability beyond this that you are very far from having known him whole and entire.

When he was alive, he did me the honor, which I count among my greatest good fortunes, of forming with me a bond of friendship so close and tight-knit that there was no slant, impulse, or motive in his soul that I was not able to consider and judge, at least unless my vision at times fell short. Now, without prevarication, taken all in all, he was so nearly a miracle that in order not to fly beyond the limits of plausibility and be completely disbelieved, I am obliged, in speaking of him, to restrain myself and say far less good than I know about him. And for the moment, sir, I will be content merely to entreat you, for the honor and reverence that you owe to the truth, to believe and bear witness that our Guienne has never come near seeing anything like him among the men of his robe.[31]

So, in the hope that you will render him this, which is very justly his due, and in order to bring him more freshly into your memory, I give you this book, which at the same time will also warrant you, for my part, that if my lack of ability did not expressly forbid me, I would be just as eager to present you with something of my own in recognition of my obligations to you and of the ancient favor and friendship that you have borne to the members of our family. But, sir, for lack of better coin, I offer you in payment a very steadfast will to do you humble service.

> Sir, I pray God to maintain you in his keeping.
> Your obedient servant,
>
> MICHEL DE MONTAIGNE

31 Men of the long robe, that is, of the legal profession.

8. *To Paul de Foix*: DEDICATORY EPISTLE
TO LA BOÉTIE'S "FRENCH VERSES"
[September 1, 1570]

To Monsieur de Foix, Councillor to the King in his Privy Council
and Ambassador from His Majesty to the Signory of Venice[32]

Sir, since I am in a position to recommend, to you and to
posterity, the memory of the late Etienne de La Boétie, both for
his extreme worth and for the singular affection that he bore me, it
has occurred to me that it shows a very consequential lack of
discrimination, deserving the constraint of our laws, to go about,
as is commonly done, robbing virtue of glory, its faithful compa-
nion, and making a present of glory, without discrimination or
judgment, to the first comer, according to our private interests;
seeing that the two principal reins that guide us and keep us to
our duty are punishment and reward, which concern us directly and
as men only by means of honor and shame, inasmuch as these go
directly to the soul and are sensed only by the inward feelings that
are most our own; whereas even the animals are seen to be somewhat
susceptible to all other, corporal kinds of reward and punishment.
Besides, it is well to see that the custom of praising even the virtue of
those who are no longer alive is not directed to them, but aims by
this means to spur the living to imitate them, just as the ultimate
punishments are employed by justice more for an example than for
the correction of those who suffer them. Now since praise and
dispraise correspond with each other and have consequences so
comparable in importance, it is hard to justify the fact that our
laws forbid us to damage the reputation of others and nevertheless
allow us to ennoble it undeservedly. This pernicious license thus to
toss to the winds as we wish the praises of one and all was once
restrained in various ways in other places. Indeed it may have helped
to put poetry in the bad graces of the sages. Be that as it may, at least
there is no hiding the fact that the vice of lying always appears most
unbecoming to a wellborn man, whatever face we put upon it.

32 Paul de Foix (1528–84), long a counselor at the Parlement of Paris, in disfavor
for a time under Henry II for his relative moderation, later an eminent public
servant, adviser to Charles IX and Henry III, archbishop of Toulouse. A serious
student of law and of letters, he was a good friend to Montaigne, who lamented
his death in the *Essays* (III: 9, p. 888).

As for this person I am speaking to you about, sir, he sends me far outside these conditions; for the danger is not that I may lend him some quality but that I may deprive him of some. And his bad luck will have it that whereas he has provided me, as well as a man can do, with very just and very manifest occasions for praise, I have just as little means and ability to render him his due – I indeed, to whom alone he communicated himself to the life, and who alone can vouch for a million graces, perfections, and virtues which molded idle in the midst of so fair a soul owing to the ingratitude of his fortune. For since the nature of things has allowed, I know not how, that however beautiful and acceptable truth may be of itself, yet we embrace it only if it is infused and insinuated into our belief by the instruments of persuasion, I find myself so very destitute both of the credit that might give authority to my simple testimony and of the eloquence to enrich it and set it off well, that I have come very close to giving up this whole effort, for I have not even anything of his left by which I can worthily present to the world so much as his mind and his learning.

In truth, sir, having been surprised by his destiny in the flower of his age and in a state of very happy and very vigorous health, he had never given less thought to anything than to publishing works that should testify to posterity what sort of a man he was in this respect. And perhaps he was strong enough, if he had thought about it, not to care very much about it. But finally I decided that it would be much more excusable for him to have buried with himself so many rare favors of heaven than it would be for me to bury also the knowledge he had given me of them. And therefore, having assiduously collected everything complete that I found among his notebooks and papers scattered here and there, the playthings of the wind and of his studies, I thought best, whatever it was, to distribute and divide it up into as many parts as I could, in order thereby to take the occasion to commend his memory to all the more people, choosing the most notable and worthy persons of my acquaintance, and those whose testimony might be the most honorable to him; like you, sir, who may have had some knowledge of your own of him during his life, but certainly too slight to reveal how great was his full worth. Posterity may believe me if it please, but I swear to it upon all the conscience I have that I knew and saw him to be such, all things considered, that even in desire and imagination I could hardly reach beyond, so far am I from assigning him many equals.

I very humbly entreat you, sir, to assume the general protection not only of his name but also of these ten or twelve French poems,

which cast themselves, as if out of necessity, under the shelter of your favor. For I will not conceal from you the fact that their publication was deferred after the rest of his works because up there[33] they did not consider them polished enough to be displayed to the public eye. You, sir, will see what the truth of the matter is. And because it seems that this judgment of theirs affects the interest of all this part of the country, from which they think nothing in the vernacular can come that does not have a wild and barbarous flavor, it is properly your responsibility – you who, to the eminence of a member of the first family of Guienne, which you received from your ancestors, have added on your own also the highest eminence in every sort of ability – to maintain, not only by your example but also by the authority of your testimony, that this is not always the case. And although doing is more natural to Gascons than saying, still they sometimes perform exploits with their tongue as much as with their arm, and with their mind as much as with their heart.

For my part, sir, it is not my quarry to judge of such things; but I have heard experts in learned matters say not only that these verses are worthy to appear on display, but that if you stop to consider the beauty and richness of the invention, they are in subject matter as meaty, full, and marrowy as any that have yet been seen in our language. Naturally each workman feels himself strongest in one certain part of his art, and the most fortunate are those who have seized upon the noblest part; for not all the pieces that are equally necessary to the construction of a building are therefore equally to be prized. Elegance of language, sweetness, and polish may perhaps shine more brightly in a few others; but in nobility of imagination, in the number of sallies, conceits, and nice touches, I do not think that any others surpass these. And moreover it should also be taken into account that this was neither his occupation nor his study, and that he hardly put his hand to his pen once a year, witness the little we have left from his whole life. For you see, sir, unseasoned and dry, all of his poetry that has come into my hands, without selection or choice, so that there is even some from his boyhood. In short, it seems as though he put his hand to it only to show that he was capable of doing anything. For as to the rest, thousands and thousands of times, even in his ordinary remarks, we have seen things come from him that were more worthy of being known, more worthy of being admired.

33 In Paris, where La Boétie's works were being published. Montaigne, after publishing the first lot, was writing this dedication from his château.

This, sir, is what reason and affection, joined together by a rare coincidence, command me to say to you about this great and good man; and if the liberty I have taken in addressing myself to you and talking to you so long about this offends you, please remember that the principal effect of greatness and eminence is to make you a target for the importunateness and involvement of other people's affairs.

Hereupon, after placing my very humble affection at your disposal, I pray God, sir, to give you a long and very happy life.

From Montaigne, September 1st, 1570.

Your obedient servant,

 MICHEL DE MONTAIGNE

9. *To His Wife:* DEDICATORY EPISTLE TO LA BOÉTIE'S TRANSLATION OF PLUTARCH'S "LETTER OF CONSOLATION TO HIS WIFE"

[September 10, 1570]

To Madame de Montaigne, my wife

My wife, you understand very well that it is not the act of a gallant man, according to the rules of the present day, still to pay court and show affection to you. For they say that an intelligent man may well take a wife, but that to espouse her is for a fool to do.

Let us let them talk. For my part I hold to the simple ways of the old days – as indeed my hair is beginning to show. And in truth innovation[34] has been costing this poor state so dear up to now (and yet I do not know if the bidding will not go still higher), that in every way and every place I give it up. You and me, my wife, let us live in the old French way.

Now you may remember how the late Monsieur de La Boétie, that dear brother and inviolable companion of mine, gave me as he was dying his papers and his books, which have since been the most treasured adornment of my library. I do not want stingily to enjoy them all alone, nor do I deserve that they should be useful only to me. For that reason I have wished to communicate them to my friends. And because I have, so I believe, none more intimate than you, I send you Plutarch's "Letter of Consolation to His Wife,"

34 Protestantism.

translated by my friend into French. Indeed I am sorry that fortune has made this present so appropriate for you, and that having no child but a long-awaited daughter after four years of marriage, you had to lose her in the second year of her life.[35]

But I leave to Plutarch the charge of consoling you and advising you of your duty in this, begging you to believe him for my sake. For he will reveal to you my views, and what can be said in this matter, much better than I could myself.

With this, my wife, I commend myself very strongly to your good graces, and pray God to maintain you in his keeping.

From Paris, September 10th, 1570.

Your good husband,

MICHEL DE MONTAIGNE

10. *To the Jurats of Bordeaux*

[May 21, 1582]

To Messieurs the Jurats of the City of Bordeaux

Gentlemen, I hope that Monsieur de Cursol's[36] trip will be of some help to the city at this time when it has in hand such a just and favorable cause. You have put all possible order into the affairs that came up. Things being in such a good state, I beg you to excuse for a little while longer my absence,[37] which I shall certainly cut short in so far as the pressure of my affairs may permit. I hope it will be brief. Meanwhile please keep me in your good graces and command me if the occasion arises for you to employ me in the public service. Your Monsieur de Cursol has also written me and notified me of his trip.

I commend myself to you very humbly, gentlemen, and pray God to give you a long and happy life.

From Montaigne, May 21st, 1582.

Your humble brother and servant,

MONTAIGNE

35 This letter is dated about two weeks after the death of their first child, Thoinette, at about two months of age. Montaigne's "second year" may well be a printer's error. They had been married about five years.

36 One of the jurats, who formed a council of six working closely with the mayor.

37 Montaigne was in his first term as mayor of Bordeaux.

11. *To Marshal de Matignon*

[October 30, 1582]

To Monseigneur de Matignon,[38] Marshal of France

Sir, since the letter I wrote you three or four days ago, in which I told you among other things that I had received no letter from you during my absence and no command to come here, nothing new has happened. I have just this moment seen the general of the Cordeliers, Gonzaga,[39] who arrived yesterday; and if his fever, for which he was bled and treated, does not prevent him, he will leave tomorrow, he told me, to continue on his way toward Spain. He had letters for you from the King, but I think they were only to recommend him. I offered him for his convenience such little power as I have in this town.

Since Monsieur de Gourgues[40] has notified me that he was writing you, I have written this note in order very humbly to kiss your hands, praying God, sir, to give you a long and happy life.

From Bordeaux, October 30th, 1582.

Your very humble servant,

MONTAIGNE

12. *To Antoine Duprat*

[November 22, 1582]

To Monseigneur de Nantouillet,[41] Councillor to the King

Sir, you wish to know from me how the King should maintain the three checks by which absolute power is controlled. Here is my feeling.

38 Jacques II de Goyon, comte de Matignon (1525–97), sire de Lesparre, prince de Mortagne, baron de Saint-Lô, marquis de Lonray, marshal of France, Montaigne's future successor as mayor of Bordeaux, at this time lieutenant-general in Guienne for Henry III. As this and the other fifteen letters to him show, Montaigne worked closely with him to defend the King's rights and keep the peace in the divided southwest of France.

39 Francisco Gonzaga, general of the Cordeliers (Friars Minor) from 1579 to 1587, later bishop of Cefalù (Sicily) and still later bishop of Mantua. He died in 1620.

40 Ogier de Gourgues, seigneur de Montlezun, vicomte de Juillac, baron de Vayres, treasurer-general of French finances in Guienne, who died in 1594. Montaigne speaks of him again in Letter 29.

41 The same Antoine Duprat, seigneur de Nantouillet, to whom Letter 1 was addressed.

First, concerning the three checks that I spoke to you about in my previous letter, by which the absolute power of the prince and monarch, which is called tyrannical when used contrary to reason, is curbed and civilized and thus reputed just, tolerable, and aristocratic: I say again that the King can do nothing more agreeable, more pleasant, and more profitable to his subjects, or more honorable and laudable for himself, than to maintain the said three things, by which he acquires the name of good king, very Christian, father of the people, and well loved, and all the other titles that a valiant and glorious prince can acquire. Such is my complaint and my opinion.

With this, sir, I pray God to give you health and a good and long life.

November 22nd, 1582.

Your servant,

 MONTAIGNE

13. *To King Henry III:* LETTER OF
REMONSTRANCE FROM THE MAYOR AND JURATS
OF BORDEAUX

 [August 31, 1583]

To the King

 Sire,

The mayor and jurats, governors of your city and town of Bordeaux, very humbly remonstrate to you that now and earlier, both for themselves and for the inhabitants of the seneschalsy of Guienne, who are all your very humble and natural subjects, they have voiced at great length to the lord commissioners, Your Majesty's deputies to the region and duchy of Guienne, their plaints and grievances concerning the burdens and surcharges that they have suffered and do suffer daily, about which they are confident that Your Majesty, using your royal and paternal kindness and inclination, will make provision so wisely and with such equity that the universal repose of this kingdom and relief of its inhabitants will ensue.

However, inasmuch as since the departure of the said lord commissioners, new circumstances and calamities have come upon the great mass of the people, and as experience, mistress of events, has made known more clearly how pernicious are innovations in

all states, may it please Your Majesty to take it in good part that the said mayor and jurats, in adding to their said first remonstrances and grievances, hereby present to you in all humility certain articles concerning the good of your service and the relief of your subjects, so that by the same means they may receive the benefit and alleviation that you may be pleased to impart to them out of your clemency and mercy, to which alone, after God, they have recourse.

And in the first place, although by the ordinances of Your Majesty, both ancient and modern, in conformity with reason, all impositions must be made equally upon all persons, the strong supporting the weak, and although it is most reasonable that those who have the greater means should feel the burden more than those who live only precariously and by the sweat of their body; yet it has happened, for some years back and especially this year, that as regards the taxes that have been imposed by your authority, besides the *taillon*[42] and property taxes and the wages of the presidial courts – those for the paying off of the export duties, for subvention, the repair of the Cordouan Tower,[43] the payment of the chamber of justice, the expenses of the army in Portugal, and the suppression of the elect,[44] as well as taxes remaining from previous years – the richest and most opulent families of the said city have been exempt from all these because of the privilege claimed by all the officers of justice and their widows, the officers of your finances and of elections, vice-seneschals, lieutenants, officers of the vice-seneschalsy, domestic officers of Your Majesty and of the king and queen of Navarre, officers of the chancellery, of the mint, and of the artillery, untaxable soldiers of the castles and provisioners of these; and besides these, by decree of your court of the Parlement solemnly pronounced on the sixth day of April of the current year, all the children of the presidents and counselors of the Parlement have been declared noble and not subject

42 A supplement to the taille, a personal tax.
43 A tower and lighthouse on the Garonne, built by the English in the fourteenth century and fallen into ruin. Henry III appointed the engineer Louis de Foix in 1581 to study the question of its repair, ordered money raised a year later, and on January 16, 1583, named Montaigne, the treasurer Ogier de Gourgues (see Letter 11), and François de Nesmond, president of the Parlement of Bordeaux, to constitute a commission for the repair of the tower.
44 Presumably ironic: keeping the Protestants in line.

to any tax; so that henceforth when it is appropriate to impose some sort of tax, it will have to be borne by the least and poorest group of the inhabitants of the cities, which is quite impossible, unless suitable remedies are provided against this by Your Majesty, as the said mayor and jurats very humbly request you to do.

May it please Your Majesty also to consider that although most of the sums destined for the repair of the Cordouan Tower have been raised and placed in the hands of your receiver-general, nevertheless there has not been a finger lifted for this repair nor provision made for preparing for it, as necessity required. And inasmuch as the money destined to this end might be employed elsewhere, to the great detriment of the public, may it please Your Majesty to ordain that restraining orders be given to the lord treasurers-general and aforementioned receivers to prevent their disposing of the said sums or using them elsewhere than for the purpose for which they are destined, to wit, for the said repair, whatever the other cause or occasion; and to order also that the ruling set forth by these letters-patent of Your Majesty about the distribution of the said moneys – to wit, that it shall be made by one of the lord presidents of the court of the Parlement, one of the said lord treasurers, and the mayor of the said city or in his absence one of the said jurats – be maintained and observed according to its form and tenor. And nevertheless, so that trade shall not be slowed up and your revenue diminished, may it please you to provide that the said repair shall be started according to the means that you have been pleased to establish.

By the privileges granted by the Very Christian Kings to the said city and confirmed not long ago by Your Majesty, the cognizance of, and provision for, the masterships of all artisans and the enforcement of the said statutes, which are registered in the said city, belongs to the said mayor and jurats, who have had this cognizance peacefully and without contradiction for all time, up to the present; and likewise, by the same instrument, that of the setting up of sworn keepers of taverns and public houses,[45] established as a corporation

45 There were 120 keepers of taverns and public houses, appointed to this minor municipal office by the mayor and jurats, in return for a sum of money. They were authorized to sell all the wine grown by the citizens of Bordeaux before any wine from anywhere else could be sold. Wine was the most important source of the city's revenue.

to sell wine in the said city, so that they form one of the main parts of the city's fiscal domain. Nevertheless, some people, desiring to reintroduce complete disorder and confusion among the artisans and make the city and its inhabitants lose their freedom to sell wine, which is their sole revenue, and without which they cannot bear the burdens ordained by Your Majesty, have managed to obtain edicts making the said masterships venal, and with them the freedom to sell wine, by establishing new groups of keepers of taverns and public houses; which is directly contrary to the tenor of the said privileges, confirmed not long ago by Your Majesty, and contrary to the express declaration of Your Majesty, granted in favor of the said mayor and jurats on behalf of the said tavern keepers, on December 21st, 1556, confirmed in your court of the Parlement. This would amount to the total ruin and overthrow of the said inhabitants, unless by your kindness provision is made, and unless the said edicts, obtained presumably by circumvention and heavy pressure, are revoked and nullified, as the said mayor and jurats and inhabitants very humbly request and entreat that they be.

As kings rule by justice and all states are maintained by it, so it is necessary that it be administered gratuitously and with as little burden on the people as possible. Your said Majesty, knowing this full well, and wishing to cut off the source of the main trouble, has by your very sacred edict forbidden all venality in judiciary offices. However, through the fault of the times, the multiplicity of offices has persisted, by which the poor people is very greatly burdened, especially in that for a year now the court clerks in the said city and seneschalsy have been established with a title of office and an increase in salary. And whereas at the beginning there seemed little likelihood of great harm to the public welfare, yet it has been learned since, and is seen every day, that this is one of the greatest burdens and surcharges on the poor people that it has suffered for some time. For what used to cost only one sou now costs two, and for one court clerk that you had to pay you have to pay three, to wit, the clerk, the assistant clerk, and the assistant clerk's clerk; with the result that the poor, not having the means to meet so many expenses, are most often constrained to abandon the pursuit of their rights; or, what should be used to support their families or to meet public necessities is by this means paid out to assuage the ambition of certain private persons, to the detriment of the public.

As for the disputes that have come up between the said mayor and jurats and the captains of the castles of this your city[46] over the matter of guards and watches and their usurpation of certain places belonging to the said city, Monsieur de Matignon, marshal of France, has sent Your Majesty the record of the whole investigation that has been made into this, by which the justice of the cause of the said mayor and jurats is clearly established. And because this affair is still undecided, and the delay is prejudicial to the good of your service and the rights that you have been pleased for all time to preserve in the said city, may it please Your said Majesty as soon as possible to give a ruling between the parties so that in the future each one shall freely perform what belongs to its charge and functions, and all things shall be restored to their first and former state, without damage to your sovereign authority or to the rights and prerogatives of your city.

And inasmuch as the misery of the time has been so great since the misfortune of the civil wars that many persons of both sexes and all ranks are reduced to begging, so that all you see in the towns and the fields is a frantic multitude of poor people – which would not happen if the edict made by the late King Charles, of happy memory, whom God absolve, were maintained: stating that each parish would be required to feed its poor, without their being allowed to roam elsewhere – for this reason, in order to remedy this disorder and the troubles that come of it daily, may it please Your Majesty to order that the said edict, which has been confirmed in your courts of Parlement, be strictly maintained and observed, with the injunction to all seneschals and local judges to lend a hand to its observation; and further, that the priors and administrators of hospitals (which are mostly of royal foundation) that are dedicated to the feeding of pilgrims going to Santiago de Compostela or other shrines, be constrained, on pain of seizure of their properties, to feed and shelter the said pilgrims for the time provided by the said foundation, so that the pilgrims shall not be constrained to go begging through the town, as is done every day, to the great scandal of everyone.

Your Majesty is very humbly entreated to receive in good part the

46 Merville, captain of the Château du Hâ in Bordeaux, was Montaigne's vehement and conniving but unsuccessful rival for the mayoralty in 1583. Vaillac (see note 116, Letter 30), a Leaguer, was in command of the other castle in the town, the Château Trompette.

aforesaid remonstrances which the said mayor and jurats, performing the duty of their charges and offices, present to you with all humility, being moved by no other zeal than that of the good of your service and the commiseration we must have for the poor populace, which, while awaiting relief from these burdensome woes – relief so much hoped for, and promised by Your Majesty – is perpetually in prayer for your prosperity and the increase of your state; and we are firmly resolved, the people and ourselves, to employ our goods and the little means we have left in your service and in keeping your city obedient to Your Majesty.

Done in Bordeaux, in council of the jurats, the last day of August, 1583.

MONTAIGNE, DALESME, GALOPIN, PIERRE RÉGNIER, DE LAPEYRE, CLAVEAU.

14. *To King Henry of Navarre:* LETTER OF REMONSTRANCE FROM THE MAYOR AND JURATS OF BORDEAUX[47]

[December 10, 1583]

This is what Messieurs de Montaigne, mayor, and de Lurbe,[48] attorney and syndic, of the city of Bordeaux are delegated and commissioned to say in remonstrance to the king of Navarre, lieutenant-general of the King in the region and duchy of Guienne, for the welfare of His Majesty's service and the relief of his subjects.

They will remonstrate to the said lord, king of Navarre, that provinces and cities cannot be maintained and preserved in good condition without freedom of commerce, which, by the free communication with each other, causes all things to abound in them; and by this means the plowman feeds and supports his family by the sale of his crops, the merchant traffics in wares, and the artisan finds a price for his work, all this to support public taxes. And since the principal commerce of the inhabitants of this city is carried on with the inhabitants of Toulouse and other towns situated on the Garonne, not only in the matter of wheat, wines, pastels, and fish, but also in wool; and since the said mayor and jurats have been informed

47 This letter explains the mission related in the following one (No. 15).
48 Gabriel de Lurbe (died 1613), a jurat, attorney and syndic of Bordeaux, author of the *Chronique bourdeloise* (1619).

by a general report that the people of the Mas-de-Verdun[49] are resolved, on the pretext of default in payments to the garrisons of the places of surety granted by the edict of pacification, to stop the boats loaded with merchandise going both up and down the said river Garonne, which would mean the total ruin of this region:[50]

The said lord, king of Navarre, shall be entreated not to allow the said boats and merchandise to be stopped either at the said Mas-de-Verdun or at other towns under his government, but to preserve and maintain freedom of commerce between all persons, in accordance with the edicts of the King.

Done in Bordeaux, in council of the jurats, the 10th of December, 1583.

MONTAIGNE, DALESME, GALOPIN, PIERRE RÉGNIER, DE LURBE, CLAVEAU, DE LAPEYRE.

15. *To Marshal de Matignon*

[December 14, 1583]

To Monseigneur de Matignon, Marshal of France, in Bordeaux

Sir, I arrived yesterday evening in this town with Monsieur de Clervant,[51] who turned up at Roquefort as I was dining, and we

49 See note 52 (Letter 15).

50 One copy or draft of this letter adds the following paragraphs at this point:

"Likewise, because the poor populace is so afflicted by the miseries of the past that it is virtually reduced to the depths of despair, and moreover because the six years' truce destined for the maintenance of the said towns of surety has expired, the said lord, king of Navarre, will be entreated to intervene with the King our sovereign lord so that henceforth the poor populace may be rid of the burden of paying the garrisons of the said towns of surety, which has been particularly oppressive to the inhabitants of the seneschalsy of Guienne who are of the third estate.

"Finally, and in consequence of the above, the said lord, king of Navarre, will be entreated to intervene with the King our lord so that the salaries of the lords of the Chamber of High Justice now at Périgueux may henceforth not be levied on the poor populace, which alone has borne this mass of surcharges for two years, which was the time set for the formation of the said Chamber; and it is not possible that the poor inhabitants of the said city can continue in the future to pay the said salaries, as they have done mainly so as not to interrupt the progress of the edict of pacification."

51 Claude-Antoine de Vienne, seigneur de Clervant, a counselor and

made the rest of the trip together. He had gone the wrong way, thinking to find the king of Navarre in Foix, and passed through Limoges and Périgueux.

Yesterday I did reverence to this prince. For the first attempt, we did not come away with much hope in the matter of your request. He wants to use all possible means to be paid.[52] We shall see tomorrow whether we can bring him down a bit.

Monsieur de Lavardin[53] leaves here today to go home; he told me that he would write you. Our ears are filled with Bazas.[54] Monsieur de Birague[55] left yesterday morning. I shall be here as short a time as I can.

Sir, I very humbly kiss your hands and pray God to have you in his keeping.

From Mont-de-Marsan, December 14th, 1583.

Your very humble servant,

MONTAIGNE

frequent negotiator for Henry of Navarre, who was then returning to his king from a mission to Henry III with the latter's instructions to work for a reconciliation between Navarre and his wife, Margaret of Valois. Roquefort is a little town about sixty miles south of Bordeaux and fifteen miles northeast of Mont-de-Marsan on the road between the two.

52 The prince, of course, is Navarre. The previous letter explains the problem. Bordeaux was complaining that Protestant troops in the Mas-de-Verdun, a small stronghold on the Garonne near Montauban, were intercepting boats bringing needed wheat from Toulouse. Navarre replied that his soldiers in the towns of surety were unpaid and hungry, and that the Bordeaux people would have to talk to those who were withholding the pay due his soldiers.

53 Jean de Beaumanoir, marquis de Lavardin (1551–1614), an officer and negotiator for Navarre, later (1595) marshal of France.

54 In reprisal for Navarre's seizure of Mont-de-Marsan, Matignon had occupied Bazas for the king of France. Philippe de Mornay, known as Duplessis-Mornay (1549–1623), a leading adviser to Henry of Navarre, wrote five letters to Montaigne that are still extant between November 9, 1583, and January 25, 1584, and mentioned a letter from Navarre himself to Montaigne, seeking to explain and justify their action to him and through him to Catholic men of good will. Navarre, though Protestant, was a loyalist, and his claims to succession were supported by Henry III.

55 Charles de Birague, called Captain Sacremore (died 1587), bastard son of Ludovic de Birague, governor of the marquisate of Saluzzo, King's lieutenant-general in Italy.

16. *To Marshal de Matignon*

[January 21, 1584]

To Marshal de Matignon

Sir, the people of this region who had gone to meet the king of Navarre have been back for two days. I have not seen them, but they have returned with only peaceful inclinations, as I wrote you. There is nothing new except a general and extraordinary assembly of many ministers, which will take place Monday at Sainte-Foy-la-Grande.[56] If a large company of people of various sorts and sexes comes in here tomorrow, as I expect, I will let you know what I learn.

I very humbly kiss your hands, praying God, sir, to give you a long and happy life.

From Montaigne, January 21st, 1584.

Your very humble servant,

MONTAIGNE

17. *To Claude Dupuy*

[April 23, 1584(?)]

To Monsieur Dupuy,[57] Counselor of the King in His Court of the Parlement of Paris, at Saintes

Sir, the action of the prisoner, the sieur de Verres, which is very well known to me, deserves that you bring to bear in judging it your natural mildness, if there is a case in the world in which you may justly bring it to bear. He did a thing not only excusable according to the military laws of our time, but necessary, and in our judgment laudable. And without a doubt he did it under great pressure and reluctantly. There is nothing to reproach in the rest of the course of his life.[58]

I entreat you, sir, to give it your attention: you will find that his deed appears such as I am representing it to you, and his prosecution for it is more malicious than the act itself. If this can also serve his

56 A Protestant town on the Dordogne about ten miles east of Montaigne.
57 Claude Dupuy (1545–94) was a member of a special court of justice sent to Bordeaux in 1582 by Henry III. At the time of this letter it was in session at Saintes, about sixty-five miles north of Bordeaux.
58 The sieur de Verres has not been identified.

case, I will tell you that he is a man brought up in my house, related to many worthy families, and, above all, one who has always lived honorably and innocently. He is a very good friend of mine. By saving him you will put me under extreme obligation. I entreat you very humbly to accept this recommendation on his behalf, and, after kissing your hands, I pray God, sir, to give you a long and happy life.

From Castera,[59] April 23rd.

Your affectionate servant,

MONTAIGNE

18. *To Marshal de Matignon*

[July 12, 1584(?)]

To Monseigneur de Matignon, Marshal of France, at Bordeaux

Sir, I have just now received yours of the 6th, and I very humbly thank you for showing a sort of sign, by the command you give me to come back to you, that you do not find my assistance disagreeable. This is the greatest benefit that I can expect from this public office of mine, and I hope to go to see you on my first day there.

All I can tell you meanwhile is that Messieurs Duplessis and de Quitry[60] and their large family left Sainte-Foy-la-Grande yesterday morning. The ladies and retinue whom they are conducting will lengthen their return to the king of Navarre.

You already know that at their interview at the baths of Encausse, Monsieur d'Epernon[61] resolved to go to Bagnères and see His Majesty on the 10th of this month at Pau, where they can confer in greater privacy. I believe that the king of Navarre will indeed see him again at the said Pau on his return from Bagnères,

59 Castera is a small place in Médoc near the left bank of the Gironde about thirty miles north-northwest of Bordeaux. It belonged to Montaigne's brother Thomas de Beauregard (see note 13, Letter 2).
The year is not given in this letter, but most editors agree on 1584.
60 For Duplessis, see note 54 (Letter 15). Jean de Chaumont, seigneur de Quitry, was counselor and gentleman of the chamber to the duke of Alençon and was later to be lieutenant-general of the King's armies.
61 Henry III, when the death of his last brother made Henry of Navarre the legitimate heir to the French throne, sent one of his favorites, Jean-Louis, duc d'Epernon (1554–1642), to urge Navarre to abjure his Protestantism. Navarre finally refused. Encausse-les-Thermes and Bagnères-de-Luchon are mineral baths near the Spanish border. "His Majesty" is Henry of Navarre.

and I do not know whether meanwhile he will be able to make a trip to Nérac. He is fully occupied in digesting the request, which is being made him by the people of the low country, to take the place of Monsieur[62] as protector of their interests, which they have reason to hope are prospering. I have no doubt that the queen of Navarre is likewise having her share of these visitations.

While waiting for an early opportunity to kiss your hands, I shall say no more, except that I pray God, sir, to give you a long and happy life.

From Montaigne, July 12th.

Your very humble servant,

MONTAIGNE

19. *To Marshal de Matignon*

[August 19, 1584]

To Marshal de Matignon

Sir, I see nothing here worthy of your notice. However, feeling justified by the favors you show me and the intimacy you grant me with you, I make bold to write you this note merely to inform you of my health, which has improved a little from the change of air.

I came here in a single stretch, which is quite long. Near my house I found that some good people of the Reformation from Sainte-Foy-la-Grande had killed a poor tailor with fifty or sixty stabs with scissors, for no other reason than to rob him of twenty sous and a coat worth about twice that.

I very humbly kiss your hands and pray God, sir, to give you a very happy and long life.

From Montaigne, August 19th, 1584.

Your very humble servant,

MONTAIGNE

62 "Monsieur" is the duke of Anjou, last brother of Henry III, whose recent death (June 10, 1584), had made Navarre heir to the throne. The "people of the low country" are the Protestants of lower Guienne, to the north.

20. *To the Jurats of Bordeaux*

[December 10, 1584]

To Messieurs the Jurats of the City of Bordeaux

Gentlemen, I have received your letter and will see about going to see you as soon as I can. This whole court of Sainte-Foy-la-Grande[63] is on my hands, and they have come to see me by appointment. When this is over, I shall be more at liberty.

I send you the letters from Monsieur de Vallées,[64] which you can decide about. My presence would add nothing but some of the irresolution and uncertainty of my choice and opinion on this matter.

With this I humbly commend myself to your good graces and pray God, gentlemen, to give you a long and happy life.

From Montaigne, December 10th, 1584.

Your humble brother and servant,

MONTAIGNE

21. *To Marshal de Matignon*

[January 18, 1585]

To Marshal de Matignon

Sir, on the strength of several accounts that Monsieur de Bissouse[65] has given me, on behalf of Monseigneur de Turenne,[66] of his judgment of you and of the confidence this prince has in my advice (though I do not build much on courtly phrases), I decided at dinnertime to write to Monseigneur de Turenne, to this effect:

63 Henry of Navarre and his court came to Montaigne for the first time on December 19 to spend two days. In his copy of Beuther's *Ephemeris Historica* Montaigne notes that Navarre slept in the same bed with him and was served entirely by Montaigne's servants.

64 Monsieur de Vallées has not been identified. Some editors read "Vallier."

65 The text reads "Bissonse," and some editors take this to be Antoine de Belsunce. It seems more likely to be Raymond de Bissouse (or Vissouse, Vysouze, or Viçoze), financial secretary to Henry of Navarre, one of those who visited Montaigne on December 19, 1584.

66 Henri de La Tour d'Auvergne, vicomte de Turenne (1555–1623), duke of Bouillon and prince of Sedan by virtue of his first marriage and father of the famous marshal by his second, was one of the principal followers of Navarre and another of those who had visited Montaigne the month before.

That I was saying good-bye to him by letter. That I had received the letter from the king of Navarre, who seemed to me to be taking good advice by trusting in the affection that you offered him to do him service. That I had written to Madame de Guissen[67] to make use of time to further her enterprise, and that I would urge you to assist in this. That I had advised her not to engage the interest and fortune of this prince in her passions, but, since she had so much power over him, to look more to his advantage than to her personal inclinations. That you were talking about going to Bayonne, where I might perhaps offer to follow you if I thought that my presence could be of even the slightest use to you. That if you went there, the king of Navarre, knowing you were so near, would do well to invite you to see his beautiful gardens at Pau.

That is exactly the substance of my letter, without any other haranguing. I am sending you the answer to it that was brought to me this evening. If I am not mistaken, from this beginning there will soon spring some scribbling. It seems to me that his letter already gives a certain impression of discontent or fear. Whatever he says, I have a hold on them at the place where they are going for more than two months, and where another sort of tone will be heard.

I beg you to send me back the enclosed letter with the other two. The bearer has no other business but your dispatch.

With this I very humbly kiss your hands and pray God, sir, to give you a long and happy life.

From Montaigne, January 18th, 1585.

Your very humble servant,

MONTAIGNE

67 Diane (better known as Corisande) d'Andoins, comtesse de Guiche (or Guissen) et de Gramont (1555–1621), mistress and adviser of Henry of Navarre. A letter of February 28, 1588, from the Spanish envoy in Paris to Philip II describes Montaigne as having great influence on the countess and as being a negotiator for Navarre with Henry III. This and other evidence suggests that Montaigne's influence on Navarre, both directly and through Corisande, may have been very important.

22. *To Marshal de Matignon*

[January 26, 1585]

To Marshal de Matignon

Sir, I have learned nothing since, although I have seen many people from this court[68] around here. I think that everyone has left, except that Monsieur du Ferrier[69] has remained to pay the servants' wages. If you would like to see a letter that the sieur Duplessis wrote me later, you will find in it that the reconciliation[70] was quite complete and full of good understanding; and I think that his master confided in him about this more intimately than in the others, knowing that this course is to his liking, as well as to that of Monsieur de Clervant,[71] who has seen you since. If I am to accompany you to Bayonne, I would like you to stick to your plan of waiting until Lent, so that I can take the waters at the same time. Incidentally, I have learned that there is nothing so distasteful to the husband as to see people on terms of good understanding with the wife.[72]

I have had news that the jurats reached a safe haven; and I very humbly kiss your hands, praying God, sir, to give you a long and happy life.

From Montaigne, January 26th, 1585.

Your very humble servant,

MONTAIGNE

Sir, you do me a great favor by welcoming the affection I show for your service, and you may be sure you have acquired no affection in Guienne that is more purely and sincerely yours; but this is a small acquisition. If you should have to give up your position, it must not be at a time when anyone can boast of having taken it away from you.

68 The court of Navarre.

69 This is the same Arnaud du Ferrier (1506–85) whom Montaigne had met (and suspected of Protestant leanings) on his Italian trip in Venice, where du Ferrier was the French ambassador. See *Travel Journal*, pp. 1121–2.

70 The reconciliation between the king of Navarre and his wife, Margaret of Valois. For Duplessis, see note 54 (Letter 15). "His master" is of course Henry of Navarre.

71 See note 51 (Letter 15).

72 The king and queen of Navarre.

23. *To Marshal de Matignon*

[February 2, 1585]

To Marshal de Matignon

Sir, the man by whom I sent you lately a letter of mine and one from Monsieur Duplessis has not yet returned. Since then I hear from Le Fleix[73] that Messieurs du Ferrier and de La Marsillière[74] are still at Sainte-Foy-la-Grande, that the king of Navarre has just sent to fetch some remainder of his retinue and of his hunting crew that he had here, and that his stay in Béarn will be longer than he thought. Following some new and favorable information from Monsieur Roquelaure,[75] he is going back again toward Bayonne and Dax to show them that the King took in very good part the entry that Navarre made into these towns. That is what they tell me. The rest of the country remains peaceful, and there is nothing stirring.

Whereupon I very humbly kiss your hands and pray God, sir, to give you a long and happy life.

From Montaigne, February 2nd, 1585.

Your very humble servant,

MONTAIGNE

73 A little town on the Dordogne about ten miles east of Montaigne, home of Montaigne's friend and sponsor the marquis of Trans, and scene of the negotiations leading to the Treaty of Fleix (November 25, 1580) between Catholics and Protestants.

74 For Duplessis, see note 54 (Letter 15); for du Ferrier, note 69 (Letter 22). Hurosius Berziau, seigneur de La Marsillière, was a secretary of state of Navarre who was quartered with his king.

75 Antoine, seigneur de Roquelaure (c. 1544–1625), was a blithe, courageous, and very distinguished officer of Henry of Navarre. Later he was mayor of Bordeaux and still later marshal of France.

24. *To the Jurats of Bordeaux*

[February 8, 1585]

To Messieurs the Jurats of the City and Town of Bordeaux, at Bordeaux

Gentlemen, I have taken my good share of the contentment which you write me you derive from the successful expeditions that have been reported to you by your deputies, and I take it as a good omen that you have successfully made your way through the beginning of this year.

Hoping to rejoice with you over this at the first convenient opportunity, I very humbly commend myself to your good graces, and pray God, gentlemen, to give you a happy and long life.

From Montaigne, February 8th, 1585.

Your humble brother and servant,

MONTAIGNE

25. *To Marshal de Matignon*

[February 9, 1585]

To Marshal de Matignon

Sir, I hope that the stone which was bothering you lately when you wrote me has by now slipped out easily, like another that I voided at the same time.

If the jurats arrived in Bordeaux the day they were expected and came by the post, they may have brought you fresh news of the court. The rumor is current here that Ferrand[76] was seized three leagues away from Nérac on his way to the court and brought back to Pau; also that the Huguenots nearly took Taillebourg and Talmont[77] by surprise at the same time; also rumors of certain other plans for Dax and Bayonne.

On Tuesday, after a troop of vagabonds that has been roaming around here for a long time had bought the favor and help of

76 Ferrand was a man whom Margaret of Valois placed as a secretary with her husband and who was arrested while carrying letters from Margaret and others to Catherine de' Medici and others at the court of France. For more on this incident, see Letter 26.

77 Places in Charente-Maritime, some fifty to sixty miles north of Bordeaux.

a gentleman of the region called Le Borgne La Siguinie to help them to get the better of some vagabonds who belong to another troop across the river in the village of Gensac,[78] which belongs to the king of Navarre, the said La Siguinie, having assembled twenty or thirty of his friends under color of going duck hunting with harque-buses, together with two or three of the said vagabonds from this side of the river, went and attacked those on the other side and killed one. The authorities of Gensac, notified of this, armed the people and came and made an attack on the assailants, captured four, one gentleman and three others, and wounded three or four more. The rest withdrew to this side of the river. There are two or three of the Gensac people mortally wounded. The skirmish lasted a long time and was very hot. The matter is open to settlement, for there is much fault on both sides.

If the sieur de La Roque,[79] who is a very good friend of mine, absolutely must fight at Cabanac du Puch,[80] I hope it may be far from you, and so advise him.

Whereupon I very humbly kiss your hands and pray God, sir, to give you a long and happy life.

From Montaigne, February 9th, 1585.

Your very humble servant,

MONTAIGNE

Sir, I was closing my letter when I received yours of the 6th and the one from Monsieur de Villeroy[81] which you were pleased to send me (by a man whom the city corporation sent me) to notify me of the successful expedition of their deputies. The sieur de Lamothe[82] sends me word that he has things to tell me that cannot be written and that I should let him know whether it is necessary for him to

78 A village to the south of the Dordogne, about ten miles south-southeast of Montaigne. Le Borgne La Siguinie has not been identified; Le Borgne, which means "one-eyed man," may be a nickname.

79 An adviser on the side of Navarre, nephew of the Cardinal de Bourbon.

80 Presumably the château of Saint-Germain du Puch near Libourne, about fifteen miles east-northeast of Bordeaux, belonging to the Cabanac du Puch family.

81 Nicholas de Neuville, seigneur de Villeroy or Villeroi (1543–1617), first secretary of state under four successive kings: Charles IX, Henry III, Henry IV, and Louis XIII.

82 Baude, sieur de Moncuq, seigneur de Lamothe (or La Mothe or Lamotte), a jurat of Bordeaux. The deputies are presumably those mentioned in the preceding letter.

come and see me here. Just now I am making no reply. But as for the command that you are pleased to give me, to come to see you, I very humbly beg you to believe that there is nothing I would do more willingly; and I shall never cast myself back into solitude so far or unburden myself of public affairs so thoroughly as not to retain a singular devotion to your service and a fondness for being wherever you may be.

At the moment I have my boots on to go to Le Fleix, where the good President du Ferrier and the sieur de La Marsillière[83] are to be tomorrow with the intention of coming here the day after or Tuesday. I hope to come and kiss your hands some day next week, or let you know if some occurrence rightly prevents my coming. I have received no news from Béarn, but Poyferré,[84] who has been at Bordeaux, has written me, so I am told, and given the letter to a man from whom I have not yet received it. I am sorry for that.

26. *To Marshal de Matignon*

[February 12, 1585(?)]

To Marshal de Matignon

Sir, I have just arrived from Le Fleix. La Marsillière was there and others of that council. They say that since the Ferrand incident and because of it Frontenac[85] has come to Nérac. The queen of Navarre tells him that if she had thought that the king her husband was so curious, she would have had all her dispatches pass through his hands, and that what was found in the letter she wrote to the queen her mother, where she spoke of returning to France,[86] was

83 For Le Fleix, du Ferrier, and La Marsillière, see notes to Letters 22 and 23.

84 In the 1580–88 editions of the *Essays*, in a passage at the end of I: 28 that introduced I: 29, Montaigne spoke of a sieur de Poiferré who had known La Boétie long before Montaigne did and who found in his own home some sonnets by La Boétie and transmitted them to Montaigne for publication. A Maître Jean de Poyferré, attorney at the Parlement, took the oath of bourgeois of Bordeaux on January 16, 1554. It seems likely that this is the same man.

85 For Le Fleix, La Marsillière, Ferrand, and later du Ferrier, see notes to Letters 22, 23, and 25. Antoine de Buade, seigneur de Frontenac, one of Navarre's most trusted followers and friends, was in the group that visited Montaigne in December 1584.

86 That is, to the north of France.

as it were in asking for advice and deliberating, not as being resolved on it; and that she raised the question because of the small account that is taken of her, so obviously that everyone sees it and is fully aware of it. And Frontenac says that what the king of Navarre did was only because he had been led to suspect that Ferrand was bearing memoranda concerning his own state and his public affairs.

They say the principal result is that several letters from the girls of this court to their friends in France – I mean the letters that were saved; for they say that when Ferrand was taken he was able to throw some papers into the fire, and they were consumed before they could be pulled out – these remaining letters are causing a lot of laughs.

On my way back I saw Monsieur du Ferrier, sick, at Sainte-Foy-la-Grande. He is planning to come to see me some day this week; others will be here as soon as this evening. I do not expect him to come; and in view of his age, it seems to me I left him in bad condition. However, I shall wait for him, and unless you give me orders to the contrary, I shall for this reason put off my trip to see you until the beginning of the following week.

Whereupon, very humbly kissing your hands and praying God, sir, to give you a long and happy life,

from Montaigne, February 12th,

Your very humble servant,

MONTAIGNE

The said Ferrand had a thousand crowns on him – so they say; for all this information is rather uncertain.

27. *To Marshal de Matignon*

[February 13, 1585]

To Marshal de Matignon

Sir, Monsieur du Ferrier has just written me that the king of Navarre is due to go to Montauban. Hereabouts they are in a state of alarm about some troop of horsemen which they say is lodged on the other side of the river in Bazadois.[87] If I learn news about this before I close this letter I will notify you and send over there tonight. It may be the company of the king of Navarre assembling to make a show; I have some of their men-at-arms here who are going to go there.

87 The area around Bazas, to the south and east of Bordeaux, south and a little west of Montaigne. For du Ferrier, see Letter 22.

You will know about the rumors that are current in these quarters, from what the marquis de Trans[88] writes me.

I saw Poyferré's letter. There is nothing in it except that he had something to speak to me about on behalf of the ladies, something I needed to know; but that he could not write it or delay his departure.

Whereupon, hoping soon to have the good fortune of kissing your hands, I pray God, sir, to give you a long and happy life.

From Montaigne, February 13th, 1585.

Your very humble servant,

MONTAIGNE

Sir, I was forgetting to tell you that the prisoners who were held at Gensac, as I wrote you, are at liberty except for the attorney of the town of Montravel,[89] who was seized only by accident and because he was with the others; for he took no part in all this and had been on the spot on some errand in the execution of justice.

28. *To Marshal de Matignon*

[February 1585(?)][90]

To Marshal de Matignon

Sir, I have just now received this Sunday morning your two letters, pursuant to which I would be mounting my horse this very hour except that President d'Eymar,[91] who left here yesterday, has

88 Germain-Gaston de Foix, comte de Gurson et du Fleix, marquis de Trans, powerful friend and sponsor of Montaigne, probably instrumental in getting him elected mayor. Montaigne, a close friend of the entire family, twice comments on Trans in the late *Essays* without naming him: on his apparent indifference to the death of his three sons in the battle of Moncrabeau in 1587 (I: 14, p. 50) and on his tempestuous but ineffectual control of his household (II: 8, p. 346). For Poyferré, see Letter 25.

89 A little town on the north side of the Dordogne about two miles south of Montaigne. For the Gensac incident, see Letter 25.

90 The letter is undated, but seems clearly to have been written in late February, 1585.

91 President of the Parlement of Bordeaux. He was elected mayor in 1575, but his confirmation in office by Henry III was at first refused and then delayed because he was not of the military but of the legal nobility. He was succeeded by Biron as mayor in 1578.

my horses, which I expect this evening, with the hope of leaving tomorrow to go to see you. And being unable at the present period to make this trip from here to Bordeaux in one day, because of the floods everywhere, I shall go to spend the night at Faubrenet, near the port of Le Tourne,[92] in order to cross your path if you leave meanwhile; and I will be able to be at Podensac Tuesday morning to hear what you shall be pleased to command me. But unless by the bearer of this you change our assignation, I will go to meet you Tuesday at Bordeaux without crossing the river until La Bastide.[93]

The news I received from Pau on the 11th is that the king of Navarre was going away a few days later to the port of Bayonne, from there to Nérac, from Nérac to Bergerac, and then into Saintonge. Madame de Gramont[94] was still in very bad health.

Whereupon I very humbly kiss your hands and pray God, sir, to give you a very happy and long life.

Your very humble servant,

MONTAIGNE

29. *To Marshal de Matignon*

[May 22, 1585(?)]

To Marshal de Matignon

Sir, this morning I received your letter, which I communicated to Monsieur de Gourgues,[95] and we dined together at the house of Monseigneur de Bordeaux.[96] As for the difficulty of transporting the money mentioned in your memorandum, you see how hard

92 A village and port on the northeast bank of the Garonne about fifteen miles southeast of Bordeaux. Podensac is a little town on the southwest bank of the Garonne about twenty miles southeast of Bordeaux.
93 Then a town right across the Garonne from Bordeaux, now a part of the city.
94 Corisande d'Andoins, comtesse de Guiche et de Gramont. See note 67 (Letter 21).
95 See note 40 (Letter 11).
96 The text reads "Monsr de Bourdeaus." This may be one of Matignon's lieutenants named Bourdeaus or Bordeaux. It seems more likely, however, that it is Antoine Prévost de Sansac, the archbishop of Bordeaux from 1560 until his death in 1591, a zealous worker for his religion and his king. The following letter, written five days later, tells of Montaigne's looking in daily at the archbishop's palace.

a thing it is to take care of; however, we will keep our eye on it as closely as we can.

I made every effort to find the man you spoke to us about. He has not been here, and Monseigneur de Bordeaux shows a letter in which he states that he cannot come to meet the said sieur de Bordeaux as he planned, since he has been informed that you mistrust him. His letter is of the day before yesterday. If I had found him I would probably have followed the milder course, being uncertain of your resolution; but nevertheless I beg you to have no fear that I will refuse anything that you have resolved on, or that I will make any choice or distinction about the affair or the person, where your command is involved. I hope you have many people in Guienne whose wills are as much yours as mine is.

There is a rumor that the galleys from Nantes are coming toward Brouage.[97] Marshal de Biron[98] has not yet moved out. Those who had the task of notifying Monsieur d'Uza[99] say they could not find him, and I think he is no longer here, if indeed he has been here.

We are busy with our gates and guards, and are watching them a little more attentively now in your absence, which makes me fear not only for the preservation of this city but also for your own preservation, knowing that the enemies of the king's service are well enough aware of how necessary you are to it and how badly everything would go without you.

I fear that affairs will come upon you from so many sides in the region where you are that you will be busy a long time in taking care of everything and will have many and long difficulties. If anything new and important comes up, I will promptly dispatch to you a man especially to let you know of it; and you are to suppose that nothing is stirring if you have no news from me. I beg you also to consider that this sort of movement is usually so unexpected that if it should happen they will have me by the throat without giving me warning.

97 A town and port near the mouth of the Charente north of Bordeaux. It was Protestant and the galleys in question were Catholic.

98 Armand de Gontaut, seigneur de Biron (1524–92), marshal of France from 1577, whom Matignon had succeeded as lieutenant-general in Guienne, and Montaigne as mayor of Bordeaux. A Catholic, he later promptly recognized Henry IV as his king.

99 Presumably the same vicomte d'Uza who had fought under Monluc in 1562 and 1570 and held a naval command before La Rochelle in 1573, and whose family (de Lur d'Uza) much later intermarried with some of Montaigne's descendants.

I will do what I can to get news from all parts, and to that purpose will visit all sorts of men and see what their feeling is. Up to this moment nothing is stirring.

Monsieur Du Londel[100] saw me this morning and we looked into some arrangements for his place, where I shall go tomorrow morning.

Since I began this letter I learned at Les Chartrons[101] that near this town there passed two gentlemen who say they belong to Monsieur de Guise and who were coming from Agen.[102] I could not find out what route they took. People at Agen are waiting for you to come. The sieur de Mauvesin[103] came as far as Canteloup and then went back from there after learning some news. I am looking for a Captain Roux,[104] to whom Masparault[105] writes to draw him into his service with plenty of promises.

The news of the two galleys from Nantes, ready to descend upon Brouage with two companies of foot soldiers, is certain. Monsieur de Mercœur[106] is in the city of Nantes. The sieur de La Courbe[107] told President Nesmond[108] that Monsieur d'Elbeuf[109] is on this side of

100 Le Londel or Du Londel Auctoville, trusty captain of Matignon's guards, who in April 1585 had assisted Matignon in the arrest of the League Vaillac and the seizure from him of the dangerous Château Trompette in Bordeaux. It is presumably the Château Trompette that Montaigne refers to as "his place."

101 Les Chartrons or Les Chartreux, the northern edge of Bordeaux, on the river.

102 Margaret of Valois was then at Agen and involved in an intrigue with the League, the party of the Guises.

103 Michel de Castillon, sieur de Mauvesin, one of Navarre's captains. Canteloup is a village about six miles south of Bordeaux.

104 Captain Roux was a Catholic career soldier fighting for Navarre. A year later he stoutly defended Puynormand against the League armies during the siege of Castillon. He became a good friend of Montaigne's and was married at his château in 1589.

105 Pierre de Masparault, member of the privy council of Henry III and Master of Requests.

106 Philippe-Emmanuel de Lorraine, duke of Mercœur (1558–1602), one of the leaders of the League.

107 The sieur de La Courbe has not yet been identified.

108 François de Nesmond (died 1616), councillor in the King's privy council, president of the Parlement of Bordeaux.

109 Charles I, duc d'Elbeuf or d'Elbœuf (1556–1605), grandson of Claude de Guise and a general for the League.

Angers and stayed with his father, and that he is coming toward lower Poitou with four thousand foot and four or five hundred horse, after collecting the forces of Monsieur de Brissac[110] and others; Monsieur de Mercœur is to join them. The rumor is also current that Monsieur de Mayenne[111] is coming to take the troops that have been assembled for them in Auvergne and that he will come through the Forez mountain region to Rouergue[112] and to us, that is to say, toward the king of Navarre, against whom all this is coming.

Monsieur de Lansac[113] is at Bourg[114] and has two armed ships with him. His responsibility is for naval matters.

I am telling you what I hear, and mingling the news of town rumors which I do not consider likely with truths, so that you may know everything; very humbly entreating you to come back as soon as your affairs will allow; and I assure you that we will meanwhile spare neither our labors, nor, if necessary, our life, to keep everything in obedience to the King.

Sir, I very humbly kiss your hands and pray God to have you in his keeping.

From Bordeaux, Wednesday night, May 22nd.

Your very humble servant,

MONTAIGNE

I have seen no one from the king of Navarre. They say that Monsieur de Biron has seen him.

110 Charles II de Cossé, seigneur de Brissac (1550–1621), a Leaguer fighting for Henry III, who was later to turn over Paris to Henry IV, and still later became marshal of France.

111 The text reads "Monsieur du Meine," and some editors interpret it as the duke of Maine. It seems, however, that the reference must be to Charles de Lorraine, duke of Mayenne (1554–1611), one of the League's top generals and its leader after the death of Henri de Guise, who was soon to lead these forces in besieging Castillon.

112 The modern department of Aveyron.

113 Guy de Lansac or Lanssac (c. 1547–1622), known as "young Lansac," son of a favorite adviser of Catherine de' Medici (see note 29, Letter 7), a predecessor of Montaigne as mayor of Bordeaux. At this point he was pillaging and ransoming river traffic on behalf of the League. Matignon soon after attacked him and drove him out.

114 A port about ten miles north of Bordeaux near the confluence of the Dordogne and the Garonne.

30. *To Marshal de Matignon*

[May 27, 1585]

To Marshal de Matignon

Sir, I wrote you at great length these past days. I send you two letters I have received for you by the hand of one of Monsieur de Rouillac's[115] men. The proximity of Monsieur de Vaillac[116] fills us with alarms, and there is not a day that does not bring me fifty urgent ones. We very humbly entreat you to come here just as soon as your affairs may permit. I have spent every night either around the town in arms or outside of town at the port, and before your warning I had already kept watch there one night on the news of a boat loaded with armed men which was due to pass. We saw nothing; and the evening before last we were there until after midnight, and Monsieur de Gourgues[117] was there; but nothing came. I made use of Captain Saintes,[118] for I needed our own soldiers. He and Massip[119] filled the three coaches for the guard inside the city. I hope you will find the city in the state in which you left it in our hands. This morning I am sending two jurats to notify the court of the Parlement of all the rumors that are current and of the obviously suspect men whom we know to be there.

Whereupon, hoping that you may be here tomorrow at the latest, I very humbly kiss your hands and pray God, sir, to give you a long and happy life.

From Bordeaux, May 27th, 1585.

Your very humble servant,

MONTAIGNE

115 Monsieur de Rouillac is not clearly identified. One editor conjectures that he is Monsieur de Raillac, seigneur de Saint-Mezard, a follower of Navarre.

116 Louis Ricard Gourdon de Genouillac, baron de Vaillac, the Leaguer who had commanded the Château Trompette in Bordeaux until Matignon ousted and arrested him. Released so that he might go and justify himself to the King, he had remained near Bordeaux and was stirring up trouble.

117 See note 40 (Letter 11).

118 Military commander of Cahors, then on detached duty at Bordeaux, a man highly esteemed by Matignon.

119 The text reads Massep. This is probably the same Massip, a counselor at the Parlement of Bordeaux, who in 1587 was sent by the Parlement to look into some troubles at Saint-Emilion, since he held property near there.

Not a day has passed that I have not been to the Château Trompette. You will find the platform made. I look in at the archbishop's[120] palace every day, too.

31. *To the Jurats of Bordeaux*

[July 30, 1585]

To Messieurs the Jurats of the City of Bordeaux

Gentlemen, I found news of you here by chance, which the marshal[121] communicated to me. I will spare neither my life nor anything else for your service and will leave you to judge whether the service I can render you by my presence at the coming election is worth my risking going into the city in view of the bad condition it is in, especially for people coming from as pure an air as I do.[122] On Wednesday I will come as close to you as I can, to Feuillas[123] if the disease has not reached there; at which place, as I am writing to Monsieur de Lamothe,[124] I shall be very happy to have the honor of seeing some one of you to receive your commands and to discharge myself of the credentials that the lord marshal will give me for the company.

Whereupon I very humbly commend myself to your good graces and pray God, gentlemen, to give you a long and happy life.

From Libourne, July 30th, 1585.

Your humble servant and brother,

MONTAIGNE

120 See note 96 (Letter 29).

121 Matignon.

122 During one of Montaigne's many and busy absences, the plague had struck Bordeaux with the greatest violence. From June to December, 1585, 14,000 inhabitants died, or almost half the population. Only two jurats out of six remained in town; most of the inhabitants left. People from outside were forbidden to enter. Montaigne's action has been much criticized, especially in the nineteenth century, when this letter was discovered; but none of his contemporaries, as far as is known, were critical.

123 A château just across the river from Bordeaux, just south of La Bastide, between Cenon and Floirac.

124 See note 82 (Letter 25).

32. *To the Jurats of Bordeaux*

[July 31, 1585]

To Messieurs the Jurats of the City and Town of Bordeaux

Gentlemen, I communicated to the lord marshal[125] the letter you sent me and what the bearer told me you had commissioned him to make me understand; and the marshal commissioned me to ask you to send him the drummer[126] that was at Bourg on your behalf. He also told me that he asks you to send him Captains Saint-Aulaye and Mathelin[127] immediately, and to get together the largest number of mariners and sailors that can be found.

As for that bad example and the injustice of taking women and children prisoners, I do not at all think that we should imitate it as others have done. I have said this also to the said lord marshal, who has instructed me to write you not to make a move in this matter until you have fuller word.

Whereupon I very humbly commend myself to your good graces, and pray God, gentlemen, to give you a long and happy life.

From Feuillas,[128] July 31st, 1585.

Your humble brother and servant,

MONTAIGNE

33. *To Marshal de Matignon*

[June 12, 1587(?)]

To Marshal de Matignon

Sir, Madame de Mauriac is arranging the marriage of her son the sieur de Mauriac[129] to one of the sisters of Monsieur d'Aubeterre.

125 Matignon.
126 Or drum. The French *tambour* could mean either. For Bourg, see note 114 (Letter 29).
127 Captains Saint-Aulaye and Mathelin have not been identified.
128 See note 123 (Letter 31).
129 Madame de Mauriac was born Jeanne de Ségur and in 1556 married Antoine de Taillefer, seigneur de Mauriac. Her mother was a La Chassaigne, as was Montaigne's wife. Her son Isaac de Taillefer, seigneur de Mauriac, a Protestant, was born in 1564; he married Isabeau Bouchard d'Aubeterre, daughter of François and Gabrielle d'Aubeterre, on August 28, 1587.

Things are so far advanced, so they tell me, that all that remains to be arranged is the presence of her eldest daughter, Madame de Brigneux, who is at Lectoure[130] with her husband. She very humbly entreats you to grant a passport to her said daughter with her small train of servants to come to Mauriac; and since I am a relative of hers and have the honor of being known to you, she wanted me to make the request of you, and has sent me a letter which she says is from Monsieur d'Aubeterre, I think for this same purpose.

I do make you this very humble and affectionate request, if it is a thing that does not displease or bother you. If not, at least this letter will serve to recall me to your memory, from which I may have been dislodged both by my scant merit and by the long time it has been since I had the honor of seeing you. I am,

from Montaigne, June 12th,

Sir, your very humble servant,

 MONTAIGNE

34. *To Marshal de Matignon*

[February 16, 1588(?)]

To Marshal de Matignon[131]

Sir, you have learned that our baggage was seized before our eyes in the forest of Villebois,[132] and then, after a long time and much confused discussion, the seizure was judged unjust by His Highness the prince.[133] Meanwhile we did not dare go on, because of uncertainty over our personal security, about which we were to be enlightened in writing on our passports. This raid was occasioned by

130 A small town in the department of Gers, on the river Gers, about twenty miles south of Agen. Anne de Taillefer's second marriage was to Jacques, seigneur de Brigneux, governor of Lectoure for Navarre.

131 In the essay "Of Physiognomy" (III: 12, pp. 990–91), Montaigne tells of a holdup in many ways so similar to this one that many readers have thought it was the same one. This one apparently occurred on the road to Paris, where, among other things, he was going to have the first three-book edition of the *Essays* published.

132 On the road to Paris, a little south of Angoulême.

133 Presumably Henri I, prince de Condé, who died a month later. But if so, since Condé was a Protestant leader, why does Montaigne blame a Leaguer? The best explanation seems to be that this was a Protestant reprisal for the seizure by the Leaguer referred to later.

the same Leaguer who had seized Monsieur de Barrault[134] and Monsieur de La Rochefoucauld.[135] The tempest fell upon me, who had my money in my strongbox. I have not recovered any of it, and most of my papers and clothes also remained with the men. We did not see His Highness. I lost fifty-odd crowns, and the count of Thorigny[136] lost a silver water pitcher and some odds and ends of clothes. He turned out of his way in great haste to go to see the mourning ladies at Montrésor,[137] where the bodies of the two brothers and the grandmother are, and picked us up again yesterday in this city, which we are leaving presently.

The trip to Normandy is put off.

The King has sent Messieurs de Bellièvre and de La Guiche[138] to Monsieur de Guise to summon him to come to court. We shall be there Thursday.

From Orléans, February 16th, in the morning.

Your very humble servant,

MONTAIGNE

35. *To Madame Paulmier*

[1588(?)]

To Madame Paulmier[139]

Madame, my friends know that from the first time I saw you I destined one of my books for you, for I felt that you had done them

134 Probably François de Jobert, sieur de Barrault, seneschal of Bazas.

135 Probably François IV de La Rochefoucauld, Protestant fighter killed in battle against the League in 1591; or possibly Jean-Louis de La Rochefoucauld, count of Randam, who died in 1590.

136 Odet de Matignon, comte de Thorigny, the marshal's only son (1559–95), later lieutenant-general in Normandy. Matignon had evidently learned of this event from him.

137 A little town about thirty-five miles southeast of Tours. The brothers are Duke Anne de Joyeuse (1561–87), a leading favorite of Henry III, and his brother Claude, both killed two months before at Coutras; the ladies are the mother and wife of Anne. Thorigny was related to Joyeuse.

138 Pompone de Bellièvre (1529–1607), future chancellor of France (1599–1604), and Philibert de La Guiche (c.1540–1607), grand master of the artillery, both trusted officers of Henry III.

139 Marguerite de Chaumont (1554–99), married since 1574 to Julien Paulmier or Le Paulmier.

great honor. But Monsieur Paulmier's courtesy deprives me of the means of giving it to you, for he has since obligated me far more than my book is worth. You will accept it, if you please, as being yours before I owed it, and will do me the favor of liking it, either for its own sake or for mine; and I shall keep entire the debt I owe to Monsieur Paulmier in order to get even, that is if I can, by some service.

36. *To Antoine Loisel:*[140] INSCRIPTION ON A COPY OF THE 1588 *ESSAYS*

[1588(?)]

This is a poor return for the handsome presents you have made to me of the fruits of your labors, but the fact is that it is the best return I can make. In God's name, sir, take the trouble to leaf through some part of this in some leisure hour and tell me what you think of it, for I fear I am getting worse as I go on.

For Monsieur Loisel.

37. *To King Henry IV*

[January 18, 1590(?)]

To the King

Sire,

It is a sign of rising above the weight and pressure of your great and important affairs to be able to stoop and lend yourself to the little people in their turn, according to the duty of your royal authority, which at every hour exposes you to every sort and condition of men and occupations. The fact, however, that Your Majesty has deigned to consider my letters and order them answered, I would rather owe to the benignity than to the vigor of your soul.

From the first I have considered you as destined for the rank you now occupy, and you may remember that even when I had to confess

140 Antoine Loisel (1536–1617), one of the leading lawyers of his time, had been advocate-general to the royal court of justice that Henry III had sent to Bordeaux in 1582 to judge all cases concerning the latest edict of pacification, and had dedicated his closing address to Montaigne in glowing terms.

it to my curate I did not fail to look upon your successes with a distinctly favorable eye. At present, with more reason and freedom, I embrace them with my full affection.

These successes serve you up north in action, but they serve you no less down here by reputation. The reverberation strikes as hard as the blow. We could not possibly draw from the justice of your cause such strong arguments to confirm or subdue your subjects as we do from the news of the prosperity of your campaigns. And I can assure Your Majesty that in producing the new changes to your advantage that you see in these parts, your happy escape from Dieppe[141] has most opportunely seconded the frank zeal and marvelous sagacity of Marshal de Matignon, from whom I like to believe that you do not daily receive so many good and signal services without remembering my assurances and my hopes.

For this coming summer I look forward not so much to the fruits that will feed me as to those of our common tranquillity, and I expect that this will spread over your affairs with the same happy tenor, dispersing, like the earlier ones, all the great promises with which your adversaries nourish the will of their men. Popular inclinations go in waves; if the leaning in your favor is once established, it will gather its own momentum and go all the way.

I would have wished, to be sure, that the individual profit of the soldiers in your army and the need to content them had not robbed you, especially in that principal city,[142] of the fine recommendation of having treated your mutinous subjects, in the height of victory, with more solace than do their protectors; and that you had shown that they were yours, not by a passing and usurped claim, but by a paternal and truly royal affection.

To conduct such affairs as those you have in hand it is necessary to use uncommon ways. Moreover, it has always been observed that where conquests, because of their greatness and difficulty, could not be thoroughly completed by arms and by force, they have been completed by clemency and magnanimity, excellent lures to attract men, especially toward the just and legitimate side. If rigor and punishment occur, they must be put off until after the possession of mastery. A great conqueror[143] of the past boasts that he has given his

141 At the battle of Arques just outside Dieppe, September 21, 1589.
142 Presumably Paris, the siege of which had not yet begun, but which Henry IV had attacked briefly (November 1–3, 1589).
143 Scipio the Elder, according to Livy. See *Essays* III: 9, p. 901.

subjugated enemies as much occasion to love him as his friends. And here we already feel a somewhat promising effect from the impression received by the towns that have strayed from you when they compare their harsh treatment with that of the towns that are obedient to you. Wishing for Your Majesty, as I do, a more present and less hazardous felicity, and that you may be rather loved than feared by your people,[144] and considering your welfare as necessarily attached to theirs, I rejoice that this same progress that you are making toward victory is also a progress toward easier conditions of peace.

Sire, your letter of the last of November has reached me only at this moment, and after the time you were pleased to set for me, when you were in Tours. I take it as a singular favor that you have deigned to make me feel that you would take pleasure in seeing me, a person so useless, but yours even more by affection than by duty. Your Majesty has very laudably adapted your outward appearance to the height of your new fortune, but you act just as laudably in not changing the good nature and ease of your inward disposition. You have been pleased to have consideration not only for my age but also for my wishes in summoning me to a place where you would be a little bit at rest from your labors and agitations. May it be soon in Paris, Sire; and there will be neither means nor health that I will not employ to come.

Your very humble and very obedient servant and subject,

MONTAIGNE

From Montaigne, January 18th.

144 Compare *Essays* II: 8, p. 345: "Even if I could make myself feared, I would much rather make myself loved." The impact of Machiavelli's *Prince* made this question a live one.

38. *To . . .*

[March or May 10, 1590]

To . . . [145]

Sir, I send you this letter, in view of my age, beyond the requirements of need, to assure you that I can recognize the fine things you said better than I showed you just now.

Now, in the uncertain state of our savings I have been attentive not to fail in regard to the care and attachment you have shown, which I know has placed me in your debt for many long years for good and loyal services. I even want so much to prove it to you that here is the claim, whose acquittance Monsieur Estienne[146] will take care of at any time you present yourself to him.

That is what I beg you to grant me as a token of your good friendship and a thing very much to my taste, the cost of which I take as a resource.

Whereupon I pray God to give you a long and happy life.
Ma . . . 10th, 1590.

MONTAIGNE

39. *To King Henry IV*

[September 2, 1590(?)]

To the King

Sire,
The letter of July 20th that Your Majesty has been pleased to write me was delivered to me only this morning and found me caught up in a very violent tertian fever that has been popular in this region since last month.

Sire, I take it as a very great honor to receive your commands, and I have not failed to write to Marshal de Matignon three times, very expressly, of my intention and obligation to go to see him, and

145 This letter was copied by a friend for Dr. J.-F. Payen, who first published it in 1855. The original has not been found since. Payen was unable to determine the addressee and whether the "Ma . . ." in the date stood for March or May. Montaigne seems to have written this in great haste and perhaps in pain or some kind of trouble, for many words are missing.
146 Monsieur Estienne has not been identified.

I even marked out for him the route I would take to go to meet him in safety if he saw fit. Having had no answer to all this, I assume that he has considered, on my behalf, the length and hazard of the roads.

Sire, may it please Your Majesty to do me the favor of believing that I will never begrudge my purse on the occasions for which I would not want to spare my life. I have never received any gift whatsoever from the liberality of kings, any more than I have asked it or deserved it; and I have received no payment for the steps I have taken in their service, of which Your Majesty has had partial knowledge. What I have done for your predecessors I will do still more willingly for you. I am, Sire, as rich as I wish to be. When I have exhausted my purse with Your Majesty in Paris, I will make bold to tell you so; and then, if you consider me worth keeping any longer in your retinue, I will cost you less than the least of your officers.

Sire, I pray God for your prosperity and health.

Your very humble and very obedient servant and subject,

MONTAIGNE

From Montaigne, September 2nd.

ABOUT THE TRANSLATOR

As well as translating the Complete Works, the late DONALD M. FRAME wrote a biography of Montaigne and a study of Montaigne's humanism. He also translated works by Voltaire, Molière and Rabelais.

ABOUT THE INTRODUCER

STUART HAMPSHIRE was born in 1914 and has been a Fellow of All Souls College, Oxford, since 1936. Other academic posts he has held during his long career are Grote Professor of Philosophy at University College, London, and Professor of Philosophy at Princeton. He is the author of *Thought and Action*, *Freedom and the Individual* and a study of Spinoza.

This book is set in CASLON, designed and engraved by William
Caslon of WILLIAM CASLON & SON, Letter-Founders in
London, around 1740. In England at the beginning of
the eighteenth century, Dutch type was probably
more widely used than English. The rise
of William Caslon put a stop to the
importation of Dutch types
and so changed the his-
tory of English
typecutting.